DEBATES AND PROCEEDINGS

OF THE

MARYLAND REFORM CONVENTION

TO

REVISE THE STATE CONSTITUTION.

TO WHICH ARE PREFIXED

THE BILL OF RIGHTS AND CONSTITUTION AS ADOPTED.

PUBLISHED

BY ORDER OF THE CONVENTION.

VOLUME I.

ANNAPOLIS:
WILLIAM M'NEIR, OFFICIAL PRINTER.
1851.

DECLARATION OF RIGHTS.

We, the People of the State of Maryland, grateful to Almighty God for our civil and religious liberty, and taking into our serious consideration the best means of establishing a good Constitution in this State, for the sure foundation and more permanent security thereof, Declare:

Art. 1. That all government of right originates from the people, is founded in compact only, and instituted solely for the good of the whole: and they have at all times according to the mode prescribed in this Constitution, the unalienable right to alter, reform, or abolish their form of Government, in such manner as they may deem expedient.

Art. 2. That the people of this State ought to have the sole and exclusive right of regulating the internal government and police thereof.

Art. 3. That the inhabitants of Maryland are entitled to the common law of England, and the trial by jury according to the course of that law, and to the benefit of such of the English statutes as existed on the fourth day of July, seventeen hundred and seventy-six, and which by experience have been found applicable to their local and other circumstances, and have been introduced, used and practiced by the courts of law or equity, and also of all acts of Assembly in force on the first Monday of November, eighteen hundred and fifty, except such as may have since expired, or may be altered by this Constitution, subject, nevertheless to the revision of, and amendment or repeal by the Legislature of this State; and the inhabitants of Maryland are also entitled to all property derived to them from or under the charter, granted by his Majesty Charles the First to Cæcilius Calvert, Baron of Baltimore.

Art. 4. That all persons invested with the legislative or executive powers of government are the trustees of the public, and as such accountable for their conduct; whenever the ends of government are perverted, and public liberty manifestly endangered, and all other means of redress are ineffectual, the people may, and of right ought to reform the old or establish a new government; the doctrine of non-resistance against arbitrary power and oppression is absurd, slavish and destructive of the good and happiness of mankind.

Art. 5. That the right of the people to participate in the Legislature is the best security of liberty, and the foundation of all free government; for this purpose elections ought to be free and frequent, and every free white male citizen having the qualifications prescribed by the Constitution, ought to have the right of suffrage.

Art. 6. That the legislative, executive and judicial powers of government ought to be for ever separate and distinct from each other; and no person exercising the functions of one of said departments shall assume or discharge the duties of any other.

Art. 7. That no power of suspending laws, or the execution of laws, unless by or derived from the Legislature, ought to be exercised or allowed.

Art. 8. That freedom of speech and debate or proceedings in the Legislature, ought not to be impeached in any court of judicature.

Art. 9. That Annapolis be the place for the meeting of the Legislature; and the Legislature ought not to be convened or held at any other place but from evident necessity.

Art. 10. That for the redress of grievances, and for amending, strengthening and preserving the laws, the Legislature ought to be frequently convened.

Art. 11. That every man hath a right to petition the Legislature for the redress of grievances in a peaceable and orderly manner.

Art. 12. That no aid, charge, tax, burthen, or fees, ought to be rated or levied, under any pretence, without the consent of the Legislature.

Art. 13. That the levying of taxes by the poll is grievous and oppressive and ought to be abolished; that paupers ought not to be assessed for the support of government, but every other person in the State, or person holding property therein, ought to contribute his proportion of public taxes, for the support of government, according to his actual worth in real or personal property; yet fines, duties or taxes may properly and justly be imposed or laid, on persons or property, with a political view, for the good government and benefit of the community.

Art. 14. That sanguinary laws ought to be avoided, so far as is consistent with the safety of the State; and no law to inflict cruel and unusual pains and penalties ought to be made in any case, or at any time hereafter.

Art. 15. That retrospective laws, punishing acts committed before the existence of said laws, and by them only declared criminal, are oppressive, unjust and incompatible with liberty; wherefore, no expost facto law ought to be made.

Art. 16. That no law to attaint particular persons of treason or felony, ought to be made in any case, or at any time hereafter.

Art. 17. That every free man, for any injury done to him in his person or property, ought to have remedy by the course of the law of the land, and ought to have justice and right, freely without sale, fully without any denial, and speedily without delay according to the law of the land.

Art. 18. That the trial of facts where they arise, is one of the greatest securities of the lives, liberties, and estate of the people.

Art. 19. That in all criminal prosecutions, every man hath a right to be informed of the accusation against him; to have a copy of the indictment or charge, in due time (if required) to prepare for his defence; to be allowed counsel, to be confronted with the witnesses against him; to have process for his witnesses; to examine the witnesses for and against him on oath; and to a speedy trial by an impartial jury, without whose unanimous consent he ought not to be found guilty.

Art. 20. That no man ought to be compelled to give evidence against himself in a court of common law, or in any other court, but in such cases as have been usually practiced in this State, or may hereafter be directed by the Legislature.

Art. 21. That no free man ought to be taken or imprisoned, or disseized of his freehold, liberties or privileges, or outlawed, or exiled, or in any manner destroyed, or deprived of his life, liberty or property, but by the judgment of his peers, or by the law of the land; provided, that nothing in this article shall be so construed as to prevent the Legislature from passing all such laws for the government, regulation and disposition of the free colored population of this State as they may deem necessary.

Art. 22. That excessive bail ought not to be required, nor excessive fines imposed, nor cruel or unusual punishment inflicted by the courts of law.

Art. 23. That all warrants, without oath, or affirmation, to search suspected places, or to seize any person or property, are grievous and oppressive; and all general warrants to search suspected places, or to apprehend suspected persons, without naming or describing the place, or the person in special, are illegal and ought not to be granted.

Art. 24. That no conviction shall work corruption of blood, or forfeiture of estate.

Art. 25. That a well regulated militia is the proper and natural defence of a free Government.

Art. 26. That standing armies are dangerous to liberty, and ought not to be raised or kept up without consent of the Legislature.

Art. 27. That in all cases and at all times, the military ought to be under strict subordination to, and control of the civil power.

Art. 28. That no soldier ought to be quartered in any house in time of peace without the consent of the owner, and in time of war in such manner only as the Legislature shall direct.

Art. 29. That no person except regular soldiers, mariners, and marines, in the service of this State, or militia when in actual service, ought in any case to be subject to or punishable by martial law.

Art. 30. That the independency and uprightness of Judges are essential to the impartial administration of justice, and a great security to the rights and liberties of the people, wherefore the Judges shall not be removed except for misbehaviour, on conviction in a court of law, or by the Governor, upon the address of the General Assembly; *provided*, that two-thirds of all the members of each House concur in such address. No Judge shall hold any other office, civil or military, or political trust or employment of any kind whatsoever, under the Constitution or Laws of this State, or of the United States, or any of them, or receive fees or perquisites of any kind for the discharge of his official duties.

Art. 31. That a long continuance in the executive departments of power or trust, is dangerous to liberty; a rotation, therefore, in those departments is one of the best securities of permanent freedom.

Art. 32. That no person ought to hold at the same time more than one office of profit, created by the Constitution or laws of this State; nor ought any person in public trust to receive any present from any Foreign Prince, or State, or from the United States, or any of them, without the approbation of this State.

Art. 33. That as it is the duty of every man to worship God in such manner as he thinks most acceptable to Him, all persons are equally entitled to protection in their religious liberty; wherefore, no person ought, by any law, to be molested in his person or estate, on account of his religious persuasion or profession, or for his religious practice, unless under color of religion, any man shall disturb the good order, peace or safety of the State, or shall infringe the laws of morality, or injure others in their natural, civil or religious rights; nor ought any person be compelled to frequent or maintain or contribute, unless on contract, to maintain any place of worship or any ministry; nor shall any person be deemed incompetent as a witness or juror, who believes in the existence of a God, and that under his dispensation such person will be held morally accountable for his acts, and be rewarded or punished therefor, either in this world or the world to come.

Art. 34. That no other test or qualification ought to be required on admission to any office of trust or profit, than such oath of office as may be prescribed by this Constitution, or by the Laws of the State, and a declaration of belief in the Christian religion; and if the party shall profess to be a Jew, the declaration shall be of his belief in a future state of rewards and punishments.

Art. 35. That every gift, sale or devise of land to any minister, public teacher or preacher of the gospel, as such, or to any religious sect, order or denomination, or to or for the support, use or benefit of, or in trust for any minister, public teacher, or preacher of the gospel, as such, or any religious sect, order or denomination, and every gift or sale of goods or chattels to go in succession, or to take place after the death of the seller or donor, to or for such support, use or benefit; and, also, every devise of goods or chattels, to or for the support, use or benefit of any minister, public teacher or preacher of the gospel, as such, or any religious sect, order or denomination, without the leave of the Legislature, shall be void; except always, any sale, gift, lease or devise of any quantity of land not exceeding five acres for a church, meeting house or other house of worship, or parsonage, or for a burying ground, which shall be improved, enjoyed or used only for such purpose; or such sale, gift, lease or devise, shall be void.

Art. 36. That the manner of administering an oath or affirmation to any person ought to be such as those of the religious persuasion, profession or denomination of which he is a member, generally esteem the most effectual confirmation by the attestation of the Divine Being.

Art. 37. That the city of Annapolis ought to have all its rights, privileges and benefits, agreeably to its Charter, and the Acts of Assembly confirming and regulating the same; subject to such alterations as have been or as may be made by the Legislature.

Art. 38. That the liberty of the press ought to be inviolably preserved.

Art. 39. That monopolies are odious, contrary to the spirit of a free government and the principles of commerce, and ought not to be suffered.

Art. 40. That no title of nobility or hereditary honors ought to be granted in this State.

Art. 41. That the Legislature ought to encourage the diffusion of knowledge and virtue, the promotion of literature, the arts, sciences, agriculture, commerce and manufactures, and the general melioration of the condition of the people.

Art. 42. This enumeration of rights shall not be construed to impair or deny others retained by the people.

Art. 43. That this Constitution shall not be altered, changed or abolished, except in the manner therein prescribed and directed.

CONSTITUTION.

ARTICLE I.

Elective Franchise.

Sec. 1. Every free white male person of twenty-one years of age or upwards, who shall have been one year next preceding the election a resident of the State, and for six months a resident of the city of Baltimore, or of any county in which he may offer to vote, and being at the time of the election a citizen of the United States, shall be entitled to vote in the ward or election district in which he resides, in all elections hereafter to be held; and at all such elections the vote shall be taken by ballot. And in case any county or city shall be so divided as to form portions of different electoral districts for the election of Congressmen, Senator, Delegate or other officer or officers, then to entitle a person to vote for such officer, he must have been a resident of that part of the county or city which shall form a part of the electoral district in which he offers to vote, for six months next preceding the election, but a person who shall have acquired a residence in such county or city entitling him to vote at any such election, shall be entitled to vote in the election district from which he removed, until he shall have acquired a residence in the part of the county or city to which he has removed.

Sec. 2. That if any person shall give, or offer to give directly or indirectly, any bribe, present or reward, or any promise, or any security for the payment or delivery of any money or any other thing, to induce any voter to refrain from casting his vote, or forcibly to prevent him in any way from voting, or to obtain or procure a vote for any candidate or person proposed or voted for, as elector of President and Vice President of the United States, or Representative in Congress, or for any office of profit or trust, created by the constitution or laws of this State, or by the ordinances or authority of the Mayor and City Council of Baltimore, the person giving or offering to give, and the person receiving the same, and any person who gives or causes to be given an illegal vote, knowing it to be so, at any election to be hereafter held in this State, shall on conviction in a court of law, in addition to the penalties now or hereafter to be imposed by law, be for ever disqualified to hold any office of profit or trust, or to vote at any election thereafter.

Sec. 3. It shall be the duty of the General Assembly of Maryland to pass laws to punish with fine and imprisonment any person who shall remove into any election district or ward of the city of Baltimore, not for the purpose of acquiring a *bona fide* residence therein, but for the purpose of voting therein at an approaching election, or who shall vote in any election district or ward in which he does not reside, (except in the case provided for in the first article of the constitution,) or shall, at the same election, vote in more than one election district or ward, or shall vote or offer to vote in any name not his own, or in place of any other person of the same name, or shall vote in any county in which he does not reside.

Sec. 4. Every person elected or appointed to any office of profit or trust under the constitution or laws made pursuant thereto, before he shall enter upon the duties of such office shall take and subscribe the following oath or affirmation: I, A B, do swear (or affirm, as the case may be,) that I will support the constitution of the United States, and that I will be faithful and bear true allegiance to the State of Maryland, and support the constitution and laws thereof; that I will to the best of my skill and judgment diligently and faithfully, without partiality or prejudice, execute the office of ——— according to the constitution and laws of this State, and that since the adoption of the present constitution, I have not in any manner violated the provisions thereof in relation to bribery of voters or preventing legal or procuring illegal votes to be given; (and if a Governor, Senator, member of the House of Delegates, or Judge,) "that I will not directly or indirectly receive the profits or any part of the profits of any other office during the time of my acting as ———." And if any person elected or appointed to office as aforesaid, shall refuse or neglect to take the said oath or affirmation, he shall be considered as having refused to accept the said office, and a new election or appointment shall be made as in case of refusal or resignation, and any person swearing or affirming falsely in the premises shall, on conviction thereof in a court of law, incur the penalties for wilful and corrupt perjury, and be thereafter incapable of voting at any election, and also incapable of holding any office of profit or trust in this State.

Sec. 5. That no person above the age of twenty-one years, convicted of larceny or other infamous crime, unless he shall be pardoned by the Executive, shall ever thereafter be entitled to vote at any election in this State, and no person under guardianship as a lunatic, or as a person *non compos mentis*, shall be entitled to vote.

ARTICLE II.

Executive Department.

Sec. 1. The executive power of the State shall be vested in a Governor, whose term of office shall commence on the second Wednesday of January next ensuing his election, and continue for four years, or until his successor shall have qualified.

Sec. 2. The first election for Governor under this constitution shall be held on the first Wednesday of November, in the year eighteen hundred and fifty-three, and on the same day and month in every fourth year thereafter, at the places of voting for delegates to the General Assembly, and every person qualified to vote for delegates shall be qualified and entitled to vote for Governor; the election to be held in the same manner as the election of delegates, and the returns thereof, under seal, to be addressed to the Speaker of the House of Delegates, and enclosed and transmitted to the Secretary of State, and delivered to the said Speaker at the commencement of the session of the Legislature next ensuing said election.

Sec. 3. The Speaker of the House of Delegates shall then open the said returns in the presence of both houses, and the person having the highest number of votes, and being constitutionally eligible, shall be the Governor, and shall qualify in the manner herein prescribed, on the second Wednesday of January next ensuing his election, or as soon thereafter as may be practicable.

Sec. 4. If two or more persons shall have the highest and an equal number of votes, one of them shall be chosen Governor by the Senate and House of Delegates; and all questions in relation to the eligibility of Governor, and to the returns of said election, and to the number and legality of votes therein given, shall be determined by the House of Delegates. And if the person, or persons, having the highest number of votes be ineligible, the Governor shall be chosen by the Senate and House of Delegates. Every election of Governor, by the Legislature, shall be determined by a joint majority of the Senate and House of Delegates, and the vote shall be taken viva voce. But if two or more persons shall have the highest and an equal number of votes, then a second vote shall be taken, which shall be confined to the persons having an equal number; and if the votes should again be equal, then the election of Governor shall be determined by lot between those who shall have the highest and an equal number on the first vote.

Sec. 5. The State shall be divided into three districts; St. Mary's, Charles, Calvert, Prince George's, Anne Arundel, Montgomery and Howard counties, and the city of Baltimore, to be the first; the eight counties of the Eastern Shore to be the second; and Baltimore, Harford, Frederick, Washington, Allegany and Carroll counties, to be the third. The Governor, elected from the third district in October last, shall continue in office during the term for which he was elected. The Governor shall be taken from the first district, at the first election of Governor under this constitution; from the second district at the second election; and from the third district at the third election; and in like manner, afterwards, from each district, in regular succession.

Sec. 6. A person to be eligible to the office of Governor, must have attained the age of thirty years, and been for five years a citizen of the United States, and for five years next preceding his election a resident of the State, and for three years a resident of the district from which he was elected.

Sec. 7. In case of the death or resignation of the Governor, or of his removal from the State, the General Assembly, if in session, or if not, at their next session, shall elect some other qualified resident of the same district, to be the Governor for the residue of the term for which the said Governor had been elected.

Sec. 8. In case of any vacancy in the office of Governor during the recess of the Legislature, the President of the Senate shall discharge the duties of said office till a Governor is elected as herein provided for; and in case of the death or resignation of said President, or of his removal from the State, or of his refusal to serve, then the duties of said office shall, in like manner, and for the same interval, devolve upon the Speaker of the House of Delegates, and the Legislature may provide by law for the case of impeachment or inability of the Governor, and declare what person shall perform the executive duties during such impeachment or inability; and for any vacancy in said office, not herein provided for, provision may be made by law, and if such vacancy should occur without such provision being made, the Legislature shall be convened by the Secretary of State for the purpose of filling said vacancy.

Sec. 9. The Governor shall be commander in chief of the land and naval forces of the State, and may call out the militia to repel invasions, suppress insurrections, and enforce the execution of the laws; but shall not take the command in person without the consent of the Legislature.

Sec. 10. He shall take care that the laws be faithfully executed.

Sec. 11. He shall nominate, and by and with the advice and consent of the Senate, appoint all civil and military officers of the State whose appointment or election is not otherwise herein provided for, unless a different mode of appointment be prescribed by the law creating the office.

Sec. 12. In case of any vacancy during the recess of the Senate, in any office which the Governor has power to fill, he shall appoint some suitable person to said office, whose commission shall continue in force till the end of the next session of the Legislature, or till some other person is appointed to the same office, which ever shall first occur, and the nomination of the person thus appointed during the recess, or of some other person in his place, shall be made to the Senate within thirty days after the next meeting of the Legislature.

Sec. 13. No person after being rejected by the Senate, shall be again nominated for the same office at the same session, unless at the request of the Senate; or be appointed to the same office during the recess of the Legislature.

Sec. 14. All civil officers appointed by the Governor and Senate, shall be nominated to the Senate within fifty days from the commencement of each regular session of the Legislature; and their term of office shall commence on the first Monday of May next ensuing their appointment, and continue for two years, (unless sooner removed from office,) and until their successors, respectively, qualify according to law.

Sec. 15. The Governor may suspend or arrest any military officer of the State, for disobedience of orders, or other military offence, and may remove him in pursuance of the sentence of a court-martial; and may remove for incompetency or misconduct, all civil officers who receive appointments from the executive for a term not exceeding two years.

Sec. 16. The Governor may convene the Legislature, or the Senate alone, on extraordinary occasions; and whenever from the presence of an enemy, or from any other cause, the seat of government shall become an unsafe place for the meeting of the Legislature, he may direct their sessions to be held at some other convenient place.

Sec. 17. It shall be the duty of the Governor semi-annually, and oftener if he deem it expedient, to examine the bank book, account books, and official proceedings of the Treasurer and Comptroller of the State.

Sec. 18. He shall from time to time inform the Legislature of the condition of the State, and recommend to their consideration such measures as he may judge necessary and expedient.

Sec. 19. He shall have power to grant reprieves and pardons except in cases of impeachment, and in cases in which he is prohibited by other articles of this Constitution, and to remit fines and forfeitures for offences against the State; but shall not remit the principal or interest of any debt due to the State except in cases of fines and forfeitures; and before granting a nolle prosequi, or pardon, he shall give notice in one or more newspapers of the application made for it, and of the day, on or after which his decision will be given; and in every case in which he exercises this power he shall report to either branch of the Legislature, whenever required, the petitions, recommendations and reasons which influence his decision.

Sec. 20. The Governor shall reside at the seat of government, and shall receive for his services an annual salary of thirty-six hundred dollars.

Sec. 21. When the public interest requires it, he shall have power to employ counsel, who shall be entitled to such compensation as the Legislature may allow in each case after the services of such counsel shall have been performed.

Sec. 22. A Secretary of State shall be appointed by the Governor, by and with the advice and consent of the Senate, who shall continue in office, unless sooner removed by the Governor, till the end of the official term of the Governor from whom he received his appointment, and shall receive an annual salary of one thousand dollars.

Sec. 23. He shall carefully keep and preserve a record of all official acts and proceedings, (which may, at all times, be inspected by a committee of either branch of the Legislature,) and shall perform such other duties as may be prescribed by law, or as may properly belong to his office.

ARTICLE III.

Legislative Department.

Sec. 1. The legislature shall consist of two distinct branches, a Senate and a House of Delegates, which shall be styled "The General Assembly of Maryland."

Sec. 2. Every county of the State and the city of Baltimore, shall be entitled to elect one Senator, who shall be elected by the qualified voters of the counties and city of Baltimore respectively, and who shall serve for four years from the day of their election.

Sec. 3. The Legislature at its first session after the returns of the National Census of eighteen hundred and sixty are published, and in like manner after each subsequent census, shall apportion the members of the House of Delegates among the several counties of the State, according to the population of each, and shall always allow to the city of Baltimore four more delegates than are allowed to the most populous county, but no county shall be entitled to less than two members, nor shall the whole number of delegates ever exceed eighty or be less than sixty-five; and until the apportionment is made under the census of eighteen hundred and sixty, St. Mary's county shall be entitled to two delegates; Kent two; Anne Arundel three; Calvert two; Charles two; Baltimore county six; Talbot two; Somerset four; Dorchester three; Cecil three; Prince George's three; Queen Anne's two; Worcester three; Frederick six; Harford three; Caroline two; Baltimore city ten; Washington five; Montgomery two; Allegany four; Carroll three and Howard two.

Sec. 4. The members of the House of Delegates shall be elected by the qualified voters of the counties and city of Baltimore respectively, to serve for two years from the day of their election.

Sec. 5. The first election for delegates shall take place on the first Wednesday of November, eighteen hundred and fifty-one; and the elections for delegates, and for one half of the senators as nearly as practicable, shall be held on the same day in every second year thereafter, but an election for senators shall be held in the year eighteen hundred and fifty-one in Howard county and all those counties in which senators were elected in the year eighteen hundred and forty-six.

Sec. 6. Immediately after the Senate shall have convened after the first election under this constitution, the senators shall be divided by lot, into two classes, as nearly equal in number as may be, the senators of the first class shall go out of office at the expiration of two years, and senators shall be elected on the first Wednesday of November, eighteen hundred and fifty three, for the term of four years, to supply their places; so that, after the first election, one-half of the senators may be chosen every second year; provided, that in no case shall any senator be placed in a class which shall entitle him to serve for a longer term than that for which he was elected. In case the number of senators be hereafter increased, such classification of the additional senators shall be made as to preserve as nearly as may be an equal number in each class.

Sec. 7. The General Assembly shall meet on the first Wednesday of January, eighteen hundred and fifty-two, on the same day in the year eighteen hundred and fifty-three, and on the same day in the year eighteen hundred and fifty-four, and on the same day in every second year thereafter, and at no other time, unless convened by the Proclamation of the Governor.

Sec. 8. The General Assembly may continue their first two sessions after the adoption of this constitution, as long as in the opinion of the two Houses, the public interests may require it, but all subsequent regular sessions of the General Assembly shall be closed on the tenth day of March next ensuing the time of their commencement, unless the same shall be closed at an earlier day by the agreement of the two Houses.

Sec. 9. No person shall be eligible as a Senator or Delegate who, at the time of his election, is not a citizen of the United States, and who has not resided at least three years next preceding the day of his election in this State, and the last year thereof in the county or city which he may be chosen to represent, if such county or city shall have been so long established, and if not then in the county from which, in whole or in part, the same may have been formed; nor shall any person be eligible as a Senator, unless he shall have attained the age of twenty-five years, nor as a Delegate, unless he shall have attained the age of twenty-one years at the time of his election.

Sec. 10. No member of Congress, or persons holding any civil or military office under the United States, shall be eligible as a Senator or Delegate, and if any person shall, after his election as a Senator or Delegate, be elected to Congress, or be appointed to any office, civil or military, under the government of the United States, his acceptance thereof shall vacate his seat.

Sec. 11. No Minister or Preacher of the gospel, of any denomination, and, no person holding any civil office of profit or trust under this State, except justices of the peace, shall be eligible as Senator or Delegate.

Sec. 12. Each House shall be judge of the qualifications and elections of its members, subject to the laws of the State, appoint its own officers, determine the rules of its own proceedings, punish a member for disorderly or disrespectful behaviour, and with the consent of two-thirds expel a member; but no member shall be expelled a second time for the same offence.

Sec. 13. A majority of each House shall constitute a quorum for the transaction of business, but a smaller number may adjourn from day to day, and compel the attendance of absent members in such manner and under such penalties as each House may prescribe.

Sec. 14. The doors of each House and of committees of the whole shall be open, except when the business is such as ought to be kept secret.

Sec. 15. Each House shall keep a journal of its proceedings, and cause the same to be published. The yeas and nays of members on any question shall, at the call of any five of them, in the House of Delegates or one in the Senate, be entered on the journal.

Sec. 16. Neither House shall, without the consent of the other, adjourn for more than three days; nor to any other place than that in which the House shall be sitting, without the concurrent vote of two-thirds of the members present.

Sec. 17. The style of all laws of this State, shall be, "Be it enacted by the General Assembly of Maryland," and all laws shall be passed by original bill, and every law enacted by the legislature shall embrace but one subject, and that shall be described in the title, and no law or section of law shall be revived, amended or repealed by reference to its title or section only; and it shall be the duty of the legislature at the first session after the adoption of this constitution, to appoint two commissioners learned in the law, to revise and codify the laws of this State; and the said commissioners shall report the said code, so formed, to the legislature, within a time to be by it determined, for its approval, amendment or rejection, and if adopted after the revision and codification of the said laws, it shall be the duty of the legislature in amending any article or section thereof to enact the same as the said article or section would read when amended. And whenever the legislature shall enact any public general law, not amendatory of any section or article in the said code, it shall be the duty of the legislature to enact the same in Articles and Sections, in the same manner as the said code may be arranged; and to provide for the publication of all additions and alterations which may be made to the said code, and it shall also be the duty of the legislature to appoint one or more commissioners learned in the law, whose duty it shall be to revise, simplify and abridge the rules of practice, pleadings, forms of conveyancing, and proceedings of the Courts of Record in this State.

Sec. 18. Any bill may originate in either House of the General Assembly, and be altered, amended or rejected by the other; but no bill shall originate in either House during the last three days of the session, or become a law, until it be read on three different days of the session in each House, unless three-fourths of the members of the House, where such bill is pending, shall so determine.

Sec. 19. No bill shall become a law unless it be passed in each House by a majority of the whole number of members elected, and on its final passage the ayes and noes be recorded.

Sec. 20. No money shall be drawn from the Treasury of the State, except in accordance with an appropriation made by law, and every such law shall distinctly specify the sum appropriated and the object to which it shall be applied, provided that nothing herein contained shall prevent the Legislature from placing a contingent fund at the disposal of the Executive, who shall report to the Legislature at each session the amount expended and the purposes to which it was applied. An accurate statement of the receipts and expenditures of the public money shall be attached, to and published with the laws after each regular session of the General Assembly.

Sec. 21. No divorce shall be granted by the General Assembly.

Sec. 22. No debt shall hereafter be contracted by the Legislature, unless such debt shall be authorized by a law providing for the collection of an annual tax or taxes sufficient to pay the interest on such debt as it falls due, and also to discharge the principal thereof, within fifteen years from the time of contracting the same, and the taxes laid for this purpose shall not be repealed or applied to any other object until the said debt and the interest thereon shall be fully discharged, and the amount of debts so contracted and remaining unpaid shall never exceed one hundred thousand dollars. The credit of the State shall not, in any manner, be given or loaned to or in aid of any individual, association or corporation, nor shall the General Assembly have the power, in any mode, to involve the State in the construction of works of Internal Improvement, or in any enterprise which shall involve the faith or credit of the State, or make any appropriations therefor. And they shall not use or appropriate the proceeds of the Internal Improvement companies, or of the State tax now levied or which may hereafter be levied, to pay off the public debt, to any other purpose, until the interest and debt are fully paid, or the sinking fund shall be equal to the amount of the outstanding debt, but the Legislature may, without laying a tax, borrow an amount never to exceed fifty thousand dollars, to meet temporary deficiencies in the Treasury, and may contract debts to any amount that may be necessary for the defence of the State.

Sec. 23. No extra compensation shall be granted or allowed by the General Assembly to any public officer, agent, servant or contractor after the services shall have been rendered or the contract entered into. Nor shall the salary or compensation of any public officer be increased or diminished during his term of office.

Sec. 24. No senator or delegate, after qualifying as such, shall, during the term for which he was elected, be eligible to any office which shall have been created, or the salary or profits of which shall have been increased, during such term, or shall, during said term, hold any office or receive the salary or profits of any office, under the appointment of the Executive or Legislature.

Sec. 25. Each House may punish, by imprisonment, during the session of the General Assembly, any person not a member, for disrespectful or disorderly behaviour in its presence, or for obstructing any of its proceedings or any of its officers in the execution of their duties; provided, such imprisonment shall not, at any one time, exceed ten days.

Sec. 26. The members of each House shall, in all cases, except treason, felony or other criminal offence, be privileged from arrest during their attendance at the session of the General Assembly, and in going to and returning from the same, allowing one day for every thirty miles such member may reside from the place at which the General Assembly is convened.

Sec. 27. No senator or delegate shall be liable, in any civil action or criminal prosecution whatever, for words spoken in debate.

Sec. 28. The House of Delegates may inquire, on the oath of witnesses, into all complaints, grievances and offences, as the Grand Inquest of the State, and may commit any person for any crime to the public jail, there to remain until discharged by due course of law—they may examine and pass all accounts of the State, relating either in the collection or expenditure of the revenue, and appoint auditors to state and adjust the same—they may call for all public or official papers and records, and send for persons whom they may judge necessary in the course of their inquiries concerning affairs relating to the public interest, and may direct all office bonds which shall be made payable to the State, to be sued for any breach of duty.

Sec. 29. In case of death, disqualification, resignation, refusal to act, expulsion or removal from the county or city for which he shall have been elected, of any person who shall have been chosen as a delegate or senator, or in case of a tie between two or more such qualified persons, a warrant of election shall be issued by the Speaker of the House of Delegates or President of the Senate, as the case may be, for the election of another person in his place, of which election, not less than ten days' notice shall be given exclusive of the day of the publication of the notice and of the day of election; and in case of such resignation or refusal to act, being communicated, in writing, to the Governor, by the person making it, or if such death occur during the legislative recess and more than ten days before its termination, it shall be the duty of the Governor to issue a warrant of election to supply the vacancy thus created in the same manner that the said Speaker or President might have done during the session of the Legislature; provided, however, that unless a meeting of the General Assembly may intervene, the election thus ordered to fill such vacancy shall be held on the day of the ensuing election for delegates and senators.

Sec. 30. The senators and delegates shall receive a per diem of four dollars and such mileage as may be allowed by law, and the presiding officer of each House shall be allowed an addition of one dollar per day. No book or other printed matter not appertaining to the business of the session, shall be purchased or subscribed for, for the use of the members, or be distributed among them, at the public expense.

Sec. 31. No law passed by the General Assembly, shall take effect until the first day of June next, after the session at which it may be passed, unless it be otherwise expressly declared therein.

Sec. 32. No law shall be passed creating the office of Attorney General.

Sec. 33. The General Assembly shall have full power to exclude from the privilege of voting at elections, or of holding any civil or military office in this State, any person who may thereafter be convicted of perjury, bribery or other felony, unless such person shall have been pardoned by the Executive.

Sec. 34. Every bill when passed by the General Assembly and sealed with the Great Seal, shall be presented to the Governor, who shall sign the same in the presence of the presiding officers and chief clerks of the Senate and House of Delegates. Every law shall be recorded in the office of the Court of Appeals, and in due time be printed, published and certified under the great seal to the several courts in the same manner as has been heretofore usual in this State.

Sec. 35. No person who may hereafter be a collector, receiver or holder of public moneys shall be eligible as senator or delegate or to any office of profit or trust under this State, until he shall have accounted for and paid into the Treasury all sums on the books thereof, charged to and due by him.

Sec. 36. Any citizen of this State who shall, after the adoption of this constitution, either in or out of this State, fight a duel with deadly weapons, or send or accept a challenge so to do, or who shall act as second, or knowingly aid or assist in any manner, those thus offending, shall ever thereafter be incapable of holding any office of trust or profit under this State.

Sec. 37. No lottery grant shall ever hereafter be authorized by the Legislature.

Sec. 38. The General Assembly shall pass laws necessary to protect the property of the wife from the debts of the husband during her life, and for securing the same to her issue after her death.

Sec. 39. Laws shall be passed by the Legislature to protect from execution a reasonable amount of the property of a debtor, not exceeding in value the sum of five hundred dollars.

Sec. 40. The Legislature shall at its first session after the adoption of this Constitution, adopt some simple and uniform system of charges in the offices of clerks of courts and registers of wills in the counties of this State and the city of Baltimore, and for the collection thereof; provided, the amount of compensation to any of said officers shall not exceed the sum of twenty-five hundred dollars a year, over and above office expenses, and compensation to assistants; and provided further, that such compensation of clerks, registers, assistants and office expenses, shall always be paid out of the fees or receipts of the offices respectively.

Sec. 41. The House of Delegates shall have the sole power of impeachment in all cases, but a majority of all the members must concur in an impeachment; all impeachments shall be tried by the Senate, and when sitting for that purpose, they shall be on oath or affirmation to do justice according to the law and evidence, but no person shall be convicted without the concurrence of two-thirds of all the Senators.

Sec. 42. That it shall be the duty of the Legislature, so soon as the public debt shall have been fully paid off, to cause to be transferred to the several counties and the city of Baltimore, stock in the Internal Improvement companies, equal to the amount respectively paid by each towards the erection and completion of said works at the then market value of said stock.

Sec. 43. The Legislature shall not pass any law abolishing the relation of master or slave, as it now exists in this State.

Sec. 44. No person shall be imprisoned for debt.

Sec. 45. The Legislature hereafter shall grant no charter for banking purposes or renew any banking corporation now in existence, except upon the condition that the stockholders and directors shall be liable to the amount of their respective share or shares of stock in such banking institution for all its debts and liabilities upon note, bill or otherwise; and upon the further condition that no director or other officer of said corporation shall borrow any money from said corporation; and if any director or other officer shall be convicted upon indictment of directly or indirectly violating this article, he shall be punished by fine or imprisonment at the discretion of the court. All banks shall be open to inspection of their books, papers and accounts, under such regulations as may be prescribed by law.

Sec. 46. The Legislature shall enact no law authorizing private property to be taken for public use without just compensation, as agreed upon between the parties or awarded by a jury, being first paid or tendered to the party entitled to such compensation.

Sec. 47. Corporations may be formed under general laws, but shall not be created by special act, except for municipal purposes, and in cases where, in the judgment of the Legislature, the object of the corporation cannot be attained under general laws. All laws and special acts, pursuant to this section, may be altered from time to time, or repealed; provided nothing herein contained shall be construed to alter, change or amend in any manner the article in relation to banks.

Sec. 48. The Legislature shall make provision for all cases of contested elections of any of the officers not herein provided for.

Sec. 49. The rate of interest in this State shall not exceed six per cent. per annum, and no higher rate shall be taken or demanded, and the Legislature shall provide by law all necessary forfeitures and penalties against usury.

ARTICLE IV.

Judiciary Department.

Sec. 1. The Judicial power of this State shall be vested in a Court of Appeals, in Circuit Courts, in such Courts for the city of Baltimore as may be hereinafter prescribed, and in Justices of the Peace.

Sec. 2. The Court of Appeals shall have appellate jurisdiction only, which shall be co-extensive with the limits of the State. It shall consist of a chief justice and three associate justices, any three of whom shall form a quorum, whose judgment shall be final and conclusive in all cases of appeals; and who shall have the jurisdiction which the present Court of Appeals of this State now has, and such other appellate jurisdiction as hereafter may be provided for by law. And in every case decided, an opinion in writing shall be filed, and provision shall be made, by law, for publishing reports of cases argued and determined in the said court. The Governor, for the time being, by and with the advice and consent of the Senate, shall designate the chief justice, and the Court of Appeals shall hold its sessions at the city of Annapolis, on the first Monday of June, and the first Monday of December, in each and every year.

Sec. 3. The Court of Appeals shall appoint its own clerk, who shall hold his office for six years, and may be re-appointed at the end thereof; he shall be subject to removal by the said court for incompetency, neglect of duty, misdemeanor in office, and for such other causes as may be prescribed by law.

Sec. 4. The State shall be divided into four Judicial districts: Allegany, Washington, Frederick, Carroll, Baltimore and Harford counties shall compose the first; Montgomery, Howard, Anne Arundel, Calvert, St. Mary's, Charles and Prince George's the second; Baltimore city the third; and Cecil, Kent, Queen Anne's, Talbot, Caroline, Dorchester, Somerset and Worcester shall compose the fourth district. And one person from among those learned in the law, having been admitted to practice in this State, and who shall have been a citizen of this State at least five years, and above the age of thirty years at the time of his election, and a resident of the judicial district, shall be elected from each of said districts by the legal and qualified voters therein, as a judge of the said Court of Appeals, who shall hold his office for the term of ten years from the time of his election, or until he shall have attained the age of seventy years, whichever may first happen, and be re-eligible thereto until he shall have attained the age of seventy years and not after, subject to removal for incompetency, willful neglect of duty or misbehaviour in office, on conviction in a court of law, or by the Governor upon the address of the General Assembly, two-thirds of the members of each House concurring in such address; and the salary of each of the judges of the Court of Appeals shall be two thousand five hundred dollars annually, and shall not be increased or diminished during their continuance in office; and no fees or perquisites of any kind shall be allowed by law to any of the said judges.

Sec. 5. No Judge of the Court of Appeals shall sit in any case, wherein he may be interested, or where either of the parties may be connected by affinity or consanguinity within such degrees as may be prescribed by law, or when he shall have been of counsel in said case; when the court of appeals, or any of its members, shall be thus disqualified to hear and determine any case or cases in said court, so that by reason thereof no judgment can be rendered in said court, the same shall be certified to the Governor of the State, who shall immediately commission the requisite number of persons learned in the law for the trial and determination of said case or cases.

Sec. 6. All Judges of the court of Appeals, of the circuit courts, and of the courts of the city of Baltimore, shall by virtue of their offices, be conservators of the peace throughout the State.

Sec. 7. All public commissions and grants shall run thus: The State of Maryland," &c., and shall be signed by the Governor, with the seal of the State annexed; all writs and processes shall run in the same style, and be tested, sealed and signed as usual; and all indictments shall conclude "against the peace, government and dignity of the State."

Sec. 8. The State shall be divided into eight Judicial Circuits, in manner and form following, to wit: St. Mary's, Charles and Prince George's counties shall be the first; Anne Arundel, Howard, Calvert and Montgomery counties shall be the second; Frederick and Carroll counties shall be the third; Washington and Allegany counties shall be the fourth; Baltimore city shall be the fifth; Baltimore, Harford and Cecil counties shall be the sixth; Kent, Queen Anne's, Talbot and Caroline counties shall be the seventh; and Dorchester, Somerset and Worcester counties shall be the eighth; and there shall be elected, as hereinafter directed, for each of the said Judicial circuits, except the fifth, one person from among those learned in the law, having been admitted to practice in this State, and who shall have been a citizen of this State at least five years, and above the age of thirty years at the time of his election, and a resident of the Judicial Circuit to be Judge thereof; the said judges shall be styled Circuit Judges, and shall respectively hold a term of their courts at least twice in each year, or oftener if required by law, in each county composing their respective circuits; and the said courts shall be called Circuit Courts for the county in which they may be held, and shall have, and exercise in the several counties of this State, all the power, authority and jurisdiction which the county courts of this State now have, and exercise, or which may hereafter be prescribed by law, and the said judges in their respective circuits shall have and exercise all the power, authority and jurisdiction of the present Court of Chancery of Maryland; *Provided*, nevertheless, that Baltimore County Court may hold its sittings within the limits of the city of Baltimore until provision shall be made by law for the location of a county seat, within the limits of the said county proper, and the erection of a court house and all other appropriate buildings, for the convenient administration of justice in said court.

Sec. 9. The judges of the several judicial circuits shall be citizens of the United States, and shall have resided five years in this State, and two years in the judicial circuit for which they may be respectively elected, next before the time of their election, and shall reside therein, while they continue to act as judges; they shall be taken from among those who, having the other qualifications herein prescribed, are most distinguished for integrity, wisdom and sound legal knowledge, and shall be elected by the qualified voters of the said circuits, and shall hold their offices for the term of ten years, removable for misbehaviour, on conviction in any court of law, or by the Governor upon the address of the General Assembly, provided that two-thirds of the members of each House shall concur in such address; and the said judges shall each receive a salary of two thousand dollars a year, and the same shall not be increased or diminished during the time of their continuance in office; and no judge of any court in this State, shall receive any perquisite, fee, commission or reward, in addition thereto, for the performance of any judicial duty.

Sec. 10. There shall be established for the city of Baltimore, one court of law, to be styled "The Court of Common Pleas," which shall have civil jurisdiction in all suits, where the debt or damage claimed shall be over one hundred dollars, and shall not exceed five hundred dollars; and shall also have jurisdiction in all cases of appeal from the judgment of justices of the peace in the said city, and shall have jurisdiction in all applications for the benefit of the insolvent laws of this State, and the supervision and control of the Trustees thereof.

Sec. 11. There shall also be established for the city of Baltimore, another court of law, to be styled the Superior Court of Baltimore city, which shall have jurisdiction over all suits where the debt or damage claimed shall exceed the sum of five hundred dollars, and in case any plaintiff or plaintiffs shall recover less than the sum or value of five hundred dollars, he or they, shall be allowed or adjudged to pay costs in the discretion of the court. The said court shall also have jurisdiction as a court of equity within the limits of the said city, and in all other civil cases which have not been heretofore assigned to the Court of Common Pleas.

Sec. 12. Each of the said two courts shall consist of one judge, who shall be elected by the legal and qualified voters of the said city, and shall hold his office for the term of ten years, subject to the provisions of this constitution, with regard to the election and qualification of judges, and their removal from office; and the salary of each of the said judges shall be twenty-five hundred dollars a year, and the Legislature shall, whenever it may think the same proper and expedient, provide, by law, another court for the city of Baltimore, to consist of one judge, to be elected by the qualified voters of the said city, who shall be subject to the same constitutional provisions, hold his office for the same term of years, and receive the same compensation as the judge of the Court of Common Pleas of the said city; and the said court shall have such jurisdiction and powers as may be prescribed by law.

Sec. 13. There shall also be a Criminal Court for the city of Baltimore, to be styled the Criminal Court of Baltimore, which shall consist of one judge, who shall also be elected by the legal and qualified voters of the said city, and who shall have and exercise all the jurisdiction now exercised by Baltimore City Court, and the said judge shall receive a salary of two thousand dollars a year, shall be subject to the provisions of this constitution with regard to the election and qualification of judges' term of office, and removal therefrom.

Sec. 14. There shall be in each county a clerk of the Circuit Court, who shall be elected by the qualified voters of each county, and the person receiving the greatest number of votes shall be declared and returned duly elected clerk of said Circuit Court for the said county, and shall hold his office for the term of six years from the time of his election, and until a new election is held shall be re-eligible thereto, and subject to removal for willful neglect of duty, or other misdemeanor in office on conviction in a court of law. There shall also be a clerk of the Court of Common Pleas, in Baltimore city, and a clerk of the Superior Court of Baltimore City, and there shall also be a clerk of the Criminal Court of Baltimore City, and each of said clerks shall be elected as aforesaid by the qualified voters of the city of Baltimore, and shall hold his office for six years from the time of his election and until a new election is held, and be re-eligible thereto, subject, in like manner, to be removed for willful neglect of duty or other misdemeanor in office on conviction in a court of law. In case of a vacancy in the office of a clerk, the judge or judges of the court of which he was clerk, shall have the power to appoint a clerk until the general election of Delegates held next thereafter, when a clerk shall be elected to fill such vacancy.

Sec. 15. The clerk of the Court of Common Pleas for Baltimore city shall have authority to issue within the said city all marriage and other licenses required by law, subject to such provisions as the Legislature shall hereafter prescribe; and the clerk of the Superior Court for said city shall have the custody of all deeds, conveyances and other papers, now remaining in the office of the clerk of Baltimore county court, and shall hereafter receive and record all deeds, conveyances and other papers, which are required by law to be recorded in said city. He shall also have the custody of all other papers connected with the proceedings on the law or equity side of Baltimore county court and of the dockets thereof, so far as the same have relation to Baltimore city.

Sec. 16. That the Clerk of the Court of Appeals, and the Clerks of the Circuit Courts in the several counties, shall respectively perform all the duties and be entitled to the fees which appertain to the offices of the Clerks of Court of Appeals for the Eastern and Western Shores, and of the Clerks of County Courts; and the Clerks of the Court of Common Pleas, the superior court, and the criminal court for Balti more city, shall perform all the duties appertaining to their respective offices, and heretofore vested in the clerks of Baltimore county court and Baltimore city court respectively, and be entitled to all the fees now allowed by law; and all laws relating to the clerks of Court of Appeals, clerks of the several county courts and Baltimore city court, shall be applicable to the clerks respectively of the Court of Appeals, the Circuit Courts, the Court of Common Pleas, the superior court and the criminal court of Baltimore city, until otherwise provided by law; and the said clerks, when duly elected and qualified according to law, shall have the charge and custody of the records and other papers belonging to their respective offices.

Sec. 17. The qualified voters of the city of Baltimore, and of the several counties of the State, shall, on the first Wednesday of November, eighteen hundred and fifty-one, and on the same day of the same month in every fourth year for ever thereafter, elect three men to be judges of the Orphans' Court of said city and counties respectively, who shall be citizens of the State of Maryland, and citizens of the city or county for which they may be severally elected at the time of their election. They shall have all the powers now vested in the Orphans' Courts of this State, subject to such changes therein as the Legislature may prescribe, and each of said judges shall be paid at a per diem rate, for the time they are in session, to be fixed by the Legislature, and paid by the said counties and city respectively.

Sec. 18. There shall be a Register of Wills in each county of the State and in the city of Baltimore, to be elected by the legal and qualified voters of said counties and city respectively, who shall hold his office for six years from the time of his election, and until a new election shall take place, and be re-eligible thereto, subject to be removed for willful neglect of duty, or misdemeanor in office, in the same manner that the clerks of the County Courts are removable. In the event of any vacancy in the office of Register of Wills, said vacancy shall be filled by the Judges of the Orphans' Court, until the general election next thereafter for Delegates to the General Assembly, when a Register shall be elected to fill such vacancy.

Sec. 19. The Legislature, at its first session after the adoption of this Constitution, shall fix the number of the Justices of the Peace and Constables for each ward of the city of Baltimore, and for each election district in the several counties, who shall be elected by the legal and qualified voters thereof respectively at the next general election for Delegates thereafter, and shall hold their offices for two years from the time of their election, and until their successors in office are elected and qualified; and the Legislature may from time to time increase or diminish the number of Justices of the Peace and Constables to be elected in the several wards and election districts, as the wants and interests of the people may require. They shall be, by virtue of their offices, conservators of the peace in the said counties and city respectively, and shall have such duties and compensation as now exist or may be provided for by law. In the event of a vacancy in the office of a Justice of the Peace, the Governor shall appoint a person to serve as Justice of the Peace until the next regular election of said officers; and in case of a vacancy in the office of Constable, the County Commissioners of the county in which a vacancy may occur, or the Mayor and City Council of Baltimore, as the case may be, shall appoint a person to serve as Constable until the next regular election thereafter for said officers. An appeal shall lie in all civil cases from the judgment of a Justice of the Peace to the Circuit Court or to the Court of Common Pleas of Baltimore city, as the case may be, and on all such appeals either party shall be entitled to a trial by jury, according to the laws now existing or which may be hereafter enacted. And the Mayor and City Council may provide, by ordinance, from time to time, for the creation and government of such temporary additional police as they may deem necessary to preserve the public peace.

Sec. 20. There shall be elected in each county and in the city of Baltimore, every second year, two persons for the office of sheriff for each county, and two for the said city, the one of whom having the highest number of votes of the qualified voters of said county or city, or if both have an equal number, either of them, at the discretion of the Governor, to be commissioned by the Governor for the said office, and having served for two years, such person shall be ineligible for the two years next succeeding; bond with security, to be taken every year, and no sheriff shall be qualified to act before the same be given. In case of death, refusal, disqualification or removal out of the county before the expiration of the said two years, the other person chosen as aforesaid shall be commissioned by the Governor to execute the said office for the residue of the said two years, the said person giving bond with security as aforesaid. No person shall be eligible to the office of sheriff but a resident of such county or city respectively, who shall have been a citizen of this State at least five years preceding his election, and above the age of twenty-one years. The two candidates, properly qualified, having the highest number of legal ballots, shall be declared duly elected for the office of sheriff for such county or city, and returned to the Governor, with a certificate of the number of ballots for each of them.

Sec. 21. Coroners, Elisors and Notaries Public shall be appointed for each county and the city of Baltimore, in the manner now prescribed by law, or in such other manner as the General Assembly may hereafter direct.

Sec. 22. No Judge shall sit in any case wherein he may be interested, or where either of the parties may be connected with him by affinity or consanguinity, within such degrees as may be prescribed by law, or where he shall have been of counsel in the case; and whenever any of the judges of the circuit courts, or of the courts for Baltimore city shall be thus disqualified, or whenever, by reason of sickness, or any other cause, the said judges or any of them, may be unable to sit in any cause, the parties may, by consent, appoint a proper person to try the said cause, or the judges or any of them shall do so, when directed by law.

Sec. 23. The present chancellor and the register in chancery, and in the event of any vacancy in their respective offices, their successors in office respectively, who are to be appointed as at present, by the Governor and Senate, shall continue in office, with the powers and compensation as at present established, until the expiration of two years after the adoption of this Constitution by the people, and until the end of the session of the Legislature next thereafter, after which the said offices of Chancellor and Register shall be abolished. The Legislature shall, in the meantime, provide by law for the recording, safe keeping or other disposition, of the records, decrees and other proceedings of the court of chancery, and for the copying and attestation thereof, and for the custody and use of the great seal of the State, when required, after the expiration of the said two years, and for transmitting to the said counties and to the city of Baltimore, all the cases and proceedings in said court then undisposed of and unfinished, in such manner, and under such regulations as may be deemed necessary and proper; provided that no new business shall originate in the said court, nor shall any cause be removed to the same from any other court, from and after the ratification of this Constitution.

Sec. 24. The first election of Judges, Clerks, Registers of Wills, and all other officers, whose election by the people is provided for in this article of the constitution, except Justices of the Peace and constables, shall take place throughout the State on the first Wednesday of November next after the ratification of this constitution by the people.

Sec. 25. In case of the death, resignation, removal, or other disqualification of a Judge of any of the Courts of law, the Governor, by and with the advice and consent of the Senate, shall thereupon appoint a person duly qualified to fill said office, until the next general election for delegates thereafter; at which time an election shall be held as herein before prescribed, for a judge, who shall hold the said office for ten years, according to the provisions of this Constitution.

Sec. 26. In case of the death, resignation, removal, or other disqualification of the judge of an Orphans' court, the vacancy shall be filled by the appointment of the Governor, by and with the advice and consent of the Senate.

Sec. 27. Whenever lands lie partly in one county and partly in another, or partly in a county and partly in the city of Baltimore, or whenever persons proper to be made defendants to proceedings in chancery, reside some in one county, and some in another, that court shall have jurisdiction in which proceedings shall have been first commenced, subject to such rules, regulations and alterations as may be prescribed by law.

Sec. 28. In all suits or actions at law, issues from the Orphans' Court or from any court sitting in equity, in petitions for freedom, and in all presentments and indictments now pending, or which may be pending at the time of the adoption of this Constitution by the people, or which may be hereafter instituted in any of the courts of law of this State, having jurisdiction thereof, the judge or judges thereof, upon suggestion in writing, if made by the State's Attorney, or the prosecutor for the State, or upon suggestion in writing, supported by affidavit, made by any of the parties thereto, or other proper evidence, that a fair and impartial trial cannot be had in the court where such suit or action at law issues, or petitions or presentment and indictment is depending, shall order and direct the record of proceedings in such suit or action, issues or petitions presentment or indictment, to be transmitted to the court of any adjoining county; provided, that the removal in all civil causes be confined to an adjoining county within the judicial circuit, except as to the city of Baltimore, where the removal may be to an adjoining county, for trial, which court shall hear and determine the same in like manner as if such suit or action, issues or petitions, presentment or indictment, had been originally instituted therein; and *provided also*, that such suggestion shall be made as aforesaid, before or during the term in which the issue or issues may be joined in said suit or action, issues or petition, presentment or indictment, and that such further remedy in the premises may be provided by law as the Legislature shall from time to time direct and enact.

Sec. 29. All elections of judges and other officers provided for by this constitution, shall be certified, and the returns made by the clerks of the respective counties to the Governor, who shall issue commissions to the different persons for the offices to which they shall have been respectively elected; and in all such elections, the person having the greatest number of votes, shall be declared to be elected.

Sec. 30. If in any case of election for Judges, Clerks of the Courts of Law and Registers of Wills, the opposing candidates shall have an equal number of votes, it shall be the duty of the Governor to order a new election, and in case of any contested election, the Governor shall send the returns to the House of Delegates, who shall judge of the election and qualification of the candidates at such election.

Sec. 31. Every person of good moral character, being a voter, shall be admitted to practice law in all the courts of law in this State in his own case.

ARTICLE V.

The State's Attorneys.

Sec. 1. There shall be an Attorney for the State in each county and the city of Baltimore, to be styled "The State's Attorney," who shall be elected by the voters thereof, respectively, on the first Wednesday of November next, and on the same day every fourth year thereafter, and hold his office for four years from the first Monday of January next ensuing his election, and until his successor shall be elected and qualified, and shall be re-eligible thereto, and be subject to removal therefrom for incompetency, willful neglect of duty or misdemeanor in office, on conviction in a court of law.

Sec. 2. All elections for the State's Attorney shall be certified to, and returns made thereof, by the Clerks of the said counties and city to the Judges thereof having criminal jurisdiction, respectively, whose duty it shall be to decide upon the elections and qualifications of the persons returned, and in case of a tie between two or more persons to designate which of said persons shall qualify as State's Attorney, and to administer the oaths of office to the persons elected.

Sec. 3. The State's Attorney shall perform such duties and receive such fees and commissions as are now prescribed by law for the Attorney General and his Deputies, and such other duties, fees and commissions as may hereafter be prescribed by law; and if any State's attorney shall receive any other fee or reward than such as is, or may be allowed by law, he shall, on conviction thereof, be removed from office.

Sec. 4. No person shall be eligible to the office of State's Attorney who has not been admitted to practice the law in this State, and who has not resided for at least one year in the county or city in which he may be elected.

Sec. 5. In case of vacancy in the office of State's Attorney, or of his removal from the county or city in which he shall have been elected, or on his conviction as herein before specified, the said vacancy shall be filled by the Judge of the county or city, respectively, having criminal jurisdiction in which said vacancy shall occur, until the election and qualification of his successor; at which election said vacancy shall be filled by the voters of the said county or city, for the residue of the term thus made vacant.

Sec. 6. It shall be the duty of the Clerk of the Court of Appeals, and the Commissioner of the land office, respectively, whenever a case shall be brought into said court or office, in which the State is a party, or has an interest, immediately to notify the Governor thereof.

ARTICLE VI.

Treasury Department.

Sec. 1. There shall be a Treasury Department, consisting of a *Comptroller*, chosen by the qualified electors of the State at each election of members of the House of Delegates, who shall receive an annual salary of two thousand five hundred dollars; and of a *Treasurer*, to be appointed by the two houses of the Legislature at each session thereof, on joint ballot, who shall also receive an annual salary of two thousand five hundred dollars; and neither of the said officers shall be allowed or receive any fees, commissions or perquisites of any kind, in addition to his salary, for the performance of any duty or service whatever. In case of a vacancy in either of the offices by death or otherwise, the Governor, by and with the advice and consent of the Senate, shall fill such vacancy by appointment, to continue until another election by the people, or a choice by the legislature, as the case may be, and the qualification of the successor. The Comptroller and the Treasurer shall keep their offices at the seat of government, and shall take such oath, and enter into such bonds, for the faithful discharge of their duties, as the legislature shall prescribe.

Sec. 2. The Comptroller shall have the general superintendence of the fiscal affairs of the State; he shall digest and prepare plans for the improvement and management of the revenue, and for the support of the public credit; prepare and report estimates of the revenue and expenditure of the State; superintend and enforce the collection of all taxes and revenue; adjust, settle and preserve all public accounts; decide on the forms of keeping and stating accounts; grant, under regulations prescribed by law, all warrants for moneys to be paid out of the treasury, in pursuance of appropriations by law; prescribe the formalities of the transfer of stock or other evidences of the State debt, and countersign the same, without which such evidences shall not be valid; he shall make full reports of all his proceedings, and of the state of the Treasury Department, within ten days after the commencement of each session of the legislature, and perform such other duties as shall be prescribed by law.

Sec. 3 The Treasurer shall receive and keep the moneys of the State, and disburse the same upon warrants drawn by the Comptroller, and not otherwise; he shall take receipts for all moneys paid by him, and all receipts for moneys received by him shall be endorsed upon warrant signed by the Comptroller, without which warrants, so signed, no acknowledgment of money received into the Treasury shall be valid; and upon warrants issued by the Comptroller, he shall make arrangements for the payment of the interest of the public debt, and for the purchase thereof, on account of the sinking fund. Every bond, certificate, or other evidence of the debt of the State, shall be signed by the Treasurer, and countersigned by the Comptroller, and no new certificate, or other evidence intended to replace another, shall be issued until the old one shall be delivered to the Treasurer, and authority executed in due form for the transfer of the same, shall be filed in his office, and the transfer accordingly made on the books thereof, and the certificate or other evidence canceled; but the legislature may make provision for the loss of certificates or other evidence of the debt.

Sec. 4. The Treasurer shall render his accounts quarterly to the Comptroller; and on the third day of each session of the legislature, he shall submit to the Senate and House of Delegates, fair and accurate copies of all accounts by him from time to time rendered and settled with the Comptroller. He shall at all times submit to the Comptroller, the inspection of the moneys in his hands, and perform all other duties that shall be prescribed by law.

ARTICLE VII.

Sundry Officers.

Sec. 1. At the first general election of delegates to the General Assembly, after the adoption of this Constitution, four commissioners shall be elected as hereinafter provided, who shall be styled "Commissioners of Public Works;" and who shall exercise a diligent and faithful supervision of all public works, in which the State may be interested as stockholder or creditor, and shall represent the State in all meetings of the stockholders, and shall appoint the Directors in every Railroad or Canal company in which the State has the constitutional power to appoint Directors. It shall also be the duty of the Commissioners of Public Works to review, from time to time, the rate of tolls adopted by any company; use all legal powers which they may possess, to obtain the establishment of rates of tolls, which may prevent an injurious competition with each other, to the detriment of the interests of the State; and so to adjust them as to promote the agriculture of the State. It shall also be the duty of the said Commissioners of Public Works, to keep a journal of their proceedings; and at each regular session of the Legislature to make to it a report, and to recommend such legislation as they shall deem necessary and requisite to promote or protect the interest of the State in the public works, and perform such other duties as may be prescribed by law. They shall each receive such salary as may be allowed by law, which shall not be increased or diminished during their continuance in office.

Sec. 2. For the election of the Commissioners of Public Works, the State shall be divided into four districts The counties of Allegany, Washington, Frederick, Carroll, Baltimore and Harford, shall constitute the first district. The counties of Montgomery, Howard, Anne Arundel, Calvert, St. Mary's, Charles and Prince George's shall constitute the second district. Baltimore city shall constitute the third district. The counties of Cecil, Kent, Queen Anne's, Talbot, Caroline, Dorchester, Somerset and Worcester shall constitute the fourth district. One commissioner shall be elected in each district, who shall have been a resident thereof at least five years next preceding his election.

Sec. 3. The said Commissioners shall be elected by the qualified voters of their districts respectively; the returns of their election shall be certified to the Governor, who shall, by proclamation, declare the result of the election Two of the said Commissioners, first elected, shall hold their office for four years, and the other two for two years from the first Monday of December next succeeding their election. And at the first meeting after their election, or as soon thereafter as practicable, they shall determine, by lot, who of their number shall hold their offices for four and two years respectively; and thereafter there shall be elected as aforesaid at each general election of Delegates, two Commissioners for the term of four years, to be taken from the districts respectively, wherein the Commissioners resided at the time of their election, whose term of service has expired. And in case of a vacancy in the office of either of said Commissioners, by death, resignation, or otherwise, the Governor, by and with the advice and consent of the Senate, shall appoint some qualified person from the same district, to serve until the next general election of Delegates, when an election shall be held, as aforesaid, for a Commissioner for the residue of said term. And in case of an equal division in the Board of Commissioners, on any subject committed to their charge, the Treasurer of the State shall have power, and shall be called on to decide the same. And in the event of a tie vote for any two of the candidates for the office of Commissioner in the same district, it shall be the duty of the Governor to commission one or the other of the candidates having the equal number of votes. And if the Governor doubt the legality or result of any election held for said Commissioners, it shall be his duty to send the returns of such election to the House of Delegates, who shall judge of the election and qualification of the candidates at such election.

Sec. 4. During the continuance of the lottery system in this State, there shall be elected by the legal and qualified voters of the State at every general election for Delegates to the General Assembly, one Commissioner of Lotteries, who shall hold his office for two years, and till the qualification of his successor, and shall be re-eligible. His whole compensation shall be paid out of the fund raised for the Maryland Consolidated Lottery grants, and shall not exceed the amount of commissions received by one of the present Lottery Commissioners out of said fund; and he shall give such bond for the faithful performance of his duties as is now given by the Lottery Commissioners. The term of the Commissioner who shall be elected at the general election for Delegates next succeeding the adoption of this Constitution, shall commence at the expiration of the commissions of the present Lottery Commissioners, and continue for two years, and till the qualification of his successor.

Sec. 5. From and after the first day of April, eighteen hundred and fifty-nine, no lottery scheme shall be drawn for any purpose whatever; nor shall any lottery ticket be sold in this State. And it shall be the duty of the several Commissioners elected under this Constitution to make such contract or contracts as will extinguish all existing lottery grants before the said first day of April, eighteen hundred and fifty-nine, and also secure to the State a clear yearly revenue equal to the average amount derived by the State from the system for the last five years; but no such contract or contracts shall be valid until approved by the Treasurer and Comptroller.

Sec. 6. There shall be a Commissioner of the Land Office elected by the qualified voters of the State, at the first general election of Delegates to the Assembly after the ratification of this Constitution, who shall hold his office for the term of six years from the first day of January next after his election. The returns of said election shall be made to the Governor, and in the event of a tie between any two or more candidates, the Governor shall direct a new election to be held by writs to the several Sheriffs, who shall hold said election after at least twenty days' notice, exclusive of the day of election. The said Commissioner shall sit as judge of the Land Office, and receive therefor the sum of two hundred dollars per annum, to be paid out of the State Treasury. He shall also perform the duties of the Register of the Land Office, and be entitled to receive therefor the fees now chargeable by said officer; and he shall also perform the duties of Examiner General, and be entitled to receive therefor the fees now chargeable by said officer.

The office of Register of the Land Office and Examiner General, shall be abolished from and after the election and qualification of the Commissioner of the Land office.

Sec. 7. The State Librarian shall be elected by the joint vote of the two branches of the legislature, for two years, and until his successor shall be elected and qualify. His salary shall be one thousand dollars per annum He shall perform such duties as are now or may hereafter be prescribed by law.

Sec. 8. The county authorities now known as Levy Courts or County Commissioners, shall hereafter be styled "County Commissioners," and shall be elected by general ticket, and not by districts, by the voters of the several counties, on the first Wednesday in November, one thousand eight hundred and fifty one, and on the same day in every second year thereafter. Said Commissioners shall exercise such powers and duties only as the Legislature may from time to time prescribe, but such powers and duties and the tenure of office shall be uniform throughout the State; and the Legislature shall, at or before its second regular session after the adoption of this Constitution, pass such laws as may be necessary for determining the number for each county, and ascertaining and defining the powers, duties and tenure of office of said Commissioners; and until the passage of such laws the Commissioners elected under this Constitution shall have and exercise all the powers and duties in their respective counties now exercised by the county authorities under the laws of the State.

Sec. 9. The General Assembly shall provide by law for the election of Road Supervisors in the several counties by the voters of the election districts respectively, and may provide by law for the election or appointment of such other county officers as may be required, and are not herein provided for, and prescribe their powers and duties; but the tenure of office, their powers and duties and mode of appointment, shall be uniform throughout the State.

Sec. 10. The qualified voters of each county and the city of Baltimore shall, at the first election of delegates after the adoption of this Constitution, and every two years thereafter, elect a Surveyor for the counties and the city of Baltimore respectively, whose duties and compensation shall be the same as are now prescribed by law for the county and city Surveyors respectively, or as may hereafter be prescribed by law. The term of office of said county and city Surveyors respectively shall commence on the first Monday of January next succeeding their election; and vacancies in said office of Surveyors by death, resignation or removal from their respective counties or city, shall be filled by the Commissioners of the counties or Mayor and City Council of Baltimore respectively.

Sec. 11. The qualified voters of Worcester county shall, at the first election of delegates after the adoption of this Constitution, and every two years thereafter, elect a Wreck-Master for said county, whose duties and compensation shall be the same as are now prescribed or may be hereafter prescribed by law. The term of office of said Wreck-Master shall commence on the first Monday of January next succeeding his election; and a vacancy in said office by death, resignation or removal from the county, shall be filled by the County Commissioners of said county for the residue of the term thus made vacant.

ARTICLE VIII.

New Counties.

Sec. 1. That part of Anne Arundel county called Howard District, is hereby created into a new county, to be called Howard county; the inhabitants whereof shall have, hold and enjoy all such rights and privileges as are held and enjoyed by the inhabitants of the other counties in this State; and its civil and municipal officers at the time of the ratification of this constitution, shall continue in office until their successors shall have been elected or appointed, and shall have qualified as such; and all rights, powers and obligations incident to Howard District of Anne Arundel county shall attach to Howard county.

Sec. 2. When that part of Allegany county, lying south and west of a line beginning at the summit of Big Back Bone or Savage Mountain, where that mountain is crossed by Mason and Dixon's line, and running thence by a straight line to the middle of Savage river, where it empties into the Potomac river; thence by a straight line to the nearest point or boundary of the State of Virginia, then with said boundary to the Fairfax stone, shall contain a population of ten thousand, and the majority of electors thereof shall desire to separate and form a new county, and make known their desire by petition to the Legislature, the Legislature shall direct at the next succeeding election, that the judges shall open a book at each election district in said part of Allegany county, and have recorded therein the vote of each elector "for or against" a new county. In case the majority are in favor, then said part of Allegany county, to be declared an independent county, and the inhabitants whereof shall have and enjoy all such rights and privileges as are held and enjoyed by the inhabitants of the other counties in this State: *Provided*, That the whole representation in the General Assembly of the county when divided shall not exceed the present delegation of Allegany county allowed under this constitution, until after the next census.

ARTICLE IX.

Militia.

Sec. 1. It shall be the duty of the Legislature to pass laws for the enrollment of the militia; to provide for districting the State into divisions, brigades, battalions, regiments and companies; and to pass laws for the effectual encouragement of volunteer corps by some mode which may induce the formation and continuance of at least one volunteer company in every county and division in the city of Baltimore. The company, battalion and regimental officers (staff officers excepted) shall be elected by the persons composing their several companies, battalions and regiments.

Sec 2. The Adjutant General shall be appointed by the Governor, by and with the advice ane consent of the Senate. He shall hold his office for the term of six years, and receive the same salary as heretofore, until changed by the Legislature.

ARTICLE X.

Miscellaneous.

Sec. 1. Every officer of this State, the Governor excepted, the entire amount of whose pay or compensation received for the discharge of his official duties, shall exceed the yearly sum of three thousand dollars, shall keep a book in which shall be entered every sum or sums of money received by him or on his account as a payment or compensation for his performance of official duties, a copy of which entries in said book, verified by the oath of the officer by whom it is directed to be kept, shall be returned yearly to the Treasurer of the State for his inspection, and that of the General Assembly of Maryland; and each of such officers, when the amount received by him for the year shall exceed the sum of three thousand dsllars, shall yearly pay over to the Treasurer the amount of such excess by him received, subject to such disposition thereof as the Legislature may deem just and equitable. And any such officer failing to comply with the said requisition, shall be deemed to have vacated his office, and be subject to suit by the State for the amount that ought to have been paid into the treasury.

Sec. 2. The Legislature shall have power to pass all such laws as may be necessary and proper for carrying into execution the powers vested by this Constitution, in any department or office of the government, and the duties imposed upon them thereby.

Sec. 3. If in any election directed by this Constitution any two or more candidates shall have the highest and an equal number of votes, a new election shall be ordered, unless in cases specially provided for by the Constitution.

Sec. 4. The trial by jury of all issues of fact in civil proceedings in the several courts of law of this State, where the amount in controversy exceeds the sum of five dollars, shall be inviolably preserved.

Sec. 5. In the trial of all criminal cases, the jury shall be the judges of law as well as fact.

Sec. 6. The Legislature shall have power to regulate by law all matters which relate to the judges, time, place and manner of holding elections in this State, and of making returns thereof, provided that the tenure and term of office, and the day of election, shall not be affected thereby.

Sec. 7. All rights vested and all liabilities incurred shall remain as if this Constitution had not been adopted.

Sec. 8. The Governor and all officers, civil and military, now holding commissions under this State, shall continue to hold and exercise their offices according to their present tenure, until they shall be superseded pursuant to the provisions of this Constitution, and until their successors be duly qualified.

Sec. 9. The Sheriffs of the several counties of this State and of the city of Baltimore shall give notice of the several elections authorized by this Constitution in the manner prescribed by existing laws for elections under the present Constitution.

Sec. 10. This Constitution, if adopted by a majority of the legal votes cast on the first Wednesday of June next, shall go into operation on the fourth day of July next, and on and after said day shall supersede the present Constitution of this State.

ARTICLE XI.

Amendment of the Constitution.

It shall be the duty of the Legislature, at its first session immediately succeeding the returns of every census of the United States, hereafter taken, to pass a law for ascertaining, at the next general election of delegates, the sense of the people of Maryland in regard to calling a convention for altering the Constitution; and in case the majority of votes cast at said election shall be in favor of calling a convention, the Legislature shall provide for assembling such convention, and electing delegates thereto at the earliest convenient day; and the delegates to the said convention shall be elected by the several counties of the State and the city of Baltimore, in proportion to their representation respectively in the Senate and House of Delegates, at the time when said convention may be called.

Done in Convention the 13th day of May, in the year of our Lord eighteen hundred and fifty-one, and the independence of the United States the seventy-fifth.

J. G. CHAPMAN,
President of the Convention.

Attest—George G. Brewer,
Secretary to Convention.

INDEX

TO THE

REGISTER OF DEBATES.

A

B

D

E

F

G

I

K

L

Q

R

S

T

V

W

GENERAL
SKETCHES OF DEBATES,
PREPARED EXPRESSLY, AS SUCH,
BY ORDER OF THE CONVENTION.

MONDAY, January 13, 1851.

The Convention met (a quorum being present.)

Prayer by the Rev. Mr. GRAUFF.

The Journal of Saturday was read and approved.

HENRY G. WHEELER, appointed under the order of the Convention, official Reporter of its debates (under certain restrictions and limitations) appeared and took his seat.

The Convention resumed the consideration of the unfinished business of Saturday, being the motion of Mr. WEEMS, to reconsider the vote of the Convention upon the order submitted by Mr. THOMAS, on the 8th instant, in relation to the preparation of the Map of the State, &c.

Mr. MORGAN moved to postpone the consideration of the same until to-morrow.

Mr. SHRIVER moved that the consideration of the same be postponed until Thursday, 16th inst.

Determined in the affirmative.

On motion of Mr. BROWN, it was

Ordered, That the Secretary of this Convention direct such of the committee clerks as he may think proper, to add up the census returns for the use of the Convention.

On motion of Mr. GWINN, it was

Ordered, That it be entered upon the Journal, that Mr. MARRIOTT, a committee clerk to this Convention, is detained from this Convention by indisposition.

On motion of Mr. HARBINE, it was

Ordered, That it be entered upon the Journal, that Mr. MICHAEL NEWCOMER, a member of this Convention, is detained from the Convention by indisposition.

On motion of Mr. HEARN, it was

Ordered, That it be entered upon the Journal, that Mr. JACOBS, a member of this Convention, is detained from his seat by indisposition.

Mr. NEILL, presented the petition of sundry citizens, members of the Menonite Church, praying that the Convention will take into consideration, the necessity of making provisions in the Constitution for such societies and such persons who are conscientious in bearing arms, swearing the oath and serving as Jurors, &c.

Which was read, and on motion of Mr. NEILL, referred to committee No. 14.

THE ELECTIVE FRANCHISE.

On motion of Mr. PHELPS, the Convention again resolved itself into committee of the whole, Mr. BLAKISTONE in the chair, and resumed the consideration of the report of the committee on the Elective Franchise.

The question before the committee being upon the amendment offered by Mr. CHAMBERS, of Kent, to insert in the first section, second line, the words "for six months," in lieu of the words "for thirty days," (which had been previously stricken out by the vote of the Convention.)

Mr. BISER called the yeas and nays, which were ordered, and having been taken, were as follows:

Affirmative.—Messrs. Dent, Lee, Chambers, of Kent, Dorsey, Wells, Randall, Kent, Bond, John Dennis, Jas. U. Dennis, Crisfield, Dashiel, Williams, Hicks, Hodson. Goldsborough, Phelps, Sprigg, McCubben, McMaster and Hearn—21.

Negative.—Messrs. Chapman, President, Morgan, Blakistone, Hopewell, Ricaud, Dalrymple, Sollers, Jenifer, Buchanan, Bell, Welch, Ridgley, Lloyd, Dickinson, Sherwood, of Talbot, Colston, Chambers, of Cecil, McCullough, Miller, McLane, Bowie, Grason, George, Dirickson, Shriver, Gaither, Biser, Annan, Sappington, McHenry, Magraw, Nelson, Thawley, Stewart, of Caroline, Hardcastle, Gwinn, Brent, of Baltimore city, Fiery, Neill, John Newcomer, Harbine, Kilgour, Brewer, Waters, Weber, Hollyday, Slicer, Fitzpatrick, Smith, Park, Shower, Cockey, and Brown—53.

So the amendment was rejected.

Mr. CHAMBERS, of Kent, moved to amend the said report, as herinafter stated.

Mr. DORSEY said that in addition to what had fallen from him on a former occasion, he would now add but a few remarks. Since the adjournment of this Convention on Saturday, he had been informed of a fact, of which he was before ignorant, that increased his convictions of the expediency, nay, necessity, of filling up the blank in the manner proposed. He had learned from a gentleman in whom he reposed confidence, that this corrupting vice, of political partizans paying out of their own or party funds raised for that purpose, the costs of naturalization papers of foreigners becoming citizens, was extending itself into the counties of this State, and was not, as he had heretofore supposed it to be, confined to the city of Baltimore. His informant stating that again, again, and again, he had seen persons thus in the possession of naturalization papers, as they are called, standing at the polls of an election district of the county of his residence, awaiting the arrival of the new made citizens, who received their certificate of naturalization from the person who gave them at the same time a ticket to vote, which the person giving it, he saw deposited in the ballot-box. That the day before the last election in this State, a friend of the informant called upon him and showed him the naturalization papers of a foreigner, for which he had paid the clerk; and that in consideration thereof, this new born citizen was, by agreement, to meet him the next day at the polls, and vote the ticket that was to be given him, upon the receipt of his papers thus paid for. My informant then observed to his friend—"But how do you know that he will not cheat you in voting the ticket given him?" The reply was, "I am to see the ticket deposited in the ballot-box, and if he does not do so, he shall not have his papers at all."

This, he was credibly informed, and verily believes, was but an ordinary transaction, occurring on every election day at the polls of the different wards in the city of Baltimore. If this Convention under such circumstances will do nothing to put a check upon such abuses of the elective franchise, such foul corruptions of the ballot-box; then indeed there is no hope of the permanency of our free political institutions; which can only exist or be preserved whilst the purity of the ballot-box is protected against fraud and corruption. In all fairness he would state that the particular instance of misconduct in a county of this State, to which he had alluded, was the act of a whig, not of what in this body has been called progressive democracy, nor had he ever intimated a belief that the similar conduct, which he had described as prevailing in the city of Baltimore, was imputable to one of the political parties only. He had always regarded the odium as justly attributable to both parties. But as to what I shall say or do in this Convention, I disclaim all party ties or obligations; I belong to no party, my sole object being, in the matters now under consideration, to purge and protect the ballot-box from all impurities, and to frame such a Constitution as will give equal security and protection to every portion of the State of Maryland, and promote its tranquility and prosperity for ages yet to come.

He was free to confess that he was not so replete with the milk of human kindness and toleration, as the distinguished member from Queen Anne, who sees nothing in the acts of those patronizers of naturalization, which he had endeavored to portray; but instances of the purest and most praiseworthy charity and benevolence. Could he view their acts in the light that he does, he should be one of the last persons in the community to complain of them. To ask him to do so, was a heavier tax upon his credulity than it is able to bear. He had so long been in the habit of judging of the actions of men by the motives which prompted them, that he wanted faith in that kind of charity and benevolence, which is barren of all fruits, is hermetically sealed up for eleven-twelfths of the years, and never discloses itself or is seen or heard of, but upon the eve of a warmly contested election. In the purity or sincerity of a benevolence so novel and extraordinary, he must confess that he reposed no confidence.

Mr. BUCHANAN said he had been under the impression that this very discursive debate had terminated on Saturday, and that he had regarded the able, patriotic, and liberal speech of the gentleman from Calvert, (Mr. SOLLERS) as entirely conclusive on the subject. It seemed, however, from the remarks which had been made this morning, that the debate was not yet to be brought to a close, and hence the necessity of a few observations from him (Mr. BUCHANAN).

His object was to say a few words to his friend from Kent (Mr. CHAMBERS). The proposition before the Convention was to engraft upon our political system a provision wholly unknown to it before—unjust—invidious—oppresssive, and in derogation of the spirit of the age. Before any such provision, emanating from so distinguished a quarter, should be incorporated in our Constitution, the Convention was entitled to hear some satisfactory reasons for the change He submitted whether his friend from Kent had not failed to make out such a case as ought to be satisfactory to the Convention—whether, in fact, he had not expected gentlemen who advocated a different system to give their reasons for the faith that was in *them*, rather than assign any sufficient reasons for his own. The gentleman presumed that frauds existed, and on the strength of that presumption, he boldly made the charge of their existence. Now, his friend well knew that no principle was better settled, than that where a charge of fraud was made, it was not to rest purely upon presumption, but the gentleman had given the Convention nothing more than the vaguest suspicion of its existence. If frauds did actually exist, and if the mode proposed by the gentleman from Kent would remedy the evil, he (Mr. B.) was quite willing that the gentleman should have his own way; but if fraud did not actually exist, then the whole basis of the complaint was taken away.

Upon what did the gentleman rest his charge of fraud? Why, upon the ground that, a short time before an election came on, when the excitement was great, when the judgments were lulled, or their cupidity awakened, frauds were not only more easily committed, but were in fact committed upon the ballot-box. The argument was not valid. Every man having any knowledge of the mode of conducting elections in the State of Maryland, (especially in that part of the State to which the mind of his friend from Kent was more particularly directed, that was to say, the City of Baltimore, where the greatest amount of the foreign population resided,) knew that the time antecedent to an election, when great excitement prevailed, and when corresponding care and vigilance were exercised, was precisely the time when such frauds could not be committed. The excitement itself prevented their perpetration; because there were so many increased means for its detection. He insisted, therefore, that his friends on the other side were mistaken in asserting, that frauds were committed to an enormous extent in the City of Baltimore. What might be the case in the counties he did not know—but so far as Baltimore was concerned, the difficulty was not to prevent frauds, but to commit them.

Mr. BUCHANAN then examined the position which had been taken, that a suspicion of fraud existed because men delayed application for their naturalization papers, in the expectation that other parties would contribute to their payment. Suppose this to be the case. He, for one would plead guilty to the charge, and would hold himself responsible for that high offence. Suppose it to be true, that a man did contribute out of his own pocket a portion of the means to enable an individual entitled to naturalization, to procure his papers. Was that wrong? Was it not in accordance with the very spirit of our institutions? Had we not invited the people of other lands to emulate our career, and take a light from the lamp of freedom which was burning here? What had we done in the case of the Greeks, and the Poles, and, more recently, in the cause of Hungary? Had we not held out to them the light of our example, and told them that they were not only entitled to be free—but entitled to the glorious liberty which we ourselves enjoyed? And had we not substantially said to them, come and cast your lot with us, and we will show you how free we are? Suppose then, that a son of Erin should make an appeal to him (and he took one of that race of men as an illustration, because in the hour of trial and of dark adversity he had ever found them true)—suppose such an individual should make an application to him (Mr. B.) He should examine into the matter and see whether he was entitled to his naturalization papers. Suppose he found him to be so—but that he was unable without aid to obtain his naturalization papers; or, at all events, that for reasons satisfactory to himself, he should call his (Mr. B.'s) aid, and he should grant it. Was this fraud? Was there any thing wrong in it? If the man was entitled to his papers, and he (Mr. B.) should choose, of his own volition, or upon the appeal of the individual himself, to aid him in obtaining his papers, was there any thing more in the transaction than any good freeman, or any generous mind, might properly and rightfully do?

Mr. B. then alluded to the general nature of the testimony on which these allegations of fraud rested—that of the Newspaper press—as being unsatisfactory and insufficient. Disclaiming any charge of corrupt motive, he submitted that newspapers did sometimes say very extraordinary things in regard to the course and characters assumed, moral and political. The Convention itself had in the course of its debates, had some experience on that point. And, in high party times especially, one newspaper might be got to advocate any one doctrine, and another to advocate another—each devoutly believing in the orthodoxy of his own doctrine. And if gentlemen were about to throw their arms around the whole press, and say that the Convention were bound to believe that these monstrous frauds existed because they were charged, he knew not where it would lead them. There was then no proof to show the existence of these frauds.

But his friend from Anne Arundel (Mr. DORSEY,) had adverted to the reports which were abroad, in Baltimore City, that these frauds were committed from time to time, and to an alarming extent. Surely no such hearsay evidence could be depended upon. Before no tribunal—and least of all before such a high tribunal as this—was any such testimony to be received. He challenged his friend from Kent to show the fact upon which, as a lawyer or as a Judge, he could pronounce that fraud did exist.

But the gentlemen from Anne Arundel came to the relief of the gentleman from Kent, and said "Oh! it makes no difference, the provision only affects a few; it has no retrospective influence." Suppose that a few persons only were to be affected. Was that any reason for the adoption of such a provision? Were the feelings of a whole class of honest men to be wounded, or were they to be disfranchised because a few might be guilty of these frauds? If there were only a few, it was more facile to discover who they were, and to punish them. But he denied that the operation of this provision will be perspective alone, and not retrospective. Even if it were only perspective it would be a flagrant act of injustice on the part of the Convention. But it was retrospective also, and Mr. B. proceeded to sustain this position; and expressed his belief that the system of buying votes was carried on to a greater extent upon the Eastern Shore than in any other part of the State of Maryland. At the same moment he paid a passing compliment to the incorruptible integrity of the people of Baltimore County, and remarked that a man might as well attempt to run away with the Washington Monument, as to approach one of them with a bribe. He took it that that county preserved within her own borders purifying influences enough to save the whole State. [Laughter.]

It behooved the Convention, whilst attempting to guard against frauds on the part of naturalized citizens, to be careful that it did not break the good faith of the State with them. The policy of the country, from its earliest days, had been to encourage immigration. In the stormy days of the Revolution, when France came to our rescue, the policy of the country was, not to repudiate and insult those of her sons who tendered their services and their lives in our cause, but to lean upon them—to put them in the van of our armies and to entrust them with the charge of our dearest and most sacred rights. He referred to the services which had been rendered to the country, previous to the adoption of the constitution, by the foreign population, and cited especially the cases of La Fayette, De Kalb, Steuben and Pulaski. In relation to Steuben, so gratified was the United States at his emigration to this country that, as was well known, Congress passed a vote of thanks to him for coming and offering himself as a private soldier in the ranks and fighting our battles—and soon afterwards he took command of the detachment and distinguished himself throughout the war. Such had been the policy not only of the Federal Government, but of the Government of the State of Maryland. The most liberal and enlarged privileges had been allowed to the freemen of that day; and that policy had been continued until the adoption of the constitution of '76. It was true, indeed, that for a time the policy of the General Government had been changed, and a restrictive policy substituted. But the latter in its turn had been repealed, and been followed by a new and most liberal system. It taught the people of foreign countries, that our policy was to admit these persons upon more liberal terms than had been held out under former laws. It would be bad faith now to turn our backs upon them, and enact odious provisions against them, calculated to deprive them not only of their rights, but of their character.

Mr. B. referred to the services which had been rendered by the foreign population, and to the debt which was due to them—instancing especially the services rendered by them after the destruction of the capitol, in the defence of Baltimore. In all our civic and military struggles, these individuals had stood manfully up, and now we were to turn upon them and insult them. Not only had they fought our battles, but they had been among the foremost in the promotion of the charities of the land. He alluded to the school-houses they had built in Baltimore, and especially to an institution in Baltimore county, which had been built by the munificence of an Irishman, and which was known as "the Orphans' Home." He also referred to the late case of the McDonough bequest, in illustration of his point. And he concluded by expressing the hope that the Convention would not only act up to the vote it had given on Saturday last, but that it would reject the proposition before it, so as to indicate to the people of the State that although they were willing to entertain it as a matter of caution and respect to those who advocated it, yet that, as a body, the Convention was utterly opposed to its adoption.

[Mr. B. spoke about 35 minutes. The above is a mere outline of his points, but is considerably longer than the limit prescribed by the contract.]

Mr. Sollers stated that the gentleman from Anne Arundel had characterized some remarks which he had made on Saturday, as wild, extravagant and not worthy of notice. He felt himself called on to refer to the fact this morning, especially as

"A chiel's amang us takin' notes."

Mr. Dorsey explained that he did not use the phrase imputed to him, "not worthy of notice," but that he did not feel himself called on to notice the remarks.

Mr. Sollers resumed. That may be true, but the gentleman from Anne Arundel stated that the remarks were extravagant. As to his political and party tendencies, whatever they may be, or whether his father was a whig or a democrat, was a matter of little import. It was not necessary to trace his lineage. But he felt called on to resist the assumption of an authority to compel the junior members of this body to sit still and say nothing. He desired to say that he had uttered not a single sentiment which had not emanated from his heart. The gentleman from Kent, the gentleman from Anne Arundel and the gentleman from Queen Anne had all introduced politics in their speeches, and in a style in comparison of which he had said nothing extravagant. He had thought it right to make this explanation, and to add that while he had no desire to assail the gentleman from Anne Arundel, he could not consent to sit silent when he himself was assailed.

The question was then stated to be on the amendment of Mr. Chambers.

Mr. Biser asked the yeas and nays, which were ordered, and being taken resulted as follows:

Affirmative—Messrs. Dent, Lee, Chambers of Kent, Dorsey, Wells, Randall, Kent, Bond, John Dennis, James U. Dennis, Crisfield, Dashiell, Williams, Hicks, Hodson, Goldsborough, Phelps, Sprigg, McCubbin, McMaster and Hearn—21.

Negative—Messrs. Chapman, President, Morgan, Blakistone, Hopewell, Ricaud, Dalrymple, Sollers, Jenifer, Buchanan, Bell, Welch, Ridgely, Lloyd, Dickinson, Sherwood of Talbot, Colston, Chambers of Cecil, McCullough, Miller, McLane, Bowie, Grayson, George, Dirickson, Shriver, Gaither, Biser, Annan, Sappington, McHenry, Magraw, Nelson, Thawley, Stewart of Caroline, Hardcasle, Gwinn, Brent of Baltimore city, Fiery, Neill, John Newcomer, Harbine, Kilgour, Brewer, Waters, Weber, Hollyday, Slicer, Fitzpatrick, Smith, Parke, Shower, Cockey and Brown—53.

So the amendment was rejected.

Mr. Brown indicated his intention to offer an amendment.

The Chair requested that the gentlemen would reduce it to writing.

Mr. Chambers interposed, and desired the opportunity to state what his amendment was.

Mr. Brent yielded the floor for the purpose.

Mr. Chambers then declared his amendment to be in the following words:

"Every free white male citizen of the United States, of 21 years of age and upwards, who shall have resided in this State," &c.

Mr. Brown referred to a case in which the amendment would operate unfairly. Suppose a man, living near the county line, acquired by purchase or bequest an estate lying over the line and in the adjoining county, and transfer his residence to the newly acquired property, is he to be compelled to remain six months at his new residence before he is permitted to vote in that county? While we ought to do all that we can to prevent persons from coming into a county for a brief residence, merely for the pupose of voting, we ought to be careful not to abridge the rights of honest citizens, whose right to vote is not questioned. The object of the constitution is to secure the full enjoyment of the right of suffrage to those who are entitled to it, not to throw obstacles in its way. A citizen entitled to his vote in one county, ought not to be deprived of his suffrage because he has removed his residence over an imaginary line.

Judge CHAMBERS stated that it was impossible in the most perfect system of legislation so to regulate its operation as to prevent the occurrence of cases of individual hardship. In the application of principles it is necessary to keep in view the interests of communities. It is owing to the unavoidable defectiveness of all human legislation, that no rule can be adopted which will work with its general equity in every individual case. He insisted on the necessity of requiring a residence of six months in a county to entitle the resident to the right of voting in that county. Without such a provision, what was there to prevent a portion of the voters of one county from passing over the line to give their votes in another county? He did not mean that we were purer or better now than we have been. Frauds were perpetrated, and their was little difficulty in obtaining witnesses to sustain them, and to screen the perpetrators. It should be our aim to adopt every mode in our power to preserve the purity of the ballot-box. He requested the gentleman from Harford to withdraw his amendment.

Mr. BROWN said it was admitted that this was a question of time; and he put it to the experience of gentlemen, whether the most stringent laws we could authorize would be sufficent to prevent the perpetration of frauds. Where you would shut out one person from the ballot-box to prevent a fraudulent vote, you would exclude two honest voters, who are entitled to the exercise of their privilege. The gentleman from Kent and himself, differed on every principle connected with this question, and at a proper time he might offer an amendment to reduce the time.

Mr. McHENRY asked if he had understood the gentleman from Kent as requesting him to withdraw his amendment.

Judge CHAMBERS replied that he had done so for the purpose of expediting the business by permitting a vote to be now taken.

Mr. McHENRY said he had no objection, if there was a general understanding to that effect.

Judge DORSEY expressed a desire to make an amendment.

Mr. McHENRY declined to withdraw his amendment.

An indistinct and irregular conversation followed, which was sustained by a number of members, as to the phraseology of the amendment of Mr. CHAMBERS, the result of which was that—

Mr. CHAMBERS read the amendment in the form in which he desired it to be submitted to the Convention, and offered it as a substitute for the first section of the Report.

The question, therefore, recurred on the amendment of Mr. McHENRY (the vote requiring that a motion to perfect a proposition shall have precedence over a motion to strike out.)

Mr. McHENRY said, that the Convention had listened to so long a discussion on this subject, that he felt no disposition to protract it, especially as he felt that he could throw no new light upon it. He explained the object of his amendment to be to substitute a residence in the district for a residence in the county. He thought that it would effectually guard the purity of the ballot box, by making it impossible for a stranger to palm himself off as a resident. He was as anxious to promote the purity of the ballot box as any man in the Convention, but at the same time he was indisposed to place unnecessary restrictions upon it.

Mr. DORSEY (interposing.) Does the gentleman designate any length of time—any number of days?

Mr. McHENRY. I have not done so. I preferred to leave it to the experience of other members of the Convention to specify what a proper limit would be.

Mr. CHAMBERS would be willing, he said, to vote with all his heart for the proposition of the gentleman from Harford (Mr. McHENRY,) if he (Mr. C.) could persuade himself that there were any thing in the proposed modification of the Report of the Committee, calculated to improve the chances of a pure election. He thought it probable that the suggestion made by the gentleman might in a certain degree effect such a result. But why not engraft it on the other? If the gentleman would superadd his proposition as a requirement, and the Convention would concur in it, he (Mr. C.) would gladly go with him. It need not displace any of the other qualifications.

Mr. McHENRY said he had already disavowed very distinctly any desire to impose unnecessary shackles on the exercise of the elective franchise. He referred to the injurious restriction which it was the object of his amendment to remove, and contended that it contemplated the substitution of something useful for that which was at present useless—that its adoption would prevent frauds and would lead to the detection of men who held themselves out as denizens when in fact they were strangers.

Mr. M'LANE asked if the gentleman from Kent had any distinct purpose in view in desiring this change from the phraseology of the old Constitution.

Judge CHAMBERS replied that he had none.

Mr. M'LANE. In that case he would move, by way of amendment to the proposition of the gentleman from Kent, to adopt the provision on this subject contained in the old Constitution, *totidem verbis.*

Judge CHAMBERS thought that the language ought to be rendered a little more explicit, or there might be some difficulty in ascertaining what sort of officers would be elected.

Mr. M'LANE did not apprehend any difficulty as likely to arise on this point by the adoption of the language of the old Constitution. Unless the Convention should desire for some distinct purpose a variation of the phraseology from the old article, he should feel some unwillingness to make a change. He would confess that he felt so much veneration for the old Constitution as to be reluctant to lay his hands upon it, although he was fully aware that whatever we do here would be in part to change its character in some degree. He looked with great respect on some of the clauses in that instrument, and thought they had worked well. Abuses, it is true, have crept in, and he was ready to co-operate with gentlemen around him in their correction where they existed. But in this article he saw no necessity for any change. He knew there had been a good deal of difference of opinion on the distinction between citizens of the State and citizens of the United States. Although he could not concur in all the views which had been thrown out in these discussions, there were some to which he gave his assent. And for the principle of obviating all difficulties he now proposed, in lieu of the amendment of the gentlemen from Kent, to insert the clause as it stood in the old Constitution, without alteration, and which he would now read.

"Every free, white, male citizen of this State above twenty-one years of age, and no other, having resided twelve months within this State and six months in the county, or in the city of Annapolis or Baltimore, next preceding the election at which he offers to vote, shall have a right of suffrage, and shall vote by ballot, in the election of such county or city, or either of them, for Electors of the President and Vice President of the United States, for representatives in this State or the Congress of the United States for Delegates to the General Assembly of this State * * * and sheriffs.

Judge Chambers reminded the Convention that the instrument from which the gentleman from Cecil had read his amendment was not the original Constitution of 1776, but was comparatively a late affair, (1809.) The language of the old Constitution was very different as may be seen by a reference to the proceedings on its adoption. The language of the old Constitution runs thus:

"All freemen, above twenty-one years of age, having a free-hold of fifty acres of land in the county in which they offer to vote and residing therein, and all freemen having property in this State above the value of £30 current money, and having resided in the county in which they offer to vote one whole year next preceding the election, shall have a right of suffrage in the election of delegates for such county."

He supposed that when the amendment was made which had just been submitted, it was because we required citizenship, which was not required in the old Constitution. That instrument only required that persons should be residents of the State—it also used only the word "free," not "free white." Conceive the phraseology altered in the slightest possible degree, what would be the effect? We have citizens of the State certainly; as nothing is more common than to pass laws to enable foreigners to hold estates. Now he did not desire to insert any language which does not convey the precise idea intended to be conveyed. He wished it to be distinctly indicated what a citizen of the State is. He hoped the gentleman from Cecil would see the propriety of reinstating the words in the original instrument which a subsequent Convention struck out. Because that Convention had thought it expedient to introduce this amendment, it was by no means necessary that we should follow in their steps. It appears to me, as it did to the Committee, that these citizens are entitled by their residence to the enjoyment of the elective franchise at all the elections.

Mr. M'Lane did not think that the fact of an individual holding land should constitute him a citizen. But he would not press his amendment now, as he would have the opportunity to offer it when the report was made to the House.

Mr. Brent, of Baltimore, asked for the reading of the section.

The section was accordingly read.

Mr. McHenry moved to amend by striking out the words from the word "election" in the third line to the word "and" in the fifth line, being as follows, "at which he offers to vote shall have a right of suffrage," and inserting in lieu thereof the words following:

"Shall, unless excluded by other provisions of the Constitution, be entitled to vote at every public election in the election district where his residence may have been established days preceding such election, and not elsewhere."

The Chair suggested that that amendment would be in order after the one now pending shall have been disposed of.

The Chair stated the question.

Mr. Donaldson proposed to insert the time, and moved to fill the blank with sixty days.

Mr. McHenry suggested that a vote should first be taken on the principle.

Mr. Donaldson. No, Sir—it is a practical matter as to the length of time.

After some conversation, Mr. McHenry moved to fill the blank with ten days.

Mr. Phelps moved thirty days.

The question was taken on inserting sixty days, and was rejected.

And the question was taken on inserting thirty days, and rejected.

And the question was taken on inserting ten days, and rejected.

Mr. Brown enquired of the Chair, whether it would now be in order to move an amendment to the proposition of the gentleman from Kent, (Mr. Chambers.)

The Chairman said it was not now in order. The pending proposition had not yet been disposed of.

Mr. McHenry enforced the propriety of the adoption of his amendment, by reference to the changes which were proposed to be made in the new Constitution, and the elections which would grow out of them; and he defended it against the supposition that there was anything in it which would interpose new restrictions upon voters.

Mr. Phelps said the object of the amendment he had proposed was to put the wards of the City of Baltimore, on a footing with the counties. We have been told that the frauds do not usually grow out of fraudulent naturalization papers, but from the same individuals casting their votes at different places. He wished to reach this evil. The amendment of the gentleman from Harford, (Mr. McHenry,) with that which he, (Mr. P.) now proposed added to it, would go far to meet the case. It would have the effect of making every one who attempted this fraud known, and be wholesome in its effect on the elective franchise. His motion was to add the words, "and the wards in the City of Baltimore."

Mr. Gwinn thought the security against fraud would not be increased by this amendment. The Judges had the power to enquire into the fact of residence. If an individual was not a resident of a ward, he could only get his vote in by a false oath, as to his term of residence. He might be asked if a man would swear falsely, that he had lived in a ward one day, would not as readily perjure himself as to a residence of thirty days. There were several large establishments in Baltimore, which employed a great number of hands There was the Clare Factory, the Canton and others. The persons employed there generally reside, while in this employ, in the wards in which establishments are established, and he considered it would be very hard upon these persons whenever they were transferred to another ward.

Mr. Phelps made a few remarks in reply, in which he stated that it was his desire to give the largest liberty to the largest number. But it had been charged against the City of Baltimore, by the gentleman from the county that frauds had been perpetrated there by double voting, he thought the amendment would check that evil.

Mr. Brent, (in the absence of his colleague,) expressed regret that his colleague was not in his seat. The gentleman who had just spoken had asserted that his colleague had charged on the City of Baltimore, that frauds were perpetrated there by double voting.

Mr. Phelps said he had so understood him.

Mr. Brent resumed. The gentleman was mistaken. His colleague did not say so. His language was that it had been stated to him as an allegation. He would now take occasion to say that he was opposed to all attempts to impose restrictions on the elective franchise. It was a restriction of freedom, and he was opposed to it. Does a man by a residence in a place for thirty or sixty days become more enlightened, than by a residence of one. He who is entitled to the right of suffrage, is as much entitled to exercise it in one county as another, and in one ward as another. Why is it considered necessary that he should have been a local resident in a particular district, to entitle him to vote? He is as much entitled to vote at a general election, after a residence of thirty days, as of six months. By the existing laws a residence in a ward, or a district, for one day is sufficient. If there was to be any difference, it ought, in his opinion, to be in favor of a commercial city, where are so many laborers who are compelled to sleep where they are employed. If the Judges do their duty all this illegal voting may be prevented. He was ready to impose any penalty to put down illegal voting; but he would never be willing to restrict the franchise. If there was to be any distinction, it should be in favor of a large commercial city.

Judge Dorsey expressed his concurrence in the views of the gentleman from Kent, (Judge Chambers,) as to the impossibility of so framing any legislative rule, as it should in no case bear hardly on an individual. If he could adopt the views of the gentleman from Baltimore, who had just taken his seat, he should be ready to vote with him throughout. But there were reasons which operated in his mind strongly in favor of a six months residence. A residence of that extent was necessary to make an individual competent to give an intelligent vote, by making him familiarly acquainted with the true interests of the county, so that he may be guided to a wise selection of a candidate. He would have been ready to vote for the amendment of the gentleman from Harford, (Mr. McHenry,) if he would have accepted two amendments, which he had thought proper to be added to it. One of these was to insert the wards in the City of Baltimore. He had understood the gentleman from Baltimore to say that the persons in the wards ought to be allowed to vote He agreed with him. As he viewed the law, no one had any right to prevent the voters in the City of Baltimore, from voting in any of the wards. It was sufficient, if he was a citizen of Baltimore But he objected to the latitude of construction which would allow the resident of a State to vote in any county he may choose. He referred to the period when a number of persons then called the blue light federalists, were brought into the City of Annapolis, for the purpose of defeating a popular candidate. They were paid so much per month, but they were treated so badly by the people, and so thoroughly hooted by the boys, and made so uncomfortable, that they violated their contract, and left the city without remaining to effect their object. They were not in force enough to carry the election of their federal representative; their funds gave out, and the opposition candidate was elected. If no residence is to be required, what will prevent the sending into any particular county as many men as might be necessary to turn the election? We ought to secure the purity of the ballot-box. We ought to insist that the voters in the counties, and City of Baltimore, shall be residents of the election districts and reside in the wards in which they vote. Without such restriction the voters may come out from the large in numbers sufficient to overwhelm the public aspirants of the small counties. Without residence, all the small counties will be made subject to the large counties, and the voice of the people will be there annihilated.

These remarks were produced by a suggestion that the required residence in the counties, and City of Baltimore should be abolished.

He referred to the practice which prevailed of raising funds for the purpose of carrying on elections. If the voters are not required to be residents of the wards in the City of Baltimore, in which they vote, what is to prevent them from voting in all the different wards? Why might not John Smith go and vote in every ward, and how could he be identified, unless he was a distinguished person who could not be overlooked, and in this way political questions of the greatest importance might be decided by these fraudulent voters. If it was true, as stated by the gentleman from Baltimore city, that an improper restriction is imposed on the citizens of Baltimore, we ought to remove it at once.

He was opposed to this double voting in the City of Baltimore, it was productive of great mischief to the whole State. And in the municipal elections, where one district may be in favor of one person, and the next in favor of another, voters from one district can turn the scale if residence in the ward be not required, the favorite candidate of the ward may be decidedly defeated by voters corruptly imported from some other ward, by moving into the other. The same may be said of Howard District, &c., where each elects its own Commissioners.

Mr. Gwinn enquired how the action of the citizens of the City of Baltimore could effect the frauds perpetrated in the counties. It might be important in its effect on the elections for municipal officers, but it could not influence the election of delegates for the counties. If the voters of the City vote only once, how is the State injured, if the votes be given in this or that ward?

Judge Dorsey replied, that if the residue of the State had no interest in the city of Baltimore there would be some reason in this view of the subject. He had been accused with applying the term "rowdy" to the citizens of Baltimore when it was well known to the Convention that he only expressed his apprehension, that a spirit of rowdyism might be provoked by the interference of the citizens of one district with those of another. Ought not the State interfere when persons, who are called in the newspapers "rowdies," go from poll to poll committing outrageous acts, and preventing the free exercise of the elective franchise? He was anxious to keep the ballot box pure, by holding in check that spirit of demagogism which was destroying the character of the city. We must take care that there is no double voting, that the residents of one ward shall not go over and give their votes in another ward also. It is by this double voting that the wishes of the citizens of one ward may be overruled by the interference of another, and that a mayor and municipal authorities not agreeable to them, may be forced upon them. He desired to protect Baltimore against herself, to preserve her from being annihilated by fraudulent voting.

He concluded with an expression of his hope that the ballot box would be preserved in its purity, and that the practice of double voting would be prevented hereafter. If the principle of admitting all to the polls without any restriction as to residence is to prevail, our institutions will not be worth a brass farthing. Yet we are told we may do what we will with the rest of the State, but we must not touch the city of Baltimore. He did not hold himself as a delegate merely for Howard District, but for all the State. And looking at the interest of the whole State, he thought a reasonable time ought to be fixed for residence, both in the districts through the State and in the wards of Baltimore city.

Mr. Brent, of Baltimore city, was of opinion that a man who moved from one county to another, carried with him the right to vote. It was said there should be some restriction, and he would be willing to agree to thirty or sixty days in the county and twelve months in the State. But he was entirely opposed to any restriction in the suffrage of those who moved merely from one election district to another. As the law now stands one day's residence in a ward is deemed sufficient. He was satisfied with that; no man can vote in any ward who has not slept in it the previous night; and any one can challenge his vote on shewing where the person did sleep the last night. He desired no further restriction. The law prescribing a residence of one day cannot be evaded without either fraud or perjury, which can always be detected by the agency of a challenger. With reference to what had been said by the gentleman from Anne Arundel as to the danger of the voters of one county going over the line to vote in other counties, he contended that no evil could result from this practice, as they could only vote once, and if they voted in another county they could not return to vote in their own. It was desirable that there should be the fullest possible expression of the public sentiment. He was opposed to any restriction which would have the effect of preventing this. If the people themselves will perpetrate frauds, it is impossible to prevent them by any restrictions we may impose. Whether we fix a residence of thirty days or of six months, the restriction will be rendered of no effect so long as there is a spirit among the people which prompts to its evasion. He was, therefore, in favor of giving the largest privilege.

He concluded with stating that he did not understand his friend from Harford (Mr. McHenry) as intending by his amendment to do any thing more than to limit the term of residence. In any remarks he had made, he desired it to be understood that he had no intention that they should be applied to that gentleman, who, he was entirely satisfied by his vote on Saturday, was in favor of the largest liberty. His remarks were only intended for those who voted in the minority on Saturday.

On motion of Mr. Phelps,

The Committee then rose and reported progress; and

The Convention adjourned until 10 o'clock tomorrow morning.

TUESDAY, January 14th, 1851.

The Convention, in pursuance of its order heretofore adopted, met at 10 o'clock.

Prayer by the Rev. Mr. Grauff.

The Roll of the members was called.

Mr. BISER said it was evident that a quorum was not present, and he would, therefore, move a call of the Convention.

The motion was agreed to.

The Secretary called the roll.

A quorum having in the *interim* appeared, all further proceedings in the call were dispensed with.

The Journal of yesterday was read and approved.

The President laid before the Convention a communication from the Treasurer of the State, (for which see Journal) in reply to a resolution heretofore adopted, calling for certain information.

On motion of Mr. BROWN, the communication was ordered to be printed (the reading having, on his motion, been in part dispensed with.)

The President also laid before the Convention a communication from the Governor of the State of Louisiana, in relation to the system of education in that State.

Mr. BROWN said, if there were no other business before the Convention, he would move that the Convention resolve itself into committee of the whole on the order of the day.

Mr. BRENT, of Baltimore city, requested him to withdraw the motion for a short time, to enable him (Mr. BRENT) to offer a resolution.

Mr. BROWN withdrew his motion.

ABSENTEES.

Mr. BRENT then offered the following order, which was read:

Ordered, That on and after Monday next, the Secretary shall enter on the journal of each day, the names of all members absent at the call of roll without leave, unless they shall on the same day before adjournment, report themselves in person to the Secretary; which was twice read.

Mr. BRENT said he had not offered this proposition with any sort of reference to Buncombe, and he believed he could conscientiously say that he had not, during the entire session of this body given one single vote with reference to that object. But he was impressed with the necessity of the Convention taking some action, with a view to enforce the attendance of its members. Before the holidays it was declared on every side that, after their termination, the Convention would, on resuming its duties, go earnestly to work. What was the actual state of facts? The Convention had been in session fourteen days after the holidays; and yet, on Saturday last, when a vote was taken upon one of the most important questions on which the Convention would be called to act, some thirty members were absent. Yesterday, he believed, a still greater number were absent. Could they all be sick, or have a valid excuse? His proposition was, not to deprive them of their *per diem*, but simply to record their names upon the Journal. If any gentleman had just cause of absence, it could not be doubted that the Convention would excuse him. He hoped that the Convention would put a stop to this system, at least so far as the object could be effected by this resolution. The people had to vote upon the adoption or rejection of the new Constitution, in June, and time ought to be allowed them to canvass its various provisions. With this view, the Convention ought to adjourn by the first of April, or, at furthest, by the fifteenth; and this would allow but little time for examination. The new Constitution would contain more than one hundred sections; yet, for fourteen days, the Convention had been engaged upon one. At that rate, when would the labors of the Convention terminate? He called upon the reformers in the body to expedite its business; and, with that end in view, he gave notice that he should follow up the resolution he had now offered by another, providing for the application of the one hour rule, at least for the present, to the speeches of members.

Mr. JENIFER said, that if the resolution of the gentleman from Baltimore city (Mr. BRENT) had been offered at an early period of the session, it might have met with his (Mr. JENIFER'S) support; but that, coming upon the Convention at this time, it seemed to him to be rather a reflection upon it. And it occurred to him as somewhat remarkable that those gentlemen who had been most often absent, and who had themselves indulged in the broadest latitude of debate, should be the first to turn round and read Puritanical lectures to the Convention upon the delay in the transaction of its business. He thought that, previous to the recess, his friend from Baltimore city had been absent as much, perhaps, as any other member, and yet nothing was said about that. In what instance had his friend ever expedited the public business by calling for the question, or withholding, for the sake of allowing it to be taken, any remarks which he might have desired to make? He (Mr. J.) protested against these *ad captandem* arguments to bring this body into disrepute. Enough had been said about this Convention in the newspapers. If the gentleman intended that the whole of the Convention should be reflected upon by this resolution, then he (Mr. J.) hoped that the gentleman would go back to the commencement of the session. He (Mr. J.) moved that the resolution be laid upon the table.

Mr. BRENT said he had been as faithful to the attendance of his duties here before the recess as after, and explained that he had never been absent except in one case of imperious necessity —an occasion upon which the Convention would have been willing to grant him leave. But he insisted that if gentlemen were to be permitted to absent themselves by thirties and forties, it was his right to reflect upon them and his duty to do so if such a proposition as this could be viewed as a reflection. He believed that the public interests would have been promoted if such a resolution had been passed long ago.

The gentleman (Mr. JENIFER) was mistaken in saying that he (Mr. B.) had not called for the question. He had often done so—and this was, therefore, an unnecessary attack upon him.

Mr. JENIFER (interposing) disclaimed any intention to attack the gentlemen, and stated that his intention was to defend him.

Mr. BROWN said that to obviate one of the many difficulties which the introduction of the resolution was designed to prevent, he would move the previous question.

Mr. JENIFER. I made a motion that the resolution be laid on the table.

Mr. BROWN suggested that the gentleman had withdrawn it.

Mr. JENIFER said he had done so only at the request of the gentleman from Baltimore city, (Mr. BRENT.)

Mr. BRENT thereupon renewed the motion to lay on the table—at the same time, of course, indicating his intention to vote against it. And, he asked the yeas and nays, which were ordered.

And the question having been taken, the vote resulted as follows:

Affirmative.—Messrs. Blakistone, Hopewell, Ricaud, Lee, Chambers, of Kent, Donaldson, Dorsey, Wells, Kent, Weems, Dalrymple, Bond, Jenifer, Ridgely, John Dennis, James U. Dennis, Williams, Hodson, Goldsborough, McLane, Sprigg, McCubbin, George, Wright, Annan and Holliday—26.

Negative.—Messrs. Chapman, President, Morgan, Dent, Mitchell, Bell, Welsh, Sherwood, of Talbot, Colston, Crisfield, Dashiell, Hicks, Eccleston, Phelps, Chambers of Cecil, McCullough, Miller, Dirickson, McMaster, Hearn, Shriver, Gaither, Biser, Sappington, McHenry, Magraw, Nelson, Carter, Thawley, Stewart of Caroline, Hardcastle, Gwinn, Brent of Balt. city, Ware, Fiery, Neill, Jr., John Newcomer, Harbine, Kilgour, Brewer, Waters, Weber, Slicer, Fitzpatrick, Smith, Parke, Shower, Cockey and Brown—48.

So the resolution was not laid on the table, and the question recurring on the adoption of the resolution.

Mr. RIDGELY, said he had desired to see the proposition laid upon the table, not because he objected to the principle of it, but because he thought that it covered too much ground.—An order had been adopted changing the daily hour of meeting to ten o'clock. The resolution now under consideration provided that the name of every member not present at the call of the roll, should be entered on the Journal unless he should report himself before adjournment. Now it was obvious, from the proceedings which had taken place this morning, that if the roll was to be called at ten o'clock, and this resolution was to be adopted, it would be found that no quorum was present, and that a portion of every day would be occupied in notifying the Secretary what members were present. He (Mr. R.) would suggest that the Convention should, in the first place, go back to a proper hour of meeting—eleven o'clock. Let that be done, and he would then go for the proposition before them, and live up to it. If members were not then present, let their names be recorded thus and so.

He thought that no great object could be effected by meeting before eleven. A number of members were upon committees which met between the hours of 9 and 11. It would be very inconvenient to gentlemen who were in the Convention five or six hours during the day, and upon committees in the morning and at night, to meet here at ten, and if this resolution was to be adopted, he hoped it would be with the qualification he suggested as to the hour of meeting. And he proposed an amendment to that effect (to precede the resolution.)

Mr. HARBINE said, he hoped that the amendment would not prevail. In his opinion, the hour of ten was not too early an hour for the commencement of the business of the Convention. He doubted whether there was any Convention now in session, which met later than ten. It was late enough, if gentlemen looked to the time that the Convention had been in session, or to the present state of its business. He disclaimed the vocation of a lecturer. It was probably as much his fault as the fault of any other member of the Convention, that things were in the condition in which they now stand. He could not claim for himself to have been altogether free from the charge of inattention to duty. He could not and would not shut his eye to the fact that very little progress had been made in the public business and he coincided entirely in the remarks which had been made on that point by the gentleman from Baltimore city (Mr. BRENT). It was that the Convention should meet at an early hour, and should go seriously to work, that its business might be disposed of.

He denied the validity of the argument which had been urged as respected the business of the committees, or the difficulty of procuring the attendance of gentlemen at the hour designated. He believed that when the hour was once known and understood, gentlemen would be punctual in the discharge of their duties; and if they would not, the fault and the responsibility would rest upon them.

Mr. HICKS sent up to the Secretary's table an amendment (by way of substitute) which he desired to offer.

The PRESIDENT thought that the amendment was not now in order.

Mr. WEBER demanded the previous question, and by ayes 34, noes 29, there was a second.

MR. DORSEY rose to move an amendment.

The PRESIDENT intimated that no amendment was now in order, the previous question having been recorded. The main question was then ordered to be taken, which main question was, first, on the amendment of Mr. RIDGELY (fixing *eleven* as the hour of meeting.)

Mr. JOHN NEWCOMER called the yeas and nays, which were ordered and were as follows:

Affirmative—Messrs. Chapman, President, Morgan, Blakistone, Hopewell, Ricaud, Chambers of Kent, Mitchell, Donaldson, Dorsey, Wells, Sellman, Weems, Dalrymple, Bond, Jenifer, Ridgely, John Dennis, Crisfield, Williams, Hicks, Hodson, Goldsborough, Phelps, Miller, McLane, Sprigg, McCubbin, Wright, Stewart of Caroline, Hardcastle, Brent of Baltimore city, Kilgour, Waters and Hollyday.—34.

Negative.—Messrs. Dent, Lee, Kent, Bell, Welch, Sherwood, of Talbot, Colston, James U.

Dennis, Dashiell, Eccleston, Chambers of Cecil, McCullough, Grason, George, Dirickson, McMaster, Hearn, Fooks, Shriver, Gaither, Biser, Annan, Sappington, McHenry, Nelson, Carter, Thawley, Gwinn, Ware, Fiery, Neill, jr., John Newcomer, Harbine, Brewer, Weber, Slicer, Fitzpatrick, Smith, Parke, Shower, Cockey and Brown.—42.

So the amendment was rejected.

The question then recurred on the adoption of the original resolution of Mr. Brent.

Mr. Dorsey desired to be informed by the chair, whether all debate was cut off.

The President replied, that it was, because the previous question had not yet been exhausted.

The question was then taken, and by ayes 45, and nays 26, the resolution was adopted,

Mr. Hicks desired to offer as an original proposition the substitute amendment of which he had given notice, and which was as follows:

Ordered, That Committee No. 14, be requested to inquire into and report to this Convention the expediency of holding three night sessions in each week, until the close of this Convention for the purpose of giving members an opportunity to make personal explanations and fancy speeches, that time and expense may thereby be saved.

The President had awarded the floor to Mr. Dorsey.

Mr. Hicks gave notice that he would offer his resolution to-morrow morning.

Mr. Jenifer (whilst Mr. Dorsey was reducing to writing the proposition he intended to offer) laid on the table the following order, which he intended to call up hereafter:

Ordered, That it be incorporated among the standing rules of this body, that no member shall speak at one time longer than one hour, nor more than one hour on the same question.

Mr. Dorsey then moved the following order:

Ordered, That the rule adopted as to the attendance of members of this Convention shall not apply to members who will state that the cause of their absence was their necessary attendance to the business of this Convention.

Mr. Dorsey said it seemed to him that the precipitation with which the Convention was required to act in its proceedings here, was not becoming such a body. They had been brought here for the purpose of deliberating calmly and acting intelligently upon every subject which might be brought before them. It was their duty to devote to every subject such portion of time as might be requisite to enable them faithfully to discharge their duty in regard to it. It appeared to him, from the discussion which had taken place, that members thought that all they had to do was to attend the committees, to agree, or disagree, to what might there be done—and that that was the scope and limit of their duties. Such was not his view. He considered it as much his duty, as a member of this Convention, to satisfy his own mind by all proper investigation, whether the Report of a Committee ought, or ought not, to be adopted in the terms and manner which they proposed, as it would be to form his own conclusions, as a member, of every particular, why he should agree or disagree to its report. Take, for example, the Report of the Committee on the Elective Franchise. If he had been called upon to vote upon that subject without having paid any attention to it, he should have been perfectly blindfold He believed that a dozen amendments were necessary to carry out the wishes of the people on that subject, and what he supposed to be the wishes of the Convention. He considered the labors which members should perform in their rooms, quite as important as any which they were called upon to perform here. They ought not to act without a minute examination of what is contained in the Reports, nor without weighing every word of every section they contained. Otherwise they might form a Constitution which the people would reject, as indeed, under such circumstances, they ought to reject it.

Mr. Brent interposed and explained that his resolution contemplated that the name of no absent member should be entered on the Journal, if he should report himself during the day.

Mr. Dorsey, expressing his entire knowledge of the import of the resolution, proceeded to say, that he was as anxious as any member of the Convention could be, that its labors should be brought to a close; but it was due to themselves, to the body and to the State, that full and perfect consideration should be given to every subject. He referred to a conversation which he had held, when last coming to Annapolis, with a gentleman who was either a member of the Virginia Reform Convention, or had been attending its sessions, in which Mr. Henry A. Wise (a member of the latter) was said to have declared in the Convention, that he would not give a fig for any Constitution which was framed in less than twelve months; and that if he had been a member of the Legislature by which the Convention was called, he would have offered a provision declaring the Convention incompetent to adjourn, or adopt a Constitution, in less than six months. He (Mr. D.) did not mean to say that this opinion accorded with his own views. But he was willing to labor as long as any man in the Convention to mature and make the best Constitution which they could. He desired to gratify each portion of the State so far as it could be done consistently with the rights of every other portion. But he thought that to meet at the hour of ten, allowing no time for exercise, and to act precipitately and without due consideration on the subjects before them, were unreasonable requirements.

Mr. McLane suggested to the gentleman from Anne Arundel (Mr. Dorsey), so to modify his proposition as to give it a retrospective action, and to call upon every member to come up and declare on his honor and conscience how long he was absent and for what purpose. And he made some remarks in support of the suggestion.

Mr. Dorsey said he would accept the modification.

Mr. Brent, of the city, replied to some of the

positions of Mr. McLane; briefly enforced the propriety and necessity of the resolution which had been adopted, and expressed his hope that the Convention would not rescind it.

Pending the question, the Convention passed to the order of the day.

THE ELECTIVE FRANCHISE.

On motion of Mr. Jenifer, the Convention again resolved itself into committee of the whole, Mr. Blackistone in the chair, and resumed the consideration of the report of the committee on the Elective Franchise.

The pending question was on the following amendment offered yesterday by Mr. McHenry:

To strike out all from the word "election," in the third line, to the word "and" in the fifth line, and insert in lieu thereof the following:

"Shall, unless excluded by other provisions of this Constitution, be entitled to vote at every public election in the election district where his residence may be established for days preceding such election, and not elsewhere."

Mr. Brown suggested to the gentleman to withdraw the amendment. The committee by three separate votes had refused to fill the blank with any specific time, and if it was not filled, of course the whole proposition was nugatory. He trusted the amendment would be withdrawn, that the Convention might get rid of the debate.

Mr. McHenry said he was willing to acquiesce in the suggestion, not only because the experienced member from Carroll, (Mr. Brown,) had made it, but because upon consultation with friends he Mr. McH. found that there was not the least probability of the adoption of the amendment, therefore he would withdraw it. He desired to say, however, that he had not in the slightest degree modified his opinion. He believed that the amendment, if it had been adopted, would effect the object he designed to accomplish; but he would be the last man in this Convention to procrastinate its action by any pertinacity of his own.

So the amendment was withdrawn.

Mr. Sappington thereupon withdrew the amendment which he had heretofore offered.

Mr. Phelps now moved the following amendment:

Insert after the words "Howard District," the following: "And thirty days in the election district or ward of the city of Baltimore."

Mr. Dorsey asked for the yeas and nays which were ordered, and were as follows:

Affirmative—Messrs. Chapman, President, Morgan, Dent, Hopewell, Lee, Chambers of Kent, Mitchell, Donaldson, Dorsey, Wells, Kent, Weems, Dalrymple, Sollers, Merrick, John Dennis, James U. Dennis, Crisfield, Dashiel, Williams, Hicks, Hodson, Goldsborough, Eccleston, Phelps, Sprigg, Dirickson, McMaster, Fooks, McHenry, Magraw, Davis and Waters—33.

Negative—Messrs. Blakistone, Sellman, Bond, Bell, Welch, Chandler, Ridgely, Sherwood, of Talbot, Colston, Chambers, of Cecil, McCullough, Miller, Bowie, McCubbin, Spencer, Grason, George Wright, Shriver, Gaither, Biser, Annan, Sappington, Stephenson, Nelson, Carter, Thawley, Stewart of Caroline, Hardcastle, Gwinn, Brent of Baltimore city, Ware, Schley, Fiery, Neill, Harbine, Kilgour, Brewer, Anderson, Weber, Hollyday, Slicer, Fitzpatrick, Smith, Parke, Shower, Cockey, and Brown.—46.

And the amendment was rejected.

Mr. Dirickson stated that he had hitherto voted with the party which had evinced a disposition to abolish all distinctions in the exercise of the right of voting. He had no idea that by any act of ours we could succeed in making men more pure, and he was unwilling to impose restrictions unless where he was satisfied that they were demanded by the public interest.—He would not be desirous to restrict even foreigners in their exercise of this high privilege. He had no prejudices against such, as foreigners; and even if he had, his sense of what was due to justice would not permit him to let such prejudices influence his actions. The general goverment had said that after a residence of so many years, foreigners should be entitled to the privileges of other citizens. Whether it was, in every view, right or not, he would not to stop to decide. Older men and sages had thought so, and he would not attempt to impugn their decision. He differed with the gentleman from Charles on this point. He had heretofore avowed a wish to see all distinctions broken down. If this was democratic doctrine, it was the doctrine in which he had been brought up. He was desirous as any one to purify the ballot box. Gentlemen all around professed an equal desire to effect this object, but all seemed to discover a great difficulty as to the proper mode to be adopted. It seemed to be generally admitted that, in every part of the State, the ballot box had been greatly corrupted. He did not believe that the evil had reached that extent which some believed, but, to some extent, he could not but allow that corruption had crept in. His objection to the course of many members was that, while they admit the existence of the evil, they reject the means for its removal, after tenaciously opposing every attempt to introduce a remedy. Will not the amendment now under consideration, work well, and produce good to the city of Baltimore?

The gentleman from Baltimore (Mr. Gwinn) had said that if a man desired to commit a fraud all he had to do was to swear that he had slept the night before in one of the wards of the city or county.

Mr. Gwinn. I never said so.

Mr. Dirickson resumed. Whether it was that gentleman who said it, or his colleague; it was an argument against the restriction which this amendment imposed. It was true that a man who would swear that he had slept one night there, might be more easily detected than if he perjured himself in reference to a longer residence. But this rendered the amendment the more necessary. There are always persons belonging to the Ward who watch for such men, and who, in consequence of this enlargement of the term required for residence would the more readily detect them. And how easy is it for individuals, or classes, to come into a ward to sleep for one night in order to be entitled to vote. This has indeed been done, if we are to believe the current reports. But the allegation is, that the frauds are perpetrated by foreigners; but they originate not with them, but with our own people who are eager to secure their votes. Another evil is that of double voting, the same persons having voted at different polls on the same day. It had been replied to this, that even if they had done so, no harm could result, that it was only a fuller expression of public opinion! But when this practice is carried into the Congressional districts in the State, the result is more important, tending as it does to change the whole character of our government. He was opposed to this system of aggregate voting. He wished to see the people represented by delegates not elected in this mode, not by an aggregated franchise, but by the votes of their own proper constituency. This was the best system. He desired an expression of the sentiments of all, on the subject, that we may, by a compromise, adopt that mode which is most approved. He wished a full expression of public opinion at the polls, and thought this amendment would effect it.

Mr. Phelps consented to modify his proposition. But a general desire being expressed to take a vote on "thirty," he adhered to his original motion.

Mr. Ridgely, in consequence of the impatience of the House to take the vote, very briefly addressed the Convention in correction of the erroneous views which he thought gentlemen had taken with regard to the question of residence. The gentleman from Dorchester (Mr. Phelps) appeared to entertain the belief that thirty days residence meant actually the presence of an individual in the ward for that time previous to the election; and that he lost his right to vote because his residence was not qualified by his presence. The fact of residence must be determined by the *quo animo*. He would illustrate, by putting a case. You bring a man desirous of voting to the Judges of election at one of the wards of Baltimore city. He may have worked twenty-nine days out of the ward, and relying on his residence, comes to vote. His vote is objected to because he has not resided the thirty days required by this proposition. He replies, that although he had been at work out of the ward for twenty-nine days and actually present in the ward only one day, yet he considers that his place of residence, and he is ready to swear to the fact. Here then the question of the *quo animo* comes up for consideration and determines his right to vote.

Hitherto, he had voted against all restrictions on the suffrage. He would continue to do so. It was his wish that the ballot-box should be preserved in all its purity. And, at a proper time, it was his intention to submit a proposition for purifying the ballot-box. He thought the familiar adage ought to be reversed, and that an ounce of cure was worth a pound of prevention in this instance. All the expedients which had hitherto been introduced, might perhaps have the effect of reaching one or two illegal votes, while they would operate against twenty legal ones. While preventing illegal voters from treading on the heels of legal ones, we may perhaps impose restrictions on legal voters. He did not think the amendment would produce good.

Mr. Merrick said his opinion was precisely in opposition to that of the gentleman from Baltimore county on this point. He believed as the old adage quoted by the gentleman runs, that an ounce of prevention is worth a pound of cure.

Mr. Ridgely explained that he wished to reverse the adage.

Mr. Merrick understood this, but differed with the gentleman, and thought now, as in times of yore, "an ounce of prevention was worth a pound of cure," and he therefore was for making provision to prevent the evil complained of. He had been altogether averse from the various propositions discussed during the last few days, making, as he conceived, invidious distinctions between different classes of citizens. The amendment of the gentleman from Dorchester did not partake of that character, and was in his opinion wise and salutary—more useful even than the requirement of the six months' previous residence within the particular county.

For what purpose is the qualification of six months' previous residence in the county, now required by your laws, and still without objection, proposed by the pending report to be continued? Certainly not for the purpose of insuring to the voter a sufficient knowledge of our interests and local institutions to enable him to exercise his right of suffrage understandingly—this purpose is accomplished by the requirement of twelve months' previous residence in the State—for what purpose then is this residence within the particular county of six months required? Plainly that the voter may have identity of feeling and interest with the community for whom he purposes to aid in electing a functionary, and also that he may become sufficiently known to the people of the vincinage to render the proof of his right to vote easy, and the avoidance of spurious voting by transient persons more certain. And for the very same reasons was the reqirement proposed by the gentleman from Dorchester of thirty days' previous residence in the particular election district necessary and proper. To give to the great body of the resident and legal voters of every district, a sufficient opportunity of knowing who were legal voters among them, and thereby protecting themselves from frauds upon the dearest and most sacred of all the freeman's privileges, the right of selecting his own functionaries, by the abominable system of colonizing voters, as it is called; that is, of sending voters for a single night before an election from one district to another, for the purpose of there voting and controling the election. Something had been said of correcting this abuse by penal enactments, to provide for the punishment of the fraudulent voter,—but he preferred the prevention of the fraud,—besides, as the laws now stood, or rather as they had been told by gentlemen learned in the law, it was practically construed—a man going from one district to the other, in the city of Baltimore, but the night before an election, was considered as having required the legal right to vote in the district into which he had gone. The practice was therefore legalized, and the person thus trampling on the right of those amongst whom he went, could not be reached by any penal law, because he had only done what it has been determined he had a legal right to do. To remedy this, we propose now to adopt a proposition making it unlawful, and to require such a length of residence as will enable the lawful voters to acquire the knowledge which will protect them against the consequences of such practices. He adverted to this practice of colonizing voters as prevailing to a considerable extent, not only in Baltimore and in some of the counties on the Chesapeake, but also as he had heard (he knew not how truly,) all along the Pennsylvania border. The measure proposed appeared to him to be a wise, and indeed, the only proper and efficient corrective, and he trusted the Convention would apply it. He was far, very far, from any desire to restrict the elective franchise—his object was to protect it in its purity. He was aware, as the gentleman had said, questions might arise as to what is meant by a legal residence, but that and similar questions can better be discussed and disposed of at another time. It was well known the abuse complained of did exist to a greater or less extent, and it certainly should be corrected.

Mr. Kilgour moved to strike out thirty days and insert five. This restriction, he thought, would be sufficient to prevent the evils complained of.

The Chairman said the amendment was not now in order.

Mr. Kilgour gave notice than when in order he would move it.

Mr. Brent, of Baltimore city, called the yeas and nays pending the amendment,lwhich were ordered:

Mr. Jenifer suggested that amidst so great a diversity of opinions as was held on this subject, gentlemen ought not to be too pertinacious about their own amendments. It was the general opinion of this body that no one who was entitled to vote, should be allowed to lose it, but that illegal votes should be excluded from the polls. These, then, are the two great objects to be accomplished. He thought that they would be most surely attained, not by grafting into the Constitution any particular term of residence, but by authorizing the Legislature to adopt regulations to that end. He had prepared a proposition on this point, which he intended to offer hereafter. He had no design to trammel the Legislature, or to restrict the franchise. So far from restricting it, he would give it the largest liberty. But it was necessary that something should be done to enable the judges of elections to decide who are entitled to vote. Without being satisfied that the judges would be qualified to decide on this point, it could not be entrusted to them to decide the question. He would be willing to place it in the discretion of the judges, if all the voters could be known to them. But as that is not likely to be the case, he desired rather that it should be left to the Legislature to regulate the mode, and such was the purport of the proposition he intended to offer. He desired that the Legislature should provide for a proper registration of the votes, and this would accomplish the object. With this impression, he intended to move an amendment to this effect to come in at the end of the section. There would then be no inquisition into the legality of the voters. He wished to have no man voting who is not a *bona fide* citizen of the State. He intended to vote against all propositions to fix a certain term of residence; and if any motion to that effect should be adopted, he would move its reconsideration.

Mr. Dorsey said that when questions of such grave importance were before the Convention, and he had information calculated to throw any light upon them, he felt himself bound to give it. As to the adage of the ounce of prevention and pound of cure, he stated that the ounce of prevention was now proposed by those who thought with him, while the pound of cure which the gentleman from Baltimore county suggested was the punishment of those who are guilty of these outrages on the ballot box. The gentleman from Baltimore who first addressed the Convention on this subject, stated that a resident of the city of Baltimore was at liberty to vote in any of the wards of the city. There is no restriction on such, in the city, as to residence, whether of a day or a year; in which he concurred with the gentleman, as the charter of the city imposed no such restriction. Each election district and ward district elects its own Commissioners, and in Anne Arundel the same practice prevails. All the candidates—Congressmen, Sheriff, members of the House of Delegates and Commissioners of Congressional elections to be voted for, are voted for on one ticket—not a Congressman in one, a Sheriff in another, and so on, but all the names are on one ballot, and that single one is deposited in the ballot box. There was nothing in the Constitution as to the qualification in respect to residence in the different election districts, to prevent voters from voting in another election district than that in which they reside, so that the vote of one might be changed by the residents of another. The mode now presented appeared to him the most judicious that had been offered, and the best calculated to prevent abuse. The term of thirty days was that which he proposed as a term of residence. A gentleman, not now in his seat, had said that it would be idle to impose any restrictions as to the period after naturalization, when foreigners might be permitted to vote; and he assigned as his reason that the judges of elections, being warm political partizans of one of the parties, would reject the votes offered by voters who were not in favor of their party. Now he would not cast any such imputation on the judges of election. They are the only persons to whom the decision of such questions was entrusted. Still he had no objection to the adoption of any rule by which the evil complained of might be prevented.

In reply to what had been said of the hardship upon a man who had removed into another ward, and was refused the right to vote, not having resided therein the required time, he stated that a much greater hardship was that upon a voter removing from one county in a Congressional district where he had resided twelve months, into another county of the same Congressional district where he may have resided above five months before the election, and yet, under the Constitution of our State, he would not be entitled to vote. But these were of those cases of individual hardships which must occur under the operation of every general rule. The Congressional candidate in a ward may be one in whose success great interest might be felt in that ward, yet the election of that candidate might be defeated by other votes coming over from the city. Modes may be suggested by which the difficulties in Howard District and Anne Arundel, which are in the same condition as Baltimore, might be obviated; but under the Constitution, as it now stands, the remedy would be impossible, as the names are all on one ticket and are voted for by every qualified voter where the election is held.

Mr. Gwinn begged to call the attention of the gentleman from Anne Arundel to the fact that the second City Ordinance says, that no man shall vote out of the ward in which he resides; and if he does, he is liable to a penalty. The last law of the Legislature makes this applicable to Congressional elections.

Mr. Dorsey resumed. We are here acting on the Constitution. It is the Constitution only which determines who shall have the right to vote. If the right is possessed by virtue of a provision in the Constitution, it cannot be changed by an ordinance of the Corporation of the City of Baltimore, or even by an Act of the Legislature. How then does this change the condition of things? Baltimore will have no reason to complain if a similar principle which she has introduced into her wards, should be introduced by the Convention into the State.

Mr. Bowie. The Constitution is silent as to to the places where the votes shall be cast. At one time they were cast at the county town. Since that time, the State had been laid out in Election Districts, and the people voted in those districts. He held the law by which this had been done to be constitutional.

Mr. Dorsey resuming. If these changes had been made by a single law, the law is unconstitutional. As regards constitutional qualifications, the law can impose no restrictions different from those in the Constitution. The changes made in the qualifications of voters by an act of the Legislature are unconstitutional. If it relates to the term of residence, an hour is equal to a night. He agreed with the gentleman from Baltimore county, that the fact of residence is not established by mere personal presence for a night, but by acts and intentions showing such residence. If a laborer from one county, worked there, and went to his home in another county on Saturday night, he was entitled to vote in the county where his home is. We must judge of residence by acts and declarations of the party in relation thereto. He was in favor of a thirty days' residence, not merely a sojourning. If one ward choose to abandon an election or to let it go by default, and should send its voters into another ward, we ought to set a guard upon that practice. The residence of six months in the county is designated that the voters may know the fitness of the candidates and to prevent frauds. He thought some residence necessary; it may be thirty days or more.

Mr. Gwinn expressed a hope that the gentleman would turn to the second ordinance of the city of Baltimore, which he presumed the learned gentleman had studied.

Mr. Dorsey resumed. He did not look to the ordinance. He looked to higher authority. He took it for granted that the gentleman who declared that a citizen of Baltimore had a right to vote in any ward, had looked to the act of Assembly. It was provided in the charter which prescribes the mode of the election, that each ward should send one member to the first, and two to the second branch of the City Council, and that each candidate must be a resident of the ward in which he is voted for, and from this it has been inferred that voters must also be residents of the ward, but such inference is not authorized. He asked the gentleman to read the law.

Mr. Gwinn read the city ordinance.

Mr. Dorsey. If the ordinance was contrary to the Constitution it was null. The voters of Baltimore city, as to Congressional elections, derive their right from the Constitution. City ordinances cannot change it. The gentleman from Baltimore said it was necessary that a voter should sleep in the ward the night before the election. This does not of itself constitute residence. We ought to require something more than mere sleeping in the ward.

Mr. Gwinn here read the act of assembly, extending the ordinances of Baltimore as to the city elections to the counties. Appeals had been made, and had gone to the judicial tribunals, yet this law had never been pronounced unconstitutional.

Mr. Dorsey expressed a doubt whether the Legislature had a right to establish as a residence in respect to a Congressional election, the mere fact of a man sleeping one night in a county. If this was to be considered a residence, it appeared to him to be the more incumbent on the Convention to exercise a revisory power. He insisted that the city authorities had no power, and that the extent of the power of the Legislature was the extension of the number of election districts from sixteen to twenty. No gentleman would maintain that the fixing of a rule of residence should be left to the authorities of the city of Baltimore. Adopt this principle, and it would not be worth while to impose any restrictions as to members of Congress; you may as well throw all restrictions off, and leave the ballot box open to every one. But it is the duty of this Convention to fix such principles as will regulate future elections.

The question was then taken on the amendment of MR. PHELPS, and the result was as follows:

Affirmative.—Messrs. Chapman, President, Morgan, Dent, Lee, Chambers, of Kent, Donaldson, Dorsey, Wells, Randall, Kent, Weems, Dalrymple, Bond, Merrick, John Dennis, James U. Dennis, Crisfield, Dashiell, Hicks, Hodson, Goldsborough, Eccleston, Phelps, Sprigg, Dirickson, McMaster, Hearn, Fooks, McHenry, Magraw, Davis and Waters—32.

Negative.—Messrs. Blakistone, Sellman, Jenifer, Bell, Welch, Chandler, Ridgely, Sherwood, of Talbot, Colston, Chambers, of Cecil, McCullough, Miller, Bowie, McCubbin, Spencer, Grayson, George, Wright, Shriver, Gaither, Biser, Annan, Sappington, Stephenson, Nelson, Carter, Thawley, Stewart, of Caroline, Hardcastle, Gwinn, Brent, of Baltimore city, Ware, Schley, Fiery, Neill, John Newcomer, Harbine, Kilgour, Brewer, Anderson, Weber, Hollyday, Slicer, Fitzpatrick, Smith, Parke, Shower, Cockey and Brown—49.

Determined in the negative.

Mr. KILGOUR then moved to fill the blank with ten days, and asked the yeas and nays, which were ordered.

Mr. HICKS began to feel somewhat alarmed, he said, at the indisposition manifested on the part of the Convention, to throw around the ballot-box those guards which were so necessary to its protection, and consequently to the safety and the perpetuity of our institutions. After the angry discussion which had taken place on another subject in this Convention, and which closed only a few days ago, he had felt disposed to congratulate himself and the Convention that a subject had at last been reached, upon which he had hoped they might agree. In this, it seemed, he was disappointed. He supposed that they had all come here with a full determination to do any and every thing in their power to prevent the perpetration of frauds upon the ballot-box. He did not design to make a set speech; he had never done so. He believed it would be for the Convention itself and for the people of the State of Maryland, if there was less of that kind of speaking and a little more plain talking.

He supposed that a majority of the members of this body had a personal knowledge of the fact that frauds upon the ballot-box were every where committed. He trusted, therefore, that there was no partizan feeling about the matter. He certainly had none; and he could say, with his hand upon his heart, that although he had voted against the call of the Convention, yet when the people of the State determined there should be one, and particularly when he had addressed himself to the voters in his county for the seat he now occupied, he had resolved fully to put aside all considerations of a party character. He did not mean to say, that he was not a party man; he spoke merely with reference to the business of this Convention. It was certainly true that, in the course of his short career, he had witnessed many disgusting scenes at the ballot-box. Mr. H. proceeded to give some illustrations of his experience, and expressed the belief that if gentlemen would come out and boldly speak the truth, instances still more flagrant than those he had mentioned might be adduced. He was in favor of some such limitation as was proposed by the amendment, and thought its operation would be effective in the suppression of fraud. The blank, he thought, should be filled with some period, if it were but twenty-four hours. He desired honestly to carry out, under the lights which he possessed, the full wishes of the people. He looked upon this question as being one of the most important which the Convention had been called to consider and decide; and he hoped and trusted that some system might be matured by which this practice of fraud upon the ballot-box, every where known to exist, might be done away with. He did not think that there was any difference of feeling in the Convention as to the necessity of obtaining that end, but there were some hundred and three members of the body, and about as many different plans to accomplish the result. Yet they had all such a practical knowledge of the subject, that it seemed to him some such system might be matured in an hour. He would go even for a registration—in short, he would go for any and every thing, by means of which the one great object—the protection of the ballot-box—might be attained.

Mr. DAVIS said that the evil which was complained of, had been felt in the county of Montgomery. In that county there was at least as great an amount of virtue and intelligence to be found among the people, without disparaging other counties, as in any of them. Commissioners of the county were formerly elected by districts. Corruption, as it was thought, made its appearance. The county became dissatisfied on account of the colonization of voters. The mode of election was then changed to the general ticket system. He hoped that some guards would be placed round the ballot-box. He desired that the voters of Maryland should be secured in the fullest enjoyment of the elective franchise. That illegal voters are to be found he had no doubt. He would give an instance of one. At the September election a man called upon him, and, although of the opposite party, offered to vote for him. He went up to the polls with him, when, after an examination, he became satisfied that he was not entitled to vote, and requested the judges not to consider him as pressing the vote, and he then withdrew from the window. This man afterwards swore that his residence was in Montgomery county and was received. He (Mr. DAVIS) had since become satisfied that the man had no right to vote in that county.

Mr. BELL stated that the district from which he came was bounded by the Pennsylvania line. So far, however, from the fact was the statement made that persons from Pennsylvania came over the line in numbers to vote in the Maryland elections, that he never knew an instance of such a case. He had a high opinion of the Pennsylvanians, and believed they would scorn to be guilty of such an act. As to the election districts, he would say that in his district, a voter four-fifths of whose land lay on one side the district line, and his residence on the other, would not be permitted to vote where the greater part of his land was, but where his residence stood.

Mr. BROWN called on a colleague to bear him out in the assertion, that no illegal voters had come over the Pennsylvania line into his district.

Mr. SHOWER declared in the most solemn and emphatic manner that so far as he knew, no Pennsylvania Democrat had ever voted in Maryland.

The question was then taken on the amendment of Mr. KILGOUR, and the result was as follows:

Affirmative.—Messrs. Chapman, President, Morgan, Dent, Hopewell, Lee, Chambers, of Kent, Mitchell, Donaldson, Dorsey, Wells, Randall, Kent, Weems, Dalrymple, Bond, Merrick, Jenifer, John Dennis, James U. Dennis, Crisfield, Dashiell, Williams, Hicks, Hodson, Goldsborough, Eccleston, Phelps, Sprigg, Dirrickson, McMaster, Hearn, Fooks, Annan, McHenry, Magraw, Davis, Kilgour and Waters—38.

Negative.—Messrs. Blakistone, Ricaud, Sellman, Bell, Welch, Chandler, Ridgely, Sherwood, of Talbot, Colston, Chambers, of Cecil, McCullough, Miller, McLane, Bowie, McCubbin, Spencer, Grason, George, Wright, Shriver, Gaither, Biser, Sappington, Stephenson, Nelson, Carter, Thawley, Stewart, of Caroline, Hardcastle, Gwinn, Brent, of Baltimore city, Ware, Schley, Fiery, Neill, John Newcomer, Harbine, Brewer, Anderson, Weber, Hollyday, Slicer, Fitzpatrick, Smith, Parke, Shower, Cockey and Brown—48.

So the amendment was rejected.

Mr. PHELPS. Let us now try five days. I move that amendment.

Mr. BROWN. I rise to a point of order. With the exception of one word, we have defeated this amendment, I know not how many times. The frame-work of the proposition is the same, with the exception only of the time that shall fill the blank, and gentlemen must perceive by this time that the Convention will not supply that blank with anything.

Mr. MITCHELL suggested that the gentleman might be mistaken. He (Mr. M.) could refer to one gentleman who would go for the provision with the limitation of five days, who had not yet voted against any other period of time. There might be other members of the Convention similarly disposed.

Mr. BROWN. I withdraw the point of order.

Mr. SPENCER was opposed to all further restrictions on the suffrage. The penal law might be strengthened, if necessary; the penalties might be increased; officers who were not vigilant in the detection of illegal voters, might be punished. But there ought to be no further restriction on the ballot-box.

Mr. PHELPS said his friend from Queen Anne said we ought to rely on the penal laws. Now he had been much engaged in politics, but he had never known an instance where a voter had been disfranchised.

Mr. SPENCER referred to an instance of a conductor of a whig paper who was rejected, although a legal voter, because he could not specify the exact term of his residence to a day.

Mr. PHELPS said that case was not in his county. In reply to which the gentleman had said concerning the penal laws, they had hitherto been inefficient. The penal laws have been long in operation. A man in his county was presented by the Grand Jury, and prosecuted for bribery, and then came to Annapolis, and obtained a *nolle prosequi.* This was not the only instance of executive interference. He knew of one case in which a whig Governor, and another in which a democratic Governor interfered. We cannot find security for the purity of the ballot-box, unless we impose some limits on the term of residence. The remarks of his colleague had deep force in them, and were strongly impressed on his mind.

Mr. MERRICK, after stating that it was better to be a listener and a learner, than a speaker, said that one idea had struck him, which he would lay before the Convention. The gentleman from Queen Anne thought the existing penal laws sufficient, and that he would go as far as any one to make them more stringent. Now, we have heard a good deal from learned lawyers and judges, who after poring over the books, tell us that if a man from an adjoining ward goes into another ward of the city, and sleeps one night, he may gain his vote in that ward. Now, he desired to give his vote to check this evil, by sustaining that amendment fixing the term of residence at five days. As we are, the law is perfectly insufficient to check the evil. He thought a residence of five days proper. A man is not bound to be there every hour, but he must have his residence there, although he may work at Washington.

Mr. BOWIE suggested that if this amendment was adopted, it would make an important change in our election laws which now require six months residence in the county, twelve months in the State, and according to the construction of judges of election and others, one day in Baltimore city. The present system has stood the test of the experience of seventy years. Originally a property qualification was required, and in consequence of the universality of the term freeman, even free negroes were included. Subsequently these provisions have been repealed, and the qualifications of residence as they now stand have been acquiesced in by the people. We are now sent here to form a new Constitution. Complaints have been made as to the working of some parts of the present constitution, but he had heard of none against that which relates to the elective franchise. He wished to ask whether it was intended to get rid of the abuse of power by getting rid of the power itself. Was not that too great a sacrifice. He then quoted the provisions of the existing Bill of Rights, in relation to the suffrage; and stated that the right was not derived from the Bill of Rights or the Constitutiom. It had a far higher origin. It existed with and belonged to the people, as members of the body politic. He did not come here to put new shackles on the right of suffrage, but to qualify it by such wholesome provisions as the public safety might require. He held that every man of twenty-one years of age had an inalienable right to vote, and it could not be restrained unless demanded by the public safety. He would not vote for this restriction of five days' residence, because it would fall on a large class of poor citizens, who had no permanent home, but were constantly moving from district to district. The amendment would deprive them of the right of suffrage. Because we have the power, it would be wrong to diminish the rights of this class. Public safety demands no such act at our hands. Something ought to be done, but the Legislature could increase the rigor of the penal laws. He was willing to increase the rigor of the penal laws if public opinion demanded it, but, (said he,) "So help me God, I will never consent to strike down the free right itself."

Mr. CHAMBERS was unwilling to remain silent and hear different gentleman again and again impute to him and those with whom he had been acting, motives and reasons utterly at variance with those which governed them. No one here was disposed to violate the fundamental principles of the Bill of Rights and the Constitution—to shackle the right of freemen to vote. He believed all desired the same object—the purity of elections. Opinions differed as to the mode of securing it. Each should adopt this charitable opinion of the intention of others. The right of voting is undoubtedly of vast importance to freemen; and why is it so? Because it enables them to select for themselves their political rulers and agents. Hence your Constitution and laws guarantee that the majority of legal voters in a particular election shall have those elected for whom they cast their votes. If persons not entitled to vote interpose and nullify the effect of legal votes, this pledge is forfeited, and your Governors, Congressmen and others, are not the persons chosen by a majority of the legal voters, but are put upon them by others not entitled to have a voice in their selection. Every false vote defeats and disfranchises a legal voter.

It is not true as has been suggested that if a man has a right to vote in one place, he may as well vote in any place. Where the right of electing an officer is given to the legal voters of a particular district, it is a violation of this right to permit any other than a legal voter to interfere. It is objected that the remedy will in some cases deprive persons of the right, who ought to vote. Every general rule must produce particular instances of hardship. It was the result of human imperfection. Yet general rules must exist. His rule of political morality was, that where an abstract right existed, but owing to particular conditions and circumstances of a community, could not be exercised without necessarily producing greater evil than the good resulting from the exercise of the right would compensate, then the right must be restrained. The greatest good for the greatest number, was the proper aim and end of our labors. If one citizen, under particular circumstances, cannot exercise the right of voting without necessarily depriving two others or more of all benefit of their right, he must not be permitted to vote; and then others are denied all effect, and of course all benefit of their votes, when each of their votes shall be neutralized by the opposite votes of persons not legally entitled. He invited all to engage in the work of arresting illegal voting. It is a question of expediency of means. There should be no harsh denunciation, where all have a common and a laudable purpose.

Those were mistaken who said this was contradicting the principles of the old constitutional doctrines. Circumstances had changed and those very principles made it necessary to change our legislation. Besides, in the good old times and amongst the pure men of the days of the Constitution, corruption in elections was unknown.—These practices, now it seems, admitted so generally to exist, were of later introduction. We are told to enact penal laws. Well, it has been done and the practice is said to increase. And now, sir, said Mr. C., allow me to say, that if not restrained here and elsewhere, the most fearful consequences may be apprehended. It was his deliberate opinion that the greatest danger to be apprehended to the perpetuity of this glorious Union was from this quarter. If ever an individual shall be put upon the people as President of these United States, who they shall be thoroughly satisfied owes his elevation to fraud in the election, what disastrous results may we not expect from the outbreak of every passion which a sense of insult and outrage can generate in minds already excited to the highest degree by political partizanship? Let us do all we can to correct even a tendency to such an issue. It is asked, why not vote as well one side of a geographical line as another? Why, because it will defect the voice of the *bona fide* residents and voters to whom you give the right of election. If a geographical line divides two counties in the same congressional district, a man must cross that line as a resident, six months before an election, to enable him to vote; but if the geographical line which divides two congressional districts runs through a county or city, then six hours residence is to entitle him. Is this agreeable to reason, consistency or equality?

To make such facilities for fraud is to invite its perpetration. He admitted, the House by refusing to fill the blank with a longer time, had diluted the proposition, which in its present form, could do but little good. Still it was a step, though a short step, in the right road and he would support this and every other proposition tending to the great result of purifying the ballot-box.

Mr. JENIFER, after stating that he had for ten days voted against all amendments fixing a term of residence, advised his friend from Dorchester to withdraw his amendment, and let the subject come up hereafter.

On motion of Mr. McHENRY, the Committee rose and reported progress,

And the Convention adjourned.

[*Explanation.* The view expressed by Mr. DIRICKSON, in relation to double voting should read as follows:

"The chief evil which this amendment is designed to prevent is that of double voting—to render it impossible for the same voters to deposit their ballots at different polls on the same day. It had been further urged, that even if persons did not vote in the same ward or district in which they lived—still, provided they voted but once, no harm could result—it being only the expression of public opinion in the aggregate. But when this practice is carried into the Congressional districts in the State or in the Commissioners' districts in the county, the crime of such a practice became exceedingly glaring, tending as it did to destroy the whole character of our general government as well as our internal political institutions and regulations."]

WEDNESDAY, January 15th, 1851.

The Convention met at 10 o'clock.

Prayer by the Rev. Mr. GRAUFF.

The roll of the members was called; and

The journal of yesterday was read and approved.

ATTENDANCE OF MEMBERS.

The President announced the unfinished business to be the consideration of the order offered yesterday by Mr. DORSEY, and which is in the following words:

Ordered, That the rule adopted as to the attendance of members of this Convention, shall not apply to members who shall state that the cause of their absence was their necessary attendance to the business of the Convention.

And the pending question was on the adoption of the said order.

Mr. DORSEY said, he should move to lay his own order upon the table. He did so in the hope that the members of the Convention might see the necessity of reconsidering the order which had yesterday been adopted.

The order of Mr. DORSEY was laid upon the table.

Mr. HICKS remarking that he was convinced that no good could result from this order, he would move that the vote by which it had been adopted, should be reconsidered.

The PRESIDENT stated the question to be on the motion to reconsider the vote by which the following order had been adopted:

Ordered, That on and after Monday next, the Secretary shall enter on the journal of each day, the names of all members absent at the call of the roll, without leave, unless they shall on the same day before adjournment, report themselves in person to the Secretary.

Mr. BRENT of Baltimore city, asked the yeas and nays on the motion to reconsider, which were ordered.

Mr. DAVIS called for the reading of the order, which was read.

Mr. WILLIAMS moved that there be a call of the Convention, which was ordered.

The roll was called and the names of the absentees were then called.

Mr. BROWN moved that further proceedings on the call be dispensed with. There were, he said, only two or three members absent which were known to be in the city.

Mr. WILLIAMS. I hope they will be sent for.

Mr. BRENT of Baltimore city. Well, I withdraw the motion.

Mr. DORSEY suggested that if a member of the Convention were to fall in the street and break his arm, he could scarcely come in under the order which had been adopted, and report himself to the Secretary.

Mr. BRENT, of Baltimore city, said that if a member broke his arm, or met with any similar accident, the fact might be stated by any gentleman, and the Convention would, of course, grant leave of absence.

A pause of some ten minutes followed in the proceedings of the Convention, the absent members having been sent for.

Mr. BROWN then said, that he believed every member was in his place. He would move that further proceedings on the call be dispensed with.

Ordered accordingly.

The question then recurred on the motion to reconsider the vote by which the order of Mr. BRENT had been adopted, and the vote stood as follows:

Affirmative—Messrs. Morgan, Blakistone, Dent, Hopewell, Ricaud, Lee, Chambers of Kent, Mitchell, Donaldson, Dorsey, Wells, Randall, Kent, Sellman, Weems, Dalrymple, Bond, Sollers, Brent of Charles, Merrick, Jenifer, Buchanan, Bell, Welsh, Chandler, Ridgely, John Dennis, James U. Dennis, Crisfield, Dashiell, Williams, Hicks, Hodson, Goldsborough, Phelps, Miller, McLane, Sprigg, McCubbin, Spencer, Grason, George, Wright, Fooks, Annan, Schley, Davis, Waters and Hollyday—49.

Negative—Messrs. Chapman, President, Sherwood of Talbot, Colston, Eccleston, Chambers of Cecil, McCullough, McMaster, Hearn, Shriver, Gaither, Biser, Sappington, Stephenson, McHenry, Magraw, Nelson, Carter, Thawley, Stewart of Caroline, Hardcastle, Gwinn, Brent of Baltimore city, Ware, Fiery, John Newcomer, Harbine, Kilgour, Brewer, Anderson, Weber, Slicer, Fitzpatrick, Smith, Parke, Shower, Cockey and Brown—37.

So the vote was reconsidered.

The question then recurred on the adoption of the resolution.

Mr. JENIFER. I move to lay the order on the table.

Mr. BRENT. I call for the yeas and nays.

Mr. JENIFER. I withdraw the motion.

And the question again recurred on the adoption of the resolution.

Mr. McLANE offered the amendment which he had yesterday indicated, to give a retrospective effect to the order, so that all members who had been absent heretofore should give notice of their absence to the Secretary, that they might appear on the same record with other members contemplated by the order.

Mr. McLane said he had not offered this amendment in any light mood, and he did not wish that it should be so considered. He thought that the whole affair was out of place, and that it ought to have been let alone. He disclaimed any intention to reflect upon the gentleman who had introduced the order; but he (Mr. McLane) felt that the result of the continued efforts made here was inevitable. They would not only take away from the Convention the respect of the public, but would in the end, if persisted in, deprive it of its own respect, and lead to every species of disorder. He thought that the true mode was to rely upon the dictates of every member's conscience and sense of duty, and to trust to an enlightened community to do them justice. If, however, the Convention was to cast a censure upon itself, he hoped that it would not be confined to the future, but that it should be retrospective also.

He did not think that any evil had resulted from the absence of members; and certainly he imputed to no gentleman who had been absent any motive or intention unworthy of him as a gentleman or a member of this body; but if any evil had resulted, it had been because the absence of members heretofore had obstructed the action of the committees and prevented them from making their reports. There were members enough to carry on the business of the Convention every day; and if gentlemen did not happen to be here at the call of the roll, he did not think that they should, for that reason, be held up to public reprobation. But if it must be so, let all stand upon the same footing.

Mr. Brent said he hoped the Convention would not be induced to retrace the step which it had yesterday taken by so decisive a vote. Why was it that a change had "come over the spirit of its dream" in the course of the night? The operation of the resolution had not yet been tested. How then could the Convention know whether it would be successful or not? It was not to go into operation until Monday next. What harm could there be in it? What was the resolution? Mr. B. explained its purposes, and proceeded to argue that if a member was called by any necessity, the Convention could, by letter or otherwise, be informed of the fact, and that the gentleman's own statement of the facts, would be taken by the Convention as a sufficient excuse.

The gentleman from Cecil, (Mr. McLane) was mistaken if he supposed that that resolution was offered because there had not been a sufficient number of members attending the Committees. He, Mr. B., had no such consideration in view in offering the resolution. He had assigned nothing in the failure of the past (melancholy as that had been) to transact the public business as the reason for the resolution. He looked only to the future; and he did not intend to stop here. If it should be found that this resolution did not answer the purpose, he should follow it up with another proposition. He would cease to throw grass, and would begin to throw stones. He would offer a resolution to dock the *per diem*. He saw that gentlemen were absent. He saw that they would continue to be so, unless something was done. The gentleman from Cecil had referred to the discredit which was brought upon the Convention, by these propositions. The highest and deepest reproach which could be brought upon the Convention, would result from the failure to present to the people, in consequence of the absence of members, such a Constitution as would command their votes.

He had introduced this order upon high considerations, as he understood them, and not from any miserable desire to cater to a morbid appetite to cast odium upon this Convention. He was not satisfied with the presence of a quorum only. The State had a right to the collective wisdom and votes of the whole body.

Mr. McLane. I withdraw the amendment which I offered. It is very possible that its purpose may not be understood; and yet it might be understood as reflecting upon the absence of gentlemen hitherto. I will withdraw it. My motive was entirely different. I believe that no gentlemen who has been absent heretofore, should in any degree be censured for it, and I am unwilling to do anything which might lead to such a result.

So the amendment was withdrawn.

Mr. Brown said he should have voted against the proposition of the gentleman from Cecil, (Mr. McLane,) and propably with as much propriety as any other member of the body, so far as the matter of absence was concerned. He Mr. B., doubted whether any member, except those immediately from the City of Annapolis, had been less frequently absent than himself. But he was willing that "by-gones should be bygones." He thought the adoption of such an order would be a reflection upon gentlemen.

Mr. McLane, (interposing.) I have withdrawn it.

Mr. Brown. I know it. I shall again vote for the resolution of the gentleman from Baltimore city, (Mr. Brent,) because I think we have a right to adopt it. We reflect upon nobody, and the punishment contemplated is but a slight one. We record the names of those who are present, but we say nothing about the absentees. I suggest, however, that the gentleman should allow the resolution to lie on the table for a short time. Perhaps the very fact of its having been offered, may produce beneficial results. I think that this body, and especially the reform portion of it, has a right to complain of the continued absence of members from their seats.

Mr. Wells said, that the effect of the proposition would be to hold up to the reproach of their constituents, gentlemen who might be unavoidably detained from their seats; and there was one great inequality growing out of it sufficient in itself to cause its rejection. If the rule was adopted, a member could come into the Convention, wait until his name was called, go out and stay out for the rest of the day. Or, he might come in one minute before the Convention adjourned, report himself present to the Secretary, and thus be recorded as having been present from the commencement of the sitting. And thus both these gentlemen, neither of whom had been present for any substantial purpose, were placed in the same position with gentlemen who had been in attendance during the whole day. There were other reasons which might be urged against the adoption of the resolution, but he thought this one sufficient.

Mr. JENIFER said, that if the gentleman from Cecil (Mr. McLANE) had not withdrawn his amendment, he (Mr. J.) should have voted for it, but with the intention at the same time to have voted against both the amendment and the resolution, if the amendment should have been adopted. He was surprised to hear the declaration that the absence of members was the cause of the delay in the public business.

Mr. BRENT explained that he had not stated that the *past* absence of members was the cause of the delay.

Mr. JENIFER proceeded to remark, that he considered it their duty to leave all these matters to their constituents. If it was intended to inflict an iron rod upon this Convention, and to make the members sit down here and listen to all the dull speeches that might be made (including his own) upon every question, he would not give his sanction to any such proceeding. He believed that if members did pair off in twenties on some occasions, it would be better for the Convention, and would expedite its motion. He thought if some of them (and he enrolled himself among the number) were sometimes out of their seats it would be all the better. He referred to the argument of the gentleman who preceded him (Mr. WELLS) in regard to the unequal operation of the rule, and showed how, under its operation, a member might be here at the call of the roll on one day—go to Baltimore—return the next day, and yet have his name recorded as present on both the days of his absence.

In regard to the morning hour more especially, he thought it would be well if most of the members were not here, for more time was taken up in the discussion of propositions such as these, than in more important matters. He referred, as an example, to the resolution of the gentleman from Batimore city, which had already been the subject of debate in two morning hours. Let every gentleman be left to his own conscience and to the judgment of his constituents. For himself he must be permitted to say, that if the order was passed he should never record his name, because, when he went home to his constituents, and when they knew that he had discharged his duty with fidelity, they would not desire that he should be brought up to the Secretary's table to record his presence, like a servant who answered to the overseer's call on Saturday night.

Mr. BRENT said some gentlemen might suppose it to be a matter of very little moment whether the Convention made a Constitution or not; for one, he desired that a Constitution should be made with as little delay as possible, and such a Constitution as the people would accept. The gentleman who had just taken his seat had remarked that if some gentlemen were absent at times, it would be all the better for the Convention.

Mr. JENIFER, (interposing.) I included myself.

Mr. BRENT. I know you did, and I am willing to include myself also—but that is a matter of taste. I say that every gentleman's constituents have a right to his full services here.

But (Mr. B. proceeded to remark) the gentleman had said that members should not be bound to sit here all day and listen to dull speeches.

Mr. JENIFER. There also I included myself.

Mr. BRENT said, gentlemen could walk out at any time they pleased; and the resolution gave the very liberty that was claimed. Again—the gentleman had remarked that he would not record his name. Let him take that responsibility on himself. He (Mr. B.) did not pretend to say, that the resolution would work successfully, but at all events he hoped the Convention would try it. If any gentleman proposed to draw a distinction between those who were here all day and those who were not, let him introduce a resolution to that effect. All he (Mr. B.) proposed, was to get gentlemen here who were in the city of Annapolis,—not gentlemen who were perhaps a thousand miles off. If they were in the city they could be sent for, or could be brought here by a call of the Convention.

Mr. SOLLERS said, he was not in his seat yesterday when the question was taken on the resolution of the gentleman from Baltimore city, (Mr. BRENT,) and if he had been, he should have voted against it. There were two objections to it. In the first place, this whole series of measures was calculated to bring the Convention into disrepute with the people of Maryland, and, he agreed with the gentleman from Cecil, (Mr. McLANE,) that, whilst they did so, they were calculated also to make it lose respect for itself. He (Mr. S.) did not see the necessity for the adoption of such a resolution.

In the second place, it was utterly inadequate to the accomplishment of the object in view. Were the members of this Convention to be tied, like children by their nurses, to a bed-post with a garter? He did not intend to be so—he was responsible to his constituents alone. The yeas and nays were taken on every important question, and the people could see who were here and who were not. He owed responsibility not to the Convention, but to his constituents alone.

But the gentleman who offered the resolution said, let us try the enforcement. It was of no practical use to do so. The penalty was insufficient. A member could not be compelled to record his name if he did not choose to do so, and he gave notice that he, for one, should never choose to do so.

Mr. HARBINE demanded the previous question, but withdrew the motion.

Mr. DASHIELL, in order, he said, to accomplish the object of the resolution more effectually, moved to amend by adding the following:

"And that the absentees hereafter shall not receive their per diem during their absence."

Mr. Dashiell asked the yeas and nays.

Mr. Jenifer moved to amend the amendment by inserting the words "or who may have been absent heretofore."

Mr. Dashiell accepted the modification.

Mr. Magraw moved further to amend by adding the words "and absentees without leave."

Mr. Dashiell accepted this modification also.

Mr. Sollers moved further to amend by embracing a provision, that so much of the *per diem* of members should be docked, as would be equal to the sum they had received during the recess.

Mr. Grason moved that the resolution and amendments be laid upon the table.

Mr. Weber call the yeas and nays, which were ordered, and being taken, resulted as follows:

Affirmative—Messrs. Chapman, President, Morgan, Blakistone, Dent, Hopewell, Lee, Chambers, of Kent, Donaldson, Dorsey, Randall, Kent, Weems, Dalrymple, Bond, Sollers, Brent, of Charles, Merrick, Jenifer, Buchanan, Chandler, Ridgely, Sherwood, of Talbot, Colston, John Dennis, James U. Dennis, Crisfield, Dashiell, Williams, Hodson, Goldsborough, Phelps, Chambers, of Cecil, McCullough, Miller, McLane, Sprigg, McCubbin, Spencer, Grason, George, Wright, McMaster, Hearn, Fooks, Biser, Annan, Davis, Kilgour, Waters, Anderson, Hollyday and Fitzpatrick—52.

Negative—Messrs. Ricaud, Mitchell, Sellman, Bell, Welch, Hicks, Eccleston, Shriver, Gaither, Sappington, Stephenson, McHenry, Magraw, Nelson, Carter, Thawley, Stewart, of Caroline, Hardcastle, Gwinn, Stewart, of Balto. city, Brent, of Balto. city, Ware, Jr., Schley, Fiery, John Newcomer, Harbine, Brewer, Weber, Slicer, Smith, Parke, Shower, Cockey and Brown —33.

And the resolution and amendments were laid upon the table.

On motion of Mr. Spencer the Convention proceeded to the order of the day.

THE ELECTIVE FRANCHISE.

The Convention again resolved itself into committee of the whole (Mr. Blakistone in the Chair) and resumed the consideration of the Report of the Committee on the Elective Franchise.

The pending question was on the motion of Mr. Phelps to amend the amendment heretofore offered by Mr. Chambers, of Kent, as a substitute for the first section of the report, by inserting after the words "Howard District," the following:

"And five days in the Election District or Ward of the City of Baltimore."

Mr. McLane obtained the floor but yielded to Mr. Chambers of Kent, who desired, he said, to supply an omission which he had inadvertantly made in the remarks which, without notes or premeditation, he had yesterday submitted to the Convention. Reference had been made to the Constitution as it had existed at the commencement of the government, and it had been alleged that according to its provisions, there never had been any requirement that a party claiming to vote should have a residence except in the State and county. He had yesterday remarked that the Constitution was formed under circumstances entirely different from those which now existed, and he intended also, but omitted to state a fact which he should now supply. It was this: When the Constitution was originally made, and as subsequently modified in 1809, the only geographical division in the State, in which votes were received, was into counties. There was no instance, he believed, in which citizens of the same county or city, or citizens of the same district were called upon, or had the privilege to vote for a different member of the Legislature, or a different Senator, or a different Congressman. Every man in his county voted at the same election for a representative for his immediate district and for none other. The result was, therefore, such as had been stated, that although from district No. 1, in county A, a voter might be translated to district No. 2, yet he had before him the choice between the same candidates, and whether his vote was cast in one district or the other, the result of the election was not changed. He meant to say that it was unimportant, that although the voter moved over-night out of one district of the county into another, yet that no one was practically injured. In the position he had yesterday assumed, therefore, he was not going in violation of any principle of the old Constitution, because a change was absolutely necessary to carry out the very principles of that instrument, since the division of one of the counties and the City of Baltimore, into different Congressional districts.

After some conversation between Mr. Bowie and Mr. Chambers,

Mr. McLane resumed the floor.

Mr. McLane referred to the legislation of Congress in passing the law establishing the district system, and contended that it was simply a direction to the States to make the elections by districts, without intending to interfere with the arrangement of the districts. To do this, Congress had no power under the Constitution of the United States. Their power was to district the States themselves and not to direct the States to do it. Their law, however, was acquiesced in by the States and the subject is not now material. The framers of our original Constitution knew that Congress had the right to establish the system of election by districts, and so they left it.

Considering the question now before the Convention as one of the highest importance, he had felt it his duty to submit the observations he was about to make. He should embrace the opportunity, however, to go beyond the immediate question, and to touch on other parts of the report. He concurred with the gentleman from Kent in many of his views. There was no question of greater importance than the purity of elections: it lies at the root of our republican institutions. Concurring in this view, with the gentleman from Kent, he was willing to go with him, so far as he could with propriety, any length to effect this object. He would not have now risen to take any part in the debate, but for the remark made by the gentleman from Dorchester, (Mr. Hicks,) which appeared to be sustained by the gentleman from Kent, that this is to be regarded as a test question, and that they who vote against this restriction are disposed to throw away all the guards of the purity of the elective franchise. Now, he begged it to be understood that he would vote against this amendment, and his objection to it is, that it was not an adequate and appropriate remedy. He would concur in any measure which, while it would prevent frauds, would, in no degree, impair the elective franchise in the hands of those who are entitled to it. But he could not vote for a proposition, which, while it aimed at the prevention of frauds, would also have the effect of restricting the right of voters legally.

He deeply regretted the state of things that had been represented as existing in this commonwealth: because, wherever his earlier lot was cast, he regarded his destiny for the future as fixed in this State. Until he came to this Convention, and heard the statements made by other gentlemen, he had formed no idea of the alleged extent to which fraud and corruption have been carried. This evil, it would appear, from these allegations, is, by no means confined to the city of Baltimore, which has been stigmatized as the sink of political iniquity, but has extended to all the counties of the State. The facts of double voting, giving money to purchase votes, giving money to obtain naturalization papers, in which men of character and standing, wealthy individuals, and even official dignitaries are alleged to have taken part, appear to be common occurrences. Who could have been prepared for such a state of things? He was not, and could not credit it to that extent. Where is the law? Is there no power to check these outrages?

He then went on to shew that bribery had been apprehended in the earlier periods of our history, as was evident from the clause in the Constitution which relates to that crime. It was feared it might reach high places; and the provision in the Constitution was a wise one. The gentleman from Kent was therefore mistaken when he said that corruption was not known to our fathers, and that they had not provided against it. The provisions inserted in our Constitution shew that it was necessary to provide against its introduction in our Judiciary and Executive officers, as well as in the elections. And while these provisions attest the apprehension that it might be practised, they also prove in what abhorence it was held by the framers of the Constitution. And now we are told publicly that bribery prevails at every election, that it pervades every district in the State. If this be true, it is indeed time that we had a Convention. There is nothing like this in England, where we have been accustomed to believe that corruption stalks abroad in open day. There is nothing like it in the history of Rome, until she had reached the zenith of her glory, and then it appeared and hastened her decline. And so it precipitated the other republics of antiquity to their ruin. And they all stand, among the wrecks of time, as beacon lights to warn those who shall come after them. If the statements made here are true, then our State is corrupt to the core. There has been nothing like it, if true. He did not say that it was true and does not believe it. But if it is true in any indirect part, it calls for a speedy and vigorous remedy; it is too dangerous to be cured by homœpathic treatment. If the disease has taken such hold in the State; if the cancer has made such progress over the body politic, it becomes our duty to take the knife and cut deep to the root, or our career will be short, and the time is not far off when we shall be stricken down by the iron hand of despotism.

And what is the remedy for this diseased condition of the State? He scarcely knew where to go for an adequate remedy—those proposed were not so. The gentleman from Anne Arundel would provide a remedy by keeping back from the poor foreigner his naturalization papers, or preventing him from receiving from others the expense of procuring them, so that he may be prevented from giving a fraudulent vote. This is certainly homœpathic and unjust treatment. While excluding two or three foreigners, we shall shut out twenty who have an indisputable right to vote. Other remedies have been proposed, all similar in their want of power to effect a cure. In all the suggestions which have been made there is a greater possibility of punishing the innocent than deterring the guilty. He would rather permit foreigners to go into our Courts, and be naturalized gratuitously. That was his remedy. Now the foreigner becomes the tool of the person who pays for his papers, and is used by him to further his purposes. Let him have his papers without cost, and he walks forth free and independent.

Another remedy looks to the question of residence. At present it is necessary that the voter shall have resided twelve months in the State, and six months in the county. The gentleman from Kent says this provision may be evaded. We have already the State residence, and the County residence. And now the district residence is wanted. These districts were established merely for the convenience of the people, and not for the better security of the ballot box. His remedy was to abolish the district elections for Commissioners, and let the whole County vote for them. This would not convert the district system, intended for the convenience of the people, into an injury.

The gentleman from Kent says, a man who has a right to his vote, is deprived of his right when an illegal vote is received; and to this he (Mr. McL.) agreed. But what remedy does he propose? He takes away from a voter who moves from one district into another, the right to vote, because there is a knave standing by him, who will be admitted to vote, if the honest voter is. All the remedies proposed, like this, would unnecessarily shackle the right of suffrage, and be ineffectual to cure the disease.

He objected to the proposition laid down by the gentleman from Kent, that every right that must necessarily be abused ought to be qualified, as fraught with mischief if carried out. What does he mean by "necessarily?" He must mean that when a right becomes very valuable, it will be seized upon by some other than the possessor, and to prevent this, it ought to be taken away. And this the gentleman puts forth as a maxim of his political morality.

Mr. CHAMBERS explained. What he said was, that where the practical exercise of an abstract right is accompanied by evils which counterbalance the benefits derived from the existence of the right, it ought to be abandoned. That was his morality, and he would stand or fall by it.

Mr. McLANE resumed. If the right of suffrage was an abstract right, what is a practical right? This is a practical right. If it be an abstract right, and the mischiefs resulting from its practical exercise counterbalance the benefits from its exercise, it is better that it be abandoned. That was the principle of the political morality of the gentleman from Kent. It was a principle unknown to any government, civil or divine. If this principle were carried out, the effect would be that all government must stand still. He then referred to the principle which was perceptible in the operations of a Divine Providence, which separated the innocent from the guilty, and to the principle of our own penal code, which lays it down as better, that ten guilty should escape than that one innocent person should be condemned. According to the argument of the gentleman from Kent, we ought to be deprived of an unquestionable right, because the exercise of that right may lead to great abuses. He could not see how this principle could apply to the elective franchise, which is, in itself, too valuable to be counterbalanced by any imaginable mischiefs. He referred to banking operations, which led to forgeries, where the forger is punished, while the innocent man is untouched. The liberty of the press was liable to great abuse, because it sometimes becomes licentious; yet we do not attempt to restrict that liberty. Formerly, indeed, restraints were imposed on the liberty of the press; and it was attempted to restrain it under a recent administration in England, and also in this country. But no one now would attempt to restrict the liberty of the press as a punishment. This liberty stands, in importance, side by side, by the elective franchise. Instead of restricting its free action, we are content with punishing those who abuse it. One great principle is, that no man shall be prevented from publishing what he pleases, but such as falsely publish are punished.

But, he went on to enquire, what are the causes of the corruption of the ballot-box in this State? Let us find out the cause, and apply the remedy to that. The cause is to be found in the unhealthy condition of public opinion. It is because public opinion winks at these corruptions that they have grown to their present enormity. Unless it is in response to public opinion, we can never make penal laws which will prove efficient to check the evil. Public opinion is not healthy on this point. His remedy was to cure public opinion, and then our penal laws will prove sufficient. This morbid state of public opinion has been produced by the strife of parties, under our conflicting State administrations. He did not mean to assail one party more than another. He condemned both parties where their conduct merited condemnation. In their eagerness for political ascendency, they have not always been careful enough to keep on the right side of the line which separates the legal from the illegal. The course of corruption is downward: it begins at the head, and descends to the feet. The example of the high, preserves or corrupts the law. And so it will ever be. We shall have a corrupt community in the mass when the heart or the head is corrupt. When men holding high stations become corrupt, we must expect the mass to be infected. When we see men of wealth and standing contributing their means to feed corruption, it is our duty to grapple with them, and shut up the source of the evil. Without the aid of money, there would be no corrupt voting.

The bitter fruit which is produced by the strife of parties is a corruption which increases until it destroys the institutions in which it is found. Such was its fatal influence on the ancient republics. Following their course of corruption their fate will be ours.

He referred to the system of gerrymandering which had on several occasions exhibited itself in the arrangement of the election districts. This vice originated not in our State; it had its origin elsewhere. But the application of it in this State has been productive of the colonization of voters, which has been so much complained of. The evil of this principle is the result of the struggle of the people to extricate themselves from the condition in which its oppressive operation has placed them. He only stated the fact; he did not justify it. It would have been better to wait patiently until it had worked its own overthrow. But if you press on any portion of the community, it will rise against the pressure. You find a people in the tranquil enjoyment of a freedom of more than half a century, and by a single law you destroy it. Were it not that thus public opinion could rectify the evil which oppresses it, a more dreadful strife would be engendered by the weak against the strong.

There is one other result, a reference to which caused him great pain. Large contributions have been made by wealthy individuals, for the purpose of carrying on elections. He had known committees formed in the City of Baltimore, for the express purpose of collecting funds, opening books, and calling on office-holders and others for contributions of ten and twenty dollars each, for the purpose of defraying the expenses of an election. A candidate for Governor has been assessed as high as $3000 or $4000, and has been told it was for the purpose of defraying the expenses of the election. Such is the condition of things, that the most respectable men have been required to give their means. And how many are there in this Hall, who can say they are free from this imputation?

Mr. CHAMBERS. I am free.

Mr. McLANE resumed, stating that money thus

raised has been sent into every part of the State. He thought all had contributed their means for one purpose or other. He himself was not so free from the charge as the gentleman from Kent. He admitted that he had contributed to the expenses of an election. It was, indeed, so common a case, that it had ceased to be regarded as dishonorable among gentlemen. Our only remedy for this evil is to correct public opinion. He would pass laws that would lead to that correction and stamp all such conduct as unworthy. He would protect the franchise, preserve the innocent from fraud, and punish the guilty. He would render bribery infamous, both to the giver and the receiver of a bribe. He knew no other way of securing the purity of the ballot-box. No law, however, could have a beneficial effect, unless it was in response to public opinion, and did not involve the innocent in a common fate with the guilty. Any law that punished the legal voter in order to reach the fraudulent, would enlist both in opposition to it, and render it ineffectual. Would this amendment of a five days residence effect the object proposed? A man disposed to do wrong would find no greater difficulty in getting over five days, than over a longer period—such as is provided by a residence of six and twelve months already in the laws. He did not expect to purify the ballot box by such measures as these; it would be just as easy a task to purge society. Frauds of a higher character exist; and when we can reach these great frauds, we may hope to be able to remedy the others. But while we leave the greater evils unremedied, it is vain to expect that we can extirpate the smaller.

Mr. Merrick expressed his regret, that concurring so fully as he did with much the greater part of the general remarks so eloquently made by the honorable gentleman from Cecil, he should find himself compelled to dissent from the conclusions to which he had come. He was not disposed to trespass on the Convention by any attempt to make a speech in reply, and indeed, were he ever so much disposed to do so, the difficulty he now had of utterance, from a severe cold, forbade such an effort.

He united most cordially with the honorable gentleman in deprecating the effects of party strife here and every where, and the honorable member could not be more deeply impressed than he was with a sense of its past and a dread of its future influence upon our republican institutions. He was fully aware that under the excitements engendered by party contentions, many good men would temporarily forget that just sense of moral and political duty, by which ordinarily they were actuated; and their evil example on such occasions had the fatal tendency of lowering and corrupting the moral tone of the whole community—of producing that unhappy state of public opinion, by which it had or might become to be regarded that in elections almost anything was justifiable which tended to secure the ascendancy of your party, that the end sanctified the means. He agreed too, that the very best means of preventing and correcting these evils was the enlightenment and purification of public opinion, and wise and patriotic men should spare no pains, leave no stone unturned both by precept and example, by general education and legislation, so to enlighten and improve the general public sentiment. He united, too, most cordially with the honorable gentleman in calling on the Convention to elevate their minds above all subordinate considerations, and come up in the spirit of liberalized and enlightened patriotism, in the true spirit of the *Patres Conscripti* of the Commonwealth, to the performance of the high duties entrusted to them, and to bring to the consideration of the great question now under consideration, a proper sense of its deep and abiding importance. True, he said, it was difficult, very difficult, to divest ourselves of the influences of long cherished associations—the ties of habit—and deal with such questions solely with reference to their own intrinsic merit—but the end was at least worthy of a vigorous effort. Such were the infirmities of human nature, that a perfect accomplishment of this object was hardly to be expected, yet an approximation to this good end was certainly to be hoped for.

Sir, said he, what is the question we now have on hand: the regulation of the exercise of the elective franchise and the protection of this most precious prerogative of freemen from frauds and abuses. Could you deal with a graver or more momentous question to a republican people? It is the foundation stone of the republic—the sheet anchor of freedom. It should not be touched with unholy hands; and the guards and securities thrown around it should be proportioned to its inestimable value—and yet gentlemen argue, or seem to argue, that because it is so valuable and precious, it must be left unguarded! And here is the point of great difference between myself and the very distinguished gentleman from Cecil. He has discoursed fluently on the subject of political morality; upon the baneful effects of party strife; upon the invaluable nature of the elective franchise; and admits that frauds are, and are likely to be, practised upon the privilege—yet he proposes no guards to protect us from these frauds, and declares himself averse to the slight dditional security which would be given by the pending amendment, requiring only five days previous residence within the district before a newcomer shall be there entitled to vote.

Mr. Chairman, as I have before said, I am utterly opposed to all improper restrictions upon the right of suffrage. I have resisted throughout all attempts to make invidious distinctions on this subject, among classes of our citizens. I have voted steadily against all amendments intended or tending to impose any other or greater restrictions upon our naturalized than are imposed upon our native citizens. I am here to advocate the extension of this sacred right equally to all our citizens of every age and condition, to whom, according to the general judgment and general sense of the people of the State it should be extended; but it must be limited; it must be guarded; it must be protected,—it is too dear, too valuable to freemen to be trifled with. Some gentlemen have said they were for giving it the widest extension. How far would these gentlemen extend it? Would they give this right to free negroes? Would they give it to all, indiscriminately? What then becomes of the qualifications of age, sex, residence within the State. I can consent to no such extension as this—but my desire is to give to this right as wide an extension as prudently and safely we can, and to secure to all to whom the right now is by law or can safely be given, as full, free, and untrammelled exercise of this invaluable right as is consistent with its preservation and the purity of the ballot box. The gentleman says we cannot fully guard against the abuses complained of, that the remedy proposed is inadequate. Admitted; but what then? Does it follow because we cannot do all we desire, that therefore we are to do nothing? Are we to conclude, because we are imperfect by nature and can in nothing attain perfection—that we are therefore not to endeavor to approximate to it? I am of a very different opinion, and think we should do all we can, to save and protect ourselves and the freemen of Maryland, and then bear the lessened evils which we cannot remedy.

Mr. Merrick said it was too true, as had been said, party strifes and political corruptions had led and were likely to lead to the destruction of republican institutions. They had produced the downfal of all that had gone before us, and their warning voice sounded in our ears to guard ourselves from a similar impending fate. "The price of liberty, we all knew, was perpetual vigilance." It becomes us, then, the chosen agents of the free people of Maryland, clothed with the high power of framing a new compact of Government for them and their posterity, now especially to exercise that vigilance and to engraft into that compact all the appropriate safeguards to that liberty which our united wisdom could devise. Nothing was dearer, nothing more precious in the eyes of a free people, than the elective franchise. It was the life-giving principle of republics, and not less dearly cherished by freemen, than the ruddy drops which warm their hearts. Protect it then—preserve it in its purity. We have had many violent party contentions; but violent as these have been, they are nothing compared with what we are reasonably to expect will arise in the distant future. The Constitution we now make is to operate for good or for evil upon that future. Its effects—its working—are to be felt when we who make it—when the parties of the present day and all who compose them, shall have passed away and been forgotten. Nothing we can do is to be of greater effect, than the means devised for the preservation of the purity of the ballot-box. While that purity shall be preserved, all will be safe, and upon it and its efficiency our habit now is, and this habit will grow and strengthen with our growth, to repose with confident security. Thus the ballot-box, if pure, has been found and will be found in future, to be the reliance of all good republicans for a redress of grievances, and to supercede the necessity of all appeals to violence. It has been and it will be to all defeated parties, even when writhing and chafing under the mortification of recent defeat,

"Hope's precious pearl in sorrow's cup,
Which unmelted at the bottom lay,
To shine again when all drunk up,
The bitterness shall pass away."

Yes, sir; reliance upon this, if its purity be preserved, will calm their angry passions, will sooth their troubled breasts. They will submit to present defeat, and trust to reason to bring about convictions of right in the minds of their fellow citizens at a subsequent trial of strength in this peaceful mode. But let frauds and corruptions creep in; let freemen be unjustly deprived of their rights in this particular; let the decisions of your ballot-box be rendered false and polluted, and the beauty of that pearl is lost; its lustre is gone—gone and forever; and with it dies the hopes of freemen and of freedom. Guard it then, and guard it well, I implore you.

Reference had been made, by the honorable gentleman from Cecil, to the act of Congress requiring members of Congress to be elected by single districts throughout the United States; and the constitutionality of that law had been questioned. He (Mr. Merrick) was a member of Congress at the time that law was passed; and he knew, plain as the language of the Constitution appeared to him to be, which conferred the power, the constitutionality of that exercise of the power, was questioned at the time. It was made a party question of—one party contending for the power as exercised, and the other contending that Congress could not require the elections to be held in the States by districts without themselves marking out the districts. The majority in both Houses of Congress thought otherwise, and the law was passed as it now stands on the Statute books. Party spirit ran high; and for a time the defeated party manifested a spirit of determined resistance to the law. But as soon as the passions and excitement of the hour had subsided and reason resumed her throne in the public mind, the law was carried into effect in every part of the Union; there was a general acquiescence under its provisions, and the members of Congress are now every where elected by single districts. This had occasioned the necessity for re-arranging the Congressional districts in Maryland, and the consequent division of some of the counties and the city of Baltimore, and the attachment of parts of each to different districts for the election of Congressmen. Up to that time the requirement of a certain length of previous residence within the district as a qualification of the voter, was not so necessary, because the county and city limits had been always respected, and the qualification of six months previous residence within the county or city was considered sufficient; but since this new division, the former requirement of six months residence has been found not to answer the purpose designed by it in the district—to form which, counties and the city are divided. And more than that, it does not operate equally and alike upon all the citizens of the State. In this way, every man having the other qualifications, is entitled, under the law, to vote at all elections in the county or city where he has resided for the last preceding six months. Different parts of the city of Baltimore now compose one entire Congressional district, and the other a portion of another Congressional district. A citizen of that city, then, (no fixed duration of residence being required, in migrating from district to district within the same county or city,) can acquire the right of voting in the district in which he has not before resided, though it be for a representative of a different people from those with whom he has before resided, by passing over the line separating the two districts only a few hours before the election; whilst another citizen of the State, equally entitled to the right of suffrage, but an inhabitant of another county, cannot come into the same district and acquire the right of voting without a previous residence of six months. This is unjust. But the worst feature is, the facility it gives to the perpetration of frauds on the elective franchise, under the system known by the name of "colonizing voters"—which facility, it is said, is extensively availed of. And it is this great evil we propose, in some measure, to correct by the pending amendment. It is not perfect I know, but it is better than nothing; and the best, it seems from the previous votes of the Convention, we can now obtain. It will answer to some degree, the object of requiring the six months previous residence within the counties, which I take it must have been in part, at least, to arm the resident legal voters with the means of protecting themselves from the perpetration of such frauds upon this their dearest of political rights. By a previous residence among the people entitled to vote at an election, the person claiming that right becomes known, and his right or the absence of it, is of easier proof by those disposed to guard the purity of this franchise, and does not, therefore, depend exclusively upon statements or proof derived from the claimant himself.

This five days does not, I admit, take away the inequality of the operations of the present system, as regards the citizens of other counties, nor is the means of self-protection it affords to the resident voters of the district perfect; but it is much better than nothing, and will prove a very great impediment in the way of the perpetration of the species of fraud complained of. Mr. MERRICK added, he would have said much more, but he really felt he was physically unable.

Mr. PRESSTMAN stated that it had been held by the judges in Baltimore, that no man is entitled to vote in a ward unless he goes to reside, previously, in the ward, with a *bona fide* intention to remain there. He must be a resident of the ward at the time of the election.

Mr. CHAMBERS. For how long before the election?

Mr. PRESSTMAN. He must have lived there the day before.

Mr. CHAMBERS. And may leave the day after—a *bona fide* intention to remain one day and go away the next.

Mr. PRESSTMAN. Could any reasonable man consider that as a *bona fide* intention to reside there?

Mr. MERRICK. Yes, the voter must have a *bona fide* intention to remain one day.

Mr. SPENCER said he had very briefly, on yesterday, expressed his opposition to the amendment under consideration. He did so, at the time, in consequence of members having imputed to those who voted against it, an indisposition to preserve the purity of the ballot box. He had, at a very early period, offered resolutions to this Convention, which afforded indisputable evidence of his feelings on that subject. He now rose to notify this body of his intention, at the proper place, to offer the following amendments, which he read, as follows:

"Insert after the second section, the following additional sections:

"Sec. 3. That every person who shall be elected to any office whatever, at any election to take place in this State hereafter, or who shall be appointed to any office whatever in said State hereafter, shall, before he enters upon the duties of the office to which he may be elected or appointed, first take and subscribe the following oath (if not conscientiously scrupulous, and in such case, affirmation) before some one of the Judges of the Court of Appeals of this State:

"I, ——, do solemnly swear, that I have not at any election held in this State since the ratification of the new Constitution of this State, or in any manner violated the provisions of the second section of the new Constitution relating to bribery, and that I have not procured or induced, by any means, any individual or individuals to vote at any such election in violation of the provisions contained in the first section of said Constitution relating to the age and residence of voters."

And any person who shall swear falsely in the premises, shall be guilty of perjury, and on conviction in due course of law, subject to all its pains and penalties.

Sec. 4. That the Judge, before whom such oath or affirmation shall be taken, shall cause the same to be subscribed by the person so swearing or affirming, in a book to be by him kept for such purpose, a duplicate of which said oath or affirmation, as the case may be, he shall transmit to the Clerk of the Court of Appeals of this State, with the name of the individual who took and subscribed the same, designating the office to which he has been elected or appointed, to be by the said Clerk, whose duty it shall be to do so, recorded in a book to be by him kept for such purpose, among the records of the said Court of Appeals, a certified copy of which said oath or affirmation, by the said Judge under his seal, or of the said duplicate by the said Clerk under his seal of office shall be had, taken and received as evidence in any of the Courts of this State having criminal jurisdiction.

Mr. CHAMBERS asked permission of the gentleman to state the fact, that the committee had a meeting yesterday, at which the principle of the amendment now suggested by the gentlemen from Queen Anne's was agreed to. He had been expected to reduce it to form, and present it as a supplementary report. It would be reported to the Convention as soon as he could prepare it.

He would only add, that the committee were prepared to act on the subject.

Mr. SPENCER expressed his gratification that the committee had come to such a conclusion. He had not seen or read the provisions from the committee, and his course would not, therefore, be changed.

He here read another of his proposed amendments, as follows:

Sec. 5. That the Governor of this State shall under no circumstances grant a *nolle prosequi* to any person, who may be prosecuted in due course of law in any of the courts of this State, for any violation of the second Section of this Constitution, nor shall he grant a pardon to any person who may be convicted in due course of law, as aforesaid, for any such violation, unless he is satisfied that the said prosecution was malicious, unfounded and untrue.

These amendments would show that so far as he was concerned, he was anxious to preserve the purity of the ballot box, by preventing bribery or the colonizing of voters. On these, and the remedies suggested by the gentleman from Cecil (Mr. MCLANE) and a proper tone in public morals will rest our security against the corruption of the elective franchise. It is not right or just to attribute them to the humble, the uninformed, the poor. They originate in more elevated sources and flow from a higher fountain—from those who occupy seats of power and who are distinguished by wealth and station. Official dignitaries have connived at, encouraged and often taken the lead in them. The humble instrument is not as much to be blamed, as the tempter who, taking advantage of his necessities, seduces him by his alluring bribe. Men of the highest talent and education in the State are implicated. It is well known that committees are appointed and money raised to immense amounts, for the purpose of controling the elections, by buying and colonizing voters. Committees to carry out purposes so discredible are raised. We must strike down this evil, in order to arrest the disease. We must interpose barriers which will prevent our public men from engaging in the corrupting schemes which are resorted to at elections. It will not do to impose restrictions upon the right of suffrage. That right is too sacred. If the amendment proposed is adopted, it will operate most unjustly and oppressively upon the laboring classes. It will effectually strike down the right of many humble and honest men every where, throughout the State, whilst it will inflict no punishment on official criminals. In the city of Baltimore it will work particularly hard. Our elections for State purposes occur early in October, the first Wednesday, and we have heard no intimation that the time will be changed. Hundreds of the honest laboring classes in that city, men who have not the substance to enable them to procure permanent residences, rent by the quarter, which will expire on the first day of October. If you pass this restriction, and their necessities, business or convenience require them to move into another ward, they will lose their votes. Five days will not have elapsed from the termination of their quarter to the day of election. It was not just to deprive this class of citizens of their rights by imposing such restrictions. It was not proper to deprive an honest man of his rights of suffrage, because another abuses it. There is no reason why a just and honest man should not vote, because dishonest men abuse the same high privilege. And yet, this is the excuse given for such a measure, by the gentleman from Kent, and others. The morals of such a sentiment cannot be appreciated. They rest upon no authority derived from any school in ethics.

It is alleged that the object was to prevent the colonizing of voters. It would have no such effect. Colonizing would be conducted on a more extensive and demoralizing scale. It is no new thing in Maryland. Many years ago, under the old divisions of party, as he had understood, and the gentleman from Kent, (Mr. CHAMBERS,) he supposed, knew of the fact, voters were colonized in Kent for six months, previous to an election.

Mr. CHAMBERS, interposing, observed the gentleman then resided in the county.

Mr. SPENCER. Yes—he was then a boy, but the gentleman was a leader of the party which was reported to be engaged in the matter. It was said that a factory was established in Chestertown for the purpose of *manufacturing* voters.

Mr. CHAMBERS in explanation said a factory was established by a company, and he was a stockholder in it, but it had no relation to the elections, as the gentleman supposed.

Mr. SPENCER was about to reply, when Mr. BRENT of Baltimore, called the gentleman to order, they being engaged in a colloquem, which was irregular.

Mr. SPENCER resumed and went on to say, that we could gain nothing by adopting the five days system. The only effect would be that voters would be colonized for five days, instead of six months; and during those five days the grossest corruption will be practised, and the largest purse will win the victory. We have had in this State proof in abundance of the power of money to corrupt and destroy; and if we adopt this restriction, we must expect to see a flood of corruption inundating the State. You can never expect to see the ballot-box purified, until the money temptation can be checked. It can never be effected by bearing down upon the poor and humble man, whose poverty lays him open to temptation. Let the humble be uninterrupted in their enjoyment of the right of suffrage; and adopt the principle that no man shall be allowed to hold office, until he shall have purified himself, on oath, from all suspicion of having been guilty of bribery or corruption. Some gentlemen admit that they had contributed to election expenses. Would these gentlemen, if elected to high office, put their hands to the book. He believed there was no man here, who would perpetrate so palpable an outrage on the laws of God and man. Candidates for office would not, could not, directly or indirectly, engage in frauds and corruptions. They would not give money to buy or colonize voters. Nor could their friends do so for them.

It would be impossible for it to be done, without the knowledge of the aspirants for office. And if it could, by possibility, be done without such knowledge, it would necessarily bring the person so elected, into suspicion and disrepute. But, besides this, each and every man in the community will know, that though he may not for the time be a candidate, yet the time may come, when he may desire to hold an office, by election or otherwise. The oath of qualification will forever stare him in the face. He will ever remember that any violation of the law, in any form, or by any means, either in buying or colonizing voters, will operate a perpetual bar to his success. To cover it, he will have to perjure himself, with all its consequences of exposure, and with all its pains and penalties, inflicted by God and man. He would enter upon his office with a violated and wounded conscience and with the harrassing terror of expected exposure.

Every argument which had been advanced in favor of restriction, had been answered already? He referred to the fact of the obtaining of the right to vote at Baltimore, by sleeping there one night, and was about to remark on it, when

Mr. Merrick interposed a remark. While a man moving from one ward to another, may require the right to vote in six hours, you and I could not obtain it without a residence of six months.

Mr. Presstman. Should it so happen that a different arrangement of the districts was to be made, the same evil would occur. What difference did it make in the right to vote, whether a man lived on one side the street or the other? Besides, the gentlemen, if he lost his vote, would do so voluntarily, by leaving his county, where he had a right to vote.

Mr. Spencer. The gentleman from Baltimore, had given the true construction of the law. The residence in the ward or district, must be real and not fictitious. Sleeping would not afford evidence of the fact. It depended on a *bona fide* intention. His exposition was received with a *smile*. He put it to the gentleman from Kent, whose *smile* he had noticed, to say whether, if as a judge, a case came before him, the evidence of which showed that the party had sworn, that he went *bona fide* to reside in a ward, or district, when the evidence proved, that he only slept a night and left it, the next day, he would not inflict punishment on him?

Mr. Chambers. If a jury convicted him, I would send him to the Penitentiary.

Mr. Spencer. And would not any intelligent jury convict?

Mr. Chambers. They ought to do so.

Mr. Spencer. The gentleman from Kent had answered. If a man swears he went with a *bona fide* intention to reside, and then went away the next day, he would be guilty of perjury. And how shall we be benefited by substituting five nights for one night. If he would perjure himself in one case, he would in another.

He went on to state that the right of suffrage was restricted in the early period of the Government. And if it should be the desire of the people to restrict it now, they have a right. But is it expedient? He held it to be inexpedient, and impolitic. He held that every man should have a right to vote. This was the position on which he stood. He would never consent to trench on the right of suffrage. He would vote against all restrictions, except those which are already in the Constitution. He, as he had heretofore said, had seen great injustice practised under the restrictions as they now existed. An election rarely occurred, at which legal voters were not rejected, by the judges of elections, urged by men who stood at their backs, and who knew better. Who knew, at the time, they were doing an act of injustice. Voters were often rejected, for partizan purposes, as well on the ground of residence as age, whose right to vote was beyond question. Other restrictions will inflict greater evils.

Mr. Davis said that after the able and eloquent speeches which had been made, he only rose to state a fact. It is well known that the great question of Reform had its origin in Frederick county; that not being able to obtain a convention to revise the Constitution, that county set about the work in her own limits through the legislation of the State. In doing so, she set an example worthy of the imitation of this Convention. In 1838, she petitioned the Legislature for a change in the mode of electing the members of the Levy Court, from the Governor to an election by the people. The county was divided into three Levy Court districts, and, as a qualification for voters to vote for members of the Levy Court, it was provided by chapter 261, section III, "that the voters in each Levy Court district in said county, who shall be qualified to vote for delegates to the General Assembly, and shall have resided *six* months in said Levy Court district in which they shall offer to vote, shall be entitled to vote for as many persons in said district as Justices of the Levy Court in said county as hereinbefore assigned to such district."

By reference to the journal of the House of Delegates of that session, he found that his honorable friend, Mr. Biser, then before him, and Mr. Schley, now a member of this Convention from Washington county, were then Delegates for Frederick county to the General Assembly. Mr. Schley reported the bill above referred to; and although he had been unable to trace the vote upon that bill, he found that Mr. Biser had introduced another bill to abolish the Commissioners of Tax and refer their duties to this same Levy Court, with the restriction of the six months residence as provided for in the said bill. The people in Frederick appeared to be so much in love with this system, that upon an enlargement of the number of Levy Court districts in 1844, from three to five, it was provided by chapter one hundred and ninety-two, section five, "that every voter in each of the Levy Court districts as described in the the third section of the act, who shall be qualified to vote for Delegates to the General Assembly, and who shall have resided at least *six* months next preceding the election in the Levy Court district in which he may offer to vote, shall in such Levy Court district, be entitled to vote," &c.

And on reference to the journal of the House, he found in addition to the gentlemen already named, that Mr. Bowie of Prince Georges, was then a member; and it no where appeared that he had raised his voice against the oppression, wrong, and injustice done to the people of Frederick county by this restriction which he now thought would be the result of the smallest restriction imposed.

Mr. Bowie interposed. It was for Frederick county only.

Mr. Davis presumed his friend would as soon raise his voice against oppression in Frederick county, as in Prince George's county. He commended this wholesome example of the Reformers of Frederick county to the grave attention of this Convention.

Mr. Spencer said Governor Grason had just been elected Governor, and this was the action of the Whigs to deprive him of the patronage.

Mr. Davis said it was well known as a matter of history, that the politics of Frederick county have vacillated with the returning season of almost every year. And although it may then have been a Whig measure, the Democrats since had had the power to change it. But so satisfactory was its operation, that it was still to be found on the Statute Book.

Mr. Biser said, the gentleman from Montgomery had held up Frederick as the great Reform county. He thanked him for the compliment, which he properly appreciated. He was sorry it was not Montgomery. He had himself introduced a bill in the House of Delegates to make the election by general ticket. It was rejected in the House. In 1838, when the gentleman from Queen Ann's was Governor, he was not in the House. A gentleman from Washington county introduced a bill, the effect of which would have been to strangle the strength of the county. The vacillation of Frederick was in consequence of the policy adopted by the Whigs.

Loud cries for the "question."

Mr. Jenifer (to whom the floor had been awarded,) said that he had not risen to make a speech, but to give notice of his intention to effect the very object which gentlemen who called for the "question" were so anxious to attain. He notified the Convention that he should to-morrow morning move a resolution, providing that the vote be taken on the amendments to this article at two o'clock.

Mr. Brent, of Baltimore city, made a brief explanation. It had been said that he had justified what is called the colonization of voters. He had not done so. He had said that in general elections, the voter might cast his vote wherever he chose, in the election district, so that he gave but one vote, as the result would be the same. He thought in the election of County Commissioners, the general ticket system the fairest, and therefore the *bona fide* removal of voters from one election district to another, should be unrestricted, except that they should only vote once at the same election. He preferred that every candidate should represent numbers rather than territory. Baltimore city formed two Congressional districts, and a voter could remove from one district to the other, and vote in his new residence without the limitation of six months residence, which is required in removals from one Congressional district consisting of counties, to another consisting of counties. So the county, of Anne Arundel is divided into two Congressional districts, and a voter could remove from Anne Arundel proper, into Howard district of the county, and vote there without previous residence.

Mr. Dorsey said it had always been held that voters so removing could not vote immediately, and they had been always excluded.

Mr. Brent, resuming, said he could not see how that was unless by the terms of the special act separating Howard district from Anne Arundel county, for judicial and municipal purposes. Neither the Constitution nor the election laws, would justify such exclusion. If we adopt these isolated cases as a rule of action, rather than the general condition of things, then we must carry out the principle whereon the distinction is found. But if a resident of Baltimore is to forfeit his right to vote, because he has changed his ward two or three times before an election, or a citizen of a county because he has removed from one election district to another, it is disfranchisement of a legal voter, for no other reason than that his admission to vote may open the way for colonization of voters from district to district, or ward to ward, for election purposes only. What right have we to do this?

He then referred to the roving character of a portion of the population of Baltimore, living by daily labor, where they could obtain it, from Fell's Point to the Western limits of the city, working and living in one ward to-day, and another to-morrow. They are citizens of Baltimore, and if they come to vote in the ward in which they are employed, it would be gross injustice to disfranchise them.

He then replied to some of the remarks of the gentleman from Kent, (Mr. Chambers) as to the effect on party candidates, which might be produced by voters changing their Congressional district, and voting without the required residence, a ground on which the action of this Convention ought not to be based. But even adopting this view, no harm could result from obtaining a full expression of public opinion among the legal voters. The gentleman from Kent said that this restriction, as to residence in wards and districts, was not in the old Constitution, because colonization was then unknown. Mr. B. said he was not old enough to speak of those times, but he had heard old men say that party spirit was fiercer then than now, and frauds were every where practised.

If the argument of the gentleman from Kent was good, what is to become of Dorchester county, one of whose delegates (Mr. Hicks) stated that when he was about to challenge an illegal voter, a friend whispered "let him alone, he votes the right ticket," and the man voted without objection?

Mr. HICKS explained, stating that it was too late to stop the voter, when he was about to attempt it.

Mr. BRENT expressed his gratification that the gentleman could acquit himself from the implication which others had understood him to admit. But were the honest voters of Dochester county to be disfranchised because some of its citizens winked at such frauds? He hoped not, and he would never consent to such a principle.

Mr. RICAUD moved that the Committee rise.

Mr. STEWART, of Caroline, asked the yeas and nays.

Mr. BOWIE. Does the gentleman ask the yeas and nays on the motion that the Committee rise?

Mr. STEWART. I will explain my reasons.

The CHAIRMAN interposing. In the opinion of the Chair, a motion that the Committee rise, is in the nature of a motion to adjourn, and is not therefore debateable.

Mr. RICAUD. I hope that the Committee will rise.

The CHAIRMAN. The Chair cannot entertain any debate.

The yeas and nays were refused.

The Committee then rose and reported progress,

And the Convention adjourned.

THURSDAY, Jan. 16, 1851.

Prayer by the Rev. Mr. GRAUFF.

The roll having been called, and a quorum being present, the journal of yesterday was read and approved.

DEBATE ON THE ELECTIVE FRANCHISE.

Mr. JENIFER offered a resolution, remarking that he thought its adoption could not fail to be attended with beneficial results.

The resolution was read as follows:

Resolved, That all debate in committee of the whole upon the first section of the report of the committee on Elective Franchise, shall cease this day at one o'clock, and the committee of the whole shall then proceed to vote upon the amendments then pending, or which may be offered,—and five minutes may be allowed to any member to explain any amendment which he may offer.

Mr. PHELPS inquired whether the terms of the resolution did not preclude debate on all the sections of the report of the committee? The committee of the whole was now engaged in the consideration of the *first* section. The whole debate for some days past had been confined to that section; and if this order should be adopted, debate would be cut off on such amendments as might be offered to the other sections. He had no disposition to delay the action of the Convention, but he thought that the greatest latitude ought to be afforded for amendments to the other sections and for enforcing by explanation the propriety of their adoption. The Convention should bear in mind that it was not engaged in the mere ordinary business of legislation, but in the formation of an organic law which might endure for ages.

Mr. JENIFER. I modify my resolution so as to make it applicable exclusively to the *first* section.

Mr. PHELPS. Then I have no objection to its adoption.

Mr. DORSEY said, he confessed he did not expect that any such proposition as this would be adopted, although the gentleman from Charles (Mr. JENIFER) had yesterday intimated his intention to offer it. It would certainly operate unfairly upon those members of the body who desired to express their sentiments, but who, not possessing the agility and activity of some others, were not always able to obtain the recognition of the Chair. He thought it due to the very important nature of the subject under discussion, that the amplest opportunity should be given to gentlemen on all sides of the Convention to express their views. Especially important was it that gentlemen should have the opportunity to answer some of the new views and arguments which had recently been thrown out, so that the discussion might not be confined altogether to one side of the question. The proposition reminded him of a story he had heard of a German living somewhere in the upper counties, who offered up a prayer something in this form:

God bless me and my wife,
My son and his wife;
Them four—
And no more! (Laughter.)

Mr. JENIFER (Mr. DORSEY yielding the floor) said, he would further amend the resolution by confining its operation to those gentlemen who had already spoken.

Mr. DORSEY, (continuing.) Subjects have been discussed in the speeches of several gentlemen, to which no opportunity for reply has been given.

The President interposed, and indicated his judgment that the amendment last proposed by the gentleman from Charles, conflicted with one of the standing rules of the body, and it was not, therefore, in order.

Mr. WEBER (to Mr. JENIFER.) Did the gentleman so modify his resolution as to make it applicable to the first section only?

Mr. JENIFER. I did.

Mr. WEBER. I then move to amend the resolution by restoring it to its original form. The object of going into committee of the whole was to take into consideration, at one and the same time, the whole subject matter of the report. The gentlemen who have taken part in the discussion have traveled over the entire ground. They have not confined themselves to any proposed amendment—but have discussed, generally, and freely, the various abuses and corruptions which are said to prevail in connection with the elective franchise, and the remedies which they deemed most appropriate to them.

We have been in committee on this report,

since the recess. It was thought that but little time would be occupied in its discussion. Matters more important remain to be acted upon; and if we are to occupy one, two, nay three weeks upon this report, the same delay in the consideration of other things will take place; and thus a month may elapse before we reach a question which was made the order of the day for yesterday. I mean the report from the committee on representation. I hope gentlemen may see the necessity of bringing this discussion to a close, but that some few hours may be allowed for the benefit of those gentlemen who have not yet been heard. After that, let us stop the general debate, and, five minutes being reserved for explanations, all the time that ought now to be given will be extended.

Mr. DORSEY regarded this subject as one of the gravest matters that could engage the consideration of the Convention, and thought that an undue advantage would be taken if gentlemen were not permitted to reply to the new facts and arguments which had been brought forward. If the Convention would exclude the views of members in this way, and hear only those of one side, he supposed he must submit.

Mr. BRENT, of Baltimore city. I have myself spoken two or three times on this report. I do not desire to speak again. It is no wish of mine to prevent gentlemen who have not spoken, from addressing the Convention; but only those who have already been heard. I am, therefore, in favor of the amendment of the gentleman from Charles.

The President explained that the Chair had ruled that amendment out of order, and stated the reasons for the decision.

Mr. BRENT. Well, sir, I can only say, I hope the Convention will put a stop to this debate. If it is to be prolonged until all the new views and arguments which may strike the minds of members, shall be delivered and answered, it is easy to see that final action on the report will be postponed for an indefinite period of time.

Mr. RIDGELY enquired of the President, what was the state of the question?

The President explained.

Mr. RIDGELY. It is necessary that something should be done to prevent the time of this body being occupied for an interminable period by some half dozen of its members, to the exclusion of all others. I am as ready and willing to listen to gentlemen as any other member of the Convention, but I protest against its time being monopolised by a few. We have a rule extending to every gentleman the right to express his sentiments, and that rule is constantly violated by members speaking three or four times.

Mr. BOWIE. Enforce your rule, then.

Mr. RIDGELY (apparently not hearing the interruption) proceeded to contest the sufficiency of the argument which had been urged, that gentlemen were not allowed to answer new views and positions, and to point out the everlasting delay which must take place in the business of the Convention, if this rule of action was to be adopted. The Convention should live up to its rule. He hoped the proposition would be agreed to. If it affected any particular gentleman injuriously, that was his misfortune; the general result of the proposition would be wholesome and effective.

Mr. BLAKISTONE (who, under the invitation of the President, has presided over the deliberations of the committee, whilst the subject of the Elective Franchise has been under consideration,) rose, he said, for the purpose of putting himself right before the Convention, for he understood this to be an indictment against him.

The President (interposing.) The Chair would not entertain any indictment against the gentleman.

Mr. BLAKISTONE. I appreciate the courtesy of the Chair. I am aware that no idea of the kind was entertained, but I speak of the effect of the remarks that have been made by the gentleman from Baltimore county, (Mr. RIDGELY.)

Mr. RIDGELY. Certainly, I had no intention to reflect upon the gentleman.

Mr. BLAKISTONE. I am sure of that. I speak only of the effect of the gentleman's observations. Mr. B. proceeded to remark on the proper construction of the rule governing debate in Committee of the Whole, and to claim that his administration of the duties of the Chair had been marked by a strict adherence to its requirements; and if he had not discharged the duties of the Chair faithfully and impartially, then, he said, let the President of the Convention note the fault and substitute for me some gentleman who may be exempt from a similar fault.

Mr. BROWN. We will not let the President supply your place.

Mr. BLAKISTONE, in some further remarks, expressed his belief that all propositions of this kind did but protract the action of the Convention. Let full latitude of debate be allowed; let gentlemen be satisfied that they had discharged their duty to their constituents by a fair and frank expression of their will, and they would then be ready to vote. He desired, himself, to express his views, but was prohibited by the position which had been assigned to him. He hoped the proposition would not prevail.

Mr. DORSEY. Upon the question before the committee of filling the blank in the amendment with five days, I have never expressed my views nor spoken a word.

The question was then stated to be on the motion of Mr. WEBER to strike out from the resolution the words "first section," so as to make it applicable to the entire report of the Committee.

Mr. SPENCER hoped the amendment would not prevail for this reason, he said, among others, that he had indicated his intention to offer certain amendments which would lead to debate, and which had never been touched at all. He was unwilling to give to the judges of election the power to determine who are *non compis mentis*.

Mr. JENIFER. I think, perhaps, that this proposition may but embarrass the proceedings of the Convention, and I therefore withdraw it.

Mr. WEBER renewed the proposition, so as to terminate debate on the whole report.

Mr. SMITH. I am sorry to differ with the gentleman from Allegany, (Mr. WEBER) in a matter of this kind. There has been a wide latitude of debate. Much poison has been sent out, and I propose that the antidote should go with it. I, therefore, move that the resolution be laid upon the table.

Mr. STEPHENSON asked the yeas and nays.

Mr. STEWART, of Caroline. I desire to say one word.

The PRESIDENT. The motion to lay on the table is not debateable.

Mr. SMITH. I withdraw the motion, to enable the gentleman from Caroline,(Mr. STEWART,) to make his remarks.

Mr. STEWART. I call the attention of gentlemen to the rules by which we are supposed to be governed. It is known, I believe, to the Convention, that I have been as much in favor of expediting its business as any gentleman here, and that I have occupied the attention of the Committee and of the Convention as little as any gentleman. I desire now to read the 20th, 23rd, and 27th rules. (Mr. S. read them.) Now, it seems to me that the adoption of this resolution will have the effect of changing or rescinding one of these rules, and if that be so, then one day's notice will be required.

Mr. BRENT, of Baltimore city. How change a rule?

Mr. STEWART. Because it stops debate.

Mr. BROWN. Suspends debate.

Mr. STEWART. Well, suspends debate.

Mr. BRENT suggested that the difficulty to which the gentlemen referred could only arise in case of collision between two gentlemen as to the right to the floor.

Mr. STEWART, in illustration of his position, contended that the adoption of this rule would preclude him from expressing his views. We propose (he said) to adopt a rule to govern men of intelligence and wisdom, which would be applicable enough to a set of school boys. Let members judge for themselves how often they shall speak. I look about me, and I see men of experience and ability, (for example, the chairman of the committee of the whole,) who have not had an opportunity to express their sentiments. I should like to speak mine. But this resolution precludes me, and will preclude others. I believe, in point of fact, that not more than a dozen members have been heard on this subject of the elective franchise. Yet, forsooth, the balance of the Convention must be stopped and not permitted to say a word. The importance of the objects for which we are here, cannot be over estimated. If the report of the committee on the elective franchise is adopted, the effect will be that we shall have judges of elections sitting as judges upon the intellects of men—we shall have them deciding whether a man is mentally capable of voting or not. Such a provision is to be incorporated into the organic law, and that, too, without debate.

Mr. CHAMBERS, of Kent. The committee never dreamed of any thing of the kind. It was intended expressly to provide that the votes of no persons should be excluded, whether *non compos mentis* or lunatic, unless under guardianship.

The President (interposing.) The merits of the bill are not under consideration. The gentleman must confine his remarks to the resolution before the Convention.

Mr. STEWART. I beg to differ with the honorable gentleman from Kent (Mr. CHAMBERS.)

Mr. CHAMBERS. I do not mean to say that that is the grammatical meaning. *That* is another affair. But I say that the committee never designed any such thing as the gentleman indicates.

Mr. STEWART. If the report of the Committee is not put in grammatical language, and is to be altered, I think it should be open to discussion. To sustain my view, I will read the section. (Mr. S. read the third section of the report.) I say that, as the section now reads, it would leave it to the judges of election, to say whether a man is *non compos mentis*, or not.

If this resolution is to be adopted, I hope it will be made applicable to the first section of the report only. I renew the motion to lay the resolution on the table.

And the question having been taken, the resolution was laid upon the table.

THE PREVIOUS QUESTION.

Mr. RANDALL. According to the twenty-seventh rule, it will be seen that no vote of this body can be rescinded or changed, without one day's notice previously given. I rise to give notice, that I shall propose a change of the seventeenth rule, which declares that the previous question shall be always in order, if seconded by a majority, &c., &c., and that the main question shall be on the adoption of the proposition under consideration, and that, in cases where there shall be pending amendments, the question shall be first taken on such amendments, in their order and without further debate or amendment.

Now, I understand by the construction given to this rule, and under the Parliamentary law, that the effect of the previous question, if sustained, is not only to cut off all debate and amendments on the question then before the Convention, but to cut off all debate and amendments on the whole subject matter. (Mr. R. gave a case in illustration.) That is to say, we have to vote upon the whole bill and amendments, at one time. I suggest to the consideration of gentlemen, that every desirable object will be effected, by confining the operation of previous questions to the actual question under consideration ; and to nothing else. Many friends more experienced than myself in such matters, have intimated their opinion, that such a change would have a happy effect ; and I propose so to amend the motion as to give it that operation.

The notice was entered on the Journal.

Mr. SOLLERS gave notice that he would to-morrow, move to amend the twenty-third rule, by striking out these words, "except that part of the twentieth rule which restricts members from speaking more than twice upon the same question. The ayes and noes shall be taken in committee of the whole, in the same manner as they are taken in Convention."

Mr. BOWIE. In committee of the whole?

Mr. SOLLERS. In committee of the whole! I do it from the best motive. We know that much of the delay in the transaction of business is to be attributed to the fact that gentlemen speak more than twice on the same subject.

On motion of Mr. MERRICK, the Convention passed to the Orders of the Day.

The President laid before the Convention a report from the clerk of the levy court of Calvert county, in obedience to the order of the Convention of 15th November, containing a statement exhibiting the aggregate valuation, rate of tax, and each general expenditure, &c.,

Which was read and referred to the committee on Representation.

Also, laid before said Convention, a report from said clerk, in obedience to the order of the Convention of the 2nd of December, relative to the fees and perquisites paid the Attorney General and his Deputies by Calvert county;

Which was read and referred to the committee appointed on the Attorney General and his Deputies.

THE ELECTIVE FRANCHISE.

The Convention resolved itself into committee of the whole, Mr. BLAKISTONE in the chair, and resumed the consideration of the report of the Committee on the Elective Franchise.

The pending question was on the motion of Mr. PHELPS, to amend the amendment offered by Mr. CHAMBERS, of Kent, as a substitute for the first section of the report, by inserting after the words "Howard District," the following:

"And five days in the election district or ward of the city of Baltimore."

Mr. RICAUD was entitled to the floor. He said, he should not have undertaken to say one word on this question, but for the peculiar circumstances by which he was surrounded. As a junior member of the delegation from the county of Kent, he had found himself differing widely not only from the other members of that Delegation, but from the party with which he had hitherto acted, and with which he hoped it might still be his pleasure to be associated. Entertaining, however, a conscientious difference of opinion with them, he felt it to be his duty, candidly and plainly to express his sentiments.

As regarded the constitutional power, he thought that if there was a question easy of solution, it was that this Convention, called together for the purpose of making an organic law, had the right to throw around the elective franchise such guards and restraints as they might think best calculated to secure the safety of that valuable right which it involved. He could not agree with the gentleman from Prince George's county, (Mr. BOWIE,) that to impose such restrictions, was to derogate from the rights of the people as to become usurpers of these rights.

Nor could he agree with the gentleman from Queen Anne, (Mr. SPENCER,) that in this matter were involved the humble rights of humble individuals only. The rights of all were concerned. It was as foreign to his (Mr. R's.) purpose, to trample upon the rights of the humble as upon those of the most exalted.

The language of the report of the committee was such as, in the opinion of a majority of the Convention, to make distinctions as to the citizens of the State. It drew a distinction between the rights of the native citizen and those of the foreign citizen. He was opposed to all such distinctions, and doubted the policy of making them. His opinion was, that after a foreigner had resided amongst us for five years, and had acquired the civil rights granted to him by the laws of Congress, the very acquisition of these rights, entitled him to his political rights, if he was ever to be entitled to them. His attachment to our institutions, if ever that attachment was to exist at all, would by that time be such as to authorise the extension of political rights to him.

Other questions had been introduced—questions which, it seemed to him, were not germane to the subject matter before the committee, and which were calculated to increase, rather than allay, the excitement which had characterised the debate. Party politics had been introduced? Why should this be so? Gentlemen came into this body, not as Democrats, nor as Whigs, but as representatives of the people, elected to carry out their views in the formation of such an organic law as would promote the best interests of the State.

Mr. R. then proceeded to trace the action of the State, from the Constitution of '76, on the subject of the elective franchise. He followed it through the imposition and subsequent revocation of the property qualification—illustrated the operation of that law—explained the modifications which had from time to time been made in the provisions regulating the elective franchise, and the reasons which had influenced the policy. He denied that there was any authority in the Constitution or the laws, for the qualification (sleeping one night) which, gentlemen had said the judges of election and the laws prescribed; contended that the only requirement was a *bona fide* intention on the part of the voter to remove from one place to another; and referred to the section of the elections laws which inflicted pains and penalties upon any one who should reside in one district, and should, without a *bona fide* intention to remove fraudulently attempt to vote in a district to which he did not belong.

But if frauds were practised—if violations of the elective franchise took place by which honest voters were cheated out of their legitimate rights, and if the elective franchise was the great constitutional basis upon which rested the liberties, the rights and the interests of every man, how were these frauds to be prevented, or these rights and liberties to be preserved by a residence of five days in the county or district? The very fact of prescribing a remedy so slight for an evil so serious, was, to his mind, sufficient in itself to induce the Convention to vote down the proposition. A man might have been a resident in a county which was the first that had been settled in the State. He might have lived there all his life; he might be a descendent of the very men who had first landed upon the shore, he might have resided in one district in a county for twenty-five or thirty consecutive years—the same district perhaps in which his ancestors had resided, and where all his own property was, and yet because upon the day of the election, or the day before, he should see fit from motives of business, or health, or pleasure, *bona fide* to remove himself and his family into another section of the county in which he had every thing at stake, and to which he had every thing to bind him, he was to be disfranchised because he had not been a resident of District No. 1, more than one day; and yet he might have resided in the adjoining district No. 2, for twenty-five or thirty years. The officers who were to be elected were men to whose hands his interests, his rights, his life, and that which was dearer to every rightly constituted mind—his reputation, were to be entrusted, and yet he was not allowed a voice in their selection. Such were the consequences, which would result from the proposition for a five days residence. He could not, under any circumstances, give it his support.

But if frauds did exist, it was more probable that they would exist in the city of Baltimore than in the counties. He made this assertion only because the larger and increasing population of that city, made it more difficult for the judges of election, or those persons interested in the election, to know who the legal voters were. He referred to the allegations of fraud and corruption which had been made against the county, which he in part represented, (Kent,) and vindicated her from these allegations. He had been a politician for twenty years; yet, he had never known a case in his county where a successful attempt had been made, either by a native born citizen, or a foreigner, to interfere with the elective franchise. In regard to colonization in that county, he could only say that it was the same kind of colonization already spoken of; it had taken place in high party times, and it was the work of the old federal party.

But, if these frauds, about which, so many confessions had been made, did exist, they were far more likely to exist in the larger counties, or in the city of Baltimore. In the smaller counties, the probability of their existence was not so great, because the people residing therein, were so much better acquainted with each other. The remedy proposed would fail to answer the object and would be a dead letter upon the Statute Book.

How, then, was the Convention to act? By prescribing and setting forth plainly and emphatically, what this great constitutional right was, and when that shall have been done, to cultivate on the part of the citizens of the State a due appreciation of its value, to make every man free to exercise this inestimable privilege, and to make it his interest and his duty to protect it alike from secret corruption or open invasion. If we had an enlightened people—if every man was made to understand his constitutional rights, and to cultivate in his bosom a love of country, and a devotion to its institutions—every man would be made the guardian of this right. We should then depend neither on courts of justice, nor jurors, nor officers for the enforcement of the right, or for its immunity from violation. His life, upon it, if the punishment were made commensurate with the offence, there need be but one or two convictions to put an end to such offences.

How were these frauds to be checked? He thought that the best protection was that which he had indicated. It was by an enlightened public opinion—it was by instructing the rising generation—by multiplying school-houses, and thus ensuring a sound, healthy, moral condition of the public mind. For wherever there was an enlightened public opinion, the rights of every man would be guarded and respected, just as wherever there was an ignorant people, there would be a people that could be led by designing men to the commission of fraud, perjury, or other crimes.

But this process might be regarded as too tedious. We should then guard against these frauds by giving to the legislative branch of the Government, power to devise ways and means, to prevent these frauds, and if they could not be prevented, they should be made the subject of exemplary punishment.

He referred to the registry law which had been passed some years ago, and to its repeal after a brief existence. It was a failure. He was a member of the Legislature, by which it had been passed and repealed. The objection against it was not that, if properly regulated, it would not answer the object for which it had been designed, but that the measure itself was unconstitutional—that the Constitution itself determined by whom, and in what manner the elective franchise should be exercised, and that the Legislature in undertaking to impose restrictions unknown to the Constitution, exercised a power not given to it, and that, therefore, the law was null and void.

Mr. R. also suggested, as a means of protecting this right, a small tax, to be laid by the Legislature, for purposes of education. He cared not how inconsiderable the sum might be.

It had been said, that "in the violent combats of party which might occur, not only this right but every other which was dear to us, might be taken away. He had no such apprehension. Such was his confidence in the general patriotism and intelligence of the people of the country, that he did not think our institutions would ever be endangered from this source; for whenever any party, however strong, should attempt to trample upon our Constitutional rights, it would soon find itself hooted into a very small minority. The whole history of the country had demonstrated that, however violent the struggles of party might be with each other, the moment the country was in peril, both were found ready to do their whole duty to it. Such, he believed, would ever be the case. The struggles of party would continue to be, as they had always been, violent and bitter; but they would pass away like the summer clouds, leaving the surrounding atmosphere purer and more serene.

For these and similar reasons, he should oppose this amendment. He did not believe it would answer the end for which it was designed, and he thought its operation would be oppressive. It did not in fact guard the elective franchise, and it was probable that, even if it were enacted, the people themselves would trample it under foot. In conclusion, he would invite gentlemen to go with him, first, in favor of the definition of the right in the Constitution, and then, in giving such powers to the Legislature as would best accomplish the great object which was desired by all.

Mr. Sollers obtained the floor; but yielded for purposes of explanation, to

Mr. Hicks, who said, he had risen to endeavor, if he could, to make himself correctly understood in regard to certain honest confessions he had made the other day, and which had been animadverted upon by several gentlemen. "Honest confessions, it was said, were good for the soul." The gentleman from Cecil had referred to one of the three cases which he (Mr. H.) had cited on a former day, as exemplifying the facility with which frauds upon the ballot-box might be perpetrated.

Mr. Sollers (interposing) said that he had yielded only to allow the gentleman to make an explanation and state a fact.

Mr. Hicks remarking that that was all he desired, proceeded to correct a misapprehension as to one of the cases referred to, and said that he had brought forward these cases with no invidious or party purpose. He had, in his remarks the other day, distinctly disclaimed all such motives, and he had endeavored in his course here, to demonstrate the sincerity with which that disclaimer had been made. His own opinion was, that there was not a county in the State of Maryland where these frauds were not practised to a greater or less degree; although he had no doubt that gentlemen were perfectly sincere in avowing a disbelief of their existence. Nor did he himself believe that they existed to the extent some gentlemen supposed. He thought, however, that these matters were not germane to the question. But the evil ought to be corrected, whatever its extent might be; and he would go for any proposition, no matter from what quarter or party it might emanate, which would effect that object. At the same time, he would be among the last to impose any improper restraints upon the honest voter.

Mr. Sollers apologized for rising to reply to the gentleman from Cecil, but he felt himself called on by an imperative sense of what was due to the State of Maryland, to vindicate her against the charges which had been brought against her. He was a Marylander, "native to the manor born," and he could not restrain himself when he heard the gentleman from Cecil arraign his native and much loved State as rotten to the core from corruption, as the victim of a foul and spreading cancer, the result of which must be fatal, unless the knife be promptly employed, and that it would require the scalpel of the most skilful surgeon to eradicate it. He knew not where the gentleman from Cecil obtained the information which he has thus communicated to this Convention. If he meant to say that he obtained it from gentlemen on this floor, he denied that any facts had been presented to justify so sweeping and severe a censure. He denied that such facts existed. He knew of no such frauds as those which had been described in such awful terms by the gentleman from Cecil. He demanded the evidence of their existence. Where was it to be found? It was not so. And it was a libel on the State to utter such things in the ear of this Convention. It might be, that all this was instigated by a jealousy of Baltimore. But whether it was so or not, he would not let the charge pass without notice; without prompt and stern denial. It was not so. And then the gentleman from Cecil, after specification of all the possible evils which could fall upon a country, held up the examples of Greece and Rome and told us that as we are following their course of corruption, we must participate in their ruin. And in this corruption, which is to destroy us, the gentleman had said that we have all participated. "Speaketh the prophet of himself or of some other man." The gentleman admitted that he had himself contributed to the expenses of an election. Surely then he ought to have been the last to come out with this general denunciation of the State.

He thought it ill became the gentleman from Cecil to stand up in this body and lecture native Marylanders and denounce them for these frauds. What right had that gentleman to say that we are on the brink of perdition? This he has told us, and that he himself aided to bring us into this condition. It might be all true that learned men from other States should be allowed to come here and teach us our duty. He could not understand it.

He accorded with the gentleman from Cecil in some things he had said. When that gentleman lectured the gentleman from Kent, he agreed with him in all he said about his political morality. But why did he tell us of the downfal of Greece and Rome, and of the probability of their fate becoming ours? What remedy has been proposed to save us in this dangerous condition? None. He felt all proper respect for the gentleman from Cecil. But had he offered any remedy? He had told us that the government was tottering. Where then was the remedy? A "masterly inactivity." He has talked of correcting public opinion. And the gentleman from Kent, who had followed him, proposed to cure the corruption by correcting public sentiment—by encouraging public schools! "By enlightening public sentiment," said the gentleman from Kent. Now, with all respect for these gentlemen, and their abstract ideas, he could not understand them.

He could not see, by the course of these gentlemen, that they are doing much towards enlightening the public sentiment when they oppose every effort to maintain the purity of the right of suffrage. When we see gentlemen acting diligently and in good faith, in this Convention, for the prevention of frauds, in such a line of conduct we shall find a greater remedy for the existing evils, than in all the opinions and denunciations they may utter here. He desired the sincerity of the opinions of the gentleman from Kent to be exhibited in his acts. Opinions without acts were, according to his view of things, of little value.

We have also heard some tremendous denunciations from the gentleman from Queen Anne's. He may be very properly called the Jupiter Tonans of this Convention. His bold and florid style of eloquence always attracts. He complained of aggressions by this Convention on the rights of tee honest voter. So desirous was he to open the polls to all, that he would perhaps even be willing to admit women—who are called the better half of creation, on which he should give no opinion—to vote. The object of laying slight restrictions on the right of suffrage is to give it a higher character, and secure its continuance.

He referred to the admitted fact, that one night's sleeping in a ward of the city of Baltimore gave a right to vote in the ward, so as to afford facilities for fraud, and thought some reform was necessary on this point. He remarked on the recent change which had taken place in the opinions of the gentleman from Prince George's, (Mr. Bowie,) who had now become a great friend of the people, and was ready to give the freedom of the elective franchise to all. The gentleman had taken an entirely new position on this subject.

He admitted that frauds exist, and he was willing to apply some remedy. But he did not believe that they existed to the extent which had been represented by the gentleman from Cecil. Wherever we find their existence, let us adopt the best means in our power to prevent them. But he refused to believe that the State was rotten to the core. He had no doubt the gentleman from Cecil believed that the condition of things was as he had represented. But he had acted on erroneous information, and his remarks, as they would go forth to the world, would be keenly felt by the people of the State. He admitted that the gentleman had, by his manner and his talents, done much to sustain the dignity of this Convention, but he ought not to have inflicted so severe a wound on the State. These declarations of the existence of gross frauds were greatly exaggerated. He gloried in being a native of Maryland. He felt for her the affection of a son to a mother; and when he heard these charges made against her,

"In thoughts that breath and words that burn,"

he would not sit silent, but would rise in her defence. Such defence would have come better from some of those who are candidates for high station. It would have better become them to defend the State over which they intend to preside.

He went on to state that he introduced the registry law, in December 1836. The gentleman from Kent, (Mr. Ricaud,) voted for it. But times have changed, and men have changed with them. Side by side, that gentleman and himself voted for that law. The gentleman had changed his course and was now opposed to it. When his friend from Charles should bring in his proposition concerning a registry law, he would go with him. And he would say in advance that it does not restrict any right, while it secures the purity of the franchise. His friend from Prince Georges went for the law.

Mr. Bowie. Was I there?

Mr. Sollers. You know very well.

Mr. Bowie. The record will show.

Mr. Sollers went on to say here was a remarkable change.

He proceeded to state the importance of securing the purity of the elective franchise. He agreed that if our institutions were ever to be destroyed, by corruption extending itself from one end to the other, it would result from the abuse of this right of voting. The time may come when the people will abandon the ballot-box for a more fearful struggle. Where then should we find the gentleman from Prince Georges, from Cecil and from Kent? Where will they be in that day when the pillars of the temple are giving way? They will not remain to fall, like Samson, but will fly from the temple to seek some quiet retreat.

Mr. McLane said that some of the remarks made by the member from Calvert, required so much of reply from him, as would put him right before the community. He was not in a state of health to permit him to deal in loud denunciations, and he was equally incapable of personalities. He had thought it the best course to hear the member speak out to the end, before he attempted any reply. The member from Calvert, in denouncing as untrue his statements of the prevalence of corruption, had, at least, abstained from any assault on his personal truth and honor.

Mr. Sollers. I intended to do so.

Mr. McLane resuming, said he thanked him. At his age, and with the character he had sustained through life, it was not probable that an assault of that kind, if made, would have produced much injury. But the disavowal of such intention did not excuse the attack. He knew the gentleman from Calvert to be incapable of assailing his character for truth. The gentleman had stated that he, (Mr. McL.) had denounced the State as corrupt to the core. It was not so. If the gentleman had listened attentively to the course of his remarks, he would have found, that he did not. Quite the contrary: he stated that he had not heard of the corruption till he came here, and that he did not believe it. He said explicitly that he did not believe the allegation. But he did proceed to say, that if the information was true, and if the evil was as great as had been represented, then the remedies proposed were merely homopœthic doses. That was what he had said. He had said further, that we ought to look for the remedy in the correction of public opinion, and that no man now thought it dishonorable to contribute, without enquiry, to the expenses of an election. He had also said that he would unite to make it disreputable, hereafter, to contribute for such a purpose.

He had risen merely to vindicate himself from the suspicion that he could have presumed to believe, that such a state of things as was represented to him, really existed. It was not for him, at this time, to bring forward any proposition on the subject, until that now under consideration is disposed of. He repeated that he made no charges against the State. If she had been libelled, it was by her own children.

Mr. SOLLERS said it was not his wish or intention to make the slightest attack on the personal character of the gentleman from Cecil. But he appealed to those around him, whether the effect of the speech of that gentleman, was not to impress a conviction on the public mind, that there was great corruption in the State. It was true he had said he did not believe it. But the gentleman drew a picture of existing frauds, calculated to strike with dismay every man in the State. If the gentleman from Cecil did not endorse these frauds, why this lengthened argument, and the reference to the fate of Greece and Rome. He must have supposed there was some truth in them; for he would scarcely have erected so magnificent a superstructure from materials furnished by fancy.

Mr. BRENT, of Charles, remarked that the principle involved in the question now before the committee was regarded as one of very high importance. It had already been very ably and eloquently discussed (as he had learned upon his return to Annapolis yesterday,) and the subject was perhaps at this advanced stage of the debate, worn somewhat "thread-bare." He wished, however, to assign in as concise a manner as possible, some of the reasons which would influence his vote, and asked the indulgence of the committee to enable him to do so.

The right of suffrage, as had been truly said, was a right dear to the freeman. It was a jewel of great value, and the greater its value the more careful we should be in properly guarding and protecting it by wholesome restrictions.

Our power to restrict the right, it seemed to him with due deference to others, was clear and undoubted. He referred to the Constitutions of the several States to show this power had been exercised and admitted from the period of the Revolution up to the present time. The first restrictions upon this right in Maryland were imposed under the Proprietary Government in 1681, and these were continued in the Constitution of 1776. In 1802 the restriction of property qualification was very properly abolished. The prohibition upon the exercise of the right of voting until the voter shall have attained the age of twenty-one years, shall have resided in the State twelve months, and in the county or city, where he may offer to vote, six months, is undoubtedly a restriction. It has been a part of the Constitution of the State since 1810, and has been engrafted already, by a large majority, upon the one, which this Convention has now in charge. The power, therefore, to restrict this right of suffrage must be conceded.

Possessing then the power to restrict, the question becomes one solely of expediency. In the formation of an organic law the rights of the citizen should be carefully guarded and protected. To guard the right of suffrage against fraud and protect it in its purity, is one of our first duties—for the channel through which the sovereign will of the people is uttered, should be pure and unpolluted.

It is true there is no specified period of residence in an election district required under the present Constitution of the State. A residence there in good faith, no matter how recent, entitles the person claiming it to vote, if he has resided in the State and county or city for the length of time designated in the provision adopted in 1810. Prior to 1841 no reason existed for such a provision. Until 1799 all elections were held at the county towns. The election district system was then established for the "better convenience of the people." Still there was no division of counties for separate elections—except in one or two instances for local officers—until after the census of 1840—when in laying off Congressional districts upon the basis of representation in Congress then adopted, it became necessary and proper for the Legislature of the State to divide Baltimore city and Anne Arundel county. By the division thus made, parts of that county and city were attached to different congressional districts. Here then, in this division by ideal lines in the same county and city exists the temptation to fraud upon the Elective Franchise by double voting, and the system of "colonizing," of which so much has been said in the course of this discussion. In the progress of time, as the basis of representation in Congress is again changed, divisions of other counties in the State may also become necessary and proper. A new feature in the division of the State has thus sprung up. Different election districts in the same county are called upon to vote for and elect different members to Congress—and hence the importance of now requiring a fixed period of residence in each particular election district. The amendment proposes five days residence, and he desired to see it adopted.

He proceeded to refer to the remarks made by the gentleman from Queen Anne, (Mr. SPENCER) yesterday, in which he understood him as intimating that the restriction proposed would be oppressive only to the man in poor and humble life.

Mr. SPENCER explained. He admitted that the Convention had the right to impose restrictions, and that the only question was one of expediency. He had said that the restriction would be particularly hard on the humble. He disavowed any intention of charging such a motive on any one.

Mr. BRENT resumed. He had not understood the gentleman as denying the power of the Convention to impose restrictions. He had, however, misunderstood him in reference to the effect of the proposition under discussion. He now understands him as having said that this measure would operate with peculiar hardship on the humble. He (Mr. B.) did not think so. It was a measure designed for the wise purpose of guarding the purity of the Elective Franchise. Its operation would be equal upon all classes, and it would enter with an impartial tread into the cottage as well as the palace. It may not be so perfect, that no case of hardship can occur under it. Perfection is not within the grasp of the human mind. Yet its general beneficial results will greatly over-balance any temporary and individual hardship it may occasion.

He proceeded to say, it had been stated that frauds upon the Elective Franchise, in the way of double voting, colonizing, bribery, and so on, existed in some parts of the State to an alarming extent. That frauds existed and had been practised, he had no doubt. He spoke in terms of high praise of his own county, and said bribery at elections there was a thing unknown. Whether these frauds existed or not, was not very important to the consideration of this question. If they did not now exist, they might hereafter, and it was the duty of the statesman to guard against them in either aspect. Whenever any measure to guard the honest voter in the exercise of his right was brought forward, it should have his support. He here referred to the supposed case, mentioned by the gentleman from Kent, (Mr. Ricaud) to shew that this amendment might operate unjustly, and stated how, in his opinion, the same state of things might occur, even to a greater extent, under the restrictions already adopted requiring a residence of twelve months in the State and six months in the county.

The object of the amendment is to prevent the ready transfer of voters from one district to another in the same county or city, and the "colonizing" of men in a certain district to influence and control the election there. The principal objection urged against the amendment is, that the means are inadequate to the proposed end. The time of residence was not as long as he desired. He would have preferred thirty, or even sixty days; but as these longer periods had been rejected, he was now willing to take the short term proposed. It certainly throws some impediment in the way of double voting and "colonizing," and will no doubt, in great measure, act as a check upon both. If a residence of five days is required, the difficulty of colonizing would be increased by that much, and men could not, on the day of election, with such facility, (as they might in the absence of such a provision,) go from district to district, voting in each one. He trusted the amendment would be adopted, and that this Convention would be able to embody in the Constitution such guards as will effectually prevent fraudulent voting.

Mr. Stewart, of Caroline, stated that after listening with great attention to the discussion, he entered into it, feeling his inability to throw any new light on the subject. But as he was desirous that his views should be understood, he would briefly give the reasons which influenced his vote. He had been induced to do this principally because he had seen a paper published in the district he represented, advocating the Registry Law. He had thought it proper through this Convention, to lay before his constituents his views on the subject. Against every attempt to impose these restrictions on the right of suffrage he had given his vote, and in order to satisfy himself of the correctness of his course, he had listened to all that had been said on the subject, and had not heard a single argument to lead him to any change of his own convictions on the subject.

He referred to the statement of the gentleman from Dorchester, (Mr. Hicks,) relative to the individual who was about to deposit an illegal vote, and the polite attempt of the gentleman from Dorchester to arrest his vote, in consequence of the interference of a friend who said the man was going to vote the right ticket; and put it to that gentleman whether he would have been more successful in preventing this illegal vote from being given, if a five days residence had been required.

Mr. Hicks hoped the gentleman from Caroline would state the other case of the man who had voted in four different places.

Mr. Stewart, resuming, disavowed any intention to make an attack on the gentleman from Dorchester. His only design was to show that there was nothing in this case to induce him to vote for the pending amendment. Neither the statement of the gentleman from Dorchester, nor the argument of the gentleman from Cecil, had brought him to that conclusion. If the gentleman from Calvert, (Mr. Sollers,) believed that there were no frauds committed in the ballot box, why does he not evince his sincerity by lending his aid to strike at all restrictions on the freedom of suffrage. He (Mr. S.) knew of no frauds of the kind spoken of in the elections in his county. He knew of no voters from Delaware coming over the line to vote in Caroline. There was, indeed, a fraud which he would not specify, but which he would be happy to contribute his aid in preventing.

He attributed this fierce tirade against the corruption of the ballot box, to the fact that Baltimore city always voted by large majorities in a certain way, and presumed that it was the wish of those who uttered these tirades, that in framing the Constitution, instead of looking to the whole State, we should have an eye to Baltimore only. He felt great respect for the city of Baltimore; she occupied a proud position for her commercial enterprise; without her, we should not have seen our flag floating on many a distant sea; she was justly the pride of Maryland, and it was the duty of every citizen of the State to unite in sustaining her character. And if he should be charged with being under the influence of Baltimore, he must bear the imputation as well as he could. He himself had connexions in that city. He knew of many instances of young men who had gone there, accumulated fortunes, and returned to their native counties, thus forming a tie between the counties and city. The effect of this restriction in the city of Baltimore would be to throw the poor into the hands ot the wealthy. By the aid of money the dwelling of the poor man might be purchased over his head, and its tenant turned out of doors five days before an election; and in this way the corrupting purse of wealth might be increased beyond what it is now. Poor tenants might be turned out, so as to prevent them from exercising their legal right to vote. The gentleman from Calvert, (Mr. SOLLERS) had said that every State had adopted this principle.

Mr. SOLLERS explained. He had said that every State had acknowledged the right to impose restrictions on the Elective Franchise by a Convention.

Mr. STEWART, resuming. So had every State acknowledged the principle of representation. One gentleman had referred to the language of the Constitutions of some of the States. Gentlemen are in the practice of quoting just so much of an authority as sustains the position they assume, while they reject what is not in conformity with their particular views. He indicated his intention at a proper time to introduce a homestead exemption in order that every man might have an interest in the State, as was designed by our original Constitution, and which would tend much to purify the ballot box, by elevating the citizens. The gentleman from Calvert, said, that the Constitution required a residence of twelve months in the State, and of six months in the county. Did the gentleman know why this residence restriction was inserted in the Constitution? It was not so much to prevent frauds, as to give every voter an interest in the State. A citizen of Delaware would not be permitted to vote in Caroline, because he had no interest in the county.

He then adverted to the distinction which exists in consequence of the division of Baltimore city into two districts, and of the arrangement of Howard District and Anne Arundel county into districts, contending that this exception to the general rule in the State, was a convenience, and did not change the result of an election, no matter in which of the districts the voter cast his vote. The fact of his residence gave him an interest there. The law of Congress prescribes five years as the term before foreigners can be naturalized, that they may acquire an interest in the country, and he was opposed to any distinction between naturalized foreigners, who had resided in the State and county the required term, and native citizens. He was aware that there were conflicting opinions on this point, some gentlemen being desirous of restricting foreigners from the enjoyment of the Elective Franchise, not reflecting that some of these may be allied by blood to some of the original framers of our Constitution.

He knew not how the five days restriction could prevent frauds, unless on the ground that by excluding all voters, you exclude the illegal. We are engaged in framing an organic law; and while we are doing this, we should secure the legal voters in their rights, and prevent those who have no legal right from participating in the Elective Franchise.

Mr. PRESSTMAN was willing to acknowledge that frauds had been committed upon the Elective Franchise in the city of Baltimore, but the great question was, is the proposed remedy likely to abate the evil? He thought it would rather tend to increase than diminish the evil. In making the admission, that election frauds had been perpetrated, he did so because he believed, to deny that would induce the Convention to receive any future statement of his in a spirit of doubt and cavil; and he was unwilling to lose even the small influence he might enjoy in that honorable body. He claimed to be well acquainted with public sentiment in the city of Baltimore, but any thing he should say was upon his own responsibility. Each member of the city delegation was alike responsible for what he should say, to his constituency. You could not find any individual in Baltimore city who would say that no fraud was committed on the ballot box, but he denied the extent to which it is alleged to be carried on there, the vigilance of party prevented. The citizens of Baltimore are not alone responsible for the fraudulent abuse of the Elective Franchise. It has been frankly admitted by honorable gentlemen on this floor, that there are fraudulent practices in the counties, and that large sums of money are contributed for electioneering purposes. Money is raised in the city of Baltimore to be used throughout the State. He believed his friend from Calvert had honestly introduced the Registry Act, and intended it not to operate in Baltimore city alone, but through the State.

Mr. SOLLERS. Through all the State?

Mr. PRESSTMAN said he so understood, and when that subject should come up he would endeavor to show that a Registry might be made a mere instrument of fraud in the hands of the party to which the Registers might belong. He adverted to the practice of bribery as the present source of evil, and which existed in the counties to a great extent. He could put his hand upon honorable gentlemen in the Convention, who had admitted the existence of this species of corruption.

Mr. SOLLERS. The gentlemen will speak for himself; he has no right to put his hand on me.

Mr. PRESSTMAN. Honorable gentleman around me have frankly made the admission, and it cannot be denied, though he believed that some few counties were not obnoxious to the charge.

He went on to state the requirements of the law as it now exists, and denies that a mere temporary residence entitled a party to vote in an election district. The residence must be *bona fide*, without the *animus revertandi*. The amendment proposing five days residence, would open the door to fraud, and render it more easy of perpetration. He was opposed to experimenting upon the right of suffrage. Like in many cases of sickness, it was better to rely upon the healthful re-action of the system, than resort to nostrums. Entire purity was not to be expected—the church itself was not pure. He regretted that the discussion had led to any disagreement between the gentleman from Calvert and the gentleman from Cecil. He did not believe that the former had intended to impute unworthy motives to the latter. In a Maryland Convention, when a gentleman designed to be personal, he would find language so to express himself as not to be misunderstood. He concluded with stating some further objections to the amendment, and his intention to vote against it.

A long interlocutory discussion followed, between Mr. SOLLERS and Mr. BOWIE, directed to the point whether the latter gentleman had, or had not, voted for a Registry Law. Mr. SOLLERS asserted that Mr. BOWIE *had* voted for a stringent bill of that character, and appealed to the journals to sustain the fact. Mr. BOWIE asserted that he did not vote for the Registry Bill which became a law, and could not so have voted, because he was absent from his seat in the Legislature at the time.

Mr. SOLLERS rejoined that, the Registry Bill for which Mr. BOWIE voted, did become a law, having passed both branches of the Legislature; but that afterwards, in consequence of imperfections in the law, another bill was introduced by Mr. SOLLERS, on which bill Mr. BOWIE did not vote because he was not in his seat.

Mr. BOWIE said he thought his friend was mistaken in supposing that the Registry Law, for which he (Mr. B.) had voted, ever became a law. The law for which he (Mr. B.) had voted, was not the one which subsequently became a law, but was one which was much milder in its provisions, and under certain circumstances, allowed every man to vote, whether his name was registered or not.

Mr. SOLLERS referred his statements to the decision of the journal.

The discussion was conducted, generally, in good temper, and both gentlemen resumed their seats satisfied, apparently, with the issue of the controversy.

Mr. BROWN said he was aware that it was the custom of all deliberative bodies to allow great latitude of debate, but in that respect, he thought this body differed from any that had ever assembled in the State of Maryland for seventy-four years. His own opinion was, that no remarks should be indulged in, in committee of the whole, that were not applicable to the question under consideration. Here we had had an elaborate history of the personal cause of votes of gentlemen upon a particular question long since decided. He gave notice of his intention to move, in Convention, an order discharging the committee of the whole from the further consideration of the bill, unless the necessity for that cause should be obviated by a general consent that the question should be taken. He would move that the committee rise.

[Cries of "question."]

Mr. TUCK expressed his desire to occupy some fifteen minutes of the time of the Convention, and would, he said, either proceed now, or in the morning, as gentlemen might prefer.

The usual hour having passed, and the committee indicating its desire to rise,

Mr. TUCK yielded the floor.

The committee thereupon rose and reported progress. And the Convention adjourned.

FRIDAY, January 17th, 1851.

Prayer by Rev. Mr. Grauff.

The roll was called, and the Journal of yesterday was read and approved.

HOUR OF MEETING, &c.

Mr. RIDGELY rose, he said, to submit a motion.

Mr. CHAMBERS of Kent, desired to be informed whether reports from committees were now in order?

The President said reports of committees would regularly be in order. But the floor had been obtained by the gentleman from Baltimore county, (Mr. RIDGELY.)

Mr. RIDGELY said his object in rising was to move that the daily hour of the meeting of the Convention be 11 o'clock, instead of ten.

Mr. BUCHANAN. I second the motion.

Mr. BOWIE. And I.

Mr. RIDGELY said that although the Convention had once or twice before refused to adopt this proposition, yet he had again presented it from a conviction that it was idle to hope for the accomplishment of any good result by meeting as early as ten o'clock. He trusted that, in consideration not only of the length of the daily sessions, but of the absolute necessity of some time for relaxation, the motion he had made would be agreed to.

The first hour of the day was generally spent in the consideration of unimportant business. It frequently happened that no quorum was present, until one half of the first hour had passed. The Convention might meet at the hour of eleven, and might immediately, if it should think proper, pass to the Orders of the Day, and thus accomplish the same object that was at present accomplished by meeting at ten. He thought he had shown by his course in this body, that he had evinced as strong a disposition as any other member, to expedite the completion of the business for which it had been called together. He had never interposed any obstacle, or countenanced any delay in the disposition of its business; and he submitted this proposition now, only because he believed it would facilitate, and not retard, the discharge of their duties. The Convention sat here from ten to three, or half-past three; night overtook them very soon after they had adjourned, and by ten o'clock the following morning, they were again to be in their seats; having no interval for ordinary and proper relaxation, to say nothing of the additional duties imposed upon them by the meetings of the Committees.

Another reason for the change was to be found in the fact that the Convention had engaged a Reporter, to furnish reports of its debates; and he referred to this point without any authority or suggestion, on the part of that gentleman. It was known that he, (Mr. R.) had opposed that measure with all the energy he possessed. But as the Convention had, by its deliberate vote, decided to adopt an order that its debates should be reported, it was due to the person whom they had assigned to that duty, that he should have some relaxation, at least, from the great physical and mental labor which were inseparable from the task. He hoped the motion would be agreed to.

Mr. HARBINE said that the gentleman from Baltimore county (Mr. RIDGELY) had made a motion which met with his (Mr. H's.) decided disapprobation. He accorded to that gentleman, however, credit for the best motives. He believed that that gentleman felt, as he (Mr. H.) felt, the stern necessity of proceeding, without further delay, to the transaction of the public business. But he submitted, in all candor and sincerity, that the motion to change the hour of meeting to 11 o'clock, was calculated not to promote the common object they had in view, but to defeat it. He declared, as he had declared a few days ago, that the motion was one calculated to frustrate the ends for which this Convention had assembled. He could not agree with the gentleman, that the change would have the effect of causing the Convention to get to its substantial work sooner and more earnestly. Why should it do so? Had the gentleman offered any resolution which would so direct the action of this body, as to have that effect? None. What were the facts? Between the hours of ten and eleven, the Convention was engaged in the discussion of motions, which were supposed to have a considerable bearing on its labors. Would not the same propositions be discussed if the Convention met at eleven? What then was gained? The change, if it had any effect, would rather tend to protract these discussions and to multiply the number of motions. Away, then, with all such arguments.

But what were the precedents? He took it for granted that if it worked well, as to other Conventions, to meet at an early hour, it would operate equally well here. If it were good policy in the Convention of the State of Ohio, to meet at ten and at nine; if it was good policy in the Convention of the State of New York, to meet at ten in the beginning of its sessions, and subsequently at nine—it was equally good policy here. After the discussion which had taken place on a former day, he had been at some trouble to see what other Conventions had done. They met at an earlier hour than this body met. How was it with the Convention which framed the old Constitution? They not only met at nine, (shortly after the commencement of the session,) and continued to do so, but they held afternoon sessions.

Mr. RIDGELY. Will the gentleman be so good as to state at what season of the year the Convention of the State of New York was in session?

Mr. HARBINE. I knew that it was at a different season of the year—the month of June or July. But at what season did the Convention that framed the old Constitution meet? How was it with the Convention of the State of Ohio now in session? It met at nine, and had afternoon sessions also. He earnestly begged of the Convention, if they valued the objects for which they had assembled to vote down this proposition.

Mr. BUCHANAN said, that as regarded the modern precedents which his friend (Mr. HARBINE) had referred, it seemed to him (Mr. B.) that they had not as yet exactly had a fair trial. As to the real and substantial precedents, they were all the other way. He would like to know from that gentleman, whether any Convention had ever assembled within the limits of the United States, composing more capable business men—men of higher intellectual endowments in every respect, than those who framed the original Constitution of the State of Virginia? Yet that body never met earlier than twelve o'clock, and yet a more perfect or stupendous work never emanated from the brains or the hearts of men. There was another precedent almost equal to that of the State of Virginia. He referred to the Constitution of the State of New York, formed in 1821. The Convention of that day, composed of men quite as industrious and quite as zealous in the cause of their constituents as this body could be, met at eleven and twelve o'clock. They made a perfect work, so much so that the members of this Convention, in the course of its discussions, had been constantly referring to the Debates in that body as guides for their own.

He did not know to what Committee the gentleman (Mr. HARBINE) belonged. But he (Mr. B.) was a member of a Committee (the judiciary) which would be constantly engaged in the business before it, not only after the adjournment, and in the evenings, but in the mornings. It could not dispose of the business before it, unless time was given. So he might say of other committees. It was idle to talk of doing business here, between the hours of ten and eleven. Every gentleman who had been present between those two hours, knew that nothing had been done. They met, and talked—talked—talked; but God knew there was time enough for talk in the other hours, during which the Convention remained in session. Deducting the one hour, they still talked from eleven to three or half past three. The Committee then rose and reported that they had made progress, but "had come to no conclusion," and they would come to none in this way. There were times when work was to be done; there were times when talking was to be done. The talking was to be done after they met here; the work was to be done after night and in the morning when the Committees met. Hence, he would cordially sustain the motion of the gentleman from Baltimore county, (Mr. RIDGELY.)

Mr. BROWN moved that the resolution be laid upon the table.

Messrs. RIDGELY, BUCHANAN and HARBINE asked the yeas and nays, which were ordered.

And the question having been taken, the vote resulted as follows:

Affirmative.—Messrs. Dent, Lloyd, Sherwood, of Talbot, James U. Dennis, Eccleston, Grason, George, Wright, McMaster, Hearn, Shriver, Sappington, Stephenson, Magraw, Nelson, Carter, Thawley, Stewart, of Caroline, Schley, Fiery, John Newcomer, Harbine, Weber, Slicer, Fitzpatrick, Smith, Parke, Cockey and Brown.—29.

Negative.—Messrs. Chapman, President, Morgan, Blakistone, Hopewell, Ricaud, Lee, Chambers, of Kent, Mitchell, Dorsey, Randall, Kent, Weems, Dalrymple, Bond, Brent of Charles, Merrick, Jenifer, Buchanan, Welch, Chandler, Ridgely, John Dennis, Crisfield, Dashiell, Williams, Hodson, Goldsborough, Chambers, of Cecil, Miller, McLane, Bowie, Tuck, Sprigg, McCubbin, Spencer, Fooks, Jacobs, Biser, Annan, Hardcastle, Gwinn, Stewart, of Baltimore city, Brent, of Baltimore city, Presstman, Ware, Neill, Davis, Kilgour, Waters and Hollyday—50.

So the resolution was not laid on the table.

The question then recurred on the adoption of the resolution.

Messrs. JOHN NEWCOMER and HARBINE asked the yeas and nays, which were ordered.

Mr. MERRICK. I suggest to gentlemen who demand the yeas and nays—

Mr. BUCHANAN. (Interposing.) And who are so anxious to save time?

Mr. MERRICK. (Continuing.) And are so anxious to save time, that we have just taken the yeas and nays on a motion to lay the resolution on the table. I hope, therefore, that the call will be withdrawn.

Mr. NEWCOMER insisted on his motion for the yeas and nays.

Mr. HARBINE. If the call for the yeas and nays should be withdrawn, the time of the Convention will be taken up in something a good deal worse.

Mr. MITCHELL. I suggest to my friend on the left, whether if he is opposed to the consumption of time, the demand for the yeas and nays upon every motion that is made, is not a very effectual mode of consuming it?

Mr. HARBINE. Assure me that the time will not be more unprofitably spent, and I will consent to withdraw the call. I feel as sure as fate what the result will be.

The question on the adoption of the resolution was then taken, and resulted as follows:

Affirmative.—Messrs. Chapman, President,—Morgan, Blakistone, Hopewell, Ricaud, Lee, Chambers, of Kent, Mitchell, Dorsey, Randall, Weems, Dalrymple, Bond, Brent, of Charles, Merrick, Jenifer, Buchanan, Welch, Chandler, Ridgely, John Dennis, Crisfield, Dashiell, Williams, Hodson, Goldsborough, Phelps, Chambers, of Cecil, McCullough, McLane, Bowie, Tuck, Sprigg, McCubbin, Spencer, Jacobs, Annan, Hardcastle, Gwinn, Stewart, of Baltimore city, Brent of Baltimore city, Presstman, Ware, Niell, Davis, Kilgour, Waters and Hollyday—48.

Negative.—Messrs. Dent, Kent, Lloyd, Sherwood, of Talbot, James U. Dennis, Eccleston, Grason, George, McMaster, Hearn, Fooks, Shriver, Biser, Sappington, Stephenson, Magraw, Nelson, Carter, Thawley, Stewart, of Caroline, Schley, Fiery, John Newcomer, Harbine, Slicer, Fitzpatrick, Smith, Parke, Shower, Cockey and Brown—31.

So the Convention decided that hereafter, until otherwise ordered, the daily hour of the meeting of the Convention should be eleven o'clock.

THE ELECTIVE FRANCHISE.

Mr. CHAMBERS, of Kent, from the Committee on the Elective Franchise, made a report, being an additional section to the first article of the Constitution heretofore reported by the same Committee.

The report was read, and—

On motion of Mr. CHAMBERS,

It was ordered to be printed.

On motion of Mr. BLAKISTONE,

The report was referred to the same Committee of the Whole, having under consideration the previous report of the said Committee.

THE PREVIOUS QUESTION.

On motion of Mr. RANDALL,

The Convention proceeded to the consideration of the amendment offered by him yesterday, to the 17th rule, &c.

Mr. R. briefly explained its object. He disclaimed any intention to call the previous question or to encourage its application, and took occasion to say, that he had not the slightest complaint to make of the course, of the debates which had taken place here. He had offered the amendment, with the concurrence of friends who were anxious for the transaction of public business, but who desired that the operation of the previous question should be so restricted, that it would apply only to one proposition, or to such portion of the pending matter as the mover might designate. And Mr. R. briefly exemplified the operation of the change which he proposed to make. The adoption of the amendment, he submitted, would expedite the business of the Convention, without depriving it, in any sense, of the full benefit of the rule.

Mr. BROWN. Your amendment can only operate in Convention?

Mr. RANDALL. Certainly.

Mr. BROWN suggested the propriety of making the previous question applicable in Committee of the Whole, so far as regarded the pending amendment. Time and trouble would be saved. He was opposed to going into committee, and should oppose going into it for the future, unless some means could be devised for arresting debate. That object could be effected under the existing rules in Convention, but not in Committee; therefore, it was, he had suggested that the previous question should be made applicable in Convention.

THE ELECTIVE FRANCHISE.

Pending the motion of Mr. RANDALL, (the usual hour having arrived,) the Convention,

On motion of Mr. JENIFER,

Resolved itself into Committee of the Whole, Mr. BLAKISTONE in the Chair, and resumed the consideration of the report of the committee on the Elective Franchise.

The question pending before the Committee was on the motion of Mr. PHELPS, to amend the amendment offered by Mr. CHAMBERS, of Kent, as a substitute for the first section of the report, by inserting after the words "Howard District," the following:

"And five days in the election district or ward of the city of Baltimore."

Mr. Tuck, was entitled to the floor.

Mr. T. assumed it as indisputable that the purity of the Elective Franchise lay at the foundation of this and all representative governments, and he expressed his surprise that where frauds were admitted to exist, efforts made to remedy the evil, should be resisted. If but one fraudulent vote had been given, it was sufficient reason for the adoption of such measures as were calculated to prevent the extension of the evil. Some who oppose this restriction have avowed themselves in favor of the largest liberty. He was an advocate for that civil liberty which we enjoy under the restraint of wholesome laws, and without which, republics cannot exist. Any doctrine of liberty inconsistent with this will ultimately reduce the government from a republic to a mere representative democracy.

He adverted to the party allusions that had been made in this debate. One gentleman had stated that the friends of this restriction were influenced by political motives, and that this cry of fraud on the ballot box was only raised when large majorities in the Baltimore elections were cast in a particular way. For himself he regretted the introduction of politics into this debate. He assailed no man's motives. Conscious of the rectitude of his own, he left others to judge of their conduct, and to settle such questions with their consciences and their constituents. But when the gentleman assigned this motive, he must have forgotten that all the questions touching the Elective Franchise, all the members of one party (except two) have united, and voted against the measures designed to protect the ballot box, whereas the other party have never united on any one question since the organization of the Convention. Mr. T. suggested that this fact might furnish some evidence of party design to those who were in search of the motives of others. Yet he made no such charge himself. Gentlemen had alluded to their democracy, and some had appealed to their ancestry to show the purity of their democratic faith. If he were judged by this test, he might claim to belong in some degree to both sides. His whiggery consisted of a proper mixture of principles for both the old parties. He certainly laid no claim to being a democrat of the present day. But it is not prudent for our democratic friends to trace back too far, they may run into a cross that was once considered quite impure, and is now generally repudiated. Many of them would find that their original politics had no better source than the federalism of 1800. Referring to this subject the other day, an honorable gentleman from Queen Anne's had prudently dated his democracy from the Jackson epoch, and disclaimed running into the Jefferson line.

Mr. T. commended the discretion of that gentleman to others of his political friends. The fact is that the times have changed, and men have changed with them. The least said on this subject the better. We are all more or less party men, and perhaps we show our feelings at times when we ought not. Where we differ let us differ as men should, who honestly disagree. Let us agree to disagree, and have no controversy about it.

It is a mistake to suppose that this amendment would operate invidiously, as regards Baltimore. It applies as well to the counties. Mr. T. had no unfriendly feeling towards that city. We all have a just pride in her growing wealth and prosperity. He would be the last to effect her interests. But the Delegates from Baltimore must remember that if they enjoy the advantage of living in the third city of the Union, and have the honor of representing her here, they must bear the inconveniences of having among their constituents a proportion of that species of population, that is common to all large cities. Mr. T. had no doubt that frauds had been committed on both sides. Proof has been demanded. It is not a case that admits of strictly legal proof. But he had heard enough to satisfy his own mind. He would not exculpate the whigs. Both he believed to be guilty. Mr. T. could mention some instances coming to his knowledge, on reliable information, implicating persons of his own party, and he had no doubt gentlemen of the other side could do the same, if they would. In 1847, a whig of Baltimore informed him that he had received an offer from members of the Empire Club of New York, to carry the election in Baltimore for the whigs for five thousand dollars, and that after conferring with some of the Central Committee, the offer was declined, but his informant thought the arrangement ought to have been made.

Mr. Brent, of Baltimore city, asked for the name of the gentleman's informant.

Mr. Tuck declined giving the name.

Mr. Presstman understood the gentleman made no charge against the Democratic party.

Mr. Tuck did not charge this against any party.

Mr. Brent wished to know the name because the gentleman said he was told by a member of the Central Whig Committee.

Mr. Tuck had not said so. He had said that his informant was a whig, and that he had mentioned it to members of the Central Committee, and that they would have nothing to do with it. His informant was not a member of that Committee.

Mr. Brent. Well—I want to know because the Empire Club is Democratic.

Mr. Biser. They are Democratic, but vote for the side that pays best.

Mr. Tuck. The gentleman's democratic friend from Frederick, (Mr. Biser,) seems to have some knowledge of that club, and I refer my friend from Baltimore to him, for further information.

Mr. T. adverted to the pipe laying fraud, that was attempted some years ago in Baltimore. There were also convictions in Baltimore a few years ago, for fraudulent voting, (which the delegates from Baltimore must remember.) The parties were fined and imprisoned. Whose frauds they were, he does not know; but they were ascribed to the Democrats. Frauds in procuring naturalization papers, are committed on both sides. Since the commencement of the Convention, he had been informed by a whig, that four Germans who had been in the country only four months, had been carried to Baltimore for the purpose, and afterwards voted the whig ticket in the county. This was a whig, and he urged the necessity of something being done to prevent it, because he said if it is done on one side, the other will resort to the same means in self-defence. If frauds have not been perpetrated in Baltimore, why did the Councils in 1838, pass an ordinance to punish fraudulent voting? Mr. T. read from the ordinance in proof of this statement. He made these statements to show that something should be done to prevent the evil. He was satisfied that there were frauds on both sides, as had been admitted frankly by the gentleman from Baltimore, (Mr. Presstman.)

Mr. T. agreed with the gentleman, that the only question was as to the efficiency of the amendment proposed. Upon this we differ. Mr. T. thought it would do much good in the counties as well as the cities. At seasons of election those best acquainted with the people were in the habit of canvassing the districts a day or two previous to the election, and ascertaining how the result would probably be. If the counties should elect their Commissioners and other officers by districts, this restriction of five days residence would prevent many fraudulent votes. If it were ascertained a day or two before the election, that either side would be in a small minority, they might import a few voters from another district able to spare them, and thus by a distribution of surplus voters from any one district, carry a majority in all the others. In most of the counties there are persons who vote where they happen to be at work, being residents of the counties, but having no fixed place of abode. In the hands of the designing, these men might be made to vote in any district, by being employed there the day before the election. And again, the judges of the elections, in some counties, hold the incorrect opinion that a man may vote where he has his washing done. If a man go to a district a day before the election and have washing done there, he might vote on the ground that this gave him residence.

Mr. Presstman. Are we to provide judges who understand their duties?

Mr. Tuck. No. But we should, if we can, save the people from the necessity of having these questions decided by them at all. Mr. T. said that the same would be the effect in Baltimore, in the city elections. It would prevent colonizing in the city and the counties; and if it did no good, as some thought, it was at least worth the trial, because no one had shown that any injury to any person was likely to result from its operation. He insisted that a partial remedy was better than to allow the evil to progress without any attempt to arrest it. He believed that the people generally would favor a restriction of this kind, even for a longer time, as tending to preserve our free institutions, the permanency of which we all have so much at heart.

Mr. Weber moved to amend the pending amendment by adding, at the end thereof, the following:

"Provided, That the voter, if required, shall make affidavit that he did not move into the election district, to effect the election then being held."

Mr. Ridgely felt compelled, notwithstanding his previous determination not to mingle in this debate, to make some remarks, in reply to the gentleman from Prince George's, (Mr. Tuck.) That gentleman expressed surprise that there should be found any man who was unwilling to sustain the purification of the ballot-box. He desired to ask that gentleman, if he could suppose that there was any gentleman in this Convention, who would oppose its purification.—There was more of the time of this Convention lost in the discussion of what are either unnecessary or irrelevant questions, than of those which are relevant and necessary.

The object of every gentleman is the purification of the ballot-box. To effect this common object, some suppose that restrictions are necessary, others think they are not. He never could have supposed that the gentleman from Prince George, would have brought up here that extraordinary story, of the attempt of the Central Whig Committee, to buy over the Empire Club of New York. The gentleman ought to, as he hoped he would, have done the Whig Central Committee the justice to say he disbelieved the story.

Mr. Tuck explained, and said the Whig Central Committee had refused to entertain the thing.

Mr. Ridgely resumed, denying that any such proposition had ever been made. No member of the Whig Central Committee ever dreamt of such a thing. He was sorry the gentleman from Prince George had brought forward this and other cases, which seemed to show that it was necessary to impose restrictions on the Whigs. He could not, after this, wonder if some Democrats voted for restrictions. He eschewed all party discussion. He came here with clean hands and a pure heart. He was unsophisticated enough to go before his constituents in Baltimore county, and ask them to elect him on the no party principle. He was so green as to believe that there might be found in a Convention selected by the people, to frame an organic law, men capable of rising above the evanescent operation of party feelings, and he had found his way into this body with that impression on his mind.

These matters are altogether irrelevant: they had nothing to do with the main question. That had been discussed and exhausted. The gentleman from Kent, (Mr. Chambers,) conceded, that the remedy had been so diluted by its reduction to five days residence, as to leave but little life in it; the gentleman from Cecil, (Mr. McLane,) had well qualified it as a homœpathic dose; and in reference to it he would ask, *cui bono*? The utmost that had been advanced in favor of the restriction now proposed, was that it might do some good; while he himself, and his friends, who stood opposed to it, contended that it would do much harm—operating more against legal than illegal voters, by disqualifying many of the former, and few of the latter.

In framing an organic law, much must be left to the discretion of the Legislature. The act of Congress directed the creation of election districts in the States, but the details were left to the Legislatures. Every local regulation as to residence in districts which are continually changing their boundary lines, should be left to the Legislature. As was suggested by the gentleman from Kent, municipal matters should be left for the action of the municipal authorities. It was proper that local regulations should be made by local authorities. Among the frauds alleged to have been committed, that of colonization was a fraud of one municipal authority upon another authority of the same character. This cannot, however, apply in cases where votes are aggregated through the State. It can only apply to elections in Congressional districts. It will apply to Baltimore, where owing to the contiguity of votes, colonization does exist; and in reference to this matter, both parties are obnoxious to censure. In the rural districts of the State, the elective franchise was in as great purity as human infirmity will permit.

The great evil exists in Baltimore city, which is divided into two districts for Congressional elections. These districts have been twice gerrymandered by the whig party. Since the year 1842, the evil has been the fruit of party legislation. The Legislature have the power to correct this evil by an honest apportionment, and to prevent the colonization of voters. It is not to be doubted these evils have arisen from the strife of parties. But we are not making a Constitution to reach every contingency which may arise. This is an isolated case in Maryland, and can be cured by the Legislature without any provision in the organic law.

This proposition of five days residence would be productive of inconvenience in the rural districts. A great number of the persons residing in the interior, are laborers who are continually passing over the lines, from one district into another. It is much worse in Baltimore, where thousands of persons who have no fixed domicil, are daily passing over imaginary lines, and it would be wiser to allow them to vote where they are, than to make restrictions which would disfranchise many legal voters.

He then put a case to shew that even if the proposition was introduced into the organic law, its effect would be different from what was contemplated by the friends of the measure, and would not prevent illegal voting.

In reply to what had been said by the gentleman from Prince George's, as to the simplicity of the judges of election, he contended that the gentleman was mistaken; that the election laws were simple, that they had been put in the hands of the judges, and that some of those judges had been judges for many years. But admitting maladministration, that was no argument against the law itself.

It had been asked on the other side, what remedy, if any, we proposed for illegal voting? And with a purpose of impugning the sincerity of gentlemen, who had voted against restrictions, it was charged that whilst we thus voted, we admitted the existence of the evil. On a former occasion, he had urged as a remedy, that fraud upon the ballot box, was an evil, which could be better reached by *cure* than by *prevention*. He then said, that illegal voting should be declared an infamous crime, that a single conviction followed up by ignominious punishment, would do much, by example, to abate the evil. This suggestion had been met by honorable gentlemen, who contended for district residence, as a remedy, or an aggravation of the evil. They had characterized it, as an invitation to illegal voting, and had appealed to the utter inefficiency of existing penal laws for such a purpose.

He was free to admit that the present penal laws against illegal voting, have supplied that experience, but such testimony served only to enforce the necessity of their repeal, and the substitution of other laws; which, recognizing the vice, as one of the deepest moral turpitude, would provide a penalty commensurate with the crime. He admitted that the existing penal laws, invite to the offence. What are they? Why, they provide a mere fine of a few dollars for a violation of that, which has been again and again characterized in this House as the dearest and most cherished right of freemen. Will any man pretend that such a penalty would for a moment restrain a person depraved enough to perpetrate the act of illegal voting? No sir—no sir! The penal laws are mere waste paper; they have proved utterly useless; and it was time to profit by the experience of the past, to provide such a punishment for illegal voting, as its frequency and enormity demands.

He was ready to make illegal voting an infamous crime, a just cause of disfranchisement; and by this remedy, rather than by the imposition of shackles upon the right of suffrage, which involve the innocent with the guilty, he hoped in some degree to purge the ballot box. He concluded by admonishing his friends, that the adoption of this restriction, would be to open the door for all the propositions to be revived, which had been rejected.

Mr. Davis rose, in the language of a distinguished Senator of the United States, "to establish the truth of history." He found in the few remarks which he had addressed the Committee a day or two since, he did injustice to the populous and distinguished county of Frederick. He wished to make the *amende* honorable. In giving the history of her efforts to reform, her own internal affairs, he made an important omission, which he now wished to supply.

He then restated the facts in relation to the action of the county of Frederick, concerning the change in the mode of appointing the levy court, in 1838, and the adoption of the six months residence as a qualification for the members of that court, and the recognition of the same feature in the law of 1844.

How was this odious, unjust, and oppressive example and action of Frederick county met? How was it answered? First, by the gentleman from Queen Anne, (Mr. SPENCER,) who said that it was a whig measure introduced to deprive Mr. Grason, the then Governor of Maryland, of the patronage of Frederick county, and —Secondly, by Mr. BISER, who declared that he opposed the measure, and introduced a bill to elect the levy court, by general ticket; but Mr. Schley, being a whig, and a majority of the Legislature being whigs, he defeated him, and carried this measure through the Legislature against his vote and against his wishes. Now he, (Mr. D.) did not say a word about this being a whig measure, or a democratic measure. He alluded to it as a reform measure of the county of Frederick, and mentioned the names of three gentlemen, members of this Convention, who were then members of the Legislature, without classing them as either whigs or democrats. It so happened that two of them were whigs, and one a democrat. Now, to weaken the force of this conservative example of Frederick county, who has given us a valuable precedent for the very measure under consideration, it is to be denounced as a whig measure, and party feeling is to be invoked to lessen its influence here, because it is a whig measure—upon no other principal than the unjust and illiberal principal, "that nothing good can come out of Nazareth."

But how stands the case with the honorable member from Frederick, (Mr. BISER.) By looking further into the history of this matter, it appears that in 1842, the honorable gentleman was elected Speaker of the House of Delegates—it is to be presumed not by whig votes—that at that session the democrats being in a majority, a bill was introduced, by a Mr. Crampton of Frederick, to change the number of levy court districts, from three to nine. Was Mr. Crampton a whig?

Mr. BISER. Mr. Crampton was a democrat.

Mr. DAVIS. Very well. That in this bill introduced by a democrat, this same restriction of a residence within the levy court district was retained, but reduced from six months to sixty days, a more reasonable time; and a further restriction of *a six months* residence within the district, to render a person elected *eligible* to the levy court.

Mr. Biser. Did this bill become a law?

Mr. DAVIS replied in the affirmative. He held the laws of 1842 in his hand, and found this bill published as a suppliment to the act of 1838.

Mr. BISER. Did I vote for it?

Mr. DAVIS would answer the gentleman. It does not appear from the journal of the House of Delegates, that the ayes and noes were called upon the passage of the bill, but he took it for granted that two such experienced and astute members, as the gentleman from Frederick, and the gentleman from Carroll, (Mr. BROWN,) who was also a member of that session of the Legislature, would never have suffered so odious, oppressive and unjust a restriction, as a much shorter period of residence is now pronounced to be, without calling the ayes and noes, to record their names against it, unless they were willing for its passage.

Mr. BISER. How could I have called the ayes and noes, when I was Speaker of the House?

Mr. DAVIS. It would have been very easy for the gentleman when he saw so obnoxous a measure, as he now considers this to be, about to pass, to have requested some friend to call the ayes and noes, that he might record his name against it. But, he asked, did the gentleman vote against it?

Mr. BISER replied in the affirmative.

Mr. DAVIS continued. Well, so this bill passed with these now obnoxous and odious features in it, and so it continued the law for Frederick county till 1844, when the whigs being again in power they altered the law so as to reduce the number of districts for the levy court to five, but so pleased were they with the new feature of restriction introduced by the democrats in 1843, that they incorporated it in the bill of 1844, and so it stands the law of Frederick county, the great reform county of the State now. He held it up as an example, from the hot bed of reform, worthy the consideration and imitation of this Committee, and if he possessed the tact and parliamentary skill and knowledge of the gentleman from Carroll, (Mr. BROWN,)—not now in his seat—and knew how to accomplish it, he would move this conservative Democratic restriction of sixty days, as a substitute for the small restriction of five days now under consideration.

He deprecated the introduction of party feeling or party action, into this debate, or this Convention. It bodes no good to a harmonious result. He was not here for any such purpose. He came not here to elevate the whig party, or to procure the downfal of the democratic party; but for higher and nobler objects. He came here to lend his feeble efforts to the formation of a Constitution for the State of Maryland which will survive the rise and downfal of parties. He was a whig, and known to be a whig. Yet, he should feel himself unworthy the name of whig, if he did not feel that he could so far elevate himself above party feeling, and party action, as to act alone for the honor, the welfare, and prosperity of the whole State, irrespective of party.

Mr. RANDALL indicated his intention at the proper time to offer the following provision, which would, he thought, meet with the views of many gentlemen who were opposed to further restriction upon the privileges of voters.

"Every free white male citizen of this State, and no other, above the age of twenty-one years, having resided twelve months *as a citizen thereof* in the county next preceding the election at which he offers to vote," &c., &c.

The amendment having been read,

Mr. R. remarked, that he wished to say a few words in regard to the universally admitted frauds which were practised upon the ballot box in the State of Maryland. He said, universally, but, perhaps, the more correct term would be, generally, because some gentlemen desired that their counties should be excluded from the charge. It seemed, however, to be a matter of general notoriety that these frauds did exist.

The gentleman from Cecil, (Mr. McLane,) had referred to the 54th article of the Constitution of 1776, by which it would be seen that the framers of that instrument did not refuse to entertain a suspicion that frauds of this kind might exist, because the design of that article was to prevent their commission. That such frauds did begin to prevail to a much greater extent about the year 1838, was manifest from the ordinance passed in May of that year, by the corporation of Baltimore. The enormity of the evil had then become so apparent that, in addition to the Constitutional provisions and to the acts of Assembly upon the subject, the corporation passed an ordinance imposing pains and penalties upon persons twice voting, or voting in the city of Baltimore without the legal right to do so.

It had been said, that the Convention was about to impose new restrictions. Surely, as the increase of population demanded such restrictions, they ought to be enacted. Previous to the year 1802, these evils did not exist to any serious extent. The property qualification was such, that owing to the permanent and known abodes of the voters, the same necessity for such enactments did not exist. Since then, the aspect of things had greatly changed. He, however, was not one of those who believed in primitive purity—and none other. He believed that there was as much purity now in the world, as there ever had been; but a different condition of things existed at the present time. There had been a great increase of population, the exigencies of which had now to be provided for. He referred to the various laws which had been passed by the Legislature at various periods to meet the requirements of the times.

So much for the *prevalence* of the frauds. What then was the remedy? The evil was plain and palpable—manifest to the eyes of all men, stalking abroad at noon-day before the eyes of men, and calling loudly for a remedy. Where was it to be found? In public opinion and in criminal laws, some gentlemen said. Were they in earnest? Had not public opinion been arrayed, and penal statutes been fulminated against this crime, and of what avail had they been? No more than so much waste paper.

When a mode of redressing one of these evils was presented, gentlemen answered: "That is not the great evil; it is some other, by which we are defrauded of our rights and illegal votes admitted." When a remedy for another fraud was presented, the same answer was given. And thus every measure looking to the cure of the disease was voted down. He had no doubt of the sincerity of gentlemen who opposed these various propositions. Their error was, that each gentleman regarded one particular mode as the *only* mode by which the evil was to be reached. And his friend from Charles (Mr. Jenifer,) erred with others, in his, (Mr. R's,) judgment. That gentleman thought that a Registry Law was the remedy—another found it in criminal laws; yet if we had them all, they would scarcely accomplish the object. We *needed* them all. He cared not what party was to be built up or put down by them, he would vote for all measures calculated to effect the object to any extent. All these measures were calculated to do so; no one of them could. But that something must be done was obvious.

He referred to the passage of the single district law by Congress—to the fact that Baltimore must hereafter be entitled to at least two representatives in that body, and thence argued the necessity of the resolution as to that city, in order that the intent of the law should not be defeated by persons in one of these districts casting votes in the other. He alluded to the course which had been adopted by Frederick county in regard to the election of certain officers there; and contended that some general restriction of the kind must be imposed. Five days, he admitted, would not accomplish the object as effectually as a longer period, but, as had been remarked by a gentleman who had preceded him, if he could not get a whole loaf he would take half a loaf, since "half a loaf was better than no bread." He desired that every restriction which promised to accomplish the great object in view, should be imposed, and even the restriction of five days residence would give an opportunity to detect and expose the false statements of men who might otherwise fraudulently attempt to vote. He should, therefore, vote in favor of that restriction, limited as it was, and should at the proper time offer the proviso of which he had given notice.

Mr. Dorsey rose; not, he said, to make a speech, but to show what seemed to be a matter of dispute, that these frauds and corruptions did exist in the State of Maryland, and had, from time to time called forth the action of the Legislature for their suppression and punishment.—He agreed with the gentleman from Baltimore county (Mr. Buchanan,) that frauds did not exist in that county. But what was the reason? The gentleman had claimed that it was because the people themselves were immaculate and incorruptible, beyond the reach of temptation or the seductions of fraud. Now, perhaps, he (Mr. D.) might assign a very different reason. In Baltimore county there was a Democratic majority of some eight or twelve hundred votes, or more. At all events, it was so enormous, that no party would throw away its money in attempting to colonize it or to commit frauds upon the franchise. (Laughter.) Therefore, it was, that these frauds did not exist in Baltimore county, or in the other parts of the State. (Renewed laughter.) He disclaimed any intention to make imputations on the city. He had never seriously heard the charge of bribery there, although he had heard of illegal voting.

But he had risen to show that this illegal voting had been a progressive kind of crime, and that it ought to be prevented. He then read from the Acts of Assembly the provisions applicable to the point, and argued that the corporation of Baltimore in the ordinances which they had made, had not kept pace with the evil as well, or seen its enormity as clearly as the Legislature had. It seemed to him that these acts, if they were evidence of any thing, were evidence sufficient to satisfy this Convention that there must have been a progressive vice of fraud and corruption upon the ballot-box, which required correction and punishment. And he insisted upon the necessity of restrictive provissions, irrespective of party acts in the past or party consideration in the future.

No member taking the floor, the Chairman stated the question.

Mr. BRENT, of Baltimore city, moved that there be a call of the Convention.

The CHAIRMAN said that the motion was not in order. The committee had no right to a call. But the gentleman could move that the committee rise, in order to make the motion in Convention.

Messrs. SHRIVER and BUCHANAN asked the yeas and nays on the pending amendment of Mr. PHELPS; which, after some conversation, were taken and resulted as follows:

Affirmative—Messrs. Chapman, President, Morgan, Blakistone, Dent, Hopewell, Lee, Chambers of Kent, Mitchell, Donaldson, Dorsey, Randall, Kent, Weems, Dalrymple, Bond, Brent of Chas., Merrick, Jenifer, John Dennis, James U. Dennis, Crisfield, Dashiell, Williams, Hodson Goldsborough, Eccleston, Phelps, Tuck, Sprigg, Dirickson, McMaster, Hearn, Fooks, Jacobs, Annan, McHenry, Davis, Kilgour, and Smith—39.

Negative—Messrs. Ricaud, Buchanan, Chandler, Ridgely, Lloyd, Sherwood of Talbot, Chambers of Cecil, Miller, McLane, Bowie, McCubbin, Spencer, Grason, George, Wright, Shriver, Biser, Sappington, Stephenson, Magraw, McHenry, Carter, Nelson, Thawley, Stewart of Caroline, Hardcastle, Gwinn, Stewart of Baltimore city, Brent of Baltimore city, Presstman, Ware, Schley, Neill, John Newcomer, Harbine, Anderson, Weber, Hollyday, Slicer, Fitzpatrick, Parke, Shower, Cockey and Brown—43.

So the amendment was rejected.

Mr. JENIFER expressed his gratification that the committee had at least progressed so far in its action to-day. And he sent up to the Secretary's table an amendment which he desired to offer, (providing for a Registry Law.)

Mr. DORSEY indicated his desire to offer an amendment.

Mr. JENIFER said, if it would not give rise to debate, he would waive his motion in favor of the gentleman (Mr. DORSEY.)

Mr. DORSEY said, he desired only to say a few words.

Mr. JENIFER withdrew his proposition for the moment.

Mr. DORSEY then moved to amend the amendment—by striking out in the first line, the words "this State," and inserting in lieu thereof, the words "the United States."

Mr. DORSEY briefly gave his reasons for moving the amendment, which was intended to make clear what might otherwise be regarded, as a matter of doubt, as it was contended by some that naturalization merely gave civil rights within the State of the citizen's residence, whilst others insisted that it conferred political, as well as civil rights.

Mr. GWINN here raised the question that this amendment had been disposed of a few days ago. But it appeared on reference to the journal, that the proposition was adopted by Mr. WEEMS as a modification of an amendment offered by him and rejected, without a distinct vote being taken on this amendment, it was again entertained.

Mr. DORSEY said he regarded it as the settled opinion of this Convention, that it has the right to preclude naturalized citizens from the exercise of the elective franchise within the State, because, by the act of naturalization, no political, but civil rights only are given. If the act of Congress, passed pursuant to the Constitution of the United States, conferred political rights, we have no power to restrict these rights. If the naturalized citizen possesses the right to vote, we cannot limit his eligibility to fill any office in the State; and by assuming the right to restrict him, we concede to him civil rights only acquired by naturalization. His object now was to remove all existing doubts on the subject. His object was not to deprive him of any right, civil or political, which he before possessed, but to secure to him the elective franchise of a native born citizen.

Mr. RIDGELY said the amendment proposed by the honorable gentleman from Anne Arundel, takes, in his judgment, a proper distinction, and he hoped will be adopted. A man may be a citizen of the State, and yet not a citizen of the United States. The act of naturalization confers only civil rights—political rights arise out of the compact of State government and its legislation. An alien may, by State legislation, be authorised to exercise citizenship for State purposes, or within the limits of the State, and yet not being naturalized is not a citizen of the United States, entitled to the immunities of citizens of other States. The State may relieve a foreigner from the disabilities, which its laws impose, but cannot make him a citizen of the United States. The amendment, therefore, is broad and comprehensive; covers the whole ground; inasmuch as if the person be a citizen of the United States, and has the residence and other qualifications prescribed in the section, he is citizen necessarily of the State.

Mr. BOWIE said no foreigner could be a citizen of Maryland who had not been naturalized. No foreigner can vote here. He may, by an act of the Legislature, be permitted to hold real estate in Maryland. But this does not make him a citizen. He cannot be a citizen of the State until he has been naturalized; when he is naturalized he then becomes a citizen of the State in which he has been naturalized, and also a citizen of the United States. We are engaged in making an organic law, not so much for citizens of the United States as for citizens of our own State. A man might be a citizen of the United States, and yet not a citizen of this State notwithstanding his residence of twelve months within the State. He might in fact reside here twenty years, and yet not be a citizen of this State. He wished to confine the right of suffrage to the citizens of the State. When any foreigner resident among us is naturalized, he becomes, *eo instanti*, a citizen of the State. There was no ground then for the new born sympathy of the gentleman from Anne Arundel, for naturalized foreigners, which he confessed himself unable to comprehend. He did not wish to open the door for the admission of voters from other States who had no right to political privileges here. He would therefore oppose the insertion of the words "citizens of the United States." He thought the term "citizens of this State" preferable.

Mr. RIDGELY repeated that an alien might by Act of Assembly be authorized to hold real estate, he, *eo instanti*, becomes a citizen of the State, except as regards the right of voting.

Mr. SPENCER inquired if a person in that position could be called on to serve in the militia.

Mr. RIDGELY supposed not. It was idle however, to waste time in describing these distinctions. The amendment of the gentleman from Anne Arundel would cover the whole ground.

Mr. GWINN put a case by way of analogy.

Mr. CRISFIELD asked by what rule a "citizen of this State" is defined? Who is a citizen of the State of Maryland? The term is indefinite. Unless defined by the Constitution, the Legislature will have power to declare who are citizens. The power of the Legislature in this respect should be limited. Unless restrained by express provision of the Constitution, the Legislature might declare that persons not naturalized should be citizens of this State. Was the gentleman from Prince Georges prepared to entrust this power to the Legislature without restraint?

Mr. BOWIE thought that his friend, who had put this question, might have learned from the elementary books what was meant by the term citizen. As soon as allegiance to a government begins, citizenship also begins. It begins with birth, in the case of the native; with naturalization, in the case of an alien. Allegiance to the United States was citizenship of the United States. He was of opinion that no unnaturalized foreigner could be a citizen of Maryland. Any law which should admit such, would be unconstitutional.. He had no doubt of it.

Mr. CRISFIELD thanked his friend, for his reference to the elementary books, but he was not satisfied with the answer. It is admitted that neither this Convention, nor the Legislature, could confer any of the rights of a citizen of the United States. But Maryland is a sovereign State, and can apportion political power at discretion, to any or all classes of her inhabitants, to be exercised within her limits. She may grant to an alien all the privileges of a citizen of the State; and allegiance will begin when the grant is accepted.

Mr. SPENCER referred to the language "free white citizen" used in the amendment of the gentleman from Kent, and also in the Constitution, and asked whether a foreigner could be a citizen of the United States? Could any law of the State make him so? The power of passing naturalization laws was ceded by the States to the General Government, and Congress alone has the power to declare who shall be citizens of the United States. No man then, who is not a native of the United States, can be made a citizen of the United States except by the United States. Then, as the gentleman from Prince Georges says, allegiance and citizenship begin together. So common sense tells us that a citizen of the State must have been born in the State, or must come in by process of laws. Every naturalized foreigner is a citizen of the United States, and of every State of the Union, and after a proper residence in Maryland would be entitled to the privileges of a citizen of Maryland. He saw no difficulty in the thing. In case of invasion, could not the United States summon these persons to the field to defend the United States?

Mr. CRISFIELD. Naturalization confers only civil and not political rights. Political rights are the fruits of State sovereignty. The arguments of the gentleman from Prince George's and Queen Anne's had failed to convince him. The States alone could apportion political power and declare what classes of persons shall enjoy it, and on what terms. In Illinois aliens are permitted to vote; and is Illinois more sovereign than Maryland? The power exists in the State, and unless restrained by the Constitution, the Legislature may exercise it.

Mr. BRENT, of Baltimore city, made a few remarks, in which he stated that it had been decided that as soon as a naturalized citizen of the United States enters any State of the Union to settle and fix his residence there, he becomes *ipso facto*, a citizen of the State, and if he conform to the terms of the law fixing the term of residence required for a qualification to vote, gains a right to vote. The course of Illinois and her construction of her power constitute no rule for our action.

Mr. RIDGELY, read from the Constitutions of six of the States, extracts to show what constructions were put on the term citizen. In these extracts the word was used in a broad sense.

Mr. JENIFER referred to the Constitution of the United States, and asked if any gentleman supposed that any question could ever arise to bring this question into dispute. He, himself, felt very clear on the subject, until the arguments he had now heard from the distinguished lawyers round him, had instilled a doubt into his breast.

Mr. DORSEY said a few words in reply to the gentleman from Prince George's, re-stated what he had before urged in defence of the amendment, and said, although he was guilty of pertinacity, as was asserted by the gentleman from Prince George's, in adhering to his opinion after its emphatic contradiction by the gentleman from Prince George's, who says, there can be no doubt on the subject. Yet, having formed his opinion on the subject, after mature deliberation, he could not be induced lightly to abandon it; and hoped he would be excused for adhering to it, after a charge of pertinacity for venturing to differ in opinion with his friend from Prince George's on a Constitutional question. Because he adhered to his amendment, he had been charged with being the champion of naturalized citizens. He was the champion of nobody; he had no political aspirations, and had the imagination of his friend been equally free from them, he never would have made such a charge. He did no more than that what he deemed his duty, to make the language of the Constitution so explicit as to prevent controversy hereafter.

Mr. Grason said, it seemed to him that, upon the question before the Convention, gentlemen on different sides came very nearly to an agreement. For his own part, he agreed in the opinions expressed by the gentleman from Queen Anne, and also with those expressed on the other side, because he was satisfied that either term would answer the purpose. In the Constitution as it originally stood, the word "citizen of the United States," or "citizen of the State" was not to be found. In that instrument we found the term used was "persons"—"people"—"freemen." But in the year 1810, when the right of suffrage was extended, there was a provision that every free white male citizen of the State should be entitled to vote. That term had stood the test of forty years without producing a single inconvenience or difficulty. It appeared to him that there could not be any objection to its use. He preferred it because he thought that the dignity of the State of Maryland would be consulted by acting up to the idea that there was such a thing as a citizen of that State. When the gentleman from Baltimore county (Mr. Ridgely) had cited the provisions of the Constitutions of other States, he (Mr. G.) had turned to the Constitution of the State of Virginia, of the history of which he had some knowledge. The words there were "every free citizen of the Commonwealth." He would barely suggest that possibly the words "a citizen of Maryland," were more appropriate than the words "a citizen of the United States." He should always contemplate with painful emotions the possibility that there ever could be a separation of the States of this Union. But it might happen that three or four of the States might withdraw—that there might be a rupture, or even a peaceable separation. The Convention was framing a Constitution which, if it should prove acceptable to the people, and calculated to promote their honor and interest, might endure for ages to come. And, looking to the possibility that either of the events to which he had alluded might occur, he would prefer that a term should be used which was applicable to the people of the State.

Mr. Bowie and Mr. Dorsey made mutual explanations.

Mr J. U. Dennis said, that some of the States had made negroes citizens, and given them the right of suffrage. If other States have this power, it is to be presumed that we have.

The question was then taken on the amendment of Mr. Dorsey, and the vote was declared to be, yeas 39, nays 30.

Mr. Spencer suggested that there was a mistake in the count (a large number of members standing up in a limited space in that extreme quarter of the hall which immediately fronts the Committee room.)

Several members called for a re-count.

The Chairman said, he was sure of the correctness of the count, but was willing to make a re-count, if desired by the Committee.

Mr. Brent called the yeas and nays.

Mr. Phelps submitted that it was not in order to call the yeas and nays, after the result of the vote had been announced.

Mr. Magraw. We were so thick in the corner here, that we could not get out. (Laughter.)

Mr. Brent, of Baltimore city. I will state the reason why the yeas and nays should be taken. If the event to which the gentleman has referred of a dissolution of the Union—

Mr. Buchanan. (Interposing.) This is clearly out of order, Mr. Chairman. The gentleman has no right to speak on that subject.

Mr. Brent. I have the right to state the reason why—

Mr. Buchanan. Oh! no, you have no such right.

Mr. Jenifer. If we adopt this principle, why may not a gentleman get up on every question and say he distrusts the count of the chair, and ask the yeas and nays.

The Chairman. The Chair presumes that every member of this body is an honorable man, and would not make such a statement unless he believed it to be true. (Laughter.)

The yeas and nays were then ordered, and being taken, resulted as follows:

Affirmative.—Messrs. Chapman, President, Morgan, Blakistone, Dent, Hopewell, Ricaud, Lee, Chambers, of Kent, Mitchell, Donaldson, Dorsey, Kent, Weems, Dalrymple, Bond, Brent, of Charles, Jenifer, Ridgely, John Dennis, James U. Dennis, Crisfield, Dashiell, Williams, Hodson, Goldsborough, Eccleston, Phelps, McCullough, Sprigg, McCubbin, Dirickson, McMaster, Hearn, Fooks, Jacobs, Annan, Schley, Fiery, John Newcomer, Harbine, Davis, Waters, Smith, Parke and Cockey—46.

Negative.—Messrs. Randall, Buchanan, Chandler, Lloyd, Sherwood, of Talbot, Chambers, of Cecil, Miller, McLane, Bowie, Tuck, Spencer, Grason, George, Wright, Shriver, Biser, Sappington, Stephenson, McHenry, Magraw, Nelson, Carter, Thawley, Stewart, of Caroline, Hardcastle, Gwinn, Stewart, of Baltimore city, Brent, of Baltimore city, Presstman, Ware, Neill, Kilgour, Weber, Hollyday, Slicer, Shower and Brown—37.

So the amendment was adopted.

The question then recurred upon the amendment as offered by Mr. Weber.

Mr. Buchanan, moved that the Committee rise.

Determined in the affirmative.

The Committee accordingly rose, the President resumed the Chair, and the Chairman reported that the Committee had in obedience to order, had the said report again under consideration, and had come to no conclusion thereon.

And the Convention adjourned until to-morrow morning eleven o'clock..

SATURDAY, Jan. 18th, 1851.

The Convention, in pursuance of its order, met this day at eleven o'clock.

Prayer by the Rev. Mr. GRAUFF.

The roll of the members was called. A quorum being present, the journal of yesterday was read, and a typographical error having, on motion of Mr. WEBER been ordered to be corrected, was approved.

The PRESIDENT said that the regular order of business would be reports of Committees.

There being no reports—

The PRESIDENT announced the unfinished business of the morning hour, to be the amendment to the resolutions of which Mr. RANDALL had heretofore given notice.

THE PREVIOUS QUESTION.

The Convention resumed the consideration of the amendment heretofore offered by Mr. RANDALL, to amend the 17th rule, which is in the following words:

"The previous question shall be always in order in Convention, if seconded by a majority; and, until decided, shall preclude all further amendment and debate, and shall be in this form: 'Shall the main question be now put?' When, on taking the previous question, the Convention shall decide that the same shall not now be put, the main question shall be still under consideration, and if the previous question is sustained, the main question shall be on the adoption of the proposition under consideration. And in cases where there shall be no pending amendments, the question shall be first taken on such amendments in their order, and without further debate or amendment."

Mr. RANDALL had moved to amend this rule as follows:

1. After the word "Convention" in the 1st line, insert the words "the mover designating whether the whole or a part and what part of the matter depending is comprehended in his motion."

2. Strike out all after the word "adoption ' in the 8th line, and insert in lieu thereof the following words, "of the special matter under consideration, and the question shall be taken thereon alone without further debate or amendment thereof, and the previous question shall be then exhausted."

Mr. RANDALL remarked, that as some members of the Convention were not probably in their seats when he made an explanation of the operation of this amendment, he would repeat that explanation, so that gentleman might understand the object which he had in view.

Mr. R. explained accordingly.

Some conversation followed between Mr. BISER and Mr. RANDALL, as to the effect of the amendment.

The question was then taken, and the first and second branches of the amendment were severally adopted.

BUSINESS OF THE CONVENTION.

The Convention proceeded to the consideration of the motion of Mr. SOLLERS, to amend the twenty-third rule which is as follows:

"The preceding rules shall be observed in a Committee of the Whole, so far as they are applicable, except that part of the twentieth rule, which restricts members from speaking more than twice upon the same question. The ayes and noes shall be taken in Committee of the Whole, in the same manner as they are taken in Convention, and a journal of the proceedings in a Committee of the Whole shall be kept. The motion to adjourn and the previous question, shall not be in order in the Committee of the Whole."

Mr. SOLLERS moved to amend the rule, by striking out these words, "except that part of the 20th rule which restricts members from speaking more than twice upon the same question. The ayes and noes shall be taken in Committee of the Whole, in the same manner as they are taken in Convention."

Mr. SOLLERS said that his only motive in proposing the amendment, was to facilitate the business of the Convention. It was well known that there had been occasions in committee of the whole, where gentlemen had spoken four or five times. If this state of things was to continue, the session of the Convention would be protracted a long time. The same motive—to save the consumption of time—had induced him also to offer the other part of the amendment, which proposed to prohibit the taking of the yeas and nays in committee of the whole.

Mr. HARBINE said that he was in favor of the first branch of the amendment, but was opposed to the adoption of the second. He believed that restriction upon debate would to some extent be necessary to prevent the discursive, wild and desultory discussions which took place in committees. As to the latter part of the amendment, he was opposed to its adoption, as he thought it important that the privilege of taking the yeas and nays in Committee, should be allowed. He could see no sufficient reason why they should not be taken in the Committee, as well as in the Convention. The only objection that could be urged was that the yeas and nays might be taken twice on the same proposition; but he submitted whether there were not some propositions voted upon in Committee, which never might be voted upon in the House at all.

Mr. PHELPS was in favor, he said, of the adoption of both the amendments of the gentleman from Calvert, (Mr. SOLLERS.) As Chairman of the Committee on the Rules, he had dissented from the proposition to take the yeas and nays in Committee. He regarded the taking of the yeas and nays there, as a work of supererogation, because they could as well be taken in Convention.

Mr. SPENCER asked for information. He did not understand that every measure offered in committee of the whole would come up again in Convention.

Mr. PHELPS. I mean to say, that it is competent for a gentleman to offer the same proposition in Convention, which may have been voted down in Committee.

Mr. SPENCER. But a great deal of time will be unnecessarily consumed in that way. I hear it suggested also, that if the previous question is called in the House, it will cut off all amendments lost in committee of the whole. Again, if a gentleman knows that a proposition has been voted down in Committee, by a record vote, he will not renew it in Convention, because no object can be attained by doing so.

Mr. SOLLERS explained that his only aim was to save time, and that when gentlemen reflected on the objects for which this Convention had assembled, it seemed to him they could not hesitate as to the propriety of adopting this amendment.

The question was then taken on the first branch of the amendment, and it was agreed to.

And the question recurring on the second branch of the amendment, (prohibiting the yeas and nays in committee of the whole,)

Messrs. JOHN NEWCOMER and HARBINE called the yeas and nays, which were ordered, and being taken, resulted as follows:

Affirmative.—Messrs. Chapman, President, Morgan, Blakistone, Hopewell, Ricaud, Lee, Chambers, of Kent, Donaldson, Dorsey, Wells, Randall, Kent, Sellman, Dalrymple, Bond, Sollers, Brent of Charles, Merrick, Jenifer, Buchanan, John Dennis, James U. Dennis, Crisfield, Williams, Hodson, Goldsborough, Phelps, Tuck, Grason, George, Wright, McMaster, Hearn, Jacobs, Annan, Hardcastle, Gwinn, Stewart, of Baltimore city, Ware, Davis, Waters, Anderson, Weber, Slicer, Fitzpatrick and Smith—46.

Negative.—Messrs. Dent, Ridgely, Lloyd, Sherwood, of Talbot, Dashiell, Eccleston, Chambers, of Cecil, McCullough, McLane, Bowie, Sprigg, Spencer, Fooks, Shriver, Biser, Stephenson, McHenry, Nelson, Carter, Thawley, Stewart of Caroline, Presstman, Schley, Fiery, Neill, John Newcomer, Harbine, Parke and Cockey—29.

So the amendment was adopted.

DOUBLE SESSIONS, &c.

Mr. FIERY offered the following resolution:

Resolved, That from and after Monday, the 27th inst., the Convention shall hold morning and evening sessions; the former commencing at ten o clock, and the latter at three o'clock.

The resolution having been read,

Mr. PRESSTMAN moved that it be laid on the table.

Mr. FIERY requested that the motion might be withdrawn.

Mr. PRESSTMAN. I am so unwilling to refuse any request which my friend may make, that I will withdraw the motion, if he will renew it after he has submitted such remarks as he may desire to offer.

Mr. FIERY. I will do so.

Mr. PRESSTMAN. I withdraw the motion.

Mr. FIERY. I simply wish to say, that this order, if adopted, will not take effect until next Monday week. I desire that the committees shall have time to make their reports, and that all the members of this Convention who are solicitous to discharge the duties for which they have been sent here, should go to work earnestly and immediately. I anticipate a great deal of talking. Certainly, if we are to judge of the future by the past, this anticipation will be realized. I desire that all gentlemen who wish to express their sentiments should have the privilege of doing so; but I think that we are in duty bound to adopt this resolution.

I do not entertain any feeling of jealousy or ill will towards any member of this body. All I desire is that we shall make the most rapid progress in the business of the Convention, that is consistent with a sound and enlightened action. Nothing, I believe, will more effectually tend to accomplish that object than that members should have the opportunities for discussion and for the comparison of their views, which my resolution proposes to give them.

Mr. BUCHANAN said it seemed to him that the committees should have time to consider and prepare their reports before they were called upon to make them. The committee on the Judiciary, for example, was in session many hours, and would have to be in session hereafter at various periods during the day, and if this proposition was to be adopted, he thought that the Chairman of the committee should ask (and if that gentleman did not, he (Mr. B.) would ask,) that the committee should be discharged from further service. Certainly, the committee never could, under a resolution of this character, discharge its duty to itself and to the Convention.

Now, he believed, that all the members of this body were anxious to save time. But there were various opinions about the mode in which that object could be effected. His proposition was, to meet together in small numbers, about the size of one of the ordinary committees, to do the *work* whilst there; and the same necessity would not then exist for the "talking" which his friend (Mr. FIERY) so much and so well apprehended the danger. Looking to the amount of business before some of the committees, it was impossible to move along if this resolution was to be adopted. He hoped that it would be withdrawn; or that, if not so, leave would be granted to the committee on the Judiciary to sit during the sessions of the Convention.

Mr. HARBINE said he would state one or two facts, in reply to the remarks of the gentleman from Baltimore county, (Mr. BUCHANAN,) as to the business before the Committee, which would he (Mr. H.) thought throw all such arguments into utter insignificance. How long would it take the Convention to get through with the reports which had already been made? If the experience of the past, formed any guide for the calculations of the future, another Summer's sun would have risen and past before these reports were disposed of; and his friend from Baltimore county, therefore, would have ample time to prepare and submit half a dozen reports if he desired to do so. What length of time did the gentleman desire to have for the preparation of the report on the Judiciary question? At the rate at which the Convention was now going on, the gentleman would have until at least the first of July; and thus, no more time would be wanted than, from the present aspect of things, the Convention was going to give. It was not that time was wanted by the Committees—but that it was wanted by the Convention. There was already business enough before them to occupy them three months, and before that time had elapsed, other business would be presented for their consideration.

He cordially sustained the resolution, and hoped it would meet with the favor of the Convention.

Mr. KILGOUR said that in voting against this resolution, as it was his intention to do, he obeyed the voice of at least one of his constituents, who told him before he left home to take care of his health. (Laughter.) And he had promised *her* that he would do so. (Renewed laughter.) Was it not enough to kill any man to sit here six or seven hours a day? Especially hard was it as concerned the reporters. Some little regard certainly ought to be shown to them. Yet so great was the labor, and so apprehensive was one of them (Mr. WHEELER) as to the result, that it was understood he was already in negociation with an undertaker as to the expenses of a decent christian funeral in the city of Annapolis. (General laughter.) Now, after the discussion had been carried on for a short time, it would be found that the Convention would grow tired of it; and the result, he thought, would be that a Constitution would be framed at an earlier date than some gentlemen anticipated.

Mr. STEWART, of Caroline, said, he did not rise so much for the purpose of saying any thing for or against the resolution immediately under consideration, as to suggest to the Convention the necessity of giving their vote only after mature reflection. How often had the rules been already changed? The whole system, as regarded the hour of meeting, had been one of constant, ceaseless change. But the procrastination which had marked the proceedings of this body, grew not so much out of the speeches that were made, as out of the want of concert of action in and out of the Convention. It was necessary that there should be such a concert of action by a majority of the Convention somewhere, either in or out of doors. He cared not how that end was to be brought about. He was ready now to go into a Reform caucus, and ascertain who were Reformers, and who were ready to do the business of the Convention. Here they were floating recklessly about on the broad waters of speculation, every man entertaining his own views and adhering to his own pre-conceived opinions; and if things were to go on in this way, it was easy to foresee that the session would be protracted to an indefinite period. He would vote for this resolution, just to try it.

Allusion had been made to the probable loss of health by the members of the Convention. He thought every gentleman looked pretty well. (Laughter.) But it was not because they sat here too long, or deliberated too intensely that danger to their health was to be apprehended. It was to be feared from the fact, that gentlemen lived too high—(general laughter)—Gentlemen came here accustomed to plain diet (renewed laughter)—and to regularity of meals. As to the latter difficulty, this resolution would set all that matter right. As to the diet, gentlemen knew very well that many of them get better here than they were accustomed to at home. (Roars of laughter.) Among this class, he had no hesitation in placing himself.

He thought that the labor of the mind should be done out of the Convention—that gentleman should reflect upon the matters before them—and that when they came here, they should be prepared to act. But he called for concert of action. Mr. S. illustrated the condition of things in the Convention, by some similes which created much amusement.

In concluding, he referred to the change which had taken place this day in the operation of the previous question. That change had been made without reflection, and would, he thought, seriously retard the action of the Convention. The one only remedy for all these difficulties was that which he had designated—concert of action.

The hour of twelve having arrived, the Convention passed to the orders of the day.

Mr. CHAMBERS, of Kent, moved that the Convention resolve itself into committee of the whole, but waived the motion to enable

Mr. MERRICK presented a communication from Joseph C. G. Kennedy, Esq., superintendent of census, covering a statement of the population of the State of Maryland.

The communication was read and, on motion of Mr. MERRICK, was ordered to be printed.

THE ELECTIVE FRANCHISE.

On motion of Mr. CHAMBERS, of Kent,

The Convention resolved itself into Committee of the Whole, Mr. BLAKISTONE in the Chair, and resumed the consideration of the report submitted by the former gentleman from the Committee on the Elective Franchise.

The pending question was stated to be on the amendment heretofore offered by Mr. WEBER, to add to the end of the amendment, offered by Mr. CHAMBERS, the following words:

"Provided, That the voter, if required, shall make affidavit, that he did not move into the election district to affect the election then being held."

Mr. BUCHANAN said, he believed he was entitled to the floor, but as there was no question pending upon which he desired to be heard, he would yield his right to any gentleman who desired it.

Mr. CHAMBERS, of Kent, said he was about to offer a proposition, which he supposed would constitute the first section, so far as the Convention had, by its votes indicated what that section should be. After conference with several gentlemen, some of whom voted on one side, and some on the other, in relation to the various propositions, which had been offered, and after hearing some difficulties expressed in relation to the effect of the vote on the proposition of the gentleman from Anne Arundel (Mr. DORSEY) which had been adopted yesterday; difficulties arising from an apprehension, that that proposition would not effect the object designed; he (Mr. C.)

was prepared to offer a first section in a form which he thought would embody the various views of the Convention.

The section was read as follows:

"Every free white male person of twenty-one years of age or upwards, who shall have been for one year next preceding the election, a resident of the State, and for six months a resident of the city of Baltimore, of Howard District, or of any county in which he may offer to vote, and being at the time of the election a citizen of the United States, shall be entitled to vote in the ward or election district in which he resides, in all elections hereafter to be held, and at all such elections the votes shall be taken by ballot."

The section having been read:

Mr. CHAMBERS withdrew his previous amendment, and offered this in lieu thereof.

Mr. WEBER's amendment thereupon fell to the ground under the operation of the Parliamentary Law; and

The question being on the adoption of the amendment last offered by Mr. CHAMBERS,

Mr. BOWIE suggested to the gentleman, so to modify it, as to insert after the words "a citizen of the United States," the words "and of the State."

Mr. CHAMBERS said, the difficulty was that there were some forty members of the Convention, who would express the same idea in different terms. Personally, he had no objection to it, except that it loaded down the section with phraseology which could have no effect upon it.

Mr. BOWIE explained, that the only difficulty he had about the matter, was that, in his judgment, it was not in fact true that every citizen of the United States was a citizen of the State of Maryland for political purposes.

Mr. GRASON said that he thought the amendment, as it now reads, was in conformity with the wishes and opinions of the Convention. He would therefore vote for it.

Mr. CHAMBERS suggested that the gentleman from Prince George's could move his amendment as a separate proposition.

Mr. STEPHENSON moved to amend the amendment by striking out the word "six" and insert "three" before the word "months," so as to make it read "three months."

Mr. CHAMBERS expressed a hope that the Convention would adopt the amendment he had offered, as a substantive proposition. He would afterwards introduce another proposition.

Mr. DORSEY rose to vindicate himself against an insinuation that he had been actuated by some sinister design in his conduct on yesterday. It seemed to have been understood by some gentlemen that the object of his amendment was to postpone the exercise of political rights by naturalized citizens, by requiring of them, after they had been naturalized here, to reside twelve months in the State, as well as six months in the county. He was informed by his colleague, after leaving the committee room last night, that such construction had been put upon his course. He was informed this morning at the breakfast table, that a sinister design was imputed to him. He then pulled out of his pocket an amendment which he had prepared with a view to set himself right before the Convention, and showed it to the gentlemen.

He could not have desired such a construction of his amendment as was charged against him, with any sinister design, because the report would have borne the same construction after, as before his amendment. It reads, "every free, white, male citizen." Who are these citizens who have come into our State and resided among us, and been naturalized here? They are all residents of the State. The objection would apply to naturalized citizens from other States. He never conceived such an idea as postponing the rights of these citizens for twelve months. He had voted for the present proposition, which carries out that which he brought forward yesterday. And he would not now have said one word but to explain his conduct.

The question was taken on the amendment of Mr. Stephenson, to strike out six months, and insert "three;" and it was rejected.

The question then recurred on the amendment of Mr. CHAMBERS, of Kent.

Mr. CHAMBERS would explain in few words. Originally every man voted in the county in which he resided, and every man in every part of the county voted for the same officers, whether for officers of the General Government or of the State. There was no such thing as a voter in one part of a county or city, voting for a representative of one district, and another voter in the same county or city, voting for a representative of another district. This arrangement was subsequently altered. Now by the act of 1843, the first eleven wards of the city of Baltimore, are thrown into one Congressional district, and the other wards into another. So Howard district being part of Anne Arundel county, forms part of one Congressional district, and the residue of that county forms part of another. Congress having full jurisdiction over the subject, has declared that each State shall be divided into separate and single districts, and it is therefore most probable that this interference between the geographical lines by which the counties are divided, and the goegraphical lines of the Congressional districts will occur in other instances, as the increasing population of the United States may continue to require an increased ratio of representation. Now then it is apparent that if a residence of six months in the county or city, shall entitle a person to vote in any part of the county in which he has his actual residence, the voters in a divided county or city, have advantages not possessed by those in other counties. Thus, a man residing in Prince George's county for six months prior to the election, must vote for the representative in Congress for the first district, and if at any time less than six months before the election, he removes into the county of Anne Arundel, he loses his vote altogether. But his neighbor, living it may be, not one hundred yards from him, yet on the opposite side of the line which divides the two counties, and thus having a residence in the first district, may by removing into Howard district the day previous to the election, obtain his vote in the third district. So a voter residing in the twelfth ward of the city of Baltimore, and entitled to vote in the third district, may by removing into the eleventh ward, over night, claim his vote next day in the fourth district. It is therefore obvious that these persons have advantages and privileges not common to other citizens, and it is admitted that a remedy is necessary to produce equality. The amendment now offered, simply proposes that in all cases a voter shall have resided in his Congressional district or the district for which any officer is to be chosen, for six months previous to the election.

An erroneous opinion seemed to prevail, that he desired to restrain or restrict the right of suffrage. It was not so. His sole object was to secure to legal, honest, fair voters, the just effect of their votes, by preventing false and fraudulent votes.

The amendment he now offered, had a further provision, which would extend the right of suffrage to a considerable class of persons, who had never before enjoyed it, but as he thought ought to have it. Where a citizen now removes from one county to another, although all the time in the same district,he cannot vote unless he has resided six months in the county to which he last removed.

By his amendment, he would have the privilege of voting always in some part of that district, if he had not removed entirely beyond it. This provision would not only remedy the evils which had been suggested as likely to be felt by men in humble life, whose necessities required them frequently to change their place of residence, but would extend the right to quite a considerable number of persons now disfranchised.

Mr. PRESSTMAN said he had a much stronger objection to this amendment than to the five days restriction, as applicable to Baltimore. The ground taken by the Baltimore delegation, was that Baltimore had a population much greater in amount, than other counties; and the hardship of the proposition bore more hardly on them than others. He instanced the operation of the restriction on the residents of Baltimore, to show the effect of the restrictions. He did not wish to encourage or countenance any frauds; and concluded with expressing a hope that the right of a legal voter might not be infringed, lest an illegal vote should be admitted.

Mr. MERRICK could not believe it possible, that this body could put all the counties of Maryland on the same footing. He instanced the inequality to which this would give rise, and contended that laws should not be so made as to have a partial operation. The amendment now offered secured equal rights to all.

Mr. RIDGELY stated that he had voted against the five days restriction; but his difficulty was entirely obviated by this amendment, which broke up colonizatson, and gave sufficient protection to the legal voters. He would go for it.

The question was then taken on the substitute amendment of Mr. CHAMBERS, and it was agreed to.

Mr. CHAMBERS then offered the following amendment:

"And in case any county or city shall be so divided as to form portions of different electoral districts for the election of Congressmen, Senator, Delegate or other officer or officers, then to entitle a person to vote for such officer, he must have been a resident of that part of the county or city which shall form a part of the electoral district, in which he offers to vote, for six months next preceding the election, but a person who shall have acquired a residence in such county or city, entitling him to vote at such election, shall be entitled to vote in the election district from which he removed until he shall have acquired a residence in the part of the county or city to which he has removed."

Which was twice read.

Mr. SELLMAN suggested that a delay of a day or two should be allowed for the consideration of this amendment, as he thought that some difficulty might exist in relation to it. It was a proposition for which all gentlemen would be likely to vote, if they could properly do so; and he cited, in illustration; a case in which difficulty might arise.

Mr. PARKE moved to strike out six months and insert "one," but, on a suggestion from the Chair, that the motion was not now in order, withdrew it.

Mr. CHAMBERS modified his amendment by inserting the word "ward."

Mr. SPENCER said that the proposition of the gentleman from Kent, struck him with great force, but he thought it was not entirely exempt from difficulties. Therefore, he asked a little more time for its examination. As the gentleman from Kent desires to promote the object we all desire in this proposition, it might be desirable to let it lie over until Monday. He stated, in brief, what were his objections, and as he wished to vote for it, if on examination these objections should be removed. He would vote that the amendment might be laid on the table and printed. It can be again offered in the House; or, after we have voted on some other amendments, might be brought up again in committee of the whole.

The CHAIR intimated that the motion was not now in order.

Mr. CHAMBERS made a further explanation, in which he suggested that as in all laws for practical purposes, hardships could not be in every case avoided. So it might possibly be in carrying out this law. The proposition now offered had been deliberated on, and the Committee had come to the conclusion that if we cannot extend the franchise to all, we may to some. He had no desire to press the vote now. It might be postponed until Monday, if the Convention was not prepared to act on it.

Mr. SPENCER did not wish to be understood as opposing the amendment. The gentleman from Kent, had forcibly presented his reasons. But his objections were not obviated. He hoped the amendment would be printed, after which he might be prepared to offer an amendment, which would obviate his objections.

The question was then taken and the amendment of Mr. CHAMBERS was agreed to.

Mr. SELLMAN enquired whether the amendment would be open to amendment in Convention ?

The reply from several quarters was in the affirmative.

REGISTRY LAW.

Mr. JENIFER said, he was gratified to find that we had gotten through with the first section. That difficulty having been surmounted as far as the Committee was concerned, he would now move the amendment which he indicated some days ago.

"That the Legislature may provide for a uniform registration of voters within the State of Maryland, which shall be taken and held as the only evidence of the qualifications of said voters, to vote at any election that may hereafter be held in the State."

Mr. J. said, it was admitted by all that under the present system frauds were committed upon the right of suffrage, and the purity of the ballot box annually invaded. It was also admitted that a remedy should be applied, but it was objected that none heretofore proposed would be adequate to correct the evil—hence, all have been rejected. A registry law, with proper provisions, seemed to him to be the best measure to accomplish the object.

The distinguished gentleman from Cecil, (Mr. McLANE,) suggests additional penal laws. The gentleman from the city of Baltimore, (Mr. PRESSTMAN,) thinks that the committees of vigilance at the polls, the most effectual preventive. The gentleman from Caroline, (Mr. STEWART,) says, give to every voter a homestead, and other gentlemen have given their views, but no definite proposition made, which has not been rejected. If then, this Convention, seeing the evils of the violation of the elective franchise, the innumerable frauds committed at every election, cannot provide the remedy, let us, at least, place it in the power of the Legislature, to make such regulations as may be adequate. The registry law of 1837-8, which was repealed in 1839, is referred to, as evidence against it. It should be recollected that that law was confined to the city of Baltimore. It was partial and invidious; many believed it to be unconstitutional, as he (Mr. J.) did. It imposed duties upon the electors of the city of Baltimore, which were not common to others of the State. The law itself was inadequate.

By adopting the amendment now proposed, it will enable the Legislature to pass a Registry Law with such provisions as may guard the ballot box from fraud and place all the voters of the State upon the same footing. The question of unconstitutionality will not arise, the experience of the past will be beneficial to the future—no honest man entitled to a vote, will be deprived of the inestimable privilege, whilst it will protect the elective franchise in its whole purity.

Gentlemen are quite indignant at the proposition to make five days residence in an election district necessary to entitle the elector to vote—and seem to think that any guards thrown around the ballot box to protect it from fraud, is a restriction upon the rights of the elector. It is stigmatized by some as oppressive, a grievous infringement of the elective franchise. How is it that five days residence in an election district in the city of Baltimore is a denial of the right of suffrage, and the requirement of six months residence in the counties should be a just and necessary restriction? Should the proposition now under consideration be adopted, it will apply to the whole State and there is nothing invidious in it. Reject it and according to the construction given to the clause in the Constitution by the gentleman from Baltimore, and others, a single night's sleep in any district will entitle the elector to vote in that district, whether for delegates to the Legislature, members of Congress, or at other elections. Mark the difference as applied to the counties. No elector can vote for a Governor or member of Congress until he shall have a *bona fide* residence of six months in the county in which he proposes to vote. He may be eligible as Governor or Representative in Congress, and elected as such, but cannot vote himself, unless he has resided six months in the county. Whereas in the city of Baltimore the elector can cross over into any election district, and by one night's residence vote in all cases of elections. Is there not a singular inconsistency in the action of gentlemen in regard to the elective franchise? No member of this body, no honorable man in the State would deprive the honestly entitled elector of his vote—no honorable man should encourage the vote of one not entitled. In either case it would be unjust and an infringement upon the rights of those entitled to suffrage. But if all the evils attendant upon illegal and fraudulent voting, cannot be arrested, does it follow that we shall not make such wholesome regulations as may prevent a portion of them.

Mr. RICAUD offered an amendment to which—

Mr. PRESSTMAN suggested a modification by the insertion of the word "unfair," &c.

Mr. RICAUD accepted the suggestion, and the amendment was read as follows:

Insert after the word "Maryland," the following:

"And from time to time thereafter, of all who may become such qualified electors;" and add at the end of the said amendment, the words following: "or some other uniform provision whereby the legal and qualified electors may be fully and truly ascertained, and the elective franchise protected from all fraud."

Mr. JENIFER accepted the first branch of Mr. RICAUD's amendment as a modification of his own.

Mr. KILGOUR said, he desired to move an amendment to the amendment of Mr. JENIFER—by striking out in the first line the word "may," and inserting in lieu thereof, "shall not." Mr. K. also desired, he said, to make a speech, but thought he could make it better on Monday than to-day. Some opportunity should also be allowed to the Reporters to bring up the proceedings, and he would, therefore, move that the Committee rise.

The motion having been agreed to—

The Committee rose, and reported progress.

Mr. CHAMBERS, of Kent, suggested that as many members were absent, or going away for the Sabbath, he would, to give them an opportunity of being here at the meeting of the Convention, move that when the Convention adjourned it adjourn to meet on Monday, at twelve o'clock.

Mr. HARBINE moved to substitute ten for twelve.

The motion of Mr. CHAMBERS (being first in order) was agreed to.

And then the Convention adjourned until Monday at twelve o'clock.

MONDAY, January 20th, 1851.

The Convention met at twelve o'clock.

Prayer by the Rev. Mr. GRIFFITH.

The roll was called and a quorum being present, the Journal of Saturday was read and approved.

The PRESIDENT announced the regular order of business to be the call of the committee for Reports.

Mr. JENIFER, chairman of committee No. 14, to which was referred the order to enquire into the expediency of reporting some constitutional enactment by authority of which the future Legislature of the State shall have power to pass laws, providing for the removal of the free colored population from the State of Maryland, "asked to be discharged from the further consideration thereof, and that the same be referred to the committee on the free colored population.

The motion was agreed to.

On motion of Mr. STEPHENSON, it was

Ordered, That the committee on Corporations enquire into the expediency of providing in the new constitution for limiting the time for which charters hereafter granted, shall endure to twenty years; also, into the the propriety of vesting the Legislature with the power of altering or revoking any charter whenever, in their opinion, the public interest may require it, but in such manner that no injustice be done to the corporators.

DOUBLE SESSIONS.

The PRESIDENT announced the unfinished business of the morning hour to be the resolution heretofore offered by Mr. FIERY, providing for morning and evening sittings of the Convention.

Mr. PHELPS suggested that, as the attendance was not very full, it might perhaps be better that the resolution should lie over until to-morrow.

Mr. FIERY acquiesced in the suggestion,

And by general consent, the resolution was laid over until to-morrow.

ORDERS OF THE DAY.

Mr. WEEMS called up the motion of which he had given notice, to re-consider the vote of the Convention adopting the resolution heretofore offered by Mr. THOMAS in relation to the preparation of a map for the use of the Convention, showing the boundaries of the several election districts, &c.

And the Convention proceeded to the consideration of the motion to reconsider.

Mr. W., in explanation, said, it seemed to him that it was impracticable to obtain the information sought by the resolution, and the only object he had in moving a reconsideration, was to enable the gentleman to make such explanations as would perhaps be satisfactory to the Convention.

Mr. THOMAS said he was under the impression that the gentleman from Calvert, (Mr. WEEMS,) upon conference with the officer of the Convention who had charge of the execution of the order, would readily learn that such progress had been made in the preparation of the map, as would satisfy his mind that all the information asked for, could be obtained within a very limited period. Most of the tabular statements called for in the order had previously been ordered by the Convention; and the only effect of his (Mr. T's) resolution, would be to append these statements to the map. The boundaries of the counties; the boundaries of the city of Baltimore, and of the several wards of the city; and many of the boundaries of the several subdivisions of the several districts were already delineated, and he was assured upon the authority of the gentleman who was making the map, and who was an experienced surveyor, that the whole of the work would be completed in a short time.

The occasion did not require, that he (Mr. T.) should assign the reasons which had led him to offer a resolution calling for this map. He supposed it would be anticipated by every intelligent gentleman, that he (Mr. T.) intended to make use of it in the contingency of a proposition to sub-divide the State into several single election districts, for the choice of members of the House of Delegates. That was his own individual preference. How far that preference would be concurred in by the members of this body, he had no means of predicting, He had conferred with very few gentlemen, but he knew that there were others besides himself, who had such a preference. If there were only a small minority here who desired at the proper time to express their reasons for prefering this mode of apportionment, they threw themselves upon the courtesy of the Convention to afford them the requisite facilities for procuring such facts and documents as would enable them to submit that preferred mode to the consideration of the Convention, if it could be done without a very large or unreasonable expenditure of the public money.

The largest portion of the cost had already been incurred by the officer having charge of the work. He had employed an experienced surveyor. The whole map, Mr. T. supposed, would not cost more than twenty dollars. After the map should have been prepared, it was his intention to submit a proposition to have it lithographed, that each member of the Convention might have one or more copies. The lithographing would be a matter of small expense.

Some four or five cents a copy would be the entire charge.

Mr. WEEMS took the floor but yielded for the moment, to,

Mr. RANDALL, who referred to an order which he had offered heretofore. It was his object, he said, to elect through districts, and that could only be accomplished by successfully carrying out the motion of the gentleman from Frederick, (Mr. THOMAS.) He (Mr. R.) submitted to the Convention that this mode of electing delegates was more truly in accordance with the plan and the spirit of representation gentlemen, than an election by the consolidated vote of the counties. It accorded also with the plan adopted by Congress for the election of Representatives to that body.

Mr. WEEMS said, it was not his object to oppose the procurement of this information. But it struck him that it was altogether impracticable to give a correct district line upon the map which was in progress. He believed also, that it was altogether impracticable to obtain another item of the information sought for—namely, the population of the several election districts in the respective counties, without incurring a very large expense.

Mr. THOMAS said, that since his return to Annapolis, the Clerk had suggested the difficulty of executing the order in the particular to which the gentleman (Mr. WEEMS) had referred. He (Mr. T.) had been under the impression, until otherwise informed, that in the Executive Department of the Government, would be found returns of the population in each of the election districts, but he had been told that the Marshal in taking the census for Maryland, had sometimes disregarded the boundaries of election districts, and that, therefore, definite information could not be had.

He (Mr. T.) had suggested a remedy for this difficulty which it seemed to him, would be satisfactory. The Secretary had sent a circular to the several Clerks of the County Courts asking them to report the aggregate vote in the election districts at the recent election for Governor. Although, upon this information, we could not have a precise account of the inhabitants of the several districts, we could approximate sufficiently near to it for any purposes which the Convention might desire to accomplish.

Mr. WEEMS. All I intended to say was, that I considered it impracticable to obtain the population of the election districts in the county from the returns of the census—that there was no data upon which that population could be ascertained. I withdraw the motion to reconsider.

So the motion was withdrawn.

Mr. MCHENRY. With great diffidence and some misgiving, I offer the following order:

Ordered, That the debate on the article of the constitution, reported by the committee on the elective franchise, shall terminate in committee of the whole on Wednesday the 22d inst., at two o'clock, P. M., when each amendment pending, or which may be offered shall be passed upon, without any further discussion than explanatory remarks, not extending beyond five minutes, by the several proposers of such amendments.

The resolution having been read—

Mr. MCHENRY said, he desired to make one remark.

Some conversation followed between Messrs. RANDALL and MCHENRY, when the latter gentleman, on a suggestion to that effect made by Mr. CHAMBERS, of Kent, and in which Mr. MCHENRY acquiesced, the consideration of the order was postponed until to-morrow.

THE ELECTIVE FRANCHISE.

On motion of Mr. PHELPS, the Convention resolved itself into committee of the whole, Mr. BLAKISTONE in the chair, and resumed the consideration of the report of the committee on the Elective Franchise.

Mr. KILGOUR was entitled to the floor, having on Saturday indicated his intention to offer an amendment of which he had given notice.

Mr. SOLLERS stated that Mr. KILGOUR was confined to his room by indisposition.

Mr. TUCK then took the floor. He had done so, he said, for the purpose of submitting a motion which would be the means, he thought, of saving much time. He had reflected upon it a good deal. It was that the committee rise and report the bill under consideration to the Convention, together with all such amendments as had been adopted. And he would state briefly his views for this course of proceeding. It was very well known that if the committee sat a month longer on this bill, all these clauses would have to come up again in Convention. Until a day or two ago, a call for the yeas and nays in committee had been in order. Gentlemen could have the same latitude in Convention that they had in committee. He took it for granted that gentlemen would not travel beyond the legitimate range of debate in Convention any more than in committee, and he was free to say that, as yet, he had heard nothing that was very wide of the legitimate mark.

Mr. T. further enforced the propriety of his motion, showing that double votes would be saved, and much time in other respects saved; and concluded by moving that the Committee rise.

But Mr. T. withdrew the motion on a suggestion by Mr. MCHENRY, that he (Mr. McH.) had waived his resolution, because the Chairman of the Committee on Elections was not present, and that reason applied still more forcibly to the present proposition than to the other.

So the motion was withdrawn.

REGISTRATION OF VOTERS.

The question was now stated to be on the amendment heretofore offered by Mr. RICAUD to the amendment of Mr. JENIFER, which last named amendment provides for a registration of the names of voters within the State, &c.

The amendment of Mr. RICAUD was as follows, (Mr. JENIFER having accepted the first part of the amendment as a modification of his own. Add the following words to the end of the amendment:

"Or some other uniform provision whereby the legal and qualified electors may be fully and truly ascertained, and the elective franchise protected from all fraud."

Mr. J. U. DENNIS gave notice of his intention to move, when in order, to amend the amendment of Mr. JENIFER, by striking out the word "may," and inserting the word "shall"—(so as to make the provision imperative on the Legislature.)

Mr. JENIFER turning to Mr. D., and therefore scarcely heard at the Reporter's desk, was understood to express his preference for the language of the original amendment, which had been inserted, he said, after due reflection and upon consultation with friends.

Mr. DENNIS said that if we were to have a Registry law at all, it seemed to him that it would be best to make it imperative. If such a law was to exist, it should be made incumbent upon the Legislature to pass it, and should not be left to the alterations of party in every successive Legislature; as it had been suggested parties alternated every two years on the oyster law.

MR. RICAUD stated his object, (in his second amendment,) to be to empower the Legislature, by Constitutional provision to pass such a law if they deemed it necessary, and thus take away the objection that the Legislature transcended its Constitutional power, if they should think this the best mode of protecting the elective franchise. If a Registry law should not be the best mode to accomplish the object, then the Legislature would have it in their power to pass such other laws as they might think proper.

Mr. SPENCER. The reason which will induce me to vote against the whole proposition is this; if it is proper that any other restrictions should be imposed upon the voters of the State, beyond those which now exist, let it be done here. I am unwilling to leave the matter to the changes and vacillations which must attend it, if it is referred to the discretion of the Legislature. If it is proper the thing should be done, let *us* do it. If it is not proper, let it go by the board.

The question was then taken, and by ayes 37, noes 17, the amendment was rejected.

The question was then stated to be on the amendment heretofore offered by Mr. KILGOUR, (which prohibits the Legislature from passing such a law.)

Some desultory conversation followed, as to the fact whether Mr. KILGOUR's amendment was or was not pending before the Committee.

Mr. DAVIS expressed the hope that the final vote on that amendment, would not be taken in the absence of Mr. KILGOUR, as that gentlemen desired to present his views.

After some further conversation,

Mr. J. U. DENNIS offered the amendment indicated by him, (making it *imperative* on the Legislature to pass a Registry law.)

Mr. MCMASTER called for the yeas and nays.

The CHAIR reminded the gentleman that, under the late change of the rules, the yeas and nays could not be taken in Committee.

Mr. MORGAN moved to amend the amendment of Mr. JENIFER, by striking out all after the words, "the Legislature," and inserting in lieu thereof the following:

"Ought from time to time to pass such laws as in their wisdom may be deemed necessary to ascertain the legal and qualified voters of the State, and to protect the elective franchise from all fraud."

Mr. MORGAN said, he was opposed to the passage of any law for a uniform system of registration. He was opposed to it: First, because he could see no reason why such a law should be passed, where it could have no proper application. He could see no reason why the Convention should incorporate in the Constitution a provision declaring that the voters in his county, where, so far as his knowledge extended, there was no fraud, should be required, simply because frauds were committed elsewhere, to go and register their names in the county town or election district of the State. It had been alleged, and in part, it was a matter of notoriety, that in other sections of the State, frauds had been committed; and wherever they *were* committed, he desired that the Legislature should have the power to apply the corrective. Hence it was, that he was opposed to the amendment of the gentleman from Charles, (Mr. JENIFER,) because he saw that it would operate unjustly. His (Mr. M's,) amendment, would cover the whole ground, and would give to the representatives of the people, who were supposed to know their wants, a sufficient grant of power to protect the ballot box from fraud, wherever it might exist. If it existed in any of the counties or cities of the State, let them pass laws applicable to those counties or cities; but let them not have the power to pass laws which would act injuriously, and in his opinion wrongfully, upon those portions of the State where no such outrages were committed.

He declared his belief that the opposition to the Registry Law formerly passed with reference to the city of Baltimore, arose from the fact, that it did not operate uniformly; that restrictions upon the elective franchise should operate alike upon all citizens of the State, whether in the city or county, and that therefore, the law itself was unconstitutional, in as much as it imposed upon the citizens of Baltimore, burthens in the exercise of their rights, which were not imposed upon the citizens of the counties. He could see the force of this objection, and he contended it was equally appropriate here, because it was proposed to make the rule apply to a people, in respect to whom the reason of the rule had no force.

He had heard different gentlemen give their testimony in regard to the illegal votes in their counties. He repeated, he had no such experience as to his own. He had no knowledge of a single illegal vote having ever been given there, which, at the time was known to be illegal. He knew that there were other counties of the State that were similarly situated. He could see very great reason why a general grant of power should be given, leaving it to the Legislature in its wisdom, to apply it where frauds existed, and where the pure voice of the people, was stifled by the corrupt practices of men, who had no legal right to vote.

Mr. JENIFER thought that there was some inconsistency in the argument of the gentleman who had just taken his seat, (Mr. MORGAN.) His objection was that the provision would operate unequally upon the State. Would not the same rule apply, according to the argument of the gentleman, to any law for the prevention or punishment of crime? And might not the gentleman, with equal propriety, say that no petty larcenies were ever committed in St. Mary's county; and, therefore, it was unjust and oppressive in the Legislature, to pass a law to punish petty larcenies in the State? So far as he, (Mr. J.) could perceive, the amendment of the gentleman would do away with any benefit that might be expected to result from the passage of the law. He wanted to have such an enactment, not for a part of the State, but for the whole of it—Charles county, Baltimore city, and every other section of the State. Any thing less than that, would fall far short of his views and wishes.

Mr. MORGAN denied the applicability of the illustration given by the gentleman from Charles, (Mr. JENIFER,) to the point under consideration, Under the proposition of that gentleman, if frauds existed in Charles county, and no where else, the Legislature could not pass a law to remedy the evil in Charles county without making it applicable to the State even though frauds did not exist, thus making no discrimination between the innocent and the guilty.

Mr. J. U. DENNIS said, he did not expect that any thing he could say would influence the opinion of any member. Still as he was in favor of any proposition which had for its aim, the prevention of these frauds, he should say a few words upon the various propositions before the Committee. He could not assent to the proposition of the gentleman from St. Mary's, (Mr. MORGAN.) He (Mr. D.) was in favor of every measure not absolutely onerous in itself which would tend to the purification of the ballot-box. The Committee had heard from other gentlemen how frauds were committed in other counties; but some of them knew nothing of frauds in their own. To hear the gentleman from St. Mary's (Mr. MORGAN) and the gentleman from Baltimore county, (Mr. BUCHANAN) speak of their counties, one would suppose that they inhabited

"A land of pure delight,
Where saints immortal reign."

For his own part, he believed that in every section of the State, more or less, these frauds prevailed. It was in the nature of the Government and in the nature of the human character, that it should be so.

What was the corrective? As one means he was in favor of the amendment, of the gentleman from Charles, (Mr. JENIFER.) He (Mr. D.) had voted, and should continue to vote for every measure which held out a reasonable hope of effecting the object in view. He believed that a Registry Law, coupled with the amendment of the gentleman from Kent, would cut up this system of bribery and corruption, root and branch. He feared, however, that no such proposition would receive the vote of the Convention. Measure after measure had been met by solid phalanx arrayed against it, and on Saturday last the gentleman from Caroline, (Mr. STEWART) had called for "concert of action." He (Mr. D.) had no doubt that the requisite numbers would come with the clansman at the sound of Roderic Dhu's whistle, and vote against this thing.

Mr. McHENRY. (Interposing.) The gentleman from Caroline, (Mr. STEWART) is not now in his seat. But the gentleman over the way. (Mr. DENNIS,) has misconceived the remark. The gentleman from Caroline called for concert of action on the part of reformers.

Mr. DENNIS. Who are they—may I ask the gentleman who represents the gentleman from Caroline?

Mr. McHENRY. Some very good reformers are among the Whigs.

Mr. DENNIS. I shall present myself as a reformer at your call—though I am apprehensive that my claim will be rejected.

Mr. D. concluded by briefly contesting the argument of Mr. MORGAN as to the unjust operation of the amendment of Mr. JENIFER, and argued that there would be much injustice in the amendment of the gentlemen from St. Mary's, (Mr. MORGAN.)

Mr. MORGAN said, that the gentleman who had just taken his seat (Mr. DENNIS) had misconceived his amendment. He (Mr. M.) had offered no amendment, making special reference to counties—or giving power to the Legislature to make local laws. His amendment gave to the Legislature the constitutional power to discriminate between the application of laws to particular sections and a uniform system. If the Legislature, knowing the wants of the people and informed of the existence of frauds, deemed it necessary to pass a uniform Registry Law, they were to do so. The power was full and ample to pass, or not to pass it, as the case might require. He would be the last man to introduce partial provisions, because he thought that the operation of laws should be uniform. If frauds existed, the Legislature would act; if such frauds were not made to appear, they would not act. The matter should be left with the Legislature, who were the Representatives of the people, and responsible to them.

Mr. PHELPS thought the proposition before the committee was so uniform and fair that no gentleman could vote against it. Every gentleman who believed that frauds did exist at the ballot box, and that the evils were such as to require a corrective, could not fail to give it his sanction. It merely gave the Legislature the right to pass such laws as in its wisdom they might think necessary and proper to correct existing evils now or in the future.

Was not every gentleman satisfied that such frauds did exist in certain sections of the State, and that they would increase unless this Convention should adopt some effective means for their detection and suppression? It seemed to him that on a proposition so little liable to the charge of being indviious, or of distinguishing between one section and another, gentlemen might meet as upon a common platform, and give their united strength to the accomplishment of the great object in view. Suppose the Convention should reject the proposition under consideration, and the proposition of the gentleman from Charles, what would be the effect? The Legislature would say that they had no power to pass such laws, and they would point to the refusal of this Convention to authorize them, as unerring evidence of the fact. He earnestly hoped that one or the other of the two propositions would be adopted.

Mr. HARBINE said that probably he did not precisely understand the proposition of the gentleman from St. Mary's, [Mr. MORGAN,] but that according to his, [Mr. H.'s] construction of it, it meant one of two things, and that, in either case, he should feel constrained to vote against it. He was in favor of such an organic law, as would not be subject to the whims and caprices, [if he might so express himself,] of the Legislature. If the object of the amendment of the gentleman from St. Mary's was that the Legislature should have the power to control the organic law, after this Convention should have defined the right of the citizen in relation to the right of suffrage, then he [Mr. H.] was opposed to it. If that was not the object, and it was solely to throw guards around the right of suffrage, then he would ask, had not the Legislature got that power already, without any such provision? He illustrated his position, and declared his intention to vote against the amendment.

Mr. WEEMS said he was as much disposed as any man to throw all proper guards and protection around the ballot-box. Such a law was either necessary or not. If it was necessary there should be no discretion on the part of the Legislature; but it should be made its imperative duty to pass such a law.

If it was not necessary, there was an end of the question. He was no lawyer, but he was altogether opposed to giving to the Legislature in the organic law of the State, (by which bounds were to be set, beyond which the different departments of the government should not go,) a discretion which would enable them to enact laws that might operate locally, unequally, or unjustly.—He was opposed to both propositions, and should vote against them; although he was in favor of a general registry law to prevent frauds. He had no personal knowledge of frauds, but he believed them to exist, not only in the city of Baltimore, but in the respective counties; and if a Registry Law would prevent them, he would vote for such a law, to operate throughout the State and to leave no discretion. He was either for letting the thing alone altogether, or for making the provision imperative and giving the Legislature no power to repeal it.

Mr. PHELPS rose to make a very few remarks on the powers of the Legislature, in reply to what had fallen from the gentleman from Washington, (Mr. HARBINE.)

Mr. HARBINE said he was speaking of the amendment of the gentleman of St. Mary's, (Mr. MORGAN.)

Mr. PHELPS so understood him. The gentleman contended that by the adoption of this amendment, we give the Legislature the right to override the Constitution. Has not the Constitution given the power to the Legislature to grant divorces, and to levy taxes; and does not every organic law grant certain powers to that body, and reserve other powers? The argument of the gentleman from Washington may be applied to all other powers, as well as that which is embraced in this amendment. The gentleman from Calvert, (Mr. WEEMS,) had taken the ground that it was either necessary to have a registration law, or unnecessary; and that if necessary, it ought to be a general law, acting uniformly throughout the State, and might be passed by the Legislature without a constitutional provision; if it was not necessary, there was no need to insert any such provision in the organic law. He reminded that gentleman that when the Registry Law of 1838 was passed, the question in regard to its constitutionality was raised, and there was at least one gentleman in this body who asserted that it was unconstitutional.

The amendment of the gentleman from St. Mary's proposes to invest the Legislature with a limited control over the elective franchise, and if this Convention now, by a solemn vote, refuse to grant this power, those who succeed us, must infer, that any attempt hereafter, by legislative enactments to prohibit illegal voting, will be an exercise of power not contemplated by the framers of the Constitution, and therefore totally unauthorized.

Mr. SOLLERS said that the question was simply of a grant of authority to the Legislature which it either did or did not now possess. He would like to hear the gentleman from Dorchester, (Mr. PHELPS,) on the power of the Legislature to pass a Registry Law without a special grant from the Constitution. He had never heard the Registry Law of 1838 objected to on the ground that it was unconstitutional. If the Legislature already have the right to pass such a law, why is there a necessity for any special grant of power? If we do insert such a provision in the Constitution, the Legislature have the power without it, and can exercise it when they think it necessary to do so. He objected to the change made by the gentleman from Charles in the original anendment, by the substitution of the word "may" in the place of "shall," and referred to the present Constitution to show that the imperative mood was used in that instrument.—The change might lead to the inference that circumstances might occur in which the exercise of the power would be inexpedient, and such a law ought not to be enacted. He thought the wisest course would be to let the matter rest as it is, and leave it to the Legislature to exercise their own discretion.

Mr. MORGAN reminded the Convention of the answer given the other day, by the gentleman from Prince George's, that he had always considered the Registry Law of 1838 unconstitutional; so that we have one gentleman in the Convention who holds that opinion.

Mr. BOWIE said his remark did not apply to a Registry Law uniform in its operations throughout the State.

Mr. MORGAN stated that his amendment granted to the Legislature the power to pass such laws as in their wisdom may be deemed necessary to ascertain the legal and qualified voters of the State and to protect the elective franchise from all frauds.

The question was then taken on the amendment of Mr. MORGAN, and the vote stood yeas 37—nays 17.

So the amendment was rejected.

The question recurred on the amendment of Mr JENNIFER.

Mr. JENNIFER asked the yeas and nays.

The CHAIRMAN said the yeas and nays could not now be taken in committee.

The question was then taken and the vote stood yeas 25—nays 21.

So the amendment was rejected.

There being no other amendment to the first section, the second section was read as follows:

"Sec. 2. That if any person shall give any bribe, present or reward, or any promise or any security for the payment or delivery of any money or any other thing, to obtain or procure a vote for any candidate or person proposed or voted for, as elector of President and Vice President or the United States, or Representatives in Congress, or for any office of profit or trust now created or hereafter to be created by the Constitution or Laws of this State, the person giving and the person receiving the same, shall, on conviction in a court of law, in addition to the penalties now or hereafter to be imposed by law, be forever disqualified to hold any office of profit or trust, or to vote at any election thereafter."

Mr. SPENCER moved to amend said report by inserting after the word "give," in the first line, the following "by himself or by any other person, or by any means direct or "indirect."

Mr. SCHLEY offered, as a substitute for said motion, to insert after the word "give," in the first line, the words "directly or indirectly."

Mr. SPENCER thought these words would not answer the purpose. Those of his own amendment, he suggested, prevented all evasions or equivocations.

Mr. SCHLEY dissented from this view, and contended that the application of other words except those contemplated in his amendment, was a mere unnecessary accumulation of language. In forming an organic law, the words used should be as few and as pithy as could be used to express the object of the provision.

Some discussion, chiefly in the nature of verbal criticism, followed.

The substitute amendment of Mr. SCHLEY, by ayes 37—noes 10, was agreed to.

And the amendment as thus amended was agreed to.

Mr. MERRICK said, the Convention had provided for the positive evil of bribery; and he proposed now to provide for a negative mode just as culpable as the other of accomplishing the same object. He offered the following amendment:

Insert in the third line of the second section, after the word "thing," the words "to induce any voter to refrain from casting his vote, or (forcibly) to prevent him in any way from voting or."

Mr. RANDALL suggested the introduction of the word "forcible"—to meet the evil of "cooping."

Mr. MERRICK accepted the modification.

Mr. BRENT, of Baltimore city, suggested that the words "with intent" should be inserted. It was the intent, he said, that should be punished.

And after some conversation, the question was taken, and the amendment as modified was agreed to.

Mr. SPENCER offered an amendment; to insert after the word "for," in the third line, the words "himself or for." Rejected.

Mr. BRENT, of Baltimore city, moved the following amendment:

Strike out in the last line the words "or to vote at any election thereafter."

Mr. BRENT, of the city of Baltimore, assigned as his reason for submitting this amendment, his unwillingness, by so severe a punishment as the original amendment prescribed, to shut out forever from so high a privilege, the person who may be guilty of the offence, and thus to render it impossible for reformation to restore him to his forfeited rights as a freeman. It inflicts disfranchisement forever, and cuts him off from every hope of being allowed again to exercise this valuable franchise. It makes him an unforgiveable offender. Believing such punishment to be too severe for the offence, he moved to strike out the words.

Mr. MERRICK expressed his opinion that any one who would prostitute this sacred right, ought forever afterwards to be deprived of it.

Mr. BRENT suggested the case of a young and inexperienced voter who had recently become possessed of the right, and, who in a moment of thoughtlessness, and under strong temptation, had been drawn for a moment from the path of rectitude. Would you inflict on him, perhaps a minor, a punishment so severe, that, when at a later period of life, he may have repented of the act, changed his course, and become a useful citizen, he shall find himself under the ban of this perpetual disfranchisement? However penitent, he must never again be permitted to vote. Now, he was not in favor of going to the whole extent of perpetual disfranchisement, because the offender had in early youth violated the law in this respect. He was perfectly willing that any punishment of a less severe character should be inflicted, but he thought that which was now proposed was altogether too severe.

Mr. MERRICK was of opinion that the very case cited by the gentleman from Baltimore would be one which ought to be marked out for an example to others. It would, he admitted, be hard on the individual himself, but it would on that account, have a more salutary efficacy in checking the growth of the crime.

Mr. RIDGELY moved a substitute for the proposition of the gentleman from Baltimore city, (Mr. Brent,) which, however, Mr. R. withdrew.

Mr. Spencer expressed a hope that the amendment of the gentleman from Baltimore county would not be adopted. To give authority to remit the penalty in a place like the city of Baltimore, where, in times of high party excitement, the offence would be the most likely to be committed, would be to open the door to its frequent repetition. It was necessary that the punishment should be severe and certain. He would be willing to abate a little from perpetual disfranchisement. But he was opposed to leaving the punishment within the reach of remission.

Mr. Ricaud moved to amend the amendment by inserting the word "for the period of five years," after the word "election," in the last line.

Mr. Crisfield said, that as the distinguished gentleman at the head of the committee was absent, as it was near the usual hour of rising, and as he (Mr. C.) thought that in deference to that gentleman an opportunity should be afforded to him to be heard on the several pending propositions, and in defence of his own—he (Mr. C.) would move that the committee rise.

The motion having prevailed, the committee rose and reported progress.

And the Convention adjourned until to-morrow at eleven o'clock.

TUESDAY, January 21st, 1851.

The Convention met at eleven o'clock.

Prayer by the Rev. Mr. Griffith.

The roll was called. A quorum was present, and the Journal of yesterday was read and approved.

Mr. Annan presented a petition of sundry tanners and dealers in leather, praying that no change may be made in the inspection of leather.

Which was read and referred to the Committee on Inspections.

Mr. Davis presented the address of the Primary School Convention, to the people of Maryland, signed by John S. Tyson, Esq., and others.

Which was read.

Mr. D. remarked that there was a large amount of important and interesting statistical information contained in the address, and that the committee had very considerately printed a large number of copies, which would be laid on the table of members to-morrow morning.

Referred to the Committee on Education.

Mr. Spencer laid before the Convention an account of James T. Wootters, clerk to the levy court of Queen Anne's county, for information furnished the Convention under their order of December 2nd.

Which was read and referred to the Committee on Accounts.

The President announced the regular order of business to be the call of Committees for Reports.

There being no reports—

The Convention, on motion of Mr. McMaster, passed to the order of the day.

THE ELECTIVE FRANCHISE.

The Convention thereupon resolved itself into committee of the whole, Mr. Blakistone in the chair, and resumed the consideration of the report of the committee on the elective franchise.

The state of the question was as follows:

Mr. Merrick had moved to amend the second section of the report, by inserting in the third line after the word "thing," the following, "to induce any voter to refrain from casting his vote, or forcibly to prevent him in any way from voting, or," &c.

Mr. Brent of Baltimore city, had moved to amend the section by striking out from the last line thereof, these words, "or to vote at any election thereafter."

And Mr. Ricaud had moved to amend said section by inserting, after the word "election," in the last line, the words "for the period of five years."

Mr. Brent of Baltimore city, expressed his willingness to adopt the proposition of Mr. Ricaud limiting the operation of the clause to the period of five years. But he, (Mr. B.) gave notice of an amendment which he intended to offer as a substitute for the whole section, as it was amended.

Mr. Merrick said he hoped the amendment to his amendment would not prevail. In our sympathies for the victims of crime, we were prone to forget the great object of punishment. It was a fault in our nature, though a fault which "leans to virtue's side." Men exercising the high functions for which this Convention had assembled, should not yield to such impressions. The great object of punishment was its example upon society—its effect in purifying and elevating the moral tone of that society. All punishments should be so framed as to have the greatest effect upon that moral tone; to preserve it pure, if it could be so, and to punish with a heavy hand all those who would attempt to pollute it. Individual sympathies should not be listened to, when the public good required that punishments should be inflicted. Vengeance, it was true, did not belong to man—but in the spirit of justice, and not of vengeance, he would act. He referred to the many cases in which every appeal which human sympathy could make had addressed itself to the hearts of some of the best and purest men that had ever lived, and yet where justice had been sternly executed. And he instanced particularly the case of Major Andre. Mr. M. called upon the Convention to imitate the example of the Father of his Country in that case.

Here was a crime which struck at the vital principle of all republican governments; and although gentlemen of good hearts might feel reluctant to inflict exemplary punishment upon those who committed it, yet, if the public good required it, that punishment should not only be severe, but should be inexorably meted out.

He referred to the condition of public opinion as evidence of the light estimate in which this crime of fraud upon the ballot box had heretofore been held, and the necessity of infusing a new pathies for the victims of crime, we were prone to forget the great object of punishment. It was a fault in our nature, though a fault which "leans to virtue's side." Men exercising the high functions for which this Convention had assembled, should not yield to such impressions. The great object of punishment was its example upon society—its effect in purifying and elevating the moral tone of that society. All punishments should be so framed as to have the greatest effect upon that moral tone; to preserve it pure, if it could be so, and to punish with a heavy hand all those who would attempt to pollute it. Individual sympathies should not be listened to, when the public good required that punishments should be inflicted. Vengeance, it was true, did not belong to man—but in the spirit of justice, and not of vengeance, he would act. He referred to the many cases in which every appeal which human sympathy could make had addressed itself to the hearts of some of the best and purest men that had ever lived, and yet where justice had been sternly executed. And he instanced particularly the case of Major Andre. Mr. M. called upon the Convention to imitate the example of the Father of his Country in that case.

Here was a crime which struck at the vital principle of all republican governments; and although gentlemen of good hearts might feel reluctant to inflict exemplary punishment upon those who committed it, yet, if the public good required it, that punishment should not only be severe, but should be inexorably meted out.

He referred to the condition of public opinion as evidence of the light estimate in which this crime of fraud upon the ballot box had heretofore been held, and the necessity of infusing a new and more healthy tone into the public mind by proper and adequate provisions. Let the present and rising generation be taught that this was not the light and trivial offence which it had hitherto been deemed, but that it was in fact a great and heinous crime. The beneficial results of such a policy would soon be made apparent.

Mr. Dorsey said, he did not precisely understand what the amendment was, and he would be glad that it should be read.

The state of the question became the subject of some conversation between Messrs. Merrick, Phelps and Tuck; after which the amendment was again read.

Mr. Chambers, of Kent, said, that he felt somewhat embarrassed by this proposition which had been offered in his absence. Undoubtedly the amendment of the gentleman from Kent, (Mr. Ricaud) was better than no provision at all. But he (Mr. C.) hoped that the Convention would not now falter in the disposition which it had hitherto manifested, to adopt the most stringent provisions against corrupt voting. He said the immediate, the avowed object—that which bore directly upon the question—had reference to corrupt proceedings at elections. On that point, he had supposed that there was no difficulty in the Convention.

He called the attention of gentlemen to the erroneous consequences which must result, if this mischief was permitted to increase and multiply, as the Convention had been told from various quarters it had increased and multiplied for some years past—and as it would continue to do if it was regarded with the least toleration. He believed that the most imminent peril to the continuation of our institutions was to be apprehended from this very source. He forbore to paint—he had not command of language to paint even the beginning of the terrible scenes which would follow, when the people should come to learn that those who had been elevated to the high places of the land, did not occupy them by the voice of legal votes. Whatever might be the reception, or the fate, of other portions of that Constitution which the Convention might present to the people, he had no doubt that any provision which might be placed in it for the purification of the ballot-box, would meet with a cordial and uniform response from one extremity of the State to the other. He should be gratified if his colleague, (Mr. Ricaud.) would withdraw his amendment until a vote should have been taken on the question as it stood.

Some conversation followed.

Mr. Ricaud remarked, that he was willing to take any plan which the Convention might suggest, if it would meet the point. And if that object could be accomplished by the withdrawal of his amendment, he would withdraw it.

But, after some conversation with Mr. Merrick—

Mr. R. adhered to his amendment.

Mr. Tuck said, all must agree that something should be done to prevent the evils complained of. But in all penal laws there was a principle of this character, that you might make the punishment so great that no jury would enforce it. Such, he thought, was the nature of the proposition before the Committee. If the argument of the gentleman from Kent, (Mr. Chambers,) had been made in favor of the punishment for the term of five years, it would have been a powerful one. The limitation of five years was sufficient for the purpose, and he was glad that the gentleman from Kent, [Mr. Ricaud] had persisted in his amendment. He [Mr. T.] should vote for it. If that was voted down, then he should vote for the proposition as it came from the Committee.

Mr. Merrick argued that there was no fear that the laws would not be enforced by one or the other party—by that party against which the votes might be cast. The preservation of the purity of the elective franchise—the preservation of Government itself, required that we should hold up to public scorn, as a terror to others, all those who might be disposed to commit a similar crime.

Mr. Tuck suggested that this law was not to be enforced at the polls, but upon conviction in courts of justice. It was the sympathy of juries, to which he had referred. His idea was that if the punishment was made too severe, convictions could not be obtained.

Mr. Chambers, of Kent, correcting a misapprehension into which, he said, his friend from Prince George's [Mr. Tuck,] had fallen, in rela-lation to his [Mr. C.'s] remarks, as to the character of the men by whom these frauds were perpetrated, proceeded to reply to the position that juries would not execute the law, if the crime was punished too severely. His, [Mr. C.'s] hope lay in this: we were taking a new start—we were about to have a new Constitution—old things and old measures were passing away. There was to be a line chalked between the time present and the time passed. He was disposed to hope, and he believed, that the honest, respectable, intelligent portion of the people, [which was the immense mass of the community,] was so satiated, so gorged with the miserable state of things which existed, and for which all former remedies had proved inefficient, that they would readily avail themselves of the means to get rid of it. He did not think that the mitigation of the punishment contemplated by the amendment, was calculated to accomplish the end sought to be attained.

Mr. Sellman desired as much as any man, he said, to prevent bribery and corruption. He did not, however, believe that these crimes existed to the extent stated. For upwards of twenty years, he had represented a constituency comprising more than three thousand voters. Nine-tenths of them, he believed were pure, and no man dare approach one of them with an improper motive.

He read the provision of the old Constitution on this subject, and asked gentlemen to state of what good it had ever been productive. Had any convictions taken place or any indictments been preferred under it? He would like his colleague, (Mr. Dorsey,) to give his experience on that point.

He thought the punishment here proposed was too great. Still, if gentlemen would show him its necessity, he would vote for it. He believed that all punishments should be so proportioned to the offence committed, that there could be no difficulty in enforcing the law.

He suggested the good results which would follow, by the constant presentation of this subject of bribery and corruption to the consideration of grand juries. He did not think that any general provision in the Constitution would reach the evil. He desired to see it put down, and thought that moderate means would be the most effectual. He preferred the amendment limiting the punishment to five years, but would vote for the other proposition if that could not be passed.

Mr. Spencer briefly recapitulated the ground he had taken yesterday on this question, and proceeded to say that he concurred in the views that had been expressed by the gentleman from Kent, (Mr. Chambers.) He [Mr. S.] would go with that gentleman to the utmost extent in crushing this evil and would vote for the clause as it now stood.

If, as had been intimated, there had been no convictions, it was not the law which prevented it, but it was the morbid sentiment that prevailed among men of position, which had led to that result. Replying to the argument as to the propriety of charging grand juries on the subject, he said that some of the most eloquent and probing charges he had ever heard from the bench, were addressed to this very evil. It was a mistake to suppose that there had been no prosecutions and convictions; but the great misfortune had been, that when courts and juries had done their duty, the Executive in high party times, had interfered to arrest the legitimate results. Carry out the principle which he had laid down upon that point, in his amendment—infuse by the action of this Convention a high moral sentiment in the public mind, and the object so long desired would at length be accomplished.

Mr. Jenifer felt, he said, that he could not give a silent vote on this question, but would detain the Convention only with a very few words. The object which all gentlemen had in view was to prevent corrupt voting. But it seemed to him that the proposition before the committee was calculated more than any other to defeat that object. He believed that the amendment limiting the term of condemnation would have a beneficial effect. Under that amendment he believed that a conviction would be obtained as soon as the case might present itself. The penalty, without the amendment, was too rigorous—so much so as, in his judgment, to prevent persons being prosecuted. Under the limited punishment, the first conviction would go far to arrest the evil. But make the punishment perpetual, and the clause would remain, as that in the existing Constitution had done, a dead letter.

Mr. J. U. Dennis thought that the heaviest brand of condemnation should be stamped upon that man who would prostitute the elective franchise. But he had risen mainly to say a word in reply to the gentleman who addressed the committee a short time since (Mr. Sellman.) Mr. D. then took up the statement which had been made by Mr Sellman as to the incorruptibility of nine-tenths of his constituents; and entered upon a mathematical calculation to show that, upon the principle that one-tenth *could* be corrupted, there were five hundred and thirty nine of his constituents that might be approached in that way.

Mr. Sellman explained that he did not intend to say that there were not more than nine-tenths that were incorruptible. He believed that there were.

Some conversation followed between Messrs. Sellman and Dennis.

Mr. Brent, of Baltimore city, stated that he should vote for the amendment disqualifying the party convicted, from voting or holding office for five years, but should afterwards rely on a substitute referring this whole subject to the Legislature and making it obligatory to pass full and suitable laws for the prevention of these offences. It seemed to him that gentleman had been so much stunned and confused by reports of election frauds all over the State, that they were running wild on the subject. One gentleman has said that the bribing of a voter was worse than murder. Mr. Brent, would not for one moment justify such an act, but if it is worse than murder, why not make it a capital offence at once, and hang the offender under the second section, for we were now at work on that section.

He would go as far as any man, in inflicting adequate punishment in all such cases, but he did not desire to see the punishment so severe and excessive, that juries would recoil from its infliction and malfactors would escape.

Nor would he consent to lay down as proposed, one undeviating, inexorable and unbending rule, punishing all offenders for life, without any sort of reference to the extenuating circumstances which might exist in many cases. It is scarcely possible that all would offend in equal degree, the inexperienced youth, led away by designing men, might be the victim equally with the hardened offender. By the proscriptive terms of the section as reported, every offender is to be disfranchised from voting or holding office for life, in addition to other penalties. Is this just or consonant to the dictates of humanity? No mercy, no forgivness for the repentant man, who by years of moral conduct, may atone for youthful crime. Mr. Brent would not thus deprive a man of every motive to become a good citizen, but would think five years disfranchisement enough. The old Constitution has disqualified such offenders from holding office, and yet no one has ever suffered under its idle restrictions. Why is this so? Because the penalty is too harsh and disproportioned for the offence. It is therefore impossible to get up a prosecution or to convict, under so penal a code, and this accounts for the morbid feelings heretofore entertained by the community as stated by the gentleman from Queen Anne's, (Mr. Spencer.) But he (Mr. Brent) would greatly prefer to avoid cumbering the new Constitution with crude and sweeping penalties. Let the whole subject of penal enactment in detail, be referred to the Legislature with a clear constitutional obligation imposed on them to pass proper laws, punishing these crimes, and disfranchising the offenders for such term as might seem proper. He was opposed to this Convention wasting its time in such matters, because to carry out such penal enactments properly requires much detail; and our Constitution, instead of being concise and simple, would become complex and voluminous.

Mr. Ridgely said he had opposed all restrictions upon the elective franchise, and had regarded the punishment to be visited upon the offender as the proper corrective of the evil. He was prepared to vote for the amendment of the gentleman from Kent, (Mr. Ricaud.) He thought that the moral effect of the two punishments would be the same; because the individual would carry a brand upon him, whether the punishment was limited or not. But he thought that the section under consideration would not accomplish the object. Convictions were wanted in order to deter others from the commission of the crime. It had been said that there had been convictions under the existing law, and that the Executive had interfered to prevent them being carried out. That was the very difficulty which he feared, and to prevent which he should offer an amendment, (which he read.)

Some conversation followed between Mr. Chambers, of Kent, and Mr. Ridgely.

Mr. Jenifer expressed the hope that if any such proposition as the gentleman from Baltimore county, (Mr. Ridgely,) indicated, was to be adopted, he hoped it would be made to apply generally or not at all.

Mr. Ridgely then offered his amendment in the following words:

Add at the end of the second section the following words:

"And over all such offences or the punishment or disability imposed thereon, the Executive of this State shall exercise no power or control."

Mr. Spencer gave notice that at the proper time he should offer the following as additional sections to the report:

Insert after the 2nd section the following:

Section 3rd. That every person who shall be elected to any office whatever, in said State hereafter, or who shall be appointed to any office whatever, in said State hereafter, shall before he enters upon the duties of the office to which he may be elected or appointed, first take and subscribe the following oath, (if not conscientiously scrupulous, and in such case, affirmation,) before some one of the Judges of the Court of Appeals of this State:

I, ———, do solmenly swear that I have not at any election held in this State, since the ratification of the new constitution of this State, or in any other way, in any manner violated the provisions contained in the 2nd section of the said constitution relating to bribery, and that I have not procured or induced by any means, any individual or individuals to vote at any such election in violation of the provisions contained in the 1st section of said constitution relating to the age and residence of voters, and if any person elected or appointed to office as aforesaid, shall refuse or neglect to take the said oath or affirmation, he shall be considered as having refused to accept the said office and a new election or appointment shall be made as in case of refusal or resignation; and any person who shall swear or affirm falsely in the premises shall be guilty of perjury, and on conviction thereof in due course of law subject to all its pains and penalties.

Sec. 4. That the Judge before whom such oath or affirmation shall be taken, shall cause the same to be subscribed by the person so swearing or affirming, in a book by him to be kept for such purpose, a duplicate of which said oath or affirmation as the case may be, he shall transmit to the clerk of the Court of Appeals of this State, with the name of the individual who took and subscribed the same, designating the office to which he has been elected or appointed, to be by the said clerk, whose duty it shall be to do so, recorded in a book to be kept for such purpose among the records of the said Court of Appeals, a certified copy of which said oath or affirmation by the said Judge under his seal, or by the said clerk of the said duplicate, under his seal of office shall be taken and received as evidence in any of the courts of this State that have criminal jurisdiction.

Mr. Dorsey, replying to Mr. Sellman's question as to convictions, &c., stated that it had been the customs of the courts to invite the attention of the grand jury to the subject of bribery and corruption, in relation to the elective franchise. The difficulty had not arisen in getting cases before the grand jury, nor from the fact that the offences could not be abundantly proved; but from the fact that the grand jury would not find bills, because so many persons were implicated, and it was believed that more injury would result from prosecuting any person, than from leaving him unpunished.

One word in answer to the statement of his colleague, (Mr. SELLMAN,) as to nine-tenths of his constituents being pure and unapproachable. If there was one-tenth of the voters in Anne Arundel county, who could be approached in this way, it was the duty of the Convention to adopt the most energetic measures to prevent bribery and corruption. Bribery was of modern origin. It was not yet at its maturity; but if his sources of information were to be relied upon, bribery would be committed on a much more extensive scale in a few years. He thought Anne Arundel might be as pure as she had been represented. The means of corruption were perhaps not as extensive in that county as might be required. He had heard less complaint of bribery in the city of Baltimore, than perhaps in any other portion of the State of Maryland, either on the eastern or western shore But he did not attribute that state of things to the fact that the people of Baltimore, more than the people of any other portion of the State, were beyond the reach of corruption. He thought there was a much more natural reason; and that was that there were so many voters—the merchantable commodity was so great—(laughter)—that it would be utterly ruinous to any party to supply the means of corruption. It would be almost an evidence of insanity to attempt it; and he spoke of both parties alike, because it was known that each party was disposed to retaliate upon the other.

The same might be said of Frederick, and the larger counties. Both parties were afraid to commence the system. In the smaller counties, where there was but a comparatively small material, the system might be exercised successfully. As to Anne Arundel county, if he could credit the statements of those who were most trustworthy, frauds did exist to a considerable extent. He had heard many enquiries, both by whigs and democrats, whether this Convention was going to do any thing to prevent and punish those frauds. That was the great question which this Convention had to settle. If they did not settle that, they scarcely need do anything. Such was public opinion.

He contested the position which had been assumed, that if severe penalties were imposed they would not be enforced. He believed that if they resorted to the proper measures, these frauds could be prevented.

He read the clause of the Constitution and stated frankly that he had never known a conviction under this clause, nor of a violation of it. The framers of that instrument had no idea that this vice would exist, as it now existed; they only provided for the case of the officers themselves, because they did not anticipate any extensive system of bribery. They proposed, therefore, a very limited remedy; in fact, no remedy at all, for the evil as it existed at the present day. So long as both parties continued this system, and until such punishments were prescribed as would deter every body from the perpetration of the crime, nothing would be expected. In his opinion, murder, arson, burglary, theft, were venial offences in comparison with this. The consequences of these crimes were comparatively nothing; and if the system was not put an end to, by the most stringent measures, it would continue so long as the government could, under such circumstances endure. And to do nothing would be equivalent to saying, that the Convention was willing that the evil should continue. He had been twenty-five years on the bench, and some fifty years at the bar; and he was satisfied that if such provisions as he had proposed were carried out, the government was safe; if not, every thing was lost.

Mr. GWINN reminded the gentleman from Anne Arundel, that the severe punishment provided for by the gentleman from Kent, (Mr CHAMBERS,) would not, of necessity, effect the purpose for which it was designed. Formerly, in England, shoplighting and many other minor offences were punishable with death; yet, in spite of this, such crimes multiplied to an incredible extent. The peril incurred seemed to dignify the crime, and it would be the case here. It was the great glory of Sir Samuel Remilly, that he introduced provisions in which some proportion was observed between the offence and punishment. The Convention might imitate him; for although a fraud upon the elective franchise is a serious evil, yet it is certainly not as dangerous. whether occurring in few or many instances, as those crimes which imperil the peace of society and the safety of human life. Lesser penalties would accomplish the same end. A jury could not be found to convict men, who, in times of high party excitement, had o'er leaped proper bounds, if the punishment was so excessive.

Mr. SPENCER offered the amendments which he had before indicated his intention to submit. He did so in order that the Convention might have the whole subject before it. They could come in at the proper place.

The amendments were read.

Mr. SPENCER resumed, expressing his belief that these amendments if adopted, by the Convention, would effect the object of reaching all those individuals who were either candidates for office, or who aspired to become candidates hereafter. He referred to his remarks of a previous day when he indicated his intention to propose these amendments, and to the reply of the gentleman from Kent, (Mr. CHAMBERS,) that the committee had come to a conclusion in accordance with the spirit of these amendments, and he was authorized to put them in the form in which they should be presented to the Convention. The proposition of the gentleman from Kent had been presented, and it appeared to him not to go far enough to effect the purpose. A more stringent oath would be necessary, and in other respects, he considered that proposition as less effective than the amendments he had now offered.

He then went on to compare the proposition of the committee as presented by Mr. CHAMBERS, with the amendments he had just read and to show wherein he thought the defects of the former were supplied by the latter.

He proceeded to state that the people everywhere were looking to the Convention to adopt measures for the greater security of the right of suffrage, and he had offered these amendments to show the earnestness and sincerity with which he sought the same object.

He was conscious that the amendment he had offered, yesterday, to the proposition of the Committee restricting the power of the Governor as to the remission of punishment for bribery, was received by some unfavorably, because he had introduced a qualification providing that the Governor should be clothed with the power of remission in cases where the prosecution was false and malicious. In his experience, however, he had known cases of this character, and that juries had sometimes rendered their verdicts under the influence of party feelings. He was willing, therefore, to deprive the Governor of the power of entering a *nolle prosequi*, or granting a pardon in these cases, except where he was satisfied by sufficient evidence that the prosecution was malicious or untrue. He was not willing to entrust these cases to the jury, or to the Legislature, but he would confer this power on the Governor, who was more likely to act with deliberation, and to remit the punishment on being satisfied that malice and falsehood were at the bottom. In such cases he was unwilling to take from the offender every chance of restoration to his position in society.

Mr. MITCHELL said he rose with very great reluctance, but as he differed from his colleague and felt conscientiously bound to support the amendment, he wished to state the reasons which induced him to do so. It was well known that in all the counties there was a large proportion of poor men. Poor men have very large families generally. (Laughter.) It is the practice among those who desire to help this class, and to stand well in their neighborhood, to give out corn about the months of June and July. I know that about that time the corn-houses are thrown open, and as the natural effect is to give them popularity at home, if they should chance to be candidates for office, the people of that neighborhood would usually vote for them. Now, if any malicious individual should lay hold of this circumstance, he might bring these gentlemen into Court, and by a jury picked by political opponents, they might, notwithstanding their known popularity would have elected them, without any such act of liberality, be convicted under this section, as it had been reported, and be forever disfranchised. He could not make a speech, because he found he was getting frightened here. (Cries, "go on, go on.") Mr. MITCHELL I cannot do it.

Mr. DIRICKSON said, that the spirit of harmony which now seemed to manifest itself in every quarter upon this subject, must be regarded as a most happy change, and one highly gratifying, alike to the Convention and the entire community. Scarce a week had yet elapsed since the fiercest battle had been waged against every proposition, designed peculiarly to purify the elections of the city of Baltimore, and to wipe away forever, the stain of fraud, so frequently and so gravely charged. Then it seemed impossible to effect any beneficial remedy. Gentlemen trembled, lest forsooth, the liberty of free suffrage should be fettered by some slight restriction, and however wholesome such restrictions were shown to be in their purifying tendency, the result had shown how willingly the responsibility had been avoided. Such, however, was not the feeling, and caution now exhibited upon the subject of bribery, an evil supposed mainly to exist in the various counties of the State, rather than in its populous towns and cities. Developments and admissions had been made most humiliating to our "State's pride," and he warned those who were making such unhappy confessions, that

> "A chiel's amang us takin' notes,
> And faith he will print 'em,"

and that their degrading aspersions would therefore go forth, telling fearfully against the purity of their constituency, and the integrity of our noble State. That this political disease might exist to some extent, it was unnecessary to deny; but, surely, it was not yet in that exaggerated form which the heated fancies of political moralists had induced them to imagine. He had from boyhood, mingled freely with his fellow men, and though he regarded the evil of bribery as baneful in its effects, he could not yet consider it as a great political cancer, devouring the body politic, and requiring so fearful a remedy as that now proposed for its suppression. The great object of all punishment was to prevent the commissions of crime, by imposing and awarding such pains and penalties as would be justified by the character and heinousness of the offence. In this view he asked whether the terrible punishment specified in the amendment of the gentleman from Kent (Mr. CHAMBERS,) was in just proportion to the character and criminality of this evil practice. It might be that the elevated position which that distinguished gentleman had so long occupied, with such signal ability, had prevented him from visiting the hustings and mingling in the exciting scenes that ever, from the very nature of our government, surround the polls. Then under the influence of intense party feeling and in the midst of great strugglings, men with the most unblemished moral character and the most spotless integrity, might almost imperceptibly be hurried into the commission of deeds, which, however improper, could scarcely under all the circumstances, be denominated even by the strictest moralist as highly criminal. He could not for an instant, concur with the honorable gentleman from Anne Arundel, (Mr. DORSEY,) in ranking this evil as above the high crimes of murder, and arson, and larceny, in its enormity. And he thought that in pursuing it with such cruel rigor, the Convention was in imminent danger of carrying its fancied detestation and horror quite too far. It seemed as tho' gentlemen all round were running a Gilpin race, seeking to elevate the political character, by the application of a remedy that caused human nature instinctively to shudder.

An additional amendment had been proposed, which went so far as to deprive the Chief Executive officer of the State, of the power of pardon upon convictions for this offence. What a spectacle would such a constitutional feature present to the world.

Murder, arson, larceny, crimes of all grades and description, might in all their horrid array stalk throughout the length and breadth of our State. And yet for them all, there was pardon However devastating and demoralizing their influence, the clemency of the Executive was still open. But for the man who dared, whatever might be the circumstances, to give or receive the most trifling bribe, there was no mercy, no hope, this side the grave. Like Cain of old, he must wander the world, bearing upon his brow the mark of shame and the impress of infamy. Surely, gentlemen would pause ere they gave their sanction to such a measure; the consequences may be of the most fearful character. Though the political Cains might be few; yet because their degredation and dishonor could not be wiped out, they would inevitably, like other desperadoes, become moral monsters—infusing their poison into the very vitals of the body politic. Let us be careful then, how we make unpardonable crimes, lest those whom we make inhuman and desperate, deal with us fearfully. The right of suffrage is the exalted privilege of a freeman and should not be lightly wrested from him.

If, then, you desire to destroy bribery, let the punishment be modified, and made proportionate to the offence. No jury (and he expressed his gratification that such was the fact,) could be induced to convict; the penalty absolutely victimized—and therefore defeated the very object sought to be obtained by its extreme and most disproportionate severity.

Before the subject was finally disposed of, he expressed the hope that gentlemen in their great zeal to prevent bribery, would again consider the propriety of prescribing some adequate punishment to destroy the system of double voting, so often alluded to in the beginning of this discussion. He regarded this evil as far the worst of the two. The man who deposits a series of votes, defrauds a whole political community of their rights, and destroys the very spirit upon which our government rests, whilst the voter who suffers himself to become the victim of bribery, deposits but one ballot to which he is legitimately entitled, and involves only himself and his tempter. He expressed the confident belief, that if the Convention was careful to proportion the punishment properly to the offence, the people every where would most cheerfully co-operate in our labors, by strictly observing the mandates of the Constitution and by seeking to purify the elective franchise in every section of the State.

Mr. Chambers regarded bribery of voters as a crime of the greatest enormity, and one of which no man who had a correct sense of honor and of right moral principle, should be guilty. He expressed his regret to see a spirit prevalent in this body, which while it admitted the magnitude and mischiefs of the crime, obstructed the adoption *seriatim* of each particular measure offered for its correction.

We shall egregiously fail in our duty, if we omit to insert in our Constitution some provision effectually to arrest this vice, which is now stalking abroad through the land, and has made its appearance, as is said, into all classes and circles of society, even amongst those who are in all other particulars elevated in their moral character and worth.

The vice of bribery could not be too soon assailed and put down. The most effectual as well as most prompt means to arrest it, ought to be employed. He was willing to adopt any suggestion, or any amendment, calculated to effect it. To most of the suggestions coming from the gentleman from Queen Anne, (Mr. Spencer,) he had no objection, but he was opposed to the modification of the executive power as proposed. The fact had been stated and was notorious, that in former instances the Governor had interposed his authority to shield offenders from punishment; in some cases by *nolle prosequi*, to prevent trial, and in others by pardon after conviction. Let this be prevented for the future. In general it might be well to leave some discretionary power with the Governor to remit penalties for crimes, but this should be an exception. It is the crying vice of the times. The rapidity with which it is spreading, and its pernicious and corrupting influence on the ballot-box, called for the utmost certainty as well as severity of punishment. We are now preparing for a fresh start in our political history, with a remodeled and renovated code of organic law ; let us move off from the beginning with a firm and decided purpose, to frown upon any and every approach to this detestable and mischievous practice, and thus enlist the great lever of public sentiment against it. Let us give the lead and the tone to that public sentiment. The people expect us to arrest this torrent of corruption, and will sustain us in our efforts to do it. Those persons, if there be such, of high and honorable feeling, who have in a moment of excitement yielded to the example around them so far as to participate, in some degree, in this vice, will give a most attentive ear to your solemn admonition. He believed most firmly that those who had been active in these practices, would be among the very first to thank us for a provision which will make it impossible to continue such a course. They all perceive, as every man must, the debasing, corrupting effects of this vice, and will be most happy to have a reason and a motive on which they can place their refusal, further to pursue a course which their feelings and their conscience detest and loathe.

It is said the modification is designed to leave

with the Governor the power to remit only in cases where he is satisfied the prosecution originates in malice and falsehood. If this can be proved to the Governor, the same testimony will prove it to the court and jury, and protect the party there. But we know—experience has taught us—that the Governor will act not upon proof, but upon *exparte* representation—upon political party representation. He alone is to judge when malice or falsehood instituted the prosecution, and how is his judgment to be impressed, but by individuals impelled by political excitement and party prejudice? Every case will be made a case originating in malice and falsehood, and thus your whole system become practically a dead letter. Against this he protested.

Mr. DIRICKSON replied that whatever might be the opinion of gentlemen, in regard to this "crying vice," as it had been styled, he was confident that very many persons of the highest respectability and of sterling honesty, had mingled in the scenes of political strife and partaken of its excitement, and might have involved themselves in this very "vice," perhaps rather from the necessity of the case, than from any deliberate design to do a wrong. Like the gentleman, he fully appreciated the consequences of the evil, and earnestly desired to see it wholly eradicated—and for that very reason he urged the Convention to apply some appropriate remedy, not to attach the punishment now prescribed, at which the very courts would look with terror, and shudder to inflict. He never could accord with the opinion that this offence was above or equal in grade to the crimes of murder and arson and those of a kindred character, and he never could agree to establish any punishment—(more especially one of so solemn a character as that now proposed,) which neither time nor circumstances could mitigate or wipe away. Disfranchisement forever! Let gentlemen pause—let them beware—behind such a provision, if it can be executed, an abyss lies open, into which many a noble, but thoughtless youth, under the influence of momentary impulses, may fall and sink to rise in this world no more forever.

Mr. J. U. DENNIS reminded the Convention, that it was committed to us to determine the question of our fitness for self government, and that this might be one of the last opportunities we may have of proving our capacity for it. He adverted to the effects of corruption on the Republics of Greece and Rome, and expressed his fervent hope, that the time would never come when the name of our country would be coupled with theirs, in illustration of the brevity of republican institutions. He trusted that America, the place of his birth, would survive to the latest period, and the people of after ages would pronounce a blessing on the State of Maryland for the successful labors of this Convention. In reply to the suggestion that we are making the punishment of bribery out of all proportion to the enormity of the crime, he referred gentleman to the book, which they had read in their infancy, about the choice between good and evil. The ballot-box was the greatest good we possessed, and he asked gentlemen whether they were ready to suffer its purity to be violated without some effort to check the evil. The extent to which it has spread is a sufficient reason to justify us in laying a strong hand upon it at once. We have been told that public opinion calls for the suppression of this vice. He considered it as worse than the leprosy, and expressed a hope that it would be eradicated. Men who would deliberately inflict a stab on the purity of the ballot-box, he would mark with the brand of Cain, and drive them with the lash of scorpions from the pale of free institutions.

The question was then taken on the amendment of Mr. RICAUD, and, by ayes 40, noes 31, it was agreed to.

The question then recurred on the amendment of Mr. RIDGELY (as to the pardoning power.)

Mr. GRASON said that the amendment of the gentleman from Baltimore county proposed to limit a power which was not yet granted. When the report on the Executive department should be before the Convention, it would be the proper time go into the consideration of this subject. But at present there is no such power existing as it is proposed here to limit. It will be time enough to discuss this question when that report comes up for action. Now, from the character of the discussion, we seem to be about sliding into a debate on the pardoning power, which may occupy the time of the Convention for some days. He hoped, therefore, that the gentleman from Baltimore county would not press his amendment at present, but let it be withdrawn until it be in its appropriate place.

Mr. RIDGELY expressed his belief that this amendment embraced the great object which the people looked for, and that unless this provision shall be inserted in the Constitution, they would not vote for it. He did not consider it as obnoxious to the criticism of the gentleman from Queen Anne's. It referred to an offence which was *sui generis*, and entirely unknown to our laws. The sense of the Convention seemed to be that the pardoning power should not be given to the Legislature or the Courts, but only to the Executive, if it could be guarded in his hands, by proper restrictions. He could not see that there could be any better plea for the introduction of his amendment than that in which the offence itself is defined. He therefore could not consent to withdraw his proposition for the purpose of introducing it in the report to which the gentlemen from Queen Anne's referred.

Mr. JENIFER was of opinion that the objection urged by the gentleman from Queen Anne's deserved consideration. There is a report on our tables on the Executive department, and that would seem to be the proper place for this amendment to come in. It may be very properly grafted on that report. But as the amendment of the gentleman from Kent, (Mr. RICAUD,) limiting the disfranchisement to five years had been rejected, he should be against the withdrawal of the amendment at this time, as he thought there should be an opportunity given to take the sense of the Convention now on the question whether the original proposition ought to be modified in the manner proposed or not.

Mr. BUCHANAN. So do I.

Mr. CHAMBERS. Concurring as he did with the gentleman from Queen Anne's, who had started this objection in his general views, thought it would be better to discuss this subject now, and it could be taken up again at some future stage of our proceedings if the Convention deemed it proper to do so. It could be again considered when the Convention comes to revise the Constitution as agreed on, and to appropriate the various powers among the several departments. If we were to adopt the suggestion of the gentleman from Queen Anne's, the effect would be to bring up again this whole discussion when the report on the Executive shall be called up for consideration.

Mr. GRASON said we had been discussing the subject of the elective franchise four or five weeks. And now a proposition is introduced which brings up the question of the pardoning power. It is a new question and must lead to a new discussion. He intended to take a part in that discussion, but he would not do it at this time, and on this report. There may be other crimes in reference to which we may think it wise to restrict the pardoning power in the hands of the Executive, and we can then embrace the whole subject in one discussion. It appeared to him that this would be a much better course than to have all these propositions, connected as they are in their character, separated in different reports.

Mr. NEILL stated that, as the limitation of the disfranchisement to five years had been rejected bythe Convention, he should feel himself constrained to vote against the original proposition, although he was in favor of inflicting some punishment for bribery. All human tribunals are liable to error; by an unjust verdict an innocent man might be convicted; and if this provision should be inserted in the Constitution, the punishment would be irrevocable. He must therefore vote against it. The innocent may make their innocence clear after the conviction and punishment may have taken place, yet it would be impossible to revoke the sentence, and the innocent would be disfranchised forever.

Mr. JOHN DENNIS said that he had voted throughout, from Alpha to Omega, for every measure calculated to throw guards round the ballot box, to preserve it in its purity. In favor of every proposition of that character he had voted, and he had been assailed by those around him, and told of the dire and certain responsibility which awaited him at the bar of public opinion. All this, however, he regarded as the idle wind which passeth by. Because he had voted that a naturalized foreigner in the State of Maryland, should reside in the State twelve months after naturalization before he could be entitled to vote, he had been charged with being an oppressor, a restrictionist, a usurper, &c. He looked into his conduct to discover what, if there could be any, analogy between his course and that of Oliver Cromwell. From the gentlemen from Baltimore county and Queen Anne's, charges of oppression and usurpation had been thundered against him. Against such charges he would always be prepared to defend himself, while he would carefully abstain from assailing others. Regarding the elective franchise as of inestimable value, he would watch over it and protect it as he would virgin chastity. All his votes had been given with that view. He had no aspirations after public station, and when he was called from his private pursuits to become a member of this body, he obeyed with reluctance. He intimated that the gentleman from Baltimore county, (Mr. BUCHANAN,) after vouching the purity of his own county, had spoken of the frauds on the Eastern Shore. He did a wrong to this part of the State which was as pure as the infirmities of human nature would permit; and had always stood high in its reputation for hospitality. He did not wish to disturb the self-complacency of his friend, but was ready to compare constituents at any moment. In reference to the Irish character, he stated, that he would not yield even to that gentleman in his admiration of the noble traits which had given to her heroes the love and sympathy of all lovers of freedom, and his estimation of the valuable services which the Irish people, who have settled among us, have rendered to our country. No one could admire more than he did the greatness of that oppressed country. He felt gratitude and admiration also for the good and generous Lafayette. But, with all these feelings, he could not conscientiously vote to admit a naturalized foreigner to the right of suffrage until he completed a subsequent residence of twelve months in the State—while the citizens of Pennsylvania, Delaware, Virginia, and all the other States of the Union must submit to that restriction. The foreigner is not compelled to bear arms, or to contribute to the defence of the country, while our own citizen must take his share of the danger. He was for even-handed justice and would put all on an equality

Mr. DORSEY said, he would move to amend the amendment as follows:

"But it shall at all times be competent for the court before which such conviction may have been had, upon being satisfied by testimony, offered for the purpose, of its being malicious and unfounded in fact, to set aside the judgment rendered on the verdict of the jury, and *nolle prosequi.*"

Mr. SPENCER said he was inclined to adopt the suggestion of his colleague, (Mr. GRASON,) and not proceed further in the discussion of this subject now. Had it occurred to him earlier, he would not have proposed the amendments at this time. He would prefer waiting the action of the Committee on the Executive department. He intended no disrepect to the courts of justice. But judges were men, and as likely to be influenced by party as well as jurors. The amendment of the gentleman from Anne Arundel, proposed to confer a power on the courts, which they have already in their hands. He hoped, therefore, that the Convention would not agree to the amendment, but would adopt the suggestion of his colleague, and let the subject be postponed until the report on the executive department shall come up. He would withdraw his amendment.

Mr. GRASON cited the amendment as proof that the Convention had not sufficiently considered the connection between this subject and the report on the executive department. The gentleman from Anne Arundel proposes that power shall be given to the courts to grant a new trial. Was it not better to remit the case to the Executive, when it appeared that the conviction had been given improperly, than to try the man over again?

Mr. DORSEY suggested that the gentleman from Queen Anne, (Mr. SPENCER,) had committed an error when he stated that the courts now possessed the power conferred by his amendment. To obtain a new trial, which can only be granted before judgment, it is now necessary to make a motion therefor within some few days after the verdict, according to the rules of the courts. But his amendment proposed to override these rules of court, and to permit the motion to be made any time; and as well after as before judgment. It was alleged by that gentleman that courts were sometimes influenced by prejudices or partialities, as well as jurors.

During his observation, when at the bar, and his experience on the bench, which was not a very short one, he had never know, had never heard of any court in this State, which had been thus influenced. It is well known that the feelings of judges are always in favor of the accused and that in trials by the court to induce a conviction full and satisfactory evidence of guilt is required. He could speak with the same knowledge of facts in exculpation of juries. He recollected but one case to the contrary, as having passed under his judicial cognizance. There the jury under mistaken influences found a verdict of guilty, when the court, after a moment's consultation, informed the counsel of the accused, that if applied for a new trial would be granted. He did not think that the Governor was so likely to be free from political influences the courts. He would further state that he, when acting as a judge, had made it a rule never to suffer any man to approach him for an appointment, on the ground that he was a Whig or a Democrat. He always replied to such applicants, that he knew no politics on the bench, and this he believed was the case of all courts in this State. The Governor on the contrary is a politician. The court when acting has heard both sides; while the Governor, after listening to the testimony on one side, only grants or refuses a pardon. It is important to a just decision, that if a punishment is to be remitted, it ought to be after an examination of the testimony on both sides.

Mr. GRASON considered it improper to commit the pardoning power to the courts, or the Legislature or the Attorney General; he did not think that it ought in all cases to be vested in the Governor. But he did not intend to make any speech. He was not prepared to go into the consideration of this subject at present.

Mr. RIDGELY regretted that he could not comply with the request of the gentleman from Queen Anne's, that he should withdraw his amendment. He would be happy to do so, from courtesy to that gentleman; but he felt himself compelled from a sense of duty to persist in it until the question should be taken He did not think the amendment was out of place.

Mr. CRISFIELD gave notice that at the proper time he should offer the following amendment:

"Laws shall be made for ascertaining by proper proof, the citizens who shall be entitled to the right of suffrage hereby established."

On motion of Mr. McHENRY,

The Committee rose, the President resumed the Chair, and the chairman reported that said committee had in obedience to order had said report again under consideration, and had come to no conclusion thereon.

The Convention then adjourned until to-morrow morning, 11 o'clock.

EXPLANATION.—Mr. SPENCER in reply to the gentleman from Dorchester, Mr. PHELPS, said, so far had the law been carried by the judges of elections, in rejecting legal voters, that he had known instances, where persons offering to vote, were rejected on the score of age, who notoriously were above the age of twenty-one years. He could mention many instances of legal voters, who had been rejected on the score of age. He could refer to the case of an individual, who was associated with a newspaper journal in Queen Annes, who had been so associated in Talbot county; who had been a farmer in Talbot county, and whose birth place was in a distant county. He offered to vote in Queen Annes and was objected to, on the score of age, and although he offered to swear that he had voted at previous elections for years antecedent, in other counties in this State, and that he had been conducting his own business for years and was of age, still because his parents and the bible in which they had registered his birth, were not at hand, and in the nature of things beyond his reach, his vote was rejected. He could recite other cases of like abuse in reference to age as well as residence.

WEDNESDAY, January 22d, 1851.

The Convention met at eleven o'clock.

Prayer was made by the Rev. Mr. GRIFFITH.

The roll was called, and a quorum was present.

The Journal of yesterday was read, and having been so amended as to correct an error in the statement of the amendment of Mr. SPENCER, was approved.

DEBATE ON THE ELECTIVE FRANCHISE.

Mr. GWINN. I move the adoption of the following order:

Ordered, That all debate on the report of the committee on the Elective Franchise, and on the pending amendments, shall cease at twelve-and-a-half o'clock to-day, and that the chairman of the committee of the whole shall report the said report of the said committee and the amendments agreed to and pending in said committee, to the Convention for its action.

The order having been read,

Mr. GWINN called the previous question.

Mr. CRISFIELD. I ask the gentleman from Baltimore city (Mr. GWINN) to withdraw the call for the previous question for a moment. I desire to suggest to him, that it would be better so to modify the order as to allow five minutes to the mover of a proposition, and no further debate. I approve the object of the order, but should be better satisfied with it, if such a modification was made.

Mr. GWINN. The gentleman will perceive that the resolution does not operate upon a subject when it comes into Convention. There a gentleman can occupy as much time as he chooses.

Mr. CRISFIELD was proceeding to reply, when

The PRESIDENT interposed and said, that all debate was precluded by the demand for the previous question.

Mr. MCLANE desired to be informed, whether gentlemen would be at liberty to offer in Convention, any amendments which had not been offered in committee of the whole.

The PRESIDENT stated his impression to be that, according to all practice under the parliamentary law, no proposition could be offered in Convention, which had not been offered in committee of the whole.

A desultory debate followed, covering a great deal of ground, and making the general application of the parliamentary law and rules of order in the House of Representatives of the U. S. and in the House of Delegates.

Mr. BISER intimated his opinion that the usage in the House of Delegates, had not been in conformity with the intimation made by the Chair; and submitted that, under such a construction, members would be prohibited from offering in Convention amendments which, had they anticipated any such course of proceeding, they would have offered in Committee.

Some conversation followed on the part of Messrs. SPENCER, BUCHANAN, BISER, JENIFER and DORSEY and the PRESIDENT.

Mr. DAVIS moved to lay on the table the motion for the previous question.

This motion was at first entertained by the PRESIDENT, but was subsequently declared out of order.

After some further conversation, the question was taken on the demand for the previous question, and there was not a second.

So the question recurred on the adoption of the order.

Mr. PHELPS moved that it be laid on the table.

Mr. GWINN called the yeas and nays.

Mr. PHELPS withdrew his motion, in order, he said, that the question might be taken on the order itself.

Mr. GWINN. I ask the yeas and nays on the adoption of the order.

Mr. CRISFIELD moved to amend the resolution by striking out so much as directed the Chairman to report the bill, with the pending amendments, to the Convention, and to insert in lieu thereof, a provision "that the Convention proceed to take a vote on the amendments pending, and on such as may be offered, and that the mover have the right of explanation."

Mr. MCHENRY alluded to a proposition which he had offered on a former day, having, he said, precisely the same object in view, but which had not yet been acted on.

Mr. CRISFIELD said if the gentleman meant his proposition as a substitute, it would meet his, (Mr. C.'s) views.

Mr. MCHENRY then offered the following substitute for the resolution of Mr. GWINN:

"Ordered, That the debate on the articles of the Constitution, reported by the committee on the elective franchise, shall terminate in committee of the whole on this day, at 2 o'clock, P. M., when each amendment pending, or which may be offered shall be passed upon, without any further discussion than explanatory remarks not extending beyond five minutes by the several proposers of such amendments."

Mr. PHELPS moved to substitute fifteen minutes for five, but withdrew the amendment.

Mr. RICAUD moved to amend by designating one o'clock of this day, as the hour at which the vote should be taken.

A long discussion followed upon the question of order, the construction of the parliamentary law, and the effect of that law upon the business of the Convention if the interpretation intimated by the President was correct.

Mr. BUCHANAN suggested either that that interpretation must be over-ruled, or that the Convention must retrace the step it had taken the other day, in prohibiting the taking of the yeas and nays in committee. Otherwise, nothing would be known to their Constituents.

Mr. MCLANE, after giving his view of the construction of the parliamentary law, expressed the opinion that it would be best, as the report of the committee on the elective franchise had been discussed in Committee, to let it run its career there; but intimated that hereafter he should be opposed to sending any subject to the Committee.

The point of order was further discussed by Messrs. JENIFER, BUCHANAN, MCLANE and BISER,

When the PRESIDENT announced that the hour assigned for the order of the day had arrived.

On motion of Mr. TUCK,

The consideration of the order of the day was postponed, that the Convention might proceed with the consideration of the pending question.

Mr. SOLLERS cited a rule of the House of Representatives of the United States, to show that the practice in that body was not in conformity with the opinion given by the President.

Mr. TUCK followed in a brief exposition of his view of the Parliamentary law.

The discussion was continued by Messrs. DORSEY, BLAKISTONE, by the PRESIDENT, (in explanation,) Mr. BRENT, of Baltimore city, SPENCER, THOMAS, CHAMBERS and BROWN.

The PRESIDENT intimated that the whole difficulty might be avoided by the adoption of a new rule (of which no notice was requisite) pending, that amendments might be offered, &c.

After which,

On the motion of Mr. Brown,

The pending proposition was informally laid upon the table, to enable

Mr. Sollers to offer the following resolution:

"After report from the committee of the whole the article shall be again subject to be debated and amended before the question upon its passage shall be taken."

The resolution was adopted.

Mr. Brown moved that the Convention resume the consideration of the proposition of Mr. Gwinn, with the pending amendments.

Some conversation followed, after which,

Mr. Brent, of Baltimore city, offered the following order:

Ordered, That so much of the 17th rule be rescinded, as prevents new amendments being ordered after the call for the previous question shall have been sustained; and be it further ordered, that all rules which allow this Convention to resolve itself into committee of the whole, be rescinded.

Mr. Randall suggested that an amendment, made to the rules the other day, provided for this very thing.

Mr. Brent explained wherein he considered the two propositions as differing from each other.

Some further conversation followed.

Mr. Brent then moved, (according to the requirement of the existing rule,) that the rules be suspended to enable him to offer the resolution. But he withdrew the motion, and intimated that he would offer the resolution to-morrow morning.

On motion of Mr. Brown,

The Convention resumed the consideration of the resolution offered by Mr. Gwinn, and of the pending amendments.

Mr. Ricaud withdrew his amendment, designating the hour of one, as the limitation of time, (that hour being already passed.)

The question was then taken on the substitute of Mr. McHenry, and it was adopted.

And the resolution of Mr. Gwinn, thus amended, was adopted.

THE ELECTIVE FRANCHISE.

On motion of Mr. Brown,

The Convention proceeded to the orders of the day.

And the Convention resolved itself into committee of the whole, Mr. Blakistone in the Chair, and resumed the consideration of the report of the committee on the elective franchise.

The pending question was on the amendment offered yesterday by Mr. Dorsey to the amendment of Mr. Ridgely.

The amendment to the amendment, by yeas 28, nays 34, was rejected.

And the amendment, by yeas 25, nays 34, was rejected.

Mr. Fooks offered the following amendment:

"After having taken an oath (if not conscientiously scrupulous, and in such case, affirmation,) that he has not received, and will not receive any fee or reward for his vote at said election, and that he has not given or offered to give, and will not give or offer to give directly or indirectly, any fee or reward to bribe, or assist in bribing, or influencing any voter at said election, or to induce any person not to vote at said election."

The question was taken and the amendment was rejected.

Mr. Kilgour offered the following amendment:

Insert in the second section, seventh line, after the word "same" the following: "And any person who gives or causes to be given an illegal vote, knowing it to be so, at any election, to be hereafter held in this State."

The amendment was agreed to.

The question now recurred on the amendments offered yesterday by Mr. Spencer, as the third and fourth sections to the Report. (See proceedings of yesterday.)

Mr. McHenry expressed a hope that the Convention would not consent to embody what was almost an entire code of laws in the shape of an amendment to the Constitution. He would not make any objection to the principle contained in this proposition of the gentleman from Queen Anne's. The details into which it had been extended were very suitable for a law. But he hoped they would not be admitted here. The provisions of an organic law should be general, plain and unmistakeable. If, following this example, we are to engraft in the organic law, all the details which would be necessary in a legislative act for the punishment of murder, larceny, and all the other classes of crimes, we shall never get through the labor before us. All that we can do, all that is proper for us to do, is to insert general provisions, leaving it to the Legislature to fill up the details. It is for us to consider the purpose for which we are sent here, and to carry out the wishes of the people; and unless we do this, they will reject the Constitution when presented to them, and all our work will fall to the ground. If there was one antipathy which was felt by the people stronger than any other, it was against any restrictions on the right of suffrage. This was a privilege which the people had a right to delegate to as few persons to exercise, as they might think best, as in other countries it is entrusted to a limited number. But so jealous are they of this power, that they will not be satsfied with any thing less than its most ample enioyment. Every restriction on this right is therefore to be avoided.

At an earlier period of the session, he had offered a provision prescribing a short residence in the district; and he had intended to follow it up with another making the election districts smaller, so that the voters in each district may be well known to each other. This, he thought, would be the best way to prevent fraud, and would be the only safeguard to the right of suffrage. Having withdrawn that proposition, and finding that numerous motions to restrict the privilege had been since offered, he would now give notice that he intended at a proper time, to renew his amendment.

This system of limiting districts to comparatively small neighborhoods would render it impracticable to commit frauds. He believed that, under its operation there would not be a solitary legal vote lost, while the qualification of a six months' residence would lead to many. He could not but express his astonishment that the Convention should have almost unanimously adopted the cramping amendment of the committee which contained this residence qualification, not only in the counties, but even in every district or ward of the city of Baltimore. He did not intend to detain the Convention by going further into the subject at present. His only design in making these few remarks was to show the ground on which he should vote hereafter. He would vote against all restrictions.

Mr. SPENCER wished to explain to the gentleman from Harford, that his amendment had nothing in it which touched the right of suffrage.

Mr. BREWER suggested to the gentleman from Queen Anne's, at the close of the first paragraph, where it prescribes that the oath shall be taken before the Judge of the Court of Appeals, to substitute a judge of the county.

Mr. SPENCER admitted that it might be proper to make some change in the amendment. He had himself thought it would require slight modification on this point. But it could be amended in the House.

Mr. KILGOUR said the amendment ought to go further. Bribery was not the only offence against which it was necessary to make provision. He was of opinion that the offence of double voting ought to be covered by this proposition.

Mr. SPENCER replied that it covered the whole ground.

Mr. CHAMBERS said that the committee on the elective franchise had reported an additional section which accomplished the object of the gentleman from Queen Anne's in much fewer words.

Mr. SPENCER answered some of the objections which had been made to the diffuseness of his amendment. He would not go into the question whether it was more condensed than the report of the committee. The report contained more words. But it did not cover the whole ground. The report only embraces those who give bribes What then was to become of those who were guilty of double voting and colonizing? Now, his amendment embraces all these offences. He would submit to the Convention, therefore, which proposition was the best

Mr. DORSEY sent up to the Chair a series of amendments, which he desired might be printed for the information of the Convention.

The CHAIRMAN said that the power to order the printing of a paper was in the Convention, and not in the Committee.

Mr. TUCK suggested that the amendment should be read, but did not press the request.

Mr. MORGAN suggested to the gentleman (Mr. DORSEY) to designate at what particular points the amendments should come in.

After some further conversation,

The question was taken on the amendments of Mr. SPENCER, and by ayes 40, noes 27, they were agreed to.

Mr. SOLLERS offered the following amendments:

Insert after the word "person," in the first line, 3rd section, the words "above the age of twenty-one years;" and after the word "crime," in the second line, insert "unless he shall be pardoned by the Executive."

Mr. SOLLERS explained his object in offering this amendment. Assault, with intent to kill, was an infamous crime. Fighting a duel was an infamous crime. But with reference to these offences, the pardoning power is left in the hands of the Executive, because the innocence of the party may be disclosed by subsequent evidence, which may satisfy the Executive that the punishment should be remitted. An infant may be convicted of an infamous crime, and it may be considered proper that the pardoning power should step in and save him from destruction.

Mr PRESSTMAN presumed that to the first part of the amendment there would be little objection. But as to the second part, he would suggest to the gentleman from Calvert, that the pardon, according to a known construction of law, purges the offence. It is the general interpretation that if an individual convicted of crime is afterwards pardoned, or has served out his term of imprisonment, he is purged of the crime. If this was not the case, he would not object to the amendment.

Mr. SOLLERS briefly explained.

Mr. SPENCER moved a substitute, for the first amendment of Mr. SOLLERS, and which was read as follows:.

"Strike out all after the word 'that' in the first line of said section, to the word 'be,' in the third line."

Mr. DORSEY said, that one of the amendments which he had sent up to the Chair, reached the point contemplated in the amendment of the gentleman from Queen Anne's, (Mr. SPENCER.)

Some conversation followed, as to the order in which Mr. DORSEY's amendments were entitled to be received.

Mr. CRISFIELD expressed great surprise that such an amendment as the one now submitted, should have emanated from such high sources. He was astonished that the gentleman from Queen Anne's, and the gentleman from Anne Arundel should have suggested it. If the right of suffrage be of such high value, are these gentlemen willing to share it with men who have been convicted of crime, and have just left the penitentiary? Are such men as these proper trustees of this inestimable right—men, who, by the sentence of the law, have been pronounced unworthy to be members of society? Are the gentlemen who support this proposition, ready to go with such men, arm in arm, to the polls? Is it safe to entrust the interests of the commonwealth in such hands? If the Convention shall be brought to this decision, the State of Maryland will stand alone on this point. He referred those gentleman to the Constitutions of all the other States, and asked if there was not in all of them, provisions excluding men of this class from the exercise of the elective franchise? The Constitution of the State of New York, which was eulogized as containing all the modern improvments in the science of government, expressly excludes them. He hoped that the Convention would not permit such persons to share in the exercise of the right of suffrage.

Mr. STEWART, of Caroline, briefly replied, explaining the reasons which had induced him to move to strike out this clause. His object was to assimilate the amendment to that which had been offered by the gentleman from Queen Anne's; not that he intended to advocate the crimes themselves, but because he felt a sympathy for fallen humanity, and was averse to putting an indelable mark of infamy on convicts. There was no distinction made between an individual sentenced to two years imprisonment, and one for fifteen. None between the highway robber, and the man guilty of a less crime. The public will set a proper estimate upon the character of these individuals. He never heard any complaining because these individuals voted. The gentleman from Somerset, (Mr. CRISFIELD,) had asked whether we, who support this amendment, would be willing to go, arm in arm, to the polls with men who had been convicted of crime, and had just left the penitentary? He would ask the gentleman, if many persons were not discarded from society, who had never fallen into such crimes, while many who had been reformed by punishment, had become valuable members of the community. In classifying offences, we ought to look at their effect on the community, and thus to estimate the degree of infamy which should attach to an offender. What is the object of punishment? It is in part, to check the propensity of the offender to commit the offence of which he has been convicted, and also to prevent others from its commission. He had known individuals who had served in the penitentiary one year, and had been in the Legislature the next; and he had been himself professionally employed in a case where a man who had been convicted of a crime and who had served his time in the penitentiary, excepting for one week, and who desired to be informed whether he had not a right to vote, and when told that he had, said "he felt as a freeman." That man, he believed, was a good citizen. [Here the hour of two o'clock arrived when all debate was to stop by resolution.]

The CHAIRMAN interposed and announced that the hour had arrived, by which, under the order of the Convention, the general debate must terminate.

Mr. DORSEY said, in explanation of the amendment, he had indicated that the object of punishment was to confine an individual who had committed crime, in a place where he could repent and reform. And unless the Convention intended to fly in the face of all the Legislation of the State, they were bound, if these individuals afterwards became good citizens, to receive and treat them as such, and to let that which had passed be forgotten. If time allowed, he could state many signal instances of this reformation.

Mr. SOLLERS repeated what he had before advanced in support of his amendment. He thought it extraordinary that the gentleman from Anne Arundel, (Mr. DORSEY,) who was willing to punish bribery at elections, by disfranchisement forever, would be willing to pardon criminals of this kind, and receive them back into society.

Mr. DORSEY said he would explain to the gentleman from Calvert. The one offence strikes at the root of our institutions, while the other injures society only in a limited degree, and is therefore, comparatively light, and he may have come out of the penitentiary, a place for repentance, a reformed man.

Mr. SOLLERS resumed. The gentleman from Anne Arundel says, the penitentiary is a place to repent in. Why then would he not send the man there who gives or receives a bribe, and give him an opportunity to repent? He could not see why the gentleman from Anne Arundel would give his arm to the one at the polls, and proscribe the other for ever. But if a few persons come out of the penitentiary reformed, it is very well known that nine-tenths of those who have been there, have come out worse than when they went in.

Some conservation followed on points of order.

Mr. SPENCER withdrew his substitute to enable the question to be taken on the first amendment of Mr. SOLLERS.

Mr. STEWART of Caroline, renewed the amendment of Mr. SPENCER, and made a brief explanation, in reply to Mr. SOLLERS, stating the reason which induced him to vote for so heavy a penalty in bribery. The punishment of other crimes was fixed by law, and this would be to add one greater of itself, than that now imposed by the act of Assembly.

The question was taken on the first branch of the amendment of Mr. SOLLERS.

And it was agreed to.

The question recurring on the second branch of the amendment,

Mr. SPENCER moved to amend it by striking out the words "be pardoned by the Executive," and inserting "unless the restriction is taken off by the Governor."

Mr. S. explained the operation of the amendment.

Mr. TUCK submitted to the Chair, that the remarks of both the gentlemen who had last spoken were out of order.

Some conversation followed as to the construction of the rule; after which, the amendment of Mr. SPENCER was rejected.

And the amendment of Mr. SOLLERS was agreed to.

The question then recurred on the amendment as offered by Mr. SPENCER, but withdrawn by him, and renewed by Mr. STEWART, of Caroline.

The amendment was rejected.

Mr. DORSEY asked, that if in order, the amendments he had offered, might be read:

The first amendment was read as follows:

Strike out from the second section, in the first line, after the word "give" the words "or offer to give."

Mr. DORSEY said, this provision was in conformity with the act of Assembly, which punished such offences. The object was to strike at the root of the evil.

The amendment by ayes 41, noes 19, was agreed to.

The second of the series of amendments offered by Mr. DORSEY, simply corrected a verbal error; and was agreed to.

The next was as follows:

Strike out in the fifth line, the words "of profit or trust," and insert in lieu thereof, "or appointment."

This amendment,by ayes 33, noes 19, was rejected.

The next amendment of Mr. DORSEY, was to insert after the word "giving," in the 7th line of said section, the words "or offering to give."

The amendment by ayes 38, noes 25, was rejected.

The next amendment was agreed to as follows:

Insert after the word "State," in the 7th line, the words, "or by the ordinances or authority of the mayor and city council of Baltimore."'

Mr. DORSEY offered the following as an additional section:

"That no person who is a candidate or has been nominated and is to be voted for to fill any office or appointment under the constitution or laws of this State, or the ordinances or authority of the mayor and city council of Baltimore, shall contribute, give or subscribe, or promise so to do, any money, or other thing of value, to be used or employed in any way, in aiding or promoting the success of his election; except some reasonable sum to be applied to the payment of the expense of printing ballots or tickets to be cast at the election. And any person herein offending shall be deemed guilty of a misdemeanor and on conviction thereof, in a court of law,shall be punished by fine and imprisonment, and forever thereafter be deprived of his elective franchise in this State and the city of Baltimore, and be incompetent to hold the office to which he may have been elected; or any other office or appointment under the constitution or laws of this State, or ordinances or authority of the mayor and city council of Baltimore, or to vote thereafter at any election therein."

Some jocular conversation followed.

Mr. DORSEY stated that in offering this amendment, his object was two-fold. First, to prevent the raising of large sums of money to be used in bribery and corruption at elections; and secondly, to make public offices the reward of merit, not of wealth. That for their attainment, the poor man and the rich man might enter into competition upon equal terms. That he belonged to that school of olden democracy which held, that "worth makes the man, and want of it the fellow."

"That honor and shame from no condition rise;
Act well your part, there all the honor lies."

That in selecting public servants or officers, wealth formed no element of preference. That superior integrity and capacity, not wealth, were the grounds upon which such selections were to be made. Suffer such enormous subscriptions to be exacted from candidates, for purposes of bribery and corruption, as they are now subjected to, to ensure a party triumph, and every poor man, no matter how pre-eminent his qualifications for office may be, is driven from the field of competition by his more wealthy competitor, with not half his merit, solely on the ground that more money will be given to secure a party triumph by bribery and corruption. The result will be, Mr. President, if no check is imposed upon this system of bribery of voters and pollution of the ballot-box, that the elective franchise will cease to be of any value in the eyes of the virtuous, patriotic portion of the community, and your public offices will virtually become a saleable commodity to be struck off to the highest bidder. Reports which defy contradiction are rife amongst us, that a candidate for office has been known to subscribe $5000, nay $7000, to be expended upon a single election, and from information, the truth of which I do not doubt, the sum of $20,000 if not $30,000, has been offered as a contribution if successful in procuring a party nomination.

The question was then taken and by yeas 33, noes 41; the amendment was rejected.

Mr. DORSEY offered the following as an additional section

Art. 5th. No person in this State not a candidate or nominated as aforesaid, shall give, contribute or subscribe any sum or sums of money, or thing of value to be used in any electioneering canvass, or to be expended in any way in relation to any election to be held under the constitution or laws of this State, or under any ordinance or authority derived from the mayor and city council of Baltimore, unless such gift, contribution or subscription be directed by its author to be exclusively applied to the giving of barbacues or treats, at which candidates for office and others may have an opportunity of addressing their fellow citizens; or to the printing of public documents or political essays, addresses or hand-bills designed for circulation among the people; or the providing vehicles for the transportation of voters to the polls or to the printing of tickets designed for the ballot box; and any person herein offending, or any person applying such gift, contribution or subscription to any electioneering purpose contrary to such direction, upon conviction thereof in a court of law, shall be fined and imprisoned as shall hereafter be provided for by the Legislature, and be thereafter incapable of voting at any election, or of holding any office or appointment of any nature or description, under the constitution or laws of this State, or under any ordinance or authority of the mayor and city council of Baltimore.

Mr. BRENT of Baltimore city, moved the following amendment to the amendment:

"Or for platforms for political speakers to stand on, music, transparencies and other incidental expenses necessary and proper."

Mr. MITCHELL desired to move further to amend by adding "and that no spirituous liquors shall be used."

This amendment was not now in order.

The amendment of Mr. BRENT by ayes 26, noes 41, was rejected

And the amendment of Mr. DORSEY was rejected.

Mr. DORSEY offered the following amendment:

No person in this State holding any office or appointment under the constitution or laws of the United States, or any of the officers thereof, shall give, contribute or subscribe any sum or sums of money or other article of value, to be used in any electioneering canvass, or to be expended in any way, in relation to any election to be held under the constitution or laws of this State, or ordinances of the Mayor and City Council of Baltimore, and any person herein offending shall, upon conviction thereof, in a court of law, be fined and imprisoned as from time to time may hereafter be provided by the Legislature; and be forever thereafter incapable of voting at any subsequent election, and of holding any office or appointment of any nature or description whatever, under the laws or constitution of this State, or under the ordinances or authority of the Mayor and City Council of Baltimore.

Mr. DORSEY stated that it was matter of public notoriety that officers of the United States had been called upon to contribute to the expenses of the elections. Levies were made on them, which they complied with under the dread of losing their offices. He desired to extricate the United States officers employed in this State, from this state of things, by exempting them from these levies. He wished to prevent the United States government from thus interfering with, and corrupting our State elections.

The question was taken, and by ayes 40, noes 41 (after a second count) the amendment was rejected.

Mr. DORSEY offered the following amendment:

No person in this State shall himself or through the agency of others, receive, use or expend any sum or sums of money, or other thing of value given, contributed or subscribed by any person or persons whatsoever living out of the State of Maryland to be made operative in any electioneering canvass, in relation to any election about to be held under the laws or constitution of this State, or of the ordinances or authority of the Mayor and City Council of Baltimore; such person so receiving, using or expending, and each and every of his agents therein, upon conviction in a court of law shall be fined and imprisoned as the Legislature may, from time to time direct; and be forever thereafter incapable of voting at any future election of any nature or kind in this State, or in the city of Baltimore, or of holding any office or appointment under either.

Mr. DORSEY explained that this amendment was intended to operate not only in the State, but on persons out of the State, and out of the United States. In former times, with what truth he could not say, we had heard of hundreds of thousands being expended by British manufacturers, for the purpose of destroying ours. He thought it right to punish any man who shall receive from any others, whether from Presidents of the United States, or of foreign countries, any sums of moneys for the purpose of bribing.

Mr. MAGRAW moved (the usual hour having passed) that the committee rise.

The motion was rejected.

The question was then taken on the amendment of Mr. DORSEY, and by ayes 30, noes 43, it was rejected.

Mr. STEWART, of Caroline, moved that the committee rise.

The motion was rejected.

Mr. DORSEY moved the following amendment:

Or appointment under the laws or constitution of this State, or the ordinances or authority of the Mayor and City Council of Baltimore, or to vote thereafter at any election therein; and the person to whom such bribe, present, reward, promise or security may have been offered or given, shall be a competent witness to prove the offence, and may be compelled to testify as such, and if so testifying should he have received the same, he shall be exempt from all punishment therefor, and the person by whom such bribe, present, reward, promise or security may have been proffered or given, shall be a competent witness, and may as such be compelled to testify, and if so testifying, he shall be exempt from all prosecution or punishment for the offence by him committed; provided always, that such exemption from prosecution and punishment shall only be extended to that party who shall first appear before the grand jury to testify against the other party, and that neither party shall be compelled to give testimony unless protected from punishment by the exemption hereinbefore provided.

Mr. DORSEY said it had been alleged, that it would be impossible to obtain a conviction in these cases, because of the difficulty of compelling one of the parties to testify against the other. Therefore, we proposed to exempt from punishment, the party which would first give testimony for the conviction of the other.

Mr. CHAMBERS called for a division of the question (which was ordered) upon the first branch of the amendment, ending with the words "at every election therein."

The first branch of the amendment was rejected.

And the second branch of the amendment was rejected.

Mr. DORSEY then moved to amend said report by adding at the end thereof, as an additional section, the following:

It shall be the duty of the General Assembly of Maryland to pass laws punishing with imprisonment as well as a fine, any person who shall remove into any election district of Howard District or Anne Arundel county, or into any ward in the city of Baltimore, not for the purpose of acquiring a *bona fide* residence therein, but for the purpose of voting therein at an approaching election, or who shall vote in any such election district or ward, in which he does not reside, except in a case provided for in the first article of this Constitution, or shall at the same election vote in more than one of snch election districts or wards, or shall vote or offer to vote in any name, not his own, or in place of any other person of the same name, or shall vote in any county in which he does not reside, or shall vote or offer to vote in virtue of a certificate of naturalization granted to another person; and any person convicted of any of the aforegoing offences in a court of law shall not only be punished as aforesaid, but shall be incapable thereafter of voting at any election in this State, or holding any office or appointment of any nature or description under the Constitution or laws of this State, or under any ordinance or laws of the Mayor and City Council of Baltimore.

The amendment was rejected.

Mr. CRISFIELD, moved to amend said report by adding at the end thereof the amendment offered by him on yesterday, being in these words:

"Laws should be made for ascertaining by proper proofs the citizens who shall be entitled to the right of suffrage hereby established."

Mr. PARKE, moved to amend said report by inserting after the word "person," where it occurs the second time in the third line of the third section, these words "legally declared."

Mr. RICAUD, (the hour growing late) desired to move that the committee rise.

Mr. TUCK moved to amend the motion so, that the committee should rise and report the bill and amendments to the Convention.

Mr. CRISFIELD had no objection, he said, to to the motion, if he did not thereby lose the opportunity of offering the amendment he had indicated.

Mr. TUCK included in his motion, he said, amendments adopted and pending.

The CHAIRMAN expressed some doubts whether the motion of the gentleman from Prince George's (Mr. TUCK) was now in order.

Mr. TUCK waived his motion, therefore, but gave notice that if the motion to rise did not prevail, he would renew his own.

And the question was taken and decided in the negative: ayes 36—noes 39.

So the committee refused to rise.

Mr. TUCK then renewed his motion that the committe rise and report the amendments pending and adopted.

The question was then taken on the motion of Mr. TUCK, and decided in the negative without a division.

So the committee rose and reported the bill and amendments to the House, and the committee of the whole was discharged from the further consideration of the subject.

On motion of Mr. CHAMBERS, of Kent, the report and amendments were ordered to be printed, and the further consideration thereof was postponed until Monday next.

Mr. BRENT, of Baltimore city, gave notice that he would to-morrow move the following order, as a substitute for that offered by him this morning:

Ordered, That the standing rules of this Convention be so amended as to apply the previous question without restriction and without debate to the matter then pending, and to such amendments thereto as may be offered consistently with existing rules, after the call for the previous question has been sustained, and in voting on the matter pending when the previous question is sustained and the amendments thereto as aforesaid, the previous question shall then be exhausted.

And be it further ordered, That all rules which allow this Convention to resolve itself into committee of the whole be rescinded.

Which was read.

And then the Convention adjourned.

THURSDAY, January 23d, 1851.

The Convention met at 11 o'clock.

Prayer by the Rev. Mr. GRIFFITH.

The roll was called. A quorum being present, the Secretary proceeded to read the journal, and made some progress when, on motion of Mr. MAGRAW, the further reading was dispensed with. Subsequently a verbal error was corrected, on motion of Mr. KILGOUR.

The President laid before the Convention a report from the clerk of the commissioners of tax for St. Mary's county, relative to fees and perquisites paid the Attorney General and his Deputies by said county.

Which was read and referred to the committee on the Attorney General and his Deputies.

The President also laid before the Convention an account of the clerk of Charles county court, for services rendered under the resolution of the Convention of 15th November.

Also, an account of the clerk to the commissioners of tax for Charles county, for services rendered under an order of the Convention.

Which were referred to the committee on Accounts.

Mr. RIDGELY presented a communication of E. Smardon and others, of Baltimore county, touching public education.

Which was read and referred to the committee on Education.

Mr. STEWART of Baltimore city, offered ithe follow order:

Ordered, That the President of this Convention be authorized to pay to the Printers and Reporter of the Convention, from time to time, such sums of money as may be due to them respectively according to their contracts, upon the certificate of the committee on Printing

Mr. CHAMBERS of Kent, asked for some explanation in regard to the delay in the *printing* of the reports.

Mr. WEBER, made an explanation as to the causes of the delay with which

Mr. CHAMBERS expressed himself satisfied.

And the order was then adopted.

THE RULES.

Mr. BRENT, of Baltimore city, called up the following order, which he had offered immediately before adjournment yesterday, as a substitute for that offered by him at an earlier period of the day.

"Ordered, That the standing rules of this Convention, be so amended as to apply the previous question without restriction and without debate to the matter then pending, and to such amendments thereto as may be offered consistently with existing rules, after the call for the previous question has been sustained, and in voting on the matter pending when the previous question is sustained and the amendments thereto as aforesaid, the previous question shall then be exhausted.

"And be it further ordered, That all rules, which allow this Convention to resolve itself into committee of the whole be rescinded."

Mr. BRENT briefly explained the principle which it was his intention to embrace in the order. He expressed the belief that there was a disposition on the part of the Convention not to go into committee of the whole, and in order that some protection at least might be given to the minority, his proposition contemplated that the pending matter, when amendable under existing rules, might be amended. In other words, he was for leaving it to the sense of the majority to say, when the debate should be closed. He illustrated the operation of the amendment. His desire was that the amendment heretofore adopted on motion of the gentleman from Anne Arundel, (Mr. RANDALL,) should be rescinded so far as it gave the mover the power to designate the matter to which the previous question should apply. He insisted on the expediency of its adoption, and the happy effects it would have on the business of the Convention. Nine-tenths of the discussions here had been but a repetition of the same ideas in a different form. If any gentleman had a better rule to suggest, he would cheerfully take it.

Mr. RICAUD moved that the order be laid upon the table.

Mr. BRENT asked the yeas and nays, which were ordered, and being taken, were as follows:

Affirmative.--Messrs. Chapman, President, Morgan, Blakistone, Dent, Ricaud, Chambers of Kent, Mitchell, Donaldson, Dorsey, Wells, Randall, Kent, Bond, Brent, of Charles, John Dennis, James U. Dennis, Crisfield, Dashiell, Williams, Hicks, Hodson, Eccleston, Phelps, Bowie, Sprigg, Bowling, Wright, McMaster, Fooks, Jacobs, Schley, Fiery, John Newcomer, Harbine, Davis, Weber and Smith—37.

Negative.—Messrs. Merrick, Buchanan, Bell, Welch, Chandler, Ridgely, Lloyd, Dickinson, Sherwood, of Talbot, Colston, Chambers, of Cecil, McCullough, Miller, McLane, Tuck, Thomas, Shriver, Gaither, Biser, Annan, Stephenson, Magraw, Nelson, Carter, Thawley, Hardcastle, Gwinn, Stewart, of Baltimore city, Brent, of Baltimore city, Presstman, Ware, Brewer, Hollyday, Slicer, Fitzpatrick, Parke, Cockey and Brown—38.

So the order was not laid on the table.

And the question recurring on its adoption,

Messrs. HARBINE and FIERY called for a division on the first and second branches, which was ordered.

Mr. MERRICK now rose and stated that he had acted under a misapprehension of the question, and asked leave to change his vote.

The PRESIDENT said it could be done only by unanimous consent.

Mr. TUCK said he had voted against laying the order on the table because he thought that these questions when once introduced should be settled, that the Convention might know what its rules were.

Mr. MERRICK said his intention was to vote for the readiest way of getting rid of the proposition.

Some conversation followed between Messrs. TUCK and BRENT as to the effect the order would have on the amendment adopted on motion of Mr. RANDALL.

Mr. TUCK then addressed a few remarks to that branch of the order which proposed to rescind all rules allowing the Convention to resolve itself into committee. Generally speaking, he said, he was as much opposed to going into committee as any member could be, but he was not in favor of abolishing the power. The debate was at all times within the control of the majority, and there might be cases in which it might be proper that the House should resolve itself into committee. He would, therefore, retain the power.

Mr. THOMAS made some remarks, in which he expressed himself in favor of the first branch of the order; but suggested to Mr. BRENT that it might perhaps be improved by adding the words "they shall be submitted and passed upon without debate."

As to the second branch of the proposition, he dissented entirely from the gentleman from Baltimore city, (Mr. BRENT.) There were advanta es in committee of the whole, (of which, he, Mr. T., should perhaps avail himself as little as any member of the body,) which could not be secured in Convention. He illustrated this opinion, and said that he could not, under any circumstances, vote for this branch of the resolution.

Mr. RANDALL suggested that the gentleman from Baltimore city, (Mr. BRENT,) would attain his end by striking out from the amended 17th rule, the words "or amendment." But Mr. R. argued that it would be better to let that rule remain as it was, until the Convention had had an opportunity of knowing something about its practical operation.

He insisted on the importance of retaining the power to go into committee, and contended that to adopt the restriction proposed, would prevent calm deliberation, and lead to precipitate action. He should vote against both propositions.

The PRESIDENT announced the hour of twelve, that being the time appointed for the consideration of the order of the day.

Mr. BISER moved to postpone it, with a view to dispose of the subject matter before the Convention.

Mr. SPENCER enquired of the PRESIDENT, what the order of the day was?

The PRESIDENT said, it was the resolution reported from the Committee on Representation.

The question was then taken on the motion of Mr. BISER, and the order of the day was postponed.

Mr. BRENT contended that the amendment suggested by the gentleman from Anne Arundel, (Mr. RANDALL,) would not accomplish the object which he (Mr. B.) had in view. This he proceeded to show. He also submitted that the amendment suggested by the gentleman from Frederick, (Mr. THOMAS,) was embraced in his (Mr. B's) proposition. He submitted with great deference to the opinions of gentlemen having more experience than himself, that there was no substantial reason for going into Committee, and that the reasons applicable in that report to ordinary parlimentary bodies, did not apply to this Convention.

The question was then taken on the first branch of the order, and, by ayes 42, noes 31, it was adopted.

Mr. BROWN suggested to Mr. BRENT to withdraw the second branch of the order.

Mr. BRENT acquiescing in the suggestion—

The second branch of the order was withdrawn.

Mr. BLAKISTONE offered the following order, which was adopted.

Ordered, That the Secretary of this Convention cause the rules as amended, to be printed for the use of the members of this body.

The Convention hereupon passed to the orders of the day.

BASIS OF REPRESENTATION.

The PRESIDENT announced the order of the day to be the following resolution reported on Wednesday, Dec. 11, by Mr. MERRICK, from the Committee on Representation.

1. *Resolved*, That it is expedient to regard federal numbers in finding the estimates and basis of representation in the House of Delegates.

2. *Resolved*, That it is inexpedient to adopt a principle of representation, based exclusively upon popular numbers in organizing the House of Delegates or the Senate.

The resolutions having been read—

Mr. SOLLERS moved that they be referred to a committee of the whole; for (said Mr. S.) if we *are* to discuss abstractions, I think we had better do so in Committee.

Mr. DENT. I hope the Convention will not agitate the discussion of this question at the present time. I do not see any good that can result from so doing. For my own part, I should greatly prefer that there should be some practical proposition submitted to our consideration before an effort is made to discuss merely abstract principles. This question of representation, is one to which more importance is attached than to any other upon which this Convention will be called upon to act.

Mr. SOLLERS. That is the very reason why it should be discussed in Committee.

Mr. DENT. I can only express the hope that my suggestion may be adopted, and if in order, I will move a postponement.

Mr. SOLLERS. I have no objection to that, and if the gentleman will make such a motion as he indicates, I will withdraw mine.

Mr. DENT. I move that the consideration of this subject be postponed until the 15th day of February.

Mr. MERRICK said, he should not object to any disposition which the Convention might think proper to make of the resolutions. They had been reported by the Committee on Representation, of which he was Chairman—the first by a unanimous vote, and the second with only one dissenting voice. The object of the Report was to endeavor to obtain the judgment of the Convention on these two controling principles as the basis of any detailed plan which might be reported here, and within the circumference of which some plan might be laid down. These two great principles would have to be fixed at last, before any plan could be decided upon. As to the mere question whether the report should be considered now, or a fortnight hence, he was indifferent.

In regard to the first resolution as to the mode of computing population, there would probably be no great diversity of opinion, for he presumed that the Convention would, by a large majority, if not by a unanimous vote, decide that it was inexpedient to have regard to federal numbers in fixing the basis of representation.

Mr. SOLLERS said, he had made the motion to go into committee, for the very reason assigned, that this was a most important and vital question—the most vital and important of all the objects for which this Convention had been called—if he knew any thing as to what these objects were. If any subject should be discussed in committee of the whole, where greater latitude of debate was allowed than in Convention, this was that very subject. He saw no reason why it should be postponed, though he was willing that it should be, if the House thought proper.

Mr. CHAMBERS, of Kent, said he thought it was impossible for the committee on representation to act until the Convention had first acted in the form of instructions to them. So conflicting were the views entertained by the members of the committee, that they could only be reconciled by some agency which would control their decision and compel the surrender of some of these opinions. That agency could only be found in the Convention itself. These principles had to be fixed. *That* was a necessary preliminary to the action of the Convention, and he could see no good reason why a decision upon it should be delayed. He admitted that the question was one of great importance, though he might not go so far as some gentlemen who thought it the most important upon which the Convention would be called to act. If, as had been said, it was an abstraction, putting it off would not make it less so. He asked the yeas and nays on the motion to postpone.

Mr. BROWN suggested that the day designated in the motion to postpone was two distant, but thought it would be well that the Convention, before taking up so important a subject, should dispose of the report of the committee on the elective franchise which had been made the special order for Monday, so that there might be no interference. In the meantime the Convention could occupy itself in the consideration of other matters.

Mr. MERRICK said, that if any postponement was to take place, he should be glad, in view of some private matters which required his attention, that the postponement should be to a less distant day than had been moved.

Mr. BROWN suggested a postponement to Thursday next.

Mr. PRESSTMAN submitted, as a question of order to the chair, whether after the resolution should have been taken up, it would be in order for gentlemen to submit plans for apportionment, and whether these plans would then be before the Convention for action, without the necessity of referring them to the committee on representation.

If so, he was in favor of taking up the resolution. He was opposed to referring the matter again to the committee in any form whatever.

The PRESIDENT said, it was his impression that it would be in order for the Convention to engraft any proposition it might think proper, on the report of the committee, without referring that proposition.

Mr. PRESSTMAN said, he was entirely opposed to the action of the Committee. He agreed with gentlemen who had expressed the opinion that this was but an abstraction. Gentlemen had been sent here for the most part with power to carry out the direct wishes of their people, and they knew as well now how they stood, as they ever would know.

The question of representation according to population, he considered as settled—settled beyond the power of resurrection. The election had settled that point. He was not in favor of discussing it; and he was opposed to all discussion upon the subject, unless directed to some practical plan. He should vote at all times for the basis of representation according to population, but he could not close his eyes to the fact, that upon that question he was in a very small minority. He preferred, therefore, that the discussion should be confined to some liberal plan of compromise, and he believed that there were gentlemen in the Convention who had such plans to offer, without the intervention of the committee. He hoped that the committee would never again have charge of the subject. And he gave notice that he should himself offer a plan, looking to a compromise.

Mr. KILGOUR was in favor of the postponement. The members of the Convention, he said, were now in good humor with each other, and the longer they remained so, the better it would be, not only for themselves, but for the accomplishment of the objects which had called them together. If there was any question which would excite the minds of members and lead to irritation and ill-feeling, it was this. And if they get mad, one with another, (laughter,) what sort of a Constitution did gentlemen suppose they would make? He hoped the consideration of the subject would be postponed until every other had been disposed of.

Mr. DASHIELL. As we have already entered upon the discussion, I hope that the motion to postpone may be withdrawn.

Mr. DENT. I do not feel at liberty to withdraw the motion. I can see no practical good that is to result from the discussion now; and I, therefore, persist in the motion.

Mr. BROWN enquired whether it would not be competent for any gentleman to submit a plan of representation, and then to move a re-commitment with instructions to report that plan.

The PRESIDENT. The Chair thinks it would be in order.

Mr. BROWN. Then I move to postpone the consideration of the subject to Thursday next.

Mr. BRENT, of Baltimore city, referred to the fact, that at an early stage of the session, he had been in favor of postponement; but the sense of the Convention had been against it. This was a most important question, and when the Convention took it up, they should give their entire and undivided attention to it. He thought the Convention was not prepared to consider it now, and he hoped that it might be postponed generally, and that the Convention would proceed to the consideration of the Bill of Rights.

Mr. SPENCER hoped, he said, that the Convention would take up the resolution reported by the chairman of the committee on representation, that it might be determined whether it would, or would not give these instructions to the committee. It was his intention. at the proper time, to move that the report be referred back to the committee, with instructions to report a specific plan. If the committee could not agree let majority and minority reports be made. He was opposed to all discussion on abstractions.

Mr. TUCK suggested that the Convention could not shut out the discussion on abstractions. If gentlemen were prepared to enter upon such a discussion, it must unavoidably come;—it might as well come now as at any time, and, when once over, gentlemen would be ready to give their votes upon some substantive proposition. He thought time would be saved by refusing to postpone the consideration of the question. He should, therefore, vote against the postponement, and in favor of all motions to take up the subject at once.

Mr. GWINN said, it was immaterial to him whether the question was referred back to the committee or not. He knew very well that that committee could not agree upon any thing, unless they should receive specific instructions from the Convention. But he must say, in reply to the remark of a gentleman who had preceded him, that there had never been in the history of the country an instance in which this question of representation had been taken up and acted upon from beginning to end without interruption. In support of this assertion, he cited the instance of the Convention that framed the old Constitution of the State of Virginia. It was not to be imagined that a question of this magnitude could be disposed of in one day. Debate must take place, and the result might be a compromise upon all matters involved. As a mere individual, he considered himself instructed to insist upon the principle of representation according to population. The people whom he represented believed that to be the true and honest doctrine; and he would never think of any plan of compromise, until it had first been ascertained that that doctrine could not be carried out. He referred to the long delay which had taken place in the British Parliament, before a similar question could be settled there. And was he to be told that he was not to urge a principle which he believed to be right, because the effort to establish it might be defeated? Or was that principle entitled to less respect and consideration, merely because it might not command the votes of a majority of the Convention?

Mr. DENT interposed to a point of order. The gentleman was gradually sliding into the discussion which it was the object of every motion to avoid.

The PRESIDENT decided that the question was debateable only to the extent of the propriety of a postponement.

Some conversation followed

Mr. GWINN resumed and briefly argued that whether these resolutions were abstractions or not, the course of proceeding indicated here was precisely that which had been adopted in the Virginia Convention and in the Convention which framed the Constitution of the United States. These resolutions contained within themselves all the elements of calculation, and if they were abstractions, he knew not what an abstraction was.

The two great issues which this Convention was sent here to try, were the questions of representation, and the election of officers. They had assembled for the purpose of making reforms. And he would ask what single reform, of all those, which, for fourteen years the people had agitated, had yet been made?

Mr. DENT again interposed to the question of order.

The PRESIDENT satisfied Mr. GWINN what the limit of debate was.

Mr. GWINN resumed. I have only followed in the track which other gentlemen have marked out. I have not made a comment that was not attacked by the remarks of the gentlemen who have preceded me. The friends of this reform are entitled to have this question brought up at an early day. And the best and wisest course, in my judgment, is first to take up a question about which there is so much dispute and feeling, and to leave all other matters to be disposed of after that shall have been settled.

Mr. HARBINE said that he did not concur in the opinion expressed by the gentleman from Baltimore city, as to the propriety of taking up this question at the present time. He believed it would be better for the Convention, and better for the people whom they represent, that the consideration of so important a subject should be postponed at least for a short time. Whether these resolutions were abstractions or concretions, was a matter of little moment to him; but he was satisfied that if the Convention should take up this great principle of representation, it would be discussed from day to day, and from week to week, for a length of time which no one could predict. He differed with the gentleman from Charles county, as to the chances of a speedy vote upon the proposition, whether or not it was expedient to adopt federal numbers in fixing the basis of representation. He (Mr. H.) thought that the discussion of that question would occupy as much time as any other. So, in relation to representation according to population. That matter was not going to be passed over slightly. How long might this single proposition occupy the attention of the Convention? So with the restriction as to Baltimore city, there might be another protracted debate. It was manifest that all these questions, from their intrinsic importance, were going to occupy a good deal of time. He was willing to fix that time. But as much local feeling might probably be excited, and as the discussion was going to be prolonged, he believed that it would be politic and prudent to postpone the consideration of the matter for the present. The Convention, he suggested, should take up the report of the Committee on the bill of rights. As to the propriety of referring the resolutions back to the committee on representation, he disagreed with the gentleman from Baltimore city. He, (Mr. H.) thought there was as much propriety in sending this subject to a committee as any other.

Mr. STEWART, of Caroline, referring to the journals of the Convention, briefly recited the history of the proceedings of the Convention hitherto, in reference to this subject, for the purpose of shewing that there was some conflict in the action of this body, and of illustrating the propriety of some remarks which he had formerly made in reference to this question. He was proceeding with some remarks in reference to the subject matter, when

Mr. BRENT, of the city, called the gentleman to order.

The PRESIDENT reminded the gentleman from Caroline, that the question was on the postponement of the subject.

Mr. STEWART resumed—suggesting that in order to show the propriety of postponement, it was necessary to understand what had been done. The committee to which the subject had been committed, had reported certain resolutions. And now, when these resolutions come up for consideration, a motion is made to postpone them. He stated that he was ready to go on now, and should vote against any postponement. He was prepared to vote for the resolutions of the Chairman of the Committee, if brought before the Convention in a proper manner. The report on the elective franchise had been discussed, and if the Convention had rejected it, there would have been an end of it, unless it was recommitted. He was fearful that such would be the effect of the postponement of this question. The gentleman from Baltimore, had said that he was in a minority on the principle of making population the basis of representation. Others were in favor of a different basis. He thought it right that we should come to immediate action on the subject and settle the principle. He thought it was the duty of the committee to report some basis of representation, upon which the Convention might act. If it would be in order, he desired to move a substitute, as follows:

"To recommit the report with instructions to report a specific plan."

Some conversation followed on a point of order.

Mr. Brown demanded the previous question, and by ayes 40, noes 31, there was a second.

And the main question was ordered to be now taken.

Mr. Chambers of Kent asked the yeas and nays on the main question, which were ordered.

And the question, "shall the consideration of the said resolution be postponed until the 15th day of February," was taken and decided in the negative as follows:

Affirmative.—Messrs. Morgan, Blakistone, Dent, Hopewell, Sellman, Dalrymple, Bond, Buchanan, Welch, Chandler, Lloyd, Dickinson, Sherwood of Talbot, Colston, Eccleston, Chambers, of Cecil, McCullough, McLane, Bowie, Sappington, Stephenson, McHenry, Nelson, Brent of Baltimore city, Fiery, John Newcomer, Harbine, Kilgour, Fitzpatrick—29

Negative.—Messrs. Chapman, President, Ricaud Chambers of Kent, Mitchell, Donaldson, Dorsey, Wells, Randall, Kent, Sollers, Brent, of Charles, Merrick, Bell, Ridgely, John Dennis, James U. Dennis, Crisfield, Dashiell, Williams, Hicks, Hodson, Phelps, Miller, Tuck, Sprigg, Bowling, Spencer, Wright, McMaster, Fooks, Jacobs, Thomas, Shriver, Gaither, Biser, Annan, Magraw Carter, Thawley, Stewart, of Caroline, Hardcastle, Gwinn, Stewart, of Baltimore city, Presstman, Ware, Schley, Davis, Brewer, Weber, Hollyday, Slicer, Smith, Parke, Shower, Cockey and Brown—56.

So the Convention refused to postpone the consideration of the order, until the 15th day of February.

The question then recurred on the motion of Mr. Brown, to postpone the consideration of the second report until Thursday next.

Mr. Brown rose to withdraw the motion.

The President said it was not in order for the gentlemen to do so, the previous question having been called.

Some conversation followed as to the effect of the new rule on the question before the House, between Messrs. Brent, of Baltimore city, Chambers, Biser, Tuck, Thomas and the President.

In reply to an enquiry by Mr. Thomas,

The President finally decided that the previous question would be exhausted on taking the question on the motion of Mr. Brown, that being the "matter pending."

Mr. Kilgour asked the yeas and nays on the motion of Mr. Brown, which was refused.

Mr. John Newcomer enquired, whether it would be in order to move an amendment.

The President said that under the rule adopted this morning, it would be in order

Mr. Newcomer thereupon moved that the further consideration of the question be postponed until the first Monday in February.

Mr. Tuck suggested that the best course of proceeding would be, that the pending motion to postpone, should be withdrawn, and that the Convention should get rid of the previous question by going into Committee of the whole.

The question was then taken and the amendment of Mr. Newcomer was rejected.

The question recurred on the motion to postpone to Thursday next.

The motion was rejected.

The question recurred on the motion of Mr. Sollers, to commit the report to a Committee of the whole.

Mr. Spencer, then moved to recommit the report to the committee on Representation, with instructions that they report articles of the Constitution on some basis of representation, fixing the representation in the House of Delegates and Senate.

Mr. Merrick stated that in the committee, the gentleman from Baltimore (Mr. Presstman) had taken his ground, and would go for nothing but the basis "of population." Others had taken their stand; and thus the committee had been distracted in their labors, and unable to agree on the principle. Now if the Convention would come to any decision which would be an instruction to the committee as to the principle on which they should found a report, the existing differences of opinion would at once be brought to a compromise. For this purpose the resolutions were reported. He believed that the sense of the Convention was against the population basis. If he was right, and the decision of this body should send back the resolutions with an instruction to that effect, it would promise a compromise of the jarring opinions of the members of the committee. They had made no report, because they could come to no conclusions; and the resolution of the Convention forbade a report of reasons, and called only for results He repeated that the sanction of the House was required for the guidance of the committee; and until that sanction was given, the committee could be brought to agree on neither of the extreme principles.

Mr. Brent, of Baltimore city said

The question now was, whether the Convention should resolve itself into a committee of the whole. I am opposed (continued Mr. B.,) to again entering into that committee on any subject whatever, but especially at this time and on this great question of representation, because I think to entertain that question now, would be premature. The labors of the Convention are not yet sufficiently matured for us to proceed to this subject. It is because I regard representation as the most momentous and and important of all questions that I do not wish to begin its discussion now, when we must break off on next Monday to resume the report on the elective franchise. Let us, when once we touch the principle of represention, devote all our energies without interruption or diversion, to its undivided consideration.

The gentleman from Charles, (Mr. Merrick,) says that the Convention is now prepared to vote on this whole subject. I regret to hear that it is prejudged. I had hoped that gentlemen were open to conviction. I am ultra and zealous for the principle of representation on the basis of population; but satisfy me that I am wrong, and I will acknowledge the error; otherwise, I shall know no compromise in my votes on this subject yet if a constitution is formed, I would look at it as an *entire instrument*, and if I should approve it *as a whole*, I reserve the right to vote for the new Constitution, though it may not give us our full and equal rights. But the new Constitution is not yet formed, and until I see it complete I cannot say whether it will receive my support. In the meantime, let us postpone this subject until we have completed our action on the elective franchise, and then let us have full and thorough discussion in all its latitude, and if we cannot change a vote here, the seed will be sown among the people, which, at some future time, will bring forth the harvest of reform, if it shall fail now.

Gentlemen who are favorable to the doctrine of representation based on population, have said that it ought to be pressed at all times and under all circumstances, and that we ought to begin its consideration even if we have to break off time and again. I beg leave to differ with them, and shall contend that more justice will be done to the subject by postponing it now and taking it up hereafter, when we can bestow on it our single and undivided attention.

One gentleman, from Caroline, has spoken of those who are for postponement now as generally acting to postpone every thing, and he has used the unsavory metaphor of a flock of sheep following the one which first bleats. If he means to apply such a comparison, however general, to me, he is much mistaken, as I am always for action, prompt and speedy, and utterly opposed to those who would procrastinate the work of reform.

Mr. PRESSTMAN wished the Convention to understand the position he occupied as a delegate from the city of Baltimore. He wished also that his constituents and his colleagues should understand it. He was against postponement. He was against the practice of members of the committee, who took an opportunity to rise in the House, and make an exposition of their views, and then to abandon the ground they had taken.

[Mr. GWINN disclaimed any such intention.]

Mr. P. said, he did not allude particularly to his colleague. He reminded his colleague, who was very fond of looking into Convention proceedings, that it had always been permitted to each member of a committee to make a report embracing his views; he might avail himself of that privilege. He referred to the statement made by the gentleman from Charles, (Mr. MERRICK,) that no agreement could take place in that committee; and stated that the views of his colleague were opposed to those of a majority. He intended, when he had the opportunity, to move to discharge the committee from the further consideration of the subject, because he wished to offer a plan, and he knew other gentlemen would offer plans, for the purpose of obtaining the vote of a majority of the Convention in favor of some principle. He thought it the proper course for every gentleman in committee, or a minority, to make separate reports, and then let them be considered by the House. He did not allow that he had been instructed to vote for the basis of population; his constituency undoubtedly preferred it; but he felt at liberty to make terms.

Mr. TUCK called for the previous question.

There was a second, and the main question was ordered to be now taken; which main question was on the motion of Mr. SOLLERS, to refer the said report to the committee of the whole.

Mr. PHELPS asked the yeas and nays which were ordered, and being taken, resulted as follows:

Affirmative—Messrs. Chapman, President, Morgan, Blakistone, Dent, Hopewell, Ricaud, Chambers of Kent, Dorsey, Wells, Randall, Dalrymple, Bond, Ridgely, John Dennis, James U. Dennis, Crisfield, Dashiell, Williams, Hicks, Hodson, Eccleston, Phelps, Miller, McLane, Tuck, Bowling, McMaster, Fooks, Jacobs, Gwinn, Stewart, of Baltimore city, Schley, Davis, and Smith—34.

Negative—Messrs. Donaldson, Sellman, Brent of Charles, Merrick, Buchanan, Bell, Welsh, Chandler, Lloyd, Dickinson, Sherwood of Talbot, Colston, Chambers of Cecil, McCullough, Bowie, Sprigg, Spencer, Wright, Thomas, Shriver, Gaither, Biser, Annan, Sappington, Stephenson, Nelson, Carter, Thawley, Stewart of Caroline, Hardcastle, Brent of Baltimore city, Presstman, Ware, Fiery, John Newcomer, Harbine, Kilgour, Brewer, Weber, Hollyday, Slicer, Fitzpatrick, Parke, Shower, Cockey and Brown—46.

So the Convention refused to commit the report to the committee of the whole.

The question then recurred on the motion of Mr. SPENCER, to recommit the said report with the instructions he had indicated.

Mr. THOMAS moved to amend said motion by striking out the instructions to the committee.

Mr. THOMAS referred to the order which had been adopted by the Convention on motion of Mr. GRASON, restricting the committees from reporting reasons; and suggested that the object of that order was to prevent any influence which a statement of opinions might have on the Convention. The committee had made no report in the shape of an argument on this, what he must call, vital question, for vital he considered it, and one on which he had taken ground which he would never abandon without a severe struggle. He thought, however, that the committee had violated the spirit of the order, by coming forward and throwing the weight of their opinions against the course which he should advocate. He desired that the resolutions should be recommitted, with instructions to report a practical measure. He deprecated discussion on the abstract propositions, whether representation should be based on popular numbers; whether it should be based on federal numbers; or on popular numbers for the House and federal numbers for the Senate. He did not wish to waste time on abstractions. The members of the committee appeared to be as various in their opinions as their numbers. They were not likely to make any report. Had the committee reported any practical plan, some progress might have been made. But constituted as the committee are, the better plan would be to discharge them if they should ask it, and then take up the subject in the House. He thought the instructions contained in the amendment of the gentleman from Queen Anne's (Mr. SPENCER) would only embarrass the committee, without leading to any practical result. It was his opinion that the committee ought to report a plan.

Mr. CHAMBERS said that the committee could report a plan directly, if they could have a vote of the Convention.

Mr. THOMAS replied that this was only a single opinion. He thought the committee might make a report without violating the order of the House.

Mr. SPENCER said he had no intention to give the committee any instruction beyond what the resolution appointing them gave.

Mr. THOMAS suggested that under the instructions of the gentleman's amendment, the committee may not report at all. His object was that they should be ordered to report a plan.

Mr. SPENCER stated that the committee was appointed to deliberate and report on the subject of representation. The amendment he had offered was to recommit with instructions to do, what the original resolution instructed them to do. The gentleman from Frederick objected to it, on the ground that they might not report at all. He wanted them to agree and ask instructions.

Mr. GWINN intimated that a majority could not agree.

Mr. SPENCER intimated that if they could not agree to ask instructions, any two of them, or even one, might make a report on which the Convention could go on. Let them separately report articles which may be taken up and considered. Unless they do this, how were any articles to come before the Convention? He said he was not tenacious about the instructions and was willing to strike them out.

Mr. PRESSTMAN concurred in the views of the gentleman from Frederick.

Mr. THOMAS moved to strike out the instructions in the amendment.

Mr. SPENCER accepted the amendment, and modified his proposition by striking out the instructions.

Mr. PRESSTMAN understanding that the gentleman from Kent, had said that some members of the committee wished to bring forwarded plans, in order to present their views to the Convention, asked if a member of the committee had any greater right to do this than any other gentleman in this body.

After a brief explanation between Messrs. CHAMBERS and PRESSTMAN,

Mr. CHAMBERS resumed. His object in rising was to urge immediate action on the report, as the safest, surest mode of expediting our work. Pass this report, and you will probably, in a few hours after the committee can be convened, have a report on the compromise plan—reject it and thereby declare your determination to take a ratio of numbers, and you must have a report accordingly.

It had been remarked that delay was desirable, because it was a subject, the discussion of which would produce angry feelings. Why should such apprehension exist? There is nothing in the question to excite angry or unkind remark—nothing. He regretted—very much regretted—to hear such anticipations. They seemed to invite such a state of irritation. Where was the occasion for it? It is a question of political expediency and policy; involving no personal imputations. We differ—differ honestly. It is fair to use arguments to convince each other; but passion is not argument, and of all means is the least likely to convert or persuade an opponent. None of us are excited now by any unkind feeling. Then why should we become so in the calm investigation of such facts, and the cool expression and consideration of such arguments as should lead us to wise conclusions? He thought this the place, now the time, and that the form in which the question should be discussed and decided.

Mr. MERRICK said that the Committee could have had no intention to violate the spirit of the order, or to bring up abstract principles. They thought the resolutions contained practical principles, such as it would be necessary for the Convention to settle, before the Convention could consider and report details. It was necessary that they should know whether popular numbers was to be the basis of representation or not, that they might go into the details under the sanction of the vote of the Convention. The committee were of opinion that the business would be expedited if they could get these principles settled. The gentleman from Frederick asked what progress could be made? He answered that they might make great progress. There must be animated discussion on the subject, and why should we not begin by making the ground clear. We should advance the business of the committee, by coming to a solemn decision as to the character of the basis. To settle that now would be to get rid of a great sub-division of the subject. And if it should appear that the Convention will adopt neither federal nor popular numbers exclusively, a compromise of opinions would take place in the committee. It was his opinion that individual members, or even a minority of the committee, had no right to make reports, but that this right was in the majority only. But a member of the House was always at liberty to submit propositions, and, as such, he had submitted a plan. He had presented it as his own, not presuming to offer it as a report from the committee. Hitherto there had been no plan suggested on which the committee had been able to agree; but hoped that they would soon come to an agreement, especially if by a vote of the Convention, the principle were to be established. The expression of the views of the House would, at once, terminate the difficulties in the committee.

Mr. GWINN offered the following amendment.

"Ordered, That the committee on Representation be instructed to report a plan of representation in the Senate and House of Delegates, giving one delegate to each five thousand of population in the counties and city of Baltimore, in the House of Delegates, and dividing no county or city of Baltimore, and to constitute the Senate of senatorial districts, of which the city of Baltimore shall be one, and to arrange the said districts in such a manner that they may be, as far as possible, equal in population—and to provide that each senatorial district should have five delegates."

Mr. CHAMBERS denied that this was an abstract question. It was eminently practical. He adverted to the common notion that this was the age of "progress," and said he believed in this country the progress in the arts and sciences, was much greater and much more useful, than progress in the science of government. In none of these was the improvement greater than in chemistry. It gave us *tests* by which in almost every case to ascertain the truth. If, for instance, the farmer desired to know whether carbonate of lime was an element in the composition of his bank, he had only to apply an acid to a portion of it, and its presence was truthfully announced by the "effervescence." There were some questions in law and logic, determinable by tests equally infallible. This was an instance. An "abstraction" is that which is by itself—it has no practical consequence or result. Now the resolution of the committee puts before the house the proposition, whether the basis of representation shall or shall not be exclusively that of a ratio of population. If you concur with the committee and say that such a basis will not be adopted, will there be no result—no consequence? If on the contrary you decide that the committee are wrong in repudiating this basis, and that it ought to be adopted, will this produce no result—no consequence? Why, sir, just so surely as you decide the one way or the other, will the committee report a corresponding system for you, and just so surely as members adhere to their opinions, will the system reported rest on that basis which this vote shall indicate, and shape be given accordingly to one of the most important articles in your Constitution. This is the "effervescene." The article in your Constitution—that's the "result."

He denied that the committee had in any degree offended against the letter or the spirit of the order requiring reports to be made without accompanying arguments. He explained the object of that order, which was not to prevent a report of *opinions* as had been said, but of arguments to sustain opinions. Every report must give an opinion. The fact that a particular provision is recommended for our adoption is the strongest form in which the opinion of its propriety can be expressed.

A report without an opinion would be that very abominable thing which is so hateful to gentlemen—an "abstraction." He vindicated the course of the committee. There was no argument here to sustain the report or prejudice the question. It was the opinion of the committee that this question should be decided as a guide to their action. There were so many and so diverse opinions amongst its members that a majority could not unite affirmatively on any plan. Some of the members would yield to no terms of compromise until the House should settle the broad question of "representation on the basis of numbers exclusively." No complaint can be made on that account. These gentlemen held themselves bound to stand upon this floor in public view in vindication of the claim of their constituents to the benefit of this principle. They thought the silence of the committee room was not the scene for their labors, as no history of their efforts would then appear. Of course the committee could not have the aid of these gentlemen in the preparation of any other plan till the House decided this question. It must be discussed. Gentlemen have said it shall not pass *sub silentio*—but must encounter opposition stern, and strong. It will occupy as little time now as ever. We are at it and why not get through it?

Mr. DAVIS moved that the Convention adjourn, but waived the motion to enable

Mr. MCHENRY to give notice, that when the report of the committee on the elective franchise came up for consideration, he should offer sundry amendments, which he moved should be printed.

Determined in the affirmative.

Mr. DAVIS then withdrew his motion to adjourn.

Mr. DASHIELL renewed the motion to adjourn, and on the question being put, it was

Determined in the negative.

The question then recurred upon the order submitted by Mr. GWINN.

On motion,

The Convention adjourned until to-morrow morning 11 o'clock.

FRIDAY, January 24, 1851.

The Convention met at 11 o'clock.

Prayer by the Rev. Mr. GRIFFITH.

The roll was called and a quorum was present.

The journal was read, and having been so amended, on motion of Mr. SPENCER, as to state the fact that he had withdrawn the *instructions* accompanying his motion to recommit the resolutions reported by Mr. MERRICK from the committee on representation, was approved.

Mr. PARKE presented the petition of seventeen officers and members of "Lippard Circle, Brotherhood of the Union, (H. F.) No. 3, of the the State of Maryland, No. 86 of the Continent of America."

Also, of seventeen other citizens of Maryland, praying that a certain portion of real estate may be exempted in the new Constitution, from any forced sale, extent or levy, on execution or decree from or by any court of law or equity.

Mr. P. simply desired, he said, to remark that the signers of the petitions were very respectable persons—that the subject was one which was attracting universal attention, and which, he thought, deserved the respectful consideration of the Convention.

On motion of Mr. P. the petitions were referred to the committee on the bill of rights.

Mr. WELLS, from the committee on accounts,

reported the following order, which was adopted :

The committee of accounts beg leave to report that the several accounts herewith filed numbered respectively, No. 1, 2, 3 and 4; have been examined by them, which they believe correct, that under resolution No. 67, passed at December session 1849, they are of opinion they should be paid by an order on the Treasury, drawn by the President of this body, they beg leave to suggest the adoption of the following resolution :

Resolved, That the amount of the accompanying accounts, being $4?8.14, be paid by an order drawn on the Treasury by the President of this Convention.

G. WELLS,
W. WILLIAMS,
EDWARD LLOYD.
ALEX. NEILL, Jr.,
ELIAS WARE, Jr.
Committee on Accounts.

MASTER AND SLAVE.

Mr. PRESSTMAN submitted the following order:

"*Resolved*, That the Legislature shall not pass any law to abolish the relation of master and slave as it now exists in this State, and that the committee on the Legislative Department be instructed to report an article to carry out this provision."

Some conversation followed between Messrs. BLAKISTONE, PRESSTMAN and the PRESIDENT, as to the fact whether a similar proposition had not heretofore been referred to Committee No. 14.

Mr. PRESSTMAN said he did not think that the subject matter embraced in this resolution had already been referred, or that any order had been submitted to the Convention going to the extent contemplated by it. If the subject had been referred in this particular form, he had no wish to press the resolution ; but he thought that no order had been referred denying to the Legislature the power to act upon the question of the relation of master and slave. His desire was to insert a guarantee in the new Constitution upon slavery as it now existed in the State of Maryland, and, providing that it should not be changed by the Legislature. In making a Constitution, he was prepared to look to compromises, with a view to obtain more confidence on the part of the counties than now existed in relation to the matter of slavery. He believed that there was no desire on the part of his constituents to interfere with the relation of master and slave as it now existed; and they would be prepared to sustain a Constitution embodying such a provision. He thought it was important that, in the early stages of the proceedings of the Convention on the subject of representation, gentlemen should understand that, whatever its basis might hereafter be, the rights of property as regarded the relation of master and slave would be secure. He intended to press the resolution with a view to obtain the speedy action of the Convention upon it, and he believed there was a large majority here ready to sustain it.

Mr. SPRIGG said, that on Wednesday, the 4th of December, he had offered the following order, which had been referred to the committee on the Legislative department:

"*Resolved*, That the committee on the Legislative department of the government, enquire into the expediency of engrafting on that branch of the Constitution, a clause prohibiting the Legislature from passing any law affecting the existing relation of master and slave in this State."

Mr. BROWN remarked that there was no such committee as a committee on the colored population. There was a committee on the free colored population. He would suggest that the resolution should be referred to Committee No. 14, and he (Mr. B.) would vote for that reform with pleasure.

Mr. PRESSTMAN said that his object was different from that of the gentleman, (Mr. SPRIGG.) The order introduced by the latter gentleman, proposed to direct the com. on the Legislative department of the government to enquire into the expediency, &c. Now, his (Mr. P's.) object was to carry out the entire view embraced in the resolution of the gentleman in the present proposition, as he (Mr. S.) would probably desire it should come from the Committee.

Mr. CHAMBERS, of Kent, (to the PRESIDENT. Is it in order for a proposition identically the same as one previously offered, to be renewed ? I hold, in justice to my friend, (Mr. SPRIGG,) that, as this is precisely the same proposition which he introduced some time ago, it is not in order now to renew it.

Mr. PRESSTMAN. I admit that the two propositions are of a similar character, but I deny that I have not the right to offer a resolution, the object of which is to take the sense of the Convention on any subject. I would not have offered the resolution if I had not known that the object it has in view is agreeable to a majority of the Convention. But if the gentleman (Mr. SPRIGG) has any objection, personally, I shall certainly withdraw the order. I hope he will understand the spirit in which I offer it.

Mr. DORSEY. I ask for the reading of the resolution.

The resolution having been again read,

Mr. CHAMBERS, of Kent, said, I withdraw all objection.

Mr. BOWIE. The gentleman from Kent, (Mr. CHAMBERS,) will, I think, perceive at once the difference between the two propositions. The one which my colleague, (Mr. SPRIGG,) submitted was a mere resolution of enquiry. The resolution of the gentleman from Baltimore city, (Mr. PRESSTMAN,) I understand to be a resolution directly instructing the Committee on the Legislative department of the government to report such a provision.

Mr. SPRIGG. Personally, I have not the slightest objection that the House should refer this proposition.

Mr. DASHIELL. It seems to me that this resolution comes from rather a suspicious source; slavery not being much in favor in the city of Baltimore. It comes from a part of the State of Maryland, which is called Western Maryland, where, I repeat, no great interest in slavery is felt. It seems from the remarks of the gentleman from Baltimore city, that he designs to gain votes and influence upon other questions, in which that portion of the State is deeply interested. I do not object to the resolution, but to the motive with which the gentleman seems to have offered it.

Mr. Presstman, interposing. I do not understand the gentleman as imputing any improper motive to me?

Mr. Dashiell. No improper motive—only—(Laughter.)

Mr. Presstman, interposing. I am surprised that gentlemen representing a section of the State particularly interested in this question of slavery should object to a gentleman, even though he might come from a suspicious quarter, advocating his own views. It is precisely because, I believe that the views of the people of the city of Baltimore are misrepresented, that I am prepared to give this guarantee, and to give it in good faith.

Mr. Brent, of Baltimore city. I hope that the Convention will adopt this resolution, and that it will be followed up by resolutions to the same effect, imposing restrictions upon the Legislature in respect to debts for works of internal improvement.

Mr. Johnson. I am not disposed to give any opinion upon this resolution at the present time; but I object to this mode of proceeding. The subject, I understand, is already before one of the committees of this body. Is it not, sir? (to the President.)

The President. It is.

Mr. Johnson, continuing. I cannot see why that committee should not make a report, and bring the subject up in due form for deliberate and proper consideration. Whether one portion of the State ownes more or less slaves than another, is a question which I do not intend to discuss here. I am, myself, a slaveholder; and I should be the last man in the State, who would wish to see that question discussed in this Hall or out of it, unless some good end is to be attained. Let then, the regular course of proceedings be adopted, as more in consonance with the usages of a body of this character. I should be glad if the gentleman from Baltimore city, (Mr. Presstman,) would withdraw his resolution. If he does not, I shall move that it be laid upon the table.

Mr. Presstman. As I cannot see the propriety of postponing this matter, I must, with all respect to the gentleman who made the suggestion, decline to withdraw my resolution.

Mr. Johnson. Does the gentleman object, so to change the form of his proposition, as to make it one of enquiry?

Mr. Presstman. Yes, I do object.

Mr. Johnson. I shall not make the motion to lay on the table, but shall decline to vote on the resolution.

Mr. Presstman. Very well, sir. I object to making the resolution a mere proposition of enquiry, because it would not at all answer the purpose which I have in view.

The question was then taken and the resolution was adopted.

BOARD OF PUBLIC WORKS.

Mr. Merrick submitted the following order:

"Ordered, That committee No. 14, be instructed to inquire into the expediency of providing in the Constitution for a Board of Public Works, to consist of a President and two members, to be chosen every third year, one member by the separate vote of each branch of the Legislature, and the President by joint ballot of both Houses, the person thus elected President of said Board to receive always the vote of the State of Maryland for the office of President of the Chesapeake and Ohio Canal Company, and the Legislature to provide suitable and adequate salaries for the persons composing said board."

Mr. Thomas suggested to the mover of the resolution, (Mr. Merrick,) to avoid contrariety of opinion by omitting the latter part of it.

Mr. Merrick replied, that the resolution was simply one of enquiry. It did not in any degree commit the Convention. The specifications in the order were nothing more than an indication of the individual preference of the member offering it.

Mr. Thomas said, he should then indicate *his* preference by moving to strike out the latter part of the order.

Mr. Merrick said, the motion would lead to discussion, and that was precisely what he wished to avoid.

Mr. Thomas said it was his desire also, by the motion he had made, to avoid the necessity of discussion.

Mr. McLane said he understood that this was a simple resolution of enquiry. According, therefore, to all courtesy and the practice of the body, it would, under any circumstances, be only proper that the order should go to the committee.

But he had risen for the purpose of saying that an order had heretofore been adopted, not exactly to the same effect or in the same terms, but on the same subject, and having in view the organization of a body similar to that which the gentleman, (Mr. Merrick,) proposed. The Committee had had a meeting, and, in the absence of its Chairman, he, (Mr. McL.) believed he might be permitted to state, that they had come to a decision, and had directed a report to be submitted to the Convention. He did not make this statement with a view to preclude the order. It was not exactly in accordance with the views of the committee, as he understood the matter. The gentleman from Frederick, (Mr. Thomas,) would see, however, that the adoption of the order would neither commit the House nor embarrass the committee.

Mr. Davis asked that the order might be again read.

The resolution was read and adopted.

INDEXES.

Mr. Tuck submitted the following resolution:

"*Resolved*, That the committee on Printing be authorised to have a suitable index made to the Journal of proceedings, and also to the debates of the Convention.

Mr. McHenry enquired as to the cost?

Mr. TUCK said he had no information on the subject. He only knew from experience that, without indexes, it was a matter of great difficulty to find any thing that might be wanted either in the journal or the laws. The same difficulty would be found to exist in regard to the debates. He had offered the resolution, because he understood that the committee on Printing did not think that they had the power, under previous orders, to carry out the design of the resolution.

Mr. PHELPS, replying to the enquiry of Mr. MCHENRY, said that one hundred dollars was about the sum paid for indexing the laws. From this standard, the gentleman could form some idea of the cost of the work.

Some desultory remarks and explanations were made by Messrs. WEBER, BUCHANAN, SPENCER and RANDALL, in favor of the resolution, and by Mr. MCHENRY in opposition to it.

Mr. THAWLEY moved an amendment, which was decided, by the President, to be out of order, (and which will be found in the proceedings of to-morrow.)

Pending the question on the resolution of Mr. TUCK,

The PRESIDENT announced that the hour had arrived for taking up the Order of the Day.

Mr. SPENCER moved to postpone its consideration, until the pending question should have been disposed of.

The question having been taken, the Convention refused to postpone.

BASIS OF REPRESENTATION.

The Convention, thereupon, resumed the consideration of the following resolutions, submitted by Mr. MERRICK, on the 11th of January, from the committee on Representation:

1. *Resolved*, That it is inexpedient to regard federal numbers in fixing the estimates and basis of representation, in the House of Delegates.

2. *Resolved*, That it is inexpedient to adopt a principle of representation based exclusively upon popular numbers, in organizing the House of Delegates, or the Senate.

The pending question was upon the motion made yesterday by Mr. GWINN, (as a substitute for the motion of Mr. SPENCER,) to recommit the resolutions, with certain instructions.

Mr. GWINN now withdrew his instructions, and said he desired that the question might be taken on the simple motion to recommit, and he hoped that that motion would prevail.

So the question was on the motion of Mr. SPENCER, to recommit the report to the committee on Representation.

Mr. CHAMBERS, of Kent, asked the yeas and nays on that motion, which were ordered.

Some conversation followed between Mr. PRESSTMAN and the PRESIDENT, on a question of order, after which

Mr. CHAMBER, of Kent, said he merely desired that the Convention should adopt such a course of proceedings, as would afford every gentleman an opportunity of expressing a distinct opinion upon the highly important question of representation. He wanted to avoid all side-blows—every thing like throwing a veil over it—though he imputed no such motive to any gentleman. He referred to the fact that gentlemen had taken the stump, and that the public mind had become excited on this question of representation, simply according to numerical force, and submitted that it ought to be settled. What the gentleman from Baltimore city, (Mr. PRESSTMAN,) had said about the slave question, he, (Mr. C.) applied to this. Let it be fixed now, and fixed forever, beyond the hope of resurrection. The battle was to be fought. We were told by gentlemen, who were known never to back out from their position, that the ground would not be yielded without a severe and a stern struggle. The sooner, therefore, that the cloud passed over, (to use the language of his friend from Carroll, (Mr. BROWN,) who said many good things,) the sooner we shall see the sunshine. And he, (Mr. C.) hoped that every proposition would be voted down until the Convention came to a direct question on the adoption of the resolutions.

Mr. THOMAS said, that he had yesterday signified his preference for the mode of disposing of this question. Reflection had but confirmed his opinion. There were peculiarities connected with this question, which belonged to no other on which it would become the duty of the Convention to act; because, in the apportionment of representatives, would come the struggle for the distribution of political power. In his judgment, the Convention would be in a better frame of mind for calm and mature action on all other questions, if this struggle were postponed until other matters had been disposed of. In this judgment perhaps he might err. But, independent of these general considerations, there were reasons which he signified the other day, and which he need not now repeat, why the Convention should recommit this resolution. He still pronounced it an abstraction. It was aside from the main question, and whatever might be the decision of the Convention, no result would be produced. It did not require the Convention to declare any thing affirmatively; it only declared what the Convention would *not* do. It laid down no rule; it prescribed no plan; and the Convention might go on, week after week, and month after month, and yet not obtain a single tangible proposition on which it could act. He earnestly hoped it would be recommitted, and that the committee would be permitted to take charge of the subject. If they could not agree, let them come into the Convention, say so, and be discharged; and then, he hoped, that some gentleman would in his place here submit a *projet*.

Mr. TUCK said, he could not perceive how any thing was to be gained by sending the resolutions back to the committee, unless the Convention should first express some opinion on the subject. They had been told yesterday that the committee could not agree on any plan. Suppose then the resolutions were recommitted. To what end? What was the committee to do? They had declared that they could not agree—they had all said so. In his opinion the Convention should either refuse to recommit, or should recommit with some positive instructions.

My desire is (concluded Mr. T.) to vote on something tangible. I hold in my hand a proposition which embodies the true republican doctrine; and which I now offer.

Mr. T. read as follows:

"With instructions to report a plan of representation in the House of Delegates on such basis of compromise as will in their judgment protect the interests of the different sections of the State."

Mr. T. then referred to the resolutions, and said that the Convention proposed to send these resolutions back without either an affirmative or a negative answer. His opinion was that in order to protect all the interests of any State, or Government, compromises on the part of the various interests involved must be made. And this he supposed to be the conclusion to which the Convention must come at last.

Mr. Spencer said, he would accept the amendment of the gentleman from Prince George's, (Mr. Tuck,) if he (Mr. S.) was at liberty to do so.

Mr. Brown thought, he said, that the proposition of the gentleman from Prince George's did not remove the difficulty. It was probable there would be as many differences of opinion under that amendment, as there had already been in committee.

After saying a few words in reply to Mr. Chambers, of Kent, and applying to that gentleman's course on this question one of David Crockett's anecdotes about a coon-fight, Mr. B. expressed the belief that the resolution ought to be recommitted; and he was sure that if the committee could not agree on a plan without the instructions of the gentleman from Prince George's, they could not agree with them.

Mr. Tuck. I withdraw my amendment.

Mr. Chambers, of Kent, replied briefly and in good humor to the coon story, and, after referring to the proceedings which had taken place in the committee upon them, said that every member of the committee agreed that it it was necessary that the Convention should pass upon the question involved in the resolution. He believed that, if the House would decide that question, a report could be made in twenty-four hours afterwards, if the committee could be got together.

Mr. Merrick could not discover, he said, any reasonable ground for the apprehension which some gentlemen had expressed that bitter and accrimonious feelings would grow out of the discussion on this question. The gentleman from Frederick, (Mr. Thomas,) had said that the question of the distribution of political power was connected with this subject, and that other questions should be disposed of first, because of the danger (as he, Mr. M, understood the gentleman,) that astrangement and alienation would grow out of the discussion. He, (Mr. M.,) hoped that their was no member of this Convention who did not feel the utmost good will towards every other member of it; and that it would be found that they could, as statesmen and philosophers (many of them with locks whitened with age,) act upon this question without being transported with that passion or ill-will to which younger men might be apt to yield. So far from thinking that this question should be postponed, because of its importance, and because it occupied a larger share of public consideration, and of the consideration of the Convention than any other, he thought it should for that very reason be the sooner disposed of.

He contested the idea that the resolutions reported from the Committee, were mere abstractions. What was the first question to be decided when the Convention came to consider the subject of representation? Was it not whether there should be representation strictly according to population, or whether there should be a modification of that principle? That was the first operation of the mind in approaching the question—one which no mind could resist. And it was emphatically and pre-eminently a practical question. Had not the Convention to determine whether it would concede the principle of representation according to population, or whether it would settle down upon something else—some modification of that principle? When that principle had once been settled, there would be no trouble. The rest was a matter of calculation and figures. Once settle the principle, and the Convention would have a practical decision which would lead to a certain result. Suppose the Convention decided this resolution negatively. Would they not even then have advanced very considerably towards an adjustment of the question? And was it not much more likely that it would be adjusted at an early day upon some proper, rational and salutary principle of compromise? He earnestly hoped that the Convention would not blink this question, but would come boldly up to it by a direct and solemn vote.

Some conversation followed on a point of order, between Mr. Gwinn and the President, after which—

Mr. Gwinn withdrew his amendment.

Mr. G. asked the House to say, whether, if they should proceed to take a vote on the resolution now pending, they would have settled any principle. He had, in committee, voted that it was inexpedient to regard federal numbers in fixing the basis of representation. With his experience of the state of things in this Convention, he considered that in giving that vote he was in fact voting for a compromise.

But so far as he was concerned, if this resolution should be set aside by the Convention, he should vote for any proposition to place it upon the basis of federal numbers. There was no necessity, as the gentleman from Frederick, (Mr. Thomas,) had said, for taking the question as it now stood, because the Convention would settle nothing by the motion. He, (Mr G.,) was willing that the matter should be recommitted, and that the committee should be discharged, because he was confident that it would never come to any conclusion.

Mr. Blakistone said, he had voted yesterday in favor of the motion to postpone the consideration of this subject, and was anxious that it should be postponed; but the Convention had decided otherwise. He was, therefore, desirous that the sense of the body should be taken upon the resolutions reported by the committee.

Several gentlemen had declared that they were in favor of representation according to population. He desired that the people of the State should understand how they were voting here. The gentleman from Carroll had said the other day, that he was anxious that gentlemen should show their hands. The time, he, (Mr. BLAKISTONE,) thought had come. He was for no dodging. He would tell gentlemen that they should not dodge. The proposition might be voted down, but it should come up in its plain and naked shape, and a vote should be taken upon it. He took it for granted that no gentleman here, was afraid. or ashamed to give his opinion upon the proposition itself. He, for one, was ready to express his. He wanted to record his name, and he desired to see other gentlemen record their's.

It had been intimated by the gentleman from Carroll, that there were some members of this body who were not ready to "toe the mark." Let it be seen who they were. Let every gentleman march up to the vote with a fixed and steady purpose, to let the people of the State of Maryland know who they were, from whence they came, who would go for this abstract proposition of representation according to population. He did not anticipate that any such scenes of excitement as some gentlemen predicted would take place here, or that any member of the body, in the expression and enforcement of the opinions he entertained, would go beyond the limits of propriety. He alluded to this doctrine of representation according to population, as a political hobby which had been ridden to death, and whose death-warrant he desired to see. Gentlemen might ride it at home if they pleased, but it should not be mounted here, or if it was, he, for one, was resolved to see how the gentleman rode, and upon what sort of pony he was mounted.

The people did not know all the reform opinions advocated in this body. He alluded to the various grades of reformers, and the kind of reform which they sustained; but declared that he had never, in his experience, heard a man in the State of Maryland, high or low, broadly advocate before the people, the principle of representation according to population. It had not even been argued here when the reform bill was up, and if it had been, the very statement of the argument would have strangled the offspring in its birth. Let the question be met. He would meet it boldly—even if alone; and if he fell, the greater glory would be his, that he had fallen, not by the hands of pigmies, but of giants.

He amused the Convention for some time by allusions to the strange combinations of the political elements which were manifested in the Convention; and described the animals, (hobbies) upon which some gentlemen were riding and the particular order in which they mounted. He then proceeded to remark, that if gentlemen had come here with a serious intention of making a Constitution, it was time they should go to work in good earnest to do so. Looking to the way in which the Convention was now going on, the people would never get a Constitution on the face of the earth. He spoke of his own constituents as among the purest in the world; and thought, that one of the strongest evidences of the fact was to be found in the steadfastness with which they had always voted for him. (Laughter.)

He desired to say one word to the gentleman from Baltimore city, (Mr. GWINN.) That gentleman had stated that the Committee could not make a report without instructions, and yet he turned around and declared his willingness to vote to recommit without instructions, when it was conceded by him that no report could be obtained. Did gentlemen expect to have a Constitution, when the sure result of attempting to carry out their own extreme views, would be to defeat the formation of any Constitution? He (Mr. B.) did not expect to gain any great degree of credit among the ultra reform members of this Convention, by any vote which he should give. He came here with a fixed determination to make the best Constitution he could, for the whole people of the State. And if he ever spoke an honest word, such was his fixed purpose now. If he could make such a Constitution before the sun went down this evening, he would do so. The time for work had come, and he called upon every member of the Convention to step boldly forward and avow his opinion.

Much had been said in the course of the recent discussions, about corruption in Maryland. Where was its paternity? This reform movement in Maryland was its father—corruption was its design. Before a sacrilegious hand had been laid upon the Constitution which our forefathers made, there was no corruption to be found in any part of the State of Maryland. And where did it now come from? From the office-seekers and their satellites. This was the origin of all the corruption.

Notwithstanding all that had been said of the fraud and corruption existing in the State of Maryland—of which there might be a good deal —he believed there was not a more honorable or chivalrous people on the face of the earth, or a people generally more free from corruptions. He passed a high eulogy upon them.

In conclusion, he appealed to the members of the Convention, whigs and democrats—for he recognized here no party but Marylanders—to come up and vote upon this question. Let there be no higgling—chaffing—or dodging—but let every man vote boldly, aye or no. The people would then have some guarantee, that the Convention intended rapidly and successfully to do the work for which it had assembled.

Mr. DAVIS corrected his friend from St Mary's, (Mr. Blackistone,) who had stated that no person could be found in or out of the Legislature, who had come out, and taken the broad ground in favor of population as a basis of representation. He pointed out his friend from Carroll, (Mr. BROWN,) as having done so, and asked his friend from Frederick, (Mr. BISER,) if he also had not advocated the principle before the Legislature.

Mr. BLAKISTONE replied that he stood corrected if he had been wrong, if his friend from Frederick had advocated that basis.

Mr. BISER said he had avocated it at home and abroad, but was compelled to yield to a modification.

Mr. PHELPS enquired if the gentleman from Frederick had supported that basis for the city of Baltimore, as well as the counties?

Mr. BISER answered, that he had advocated it for the whole State, Baltimore included.

Mr. DAVIS resumed, expressing a wish to do full justice to his friend from Frederick. He felt, as Montgomery was the daughter of Frederick, a strong desire at all times to carry out his feeling of respect and veneration for his maternal ancestor. He had come to her aid in this convention, in endeavoring to obtain a reform of the constitution; nor did he intend to restrict himself to the two questions, as stated by the gentleman for Baltimore—the basis of representation and an elective judiciary. He wished to extend reform beyond these two important principles and to put additional guards round the treasury; and also to put guards and restraints round the commissioner of loans as had been proposed. All these substantial reforms he advocated. He had taken his course from the example of Frederick, and he would go to her again when he wanted further promptings. He referred to a speech made by his friend from Frederick, when in the Legislature several years ago, in which that gentleman had stated that the effect of the establishment of the popular basis, would be to legislate the small counties out of existence. Now, Montgomery, St Mary's and Talbot would scarcely suffer themselves to be legislated out of existence. The gentleman from St Mary's had not gone far enough back when he fixed the origin of the reform excitement. In Baltimore, in 1845, the license law of 1831, was denounced as unjust and oppressive, as well as the appropriation of the auction duties by the Legislature, and the passage of the stamp tax. It was in consequence of the discontents growing out of these measures that the banner of repeal and reform was unfurled together, repeal being coupled with reform. The city of Baltimore complained that she contributed beyond her share to the public treasury, and determined to remove the weight from her own shoulders, and as a necessary consequence it must fall upon the counties. To show that a disinterested gentleman, a citizen of another State, and an officer high in civil station under the United States, had been led to a different conclusion, he read an extract from an address delivered by Mr. E. WHITTLESEY, in Montgomery county, in which he states that the State of Maryland had submitted to many voluntary sacrifices for the benefit of Baltimore and the western country.

Mr. HARBINE called the gentleman to order, which caused a slight interruption.

Mr. DAVIS resumed, stating that his object was to show that Baltimore was not exclusively entitled to a reputation for patriotism as had been claimed for her on this floor. The counties were entitled to a share in this reputation, for they without benefit had submitted to the burden of taxation. To show that the reform question had been agitated in the city of Baltimore at the time he had stated, he referred to a preamble and resolutions adopted by the City Councils, in which the license law, the auction duties, and the stamp tax were denounced as oppressive, and the idea was thrown out that Baltimore was likely to be crushed beneath the weight of these burdens. It was alleged that if she had been properly represented in the Legislature these odious laws would not have passed. If the basis on population should be adopted by the Convention, Baltimore would be able to accomplish all she proposes—repeal as well as reform.

It had been already hinted that the Maryland canal, which Col. Abbot has ascertained by instrumental surveys will cost $11,000,000, will have its termination there, and although you may cut up Baltimore into districts, as many as you please, as has been proposed by the distinguished gentleman from Frederick, (Mr. THOMAS,) whenever any scheme of commercial enterprise is started, you will find party differences obliterated, and her representation united as one man. Every effort would be made to secure and advance the interest of Baltimore, whatever sacrifice it might, as Mr. Whittlesey has shown it has been, to the rest of the State.

Mr. SPENCER moved the previous question, but withdrew it at the request of

Mr. BISER, who said a few words to extricate himself from a false position in which he complained that the gentleman from Montgomery had placed him. The gentleman had asked him if he approved the principle of representation on the basis of population; and when he had answered in the affirmative, the gentleman from Montgomery had quoted from a speech of his (Mr. B's.) in 1845, to prove that he had been guilty of inconsistency. He explained by stating that the quotation was not a fair exposition of his views, as they had relation only to the question then before the House, which led him to show what would be the effect of a mixed basis on different counties. He did not abandon the ground of representation on population, nor would he abandon it now. Nor did he give it up in 1849, but that he thought half a loaf better than no bread. He concluded with renewing the motion for the previous question.

Mr. DAVIS interposed, and said that he stated that the gentleman's calculations had brought him to see that the small counties would be legislated out of existence—and fearing the effect of that result, he added, "I am not to be understood as advocating representation according to population, I am willing to leave that question to a Convention."

The call for the previous question was seconded.

And the main question was ordered to be now taken.

Mr. DORSEY inquired what the main question was.

The PRESIDENT explained that, under the amendment to the rules, it would be on the motion to recommit.

The yeas and nays (which had heretofore been ordered) were taken and resulted as follows:

Affirmative—Messrs. Buchanan, Bell, Welch, Chandler, Lloyd, Dickinson, Colston, Miller, McLane, Spencer, Wright, Thomas, Shriver, Johnson, Gaither, Biser, Annan, Sappington, Stephenson, McHenry, Magraw, Nelson, Hardcastle, Gwinn, Brent of Baltimore city, Presstman, Ware, Brewer, Weber, Hollyday, Slicer, Fitzpatrick, Parke, Shower, and Brown—35.

Negative—Messrs. Chapman, President, Morgan, Blakistone, Dent, Hopewell, Ricaud, Chambers of Kent, Donaldson, Dorsey, Wells, Randall, Sellman, Dalrymple, Bond, Sollers, Brent of Charles, Merrick, Jeifer, John Dennis, James U. Dennis, Crisfield, Dashiell, Williams, Hicks, Hodson, Phelps, Bowie, Tuck, Sprigg, Bowling, McMaster, Fooks, Jacobs, Thawley, Schley, Fiery, John Newcomer, Harbine, Davis, Waters, and Smith—41.

So the motion to reconsider was rejected.

Mr. Spencer then moved to recommit the report to the committee on representation, with instructions to "report a basis of representation in some fair principle of compromise."

Mr. Spencer said, he would make no speech, unless any gentleman should attack his motion. In that case, he should feel himself called on to defend it. He had submitted it, because it appeared to him to be proper, and also, because he believed it would have had the endorsement of a large majority of the Convention.

Mr. Schley was of opinion that this proposition would not at all facilitate the action of the Committee, because it had been represented that the Committee cannot agree upon any report, until the House shall come to a vote on the resolutions. He did not look on these resolutions as mere abstractions. They are intended to evoke an expression of the opinion of the Convention. For instance, if the second resolution be passed, it will be the deliberately expressed opinion of the House, that the popular basis will not be adopted. The gentleman from Queen Anne's now proposes an instruction to the Committee to report the plan of a compromise, but it omits to specify what kind of compromise. Now he, (Mr. S.,) was ready, at once, to vote on the second resolution which had been reported. He was prepared when he came to the Convention; the subject had been well discussed among the people, and he had been instructed by the county of Washington. That county he described as opposed to representation according to population, and that he would prefer the Constitution as it is, to the adoption of that basis. He was not so well prepared to vote on the other resolution; on that he desired the light of a further discussion. But he could not see the propriety of sending the resolutions back to the Committee, when the Committee say that they cannot agree. What did the gentleman from Queen Anne's mean by a fair compromise? Would the adoption of the popular basis in the counties, and restricting the city of Baltimore, to the representation of the largest county, for which he, (Mr. S.,) would be willing to vote, be regarded as such by that gentleman? If the resolutions should be recommitted with this instruction to report a fair compromise, what in the Committee might be regarded as fair, might not be so considered in the House. The Committee certainly *would not* report the popular basis—that point would have been settled.

It had been said that this Convention is doing nothing, idling away its time, and spending the people's money. This was not so, and he repudiated the charge as unworthy of a moment's consideration. The Convention has been, and is busily employed in its laborious and difficult work, and now that these resolutions are before us why should we procrastinate? Why should we delay when there is work before the Convention, as the gentleman from Frederick has given notice that he will not abandon his position without a stern and steady fight. Discussion must take place now or hereafter. He thought it better that it should begin now, and that the Committee should be instructed by a vote of the House. He wished that there should be ample discussion, and he would not stop it by calling for the previous question. He would not shut out a single gentleman, who desired to participate in debate, although the gentleman from Baltimore, (Mr. Brent,) had ridiculed the idea of the whole hundred and three members of the Convention being permitted to take part in the debate. Whilst he would restrict debate within proper limits, he would not deny to any member the exercise of his right to proclaim and enforce his views.

Mr. Brent, of Baltimore city, said that he was for a postponement of the subject of representation, as he had always been, and he still thought that all the constitutional safeguards which were just and proper, should be adjusted before we act upon this, the greatest of all questions.

But he protested against the course of the anti-reformers, who have availed themselves of this occasion to lay down their platforms in advance of the main question; still he hoped the speeches already made by anti-reformers, might be suffered to go before the public for what they were worth, and that the reformers in this body would forbear until the question came up at a proper time on its merits.

He was not willing to discuss the question now although he disclaimed any disposition to gag other gentlemen. In reply to the remarks of the gentleman from Washington Co., (Mr. Schley,) he, (Mr Brent,) would reiterate what he had said before, denying that we were to discuss every question until every member had spoken. He insisted that no true reformer should desire to hear one hundred and three members on every question that might be started, because, at that rate, it would take several years to finish our labors, and such procrastination would effectually kill the present reform movement.

Members must take their chances in securing the floor, and after a reasonable debate has been allowed, it should be stopped by the previous question. Look at the long and protracted debate which has happened on the elective franchise. He meant no disrespect, but for more than a week we had heard very little but a repetition of what had already been said. If this evil was not arrested, he, for one, was prepared to throw up his commission and go home in disgust. He understood reformers to come here from Western Maryland and say, as the gentleman from Washington county, (Mr. SCHLEY,) had said, that they were instructed to claim representation, based on numbers, for themselves, and to deny it to Baltimore city.

Mr. B. could not but regard this as a monstrous proposition, and he, for one, would never sanction it by his vote. Other gentlemen might do as they please, but he would make no compromise on this subject by his votes, which should be given to confer equal rights on all, and if defeated in that object by the votes of western reformers, he would vote to deny them what they denied to Baltimore city. He wished, therefore, to be distinctly understood, he had no compromise in his votes on this subject, but if a compromise be made by the Convention on this subject without his vote, he then reserved the right to look at the new Constitution when completed as *a whole*, and to vote for or against it as his judgment then dictated ; so that while making no compromise himself, he might or might not vote for a new Constitution containing some adjustment of this question, along with other great and salutary reforms, but certainly the rejection of the popular basis would be a great objection to the new Constitution, however liberal the compromise might be.

The gentleman from St. Mary's, (Mr. BLAKISTONE,) had desired the privilege at once to record his vote on representation, and Mr. B. was as ready to register his vote as that gentleman, but he thought that gentleman came here to compare opposing views as well as to record votes.

Mr. BLACKISTONE explained that he came here to aid in making a Constitution. He wished to record his vote on that question and so did others, and he complained that Mr. BRENT did not state all that he had said.

Mr. BRENT replied, that to state all that the gentleman from St. Mary's, (Mr. BLAKISTONE,) had said, would take an hour or more. He, (Mr. B.,) thought they had higher duties to perform here than merely voting. He desired an interchange of views, that if they failed to establish right and justice here, the seed sown in this hall should germinate broad-cast through the State. In conclusion, he hoped that as the subject of the elective franchise was fixed for Monday, we should postpone the matter of representation until after we had completed that subject. Let us, not begin this important discussion for two or three days and then leave it incomplete to retrace our steps to other unfinished business. Let us when we begin it, devote all our time and efforts to its demands.

Mr. SPENCER briefly defend his proposition against the attacks which had been made upon it. The committee had asked of the Convention to adopt their first resolution, declaring it inexpedient to establish federal numbers as a basis of representation ; and also their second resolution declaring it inexpedient to adopt the popular basis. If the Convention should pass these two resolutions, the committee will necessarily be driven back on a compromise. For this reason he thought his proposition ought to be adopted. There was another reason for the adoption of the amendment On one side it was contended that popular numbers should be wholly disregarded; and on the other, that they constituted the true basis of representation. It was clear, from the indications around us, that neither extreme would succeed.

A compromise would be necessary. This question then would have to go to the committee to be settled on a principle of compromise. He saw no good which could rise out of the discussion now. One part of the State was opposed to the popular basis, while another part was in favor of it. How then, in this state of things, could the question be forced on the House? The member from Baltimore city, had admitted that popular numbers was his own choice, but that he would be willing to yield his preference, in a spirit of compromise. He was gratified that the gentleman from Baltimore took that ground. He stated, that by the adoption of his amendment, the Convention would, by their vote, say that the question ought to be compromised. He had no fear of any excitement. He saw round him familiar faces, and he could not be apprehensive of any danger. But if any gentlemen feel any apprehension of this kind, he would ask them to vote for his amendment, and thus give evidence that they were desirous to have a compromise. He was willing to go for a liberal compromise, as regards the city of Baltimore.

Mr. JENIFER was in favor of immediate action on the subject He had, at one time, been disposed to postpone the subject, and had voted for postponement. But times had changed since that vote was given ; reports had been made; the subject had been fully considered, and all were now ready to vote. For what purpose should the subject be sent back to the committee, when it has been told the House that the committee cannot agree. It would be the better course to vote at once on the question, and determine whether the Convention will take population as the basis of representation, and, that question decided, the House will have advanced a step. Without action of this kind, on the part of the House, the committee cannot be brought to an agreement ; but let either, or both of these resolutions pass, and there will be a ground established on which the committee can act.

Mr. PRESSTMAN, of Baltimore city, said, he rose to offer an amendment, in order to hinder the call of the previous question, on the resolution from the Committee, which he anticipated was about being made by the gentleman from Kent, (Mr. RICAUD,) and at the same time, in a few remarks, to indicate a spirit of compromise upon this vexed question of representation.

He read the following amendment :

"That the committee on Representation and Apportionment be requested to report a plan of apportionment and representation, making numbers the basis of representation to the House of Delegates, and of mixed basis of population and territory as for representation in the Senate."

He would be willing to meet all true reformers at a point short of representation according to numbers and was willing still further to modify his proposition should any suggestion be made by any one in whose attachment to the cause of reform he had confidence. Before proceeding to a discussion of the amendment, he desired to comment upon the course adopted by the committee in presenting an abstract proposition, and endeavoring to force the House to a vote which when taken, could not in the nature of the case accomplish any practical result. He emphatically denied the right of the Committee, to submit such a resolution, under the terms of the order originally submitted by himself and amended by the distinguished gentleman from Queen Anne's, (Mr. Grason,) requiring the Committee to report by articles. He protested against the right of the Committee to shield any one or more of its members from the responsibility of a report until a decision should be first had upon such interrogatories, as they chose to submit to the Convention. The chief, if not sole object of the formation of Committees, is to expedite the business of the Convention by proposing plans for the adoption or rejection of that body. This was the only Committee which had taken a different course. They seem to think that the task of perfecting a plan was committed to them. Not so. Their usefulness would be better exemplified by bringing forward their plans that the Convention might shape them to meet the views of a majority. If there were no two of them who could agree, let each member report separately as had been done in New York and other State Conventions. He did not charge it as a motive with the Committee, but the resolution seemed to invite a spirit of partyism, an arraignment of county prejudices—the smaller against the larger, and both against the city of Baltimore. So much, sir, as to my objections to the course of the Committee. Let us look to the resolution itself, and its merits. Are gentlemen called upon to commit themselves upon isolated propositions before they had surveyed the whole ground? For himself, he never meant to contend under all circumstances for the principle of representation according to numbers, as a *sine qua non* to be inserted in the new Constitution. He was free to confess, that when he came to the Convention he did not expect to find the opponents of that principle, willing to yield every thing on that point.

The act itself under which this Convention was called, when it fixed the basis of representation in this body, was a virtual acknowledgement that the Constitution was to be a work of compromise. If not, why place us here a minority of Delegates representing an overwhelming majority of the people, "to be laughed to scorn," when setting up such pretensions. He avowed himself unwilling to support a Constitution, however acceptable in other respects, unless much was yielded on the basis of representation. The present basis is in derrogation of the equal rights of American citizens. Let all true reformers unite and fashion a Constitution, which, like the great federal compact of the Union, shall contain compromises to protect the weak, and do justice to the great majority principle which should lie at the foundation, as a corner stone, of all representative government. He desired to say a few words to his friends from Somerset, (Mr. Dashiell,) and St. Mary's (Mr. Blakistone,) who appear to regard the proposition he had the honor to submit, in relation to a constitutional guarranty upon the subject of slavery, as a sort of Trojan horse.

The gentleman from St. Mary's was fond of speaking of hobbies—*de gustibus non est disputandum.* If he had jostled the hobby (slavery) on which he so gracefully rides, he must beg pardon. In seriousness, sir, that proposition was but one of a series of constitutional guaranties he designed to propose to insure greater confidence in those who represented minority interests, and thereby lead to an honorable adjustment of the question of representation. He announced that he would not pertinaciously adhere to the principle of representation according to population, and he believed the constituency he had the honor to represent in part, would hold any one of their delegates to strict accountability, if by any extreme demands, the Constitution itself was to be defeated. There is a path of duty to be trod within these walls, in which a consciousness of honest motive, and a confidence not feigned but real, in the virtue and intelligence of the people can alone support us. That path is not a hidden one, it is to be reached not by windings, but by the avoidance of extremes. Practical men look anxiously to a radical reform in all the departments of the government. It is in no martyr's spirit, that he avowed himself in favor of a fair and liberal compromise; he expected the cordial support of his constituency, who were a chivalrous and high-toned people, who did not expect their delegates to accomplish impossibilities. The gentleman from St. Mary's had again and again called upon members to show their hands upon the question of popular representation; to use his own language, to "toe the mark."

Why, Mr. President, what does this all amount to? Does it require any peculiar strength of nerve for a gentleman from a small county to cry out lustily against numerical representation? Far from it; to do otherwise might require a high degree of moral courage. Or, what merit should he claim as a representative in part, of one hundred and seventy thousand souls, "to toe the mark," upon the extremest line of popular representation. Let us, sir, act as becomes Marylanders, freed from sectional prejudices and having a single eye to the public good.

Mr. Hicks asked for some information from the chair. Was it competent to offer a substitute to the pending amendment?

The chair replied in the negative, two amendments being now pending.

Mr. Hicks then read a proposition which he intended to offer when he could get the opportunity.

Mr. MERRICK expressed surprise at the reluctance of the House to come to a direct vote. He had not expected that any opposition would have risen, or he would not have reported these resolutions. He was astonished when some gentlemen say they were not prepared to vote. He felt apprehensive that there was something behind, which he was unable to comprehend. It was the desire of the committee that the House should say if they would adopt either of the basis in the resolutions. He believed that every gentleman was prepared to give his vote; that the opinions of all were made up on the subject before they came to the Convention;—and all that the committee asked was that this opinion should be expressed by the House. He did not believe any gentleman on this floor was influenced by fear. It was necessary that the House should agree as to the basis, and having settled this great controling principle, the committee would be able to agree on a report. Then the subsequent action of the House also would be rendered easy. It will become a mere matter of figures if numbers should be decided on, and if not, it would be a plan of compromise. The settlement of the question by the Convention would also have the effect of settling public opinion on this subject.

Mr. TUCK. I call for a division on the amendment. It is nothing more nor less than an affirmation of that which the committee have called upon us to deny.

Mr. PRESSTMAN suggested that his amendment was not susceptible of division. It would be seen that it required the population basis in the House, and a mixed basis in the Senate. The two basis were embraced in one proposition, in order that they might not be separated. He wished to have the sense of the House on the basis of population in the House of Representatives, and of territory and population in the Senate, and he thought the two propositions could not be divided. He would withdraw his amendment.

The PRESIDENT (in reply to the enquiry of Mr. PRESSTMAN) stated that the amendment offered by him, (Mr. P.,) was divisable.

Mr. PRESSTMAN. Then I withdraw it.

Mr. BLAKISTONE. I then offer the first part of that amendment as my own proposition.

The amendment was as follows:

"That the committee on representation and apportionment be requested to report a plan of apportionment and representation, making numbers the basis of representation to the House of Delegates."

Mr. CHAMBERS, of Kent. I suggest to the gentleman (Mr. BLAKISTONE) to modify the proposition so far as to introduce the word "exclusively."

Mr. BLAKISTONE modified the amendment accordingly, and demanded the previous question.

Mr. JOHNSON called for the reading of the amendment, which was again read.

Some conversation followed on a point of order.

Mr. BROWN enquired of the PRESIDENT what would be the question if the previous question was sustained?

The PRESIDENT said that under the rule as amended, the question would be simply on the amendment of the gentleman from St. Mary's, (Mr. BLAKISTONE.)

The question was taken, and by ayes 41, noes 34, the previous question was seconded. And the main question was ordered to be now taken.

Mr. SPENCER asked the yeas and nays on the amendment, which were ordered.

Mr. BRENT, of Baltimore city. I move that the Convention now adjourn.

Mr. GWINN. I ask the yeas and nays.

Mr. BOWIE. I rise to a point of order. Is it in order for any gentleman to move an adjournment when the Chair is in the act of putting a question?

The PRESIDENT. The Chair had put the question.

Mr. BOWIE. The yeas and nays have been ordered.

The PRESIDENT. Yes, but the Secretary had not commenced calling the roll. The motion to adjourn is a privileged motion, and may be made at any time except when the Convention is in the act of dividing or of taking a question.

The question then recurred on ordering the yeas and nays on the motion to adjourn.

The yeas and nays, the PRESIDENT said, were refused.

Mr. BRENT. There are two more up.

The PRESIDENT. It is too late.

The question was then taken, and the House refused to adjourn.

The question then recurred and was taken on the amendment of Mr. BLAKISTONE, and was decided in the negative, as folllows:

Affirmative.—Messrs. Buchanan, Bell, Welch, Thomas, Shriver, Johnson, Gaither, Biser, Annan, McHenry, Gwinn, Brent, of Baltimore city, Presstman, Ware, Parke, Shower and Brown—17.

Negative.—Messrs. Chapman, President, Morgan, Blakistone, Dent, Hopewell, Ricaud, Chambers, of Kent, Donaldson, Dorsey, Wells, Randall, Sellman, Dalrymple, Bond, Sollers, Brent, of Charles, Merrick, Jenifer, Ridgely, Lloyd, Dickinson, Colston, John Dennis, James U. Dennis, Crisfield, Dashiell, Williams, Hicks, Hodson, Phelps, Miller, McLane, Bowie, Tuck, Sprigg, Bowling, Spencer, Wright, McMaster, Hearn, Fooks, Jacobs, Sappington, Stephenson, Nelson, Thawley, Hardcastle, Schley, Fiery, John Newcomer, Harbine, Davis, Brewer, Waters, Weber, Hollyday, Slicer, Fitzpatrick, Smith, and Cockey—60.

So the amendment was rejected; and, thereupon the Convention adjourned.

SATURDAY, January 25, 1851.

The Convention met at eleven o'clock.

Prayer was made by the Rev. Mr. GRIFFITH.

The roll was called, and a quorum was present.

The Secretary read the journal in part, when, on motion of Mr. WRIGHT, the further reading was dispensed with.

The President announced the regular order of business to be the call of the committee for reports.

THE LEGISLATIVE DEPARTMENT.

Mr. JOHNSON (Chairman of the committee on the Legislative Department) said, he was instructed by that committee to make a report.

The committee (Mr. J. said) had given as much time as could well be spared to the consideration of the subject matter of this report. They had found some difficulty in defining the line where their appropriate duties began and ended. So multifarious had been the matters referred to them by the Convention—some belonging to the committee on the Legislative Department, and some to other committees—that it had not been an easy task to escape encroachment upon the prerogative of other committees. So far as was possible, however, they had done so.

In the report now presented, the committee had embodied many suggestions drawn from the references made to them by the Convention, but had not made a special report upon each special reference. He presented it as a report in part, inasmuch as there were one or two subjects which had not yet been acted upon, and upon which a report would be made when the action of the committee had been matured upon them. And each member of the committee, so far from being considered as committed to the report, would feel himself privileged to offer any amendments which he might think proper at any time in the course of the discussion. Many such amendments would no doubt be offered—the common desire of all gentlemen being to perfect the Legislative Department so far as practicable. Mr. J. then presented the following

REPORT:

Section 1st. The Legislative power of this State shall be vested in two distinct branches, the one to be styled the Senate, the other the House of Delegates, and both together "the General Assembly of Maryland."

Sec. 2d. The Senators shall be elected by the qualified voters, for the term of four years, and the Delegates for the term of   from the day of the general elections.

Sec. 3d. The first election for Senators and Delegates shall take place on the first Wednesday of October eighteen hundred and fifty-one, and on the same day in every second year forever thereafter the general elections for Delegates; and for one-half of the Senators as nearly as practicable, shall be held.

Sec. 4th. Immediately after the Senate shall have convened after the first election under this Constitution, the Senators shall be divided by lot into two classes as nearly equal in number as may be, the Senators of the first class shall go out of office at the expiration of two years, and Senators shall be elected on the first Wednesday of October eighteen hundred and fifty-three, for the term of four years, to supply their places; so that, after the first election one-half of the Senators may be chosen every second year. In case the number of Senators be hereafter increased, such classification of the additional Senators shall be made as to preserve as nearly as may be, an equal number in each class.

Sec. 5th. The General Assembly shall meet on the first Wednesday of January eighteen hundred and fifty-two, and on the same day in every   year forever thereafter, and at no other time unless convened by the proclamation of the Governor, who shall have power to convene the same whenever he may deem it expedient and proper.

Sec. 6th. The General Assembly may continue their first two sessions after the adoption of this Constitution as long as in the opinion of the two Houses, the public interest may require it, but all subsequent regular sessions of the General Assembly shall be closed on the tenth day of March next ensuing the time of their commencement, unless the same shall be closed at an earlier day by the agreement of the two Houses.

Sec. 7th. No person shall be eligible as a Senator or Delegate who, at the time of his election, is not a citizen of the United States, and who has not resided at least three years next preceding the day of his election in the State, and the last year thereof in the   which he may be chosen to represent, if such   shall have been so long established, and if not, then in the county from which in whole or in part, the same may have been formed; nor shall any person be eligible as a Senator unless he shall have also attained the age of   years, nor as a Delegate unless he shall have attained the age of twenty-one years at the time of his election.

Sec. 8th. No member of Congress, or person holding any Civil or Military office under the United States, shall be eligible to a seat in the General Assembly, and if any person shall after his election as a member of either House of the General Assembly, be elected to Congress or be appointed to any office, Civil or Military, under the government of the United States, his acceptance thereof shall vacate his seat.

Sec. 9th. No Priest, Clergyman or Teacher of any religious persuasion, society or sect, and no person holding any civil office of profit under this State, except Justices of the Peace, shall be capable of having a seat in the General Assembly.

Sec. 10. Every Senator and Delegate before he acts as such, shall take and subscribe the following oath or affirmation, viz: "I do solemnly swear, (or affirm as the case may be,) that I will support the Constitution of the United States, and the Constitution of the State of Maryland, and that I will faithfully discharge my duties as Senator, (or Delegate as the case may be,) without prejudice or partiality, and to the best of my ability."

Sec. 11th. The Senate, upon assembling, shall choose a President and its other officers, and the House of Delegates when assembled shall choose a Speaker and its other officers—each House shall be judge of the qualifications, elections and returns of its members, but a contested election shall be determined in such manner as shall be directed by law.

Sec. 12th. A majority of each House shall constitute a quorum for the transaction of business, but a smaller number may adjourn from day to day, and may compel the attendance of absent members in such manner and under such penalties as each House may prescribe.

Sec. 13th. The doors of each House and of committees of the whole shall be open, except when the business is such as ought to be kept secret.

Sec. 14th. Each House shall keep a Journal of its proceedings and cause the same to be published—the yeas and nays of the members on any question shall, at the desire of any five of them, be entered on the journal.

Sec. 15th. Neither House shall, without the consent of the other, adjourn for more than three days, nor to any other place than that in which the houses shall be sitting, without the concurrent vote of two-thirds of the members present of both Houses.

Sec. 16th. The enacting clause of every bill shall be, "Be it enacted by the General Assembly of Maryland," and no law shall be enacted except by Bill.

Sec. 17th. Any bill may originate in either house of the General Assembly, and be altered, amended or rejected by the other, but no Bill shall have the force of a law until it be read on three different days in each House, unless in case of urgency three-fourths of the House, where such bill is depending, shall dispense with this rule.

Sec. 18th. No Bill shall become a law unless passed in each House by a majority of the whole number of members elected, and on the question of its final passage the ayes and noes shall be recorded.

Sec. 19th. No money shall be drawn from the Treasury of this State but in consequence of appropriations made by law, an accurate statement of the receipts and expenditure of public money shall be attached to and published with the laws after each regular session of the General Assembly.

Sec. 20th. No divorce shall be granted by the General Assembly, nor any tax or other burden be levied on the persons or property of the people, for the support of any religious sect or denomination.

Sec. 21st. No loans shall be made upon the credit of this State which are not redeemable at the pleasure of the State: except such as may be authorized by an act of Assembly, passed at one session and ratified and confirmed at the next succeeding regular session of the General Assembly.

Sec. 22nd. No extra compensation shall be granted or allowed by the General Assembly to any public officer, agent, servant or contractor after the services shall have been rendered, or the contract entered into, nor shall the salary or compensation of any public officer be increased or diminished during his term of office.

Sec. 23rd. No county now established by law, shall ever be reduced by the establishment of any new county, to a population of less than thousands, nor shall any new county be hereafter established with a population of less than thousand.

Sec. 24th. No senator or delegate shall during the term for which he shall have been elected, be appointed to any civil office in this State, which shall have been created, or the salary or emoluments of which shall have been increased during such term: and no senator or delegate during the time he shall continue to act as such, shall be eligible to any civil office.

Sec. 25th. Each House may determine the rules of its own proceedings, punish a member for disorderly or disrespectful behavior, and with the consent of two-thirds expel a member; but no member shall be expelled a second time for the same offence.

Sec. 26th. Each House may punish by imprisonment during the session of the General Assembly, any person not a member, for disrespectful or disorderly behavior in its presence, or for obstructing any of its proceedings, or any of its officers, in the execution of their duties; provided, such imprisonment shall not at any one time exceed ten days.

Sec. 27th. The members of each House shall in all cases, except treason, felony or breach of the peace, be privileged from arrest during their attendance at the sessions of the General Assembly, and in going to and returning from the same, allowing one day for every thirty miles such member may reside from the place at which the General Assembly is convened.

Sec. 28th. No senator or delegate shall be liable in any civil action or criminal prosecution, whatever, for words spoken in debate.

Sec. 29th. The House of Delegates may inquire on the oath of witnesses into all complaints, grievances and offences, as the grand inquest of the State, and may commit any person for any crime to the public jail, there to remain until discharged by due course of law—they may examine and pass all accounts of the State relating either to the collection or expenditure of the revenue, or appoint auditors to state and adjust the same,—they may call for all public or official papers and records, and send for persons whom they may judge necessary in the course of their enquiries concerning affairs relating to the public interest, and may direct all office bonds, which shall be made payable to the State, to be sued for any breach of duty.

Sec. 30th. In case of the death, disqualification, refusal to act, expulsion or removal from the county or district for which he shall have been elected, if any person shall have been chosen as a Delegate or Senator, or in case of a tie between two or more qualified persons, a warrant of election shall be issued by the Governor, or person exercising the functions of Governor for the time being, for the election of a Senator or Delegate as the case may be, to supply the vacancy, of which not less than ten days notice, exclusive of the day of notice and day of election shall be given; provided, however, that unless a meeting of the General Assembly may intervene, or the vacancy shall occur during the session of the General Assembly, the election to fill the same shall take place on the day of the ensuing general election.

Sec 31st. The senators and delegates shall receive such compensation for their services as may be allowed by law; but no law increasing or diminishing the compensation shall be made to take effect until after the general elections next ensuing the passage thereof. No book or other printed matter not appertaining to the business of the session, shall be subscribed for, for the use of the members, or be distributed among them.

Sec. 32nd. No law passed by the General Assembly shall take effect until the expiration of days, from the closing of the sessions at which it may be passed, unless it be expressly declared on the face of the law, that it shall take effect on or after a different day; and no law of a public nature shall take effect until the same shall be published.

Sec. 33rd. The General Assembly shall have full power to exclude from the privilege of voting at elections, or of being elected to either House, or of being elected or appointed to any civil or military office in this State, any person convicted of perjury, bribery, or other infamous crime.

Sec. 34th. The General Assembly may confer upon of the several counties such powers of local legislation and administration as they may prescribe, provided however, that all laws conferring such powers shall be general in their nature, and shall extend to all the counties of the State.

Sec. 35th. Every bill passed by the General Assembly, when engrossed, shall be presented by the Speaker of the House of Delegates, in the Senate chamber, to the Governor for the time being, who shall sign the same, and thereto affix the great seal in the presence of the members of both Houses; every law shall be recorded in the office of the court of Appeals of the Western Shore, and in due time be printed, published and certified under the great seal to the several county courts in the same manner as has been heretofore usual in this State.

Sec. 36th. No person who may hereafter be a collector, receiver or holder of public moneys, shall have a seat in either House of the General Assembly or be eligible to any office of profit or trust under this State until he shall have accounted for and paid into the Treasury all sums for which he may be liable.

Sec. 37th. All laws and parts of laws not inconsistent with this constitution, shall continue in force according to their respective provisions, subject nevertheless to be altered, amended or repealed by the General Assembly.

MASTER AND SLAVE.

Mr. Jenifer rose, he said, to make a report from Committee No. 14, (being the Committee to consider and report such provisions proper to be embodied in a Constitution for the State, as had not been embraced in resolutions referred to other Committees.)

He was not in his seat yesterday, at the time the gentleman from Baltimore city, (Mr. Presstman,) offered a resolution in the following words:

"*Resolved*, That the Legislature shall not pass any law to abolish the relation of master and slave, as it now exists in this State, and that the Committee on the Legislative Department be instructed to report an article to carry out this provision."

I take it for granted [continued Mr. J.] that my friend from Baltimore city was not aware of the fact, that a similar resolution which I will now read, was offered by myself some time since, and referred to the Committee No. 14. It is in these words:

"*Resolved*, That Committee No. 14, consider and report upon the expediency of engrafting in the new Constitution, the same or a similar article as is contained in the present Constitution, respecting the relation of master and slave." [See Journal, Dec. 16, page 173.]

Mr. Presstman. Mine was an entirely different proposition

Mr. Jenifer (apparently not hearing the interruption) proceeded to say, that the Committee had had the subject under consideration, and had instructed him to make a report.

Mr. J. presented the following report:

"The relation of master and slave in this State shall not be abolished, unless a bill to abolish the same, shall be passed by a unanimous vote of the members of each branch of the General Assembly, and shall be published at least three months before a new election of Delegates, and shall be confirmed by a unanimous vote of the members of each branch of the General Assembly, at the next regular constitutional session, after such new election, nor then without full compensation to the master for the property of which he shall be thereby deprived."

Mr. Presstman explained, that the subject matter had, in the first place, been referred to the Committee on the Legislative Department and had subsequently, on the gentleman's own motion, been sent to the Committee of which the gentleman himself was Chairman, and, besides that, the resolution which he, [Mr. Presstman,] had yesterday introduced, was not similar either in principle or phraseology to the order which the gentleman had read. His [Mr. P's.] resolution did not propose to engraft upon the new Constitution a provision similar to that which now existed, but went a great deal further and declared that there should be no alteration by the Legislative Department in the relation of master and slave.

Some conversation passed between Mr. Jenifer and Mr. Presstman, of which the Reporter [having been interrupted] knows nothing.

On motion of Mr. Jenifer, the report was made the order of the day for Monday the third day of February.

BOARD OF PUBLIC WORKS.

Mr. Jenifer also referred to the resolution which had yesterday been adopted on motion of Mr. Merrick, directing Committee No. 14, to enquire into the expediency of providing in the Constitution for a Board of Public Works.

He [Mr. J.] was not in his seat when the resolution was offered. He understood that the gentleman from Cecil, [Mr. McLane,] had stated that an order on the same subject had heretofore been passed. He, [Mr. J.] desired now to state, in justice to the gentleman from Alleghany, [Mr. Fitzpatrick,] that the Committee were prepared to make a report. But in view of the order adopted yesterday, it might be proper that the Committee should again be called together, before any report on the subject was presented.

Mr. Williams offered the following resolution, which was adopted:

"That the President of this Convention request the Treasurer of State to furnish each of the members of the Convention with a copy of his Annual Report."

Mr. Parke gave notice of certain amendments which he intended at the proper time to offer to the Bill or Rights.

Mr. Chambers, of Kent, offered the following resolution:

"That the committee No. 3, inquire into the expediency of prohibiting the passage of any law imposing a tax on money or debts due and owing by persons out of the State to persons residing in this State."

Mr. Chambers said that, in presenting this resolution, he was not to be understood as doing more than obeying what he conceived to be some sort of a duty in desiring to give every one an opportunity to be heard, and evincing towards his correspondent a disposition to extend to him any courtesy which he reasonably could. He (Mr. C.) disclaimed for herself any purpose to interfere with any existing tax laws designed to relieve the State from her incumbrances. It was proper, however, that the proposition should be referred, in order that, if there was any merit in it, it might be discussed and decided.

INDEXES.

The President announced the unfinished business of the morning hour to be the following resolutions submitted yesterday by Mr. Tuck:

"*Resolved*, That the Committee on Printing be authorized to have a suitable index made to the Journal of Proceedings, and also to the Debates of the Convention.

Mr. Thawley offered an amendment, providing that the printing of the extra copies of the Journal should be discontinued, and that the money which would have been directed to that object, should be applied towards the payment for the Indexes.

The President thought the amendment not germane to the resolution, and suggested to the gentleman from Caroline, (Mr. Thawley,) to withdraw it for the present, and to offer it again when the pending question should have been disposed of.

Mr. Thawley, with that purpose, withdrew his amendment.

The question then recurred on the original resolution.

A brief and desultory discussion followed, in which Messrs. Tuck, Brown, Hicks, Weber, and Presstman, took part.

A division of the question was called for and ordered; first, on ordering an Index to the Journal, and then of the Debates.

The question was taken, and both branches of the resolution were adopted.

Mr. Thawley now renewed his proposition in the following words:

"Ordered, That the order adopted some weeks past, authorizing the printing of four extra journals for each member of this Convention be rescinded."

Mr. T. asked the yeas and nays on his resolution, which were ordered.

Some further discussion followed, in which Messrs. Phelps, Ridgely, Spencer, Brown, Buchanan, Ricaud, Tuck, Randall and Hicks, took part;

When Mr. Spencer, in order to give an opportunity to the Chairman of the committee on printing, to make an explanation, moved that the resolution be laid upon the table for the present.

Pending the question,

The President announced that the hour had arrived for taking up the order of the day.

Mr. Bowie moved to postpone the consideration of the order of the day, that the Convention might dispose of the pending resolution.

The question having been taken, the Convention decided that the order of the day should not be postponed.

The President, by general consent, laid before the Convention a report from the Treasurer of this State, in obedience to the order of the Convention of the 2nd ultimo; which was read and ordered to be printed.

The Convention then passed to the order of the day.

SUFFOCATION BY GAS.

Mr. Brent, of Baltimore city, by general consent, called the attention of the Convention to the deleterious effects produced upon the health of the members, (many of whom were complaining,) by the gas that escaped from the furnace, by which the Hall was heated, and hoped that some step would be taken to remedy the evil. There must, he suggested, be a defect in the furnace.

The President. The gentleman had better suggest some course of proceeding.

Mr. Brent. Well—I move the appointment of a Committee.

Mr. Morgan. A Committee on Gas! (Laughter.)

Mr. Brent. A Committee on Gas.

The President. To be composed of three members?

Mr. Brent. That will do.

The committee was accordingly ordered to be appointed, and the following gentlemen compose it:

Messrs. BRENT, of Baltimore city, RANDALL, and SAPPINGTON.

BASIS OF REPRESENTATION.

The Convention thereupon resumed the consideration of the resolutions reported by Mr. MERRICK, from the committee on representation.

The pending question was on the motion of Mr. SPENCER, to recommit the report to the committee on representation, with instructions to report a basis of representation on some fair principle of compromise.

Mr. CHAMBERS, of Kent, enquired of the President, whether it would now be in order to move an amendment.

The PRESIDENT replied in the affirmative.

Mr. CHAMBERS. Then I move the following amendment:

"In such manner that the city of Baltimore shall be entitled to the same number of representatives in the House of Delegates, as may be allowed to the largest county in the State."

I have no desire, (remarked Mr. C.,) to discuss this question at the present time, but I hope that it will be left open to discussion, and that the previous question will not be called; so that if gentlemen desire to discuss it, they may have the opportunity to do so.

Mr. THOMAS said, he would make a last effort upon this point, as to the mode of proceeding, which should be adopted. He entered his protest against permitting one particular committee to depart in any way from the rule prescribed by the Convention for the government of all its committees.

Mr. THOMAS stated that the committee on Representation had departed from its proper course. For several long, tedious weeks, the Convention had had no report of a practical character before them, nothing but these abstract resolutions. And if the Convention were about to go into the discussion of them, long, tedious weeks might again be wasted without reaching any result. He objected to the way in which the members of the Judiciary came in, for the purpose of feeling their way by offering amendment after amendment, until they could shape the resolution to their wishes. Had the Legislative committee, of which his colleague was a member, pursued a similar course, a great deal of time would have been lost in settling negative propositions, which, ingeniously introduced, necessarily lead to new discussions. The clear-headed gentleman from Queen Annes, (Mr. GRASON,) had introduced a rule, which was adopted by the Convention, restricting the reports of the committees to mere results. The object of this rule was to expedite the work. He illustrated the evil which would result from adopting the course proposed by this amendment. The Convention would make little progress; amendments would be offered, and the representation of a single county would occupy one day, and another would consume the next day, and so the Convention would go on. He wished the Committee to execute the order of the Convention. He replied to the remark of the gentleman from Kent, (Mr. CHAMBERS,) that the responsibility of making the report rested on him, and that the Convention was not bound by it, by reminding that gentleman of the practice of the Senate and House of Representatives of the United States, where the Chairman of a committee makes an elaborate report, which he has prepared on his own responsibility, while every individual member of the committee may rise in his place and make any objections in the form of explanation. If the gentleman from Kent was permitted to hold the Convention, until he could produce the effect he desired by the propositions he offered, he, [Mr. T.] might be compelled, in consequence of the introduction of matter, which, in his opinion, was objectionable, to vote against the Constitution altogether, when the Convention closed their work. He might refuse to receive the little good which was mixed up with so much evil. What then was the use of keeping these propositions back in the committee? Let them be brought before the House.

He adverted to the various propositions now before the House, and asked what real progress would have been made, if any of them were adopted. He desired that the Committee should come in with a report, and that every member of it, who objected to it, should state what those objections were. With a report from the committee in a proper form, the House would have something to act on.

Mr. THOMAS moved the previous question, but,

The PRESIDENT having stated that, under the amendment recently adopted to the rules, the previous question would operate not on the motion to commit but on the amendment of Mr. CHAMBERS.

Mr. T. disclaiming any intention to cut off debate on the amendment, withdrew the demand for the previous question.

Mr. GWINN accorded with the views thrown out by the gentleman from Frederick, and expressed his hope that the senior member of the Committee would make a report, and that any member of the Committee would be permitted to rise and explain his objections. He believed that was the course approved by a majority of the Committee, several of whom were now absent. He thought the proposition of the gentleman from Kent was of an uncertain character. That gentleman had denominated his (Mr. G's) proposition an abstraction, but would the amendment offered by the gentleman himself, lead to a practical result? He was yet unable to perceive the trap which was contrived by the amendments. The object, evidently, was to produce combinations among the counties, the effect of which would act injuriously on the prospects of Baltimore in the State. Long experience had made the gentleman from Kent a great tactician, but ingenious as he was in his movements, the object of the present amendment was very palpable. He believed that if the report was now recommitted, there would be a speedy report. Some of the members are indeed away, but they would be back on Monday morning, and he thought they could come to an agreement.

Mr. McLANE, without intending to enter into

the discussion, desired to present a view of the subject which might have the effect of arresting the course of proceeding. When the motion was made to postpone these resolutions, he had voted in the affirmative, on two grounds: first, that it was not a final report of the committee which should be considered and discussed in committee of the whole; the other ground was, that it was intended by the committee as an application for instructions, without which the committee could not agree on any report. In this view of the subject he considered that to take up the resolutions would have led to great embarrassment, and might have established a precedent which might have led to greater difficulties. It might frequently occur that a committee might find itself in difficulty, and if allowed to come in and ask for instructions, it would lead to discussion of the subject. Suppose the instructions are given, and the committee report in conformity with them, the House is not concluded by its previous action from giving a different vote when that report shall have been considered.

The whole question comes up again, the House may be plunged into a controversy, and angry feelings might lead to an angry debate. He was ready to adopt the opinion of the gentleman from Kent, that we should come to a compromise of views. It was clear that neither of the extreme principles could prevail. It would be inexpedient now to go into the discussion of the subject. He had voted against the postponement of the resolutions on this ground. What did the committee ask? The committee came here, in the first instance, unable to agree in a report of any plan, because they could not unite in deciding upon an important principle lying at the foundation, and they asked for instructions from the House. They have told us that they cannot get a majority to agree. He wished, therefore, that when the House should go into the discussion of this fundamental principle, instead of deciding it for the instruction of the Committee, it should finally decide it for the House. This might not suit the committee. It had been said by the gentleman from Kent, that if the House come to a vote on the resolutions, the committee would report immediately.

Mr. CHAMBERS explained. He had said they would be unabled to make a report if they had the sanction of the House.

Mr. McLANE replied, that the question had been decided by a vote of 60 to 17.

Mr. CHAMBERS did not consider that vote an exponent of the ultimate decision of the House.

Mr. THOMAS enquired whether when he had voted on a proposition, he was not bound by that vote.

Mr. CHAMBERS explained that a gentleman might give a vote in accordance with his present views, and might then move a reconsideration of the vote. His vote simply expressed his opinion according to the view he took at the time.

Mr. THOMAS replied, that he wished to act here not as a Baltimorean, nor for the counties alone, but as a Marylander, looking at the interests of the whole State. He desired to see these county divisions cut up by the roots; and to establish districts of contiguous territory, and to sub-divide Frederick and the largest counties, as to give equality to all. He desired to put an end to all these contests which were mere questions of the distribution of political power.

Mr. CHAMBERS. And of offices.

Mr. THOMAS granted that. But he desired that the same principle should apply in Baltimore and in Talbot county. He did not wish that Baltimore should have a representation too disproportionate to Talbot, or give Talbot a power below what she ought to have. He disavowed acting for any party, or for the policy of the hour, but so that he might see the State prosperous during the residue of his days. From his present position, he could not take any report likely to emanate from the Committee without amendment.

Mr. McLANE did not wish to interfere in this dispute—*non nostrum tantas componere lites.* It had been his wish to restrict discussion, instead of which he had provoked it. He insisted that the question had been decided, so far as regards the popular basis. The gentleman from Kent he could not permit to be the exponent of his [Mr. McL's] opinions. Notwithstanding the decision of the House, when the report of the Committee comes in, the subject would be as open to discussion as it was before.

What was the proposition now brought forward? Emanating from the head of the committee it brought up the discussion on one of the most difficult points in controversy. He could not coincide in the propriety of this course. Instead of deciding what should be the delegation of Baltimore, and then sending the subject to the Committee, he would prefer to re-commit the whole matter, if the Convention could make an immediate report. If gentlemen did not approve of that course, let the House go into Committee of the whole on the resolutions, when amendments could be offered. The admission of the present amendment would lead to the introduction of numerous others, and all should be offered in Committee, not to the House. He did not believe that the Convention would decide so grave a question, without going into committee of the whole.

Mr. JENIFER thought the amendment had been merely to enquire into the expediency of inserting the provision, but he found it to be a positive instruction. He was willing to send it to the Committee, but he would not give the instructions. The vote of yesterday settled the question as to popular basis: the House must take the other principle or a compromise. Instead of sending instructions to the Committee, let the House decide the question *instanter*. He was disposed to yield some of his wishes rather than go home, because he could not get exactly such a Constitution as he would like.

Mr. CHAMBERS disclaimed all pretensions to the character of a tactician. He had altogether retired from the political field more than sixteen years ago when he went on the bench, and had taken no part whatever since, except to vote.

The gentleman from Baltimore, would learn when he had the benefit of larger experience, that the only safe and sure way to success, is by a straight forward, plain, direct and honest course to the object candidly avowed. The crooked, tortuous path in which that gentleman travelled, occasionally crossed this straight track and brought him in his view, and the gentleman was hence induced to think that he (Mr. C.) was also out of line. It was only an optical illusion. . If the gentleman would march boldly, right onward, disregarding the clamors of that large family in Baltimore, alluded to by his colleague, or from any other quarter, his own intelligence would take him in the direct road.

Mr. Gwinn asked if the gentleman would point out the direct course.

Mr. Chambers. "Follow me." (a laugh.)

He said the gentleman from Frederick, [Mr. Thomas,] had renewed the charge against this resolution, that it was an abstraction. He vindicated it at length from this imputation, and maintained that it was eminently practical. That gentleman had indulged in an elaborate address to the House, avowedly to convince them of the great error they had committed by their vote of sixty odd to seventeen, and yet concluded by assuring us that the vote "amounted to nothing." It was very true, as stated that members of a committee, from courtesy to a chairman, often permitted him to report propositions they did not approve. It often occurred too that members presented propositions they did not mean to sanction by their votes.

But in all such cases the fact was announced and known, and the sole object was to bring the House to a vote in which every member could express his actual opinion. It was certainly the first time in the experience of some years he had ever heard it said that on the final passage of a resolution by yeas and nays, the vote was no evidence of opinion, and he was glad to have the endorsement of the gentleman from Cecil, (Mr. McLane,) who had so fully concurred in this view. He had no doubt there would be found of the members voting on that proposition, no more than seventeen, to go for the broad doctrine of representation on the basis of numbers alone.

He repeated the ground he had heretofore urged as to the *cui bono*. Two gentlemen on the Committee would agree to nothing till driven by the House from this claim of a popular basis. When that was disposed of, as it would be by passing this resolution, there remained the alternatives of compromise or the *status anti belum*—the present arrangement. Compromise was an indefinite term. On that subject too the Committee was a divided family. We had a compromise in 1836—the city of Baltimore had the "lion's share." We are now to compromise again and another "lion's share" is to be taken from what was then left us. The House should indicate their views in regard to this one most important item in the compromise. The last vote decides that a reduction must be made from the immense number which would be given to the city by a basis purely of numbers. What was to be the limit? He supposed it must be to an extent which would avert the danger of bringing the counties entirely under the control of the city. He illustrated how this would be the case if no limit was imposed. This amendment was offered by him in Committee—it was now before the House, and he would stand by it. If the House thought it proper to make the limit that which was allowed to the largest county, then they should adopt this amendment; if they determined any other to be proper let it be made, and the Committee will regard it as an instruction.

Mr. McLane and Mr. Chambers said each a few words in explanation.

Mr. Thomas stated, that he had considered these resolutions as presenting merely a negative question until yesterday. The amendment now proposed by the gentleman from Kent, giving Baltimore a specific number of representatives was an affirmative question. So was the vote of yesterday, deciding that population shall not be the basis of representation in the House of Delegates. By that vote the House had fixed one principle: and if it should be decided that Baltimore shall have a representation equal to the largest county in the State, another principle will be fixed.

He went on to state the parliamentary practice in relation to amendments and the manner in which they might be introduced; and asserted that any gentleman had a right to get up and contradict to-day any position which he might have taken yesterday; and even to record his vote in one way, and to argue in another. No gentleman could be required to redeem any supposed pledge contained in his vote of the day preceding.

Mr. McLane explained.

Mr. Johnson asked if the gentleman from Kent objected to going into committee of the whole.

Mr. Chambers said he would not object to that course.

Mr. Thomas resumed, explaining more fully his views as to the binding effect of the vote of a gentleman in his future action. He adverted to the contemplated reforms which extended to the Executive, the Judicial, and the Legislative departments. It was intended to take away almost all power from the Executive; and he stated that he would not object to this if to that reform were connected an extension of power to the Legislative branch. He stated that he represented a large population, and he would not pledge them or himself to the course they should take when the Constitution was presented to them for acceptance. There might be provisions engrafted in it, such as would compel him to give his own vote against it, and to admonish the people from the hills and the house-tops to reject it.

He concluded with some further remarks, generally reiterating what he had previously said as to the inefficiency of votes given on isolated questions to stand as a true exponent of the final vote of gentlemen on the report as a whole. He considered himself as entirely free to move to amend the report hereafter by the introduction of a provision establishing representation on the basis of population.

And, pending the question, (and Mr. CHAMBERS, of Kent, being entitled to the floor,)

The Convention adjourned.

MONDAY, January 27th, 1851.

The Convention met at 11 o'clock.

Prayer by the Rev. Mr. GRAUFF.

The roll was called, and, after some time, a quorum being present, the journal of Saturday was read and approved.

BASIS OF REPRESENTATION.

Mr. DIRICKSON said, that before the Convention proceeded to the consideration of the business before it, he desired to submit an order with a view to its being entered on the journal. On Friday last, he and a friend who accompanied him, had been unavoidably detained from their seats. He saw that, in his absence, a most important vote had been taken. He referred to the vote upon the proposition of the gentleman from St. Mary's, (Mr. Blakistone,) in regard to the basis of representation. As he, (Mr. D.) regarded this as one of the most important and vital questions that would agitate this body, and as one upon which, therefore, every member ought to be heard, at least so far as his vote was concerned, he would ask that the votes of himself and the gentleman from Kent, (Mr. Lee,) might be permitted, under the courtesy of the Convention, to appear upon the journal; and with this object in view, he would offer the following order:

"Ordered, That it be entered upon the journal that Messrs. John Lee, of Kent, and L. L. Dirickson, of Worcester, vote in the negative upon the proposition submitted as a substitute by Mr. Blakistone, of St. Mary's, on Friday last, which said motion is in the following words—That the committee on Representation and Apportionment be requested to report a plan of apportionment and representation—making numbers exclusively the basis of representation to the House of Delegates."

The order was adopted.

Mr. PARKE called the attention of the Convention to the fact, that he had on Saturday last, given notice of sundry amendments to the report of the committee on the Bills of Rights. His object in so doing, he said, was to have them put upon the journal, in order that members might have an opportunity of examining them. He found that they had not been spread upon the journal, and he would now offer the following order:

"Ordered, That the proposed amendments to the report of the committee on the Declaration of Rights, submitted by Mr. Parke, on Saturday last, be entered on the journal."

The PRESIDENT, after an explanation as to the course adopted in relation to such matters, desired that the sense of the Convention should be taken, whether such amendments should be printed upon the journal, and in bill form likewise.

Some conversation followed.

Mr. SPENCER made a suggestion in relation to the appropriate distribution of matter, ordered to be printed to the several contractors.

This led to some further conversation, when

Mr. WEBER offered the following as a substitute for the order of Mr. PARKE:

"Ordered, That all reports of articles for the Constitution, and all proposed amendments, shall be printed on the journal."

Mr. WEBER briefly stated his reasons, after which

Mr. PARKE accepted the substitute as a modification of his own proposition.

And, after some further conversation, the substitute was rejected.

On motion of Mr. CHAMBERS, of Kent, the Convention reconsidered the said vote.

On motion of Mr. C., the said order was amended by striking out the words "and all proposed amendments;"

And, as thus amended, the order was adopted.

THE EXTRA JOURNALS.

The PRESIDENT announced the unfinished business of the morning hour to be the consideration of the following order heretofore offered by Mr. THAWLEY:

"Ordered That the order adopted some weeks past, authorising the printing of four extra journals for each member of this Convention be rescinded."

Mr. SPENCER had, on Saturday, made a motion to lay the order temporarily on the table, in order to give to the chairman of the committee on printing, (Mr. Stewart, of Baltimore,) who was not then in the city, an opportunity to make an explanation upon one point as to which a difference of opinion seemed to exist, to wit—whether or not there was any contract with the printers. Mr. STEWART being now in his seat, Mr. SPENCER withdrew his motion to lay on the table.

Mr. STEWART, of Baltimore city, made an explanation, setting forth the action of the committee upon the matter of the extra journals. The point of it was this; no contract had been made (Mr. S. said) with the printers. Before the recess, he had informed them that they must not supply these extra copies under any impression that there was a contract—the whole matter being within the control of the Convention. After the Convention had re-assembled, he told them, as no reporter had yet been appointed, that they might go on and still supply them. Subsequently, some ten days since, he had brought the subject to the consideration of the Committee as he felt it his duty to do. A reporter had been appointed; the system of reporting the debates and proceedings was in full operation; and he (Mr. S.,) did not suppose that the same necessity existed for the extra journals. The committee, upon a computation of the cost, which was not large, came to the conclusion that they would allow the printing of the extra copies to be continued, until such time as the Convention should think proper, by its higher authority, to nterfere and arrest it. Personally, he had no need of these copies; but the committee thought that as nine copies only of the Register of Debates were apportioned to each member, it might be well that these extra Journals should be continued.

After some conversation the question was taken on the motion of Mr. THAWLEY, (the yeas and nays having heretofore been ordered,) and resulted as follows:

Affirmative—Messrs. Chapman, President, Morgan, Ricaud, Sellman, Buchanan, Bell, Welch, Dickinson, Colston, John Dennis, James U. Dennis, Dashiell, Williams, Hodson, Phelps, Miller, Spencer, George, Wright, Dirickson, Hearn, Shriver, Biser, Annan, Sappington, Stephenson, McHenry, Nelson, Thawley, Stewart of Caroline, Hardcastle, Gwinn, Stewart of Baltimore city, Ware, Schley, Fiery, Neill, John Newcomer, Brewer, Hollyday, Slicer, Fitzpatrick, Smith, Parke, Shower, Cockey and Brown.—47.

Negative.—Messrs. Blakistone, Dent, Hopewell, Lee, Chambers of Kent, Wells, Randall, Jenifer, Lloyd, Hicks, Goldsborough, McLane, Sprigg, McCubbin, McMaster, Fooks, Jacobs, Gaither, Magraw, Presstman, Harbine, Waters and Weber—23.

So the order to rescind was adopted.

Mr. BLAKISTONE rose, he said, to offer a resolution rendered absolutely necessary, in his judgment, by the order which the Convention had just adopted; unless the Convention agreed to some such proposition, he did not know how prompt and immediate information of the proceedings here, could be given to the people throughout the State.

The order was read as follows:

"Ordered, That the committee on Printing be instructed to direct the printer of the journal to forward one copy of the journal of proceedings of the Convention, to the editors of newspapers in the several counties in this State and the city of Baltimore."

Mr. BROWN. How many newspapers are there?

Mr. BLAKISTONE. I do not know, nor do I care.

Mr. STEWART, of Baltimore city. I am happy to have it in my power to give some information on this point from the committee on Printing. I think the object of my friend from St. Mary's (Mr. Blakistone,) good and proper, and such as should recommend his proposition to the favor of gentlemen on all sides of the House. That object, however—the diffusion of knowledge of our proceedings among the people—will be accomplished in a better way, by an expedient to which the committee on Printing has already resorted. The committee set apart, out of the surplus numbers left of the copies printed under the order of the Convention, one copy of the Register of Debates, for every newspaper in the State—amounting, I believe, to an aggregate of fifty-five. The clerk of the committee has made out a list, and been specially charged with the performance of this duty; so that the people will be furnished day by day with accurate knowledge of every step of our progress here. This was done ten days ago, and it seems to me, therefore, that the adoption of the resolution of the gentleman from St. Mary's is unnecessary.

Mr. DENT suggested, that the newspapers could obtain an out-line of proceedings here sooner from the Journal, than from the Register of Debates.

The question was then taken, and by ayes 34, noes 26, the order was adopted.

The PRESIDENT announced that the hour set apart for the consideration of the order of the day, had arrived.

Mr. BLAKISTONE, by leave, gave notice that he should, to-morrow, move to change the 17th rule, and also to rescind the 29th rule.

THE ELECTIVE FRANCHISE.

The PRESIDENT announced that the first in the order of the day, was the report of the committee on the elective franchise, the consideration of which, had been postponed to this day.

Mr. MCLANE hoped, he said, that the gentleman from Kent, (Mr. Chambers,) would consent to postpone the consideration of this report until to-morrow. The printed report had been laid on the tables of the members only this morning, and no time had been afforded for an examination of it. He, [Mr. McL.,] desired to offer an amendment, but was not able to do so without paying more attention to the report than he could at present; and he was not sure that, after a proper examination, he should be disposed to offer any amendment.

He would also suggest, that the report did not appear to contain the amendments of the gentleman from Anne Arundel, not now in his seat. It was, therefore, imperfect; and he, (Mr. McL.,) wished to have an opportunity of passing upon these amendments.

Mr. STEWART, of Baltimore city. To what amendments does the gentleman allude?

Mr. MCLANE. To the amendments of Mr. DORSEY.

Mr. STEWART. They were rejected in committee of the whole, and not, therefore, reported to the Convention.

Mr. CHAMBERS, of Kent. I have only to say that I concur entirely in the opinion of the gentleman from Cecil, [Mr. McLane.] I would, however, suggest a general postponement, instead of a postponement until to-morrow.

The PRESIDENT. The amendments which were offered by the gentleman from Anne Arundel, (Mr. Dorsey,) were acted upon in committee; and are no longer before the Convention; and the Secretary did not think it necessary or competent for him to have them printed. The order embraced only pending amendments, or amendments that might be offered, and of which notice was given.

Mr. MCLANE, (to the President.) Are the amendments of the gentleman from Anne Arundel on the Journal?

The PRESIDENT. The Secretary informs the Chair that they are.

Mr McLane. That will answer my purpose.

After some conversation on a point of order, between Mr. Chambers, of Kent, and the President, the question was taken and the consideration of the report was postponed.

BASIS OF REPRESENTATION.

The President announced that the next in the orders of the day was the report of Mr. Merrick from the committee on representation.

The pending question was on the amendment offered by Mr. Chambers, of Kent, to the amendment prepared by Mr. Spencer, to re-commit the Report with instructions.

Mr. Fitzpatrick. I fear that this question is going to lead to a very long and tedious debate. I think that such a discussion can result in no practical good, and I therefore move that the whole subject be laid upon the table.

Mr. Buchanan. Will the gentleman oblige me by withdrawing the motion for a few minutes? I am desirous of saying a very few words on the motion of the gentleman from Queen Anne's, (Mr. Spencer,) as proposed to be amended by the gentleman from Kent, (Mr. Chambers.)

Mr. Fitzpatrick. If I withdraw the motion, will the gentleman renew it.

Mr. Buchanan. If the gentleman requires me to do so, I will renew it.

Mr. Fitzpatrick. I withdraw the motion.

So the question recurred on the amendment of Mr. Chambers, of Kent, to the amendment proposed by Mr. Spencer to re-commit the report with instructions.

Mr. Buchanan said he had no opportunity on Friday or Saturday last to present his views upon the questions pending; but he had felt as acutely as any member of the Convention could feel, that some things had occurred in the course of this debate which ought not to pass by, and which he was not disposed to pass by without notice. He should vote against the proposition of the gentleman from Kent, (Mr. Chambers.) He should vote for the proposition of the gentleman from Queen Anne's, (Mr. Spencer) not because he (Mr. B.) altogether concurred in it, but because it would in part effect the object which he had in view—delay in respect to this question of representation. His impression was that no conceivable good could grow out of its discussion at this stage of the business of the Convention. It would swallow up all other matters, and the Convention would not take one forward step from the time it was taken up, until, perhaps it was too late to do any thing in the way of forming a constitution.

But his main object in rising was, to say a few words in reply to the very distinguished gentleman from Frederick, (Mr. Thomas,) whom he (Mr. B.) regretted not to see in his seat. That gentleman in endeavoring to effect a postponement of this question had thought proper, in the course of his remarks, to refer to the neglect, (for the charge amounted to that,) on the part of the Convention to do the work which the Convention had assembled here to do. In other words, the Convention had, to use the gentleman's own emphasised and expressive language, been here "eight long tedious weeks,"—and, done nothing. Sir, continued Mr. B., we have been here *twelve* long, tedious weeks and done *much*, and I call upon gentlemen who have been here with us week after week and month after month, steadily discharging the duties which have devolved upon us, to bear me witness when I say that we *have* done much. These statements thus made here, echoed by the people and published by the newspapers, are doing this Convention essential and serious wrong. Talk only—debate only—nothing more than that! By what warrant does the gentleman say it? Has *he* been here? Has *he* been amongst us? Is *he* now with us? How does *he* know that the whole time of this body has been passed away in mere talk? I point him to the works which have been done here, and then let him answer to his constituents and to mine, and say, whether these works are not extremely important.

Mr. B., to sustain this position, recapitulated the various measures which had been prepared for the action of the Convention, and asked, by what right the gentleman took his seat here, and before the people of the State, told this Convention that they had been here all the time doing nothing—that they were false to their duty and faithless to their trust? He [Mr. B.] would submit to such a charge from no man. He had given up home, occupation, interest, every thing to the service of the State; and having done so, he was to be told that he was reckless of his duty and false to his trust.

He had now a word to say to his excellent friend from Kent, [Mr. Chambers] whom he, [Mr. B.,] confessed he approached with proper caution; for that gentleman, when he undertook to do execution upon those who might be so unfortunate as to invoke his wrath, did not kill them with the stroke of a cleaver or a broad-axe, but put them to death in the most delicate manner, by piercing them through and through with a well-polished small-sword.

Mr. B. then proceeded to refer to the remarks made by Mr. Chambers on a former day, in which the latter gentleman had called upon the Convention to meet this question of representation, and had declared that it was not to be "shyed"—as if, [Mr. B. said,] we were running away from it. He was actuated by the kindest feelings towards the gentleman, [Mr. Chambers,] because he was the first man who had made a report in part, and upon which the Convention had been zealously and laboriously engaged week after week. And now that they were ready to act upon that question, another exciting subject came in, and all that had been done was to go for naught. He, [Mr. B.,] had desired to aid that gentleman who had hewn out and polished the first block upon which was to rest the glorious fabric of the Constitution. He, [Mr. B.,] did not wish to see it cast aside—he wanted to protect the gentleman against himself—he desired that his work should be made perfect. The original report of his honorable friend was in itself of the highest importance, and the gentleman from Anne Arundel, [Mr. Dorsey,] not satisfied with what had been done, came in and by the side of it, piled up amendment upon amendment, until his Ossa stood "like a wart," wholly overwhelmed. And while this was going on, before any final action could be taken, *presto*, [as the gentleman from Caroline, Mr. Stewart, would say,] in came a new subject, and the Convention was turned entirely into a new track. This he [Mr. B.] was desirous to avoid.

Mr. B. proceeded to refer to the remarks made on a previous day by his friend from St. Mary's, [Mr. Blakistone,] when, in alternate tones of the softest persuasion and the loftiest command—that gentleman had summoned the members of the Convention to the discharge of their duty. Mr. B. reminded him that the motion to postpone the representation question to the 15th of February, did not come from his, [Mr. Buchanan's,] side of the House, and admonished him that he should be careful how he assailed others, lest, as in this instance, the arrow should fall upon his own house, and hit his own brethren.

He, [Mr Buchanan.] desired delay, because he thought it would ultimately result in expedition. He called attention to articles in the morning papers, asking whether the Convention had yet done any work. He was desirous to hold up to them the handiwork of the admirable artificer from Kent, [Mr. Chambers.] For his own part, he, [Mr. B.] had been almost stationery here. He intended to remain so until the work was performed—or nearly so, and he protested against any individual undertaking to denounce him as derelict to his duty, or as one who had done nothing. He would only say, in conclusion, that he would vote against the amendment of the gentleman from Kent, [and no one could ever have supposed that he, (Mr B.) would vote otherwise,] and in favor of the amendment of the gentleman from Queen Anne, [Mr. Spencer.]

Mr. SPENCER obtained the floor.

Mr. BELL interposed with the remark, that his object in making the motion to lay the subject on the table, had been to avoid the very discussion into which the Convention was now going.

Mr. SPENCER. The floor was assigned to me. I am not disposed to throw any impediment in the way of the gentleman. But I stated on Saturday last, that I desired to hear from the gentleman from Kent, [Mr. Chambers,] the reasons for the proposition he had submitted, in order that I might have an opportunity to reply. I rise now for the purpose of redeeming the pledge which I then gave.

The PRESIDENT interposed and stated that when the order was announced, the fact had for the moment escaped his attention, that, at the time of adjournment on Saturday, the gentleman from Kent, [Mr. Chambers,] had the floor, was addressing the Convention, and yielded for a motion to adjourn.

Mr. BUCHANAN. I beg the gentleman, [Mr. Chambers,] ten thousand pardons, but my word is pledged to renew the motion of the gentleman from Alleghany, [Mr. Fitzpatrick,] for upon that pledge alone it was that I obtained the floor.

Mr. FITZPATRICK. I will releave the gentleman from his embarrassment. Certainly, I never would have made the motion to lay on the table, had I known that the gentleman from Kent, [Mr. Chambers] was entitled to the floor.

Mr. CHAMBERS thereupon took the floor and said:

When the House adjourned he had not intended to occupy ten minutes more of its time. He was quite inclined to gratify the suggestion made by the gentleman from Frederick, to have this debate continued in committee of the whole, and have every gentleman to submit his plan and enable us to select some one, or compound one out of the mess. He would, however, avail himself of the opportunity to add a word in vindication of his amendment.

The idea of giving to Baltimore a representation equal to the largest county, did not originate with him. The reform committee and the reform legislature of 1836, adopted it, recommended it to the good people of the State, who confirmed it by their representation in 1837. It was the basis of compromise; Baltimore agreed to it, and was willing to increase her delegation with the increase of the largest county. It was a reasonable compromise. It was known that from the early days of the colonial government the counties had been *equally* represented. The State had prospered and all its political interests had been faithfully and usefully attended to; practically, every thing worked well in the machinery of the government. But the large counties and Baltimore desired to have more political power, or at least, more political offices, and the compromise was made, by which the small counties were greatly reduced in their comparative numbers and power.

The census of 1840 was made the basis of the first adjustment of the number of representatives to the counties respectively, and it was to be thereafter altered and made to conform to the population ascertained by every *second* census thereafter, but the same principle was solemnly agreed on, as the mode of adjustment. Baltimore was still to be equal to the largest county in the number of her representatives. The first census, therefore, which was to occasion a re-adjustment was that of 1860, but now in 1849, before the revolution of one-half of the period which is to bring 1860 into being, this compromise is disregarded, and the diminished small counties must again submit to be shorn of a portion of their reduced power, and Baltimore is no longer to be kept equal to the largest county, but, as some of her divided delegation on this floor claim, is to have a number of delegates in exact proportion to her numbers—that is to say, Baltimore is to have thirty-three members of the House of Delegates, while Kent county has two. To deny the policy and expediency of this, was charged upon him as a great heresy. He did not refer to the abusive newspapers, to which his friend from Baltimore county, (Mr. Buchanan,) had alluded. He regretted being obliged to say, that some of these could not be touched without defiling a gentleman's hands, nor their language repeated without polluting his lips.

His opinions had been assailed from higher

sources. He had been supposed to impute an especial degree of corruption to the city of Baltimore. He never had said one word like it. He regarded Baltimore precisely as he did other cities. Certainly he agreed with Mr. Jefferson that the country air, country occupation and country associations, are at least equally congenial to the growth of pure morals and patriotism, but he was willing to concede to Baltimore, as much of both as to other cities.

Yet did we not all know the power of concentration? It is as operative in the political as in the physical world—it operates every where. What is the mighty torrent that sweeps before it every opposing barrier? It is but the aggregation of drops. There were some farmers who heard him; they know how effectually a few individuals acting in concert could operate. The few millers and grain buyers in the city could do more to effect the market than all the farmers in the country, simply because they could *combine*, while these acted separately, in atoms. Every body knew the superior power of a few disciplined soldiers over a dispersed mass of men with no organization or concert.

But besides this, Baltimore had an interest in every county in the State. It was the centre of business—the heart of our trade and commerce, and its pulsations were felt through every artery, tendon, muscle and nerve, of the whole body of the people. She had never earnestly desired any thing without getting it. Delegates from all parts of the State were to some extent, delegates for the city. To ask for a representation then rateably, one for every five, six or seven thousand, is idle. No one here can expect it. Even the gentleman from Frederick, (Mr. Thomas,) proposes a limitation in the way of equal districts—a limitation as he, (Mr. T.,) regards it, not as regarded by him, (Mr. C.) Why then was he less orthodox than otners, who were allowed to be good reformers, yet insisted on a limit?

To enable gentlemen to submit their several views, and thus place the House in a condition to act intelligently, and also to gratify a request made by a gentleman from Frederick, (Mr. Johnson,) he would conclude by moving that the House now resolve itself into a committee of the whole.

Mr. Spencer said the committee on representation had reported to the Convention on the 11th of December,

1st, "That it is inexpedient to regard federal numbers in fixing the estimates and basis of representation in the House of Delegates;" and,

2nd, "That it is inexpedient to adopt a principle of representation based exclusively upon popular numbers, in organizing the House of Delegates or the Senate."

He had great objection to receiving such a report. It was not consistent with the duty for which the committee was appointed. It was the purpose and design of this Convention, in appointing the committees, to expedite its business by reports in full from them, in the form of articles to be incorporated in the Constitution. And if we depart from the purpose contemplated, we shall be greatly delayed in our proceedings. He had, therefore, moved that the report be re-committed to the Committee. That proposition had been rejected. He then moved to re-commit it "with instructions to report a basis of representation on some fair principle of compromise."

To this, the gentleman from Kent, (Mr. Chambers,) offered the following as an amendment:

"In such manner, that the city of Baltimore shall be entitled to the same number of representatives in the House of Delegates as may be allowed to the largest county in the State."

That honorable member had given to the Convention the reasons which induced him to offer an amendment which entirely excludes the city of Baltimore from all participation in the compromise of this agitating and exciting question.

Mr. Chambers explained his amendment.

Mr. Spencer resumed. The gentleman was from one of the smaller counties, and his voice had announced that the largest portion of the State, in numbers and in wealth, in the adjustment of a question so vital as the one under consideration, was not to be heard. The counties from the mountains to the sea were to compromise this matter, and then arbitrarily say to Baltimore, "we will allow you what we choose and no more." He, Mr. Spencer, was also from a small county, contiguous to the county of the gentleman, and in response, he desired to say, that he was for compromising with each and every portion of the State. Not with one part to the exclusion of the other; but with each and all. Situated as Baltimore was—a large and increasing city, in a very small State—self-defence made it necessary for the counties to resist representation based on population exclusively. But as this is denied to Baltimore, who claims it, the question must be compromised with her, and as far as can be done, an equivalent ought to be given to her.

He deprecated delay. He knew that efforts were being made to render this Convention odious, and he had no doubt if the resolutions, as reported by the committee, were passed without any qualification, they would tend to produce popular excitement. There are two great parties here; one representing the interest of Baltimore; the other, the smaller counties. Every candid mind must admit that neither extreme will prevail. His proposition would show that there existed in this body a spirit of compromise under which we could all fraternize, and the question be settled with harmony.

To his regret, the gentleman from Kent, had offered his amendment, which, while we are striving to cultivate a spirit of concession and concord, throws Baltimore off altogether. His objection to giving her a representation greater than the largest county, is on account of her concentrated position. We must all admit the commanding position which her concentrated power gives her, and he was unwilling to let the smaller counties be over-ridden by that great city. But at the same time it is right to say, that whilst we withhold from her the application of the great principle of popular representation, owing to her peculiar position to the counties, as far as we can go, we will go, in yielding to her an equivalent. What that is to be, must depend upon the compromise which must take place.

Pass the amendment of the gentlemen from Kent, and *carry it out*, and you had better adjourn at once. The Constitution which we may adopt has to be ratified by the people. If you set Baltimore against it, what prospect of ratification is there. It is too important an interest to be overlooked. It is entitled to the highest respect, and demands our serious consideration. We must not neglect it. If you pass the amendment of the gentleman, and say to her, that she is not to be heard in this compromise, her entire weight will be put in opposition to your Constitution. And so, in the same spirit, he said to the gentlemen from Baltimore, and the larger counties, if you adopt the rule of representation according to population, and attempt to force it, on the smaller counties, then you will array them against our proceedings, and raise, in them, one united army of opposition, who will stop at no point short of a total overthrow of the Constitution, which we may recommend. I appeal then to the *reformers* in this House, who are truly desirous to get rid of the abuses and inconveniences of the old Constitution, and to adopt one in conformity with the progressive spirit of the age, and which will give to you a more economical, a better, and a purer government, to vote down the amendment of the gentleman from Kent, and unite in a spirit of conciliation. Let it go forth from these Halls, that we will fraternise on this great question, and we will still the storm of passion, and prepare the public mind to accept with favor the work of our hands.

The gentleman from Kent, is further opposed to extending the compromise to Baltimore, because the original Constitution fixed a ratio of representation which was just, and which, by subsequent compromises, has tended to the injury of the counties.

The gentleman can find nothing to sustain him, in the ratio of representation, as adopted in our Constitution of seventy-six. At that time, we had no large city within our limits. The counties, which now constitute the smaller counties, were then the important sections of the State, and very much equal; and there were several commercial points on the Eastern Shore, of far greater magnitude than Baltimore town, as it was then known. Besides, our government was then one of experiment, and framed in the very midst of war. The gallant spirits who framed it, are entitled to our highest praise, and should ever be remembered with tears of gratitude and smiles of admiration. Under the circumstances which gave it birth, it was admirably suited to the crisis, but still it was imperfect, necessarily imperfect. The defects soon became manifest, and from that time to the present, have been undergoing changes. It is unnecessary to enumerate them all. But he might ask, what were the restrictions on the right of suffrage, and on public officers, from a Sheriff to a Governor? A property qualification was essential in every case. Again; how imperfect was our Judiciary system, and the mode of appointing the Governor? Time has corrected many of the evils, and this Convention has met to correct *them all*. And yet the gentleman refers to that Constitution as his guide, on this great question. He could not consent to do so.

The gentleman said that Baltimore had got all she claimed; had fixed the public taxes upon us, and was now anxious to throw off her share of them. He thought this was unjust. Baltimore was not alone responsible for the system of internal improvements and the public debt. The Potomac and the Chesapeake counties, had their share of the reproach. In the Potomac counties the strongest champions of the system were to be found. Nor was there any deficiency on the Eastern Shore. It was made a question, in his, (Queen Anne's) county. He had canvassed every part of it in opposition to the system, not as a candidate, but as one of the people. He had predicted what would be the result, and that every species of property, would be taxed to pay for the system. But the people sustained it and went for the measure, as they did in other counties on that shore. Let no unjust censure then be imposed on Baltimore for this measure, and remember too, that one of the great public works of the State—the Chesapeake and Ohio Canal—is antagonist, in every respect to the city of Baltimore, and always was. Its outlet is in the District of Columbia, where all its commerce must find its way. And this is the great work of the State, from which the people were led to expect such rich returns and so golden a harvest. He hoped it would be realized, though the hope has been long deferred.

We should have no unkind feelings towards the city of Baltimore. It was the heart of the State, diffusing vigor into every part. Into her was pouring the wealth of other States, and other counties. We furnished her with the rich and varied products of our fertile lands, whilst she furnished us in return with her comforts and luxuries. Let us then forget all sectional discord and meet on common ground, in a spirit of just and honorable concession, each to the other. Whilst we say to Baltimore, we cannot give you a representation to which you would be entitled on the basis of population, because to do this would confer on you the means of absorbing all the political influence of the State, yet we are willing to yield you an equivalent, one which will make you stronger than you now are, and as far as possible *balance the power* in the State, without detriment to any.

Mr. Neill suggested to Mr. Chambers, of Kent, so to modify his amendment as to add the words, "and that representation in the counties shall be according to population."

Mr. Chambers declined, remarking that the gentleman could offer his amendment as a separate proposition.

Mr. Neill supposed it would not be in order for him now to do so.

The President, [Mr. Ricaud, *pro tem*,] said it would not be in order.

Mr. NEILL said he should then feel himself constrained, if the amendment of the gentleman from Kent, [Mr. Chambers,] should be brought to a direct question, to vote against it.

Mr. NEILL felt himself compelled, under the circumstances, to vote against the proposition of the gentleman from Kent. As one of the representatives of Frederick county, he was not disposed to give Baltimore more representatives than she was justly entitled to. He was prepared to increase the representation of the largest counties in proportion to the increase of their population as exhibited by the new census. The gentleman from Kent had declined to modify his proposition, and he, [Mr. N.] could not vote for it as now presented. He thought it objectionable that the committee should come before the House with these isolated propositions, instead of bringing forward some general proposition. The amendment of the gentleman from Kent was calculated to win the large counties; but such isolated propositions did not embody the general sentiment of the State. He was therefore compelled to give his vote against it.

Mr. CHAMBERS could not agree with the gentleman from Washington, (Mr. Neill,) whose proposition related to a subject not at all involved in the amendment now before us and in regard to which not a word of discussion had been had.

He certainly understood his amendment as the precise principle of the Washington county platform. It looked to no particular limitation of number for the larger counties, nor to any principle on which these numbers were to be based, but solely to the equality in the delegation of the largest county and the city. If one was increased, the other would be, and there was nothing in this to commit any one to such increase in the counties or against it.

Mr. BROWN withdrew his motion. He was of opinion that whatever was the intention of the gentleman who introduced this amendment, the effect would be to array Baltimore city against the counties, or, *vice versa,* the counties against Baltimore. He believed that the greatest part of the delegates from Western Maryland were committed, when they came here, to give Baltimore a representation equal to the largest counties of the State.

The amendment of the gentleman from Kent therefore decided nothing. It settled no principle but that Baltimore shall be limited in the number of her delegates to the representation of the largest counties. He referred to the original position of the counties, and asked if it was intended that they should be kept in the nursery for ever. He alluded to the seventeen who had voted for the basis of population, and stated that they embraced more than half the representation of the freemen of the State. If Western Maryland did not exhibit some energy, and throw off the shackles which bound her, he should lose all his respect for her. He hoped the gentleman from Kent would not consume any more of the time of the House by discussing abstractions. The proposition which had now been offered, he could not think quite germane to the subject. The resolutions from the Committee contained two great general principles, while the amendment of the gentleman from Kent is confined to a single proposition; and if it should be adopted, what would have been effected by its adoption? He concluded with protesting against any further waste of time; he was desirous to make a Constitution—to go home and to save the money of the people.

Mr. CHAMBERS now renewed the motion that the Convention resolve itself into committee of the whole, for the purpose of taking up the subject.

Some conversation followed on a point of order, between Messrs. BUCHANAN, CHAMBERS, JENIFER and the PRESIDENT.

After which,

Mr. BROWN enquired of the Chair, whether a motion to lay the proposition on the table was in order, pending a motion to go into committee?

The PRESIDENT stated that that motion was in order, and would take precedence over the motion to go into committee.

Mr. BROWN moved that the whole subject be laid on the table, and asked the yeas and nays, which were ordered.

Mr. HARBINE was proceeding to speak, when,

The PRESIDENT interposed and said that no debate could be entertained on a motion to lay on the table.

Mr. HARBINE. I was only going to remark that I hoped the motion to lay the whole subject on the table would be agreed to.

Mr. FITZPATRICK. As I have been adverted to, I should like to explain the motion that I made, and I hope that the gentleman from Carroll, (Mr. Brown,) will withdraw his motion to enable me to do so.

Mr. BROWN. I will withdraw for that purpose.

Mr. FITZPATRICK said, he wished to place himself right in reference to the motion made by him, to lay the whole subject on the table. He was far from being opposed to a thorough discussion of this question, or of giving his vote upon it, when it should come up in some distinct and tangible form; but in its present shape, being a mere abstract proposition from which no practical result was likely to be deduced, he thought it a mere waste of the time of the Convention and of the people. He wished the matter sent back to the committee for some definite and practical report; or that failing to agree upon any basis of settlement, they might be discharged by the House. He, therefore, moved to lay the whole subject on the table.

The question then being on the motion to lay the whole subject on the table,

The yeas and nays were called and ordered, and being taken, resulted as follows:

Affirmative—Messrs. Sellman, Buchanan, Bell, Welch, Lloyd, Dickinson, Colston, Miller, McLane, Spencer, George, Wright, Shriver, Gaither, Biser, Annan, Sappington, Stephenson,

McHenry, Magraw, Nelson, Thawley, Stewart of Caroline, Hardcastle, Stewart of Baltimore city, Ware, Neill, John Newcomer, Harbine, Michael Newcomer, Brewer, Weber, Hollyday, Slicer, Fitzpatrick, Parke, Shower, Cockey and Brown—39.

Negative—Messrs. Chapman, President, Morgan, Blakistone, Dent, Hopewell, Ricaud, Lee, Chambers of Kent, Mitchell, Wells, Randall, Kent, Jenifer, John Dennis, James U. Dennis, Crisfield, Dashiell, Williams, Hicks, Hodson, Goldsborough, Phelps, Sprigg, McCubbin, Dirickson, McMaster, Hearn, Fooks, Jacobs, Schley, Fiery, Waters and Smith—33.

So the whole subject was laid on the table.

Mr. Spencer, [to the President.] What is the next order of the day?

The President. It is the report made by the Chairman of the committee on the executive department, (Mr. Grason.)

Mr. Spencer. The Chairman of that committee is not now in the city. It is probable he may be here to-morrow. I move that its consideration be postponed, and that, in the meantime, the Convention proceed to the consideration of the bill of rights.

Several voices. The Chairman of the committee on the bill of rights (Mr. Dorsey) is also absent.

There being no further business before the Convention at this time,

The Convention adjourned until to-morrow at eleven o'clock.

TUESDAY, January 28, 1851.

The Convention met pursuant to adjournment.

Prayer was made by the Rev. Mr. Grauff.

A quorum being present, the journal of yesterday was read.

THE PREVIOUS QUESTION, &c.

Mr. Blakistone, in pursuance of the notice he had yesterday given, moved to strike out the 17th rule of the Convention, and substitute in lieu of it the following:

"The previous question shall be always in order in Convention, if seconded by a majority, and until decided, shall preclude all further amendment and debate, and shall be in this form: "shall the main question be now put?" when on taking the previous question the Convention shall decide that the same shall not now be put, the main question shall be still under consideration, and if the previous question is sustained, the main question shall be on the adoption of the proposition under consideration, and in cases where there shall be pending amendments, the question shall be first taken upon such amendments in their order, and without further debate or amendment.

Mr. B. in support of his motion, referred to the changes which had taken place in the rule which regulates the previous question, by the adoption of the amendments of the gentleman from Anne Arundel, (Mr. Randall,) and the gentleman from Baltimore city, (Mr. Brent.) He (Mr. Blakistone,) thought that the Convention must be satisfied that these changes did not affect the good which seemed to be anticipated from their adoption; because, under the construction which the Chair had given to the rule as amended, the Convention could not come to a definite conclusion upon any subject, if a minority was disposed to prevent it. He illustrated its operation. His desire was that the rule should be so amended as to give power to a majority at all times to come to a vote upon any original proposition. He thought that the dispatch of the public business would be greatly facilitated by the adoption of his amendment.

Mr. B. thought it was necessary also, to restore the power which had recently been taken away, to call the yeas and nays in committee of the whole; so as to give gentlemen an opportunity to spread their votes before their constituents upon every important proposition which might be offered there.

Mr. Biser desired to ask a question of the Chair, the answer to which, he said, would control his vote. It was this: Was it in order to call the previous question at any stage of a bill under consideration? And, if sustained, would the Convention be brought without further debate, to a direct vote on the proposition and the amendments pending?

The President stated that, in his judgment, the previous question, under the rule as it now stood, would apply to the pending matter, whether it was an amendment or the whole bill. But the moment the previous question was taken upon the question then under consideration, the previous question was exhausted.

After some explanation between Mr. Biser and the President, on the point of order,

Mr. Biser said he should vote for rescinding the rule.

Mr. Brent, of Baltimore city, replied briefly to Mr. Blakistone, and in defence of the amendment adopted on his, (Mr. Brent's,) motion. After alluding to the tendency manifested by the Convention towards a constant change of rules, he submitted that no evidence had been afforded of a disposition on the part of a minority of the Convention to offer amendments, frivolously and wantonly, merely for the purpose of delay, and until he should see such a spirit manifested here, he was not inclined to favor any further change. He denied that the least inconvenience had as yet resulted from the amendment. He disputed the correctness of the operation of the rule as illustrated by Mr. Blakistone, and thought it was a reflection upon the Convention, to suppose that a minority would trifle with the time of the body, or offer amendments for the purpose of defeating its action. The evil complained of by the gentleman, (Mr. Blakistone,) was as yet quite speculative, and it would be time to apply the remedy when the evil was known to exist.

As to the defect in the twenty-ninth rule, Mr. B. read an amendment which he intimated, would perhaps, obviate the difficulty, and he explained its purport.

Mr. BISER with a view to allow an opportunity of testing the practical operation of the existing rule, moved to lay the motion to amend on the table, but withdrew the motion at the request of—

Mr. BLAKISTONE, who replied to Mr. Brent.

After some further remarks from Mr. BRENT,

The motion to lay the proposition of Mr. BLAKISTONE, on the table, was renewed, and was decided in the affirmative—ayes 40, noes 30.

So the proposition was laid on the table.

THE LEGISLATIVE DEPARTMENT.

Mr. PRESSTMAN, from the committee on the legislative department, submitted the following additional provisions:

"No person shall be imprisoned for debt.

"The Legislature shall not pass any law abolishing the relation of master and slave, as it now exists in this State.

"That the Legislature at its first session after the adoption of the Constitution, shall appoint one Commissioner to revise, digest and arrange the statute laws of the State, civil and criminal, and one commissioner to revise, simplify and abridge the rules and practice, pleadings, forms and proceedings of the courts of record of this State.

"The Legislature shall have power to protect by law from forced sale, a certain portion of the property of all heads of families.

"Taxation shall be equal and uniform throughout the State."

Mr. P. repeated the statement which had been made on a former day by the Chairman of the Committee on the Legislative Department of the Government, (Mr. Johnson) that it was understood that no member of the committee was in any way bound to adhere to the provisions reported.

Mr. STEWART, of Baltimore city, (to the President.) Will the report go on the journal under the order adopted yesterday?

The PRESIDENT. It will go upon the journal, and also be printed in bill form.

Mr. JOHNSON suggested whether it would not be well that all the reports should go upon the journal, including those which had been made before the order of yesterday, as well as those which might be made subsequently?

Some conversation followed, in which Messrs. SPENCER, COST JOHNSON and the PRESIDENT took part, when

Mr. MCLANE suggested that the reports referred to should be recorded on the journal when they came up for consideration.

Ordered accordingly.

Mr. BROWN moved that the Convention proceed to the consideration of the order of the day—the Report of the Committee on the Executive Department—but waived the motion at the request of Mr. JENIFER.

MASTER AND SLAVE.

Mr. JENIFER asked the Convention to take up at this time, by unanimous consent, the article which he had reported on Saturday last, from the Committee No. 14, on the subject of master and slave.

The report was read as follows:

"The relation of master and slave in this State shall not be abolished, unless a bill to abolish the same shall be passed by a unanimous vote of the members of each branch of the General Assembly, and shall be published at least three months before a new election of delegates, and shall be confirmed by a unanimous vote of the members of each branch of the General Assembly, at the next regular constitutional session, after such new election, nor then without full compensation to the master for the property of which he shall be thereby deprived."

Mr. JENIFER said, he supposed that the Convention would not occupy more than five minutes in the discussion of this report. It was a mere re-enactment of the provision of the old Constitution. It had been reported under the unanimous sanction of the committee, and there would not, he presumed, be a dissenting voice in the Convention. The prompt and ready action of the Convention upon a proposition which he believed would unite all voices, would be attended with at least this advantage—it would shew that one decisive step had been taken towards the enactment of a new Constitution.

Mr. BOWIE said, he hoped that his friend from Charles (Mr. Jenifer,) would consent to let this report lie on the table for the present. He (Mr. B.) much preferred the substance of the order introduced a day or two since, by the gentleman from Baltimore city, (Mr. Presstman,) which declared that the legislature should not have the power to abolish slavery in this State.

Mr. JENIFER repeated the statement he had made, that the report had been made by the unanimous vote of the Committee.

Mr. BOWIE said, he was not the less opposed to it on that account. He thought that the Legislature had just as much right to take his farm and give it to another man, by a unanimous vote, as they had to take any other property. He could see no distinction between the two cases. If no other gentleman, (continued Mr. B.) moves a substitute, I will.

Mr. JENIFER. I think my friend from Prince George's, (Mr. Bowie,) on looking over the report, will find that the provision is as comprehensive as any thing can be.

Mr. BOWIE. My objection to the clause is not captious. I do not quarrel with the phraseology, but with the idea. I regard it, as contrary to the bill of rights. I hold that no State or Government has the right to take private property, except for public use, and then only upon compensation made. I hold that the Legislature has no right from mere motives of caprice, merely in the exercise of a false and arbitrary power, to deprive a citizen of his property, and that it can only be done when the exigencies of the Government require that that property should be converted to its own use. I say, I know of no principle short of that, upon which this power can be exercised. If the whole Legislature of the State, by one compact, unanimous vote, should undertake to invade private rights, I will never give my sanction to the proceeding. Therefore, I desire to strike at the root of this power, and to substitute for the report of the committee, the provision reported by the gentleman from Baltimore city, (Mr. Presstman.) He has struck the idea precisely. If the State of Maryland needs the use of our slaves, she can have them, just as she can have any other property. But I will never concede that the Legislature can take away private property, except for public use, although every other member of this Convention should sanction the doctrine.

Mr. Brent, of Baltimore city. Will the gentleman read his substitute?

Mr. Bowie. I have not yet offered it, but I shall do so, unless the gentleman, (Mr. Jenifer,) will consent to let the report lie over.

Mr. Brown. This debate is altogether premature, and I do not think the point of the case is seen by either gentleman. The report of the gentleman from Charles, (Mr. Jenifer,) is copied from the provision of the existing Constitution, which declares that the relation of master and slave shall not be changed except by an amendment of the Constitution. Now, suppose that when we make our Constitution, we do not leave the amending power with the Legislature, and I for one, shall go against leaving it with them—no Government has a right to take property except for public use; but does not the gentleman from Charles, see that if we make a Constitution by which the right of the Legislature to amend, is taken away, a portion of this report falls to the ground. Or, is the gentleman willing to say that the Legislature shall have the power to amend as to one particular species of property, and as to no other? I want to take that power away. I think the best plan would be to lay this proposition on the table until we can see what the Convention will do with the amending power.

Mr. Bowie. I now offer my substitute.

The substitute was read as follows:

"The Legislature shall not pass any law to abolish the relation of master and slave as it now exists in this State."

Mr. Jenifer. If I could perceive that the substitute proposed by the gentleman from Prince George's, (Mr. Bowie,) would be of any greater effect than the provision which I have reported, I would not object to its adoption. I shall not, under present circumstances, press this question to a vote. I rose merely for the purpose of saying, that if the gentleman from Prince George's supposes that the committee in directing this report to be made, contemplated any thing like a sanction to an infringement upon the rights of the citizen, or that they would not guard those rights with as strong a will and as devoted a purpose as the gentleman himself, he is greatly mistaken. The committee believed that the clause, as it now stands, was as stringent as it could be made. And I am very much mistaken if the gentleman from Carroll, himself, (Mr. Brown,) did not engraft this very provision on the Constitution.

Mr. Brown. It was placed there at my instance.

Mr. Jenifer. The clause makes this principle in fact a part of the Constitution, which cannot be altered except by another Constitution. Does the gentleman mean to say that we are to make a Constitution which shall remain for ever just as it is—that it shall never be altered or changed? I shall say no more now; but, as the report has not been printed, I am willing that its further consideration shall be postponed to Monday next.

Mr. Brown. I desire that the gentleman should understand the point of my remarks. I say that if the amending power of the new Constitution remains with the Legislature, the course of the gentleman from Charles, (Mr. Jenifer,) will be all right. I do not take back a word I said in 1836. No, I would strengthen it if I could.

The further consideration of the subject was then postponed until Monday next.

THE HALL.

Mr. Brent, of Baltimore city, from the commitee heretofore appointed on the subject of the furnaces, &c., made the following report, which, after a few words of explanation from him, was adopted:

"*Ordered*, That this House will on Friday next, adjourn to the Monday following, in order to allow the furnace to be repaired, and that the committee appointed to superintend the comfort of the Hall, be authorised to contract with some suitable person to examine and repair the furnace and to ventilate the room properly."

Mr. Brown moved that the Convention proceed to the consideration of the report of the committee on the executive department.

This motion led to some conversation as to the order of business, between Messrs. Spencer, Blakistone, Phelps, Grason and the President, after which, on a suggestion made by

Mr. Tuck, that the Convention proceed to the consideration of the report of the committee on the elective franchise;

Mr. Brown withdrew his motion.

Mr. Tuck then submitted his motion.

The first section of the report was then read.

A desultory conversation followed as to the order of proceeding.

Mr. Dorsey suggested that the report should lie over, so as to give gentlemen an opportunity of examining the printed report as it came from the committee of the whole, and he made a motion to that effect.

Mr. Tuck. I suggest to the gentleman to name a day—say to-morrow.

Mr. Dorsey. I accept the suggestion.

Mr. Brent, of Baltimore city, opposed the postponement, on the ground that it would be better that the Convention should go on and complete one part of the Constitution, before commencing on another.

Some conversation followed between Messrs. Brent, of Baltimore, and Chambers, of Kent.

COMMITTEE OF REVISION.

Mr. JOHNSON said he had been a good deal absent from the Convention, and now, for the first time, saw the report of the committee on the elective franchise, as it had come from the hands of the committee of the whole. I was about to make a suggestion, (continued Mr. J.) which, if it should meet the views of more experienced gentlemen, will, I think, have a salutary effect on the business of this Convention. It is that a committee of revision be appointed, whose duty it shall be to take charge of bills after they have been reported from the committee of the whole, correct and, if need be, condense their phraseology, and report them back for the action of the Convention. If objection is made, I will withdraw the resolution.

The PRESIDENT intimated that such a resolution pending, a motion to postpone was not in order.

Mr. JOHNSON waived his motion for the present.

THE ELECTIVE FRANCHISE.

The question then recurred and was taken on the motion to postpone the consideration of this report, and it was decided in the affirmative.

So the further consideration of the report was postponed until to-morrow.

THE BILL OF RIGHTS.

Messrs. BLAKISTONE and BROWN moved that the Convention proceed to the consideration of the bill of rights.

Mr. PARKE. I feel some objection to that motion, because, having given notice of amendments which have not yet been printed for the use of the Convention, I shall enter upon the consideration of the subject at a disadvantage. I think it would be better to postpone the consideration of the bill, though if it is the pleasure of the Convention now to take it up. I suppose I can send to the Printer and withdraw my amendments from his hands.

Mr. TUCK. Probably the gentleman's amendments do not come in at the first part of the bill.

Mr. PARKE. One of them is an amendment to the preamble.

SEVERAL VOICES. "Well, then, the question on the preamble will be taken last!"

Mr. GRASON. I was willing that the report of the committee on the elective franchise should be taken up and finally acted upon, but as it is postponed, I think that the Convention should now proceed with the regular order of business. That is the report of the committee on the executive department. I think the bill of rights one of the very last subjects which should be considered by the Convention. After we have framed the other parts of the Constitution, and have decided what powers shall be vested in the different departments of the government—legislative, executive and judicial—we shall be better enabled to judge what provisions should be placed in the bill of rights for the purpose of restraining them. Besides, I think, that if the bill is taken up now, the debate upon it may occupy a month; whilst if its consideration is postponed until other subjects have been disposed of, the Convention, under the pressure of an earnest desire on the part of the members to go home, will be content with a much shorter discussion.

Mr. BOWIE. It seems to me to be most appropriate that the bill of rights should be taken up first. Our Constitution is to be grounded upon the great fundamental principles of liberty, set forth in that declaration. It is important first to settle the great cardinal republican principles upon which we will base a Constitution, before we attempt to raise the superstructure. Otherwise, we may have conflicting provisions. I know of no subject on which we all agree better than on these general abstract principles embodied in the bill of rights. A few amendments may perhaps be offered, but not many. I have, myself, none to propose. I hope we shall take up the bill and continue its consideration, until we have finished it. I cannot concur with gentlemen in the idea of taking up things by piece-meal. Let us take up one subject at a time, and continue upon it until it is disposed of. If we come to that determination, we shall move on in something like harmony and order—efficient order.

COMMITTEE OF REVISION.

Mr. JOHNSON desired at this time to offer the order indicated by him, providing for the appointment of a committee of revision. If the resolution gave rise to debate, he would, he said, withdraw it.

Mr. BLAKISTONE, for the moment, withdrew his motion to proceed to the consideration of the bill of rights.

Mr. JOHNSON then offered a resolution providing for the appointment of a committee for the purpose he had indicated.

Mr. JENIFER, enquired of what number the committee should be composed.

Mr. RANDALL suggested that it should consist of the Chairmen of all the committees.

Mr. JOHNSON said, that as Chairman of one of the committees, (the committee on the legislative department,) he must ask to be excused, as he would be unavoidably absent for some time.

Some conversation arising, Mr. JOHNSON withdrew the resolution.

THE BILL OF RIGHTS.

The motion was then renewed that the Convention take up this bill.

The motion having been agreed to, the Convention proceeded to the consideration of the following report, submitted by Mr. DORSEY, on the 11th instant, as Chairman of the Committee on the

DECLARATION OF RIGHTS.

We, the Delegates of Maryland, in Convention assembled, taking into our most serious consideration, the best means of establishing a good Constitution in this State, declare:

Article 1. That all government of right originates from the people, is founded in compact only, and instituted solely for the good of the whole.

Art. 2. That the people of this State ought to have the sole and exclusive right of regulating the internal government and police thereof.

Art. 3. That the inhabitants of Maryland are entitled to the common law of England, and the trial by jury according to the course of that law and to the benefit of such of the English statutes as existed at the time of their first emigration, and which by experience have been found applicable to their local and other circumstances, and of such others as have been since made in England or Great Britain, and have been introduced, used and practiced by the courts of law or equity, and also to all acts of assembly in force on the first Monday of November, 1850, except such as may have since expired, or may be altered by acts of this Convention, or this Declaration of Rights, subject, nevertheless, to the revision of, and amendment or repeal by the Legislature of this State, and the inhabitants of Maryland are also entitled to all property derived to them from or under the charter granted by His Majesty, Charles the First, to Cæcilius Calvert, Baron of Baltimore.

Art. 4. That all persons invested with the Legislative or Executive powers of Government, are the trustees of the public, and as such, accountable for their conduct; wherefore, whenever the ends of Government are preverted, and public liberty manifestly endangered, and all other means of redress are ineffectual, the people may, and of right ought to reform the old or establish a new government; the doctrine of non-resistance against arbitrary power and oppression is absurd, slavish and destructive of the good and happiness of mankind.

Art. 5. That the right of the people to participate in the Legislature is the best security of liberty, and the foundation of all free government, for this purpose elections ought to be free and frequent, and every free white male citizen having the qualifications prescribed by the Constitution, ought to have the right of suffrage.

Art. 6. That the legislative, executive and judicial powers of Government ought to be forever separate and distinct from each other.

Art. 7. That no power of suspending laws, or the execution of laws, unless by or derived from the Legislature, ought to be exercised or allowed.

Art. 8. That freedom of speech and debates, or proceedings in the Legislature, ought not to be impeached in any court of judicature.

Art. 9. That Annapolis be the place for the meeting of the Legislature; and the Legislature ought not to be convened or held at any other place but from evident necessity.

Art. 10. That for the redress of grievances, and for amending, strengthening and preserving the laws, the Legislature ought to be frequently convened.

Art. 11. That every man hath a right to petition the Legislature for the redress of grievances in a peaceable and orderly manner.

Art. 12. That no aid, charge, tax, burther, fee or fees, ought to be set, rated or levied, under any pretence, without the consent of the Legislature.

Art. 13. That paupers ought not to be assessed for the support of Government, but every other person in this State, or person holding property therein, ought to contribute his proportion of public taxes, for the support of Government, according to his actual worth in real or personal property; yet fines, duties or taxes may properly and justly be imposed or laid, on persons or property, with a political view, for the good government and benefit of the community.

Art. 14. That sanguinary laws ought to be avoided, as far as is consistent with the safety of the State; and no law to inflict cruel and unusual pains and penalties ought to be made, in any case, or at any time hereafter.

Art. 15. That retrospective laws, punishing acts committed before the existence of such laws, and by them only declared criminal, are oppressive, unjust and incompatible with liberty, wherefore, no *ex post facto* law ought to be made.

Art. 16. That no law to attaint particular persons of treason or felony, ought to be made in any case, or at any time hereafter.

Art. 17. That every free man, for any injury done to him in his person or property, ought to have remedy by the course of the law of the land, and ought to have justice and right, freely without sale, fully without any denial, and speedily without delay, according to the law of the land.

Art. 18. That the trial of facts where they arise, is one of the greatest securities of the lives, liberties and estate of the people.

Art. 19. That in all criminal prosecutions, every man hath a right to be informed of the accusation against him; to have a copy of the indictment or charge, in due time (if required) to prepare for his defence; to be allowed counsel, to be confronted with the witnesses against him; to have process for his witnesses; to examine the witnesses for and against him on oath; and to a speedy trial by an impartial jury, without whose unanimous consent he ought not to be found guilty.

Art. 20. That no man ought to be compelled to give evidence against himself in a court of common law, or in any other court, but in such cases as have been usually practised in this State or may hereafter be directed by the Legislature.

Art. 21. That no freeman ought to be taken or imprisoned, or disseized of his freehold, liberties or privileges, or outlawed, or exiled, or in any manner destroyed, or deprived of his life, liberty or property, but by the judgment of his peers, or by the law of the land.

Art. 22. That excessive bail ought not to be required, nor excessive fines imposed, nor cruel or unusual punishment inflicted by the courts of law.

Art. 23. That all warrants, without oath, or affirmation, to search suspected places, or to seize any person or property, are grievous and oppressive; and all general warrants to search suspected places, or to apprehend suspected persons, without naming or describing the place, or the person in special, are illegal and ought not to be granted.

Art. 24. That there ought to be no forfeiture of any part of the estate of any person for any crime, except murder or treason against the State, and then only on conviction and attainder.

Art. 25. That a well regulated militia is the proper and natural defence of a free Government.

Art. 26. That standing armies are dangerous to liberty, and ought not to be raised or kept up without consent of the Legislature.

Art. 27. That in all cases and at all times, the military ought to be under strict subordination to, and control of the civil power.

Art. 28. That no soldier ought to be quartered in any house in time of peace without the consent of the owner, and in time of war, in such manner as the Legislature shall direct.

Art. 29. That no person except regular soldiers, mariners and marines, in the service of this State, or militia when in actual service, ought in any case to be subject to, or punishable by martial law.

Art. 30. That the independency and uprightness of Judges are essential to the impartial administration of justice, and a great security to the rights and liberties of the people; wherefore the Chancellor and Judges shall not be removed except for misbehavior, on conviction in a court of law, or by the Governor, upon the address of the General Assembly; *provided*, that two-thirds of all the members of each House, concur in such address; that salaries, liberal, but not profuse, ought to be secured to the Chancellor and Judges during the continuance of their commissions, in such manner and at such time as the Legislature shall hereafter direct, upon consideration of the circumstances of this State; no Chancellor or Judge ought to hold any other office, civil or military, under the Constitution or Laws of this State, or of the United States, or of any member thereof, or receive fees or perquisites of any kind for the discharge of his official duties.

Art. 31. That a long continuance in the first executive departments of power or trust, is dangerous to liberty; a rotation, therefore, in those departments is one of the best securities of permanent freedom.

Art. 32. That no person ought to hold at the same time more than one office of profit, created by the Constitution or Laws of this State; nor ought any person in public trust to receive any present from any Foreign Prince or State, or from the United States, or any of them, without the approbation of this State.

Art. 33. That as it is the duty of every man to worship God in such manner as he thinks most acceptable to him, all persons are equally entitled to protection in their religious liberty; wherefore, no person ought by any law to be molested in his person or estate, on account of his religious persuasion or profession, or for his religious practice, unless under color of religion, any man shall disturb the good order, peace or safety of the State, or shall infringe the laws of morality, or injure others in their natural, civil or religious rights; nor ought any person, to be compelled to frequent or maintain or contribute, unless on contract, to maintain any place of worship or any ministry.

Art. 34. That every gift, sale or devise of lands, to any minister, public teacher or preacher of the gospel, as such, or to any religious sect, order or denomination, or to, or for the support, use or benefit of, or in trust for any minister, public teacher or preacher of the gospel, as such, or any religious sect, order or denomination, and every gift or sale of goods or chattels, to go in succession, or to take place after the death of the seller or donor, to or for such support, use or benefit; and also every devise of goods or chattels to or for the support, use or benefit of any minister, public teacher or preacher of the gospel, as such, or any religious sect, order or denomination, without the leave of the Legislature, shall be void; except always any sale, gift, lease or devise of any quantity of land, not exceeding five acres for a church, meeting or other house of worship, and for a burying ground, which shall be improved, enjoyed, or used only for such purpose; or such sale, gift, lease or devise shall be void.

Art. 35. That no other test or qualification ought to be required, on admission to any office of trust or profit, than such oath of support and fidelity to this State and the United States, and such oath of office as shall be directed by this Convention, or the Legislature of this State.

Art. 36. That the manner of administering an oath to any person ought to be such as those of the religious persuasion, profession or denomination of which such person is one, generally esteem the most effectual confirmation by the attestation of the Divine Being; and that the people called Quakers, those called Tunkers, and those called Menonists, and all others conscientiously scrupulous of taking an oath on any occasion, ought to be allowed to make their solemn affirmation in the manner that Quakers have been heretofore allowed to affirm, and to be of the same avail as an oath, in all such cases as the affirmation of Quakers hath been allowed and accepted within this State, instead of an oath. And on such affimation, warrants to search for stolen goods, or the apprehension or commitment of offenders, ought to be granted, or security for the peace awarded, and Quakers, Tunkers, Menonists and such others ought also, on their solemn affirmation as aforesaid, to be admitted as witnesses in all criminal cases.

Art. 37. That the city of Annapolis ought to have all its rights, privileges and benefits, agreeable to its charter, and the acts of Assembly confirming and regulating the same; subject, nevertheless, to such alterations as have been made by the Legislature or as may be made by this Convention or any future Legislature.

Art. 38. That the liberty of the press ought to be inviobably preserved.

Art. 39. That monopolies are odious, contrary to the spirit of a free government and the principles of commerce, and ought not to be suffered.

Art. 40. That no title of nobility or hereditary honors, ought to be granted in this State.

Art. 41. That this Declaration of Rights, or the Form of Government to be established by this Convention, or any part of either of them, ought not to be altered, changed or abolished, but in such manner as this Convention shall prescribe and direct."

The report was read through, and was then taken up by sections.

The first article being under consideration as follows:

"*Art.* 1. That all government of right originates from the people, is founded in compact only and instituted solely for the good of the whole."

Mr. PRESSTMAN moved to amend said article by adding at the end thereof, the following:

"And they have at all times the inalienable right to alter, reform, or abolish their form of government, in such manner as they may think expedient."

Some conversation followed between Messrs. PARKE, BISER and PRESSTMAN as to the most appropriate place for the amendment.

Mr. CHAMBERS had hoped, after occupying so much of the attention of the House on matters more immediately confided to his care, to take no part in the debate on the bill of rights. But he felt it to be his duty, and he supposed every other member did also, to understand what he was about.

The second article of the bill, as reported, recognizes fully the right of the people—the sole and exclusive right—to regulate the internal government of the State. What more is to be the effect of this amendment? If it is designed to admit the power and right of the people in a constitutional and legal mode, to effect changes in the government, it is submitted that this is already there, in terms as strong as language can ex press it. Is any other power intended? Is it to countenance the doctrine that under any sudden impulse, regardless of the legal forms which they themselves have prescribed, and by any tumultuous movement, the people might rise and by violence effect a change in the existing government? If that was the power intended to be asserted, he denied that it had ever been recognized by any government. The exercise of such a power would be fatal not only to property, but to the life of every citizen. It could not fail ultimately to be exerted by a lawless and infuriated assemblage. He hoped the gentleman who offered the amendment would explain his object. We had hitherto lived happily under the present bill of rights, which has been every where respected, and if we are to adopt a new principle by which any self-constituted body of men choosing to call themselves "the people," can assume the power to subvert, when and as they please, the whole social and political fabric, let us at least understand it. Let it be in terms plain and distinct, that neither this Convention or those who are to pass upon our work, may be in any doubt or error in regard to it.

Mr. PRESSTMAN said:

That when he offered the amendment to the first article of the bill of rights, he would take occasion to say to the several gentlemen who have suggested the propriety of presenting it to certain other articles, or as an additional one to the report of the committee, that he had weighed well the purport of his amendment, and after mature reflection thought, (and he had as yet seen no reason for a change of that opinion,) that there was a peculiar and fitting appropriateness in the position where he now sought to place it. He did not think that the provisions of the 4th or 41st articles, in the report of the gentleman from Anne Arundel, (Mr. Dorsey,) embraced the principle he sought to engraft upon the bill of rights; one looks to the naked revolutionary right which exists under all governments in the people, to resist tyranny and throw off the yoke of oppression. The language employed in that article is "that whenever the ends of government are perverted, and the public liberty manifestly endangered, and all other means of redress are ineffectual, the people may, and of right ought to reform the old or establish a new government." And that, sir, is the identical language of the present bill of rights of Maryland. The other refers to the mode of change which this Convention may or *may not* adopt, when we come to establish the Constitution itself. Possibly, sir, that mode may be the one now prescribed by the 59th article of the existing Constitution, which declares "that no change shall be made without the vote of two successive Legislatures." He was admonished by the lessons of experience, that the people, in trusting to that mode, had for years leaned upon a broken reed, which had pierced them. He hoped never to hear again of legislative reform. He could see in that, nothing but disappointment,—

"The serpent coil of future faithlessness."

Before making a more explicit annunciation of the object of his amendment and the doctrine it contained, he wished to relieve himself of the effect of an impression which seemed to be in the mind of the gentleman from Kent, that this was an unmatured proposition. He had nothing of that kind to say in extenuation of his position. What he had done, he had done with deliberation. The uncertainty which had existed as to the true construction of the present bill of rights and Constitution, when taken separately or as a whole, as to the time when, and the means and measures required to effect a change by the people in their organic law, and above all, the unwillingness of many to recognize this inalienable right in them, except in a manner and form so mutilated, as to peril, if not to deny its very existence, impelled him to insert the principle contained in his amendment as a cardinal one, in clear and unambiguous language, in the bill of rights now to be adopted, and that, too, unrestrained by the terms employed in the present bill of rights. The phraseology of the present article, stringent as it is, implying, in the minds of some men, no change short of a revolution by physical violence. He regarded the principle of peaceable revolution, (such as that now going on) as a precious one; it would be a jewel that would attract the affections and confidence of the people, if placed in our bill of rights, while, without it, sir, that bill of rights would be but an empty casket, unseemly and valueless. Change without civil war—adaptation of the government to the wants of the people without bloodshed! This, sir, is the whole end and purpose of my amendment. But, sir, the gentleman from Kent, (Mr. Chambers,) "scents treason in the wind." This does not surprise me, neither would it fright me from my propriety, if he should discover "it was flat burglary." The amendment he had offered was like the line and plumet, it would separate the reformers and the anti-reformers of that body, and with great deference, he placed the gentleman from Kent at the head of the latter. He had been called upon to unveil the monster which which lurked under the drapery of his amendment.

Now, sir, let me first premise if the principle is a good one; if it be just and true, let it be inserted in the bill of rights. Nothing that he could say, would add to its intrinsic merit, and surely it should not be allowed to lose its force by any attempt on his part to illustrate it. But, sir, the gentleman from Kent, in putting inquiries, seeks a full and frank disclosure of the scope and objects designed by me. The Convention will remember this amendment was offered without comment, and he was willing that the Convention should vote "aye" or "noe" upon it, as the principle itself should inspire confidence or alarm. The gentleman from Kent, has indeed taken high ground; he denies, with great emphasis, that such a principle has been adopted in any form of Government, with which he has been acquainted, that it is a monstrous proposition. Before this discussion closes, he will perhaps recognise his present position, while holding a seat on this floor, as alone justifiable in the doctrine of peaceable revolution, by the will of the people, which he, (Mr. P.) was struggling to maintain. He will pardon the resort to the *argumentum ad hominum*. The proposition submitted by him was not an original one, either in the idea or the language in which it is expressed. It shines in letters of living light upon the face of many, if not the greater part, of the bills of rights of the several States of this glorious Union. In the constitution of Virginia—the mother of States, as she has been justly styled—the following language is employed:—"That government is, or ought to be, instituted for the common benefit, protection, and security of the people, nation or community. Of all the various forms of government, that is best which is capable of producing the greatest degree of happiness and safety, and is most effectually secured against the danger of mal-administration, and that when any government, shall be found inadequate or contrary to these purposes, a majority of the community hath an indubitable, unalienable right to alter, reform or abolish it, *in such manner* as shall be judged most conducive to the public weal." Indeed, sir, the absence of such a provision in the several Constitutions constitute exceptions. A similar feature to that he had quoted is to be found in the Constitutions of Maine, Vermont and other of the older States, and it is incorporated in most, if not all of the new States. Bear in mind, sir, *no other mode* is prescribed in the Constitution of Virginia and several other States of the Union, for the reform or alteration of their organic law. All is wisely left to the wisdom, patriotism and sound common sense of the people. Did the illustrious men who framed that Constitution contemplete a bloody revolution as the appropriate mode? It is not for us to set limits upon the action of the people. Let not the agent lord it over his principal.

In the Virginia Convention of 1830, the following resolution was offered:

"*Resolved*, That in the opinion of the committee that the Constitution of this State ought to be so amended, as to provide a mode in which future amendments shall be made therein."

It was voted down, ayes 28, noes 68.

John Randolph addressed the Convention in opposition to its adoption, in the following significant language. "I shall vote against this resolution, and I will state as succintly as I can, my reasons for doing so. I believe they will in substance be found in a very old book, and conveyed in these words, 'sufficient unto the day is the evil thereof.' Sir, I have remarked since the commencement of our deliberations, and with no small surprise, a very great anxiety to provide for *futurity*. Gentleman, for example, are not content with any present discussion of the Constitutiou, unless we will consent to prescribe for all time hereafter. I had always thought him the most skilful physician, who, when called to a patient, relieved him of the existing malady without undertaking to prescribe for such, as might by possibility endure thereafter." And yet, sir, in the face of all this, gentlemen say the necessity is urgent and cannot be avoided, that some mode of change must be fixed by the Constitution. If so, which he denied, it would be time enough to consider that after we had set forth the bill of rights.

In the language of the bill of rights of Texas, which, if report be true, is the work of that illustrious statesman, John C. Calhoun, and which, in its features show the chisel of a master's hand, is the identical language embodied in my amendment He had had it demanded of him, in terms and tones indicating anticipated annihilation, whether he designed to uphold the doctrine that the people are not bound to adhere to the terms of the compact to which they are parties. His plain answer was this: that no Convention that ever sat or ever will sit in this republican land have the right to bind posterity. The people are omnipotent, and when they speak it is "the delegated voice of God." The creature is not above the Creator. The compact is binding so long as the sovereignty who framed it, wills it and until revoked, is supreme over all and must be obeyed; but it cannot survive one moment longer than the people ordain that it should last.

He held that the theory of compact between counties in a State, or the minority with the majority, requiring the assent of all to change their Constitution, to be founded in error—gross error. There is but one party—the people. The majority of the people can make or un make it. If otherwise, then our ancestors who formed this Constitution must have expected that the right of the majority could alone be secured by bloodshed—experience was not necessary to inculcate the lesson that a minority never surrender power by voluntary action. Gentlemen will perceive, that the doctrine he was seeking to maintain, was this, that the people had intelligence enough to make or unmake a Constitution without a resort to pikes and guns. Aye, sir! without being ground to the earth by the iron heel of despotism; without being the victims of tyranny; the people may, and of right ought to, alter their form of government, with a view to the adoption of a better system of government; to avail themselves of the improvements daily made in the science of government; to keep pace with the onward progress of free principles. While he spoke, we were in the midst of a revolution, not only "bloodless as yet," but, to borrow a familiar phrase, all is "as calm as a summer's morning."

Without the machinery of a legislative act, or forms prescribed by the Constitution, he insisted, that the people might take into their own hands the work of reforming the Constitution, and they would be seldom found to act on light and trivial grounds. He supposed a case, that the people of Kent county chose to meet together for the purpose of framing a Constitution, and that instrument was proclaimed by that meeting and submitted to the people of the State, would they have a right to adopt it? and if assented to by the political power of the State, would it not be valid and binding? All forms are mere matters of conveience, and are not obligatory.

Mr. Crisfield asked by what process this Constitution of the people, if ratified, was to be carried out? How did he propose to ascertain if it was ratified by a majority?

He should come to that presently, and in passing, need only say that when the gentleman from Somerset, (Mr. Crisfield,) and the gentleman from Kent, (Mr. Chambers,) both denying the constitutional right of the Legislature, (as did the party to which they belong, in many a hard fought contest,) to pass the very act which called this Convention into being, and likewise denying that "the ends of justice have been perverted, and liberty manifestly endangered," (the revolutionary right,) and pass through the fiery ordeal with their robes unscorched; (it will not do to say, that they hold their places by as good a title "*as any one else*," possession not being a good plea in *foro conscientiæ*,) it will be time enough for them to set in judgment upon the modes the people may hereafter adopt, to declare their will, and when they do so declare, possibly, these gentlemen may be members of the Convention.

But, sir, for the sake of the great principle he would be more explicit. He held the doctrine that the people—that is, a clear and unquestionable majority—have a right to determine in what mode their will is to be proclaimed, and permit him to say, that whenever they shall speak in thunder tones and adopt a Constitution in such mode and manner, as to evince to the world that it is the expression of a majority, no political Canute can be found to stay the onward tide of public sentiment; it will come to the practical test of public opinion, and as was admitted by the gentleman from Kent in a former discussion, when he held this Convention to be unauthorized by any recognized form of law, that, nevertheless, the Constitution which they should present, none but a madman would dare oppose, after it had met the sanction of the people. He did not expect that there would be found any man bold enough to say that such a movement should be put down by executive batteries.

If the proposition he sought to maintain was regarded as unsound, let some gentleman bring forward a proposition disaffirming it. The difference between himself and those who opposed the amendment was this: They no doubt entertain a fear that if we recognize this principle, that the people have the right to alter or change their Constitution at will and pleasure; that they will abuse that right, and that it will be exercised without sufficient reason, and for light and trivial causes. By what authority is this judgment pronounced against the virtue and intelligence of the people? He entertained no such opinion as to the great mass of the people. If he thought so he would openly confess that the great experiment which was being tried, whether man was capable of self-government had proved a miserable failure. Gentlemen must not confound the term *people* with that of *mob*. Give them, sir, a good Constitution, and they will appreciate it as an unpurchasable treasure. They will cling the closer to it when the tempest of passion is aroused by demagogues, and in the full enjoyment of liberty and happiness, they will not exchange the tried gold for the counterfeit presentiment.

Mr. P. having concluded,

Mr. Chambers obtained the floor, but yielded for the moment to

Mr. Hicks, who said he wished to offer an amendment, but not to make a speech upon it. He desired simply to state that if the proposition of the gentleman from Baltimore city, (Mr. Presstman,) was adopted, that contained in his (Mr. H.'s) amendment, must necessarily go with it.

Mr. H.'s amendment was read as follows:

Amend said amendment by adding at the end thereof, the following:

"And that any portion of the people of this State, shall have the right to secede and unite themselves, and the territory occupied by them, to such adjoining State as they shall elect."

Mr. Chambers said in reply to the call for his opinion. Why if the people were supreme, the act convening the Legislature was not constitutional, he had only to repeat, as he had before said, it was because the bill of rights and the constitution positively forbid any change in the organic law, except in the mode prescribed in the 59th article. He did not mean to enter upon a discussion of the doctrines of the reform party. He would, however, say, they take their origin long since the period assigned by the gentleman, (Mr. Presstman.) Many years rolled on and many changes in parties occurred before ever a whisper was heard that a Convention could be called by a single act of the Legislature, and indeed before a Convention, called in any way, was heard of. As to the right of the people to administer, reform or alter their Constitution whenever they may think proper, he never doubted or denied it. No man in this age and country does or can doubt or deny it. He asked if that was not genuine democratic doctrine. But *how* was it to be done? When on this point they compared notes, it would be found he was a better democrat than the gentleman was. I, (said Mr. C.,) give more power to the people and say they can prescribe—the "*how*" they can "bind themselves." while he says they have no power to do so. The gentleman admits the language of his proposition is cloudy, and he says let those that come after us find out for themselves its true construction. No, sir, let us make ourselves clearly understood—let every thing be plain, not a puzzle to those who are to come after us. The Constitution is not for lawyers and the courts only, but for all classes and descriptions of citizens.

The 1st article in the bill of rights is in these words,"all government originates from the people, is *founded in compact*, and instituted solely for the good of the *whole*." What meant these words, "founded in compact?" Were they senseless? No—but full of meaning. Government was a compact and for the *whole*. Yet, says the gentleman, a part may, at their will and pleasure, violate its most solemn engagements. True it is, there is no judicial tribune before which a breach may be prosecuted, but the moral and political obligation to observe its terms is none the less for that.

Mr. Presstman wished to hear the reasons on which this view was founded. The gentleman from Kent admitted the right of the people to make the compact. Had they not then an equal right to change the compact?

Mr. Chambers replied, he had said so in "*totti-dem verbis*," and he now repeated it. (Here, with a pause after every word, he said in a very slow and deliberate manner.) I admit the right of the sovereign people to change the Constitution whenever they think proper to do so. Was that emphatic enough? But yet they must do it legally.

When they have themselves declared the mode and manner, and the only mode and manner, they must pursue it. Here they divided. The gentleman says they may do it in despite of the compact without Constitution or law, against Constitution and law. Well, he should not argue against this doctrine. He would as soon enter into an elaborate logical argument with the most nervous, timid child, to persuade it to be alarmed when suddenly brought into the immediate presence of a hideous monster, as he would to persuade the people that they ought to dread this political monster; and he was free to say that of all the horrible monsters that ever presented themselves to his political vision, the most horrible was a mob, and as he had before said, such a doctrine, if sanctioned, would ultimately lead to that—the exercise of this lawless power by a mob.

He had been asked, Why not provide for a Convention?

He would say it was not only proper, but it was our duty to do this. We represent the people—we are forming the compact. Now is the time to do it, and if no one else does, (Mr. C.) said, he pledged himself to offer a provision regulating the mode of calling a Convention. This mode of proceeding had lately become quite fashionable, and if the good people of Maryland chose to follow it, they must be indulged. Only let every thing be done "decently and in order." Let it be done according to the form of law. Have a Convention once a year, if it be deemed proper—name a commission to call it at pleasure—give to the City Council of Baltimore, if it must be so, the power to convene a Convention; but let it be done "according to the Constitution and Laws of the land." Never sanction the idea that an irresponsible self-created body of men, excited by the fiercest passions, wounded by defeat and disappointment, embittered by party collisions and animosities, and enflamed by selfish unprincipled demagogues to a state of madness as well as folly—never tolerate the idea that such an assemblage, itself the sole judge of its own numbers, of its own powers, its own mode of proceeding, without any rule to guide or any authority to restrain its action, but its own unbridled will—is the power competent to rule—to put down an existing government and found a new one. He described the proposition, with its "Gorgon head" as an alarming heresy which should be abjured by every wise and prudent man.

Mr. Johnson said, he was in favor of both these propositions, and that if he were in his seat when the question was taken, he should vote for both with infinite pleasure. The first [continued Mr. J.] is a self-evident proposition. I cannot see that it requires a moment's discussion. In the nineteenth century, with thirty republican constitutions before our eyes in which it finds a place, it is an axiom—and it is two late for me, at least, to discuss it. The history of our own country and of France, demonstrates that oppression, intolerable oppression, may be thrown off by the people whenever they choose to rise up in their majesty and assert their rights. It is a power which cannot be taken away from the people, and of which they cannot even divest themselves And if this Convention should form a Constitution, one of the provisions of which should declare it to be unalterable for ever—and if that Constitution, thus stamped with a perpetual existence, should be ratified by a unanimous vote of the people of the State of Maryland, it would be an absurdity so gross, that in fifty years hence or less, when its provisions might have ceased to be applicable to another, and a different condition of things, the people would cast it indignantly aside, and substitute for it an organic law better suited to their wishes and necessities. Men would be worse than slaves if they were to hold themselves bound by such decrees, or yield a tame acquiescence in them.

The people are eternal—immortal. Government is immortal—though its peculiar form and features must be changed, so as to be adapted to the fluctuations of human life and the vicissitudes of human affairs. I will not go into a puzzle. It is admitted that the people have a right to make, and to change their Constitution. I will not go into dialectics to show, that when I admit a board principle, and say "yes, you may do this thing for yourself to-day," I cannot cripple and invalidate that very principle by adding, "but you cannot let the people do it for themselves to-morrow." I belong to no such school of tactics. If the people have the right to-day to change their Constitution, they have the right to-morrow. As their minds and the circumstances by which they are surrounded change, they may so change their Constitution, as to give it a more perfect adaptation to the new condition of affairs. Take an illustration—it may, perhaps, at this time of day, be regarded as an absurd one; but it will answer for the occasion. Let us imagine all the departments of the government—legislative, executive and judicial—conspiring to overthrow the influence of the people, and to monopolise all power within their own hands. Is there a man with a human heart beating in his bosom, or a mind that yet retains one lingering impression of the great principles of human freedom, that would not rebel—instantly, wildly rebel against such outrages? The people—the people alone—are to direct and control these things; and I will not desecrate their cause by calling them a "mob."

Mr. CHAMBERS, of Kent, interposed and said, that he had applied the term to a certain class of lawless men, and hoped he was not understood as applying it to all popular assemblies. If the gentleman from Frederick, (Mr. Johnson,) had understood him as saying one word either in opposition to the right of revolution, or in relation to that right at all, the gentleman was mistaken. He was fighting a shadow. Whenever oppression justified revolution, that was another affair.

Mr. JOHNSON, (continuing.) I was not answering the argument. I do not intend to do so, nor to go into a skirmish. I consider the term inappropriate to the people of Maryland. What *is* revolution? What is meant by the term? Let us come to the meaning of words and define them. All change is revolution.

Mr. CHAMBERS, of Kent, (in his seat.) Forcible charge.

Mr. JOHNSON, (continuing.) That is another thing. I am not to be drawn off in that way. I say, revolution is change, alteration, mutation. Revolution is going on daily, hourly, in our own nature. All the elements are in a state of revolution. The seasons gracefully revolve. I am not going to discuss what is revolution. Let not that be presented as a bug-bear here. It is not flood—it is not fire—it is not sword—it is not cannon. Revolution is alteration. We are in the progress of revolution at this moment. We are changing, or attempting to change a past state of things to a present, and a future; and I suppose that those who come after us will be as wise as we are, with all of our experience, and, at the same time, more than our knowledge. I pass over the first and second articles of the bill of rights. The fourth article teaches revolution. Human language cannot be stronger. It teaches us that whenever the people are oppressed, it is their high and holy duty to turn out their rulers and kick off a government that galls them. That duty is inscribed upon the decrees of the political Decalogue of Maryland. It is already spoken. It is already proclaimed.

How then may you do this thing? If the people have the power, and *that* is conceded, then I agree with the gentleman from Baltimore, (Mr. Presstman,) that they will always have good sense enough to exercise the power discreetly and wisely. It is not for me to hold up the feeble light of my pale candle—it is not for me to confine within the compass of my own limited horizon, the desires, the hopes, the interests, the necessities of those who may follow me, and whose expanse of vision may perhaps leave my own in comparative darkness. The question is plain. I will not argue it. I will vote "aye," from morning to night, and from night to morning on such propositions. I recollect that when a boy, some twenty years ago, in the city of New York, the American Historical Society held a meeting for the purpose of organization. I attended it. The venerable John Quincy Adams was made President, and the first duty was to form a Constitution. Article by article was adopted; and finally a young lawyer rose in his place, and offered an article, declaring that a majority of the society could change their Constitution whenever they pleased. He was about addressing the Chair, when the venerable old man said to him, "Sir, it is useless to incorporate such an article in the Constitution; for in the nineteenth century, in America, it would be ridiculous to assert a power which no one dare deny, and in which the whole world concur."

Therefore, whether we insert in our Constitution those declarations, as to what the people may do, or whether we do not insert them, they can, and will, whenever they are in a majority, correct the abuses of their government. I say, they always will do it. There is not in the wide world a people more forbearing, more orderly, more law-loving, more attached to the true principles of republican government, than the people of this brave old State of Maryland. If any evidence of this truth is needed, we have but to point to the patient endurance with which they have consented to live under their old Constitution, without suffering themselves to be quickened to rash or evil acts.

But I will say no more. I rose to give an opinion—not to make an argument. Nor do I desire to do so; for I do not believe that any converts are to be made on this question by discussing it.

Mr. BRENT, of Baltimore city, admitted that

the people had a right to change their Constitution. No man could deny or fetter this right. But he entered his protest against some of the doctrines which had been laid down, and the effect of which might be the substitution of tyranny in the place of our free institutions. Admitting the abstract doctrine, the question is, who are the people of Maryland who are to be empowered to make a Constitution? Are they a multitudinous assembly, or are they agents, legally elected by qualified voters? It can only be ascertained by the ballot-box who are the repositories of this power. It is the ballot-box that overthrows all the abstractions of the gentleman from Kent. He differed from his colleague who had expressed his opposition to the action of the legislature in framing a Constitution.

Mr. Presstman asked his colleague if he thought there was no other way of obtaining a change of the Constitution, but by a legislative act?

Mr. Brent replied, there was none. All must be orderly and legally done. That done, he was ready to go with his colleague through all the danger which was anticipated by some, from beginning to end. But there was no other way, except through the law. How could it be proved that there was a majority of the people in favor of any movement, but through the ballot-box; and the ballots must be deposited by qualified voters, before legally appointed judges of elections, and according to the prescribed forms; and when, in this way, the votes of the people shall be given in favor of the Constitution on which we are now engaged, it will have all the power of an organic law. The influence of the people is omnipotent, in a moral sense, at the ballot-box; and in a physical sense, when a resort to violence is resolved on. The majority which has made the compact has the right to revoke it. It is not like a compact made between two sovereign States; it is an agreement made among each other, and therefore may, at any time, be changed by the people who made it. It is not like the laws of the Medes and Persians. It may be altered at any time. If the people choose to say this Constitution shall not be revoked, still the same people may revoke it at any time by a resort to the ballot-box, or by physical force. While he would vote for the proposition, he differed from his colleague in his view of the manner in which the Constitution may be altered. There was no way to ascertain the sense of the majority of the people but by the ballot-box.

Mr. Presstman asked, supposing that the Legislature thought inexpedient to call a Convention, was there no such thing as a peaceable revolution? And if there is no provision inserted in the bill of rights to meet this case, the effect would be, that, in such extremity, the people might be driven to a bloody revolution, which if unsuccessful, would bring on all engaged in it, the penalty of treason. He wished to know if there was no mode of bringing about a peaceable revolution?

Mr. Brent replied, that there was no such thing as a peaceable revolution. He asked his colleague if a company of individuals were to get together, and take possession of the polls, and appoint the judges of election, would they not violate the law, and render themselves liable to punishment? The ballot box would be corrupted by such conduct, and no one could foresee the evils which would result from this kind of revolution. The only way in which the people can secure future Conventions, without legislative action, is to insert a provision that a Convention shall be held every seven years; and if the legislature is not to be permitted to act, he could devise no other mode by which it could be effected. Otherwise, it must be brought about hereafter, as it had heretofore been, by an act of the legislature. There was only one other peaceable mode, if such it could be called, that is, if the people should rise in the majesty of their power, and present themselves in such overwhelming numbers that those who had been entrusted with the charge of the Government should quietly yield and abandon their posts without resistance.

And then pending the question,

The Convention adjourned until to-morrow at 11 o'clock.

WEDNESDAY, January 29, 1851.

The Convention met at eleven o'clock.

Prayer was made by the Rev. Mr. Griffith.

The roll was called, and a quorum being present, the journal of yesterday was read and approved.

The President stated that reports from committees were now in order.

No reports were made.

Mr. Dorsey presented the petition of James Sykes and others, praying that Howard District, of Anne Arundel county, may be made a separate county, to be called "Howard county."

The petition having been read,

Mr. Dorsey moved its reference to the committee on representation.

Mr. Bowie moved its reference to a select committee.

The propriety of the reference was briefly spoken to, by Messrs. Gwinn, Bowie, Smith and Harbine.

The question was then taken and the petition was referred to a select committee.

The President announced the following gentlemen as composing the said committee:

Messrs. Dorsey, Bowie, Smith, Harbine, and Ricaud.

THE HALL.

Mr. Magraw called the attention of the Convention to the order which had yesterday been adopted, providing for an adjournment over Saturday for the purpose of repairing the furnaces.

Mr. M. referred to the inconvenience to which

those members were subjected, whose seats were in that quarter of the Hall opposite the committee room, by the constant passing and re-passing of members and others, and he moved the appointment of a committee of three, whose duty it should be to ascertain what alteration could be made in the Hall that would add to the comfort and convenience of the members.

Ordered accordingly.

The committee was ordered to consist of the following gentlemen:

Messrs. MAGRAW, DIRICKSON, and SAPPINGTON.

HOUR OF MEETING.

Mr. STEPHENSON offered the following order.

"*Ordered*, That from and after the third day of February next, this Convention will meet daily at 10 o'clock, A. M., except Mondays, on which day the hour of meeting shall be 11 o'clock."

Mr. RIDGELY moved that the order be laid upon the table.

Mr. HARBINE asked the yeas and nays, which were ordered, and being taken, were yeas 35, nays 37.

So the motion was not laid on the table.

Mr. WARE moved to amend the order by making the hour of meeting on Monday 12 o'clock.

Mr. STEPHENSON accepted the amendment.

Mr. JOHN NEWCOMER moved to amend, by making the hour of meeting on Monday *ten* instead of *twelve*.

Mr. STEPHENSON accepted the amendment.

And by ayes 21, noes 34, the amendment was rejected.

The yeas and nays were called for by Mr. DASHIELL, and after some conversation on a point of order, were taken, and were yeas 40, nays 37.

So the amendment was adopted.

Mr. MORGAN moved a call of the House.

Mr. BUCHANAN seconded the motion.

The call was ordered, and the roll of the members was called.

On motion of Mr. MCHENRY, all further proceedings on the call were dispensed with.

After some further conversation, the reading of the resolution was called for, and its confused phraseology, as amended, give rise to some merriment.

Mr. TUCK moved to amend by substituting the hour of half-past eleven on Monday.

The amendment was rejected.

Mr. MCMASTER moved to lay the whole subject on the table.

Mr. STEPHENSON asked the yeas and nays.

Mr. MCMASTER withdrew his motion.

Mr. MORGAN renewed it.

Mr. HARBINE asked the yeas and nays, which were ordered, and being taken, were yeas 35, nays 40.

So the subject was not laid on the table.

The question recurred on the passage of the resolution.

Mr. PHELPS proceeded to refer to the continual changes of rules which the Convention made, and to the consumption of time which resulted from Buncombe speeches made on propositions of this description, when

The hour of twelve having arrived,

A motion was made by Mr. HARBINE, to postpone the orders of the day, for the purpose of disposing of the pending question.

The Convention refused to postpone.

And thereupon the Convention passed to the orders of the day.

MASTER AND SLAVE.

Mr. JENIFER, by general consent, called the attention of the Convention, to the proceedings which had taken place yesterday on the report of Committee No. 14, upon the relation of master and slave. The Convention would recollect, he said, that he had moved that the consideration of the report be postponed until Monday next. The committee had met last night, and were unanimously of opinion that it would be better to accept the amendment of the gentleman from Prince George's county, (Mr. Bowie,) in lieu of their own report. The amendment proposed by that gentleman, was in the following words:

"The Legislature shall not pass any law to abolish or change the relation of master and slave, as it now exists in this State."

The only words added by the committee, (continued Mr. J.) are the words "or change," after the word "abolish."

Mr. BOWIE. That will do.

Mr. JENIFER, continuing. I believe that this will meet with the unanimous approbation of the Convention. At the same time, I must say that in the judgment of the committee, the provision which they had reported, did, in fact cover the whole ground. They have instructed me, however, to report the amendment, and I hope it will be adopted.

Whilst I am on the floor, I will say that I hope we shall not hereafter hear any denunciations as to the action of the committees of this body, unless gentlemen are perfectly sure that they stand in a position which entitles them to make charges of dereliction of duty. The meetings of the committee, at the head of which I have been placed, have always been attended by such members as were in the city, and last night, inclement as the weather was, the venerable and distinguished gentleman from Anne Arundel, (Mr. Dorsey,) was in attendance, as was also every other member. Every proposition which has been referred to that committee, has been considered, and though of course there have been differences of opinion, yet every subject has been acted on, so far as it was possible to act. I have felt it due to myself to make this brief statement of facts.

I hope the orders of the day will be postponed to enable the Convention to act upon this report.

The PRESIDENT. The Convention having refused to postpone the orders of the day, the motion can only be received by unanimous consent.

[Cries of "consent"—"consent."]

Mr. Jenifer. I think that as this is a mere isolated proposition, as to which, I believe, there will be great unanimity in the Convention, it will be well that we should act upon it at once, and show to the State and to the world, that this proposition has met with but one response in this body.

Mr. Bowie. Let us take the vote.

Mr. Spencer. I move that by unanimous consent, the orders of the day be postponed, for the purpose of considering the report of the gentleman from Charles, (Mr. Jenifer.)

The motion was agreed to.

The question then recurred on the adoption of the amended report of Mr. Jenifer.

And, without debate, motion or question, the report was adopted *unanimously*.

The President directed that fact to be entered upon the journal.

The Convention then proceeded to the orders of the day.

THE BILL OF RIGHTS.

The Convention resumed the consideration of the report of the Committee on the Declaration of Rights of the State of Maryland.

And the state of the question was this:

Article 1st being under consideration yesterday, in the following words:

"That all government of right originates for the people, is founded in compact only, and instituted solely for the good of the whole."

Mr. Presstman had moved to amend the said article, by adding at the end thereof the following:

"And they have at all times the inalienable right to alter, reform, or abolisn their form of Government, in such manner as they may think expedient."

And Mr. Hicks had moved to amend the said amendment, by adding at the end thereof the following:

"And that any portion of the people of this State shall have the right to secede and unite themselves and the territory occupied by them to such adjoining State as they shall elect."

And the pending question was on the amendment of Mr. Hicks.

Mr. J. U. Dennis was entitled to the floor. He said, that whenever there was a controversy between parties, the specific matter in dispute should first be well ascertained and understood, and the points of difference fairly and plainly laid down, so that there might be no misapprehension in regard to them. He read the proposition of Mr. Presstman, and said he, (Mr. D.) understood that gentleman as saying that a majority had at all times the power under all Governments without any law or sanction in the Constitution—without and beyond the Constitution—if they saw fit, to alter, and change their form of Government. I understood this (continued Mr. D.) to be the sentiment expressed by the gentleman from Baltimore city, and also by the gentleman from Frederick, (Mr. Johnson,) not now in his seat. Am I right?

Mr. Presstman. I prefer that the amendment I have offered should speak for itself, because I might interrupt the gentleman longer than either of us should desire, by undertaking to explain it. But I do mean to say, that the people have the right to say in what mode their Constitution shall be changed. I have never said that they should not determine that matter in a legal mode, or in such a manner as might be consistent with the bill of rights. The difficulty lies in this—what the legal mode is.

Mr. Dennis continued. The gentleman said "the people." If, by that term he meant that the entire people of the State had the right to change their government in a manner, and according to the provisions to which they themselves had assented, then there was no dispute between them. But if the gentleman meant to say that the majority of any community had the right, in opposition to the provisions of the Constitution, to assemble and make a Constitution in any way they might see fit, then he, (Mr. D.,) took issue with him.

The first question which presented itself was, What is a government? He defined his understanding of the term. It was a compact. And what was essentially necessary to a compact? Must there not be contracting parties? Then the proposition of the gentleman from Baltimore city was, that one party to a contract, simply because it found itself in a numerical majority, might annul the contract, substitute another, and thus enforce a new government upon the other party. If one party was at liberty to annul the provisions of this compact, it ceased to be of any binding force. And, he would ask, what right had a majority to say to the minority, you shall be bound by whatsoever terms we may impose. He illustrated this case, and said, some propositions were so plain that it was only necessary to state them, in order to show their absurdity. This he apprehended to be one of them. In a few years the city of Baltimore would possess a numerical majority of the whole State.

He had been told once, in reference to this Convention, that unless the principles which it might engraft upon the Constitution, should meet the concurrence of the inhabitants of Baltimore, they would make a new Constitution, and that, with a numerical majority in the State, they would enforce that Constitution upon the whole State. And such was the conclusion to which the gentleman's argument must inevitably carry us. He could foresee no other result.

The gentleman had referred to the bills of rights in the various States. In all of them the same abstract principles were found. Yet he, (Mr. D.,) would venture to assert that in no instance, excepting one, had the doctrine been carried out to the extent to which the gentleman asserted it. That one exception was the State of Rhode Island, under the lead of Governor Dorr—and he had been sent to the Penitentiary. Mr. D. read the provisions in the Constitutions of different States of the Union, to sustain his position. The assertion of these abstract principles was never intended to confer on a mere majority, the power of making a Constitution and enforcing it over a whole State. It was a doctrine unknown and unheard of in the United States except in Rhode Island, and as the doctrine of the gentleman from Baltimore city, (Mr. Presstman.)

He, (Mr. D.,) designed no reflection upon gentlemen, but he must say, that in every age of the world, persons were found ever ready to minister to the popular cry and popular caprice. It was an old saying "*vox populi, vox Dei.*" He (Mr. D.,) would run after no masses—he would minister to no morbid sentiments. He referred to the effects which a similar doctrine had produced in former ages of the world, and more recently in France; and to the various forms and *isms* which it had assumed in our own country. He was no advocate of this absolute and uncontroled license of the mob; and he hoped the day would never come when the sound and reflecting portions of any community, were to give up the restraints of law, and submit to the rule of a violent and unprincipled mob.

Mr. Hicks said, he did not like to detain the Convention by any remarks of his, but it might probably be expected that he would say a few words on the proposition he had submitted. He was perfectly serious in offering that proposition. He thought it legitimate and proper; and it was no new idea. It had not originated with him. If gentlemen would refer to the proceedings of the Convention of '76, they would find that a similar effort was made in that body, and although the provision was not inserted in the Constitution, yet the 59th article was adopted as a compromise. How? Why, by declaring that any part of the organic law, directly affecting the interests of the Eastern Shore, should be changed by a two-thirds vote of the legislature.

It must be apparent to every gentleman that, owing to the peculiar geographical position of the State of Maryland, some such arrangement seemed to be demanded by the different interests of the Eastern and Western Shores. And it seemed to him, that, whilst the work of reform was going on, it might be as well to guard every point. He had not the slightest ill-feeling towards the Western Shore—nor any desire, if he had the power, to withdraw the Eastern from the Western Shore. But his object was to provide for a crisis such as might occur in the history of those who were to come after us—by asserting the right of the Eastern Shoie to withdraw—not by means of revolution, but peaceably; and to unite herself with Delaware or Virginia, whenever the interests and happiness of the people might require it.

We had been told that the only question was one of political power. This did not alarm him as much as it seemed to have alarmed others. Baltimore was increasing largely—she would continue to increase—and, as a matter of course, would look vigilantly to her own interests. She wanted the construction of a number of public works, in order that the various interests which must always cluster around a large and growing city, might be drawn together and concentrated for her benefit. To all this, he had no objection; but the old adage that "a burnt child dreads the fire," was as true as it was trite. He and his people had no desire to trammel the interests of Baltimore; they were proud of her; they cared not to what extent her public works might be carried on, provided they were not taxed heavily for them. They had no prejudice towards her—their object, no less than their duty was, self-preservation alone. All they asked was that power should not be given to one part of the State to oppress another, and that, if such a time should every arrive, the people of the Eastern Shore might be permitted, quietly if they could, to make such an arrangement as would secure their own protection.

Allusions had been made to his opinions on the subject of reform, and he had been taunted with being an anti-reformer. There was no foundation for the charge. For twenty-five or thirty years his name had been recorded in favor of all the most important reforms in the State. But some gentlemen here seemed to think that no man was to be regarded as a reformer, unless he chose to follow them to the bitter end of all their wild and ultra schemes of reform.

He repeated, what he had on a former occasion stated, that he had voted against the call of this Convention; yet that call having been determined upon, he had come here honestly to give to the people all such reforms as he thought they needed. He wished Baltimore to prosper, but he was not willing to concede to her all the reforms that she demanded. He was not willing to award undue political and legislative influence to her, and thus to place other parties of the State at her mercy, or within her control. When he came here, he was disposed to give her and the larger counties of the State, an increased representation; but he had found opinions so various and conflicting, that he thought the best course now might be to settle down upon the old basis, or upon some other approximating to it.

It has heen hinted to me this morning (concluded Mr. H.) that if the time should ever come when we, of the Eastern Shore, should avail ourselves of the right which this provision would guarantee, we ought at least to carry with us our portion of the debt of the State of Maryland. Sir, I scorn the idea that we would ever withdraw, without paying the last dollar of our due proportion of that debt. I should feel ashamed of the people of the Eastern Shore, if I believed that there was a man amongst them who would entertain such a proposition. I have only to add that I hope my amendment may be agreed to, whether that of the gentleman from Baltimore city, (Mr. Presstman,) is rejected or not.

Mr. Stewart of Caroline, said, it seemed to him that the right claimed by the amendment o the gentleman from Dochester, [Mr. Hicks,] was within certain restrictions and limitations, already recognized. The amendment provided "that any portion of the people of this State, shall have the right to secede and unite themselves and the territory occupied by them to such adjoining State as they shall elect." Secede from what? He supposed from the other part of the State—that the Eastern Shore should have the right to cut loose from the Western Shore, and attach herself to some other State.

Now, by looking at the 3d section of the 4th article of the Constitution of the United States, gentlemen would see that it was declared that "new States may be admitted by Congress into this Union: but no new State shall be formed or erected within the jurisdiction of any other State." That was to say, for example, that the Eastern Shore could not he erected into a new State within the jurisdiction of the State of Maryland.

Mr. Hicks interposed and said, that he had forgotten in the remarks which he submitted to the Convention, to call its attention to an order which he had introduced some weeks ago, and which was referred to Committee No. 14, in relation to the grant of this power in the bill of rights. It was not to form a new State, but to unite the Eastern Shore to the States of Virginia or Delaware, upon such terms as might be mutually agreed upon.

Mr. Stewart, of Caroline, resumed. To unite the Eastern Shore to the State of Delaware was just as much the creation of a new State, as the admission of Texas was the admission of a new State: because the word "State," as he understood it, referred not so much to the territory as to the government. The people and the government, taken together—laws, property, &c.,—all these things constituted a State. So, if the Eastern Shore were united to Delaware, such a union would be just as much the creation of a new State as if Delaware and the Eastern Shore were now a territory, and should be received into the Union as a new State.

But he would not be diverted from the purpose for which he had risen, which was to show that we already possessed the right asserted in the amendment; for the latter clause of the same section of the Constitution of the United States, which he had already cited, went on to say, "nor any State be formed by the junction of two or more States, or parts of States, without the consent of the Legislatures of the States concerned, as well as of Congress."

If Delaware and the Eastern Shore agreed that the Eastern Shore should become a part of Delaware, and made application to Congress and Congress gave its consent, and if a like consent should also be given by the Legislatures of the two States, then the union might take place.

But where was the licensed high priest to marry the Eastern Shore to Delaware or Virginia? He had heard of the union of individuals brought about by money, where it was considered that a most beneficial arrangement had been effected. But here we proposed to offer ourselves as a virgin arrayed in matrimonial garments—with what recommendation? Why, the recommendation of an enormous debt. He was afraid that our charms would be disregarded; and he did not wish that any portion of the State should put herself in such a position. It seemed to him that it would be well to amend the proposition of the gentleman from Dorchester, (Mr. Hicks,) by adding the words "provided we can get any State to accept of us." There must be a mutual bargain, and it might happen that the State to which the Eastern Shore desired to unite herself would not accept her.

But he thought it was too late to ask that the Eastern should secede from the Western Shore. He alluded to the dark clouds which had overshadowed the horizon of Maryland, as having passed away, and being followed by the promise of calmer skies and brighter hopes.

He characterized, as a strange doctrine, the principle which had been asserted here, that it was necessary to engraft upon the Constitution a provision specifying the mode in which the organic law should be changed. He held that the people were just as sovereign, and, he might say, as divine over their government, as the Great Ruler of the Universe, was over His. They were sovereign—supreme—uncontroled.

As to the argument that Government was a compact, he regarded it as just such a compact as a man might make with himself. He might resolve and re-resolve; he might form his own government, and change it as he thought proper. So it was with the people. He cared not whether the provision was in or out of the Constitution, if the people said they would change their government, they could do so—they would do so—and they ought to do so. He proceeded to examine and illustrate the consequences to which a contrary doctrine would lead, and to argue that its result would be a Constitution so framed as to stand through all changes and though all time, without regard to the wants or the wishes of the people. Such was not his doctrine, or the doctrine of the people of Maryland.

He should, therefore, vote against the amendment of the gentleman from Dorchester (Mr. Hicks,) not because he, (Mr. S.) had any objection to doing this act, if it were deemed proper and right, but because he thought that the power already existed under the Constitution of the United States. As to the proposition of the gentleman from Baltimore city, [Mr. Presstman,] he [Mr. S.] could see no objection to it. It was a principle to which all must subscribe. He was not in the habit of citing authorities, and would not now trouble the Convention with them; but he thought that gentlemen would find, that in the Constitutions of almost every State in the Union, the same principle was contained, and not only so, but that the framers of the Constitutions of Virginia and other States, had gone so far as to declare that a majority of the people had a right to alter and change their Government, in any way they might think proper.

Mr. Jenifer said, he did not rise to controvert the principle involved in the proposed amendment of the gentleman from Baltimore city, (Mr. Presstman.) He did not believe there was an intelligent man in the community, who would deny that the proposition, in the abstract, and standing alone, was the true republican doctrine. But it had been embarrassed, and its meaning perverted by the arguments of gentlemen, and especially by the speech of the mover of it. The amendment assumed the right of the people to alter, change or abolish their Constitution. The gentleman from Baltimore goes a step further, and desires it to be recognized in the bill of rights, that after a Constitution is established, approved by the people of the State, and becomes the organic law of the land—a bare majority, regardless of the provisions of the Constitution from caprice, or inflamed by popular excitement, have a right to overthrow the Constitution without the forms of law. In this he is supported by his eloquent friends from Frederick, (Mr. Johnson and Mr. Thomas,) the former of whom, so emphatically expressed his opinions, "that the people, the *immortal*, the *eternal* people, could do what they pleased."

Mr. J. said, he would ask his friend from Baltimore, whether the Constitution about to be adopted, should it be confirmed by the people of the State, would not become the law of the land?

Mr. PRESSTMAN replied, that it would—but that the people had a right to change it.

Mr. J. said, he conceded that right to the utmost extent, and read the 1st, 4th, and 41st articles of the bill of rights, to show that it was *recognized in express terms.*

The 1st article provides, "That all government of right originates from the people, is founded in compact only, and instituted solely for the good of the whole."

The 4th article: "That whenever the ends of government are perverted, and public liberty manifestly endangered, &c., the people may, and of right ought to do, reform the old, or establish a new government." And the 41st provides for the manner of altering or abolishing the Constitution.

Mr. J. asked, what language can be more explicit? Here the rights of the people are protected for the good of the whole. But a mere majority tumultuously assembled from the city of Baltimore and the adjoining counties, without form of law—without "the ends of government being perverted, or public liberty endangered," assuming to control the whole State for political or worse purposes, should not be recognized in a bill of rights.

If the people—the "eternal, the immortal people," can abolish their own Constitution, and establish whatever they please, whenever they please, regardless of law and order, what becomes of the rights of the minority, which, perhaps, may be only a few thousand or a few hundred less than that majority?

Look at the populous city of Baltimore now numbering 170,000 souls; Baltimore county near 42,000; Frederick county near 40,000; their interests in many respects identical. By the facility of your railroads and other works of internal improvement, the whole population may be collected in a mass, in twenty-four hours. This assembled multitude without law or order—without even the knowledge of the distant counties of the State, being the "eternal people," may "throw off the existing and establish a new Constitution." Such is the construction which the remarks of gentlemen justify.

The gentleman from Baltimore city, (Mr. Presstman,) in a former speech, took a statesman-like view of the question of reform, and expressed his opinion that there was not an intelligent man in Baltimore, under existing circumstances, who expected or desired representation based exclusively on numbers. He has been justly complimented for that speech. But now the ground he takes is infinitely more objectionable, (Mr. J. said,) and he might add, dangerous to the interests of the counties of the State.

You have, Mr. President, only this morning engrafted the first article in the new Constitution about to be formed: "That the Legislature shall pass no law affecting the existing relation of master and slave in this State." This article has been adopted by a unanimous vote of the Convention. This was intended to put to rest the fanaticism as regards this question in Maryland, and would do so, as long as the Constitution and laws are respected.

But, if you recognise the right of a bare majority, "at all times, and in any manner they deem expedient," to abolish the existing and establish a new system—what becomes of the rights this day guarantied by the unanimous vote of this Convention? Where is the security for a month's continuance of it? If the city of Baltimore with the two counties referred to, who have less interest in this species of property than any other portion of the State, should deem it expedient to abolish it—what are the modes of preventing it? The lower counties cannot rise up in mass, as can be done in the others. It is true, that the gentleman from Dorchester county (Mr. Hicks,) perhaps, apprehending this state of things, has offered an amendment that the Eastern Shore should have the right to secede and unite with another State.

Mr. President, the time has been when the word "disunion" applied to the general government, or "secession" to the counties of a State, fell upon my ear as the words of a traitor, but occasions may arise, when they may become the language of patriotism.

Once admit that a dense mass congregated together without the forms of law, "whenever they deem it expedient," may abolish your Constitution, that doctrine advocated in this Convention by gentleman representing a high minded, intelligent and law abiding constituency—the right of secession, should go "*pari possa*," with it. It would become the duty of the Eastern Shore and of the lower counties of the Western Shore to adopt any means to protect themselves, their liberties and their property, from revolution and anarchy.

Mr. J. said we should not shut our eyes or ears to the warnings of experience. Massachusetts has had to contend with lawless spirits parading portions of her heretofore quiet State. Rhode Island has been the theatre of anarchy.

The populous cities of New York, Philadelphia and Baltimore, have at different times felt the effects of an uncontroled and excited populace. Similar scenes may again be inflicted upon them. But none have ever, until now, advocated it as a right.

A few years since the whole of Maryland felt as Baltimore, experienced the want of salutary laws, or a proper execution of them, to protect the rights and property of her citizens. For three days was that noble, gallant city under the control of a lawless, though "immortal power." Nor was it restrained until the venerable patriot of the Revolution, Gen. Samuel Smith, was called from his quiet abode to take command, and rescue his native city from anarchy and bloodshed. The Legislature of Maryland at its next session passed the indemnity law, by which the sufferers were compensated for the loss of property. Do gentleman desire that such scenes should recur again? If not, encourage not this morbid appetite for unrestrained license which must result in anarchy.

The gentleman from Frederick, (Mr. Johnson,) asks, would you deny to the people of Maryland, what has been done in the monarchical governments of Europe, the right to overthrow their government?

Mr. J. said the gentleman should recollect that our institutions were established by ourselves, and are very different from the monarchical or absolute governments of Europe. Here the people formed their own Constitutions, in their own way; enacted the laws by their accredited agents; prescribed the manner in which those Constitutions should be framed and altered. It required no revolution to accomplish this—it was the free action of the poeple—their Constitution—*their* laws. He was surprised that comparison should be attempted between the State of Maryland, and any of the oppressed subjects of Europe. His friend had referred to "France whose people had hurled from power those tyrannical rulers, and taken the government into their own keeping." There was no analogy between the government of France, and the government of Maryland, and, however much he desired to see republican principles prevail, he should not look to the present state of France, as an example worthy of imitation. It is true she had dethroned her monarch—it was equally true that her present condition evinced but little of republican government. At peace with all the world, an army of four hundred thousand soldiers are held in arms to preserve the peace of her own citizens, and it is generally admitted that at no period during Louis Phillipe's reign, was the press under so rigid a serveilance as at the present moment. The government is unstable—her citizens in constant dread of revolution. This, Mr. J. believed to be attributed to the organization of her government, in having but one Assembly, uncontroled, except by popular will. So long as this state of things existed, Mr. J. had but little hopes of a pure republican administration of the French government. Engraft similar principles upon Maryland, and anarchy will subvert the Republic.

The proposition of the gentleman, as explained by himself, will be productive of revolution; and here, Mr. J. said, he would do justice to his colleague from the city of Baltimore, (Mr. Brent,) who, in his argument yesterday, had taken a sound, statesman-like view of the subject as regards the manner of altering or abolishing the Constitution. It must be done by the provisions of the Constitution and laws, or by revolution. On the two important questions those gentlemen differ, though representing the same constituency. The one, (Mr. Brent,) an advocate for representation exclusively on the basis of numbers. Whilst his colleague, (Mr. Presstman,) does not think there is a sensible man in the city of Baltimore in favor of, or who expects the apportionment to be based exclusively on population.

Mr. Presstman said such was the feelings of his constituents, although since he came here he had expressed a willingness to agree to a compromise.

Mr. J. resumed. So far his friend was right, and held sound doctrine, and Mr. J. regretted that he did not go with his colleague, (Mr. Brent,) in favor of "changing or abolishing the Constitution according to the laws of the land."

Mr. Stewart, of Caroline, here asked if the new Constitution would be in accordance with the frame of the old Constitution?

Mr. J. replied that the gentleman from Caroline was as competent to answer that question as he was. As for himself, Mr. J. said, he was for such changes in the Constitution as might contribute to the interest and benefit of the whole State, giving to a majority a proper influence; to the minority a safe and efficient protection. With such land-marks, he would not be fastidious as to minor questions.

Mr. J. concluded by saying it was far from his intention to discuss at length all the questions involved in the bill of rights. He believed that, as reported by the Committee, it embraced and breathed throughout, sound, republican, democratic doctrines. He would not, as others had done here, make professions of his love for the people; he distrusted and doubted the sincerity of some of those who were constantly proclaiming their devotion to the rights and will of the people. He preferred to guard the people against the professions of those who were loud in denouncing as enemies those who did not unite with them in administering to popular clamor.

Mr. Wright, without making a speech, felt himself bound to state his sentiments. His friend from Baltimore had expressed opinions in regard to the rights of the people, and he desired to say that he concurred in every word which had fallen from that gentleman. The people have a right to alter, modify or change their Constitution, in any way which they may deem consistent with their interests. But the gentleman from Baltimore did not go far enough. The people would not be sufficiently vigilant over their own rights, if they did not take care to have a clause in the Constitution which would place in their own hands the power to change or alter the organic law at their will. It is our duty, as their agents, to make such provision. But the gentleman from Baltimore did not go far enough; he was for cutting the dam, and letting lose the water, before the reservoir was prepared for its reception. The other gentleman from Baltimore, had gone further; he went about as far as this Convention should go. He would go with both these gentlemen, who had stood boldly forward to assert that the people had rights, and told them how they ought to exercise those rights. The gentleman from Dorchester, (Mr.

Hicks,) had offered an amendment, either in jest or for the purpose of consuming time. He regarded that amendment as a rider intended to clog and break down the original proposition. He repelled the idea that Baltimore would oppress the counties. She had too many ties which bound them to her. She was the ornament and pride of the State. Still he did not blame the gentleman from Dorchester, who sought to delay the action of the House. He hoped the Convention would go to work, not like lawyers, but in the course suggested by common sense.

Mr. Hicks assured his friend from Queen Anne's, that he had not offered his amendment in jest, and if that gentleman would go among his, (Mr. H.'s) constituents, he would find there was no jest in it. He was a friend of the people, and so was the gentleman from Queen Anne's, and he reminded that gentleman that back-sliders were the worst of sinners. He looked on himself as representing as noble a constituency as can be found in Maryland, and he came here to do his duty to them. He had never desired to come here. He never believed there was any necessity for this Convention. He had thought that the Constitution under which we have lived so long, was good enough, and that the provision contained in it relative to its change was sufficient. But he had been sent here, and he would now do his duty. He was as proud of Baltimore as his friend from Queen Anne's, and would not throw a straw in the way of her prosperity; but while he agreed to all his friend had said about the change of seasons from summer to winter, he was not convinced that the State should give way to the city of Baltimore. His friend from Caroline, (Mr. Stewart,) had also spoken in a similar strain. Now he desired to say to that gentleman, that he had no desire to separate the Eastern Shore from the State. His friend from Caroline was the only one, he believed, who thought that the gloomy days were all past. He seemed to forget that there is a heavy debt hanging over the State, and that the counties are suffering under the burden. It would be better, perhaps, to look round the horizon, and see if there are no new storms gathering. How long it would be before new troubles would come, he could not predict. He referred to the language of the reformers in Baltimore, before this Convention was called, when they asserted that their wishes were very moderate and reasonable. Previous to 1836, the city had but two delegates, and he believed she got along just as well as when she has had more. He assured the House, that if ever the time should come, when the State should fall under the dominion of Baltimore, if he should not have left the world, he would never give his consent that the counties should be placed in a position to be used by Baltimore at her pleasure. When he came from home, he felt a disposition to give a larger representation to the city, but he felt less disposition to do it now that he saw she was never to be satisfied. He agreed with the gentleman from Baltimore, that we have the power in our hands; but as all power is to be given by the Constitution, he hoped it would be made to operate equally. He believed that without the provision contained in his amendment, it would be in the power of part of the Western Shore of Maryland, to unite herself with the State of Virginia, and of the Eastern Shore to unite herself to Delaware, by agreement with the States, and with the consent of Congress, but he desired to have such privilege or right recognized and countenanced by the Constitution, which we are now framing, that it may not be considered as revolutionary hereafter.

Mr. Phelps would not now address the Convention, or attempt to say one word, had he not felt impelled to do so, from a high sense of public duty. The amendment offered by the gentleman from Baltimore city, (Mr. Presstman,) in the sense in which that honorable gentleman has explained it, would in his humble estimation, if acted upon, at all times, be liable to subvert the foundation of the government, and to encourage a lawless opposition to the Constitution itself.

This amendment, we have been informed, is taken from the Texan bill of rights, and was drawn up by Mr. Calhoun himself—that the same amendment has been incorporated in many other State Constitutions. As positive proof, that the construction given this article, is not correct, but was intended to be exercised as an *extreme* right, Mr. Phelps read the 37th article of the Texan Constitution, which provides that the Constitution shall not be altered, except by a vote of two-thirds of the Legislature in favor of the proposed amendments, and which amendments shall be published, and voted upon by the people, and if opposed by a majority *of all the votes* the amendments shall not even then be adopted, unless confirmed by *two-thirds* of the next General Assembly. This provision, Mr. Phelps repeated, was proof positive, that Mr. Calhoun, nor the people of Texas, never intended to claim the lawless and most dangerous right to abolish their organic law, in the manner contended for by the mover of this proposition. Such doctrines, Mr. President, should not be countenanced in this Hall, or elsewhere. Besides, you find similar provisions incorporated in the Constitutions of Missouri, Michigan, Arkansas and other States, supposed to be thoroughly indoctrinated with the spirit of progressive democracy. Even South Carolina contends for no such right. In fact, no State in this broad Union would dare contend that the people in lawless assemblies and in a lawless manner, could proceed to form a new Government, upon the ruins of the old one, unless it be by revolution. Mr Phelps insisted earnestly that this doctrine, if acted upon, would prove most disastrous in its consequences. A Constitution is the foundation of all law. It is the bulwark of all our civil and religious rights. Its foundations should be broad and strong, else the whole edifice might tumble into ruins. Constitutions, Mr. President, are the results of compromise. Minorities, as well as majorities, have rights by virtue of this agreement, and both alike should be held sacred and inviolable. This provision requiring a two-third vote, and the action of two consecutive sessions of the General Assembly to alter or amend the Constitution, you find incorporated upon the organic law of nine-tenths of all the States of this Union.

Mr. Phelps said, before he proceeded to discuss the second branch of this proposition, it being the amendment offered by his friend and colleague, Mr. Hicks, he would say one word by way of defining his position. Those from the Eastern Shore, and the smaller counties, had over and again been denounced as anti-reformers. For himself, he acknowledged he voted against calling a Convention in the Senate, and also at the ballot-box. He had done so upon high constitutional grounds, as well as from expediency. He had witnessed nothing in these Halls to convince him that he was wrong. But if gentlemen suppose he was here to oppose all needful reform, they have mistaken their man. He declared himself a *bona fide* reformer. He intended to be second to no man upon that subject. The Constitution on which they were engaged was intended not only for themselves, but for posterity, and so far as his humble abilities could serve, the work shall be perfect, and shall secure the greatest good to the greatest numbers. It should be the pride of every man here, to give the people the best possible government.

But, Mr. President, what is reform? Does it *consist alone*, as has been urged here, of representation, based exclusively upon population? If so, we have only, as indicated by the vote a day or two since, but seventeen in this body, seventeen out of one hundred and three members. These seventeen are the Simon Pures; fine gold, tried in the fire.

Mr. Chambers, (interrupting.) And some of them are backing out.

Mr. Phelps, (resuming.) Well, let them back out—he was proud to hear it.

Here some explanations took place, in which Mr. McHenry, Mr. Chambers and Mr. Brent, of Baltimore city, took part, and in which Mr. McHenry and Mr. Brent repelled the charge implied in the words, "back out," if directed against them.

Mr. Chambers disclaimed any personal allusions.

Mr. Phelps resumed, and said, notwithstanding the declaration of his principles, he would doubtless still be denounced by those seventeen gentlemen as opposed to reform. The right, upon the happening of certain contingencies, of the Eastern Shore to secede, was urged before the people of Dorchester during the last campaign, and the proposition has been offered by his colleague in good faith, and he hoped the amendment would prevail. Mr. Phelps described the Eastern shore as a beautiful champaign country, intersected with beautiful rivers and creeks, penetrating the whole country, and winding around the homestead of almost every man. He contended the interests of the two shores were essentially different. Whilst the Western Shore was greatly dependent upon works of internal improvement for her prosperity, the Eastern Shore required no such public expenditures for her benefit. Already you have your great works of internal improvement, reaching far to the west, and intersecting the State in other directions, bringing into direct competition with our products the products of other and distant States. For one, he denied the almost universally received dogma, that by making the city of Baltimore the great grain market of the West, you would increase the price of our own products. These great works have been constructed by the common treasure of the whole people. The Eastern Shore was made tributary to these works—was taxed to accomplish that which daily contributed to her injury. Mr. Phelps said he had never assisted to incur the present debt of Maryland, but he was proud to say he had sustained the faith and honor of the State in her darkest hours of adversity, at a time when repudiation found a resting place even in these halls. Mr. Phelps said the time, in his judgment, for a separation had not yet come; but he desired the Convention to recognize the right we contend for. Whenever representation, according to population, shall be engrafted upon the Constitution of the State, for one, he was prepared to say, the day and the hour of our separation is at hand. He never could, and never would consent, that the Eastern Shore should be compelled to sit powerless at the feet of the city of Baltimore and Western Maryland.

Mr. Brown said he would make no reply to the gentleman who had referred to the revolutionary movement of Dorr: there was nothing in the condition or character of the State of Maryland to justify any parallel. Nor would he answer the insinuation of the gentleman from Charles, (Mr. Jenifer,) that a time might come when Baltimore might call in the aid of Charles county to protect her against her own friends.

These were questions unworthy of notice. Sneers had been thrown out by gentlemen against the seventeen who had voted on Friday for the popular basis of representation. It was true, it was a very small minority. But he would inform those gentleman, that the number of them was great—that their name was "Legion." These seventeen represented 227,000 of the voters of Maryland. Yet their fewness on this vote was made a subject of ridicule. But the effort which had been made, and the names of those who sustained it, will appear on the record, and not all the waters which separate Maryland from Delaware and Virginia will wash it out.

He moved the previous question.

The question was taken, and decided in the negative.

So the Convention refused to second the demand for the previous question.

Mr. Brent, of Baltimore city, desired to offer an amendment.

The President said, it was not now in order, there being two amendments already pending.

The question then recurred on the amendment of Mr. Hicks.

Mr. Presstman asked the yeas and nays, which were ordered, and being taken resulted as follows:

Affirmative—Messrs. Lee, Mitchell, Buchanan, Bell, Welch, Ridgely, Dickinson, John Dennis, Dashiell, Hicks, Hodson, Goldsborough, Phelps,

Bowie, McCubbin, Dirickson, McMaster, Hearn, Fooks, Jacobs, Shriver, Biser, Thawley, Michael Newcomer, Smith, Shower and Brown—27.

Negative—Messrs. Chapman, President, Blakistone, Dent, Hopewell, Ricaud, Chambers, of Kent, Donaldson, Dorsey, Wells, Randall, Kent, Weems, Williams, McCullough, Miller, McLane, Tuck, Sprigg, Bowling, Spencer, Grason, George, Wright, Gaither, Annan, Sappington, Stephenson, McHenry, Magraw, Nelson, Stewart of Caroline, Gwinn, Stewart of Baltimore city, Brent, of Baltimore city, Presstman, Ware, Schley, Fiery, Neill, John Newcomer, Harbine, Davis, Kilgour, Brewer, Waters, Weber, Hollyday, Slicer, Fitzpatrick, Parke, and Cockey—51.

So the amendment was rejected.

The question then recurred on the amendment of Mr. Presstman.

Mr. Dirickson took the floor, but yielded to Mr. Chambers, of Kent, who desired to offer an amendment.

Mr. C. said, that the question involved in the amendment offered by the gentleman from Baltimore city, (Mr. Presstman,) was, or was not, in his, (Mr. C's,) humble judgment, proper to be adopted or not, according to the construction put upon it.

Mr. Chambers said, that the main objection to the proposition of the gentleman from Baltimore city was, that the argument by which it was sustained, had very much embarrassed the question. Constructions had been put upon the amendment which would render it of doubtful meaning. It was evident that the opinions of gentlemen who had discussed it, differed widely from each other; and so the constructions put upon it by the people would be indistinct and discordant. Whatever is inserted in the Constitution ought to be clear and indisputable. He intended to vote against the amendment in its present form, and with a view to make it more acceptable, he proposed to move an amendment. By one party it had been held, that, without Constitutional enactments or against them, classes of men might resolve themselves into a meeting, and set up a Constitution of their own. Another class insisted that it was the right of the people to change the Constitution by any process, and in any way they might think best. With a view to clear the amendment of all mistiness, and make it clear to every comprehension, he moved to amend by adding the following words:

"According to the mode authorized by the Constitution or laws of the land."

Mr. Ridgely was of opinion, that the amendment of the gentleman from Kent, was not calculated to meet the object he had in view, but rather to embarrass the question. The proposition of the gentleman from Baltimore city, (Mr. Presstman,) asserts a mere truism, an abstract political truth, which no one would deny, to be embodied in that category of rights, in which is usually presented the analysis, or general principles of republican government. All such general declarations of popular rights, contemplate the last resort of a people to throw off oppression, "when the end of Government is perverted, and the public liberty is manifestly endangered," they mean in plain terms, revolution. That this power is inherent, inalienable, and would as well exist without, as by its assertion in, the bill of rights, is indisputable. No body can deny such a right as inherent in the people and inseparable from all free government.

The present declaration of rights so recognizes it; and this proposition is but a reiteration of the truth. What does the amendment of the gentleman from Kent propose? To strip this abstract declaration, of its abstract character; to seize upon an abstract truth, which contemplates revolution only, as I have already said, and to apply it to a totally different purpose, to wit: to make it, in its connection, as a part of the bill of rights; in fact a constitutional restraint, as to the manner of altering the civil compact. Is such the proper place—is this the proper connection for such a proposition? Is there propriety or fitness of things, in such antagonist association of civil and revolutionary means of changing or altering the form of Government? It seems to me not. When we reach the amendatory clause in the Constitution, there will be the proper place to put restraints upon its amendment, and to define and prescribe the manner of its change. There would doubtless be difference of opinion on that subject—that was a vital question—but here, in the bill of rights, there could be no difference of opinion, upon abstract truths—truths which had been utterred by our fathers seventy years ago, were still truths and would forever remain truths. How and when to be exercised, or restrained by the civil compact, is a question for detail in the Constitution proper. What difficulty could there be in voting for such a broad proposition. He could see none. Let it go into the bill of rights, as an abstract declaration, in company with all other articles *ejusdem generis*. There it will be qualified and restrained, by the defined terms of the Constitution proper, in which he was ready to unite with the gentleman from Kent. There was no fear of misapprehension upon this subject: the bill of rights and the Constitution must go together, as a whole, and be expounded in connection. He hoped therefore the amendment would be withdrawn, and the proposition of the gentleman of Baltimore city be agreed to.

Thereupon the Convention adjourned until tomorrow at 11 o'clock.

THURSDAY, January 30th, 1851.

The Convention met at eleven o'clock.

Prayer was made by the Rev. Mr. Grauff.

The roll having been called, the Secretary proceeded to read the journal of yesterday.

Mr. Phelps moved that the reading be dispensed with.

Mr. Spencer thought the precedent a bad one, and hoped the motion would not prevail.

Mr. Phelps, not pressing his motion, the journal was read, and having been amended so as to correct an error in Mr. STEPHENSON's resolution, was approved.

Mr. PRESSTMAN offered the following order which was adopted:

"That the committee on the Judiciary inquire into the propriety of reporting a provision that the rights and interests of parties to a suit shall not be affected by any law passed during the pending of said suit in any court of law or equity in this State."

The PRESIDENT announced that reports of committees were now in order.

No reports were made.

Mr. MICHAEL NEWCOMER, presented a petition of sundry citizens interested in the inspections of Tobacco, Flour, Liquors, Fish, Lumber, Wood, Anthracite and Bituminous Coal, Plaster of Paris, Lime and Guano, praying that the principles of a free inspection may be engrafted in the Constitution.

The petition was read and referred to the committee on Inspections.

HOUR OF MEETING.

The PRESIDENT announced the unfinished business of the morning hour to be the resolution offered by Mr. STEPHENSON yesterday, (as amended,) which provided that from and after Monday next, the daily hour of the meeting of the Convention, shall be ten o'clock.

Mr. SAPPINGTON, suggesting some doubts as to the presence of a quorum, moved that there be a call of the Convention.

The motion was agreed to.

And the roll was again called.

A quorum having been ascertained to be present,

On motion of Mr. BROWN, all further proceedings on the call were dispensed with.

And the question recurring on the adoption of the resolution,

Mr. JOHN NEWCOMER asked the yeas and nays, which were ordered, and being taken, were yeas 43, nays 26.

So the Convention decided that from and after Monday next, the daily hour of the meeting of the Convention should be ten o'clock.

Mr. BROWN said that as there seemed to be no morning business before the Convention, he would move that the Convention resume the consideration of the unfinished order of yesterday.

The motion was agreed to.

THE BILL OF RIGHTS.

The Convention thereupon resumed the consideration of the report of the committee on the declaration of rights of the State of Maryland.

The pending question was on the amendment offered by Mr. CHAMBERS, of Kent, to the amendment of Mr. PRESSTMAN.

Mr. FIERY said, that if the gentleman from Baltimore county, (Mr. Ridgely,) did not desire to speak, he, (Mr. F.,) would move the previous question..

Mr. SPENCER suggested that as he understood, the gentleman from Worcester, (Mr. Dirickson,) was entitled to the floor, that gentleman having yielded to a motion to adjourn by the gentleman from Baltimore city, (Mr. Brent.)

Mr. DIRICKSON. I believe that the gentleman from Queen Anne's (Mr. Spencer,) is correct; but if there is a great anxiety on the part of the Convention that the question shall be taken, I have no desire to delay its action by any remarks of mine.

Mr. RIDGELY. I have not entirely closed the remarks which I intended to make yesterday. But a suggestion has been made to me, that the Convention is anxious to take the question; and, if so, I will not trouble it with any additional remarks. If not, I should be glad to have an opportunity of concluding my remarks. I shall, however, be perfectly satisfied that the previous question shall be taken, if such is the disposition of the Convention.

Mr. FIERY. No gentleman in this body is more anxious to accord to every member the privilege of speaking upon every question than myself. But what is the condition of things here? For the last three months, we have been discussing different propositions, and up to this hour, not one report has been adopted by the Convention.

Mr. MORGAN, interposing. I rise to a question of order? "Is the previous question debateable."

The PRESIDENT. The previous question has not yet been moved, because the gentleman from Washington county, (Mr. FIERY,) is not in a position to move it, until it is ascertained whether the gentleman from Baltimore county, (Mr. Ridgely,) desires to conclude his remarks.

Mr. FIERY. I understood that I had the consent of the gentleman from Baltimore county, (Mr. Ridgely.)

Some conversation followed.

Mr. FIERY (resuming.) I simply desire to set myself right before the Convention. I do not wish to be discourteous. I state, upon the pledge of all the honor I possess, that I am solicitous to afford every gentleman an opportunity to do justice to his own views and to the sentiments of his constituents. But gentlemen will bear in mind that, by the very act of moving the previous question, I deny to myself, as well as to others, the privilege of discussion. But I do not desire to speak on every subject. I want action—immediate action. It is my firm belief that if we do not place some limit upon the discursive and latitudinous debates which continually take place in this body, we can never arrive at any successful result. I am conscientiously of opinion that it is my duty to enforce the necessity of action by all proper means within my reach. My constituents demand it, and when my duty directs, I shall not hesitate as to my course. Whatever may be the odium which I may bring upon myself, in this body or out of it, I shall not skulk from responsibility here or elsewhere. I take this course in good faith, and with no feeling of ill-will to any member of this Convention. My sole object is to expedite the transaction of its business. As to the question which we have had under discussion for a day or two past, the principle involved in it must come up for future discussion on the question of representation. I see no good to be attained by its continued discussion now. I confess I have borne it until my patience is totally exhausted, and I must protest against the continuation of a state of things calculated to protract the session of the Convention to an indefinite period.

The PRESIDENT (to Mr. Ridgely.) Does the gentleman from Baltimore county claim the floor?

Mr. RIDGELY yielded the floor.

Mr. DIRICKSON took the floor, and remarked that he felt himself placed in an awkward position.

Mr. BLAKISTONE interposed, and suggested that the gentleman from Worcester, (Mr. Dirickson,) should permit the question to be taken on the previous question, (there being an evident disposition on the part of the Convention not to second the previous question at the present moment.)

Mr. DIRICKSON yielded the floor.

Mr. SCHLEY. I hope that the Convention will not second the demand for the previous question.

I regard the subject which is now engrossing our consideration, as one of grave importance, and think that the gentleman from Washington county, (Mr. Fiery,) is mistaken in supposing that the same principle will again come up for discussion on the question of representation. I cannot see the connection between the two. But apart from that consideration, if it were time that this question is again to come under our revision, I, for one, am disposed to avail myself of all the light I can obtain by discussion among the members of this Convention. I care not if we remain here six months; my constituents will not make any unreasonable demands upon me. As their representative here, I have a duty to perform as well as rights to protect. It becomes me so to discharge my duties here as that when I go home, I may tell my constituents that I have accomplished the objects for which I came here.

There are some gentlemen in this body—I do not wish to specify—who seem to understand by intuition all the matters that come before us, and are ready to give their votes the moment a question is broached. I am not one of that number; and I am anxious to give to every gentleman who is disposed to speak, an opportunity to do so, that I may myself enjoy the benefit of his views. Whilst I should be glad to see more rapid progress than we have hitherto made, in order that we might perfect, as soon as possible, the work for which we have assembled, yet I am very sure that, to the satisfactory accomplishment of that work, debate is necessary. Gentlemen must be permitted to express their views, and those gentlemen only who are perfectly cognizant of every subject, are prepared to vote in the beginning, without examination and without discussion. As I am not one of them, I desire to move not at a gallop, but at a more reasonable speed. I wish to accord to every gentleman the right to express his opinions and views. I have been a long time a listener to debates at the house and elsewhere, and I cannot see that the latitudinous and irrelevant debate which gentlemen speak of here, has in fact taken place. I think that gentlemen have confined themselves pretty closely to the legitimate subject matter under discussion. I, therefore, hope that every gentleman, who desires it, may have an opportunity of being heard.

Mr. TUCK, (to the Chair.) What is the question before the Convention?

The PRESIDENT. It is on the amendment of the gentleman from Kent, (Mr. Chambers.)

Mr. DIRICKSON took the floor.

Mr. FIERY. I move the previous question.

The PRESIDENT. The gentleman has not the floor to make the motion.

After some conversation, the floor was yielded by Mr. DIRICKSON, for the motion for the previous question.

But the Convention refused to second it.

So the question again recurred on the amendment of Mr. CHAMBERS, of Kent.

Mr. DIRICKSON said:

He had listened calmly and patiently to the debate which for the past two days, had occupied the grave attention of the Convention. He had listened with somewhat more than his usual earnestness, seriously regarding the amendment offered by the gentleman from the city of Baltimore as not only of the highest and most solemn importance, but as involving principles which might shake our whole government to its inmost centre, and in a moment of time crumble its fair fabric into dust and ruin. Little did he expect to hear in this Hall, consecrated by so many patriotic and historic associations, sentiments like those which but recently had come from more than one quarter of the wise assemblage now around him—sentiments which but for the great respect and high regard he entertained for the sources from which they emanated he would denounce, as they deserved to be, as moral treasons against the fair fame and dignity of our noble State, and the peace, happiness and security of her sovereign people. There might be times and places, when and where, the enuniciation of such political heresies however agrarian in their tendencies and red-republican in their odor, would be entirely harmless and unimportant.

But such was not the case with emanations from this body. He saw around him many among the most eminent and distinguished of the land—men whose past lives and intellectual labors had already become a part of the history and pride of their country; and to an assembly graced and adorned by such a presence, the people might look with more than wonted confidence and hearken with a willing ear to its political teachings.

He did not wish to interfere with those who, by the utterance of new, and to him strange creeds, sought to place themselves in a popular attitude before their peculiar constituency. The ascent of the politician is ever steep and toilsome—ways new and untried—crooked and tortuous are frequently pursued ere station and pomp and power and all the bright baubles that dazzle around ambition's goal are fairly won. And was this an ordinary political assembly collected together for the ordinary purposes of legislation, he would be the last to complain of the mere vagaries of gentlemen, however wild and fanciful. They should be free to seek their own objects in any innocent manner which their hopes and fears might suggest. But the Convention now holding its sittings was not of that character. It had met to frame a new organic and fundamental law—to wipe away the aristocratic features and fettering restrictions that belonged to the past generation, and in their place, provide new systems better suited to the intelligence and necessities of the people, and more in harmony with the wants and progressive spirit of the age. The task was one of no little labor or light responsibility, and he earnestly invoked gentlemen to abandon Eutopian and undigested theories and bring to the work before them all the wisdom, dignity and solemnity which the subject and the occasion alike, imperatively demand.

The proposition before us was in the following words: [Here Mr. D. read the amendment offered by the gentleman from Baltimore city.] It asserted the unrestricted and unqualified power of the people in its broadest and most extended sense; and in his judgment, was evidently not designed to be followed by any limited and wholesome constitutional restraint.

This question of inherent power of the people had already been well and ably explained, and indeed from the first slight examination, had seemed so clear and plain, as to require no masterly argument to bring it within the grasp of the humblest comprehension. No one imbued with the philosophy of our form of government, and understanding the great moral principle upon which it rested, had ever denied the fact, that all power was in the people, and that from them, as the great inexhaustible source, all power flowed. The very existence of our Government, the creature of their hands, and the offspring of their combined intellect, gives the happiest and noblest evidence of their free and glorious sovereignty. They, and they alone, can bind themselves, and it is in this very power of binding themselves that all free government has its strength and origin. It is this power that ushers into being great compacts, and develops itself in the form of Constitutions and solemn agreements, by which the whole people are bound up into a mighty body-politic, under the most sacred obligations and guaranties to secure each and all in the mutual enjoyment of every civil right and political liberty. He conceded to the people even greater power than the amendment proposed was designed to indicate—for he conceded the power of binding themselves by a compact of as much moral force as though executed between individuals—by a compact infinitely more sacred, because its violation, either in letter or spirit, would involve the happiness and peace of a whole people. It was because he entertained this great fundamental maxim as part—aye, as the foundation of his political faith, that he was compelled to take issue with the sentiments now boldly announced—that the people, or rather that majorities, could not be morally bound by the most solemn contract—nay could not even bind themselves—but that having the physical power they must necessarily have the political right at all times, and in any manner they may choose, to break down every restriction, independent of the most sacred constitutional compacts, and in defiance of the violated rights of a down trodden and oppressed minority. If such was indeed the correct theory of government, every consideration of social and individual security rendered it imperative that some new and more powerful restraint should be devised—something more stable than might be its whims—and more secure than might be its mercy. Happily such has never been the design of the intelligent citizens of Maryland. The Constitution now in being—the creature of their formation—contains the very idea of compact, and recognizes its binding power to the fullest extent. 'Tis every where filled with conditions and restrictions—mere contracts of majorities with minorities, imposed, doubtless, for the protection of sections and communities, and tending to the general benefit of the whole. The doctrine now urged was a new one—and he indulged the hope would have passed away, long before it could work out its legitimate and ruinous consequences.

He regarded every provision and guaranty that had been or might hereafter be inserted in the Constitution, of as much moral and binding force, as it was possible for anything to be under the canopy of high heaven, and they could not be abolished save in the manner designed, or violated without the assumption of the most tyrannical and arbitrary power, and without open and flagrant abuse of all individual and political honesty. True, there was a mode by which every feature of an existing government could be thrown aside, without consulting the established method. But that was revolution—an expedient not contemplated or provided for in a Constitution, or by laws. It was a something without, above, and beyond them all—a fearful remedy left to man to protect him from tyranny and oppression, and always to be used under a high and awful responsibility to the great God of the Universe.

But it had been gravely argued by a gentleman from the city of Baltimore, "that the term 'compact,' in government, implied nothing more than agreement, and might at any time be changed by a mere majority without regard to restrictions." And pray, sir, what is the difference between the words "compact" and "agreement?" What force does the one carry that might not legitimately be deduced from the other. When he heard this fancied difference urged with so much earnestness and gravity, the old and oft quoted couplet came instinctively to his mind, and he could not forbear repeating

"Strange what difference there should be,
'Twixt tweedledum and tweedledee."

Mr. Brent here arose and said he hoped the gentleman would state his position correctly, before he likened it to tweedledum and tweedledee. He had said that the word *compact* in the bill of rights, did not mean *contract*.

Mr. Dirickson resumed. He was still unable to perceive the nice distinction which the honorable gentleman had in fancy drawn. To his mind the terms compact, contract, and agreement had one common and general meaning, conveyed one general and common idea. If there was the least distinction, it was certainly too slight to hang an argument upon. The same reasoning would apply as properly to the one as the other. Among men, as individuals, an agreement was styled a contract, and it only assumed the more dignified and sounding appellation of compact, when inserted in the more solemn instrument that bound together a sovereign people. Sir, we are not here to discuss such slight and trifling distinctions—but for the higher and loftier purpose of framing a Constitution for a prosperous and growing people. And what, he asked, is the object and end of all Constitutions? To draw men together by a closer bond of union—to harmonise the social world—to secure individual rights, and more than all, to protect minorities from the strong arm of the many. This was its hallowed purpose and glorious design. Are gentlemen then willing to give countenance to a principle, that must defeat its every object—recognize without limitation the power of a lawless majority, which may set at defiance every right by us prescribed? If this new doctrine is to meet your sanction and approval, why are we here to reason together? Why has every community and section of Maryland, sent forth its Delegate to this high and wise conclave? Why have the venerable and the venerated been invoked to perfect our councils by their experience and maturity? Why, in short, this most expensive and "solemn farce," if you are about to recognize a principle which may—though the instrument you are now perfecting, receives the sanction of the people—tear it asunder and rend it into a thousand fragments, in its own time, in its own way—above all Constitution, and beyond all law? Such was not the sort of power he had been taught to respect and cling to, as the great feature of republican institutions. He believed that Constitutions were devised mainly to protect minorities, and that to adopt any political vagary which over-rode and tended to their entire subversion, was to make them little less than the merest mockery. Talk of organic and statute laws—where was their efficacy? Where were minorities to look for protection? Solely to the clemency of the majority, and with uplifted hands, ask as a boon what they should demand as a right! Such innovation upon the science of government, could not well be tolerated in the nineteenth century. The day, (if ever it existed,) had gone by when the power of numbers alone was intended to govern the world.

But there seems to be some gentlemen, who regard the amendment as asserting, harmlessly, nothing more than a mere abstract right; and, as such, avow their willingness to support it. Sir, abstractions are dangerous things to insert in the great organic law. Upon them new theories may be built, and around them novel doctrines generated, which may, in time, destroy all the fair proportions and harmony of the law itself, and finally war with its very vitality. He desired that the instrument, which should be submitted for ratification, should be clear and explicit—free from all abstraction—free from all doubt and obscurity—so plain that he "who runs might read," and at a glance comprehend all its simple provisions. But he did not consider the amendment as a mere abstraction, however cunningly cloaked. An idea lurked amid its folds, which might speedily and easily develop itself into that doctrine, so acceptable to those sections and communities now clamoring for power. There was in it the admission of a lawless might and an overwhelming right, to which this Convention would hardly be willing to give its endorsement. There was about it the ghostly shadow of another Convention, called by a different power from that by which the present had its origin, and upon a basis ensuring a result not now anticipated. Gentlemen, when too late, would learn that so far from being an unmeaning abstraction, it was, in truth, a stern and practical reality; offered with deep design and significant meaning; that upon it, as a basis, new and startling systems might be wakened into life and energy. He trusted no such supicious and uncertain feature, would be written upon the pages of our future Constitution. Let its mode of change and alteration be prescribed clear, explicit, and direct. The interest of every community, and individual, eminently demands that the manner of changing the organic law, under which their lives, their honor, and their property are secured and protected, should be, without doubt and without obscurity. Mystery should not shroud with darkness, a single word or line of that instrument, under which a free people are to live and exercise their inestimable privileges.

In his judgment, the gentleman from Caroline, (Mr. Stewart,) had in a slight degree at least misapprehended the real issue now under discussion. He had argued the question as though it was one of mere physical strength—and not solely of constitutional right. No one doubted but that power was the prerogative of numbers—nor denied but that they might exercise it in its wildest and most destructive form. That was revolution, soaring above all order—and far from the idea sought to be established by the amendment at present occupying our attention. The effort now made was not only to elevate the majority power to a lawless position, but to give it form, and place, and constitutional being in this very instrument we are framing. It was our duty to recognize the power, and at the same time to guard and secure it by proper moral and legal restrictions; and in the solemn compact, now to be ordained, we could not be too careful to so distribute this inherent power, that whilst the rights of none are crushed, the general interests of the whole State and community should be placed in the happiest and most prosperous condition. There was a great morbid and feverish excitement pervading every quarter of Maryland, and he respectfully warned gentlemen to abstain from startling and terrifying doctrines, lest by their unpropitious introduction they should discolor the whole public sentiment, and force the already too tender sensibility into disease in its most aggravated form. There was an idea abroad that *might* alone would triumph, and that the counties with their sparse population were to be trodden down and robbed of their political existence. He trusted no such destiny was in store, and he would see oil poured upon the troubled waters—calming and restoring their deep agitation. Again he invoked the Convention to abandon abstractions that might have such fearful tendencies. And he respectfully asked the gentleman who had introduced this amendment, what good result he expected from the proposition inserted in the unguarded form in which he had offered it for consideration?

Mr. Presstman here said he was not apprised of the best mode of carrying it out at present.

Mr. Dirickson resumed. He understood the gentleman then to express a willingness to take a leap fearlessly in the dark—to urge the adoption of theories, the tremendous consequences of which no man had anticipated or could begin to realize until the very crisis was upon him. Born of the people, he sympathised in all their hopes and wishes. He was part and parcel of them. He would have their every right so solemnly shielded that the very tyranny of numbers itself would stand abashed and rebuked whenever tempted to break down the sacred barriers by which they were guarded and preserved.

He had heard with great pleasure the very able remarks which had fallen from his honorable and highly esteemed friend from the county of Dorchester, (Mr. Hicks.) He had alluded to the peculiar legislation of 1836, as affording the most distinguishing evidence of the spirit of reform which had ever marked his whole political career. So far as the policy of that period had manifested itself in weeding out ancient drawbacks upon the rights and privileges of the people, and in more thoroughly republicanising our present form of Government, it merited and received his gratitude and approbation. But to his deep regret he was compelled to say, that when he remembered the innovation then made upon the representative system, he was compelled to regard it as the darkest hour in the modern annals of our State.

It was then that the principle of the amendment now submitted, received, in its most modified and limited form, a sort of *quasi* adoption. Then the entering wedge was pointed—and, under the specious and deceptive guise of compromise, a change was effected, which, if now expanded to the extent advocated, might rend the State to fragments. The idea here sought to be engrafted in the bill of rights, was nothing less than the basis upon which certain gentlemen might rear their darling hobby—"representation based purely upon population." He could not for an instant give countenance to any scheme with such an aim in view. Neither the past history of our State, nor its present condition and geographical position, warranted or justified it. The statesman who would provide wise laws for the government of a large community, must not be swayed in his judgment by mere abstract rights, but looking calmly over the whole field and weighing every circumstance in the balance, so draft his code that, whilst the interests of all received its beneficial influence, individual liberty and sectional independence, should be every where plainly and distinctly secured. The legislation of past days had shown no disposition upon the part of the smaller counties to use their present power detrimental to the prosperity of other portions of the State; on the contrary, they now exhibited the noble spectacle of an honest people cheerfully discharging every obligation made essential by our common debt, without present benefit or future hope.

By their combined aid and assistance, the mountains have been divided—canals opened—railroads created, and a great city reared up in all its magnificent proportions. Why then, this continued and ungrateful clamoring against the power essential to their security and independence? Why, to illustrate a mere abstraction, seek to humiliate their pride by placing them in a position but little short of mere colonial depencies?

A distinguished gentleman from Carroll county, some days since, in speaking of that small minority of the Convention who had voted for representation upon a purely popular basis, had said, with a manner and a menacing expression, that might indicate a threat, "that their constituency was named 'Legion.'" Sir, the day of menace and threats had gone by. The duty of those who represented the smaller counties was plain and open before them. The magic of the word "Legion" could not deter them from their high and resolved purpose. They could not now desert, in the hour of peril, without proving shamefully recreant to the sacred trusts which had been confided to them by a generous people.

To the words of the honorable gentleman from Dorchester, (Mr. Phelps,) whilst speaking of the fertility and beauty of the Eastern Shore, in view of a separation that might too soon be hurried upon us, he had listened with mingled emotions of pleasure and pain. With pleasure he felt the consciousness that there was no land upon which Heaven had smiled more kindly, and surely no people more open hearted in their generous hospitality. He trusted the hour of separation and sesession would never come. He was a Marylander by birth—a Marylander by nature and by habit. Every association of the past, and every hope of the future, entwined his affections about his native State. There was not within her whole borders one spot, from the topmost peak of the Alleghanies to yon distant shore, upon which the eternal thunder of the Atlantic's roar is unceasingly heard, which he did not love and cherish as consecrated ground. The deeds of her patriots and sages—of her warriors and statesmen, were one common property, and one common inheritance. No community or brotherhood was ever bound by stronger ties or happier reminiscences; and, fratricidal indeed would be that policy which, tearing asunder these bonds, would make one of the brightest of the old thirteen, a "Niobe" amid the brilliant galaxy of her sister States. He indulged the hope that gentlemen would refrain from expressions which grated harshly upon the feelings of so large a portion of the community. Outrage, heaped upon outrage, might compel them, however reluctantly, to begin to think seriously of separation. Leave them in their present position of independence, and peace and harmony would dwell forever in our borders. Reduce them to the condition of colonies, and no man could tell the end. They had lived too long as freemen, ever to exist quietly and tamely as bondsmen.

Ere concluding his remarks, he desired to say, that in his own county, among his own people, and in his own humble way, he had, for years past, been regarded as a reformer. Great as was the respect and veneration cherished for those noble ancestors who had transmitted the present Constitution under which we had so long and so happily lived, he thought many and great changes might be effected, conducive to the general interest and public welfare. He did not regard the science of government as perfected and finished, but believed, that like all other sciences, and like man himself, would be constantly undergoing improvements—constantly advancing toward that high state of perfection which was evidently designed by the God of the Universe. Our fathers had made great strides and done nobly in their day—let us show ourselves worthy of such paternity—worthy of their approbation, by seeking a still more elevated degree of political knowledge. The instinct of the beast might remain still, but 'twas the province of man and intellect ever to be moving onward to an higher and loftier sphere. He was ready to co-operate with gentlemen every where in the great work of reform before them. He was ready to abase the aristocrat and exalt the people, and to infuse the spirit of equality into every branch and department of our government. But he never could consent to give his sanction to the principle contained in the amendment of Mr. Presstman, under discussion, even though gentleman assumed for it the name and garb of reform. He never could aid in the forging of chains destined eventually to fetter and bind the liberties of his own generous and noble constituency.

Mr. Brown followed in some remarks, which are withheld for the purpose of his revision, (he being detained by sickness at home.) The remarks will be published as soon as possible.

Mr. Spencer expressed his regret, that the debate had taken such a wide range, and that the subject of representation should have been brought into it. For the first time, in his life, he had heard that the Constitution was to be regarded as a compact, and to be treated in the same manner as a contract, or agreement between parties. There were statesmen, who contended that the Constitution of the United States was a compact, but no such proposition had ever been urged in relation to the State Constitutions. In order to show that this was an incorrect view, he quoted from Chitty's Blackstone, vol. i, p. 44, the following definition of the word "compact:"

Law "is a rule of civil conduct prescribed by the supreme power in a State, commanding what is right and prohibiting what is wrong." "It is a *rule* to distinguish it from a compact or agreement. A compact is a promise proceeding from us—law is a command directing us."

He had looked for other authorities on the subject, but they were all out of the library—such as Story, Rawle, Wilson, Madison, and others. But, if this was to be considered as correct authority in reference to our political institutions, it will be seen that this Constitution instead of being a compact, or contract, is a "rule of action," prescribed by the supreme power in the State. If this be the case, how stands the question? The gentleman from Baltimore, had offered an amendment which was now before the the House, a simple, plain, intelligent proposition. In whom is power vested? Who has the right to change the Constitution? The people constitute the supreme power of the State, and *the right is in this supreme power alone*, and yet the assertion is made, that they cannot exercise their own discretion in effecting the object, owing to the compact contained in the Constitution. He could readily understand how, between different sovereignties, compacts of a binding force may be made; but the people, by whom our Constitution was made, being the sovereign power themselves, cannot bind themselves and posterity, by any compact in the form of a Constitution. The proposition before the House was a naked one. The gentleman from Kent has thrown in an amendment, which entirely destroys the original proposition. He contends that the people have not the power to change the Constitution in any other way than in the manner prescribed by the Constitution.

Mr. Chambers explained, that when the gentleman from Baltimore offered his amendment, he had asked him to explain it. The gentleman from Baltimore, replied that it was his impression that the people, without consent of law, in disregard of the Constitution, in any way, by any mode, might upset the existing government, or put in operation a new system, and that this was the right he intended to recognize, and that those who came after us, could put their own construction on the article.

Mr. Spencer stated what he had understood to be the course of the interrogatory; and then proceeded to defend the proposition of the gentleman from Baltimore, which was to be found embodied in the Constitutions of eighteen of the States of the Union. What reason then, he asked, was there to dread its operation in Maryland, more than it had been dreaded in other States? Was there more of a mob spirit here? Was not the people of our State orderly citizens abiding by law, and governed by a Constitution? Had they not given the strongest evidence of their love of order, in their long submission to the old Constitution? How often had the public will been thwarted by the legislative power? Yet they had borne the outrages long and quietly. The amendment of the gentleman from Kent, involved both an admission and a denial of the right of the people. It asserts that they have the right, but provides that they shall only exercise it in the way prescribed for them, and if they use it in any other way, they shall be adjudged guilty of treason. Thus the first principle of popular right is denied. Now he could never admit that the Constitution and laws possess a power above the people.

Mr. Tuck asked if he understood the gentleman from Queen Anne's, as saying, that when the Constitution has provided a mode by which the people may change the Constitution, they have a right to change it in any other way than the legal way?

Mr. Spencer said the people might change their Constitution, in any way they might think best. The right is inalienable. He would not not now go into the question, how the people might carry out their will; but he could make it clear that, when necessary, it might be done by a peaceful, tranquil process.

He had only risen, however, for the purpose of stating what was his understanding, as to the meaning of compact and law. So far as he was concerned, he would never consent to let the Constitution go out to the people in such vague and undefined terms, as are to be found in the old Constitution. He wished all the rights and powers conferred or recognized in it, to be so clearly defined and expressed, that no one hereafter could misunderstand them. He was ready, at any moment, to sustain his position. He was prepared for any argument on the subject, and if it was denied, he should hereafter defend it.

Mr. Donaldson said, he was in favor of the amendment of the gentleman from Kent, [Mr. Chambers,] and against the admission into the bill of rights of any such provision as had been offered by the gentleman from Baltimore city, [Mr. Presstman.] He, [Mr. D,] thought it had been demonstrated, in the progress of this discussion, that the incorporation of such a principle into the organic law, would be improper, and highly inconsistent with those principles by which the State of Maryland had been governed from the beginning, and with the true principles of Government every where. It was, in fact, the construction put upon the article which gave it a beneficial or an injurious influence, and if it was to be left in such a condition that it might become a ground of quarrel hereafter—if it was not made so explicit one way or the other as to place it beyond the reach of those agitating discussions which work injury to every community in which they exist—then it ought not to be there in any form. He felt surprised that gentlemen, who were the advocates of the unlimited power of the majority, should desire to avoid expressing their meaning in terms which could not be misunderstood. Those with whom he, [Mr. D.] acted, had no desire that their views should be misapprehended. They did not wish that any article of doubtful import should find its way into the Constitution.

The gentleman from Baltimore county, [Mr. Ridgely,] had stated that the amendment of the gentleman from Baltimore city, was an abstract proposition, and that, therefore, he was opposed to any qualification being annexed to it in the bill of rights; thus assuming that the bill of rights was a mere statement of the abstract principles of Government, subject to such qualifications as might be imposed by other clauses in the Constitution. If the gentleman would examine the bill of rights, he would find that it was full of practical principles intended to be applied to the legislation of the State. Would the gentleman say, that the provision which declared, that excessive bail should not be required, was a mere abstract principle? Or that trial by jury was so? Or the provision which declared that property should not accumulate in a religious corporation? And so as to numerous others. Mr. D. traced the bill of rights to its early history—showing the causes which had called it into being, and that, from the altered condition of things, the necessity for such a declaration had passed away; but expressed his unwillingness to part with it, for no other reason than its historical interest. The practical parts of this declaration might otherwise be incorporated under various heads in the body of the Constitution. He insisted that the proposition of the gentleman from Baltimore, [Mr. Presstman] in any good sense that could be attached to it, was already set forth in the bill of rights. The proposition was susceptible of three constructions. The first was consistent with our views of Government, and with the principles embodied in the bill of rights: that was to say, that the whole people might, at any time, change their form of Government; that all the parties making a compact, might make a new one; *that* was not, and could not be denied. Another ground was, that a majority of the people (and he wished this distinction to be observed,) had the right to call a Convention and to alter the Constitution by the bare right of a numerical majority, without any forms of law. The gentleman shakes his head. Whether this is his view or not, it is certainly the view of many gentlemen on this floor.

Mr. Presstman. Whatever I may think of the power of a majority, my amendment speaks for itself.

Mr. Chambers. But I want to know *your* meaning?

Mr. Presstman. You wish to know more than I am willing you should know at this time.

Mr. Donaldson proceeded. He did not say this was the exclusive meaning, but this was one of the meanings.

There was another class of gentlemen who said there must be a legal mode of carrying out this principle at the ballot box. To that class belonged the colleague of the gentleman from Baltimore city, (Mr. Brent,) and he, (Mr. D.,) placed himself among those who said, that the object must be effected according to the fundamental rule prescribed by the compact. He had been much pleased to hear the remarks of the gentleman from Baltimore city, (Mr. Brent,) on that point, because that gentleman was much less radical, (not using the term in any offensive sense,) than his colleague. In this respect, (said Mr. D.,) "not to be worst, stands in some rank of praise."

Here then, was a proposition that was open to three distinct interpretations. Ought it not to be made explicit? The evil to be apprehended was that the clause would receive its interpretation, from the sources from which it emanated; from the opinions of those who sustained it, and whose views, as the gentleman from Carroll, (Mr. Brown,) had yesterday remarked, would go "upon the record which all the waters of the Chesapeake could never wash out." *That* would be looked to as its contemporaneous exposition. The most innocent proposition in the world might, in such a way, become most noxious. The principle, that a mere numerical majority should in all cases rule, was one which he had never pretended to acknowledge. It seemed to him, that the proposition, interpreted as it had been by gentlemen who advocated its adoption, was identical with that which had been voted down the other day, in respect to representation according to population. If a mere numerical majority, as such, had the right at any time to annul the Constitution and the Laws, then that majority had a right to be represented according to their numbers. The one was a necessary corollary from the other.

Mr. D. proceeded to express the extreme surprise with which he had heard the gentleman from Queen Anne's, (Mr. Spencer,) argue that the Constitution was not founded on compact; when the very first article of the bill of rights declared, "that all government of right originates from the people, *is founded in compact only*, and instituted solely for the good of the whole."

Now, whatever that might mean, or however "absurd" it might be, it was there; our forefathers had placed it there, and there it had remained for seventy-five years. Whether it was a sound principle or not, it came from a high source—a source from which all the principles of modern political liberty were derived; and the gentleman from Queen Anne's, (Mr. Spencer,) knows that it was the very principle established by John Locke, and adopted into our Constitution as a protection against arbitrary power. His, (Mr. D's,) doctrine was that the consent of all the individuals of a community was necessary to form a government, and that it was a compact of the whole. The terms of the compact were binding. A compact, if he understood the term, was something that bound together. The differences between law and compact,as defined by the gentleman from Queen Anne's, (Mr. Spencer,) were entirely aside from the subject. They had nothing to do with it. Mr. D. illustrated this position, and proceeded to show that a compact was no compact at all, if it could at any moment be annulled without the consent of the parties making it.

He had stated the meaning of the amendment of the gentleman from Baltimore city, (Mr. Presstman,) under the different constructions that might be put upon it; and that there was a certain class of gentlemen (amongst whom, as he understood the gentleman from Baltimore city, Mr. Presstman, was to be placed,) putting a large and radical construction upon it—a construction against which, he, (Mr. D.,) protested, and which he did not desire to see sent out from this Convention, without the addition contemplated by the amendment of the gentleman from Kent, (Mr Chambers.)

The gentleman from Baltimore city, (Mr. Presstman,) in his remarks, had cited the authority of the late John C. Calhoun. However much he, [Mr, D.,] might disagree with that great man in some of the principles he had maintained, as to the relative powers and duties of the general and State governments of the Union, yet he, [Mr. D.,] declared that illustrious statesman's theory of government were identical with that which he, [Mr. D.,] had avowed, and in direct opposition to that of the gentleman from the city of Baltimore. Mr. D. read several extracts from the speeches of Mr. Calhoun in support of this position; and asked whether any thing could be more explicit? [Calhoun's Speeches, pp. 29, 65, 247, ed. of 1843.] However much the opinions of Mr. Calhoun might have changed, or seemed to have changed, upon other questions, he had in this stood from the beginning, firm and immovable, "like a great sea-mark standing every flaw."

According to the argument of gentlemen, this Constitution was not to bind us a single moment, if a bare numerical majority should decree its destruction. Of course, then, the protection of the minority was gone. Now, the true principle was, not that numbers should have no weight; not that wealth should have no weight; not that territory should have no weight; not that other considerations growing out of divided or aggregated interests should have no weight; but that, when a government was to be made for the people of a State, all these interests should be considered. Upon this question of representation, for instance, he was for a compromise—but against the principle for ever, that a mere majority of numbers should have the right to govern the rest absolutely. The advantage and the interest of the whole were to be consulted, and he had not the slightest idea that any interest would be injured when such a compromise was made. Wherever there is danger of one aggregated interest possessing the whole power in a State, it was wrong and must lead to injustice. He stated that the decision of political questions and elections by majorities, was merely a rule of convenience; and that, for the same object, the power of deciding such questions, was often given, as in this State, to mere pluralties.

He then proceeded to reply to the argument of Mr. Johnson, made a day or two since. That gentleman had said that a bare numerical majority of the people had a right at any moment, and in any manner, to annul the whole or any part of the Constitution, because, in his own words, "the eternal people were immortal." Now, if the people, in all its component parts, were eternal, then they were eternally bound by any compact. If, however, the gentleman's reasoning on that point was sound, it would lead directly to the result of repudiation; because, if the compact of the people with each other was not binding for a single day, neither could the contract of the whole, with any creditor of the State, be binding for a longer time. He knew that there was a question, how far this power of binding a community from generation to generation could be exercised, yet it presented no practical difficulty, because we are bound to place such provisions in the Constitution as will prevent the existence of such a difficulty. Some method must either be provided there, or the matter must be left to that common law which the great expounder of the Constitution has laid down in the case of Luther *vs.* Borden, as the American doctrine. There is no practical difficulty, however; for, in this age of the world, no man will so clog the wheels of goverment as to stay progress or prevent improvement. With us, danger is to be apprehended rather from a contrary source. We need brakes—we are going too rapidly.

Mr. D. then proceeded to speak of the right of revolution, as recognized (for extreme cases,) by the Constitution,

But gave way to a motion that the Convention adjourn.

The motion having been agreed to, the Convention adjourned until to-morrow morning at 11 o'clock.

FRIDAY, January 31st, 1851.

Prayer by the Rev. Mr. Grauff.

The roll having been called—no quorum was present.

Mr. Michael Newcomer. I move a call of the Convention.

The President. The roll has just been called.

Mr. Newcomer. How then are we to get the members here? I suppose the proper plan will be to send the officers of the Convention for them.

After some conversation, the President directed the Secretary again to call the names of those members who had not answered on the first call of the roll.

The names having been accordingly called, and a number of members having entered the hall, *ad interim*, a quorum was found to be present.

The journal of yesterday was read and approved.

The President laid before the Convention a communication from the Treasurer of the State, relative to the interest on taxes which has been remitted by the Executive under the provisions of chapter 207, of December session 1842, as required by the order of the Convention of 3rd inst.

Which was read, and

On motion of Mr. Brown,

Ordered to be printed.

TREASURY DEPARTMENT.

Mr. McLane, chairman of the committee on the Treasury Department, submitted the following report:

The committee appointed "to consider and report respecting the Treasury Department,"

REPORT.

Article 1st. There shall be a Treasury Department, consisting of a Comptroller chosen by the qualified electors of the State at each election of members of the House of Delegates, and shall receive an annual salary of three thousand dollars; also of a Treasurer to be appointed by the two houses of the Legislature at each session thereof on joint ballot, who shall receive an annual salary of two thousand dollars; and neither of the said officers shall be allowed or receive any fees, commissions or perquisites of any kind in addition to his salary, for the performance of any duty or service whatever. In case of a vacancy in either of the officers, by death or otherwise, the Governor, by and with the advice and consent of the Senate, shall fill such vacancy by appointment to continue until another election by the people or a choice by the Legislature as the case may be. The Comptroller and the Treasurer shall keep their offices at the seat of Government, take such oath and enter into such bonds for the faithful discharge of their duties as the Legislature may prescribe.

Art. 2d. The Comptroller shall have a general superintendance of the fiscal affairs of the State; digest and prepare plans for the improvement and management of the revenue, and for the support of the public credit; shall report estimates of the revenue and expenditure of the State, and superintend and enforce the collection of all taxes and revenue; adjust, settle and preserve all public accounts, decide on the forms of keeping and stating accounts, and grant, under regulations prescribed by law, all warrants for moneys to be issued from the treasury, in pursuance of appropriations by law, prescribe the formalities of the transfer of stock or other evidences of the State debt, and countersign the same, without which such evidences shall not be valid; he shall make full reports of all his proceedings, and of the state of the Treasury Department within ten days after the commencement of each session of the Legislature, and perform such other duties as shall be prescribed by law.

Art. 3d. The Treasurer shall receive and keep the moneys of the State, and disburse the same upon warrants drawn by the Comptroller and not otherwise; he shall take receipts for all moneys paid by him, and all receipts for moneys received by him shall be endorsed upon warrants signed by the Comptroller, without which warrant so signed, no acknowledgement of money received into the Treasury shall be valid. Upon warrants issued by the Comptroller; he shall make arrangements for the payment of the interest of the public debt, and for the purchase thereof on account of the sinking fund. Every bond, certificate or other evidence of the debt of the State, shall be signed by the Treasurer and countersigned by the Comptroller, and no new certificate or other evidence intended to replace another shall be issued until the old one shall be delivered to the Treasurer, and authority executed in due form for the transfer of the same, shall be filed in his office, and the transfer accordingly made on the books thereof, and the certificate or other evidence cancelled; but the Legislature may make provision for the loss of certificates or other evidences of the debt. The Treasurer shall render his accounts quarterly to the Comptroller; and on the third day of each session of the Legislature, shall submit to the Senate and House of Delegates, fair and accurate copies of all accounts by him from time to time rendered and settled with the Comptroller. He shall at all times submit to the Comptroller the inspection of the moneys in his hands, and perform all other duties that shall be prescribed by law.

The report was read, and on motion of Mr. McLane, was ordered to be printed.

INTERNAL IMPROVEMENTS, &c.

Mr. McLane, chairman of the committee on the Treasury Department to which was referred the order requiring said committee to inquire into the expediency of incorporating in the Constitution a clause prohibiting the Legislature from creating debts, appropriating the public funds for works of internal improvements or other objects not connected with a strictly economical administration of the State government, &c., asked that said committee be discharged from the further consideration thereof, and that the same be referred to the committee on the Legislative Department.

Mr. McLane remarked that the Committee did not consider this subject as coming within the legitimate range of their duties, and had therefore instructed him to move that they be discharged from its further consideration, and that it be referred to the Committee on the Legislative Department of the Government. It was also understood that the subject was embraced in a report already submitted by the last named Committee.

The change of reference was ordered accordingly.

On motion of Mr. McMaster, the Convention passed to the orders of the day.

THE BILL OF RIGHTS.

Thereupon, the Convention resumed the consideration of the Declaration of Rights of the State of Maryland, and of the amendments pending thereto.

Mr. Donaldson, who was entitled to the floor from yesterday, resumed and concluded his remarks.

After briefly re-capitulating the points of objection which he had made yesterday against the amendment of the gentleman from Baltimore city, (Mr. Presstman,) and the reasons which led him to think that that amendment should be qualified by the restriction contemplated in the amendment of the gentleman from Kent, (Mr. Chambers,) Mr. D. proceeded to cite the authority of Washington, which he had yesterday overlooked, to sustain his, [Mr. D's] position, that a compact signified a compact of the whole, of every part with every other part. And this, it seemed to him, was the only sound view to adopt in any Constitution.

He had also omitted yesterday, he said, to notice an objection which might be made to his construction of the compact of government. That objection was, that it would be impossible to carry out the theory, because any single individual would then have the right, when a new compact was to be made, to say he would not enter into it; and could thus, by a factious opposition, impede the will of an overwhelmning majority of a community. To this, as to all other general principles, the qualification was to be attached, that a theoretical right could not always be enforced. A man who would proceed factiously to assert a right where an immense majority of the community was against him, might commit a moral wrong; and in this case it would be an act of madness. So that no practical difficulty could, in fact, ever arise. Still, the theoretical right was there. None of these metaphysical rights could be taken abstractly, but must be modified according to the circumstances of the case. Mr. D. further illustrated the argument by showing that the principle claimed on the other side of the absolute power of the majority, is necessarily subject to many qualifications in practice.

He had yesterday stated (though he could not go fully into the question,) that there was no practical difficulty in relation to this matter. The gentleman from Frederick, [Mr. Johnson,] had declared that he could not bind the people of the next generation as to matter of politics—as to Constitutions. He [Mr. D.] argued that the people, if they were "eternal," could so bind themselves. If our new Constitution shall provide, as he presumed it would. for future amendment by means of Conventions, or if the 59 article prohibiting the legislature from taking any such action were stricken out, [and he persumed no one was in favor of retaining it,] then all danger would be averted.

Had not this Convention assembled in pursuance of a law passed in the face of that very article? That law would be right and constitutional and by no means revolutionary, if the 59th article were not in existence; but it seemed to him, under present circumstances, that the act was revolutionary, although in this particular case it had taken the forms of law, and had been acquiesced in by the whole people. He did not wish again to subject the community to any such danger—because, of late years, the popular impulses had become too strong for such trials.

So in relation to the question of the public debt—as to how far one generation could bind another to repay the money which it had squandered. There, he thought, was room for argument—but still, the error should always be upon that side which maintained the public faith without the slighest blur. He supposed it to be an almost unanimous feeling in this body, that restrictions should be placed in the power of the Legislature to contract public debt; that the property of our descendants should not be thus deeply mortgaged, but that provision should be made for the payment of the debt within a reasonable time. Adopt the principle maintained by the gentleman from Frederick, (Mr. Johnson,) and there would be no such thing as faith in a political community; there would be no power to bind even for a day. That was one extreme. The other extreme was binding a people forever, for any amount of debt which the State might choose to incur. Still, this was not a practical difficulty, because the remedy was easy, and sure to be applied.

A few words as to the right of revolution: There was an admirable article, (the 4th,) in the bill of rights of the State of Maryland, (which Mr. D. read.) There was embodied the true principle which lay at the foundation of all our rights, and which constituted our true security for the future, It was all that we wanted of the right of revolution—more would be dangerous.

Mr. D. dwelt at some length upon the confusion of terms, and consequent confusion of ideas of those gentlemen who had spoken of all political changes, however slight, as being revolutions —as taking from the word "revolution," all its true political meaning—and giving the same significance to things that were the most beneficial and the most noxious. Revolution in *physics* and revolution in *politics*, were things widely different in their nature. Unless the method prescribed in the Constitution was adopted, or in case none such were provided, unless the American doctrine of Mr. Webster were applied, no changes in the Constitution could, in his, [Mr. D's,] opinion be made, except there were such a degree of oppression as would authorise a resort to the right of revolution, as defined in the fourth article of our bill of rights.

Gentleman might say, must we then suffer, and continue to suffer, under mis-government? He would answer boldly, yes! so long as we could endure it—so long as there were legal modes of redress—so long as there was any hope that liberty might be preserved and property protected. The regular operations of time, and of public opinion would effect the requisite changes. He illustrated this point. He had been supposing, (he said,) a case where civil rights were invaded, but where mere abstract political rights were concerned—as, for instance, where the right to a certain numerical proportion of reppesentation was not enjoyed to the extent claimed by certain parts of the State—in such a case he clared it criminal to change or overturn the government in a revolutionary manner. Our political rights were only valuable as they secured to us our civil rights. And so long as our civil rights were in no danger of invasion, there was nothing to justify revolution. The political objects avowed here were made of undue importance. He admired, the other day, the candor of the distinguished gentleman from Frederick, (Mr. Thomas,) formerly Governor of the State, when he declared that this question of representation was a mere question concerning the distributionof political power, and quickly added, at the suggestion of another gentleman, "and of office." The greater part of the people were sublimely indifferent to mere politics and politicians, unless in cases where substantial rights were involved. Mere politics—as such--the struggle who should have one office or who should have another, had become offensive to the people of the State. The true objects of reform, in his opinion, had no reference to mere political rights. And he asserted, without fear of contradiction, that this question of representation according to population, or the right of a majority to rule, never could have procured the call of this Convention.

If reform meant improvement, he hoped that no gentleman had a seat in this Convention, who was not ready to make a great many reforms; but this "concert of action," which had been called for, could not be obtained by those who arrogated to themselves exclusively the title of reformers, and strove to inflict on others the odium of being anti-reformers. In almost every county in the State, the question of representation according to population, was either not broached, or was disavowed; the friends of the principle tried to avoid declaring themselves in fevor of it, and put the question of a Convention upon other grounds. They said, we must reform the Judiciary; we must place checks upon the Lelature, in relation to the exercise of this or that power; and they pointed out quite a variety of reforms, some of them good enough, and others from which he hoped we might be delivered. This reform party was something like the share which the subtle Jacob secured of his father-in-law Laban's flocks, "ring-straked, speckled and spotted:" it had as many colors as Joseph's coat. There was no such thing as concert of action among reformers. They disagreed upon every proposition, and they ought to disagree, because out of that conflict good might ultimately come.

If the Convention could succeed in establishing such a system of reform as that justice, rigid, prompt, efficient justice might be brought within the reach of every man; if it should check the power of the Legislature to contract debts; if it should arrest special legislation by which general rules and rights were disregarded for particular purposes; if it should take away from the Legislature the power of divorce, which was now used wantonly, recklessly, and even shamelessly, to cancel and tear to pieces, the bond that made man and wife one; if it should give to the State a substantial and well-regulated common school system; organise the treasury department on a proper basis, and accomplish other objects which he detailed; if these things should be done, and be done well, there was no ground for apprehension that the people would have a revolution, or even a new Convention very soon.

He pointed out briefly the evils which would result to society from the principle contended for, that a bare majority had a right, at any moment, and in any way, to change their Constitution; and said, this was in fact confounding right and power, and the practical operation of that principle would realize with us a state of things graphically depicted by the great poet of the human race—poet, historian, and prophet:

Force should be right, or rather right and wrong
(Between whose endless jar justice resides,)
Should lose their names, and so should justice too,
Then every thing resolves itself in power,
Power into will, will into appetite,

And appetite, an universal wolf,
So doubly seconded by will and power,
Must make, per force, an universal prey,
And last, eat up itself."

Yes, "last eat up itself!"—for such a principle must die of its own excess. It leads directly to anarchy; and anarchy never did last long—in the very nature of things it cannot last long. But in the mean time a very severe crisis might occur, which might lead to disastrous consequences. The revolution is peaceful to-day, but no one could say that it would not be bloody to-morrow.

Mr. McLane spoke at some length, but the sketch which was prepared, is kept back for revision. It will be published early.

Mr. Gwinn, stated that the House had been told in the commencement of this discussion, that the proposition of his colleague, (Mr. Presstman,) undeniable as it was in the abstract, was embarrassed by the differing sentiments expressed by those who supported it. The gentleman from Worcester had argued against its insertion in the bill of rights as radically wrong, because it was a mere abstraction declaring only that which was self-evident, and that it was therefore, unnecessary to adopt it as an article. The gentleman from Anne Arundel on the other hand, was prepared to vote against it as an abstract idea, which was dangerous in its tendency. He could not attempt to calculate the extent to which these different opinions would influence the House in its decision.

He desired, however, to say, that there was no historical proof to sustain the idea that the present Constitution was a compact among the counties, and therefore, the resolution was not objectionable on that account. But the true relation of the counties to the State would be discussed hereafter, with reference to the question of representation, when that subject came up.

The gentleman from Anne Arundel thinks that our Constitution will derive its sole validity from the ultimate ratification by the people. If this be true, and the Constitution be adopted, it is an admission of the right of the majority to frame a government, binding on the minority; and this must be the result. Whatever basis of representation is adopted, or whatever relation between the counties is established, the Constitution will be the ordinance of the majority.

It seemed to him that if the Constitution they were framing, derived all its vitality and force from the assent of a majority of the people, that this House had no right to reject the proposition which asserted that the people could exercise the same power hereafter.

He maintained that every republican Constitution contains within itself, expressed or unexpressed, the principle that all power resides in the people, and that the government which proceeds from them, is revisable by the same authority. For if it is intended for their advantage only, and originates in their consent, they can take its exercise into their own hands, as readily as a principal can revoke a power of attorney; and it does not necessarily follow that the exercise of this power would be an act of revolution.

He then referred, as an illustration of the impropriety of quoting English statesmen on such points, to the history of the vacation of the throne by James the Second, on the invasion of William, Prince of Orange, and to the reason of the difficulties in which the Parliament was involved. The discussion given in Grey's Debates, shows that they were embarrassed by the highly artificial nature of their Constitution, and all their procceding is explicable only by reference to the fictions of that Constitution. Our case was different, and different rules and maxims should govern our decision.

Mr. Chambers, of Kent, took the floor, but yielded to a motion for adjournment.

The motion was waived for the moment, to enable

Mr. C. to move, that when the Convention adjourns, it adjourn to meet at *twelve* o'clock on Monday.

Ordered accordingly.

And thereupon,

The Convention adjourned until 12 o'clock on Monday next.

MONDAY, February 3rd, 1851.

The Convention, pursuant to its order of Friday last, met this day at 12 o'clock.

Prayer was made by the Rev. Mr. Griffith.

The roll having been called, the journal of Friday was read.

The President announced that reports of committees were in order.

No reports were made.

DESKS, ETC.

Mr. Mitchell rose to offer an order, in regard to which, he said, he had not consulted any other members of the body. He thought, however, that the opinions of gentlemen who had had any experience here, would concur with his own, as to the propriety of the adoption of the resolution.

The order was read as follows:

"*Ordered*, That all the desks be removed from the hall, and that a large table be substituted where members can write, and that the committee appointed for the purpose of examining the condition of the Furnace, be instructed to have the flues closed, and that the old fire place be substituted."

Mr. Magraw rose to enquire whether there was any such committee as a committee on gas.

Mr. Mitchell suggested that it would be well so to modify the resolution, as to provide that gentlemen who might address the Convention, should, if they thought proper, speak from the platform on which the President's desk stood, instead of speaking from their own places.

Mr. McMaster moved that the order be laid upon the table.

And accordingly,

On motion of Mr. Brent, of Baltimore city, the Convention proceeded to the consideration of the unfinished business of Saturday last.

THE BILL OF RIGHTS.

The Convention resumed the consideration of the order of the day, being the report submitted by Mr. DORSEY, on the 11th instant, as chairman of the committee on the declaration of rights.

The question pending before the Convention, was on the amendment offered by Mr. CHAMBERS of Kent, on the 29th instant, to the amendment offered by Mr. PRESSTMAN, on the 28th instant.

Mr. CHAMBERS, of Kent, was entitled to the floor.

Mr. C. said that, in order to enable the gentleman from Baltimore city, (Mr. Gwinn,) whose argument had been broken off by the near approach of the hour of adjournment, to conclude his remarks, he, (Mr. C.) would waive his right to the floor.

Mr. GWINN thereupon took the floor.

Mr. GWINN said he would take advantage of the kindness of the gentleman from Kent, to conclude the remarks, which, in consequence of his state of health and the weariness of the House, induced him to omit pressing on the Convention at its last sitting. He would promise to repay that kindness, by occupying no more time than was necessary, to express his views on the subject under discussion. The amendment of his colleague was, to insert in the bill of rights, a declaration of the inalienable right of the people to change, alter or abrogate their form of government. The gentleman from Kent, (Mr. Chambers,) had moved to amend the proposition, by adding the words "according to the law or Constitution of the State." This amendment was directly in contradiction of the original proposition. If the right was inalienable in the people, it could not be definitively surrendered to a body which was not the people, and which, as it was part of the government, might be interested in resisting that power of reformation which it was the object of the article to recognise. The proposition involved no danger. The right must be exercised with moderation, and within the limits of that "moral competence," which restrains every legislative body.

The article, as proposed by his colleague, did not assert a revolutionary principle. That principle exists in all governments, without provision made for its exercise. The object of the amendment was not to assert a right of revolution, but to compel the recognition by the existing government, of the source of power, in the State, and to constrain it by moral force to accommodate itself to their varying wants and situation. Where this is done, revolutions, even if they occur, are comparatively harmless. There is no better instance than that of England in 1688, as contrasted with the result of the less flexible system of France, which was upturned in the last century.

There was no reason to object to the majority principle which the article recognised. The peace and happiness of the greater number are interested in a stable government. They are sureties for its existence. Much more evil is to be apprehended from the obstinacy with which minorities adhere to power. The whole proceeding under our Convention bill, recognises the majority principle. The Constitution which we make, may be carried here by a majority of counties, if the majority of a delegation were entitled to cast the vote of a county, voted against by a majority of the counties, and yet be ratified by the popular vote of the city of Baltimore and the larger counties. The Convention are but agents in the business—after they have concluded their work, it is submitted to the people, and, by force of their majority vote, becomes a supreme ordinance.

Illustrations drawn from English constitutional law were not applicable. The arguments of Fox, Grey, Erskine and Sheridan in the movements in the British Parliament, on the subject of reform, in the year 1797, went on the ground of convenience and not of right. The Constitution of the State did not recognize the principle of popular rule, and Mr. Pitt was able to resist all claim which was put on this ground. So too, in 1688, when the Parliament met to remedy the state of things ensuing on the flight of James I., it was seriously embarrassed. "The King can do no wrong," and, "the King never dies," were maxims, which utterly contradicted all notion of right to fill the throne, or to consider it vacated. It was compelled to adopt an extraordinary and utterly inconsistent resolution, to arrive at any result. After examining, critically, this resolution, he showed that no such difficulty could occur under the doctrine of a majority. It arose out of their artificial system. But there was an intrinsic right in the doctrine of a majority power. Those who had the most numerous interest in life and liberty were certainly entitled to prescribe the laws by which they should be governed. It was the rule of every deliberative body—it should be the rule of that supreme Parliament of which all, who have an interest in the State, are members.

He stated that seventeen or eighteen States had adopted the principle of the amendment of his colleague, without the modification of the gentleman from Kent; and these were not new States, animated by a desire to overleap the ancient land-marks, in their eagerness after novelty. Among them were old, discreet and orderly, and what were esteemed conservative, States. They had adopted the principle, and no danger or inconvenience had resulted. Yet the cry had been raised that its introduction here was warrant for a revolution. In conclusion, he was in favor of the proposition, for two reasons: first, because the right to alter, amend or abolish the Government is in the majority of the people, and it is proper that it should be specifically recognized in the organic law; and secondly, that it is a right that cannot be absolutely surrendered, and it is useless to adopt a form of words which would imply such a surrender. The amendment of the gentleman from Cecil, (Mr. MCLANE,) because a mode should be prescribed for ascertaining, from time to time, whether the people desired a change or not. For whenever, this was ascertained, it was the duty of a popular government to lend all its energy to promote this end.

It was the duty of the Government to give a proper control and direction to popular excitement, and to keep it always in the bounds of order. They did not accomplish, by what was called "the doctrine of acquiesence." This was certainly a strange creed. He could understand the consistency of a doctrine which recognizes the right of the people to reform their government, and which declared, that all offices created by the old Constitution were *ex-necessitata* vacated, when the people established a new order of things. But he could not understand this doctrine of assent, by the officers of the old Government, to an order of things which they believed illegally ordained. The judges under the present Constitution might resign, but if they thought that the new officers were chosen in contravention of that authority which they had sworn to sustain, how could they acquiesce? And even if they did, how could they do more than resign, and leave their office vacant indeed, but still in legal existence. Acquiescence in the existing government, if it believes that its authority was encroached upon, or unduly subverted, might be treason to the Constitution—but it could be nothing more. The difficulties of the creed held by gentlemen on the other side were inevitable.

Mr. PRESSTMAN followed in some remarks, a report of which is withheld for revision.

Mr. BUCHANAN said, he did not design to trouble the Convention with any remarks at this time. He thought that the question would come up hereafter. But he felt it his duty, before his friend from Kent, (Mr. Chambers,) proceeded with his remarks, to exhibit to him certain authorities, from the examination of which he, (Mr. B.) had come to the conclusion that there was no doubt whatever, of the correctness of the doctrine set forth in the amendment of the gentleman from Baltimore city, (Mr. Presstman.)

He, (Mr. B.) had come to the conclusion, from a full examination of those authorities, that the people had an undoubted, an inalienable, and indefeasible right to amend their Constitution at any time, and in any manner they might think proper; and he would go further and say, on authority, that this was an inalienable right, of which it was doubtful, whether or not, the people could even divest themselves, if they desired to do so. He agreed with the gentleman from Baltimore city, (Mr. Presstman,) that it was not important, so far as the rights of the people were concerned, whether a provision was embraced in the Constitution, authorizing the people at specified times, to reform their Constitution or not. He, (Mr. B.) would vote for such a provision. Still it was unimportant. The people could do this thing, by virtue of their inherent sovereignty. Now, although the doctrine seemed to be broad, and although he could not, until he had examined the authorities, go to the extent to which he would now go, yet he had come to the conclusion, that this power did exist in the people, no matter what the Constitution might say. Under monarchical governments, the absolute sovereignty rested in the monarch, but with us the sovereign authority was in the people; and if the people themselves—a majority of the people—should at any time think it expedient to remodel their form of Government, they had a right to do it *non obstante*, any other power upon earth.

Mr. JENIFER. Does the gentleman mean to say, that if a provision should be inserted in the new Constitution, declaring that hereafter the Constitution may be altered by a Convention, and that Constitution should be ratified by the people, does the gentleman say, that notwithstanding that article, the people may, through all time, and without a revolutionary movement, change their government?

Mr. BUCHANAN. At any time. The people—a majority of the people—have at all times the right to remodel or change their government.

Mr. SOLLERS. How is that majority to be ascertained?

Mr. BUCHANAN. That is a matter for their consideration.

One word, (Mr. B. said,) as to what might he regarded as the sentiment of the people of the United States, on the subject. There were some twenty-four States which embraced, substantially, this very doctrine in their Constitutions—most of them, the very words. But he rested on the example of that proud old State of Virginia—he rested upon a principle which was there promulged by Marshall, Madison and Monroe, and their compatriots in the Convention which formed the Constitution of '76, where phraseology, even stronger than that of his friend from Baltimore city, (Mr. Presstman,) had been employed. The original Constitution of Virginia, asserted the inalienable right of *a majority* of the people—not the aggregate people—but of a majority of the people to remodel and change their government. That doctrine had been ratified and re-affirmed by the Convention of '30. The same principle had been adopted by Texas, Florida, and Iowa.

Mr. B. then read the following authorities, which he handed to the Reporter, as a substitute for his intended argument.

The Declaration of Independence:—

"We hold these truths to be self-evident, that all men are created equal; that they are endowed by their Creator with certain inalienable rights; among them are life, liberty and the pursuit of happiness. That to secure these rights, governments are instituted among men, *deriving their just powers from the consent of the governed*; that when any form of government becomes destructive of these ends, *it is the right of the people* to alter or abolish it, and to institute a new government, laying its foundation on such principles, and organizing its power in such forms, as to *them* shall seem most likely to effect their safety and happiness."

Mr. Jefferson says:

"It is not only the *right*, but the *duty of those now on the stage of action*, to change the laws and *institutions* of government, to keep pace with the progress of knowledge, the light of science, and the amelioration of the condition of society. Nothing is to be considered unchangeable, but the inherent and inalienable rights of man."

Justice Iredell, of the Supreme Court, (vol. iii, Elliott's debates,) says:

"Our government is founded on much nobler principles. The people are known with certainty to have originated it themselves. Those in power are their servants and agents; and *the people without their consent*, may remodel the government whenever they think proper, not merely because it is oppressively exercised, but *because they think another form is more conducive to their welfare*."—[Story's Commentaries, vol. i, page 326.]

Hamilton (Federalist, No. 22,) says:

"The fabric of American empire ought to rest on the solid basis of the *consent of the people*. The streams of national power ought to flow immediately from that pure original fountain of all legitimate authority."

Jay, chief justice of the United States Supreme Court, says:

"At the revolution, *the sovereignty devolved on the people*, and they are truly the sovereigns of the country; but they are sovereigns without subjects, (unless the African slaves among us may be so called,) and have none to govern but themselves; the citizens of America are equal as fellow-citizens, and as joint tenants in the sovereignty."—[2 Dallas' Reports, 419.]

Marshall, chief justice United States Supreme Court, says:

"It has been said that the people had already surrendered all their powers to the State sovereignties, and had nothing more to give. But, surely, the question whether they may resume and modify the powers granted to government, does not remain to be settled in this country. [4 Wheaton's Reports, 405.]

Justice Wilson, a signer of the Declaration of Independence, a member of the Convention of 1787, which framed the Constitution of the United States, and afterwards a judge of the Supreme Court of the United States, says:

"Of the right of *a majority* of the *whole people* to change their government *at will*, there is no doubt."—[1 Wilson, 418; 1 Tucker's Black. Comm. 165, cited 324 p., vol i, Story's Comm.]

Again he says:

"Perhaps some politician, who has not considered with sufficient accuracy, our political systems, would answer in our government, the supreme power was vested in the Constitution. This opinion approaches a step nearer to the truth, (than the supposition that it resides in the Legislatures,) but does not reach it. The truth is, that, in our government, the supreme, absolute, and uncontrolable power *remains* in the people. As our Constitutions are superior to our legislatures, so the people are superior to our Constitutions. Indeed, the superiority in this last instance is much greater; for the people possess, over our Constitutions, control in act as well as right."—[Wilson's Works, vol. iii, p. 292.]

Again he says:

"The consequence is, that the people may change the Constitution *whenever* and *however* they please. This is a right of which no positive institutions can deprive them.

"These important truths, are far from being merely speculative; we, at this moment speak and deliberate under their immediate and benign influence. To the operation of these truths, we are to ascribe the scene, hitherto unparalleled, which America now exhibits to the world, a gentle, a peaceful, a voluntary and a deliberate transition from one Constitution of government to another, (from the confederation to the Constitution of the United States.) In other parts of the world, the idea of revolution in government is by a mournful and indissoluble associations, connected with the idea of wars, and all the calamities attendant on war.

"But happy experience teaches us to view such revolutions in a very different light—to consider them as progressive steps in improving the knowledge of government, and increasing the happiness of society and mankind.

"Oft have I viewed with silent pleasure and admiration, the force and prevalence through the United States of this principle—that the supreme power resides in the people, and that they never part with it. It may be called the *panacea* in politics. If the error be in the Legislature, it may be corrected by the Constitution: if in the Constitution, it may be corrected by the people. There is a remedy, therefore, for every distemper in government, if the people are not wanting to themselves."—[Wilson's Works, vol. iii, p. 293.]

Again, he says:

"A revolution principle certainly is, and certainly should be, taught as a principle of the Constitution of the United States, and of every State of the Union. This revolution principle—that the sovereign power residing in the people, they may change their Constitution and Government whenever they please—is not a principle of discord, rancor or war; it is a principle of melioration, contentment and peace."—[Wilson's Lectures, vol. 1., p. 21.]

And, again:

"A proper regard to the *original*, and *inherent*, and *continued* power of the *society to change its Constitution*, will prevent mistakes and mischief of a very different kind. It will prevent giddy inconsistency; it will prevent unthinking rashness; it will prevent unmanly langor:"—[Wilson, vol. 1, p. 420.]

Justice Patterson, of the United States Supreme Court, says:

"The Constitution is the work of the people themselves, in their original, sovereign and unlimited capacity." "A Constitution is the form of Government delineated by the mighty hand of the people," is "paramount to the will of the Legislature," and is liable only "to be revoked or altered by those who made it."—[2 Dallas' Rep. p. 304.]

The Supreme Court of the United States, through Judge Marshall, says:

"That the people have an original right to establish, for their future Government, such principles as, in their opinion, shall most conduced to their own happiness, is the basis on which the whole American fabric has been erected. The exercise of this original right is a very great exertion; nor can it, nor ought it, to be frequently repeated."—[1 Cranch, 157, cited 431 Story's Comm. vol. 3.]

Rawle, an able commentator on the Constitution, says:

"Vattel justly observes, that the perfection of a State and its aptitude to fulfil the ends proposed by society, depend upon its Constitution. The first duty to itself is to form the best Constitution possible, and one most suited to its circumstances; and thus it lays the foundation of its safety, permanence and happiness. But the best Constitution which can be framed, with the most anxious deliberation that can be bestowed upon it, may, in practice, be found imperfect and inadequate to the true interests of society. Alterations and amendments then become desirable. *The people retain—the people cannot, perhaps, divest themselves of the power to make such alterations.* A moral power, equal to, and of the same nature with that which made, alone can destroy. *The laws of one legislature may be repealed by another legislature*, and the power to repeal them cannot be withheld by the power that enacted them. *So the people may, on the same principle, at any time, alter or abolish the Constitution they have formed.* This has been frequently and peaceably done by several of these States, since 1776. If *a particular mode* of effecting such alterations has been agreed upon, it is *most convenient* to adhere to it, but it is *not exclusively binding.*"—[Rawle on the Constitution, p. 17.

Justice Story, of the supreme court of the United States, says, in his commentaries on the Constitution:

"The declaration puts the doctrine on the true *ground*—that government derives its powers from the *consent* of the governed. And the people have a right to alter it," &c.—[page 300, vol. I.

Again, Judge Story, in speaking of the Declaration of Independence, says:

"It was not an act done by the State governments then organised, nor by persons chosen by them. It was emphatically the act of the whole people of the united colonies, by the instrumentality of their representatives, chosen for that, among other purposes. It was an act not competent to the State governments, or any of them, as organised under their charters, to adopt. Those charters neither contemplated the case, nor provided for it. It was an act of original inherent sovereignty by the people themselves; resulting from *their right to change their form of government, and to institute a new government, whenever necessary for their safety and happiness.*"—[Story's Com. on Con., vol. 1, page 198.

Mr. Locke, in his work on civil government, says:

"For where any number of men have, by the consent of every individual, made a community, they have thereby made that community one body, with a power to act as one body, which is only by the *will and determination of the majority;* for that which acts in any community, being only the consent of the individuals of it, and it being necessary to that, which is one body, to move one way, it is necessary that the body should move that way, whither the great force carries it, which is the consent of the majority; or else it is impossible it should act or continue one body —one community—which the consent of every individual that united into it agreed that it should; and so every one is bound by that consent to be concluded by the majority. And therefore, we see that, in assemblies empowered to act by positive laws, where no number is set by that positive law which empowers them, the act of the majority passes for the act of the whole, and of course determines as having, by the law of nature and reason, the power of the whole; and thus every man, bv consenting with others to make one body politic, under one government, *puts himself under an obligation to every one of that society to submit to the determination of the majority, and to be concluded by it.*"

Mr. Madison, in relation to the same subject says:

"If we resort for a criterion to the different principles on which different forms of Government are established, we may define a republic to be, or at least may bestow that name on a Government *which derives all its powers, directly or indirectly, from the great body of the people.*" * * * * *

"It is essential to such a Government that it be derived from *the great body of the society*, not from an *inconsiderable proportion* or a *favored class* of it; otherwise, a handful of tyrannical nobles, exercising their oppressions by a delegation of their power, might aspire to the rank of republicans, and claim for their government the honorable title of republic.

"It is essential for such a Government that persons administering it be appointed, either directly or indirectly, *by the people;* aud that they hold their appointment by either of the tenures just specified; otherwise, every Government in the United States, as well as any other popular Government that has been, or can be well organized, or well executed, would be degraded from the republican character."—[Federalist, No. 39.

The Declaration of Rights of a large majority of the States of the Union, contain a provision analagous to that proposed here.

The bill of rights of Virginia of 1776, which was unanimously adopted, contained the following provision.

That Government is or ought to be instituted for the common benefit, protection and security of the people, nation or community. Of all the various modes and forms of Government, that is best which is capable of producing the greatest degree of happiness and safety, and is most effectually secured against the danger of mal-administration. And that when any government shall be found inadequate or contrary to these purposes, *a majority* of the COMMUNITY hath an indubitable, inalienable and indefeasible right to *reform, alter or abolish it in such manner as shall be judged most conducive to the public want.*

This provision was again adopted in Virginia in the bill of rights of 1830.

In the Convention of Virginia a proposition was made to engrrft a clause on the Constitution, providing for its future amendment. This was rejected on the ground that *a majority of the people had the power at any time, and in any manner they pleased, to amend their Constitution, or to make a new one.*

Among those voting against the provision, were James Madison and John Marshall.

Some conversation followed on a point of order, in which Messrs. BRENT, of Baltimore, SPENCER and the PRESIDENT, took part.

Mr. SPENCER then proceeded to remark, that he should vote in favor of the proposition of the gentleman from Cecil, (Mr. McLane,) and he, (Mr. S.) maintained the proposition of the gentleman from the city of Baltimore, (Mr. Presstman,) in all its integrity. He should go further than that gentleman, according to the views he had submitted this morning. He was in favor of the proposition of the gentleman from Cecil, (Mr. McLane,) because it declared it to be the duty of the Convention to carry out that great cardinal principle, which lay at the foundation of all government. The mode pointed out by the gentleman from Cecil, was good, and should receive the approbation of every member—certainly every reform member of the Convention.

Mr. SPENCER said he did not intend to go into any elaborate argument. He should vote with all his heart for the amendment of the gentleman from Cecil, and for the proposition of the gentleman from Baltimore, [Mr. Presstman.] He desired also to add a few authorities to those which had been brought forward by the gentleman from Baltimore county, [Mr. Buchanan.] He then proceeded to read extracts from No. 84 of the Federalist, from Judge Story's commentaries, and from Davis' abridgement, for the purpose of sustaining the position, concerning the meaning of compact and the right of the people to alter, amend or abolish their form of government. He had cited these authorities to sustain the position he had started in the beginning of this debate.

Mr. MITCHELL begged leave to ask the gentleman from Queen Anne's, a single question. That gentleman, as well as himself, represented one of the small counties of the State. Was the gentleman prepared to throw the whole power of the State, into the hands of the people of Baltimore?

Mr. SPENCER replied that he had no fear of the power of Baltimore, or of her hostility to the counties. He was of opinion that whenever Baltimore should attempt to exercise a power over the counties, she would find in the counties power and energy enough, to oppose an effectual resistance to the attempt. The fact of the existence of a city like Baltimore in the State, did not draw him off from the republican faith. He was proud of such a city, and if the gentleman, who was from a smaller county, had a smaller share of that faith, it could not be helped. He hoped that the gentleman was answered.

Mr. MITCHELL. I am answered.

Mr. SPENCER resumed, in conclusion. He had not intended, when he rose, to make a speech. He would only add, that he intended to vote for the amendment of the gentleman from Cecil; and whenever it should be necessary for him to do so, he was ready to defend the position he had taken.

Mr. CHAMBERS said nothing was more important, in all controversies, than a distinct statement and understanding of the exact points in issue. From what was passing around us, he was led to think we were in great danger of fighting shadows. He very much regretted the apparent unwillingness of gentleman, to explain their positions precisely. It had even been said to be "unfair," to ask gentlemen distinctly to explain the object and design of their propositions submitted for our action. He regarded such notions as utterly out of place here.

Our proper duty here was to form such a Constitution, as would best secure to the people of Maryland—the whole people—the full and safe enjoyment of life, liberty and property, for all time, and not to elevate one class or party in the community, and depress another. Its provisions should be not only just and equal, but as plain and intelligible, and as free from doubt or obscurity as possible, so that those who administer the Government, and all intelligent persons, may comprehend its import. It would be a poor boon to the State, if our labors resulted in an instrument calculated to produce doubts and difficulties, and expensive litigations. He adverted to the history of this debate. When the section in the bill of rights, reported by the committee, which declares in the most expressive terms, the supreme sovereignty of the people, as the source of all political power, and their right to control and alter the government, was under consideration, the resolution now before the chair, was offered by the gentleman from Baltimore, [Mr. Presstman.] He had not perceived the necessity for any additional declaration of the kind, and enquired of the gentleman why he considered it requisite. To this it was answered that the object was to introduce the doctrine, distinctly avowed as his creed, that the majority of the people, at any time, in any mode they pleased, and without any previous constitutional or legal provision—nay, against and in opposition to constitutional or legal provision, could remodel the government or form a new one. Against this doctrine he had entered his solemn protest, and had ventured to read the first article of the present bill of rights, which declared that "all government is founded in compact only and instituted solely for the government of the whole." Another gentleman from Baltimore, [Mr. Brent,] had controverted the doctrine of his colleague, so far as related to the necessity of some legal provision, declaring the mode of proceeding. A gentlemen from Queen Anne's, [Mr. Wright,] in a very clear and concise speech, had objected, in like manner, saying the gentleman was right as far as he went, but that something more was necessary. That "something more" it was the object of his amendment to supply. Another gentleman from Queen Anne's, [Mr. Spencer,] had declared "it was the first time in his whole life, he had ever heard it claimed that government was founded in compact."

Here Mr. SPENCER explained that he had not intended to use language so broad, but to say that the Constitution was not a compact.

Mr. C. resumed. Upon this, his friend from Anne Arundel, (Mr. Donaldson,) had delivered an argument as lucid and logical, and to his mind, as conclusive, and if he were not present, he would add, as statesman-like as any he had listened to in this House. Other gentlemen had expressed conflicting opinions upon the subject. The elaborate argument of the gentleman from Cecil, (Mr. McLane,) was not professedly in reply to that of his friend near him, (Mr. Donaldson,) but was directed against the positions which he, [Mr. C.,] had previously and briefly urged; and these he now begged leave so to restate as to leave no room for misconception.

1st. He maintained, that according to our theory, government was founded in compact; and

2ndly. That the acknowledged sovereign power of the people, to alter and reform the Constitution and form of government, must be exercised by a mode prescribed by the Constitution itself, or by a law pursuant thereto, or it must be by revolution.

As to the first proposition, he begged to be distinctly understood, as not holding the "compact" to be of such a character, as to justify an action at law, by an individual who might allege a particular violation to his detriment. The very nature of the agreement and the parties to it, forbid any such idea. Amongst individuals entering into compacts, there was always a clear understanding, that the courts of justice would administer relief to a party injured by the violation of its terms.

In the formation of a government there were no tribunals superior to the government, and the only redress to which an individual could look, was the moral obligation to perform the stipulations of the agreement in good faith. Except, indeed, where one branch of the government might be appealed to, as a check upon the attempt of another branch to commit such a violation. Thus the courts frequently interposed to arrest the execution of a legislative enactment, which was in violation of individual rights, secured by the organic law.

Nor did he mean a compact in the sense of a treaty amongst nations, sovereign and independent, which having no higher power to decide in questions of alleged violations of their agreements must of necessity, each decide for itself, and recede from the agreement, when a violation was committed.

He had supposed that the express and emphatic declaration in our bill of rights would have been sufficient authority for any Maryland lawyer, but he would be able to show abundant authority for the truth of his proposition without going farther than to the pages of the book relied on by the gentleman from Cecil—Justice Story's Commentaries on the Constitution. Judge Tucker in his commentaries on Blakistone—a book in the hands of every law-student—has minutely entered into this subject. He maintains the doctrine in the strongest terms. Judge Story in the book relied on, reviews at length, Judge Tucker's remarks, and in the course of his examination, refers as is usual with him, to all the leading authorities. Mr. C. here read from various pages, the quotations from Madison, Jefferson, Jay, John Quincy Adams, Mr. Dane, the Constitution of Massachusetts, the resolutions of Virginia and of Kentucky, all in "*tottidem verbis*," expressing the distinct doctrine, that Government was founded in compact.

He averred that Justice Story himself maintained this doctrine, and was misconceived by the gentleman from Cecil. It must not be lost sight of in this inquiry, what Justice Story was discussing. The doctrine of the right of secession of one State from the Union, for a violation of the terms of the Constitution had been openly avowed. South Carolina had maintained her right to nullify—to treat as void—any law which she considered contrary to the letter or spirit of those terms. Her senators in Congress had maintained the same claim, and the subject filled the minds of political men all through the country. This right was based upon the ground, that the States as sovereignties were parties to the compact, which, therefore, was to be regarded as a treaty amongst independent nations.

Against this doctrine, Mr. Webster had raised his powerful logic; and his efforts to put down that mischievous creed would have immortalized his name, had he no other claim to the gratitude of the latest posterity. Justice Story, in his treatise, is examining into this question. After expending some five and forty pages in reviewing the authorities on either side, he says, in page 304, sec. 335, "It is easy to understand how compacts between independent nations are to be construed, and violations redressed." "There are but three modes in which these differences can be adjusted:" they are by "new negotiations," "reference to a common arbiter selected *pro hac vice*," or, "a resort to arms." In the following section, 336, he continues, "it seems equally plain that in our forms of Government the Constitution cannot contemplate either of these modes of redress. Each citizen is not supposed to enter into the compact with all the others *as sovereign, retaining an independent and co-equal authority to judge and decide for himself. He has no authority reserved to institute new negotiations; or to suspend the operations of the Constitution, or to compel the reference to a common arbiter; or to declare war against the community to which he belongs.*"

Then follows immediately the section, 337, page 305, triumphantly relied on by the gentleman from Cecil. "No such claim has ever (at least to our knowledge) been asserted by any jurist or statesman in respect to any of our State institutions." Let us pause here a moment. The gentleman would have us suppose that which Judge Story never heard of, as being claimed, was the idea of Government being founded in compact. A greater mistake never was made. He had quoted throughout the whole chapter, name after name, book after book—amongst them the Constitution of his own State, saying, "it is a social compact, by which the whole people covenants with each citizen, and each citizen with the whole people. "And had he never heard of that? The gentleman will find by reading the preceding pages of that chapter, or even the last few antecedent lines, that the "*no such claim*" refers to a claim like that of independent nations—a claim to "negotiate anew," "select an arbiter" or "declare war." To make it mean any thing else, is to make Justice Story to stultify himself. Why, in this *self-same section*, 337, a few lines below, he repeats the same doctrine, and yet expressly treats of the "compact" as recognizing it. "No right exists or is supposed to exist on the part of any town or county, or other organized body within the State, short of a majority of the whole people of the State, to alter, suspend, resist or dissolve the operations of that Constitution, or withdraw from it. Much less is *the compact* supposed liable to interruption, at the will of any private citizen, and this according to Mr. Locke, is the true sense of *the original compact* by which every individual has surrendered to the majority the right to control," &c.

Why talk of the qualities of a *compact* if there be none? How, sensibly speak of the sense of the *original compact*, if no such thing can be alleged? No, sir, it is the nature and effect of that very thing of which he had so long and so ably been discoursing, and let gentlemen think as they may on other matters, every one who would carefully examine the pages of Justice Story, would look in vain at the 337th section of his 1st vol. on the Constitution, for any authority against the doctrine that government was originally founded in compact, nor did he admit that the high authority of Mr. Webster was in any degree opposed to him. He did not allege the Constitution to be *technically* a contract or compact. It could not be enforced in a court of law. What says Mr. Webster in the speech referred to? After saying "in *strictness*," the Constitution is not a compact," he adds, "I believe it is founded in consent or agreement, or on *compact*, if the gentleman prefers that word, and means no more than *voluntary consent* or *agreement*." Indeed the gentleman from Cecil comes to this conclusion at last—that it is founded on assent and agreement. It is then but a philological difference between us, and I rather think that Noah Webster, as well as his great namesake, will show that agreement is but another word for compact.

But, after all, the question is of comparative unimportance. The great and interesting point is, as to the force and effect of a Constitution as a mode of executing the sovereign power of the people.

The absolute right is one thing, but the mode of enforcing it another. If a trespasser takes my farm or my horse, I have a perfect right to repossess myself, but I may not go on the premises and with a bludgeon knock out the brains of the one, or seize a revolver and shoot six bullets through the vitals of the other. That is not the mode in which the right is to be exercised.

At this point of his remarks, Mr. C. gave way to a motion that the Convention adjourn.

Which motion having been agreed to,

The Convention adjourned until to-morrow morning at ten o'clock.

TUESDAY, February 4th, 1851.

The Convention met at eleven o'clock.

Prayer was made by the Rev. Mr. GRIFFITH.

The roll was called, and no quorum being present,

Mr. RIDGELY moved that the Convention adjourn, (with a view to give time for members to come in,) and asked the yeas and nays, which were ordered, and being taken, were yeas 0; nays 39.

So the Convention refused to adjourn.

Mr. KILGOUR moved a call of the House.

The motion was rejected.

A quorum was now present.

HOUR OF MEETING.

On motion of Mr. WEEMS,

It was ordered,

That the daily hour of meeting hereafter, be 11 o'clock, A. M.

The PRESIDENT laid before the Convention the following communication from Jos. C. G. Kennedy, Esq., Superintendant of Census.

CENSUS OFFICE,
Washington, Feb. 3rd, 1851.

To the President of Maryland State Convention:

SIR: I find by an examination of the official returns (to which my attention was called by a newspaper statement,) that an error exists in the returns made for Frederick county, of which the total population will not vary much from 40,941. I will send a more particular statement to-morrow. We have been much delayed in reconciling the inconsistencies existing between the returns made by the marshals of the population in the several sub-divisions, and the number exhibited by the returns themselves.

I regret that the return has been made for Frederick, so much at variance with the facts, and hope no great inconvenience has resulted therefrom.

I have the honor to be, sir,
Very respectfully, your ob't serv't,
JOS. C. G. KENNEDY,

Which was read, and

Referred to the committee on representation.

The PRESIDENT also laid before the Convention a communication from E. Root, Esq., State Superintendent of Public Instruction of the State of Wisconsin, covering the reports of the State, of the Board of Regents of the State University.

Which was read, and

Referred to the committee on Education.

On motion of Mr. STEWART, of Baltimore city, the Convention proceeded to the consideration of the unfinished business of yesterday.

THE DECLARATION OF RIGHTS.

The Convention resumed the consideration of the order of the day, being the report submitted by Mr. DORSEY, on the 11th ult., as chairman of the committee on the declaration of rights.

The state of the question was as follows:

The first article of the report being under consideration in the words following:

"That all government of right originates from the people, is founded in compact only, and instituted solely for the good of the whole."

Mr. PRESSTMAN had moved to amend the said article, by adding at the end thereof the following words:

"And they have at all times the inalienable right to alter, reform, or abolish, their form of government, in such manner as they may think expedient."

And Mr. CHAMBERS, of Kent, had moved to amend said amendment by adding, at the end thereof, the following words:

"According to the mode authorized by the Constitution or laws of the land."

And the question was on the amendment to the amendment.

Mr. CHAMBERS, of Kent, who was entitled to the floor from yesterday, resumed and concluded his remarks.

Mr. CHAMBERS alluding to his remarks of yesterday in relation to the question of "compact," said there were other authorities which would sustain him, but he had thought it sufficient to show the error of his friend from Cecil, in supposing Justice Story to deny this doctrine. He thought it quite as much an error to ascribe the origin of this notion of "compact" to the advocates of the Divine right of kings, and not less an error to suppose that Justice Story had so asserted. The doctrine of the Divine right of the king to govern, is as opposite to that of compact or agreement of the people as to the terms of government, as darkness is to light.

The Divine right to rule *necessarily* leaves nothing to the people but the Divine obligation *to be ruled*. The decrees of the Deity cannot be controled by the agreements of men. His friend, (Mr. Donaldson,) had fully shown that the doctrine was introduced by Locke, Sidney and others, who were the patriots of their day and antagonists to the Divine right of kings—and so said Justice Story, p. 293, sec. 325. And in p. 313, sec. 343, he concludes, after examining the debates in Parliament on the abdication of James the Second, by saying, "it is apparent from the whole reasoning of the parties, that they were not considering how far the original institution of government was founded in compact," &c.

He would now proceed to examine the other proposition which he regarded as of the very greatest importance to the very existence of government—the binding obligation on all—the whole community of the Constitution or organic law, until altered by a Constitutional or legal mode. He did not profess to give the authority of Conventions or Legislatures, in which this subject had been directly discussed. It was the duty of his antagonists on this occasion to produce some authority for their new doctrine which was at war with long settled opinion, and doubtless, if authority existed, it could not have escaped the extensive information and industrious research of the several gentlemen who have urged it. The gentleman from Baltimore county, (Mr. Buchanan,) supposes he has the authority of Mr. Burke. It was not the celebrated and justly celebrated orator and patriot, Edmund Burke—but a name-sake. He had not been sufficiently attentive to the political operations of the last few years, to know much of such matters, and he confessed he had not heard of this report until it was now produced by the gentleman, nor did he know where Mr. Burke came from.

[SEVERAL VOICES. "From New Hampshire."]

Well, it seems Mr. Burke is, at least, of importance enough to have it known what State he represents. Most certainly he had evinced a commendable share of industry in the collection of writings, on the question of the rights of the people. But did not his friend perceive that each of these writers expressed the very doctrine which our bill of rights announces—which every Constitution in this broad land declares, which he had repeatedly said, none but a madman would deny—that is, that the people are the source of all power, and have the right to alter and change their form of government? This only left us where we were; they do not say the people, or a portion calling itself a majority, may do this without law—against law. Mr. Burke, indeed, does say, *he* thinks his is the true interpretation, and the authority of this opinion is against us. On looking over the journal, it will be seen that he came to the conclusion that the Dorr revolution or rebellion, was strictly justified, and that the general government should not have interposed to restrain, or the courts to punish it, and on the same day on which his report was presented, it was postponed to the next session of Congress, and he was not aware it had ever been heard of since.

Neither the President with his Cabinet, or the courts of Rhode Island, or the Supreme Court, so thought.

Mr. BUCHANAN remarked, he had not relied on the authority of Mr. Burke, but on the books he had cited from his report, and which were not in the library.

Mr. McLANE, asked leave to make an explanation. He had not intended to evince any indisposition to be interrupted, but was always ready to hear what any gentleman might say to him. He desired to ask the gentleman what was the doctrine to which he referred, as having never been broached before, since the commencement of our government.

Mr. C. referred to the proposition he had endeavored distinctly to state, that a Constitution was binding on the whole people, and could not be changed in a mode prohibited by its own terms, but only in conformity to a legal provision—in short, that in this respect the people could bind themselves. This had been received as a settled doctrine. It was but lately that any one had controverted it. The argument of the gentleman from Cecil, himself, ended in a proposition to introduce into the Constitution a mode of amending it—amending it by Conventions.

There was no collision with the sovereign rights of the people. He termed it a *limitation* or *restriction* of the right, to a particular mode of amendment. The gentleman from Cecil termed it a "*regulation*," by which a particular mode was to be pursued. The difference seemed to be verbal, as explained by the gentleman, and he inclined at present to withdraw his own amendment, and allow that of his friend to replace it, being much more anxious to accomplish the object, than to be the author of the resolution.

Agreeing so nearly, in conclusions, he felt no disposition to assail the arguments by which the gentleman had arrived at his, though he must say they were unlike those on which he rested his own opinions. All the gentlemen who have taken the opposite view, have reiterated the sovereign rights of the people. The "eternal people are immortal," says one gentleman. Yes, and he might have added, practically invisible and intangible. Who denies the supreme, sovereign, political power of the people? Most certainly no one on this floor. But may not political right, like any other rights be controled, regulated by self-imposed restraints or regulations? Why else do we make a Constitution? Why all this expenditure of time and money? Is it to prepare an instrument to be submitted to the solemn consideration of the whole people, for their agreement and assent to it, as the terms on which they will continue the government for all time? Is all this expensive, tedious and solemn form of proceeding to be gone through, to produce a government, and yet in one year, or month, or week, an irregular unauthorized mass of men, calling themselves a majority, may decree its termination? Aye, rightfully and without acting in violation of law, annul and destroy it.

What, sir, is a Constitution? Why is it proper to have one? Chief Justice Marshall has said "a Constitution is framed for ages to come, and is designed to approach immortality as nearly as human institutions can approach."—[6 Wheaton, 384 Cohen on Virginia.] But if this assemblage can convene at one time, it can at another. It is said to require no provision for its terms, mode of organization or action—all are to be self-imposed, self-decided—all, on an impulse, which may happen in ten years or one—at any hour of any day. If there was nothing else to condemn this heresy but its mischievous consequences, its unmixed evils, these should make it odious. All the laws of the Great Eternal source of truth, are in beautiful harmony—all most wisely destined to continue the harmonious action of man, and all creation around him.

The source of infinite order never could be the birth-place of confusion and strife. He feared this doctrine came from below, and tended downward. Wise men and patriots had anticipated the difficulties now urged on the other side as growing out of the concession of the sovereign power of the people. His friend near him, (Mr. Donaldson,) had made full reference to the various speeches of Mr. Calhoun, to show his utter abhorence of the doctrine of the absolute, unrestrained rule of bare majorities. The gentleman from Cecil, had spoken of the events of Mr. Calhoun's life, as weakening his claim to authority, after 1828. He must be permitted to say, from personal associations with Mr. Calhoun, to whose intellectual and high moral worth, he bore the warmest testimony, that these opinions were not adopted for the first time after 1828—they were those which he had always maintained.

He claimed the authority of Judge Story, that a Constitution should not be altered, but by previous provision. He read from page 305, sec. 337: "The understanding is general, if not universal, that having been adopted by the majority of the people, the Constitution binds the whole community, *proprio vigore*, and is unalterable, except by the consent of the majority of the people, or at least of the qualified voters of the State.

[Here several gentlemen were seen to laugh and produced a slight interruption.]

Mr. C. said, wait a moment and instead of "*visum teneatis*," he might have occassion to remark "*hinc illæ lacrymæ*."

Justice Story continues, "in the manner *prescribed* by the Constitution, or otherwise *provided for* by the majority. Now, "provision" implies previous arrangement—preparation. It is to be done by the Constitution, or by the authority of those who make it. This is precisely the language of my amendment, "by the Constitution or law of the land," and there can be no law of the land on this subject, but an act of the Legislature authorised by the Constitution. No other meaning could be attributed to such language. What sort of legal provision could be made by this assemblage of people, who were to wield the sceptre and rule the State? They, the people, had been presented in all sorts of shapes and described in softest, sweetest phrases, but he had not yet heard the idea suggested that they were to become a regular Legislature to pass laws and make "provision" for changes in the government. The very etymology of the word "provision," implied a "previous" preparation. The gentleman from Cecil is for "previous provision," and his is a more stringent plan. *He* would not not allow the Legislature to provide.

Mr. McLane. "No, it ought to be in the Constitution itself."

Mr. CHAMBERS. In that case the only difference between the two propositions is, that mine looks to a legislative provision, while his, does not. The gentleman will not entrust the power to the Legislature.

Mr. McLANE said the gentleman from Kent did not do justice to his argument. He explained that his idea as to the manner in which provision should be made in the Constitution, was, to give the Legislature the power only to specify such details for carrying out the provision as circumstances called for. His objection to the amendment of the gentleman from Kent was, that it vested all the power of calling a Convention, in an act of Assembly, as the amendment read, "according to the Constitution *or* laws of the land." The expression, he thought too vague and admitted of too comprehensive a construction. Act of Assembly was more definite. He did not know that he had ever read in any Constitution, the phrase, "laws of the land," except in reference to criminal cases. What, he asked, was meant by "the laws of the land?"

Mr. CHAMBERS replied. The statute and common law.

Mr. McLANE. This did not include all the laws of the land. All the ordinances of the city of Baltimore are laws of the land. He gave a brief exposition of his own views as to the operation of the civil and statute law.

Mr. C. suggested there was no such thing as the civil law in Maryland.

Mr. McLANE replied, there certainly was civil law and admiralty law also.

Mr. C. remarked. Neither have we admiralty law.

Mr. McLANE said there certainly was admiralty law in the code of the United States. He proceeded to say, he would not give the Legislature the power to call a Convention. His idea was, to engraft in the Constitution a power to the Legislature to pass a law to carry out that specific provision. If that was the meaning of the gentleman from Kent, there was no disagreement between them. He would only empower the Legislature to carry out the provision in the Constitution.

Mr. CHAMBERS resumed and said, the phrase, "laws of the land," was designed to mean exactly an act of Assembly, passed pursuant to authority given in the Constitution. He vindicated the expression, and said it occurred *frequently* in the bill of rights and Constitutions, and in his acquaintance with the courts, at the bar and on the bench, for a period of more than forty years, he had not heard such an interpretation as is now given to these words. The ordinances of Baltimore were, in his opinion, no more alluded to than the bye-laws of the Farmer's bank, over which his friend near him, (Mr. Wells,) presided. Being sort of "house-hold" terms with the profession, they had occurred to him at the moment. Whatever words were used, he insisted on some provision as the mode of ascertaining the popular will—the will of the majority.

Mr. PRESSTMAN asked if there was a general acquiesence, what reason was there for ascertaining a majority?

Mr. C. None—not the least. And if a meeting of fifty men, under the lead of the gentleman, shall form a Constitution, and induce the people to proceed to administer the government under it, by electing officers at the times, and in the manner provided, and those who legally rule the State in its various departments, choose to retire and acquiesce in the usurpation of these officers, it will become the existing government of the State; and when established as such, will be protected by the military arm of the United States.

Mr. PRESSTMAN said, "That's all I contend for."

Mr. C. said, it was not all *he* contended for. He had a right to the coat on his back. If another in his presence assumed the ownership and disposeses him of it, and he *acquiesced* in it, he might be concluded. It did not follow that the conduct of the man who had possessed himself of his coat by force or fraud, was justifiable and proper. He claimed that the change in the government should be made by a provision in the Constitution or by a constitutional law, and then the rulers would be *bound* to retire. It would no longer be at their option to acquiesce or resist.

Mr. Webster's name and authority had been invoked. He had long known Mr. Webster, and at one period intimately. He knew something of the character of his gigantic mind—the course of his political opinions—the current of his feelings.

The more these were known, the more that great man would be admired. With such knowledge he could say, that he who looks to Daniel Webster to countenance confusion, discord and civil strife, will be sadly disappointed. His tongue and his pen teach other lessons. Like his familiar friend, Judge Story, he belongs to another school. His claims to the heartfelt gratitude of the last man that lives under, and loves the American Constitution, rest on his uniform defence of well defined, national, constitutional principles of *free government* and *good order*.

What says Mr. Webster? Why in the very speech cited, the Dorr case, p. 14, he meets the objection so continually and repeatedly pressed upon us as conculsive—the implied control of what *he* admitted as fully as we do "the sovereignty of the people." It was urged then, as now, it was to control, to check these right. It is now said we "shackle" them. Hear him, "my adversary says, if so, and the Legislature would not call a Convention, and if when the people rise to make a Constitution, the United States step in and prohibit them; why the rights and privileges of the people are checked—controled." That was the objection then, precisely as it is now. Very well, now for the answer; "undoubtedly!" "The Constitution does not proceed on the *ground* of *revolution;* it does not proceed on any *right* of revolution; but it does go on the idea that *within* and *under* the Constitution no new form of government can be established in any State *without the authority* of the existing State." It must be so. All the notions we have ever entertained, concur to demand it to be so.

You find the different States accordingly giving *authority* to make new governments or to alter the existing one.

Any other doctrine consigns to us anarchy. He then went into a detail of the early incidents of the French Revolution of 1793, and read a number of passages from the speeches of the Jacobins to show how the worst men will act in the name of the "*dear people.*"

At first all France was the "people." It was soon notorious that Paris was France—presently the constituent assembly was Paris—then the Jacobin clubs were the assembly, then Robespierre and the bloody guillotine were the fit representatives of the clubs—to these succeeded a first Consul—a King and an Emperor. He did not mean to say, the succession of events would be as rapid here. Our people had too long been acquainted with the principles of civil liberty. He had regretted to hear the gentleman from Cecil say, our fathers knew nothing of these principles at the revolution. He believed that as pure a representative democracy—republicanism—was to be found in the towns of New England, before the revolution, as now. Those who framed our Constitutions had at least as just conceptions of civil liberty as we have. He read from the Constitution of Virginia, of 1830, of which all the great men of their State were said to be members, the express declaration, that "the declaration of rights made on the 12th of June, 1776, as the basis and foundation of government" "required no amendment," and should be perfixed to the new Constitution. And here, and every where, these principles were understood; so that as "John Randolph" had said, "we had only to throw King George overboard" and every thing was right. But if our ruin would not be as rapid it might be as certain. The population of Baltimore would be larger in respect to the other parts of the State, than Paris was to France. Men in all ages and counties have the same infirmities and unfortunately the same class of artful, designing demagogues to stimulate them.

The final catastrophe was inevitable, if once we were set afloat on this wild and perilous ocean of popular prejudice, passion and excitement. Edmund Burke had beautifully said, "Justice required protection from power." If now amongst us, might he not add—our weakness requires protection against oppression; our moderation against extravagant ultraism; our minorities, protection against majorities; and the rational civil liberty, we now all love, will e'er long require protection against anarchy? It will then be too late.

Mr. Spencer said, his friend from the city of Baltimore, (Mr. Presstman,) had offered to amend the first article of the declaration of rights by adding the following:

"And they, (the people,) have at all times the unalienable right, to alter, remodel, or abolish their form of government, in such manner as they think expedient."

The question presented is, one of great interest and magnitude. For thirty years or more it has agitated this State, and it is high time to be put at rest. It must be settled. A very large portion of the people have contended for the right, whilst another portion have resisted it. At one time so intense was the excitement, growing out of the question, and the bold resistance which was made to all reform, that we were seriously threatened with intestine war.

What objection is there to engrafting such a principle in our declaration of rights? Is there any thing wrong in it? The honorable gentleman from Kent, (Mr. Chambers,) tells us, he is the friend of the people, but he objects to it, because he is fearful of popular excitement—is apprehensive of the mob. He has pictured to us the character of Robespierre, his professed attachment to the people, and his profligate hypocrisy. Was this done for the purpose of casting a satire on those in this House, who contend for this unalienable and sacred right? If so, the shaft was harmless. There are those to be found in every community who cover their vices by the cloak of hypocrisy—such as profess to be the true friends of the people, and yet embrace every opportunity to stab and to deprive them of their rights. He tells us, too, that in the excitement throughout France, Paris controled everything—that Paris was France and as Robespierre managed Paris, therefore, he was France. And then the gentleman tells us, that as Paris stood to France, so does Baltimore to Maryland. Does he mean to caution us against Baltimore influence and insubordination, and to tell us that in her city, some Robespierre will spring up, who, holding in his hands her destiny, will thereby control the State, and in fact, *be the State.* Such apprehensions had no terror in them for him. He had no such fear. None which would drive him from a just and correct position. Nor did it concern him, that an effort should be made, to drive the friends of popular rights in this House, from their true ground, by pictures of such a character. The true and sincere advocate of the rights of the people, was always known and appreciated. It it true, the purest are sometimes traduced by the friends of power. Even a Henry was branded as a traitor, and would have been hung, had the Revolution proved unsuccessful.

In advocating the doctrine, which is now before us, we stand on no isolated ground. It was the doctrine of our gallant forefathers, and has been incorporated into the Constitution of a large majority of the States of this Union. And in many of them, in the very language submitted by the gentleman from Baltimore. Eighteen of the States have recognized it.

The 1st article of the declaration of rights of Tennessee, concludes as follows: "They, (meaning the people,) have at all times an unalienable and indefeasible right to alter, reform, or abolish their form of government, in such manner as they may think proper."

And for the same purpose he referred to the following authorities:

1st. Maine—declaration of rights, 2d sec.

2rd. Massachusetts—preamble to Constitution.

3rd. Vermont—article 7th, Constitution.
4th. Connecticut—article 2d, do.
5th. New Jersey—article 2d, do.
6th. Virginia—article 3d, do.
7th. Indiana—article 2d, do.

He would not detain the Convention by reading the Constitutions of the several States. They would be found, in very many cases, to embody the *very language* submitted by his friend. It was too late to question a doctrine so true, and which constitutes the very foundation stone, on which our whole republican system of government is built. But the gentleman from Kent, is afraid that it may be abused, and that popular frenzy may become excited. Has it produced any evil in the other States of the Union? Why is it that such danger is to be apprehended in Maryland?

The gentleman has said that there was no authority to sustain the doctrines that the people have the right to remodel their government, except in the mode prescribed in the Constitution; that no statesman had contended for such a proposition. To shew that the gentleman was wrong, he referred to the following authorities: Story, in his Commentaries on the Constitution of the United States, section 337, in speaking of our State Constitutions, says: "The understanding is general, if not universal, that having been adopted by the majority of the people, the Constitution of the State binds the whole community, *proprio vigore;* and is unalterable unless by the ansent of the majority of the people, or at least of the qualified voters of the State, in the manner prescribed by the Constitution, or otherwise provided for, by the majority."

Mr. Rawle, who is another distinguished writer on the same subject, says: "The people retains—the people, perhaps, cannot divest itself of the power to make such alterations. If a particular mode of effecting such alterations be agreed on, it is most convenient to adhere to it, but it is not exclusively binding."

Judge Wilson, says: "Permit me to mention one great principle—the vital principle I may well call it, which diffuses animation and vigor through all others—the principle, I mean, is this, that the supreme or sovereign power of society, resides in the citizens at large, and that therefore they always retain the right of abolishing, altering or amending the Constitution at whatever time, and in whatever manner they may deem expedient." And again he says, "As to the people, however, in whom the sovereign power resides, from their authority the constitution originates; for their safety and felicity it is established; in their hands it is as clay in the hands of the potter."

Mr. Madison, in his report upon the Virginia resolutions of 1798, says: "The authority of Constitutions over governments, and of the sovereignty of the people over Constitutions, are truths which are always to be kept in view."

Mr. Chambers here said, that at the outset he had said and now repeated, that he did not deny the inherent right of the people, and that it was the bounden duty of this Convention, to introduce into the Convention, some provision by which, without doubt or difficulty, a convenient mode for the assembling of future Conventions might be designated.

Mr. Spencer. Then why object to the insertion of the doctrine of *right in the people*, in this, its proper place? Why clog it with restrictions? We are now laying down the platform of a Republican government. There was nothing in the doctrine which would prevent us from prescribing a mode for calling Conventions in future. He advocated such a course. But he would never consent to place the Constitution in the hands of the Legislature. This was the ground on which he stood before the people of his county.

The authorities which he had quoted were right up to the point. They are too clear to require elucidation. The commonest mind can understand them. Story says, the Constitution may be altered in the manner presribed in it, *or otherwise prescribed by the majority.* Then, according to him, it may be done in a manner *other than that in the Constitution.* If so, how? *In a manner prescribed for by a majority of the qualified voters.* And on this point Mr. Story is fully sustained by Mr. Rawle, who says, if a particular mode be agreed on, it is most convenient to adhere to it, *bnt it is not exclusively binding.* Let it not then be said by the gentleman, that we are contending for a principle, new and unheard of—one unsustained by authority.

The gentleman has asked, as has also the gentleman from Anne Arundel, (Mr. Donaldson,) his friend Mr. Presstman, how the government is to be altered by the act of the people, unaided by a constitutional provision, or a legal enactment? He says he likes to meet an intelligible proposition. Is there any obscurity in this? "He who runs may read." His, (Mr. Spencer's,) friend had answered with sagacity, that it was not for him to indicate how the people were to carry out and exercise their power. That would be determined when the crisis arose. He would, however, refer the gentlemen from Kent and Anne Arundel to Story to settle their difficulty. The gentleman from Anne Arundel had asked whether the whole people were to be consulted, whether women were to vote, and who was to fix and determine the capacity of voters, the question of age and incompetency from idiocy, infamy or other cause?

Judge Story, in sect. 327 of his commentaries, says, "Every State, however organised, embraces many persons in it who never assented to its form of government, and many who are deemed incapable of such assent, and yet, who are held bound by its fundamental institutions and laws. Infants, minors, married women, persons insane, and many others, are deemed subjects of a country and bound by its laws, although they have never assented thereto, and may, by those very laws, be disabled from such an act."

And again, in the same section, he says, "a majority only of the qualified voters is deemed sufficient to change the fundamental institutions of the State, upon the general principle, that the majority has at all times a right to govern the minority, and to bind the latter to obedience to the will of the former."

It is hoped, that the two honorable members are answered, and that their difficulty has vanished.

The gentleman from Kent, in order to justify himself in the position which he occupies on this question, as he has done on another occasion, contends that a State Constitution is to be considered as a compact or contract. If he can make this out, then it is clear that the people cannot alter it, except in the mode provided. But if he fail in this, then his whole ground is taken from under him, and the point must be given up. It will be remembered, that he, (Mr. S.,) some days ago, stated that it appeared to him strange that our State Constitutions were treated as *compacts* or *contracts*. It was new to him, and the idea was all wrong. He then referred to Justice Blackistone to define the difference between law and compact. His point was, that governments were founded in compact, but as soon as organised, they cease to have such a character and become fundamental law. He also then said, that in reference to the Constitution of the United States, there was, in this country, many who held *it* to be a compact. The distinguished member from Cecil, had taken the same position with him, as to the foundation of government, and had asserted, that after it was organised, it became organic law and was no longer a compact. In this, his friend from Cecil, was too explicit to admit of doubt. He had never held that government was not founded on agreement. His doctrine was, that the agreement terminated when the government was ordained, and yet, the gentleman from Kent, (Mr. Chambers,) had spent along time in asserting a proposition which no one disputed, that government was founded in compact; and then in order to sustain his idea that the State Constitutions are compacts, he had departed from the question, and sought authority in the conflicting doctrines of distinguished statesmen, as to whether the Constitution of the United States were a compact. It is unquestionably true, that this is the doctrine of very many of the most distinguished statesmen of the southern school. But does Judge Story assert such a proposition? Does he any where hold to such a doctrine, in reference to the Constitution of the United States? It is true that he has elaborated the subject, and has devoted many pages to the notice of Judge Tucker, and other writers. But after having shown his, (Judge T's,) opinions, he proceeds to criticise and to show their error. In section 319 of his commentaries, he says, "such is a summary of the reasoning of the learned author, (Judge Tucker,) by which, he has undertaken to vindicate his views of the nature of the Constitution." And again in section 320, he says, "it will be sufficient for all the practical objects we have in view, to suggest the difficulties of maintaining its leading positions, to expound the objections, which have been urged against them." He then proceeds in the following sections, to point out the consequences which must flow from such premises, and the obvious deductions, that "if it be a compact between the States, it operates as a mere treaty, and binds such State only, so long as its consent continues; that such State has the right to judge for itself, in relation to the nature, extent and obligations of the instrument, without being at all bound by the interpretation of the Federal Government, or by any other State; and that each retains the power to withdraw from the confederacy, and to dissolve the connection when such shall be its choice, and suspend the operations of the Federal Government, and nullify its acts when in its own opinion, the exigency of the case may require." Will the learned gentleman consent to adopt such conclusions as these. He has cited Judge Story to prove his position, that the Constitution is a compact. But it will be found, on examination, that it is not the opinion of Judge Story from which he can derive support, but on the contrary, the doctrines of jurists whose views are controverted throughout by the distinguished author—will the gentleman hold to *them*, or to Judge Story? To which class does *he* belong? Is he willing to take the consequences, as illustrated by Judge Story of the doctrine of compact? That distinguished jurist, leaves no doubt upon this question. He positively negatives the idea of the Constitution, being treated or considered as a compact. In sec. 339, he says, "a Constitution is in fact a fundamental law or basis of government, and falls strictly within the definition of law, as given by Mr. Justice Blakistone." It will be borne in mind, that *this* is the very authority which was quoted by him, (Mr. S.,) in the earlier part of this debate. "It is, (says the author,) "a rule of action prescribed by the supreme power in a State: regulating the rights of the whole community. It is a *rule* as contra-distinguished from a temporary or sudden order—permanent, uniform and universal. It is also called a *rule* to distinguish it from a compact on agreement; for a compact is a promise proceeding from us; law is a command directed to us." And in sec. 340, he says, "it is in this light that the language of the Constitution of the United States, manifestly contemplates it; for it declares, (article 6th,) "that this Constitution and the laws, made under the authority of the United States shall be the supreme *law* of the land."

And so at sec. 348, in speaking of the manner in which it was understood by the great men who accomplished the revolution, he says, "they supposed from the moment it became a Constitution it ceased to be a compact and became a fundamental law." And in sec. 352, he emphatically says, "there is nowhere found upon the face of the Constitution, any clause intimating it to be a compact, or in any wise providing for its interpretation, as such."

Such are the conclusions of the author on whom the gentleman relies. He utterly annihilates the idea of a Constitution being considered a compact. It is not for him, (Mr. S.,) to express any opinion of the soundness of Judge Story's conclusions, as to the character and effect of the Constitution of the United States. His only purpose now, was to show, that the gentleman is not sustained by the author in his position.

Mr. S. then said, his learned friend, from Cecil, had cited the opinions of Mr. Webster on this subject, to show their conformity with his, (Mr. McLane's.) The gentleman from Kent had denied that Mr. Webster had sustained any such doctrine. He knew him, he said, too well, to believe for a moment that any thing could be found in a speech of his, sustaining the gentleman. He had read the speech, and nothing like it could be found in it. Mr. S. thought the gentleman was mistaken, and had not read far enough or with proper care. He begged leave to refer him to the same speech, delivered by Mr. Webster in reply to Mr. Calhoun, February 16th, 1833, on the bill "further to provide for the collection of duties on imports." He particularly invited the attention of the gentleman to that part of it, found on page 176, of the 2nd volume of Webster's speeches.

It is as follows:

"Mr. President, I concur so generally in the very able speech of the gentleman from Virginia near me, (Mr. Rives,) that it is not without diffidence and regret that I venture to differ with him on any point. His opinions, sir, are redolent of the doctrines of a very distinguished school, for which I have the very highest regard; of whose doctrines I can say, what I can also say of the gentleman's speech, that, while I concur in the results, I must be permitted to hesitate about some of the premises. I do not agree that the Constitution is a compact between States in their sovereign capacities. I do not agree that in strictness of language *it is a compact at all.* But I do agree *that it is founded on consent or agreement, or on compact*, if the gentleman prefers that word, and means no more by it than voluntary consent or agreement. The Constitution, sir, is not a contract, but the result of a contract, meaning by contract no more than assent. Founded on consent, it is a government proper. Adopted by the agreement of the people of the United States, when adopted, it has become a Constitution." And again, he says, in the same place, "So the Constitution of the United States founded in or on the consent of the people, may be said to rest on compact or consent, but is itself not the compact, but the result. When the people agree to erect a government, and actually erect it, the thing is done and the argreement is at an end. The compact is executed and the end designed by it, attained. Henceforth the fruit of the agreement exists, but the agreement is merged in its own accomplishment"

Can language be more explicit? And does not the authority cover the whole ground of the debate, and leave the gentleman without a spot to rest on? But the authorities are more explicit, if possible, still. Remember that the point under consideration, is, whether our State Constitution can be considered and treated as a contract. This is the true point. This is the point, without which the gentleman's whole fabric crumbles and falls. He has said, very emphatically, in reference to a remark uttered by the gentleman from Cecil, that he never before had heard such an opinion expressed, until this day, *Anno Domini eighteen hundred and fifty-one!* With the same emphasis, he, Mr. SPENCER, would repeat, that he had never before heard any *statesman* or *jurist* contend that our State Constitutions were to be continued as compacts or agreements, and he was glad to find, that in this, Judge Story sustained him. He then cited and read from sec. 337 of his, (Story's,) commentaries.

Mr. CHAMBERS here said, I deny that Judge Story says any such thing.

Mr. SPENCER. I say he does.

Mr. CHAMBERS read the preceding sentence.

Mr. SPENCER. It would be necessary for him to read a number of pages to show that Judge Story was treating the question of *compact* in government. He, (Mr. S.,) would assert without fear of successful contradiction, that he was fully sustained by him. At the section referred to, Judge Story says, after elucidating the question of compact, and the views of distinguished men, "no such claim has ever, (at least to our knowledge,) been asserted by any jurist or statesman, in respect to any of our State Constitutions." Again in sec. 338, he says, "the true view to be taken of our State Constitutions, is, that they are forms of government, ordained and established by the people in their original sovereign capacity. The language of nearly all these State Constitutions, is, that the people do ordain and establish this Constitution." And again, at sec. 349, he says, "the subject has been thus far considered chiefly in reference to the point, how far government is to be considered a *compact*, in the sense of a contract, as contra-distinguished from an act of solemn acknowledgement or assent, and how far our State Constitutions are to be deemed such contracts, rather than fundamental laws, prescribed by the sovereign power. The conclusion to which we have arrived, is, that a State Constitution is no further to be deemed a compact, than it is a matter of consent by the people, binding them to obedience to its requisitions, and that its proper character is that of a fundamental law, prescribed by the will of a majority of the people of the State, (who are entitled to prescribe it,) for the government and regulation of the whole people." And again at sec. 340, he says, "a State Constitution is then in a just and appropriate sense, not only a *law*, but a *supreme law*, for the government of the whole people." And again, "it would be an extraordinary use of language, to consider a declaration of rights in a Constitution, and especially of rights which it proclaims to be unalienable and indefeasable, to be a matter of *contract.*"

How now does the question stand. The gentleman, in order to show that the majority have no right to change their form of government, except in the prescribed mode, took the ground that they could bind themselves by a Constitution, which became a compact or contract. But he is contradicted by the authorities. They all show that government is not a compact, but a fundamental law, prescribed by the supreme power of the State—that the supreme power have at all times a right to change and remodel their form of government in the manner they may appoint—and that the people constitute *the supreme power*. And is there anything novel in such a doctrine? Do not the authorities all sustain it? Is it not the doctrine of the first and best men of the country? Was it not endorsed by the statesmen of the revolution? It is the foundation on which our whole system rests. It is the rock on which he rested all his faith. By what authority are we now convened in this Convention? Is it not by virtue of the will of the majority? Will any one say that we are assembled in Convention, under the Constitution? Certainly the gentleman from Kent, will not say so, for he looks to the majority of the people to sanction what we may do, and to acquiessence by the government to give it validity. Has the spirit of insubordination exhibited itself here? Are we the creatures of the mob? And if we, the representatives of the people, can thus assemble to deliberate peacefully on the change of government, and the formation of a new organic law, what right have we to distrust the same quiet exercise of the same power in future? Thrice have the people of this State, met in Convention, above and without any constitutional provisions to guide them. Amidst the war of the revolution, they framed the Constitution under which, with alterations, we have lived to the present. In 1788, they ratified, in Convention, the Constitution of the United States. And they have again met in this Convention. Each and all of these Conventions were by virtue of the supreme power of the people. In each case it was discreetly and prudently exercised. Why then distrust the prudence of the people? I have no fear of the result. He would then unhesitatingly support the amendment of his friend, (Mr. Presstman.) And he would, with equal pleasure, support the amendment of the gentleman from Cecil, (Mr. McLane.)

The first amendment asserts the right of the people, and the second declares it to be our duty to provide a remedy, for the exercise of the right. This was what he desired. He was for indicating and following the mode prescribed in the Constitution. It was convenient and desirable, and he had no doubt would prove satisfactory to the people—*the whole people*. To the amendment of the gentleman from Kent, he was opposed, because, whilst it admits the right, it fetters it in its exercise. In the same breath that it admits, it denies and restricts it.

Mr. BRENT of Baltimore city, said, he had desired and intended to have submitted some remarks. But as he supposed that the Convention must be wearied of the long discussion which had taken place on this question, he would forego his right, and call for the previous question.

Mr. McLANE enquired of the chair, what the main question would be.

The PRESIDENT replied, that the pending question was on the amendment of the gentleman from Kent, (Mr. Chambers.)

Mr. McLANE. I can only say that if that proposition should not prevail, I shall offer the amendment which I indicated on Friday last.

Some conversation followed when, for pur poses of explanation,

Mr. BRENT withdrew the demand for the previous question.

Mr. CHAMBERS of Kent, withdrew his amendment for the purpose of enabling the gentleman from Cecil, (Mr. McLane,) to offer the proposition he had indicated.

Mr. C. in withdrawing the amendment, gave notice that he should vote for the amendment of the gentleman from Cecil, (Mr. McLane,) with the intention, after that had been adopted, of voting against the whole proposition.

So the amendment of Mr. CHAMBERS was withdrawn.

And therefore, the question recurred on the amendment of Mr. PRESSTMAN.

Mr. McLANE then moved to amend that amendment, by adding at the end thereof, the following:

"Provision ought therefore to be made in the Constitution now to be formed, whereby the exercise of such right, at reasonable periods, and in Conventional Assemblies, would be secured and regulated."

Mr. PRESSTMAN accepted this amendment, as a modification of his own proposition.

Mr. JENIFER said, he had intended to vote for the amendment of the gentleman from Cecil, (Mr. McLane,) and then to vote against both propositions. He also intended to vote against the amendment of the gentleman from Kent, (Mr. Chambers,) because he, (Mr. J.) believed the whole provision to be in the bill of rights.

Mr. DORSEY proposed to offer an amendment upon which he was proceeding to make some remarks—

Mr. BRENT of Baltimore city, submitted that the previous question had been withdrawn by him, not for the purpose of general discussion, but for explanation merely.

Mr. DORSEY yielded the floor.

Mr. BRENT moved the previous question.

And the question having been taken the Convention refused to second the demand for the previous question.

The question then recurred on the modified amendment of Mr. PRESSTMAN.

Mr. DORSEY then offered the following as an amendment to the modified amendment of Mr. PRESSTMAN.

Insert after the words "they have," in the first line the following: "according to the mode prescribed in this Constitution, and the laws made in pursuance thereof."

Mr. DORSEY desired to say a few words on the subject of his amendment. The amendment of the gentleman from Cecil did not, in his opinion, accomplish the object which that gentleman, as he understood him, professed to have in view. The proposition he now offered, was restriction of the manner in which the Constitution might be amended. He asked the gentleman from Cecil if it was acceptable to him. (Mr. McLane indicated his dissent.) He understood that it was not. He knew not why, unless the gentleman from Cecil was aiming at a different object from that of which he supposed him to be in the pursuit. He does not say that the people may not alter the Constitution, except in accordance with the Constitution and law, but that they may enjoy the full right of changing it in their own way; but he recommends it to them, to exercise their right in a particular manner.

As he understood this proposition of the gentleman from Baltimore, after its amendment by the gentleman from Cecil, if the people of Baltimore were to call a meeting at the market house, without any authority of law or public notice for that purpose, and should make a new Constitution, and a majority of the people of the State, being there in attendance, should adopt the Constitution thus formed, it would become the law of the land. It was said that this inalienable right of the people, declared in the amendment of the gentleman from Baltimore, was recognized in other State Constitutions, and that it did not imply revolutionary action.

He understood the gentleman from Cecil to say, that as he understood the amendment of the gentleman from Baltimore it meant nothing more than that the people might assemble, but that their assemblies must be provided for by the then existing Constitution or some Legislative enactment in conformity thereto. If that was the view of the gentleman from Cecil, and his amendment sustained it, he concurred with him; and would desire that his amendment might be adopted in order that the public mind might be relieved on the subject. If the House would adopt an amendment, by which it is provided that any change must be made according to the Constitution, or act of the Legislature passed for the purpose, the American principle on this subject would be carried out.

If the the gentleman from Cecil designed to establish such a course of proceeding, his amendment was wholly inadequate to the accomplishment of his object. It was important to have a stable government. But if you adopt the amendment of the gentleman from Baltimore, with that attached to it by the gentleman from Cecil, you recognize the power in an assembly of the people, called without public notice, by the secret concert of individuals, held, if you please, at the market house of Baltimore, to change or abolish the form of government, without complying with any legal sanction whatever. They may do this, and in a week after may call another meeting and have a new Constitution, and thus they may go on, changing the government, week after week, and year after year. With a government of such a character, no one would consider himself safe in living under it. Yet the gentleman from Cecil thinks his proposition sufficient. If the gentleman from Cecil would agree to the modification now proposed, he, (Mr. D.,) would accede to his amendment and admit its sufficiency. Without it, the amendment of the gentleman would be entirely insufficient. If the gentleman means that the Constitution shall only be changed in the manner he proposes, and will so frame his amendment, then he would agree with him. But if it is intended, as its perusal would indicate, to admit the principles of the amendment of the gentleman from Baltimore, then the gentleman from Cecil seems rather to recognize than defeat their object. The original proposition only asserts the broad principle that the people have the inalienable right to alter or amend or make a new Constitution; the amendment of the gentleman from Cecil only points out one way in which this may be done; it imposes no restriction on the original right being exercised by the people in any other way. The lawless exercise of such a power was attempted in Rhode Island, where, perhaps, a bloody war was only prevented by circumstances that might not again occur. And it should be remembered, that some persons, but a few years past, called a like meeting of the people at Annapolis, to make a Constitution, and, but for the vigor of Governor Veazy, there might have been a civil war here.

If the gentleman from Cecil would adopt the amendment now offered, prescribing the mode in which only a change of the Constitution must be made, he would be highly gratified; otherwise the gentleman's amendment amounts, only, to a recommendation to adopt a particular mode; not excluding the people from the practice of any mode they might see fit to select.

The difference of opinion which exists as to the meaning of the amendment of the gentleman from Cecil, shows how necessary it is that our constitutional provisions should be so explicit as to preclude all contrariety of interpretation upon the subject; such would be the result of the amendment I propose, and which the gentleman from Cecil thinks is, in effect, identical with his own. My objection to the gentleman's amendment, is, that it will leave the door open for frequent and sudden changes of the Constitution at the will of a majority of the people, formed under sudden excitement, without time for deliberation or any of the formalities of law. As a compromise, he would be willing to take a provision that the Legislature should prescribe the necessary formula to the convention of the people, or their representatives. The Legislature, perhaps, might exert the abstract right without such provision, but he would prefer making it plain by a provision in the Constitution. He repeated, that the amendment of the gentleman from Ceicl left the people free, in their primary assemblies, to alter, change or abrogate the Constitution, as in the original amendment of the gentleman from Baltimore. And the effect would be, that whenever Baltimore shall have a population greater than all the other parts of the State, as must soon be the case, they may get up a meeting at the market house, give no notice to the other parts of the State, and thus change the whole form of government. At some future period, Baltimore might thus, in a single day, overthrow the Constitution. This, he would guard against. He was sorry the gentleman from Cecil would not unite with him in his effort to do so by accepting his amendment.

Mr. Brent, of Baltimore city, said, he felt a strong temptation to make some remarks, but he was so anxious that the question should be taken on these abstract propositions, that he would again call for the previous question.

Some conversation followed.

After which,

The question was taken; and

There was a second to the demand for the previous question.

And the main question was ordered to be now taken.

Which main question was first on the amendment of Mr. Dorsey.

Mr. Stewart, of Baltimore city, asked the yeas and nays which were ordered, and being taken, were as follows:

Affirmative—Messrs. Chapman, President, Morgan, Blakistone, Dent, Hopewell, Lee, Chambers, of Kent, Mitchell, Donaldson, Dorsey, Wells, Randall, Kent, Weems, Dalrymple, Bond, Sollers, Brent of Charles county, Merrick, John Dennis, Crisfield, Dashiell, Williams, Goldsborough, Eccleston, Phelps, Bowie, Sprigg, McCubbin, Dirickson, McMaster, Hearn, Fooks, Jacobs and Kilgour.—35.

Negative—Messrs. Jenifer, Buchanan, Bell, Welch, Ridgely, Colston, Chambers of Cecil, Miller, McLane, Spencer, Grason, George, Wright, Shriver, Sappington, McHenry, Magraw, Nelson, Thawley, Hardcastle, Gwinn, Stewart of Baltimore city, Presstman, Ware, Fiery, John Newcomer, Brewer, Weber, Hollyday, Slicer, Fitzpatrick, Shower and Cockey—34.

So the amendment was adopted.

The question then recurred on agreeing to the modified amendment of Mr. Presstman, as thus amended.

Mr. Jenifer, (to the President.) Is it in order now to move that the whole subject be laid on the table?

The President. The motion is not now in order.

Some conversation followed on a point of order, in which

Messrs. Brent, of Baltimore city, Jenifer, and the President took part.

Mr. Spencer, when his name was called, gave notice that he should vote in the affirmative on the amendment, as also upon the amendment as amended, for the purpose of enabling him hereafter to move a reconsideration of the vote thereon.

The question then recurred and was put upon the amendment as amended; and

Determined in the affirmative.

The yeas and nays were ordered and appeared as follows:

Affirmative—Messrs. Morgan, Blakistone, Dent, Hopewell, Lee, Chambers of Kent, Mitchell, Donaldson, Dorsey, Wells, Randall, Kent, Weems, Dalrymple, Bond, Sollers, Brent of Charles, Merrick, Colston, John Dennis, Crisfield, Dashiell, Williams, Goldsborough, Eccleston, Phelps, Bowie, Sprigg, McCubbin, Spencer, Wright, Dirickson, McMaster, Hearn, Fooks, Jacobs, Fiery, John Newcomer, Kilgour and Cockey—40.

Negative—Messrs. Chapman, President, Jenifer, Buchanan, Bell, Welch, Ridgely, Chambers of Cecil, Miller, McLane, Grason, George, Shriver, Sappington, McHenry, Magraw, Nelson, Thawley, Hardcastle, Gwinn, Stewart of Baltimore city, Brent of Baltimore city, Presstman, Ware, Brewer, Weber, Hollyday, Slicer, Fitzpatrick and Shower—28.

So the amendment as amended was adopted.

And then the first article of the Report, as thus amended, was adopted.

The second article of the Report was read as follows:

Art. 2. That the people of this State ought to have the sole and exclusive right of regulating the internal government and police thereof.

No amendment having been offered, the article was adopted.

The third article of the Report was read as follows:

Art. 3. That the inhabitants of Maryland are entitled to the common law of England, and the trial by jury according to the course of that law and to the benefit of such of the English statutes as existed at the time of their first emigration, and which by experience have been found applicable to their local and other circumstances, and of such others as have been since made in England or Great Britain, and have been introduced, used and practiced by the courts of law or equity, and also to all acts of assembly in force on the first Monday of November, 1850, except such as may have since expired, or may be altered by acts of this Convention, or this Declaration of Rights, subject, nevertheless, to the revision of, and amendment or repeal by the Legislature of this State; and the inhabitants of Maryland, are also entitled to all property derived to them from or under the charter granted by his Majesty Charles the First, to Cæcilius Calvert, Baron of Baltimore.

No amendment having been offered, the article was adopted.

The fourth article of the Report was read as follows:

Art. 4. That all persons invested with the Legislative or Executive powers of government are the trustees of the public, and as such accountable for their conduct; wherefore, whenever the ends of government are perverted, and public liberty manifestly endangered, and all other means of redress are ineffectual, the people may, and of right ought to reform the old or establish a new government; the doctrine of non-resistance against arbitrary power and oppression is absurd, slavish and destructive of the good and happiness of mankind.

No amendment having been offered, the article was adopted.

The fifth article of the Report having been read as follows:

Art. 5. That the right in the people to participate in the Legislature is the best security of liberty, and the foundation of all free government, for this purpose elections ought to be free and frequent, and every free white male citizen having the qualifications prescribed by the Constitution, ought to have the right of suffrage;

Mr. Bowie moved to amend the said article by inserting after the word "having," in the fourth line, the following:

"A common interest with, and an attachment to the community;—and"

Mr. Bowie said he hoped the amendment would be accepted by the Chairman of the committee on the declaration of rights, [Mr. Dorsey,] and that it would be adopted without discussion.

Mr. Dorsey said, the only objection to the amendment was that it was unnecessary, and might lead to some difficulty, because, although the voter might have every other qualification, yet a question might arise with the judges of election, whether he did, in fact, possess a common interest with, and an attachment to the community.

The question was then taken, and the amendment was rejected.

And the fifth article was then adopted.

The sixth article was read as follows:

Art. 6. That the legislative, executive and judicial powers of government ought to be forever separate and distinct from each other.

Mr. Brent, of Baltimore city, moved the following amendment:

Add at the end of the article the following words:

"And no person or persons exercising the functions of one of said departments, shall assume or discharge the duties of any other."

Mr. Dorsey suggested that there was one difficulty which presented itself to his mind, if this amendment should be adopted. It might exclude the Senate of Maryland, that highest tribunal, appointed by the Constitution of Maryland, from sitting as a court of appeals.

Mr. Brent said he presumed that the Constitution would make provision for that case. He had offered his amendment, because the old article in the bill of rights did not prevent a member of the Legislature from being a judge, or even the executive. He, therefore, desired to exclude from the Legislature, any member of the judiciary, and from the judiciary any member of the Legislature. The subject had been discussed here at an earlier stage of the session; and he saw no harm that could result from his amendment.

The question was then taken, and by yeas 34, noes 26, the amendment of Mr. Brent was adopted.

And the sixth article, as thus amended, was adopted.

The 7th, 8th, 9th, 10th, 11th, and 12th articles were severally read and adopted, as follows:

Art. 7. That no power of suspending laws, or the execution of laws, unless by or derived from the Legislature, ought to be exercised or allowed.

Art. 8. That freedom of speech and debates, or proceedings in the Legislature, ought not to be impeached in any court of judicature.

Art. 9. That Annapolis be the place for the meeting of the Legislature; and the Legislature ought not to be convened or held at any other place but from evident necessity.

Art. 10. That for the redress of grievances, and for amending, strengthening and preserving the laws, the Legislature ought to be frequently convened.

Art. 11. That every man hath a right to petition the Legislature for the redress of grievances in a peaceable and orderly manner.

Art. 12. That no aid, charge, tax, burthen, fee or fees, ought to be set, rated or levied, under any pretence, without the consent of the Legislature.

The thirteen article was read as follows:

Art. 13. That paupers ought not to be assessed for the support of Government, but every other person in the State, or person holding property therein, ought to contribute his proportion of public taxes, for the support of Government, according to his actual worth in real or personal property; yet fines, duties or taxes may properly and justly be imposed or laid, on persons or property, with a political view, for the good government and benefit of the community.

Mr. Kilgour moved to amend the said article by inserting the following words immediately preceding the first word of the said article:

"That the levying taxes by the poll is grievous and oppressive, and ought to be abolished."

Mr. Dorsey stated that this subject had been before the Committee. There was a question under consideration, on the subject of raising a capitation tax, or poll tax, for the purpose of education. The Committee had thought it best to strike it out, and leave it to the Legislature to act. It was for the Convention to decide this question. There was a great deal of contradictory opinion on the subject among the people. Many persons who subsisted on their labor were willing to be taxed for this object, while others were not. If the tax was laid under a constitutional provision, it must remain. If the Legislature imposed the tax, and it proved unacceptable to the people, it could be repealed.

Mr. Magraw asked the yeas and nays on the amendment, which were ordered, and being taken, resulted as follows:

Affimative.—Messrs. Morgan, Weems, Dalrymple, Sollers, Jenifer, Buchanan, Welch, Colston, Eccleston, Phelps, Miller, Bowie, Spencer, Grason, George, Wright, Dirickson, McMaster, Shriver, McHenry, Magraw, Nelson, Thawley, Hardcastle, Gwinn, Stewart of Baltimore city, Brent of Baltimore city, Presstman, Ware, Fiery, Kilgour, Brewer, Weber, Hollyday, Slicer, Fitzpatrick and Shower—38.

Negative.—Messrs. Chapman, President, Blakistone, Dent, Hopewell, Lee, Chambers of Kent, Mitchell, Donaldson, Dorsey, Wells, Randall, Kent, Bond, Brent of Charles, Merrick, Bell, Ridgely, John Dennis, Crisfield, Dashiell, Williams, Goldsborough, Chambers of Cecil, McLane, Sprigg, McCubbin, Fooks, Jacobs, Sappington, John Newcomer and Cockey—31.

So the amendment was adopted.

And the question recurring on the adoption of the article as thus amended:

Mr. Randall moved the following amendment:

Insert in the fifth line of the article after the word "property," the words "within the State."

Mr. Randall said, that his amendment proposed to re-enact the clause of the old Constitution. The difference between that and the article as proposed, was a substantial one. The amendment inhibited the Legislature from passing any law, taxing property beyond the limits of the State. The attempt to tax property without the State, must, it seemed to him, be a failure in nine cases out of ten. Those upon whom the exercise of the power devolved, had no means of ascertaining the value, or even the existence of that property; and thus the system led to perjury, and to frauds upon the revenue, and hence was wrong in itself.

Another, and an unanswerable argument was, that property was responsible for taxes in the community in which it existed. Surely, it was wrong, that a man should be compelled to pay taxes both in and out of the State for the same property. It seemed to him, that there could be, and ought to be no distinction between real and personal property in the State of Maryland. If there was the power in the one case, why should there not be in the other? He contended also, that the system was not courteous to our sister States. He alluded to the injurious operation which this example would have upon our own State stocks, if other States should, in retaliation, follow this example; and argued that no such tax ought to be laid, whether regarded either in the light of justice, or of sound policy. And he referred the Convention to a letter which had recently been presented by Mr. Chambers of Kent, from Mr. Hall, setting forth the evils which resulted from the taxation of property thus situated, and its injurious operation upon the people of Maryland.

Therefore, pending the question,

The Convention adjourned until to-morrow at eleven o'clock.

Sketch of the Remarks of Mr. Brown, *of Carroll, on the 30th of January.*

The pending question being on the amendment offered by Mr. Chambers, of Kent, to the amendment of Mr. Presstman.

Mr. Brown, said: he came to the House without any intention to make a speech. He usually contented himself with saying what he thought, and sometimes he spoke earnestly, and after expressing what he had to say, he sat down. He recapitulated what he had said yesterday in reply to the reference made to the Dorr case in Rhode Island by the gentleman from Somerset. He adverted to the ridicule which had been cast on the seventeen gentlemen who had voted for the popular basis of representation by the gentleman from Dorset and others; and then went on to state that he had replied that although seventeen was a small minority out of seventy-seven votes, yet the name of the constituents of these seventeen, was "legion." They represented in fact a majority of the white population of the State. The gentleman from Worcester had spoken of the tyranny of a majority. The phrase was entirely new to him; he had never read of it, had never heard of it until he came into this hall; and he was unable to convince himself that there was any truth in it. But he had heard of the tyranny of a minority. It so happens, that the majority of members of this body represents less than one-third of the people of the State. He could not comprehend how government, based upon the majority, could be called a tyranny. One of our leading principles is, that majorities shall govern; and that these majorities were tyrants, was an entirely new doctrine. He could easily imagine how a minority could usurp the rights and trample on the rights and feelings of the majority; and this sort of tyranny was the first step to monarchy.

Our forefathers were induced to take up arms, and to resist tyranny to obtain political rights for all! They fought to throw off the yoke of a few who tyrannized over them. He expressed his inability to comprehend some of the doctrines and some of the phrases of the gentleman from Kent. If the doctrines laid down by that gentleman were correct, they should prevail. But the language of that gentleman was new to him. The gentleman spoke of giving the people their rights. He could only reply that his constituents did not come here to ask alms. They understood what were their rights, and those they would not beg for, but demand.

He went on to state that his ancestors settled where, he now resides, when it was called the back woods, and Baltimore was a small town. The population of the State was then principally to be found on both sides of the Chesapeake Bay, and below its head. The Allegany mountains had probably, at that time, never been trodden by the foot of a white man. And what is now the condition of that part of the State? Baltimore city and Western Maryland contain a large majority, (perhaps two-thirds,) of the wealth and population of the State.

Our forefathers had lived under the rule of a monarchy, but they had fought for their liberties, contending against the most powerful nation on earth. The freedom which they achieved, they had handed down to us, and we should hand it down to our children.

He would tell the gentleman from Kent, how this reform question could be settled certainly and quietly. Give us a Constitution that will secure to the people their rights, and nothing more will be heard in the way of complaint.

The state of things was this: two-thirds of the people of the State have no political rights. Could any one suppose they would remain quiet? Could it be permitted that the one-third should tie down and control the two-thirds? Further to illustrate the principle for which he contended, he read an extract from the works of Mr. Jefferson on the subject of Constitutions, and the necessity of changes in laws and institutions to keep pace with the times. That was the principle for which his constituents were contending. They asked no favor of the Eastern Shore. "We out-number you, and we think we are able to take care of ourselves." But there is no disposition among them to exercise tyranny over the small counties; and was it not an insult to them, when a minority undertook to control and govern them, and talked of giving them their rights?

As to the amendment of the gentleman from Kent, it was precisely the 59th article of the old Constitution. It re-enacts that article without the restriction in the 42nd article of the bill of rights.

Mr. CHAMBERS interposed a remark, that this was a total misapprehension of his purpose. He thought it proper that the mode of changing the Constitution should be specified. But when the gentleman from Carroll says, that the proposition is restrictive in its effect, the gentleman from Carroll attributed to him a purpose he never intended.

Mr. BROWN, in conclusion, stated that he merely spoke of the effect of the amendment—of the intention of the gentleman from Kent, he would say nothing. It did, in effect, say to the people, "thus far shalt thou go, but no further." If it were to be adopted now, it would be rendered nugatory in its operation, before a new generation would pass away. He looked upon it as merely a re-enactment of the 59th article. This was all he proposed to say, and he had not intended to say this; but after the hard blows he had received from the gentlemen on the other side, he could not remain silent.

Sketch of the Remarks of Mr. PRESSTMAN, *Feb.* 3,

On his amendment to the Bill of Rights, as to the right of the people to alter their form of government, &c.

Mr. CHAMBERS, of Kent, again took the floor, but said that if there was any gentleman who adopted the views of the gentleman from the city of Baltimore, [Mr. Presstman,] and the gentleman from Cecil, [Mr. McLane,] and who desired to be heard, he, [Mr. C.] would cheerfully yield the floor.

Mr. PRESSTMAN said, he desired to say a very few words, in order to put himself right before the Convention. It was not his intention again to trespass upon its time. All he desired was that, before the gentleman from Kent, [Mr. Chambers,] proceeded with his remarks, he should understand precisely the position which he, [Mr. P.] intended to take at the commencement.

As he had heretofore stated, the amendment he introduced embodied precisely the same language as that contained in the bill of rights of several of the States of the Union, and he would now frankly state to the Convention, that the views which had been presented, in part, upon his side, were not the views which he designed to hold at the commencement of the debate. He intended to say that if the amendment should be adopted, following, as it did, the form of the Virginia bill of rights, and of the bills of rights of Maine, and other States, there should be no provision in any manner in the Constitution, which was about to be made, prescribing any particular mode in which that Constitution should be changed.

It would, therefore, be in harmony with his idea, that hereafter, in forming a Constitution, no mode should be pointed out by which it should be changed. It was not necessary for him, in the view which he designed to present, to assert the doctrine that the right was to be exercised against the particular forms of the Constitution which might or might not be adopted. On that point, he had as yet reserved his opinion.

If the amendment of the gentleman from Cecil, (Mr. McLane,) should be brought to a vote, he, (Mr. P.,) might feel himself constrained to vote for it; not because he had abandoned the ground which he had originally taken, but because there was not one single word in that amendment which denied the principle of his own. If there were, he would vote against it. He understood that amendment to be a mere assertion that the right exists, and to point out a mode in which that right may be exercised on the score of expediency. If the gentleman from Cecil had, in any degree, denied that right, he, (Mr. P.,) repeated that he could not have voted for the amendment. He did not now pledge himself to do so—nor would he, until he had heard the discussion. If, however, he should do so, he meant it to be understood, that he voted for it as a compromise, looking to conventional reform; and if it did not contain the germ of conventional reform as contra-distinguished from legislative reform, he would not vote for it under any circumstances. He wished, therefore, that the gentleman from Kent, (Mr. Chambers,) should bear in mind that although gentlemen had charged him, (Mr. P.) with setting up the doctrine of the right of the people, short of the revolutionary right, to change their government in a manner different from, and in violation of the mode pointed out by the Constitution, he never had asserted that doctrine, as it was unnecessary for him to do so. He had proposed his amendment in the event of no mode being pointed out in the Constitution, and leaving it, therefore, to the people to provide a mode for themselves. He did not hold with his colleague, (Mr. Brent,) nor with the gentleman from Cecil, (Mr. McLane,) that there was no mode by which the people could adopt a new Constitution, except according to provision made by the Legislature. The doctrine which he maintained, he held to be identical with that upon which some gentlemen had contended that they held their seats here, that is to say, the general acquiesence of the people, independent of legislative acts.

WEDNESDAY, February 5th, 1851.

The Convention, pursuant to its order of yes terday, met this day at 11 o'clock.

Prayer was made by Rev. Mr. GRIFFITH.

The journal of yesterday having been read,

Mr. WEBER moved so to amend it as to state the fact that he had called the yeas and nays, on the motion of the gentleman from Calvert, (Mr. Weems,) that the hour of meeting be eleven o'clock.

Some conversation followed.

It appeared that when the yeas and nays were asked, but *not ordered*, it was not usual to enter the motion on the journal.

Mr. DORSEY presented a memorial of sundry citizens of Howard district, of Anne Arundel county, praying that said Howard district may be constituted a separate county.

Referred to the select committee appointed on new counties.

Mr. DONALDSON also presented a petition of sundry citizens of said district, of similar import.

Referred to the same committee.

Mr. D. said he would take occasion to remark that he heartily concurred in the prayer of the petitioners.

The Convention therefore passed to the order of the day.

THE BILL OF RIGHTS.

Then Convention then resumed the consideration of the order of the day, being the report submitted by Mr. DORSEY, on the 11th ult., as chairman of the committee on the declaration of rights.

The immediate question was on the amendment offered by Mr. RANDALL, yesterday, and pending at the hour of adjournment, to the 13th article.

Mr. DONALDSON held the floor, but, on his suggestion, the article was informally passed over for the present, (Mr. Randall being engaged in the argument of a case in court.)

The fourteenth article was then read as follows:

Art. 14. That sanguinary laws ought to be avoided, as far as is consistent with the safety of the State; and no law to inflict cruel and unusual pains and penalties ought to be made, in any case, or at any time hereafter.

No amendment being offered, the article was adopted.

The fifteen article was read as follows:

Art. 15. That retrospective laws, punishing acts committed before the existence of such laws and by them only declared criminal, are oppressive, unjust and incompatible with liberty; wherefore no *ex post facto* law ought to be made.

Mr. DENT moved to amend the article by striking out the words "*ex post facto*," (which, he said, was mere vulgar Latin,) and to insert the word "such," in lieu thereof.

Mr. DORSEY thought it would be better that the amendment should not be adopted. The expression "*ex post facto*," was so well understood by the profession, and by all law-givers, and he thought it would be inexpedient to change it. The word "such," was more indefinite.

Mr. DENT withdrew his amendment.

No further amendment having been offered, the fifteenth article was adopted.

The sixteenth, seventeenth and eighteenth articles were read, and, no amendment having been offered thereto, was adopted, as follows:

Art. 16. That no law to attaint particular persons of treason or felony, ought to be made in any case, or at any time hereafter.

Art. 17. That every free man, for any injury done to him in his person or property, ought to have remedy by the course of the law of the land, and ought to have justice and right, freely without sale, fully without any denial, and speedily without delay according to the law of the land.

Art. 18. That the trial of facts where they arise, is one of the greatest securities of the lives, liberties and estate of the people.

The 19th article of the bill was read as follows:

Art. 19. That in all criminal prosecutions, every man hath a right to be informed of the accusation against him; to have a copy of the indictment or charge, in due time (if required) to prepare for his defence; to be allowed counsel, to be confronted with the witnesses against him; to have process for his witnesses; to examine the witnesses for and against him on oath; and to a speedy trial by an impartial jury, without whose unanimous consent he ought not to be found guilty.

Mr. MERRICK moved to amend it, by striking out the words "if required."

Some desultory conversation followed, in which Messrs. BLAKISTONE, MERRICK, BUCHANAN, DORSEY, GWINN and BOWIE took part—after which

Mr. MERRICK withdrew his amendment.

Mr. MITCHELL moved an amendment, inserting after the word "counsel," the words, "whether admitted to the bar or otherwise."

Mr. MITCHELL said, he made the amendment, in behalf of a very modest class of persons, who might not be able, often, to avail themselves of the privilege contemplated by it—but he desired that the privilege should at least be extended to them.

Some conversation followed between Messrs. PHELPS and MITCHELL.

Mr. DORSEY thought this was rather an extraordinary amendment. There was an old saying at the bar, that a suitor who was his own counsel, had a fool for his client. He cited a case within his own experience in which a distinguished citizen of Anne Arundel had undertaken to manage his own case, which was unquestionably good in itself—but which became so involved by the manner in which it was conducted, that the jury must have given a verdict against him. (Laughter.) The court then recommended him to let his counsel take charge of the case.

Mr. D. thought that the adoption of such an amendment would be attended with very injurious effects, and that, not for the sake of the profession, but of the parties themselves, it ought not to be adopted.

Mr. MITCHELL. I withdraw the amendment. I feel that I should be in a very bad perdicament myself. (Laughter.)

So the amendment was withdrawn.

And then the 19th article was adopted.

Mr. DIRICKSON rose to offer an amendment to it.

The PRESIDENT said, the question had been finally taken, and the article adopted.

Mr. DIRICKSON. I was desirous to offer an

amendment providing that the counsel for the prisoner shall have the right to close the argument.

Mr. Bowie. Move a separate article.

Several Voices. Move a re-consideration.

Mr. Dirickson. I did not vote for the article.

Mr. Phelps. I did—and I move a re-consideration, so that the gentleman, (Mr. Dirickson,) can offer his amendment.

Mr. Dirickson offered the following amendment.

Add at the end of the article, the following:

"And upon his trial, his counsel shall have the privilege of making the closing address to the court or jury."

Mr. Jenifer suggested, that perhaps the proper place for this amendment would be the judiciary bill.

Mr. Dorsey moved to amend the amendment by adding at the end thereof, the following:

"And that the State have the same right of challenging jurors that the accused has."

And the question being on the amendment to the amendment,

Mr. Stewart, of Baltimore city, asked the yeas and nays, which were ordered, and, being taken, were as follows:

Affirmative—Messrs. Morgan, Blakistone, Dent, Chambers of Kent, Mitchell, Donaldson, Dorsey, Wells, Kent, Weems, Sollers, Brent of Charles, Merrick, Jenifer, Chandler, John Dennis, Williams, Goldsborough, Bowie, Sprigg, McCubbin, Gaither, Presstman, Davis, and Hollyday—25.

Negative—Messrs. Chapman, President, Lee, Dalrymple, Bond, Buchanan, Bell, Welch, Ridgely, Colston, Dashiell, Eccleston, Phelps, Chambers of Cecil, Miller, McLane, George, Dirickson, McMaster, Hearn, Fooks, Jacobs, Shriver, Sappington, Magraw, Nelson, Carter, Thawley, Hardcastle, Gwinn, Stewart of Baltimore city, Brent of Baltimore city, Ware, Fiery, John Newcomer, Michael Newcomer, Kilgour, Weber, Slicer, Fitzpatrick, Ege, Shower, and Cockey—42.

So the amendment to the amendment was rejected.

The question then recurred on the amendment of Mr. Dirickson.

Mr. Donaldson, said: it was proper that we should know clearly what we are about when we propose radical changes in the law. We live in a community of honest men; and it is not the fact that injustice was done to accused persons, in our administration of the criminal law. When a man charged with crime is put upon his trial, his right of challenge is so extensive as in effect to give him the choice of his own jury, whilst the State can only challenge for cause. He thought that we ought not to extend the right of challenge to the State, as the practice now exists. He had voted for it as an amendment to the amendment of the gentleman from Worcester, (Mr. Dirickson,) because he feared that amendment might prevail, although he hoped it would not. If the counsel for the accused was to have the closing speech, he was in favor of allowing the State the right of peremptory challenge. Every facility is already afforded to an accused person, to enable him to prove his innocence. All presumptions of law are in his favor, and he has the advantage of every technical defect which astuteness may detect in the proceedings. When his case comes up, even should the charge be most heinous, the sympathy is almost always on his side; counsel is provided for him, if he is unable to pay for such services. The Attorney General or his deputy is actuated by no vindictive feelings; he is not like the avenger of blood in the old testament, pursuing the slayer to the cities of refuge. He stands in the position not of counsel, but of judge advocate. He opens the case with a description of the offence and its circumstance, and states the law and its application. The prisoner's counsel follows, examining and often preventing the facts in evidence, and answering the arguments of the prosecutor. And although the prosecuting attorney follows in reply, he is not permitted to introduce any new matter; and not being an advocate, as his opponent is, but representing the dignity of the State, he is bound not to descend to any unworthy artifice. Great complaints have been made of the extent to which the counsel for a prisoner frequently goes in order to obtain an acquittal; and if the advantage proposed by this amendment be added to the facilities already allowed—if the prisoner's counsel is to have the final speech and thereby have full license, without contradiction, to state such principles of law, and place such a construction on facts as may most favor his end,—it would be the means of throwing back into the community a still greater number of persons who ought to have been convicted. He knew that the gentleman from Worcester was actuated by pure motives when he offered this amendment, but believing it would be mischievous, he felt bound to oppose it.

Mr. Dirickson said:

He did not claim the entire credit of the amendment which he had just submitted to the Convention—it having been in part, suggested by the honorable gentleman from Harford county, (Mr. Magraw,) now upon his right. Familiar with the proceedings of courts of justice from his earliest manhood, it had been his fortune to witness many prosecutions for criminal offences, and he had often observed the terrible effect of the last uncontradicted speech against the accused. The motive that had induced the offering of the proposition, was in perfect harmony with the humane spirit of that principle which was eminently the characteristic of all criminal law in all Christian lands. And when he said, it was better "that ninety and nine guilty persons should escape, rather than one innocent man receive unmerited punishment," he uttered a doctrine familiar to all—and one, the justice and propriety of which, no one for a moment doubted. It had been argued by the gentleman from Anne Arundel connty, that the prosecuting attorney acted both as prosecutor and judge advocate. That such ought to, and might occasionally, have been the case, he did not deny—but he was induced to believe that professional pride, must often became aroused and sought by a triumphant prosecution, to display all its distinguishing ability. Sometimes, too, it might occur that other counsel might be employed by those who imagined themselves aggrieved to aid the regular prosecutors in the trial, and thus an additional stimulant lent its powerful influence.

Mr. DONALDSON asked if he understood the gentleman from Worcester as saying that the Attorney General, or any of his deputies were in the habit of receiving fees?

Mr. DIRICKSON replied. Certainly not. He had not said so—nor did he believe the Attorney General or his deputies, ever had received fees for doing their duty as prosecutors. He had alluded solely to the other counsel, who might be retained to assist them.

He then continued his remarks by saying, that the persons accused not unfrequently, were suffering under the very extreme of poverty and want—that they were wholly unable to obtain the influence of able and eminent men, (unless the spirit of sympathy was awakened,) and that the counsel assigned for their defence by the court might be from among the youngest and least experienced of the bar. Under such circumstances, the odds were fearful indeed; and when it was remembered that degredations and infamy, and liberty—nay, life itself, might depend upon the issue, the highest dictates of humanity urged the adoption of every measure consistent with the ends of justice, by which the unfortunate might be rescued from so awful a peril. Entertaining such sentiments, he earnestly hoped the Convention would regard the amendment with favor, and cheerfully accord to the accused, the last appeal to that jury upon whose verdict, his all of reputation and happiness might depend.

Mr. JENIFER expressed his apprehension that gentlemen were permitting their feelings of humanity to outrun their discretion. So far as his experience went, he had never known any instance of a criminal being convicted, without full proof of his guilt, after every opportunity had been given him for his defence. He was not aware of the existance of any law, which precluded the counsel for the accused from having the closing appeal to the jury.

Mr. BRENT, of Baltimore city, said it was the practice in all the courts.

Mr. JENIFER replied that it might be the practice, but he knew of no positive rule to preclude the accused from the advantage. He thought the effect of the amendment now proposed would be to give an advantage to guilty criminals over honest men.

Mr. BRENT, of Baltimore city, thought the amendment a proper one, because it carried out the benign object of our laws. He considered, from his experience, that the closing speech to the jury added 33 per cent. to the chance of the verdict. The eagerness to obtain this advantage was evident from the constant wrangling at the bar, to see who shall open and conclude a case, even before the court, on a law point. It ought to be a main object of the State, that no man should be falsely convicted; and, for this purpose, every facility should be afforded the accused. It was often the practice to employ, as an assistant prosecutor, some young lawyer whose duty it was to open the case, and the weakest argument was always in the opening, and it is to that only that the counsel for the accused is permitted to reply. The evil of this practice he had felt both in Maryland, and in the courts of the District of Columbia. He gave some reasons to show that the State had now a sufficient right of challenge and that the right ought not to be extended. Innocent men had been convicted in Maryland, as well as in other places.

Mr. CHAMBERS wished to say a single word. He had filled the office of Prosecuting Attorney, and had tried as many cases as any gentleman here, in a long course of practice. During all that period, there were very few criminals tried in whose trials he did not take part. He had only risen to say, that in all his long experience, he had never known one solitary case in which, with the present advantages allowed an accused person, of an innocent man suffering from an unjust conviction. He had acquitted scores of men who were guilty, and he had known other gentlemen at the bar who had acquitted as many. If, with these facts before its eyes, the Convention think it necessary to provide further facilities for persons brought into Court for trial, so let it be.

Mr. DORSEY said, he also would State the result of his observation and experience. He had been Attorney General of the State of Maryland, before he had a seat on the Bench, and had been on the Bench twenty-five years, and he could reiterate all which had been said by the gentleman from Kent. He had never known but one case of improper conviction, and that was since he had been on the Bench. When Attorney General, he had always felt it his duty when the evidence of guilt was insufficient to warrant the conviction of the accused, to make such statement to the jury, and an acquittal always followed. There was one case in which an innocent man tried before him, was convicted, and he, without any application made to the court for the purpose, informed the counsel of the accused that if moved for, a new trial would be granted.

Mr. BRENT stated that the feelings of old practioners were less acute on this subject than those of younger men. He referred to the case of young Stewart, of Baltimore, tried for the murder of his father, and after doubt and hesitation on the part of the jury, was convicted of murder in the second degree. The young man had since died, calmly protesting his innocence; and facts which have subsequently come out, have attested the truth of that confession.

Messrs. MAGRAW and DIRICKSON asked the yeas and nays on the amendment, which were ordered, and being taken, resulted as follows:

Affirmative—Messrs. Morgan, Hopewell, Buchanan, Bell, Welch, Chandler, Ridgely, Dashiell, Chambers of Cecil, Miller, Spencer, George, Dirickson, McMaster, Hearn, Fooks, Jacobs, Shriver, Sappington, McHenry, Magraw, Nelson, Carter, Thawley, Gwinn, Stewart of Baltimore city, Brent of Baltimore city, John

Newcomer, Michael Newcomer, Kilgour, Ege, Shower, and Cockey—33.

Negative—Messrs. Chapman, Pres't, Blakistone, Dent, Lee, Chambers of Kent, Mitchell, Donaldson, Dorsey, Wells, Kent, Weems, Dalrymple, Bond, Sollers, Brent of Charles, Merrick, Jenifer, Colston, John Dennis, Williams, Goldsborough, Eccleston, Phelps, McLane, Bowie, Sprigg, McCubbin, Thomas, Gaither, Hardcastle, Presstman, Ware, Fiery, Davis, Weber, Hollyday, Slicer, and Fitzpatrick—38.

So the amendment to the amendment was rejected.

Mr. Brent, of Baltimore city, moved to amend the amendment, by adding at the end thereof, the following:

"And in all criminal trials, the jury shall decide the law, as well as the facts in evidence, and the truth shall always be admissible in evidence."

Some conversation followed, after which the amendment was again read.

Mr. Spencer moved to amend said amendment, by adding the following:

"And to have all questions of law, arising in the course of his trial, explained by the court before his defence shall be stated by his counsel."

Mr. Brent, of Baltimore city, accepted this amendment as a modification of his own.

Mr. Brent rose to say, in justification of his amendment, that there was a difference of opinion on the Bench in reference to this matter. Some of the judges now carry out the spirit of this proposition; but there are others, who doubt the right of the jury to be judges of the law. Such was the rule in the Courts of the District of Columbia. It was not in the old bill of rights; and many gentleman thought it would be a great improvement. He had, therefore, submitted the amendment.

Mr. Chambers was not acquainted with the practice elsewhere. But, if the amendment were adopted, he thought it would operate against the accused in his district. If the counsel for a criminal thinks it desirable, he may send the law to the jury, on an instruction from the court. He thought also, that the amendment might produce some difficulty in practice. The prisoner's counsel could now ask instructions as to the law for the government of the jury; or the court, as he himself had done, might gratuitously interpose his opinion that the law is against the prosecutor, and dismiss the case.

Mr. Presstman could not give his assent to the amendment, especially was he opposed to some parts of it. He thought that the doctrine that the jury should decide as to the law, as well as the facts—if it had not been long settled in Maryland, ought not to prevail. Such a practice would never have found its way here, but for the transcendent abilities of that distinguished man, Wm. Pinckney. But as the rule has been so long in operation, he did not desire to disturb it. What are the facts which ought to go before the jury, as proper evidence, is for the court to determine. He objected to the words "facts in evidence," in the amendment of his colleague, as liable to the objection of uncertainty as to their true meaning. He thought it of great importance in times of excitement, that the power should be vested in the Judge to expound the law, because his calm and deliberate judgment would be a shield to the innocent. He did not disturb the rule as it now prevails, but if twelve men ignorant of the law were on a jury, they ought to be instructed, so that the verdict might be according to the law and the evidence.

Mr. Spencer expressed his intention to vote for the amendment, because, in some parts of the State, it was doubted whether the juries are to be judges of the law as well as the fact. He would go still further, and he intended to submit an amendment providing that the prisoner shall be entitled to have the law expounded to him before his counsel closes his defence. At present, the exposition of the law is not made by the court until the counsel for the defence has closed. It was not so, when he acted as a deputy of the Attorney General. The court then expounded the law, and the counsel for the defence closed afterwards. Now a different practice had grown up. The court gave the instructions after the counsel for the accused had closed his defence.

Mr. Dorsey said, that such was not the practice in his district.

Mr. Spencer said, it was the practice in his district, and he wished to have the principle fixed.

Mr. Brent accepted the proposition of the gentleman from Queen Anne's, as a modification of his amendment. He intended that the counsel for the prisoner should have a right to ask the advice of the court. He wished to see the largest liberty given to persons brought up for trial, and that the jury should decide both the law and the fact. His colleague had referred to Mr. Pinckney, as the originator of the jury. The practice began on the other side of the water. Previous to the days of Erskine, it was otherwise, but through his efforts aided by others, the present practice was established. It began to be fully discussed, he believed, with the case of Buchnel. There could be no difficulty in inserting a declaratory article on the subject in the bill of rights. His proposition was simple and plain. He referred to the trial of the Rev. Mr. Breckenridge, on a charge of libel. One of the Judges insisted that the truth should not be admitted in evidence, but he was overruled by the other two judges associated with him—this therefore, showed that there was judicial doubt, whether the truth could be admitted in cases of libel, and therefore be proposed to settle this doubt.

Mr. Presstman offered the following amendment which he asked his colleague, (Mr. Brent.) to accept as a modification of his amendment.

Insert between the amendment offered by Mr. Brent of Baltimore city, and the amendment offered by Mr. Spencer, and accepted by Mr. Brent, the following:

"And that the court may determine what is evidence proper to go before the jury."

Mr. Brent accepted the modifications.

Mr. CHAMBERS desired to say one word, in order that he might not be misunderstood. The present proposition was likely to be troublesome. He differed in opinion with the gentleman from Baltimore. Buchnel was imprisoned because he rendered a verdict contrary to the law as laid down by the judge. He stated that the practice of the courts now was introduced partly for the purpose of preventing the frequent altercations which formerly took place between the counsel and the court. He set forth the changes which had taken place in the manner of conducting criminal cases, and the contradictory opinions which had been entertained of the effect of these changes. He felt no particular earnestness about the amendment, but he thought it was likely to lead to difficulty, without a probability of much benefit.

Mr. SPENCER gave his recollection of the course pursued by the court in the case of Buchnel, and expressed his belief that the amendment would be beneficial.

Mr. BRENT said, he had, in company with a friend, been searching the library, but had not been able to find any report of Buchnel's case.

The question was then stated to be on the amendment of Mr. BRENT, as modified.

Messrs. BRENT and SPENCER asked the yeas and nays, which were ordered.

Mr. MERRICK said he thought that amendments of this description were more apt to incumber the bill of rights, than to accomplish any good. We had moved along for many years with the bill of rights as it stood. No evil had been wrought, or injustice done, and he thought it would be wise and prudent to let very well alone. He preferred that the law should stand as it was, and he hoped the Convention would so determine.

The question on the amendment was then taken, and resulted as follows:

Affirmative—Messrs. Welch, Colston, Miller, McLane, Spencer, George, Fooks, Thomas, Shriver, Gaither, Sappington, McHenry, Magraw, Nelson, Carter, Thawley, Gwinn, Brent of Baltimore city, Presstman, Ware, Fiery, Michael Newcomer, Weber, Hollyday, Slicer, Fitzpatrick, Ege, Shower and Cockey—29.

Negative—Messrs. Chapman, President, Morgan, Blakistone, Dent, Hopewell, Lee, Chambers of Kent, Mitchell, Donaldson, Dorsey, Wells, Kent, Weems, Dalrymple, Bond, Sollers, Brent of Charles, Merrick, Jenifer, Buchanan, Bell, Chandler, Ridgely, John Dennis, Dashiell, Williams, Goldsborough, Phelps, Bowie, Sprigg, McCubbin, McMaster, Hearn, Jacobs, Stewart of Baltimore city, John Newcomer, Davis and Kilgour—38.

So the amendment was rejected.

Mr. SPENCER moved to amend the said nineteenth article, by adding at the end thereof, the following:

"And to have all questions of law arising in the course of his trial explained by the court, before his defence shall be stated by his counsel."

Mr. SPENCER, referring to the practice as it had been stated by Mr. DORSEY, to exist in his district, said that the practice in his, (Mr. S.'s, district, was different. He declared the fact to be, that the right of the jury to pass upon the law as well as upon the first, had become almost universal; and he desired that the question should be settled finally throughout the State.

Mr. RIDGELY said, that as a rule of practice for the courts, the theory of the gentleman from Queen Anne, (Mr. Spencer,) was undoubtedly good. But the question for the Convention to determine, was whether the bill of rights ought to be loaded down with matters belonging to the practice of the courts. With perfect respect, therefore, to the gentleman from Queen Anne's, (Mr. Spencer,) he, (Mr. R.) would move that amendment be laid upon the table.

The PRESIDENT stated that the motion of the gentleman from Baltimore county, (Mr. Ridgely,) if it prevailed, would carry the whole report with it.

Mr. RIDGELY thereupon withdrew his motion to lay upon the table, and substituted a demand for the previous question.

And the question having been taken, there was a second; and the main question was ordered to be now taken.

Mr. SPENCER asked the yeas and nays on his amendment, which were ordered, and being taken were as follows:

Affirmative—Messrs. Colston, Miller, McLane, Spencer, George, Shriver, Sappington, Nelson, Carter, Thawley, Gwinn, Brent of Baltimore city, John Newcomer, Weber, Hollyday, Slicer, Ege, Shower and Cockey—19.

Negative—Messrs. Chapman, President, Morgan, Dent, Hopewell, Lee, Chambers of Kent, Donaldson, Dorsey, Wells, Weems, Dalrymple, Bond, Brent of Charles, Merrick, Jenifer, Buchanan, Bell, Welch, Chandler, Ridgely, John Dennis, Dashiell, Williams, Hicks, Goldsborough, Eccleston, Phelps, Sprigg, McCubbin, McMaster, Jacobs, Thomas, Gaither, Stewart of Baltimore city, Presstman and Michael Newcomer —36.

So the amendment was rejected.

The question was then taken on the nineteenth article, and it was adopted.

The twentieth article of the report, was read as follows:

Art. 20. That no man ought to be compelled to give evidence against himself in a court of common law, or in any other court, but in such cases as have been usually practised in this State, or may hereafter be directed by the Legislature.

No amendment having been offered, the said article was adopted.

The twenty-first article of the report was read as follows:

Art. 21. That no freeman ought to be taken or imprisoned, or disseized of his freehold, liberties or privileges, or outlawed, or exiled, or in any manner destroyed, or deprived of his life, liberty or property, but by the judgment of his peers, or by the law of the land.

Mr. BRENT, of Baltimore city, moved to amend the article by striking out the word "freeman," and inserting the word "citizen."

Mr. Brent said, the Convention was making a bill of rights for the citizens of Maryland, and a contingency might arise, in which it might be necessary to banish a certain portion of our population. This amendment would meet the case.

Mr. Presstman hoped the amendment would not be adopted. There may be white persons resident in Maryland, who are not entitled to citizenship. His colleague had stated his object to be to leave it in the power of the Legislature, to banish colored persons, if ever a state of things should arise which would render it expedient to do so. But there may be white freemen, as well as colored, and they ought not to be placed in a position in which their right to remain in the State, should be made to depend on the will of the Legislature. He hoped the amendment would not pass.

Mr. Brent said he must adhere to his amendment. His colleague seemed to think that the rights of white freemen, who are not citizens, who are not freemen, might be affected by the amendment. They are protected by the common law. This House is engaged in making a bill of rights, not for sojourners, but for citizens of the State. The new census exhibits the alarming fact, that while the number of slaves has diminished, that of the free colored persons has increased. He did not ask for any affirmative action, but a time may come, when it will be necessary for our tranquility and security, to banish these persons; while the bill of rights, as it stands, prohibits the Legislature from exiling these colored persons who are free.

Mr. Gwinn said the freedom and security of all the people of the State, were secured by the bill of rights. Should a time arrive when it will be thought expedient to banish this class of persons, the Legislature has the power to do it.

Mr. Brent thought the Legislature had not the power.

Mr. Gwinn suggested that the Legislature might reach this class of persons. He had no fear that the increase of the colored population would be such as to give reasonable ground for alarm, but if it should, the Legislature would have the power to check it without this amendment.

Mr. Jenifer agreed that a time might possibly arrive when the State would have to send away this class of our population, but as the power is already vested in the Legislature to do this, he would not be willing to make a more stringent provision.

Mr. Brent contended that the Legislature could not exile any citizen, unless judgment had previously been obtained against him. The bill of rights made no distinction between free colored people and white citizens unless it is amended. He disdained any intention to inflict cruelty on these harmless people. But he believed a time would come, when there will be a death struggle between the castes. The effect of the abolition movement on our slave population, may be their banishment. He would not tie up the hands of the Legislature so as to prevent them from acting in case of necessity. No new power is desired for the Legislature, so long as these persons peaceably remain in the enjoyment of the rights which the laws guarantee to them. But he would give the Legislature power, in case of necessity, to banish them. He regarded this population as an incubus on the prosperity of the State.

Mr. Gwinn referred to cases in which the power had been exercised.

Mr. Brent modified his amendment so as to read as follows:

"Nothing in this article of the bill of rights to apply to the free colored population of this State."

Mr. Blakistone made some remarks against the amendment, the sketch of which is reserved for publication in a future number.

Mr. Dorsey said, he acquiesced in the exposition given to this article by the gentleman from Baltimore. He did not accord with the view of the other gentleman from Baltimore, as to meaning of the words "the law of the land." If law of the land meant any act of assembly that might be passed by the legislature, this article of the bill of rights, would give to us none of the protection for which it was designed.

Mr. Gwinn asked whether, if the colored people became turbulent, the legislature had not the power to banish them?

Mr. Dorsey replied, that if the gentleman from Baltimore merely asked his private opinion, he should say that the legislature had no such power under the Constitution. If the legislature has a right to pass such law as to negroes it has an equal power to pass a similar law as to the white residents. It had the same right in the one case as in the other. If it be expedient to give the power to the legislature, to carry out in the case supposed by the gentleman from Baltimore city, (Mr. Brent,) then the amendment now proposed by him is a proper one. He had no fear that the legislature would not make proper laws, and he would willingly leave the power with that body to make such laws as might be called for, but he would not give the power to banish freemen. He believed the legislature had the power to regulate these people, but it had never, to any extent, been exercised. He did not see that this amendment would in any way authorize lawless bands of men, to violate the rights of our colored population, as had been stated, would be the consequence of this amendment. They are entitled to protection, and they will be protected. It gives no power to kidnappers which they do not already possess, and if they attempt to violate the rights of colored people, they are liable to punishment now, just as they will be if the amendment is adopted.

Mr. Gwinn referred to the alien and sedition laws, and to the discussion which formerly took place here, and asked if aliens could be banished by the United States.

Mr. Dorsey replied, by asking, if the Constitution of the United States gave Congress the power to banish aliens? If not, there was no analogy between the cases.

Mr. Gwinn said:

That he could not support the proposed amendment. As the article now stands, no *freeman* can be taken or imprisoned, or deprived of his freehold, liberties or privileges, or out-lawed, or exiled, or be deprived of his life, liberty or property, but by the judgment of his peers, or by the law of the land. And it is proposed to add to these words, the limitation that the article should not be considered as applying to the free colored population of the State.

It is said that this is proper, because an occasion may arise for sending this people beyond our limits, and that it is wisest to provide for such a contingency. If this be the only reason, the addition is unnecessary. Under the old Constitution there seems to have been no difference in the quality of citizenship between freemen of whatever color; but in 1809 the political power of the State was vested in free white male citizens only, and the whole subsequent history of our legislation, demonstrates that the free colored population have been regarded as denizens only, who are entitled to no other privilege, or domicil, than such as the law of the State accords. The words in the article contained in the bill of rights, as reported from the committee, *confer* no new civil powers—but provide only, that they shall not be deprived of those which they have obtained, under the sanction of the public law, by other means than the law itself shall prescribe. And if it be adopted, one, or all of the class referred to, can be separated from the community, and sent beyond its limits, by the formal exercise of the power of the State. It is but the retraction of a privilege, which was a gift only, and not the result of any compact, expressed or implied; for this people bear no relation to the government, except in being subject to its laws.

The free colored population of the State is, indeed, already a great inconvenience, and may soon become a serious evil. This result was long ago foreseen, and the Legislature, with benignant care, has established a colony which, among other uses, is opened as an asylum to them. It has been the policy of the State to encourage emigration by promoting a kind relation between ourselves and this people in order that they might feel we had their good at heart, and thus enter, cheerfully, into our plans. There was reason, no less than humanity in such a course; and their history confirms it. Because, although their presence is a disadvantage, they are not with us of their own choice; and the very liberty which they enjoy, or misuse, was given under sanction of our public law.

The period is now at hand when a just regard for the interests of our white population will compel us to remove a class, who compete with them in many of the walks of labor, and yet can have no share or interest in our government. But we owe it to ourselves to perform this task with humanity and gentleness, and we should keep around them the protection of the law, until we are prepared to remove them to another land. Their fathers have served our fathers,—and our justice, stern as its requirement will ultimately be, should be tempered with charity and moderation.

This right to remove them, is a power in the State to preserve itself, and is no novelty in doctrine. It does not consist only in the making and enforcement of general laws, nor are its processes limited to the arraignment or conviction of individual offenders. Whenever classes, sects, or races grow up in a commonwealth, whose habits of life, or practices endanger the general interest and prosperity, the Legislature in virtue of its supreme power in the State, ought to, and can by the formality of law, and the use of the civil power, regulate their conduct, limit their privileges, and provide for their gradual removal. There are in history many such instances of the exercise of power. Most have been tyrannical, as was the statute banishing the Jews from England in the time of Edward I., but where the right is calmly and dispassionately exercised, with an eye single to the public good,—its existence and propriety cannot be questioned. A nation is in as much, and more, danger of slow corruption than of sudden out-break; and self-preservation as imperatively demands the use of the power of the State in seasons of apparent tranquility, as in times of impending revolution. And if it should appear to any Legislature, hereafter, that the free colored people of this State paralyze the industry of our white population,—promote discontents, or disorder among the slaves,—or corrupt the springs of public morality,—it will be necessary to take all steps which may accomplish their peaceable removal. But the responsibility should be assumed and borne by the Legislature. They ought not to look to us for a sanction. And when that period arrives, they will owe it to themselves, while they perform their duty with unshrinking hands, to make the Exodus of this people a season of charity and forbearance, which will justify the necessity to themselves. That the period is not remote at which this necessity will occur, the commonest observer may determine. The walks of labor are becoming thronged. The white and black races jostle upon our thoroughfares. And there can be no question that the power of the State must be, and ought to be, ultimately used in the upholding of its white population, and in the removal of the free blacks.

But, in the mean time, since this power is undeniable it is unavailing to parade it on our statute book. While they remain, let there be no inference even that their labor and property are placed without the shelter of the law. For, although their physical power in the State is beneath apprehension, yet, as a class, if outlawed by our statutes, they would become a source of perpetual mischief; crowding our prisons with petty offenders, who seek their daily bread by thefts and violence.

Some allusion has been made in this debate to the vote given by this Convention on the article withholding from the Legislature all right to alter the relation between master and slave. The cases bear no analogy. Slavery has existed in this State, almost ever since its foundation, with its benefits or evils, as a mode of culture, we have nothing to do. If it was injurious, the harm recoiled in the first instance upon the proprietors and complaint would proceed, naturally, from him. As property, it was, under the practice of government, and by the sanction and example of our greatest and purest men, recognized as equal, in degree, to any other in the State. And since it was subject to assaults from within and without, and might, in some season of strong excitement, be placed in sudden peril, it was not improper to impose a check upon the legislative power of the States. Slavery does not thus become eternal, because those who will adopt the new Constitution, may annul it, but it was just and wise in seasons of high political excitement to keep this element of discord out of our frequent legislative contests—so that fanatacism may find no foothold in the State, and that those most concerned shall be left to pursue that course, which interest, wisdom and humanity may dictate for their guidance. Above all, ought we to refrain from any measure which will create within our own limits, a pretext even for those dangerous opinions which are freely canvassed in the northern States?

Maryland is a border State, and is from her position, exposed to the chiefest ills which would ensue upon a disruption of the Federal Union. Her internal harmony creates a bond between the north and south, and the growth of fanatical opinion within her territory, would do more towards the dissolution of the Union, than all the wickedness and perversity of external influence could accomplish.

Mr. Merrick, (with a view, he said, to remove all doubt,) offered the following amendment.

"Provided that nothing in this article shall be so construed, as to prevent the Legislature from passing all such laws for the Government, regulation and disposition of the free colored population in this State as they may see fit."

Mr. Brent of Baltimore city. That amendment carries out my own view, and I accept it as a modification of my own.

Mr. Bowie suggested to the gentleman from Charles, (Mr. Merrick,) to substitute the word "regulation," for the word "disposition."

Mr. Merrick thought, he said, that the word "disposition" was better. The object was to retain the whole power (in case the necessity for its exercise should arise,) to remove these people from the limits of our State, or to dispose of them in such manner as the public interests and safety might require.

Mr. McMaster desired to be informed by the gentleman from Charles, (Mr. Merrick,) whether his amendment went so far as to allow the Legislature to impose a tax on free negroes?

Mr. Merrick assented.

Mr. McLane asked the gentleman from Charles to modify his amendment.

Mr. Merrick declined to modify the amendment.

Mr. McLane said, he was not disposed to embark to much extent in the discussion. He acknowledged that it was a subject of delicacy and importance; at the same time, it was one on which be had a fixed opinion. He believed that we had the power to deal with these people, as we may think proper. He objected to the amendment as it was first proposed by the gentleman from Baltimore, because it made the distinction too broad, and opened the way to oppression. It may he proper for the State to remove the colored people before the danger is so imminent as some have contemplated; but, until that time shall arrive, they ought to be protected and succured. Any other course would, in his opinion, be cruel to them, and unsafe to the white population.

If the amendment does not place them out of the pale of legal protection, he would be satisfied.

Mr. Merrick said, his amendment was offered with no idea of placing these people out of the pale of the law, but merely to empower the legislature to make such laws in relation to them as the public interests might require, to leave them in the hands of the legislature.

Mr. McLane said, that the gentleman from Charles, concurred with him as to the impropriety of subjecting the colored people to disabilities. But did not this amendment put it in the power of the legislature to subject them to these disabilities? Might it not even proceed so far as to take from them their property? He objected to placing them in a situation in which they would be liable to this. He, therefore, wished that the amendment should be modified in this respect. He thought these people ought to be removed as soon as it can be done with propriety, and that we are not bound to wait until the danger becomes more imminent. The gentleman from Baltimore asked, what we owe to the principle of abolition? Owe to abolition! Could that question be put to this Convention at this day? What do we owe to abolition? We owe to it the spirit of discord, the spirit of hatred, the danger of disunion.

Mr. Gwinn said, he alluded to it for the purpose of saying, we should do nothing to strengthen it in our own borders.

Mr. McLane agreed as to this. But this abolition principle has operated on the colored people, and he was ready to adopt any humane provision for their removal, although he would protect them while here.

Mr. Merrick said, that to his mind, no question could be more deeply interesting to the State than this. We had amongst us a numerous class of persons, who, by nature, were inimical to the great body of the people of the State. We were in the same condition towards them, in which other classes had been towards each other in times gone by. We saw it written by the hand of God, that the two races could not exist in harmony in the same country. The time must come when a separation, peaceably or forcibly, must take place. No two distinct races could, or ever would, inhabit the same land, except in the relative condition of master and slave—of the ruler and the ruled. Sooner or later they must separate, or extermination of the one or the other must take place. In making an organic law, therefore, it became the duty of those who formed it, to look to futurity. It was true, that there was no present danger of any terrible calamity, arising from a proposed separation, and he hoped that the wise and patriotic action of this Convention might afford efficient aid in effecting that separation, whenever it must come, peaceably and happily to both parties. For it *must* come, as certainly as there was a God in Heaven.

The black race could not remain here. They were multiplying too fast. The two races could not amalgamate, it was horrible to the soul and spirit of the white man even to talk of amalgamation. The black race, therefore, must either go to their own original home or remain here as slaves. Whilst they *were* here, he would go as far as the gentleman from Cecil, (Mr. McLane,) or any other gentleman, to treat them with all the lenity, forbearance, and kindness which were consistent with their relative position, and with that one great object of separation which must ultimately ensue.

His amendment did not contemplate imposing any painful disabilities upon them—it did not propose to place them beyond the pale of the law. Not at all. On the contrary, it gave them all the protection which they now enjoyed. The only design was to leave them subject at all times to legislative control, in any of those emergencies which could not now be foreseen, but which might arise in the progress of time. That the Legislature of the State would act humanely towards them, no man could doubt. And it would be unwise to tie up their hands.

The gentleman from Cecil (Mr. McLane) had expressed himself willing to vote for an amendment which should provide only for the power of removal. Why not also provide for the government of these people whilst they were among us? The gentleman had said that the Legislature had the power here contemplated without the amendment and independent of the bill of Rights. Be it so. Even if the Legislature had the power, no harm could be done by the insertion of these words. There were other gentlemen, however, who had doubts as to the present existence of the power. The only design of the amendment was to leave in the hands of the Legislature of the State, the power hereafter to enact such laws as the public safety might require. This was its whole scope and import.

The gentleman had asked whether, under this clause, the Legislature would not have the power to disfranchise these people. It was so. That was precisely what he aimed at; because the emergency might arise when the public safety would demand that their rights and privileges should be dealt with by the Legislature. The amendment gave that power to the Legislature, confiding in the wisdom and forbearance of that body—and trusting that they would never forget the past history of the State, nor be false to the dictates of duty and humanity. It was indeed much more likely that that body would forbear too long, than that they would act too rashly. We could not be blind to the dangers which surrounded us. We could not be blind to the fiendish acts of the abolitionists, nor to the bitter seeds of discord which they were sewing between the master and the slave. It was the solemn duty of the State to be prepared to meet the danger, into whatever form it might present itself.

Mr. Brent, of Baltimore city, asked whether it could be regarded as unchristian to protect ourselves. Self-preservation was the first principle in our nature. He looked on this as a mere question of police. He had been induced to introduce his amendment, because it had been said here that there were many abolitionists in the city of Baltimore. It was no such thing. The abolitionists there are very few. His amendment only reserved to the Legislature, the power to rescue the people, if it should ever become necessary, for the safety or tranquility of the State. His colleague had said we should do nothing to build up abolition in other States.

Mr. Gwinn contended that we had no right to do any thing to violate the rights of the colored people among us, while they conduct themselves peaceably, or to strengthen the principle of abolition in this State.

Mr. Brent replied, that we could not now, by any legislative provision, carry away these colored people out of the State. The only way was to leave them in the hands of the Legislature. The gentleman from Cecil, thought his, (Mr. B.'s) original proposition cruel, because it takes away the rights of this class of our population, and leaves them at the mercy of a ruthless Legislature. It was not so.

Mr. McLane stated that he only meant to say that the amendment proposed to deprive them, by giving the Legislature the power to do so, of the rights to which they were entitled by another article in the bill of rights.

Mr. Brent replied, that it only gave the Legislature the power to remove them, whenever it shall become necessary for the safety of the State, and every consideration required that the Legislature should have this power for our self-preservation. We should at all times guard against the torch of the incendiary being applied to the magazine; and here was a class of people, which at some time, might become a moral magazine, fraught with our destruction.

The question was then taken on the amendment of Mr. Brent, as modified by the acceptation of the amendment of Mr. Merrick, and was decided in the affirmative.

So the amendment, as modified, was agreed to.

And the Convention adjourned until to-morrow, at eleven o'clock.

THURSDAY, February 6th, 1851.

The Convention met at eleven o'clock.

Prayer was made by Rev. Mr. Griffith.

The journal of yesterday was read and approved.

PERSONAL EXPLANATION.

Mr. Chambers of Kent, rose to make a personal explanation. A friend had informed him last evening, that his language reported in the debates of Saturday last, had been understood in a sense, which he was not willing to have imputed to him, and which it was not his design to convey. The gentleman from Baltimore city, (Mr. Gwinn,) had been understood, in the committee room, as expressing his fixed determination to make an argument in the House, on the question of popular representation. He understood the gentleman afterwards to have announced his determination, on the floor of the House, to the same effect. Subsequently, when the gentleman united in the effort, made by other members to have the subject recommitted, without discussing the merits of the general question, he had thought it fair to retort this change of position upon the gentleman, in reply to his assault, (if he might so term it,) upon him. It was to this, and this alone, he designed to refer as the "crooked and tortuous course," of the gentleman. The charge of the gentleman, on Saturday, and his defence, were both made in good temper, and certainly nothing would be more foreign to the fact, or more unpleasant to him, than to have it supposed he designed to impute to that gentleman, any habitual evasion of duty or responsibilty. Their relations had always been most friendly, and had not been in the slightest degree interrupted by the little good humored pass between them on Saturday, and he hoped nothing would occur to change these relations, as he professed high respect, both for the intellectual and honorable character of the gentlemen. It was with regret, therefore, he had heard that in the incompleteness, necessarily growing out of the parsimonious mode of reporting, there had been found room for a construction of his remarks, which would be as unjust to him, as to the gentleman. Of course he had resolved to correct any error on this subject, the moment it had been suggested to him, by the kindness of a riend.

Mr. Gwinn said that he was satisfied with the explanation of the gentleman from Kent. When the debate referred to was in progress, he had risen to an explanation, without attending to the peculiar language in which the observations of the gentleman were couched. Yesterday, however, he had read the printed report of his remarks, and perceived that the language was capable of a graver meaning than he had supposed, and has therefore requested a friend to call the attention of the gentleman to the passage in question, in order that he might explain its true meaning. He did not suppose that the gentleman ever designed any unpleasant imputation, and took it for granted that he would place it in a proper light, when he was made aware of the circumstance. His ready courtesy had shown him that he was not mistaken.

For himself, he could only say, that, if in the debate of the many exciting topics which might arise, he encroached in any manner, however slight, upon the feelings of any gentleman, he would be glad to have his attention called to the circumstance, in order that he might accord that explanation which he should always take the privilege of requiring from others.

The President called for reports of committees.

Their being no reports,

Mr. Ridgely moved that the Convention proceed to the orders of the day.

THE BILL OF RIGHTS.

The motion having been agreed to, the Convention resumed the consideration of the order of the day, being the report submitted by Mr. Dorsey, on the 11th ult., as Chairman of the committtee on the declaration of rights.

The pending question was on the adoption of the 21st article, as yesterday amended.

The question was taken, and the amendment wasadopted.

The 22nd and 23rd articles of the bill were read and adopted as follows:

Art. 22. That excessive bail ought not to be required, nor excessive fines imposed, nor cruel or unusual punishment inflicted by the courts of law.

Art. 23. That all warrants, without oath, or affirmation, to search suspected places, or to seize any person or property, are grievous and oppressive; and all general warrants to search suspected places, or to apprehend suspected persons, without naming or describing the place, or the person in special, are illegal and ought not to be granted.

The 24th article was read as follows:

Art. 24. That there ought to be no forfeiture of any part of the estate of any person for any crime except murder, or treason against the State, and then only on conviction and attainder.

Mr. Jenifer moved to amend the said section, by striking out all after the word "crime."

Mr. J. said he did not see that any case could arise in the State of Maryland where a forfeiture of property should take place after a criminal execution. It would be a hard case that a family already suffering the bitter results of the criminal acts of its head, should be visited also with this additional infliction.

Mr. Dent offered a substitute for the said motion, to read as follows:

Strike out all the 24th article to the word "treason," in the second line, and insert in lieu thereof, the following:

"That no conviction shall work corruption of blood, or forfeiture of estate except for."

Mr. Jenifer expressed his willingness to accept the substitute as a modification of his own proposition.

Mr. Merrick desired to suggest to his colleague, (Mr. Jenifer,) that it might possibly be well that he should modify his amendment. He, (Mr. M.,) did not know exactly the scope of his colleague's views. But he, (Mr. M.,) would suggest, that the time might come when it not only might be good policy, but due to justice, that there should be a forfeiture of property in case of treason. If it met the views of his colleague, he, (Mr. M.,) thought that the object might be answered by simply striking out the words, "murder or."

He could not contemplate any crime as to

which it was at all probable that the Legislature would at any time decree a forfeiture of estate.

Mr. JENIFER said, that he would with pleasure accept the suggestion of his colleague, (Mr. Merrick.) But he, (Mr. J.) could not see any great distinction between the crime of murder and that of treason, so far as the principle involved in this amendment was concerned. His great object was to provide that no family should be deprived of its property, by reason of crimes committed by its head. He would have preferred that the whole article should be stricken out; but was willing to accept the proposition of the gentleman from Charles, (Mr. Dent.) The object was to punish the criminal, but not to punish an innocent and unoffending family.

Mr. DENT read the sixteenth and twenty-fourth articles, to show that the amendment of the gentleman from Charles, (Mr. Jenifer,) if adopted, would conflict with the former. If that amendment should be adopted, it would be requisite to strike out the 16th article.

Mr. DORSEY thought, he said, that it would be rather unsafe to strike out the word "treason." He was in favor of striking out the word "murder," but thought that "treason" ought to be retained. During our revolutionary struggle, we found the Legislature constantly passing laws under which a considerable portion of the most valuable real estate in the State of Maryland, was sold—the property of tories—of those who abandoned their country in the hour of her peril, and fled to the enemy. A crisis might arise in the history of this country, where a similar necessity would exist. He believed that under every government, treason was punished by forfeiture of property, as a matter of course.

Mr. D. explained that the conflict between the several articles of the bill of rights, which the gentleman from Charles, [Mr. Dent,] supposed would exist under the amendment, would not in fact take place.

Mr. MERRICK said, he thought that this power to punish treason by forfeiture, was a matter of some importance to the goverment, and ought to be retained. This punishment was intended to operate, not upon the subordinate portion of the community, but upon the wealthy and powerful traitor. He had the means of eluding the criminal law, and it was only by an infliction of this character that he could be reached. This power constituted a check upon him for which no adequate substitute could be found. There was no other punishment applicable to them. The crime of treason was a high public crime, which could not otherwise be reached.

Mr. DENT said, he stood corrected as to the supposed conflict between the two articles. He found they would not conflict. He had no objection to forfeiture for treason, and he then modified his amendment.

After a few words by Mr. CHAMBERS, of Kent, and Mr. DORSEY, as to the construction to be given to the article—

Mr. JENIFER remarked that this clause was engrafted on the Bill of Rights just at the moment when we were emerging from the Revolution. It was not probable that any such events would happen again. Why then were we to punish an innocent family for the guilt of a single individual? Upon reflection, he felt constrained to adhere to his original motion to strike out all the clause after the word "crime."

The PRESIDENT. Does the gentleman move that amendment?

Mr. JENIFER. I do.

Mr. MERRICK rose and was proceeding to address the Convention—when

Mr. CHAMBERS, of Kent, interposed, and suggested to him that he (Mr. M.) could attain his object, by calling for a division on the motion of the gentleman from Charles, (Mr. Jenifer,) to apply to the words "murder or."

Mr. MERRICK intimated his intention so to do. His object, he said, was to retain in the Legislature the power to punish the crime of treason by forfeiture of estate. It was wise and prudent that the power should be retained in the hands of a body to which the people of the State were to look for all their future well-being, to reach a crime in the only way in which it ever could be reached.

Some conversation followed between Messrs. JENIFER and MERRICK—after which

The question was taken on striking out from the section, the words "murder or."

And it was agreed to.

So the said words were stricken out.

The question then recurred and was taken on the amendment of Mr. JENIFER, and, by ayes 34, noes 21, the said words were stricken out.

Mr. DENT now moved to strike out the article, and insert the following substitute:

"That no conviction shall work corruption of blood or forfeiture of estate."

The question was taken and the substitute was adopted.

The twenty-fifth article, as amended, was then read.

Mr. THOMAS suggested, that this article frustrated one of the objects he had in view, in the vote which he had just given. He desired to strike out all that part of the article, which forfeited the estate for treason or murder. He desired to deny to the Legislature the power to declare by law, that either of these crimes should work a forfeiture of estate. If the amendment of the gentleman from Charles, (Mr. Dent,) prevailed, his, (Mr. T.'s) object in the vote he had given, was defeated. The conviction itself might not work a forfeiture; but the Legislature might provide by bill of attainder, for a forfeiture.

Some explanation followed.

Mr. THOMAS hoped some gentleman would move a reconsideration of the vote just taken.

Mr. DORSEY suggested, that the sixteenth section, accomplished the object which the gentleman from Frederick, (Mr. Thomas,) had in view.

Mr. THOMAS acquiesced, remarking that he was not here at the time the report was made, and had not, therefore, had an opportunity of examining it.

The question was then stated to be on the twenty-fourth article, as amended.

Mr. McMaster said he was opposed to the amendment, because he thought that the language of the original article was more plain and comprehensive. He hoped it would not be adopted.

The question was taken and the article was adopted.

The 25th, 26th, and 27th articles were severally read, and no amendment having been offered thereto, were adopted, as follows:

Art. 25. That a well regulated militia is the proper and natural defence of a free government.

Art. 26. That standing armies are dangerous to liberty, and ought not to be raised or kept up without consent of the Legislature.

Art. 27. That in all cases, and at all times, the military ought to be under strict subordination to, and control of the civil power.

The twenty-eighth article of the report was read as follows:

Art. 28. That no soldier ought to be quartered in any house in time of peace, without the consent of the owner, and in time of war in such manner as the Legislature shall direct.

Mr. Dent said it seemed to him that there was a word wanting in this article. And he moved to amend it by adding, after the word "manner," the word "only."

The amendment was agreed to.

And the article, as amended, was adopted.

The 29th article of the report was read, and, no amendment having been offered thereto, was adopted as follows:

Art. 29. That no person except regular soldiers, mariners and marines, in the service of this State, or militia when in actual service, ought in any case to be subject to, or punishable by martial law.

The 30th article of the report was read as follows:

Art. 30. That the independency and uprightness of Judges are essential to the impartial administration of justice, and a great security to the rights and liberties of the people; wherefore the Chancellor and Judges shall not be removed except for misbehaviour, on conviction in a court of law, or by the Governor, upon the address of the General Assembly; *provided*, that two-thirds of all the members of each House, concur in such addresss; that salaries, liberal, but not profuse, ought to be secured to the Chancellor and Judges during the continuance of their commissions, in such manner and at such time as the Legislature shall hereafter direct upon consideration of the circumstances of this State; no Chancellor or Judge ought to hold any other office, civil or military, under the Constitution or Laws of this State or of the United States, or of any member thereof, or receive fees or perquisites of any kind for the discharge of his official duties.

Mr. Brent, of Baltimore city, moved to strike out the words "ought to" and insert "shall,"

So as to make the provision, (Mr. B. said,) expressly prohibitory.

The amendment was agreed to.

26

Mr. Bowie moved to amend the article in the sixth line, by striking out "two-thirds," and inserting a majority.

Some desultory discussion followed between Messrs. Dorsey, Bowie, Jenifer and Weems, directed, for the most part, to the proper construction to be given to the article, when

Mr. Bowie withdrew his amendment.

Mr. Ridgely moved to amend the 30th article, in the eleventh line, by inserting after the word "office," the words "of public trust or emolument of any kind whatever."

Mr. Brent, of Baltimore city, said, that so far as such offices were concerned, the gentleman from Baltimore county, (Mr. Ridgely,) could accomplish his object by inserting in the thirty-second article, the words, "trust or emolument."

He, (Mr. B.,) would now propose to amend the section, by adding the words:

"Nor shall any person hold a commission as Judge or Chancellor, at any time after such person has qualified or acted as a member of any Convention, to revise or alter the Constitution of this State, but thereupon such commission as Judge or Chancellor shall be vacated."

Mr. Ridgely said, that the proposition of the gentleman from Baltimore city, (Mr. Brent,) was specific in its character, and he, (Mr. R.,) had no objection to its being added as an amendment, at the end of his amendment. The latter, however, was broader, and covered more ground.

Mr. Ridgely then modified his amendment, by striking out the word "public," and substituting the word "political."

Mr. Chambers, of Kent, said, that of course, the members of this Convention would make such a Constitution as they might think right; but, as he had before said, the Convention should know and consider well what it was doing. He referred to his own position. He lived in a small town, where, as was the case in all such places, important gentlemen like himself were scarce. (Laughter.)

He was overpowered with offices of public trusts. [Mr. C. ran over the roll of them in a good-natured way.] He was incumbered with offices, and his personal convenience would be much promoted by the adoption of the amendment of the gentleman from Baltimore county, (Mr. Ridgely.) But he, [Mr. C.,] thought that the gentleman should give a bill of particulars.

Mr. Ridgely interposed, and said, he had substituted the word "political," for "public."

Mr. Chambers remarked, that the proposition was still indefinite.

In regard to the amendment of the gentleman from Baltimore city, (Mr. Brent,) he, [Mr. C.,] thought that this was not the proper time to discuss that question. The proposition opened up the whole subject matter, just where it had been left a number of weeks ago. It would be better to let it pass and not to rake up matter for future discussion.

Mr. Brent, of Baltimore city, said:

That in offering this amendment, he did not design to reflect injuriously on Judges in this Convention, but to be consistent with the principle assumed by him, in objecting to the seats of Judges, he must insist on his amendment.

He referred to the fact, that the report of the committee on credentials, had expressly admitted the judges to seats on this floor, because the old bill of rights did not apply in its terms, to a Convention; and therefore, he wished to make the new bill of rights explicit on this subject.

Other gentlemen thought that we had no power to decide who should come into future Conventions, but he was for passing the prohibition now, and leaving to posterity to decide our power to do so. It would, at least, be a declaration of the moral sense of this Convention.

Mr. B. then referred to the positions taken by him when on the committee of credentials, (before a Reporter was appointed,) that a judge should be far removed from any exciting element of party strife, and if possible, isolated in his sublimity—that he should devote all his time and energy to his judicial labors, which his oath requires him to administer "without delay." If judges were in future times, to come here, they would soil the ermine of justice. Referring to this Convention, through no disrespect to the judges personally, who were here, what have we seen? We have seen judges here for weeks and months, necessarily absent from their duties in the courts, in proportion as they were faithful here—we have seen them going into party caucusses.

[Here Mr. Chambers inquired, if he had gone into any caucus about principles of the new Constitution?]

Mr. B. said, he did not mean to charge that, but would the gentleman deny that he had gone into a whig party caucus, with a view to an organization of the House?

If he would not deny that, it was the same thing in principle, as it proved that the judge was a party man.

Again, judicial reform, even to the uprooting of the whole system, was one of the questions to decide, upon which this Convention has assembled. To allow men holding high judicial places, in all future time, to be present acting upon their own tenure of office, would be greatly calculated to depreciate the office of judge. I do not mean to disfranchise judges—but let them resign their judicial commissions before they can serve in a Constitutional Convention

The gentleman from Kent, (Mr. Chambers,) says, there are but few important men in his county. [Here Mr. Chambers interposed and said in *his town*.] But few important men in his town, and therefore, he says, that he is overburdened with a multiplicity of small offices of various kinds.

Mr. B. was sorry to hear that important men were so scarce in Chestertown, but the very fact of the gentleman's being assessed with so many offices, proved that he could not properly attend to all. [Mr. Chambers enquired if Mr. Brent meant to say that he had neglected his judicial office.]

Mr. B. replied that he had not so said, but he did say that a man who had even that gentleman's dispatch for business, could not properly attend to all the various offices he had assumed, and he must necessarily neglect some one or more, in proportion as he attended to the rest. But he, (Mr. B.) wished to be understood as laying down, in the Constitution, no rule for the gentlemen who were here. He did not dispute their integrity or merits, but he wished to lay down a rule of public policy, based on human experience of the weakness of mankind, and on the average of human character.

Mr. Chambers said the gentleman has informed us what he thinks human nature can do and cannot. There were a great many sorts of human nature, and he was quite sure his human nature differed from the gentleman's. We have been plainly told by the gentleman, that political organization and party interests, directed the votes of members of this body. He much regretted to hear it. He had not allowed party influences to regulate his votes here, nor should he do so. The gentleman still harps upon his old tune about the judges, and the neglect of their duties. He acknowledged no higher duty than to assist in making a Constitution, and to that duty he had most assiduously applied himself. It was but an act of justice to his brethren, who, since the first of December, were in session in the supreme court, to say that the business of that court had not been neglected. They had faithfully, wisely and usefully performed the duties of that court, and he believed he might say satisfactorily. The gentleman had assumed the large license of censuring, not only the judges, but the Legislature and the people of his county. He was here by the authority of the Legislature—if they had any authority. He was here by the selection of the freemen of his county, and he inclined to think it was not a matter of very deep regret to them that the gentleman supposed they acted very unwisely in sending him here. How far this dictation to the sovereign people—this refusal to allow them to judge for themselves, who should represent them, was consistent with the high-toned notions of democracy, it was not for him to decide.

The gentleman thought the judicial ermine could not escape a stain in this collision and strife—that it was not in human nature. Now it was in this, he supposed, his human nature differed from that of the gentleman. He could lay his hand on his bosom, and aver that his opinions were uninflenced by motives of interest. If he could not, he would not be here. Why what is there in the paltry salary of a Judge of your Supreme Court, compared with his labors, to make him so earnest in holding on to it? He denied, in the boldest terms, that after filling the office for more than sixteen years, he was not indebted to the State on a fair account, one dollar.

He had rendered services fully equivalent to every cent and more. The same services at the bar, would have secured him five times the amount of pecuniary compensation. Let the debtor and creditor sides of the account be fairly stated, and the balance sheet would not be against him. He could leave the bench to-morrow, without the least apprehension of making a bad bargain. In saying this, it was proper for him to add that he felt the most profound sense of obligation to the State for the confidence which had placed him in the various high and important trusts to which he had been called. No one knew so well as himself, how far it exceeded his claims, and none knew better that it was the result of kind and generous feelings by many personal friends whose partiality concealed his infirmities. For these repeated instances of confidence and respect, he could never cease to cherish the warmest return of gratitude and thankfulness.

But there is nothing in the value of a judgeship to make an intelligent man a fool, or an honest man a knave. This was no place for party. What is party—political party? The creature of a day. One man uppermost to-day, at the bottom to-morrow. Who could tell how long parties, as now arranged, were to continue? They were now in a crysalis state, and as the gentleman from Cecil said the other day, promising an early re-organization. He thought there could be no greater misconception of duty than to suppose we are here to promote any political party. As to the influence of office, he was not quite sure, whether after a full and fair estimate, it would be found to operate more strongly on some half dozen who held the offices, and wished to retain them, or on five times that number who desired to put out the incumbents to put themselves in.

Mr. BRENT, of Baltimore city, stated that he was surprised at the gentleman from Kent (Mr. Chambers) speaking of some cause outside of this House if not in it, for his (Mr. B's.) course.

Here Mr. CHAMBERS interposed, and disclaimed any such meaning, as his relations with Mr. BRENT had always been friendly—to which he (Mr. B.) assented.

Mr. B. said, he admited that the gentleman from Kent had fully and honestly earned his salary since he had been upon the bench, but could this be said of all judges? He did not question their honesty, but had all judges in this State, been able to earn their salaries? He should think not. But the gentleman from Kent says he has neglected no duty by coming here, and the Courts were in progress now, the same as if this Convention were not sitting. Now, I have it on respectable authority, that the Court of Appeals sitting over our heads, has been sometimes compelled to adjourn for want of a quorum, while we have been sitting here.

When he spoke of caucus, he had referred to one for party organization of the House. But the gentleman from Kent had come here on a party organization, and had voted in this Convention, side by side, with the party column to which he was attached. He might not suppose he was as much touched with party here as other men, but he was never found voting with the political party to which he (Mr. B.) belonged. What right has a judge, to know party in any shape, while he holds his commission? And what has a judge to do with party operations? If the gentleman from Kent went into a party caucus, he knows something of party, and is *exposed to party taint.* That gentleman had spoken of party tendencies here, and had lectured us for those tendencies, and yet his course showed that he was not perhaps more free from those party influences than others. Mr. B. concurred, that party lines were out of place here, and he deplored this unhappy condition of affairs. When he spoke of judges being influenced by sordid motives, he meant no personal application to any gentleman, but he spoke rather of human nature as found in the aggregate, and which according to all experience is generally prone to selfish and personal considerations, and against which tendencies it should be the policy of the laws to guard.

Mr. B. admitted, that invited by the honest Democrats of Kent, he had gone over last summer and addressed the people of one election district near Cook's Old Fields, where Sir Peter Parker was killed. He (Mr. B.) had there harangued against the election of the gentleman from Kent, (Mr. Chambers,) who now says, that the people of Kent county had turned a deaf ear to my appeals. But I will ask that gentleman if he was not greatly disappointed when the returns from that election district came in, showing the loss of some fifty or sixty votes which the gentleman calculated on—a result which he (Mr. B.) did not claim as caused by his appeal or that of another gentleman who spoke, but rather by the good sense of the people.

It did not, however, look much like turning a deaf ear, when the gentleman (Mr. Chambers) with his commanding talents and high personal character, was only elected by some *seven votes* in a county which generally gives from one hundred and fifty to two hundred Whig majority. The gentleman from Kent has said that he is here and holds his seat by authority of the people and the Legislature. [Mr. Chambers explained and said "by authority of the Legislature if it had any authority."] And yet, said Mr. B., the gentleman early in the session emphatically denied that the Legislature had any authority to call a Convention, or that the people could ever give any validity to the new Constitution by adopting it at the ballot box in June next. According to the gentleman's notions the new Constitution would be a nullity until the existing State authorities should choose to acquiesce in the new Constitution.

If the new Constitution should disqualify judges sitting in future Conventions, it would certainly bind the Legislature not to pass any act to qualify them.

In pursuing the course he had done he was not actuated by hostility towards the judges, and he claimed no other judgment for his acts but that he had acted from a conscientious sense of duty—even against all the motives of human interest which would have restrained him in his course.

Mr. SPENCER here made a suggestion as to the propriety of passing this article by informally. It would more properly come up, when the judicial report was under consideration; and he had been given to understand that that report was ready.

Mr. BRENT thought the subject was in its proper place.

Mr. MERRICK said he thought this was the place to discuss it.

Mr. RIDGELY said that when he had offered the amendment which had given rise to this debate, he intended it to have a general, not a special application. He supposed that it was conceded on all hands, that the judicial officers should be kept distinct from all other officers. He had not anticipated the opposition which had risen up to his proposition. It had been doubted by some, whether a judge ought to have a seat in this Convention. His object was to prevent a judge from holding any political trust or employment; that it may be distinctly understood hereafter, that no person sitting as a judge, should be a member of any political body. He thought his object could not be misunderstood.

Mr. CHAMBERS said he had no objection.

The question was then taken on the amendment of Mr. RIDGELY, and it was rejected.

The question then recurred on the amendment of Mr. BRENT, of Baltimore city.

Mr. McMASTER moved that the amendment be laid on the table.

The PRESIDENT said, that that motion, if it should be insisted on, and should prevail, would carry with it the whole report of the committee on the bill of rights.

Mr. McMASTER thereupon withdrew his motion.

Mr. BRENT asked the yeas and nays on his amendment.

Mr. SPENCER made a few observations to the effect, that he held the people to be supreme. If a majority of the Convention intend to say the people shall not change the Constitution, except in the mode here pointed out, then this amendment is proper to carry out that intention; but if the Convention should declare that the people have the right to change the Constitution at their will, and in their own way, that would settle the matter. He gave notice that he intended to move a reconsideration of the amendment of the gentleman from Anne Arundel, (Mr. Dorsey,) and he would do it. With such a modification, he would feel himself compelled to vote against the amendment of the gentleman from Baltimore, (Mr. Presstman.) But, he repeated, if the doctrine is to be established that the people are to be bound to act in the mode prescribed by this Constitution, then this proposition is right; if not, it ought to be rejected.

Mr. HICKS moved an amendment to the amendment, which was modified once or twice, and finally assumed the form hereafter given.

[The Reporter cannot make the proceedings on the amendment intelligible, as he has no means of tracing the proposition. It appears upon the journal only in the form which it finally assumed. The same difficulty exists in regard to the other propositions.]

The question then came back to the modified amendment of Mr. BRENT.

Mr. JENIFER suggested to Mr. BRENT, to include *all* offices, and expressed his surprise at the speech which the gentleman had made to-day—seeing that that gentleman had gone as far as the furthest in giving the election of judges, and all other offices, to the people; and yet now the gentleman proposed to forbid the people exercising the very power which he was so anxious to give to them. It seemed like "keeping the word of promise to the ear, and breaking it to the hope."

Mr. BRENT replied to the suggestion, as to making the amendment general, that the article which he proposed to amend related to no other subject matter than that of judges.

Mr. JENIFER indicated his intention to go against the proposition.

Mr. THOMAS said, he took no pleasure in discussions of this character, and would not participate if he was at liberty to avoid voting. But, as he must vote, and intended to vote against the proposition of the gentleman from Baltimore city, he felt constrained to say a few words, that his reasons for that vote might not be misunderstood. By a silent vote against that amendment, he might leave room to have it supposed, that he did not feel the force of what had been said, as to the inconvenience parties to appeals, before the Supreme Court of the State, might experience by the absence of two of the judges of that Court, in attendance as members of this Convention. He would say that there was much force in what had been said on that subject. But in saying this, he desired to disclaim all wish to make the attendance here, of two gentlemen who were distinguished by a long career of useful public service, in any degree unpleasant. They were here in pursuance of the provisions of the law, under which this Convention had assembled. That law authorized the judges to take seats as members of this Convention. The law had been submitted to the people of the whole state for their sanction. A large majority of the people had accepted the law, and we were all here in obedience to its privileges and requirements. Indeed, but for the requirements of that law, Frederick county would never have consented to meet her sister counties in a Convention such as this, where the people are not fairly represented. The Legislature of the State had proposed to the people to meet in Convention, with representatives apportioned as they are under this law. The people had no alternatives, but submission to the Constitution as it is, or, to meet in Convention on the conditions that the Legislature had imposed. The majority made choice of the last alternative, and we were all here under the law, the judges being here with as much title as other members.

Now the gentleman from Baltimore proposes to insert in the Constitution we are to frame, a provision denying to Judges in this State hereafter, a right to take seats in any future Convention, that may be assembled to change or abolish this Constitution. For this, Mr. THOMAS said he could not vote. We had no power to come after us in this respect. Such an article in the Constitution could have no effect. The generations of men who are to succeed us as residents of this State, will have a right to meet in Convention, and disregard such a restriction. If we were to declare in this Constitution, that the people of Maryland should not, hereafter, meet in Convention to abolish or change that instrument, such a declaration would be a nullity. There is a well-known destination, however, as to the power we have over the officers, we may authorize to hold appointments under this Constitution, and the power we have to restrain our posterity in the exercise of the right of self-government. We may attach conditions to the tenures of these offices. We may declare that a Judge, the Attorney General of the State, or other officer under this Constitution, shall not take a seat in a future Convention until he has first resigned his office. And in such a provision there would not be injustice or hardship. It would have the effect to put all members of a future Convention, on a footing of perfect equality.

For an article in the Constitution having for its object such an end, he could consistently vote. He could readily see that the public interest might require the constant attention of high officers, such as Judges of our Supreme Court, and the Attorney General of the State. He did not object to such functionaries being here, however, on the ground that they might be interested in defeating changes in the form of the government. He would not suppose that any one could be elected as a member of a body of this character, who would be intent upon the promotion of his personal interests only. And agreed with the gentleman from Kent, (Mr. Chambers,) in supposing that aspirations for offices, had full as much influence on the conduct of men as the disposition to retain offices already held. Believing this, he (Mr. T.) was not very unwilling to leave the people of the State at perfect liberty to send to any future Convention, officers who held commissions under the Constitution which was to be changed. Still he would vote with the gentleman from Baltimore city, if he would modify his amendment so as to make it a limitation on the tenures of offices we were about to establish. But he could not vote to incorporate any article in the Constitution that had for its object a limitation on the power of the people, to change, alter or abolish their form of government whenever they may think proper to do so, to promote their safety and happiness.

Mr. Chambers rose merely to remove the impression which might otherwise be produced, if no other reasons were assigned, for those who voted for the amendment, except those assigned by the gentleman from Frederick, (Mr. Thomas,) and others who preceded him.

He differed altogether from some of the proposition of the gentleman from Frederick, and, at a proper time, would repeat and enforce his own opinions in relation to them. He was an humble advocate of the doctrine that the Constitution could bind the whole community. His object was to excuse himself and his friends from any erroneous inference. There were two sides to these questions. He did not wish to allow *judgment by default* to be entered against him.

After some desultory proceedings,

Mr. Brent, accepting the suggestion of Mr. Thomas, modified his amendment by adding after the word "Chancellor" the following:

"Attorney General, or of any other civil officer under the Constitution of this State."

Mr. Hicks now moved the following modified amendment, to the amendment of Mr. Brent:

"Nor shall any member of this Convention accept any office or appointment under the new Constitution, for ten years after its adoption."

Mr. Hicks asked the yeas and nays, which were ordered, and

After some conversation, were taken and resulted as follows:

Affirmative—Messrs. Chapman, President, Morgan, Lee, Chambers of Kent, Dorsey, Wells, Kent, Bond, Sollers, Jenifer, Buchanan, Ridgely, John Dennis, Crisfield, Dashiell, Williams, Hicks, Goldsborough, Eccleston, Phelps, Sprigg, Dirickson, McMaster, Hearn, Jacobs, Gaither, Fiery, John Newcomer, Michael Newcomer, Davis, Shower and Cockey—32.

Negative—Messrs. Dent, Mitchell, Donaldson, Weems, Dalrymple, Brent of Charles, Merrick, Bell, Welch, Sherwood of Talbot, Colston, Chambers of Cecil, McCullough, Miller, McLane, Bowie, Spencer, Thomas, Shriver, Biser, Sappington, Stephenson, McHenry, Magraw, Nelson, Carter, Thawley, Hardcastle, Gwinn, Stewart of Baltimore city, Brent of Baltimore city, Presstman, Ware, Kilgour, Anderson, Weber, Hollyday, Slicer and Ege—39.

So the amendment to the amendment was rejected.

The question then recurred upon the amendment as offered by Mr. Brent, of Baltimore city.

Mr. Thomas moved to amend said amendment by inserting after the word "Chancellor," the following:

"Attorney General or of any other civil officer under the Constitution of this State."

Which amendment was accepted by Mr. Brent of Baltimore city.

Mr. Parke was excused from voting, having paired off for a limited time, (not yet expired,) with Mr. Ricaud.

The question then recurred on the modified amendment of Mr. Brent.

Messrs. Buchanan and Hicks asked the yeas and nays;

Which were ordered.

Mr. Thomas said:

He had not given—he did not propose to assign any reasons in support of the opinions he had expressed, as to our entire want of power to limit or restrain the people of Maryland, who are to succeed us, in the exercise of that inalienable right that exists in all political communities, to form for themselves a government. He did not desire to discuss a proposition so universally admitted to be true in this country. He referred to an incident in the Virginia Constitutional Convention of 1829, to show the opinion entertained on that subject by distinguished members of that body, then present.

At the close of that Convention, one of the members proposed to insert an article in their Constitution, giving power to the people of Virginia to meet by their delegates, in a future Convention. Mr. John Randolph opposed and ridiculed the proposition, saying that the majority of the people would have that right, without such an article, and could not be deprived of that right, by an article in the Constitution expressly forbidding them to exercise such a power. He said that article in the Constitution, declaring that that Constitution should be perpetual, would be of no more binding force on the people of Virginia, than the concluding words often found in a treaty of peace, when it was declared that the articles of the treaty should be a perpetual league and covenant, between the high contracting parties. And that every man knew, that notwithstanding this "perpetual league and covenant," the "high contracting parties" were often at war again in a very short time after such treaties had been signed, without being charged even with any breach of moral obligations; and why is this true?

Because, Mr. President, every community has an inalienable right to seek its own safety and happiness.

In these opinions of Mr. Randolph, Mr. THOMAS said the Convention of Virginia with great unanimity concurred. Chief Justice Marshall, Mr. Madison, Mr. Giles, Watkins Lee, Mr. Mercer, and numerous other distinguished men being present. The article authorising the people to meet in Convention was rejected, notwithstanding which, the people of Virginia by their delegates are now in Convention assembled to change or abolish their Constitution.

Mr. CHAMBERS inquired of Mr. THOMAS whether, if by virtue of the supreme power of the people, a law, which had been unconstitutionally passed by the Legislature, had been made valid by the acquiescence of the people, and their subsequent action under it, it might not again occur, that the Legislature might pass an act, calling a Convention, and provide therein that these officers should be eligible to seats there, which by the acquiescence of the people might also be rendered valid?

Mr. THOMAS replied that at a proper time he would discuss that point. He was ready.

Some desultory conversation followed—after which,

Mr. JENIFER moved to amend the amendment, by adding the words "or practising lawyers."

Mr. BRENT, of Baltimore city, asked the yeas and nays, which were ordered, and being taken, were as follows:

Affimative.—Messrs. Dent, Lee, Chambers of Kent, Mitchell, Wells, Kent, Bond, Brent of Charles, Merrick, Jenifer, Buchanan, Bell, Ridgely, John Dennis, Crisfield, Williams, Hicks, Goldsborough, Eccleston, Phelps, Jacobs, Gaither, Stephenson, Hardcastle, Fiery, Michael Newcomer, Davis, Weber, and Slicer—29.

Negative.—Messrs. Chapman, President, Morgan, Donaldson, Dorsey, Sellman, Weems, Dalrymple, Sollers, Welch, Sherwood of Talbot, Colston, Dashiell, Chambers of Cecil, McCullough, Miller, McLane, Bowie, Sprigg, Spencer, George, Dirickson, McMaster, Hearn, Thomas, Shriver, Biser, Sappington, McHenry, Magraw, Nelson, Carter, Thawley, Gwinn, Stewart of Baltimore city, Brent of Baltimore city, Presstman, Ware, John Newcomer, Kilgour, Anderson, Hollyday, Ege, Shower, and Cockey—44.

So the amendment to the amendment was rejected.

The question then recurred and was taken on the modified amendment of Mr. BRENT, of Baltimore city, and resulted as follows:

Affirmative—Messrs. Sellman, Welch, Ridgely, Sherwood of Talbot, Colston, Chambers of Cecil, McCullough, Miller, McLane, Bowie, Spencer, George, Thomas, Shriver, Biser, Sappington, Stephenson, Magraw, Nelson, Carter, Thawley, Hardcastle, Gwinn, Stewart of Baltimore city, Brent of Baltimore city, Presstman, Ware, Fiery, John Newcomer, Michael Newcomer, Anderson, Hollyday, Slicer, Ege, Shower, and Cockey—36.

Negative—Messrs. Chapman, President, Morgan, Dent, Lee, Chambers of Kent, Mitchell, Donaldson, Dorsey, Wells, Kent, Weems, Dalrymple, Bond, Sollers, Brent of Charles, Merrick, Jenifer, Buchanan, Bell, John Dennis, Crisfield, Dashiell, Williams, Hicks, Goldsborough, Eccleston, Phelps, Sprigg, Dirickson, McMaster, Hearn, Jacobs, Gaither, McHenry, Davis, Kilgour, and Weber—37.

So the amendment was rejected.

And the article was adopted.

The thirty-first article was then read and adopted as follows:

Art. 31. That a long continuance in the first executive departments of power or trust, is dangerous to liberty; a rotation, therefore, in those departments is one of the best securities of permanent freedom.

The thirty-second article was read as follows:

Art. 32. That no person ought to hold at the same time more than one office of profit, created by the Constitution or Laws of this State; nor ought any person in public trust to receive any present from any Foreign Prince, or State, or from the United States, or any of them, without the approbation of this State.

Mr. PARKE moved to amend by inserting after the word "that" in the second line, the following:

"Except as allowed elsewhere in this Constitution."

The amendment was rejected.

And the article was adopted.

The thirty-third article was read as follows:

Art. 33. That as it is the duty of every man to worship God in such manner as he thinks most acceptable to him, all persons are equally entitled to protection in their religious liberty; wherefore, no person ought by any law to be molested in his person or estate, on account of his religious persuasion or profession, or for his religious practice, unless under color of religion, any man shall disturb the good order, peace, or safety of the State, or shall infringe the laws of morality, or injure others in their natural, civil or religious rights; nor ought any person to be compelled to frequent or maintain or contribute, unless on contract to maintain any place of worship or any ministry.

Mr. RIDGELY moved to amend the said article, by inserting after the word "estate," in the fourth line, the following:

"Or suffer any civil or political incapacity."

Mr. RIDGELY explained his object. A fuller

explanation, made on the following day, will appear in the proceedings of that day.

Mr. WEEMS dissented from the views of Mr. RIDGELY. It was not required that persons should believe in the Christian Religion, but he thought that every individual should be required to declare his belief in a future state of rewards and punishments, and that, if they would not do so, they should not be allowed to testify.

After a few remarks from Messrs. DONALDSON and RIDGELY,

The Convention adjourned until to-morrow at eleven o'clock.

FRIDAY, February 7th, 1851.

The Convention met at eleven o'clock.

Prayer by the Rev. Mr. GRIFFITH.

The journal of yesterday was read and approved.

Mr. BISER enquired of the chair, whether it was in order to offer a resolution.

The PRESIDENT said it would be in order if there were no reports from committees.

Mr. JENIFER, chairman of committee No. 14, submitted the following

REPORT.

Article 1. There shall be a Board of Public Works, consisting of three commissioners, who shall be elected as herein provided, and to receive a salary to be fixed by law, but not liable to be increased or diminished during their continuance in office.

Art. 2. At the first general election of Delegates to the General Assembly, after the adoption of this Constitution, these commissioners, as aforesaid, one from the Eastern Shore, and two from the Western Shore, shall be elected by the qualified voters of the State, (the returns of which election shall be made and certified to the Governor,) one of whom shall hold his office for years, from the first Monday in the month of November ensuing his election, one for years, and one for years, from the same period; and at their first meeting, or as soon thereafter as practicable, they shall determine, by lot, which of their number shall hold his office for years respectively, and thereafter there shall be elected, as aforesaid, at each general election of Delegates, one commissioner for the term of years, to be taken in the proportion aforesaid from the Eastern and Western Shores, and in case of a vacancy in the office of either of the commissioners by death, resignation or otherwise, the Governor, by and with the advice and consent of the Senate, shall fill the same until the next general election.

Art. 3. The said commissioners shall exercise a diligent and faithful supervision on all public works in which the State may be interested as stockholder or creditor; shall represent the State in all meetings of Stockholders, and perform such other duties as may be prescribed by law.

Which was read, and

On motion of Mr. JENIFER,

Ordered to be printed and made the order of the day for to-morrow, the 8th inst.

Mr. TUCK rose to make an enquiry as to the motion which the gentleman, (Mr. Jenifer,) had made for the disposition of the report.

The PRESIDENT explained, that the report, in parliamentary phrase, had been made the order of the day, for to-morrow; that was to say, it would take its place in the order of business on the calendar, and would come up when previous orders had been disposed of.

THE HALL.

Mr. BISER offered the following order.

"*Ordered*, That a committee of three be appointed to make such suitable arrangements of the seats in the South-west section of the House, as would better promote the convenienee and comfort of the members occupying them."

Mr. SOLLERS offered an amendment, including in the Order, the part of the Hall in which he was seated.

Some difference of opinion as to the points of the compass, led to some amusing attempts to box it, after which,

Mr. SOLLERS withdrew his amendment,

And the order of Mr. BISER was adopted.

Thereupon, Messrs. BISER, TUCK and MCLANE were appointed the committee.

MR. BROWN, OF CARROLL.

Mr. COCKEY offered the following order, which was adopted:

Ordered, That it be entered upon the Journal, that Mr. BROWN is detained from his seat in this Convention, by indisposition.

THE HALL.

Mr. BRENT, of Baltimore city, presented the account of Messrs. Haywood, Bartlett & Co., for repairs and alterations made to the furnace, under the order of the Convention.

Which was read and referred to the committee on accounts.

Mr. RANDALL offered the following order:

Ordered, That the committee on Printing prepare, for the use of this Convention, a synopsis of the relative increase or dimunition of the slaves and free colored population of this State, as far as convenient from the various census.

Mr. R. explained that the enquiry contemplated by the order, was a very important one, and that the cost would be no more than the printing of one page of the journal, and an hour or two's labor on the part of the clerk of the committee on printing.

The order was adopted.

The PRESIDENT laid before the Convention the following communication from Jos. C. G. Kennedy, Esq., Superintendant of Census:

CENSUS OFFICE, Dep't. of Interior,
February 6, 1851.

Sir:—Enclosed I send you a corrected statement of the population of Frederick county, Md.

The statement previously sent was taken from the certificates of Assistant Marshals, which were in many instances incorrect.

I have the honor to be, sir, very respectfully, your obedient servant,

JOS. C. G. KENNEDY,
Sup't. of Census.

Hon. J. G. CHAPMAN., Pres. Con., Annapolis.

Which was read and referred to the committee on representation.

The PRESIDENT also laid before the Convention a report from the clerk of Worcester county court, relative to fees paid the Deputy Attorney General of said county, in obedience to the order of the Convention;

Which was read and referred to the committee appointed on the Attorney General and his Deputies.

On motion of Mr. BISER, the Convention proceeded to the orders of the day.

THE BILL OF RIGHTS.

The Convention resumed the consideration of the order of the day, being the report submitted by Mr. DORSEY on the 11th ult., as chairman of the committee on the declaration of rights.

RELIGIOUS TESTS.

The article under discussion yesterday, was the thirty-third article in the words following:

Art. 33. That as it is the duty of every man to worship God in such manner as he thinks most acceptable to him, all persons are equally entitled to protection in their religious liberty; wherefore, no person ought by any law to be molested in his person or estate, on account of his religious persuasion or profession, or for his religious practice, unless under color of religion, any man shall disturb the good order, peace, or safety of the State, or shall infringe the laws of morality, or injure others in their natural, civil or religious rights; nor ought any person to be compelled to frequent or maintain or contribute, unless on contract to maintain any place of worship or any ministry.

And the pending question was on the motion of Mr. RIDGELY, to amend said article by inserting after the word "estate," in the fourth line, the following:

"Or suffer any civil or political incapacity."

Mr. RIDGELY said, the amendment under consideration he had endeavored to explain on yesterday at the time of adjournment; he would now ask the indulgence of the house, to state more fully its purpose. It was intended for a two-fold object. The article is designed to secure to every citizen the rights of conscience, the privilege unrestrained of religious worship, and to protect him in person and estate from molestation, in the exercise of those rights; here the amendment comes in, and enlarges the language of the article, by providing also, that he shall "suffer no civil or political incapacity" on account of his religious opinion; the right to form and enjoy which, it is intended to secure to him. He had stated on yesterday, that his purpose was by this amendment, to relieve a large and highly respectable class of people who did not believe in a state of future rewards and punishments, from a civil disability, now resting upon them, and also to dispense with all tests for office, which imposed belief in future rewards and punishments as a qualification for such office. The latter purpose it was said was obviated by the 35th article. He thought not, but if he was mistaken in opinion, he was willing to modify his amendment to that extent, although, he could see no propriety for a distinct article on that subject, when the words "civil or political incapacity" would cover the entire ground. It had been argued yesterday by the gentleman from Anne Arundel, (Mr. Donaldson,) that there was no necessity for the first branch of the amendment, because, as the law now stood, any person was qualified as a witness, who believed in a Supreme Being, and moral accountability to that Being under pain of punishment in this, or a future world. Such he begged to say, was not the law of Maryland, however it may be elsewhere. In the courts of Maryland, the question usually propounded to a witness was, Do you believe in a future state of rewards and punishments? If the witness answered in the negative, he was rejected as incompetent on account of his religious belief. Such had been the practice in Baltimore county, in Frederick and in Washington, and as he understood from the honorable gentleman from Kent, (Mr. Chamhers,) in his district. He was not prepared to say, whether this was a proper exposition of the common law, from which the principle was derived; he spoke of it only as it existed in Maryland, as a serious, and oppressive civil, disability operating upon many conscientious and worthy citizens. He said he was aware that a much more enlightened application of the common law rule now prevailed in England, and in many of the States; that the rule had been much relaxed elsewhere; and the modern doctrine out of Maryland now was, that belief in a Supreme Being, and the certainty of punishment by that Being for human acts in this world or in the world to come, was all that was required, but he repeated that the old English doctrine of belief in rewards and punishments in a future world, still prevailed in some of the courts of the State. It was to relieve from this civil disability citizens who did not entertain such religious belief, that the amendment was designed. He would have employed the language, which was used in the New York Constitution, "that a man's religious opinions should not render him incompetent as a witness in any court of law or equity;" but he had doubts, whether incompetency as a witness was the only civil disability, which might arise on account of religious opinions, under the rule of law which obtained in some of the county courts. He did not know whether the question had ever been raised, or decided, whether disbelief in a state of future rewards and punishments, would disqualify a juror, but he could well imagine that the rule would equally apply to a juror, as to a witness; and would, under the existing exposition of the law, be a good ground of challenge. He had, therefore, used comprehensive language, so as to include every possible civil disability which might arise.

It was remarkable that whilst a witness was disqualified under such a religious belief, that as far as he had been able to learn no objection had ever been taken to jurors on such a ground, and in fact a juror, or a judge might be an infidel.

Mr. CHAMBERS desired to correct the gentleman from Baltimore county. So far as regards a judge, the Constitution provides a test of belief in a future state of rewards and punishments, for all civil officers, and also for Jews.

Mr. RIDGELY resumed. He was then in error in relation to a judge, but he could not be mistaken as regards a juror; and in fact a judge of loose morals, a mere nominal professor in such religious belief, may sit as the arbiter of life and death, whilst a citizen of undoubted character of the opposite faith, may be rejected as a witness. He desired to give to christians, the benefit of the exemption, which the Constitution interposes for the Jew. The Jew was protected in his religious belief—his conscience was respected. He could not swear upon a Testament, which he disbelieved; he could not imprecate Deity upon a religious belief which he rejected, and the Constitution was altered to take this civil disability from him. Citizens, many of whom believe in Christ and his religion, are now under civil disability, because in their conscience, they cannot believe in a future state of rewards and punishments. Why not give such the same constitutional religious protection? Will you deny to a Christian, what you have granted to the Israelite? The effect of such discrimation, will be to decide, that no man is a Christian, who rejects future rewards and punishments as a religious belief.

The gentleman from Queen Anne's, (Mr. Spencer,)—not now in his seat—had objected, that the amendment, if adopted, might admit ministers of the Gospel to seats in the Legislature. Such was no part of his purpose, he could not consent to change the existing constitutional provision in that respect. His object was to protect a man's religious opinions, and to remove a disability, which the law imposed upon them; not to relieve ministers of the gospel from their civil incapacity under the Constitution. To remove all doubt upon the subject, it was his intention, to move a further amendment to the article, in the following line, by striking out the word "*profession*," so that the word "*persuasion*" only would remain. It would then read, "or suffer any civil or political disability on account of his religious persuasion." There ought, it appeared to him, in this enlightened age, to be no hesitation, in conforming the practical truth of the liberty of conscience, proclaimed in the bill of rights, to its theory. He was not willing that any human tribunal should set up restraints upon the conscience of men. Such was the theory of the bill of rights, but judicial exposition of the law had denied to many citizens the free benefit of this Constitutional guaranty. He was, therefore, for putting this cherished prerogative beyond all doubt, by the amendment he had proposed. He was pained to hear the gentleman from Calvert, (Mr. Weems,) on yesterday, boldly assert in this House, that every man, who disbelieved in a future state of rewards and punishments, should be driven from the witness stand, as unworthy of belief. It was a harsh, and he would add, and an intolerant sentiment; and he was especially surprised that it should have been uttered by a representative from Calvert, the daughter of old St. Mary's, on whose plains the banner of religious and political liberty, was first unfurled, by the tolerant Catholic, Calvert. He would say to that gentleman, that hundreds of people entertaining that disbelief, were to be found in Baltimore city and county, who were among the most conscientious, respectable and worthy citizens of that community; men exemplary in every relation of life; of irreproachable character, and worthy of comparison with the best and purest of the orthodox faith. His attention had been called to this subject, in the early part of the session, by one of his constituents—a gentleman wherever known, universally respected for his high moral worth, and spotless honor; who had passed many years of his now advanced life, in the service of the State; had been for twenty years returned to the Legislature by the people of that county, and held many offices of public trust—and had gallantly served his country during the war of 1812. He did not design to open the subject of religion in this House, he hoped the debate would not take that direction, but he could not refrain from saying, that in his opinion, the oath of that man, who recognized the certainty of punishment in this world, for acts done in the body, was equally as reliable, if not more reliable, than the oath of one, who repudiated all punishment by Divine authority in this world, and deferred his fears of punishment for moral or religious guilt to another world; with the contemplation of which, men were little disposed to familiarize themselves. He confessed, that it required some nerve for a man to avow his disbelief in future rewards and punishments in view of the general opinions of the world, yet the very avowal of such an opinion commended itself to him as indicating at least an independence, which, in his judgment, went far to attest its perfect honesty and sincerity. The principle of this amendment is not new; it had been introduced into some of the old Constitutions, and he believed into all the new ones, although the languages employed might differ. The section under consideration without this amendment, whilst it proclaims the largest religious liberty and the right to worship according to the dictates of conscience, exposes in fact, as the price of that liberty, all who disbelieve in a future state of rewards and punishments, to the existing civil disabilities, which the courts have decided to attach to such disbelief, and which is utterly incompatible, with the freedom of conscience. He trusted that the House would not, in this nineteenth century, by rejecting this amendment, perpetuate so odious a religious discrimination upon the people of the State.

Mr. WEEMS said, that nothing could have been further from his intention, in the remarks he had submitted yesterday, than to denounce any sect or branch of the Christian church. He was no sectarian. Believing himself in the doctrines of Christianity, he had always entertained the opinion that every civil officer of the State of Maryland, when entering upon the discharge of his duties, had to subscribe to a belief in the Christian religion, or at least in a state of future rewards and punishments. And when the gentleman from Baltimore county, (Mr. Ridgely,) offered an amendment, the object of which, as he, (Mr. W.) conceived, was to depart from the good old system which had so long existed in our State, he felt it to be his duty to oppose it. He was also of opinion that it would open the door to the admission of ministers of the gospel into our legislative halls. He intended to vote against any such innovation.

He did not pretend that his opinions upon this or any other question were infallible, but, he believed, that if no restraints were to be imposed—if a man did not so far believe in the doctrines of Christianity, as to have some dread of eternal retribution—the result would be, that the better portion of mankind would be placed at the mercy of that corrupt and depraved portion, who would not hesitate to swear to any thing, however diabolical, which might subserve their own purposes of interest, malice, or revenge. He had declared yesterday, and he now repeated, that, in his opinion, all those persons who were so callous as to proclaim their disbelief in a state of future rewards and punishments, should be excluded from testifying. This was his judgment. He had declared it yesterday, and would acknowledge it any where. This, however, was a mere matter of opinion. He would go as far as any gentleman, to promote and secure religious toleration, but he thought that the adoption of this amendment would open wide the door for immorality, and lead to a total disregard of the solemn obligations of an oath. For these reasons he should vote against the amendment.

Mr. Donaldson suggested a contingency in which, under the amendment of the gentleman from Baltimore county, (Mr. Ridgely,) difficulty might arise; and said, he, (Mr. D.,) thought the amendment went beyond the gentleman's own meaning or intention. To avoid ambiguity, and make the amendment more explicit, he suggested to the mover to place it at the end of the section, though he, (Mr. D.,) was of opinion that it would come in better as an amendment to the thirty-sixth article.

Mr. Brent, of Baltimore city, offered an amendment, to come in at the end of the section, [and which as subsequently modified by Mr. Ridgely, read as follows:]

"*Provided*, That nothing herein shall be construed so as to qualify as witnesses, jurors or judges, or other officers under the constitution and laws of this State, any Atheist or other person who does not believe in any accountability to the Supreme Being for his acts."

Mr. Ridgely said that this amendment suited his views, and he would therefore accept it as a modification of his own.

And the question being on the modified amendment,

Messrs. McLane and Ridgely asked the yeas and nays, which were ordered.

Mr. McLane called for the reading of the article, as it would stand with the modified amendment.

And it was read.

Mr. Randall suggested that the gentleman from Baltimore county, (Mr. Ridgely,) had confined the application of his amendment to two classes, whereas there were hundreds of officers who were to take the oath. Did the gentleman intend that the amendment should apply to all, or only to a part?

Mr. Ridgely modified his amendment to meet this suggestion.

Mr. Chandler thought that the Convention should be very cautious in throwing off the moral restraints, which should guide and control men when about to give their testimony upon the witness stand. It was contended that every man had the right to worship God according to the dictates of his own conscience. This doctrine was believed by every branch of the christian church; and no law, no organic regulation should be introduced, the effect of which, would be to deprive men from the exercise of that sacred privilege. But there were classes of men who did not believe in God, nor worship him, nor acknowledge any responsibility to him. He was opposed to such men being called upon to give testimony in any case—because, there was no moral restraint to guide them in bearing testimony to the truth. It might be said, that such men might be thrown on their honor. Why not then throw all men upon their honor, and allow the most reckless and abandoned characters to come in and bear testimony without check, responsibility, or restraint of any kind?

The gentleman from Calvert, (Mr. Weems,) had objected to the amendment, because he thought that, under its provisions, a minister of the gospel might find his way into our legislative halls.

He, (Mr. C.,) opposed the amendment on no such ground. He did not think that, in the part which he had taken in the deliberations of this body, he had given much evidence of being a dangerous man; and, in taking a view of our fellow citizens generally, he thought that ministers of the gospel were found to be as quiet and peaceable as any other class.

He repeated, therefore, that he did not oppose the amendment on that ground; but he thought that ministers had equal rights in every respect, with other citizens. As to the expediency or propriety of their serving in the legislative halls, that was a question to be left to the judgment of their own consciences, and to the decision of the people at the ballot box.

He proceeded to refer, in language of high eulogy, to the patriotism, the fortitude, and the self-sacrificing devotion with which this class of our citizens, had stood forward in the front of the battle during our revolutionary struggle, and asked, whether we were now to be told that ministers of the gospel, were not entitled to equal privileges with ourselves, and that they were only to breath, as it were, by permission of the civil authorities?

Mr. McLane said:

He felt somewhat embarrassed as to the vote he might be called upon to give, not understanding precisely the effect of it. His own impression would be to leave things as they are. He thought we had gone on well, under the old bill of rights. He had not heard any thing to satisfy his mind, that any great necessity existed for material change.

The amendment, as he understood it, declared that nothing in the old bill of rights should be construed "to qualify" a certain class of persons as witnesses. If he voted against that amendment, in what position was he placed? The inference must be, that he meant them to be qualified. If he voted for the amendment, he knew not what inference might be drawn from the vote. It might be, to qualify others whom he did not think it right to qualify.

He would be glad if the gentleman would put his amendment into such a form as would enable him, (Mr. McL.,) to give a vote which should not convey any misapprehension as to his opinions. And he desired that the gentleman from Baltimore county, (Mr. Ridgely,) would state what the effect of the amendment was to be. He, (Mr. McL.,) did not desire to disturb the question. He did not wish to interfere with any man's rights of conscience. He was, himself, very independent in his opinions—trusting always that they were sound enough for his own welfare, and he desired to extend the same liberty to every other man. But when he was called upon to guard the rights of others, he was unwilling to cast aside any of the restraints, which, by the law of the land, or by a sound morality, might be imposed upon a man who was called upon to testify as to those rights. He wished that it should be done under all the responsibility which could be imposed by laws—human and Divine.

Mr. Buchanan, (to the President.) Is it in order to move to lay the amendment on the table?

The President. The motion is not in order.

Mr. Ridgely. My object is to place the law of the land, in relation to the religious opinions of witnesses beyond controversy. Mr. R. further explained his amendment, and recapitulated his reasons for its adoption. His object simply was, that no individual who believed in a Supreme Being, and acknowledged his accountability for his acts, should be disqualified as a witness in a court of justice.

Mr. McMaster, (to Mr. Ridgely.) Will the gentleman from Baltimore county allow me to ask him one question?

Mr. Ridgely. Certainly, sir.

Mr. McMaster. Does the amendment qualify persons who do not believe in a future state of rewards and punishments, to hold office and give testimony?

Mr. Ridgely. That is the object.

Mr. McMaster. Then I shall vote against it.

Mr. Merrick said, that he felt some reluctance to vote for this proposition. He felt disposed to leave the provision as it was; and it seemed to him that the legislature could hereafter regulate the competency of witnesses. It would be better that the Convention, should confine itself to doing that, which more appropriately belonged to it. He might be right or he might be wrong. He did not profess to know much about these things, and he would rather not touch them. We had gone on well under the law as it stood, and he thought it would be better to suffer the bill of rights to remain as it was. If there was a contradictory practise in the courts of the districts, let these matters be left to the supervision and regulation of the legislature.

Some conversation followed between Messrs. Ridgely and Merrick.

Mr. Presstman referred to his own experience as to the practice in the courts. He did not think that any other men than Atheists had been excluded from testifying—nor that any sect in this country, as a sect, had been excluded in any of our courts of justice for their particular opinions. If it were so, he should undoubtedly vote for the amendment of the gentleman from Baltimore county, (Mr. Ridgely.) He, [Mr. P.,] thought, however, that there was some misapprehension about the matter. A single individual, perhaps, might have gone further than his sect, and therefore, been excluded; but he did not think that the disqualification had been carried any further.

Mr. Fiery said he had no desire to protract this discussion; it was with some reluctance that he rose to respond to the appeal made to him by the gentleman from Baltimore city. He took occasion on yesterday to suggest to the gentleman from Anne Arundel, that an instance had occurred in Washington county, in which the testimony of a Universalist was refused, because he avowed his disbelief in the doctrine of future punishment. He now repeated the fact, upon the authority of men of undoubted veracity, who were witnesses of the whole transaction. The distinguished gentleman from Kent, (Mr. Chambers,) also states, that this has been the uniform practice in the judicial district in which he has the honor to preside.

Now, sir, said Mr. F., it is not my purpose to discuss the doctrines of this church, nor did he profess to be a disciple of their school; but from a long and an intimate acquaintance with this class of his constituents, he must say, that they rank among the most honest and respectable citizens of that county which he had the honor in part to represent. Whatever may be their religious opinions, Mr. F. declared in the presence of this Convention, that he would be willing to stake all he had in the world upon the oath of any Universalist within the circle of his acquaintance.

And yet, sir, (said Mr. F.) it has been avowed in this House, that such men are unfit to testify in our courts of justice. It has been gravely argued that those who do not believe in a future state of punishment, have no just sense of moral responsibility. He confessed he was suprised to hear such sentiments.

Moral responsibility! Why sir, a sense of moral responsibility, is as omnipresent as the Deity Himself. Where can we go to escape it; where is the asylum upon this vast globe, or in the boundless regions of infinite space, to which we can flee from the torments of a guilty conscience. If we travel beyond the pale of civilized man, even there the poor savage unconscious of the light of Divine Revelation, acknowledges his responsibility to that Great Being, whose voice is heard in the howling of every tempest, the rustling of every leaf, and the murmuring of every stream. It is a mistaken idea to suppose, that the Universalist has no just sense of moral obligation, because he is not actuated by a slavish fear of eternal punishment. For although he may not be frightened into a sense of duty, by the fear of Hell, of "gorgons, hydras, chimeras dire," may he not be governed in his conduct by that higher and nobler motive—a sense of duty to his fellow and his God?

It is an outrage upon the feelings of this highly respectable class of our fellow-citizens, that they should be driven from our courts of justice, whilst the most abandoned men in the community, are dragged forth from the gutters and sewers of our cities, to stand up as competent witnesses, merely because they profess to believe in a future state of rewards and punishments. For his part Mr. F. protested against any such invidious distinctions. He was opposed to any proscription on account of religious opinions. And whilst he had a high regard for the Christian religion, he was disposed to be liberal towards all denominations, with the confident expectation that the same charitable feeling will pervade this Convention.

We should be the last, sir, (continued Mr. F.) to encourage any thing like a feeling of intolerance, for if there be any spot upon this broad earth, which has been consecrated to the spirit of genuine freedom, it is here upon the soil of this glorious old Commonwealth, where the standard of religious liberty, was first reared in the Western world.

Mr. BISER said that in advocating this amendment, as it was his intention to do, he felt that he was treading upon delicate and dangerous ground. He knew that he was speaking in favor of a proposition which would subject those who sustained it to animadversion and criticism beyond these walls; and he desired, therefore, that the motives for the course he might take, should be understood so explicitly, as to leave no room for mis-apprehension or mis-statement.

He disclaimed any desire or intention to make invidious distinctions in matters of religion. No man here or elsewhere respected religious institutions, and religion itself, more sincerely than he did.

At an early period in the session of this Convention his attention had been called to this subject by a numerous, respectable and intelligent portion of his constituents. They desired that a provision might be inserted in the Constitution, dispensing with religious tests either as a qualification for office, or as rendering persons competent witnesses in our judicial tribunals. He had no particular acquaintance with the creed of the Universalists; (for, from that sect it was that the application to which he referred had been made,) but he took occasion, by means of letters to members of their society, and in other ways, to inform himself as to the precise character of their doctrines. The result of his investigation had led him to the conclusions which he would now state. They believed in a Supreme Being; they believed in rewards and punishments, either in this or a future world; they believed that no man would go unpunished for his misdeeds, and that the punishment must come at some time; but they did not believe in perpetual punishment.

Upon ascertaining these facts, he had looked into the Constitutions of the different States of the Union, and had found that in nearly all of them, religious tests were dispensed with. The fourth section of the declaration of rights of the State of California, had met his views more fully than any other. As an humble member of the committee of which the venerable gentleman from Anne Arundel, (Mr. Dorsey,) was Chairman, he, (Mr. B.,) had submitted that as his own proposition. But it had found no favor. A majority of the committee had voted it down. And it would be in the recollection of the Convention that he had yesterday offered the same section, but had been informed by the President, that it was not then in order.

He felt disposed to vote for the amendment of the gentleman from Baltimore county, (Mr. Ridgely,) though he, (Mr. B.,) must say, that he was better satisfied with the first amendment, than with this. He yielded, however, to the better judgment of the gentleman, who entertained the opinion that the pending proposition would cover the whole ground, and answer every object which he had in view. If that proposition should fail, he would then offer the amendment which he had yesterday indicated.

The gentleman from Washington county, (Mr. Fiery,) had, given his experience as to the operation of the existing provision in his own district. He, (Mr. B.,) could go even beyond the limits of his own county. He had seen a Justice of the Peace reject the testimony of a Universalist on account of his religious opinions, when the community at large would have taken the *word* of the witness in preference to the *oath* of the Justice of the Peace. And similar evidences of injustice and of wrong he had seen time and again. He declared himself the friend of religious toleration and equality, under all circumstances and in every aspect. He believed that more danger, far more danger, was to be apprehended from those who, under the false garb of religion, made themselves competent witnesses, than from that respectable and intelligent class of our citizens who had the independence to come forward and proclaim the doctrines in which they conscientiously believed. To use the language of the gentleman from Calvert, (Mr. Weems,) he, (Mr. B.,) was "no sectarian;" still he had his prepossessions. But it would be congenial to his own feelings, as it surely would be to the spirit of the age in which we lived, that all these harsh and invidious restraints should be blotted out from our statutes. He referred to the former history of the State, to show how little sympathy her people had manifested in that bigoted and intolerant spirit which would inflict punishment upon men for the mere sake of religious opinion, and expressed the hope that the Representatives here assembled, for high and solemn purposes, would follow the glorious example held up to them by our sister States, and place upon an equality all men who believed in the existence of a Supreme Being.

Mr. Merrick obtained the floor, but yielded for the moment to,

Mr. Tuck, who suggested to the gentleman from Baltimore county, (Mr. Ridgely,) that the more appropriate place for his amendment, would be the thirty-sixth article.

Mr. Ridgely intimating his intention to adhere to the amendment at this point.

Mr. Tuck proceeded to remark, that the question involved in it, was one of much delicacy and importance, and that any provision, in relation to it, which might be engrafted in the Constitution, should be drawn with great circumspection and care. It seemed to him, however, that the most appropriate place for the amendment, was the thirty-sixth article, and he would, therefore, move that the pending article be informally passed over, (as had been done with a previous article, on a former day,) in order that it might hereafter be taken up.

My own opinion, (continued Mr. T.) is that the true question to be put to a witness, should be whether, according to his religious faith, whatever that faith might be, he believed in a state of future rewards and punishments. Every man ought to be presumed to have some religion—a religion which teaches him to look up to a Divine Being—to a First Great Cause—and to acknowledge his belief in Him. And I say that every man who comes upon the stand, and avows his belief in a Divine Being—who acknowledges himself responsible for deeds done upon earth—ought to be allowed to testify, for, as has been well said, the most respectable men in the community, whose word, in any matter of business, would be taken in preference to the oath of some men, are turned from the witness stand, whilst the testimony of any one, however worthless, is admitted, if he will only say that he believes in a future state of rewards and punishments.

Mr. T. thought that the better way was to leave these questions, as to the competency of witnesses, to be regulated by the Legislature. But if this Convention is to pronounce its judgment of the question, he thought the appropriate place was the thirty-sixth article, and he therefore moved to lay aside this amendment for the present.

Mr. Merrick said, that gentlemen had argued the question as if this were a proposition to engraft on the Bill of Rights, a religious test. No such idea existed. On the contrary, the whole scope and object of the article was to proclaim the largest possible latitude to all persons as to their religious opinions. Gentlemen get up, talked about religious liberty, and invoked the genius of Maryland, as if some great outrage were in contemplation. Such arguments were totally inapplicable. The amendment actually proposed to restrict and limit the natural force and efficacy of the article as it stood in the Bill of Rights. Such, was the import of the language of the amendment, whatever its object might be. Whatever evils existed could be better left to the general action of the Legislature, than be specially provided for by the organic law. God forbid that it should be supposed that he would place restrictions upon any class of our citizens on account of their religious opinions. Nothing could be further from his wishes. All he desired was to bring the Convention to consider the nature of the work they had in hand, in order that they might confine themselves to it—and leave all matters proper for future deliberation and general legislation to the action of the Legislature. This was certainly one of these matters.

Mr. Chandler desired to say a few words in explanation. He held that every man had the right to worship God, according to the dictates of his own conscience. To whichsoever of the many religious creeds into which men have divided themselves, he may belong, he has this right. But the object of the remarks he had made was that those who do not worship God in any form, and who have no hope of future rewards, nor fear of future punishments to influence their conduct, ought not to be permitted to act as jurors. He did not concur in opinion with the gentleman from Frederick, that persons who acknowledge no moral responsibility are more to be relied on than those who do.

Mr. Harbine stated his intention to vote against the amendment, not because he was opposed to the fullest extent of religious toleration, or to the principle that every man should be permitted to exercise his own conscience in matters of religious faith, without forfeiting any of his rights; but for the reason assigned by the gentleman from Charles (Mr. Merrick) that it was not necessary to engraft such a provision in the organic law. It was a power within reach of the Legislature. It had been said by his colleague (Mr. Fiery) that it has been used for the purpose of preventing a respectable class of citizens from being sworn as witnesses. If he thought such a construction would be put on the provisions of the new Constitution, he would go in favor of the amendment. But the new Constitution will not admit of the same construction as the old one. He referred to the change which had been made in the thirty-third article of the Bill of Rights to shew that the construction put on that article in the old Constitution would not be applicable to the new one. The other reason for opposing the amendment had been better explained by the gentleman from Charles than he could explain it. It is within the competence of the Legislature to make such laws on the subject as may be necessary. It relates to a mere rule of evidence, which can be settled by law; and if we are to go on and insert in the Constitution provisions regulating all the rules of evidence in dispute, the instrument will be very greatly and unnecessarily encumbered, while its adoption by the people would be greatly endangered. Such a result, he had no doubt, was not desired by the members of this Convention and should be avoided, especially if it could be done (as in this instance) without the denial of a single right to the people. He would vote against the amendment.

The question on the amendment was then taken, and resulted as follows:

Affirmative—Messrs. Morgan, Hopewell, Bell, Welch, Ridgely, Eccleston, Chambers of Cecil, Miller, Bowie, McCubbin, Thomas, Shriver, Gaither, Biser, Sappington, Gwinn, Brent of Baltimore city, Fiery, John Newcomer, Michael Newcomer, Weber, Parke, Ege, Shower, and Cockey—25.

Negative—Messrs. Chapman, President, Lee, Chambers of Kent, Mitchell, Donaldson, Dorsey, Wells, Randall, Kent, Sellman, Weems, Dalrymple, Merrick, Buchanan, Chandler, Sherwood of Talbot, Colston, John Dennis, Crisfield, Dashiell, Williams, Phelps, McLane, Sprigg, George, McMaster, Fooks, Jacobs, Stephenson, McHenry, Nelson, Carter, Stewart of Caroline, Harbine, Davis, Anderson, Hollyday and Slicer—38.

So the amendment was rejected.

Mr. BISER now offered the following amendment which he had yesterday indicated his intention to offer:

"Strike out from the word 'liberty,' in the third line, to the end of said article, and insert in lieu thereof, the following:

"Therefore, no religious test shall be required as a qualification for any office of public trust, that the free exercise and enjoyment of religious profession and worship without discrimination or preference shall ever be allowed in this State, and that no person shall be rendered incompetent to be a witness on account of his opinion on matters of religious belief, but the liberty of conscience hereby secured, shall not be construed as to excuse acts of licentiousness, or to justify practices inconsistent with the peace or safety of this State."

Mr. DORSEY offered the following substitute, which (he said) he would be glad if the gentleman would accept;

Add at the end of the said article, the following:

"Nor shall any person be deemed incompetent as a witness or a juror, or disqualified to hold any office under the laws or Constitution of this State, except as hereinafter provided by the Constitution of this State, who believes in the existence of a God, and that under his dispensation such person will be held morally accountable for his acts, and be rewarded or punished therefor, either in this world or in the world to come."

Mr. BISER accepted this proposition as a modification of his own.

Mr. RANDALL called for the reading of the substitute, which was again read.

Mr. MORGAN said, he would not to be willing to admit ministers to hold seats in the House of Delegates or any political body. The amendment seemed to him to go further than the gentleman from Anne Arundel intended. He, (Mr. M.) said that he was willing to admit as witnesses all who believed in a future state of rewards and punishments,

Mr. DORSEY modified his substitute so as to insert the words "except as hereafter provided by the Constitution."

Mr. RANDALL said, it had been generally conceded, according to modern decisions, that a man is a competent witness who believes in a future state of rewards and punishments, whether here or hereafter. He thought the Convention generally acquiesced in this opinion. The question is, where should this provision be placed? It refers to the right of conscience, and he thought the proper place for it would be in the thirty-sixth article. It was cognate to the place where it is now introduced. The thirty-sixth article relates to the oath and to the manner in which it shall be administered. He was disposed to amend the thirty-sixth article so as to make it more specific. The thirty-third article refers to the duty of every man to worship God in such manner as he pleases. The thirty-sixth article relates to the qualification of a witness, to his rights as a citizen of the State. He thought, therefore, that the best course would be to reject the amendment now proposed, and to insert, in lieu of it, the substitute which he now offered to come in at the head of the thirty-sixth article.

Mr. DORSEY differed from his colleague. He thought the provision more appropriate where it was now proposed, than where his colleague wished to place it. It did not apply to official oaths but was a general provision that those who were presented as jurors or witnesses, should not be excluded if they entertained a belief in a state of future rewards and punishments, He thought, therefore, that the provision was better where it now is, and where it is entirely appropriate. He did not concur in the statement that the practice is settled in England, that none but one who believes in a future state of rewards and punishments is a competent witness. He did not so understand it. Some of the Judges in this State are of opinion, that a man must believe not in a state of future rewards and punishments, but in a future state of rewards and punisnments. The object of the amendment is to remove that difficulty. He had no particular wish to place it in this section, but he thought it the most appropriate place for it.

Mr. RANDALL thought the thirty-fifth article was a very proper place, as it relates to the test or qualification required on admission to any office of trust. The thirty-third article sets forth the duty of every man to worship God in such manner as he thinks most acceptable; and the thirty-sixth article prescribes the manner of administering an oath to witnesses. These are the three articles which relate to the subject, and it was his object to keep them distinct. He thought it more cognate in the thirty-sixth article. It would be more consistent if every thing relating to the oath were put in the thirty-sixth article. He would now offer his substitute.

Mr. RANDALL then offered the following as a substitute for the amendment of Mr. DORSEY:

"*Provided*, That an oath may be legally adminstered to any person who believes in a state of future rewards and punishments, by a Supreme Being, in this life or in the life to come."

Mr. R. said he did not think that this was the proper place for the amendment. But he would offer it again to the thirty-sixth section, and could then move to strike it from this article, if it should be adopted here.

Mr. MCHENRY said he should vote against both the substitute and the amendment, and he should be constrained to vote against every amendment which adds to the bulk of the bill of rights. When our ancestors framed the present bill of rights, they were in the midst of a severe struggle ; and the circumstances in which they acted, made them careful so to construct it, as that its great principles should be stamped on the minds of those for whose benefit it was made. But now, when the sovereignty of the people is universally acknowledged, this minute elaboration of their rights is unnecessary. It seemed to him that a few brief and comprehensive articles illustrating our position as contrasted with foreign governments, and as to our internal relations, and laying down the principles which should regulate the conduct of the officers of the government, who are the agents of the people, in their official capacities, should be deemed sufficient. When other matters are introduced, it should be in the Constitution itself—the consideration of which will come up hereafter. To insert these provisions in the bill of rights, he thought would be entirely superfluous.

Mr. CHAMBERS said, reluctant as he was to obtrude any remarks upon the House, he could not give a silent vote on this subject. One of the proposed amendments, opened a question of the utmost concern—a question not new to him.

It would be recollected that originally, no other than one professing to be a Christian, could hold office. Some thirty years since, while he was a member of the State Senate, a clamor was raised against the Constitution, because it excluded Jews. Under pretence of admitting Jews, the attempt was made to admit infidels. It failed, and after a long struggle, the Constitution was so far changed, as to admit a Jew to hold office, who would profess his belief in a future state of reward and punishments. It was no part of his purpose now to renew the discussions in which he, at that time, participated. A proposition is now before the chair, which he deeply regretted to see the learned gentleman from Anne Arundel, (Mr. Dorsey,) submit—the direct effect of which would be, to demolish the partition which divided the Christian and the unbeliever. Sir, (said Mr. C.) this is a Christian community—the Holy Bible, as the revelation of God's will and word, is a part of the law of the land, adopted by the common law of England, and with the other parts of that law, received by us. Our statutes enact penalties against *blasphemy*, and all our laws proceed on the assumption that they are to regulate a Christian people.

We afford protection to all : to those who have any religious worship, we secure the form of worship which their conscience or tastes approve; to those who have no sense of religion or of obligation to worship the Deity, we guarantee exemption from coercion. But in the privilege of holding office, the privilege of ruling in a Christian community, we have never allowed unbelievers to participate. Professed unbelievers were, in this respect, on the other side of the wall or partition, and while he had breath in his body, he would use it to protest against any and every attempt to prostrate this partition. There might be some few men deluded and most mistaken on this subject, in his poor judgment—there might be some amongst the acquaintances of the gentleman from Washington, (Mr. Fiery,) who might for aught he knew, punctually discharge the duties of some of the offices of the State, but it was better, far better, that those few persons should give place to others, than to demolish this time-honored doctrine, which, in some sort, sanctifies our system. Every general rule must, of necessity, produce an individual instance not absolutely within the expediency of the rule. Here the general rule was, that our State being a Christian community, our laws suited to the government and conduct of Christian men, Christian rulers, and none others, ought to rule such a land and people, and no power on earth could ever induce him to turn his back upon the faith of his forefathers. Educated in a Christian community, they came to this continent to establish a *Christian government* here, and as such it has hitherto been maintained.

Sir, said he, by God's blessing, I have been educated in the Christian faith—the faith of the Bible—by God's grace, I hope to live a Christian's life and die the Christian's death—by God's mercy I have been born in a Christian State and here have passed my three score years and more, and so sure as my soul lives, I will peril the loss of every temporal hope before I will act or aid in any declaration that Maryland withdraws herself from the Christian families of the earth.

Mr. RANDALL said this was a provision similar to that which prevailed in England, where there was an established church, and that country had not been unchristianized, as the gentleman from Kent, (Mr. Chambers,) apprehended we were about to be by adopting this amendment. As there seemed to be some doubt as to the law which governed this matter in England, he would read one or two authorities on the subject. He then read extracts from Greenleaf, Smith's leading cases, and other law writers, sustaining him in his position that a witness was competent who believed in the existence of a Supreme Being, who would punish perjury whether that punishment would be in this world or in the world to come. If the principle had not proved dangerous in England, he saw no reason to apprehend that its operation would be dangerous here. In almost all the States of the Union, and in England, laws have been passed enlarging the competency of witnesses and refusing the objection to their credibility. So that in adopting it here, we are only keeping up with the progressive spirit of the age.

Mr. DORSEY objected to the substitute as insufficient to carry out the purpose which the mover had in view. When all that it proposed to accomplish was effected, a great part of the ground would have to be gone over again. He thought the subject of religion should not be mixed up with legislation. We live in a country of universal toleration, and that principle ought to be carried out in relation to the competence of witnesses, and also with reference to persons who may be selected by the people as their agents, without attempting to restrict them in their choice. He should vote against the substitute.

The question was then stated to be on the substitute of Mr. RANDALL.

Mr. WARE asked the yeas and nays, which were ordered, and being taken, resulted as follows:

Affirmative—Messrs. Donaldson, Randall, Sellman, Bond, Brent of Charles, Merrick, Buchanan, Welch, Crisfield, Eccleston, Miller, Tuck, George, Dirickson, Sappington, Magraw, Gwinn, Fiery, Hollyday, Ege and Shower—21.

Negative—Messrs. Chapman, President, Morgan, Hopewell, Lee, Chambers of Kent, Mitchell, Dorsey, Wells, Weems, Dalrymple, Bell, Chandler, Ridgely, Sherwood of Talbot, Colston, John Dennis, Dashiell, Williams, Hicks, Phelps, Chambers of Cecil, McLane, Bowie, Sprigg, McCubbin, McMaster, Fooks, Shriver, Gaither, Biser, Stephenson, McHenry, Nelson, Carter, Stewart of Caroline, Hardcastle, Brent of Baltimore city, Ware, John Newcomer, Harbine, Michael Newcomer, Davis, Slicer, Parke and Cockey—45.

So the substitute was rejected.

The question then recurred on the amendment of Mr. DORSEY.

Mr. CHAMBERS asked the yeas and nays:

Which were ordered.

Mr. BOWIE called for the reading of the amendment;

Which was again read.

The question on the amendment was then taken, and resulted as follows:

Affirmative—Messrs. Morgan, Hopewell, Mitchell, Dorsey, Wells, Randall, Kent, Sellman, Bond, Sollers, Brent of Charles, Buchanan, Bell, Welch, Ridgely, Colston, Eccleston, Chambers, of Cecil, Miller, McLane, George, Dirickson, Thomas, Shriver, Gaither, Biser, Sappington, Magraw, Nelson, Gwinn, Brent of Baltimore city, Ware, Fiery, John Newcomer, Michael Newcomer, Weber, Hollyday, Slicer, Parke, Ege, Shower and Cockey—42.

Negative—Messrs. Chapman, President, Lee, Chambers of Kent, Donaldson, Weems, Dalrymple, Merrick, Chandler, Sherwood of Talbot, John Dennis, Crisfield, Dashiell, Williams, Hicks, Phelps, Bowie, Tuck, Sprigg, McCubbin, McMaster, Fooks, Stephenson, McHenry, Carter, Stewart of Caroline, Harbine and Davis—27.

So the amendment was adopted.

The question then recurring on the adoption of the thirty-third section, as amended,

Mr. JOHN NEWCOMER moved to amend it, by striking out the word "duty," and inserting the word "privilege."

Mr. N. said, it seemed to him that "privilege" was the better word.

The question was taken, and the amendment was rejected.

And then the article as amended, was adopted.

The thirty-fourth article was read as follows:

Art. 34. That every gift, sale or devise of lands, to any minister, public teacher, or preacher of the gospel, as such, or to any religious sect, order or denomination, or to or for the support, use or benefit of, or in trust for any minister, public teacher or preacher of the gospel, as such, or any religious sect, order or denomination, and every gift or sale of goods or chattels, to go in succession, or to take place after the death of the seller or donor, to or for such support, use, or benefit; and also every devise of goods or chattels to or for the support, use or benefit of any minister, public teacher or preacher of the gospel, as such, or any religious sect, order or denomination, without the leave of the legislature, shall be void; except always any sale, gift, lease, or devise of any quantity of land, not exceeding five acres for a church, meeting or other house of worship, and for a burying ground, which shall be improved, enjoyed, or used only for such purpose; or such sale, gift, lease or devise shall be void.

Mr. PHELPS moved to strike out "five" acres, and insert "thirty."

Mr. P. said, he had had some experience in these matters, and he thought it necessary to increase the number of acres which may be granted, "for a church, meeting, or other house of worship, and for a burying ground." It had of late years become very fashionable and proper to lay out cemeteries, and "five" acres was not sufficient for the purpose. He had been told that Greenwood Cemetery occupied one hundred acres.

Mr. MICHAEL NEWCOMER opposed the motion of Mr. PHELPS, and suggested that one acre of land in the county which he, [Mr. N.,] represented, was worth thirty in the county of Dorchester. (Laughter.)

Some conversation followed.

Mr. BLAKISTONE moved to strike out the whole section.

Mr. PHELPS said that scarcely a year passed, without an application being made to the Legislature, for an appropriation for the enlargement of grave yards. There was certainly nothing improper in such an object, and the spirit of beautifying and improving these grave yards, ought to be encouraged by every gentleman on this floor.

Mr. STEPHENSON called for a division on the motion of Mr. PHELPS, so that the question should be taken, first, on the motion to strike out.

A division was ordered.

The question having been taken, the Convention, by ayes 27, noes 32, refused to strike out.

The question then recurred on the motion of Mr. BLAKISTONE to strike out the thirty-fourth article.

Mr. STEPHENSON called the yeas and nays.

Mr. LEE offered the followed amendment.

"Insert after the word 'worship,' in the twelfth line, the words 'or parsonage.'"

The amendment was agreed to.

The question again recurred on the motion of Mr. BLAKISTONE.

Mr. PARKE moved to amend said article by inserting after the word "acres," in the twelfth line, these words, "or the value of ten thousand dollars."

Mr. BLAKISTONE said, by the advice of gentlemen around him, he would withdraw his amendment.

So the motion to strike out the thirty-fourth article was rejected.

The question then recurred on the amendment of Mr. PARKE.

Mr. DORSEY expressed his belief, that if this amendment should be adopted, it would be an abandonment of the principle of prohibiting gifts or devises of lands to churches, ministers of the gospel, &c., and would lead to the engrossing of a large portion of the real property of the State by the clergy. We have made a more liberal allowance of such gifts and devises, than was tolerated in the last bill of rights. If, as is proposed by the amendment offered, a devise of lands, worth ten thousand dollars, by one testator, to a priest or other minister of the gospel, is tolerated, by a succession of such devises, lands to an indefinite amount in quantity and value, may be placed in *mortmain*, in violation of the best interests of the State, and against every principle of public policy.

The question was then taken on the amendment of Mr. PARKE, and it was rejected.

Mr. JOHN NEWCOMER now renewed the motion of Mr. BLAKISTONE, to strike out the thirty-fourth article.

Mr. HARBINE said he hoped the motion of his colleague, (Mr. John Newcomer,) to strike out the entire section, would prevail. The section denied the rights of persons to give, sell or devise, and of religious corporations and clergymen as such, to receive of such persons, lands, goods, and chattels. He held that every owner of property had the right to make whatever disposition of it he pleased, provided such disposition, did not injure the community at large. He also held the right of corporations and individuals to receive, and purchase property subject to the same condition. These principles of right were so plain as to require no discussion. All institutions and persons should, as near as circumstances will possibly permit, be placed upon the same broad principles of right and equality. Any other doctrine at this era of progress, was behind and unworthy of the age. But is it in any manner probable, that the exercise of these rights, prohibited by this section, would operate to the injury of the people and institutions of this State? If there was, he (Mr. H.) was prepared to vote for the section. But he could see no possible danger. That age had long, long, since passed away. True, the old Constitution had a similar provision, but then it was formed when times were very different from what they are now. Religious prejudices then weighed powerfully; bigotry and superstition, the relic of ages gone by, still had their influences, hence it was natural that men of that day, should have great dread of the property monopolies of religious persons and corporations. Yet even in the old Bill of Rights, it was provided that by leave of the Legislature any amount of property might be given and sold, purchased and received, and when has the Legislature refused to grant such leave? Mr. H. said this question had arisen at a time he had not anticipated, and therefore he had not examined it fully, but he was prepared to say, that in very many, if not in the Constitutions of all the other States of this Union, no such provision as the section under consideration could be found. He would then ask that if not necessary in other States, was it necessary in ours? If the evils which this provision was intended to prevent did not exist in other States, whose organic law contained no clause of this character, would such evils exist among our people without it? Most certainly not. Why then encumber our Bill of Rights with such a provision? Why have such restrictions—why make such distinctions without causes that fully justify?

Mr. STEPHENSON asked the yeas and nays on the motion of Mr. JOHN NEWCOMER, which were ordered.

Mr. WEEMS expressed his intention to vote against the amendment. He had no objection to the Church holding as much property as migh- be desired. But as there are so many sects al; ready in existence, and others might arise, they might, in process of time, run all over the State, and possess themselves of all the most valuable land. And as he believed that all Church property was exempted from taxation, the effect might be to produce a great diminution of the revenue which the State derives from taxes. For this reason and not from any hostility to the Church, he should vote against the amendment.

The question was then taken, on the motion of Mr. JOHN NEWCOMER, to strike out the section, and the result was as follows:

Affirmative.—Messrs. Randall, Kent, John Dennis, Hicks, Eccleston, Phelps, Miller, McHenry, Ware, Jr., John Newcomer, Harbine and Shower—12.

Negative.—Messrs. Morgan, Hopewell, Lee, Chambers of Kent, Mitchell, Donaldson, Dorsey, Wells, Sellman, Weems, Dalrymple, Brent of Charles, Merrick, Buchanan, Bell, Welch, Ridgely, Sherwood of Talbot, Colston, Crisfield, Dashiell, Williams, McLane, Bowie, Tuck, Sprigg, McCubbin, George, Dirickson, McMaster, Fooks, Jacobs, Thomas, Shriver, Gaither, Biser, Sappington, Stephenson, Magraw, Nelson, Carter, Stewart of Caroline, Hardcastle, Gwinn, Presstman, Fiery, Michael Newcomer, Davis, Weber, Hollyday, Slicer, Parke, Ege and Cockey—55.

So the Convention decided that the section should not be stricken out.

The question then recurred and was taken on the adoption of the said thirty-fourth article, and having been decided in the affirmative, the article was adopted.

The thirty-fifth article was then read, and no amendment having been offered thereto, was adopted as follows:

Art. 35. That no other test or qualification ought to be required, or admission to any office of trust or profit, than such oath of support and fidelity to this State and the United States, and such oath of office as shall be directed by this Convention or the Legislature of this State.

The thirty-sixth article was read as follows:

Art. 36. That the mannner of administering an oath to any person ought to be such as those of the religious persuasion, profession or denomination of which such person is one, generally esteemed the most effectual confirmation by the attestation of the Divine Being, and that the people called Quakers, and those called Tunkers, and those called Menonists, and all others conscientiously scrupulous of taking an oath on any occasion, ought to be allowed to make their solemn affirmation in the manner that Quakers have been heretofore allowed to affirm, and to be of the same avail as an oath, in all such cases as the affirmation of Quakers hath been allowed and accepted within this State, instead of an oath. And on such affirmation, warrants to search for stolen goods, or the apprehension or commitment of offenders, ought to be granted, or security for the peace awarded, and Quakers, Tunkers, Menonists and such others ought also, on their solemn affirmation as aforesaid, to be admitted as witnesses in all criminal cases.

Mr. PARKE moved to amend it by striking out all after the word "being," in the fourth line, to the end of the said article, and inserting in lieu thereof the following:

"And all persons who are conscientiously scrupulous about taking an oath on any occasion, shall be allowed to make their solemn affirmation, in the manner heretofore practised, which shall be in all cases of the same avail as an oath.

Mr. BOWIE said he understood that the religious creeds of some sects interdicted them from taking an oath. These had therefore been permitted to substitute their solemn affirmation. Formerly, every man was obliged to take an oath. Any man who may choose to say that he is connected with a certain sect, and that his scruples of conscience forbid him from taking an oath, may now escape. It was likely, in his opinion, to open the door to great frauds.

Mr. DONALDSON stated that on reference to the old Constitution, it would be found that all the different sects were enumerated. Quakers, Tunkers or Menonists, are all embraced in the old bill of rights.

Mr. PARKE said that he did not wish to keep this array of names in the bill of rights. He desired to embrace all who were conscientiously scruplous on the subject of taking an oath. Besides this, he saw no necessity for retaining the last part of the article. That part of the article seemed to him to be entirely unnecessary. His amendment, if properly understood would be found to contain all that the previous article had contained, and it would have this advantage, that it greatly simplified the former provision.

The question was then taken, and, by ayes 24, noes 32, the amendment was rejected.

The question then recurred on the adoption of the said thirty-sixth article.

Mr. CHAMBERS, of Kent, moved to amend the said article by striking out all after the word "oath," in the tenth line, to the end thereof.

The question was taken and the amendment was agreed to.

Mr. RANDALL moved to amend the said article by adding at the end thereof, the following:

"And that an oath may be legally administered to any person who believes in a state of future rewards and punishments by a Supreme Being in this life or in the life to come."

The PRESIDENT, *pro tem.*, intimated his opinion that the amendment having been once voted down, was not in order.

Some conversation followed on the point of order, when,

The PRESIDENT, *pro tem.*, said he would put the question.

After some further conversation,

The question was taken and the amendment of Mr. RANDALL was rejected.

And then the article, as amended, was adopted.

The thirty-seventh article was read as follows:

Art. 37. That the city of Annapolis ought to have all its rights, privileges and benefits, agreeable to its Charter and the Acts of Assembly confirming and regulating the same; subject, nevertheless, to such alterations as have been made by the Legislature or as may be made by this Convention or any future Legislature.

Mr. BISER moved to strike out the said article.

A motion was made that the Convention adjourn.

The convention refused to adjourn.

After some conversation,

The question was taken on the motion of Mr. BISER;

And the amendment was rejected.

The thirty-seventh article was then adopted.

The thirty-eighth, thirty-ninth, and fortieth articles of the report were then read, and no amendment having been offered thereto, were adopted as follows:

Art. 38. That the liberty of the press ought to be inviolably preserved.

Art. 39. That monopolies are odious, contrary to the spirit of a free government and the principles of commerce, and ought not to be suffered.

Art. 40. That no title of nobility or hereditary honors, ought to be granted in this State.

The forty-first article was read as follows:

Art. 41. That this declaration of rights, or the form of government to be established by this Convention, or any part of either of them, ought not to be altered, changed or abolished, but in such manner as this Convention shall prescribe and direct.

Mr. THOMAS gave notice that he should make no objection to the adoption of this article, but should vote for it, with a view of enabling him at the proper time to move a reconsideration of the vote of the Convention thereon.

Mr. PRESSTMAN gave notice that it was his intention to have voted with a similar design, if the gentleman from Frederick, (Mr. Thomas,) had not indicated his purpose to do so.

The question was then taken,

And by ayes 43, noes 14, the forty-first article was adopted.

Mr. DAVIS offered the following amendment:

Art. 42. The legislature shall encourage by all suitable means, associations for the diffusion of knowledge and virtue, for the promotion of literature, the arts and sciences, agriculture, commerce and manufactures and for the general melioration of the wants and conditions of the people.

Mr. PRESSTMAN moved to amend the amendment, by striking out the word "suitable," and inserting the word "Constitutional."

After some conversation,

Mr. PRESSTMAN withdrew his amendment.

The question then recurred on the amendment of Mr. DAVIS.

And pending the question:

The Convention adjourned, until to-morrow morning at 11 o'clock.

SATURDAY, February 8th, 1851.

The PRESIDENT, *pro tem.* (Mr. Tuck, of Prince George's,) called the Convention to order at eleven o'clock.

Prayer was made by the Rev. Mr. GRIFFITH.

The roll was called.

The journal of yesterday was read and approved.

Mr. JOHN NEWCOMER said, that if there was no other business before the Convention, he would move that the Convention proceed to the orders of the day.

HOWARD DISTRICT.

Mr. DORSEY, chairman of the select committee respecting the formation of New Counties, submitted the following report:

The select committee appointed to consider and report respecting the formation of new counties in this State, beg leave to make the following report, and recommend its adoption as an article of the Constitution about to be formed.

THOMAS B. DORSEY, Chairman.

Article. That part of Anne Arundel county called Howard District, is hereby erected into a new county to be called Howard county; the inhabitants whereof shall have, hold and enjoy all such rights and privileges as are held and enjoyed by the inhabitants of the other counties in this State; and its civil and municipal officers at the time of the ratification of this Constitution shall continue in office until their successors shall have been elected or appointed, and shall have qualified as such; and all rights, powers and obligations incident to Howard District of Anne Arundel county, shall attach to Howard county.

The report having been read,

Mr. DORSEY moved that it be printed, and

Made the order of the day for Wednesday next.

Mr. SPENCER, (to Mr. Dorsey.) Is it likely that any objection will be made to the report, or that it will lead to debate?

Mr. DORSEY said, he could not hear the gentleman from Queen Anne's, (Mr. Spencer.)

Mr. SPENCER repeated his question.

Mr. DORSEY said, he had no information which would enable him to answer the enquiry.

Mr. SPENCER suggested that if debate was not likely to arise, it would be better that the Convention should act upon the report at once. Were there, he enquired, any other gentlemen here from Anne Arundel, who could answer the question?

Mr. SELLMAN speaking from the frontier seats was understood to say, that, so far as his knowledge extended, the report met with the approbation of the people of Anne Arundel county proper. He had never heard any objection to the proposition.

Mr. PHELPS said, the question involved in the report, was an important one, and that he wished it postponed until after the representation question should have been settled.

The question was then taken on the motion of Mr. DORSEY; and

Was decided in the affirmative—ayes 44, noes 8.

So the report was ordered to be printed, and

Was made the special order of the day for Wednesday next.

THE LEGISLATIVE DEPARTMENT.

Mr. PHELPS gave notice that he would at the proper time, offer the following amendments to the report of the committee on the legislative department of the government:

Strike out sections second, seventeenth and eighteenth, and insert the following sections, as numbered, in their stead; also, insert sections thirty-seventh, thirty-eighth, thirty-ninth, and fortieth, to come in between the thirty-sixth and thirty-seventh sections of the report.

Sec. 2nd. The Senators shall be elected by the qualified voters of this State, for the term of four years, and the delegates in like manner, for the term of two years from the day of the general election; and the regular session of the General Assembly shall be biennial.

Sec. 17th. Bills for raising revenue or levying taxes, shall originate in the House of Delegates, but the Senate may alter, amend or reject them as other bills. All other bills may originate in either House, and be amended, altered or rejected by the other, but no bill shall become a law without being read upon three several days in each House, only in cases of great urgency, two-thirds of the House in which the bill shall be pending, may dispense with the rule herein provided for the reading of the bill upon three several days.

Sec. 18*th*. No bill shall become a law unless it receive the concurrent vote of a majority of the members present in both Houses.

Sec. 37*th*. Any citizen of this State who shall after the adoption of this Constitution fight a duel with deadly weapon, or send, or accept a challenge to fight a duel with deadly weapons, either in or out of the State, or who shall act as second, or knowingly aid or assist in any manner those thus offending, shall be deprived of holding any office of trust or profit under this State.

Sec. 38*th*. No new lottery grant shall be authorized by the Legislature of this State.

Sec. 39*th*. It shall be the duty of the legislature to pass such laws as may be necessary and proper to decide differences by arbitration when the parties may elect that method of trial.

Sec. 40*th*. All property both real and personal, of the wife owned or claimed by her before marriage, and that acquired by gift, devise or descent, shall be her separate property, and laws shall be passed by the legislature, more clearly defining the rights of the wife in relation to her separate property.

Which was read.

Mr. P. said he gave this notice now, in order that the Convention might have an opportunity to examine the amendment.

CHURCHES AND CHURCH GOVERNMENT.

Mr. Buchanan enquired of the chair, whether there was any business before the Convention?

The President, *pro tem*, answered in the negative.

Mr. Buchanan said, he had received a petition from a very respectable citizen of the city of Baltimore. He, (Mr. B.,) declared that he did not know exactly what to do with it. It seemed to him that the petition was respectful. The petition was entitled to be heard, and he, (Mr. B.,) could see no reason why he should not be heard. He did not know precisely to what committee it should be referred. [Mr. B. explained the petition. It came from James P. Kennedy, and related to the building of churches and to church government.]

Mr. B. moved its reference to committee No. 14—(not knowing, he said, any other committee to which it more appropriately belonged.)

Mr. Mitchell called for the reading of the petition.

The petition was read and created much amusement.

The propriety of the reference of the paper, gave rise to some desultory discussion, in which Messrs. Jenifer, Buchanan, Thomas and Sollers took part, when

Mr. Jenifer moved that the petition be laid on the table.

The question was taken, and, by ayes 23, noes 25, the Convention determined that the petition should not be laid on the table.

And then the petition was referred to committee No. 14.

PERSONAL EXPLANATION.

Mr. Dorsey rose and said:

It is with extreme reluctance that, in consequence of the remarks made by the gentleman from Baltimore, in which I am held up before this body, and intended so to be held up, I presume, before the public, as guilty of the grossest dereliction of official duty as one of the Judges of the Court of Appeals, I rise to communicate a few facts within my own knowledge; but which are unknown, for the most part to the members of this Convention. I should, in immediate response to the gentleman from Baltimore, have given the explanation I now offer, but I did hope that he would have made such inquiries above stairs, (where the means of information were abundant,) as would have enabled him to ascertain the correctness of the information received by him from his informant; and in that event, I expected from him such explanatory statements as would have rendered any remarks from me on this subject, wholly unnecessary. But in this expectation I have been, to my regret, disappointed.

The impressions made upon this body by the statements of the gentleman, were, I have no doubt, not only that the Court of Appeals had been adjourning day after day from the want of a constitutional quorum for the transaction of its business, to the great hindrance and delay of the administration of justice; and that I had greatly contributed to produce this inconvenience by wholly absenting myself from the Court and having no participation in its labors; or paying any attention to its progress with the business before it. Sir, this could not have been the meaning of the gentleman, for he well knows that since this Convention has been assembled, he argued before me, as one of the Court, with two other counsel, a case of no inconsiderable length, difficulty and importance; that I participated in its decision, and drew the opinion of the Court in the case which has been for sometime filed. And the informant of the gentleman on whose statement his remarks were predicated, since the Christmas recess, argued also a case before me, in which I believe his speech consumed an entire day.

I understood the gentleman to say, that I am not here as a representative of the sovereign people of the State; but was only selected by a portion of the people of Anne Arundel county. This assertion proves rather too much. If true, it shows that the people of the State have no representatives in this body; although we are sitting here preparing a Constitution for their adoption and government. It proves that our Revolutionary ancestors in 1776, who framed our Constitution at that period, were not the delegates of the people of the State; that no Constitution perhaps of any State in the Union was framed by the representatives of the sovereign people. Such a doctrine has nothing to sustain it. Each and all of us in this body are as much the representatives of the people of the State as if elected by a general ticket or popular vote of the whole people of Maryland. My authority to withdraw from the Bench of the Court of Appeals to serve as a member of this body, I believe to be as fully established, by the passage of the Act of Assembly, its adoption by the people, their subsequent elections and our Convention thereunder, as if this Convention had been assembled after the most successful, forcible, and revolutionary struggle.

But when I came here I made up my mind that my attendance on the Convention should not prevent there being a constitutional quorum for the dispatch of business in the Court of Appeals. Of that determination I notified the Court, and requested that I might be sent for when an emergency required it. And day after day, and longer than there was any occasion for it, I visited the Court, and from time to time sat therein when it was necessary for me to do so. I have no knowledge of the Court being adjournnd for want of a constitutional quorum; nor do I believe that any such adjournment ever took place. Of my determination in relation to the Court of Appeals I made no communication to my friend from Kent; being apprehensive if I did so, that he might have offered to alternate with me. I was unwilling that he should have done so; being of opinion that his services here were more valuable and important to the business of this Convention than mine were. On one occasion, and only one, when I visited the Court of Appeals at about its hour of meeting, I found that it had adjourned a few minutes before; and fearing, that my absence had caused its adjournment, I expressed my regret and asked why I had not been sent for according to my request; when I was informed that the court had adjourned, not because it was not in a condition to proceed with its business; but because counsel had asked the indulgence, not being prepared to argue the case which had been called up for argument.

Mr. Brent, of Baltimore city, said that he regarded the statement of the gentleman from Anne Arundel County as calculated to impeach the statement made by him the other day.

Mr. Dorsey explained that nothing was further from his intention, as he was sure the gentleman from Baltimore fully believed his statement to be correct.

Mr. Brent resumed, that he did not suppose that the gentleman meant to charge him, with intentional mistatement. But until he was satisfied he must believe and reaffirm that the business of the Court of Appeals had been delayed for want of a quorum. He doubted whether Mr. Dorsey's explanation would bear investigation. The solution of the matter I suppose to be this, that as the cases were reached in *their order*, there was no quorum, because one of the three judges in attendance, was disabled from sitting, owing to his having decided the case below. In that condition of things there was no Court to try the cases as the counsel came to argue them under the rules of Court, but the Court looking ahead on the docket and seeing a remote case in which the three judges could sit, would agree to take up that case out of its order, but the counsel being of course unprepared to argue that case, the Court was compelled to adjourn over without any fault of counsel as intimated by Mr. Dorsey, but really because there was no quorum—so that Mr. B. regarded his statement as correct, and that no such adjournment would have taken place but for the presence of two of the Judges in this Convention.

In making these remarks previously, he wished every one to observe that he had only done so in *answer* to Mr. Chambers' assertion that there had been no delay, and he Mr. B. wished it to be understood that there was no blame on the judges who were out of the Convention. He had written to his informant, and if he had done injustice he would publicly acknowledge it.

The President, *pro tem.*, announced the orders of the day.

THE BILL OF RIGHTS.

The Convention proceeded to the consideration of the Report of the Committee on the Declaration of Rights.

The pending question was on the amendment offered yesterday by Mr. Davis.

Mr. Davis was entitled to the floor.

Mr. Crisfield suggested that, as the gentleman from Montgomery (Mr. Davis) was indisposed, and could not, therefore, proceed with his remarks to-day, the Convention should take up some other business.

Mr. Sollers alluded to the fact that a committee had been appointed to arrange the seats in a certain quarter of the hall, and said, that as time would be required for the purpose, he would move that the Convention adjourn until twelve o'clock on Monday next.

But Mr. S. waived the motion to enable

Mr. George to give notice of his intention to offer the following articles as amendments to the Bill of Rights:

Art. 43. The amount of debts hereafter contracted by the Legislature, shall never exceed one hundred thousand dollars, except for the defence of the State; unless such debt shall be authorized by a law for the collection of an annual tax or taxes, sufficient to pay the interest on such debt as falls due, and also to discharge the principal of such debt, within fifteen years from the time of contracting the same, and the taxes laid for the purpose shall never be repealed or applied to any other object, till the said debt and the interest thereon shall be fully discharged.

Art. 44. The assent of two-thirds of the members elected to each branch of the Legislature, shall be requisite to every bill appropriating the public money, or pledging the public faith, for local or private purposes; and the Legislature shall not have the power to make appropriations, loans or subscriptions to any work of internal Improvement.

The question then recurred and was taken on the motion of Mr. Sollers, and, having been decided in the affirmative,

The Convention adjourned until Monday morning at twelve o'clock.

MONDAY, February 10th, 1851.

The Convention met at twelve o'clock, in pursuance of the order of Saturday last.

Prayer was made by Rev. Mr. Grauff.

The journal of Saturday was read and approved.

MR. CHANDLER, OF BALTIMORE COUNTY.

On motion of Mr. BUCHANAN, it was ordered that it be entered on the journal, that H. J. Chandler, Esq., is detained from his seat in the Convention, because of sickness in his family.

The PRESIDENT, *pro tem.*, [Mr. TUCK, of Prince George's,] called for reports from committees.

No reports were made.

Motions, resolutions, and notices were also called for.

There being no other business before the Convention,

The PRESIDENT, *pro tem.*, announced the unfinished business of Saturday, being

THE BILL OF RIGHTS.

The Convention resumed the consideration of the order of the day, being the report submitted by Mr. DORSEY, on the 11th ult., as chairman of the committee on the declaration of rights.

The pending question was on the following amendment of Mr. DAVIS:

Insert as an additional article the following:

"The Legislature shall encourage by all suitable means, associations for the diffusion of knowledge and virtue, for the promotion of literature, the arts and sciences, agriculture, commerce and manufactures, and for the general melioration of the wants and conditions of the people."

Mr. DAVIS was entitled to the floor. He said:

Mr. President: I beg leave to return my acknowledgments to the Convention, for their kind consideration in not forcing me into this debate on Saturday, when I was physically unequal to the task. Although still unwell, I cannot presume longer on the indulgence of this body—but will endeavor to requite its kindness by being as brief as possible.

Never, Mr. President, have I risen undermore embarrassment, than on the present occasion. An embarrassment produced, first by the variety and importance of the questions which I have had the honor to present—and secondly by my utter inability to do any thing like justice to them. I must then claim the patient indulgence of this body, while I present a few facts and considerations in favor of the adoption of the article I have offered.

We are assembled here, Mr. President, to form a new Constitution—the foundation of a Government. What is a Government? It is the head—the common protector and defender of the State. For its support, we surrender a portion of our personal interest, and of our individual rights.

If I am correct, in thus briefly defining the true meaning of Government, that it is the common head and protector of all classes and all interests in the State—and that it is supported by all classes and all interests, I cannot be wrong in claiming, that it shall be impartially administered, as far as possible, for the benefit of all classes and all interests.

Well, sir, what do we find by looking into the past history of the State? Why nothing but partial legislation—profuse, wasteful, prodigal, legislation, for some interests, while others are almost, if not totally neglected—and in some instances an indisposition even to recognize that there is such an interest in the commonwealth. To prove that I am correct, I shall be obliged to refer to past legislation, and this will bring me in contact with the representative from the city of Baltimore, whose opposition I regret to find I have already encountered.

In referring to the past legislation of the State, and tracing, as the history of the times, leads me at almost every turn to the city of Baltimore, I beg distinctly to disclaim any feeling of hostility to that city. My associations and my connections are there—and what little of this world's goods I possess, is mainly dependent for its value upon her prosperity. And, sir, as a Montgomerian, I claim that Baltimore is largely indebted to her for her present rapidly growing prosperity. Proud as she is, and ought to be, of her monuments, whenever future generations shall decide upon her greatest and noblest monument, her *rail road*, its founder and projector will be found to be a *Montgomerian*, and posterity will ackowledge him to have been one of the greatest benefactors of your city. If I go into some of her churches, adorned with skill and ornament and convenience, and enquire into its history, I am told, this is the munificence of a *Montgomerian.* If I inspect some of your noblest warehouses, in Market, in Hanover and in German streets, I am told, they are the property of a *Montgomerian.* If I stroll to the *Park*, there to admire her stately mansions, I am told, these, that and yonder, are all owned and built by a *Montgomerian.* If I go further west, and stop to look at a large excavation—with foundation walls thick and heavy, and with strength sufficient for a massive superstructure, I am told, here too, the munificence of a *Montgomerian* is conspicuous—and if I return to the city, and begin to count your houses—to inspect the solid material from which they are constructed, I am told this too gives evidence of the skill, the industry and fidelity of a *Montgomerian.* It is impossible then, with recollections like these—with associations and ties of interest—for me to entertain any other feeling, than that of respect, for her people, and admiration at her growth, her enterprise and her intelligence.

But while I cheerfully accord all this to Baltimore, she has a quality which I feel bound to say I cannot admire. I mean her commercial selfishness—nay, sir, I may add, her political selfishness. When I see her representatives here, seeking for Baltimore, *political*, as well as commercial aggrandizement, at the expense of the rest of the State, I should be false to my duty, as an humble representative from one of the counties, if I did not enter against it my deliberate protest.

Well, Mr. President, what do we find. I have proposed that we shall insert an article in the *bill of rights*, to encourage associations, whose object is to advance and promote the various interests in all classes, and of all parts of the State. I do not propose even to exclude associations which heretofore have been so liberally patronized. I do not wish, however, to be understood as advocating a profuse expenditure of public money for any of those objects—far from it. At a proper time I shall vote for a limit upon the powers of the Legislature over State credit. But I do advocate by the Legislature a *recognition* of any and every interest which contributes to make up the whole body politic, and to sustain and support the Government. Nay, farther; I advocate such an employment of the means of the State, as in the judgment of the Legislature may be necescary to aid useful associations, whose object and tendency is to make us more intelligent, more virtuous, more useful and happier, and better citizens. That some of the objects enumerated in the article proposed have been well patronized by the State, is abundantly proved by an examination of the past acts of Assembly. *Literature*, for example, including law and medicine, has received a very large share of patronage from the State, while associations for the general diffusion of knowledge and virtue among the people have been neglected. It may perhaps be new to some to learn, that the State has endowed a professorship of law to the tune of $14,200.

And here, Mr. President, permit me to remark, that if I could believe, that human nature were as weak as has been argued upon this floor, I possibly might be induced to vote to exclude a much larger class, from all future Conventions, than has been proposed. But I believe no such thing. And while I admit the weakness and frailty of human nature, unaided by reason, by judgment, and by conscience. I must know that these faculties are given to us to check and control the waywardness of our nature. I can then well understand, where reason and judgment are directed by sound principles, how man can act superior to his nature; and from a sense of justice, and lofty motives of patriotism, rise superior even to his own personal interest or partizan feeling.

But to return from this digression.

For a professorship of law, - -	$14,200
Of medicine, for chemical apparatus -	6,500
For arts and sciences, - - - -	2,000
For infirmary, - - - - - -	3,800

Besides this the State has granted to the same University, located in the city of Baltimore, a lottery for - - - - - - $100,000

And a loan of State bonds to the amount of - - - - - - - - 30,000

And at a period of her heaviest financial depression, relinquished an annual interest of about $1500 upon this loan; which is equivalent to an annual donation of that amount.

Why the law school has never gone into operation, I leave the gentlemen of the bar from the city to answer—it is certainly no fault of the legislature.

Besides this, State bonds to the amount of $97,-947 30, have been issued for the Penitentiary, also located in Baltimore, and I apprehend chiefly for the accommodation of her citizens. In addition to this, $3,000 have been appropriated by the State to build the greatest ornament to your city—the lofty column raised to perpetuate the memory of the father of his country.

Against all this, I utter not one word of complaint.

Again, sir; the inspection laws. For whose benefit are they? For the farmers or for the merchant; and who pays the cost? If I buy and sell in the country, as farmers and millers sometimes do, I have to depend upon my own judgment; but if I take a load of flour to Baltimore before I can sell it, I must pay for its inspection; and when I buy plaster or guano in return I find inspection charged upon my bill. So all this handsome revenue from the city of Baltimore, which entitles her to so much credit for patriotism and distinction upon the books of the Treasury, as had been claimed, will be found to have been wrung from the hard earnings of the farmer, to save your citizens the trouble of exercising a little judgment for themselves.

From an examination of the Treasurer's report, it appears that the State received—

For wood hucksters, paid by the seller, ...	873 00
Hay scales, paid by the seller, .	854 95
Live stock scales, paid by the seller,	15,018 58
And from the tobacco inspection, clear nett revenue, . .	30,217 00

This latter fund is exclusively devoted to building up large warehouses to adorn and add to the wealth of your city. The inspection of one dollar per hogshead has been removed to gull the planters, but the *outage* of $1.25 from which this fund is derived, is retained and constitutes a charge against the price of the article, when the planter goes to sell.

Against the injustice and practical working of these inspection laws I do object. Again, sir. We come to *commerce: Commerce*, is defined by lexicographers, to be the exchange of commodities or the connection of one section of country with another. And how shall I begin to count the State's patronage and encouragement to this branch of my article? Neither by hundreds or by thousands, or by tens of thousands or hundreds of thousands—but by millions.

For the encouragement of commerce the little State of Maryland has gone in debt $15,424,-381 46.

For the encouragement of agriculture, $1,-000,000.

Except an appropriation of $500, ($6,000 00 less than was given to the Medical University as has been shown.) to purchase an apparatus for the State Chemist, and his salary since his appointment, only three years ago up to last year, of but $1,500.

What a miserable, pitiful, niggardly exhibit is here presented against *agriculture*—the great leading interest of the State—the interest which has built up your city, freighted your ships, and sustains your lines of internal commerce. And how soon is this pitiful encouragement to agriculture swallowed up for the benefit of commerce? Let the tax bills from Worcester to Allegany answer. They furnish an array of living witnesses, a mountain of certificates, which all the eloquence and ingenuity of her bar, distinguished as it is, cannot weaken or obliterate.

Again, *Manufactures*, I also include in my objects of encouragement—not because it has been neglected, but because in framing a new government for the State, I do wish to preserve equal and impartial justice to each and every interest. The liberal charters, and in some instances direct subscriptions to stock, ($10,000 to the Union Manufactory Company,) will show the paternal regard, the State has had for this important branch of industry. *Mechanics* is so intimately connected with manufactures that it is impossible to separate them. To this branch also, or rather to the mechanics of Baltimore, a generous and paternal care has been shown by an annual donation to the Mechanics' Institution of Baltimore of $500.

A similar donation was applied for at the same session of the Legislature for the great State Agricultural Society, and was refused.

It now remains for me to show authority, or precedent for the proposition I have had the honor to submit. And the first, because the most recent, to which I will call attention, is found in the California Constitution. The glittering gold of her hills and valleys has not even dazzled the eyes of her law makers to what is just and right and proper to the varied interests which may spring up in this land of promise. She has provided in her fundamental law that "the Legislature shall encourage, by all suitable means, the promotion of intellectual, scientific, moral and agricultural improvement."

Almost identically the language, though I was not aware of it when I drew my article, which I have employed—and this language appears to have been copied *verbatim* from the Michigan Constitution—which I have reason to believe was drawn by that eminent statesman, Gen. Cass, now so conspicuously before the country—for within a few days past, I have had the honor to receive from him an able and eloquent address delivered by him in October last, before the Agricultural Society of *Calamazoo* county, Michigan, in which I find the following cutting and well merited rebuke to the members of the National Legislature. He says in his conclusion: "My fellow citizens, I come to you from a far different scene from this; from a scene where there was neither *eye* nor *heart* for the peaceful and prosperous labors of agriculture."

Neither an eye nor heart for the peaceful pursuits of agriculture! What a censure upon a Legislature, three-fourths of which were composed of the immediate representatives of the agricultural interest. I trust, Mr. President, that this Convention will merit no such rebuke, but that we will show, by our action, that we have both an eye and a heart for the peaceful pursuits of agriculture, as well as all other interests in the State.

Mr. President, I could multiply authority. I could read from the Constitution of the granite State of New Hampshire—from Old Massachusetts—from Maine—from Indiana—I could give the example of New York and New Jersey—I could weary this body and exhaust myself with the reading of them, were it necessary. But I forbear—I am sure more cannot be necessary.

I have thus, Mr. President, as briefly as I could, in my plain way, shown what interests have been fostered and encouraged by the Legislature and what neglected, and authorities for my proposition, from the constitutions of many of our sister States. I have shown, I hope, conclusively so, that while literature, including law and medicine, have been patronized and encouraged, and commerce lavishly so, agriculture and associations for the diffusion of knowledge and virtue, have been neglected. Shakspeare says, "Ignorance is the curse of God, *Knowledge* the wing wherewith we fly to Heaven."

And its kindred *virtue*, as compared with religion, is beautifully put by Dr. Watts, who says: *Virtue* teaches us our duty towards man—Religion our duty towards God."

Shall these innocent and useful associations continue longer to be neglected. Will Maryland suffer the reproach of continuing to be behind the times, in moral and social culture? Will she in this enlightened age, at this period of moral, intellectual and physicial improvement, falter in her duty? For one, I trust not—I hope not. Let us for a moment forget party strife—political aggrandizement—and apply ourselves to the peaceful pursuits of life. Let the people of all classes, and all interests, throughout the length and breadth of Maryland, see that their wants, their wishes, and their interests, are thought of; are cared for—are provided for.

We then shall have proved ourselves, to be in fact, as well as profession, their true representatives. We then shall entitle ourselves to the commendation of "well done good and faithful servants." Mr. President, my task is done—*my* duty performed—and in the language of the poet I will say in conclusion,

"To you the polished judges of our cause,
Whose smiles are honor, and whose nods applause,
Humbly we bend, *encourage* arts like these,
For though the actor fails, he strives to please."

NOTE—The Legislature of NORTH CAROLINA, at its recent session, passed a bill authorizing an agricultural, mineralogical, and botanical survey of the State. The Governor is to make the appointment, and the surveyor is required personally, or by his assistants, "to visit every county in the State, and examine every thing of interest or value in either of the above departments, to ascertain the nature and character of its products, and the nature and character of its soil, as well as to give an account of its minerals."

Mr. JENIFER said that the views presented by the gentleman from Montgomery, (Mr. Davis,) were well worthy of consideration here and throughout the State; but he, (Mr. J.,) thought that it was questionable whether the bill of rights was a proper place for the provision. He thought that the bill of rights should stand as a declaration of rights, without the introduction of matters into it which belonged properly to the Legislature. It would be better, Mr. J. thought, that the amendment should be permitted to lie over for the present, and that it should be appended to some other portion of the Constitution.

Mr. Spencer stated that he had but one objection to the amendment, and that was to the expression "by all suitable means." To the general object itself, he was favorable, but he thought the phrase to which he took exception, was to loose and capable of too latitudinous a construction. The Legislature might regard it as a sanction to a pledge of credit of the State, or for appropriations of money. If the gentleman from Montgomery, would so modify his proposition, as to prevent the danger of such a construction, he would feel disposed to vote in favor of it. A friend near him had suggested that the object he had in view, would be effected by striking out the words "by all suitable means." Would the gentleman from Montgomery, accept that modification?

Mr. Davis replied that he had no great tenacity to any particular phraseology. His great desire was to make it so far conform to the general sentiment of the Convention, that he might obtain a vote, as nearly as possible approaching to unanimity. He would be very happy to accommodate the gentleman from Queen Anne's, but he preferred the language as it stood. He had employed the terms which he found in the other State Constitutions. He asked the gentleman from Queen Anne's, if he knew of any abuses to which that language had given rise in any of the States, in whose Constitutions, it had been adopted?

Mr. Spencer did not know of any abuses in the other States, but we have had one awful lesson, in relation to Legislative appropriations, when the Legislature made large appropriations for internal improvements. He had always doubted the power of the Legislature to make such appropriations, and when the Legislature enacted the first law for a direct tax, they outraged the people by putting a provision in the bill, which prohibited any one from bringing the question before the court of appeals, to test the constitutionality of the act. The meaning which might be generally given to the words "by all suitable means," is that the Legislature may give money, or raise loans for this object. He thought the people ought to encourage these objects, but he thought, when his friend would reflect a moment on what might be the effect of the words, he would consent to change the phraseology.

Mr. Tuck suggested a modification of the article proposed. He was decidedly in favor of the object contemplated. It was the duty of the State, to give attention to these subjects. They lie at the foundation of all good government, and although the Legislature would have the power, without this clause, he thought it proper that the declaration of rights should enjoin it as a duty. He would leave out the words *associations* and *suitable means*. It might be said hereafter that the Legislature could promote these objects in no other way than by authorizing corporations, associations, &c. He was for the largest exercise of the power—the mode and the means, he would leave to the Legislature. If the gentleman from Montgomery, would modify his amendment as suggested, Mr. Tuck thought the Convention could do no otherwise than adopt it.

Mr. Davis accepted the proposition of Mr. Tuck, (as a modification of his own amendment,) and it was read as follows:

"*Article* 42. The Legislature ought to encourage the diffusion of knowledge and virtue, the promotion of literature, the arts, sciences, agriculture, commerce and manufactures, and the general melioration of the wants and condition of the people."

After a brief conversation between Messrs. Jenifer and Davis;

The question was taken, and the modified amendment was adopted.

The Convention proceeded to consider the amendments offered on Saturday last by

Mr. George, as additional sections—to be numbered articles forty-three and forty-four.

The amendments having been read—

Mr. McHenry suggested to the gentleman (Mr. George,) that this proposition would come in more appropriately as an amendment to the Report of the Committee on the Legislative Department.

Some conversation followed.

Mr. George said, that as there seemed to be some objection to the incorporation of the amendment in the Bill of Rights, he would accept the suggestion of the gentleman, (Mr. McHenry,) and would withdraw the amendment, as also the other amendment of which he had heretofore given notice, as an additional section to be numbered article forty-four. And he gave notice that he would offer these amendments when the Report of the Committee on the Legislative Department should come up for consideration.

The next question was on the amendment of which

Mr. Parke had heretofore given notice, and which he now offered in the words following:

"*Article* 43. This enumeration of rights shall not be construed to impair or deny others retained by the people."

The amendment having being read,

Mr. Parke said that it was a mere assertion that there were rights not enumerated in the declaration of rights, and that they were retained by the people. There could not, he thought, be any impropriety in its adoption.

Mr. Schley invited the gentleman, (Mr. Parke,) to specify what the non-enumerated rights were.

Mr. Parke said it was impossible for him to do so. He presumed that they were very numerous—so much so as to render it impossible to include them in the bill of rights. A bill of rights, probably, might not be absolutely necessary, yet it was customary to have such a declaration. We all know that all the rights could not be set forth, and he thought it would be best to make a declaration that there were other rights which were not enumerated.

Mr. Jenifer thought that such a declaration would be entirely out of keeping in this place. If, as was conceded, the bill of rights took away no rights, of course every thing which was *not* taken away, remained.

The PRESIDENT, *pro tem.*, stated the question.

Mr. KILGOUR asked the yeas and nays.

Mr. MERRICK said he hoped the gentleman, (Mr. Parke,) would withdraw his amendment. It certainly was unnecessary. It could effect no great good, nor, indeed, could it do any harm.

Mr. PARKE said if it was the wish of the Convention that the amendment should be withdrawn, he, (Mr. P.,) would withdraw it. He did not see that it could make any great difference, whether the amendment was incorporated in the Constitution or not. He had seen it in other Constitutions—he had seen it in the Constitution of California. He was willing, however, to withdraw the amendment.

But, after a moment's reflection,

Mr. PARKE stated that he preferred to adhere to his amendment.

The PRESIDENT, *pro tem.*, then put the question on the demand of Mr. KILGOUR for the yeas and nays.

The Convention refused to order the yeas and nays.

The question was then taken on the amendment and no quorum voted.

Mr. MITCHELL called for the yeas and nays.

The PRESIDENT, *pro tem.*, said he had some doubts whether the motion was in order, as the Convention had once refused to take the yeas and nays.

The question was then again taken on the amendment of Mr. PARKE, and was decided in the affirmative : ayes 30, noes 25.

So the amendment was adopted.

The bill of rights had now been gone through with.

But on a former day the Convention had informally passed over the thirteenth article of the said bill, which is in the following words :

Art. 13. " That paupers ought not to be assessed for the support of government, but every other person in this State, or person holding property therein, ought to contribute his proportion of public taxes, for the support of government, according to his actual worth in real or personal property ; yet fines, duties or taxes may properly and justly be imposed or laid, on persons or property, with a political view for the good government and benefit of the community."

The pending question was on the amendment heretofore indicated by Mr. RANDALL, to insert after the word "property," the words "within this State."

Mr. DONALDSON was entitled to the floor, but said that, as he understood it was the desire of his colleague, (Mr. Randall,) to express his views more fully than he had heretofore done, he, (Mr. D.,) would yield the floor.

Mr. RANDALL rose and said that, in order to present his views in reference to his amendment, he would avail himself of the offer of his colleague (Mr. Donaldson) to yield the floor to him for that purpose. He read a portion of the thirteenth article in the old Bill of Rights, and stated that the new declaratory article proposes to omit the words "within this State," so as to give the power to the Legislature to levy taxes on real and personal property whether in or out of this State. The former Bill of Rights is framed with the express limitation that the taxing power is confined to property within the limits of this State. Such may have been the presumption without that express limitation. If the words "within this State" are now, however, stricken out, it would manifest clearly the intention to take away this limitation, and that the Legislature shall hereafter tax all the property, real and personal of its citizens lying out of this State. Is the Convention, he asked, prepared to say that taxes shall hereafter be imposed by the Legislature on the property of the citizens of this State all over the world? We are necessarily brought to this point by the difference found to exist between the two Bills of Rights. When he put the question to his distinguished colleague, not now in his place, (Mr. Dorsey,) how he proposed to tax *real* estate which might be situated in Florida, or Mississippi, or Europe—that gentleman informed him that it was not intended to tax *real* estate out of this State. In that case the change in the article effects what it was not intended to do, and should therefore remain as it is. Was it just, he would ask, to tax the property of our citizens lying beyond the limits of this State? He did not deny the existence of the power—the State had power over its citizens and their property of every description wherever it might be, unless prohibited by the Constitution. He did not therefore deny the power of the State to tax real property lying out of this State, but he did deny the justice of the exercise of such a power. Whether taxes are laid for carrying on internal improvements, or for any other object, all its expenditures are confined within its own limits, to benefit property in the State. Is it just that the property of the citizen lying out of the State should be taxed for any action in the State which in no manner adds to the value or utility of property out of this State. All our State legislation ought to be characterized by justice, that virtue which should be the guide of government, and faithfully administer in all its departments. The government should be a bright example to its citizens of justice. Within the State, where the property to be taxed will be improved by the contemplated action of the Legislature, it may be just to impose the tax, but where the property lies beyond the limits of the State and out of the reach of the improvements of the State's action, where its legislation can have no operation, its courts are not invoked to protect it or add to the facilities of its enjoyment—it is manifestly unjust to make it the subject of taxation by this State.

But there was another point in which it is unjust; it is unjust to the other States of the Union. If it were a mere proposition whether all the States of this Union shall tax all the property of their respective citizens, whether that property lie in or out of their respective limits, it would be another question—each State by its own action equalizing its own benefits by its losses, but that is not the case. Maryland alone I believe imposes such taxes on property beyond its limits—thus other States are unjustly treated, as we derive benefit from their property—they none from' our. But this injustice cannot continue, we must not flatter ourselves, if we tax the property of our citizens within their limits, that they will not also tax the property of their citizens within our State. It is not just to those States who only levy taxes on property within their limits. Where is the justice of making our citizens pay taxes for lands and slaves or other property, in another State, when they can derive no consideration in return from our State in the way of protection or other advantage. That property of our citizens is already taxed in the State where it lies. An injustice also is done to our citizens, because by imposing a tax on the property, we lessen the value of the property where it is situated, and thus the same property pays double taxes—taxes to the community in which it lies—taxes to this State where its owner resides. Again such a system will provoke retaliation—nothing ought to be done by us which may have the effect of provoking jealousies between States or a conflict of laws which will tend to destroy the harmony of our State laws. Let each State tax only the property within its own limits over which it has a more direct and complete control, and whose action and protection justify such an exercise of power.

But there was another view in which he desired to place this subject. It would be found impracticable to execute this law. It is wise to abstain from the exercise of a power which it may be difficult or impracticable to carry into effect. How is this property to be rated? Within the State we have a mode of assessing the value of real or personal estate. But how can this be done in Mississippi or Europe? How can you send there and have assessments made of the value of property? With regard to the property which consists of public stocks—although the value of these stocks are more easily known by the market price, how is it possible, or by what process could we proceed, to discover what citizens of Maryland are the true owners of such stocks. The laws and courts of Maryland are called upon to exercise no jurisdiction there, its citizens are not cognizant of what takes place there. And there can be devised no mode of taxing such property, the carrying out of which would but open the door to frauds and perjuries innumerable. A few years ago, a law was enacted to collect an income tax within this State; but it entirely failed. It was only in one or two of the counties, that the effort was made to execute its provisions when it was abandoned, and the act imposing it was shortly afterwards repealed, because of its inquisitorial character, its impertinent scrutiny into the affairs of private life and of other difficulties which it had to encounter, and the frauds and impositions it caused, and above all, and the combined effects of all—its utter failure to produce a sufficient sum. He stated this fact for the purpose of illustrating the probable result of any attempt to impose a tax when there was such difficulties in carrying out its execution as in this now contemplated.

Mr. SPENCER moved that the further consideration of the bill of rights be postponed, in order that it might be printed with the several amendments.

Mr. PARKE said he was absent when the first part of the bill of rights was under consideration. If it was now to be printed, he would offer an amendment, (with a view that it might be printed with the other amendments,) upon which he desired to have a vote of the Convention.

Some conversation followed as to the propriety of the postponement, in which Messrs. MAGRAW, SPENCER and JENIFER took part.

The result was, that

Mr. RANDALL proceeded with his remarks.

It would be perfectly acceptable to him, whatever course the House might determine on. The question was a very important one, and he hoped it would be examined carefully. He had no doubt the Convention would come to a correct decision upon it. He had endeavored to show that the change was both unjust and impracticable. He would now call attention to its policy. He had no means of knowing the extent of the property lying out of the State, which would be liable to taxation, if the measure was to be carried into effect. He presumed it was now very limited in its extent, although it could not well be ascertained what it was. But if the principle should be carried out in the other States, and surely we are not to expect that we can carry out a law taxing the property of our citizens in other States, without exciting retaliating legislation by other States, in taxing the property of their citizens lying in the State of Maryland. They surely will do so in relation to any property their citizens may have within our limits. It is mere justice to themselves to do this. What position then, will Maryland take if all the other States adopt this principle of retaliation, and say that the property of their citizens lying within the limits of this State, shall be taxed? Then all the citizens of those States having property lying in the State of Maryland, will be liable to double taxation on such property, as if citizens of the State of Maryland, by our laws, and as citizens of the respective States in which they reside, by the laws thereof. We must concede the same propriety and policy to other States which influence ourselves—what will be its operation? The stock of the State of Maryland is relatively larger in proportion to its population and resources perhaps, than any State in the Union—certainly not far from it. Let other States whose citizens hold your State stocks impose another tax upon it in addition to that which you impose, and its value would be essentially impaired; vast quantities of it are held by citizens of other States, in our canals, rail roads, mining companies, and in our city stocks, bank stocks, &c. We have an immense banking capital, and a good deal of it is owned out of the State. We have numerous stocks of companies associated for internal improvements, a great deal of which is held by citizens out of this State. In Allegany, I understand, the stock of many companies is held almost exclusively by persons living out of this State.

If we impose a tax on these capitalists, and they are taxed also by the States in which they live, they will be burdened with a double tax, and perhaps, have their capital driven out of this State. And he believed that, in carrying out this policy, it would be found in the end, that Maryland had lost more than she had gained. We are surrounded by other States. Property is held within our limits by citizens of the adjoining States of Delaware, Pennsylvania and Virginia; and if we tax the property in this State belonging to the citizens of either of those States they will also be taxed at home, and thus have to pay a double tax, or else remove out of this State, which is likely to be one result or another, that he would cease to be a holder of property in our State.

Suppose a citizen of Boston comes into Baltimore to reside, and carry on trade with a part of his capital, you tax not only all he owns in Baltimore, but all the property he has elsewhere—even though this property is elsewhere taxed—subjecting him to double tax, because you declare that your citizens shall pay a tax on all the property they possess throughout the world.

The effect of this would be to drive all such citizens out of this State, and to prevent others from coming in to settle among us. I have personal knowledge of one such case where a citizen of Georgia was prevented from settling in Baltimore, because his property consisting of debts in Georgia, for property he had sold there, would be taxed. He went to Georgetown, and there settled to avoid this tax.

He was perfectly contented with the bill of rights as it stood. As it stood it was just; now in its changed form, it would be unjust. What reduction would be made from the revenue of the State by this measure, he knew not. But he would say that if the other States of the Union should carry out this principle, and there is no reason to expect that they will not—it is but just to themselves that they should—it will be followed by inconveniences to us, which will more than counterbalance any good which can possibly result from it; and we shall actually lose in a pecuniary point of view, more than we gain by it. He had now discharged his duty in bringing the subject before the Convention, and he left it with this body to act as it may deem best.

Mr. Donaldson expressed his regret at being compelled to disagree with his colleague, (Mr. Randall,) for whose clearness of judgment and uniformly conscientious motives, he entertained the highest esteem. It was from the strength of his honest convictions, that his colleague had spoken with such warmth of what he considered the injustice of the existing system of laws, by which stocks held by citizens of this State, in the public loans of other States, and in the institutions of other States, were subject to taxation. As an act of justice, he, (Mr. Randall,) demanded the exemption of such property. He, (Mr. D.,) considered that both policy and justice were against such an exemption. If he thought there was a departure from justice, he would not argue in favor of the policy of a measure, but where both stood on the same side, they might well fortify each other.

What is the injustice complained of by the mover of the amendment? A citizen of this State, residing here, owning stocks in other States, has to pay a tax according to his actual worth, including those foreign stocks. Compare him now with his neighbor, all whose property is invested within the limits of Maryland. Both have the same protection from the laws—both have the same advantage in their business, from those great works of internal improvement, the construction of which has produced almost all our taxation. One pays for that protection, and those advantages in proportion to his property, and the others does not.

But, it is said, the present system leads to double taxation. A man may be taxed on the same property in two States. This does not follow. In many States there is no direct taxation; in others it is very small. Very few of them tax stocks held by non-residents. A citizen of Maryland, holding a million dollars of the State stock of Virginia, pays not a cent of tax in Virginia, and if this proposition to exempt should prevail, he would pay not a cent on that stock here. Besides, it must be remembered, that all this is voluntary. No man is obliged to invest in these foreign stocks; and if he becomes liable to double taxation, he can easily change his investment, and purchase stocks, or other property, here. Then he would be on a perfect equality with his neighbors. If there is any injustice, he need not suffer it for an hour. If he retains it, it is because he finds it more profitable, in spite of its liability to our taxation, than the investment of his neighbors at home, liable to the same taxation.

Real estate beyond our limits, has never been considered as liable to our taxation, because it has a locality, whereas stocks, being personal property, are considered in law as following the person.

So much in answer to the charge of injustice made against the present system. Now, let us look at the other side of the question. What would be the consequence of the exemption from taxation of stocks, in other States, held by citizens of our own. Almost all the surplus wealth of this State, would be withdrawn from taxation, both for State and county purposes, and invested in the stocks of States, where there is no taxation, or but little. This would be done, as a matter of course, by those possessing the greatest wealth. Such are the men who try every device to escape their proper share of the burdens of the State. It is a trait of human nature, not to be denied, although noble exceptions exist, that wealth generates this kind of selfishness. There is no estimating how much might, in this manner, be lost to the State and counties. The abstraction of ten millions of capital, from the city of Baltimore, for instance, would make to State and city, together an annual loss in taxes, of upwards of one hundred thousand dollars. Necessarily, those who did not so remove their capital, and the property holders who had no surplus capital to invest, would have to pay a higher rate of taxation, to make up for the deficiency thus caused. Could anything be more manifestly unjust?

Mr. D. then proceeded to state several cases by way of illustration. A man engaged in a successful business in the city of Baltimore, may accumulate, from year to year, vast profits, growing rich from the great advantages he derives from the system of internal improvements, which has cost the State and city together, upwards of twenty millions of dollars, and from all that the city has spent in the improvement of her harbor; whilst he is protected in person, in property and in the quiet pursuits of his business, by the laws of the State and city. All his profits, as fast as they accumulate, he may, if the amendment prevails, invest in stocks of other States, and he may thus convey out of the reach of taxation, say four-fifths of his property. On the other hand, a man of small property, whose earnings barely support and educate his family, must pay taxes on the whole of his worth. A farmer, who expends his profits, not generally very large, in improving his land, and adding to his buildings and stock, finds that the increased value is added to his assessment. He must pay a tax on the whole. Thus those most benefitted by the expenditures of the State, and most able to bear the burden, would have to pay far less, in proportion, than their proper share; and their deficiency must be made up by an increased tax, on men more honest and poorer. To make this exemption, would create the greatest inequality, and directly encourage the dishonest evasion of taxes.

But, (continued Mr. D.) this exemption would injure all the holders of public and private stocks here, by diminishing their market value. It would discourage the investment of our home capital, in the improvement of our lands, in building up factories and furnaces, and in various industrial occupations; for all these are subject to taxation here, whilst the same capital invested abroad, would enjoy an exemption.

It is said that the present state of the law, or of legislative practice, prevents men of capital from coming into the State, and bringing part of their means with them. A Boston capitalist, worth five hundred thousand dollars, may wish to bring one hundred thousand dollars here, and leave the remainder invested at his former home. There might be such a case, but it is merely exceptional. Very few men will come here merely for the sake of a fancy residence; and the amount of capital excluded in this way, is but trifling compared with what would be driven out by the exemption proposed. Undoubtedly the fact that we suffer such heavy taxation, does tend to discourage men of capital from settling here. It cannot be otherwise, and it is certainly to be regretted; but the great growth of Maryland, within the last ten years, in wealth and population, demonstrates that the effect of our works of internal improvement, has been to make the State more desirable, as a residence, for active and enterprising men, than it would have been if no such works had been projected; and, consequently, no such taxes levied. Active, enterprizing, business men, of small capital, are those who come from other States, to seek a residence among us; and such men are the most valuable accessions to our community.

Mr. D. concluded by saying, that we had not a great many years longer to bear the weight of our taxes. The public mind had become content under them, and, at present, it would be unwise in any essential particular, to change the system.

Mr. Thomas stated that, until this morning, he did not know that such an amendment as this was pending. It was a very important proposition, and he had been turning it over in his mind, and had satisfied himself that it would produce a change in our policy which would work injustice. He would take an illustration, by applying the new principle to the localities with which he was familiar. He would take, for example, the counties of Harford, Cecil, Frederick, Carroll, Washington and Alleghany, in all these there were numerous landholders who possessed property over the line of one of the adjoining States. What would be the response from these counties, if we were to impose a tax on our citizens for this property lying beyond the limits of the State? It would be repudiated. For what reason do we impose a tax on property within the State? It is because the State gives it in return protection against robbery and other dangers to which it is liable in an unprotected state. So, in regard to personal property, we make laws for the enforcement of contracts, and in other ways to secure this kind of property, and we tax personal property on the principle of protection. Maryland has, in her exigency, been compelled to resort to heavy taxation, and the change of policy looks to the taxation of the property of our citizens, personal as well as real, lying without the limits of the State. If one of our citizens had left the State and gone to California, and obtained property there, would it be right to tax his property there for the purpose of keeping up in this State, roads and highways in which he was not interested, and would he not refuse to pay such tax? He, (Mr. T.,) would vote against any attempt to impose a tax on real estate lying out of the State, because, it ought only to be taxed where its rights are protected by law. So ought personal property to stand in the same position. We cannot change the policy of Virginia and of the other States of the Union. Maryland may adopt the policy of taxing her State stocks, and he would vote for it; or she might impose a tax on the banking capital in the State, or on insurance stocks, or any other personal property within the State. That is, all stock in the State of Maryland, and we have a right to tax it. But it would be injurious to Maryland, if holders of foreign stock were taxed here, because there is more stock held by foreign holders in Maryland, than by citizens of Maryland in foreign stocks. He did not believe that other States would tax these stocks, and the effect of taxing the stocks of other States in the hands of our citizens, would be to drive them beyond the reach of our taxation. Tax the amount of the certificate of stock in his hands, and you drive him from your State. If his income be $30,000 a year and he has employed it in diffusing benefits round him, you deprive the State of those benefits hereafter. So as to bank stocks, a great deal of it is held by persons who are not citizens of Maryland, which is taxed twenty cents upon every hundred dollars for the school fund, and which has been in operation for forty years, during which time all holders of this stock have contributed, because the banks are obliged to pay over this tax to the school fund, out of the profits, before any dividend is made to the stock holders. Should the Legislature attempt to tax the real estate of her citizens beyond the limits of the State, and that should fail, he did not see with what propriety it could be attempted to tax personal property out of the State. In his opinion, the same principle should govern whether as to real or personal estate.

Mr. Tuck said, he desired to offer an amendment of which he had given notice on a former day, and which, as modified, read as follows:

Article 13*th*. "That taxes for the suppoit of government, and fines, duties and taxes, with a political view for the good government and benefit of the community, may be imposed or laid on property within this State, and the legislature ought to declare the objects for laying or imposing the same."

Mr. Tuck would state briefly his reasons for offering the amendment.

He desired to leave the power to the legislature with as few restrictions as possible. In times of difficulty and financial embarrassment, it is easy to find means to avoid the restrictions; and thus the spirit of the bill of rights, might be violated without any redress to the tax payer.

The opinion is entertained by many persons, that this had been done by some of the tax laws passed since 1840. It is very well known that all these laws were passed for the purpose of raising revenue for the support of government—that is, for the purpose contemplated by the first clause of the thirteenth article of the present bill of rights. The taxes were designed "for the support of government," and not "with political view;" yet, they were not assessed according to each man's "worth in real and personal property, within this State," as required by that article. He alluded to the tax on collateral inheritances; the tax on the commissions of executors and administrators—the tax on the public offices—the stamp tax, &c.

He did not mean to say that these taxes were wrong in themselves. All he meant to say, was, that they were laid to raise revenue for the support of government; that that was the design and no other. And in that view he thought the legislature had done wrong in not declaring the objects for which these bills were past.

He admitted that the legislature should have the power to levy taxes "with political view." The peace and welfare of society required this. The license system, lottery taxes, auction duties, and such other taxes were referable to this power. These required regulation.

But no such necessity existed when the bills to which he had referred were passed. It was not pretended that collateral inheritances, commissions, promissory notes, &c., needed regulation. The Treasury needed the revenue, and thus the latter clause of the thirteenth article was involved in aid of the purpose contemplated by the first clause.

His amendment required that the laws should state the object for which the taxes were laid—whether to raise revenue for the support of government or with political view, so that the tax payer might have the validity of the tax tried by the courts. This could not be done under the present laws, because the acts do not disclose the object for which the taxes are laid, and being within the provision of the latter clause of the thirteenth article, though passed for a different purpose, the courts can do no otherwise than say that they are constitutional. The power of Congress to pass tariff laws for the protection of domestic labor has been, and is now denied by a large party in the country. But this power can never be tested in the United States courts, so long as the laws profess to be mere revenue laws. The power to raise revenue being conceded, the courts are bound to declare all such laws to be constitutional, unless they are in terms against that instrument. The courts cannot go behind the laws, and decide according to what may be the motive of the legislature in passing them.

Mr. T. said that his amendment would allow these questions to be settled by the judicial tribunals, by shewing to the court the object and purpose of the law—and if these were not warranted by the Bill of Rights the act would be declared void. He had no disposition to disturb the present tax system. That system will remain until repealed by law. But cases under that system had been carried to the Court of Appeals. This showed doubt and dissatisfaction. And when this is likely to occur by the exercise of uncertain powers, the people should have an opportunity of testing the question. Nothing is more unwelcome to the people than heavy taxes. But they will submit when they are satisfied that a necessity exists, and that the power to impose the burden is vested in the Legislature. He had said that he would confide this power to the Legislature without restriction. But if we are to say any thing on the subject in the Bill of Rights he would prefer plain and definite language, not only to indicate to the Legislature the limits of their powers, but to allow the tax-payer to have his case properly tried, if complaint were made.

He had also inserted the words "in this State," so as to prevent the Legislature from taxing property beyond the State. He never could understand by what authority the Legislature taxed Bank and other Stocks, beyond the State, for the support of our Government, when the thirteenth article of the Bill of Rights declares that "every man shall contribute according to his actual worth in real and personal property *within the State*." The Stocks of foreign Banks are not within this State. The gentlemen from Frederick and from Anne Arundel had made arguments on this point which have not been and cannot be answered. The true doctrine is taxation according to protection. Why does a man pay taxes on his property? On what theory is this required? Only because justice suggests that his property shall pay according to the protection it receives. He would not multiply words on this point. The gentlemen who preceded him had said all that could be said on the subject. He would however notice in a few words, some of the positions of the gentleman from Anne Arundel, (Mr. Donaldson.) The case put by him of the capitalist who lives among us while his estate is located elsewhere, does not meet the argument. In the first place he pays taxes on his property under the laws of the State in which it is located, and in the next place he spends all his income among us. It is better, to be sure, for us to have capital and men both, but I am not for driving away or taxing a man who is willing to spend large revenues among us merely because his property is not here. If we cannot have the man with his capital, I will take him with his revenues. These go into circulation and trade, and are thus of advantage to us. The gentleman says his certificate of Stock in his pocket or drawer is property in the State. Mr. T. disagreed. But if the certificate is property here because of his possession of it, suppose he leaves it in the hands of his agent or broker in the State where the Stock is, what protection is allowed him then? The same argument may be made as reasonably, and be as well met in regard to any other property beyond the State. If one holds a bond of a person in another State our courts afford no remedy for recovering the debt, and yet the bond is taxed for the support of government here.

And again, if the certificate is the property, a man who holds stock in one of our banks, should pay double taxes; first, on the stock itself, because that is property—another on the certificate, because that is the evidence of his property.

According to the gentleman's theory, a man should not pay any tax on his bank stock located here, if he happened to reside beyond the State, because the tax must be paid where the certificate is held. A man who has stock in another State, and lives among us, is taxed because he does not invest here—while one who lives in another State, and holds stock here, is taxed because he has invested here. You tax the property in one case for being in the State—and you tax the man in the other case, because his property is not here. In the former case we tax him for the protection actually afforded, and in the other respect of the benefits he might derive from our institutions, if the property were here. It is said this is necessary to prevent persons sending their capital beyond the State. This is no answer to the injustice of the act; and besides, instead of bringing property here for investment we are likely to drive the man away too—thus losing a citizen with all the advantages to be derived from the expenditure of his revenues among us. All these taxes can be put on another ground, not liable to any objection.

Let us provide for an income tax which will reach the revenues, and salaries and income of all who have no property here, or which the tax laws can operate. We shall then make persons contribute for the support of government, in respect of the protection afforded to their persons as well as property.

Mr. T. repeated that he had no intention to interfere with the present system of taxation. We are providing for the future He was for leaving the power with the legislature. But, if we make any declaration on the subject, let it be clear and explicit, so as to prevent the complaints that were made against some of the present laws.

Mr. Donaldson replied briefly to gentlemen, who had spoken in favor of his colleague's amendment. After hearing their arguments, his opinion remained unchanged. He recapitulated the points on which he based that opinion. The gentleman from Frederick, (Mr. Thomas,) did not seem to be aware that we already taxed the public loans of our State, and the stocks held by non-residents in our State corporations. Such was the fact. He seemed to think, also, that we were endeavoring to subject to taxation, property which heretofore had been exempt. But the laws of the State have all along taxed such property, and the tax has been regularly collected. Whether the law was consistent with the meaning of the old bill of rights, was a point which had never been contested, and, therefore, there had been no decision upon it, in our supreme court. The ground of the law was that all personal property, followed by the person; and the words "within the State," in the old bill of rights, had been struck out by the committee, in order to exclude a doubt. It must be remembered, further, that the certificate of stock, the evidence of the debt, was actually in the possession of the owner.

Mr. D. said, that he differed from the gentleman from Frederick, (Mr. Thomas,) and the gentleman from Prince George's, (Mr. Tuck,) who regarded protection to the particular property itself, the sole ground of taxation. Protection to the person—protection in the prosecution of his business—the advantages derived from the public expenditures that create or foster, the mode from which the citizen is enabled to accumulate wealth—all must be considered as the sources of the power to impose taxation. If a State had not power to prevent immense masses of wealth accumulated here, from being put out of the reach of taxation, whilst its possessor still enjoys all the advantages of his residence and citizenship, then there can never be an approach to equality in the distribution of the burdens of government. The honest and patriotic must pay for the dishonest and the selfish. If such an exemption, as that proposed, is adopted, we shall be obliged, before a great while, to resort to an income tax as the only adequate remedy for such injustice.

It had been said that the collection of the tax was impracticable. This was a mistake. Some frauds and evasions would take place under every system of tax laws. The honest always have to contribute more than their due proportion; but with the present provisions of our law, it would be impossible to dispose of one specific piece of property, and get a deduction on the assessment books on account of it, without answering, on oath, as to the manner in which the purchase money received has been applied, and the new investment would be at once changed on those books. If, however, this exemption prevails, any amount of property may be deducted from the assessments, provided the proceeds are to be invested in stock of other States.

In regard to the policy of these tax-laws, he differed *toto cœlo*, from the gentleman from Frederick, (Mr. Thomas.) That gentleman thought the exemption proposed, was good policy, and that it was good policy to tax the public loans of our own State, and the stocks of our State institutions held by non-residents. He, (Mr. D.,) had already endeavored to show the impolicy of exempting, from taxation, stocks in other States, held by our own citizens; and it seemed to him clear, that to tax the investments of non-residents in our State, had the direct effect of discouraging foreign capitalists, from sending their capital here to assist us in the various enterprises, roads, canals, factories, furnaces, and the like, which require associated wealth. He thought such discouragement injudicious. In regard to taxing our own Maryland stock, it always seemed to him a breach of faith with our creditors. Before any direct tax existed here, we borrowed millions of dollars, on a solemn pledge to pay a stipulated interest, and after the money was received and expended, we said, we will not pay you the stipulated interest, but will deduct a portion of it in the shape of taxation. In this he agreed entirely with the gentleman from Prince George's, [Mr Tuck,] and stated that if he could have accomplished the repeal of the tax on State stock, when he was in the Legislature, he would have done so.

Mr. Gwinn said, that he was opposed to the amendment of the gentleman from Anne Arundel. It was true that the words "within the State" were in the old Bill of Rights, but it did not follow that it was prudent to retain them. The reason of the case should be considered.

The right to tax property, real or personal, is derived from the necessity of supporting the government, by which protection is afforded. It cannot exist without such aid, and it must be derived from the individuals over whom its rule is extended, or from the property which lies within its jurisdiction. Protection to property, is as essential as protection to persons, for the peace, good order, and duration of society; and protection to property is not only extended by the State over that which lies within its own borders, but, from the nature of our confederacy to that also which is beyond its borders. If a citizen of Maryland is deprived of property situated in another State, he is enabled, by virtue of this privilege, to use the judicial power of the Federal Union, and to enforce his rights by its aid, if need be. It is right therefore, that he should contribute his share towards the support of that State Government from whose existence he derives this privilege. The same argument, which makes it proper that the citizen should contribute to the protection of the State, which affords shelter to the property within its limits, renders it proper also that he should contribute towards the upholding of the civil power of that State, which as a party to the Union, gives him a right to resort to the Federal power of all the States.

The objection has been urged that the same property would be doubly taxed,—in Virginia, for instance, if located there,—and in Maryland, if the owner resides in this State. If it were, this would constitute no objection. Our citizens obtain the protection of the Virginia courts, and should pay their share towards their support. They have protection also to themselves, while resident here, from the power of the State of Maryland, and should contribute to its support also.

The argument turned chiefly upon the propriety of taxing personal property. This suggests itself most readily as a subject of taxation, because it follows the person in the contemplation of law. But the *reason* of the rule is the same with relation to real property as in reference to personal. If the Legislature chooses to discriminate, it is in its discretion; but no argument can properly be founded on the preference which they may accord to this source of revenue.

It has been said that the State and municipal authorities should be deprived of the power of taxing the stock of the State. He could see no reason for this. It is true that it is a debt of the State. But, nevertheless, it is property, created by the State fo rthe common advantage which derives protection from the public law, and the value of which, moreover, is sustained by our whole system of State government. It is right and proper, therefore, that it should do something towards the support of that government from which it derives its annual increase and protection.

The same argument applies to the city of Baltimore. It contributes largely to the prosperity of the whole State, and it accomplishes this end by the influence, which, in its municipal capacity it exercises over the form and growth of that wealth and labor, which it centers within its limits.

It is right and proper that those who hold the State stock, and who have all the benefit of that personal security and comfort which the ordinances of a city afford, should contribute to th maintenance of the civil power of the communit itself. There is reason and justice in the rule and it should not be interfered with.

Mr. Tuck said, the first part of the gentleman's argument answered the last. He now considered that gentlemen on the other side had abandoned the argument. You cannot tax the land of your citizens in Virginia, or the negroes on it, because you cannot get at them to collect the tax. Taxation and protection go hand in hand. You cannot tax where you cannot protect.

Mr. Gwinn explained.

Mr. Tuck said, the gentleman from Anne Arundel, referred to the money spent in Baltimore on harbors. The property out of the State derives no protection from these harbors, no benefit from them whatever; yet, it is taxed for their support. An individual is taxed properly so far as he is protected in his trade or occupation. But it is unjust to tax him further. If the legislature thought proper to lay a tax on dogs for the benefit of sheep, let them do it. The proceeds of a dog tax have been estimated at $50,000 a year, at one dollar per head. Let the legislature impose such a tax, and if the people are dissatisfied, it will give them an opportunity to carry the question of the constitutionality of the law to the competent legal tribunal.

Mr. JOHN NEWCOMER desired the gentleman from Prince George's, (Mr. Tuck,) to answer one question. It was this: whether the gentleman considered stocks or certificates of stocks of other States, held here as personal property within the State?

Mr. TUCK said, he did not.

Mr. JOHN NEWCOMER. If I hold a private security of a gentleman in Virginia or Pennsylvania, is that personal property within the State?

Mr. TUCK. I do not so consider it—nor regard it as subject to taxation.

Mr. WELLS, of Anne Arundel, asked the indulgence of the Convention for a few minutes, as he was of opinion that difficulties, not belonging to the subject had surrounded it, and that members might be embarrassed in their vote by a misapprehension of the question. Some gentlemen seemed to think that we were about to introduce a *novel* mode of taxation; but this was altogether a mistake. So far as the stocks of other States, bonds, notes, &c., were concerned, the *effect* of the article, as reported, being merely to continue the system, now in existence, in relation to the right of the State to tax the stocks, &c., of other States, which is now done, and from which the State derives considerable revenue, the whole of which will be lost, and much more, if the amendment should prevail, because it will necessarily drive a large amount of capital from our State; for it cannot be expected, and will not, he thought, be contended, that capitalists will invest their money in our stocks, which are burthened with a considerable tax, when they can purchase good stocks in other States, free from taxation. And, therefore, the deficiency produced in the receipts into the treasury, will be materially increased by adding to the loss occasioned by releasing from taxation the stocks which are now taxed, the loss of tax on the amount of capital which by this course of proceeding will seek investment elsewhere. And he desired to impress upon the consideration of the Convention, the fact, that all this loss may have to be supplied by an additional tax on the landed interest, and the amount was much more considerable than gentlemen seemed to suppose, for he had known upwards of one hundred thousand dollars invested by citizens of Annapolis in foreign stocks; and, therefore, gentlemen could estimate for themselves the probable total amount throughout the State, thus invested.

As to the right of the State to tax this description of property he had no doubt, for in contemplation of law, it is attached to the person of the owner, and when he dies, his executor or administrator returns it to the Orphan's court as a part of his assets, and it is distributed to his representatives, not according to the laws of the State from which the stock issued, but in conformity with the laws of the State of which the owner died a resident; and so, also, with regard to bonds and notes and other evidences of debt due by citizens of other States to citizens of this State.

Mr. TUCK asked if it would not be necessary to take out letters of administration in the State from which the stock issued, in order to transfer it to the representatives of the deceased, or to collect it.

Mr. WELLS resumed, and said that it would be necessary, but that in such cases, letters, he believed, were always granted to the person charged with the administration of the estate in the county of that State of which the owner died a resident, and this was only necessary in some cases, for it did not apply at all, as he conceived, to that class of stocks of which bonds with coupons attached was the evidence, for as no record of them was kept, no transfer was necessary, and passing as they did by delivery, possession conferred the power on the executor or administrator to sell them and to distribute them, and a large portion were of this description, they being invented and used expressly with a view to prevent the residence of the owner being known, and in order that the laws might be evaded.

But it has been urged that you should not tax this description of property, because our laws could not protect the citizen in the enjoyment of it; but this he denied, because if your certificate of stock or bond, or other evidence of debt, was stolen, the courts were open to redress as much so as if you were robbed of any other species of personal property that might be in your house, or upon any part of your premises. And if a forgery was committed, the protection afforded by the laws did not distinguish between the rights belonging to you as the owner of stocks, or other private securities due from other States, or corporations or citizens of other States, or of this State.

In conclusion, he repeated, that the effect of the article was not to introduce a novel mode of taxation and unsettle the present system, but quite the reverse; for if the amendment was adopted, a change would indeed follow, for additional revenue laws would have to be passed to supply the deficiency which would be produced in the receipts of the treasury by this change, and the landed interest would have to be taxed to meet the deficit.

Mr. BOWIE said, it seemed to him that we ought to adopt this amendment. If he understood the matter, the Court of Appeals has decided that, under the Bill of Rights, the Legislature had the power to impose these taxes. It would be competent for the Legislature, under this Bill of Rights to tax the real estate of a citizen of Maryland, lying out of the limits of the State. The fact of its being out of the State would not affect this power of the Legislature; and the Legislature might prescribe a mode in which the value of such property could be ascertained. Now he never could consent to such a proposition with such a result. He thought stocks or bonds might be taxed, but that bonds out of the State ought not. Foreign stocks are now taxed under the old Bill of Rights. The constitutionality of the law has never been tested. If the gentleman would include the idea that land and negroes should not be taxed out of the State, but that property in stocks and bonds should, it should have his support. But if the proposition is that the Legislature may tax real estate out of the State he could not vote for it.

Mr. MERRICK thought it would be best to leave the article as it is. There are kinds of stocks out of the State which it is impossible to reach. The effect of the clause would be to leave it to the Legislature to decide what kind of property ought to be taxed. You thus leave it to the discretion of the Legislature to tax property beyond the limits of the State, while you tie it down from taxing within the State. It does not necessarily follow that the Legislature will do a foolish thing, but it would be much better to leave the clause as it is. By grafting on the provision the word "propose," you tie up the Legislature. He had heard of citizens of Maryland who had exchanged their property within the State for property out of its limits to avoid the taxes. This was very wrong, and ought to be prevented if the Legislature can prevent it. He would vote against all amendments, and for the clause as it stands.

Mr. SPENCER expressed his hope that the suggestion of the gentleman from Charles (Mr. Merrick) would be acquiesced in. He thought it dangerous to touch the article. It was in conformity with our revenue system. Our State has had an arduous struggle to get through her financial difficulties. She has, however, sustained herself, but if we change the article and take the amendment proposed, we may be involved in difficulty. He had not the slightest doubt as to the power and the policy to tax stocks out of the State held by our own citizens. These stocks are protected as efficiently by our laws as the person of the owner, or the horse which belongs to him. The law gives him full protection for his property.

The gentleman from Annapolis had well defined the protection which is afforded by the law, against larceny, forgery, or any tort in the way of trespass or trover. He had, therefore, no doubt as to the legal right. Nor did he, for a moment, hesitate as to the policy of exercising it. If you tax your State stocks, and exempt certificates of foreign stocks, held by resident citizens, you will drive every capitalist out of the State, to invest his money in other stocks. Thus our stocks would be depreciated and comparatively valueless, and the further effect would be, that wealth and luxury would escape taxation, whilst it would fall on those less able to bear it—principally on the landholder.

The gentleman from Prince George's, (Mr. Tuck,) is also opposed to taxing our public stocks. He, (Mr. S.,) saw no reason why they should not be taxed. If they were now in the hands of the persons who had loaned their money upon them, at first view, there might appear to be some conscience in the proposition. But even this would not stand the test of scrutiny. It was but an investment of capital in one kind of security in preference to another, and there was no reason why capital invested in one mode should be taxed, and not in another. It was the same luxury wherever found, and the rule in reference to it should be universal. But, in addition, this very stock has, to a great extent, passed into other hands, than the original holders. At one time it was at a very low value in market, and a subject of speculation. Immense investments have been made in it, and at enormous profit. In every view of the case, it was just and right to tax it.

Mr. DORSEY stated that he was not disposed to make a speech at this late hour of the day. The question is, if we shall be allowed to tax property belonging to citizens of this State, lying in other States, and stocks of other States held by citizens of Maryland? He would give an affirmative answer. What injustice was there in doing so? If our capitalists sent out their money to buy the stocks of other States already there taxed, they would be able to purchase at lower rates; no injustice would be done them. The question is, if persons who send their capital out of the State to loan on security, or buy stocks, may be taxed on such property? Of the constitutionality of such tax, he had no doubt. The only question relates to its expediency. The constitutional right to impose such tax cannot be doubted. He had no doubt of the policy of the act, and he was not aware that any injustice would be done to the purchaser of such stock. Sound policy dictates to us, to encourage the institutions of our own State, and not to drive capital away from us, for investment in other States. We ought to be careful not to insert in our bill of rights an article which would prevent the prosperity of the institutions of our own State.

Mr. THOMAS said, that we were now about to decide, if we will insert an article on the subject of the taxation of real and personal property, which shall bind the legislature and our posterity, and in doing which we are fixing an eternal rule of right. We ought, therefore, to proceed with great caution, not suffering our judgment to be misled by the excited and overdrawn pictures which have been presented us of stockholders, made wealthy by speculations in stocks, and living in luxury, and of poor men contributing from their small means to the revenue of the State; but to act with clear and correct views of the effect of the measure. He thought the legislature might devise a mode of assessing the value of real estate held by any of the citizens of Maryland out of the State; it might, for instance, require the oath of the owner to a statement of its value. He could not vote for the clause, because it gives a discretion to the legislature to tax real estate beyond the limits of the State, as well as stocks and foreign securities.

Mr. RANDALL, at a late hour, took the floor, and yielded to a motion that the Convention adjourn.

The Convention refused to adjourn.

Mr. RANDALL not pressing his right to the floor,

Mr. MICHAEL NEWCOMER demanded the previous question.

But, by general consent, the question on the amendment was taken, and the amendment was rejected.

And the substitute of Mr. TUCK was rejected.

The question then recurring on the adoption of the thirteenth article of the report of the committee,

Mr. Schley moved to amend the said article by striking out in the fourth line thereof, the words "actual worth in."

The amendment was rejected.

Mr. Schley moved to amend the said article by inserting after the word "property," in the fifth line thereof, the following:

"And the legislature shall, at its first session after the adoption of this Constitution, provide a convenient mode by which the actual worth in real and personal property of any individual in the State shall be ascertained."

After some explanations by Messrs. Schley, Dorsey and Merrick,

The question was taken, and the amendment was rejected.

The thirteenth article of the report was then adopted.

And the Convention adjourned, until to-morrow at eleven o'clock.

TUESDAY, February 11th, 1851.

The Convention met at eleven o'clock.

Prayer by the Rev. Mr. Grauff.

The roll of the members was called.

The journal of yesterday was read, and on motion of

Mr. Schley, was amended by substituting, in his amendment, the word "every," in lieu of "any," as erroneously recorded.

MR. M'CULLOGH, OF CECIL.

On motion of Mr. Miller, it was

"*Ordered*, That it be entered upon the journal, that Mr. McCullough, is detained from his seat in the Convention by the severe illness of a member of his family."

On motion of Mr. McMaster, it was

"*Ordered*, That it be entered upon the journal Samuel I. Lambden, an officer of this Convention, is detained at home in consequence of the illness of his wife."

Mr. Gwinn, presented a memorial of H. J. Scarff, Robert White, Peter F. Young, William H. H. Turner, and others of the Marion Total Abstinence Society, praying some constitutional protection for the cause of Temperance;

Which was read, and

On motion of Mr. Gwinn,

Referred to the committee on the Legislative Department.

Mr. Morgan presented an account of G. J. Spalding, clerk to commissioners of tax for St. Mary's county;

Which was read, and

On motion of Mr. Morgan,

Referred to the committee on Accounts.

On motion of Mr. Phelps, it was

"*Ordered*, That the committee upon apportionment and representation be, and they are hereby directed, to enquire into the propriety and expediency of so changing the present basis of representation in the House of Delegates, as to deduct one member from each county, and the city of Baltimore.

The President, *pro tem.*, called for reports of committees, and also for motions, notices and resolutions, but none were presented or made.

THE BILL OF RIGHTS.

The Convention resumed the consideration of the order of the day, being the report of the committee on the declaration of rights.

The question was on the adoption of the following preamble:

"We, the Delegates of Maryland, in Convention assembled, taking into our most serious consideration, the best means of establishing a good Constitution in this State, DECLARE."

Mr. Dashiell moved to amend the said preamble, by inserting after the word "Maryland," in the first line, these words, "representing the counties and city of Baltimore."

The preamble, as amended, would then read as follows:

"We, the Delegates of Maryland, representing the counties and the city of Baltimore, in Convention assembled, taking into our most serious consideration, the best means of establishing a good Constitution in this State, DECLARE."

Mr. D. said his object in proposing this amendment, was to place upon record a fact which existed, and by so doing he relieved the preamble, as reported by the committee, of all ambiguity. The preamble, without the amendment, admits of a construction which the facts do not warrant, and he thought it expedient and wiser to place it beyond the possibility of cavil and doubt. He wished it to tell but the one tale, and that the truth. No one can deny the fact, that we are here as Delegates of Maryland, representing the counties and the city of Baltimore—that we, in the aggregate, are the result of an apportionment—that each county has upon this floor a separate and distinct delegation. Mr. D. adverted to the fact that the preamble to the Constitution of the United States had been a matter of great controversy, and from it the advocates of two great doctrines, deduced arguments in favor of each. One he believed, had the letter in its favor, the other, the facts. One favored consolidation, the other, confederation. Now the preamble as reported by the committee will admit of a like double construction. He hoped the Convention would see the propriety of adopting the amendment and thereby rid the preamble of its present ambiguity.

Mr. Gwinn expressed his unwillingness that the Convention should act upon a proposition of this character without some consideration. It seemed to him that it was not only a change of phraseology, but that it involved some assertions as to the political relation which the counties bore to each other utterly at variance with the fact. The members of this Convention were not delegates of the counties, but of the State of Maryland. And if the inference was to be drawn that they were here as the representatives of distinct municipalities, the idea was an erroneous one, and should not be tolerated for a moment by this Convention. They were not here as representatives of the counties, but as representatives of the State of Maryland, returned merely by its municipal divisions. Before the Convention was called upon to vote, he desired the gentleman to state what theory he proposed to inculcate by the amendment.

Mr. Parke gave notice that he should offer the following as a substitute for the said preamble:

"We, the people of Maryland, grateful to Almighty God for our own freedom, in order to establish justice, maintain public order, and perpetuate liberty, do ordain this Constitution.

ARTICLE ONE.

"*Section* 1. That the essential principles of liberty and free Government, may be truly recognised, and unalterably established, we declare."

Mr. Dashiell then spoke in reply to the inquiry of Mr. Gwinn, and in vindication of the principle intended to be asserted by his (Mr. D's.) amendment. The sketch of his remarks will be published hereafter.

Mr. Jenifer could not discover any beneficial effect, he said, that could result from the amendment. He went for the substance, not for the shadow. He would go as far as any man to protect the interests of the counties, but he was not willing to admit that he came here as a representative from Charles county only. If the gentleman intended that a new principle was to be engrafted on the Constitution, he (Mr. J.) would like to understand precisely what it was.

Mr. Gwinn said:

That the phraseology which the gentleman proposed, was ambiguous in meaning. If intended only as a designation of the localities from which we came, there was no serious mischief in the words—but if, on the other hand, it was meant as an assertion of the theory that the counties and city of Baltimore, were parties to the old compact and to the new arrangement in their municipal capacities—it was utterly unfounded. And since the words which the gentleman proposed to insert, were of a doubtful meaning, it was better to adhere to terms, about which there could be no mistake.

The theory of county compact had been urged many times in the legislature. It had been remotely hinted at during the last session. But it was strange that any one who took the least pains to examine the history of the State, could use language which admitted by construction, of such a theory. He would state a few facts, which would place the counties in their true light, as constituent portions of the State.

The county of St. Mary's was undefined by any boundaries when first alluded to in our early records. It was the part of the Province which lay around the infant colony.

The lines of Kent county were equally uncertain. It was the whole shore opposite to Kent Island, which was then a commanderate, as it was termed. They were so termed only to distinguish the localities to which reference was made. The assembly, which sat in 1650, was composed of fourteen members, chosen by eight hundreds. It was in this year that the upper and lower Houses were separated. The counties existing at that time were geographical divisions only. The political power residing in the hundreds, into which they were divided. In 1659, the lower House, until then occasionally occupied by some members, who were summoned by the proprietor, was made to consist of delegates only, and four were called from each county. This county system continued until 1681; and in the interval, two, three, or four, were called from each county at the pleasure of the proprietor. In 1682, the number was reduced to two in each county by ordinance; and in 1692, four were allowed to each county in the lower House; and in 1716, four was adopted as the permanent number for each county, and two for each city or borough, which might be created. The Constitution of 1776 adopted this law of 1716, in the organization of the lower House. The counties were then, what they had been in 1716, only corporations—some created by mere order in council, and some by act of the assembly. The idea of their political independency is utterly unfounded.

The history of the Convention which adopted the Constitution, shows this. The counties were represented in the Convention equally, because they were equal in the representation allowed under the law of 1716. The same system was adopted, because the inequality in population was not then very marked, and for the reason, also, that the existence of a war in which the common safety was involved, made it inexpedient to quarrel about details of power.

In the early Conventions, the counties voted as counties. But it will be seen by reference to page 176, of the journal of that Convention, that the Constitution was adopted by a very different rule. Until the 22d June, 1776, all votes were determined by a majority of counties, and the majority of a county delegation, had the right to cast the vote of the county. Now, on the day referred to, it was resolved, that all votes should be determined by a majority of members. Under this rule any article could have been carried, and the whole Constitution adopted by a minority of counties. For instance, say there were twelve counties—seven would be a majority. If three, out of five delegates, could cast the vote of a county, twenty-one would carry a measure, against the fourteen negatives in the seven counties, and the twenty-five negatives in the five counties, supposing them all to vote the same way, making in all thirty-nine. But, when the majority rule was adopted, this could no longer be; and the minority of the counties might rule the majority. These enquiries had been entered into, when the reform bill was under discussion, in the House of Delegates last year; but he made no apology for renewing references which were perhaps information to some present, and which the theory stated, made necessary.

This theory of the political individuality of the counties, was disproved by other circumstances also. Most present were familiar with the suit brought by Washington county against the Baltimore and Ohio Rail Road company, to recover the penalty of one million dollars, which that company was to have paid to the use of Washington county in the event of failing to pursue a specified route. This might have been regarded as a contract with the county if the Legislature represented parties dealing for it, and with it, as corporate agents. And this necessarily would have been the construction, if there had been a particle of truth in such a theory. The Legislature remitted the penalty, and Washington county failed to show that the law was unconstitutional.

The gist of the decision was the merely political character of the county organization. They are municipal corporations—nothing more. They can be divided, and sub-divided—new arranged—obliterated even, at the pleasure of the political power of the State. Why then encourage a theory that will lead only to mischievous results?

Mr. John Newcomer gave notice of an amendment which will be found hereafter.

Mr. Bowie suggested a modification of his amendment to Mr. Dashiell, which was accepted.

Mr. Thomas said, that the amendment of the gentleman from Somerset,(Mr. Dasheill,) was in direct conflict with the language of the law under which we had assembled. It would be seen, by reference to the first section of the law calling this Convention, that the people of Maryland, in the aggregate, were invited to vote for and against the Convention; and in the third section of the same law, it is declared; that the Convention shall assemble, if a majority of all the people of the State, declare in favor of such an assemblage. We are here, then, at the instance of and with authority of the people of Maryland. The sense of the several counties and of the city of Baltimore, was not taken separately. And it cannot, with any propriety, be denied that the language, as it is now in the preamble to the bill of rights, is true and applicable to our proceedings.

But, says the gentleman from Somerset, the Convention who adopted the present Constitution of Maryland, voted on questions arising therein, by counties, each county being entitled to one vote. Even if that was so, it would not effect the question now before this Convention. We are not adopting a preamble to the old Constitution, but we are proposing to prefix one to the Constitution which we are about to form. The law calling us together, having been passed by the members of the Senate and House of Delegates, voting *per capita*, and having been sanctioned by a majority of all the people of this State, that majority being ascertained by their aggregated votes.

If the gentleman from Somerset, would look a little further into the proceedings of the Convention of 1776, he would discover that in adopting the Constitution for this State, the members of the Convention voted *per capita*. On some questions for convenience, the Convention had given to each county a vote, but on the final vote for and against the adoption of the Constitution, every member of the Convention gave an individual vote. As to the supposition, that the gentleman from Somerset, seems disposed to encourage, that the Convention of 1776, considered our old Constitution as a "quasi confederacy," as Mr. McMahon, has expressed it, it is altogether inconsistent with the conduct of that Convention, in having, without asking consent of Frederick county, carved out of that, then very large county, the counties of Montgomery and Washington. Now we all know that the Constitution of the United States, which is a government for a confederacy, expressly denies to the general government the power to disturb the boundaries of any one State of the Union, without its consent.

Anticipating that the Convention would do nothing to countenance the idea that the old Constitution was nothing more than articles of confederation between the counties of the State and the city of Baltimore, Mr. Thomas contended that there was nothing in the history of its adoption that would justify a further continuance of that rule of apportionment, which gave to the counties and the city of Baltimore the representation they now have, respectively, in the House of Delegates and Senate, and upon this floor.

We had no census showing accurately the population of the several counties in the State in 1774. We had the census taken by the United States in 1790. By referring to that census it would be found that the population residing in that section of the State who desire to have a new Constitution, exceeded by a few thousand only, the number of the population in that part of the State where an amendment of the old Constitution had been uniformly resisted. From this fact it is not unreasonable to suppose, that sixteen years before that census was taken, in 1774, the majority of the people of Maryland resided in the counties who have a majority of the members of the House of Delegates and of the Senate, and a majority of the members of this Convention. And we may infer that the Convention of 1774, in giving to each county an equal vote on some questions, acted with great magnanimity in permitting the western counties of the State to have more votes than their population then justified. How different is the scene now? The population on one border of Maryland is three times as great as the population in the counties on the eastern and western side of the bay. Nevertheless this last named section controls the Legislature, and has control in this Convention. Against this state of things the people of the western counties came here to remonstrate. They admit that those brethren who had the legislative branch of the government in their hands are patriotic, honest, and capable. They claim to be possessed of the like qualifications to make good citizens. And are not willing to pass their right of self-government to others. They are willing to be governed by a majority, and consider that to be the only power to which men of free wills can properly submit.

Mr. T. invited the gentleman from Somerset, to look a little further into the early history of Maryland; saying, that he would willingly adopt the rule by which the first settlers of Maryland apportioned the members of the legislature. At that time, there were but two counties in the State—

St. Mary's and Kent Island counties. An equal representation was not given by St. Mary's to Kent Island. One representative was given to one—two to another—three to a third election district, in St. Mary's, and the whole apportionment appeared to have been made with strict reference to population. This example of our fathers, he, (Mr. T.,) was ready and willing to follow, so far as respect was paid to the number of the people, in distributing to them political power. And if other members of the Convention would consent to act on the same obviously fair principle, the Constitution could readily be formed.

After some further remarks from Mr. Dashiell,

Mr. McHenry rose, not for the purpose, he said, of prolonging the discussion, but to call the attention of the gentleman from Somerset, (Mr. Dashiell,) to the fact that the old bill of rights, framed in 1776, opened with the very words which were reported by the committee on the bill of rights, as a part of the new Constitution. And if it was not thought ambiguous then, was it more so now?

Mr. Dashiell said, that no such theory as he referred to, was then dreamt of.

Mr. McHenry said, nor was it dreamt of now, except, perhaps, by a very few persons.

But, Mr. McH. said, he had risen to demand the previous question.

Mr. Merrick desiring to say a few words,

Mr. McHenry withdrew the demand for the previous question.

Mr. Merrick then said:

He should vote against the amendment for a very plain reason. He thought it wisest and best to adhere, as closely as possible, to the language of the old Constitution.

The preamble reported by the committee was as near to the language of the old Constitution, as it well could be. It was abridged by leaving out two or three words, but the substance remained the same. The two preambles, in substance, were identical.

He had never regarded the counties as independent political communities—he had never regarded them as a federative system; and the discussion of the principle upon which the political power of the State was to be apportioned, was inappropriate here.

Mr. McHenry now renewed the demand for the previous question.

There was a second; and

The main question was ordered.

Mr. Dashiell asked the yeas and nays;

Which were ordered, and having been taken, resulted as follows:

Affirmative—Messrs. Morgan, Hopewell, Chambers of Kent, Kent, Bond, John Dennis, Dashiell, Hodson, Bowie, Sprigg, Bowling, Dirickson, McMaster, Hearn, Fooks, Jacobs and Kilgour.—17.

Negative—Messrs. Ricaud, Donaldson, Wells, Randall, Brent of Charles, Merrick, Jenifer, Buchanan, Bell, Welch, Dickinson, Sherwood of Talbot, Chambers of Cecil, Miller, Tuck, McCubbin, Spencer, Grason, George, Thomas, Shriver, Gaither, Biser, Stephenson, McHenry, Magraw, Nelson, Carter, Stewart of Caroline, Gwinn, Stewart of Baltimore city, Brent of Baltimore city, Ware, Schley, Fiery, Neill, John Newcomer, Harbine, Michael Newcomer, Davis, Waters, Anderson, Weber, Hollyday, Slicer, Smith, Parke, Shower and Cockey—49.

So the amendment was rejected.

The question was then stated to be on the substitute amendment of Mr. Parke.

Mr. Jenifer thought that the preamble as it stood, embraced every thing essential. We had lived under it sixty or seventy years without inconvenience, and could still continue to do so.

Mr. Randall desired, he said, to point out a substantial difference between the declaration which the Convention was now making, and that which our fathers made in '76. The amendment was in strict conformity with the powers under which this Convention was acting. The delegates of '76 made a Constitution. The delegates in this Convention were to make one, but only to recommend it to the people. The first was the declaration of the delegates; *this*, if ever it became a declaration, was to be the declaration of the people themselves. In adopting the amendment, the Convention would be following a safe precedent, that of the Constitution of the United States, and of the Constitution of several of the States.

Mr. R. then moved to amend the preamble of the report of the committee, by striking out all of said preamble, and substituting in lieu thereof, the following:

"We, the people of Maryland, grateful to Almighty God for our civil and religious liberty, in order to secure the perpetuity of these blessings, do declare."

Mr. R. said, that the provision was similar to that which had been adopted in seven or eight of the Constitutions of the States. He thought the recognition of our gratitude to Almighty God, for the blessings he had bestowed upon us as a people, would come with a high and holy operation upon the public mind.

Mr. Parke said, that the great object of his amendment, was to acknowledge our gratitude to Almighty God for the signal blessings which he had bestowed upon us, and to use the words, "we the people," in connection with the declaration of rights. To ensure the success of that object, he was willing to accept the amendment of the gentleman from Anne Arundel, (Mr. Randall.) The law which called this Convention together, got its vitality by the will of the people. The Constitution which this Convention might make, could receive its vitality only in the same way. And when the members of this Convention were in their graves, this declaration would still stand as the declaration of the people.

Mr. John Newcomer now offered his substitute for the preamble, as follows:

"We, the people of the State of Maryland, by our delegates in Convention assembled at the city of Annapolis, taking into our most serious consideration the best means of establishing a good Constitution in this State, declare :"

Some conversation followed.

Mr. CHAMBERS preferred the amendment of the gentleman from Washington. At any time prior to the vote of Friday last, he should have concurred in the view taken by the gentleman from Anne Arundel. He regarded that vote as changing our condition in this respect. Our Constitution no longer recognizes the God of the Christian or the God of the Jew. The invocation of an *Almighty* God is now out of place in our Constitution. We recognize "a" God—any God under whose dispensation his worshipper may look for reward or punishment in this life or the next.

The Indian, the Hindoo and numerous classes of heathens, put faith in "a" God, who, though sometimes he sleeps, or is engaged in indulgences which call off his attention, yet, when aroused, is able to punish disobedience to his will. Some worship the great spirit of evil to deprecate his wrath. All such are now made capable of holding the highest offices in the government. Let the Convention be consistent in this respect.

As to the verbal criticism of the gentleman from Anne Arundel, he dissented from his opinion. We are now *making* a Constitutlon, if we succeed in our object—if we do make a Constitution, it is for the people to *ratify* or *reject* what their delegates have done.

The question was then stated to be on the substitute of Mr. JOHN NEWCOMER.

Mr. N. asked the yeas and nays, which were refused.

The question was then taken, and by ayes 33, noes 21, the substitute was adopted.

And the preamble, as thus amended, was adopted.

Mr. SPENCER moved that the bill of rights, as amended, be printed.

Ordered accordingly.

THE JUDICIARY.

Mr. BOWIE, Chairman of the Committee on the Judiciary Department, submitted the following report:

The committee on the Judiciary, beg leave to make the following

REPORT :

Section 1. The judiciary Power of this State shall be vested in a Court of Appeals, in County Courts, in such courts for the city of Baltimore as may be herinafter prescribed, and in justices of the peace.

Sec. 2. The Court of Appeals shall consist of a Chief Justice and two Associate Justices, any two of whom shall form a quorum. The Governor by and with the adviceof the Senate, shall designate the Chief Justice.

Sec. 3. The Court of Appeals shall be co-extensive with the limits of the State, but in criminal cases, and in appeals from interlocutory judgments and decrees, with such exceptions and under such regulations as may be prescribed by law, and the Court of Appeals and judges thereof shall have power to issue writs of *Mandamus* and writs of *Diminution*, and such other writs as shall be necessary to enforce its own jurisdiction, and may also compel a judge of a county court or other inferior court to proceed to trial and judgment in a cause—and the Court of Appeal shall hold its sessions at the city of Annapolis on the first Monday of June and the first Monday of December in each and every year.

Sec. 4. The Court of Appeals shall appoint its own clerk, who shall hold his office for six years, and may be re-appotnted at the end thereof; he shall be subject to removal by the said court for incompetency, neglect of duty, misdemeanor in office, and such other causes as may be prescribed by law.

Sec. 5. The State shall be divided into three Judicial Districts, one on the Eastern and two on the Western Shore, which said districts shall be laid off as the Gubernatorial districts are, and one person from among those learned in the law, having been admitted to practice the law in this State, and who shall have been a citizen of this State at least five years, and above the age of thirty years at the time of his election, and a resident of the judicial district, shall be elected from each of said districts by a plurality vote of the legal and qualified voters therein, as a judge of the said Court of Appeals, who shall hold his office for the term of ten years from the time of his election, or until he shall have attained the age of seventy years, which ever may first happen, and be re-eligible thereto until he shall have attained the age of seventy years, and not after ; subject to removal for incompetency, wilful neglect of duty, misdemeanor in office, and such other causes as may be prescribed by law, by presentment of the Grand Jury and conviction of a petit jury of the county in which he may reside, or by the Governor upon the address of the General Assembly. two-thirds of the members of each house concurring in such address. The salaries of the judges of the Court of Appeals, shall be two thousand five hundred dollars annually, and shall not be diminished during their continuance in office.

Sec. 6. The Legislature may hereafter, should the public convenience require it, increase the number of judges of the court of appeals to five ; in which event, a new division of the State into five judicial district, shall be made in such manner as to secure two to the Eastern and three to the Western Shore.

Sec. 7. No judge of the Court of Appeals, shall sit in any case wherein he may be interested, or where either of the parties may be connected with him by affinity or consanguinity within such degrees as may be prescribed by law, or where he shall have been of counsel in the cause. When the Court of Appeals, or any two of its members shall be thus disqualified to hear and determine any cause or causes in said court, or when no judgment can be rendered in any case or cases in said court, by reason of the equal division of opinion of said judges, the same shall be certified to the Governor of the State, who shall immediately commission the requisite number of persons learned in the law for the trial and determination of said case or cases.

Sec. 8. All judges of the Court of Appeals, of the county courts and of the courts for the city of Baltimore, shall by virtue of their offices, be conservators of the peace throughout the State. The style of all laws shall run thus: "Be it enacted by the General Assembly of Maryland;" all public commissions and grants thus: "The State of Maryland, &c.;" and shall be signed by the Governor, with the seal of the State annexed; all writs and process shall run in the same style, and be sealed and signed as usual, and all indictments shall conclude, "against the peace, government and dignity of the State."

Sec. 9. There shall be a county court in each county of the State, to consist of one judge, who shall be elected by a plurality vote of the qualified and legal voters of said county, from among those learned in the law, having been admitted to practice the law in this State, and who shall have been a citizen of this State at least five years, and above the age of thirty years at the time of his election, and a resident of said county. The said judge shall hold his office for the term of ten years from the time of his election, or until he shall have attained the age of seventy years, whichever may first happen, and be re-eligible thereto until he shall have attained the age of seventy years, and not after, subject to be removed for incompetency, wilful neglect of duty, misdemeanor in office, and such other causes as may be prescribed by law, by presentment of a Grand Jury and conviction of a petit jury of said county, or by the Governor, upon the address of the General Assembly, two-thirds of the members of each House concurring in such address. His salary shall be two thousand dollars annually, which shall not be diminished during his continuance in office. He shall reside in or near the county town, and shall hold two common law terms in each and every year, at such times and places as may be prescribed by law, and attend at the court house of said county as often as the Legislature may prescribe by law for the transaction and despatch of judicial business.

Sec. 10. The said county courts, or the judges thereof respectively, shall be courts of law and equity, and have original jurisdiction in all civil and criminal cases arising in their respective limits; and in all respects have the same powers and jurisdiction that the present county courts of this State now have, or which shall hereafter be prescribed by law. They shall also have exclusive jurisdiction in all matters relating to last wills and testaments, executors and administrators and guardians, within their respective limits, and all and every other power which the orphans' courts of this State now have, or which may be hereafter prescribed by law. They shall also have and exercise appellate jurisdiction from the judgments of justices of the peace, subject to such rules and regulations as may be prescribed by law.

Sec. 11. There shall be established for the city of Baltimore, one court with common law jurisdiction, to be styled the court of "Common Pleas," which shall have civil jurisdiction in all suits where the debt or damage claimed, shall not exceed five hundred dollars.

Sec. 12. There shall also be in said city, another common law court, having jurisdiction over all suits where the debt or damages claimed, shall exceed the sum of five hundred dollars; and each of said courts shall be vested with all powers now held and exercised by Baltimore county court, as a court of law; and this last court shall be styled "the Superior court of Baltimore city."

Sec. 13. There shall also be established a court having equity jurisdiction, for the city of Baltimore, whose style shall be "the Chancery court of the city of Baltimore," and which shall have and exercise the equity jurisdiction now exercised by Baltimore county court, sitting as a court of equity. Each of the said three courts shall consist of one Judge, who shall hold his office for the term of ten years, subject to the provisions of this Constitution, with regard to the election, and qualification of Judges and their removal from office; and the salary of each of the said Judges shall be twenty-five hundred dollars per year.

Sec. 14. The court of common pleas shall have jurisdiction in all appeals from Magistrates' decisions in the said city, and the said appeals shall be made to the said court; and the Chancery court shall have jurisdiction in all applications for the benefit of the insolvent laws of this State, and of the administration of the estates of insolvent debtors, and the supervision and control of the trustees thereof.

Sec. 15. There shall be established an orphans' court for Baltimore city, which shall consist of one Judge, who shall hold his office for the term of ten years, and who shall have all the powers now vested in the orphans' court of Baltimore county, within the limits of said city, subject to such regulations as the Legislature may establish for the conduct of the ordinary business of the said court, by the Register of Wills of the said city; and who shall be subject to the provisions of this Constitution, as to the election and qualifications of Judges and their removal therefrom; and the salary of the said Judge shall be two thousand dollars per year.

Sec. 16. There shall also be a criminal court for the city of Baltimore, to be styled "the Criminal court of Baltimore city," which shall consist of one Judge, and shall have and exercise all the jurisdiction now exercised by Baltimore city court, except so far as the same may be vested in the police court hereafter to be established, and shall have exclusive jurisdiction in cases of petition for freedom, and in all cases of petitions to cancel or enforce contracts of apprenticeship—and the said Judge shall receive an annual salary of two thousand dollars per annum, and shall be subject to the provisions of this Constitution, with regard to the election and qualification of Judges and their removal from office.

Sec. 17. There shall also be established a court to be styled "the Police court of Baltimore city,", to consist of one Judge, who shall hold this office for the term of ten years, and who shall be subject to all the provisions of this Constitution with regard to the election and qualification of Judges and their removal from office; and the said court shall have jurisdiction in all prosecutions for assault and battery—for keeping disorderly houses—for larceny where the property stolen does not exceed in value the sum of twenty dollars—in all prosecutions for receiving stolen goods, knowing them to be stolen—and for selling goods without license: and it shall be the duty of the Legislature to provide for quarterly sessions of the said court for the purpose of trying those cases in which a trial by jury may be demanded by the accused; and also to provide that the said court shall hold frequent sessions for the trial of cases, subject to its jurisdiction in which the accused may not demand a jury trial; and the Judge of the said court shall receive an annual salary of fifeen hundred dollars.

Sec. 18. There shall be a clerk of each county court, who shall be elected by a plurality vote of the qualified voters of each county, and who shall hold his office for the term of six years, from the time of his election and until a new election is held, and be re-eligible thereto, subject to removal for wilful neglect of duty, or other misdemeanor in office by presentment of a Grand Jury and conviction of a Petit Jury, of the county in which he shall reside. There shall also be a clerk of the Court of Common Pleas in Baltimore city, who shall also be the clerk of the Superior Court of Baltimore city, and the Register in Chancery of the Chancery Court of the city of Baltimore, and there shall also be a clerk of the criminal court of Baltimore city, who shall also be the clerk of the police court of Baltimore city, and each of said clerks shall be elected by a plurality vote of the qualified voters of the city of Baltimore, and shall hold his office for six years, from the time of his election, and until a new election is held, and be re-eligible thereto, subject in like manner to be removed for wilful neglect of duty or other misdemeanor in office by presentment of a grand jury and conviction of a petit jury of said city. In case of a vacancy in the office of a clerk, the judge or judges of the court of which he was clerk, shall have the power to appoint a clerk until an election can be held, which shall take place under the directions of the Sheriff upon giving thirty days public notice thereof.

Sec. 19. The Legislature shall provide by law, some plain, intelligible and simple mode of compensation to the clerks of the several courts in this State, in lieu of the existing mode of fees.

Sec. 20. There shall be a Register of Wills in each county of the State, and in the city of Baltimore, to be elected by a plurality vote of the qualified voters of said counties and city respectively, and who shall hold his office for six years from the time of his election, and until a new election shall take place, and be re-eligible thereto, subject to be removed for wilful neglect of duty, or other dismeanor in office, in the same manner that the clerks of the county courts are removable. The Legislature shall provide by law, suitable annual salaries for such Register of Wills, to be levied on the assessable property of said counties and city respectively, in lieu of all fees and perquisites as now established by law. In the event of any vacancy in the office of Register of Wills, said vacancy shall be filled by the judge or judges of the court, until an election can be held, which shall take place under the directions of the Sheriff, upon thirty days public notice thereof.

Sec. 21. There shall be five Justices of the Peace, in each election district of every county of the State, and two in each ward of the city of Baltimore, to be elected by a plurality vote of the qualified voters in each of said districts and wards respectively, who shall hold their offices for two years, from the time of their election and until a successor in office is elected. They shall be, by virtue of their offices, conservators of the peace in the said counties and city respectively, and shall have such civil and criminal jurisdiction, as shall be provided for by law. In the event of a vacancy in the office of a Justice of Peace, a new election shall be held under the directions of the Sheriff of the county or city where such vacancy occurs, upon ten days notice thereof; an appeal shall be in all civil cases from the judgment of a Justice of the Peace, to the judges of the county courts and of the court of common pleas for Baltimore city, as the case may be, and on all such appeals, either party shall be entitled to a trial by jury, where the amount in controversy shall be above ten dollars.

Sec. 22. Sheriffs shall be elected in each county and in the city of Baltimore, every third year, that is to say: two persons for the office of sheriff for each county, and two for the said city, the one of whom having the highest number of votes of the qualified voters of said county or city, or if both have an equal number, either of them, at the discretion of the Governor, to be commissioned by the Governor for the said office, and having served for three years, such person shall be ineligible for the four years next succeeding; bond with security to be taken every year as usual, and no sheriff shall be qualified to act before the same be given. In case of death, refusal, disqualification or removal out of the county, before the expiration of the three years, the other person chosen as aforesaid, shall be commissioned by the Governor to execute the said office, for the residue of the said three years, the said person giving bond with security as aforesaid. No person shall be eligible to the office of Sheriff, but a resident of such county or city respectively, and who shall have been a citizen of this State at least five years preceding his election, and above the age of twenty-one years. The two candidates properly qualified having the highest number of legal ballots, shall be declared duly elected for the office of sheriff for such county or city, and returned to the Governor with a certificate of the number of ballots for each of them.

Sec. 23. Constables, coroners, and elizors, shall be appointed for each county and the city of Baltimore, in the manner now prescribed by law, or in such other manner as the General Assembly may hereafter direct.

Sec. 24. No Judge shall sit in any case wherein

he may be interested, or where either of the parties may be connected with him by affinity or consanguinity, within such degrees as may be prescribed by law, or where he shall have been of counsel in the cause, and whenever any of the judges of the county courts, or of the courts of Baltimore city, shall be thus disqualified, or whenever by reason of sickness or any other cause, the said judges, or any of them, may be unable to sit in any cause, the parties may, by consent, appoint a proper person to try the said cause, or the judges shall exchange districts, and hold courts for each other, when they may deem it expedient, and shall do so when directed by law.

Sec. 25. No new original bill shall be filed or received in the High Court of Chancery of this State, from and after the ratification of this Constitution, by the people of this State, nor shall any cause be removed from any other court in the State, to the said court of Chancery from and after the said ratification; but all causes and proceedings now pending, or which may be pending in the said court of Chancery at the time of the said ratification, shall be heard, determined and proceeded with, by the present Chancellor or his successor in office, until they shall be brought to a final close, provided the same be done in five years, from the time of said ratification, and at the end and expiration of said five years, from the time of the said ratification, or sooner if the said business in chancery be sooner disposed of, the office of Chancellor of this State, and the office of Register in Chancery, shall be,and they are hereby abolished. The present Chancellor and Register in Chancery, and in the event of any vacancy in their respective offices, their successors in office respectively, to be appointed, as at present, by the Governor and Senate, shall, during said five years, or other shorter period, receive the same salary and compensation, which they now receive. The Legislature shall provide by law, for the recording, safe keeping, or other disposition of the records, decrees and other proceeding of the said court of Chancery, at the end and expiration of said five years or other shorter period, and for the transmission to the several counties of the State and city of Baltimore, of all such causes and proceedings in said court, as may be then undisposed of and unfinished, in such manner, and under such regulations as may be deemed necessary and proper.

Sec. 26. The present judges of the county courts, of the orphan's courts, of Baltimore city court, and of the magistrates' courts, and of the commissioners of insolvent debtors for the city of Baltimore, and justices of the peace shall remain in office until the election and qualification of the judges, and justices of the peace whose election is provided for by this Constitution and no longer.

Sec. 27. The first election of judges, clerks, registers and justices of the peace, and all other officers whose election by the people is provided for in this article of the Constitution shall take place throughout the State on the first Wednesday of October next, after the ratification of this Constitution by the people.

Sec. 28. Whenever lands lie partly in one county, and partly in another, or whenever persons proper to be made defendants to proceedings in Chancery, reside, some in one county and some in another, that court shall have jurisdiction in which proceedings shall have been first commenced, subject to such rules, regulations and alterations as may be prescribed by law.

Sec. 29. In all suits or actions at law, and in all presentments and indictments, hereafter to be commenced or instituted in any of the courts of law of this State, having jurisdiction thereof, the judge or judges thereof, upon suggestion in writing, if made by the Attorney General, or the prosecutor for the State, or upon suggestion in writing supported by affidavit, if made by any other of the parties thereto, that a fair and impartial trial cannot be had in the court where such suit or action at law, or presentment and indictment is depending, shall and may order and direct the record of proceedings in such suit or action, presentment or indictment, to be transmitted to the judge of any adjoining county for trial, who shall hear and determine the same in like manner as if such suit or action, presentment or indictment, had been originally instituted therein; provided nevertheless, that such suggestions shall be made as aforesaid, before or during the term in which the issue or issues may be joined, in said suit or action, presentment or indictment. And provided also, that such further remedy in the premises, may be provided by law as the legislature shall from time to time direct and enact.

Sec. 30. All elections of judges and other officers provided for under this article of the constitution shall be certified, and the returns made by the clerks of the respective counties to the Governor, who shall issue commissions to the different persons for the offices, to which they shall have been respectively elected.

ESTIMATES

Submitted by the Committee on the Judiciary.

Costs of the present Judiciary of Maryland under the old Constitution:

Twelve associate judges of county courts, at $1,400 per annum, . . .	$16,800
Six chief justices of county courts at $2,200, . .	13,200
One chief judge of Court of Appeals, (extra pay allowed by law,) . . .	300
Extra pay allowed by law to judges of Baltimore county and city, . . .	8,000
The Chancellor's salary, .	3,000
Sixty-six judges of Orphans' courts in the counties and city of Baltimore, at an average by actual returns of $300, to each judge, . .	19,800
Salary of the commissioners of insolvent debtors for the city of Baltimore, at $2,000 to each, ...	6,000

Salary of the judges of Baltimore city court, . .	4,100	
Total costs of the present system, ...	———	$71,200
Costs of the judiciary system reported from the committee on the judiciary, under the new Constitution:		
Three judges of Court of Appeals, at $2,500 to each, .	7,500	
Twenty judges of county courts, at $2,000, . .	40,000	
Four judges of law and equity for Baltimore city, at $2,500 to each, . .	10,000	
One judge for orphans' court business for the city of Baltimore, at 2,000, . .	2,000	
One police court judge for Baltimore city, . . .	1,500	
Total cost of system under new Constitution, . .	———	61,000
Difference in favor of new system, ...		10,200
If to this be added the am't of fees of two hundred and sixty-nine judges of magistrates' courts, now in commission, and proposed to be abolished, estimated at $100 to each, equal to .		26,900
The difference will be, .		37,100

Mr. Smith offered the following order which was adopted:

Resolved, That the committee appointed by the order of the gentleman of Anne Arundel, (Mr. Dorsey,) on page 269 of the Journal, be a committee upon the subject of new counties; and the order of inquiry submitted by Mr. Smith of Allegany, on page 166 of the Journal, upon the subject of a division of Allegany county, be referred to said committee.

Which was twice read and adopted.

THE ELECTIVE FRANCHISE.

Mr. Morgan moved that the Convention proceed to the consideration of the Report of the Committee on the Elective Franchise.

Mr. Chambers, of Kent, suggested that the bill had been put into a shape by himself and the gentleman from Cecil, (Mr. McLane,) which he (Mr. C.) hoped might be acceptable to the Convention; but as that gentleman was confined to his room by sickness, he (Mr. C.) hoped the motion would be withdrawn.

Mr. Morgan withdrew the motion.

THE LEGISLATIVE DEPARTMENT.

Mr. Harbine moved that the Convention proceed to the consideration of the Report of the Committee on the Legislative Department of the Government.

The Report was announced—when the Chairman of the committee, not being in the city, a motion to postpone was made.

A discussion of some length followed, having reference to the propriety of the postponement.

The result was that the Report was read through, and its further consideration was then postponed (as a special order) until to-morrow.

THE JUDICIARY.

Pending this discussion,

On motion of Messrs. Bowie and Buchanan,

The Report of the Committee on the Judiciary was read.

And the said Report was made the special order of the day for Monday week.

And then the Convention adjourned until to-morrow at eleven o'clock.

WEDNESDAY, February 12th, 1851.

The Convention met at eleven o'clock.

Prayer was made by the Mr. Rev. Grauff.

The Journal of yesterday was read in part, when, on motion of

Mr. Magraw, the further reading was dispensed with.

THE JUDICIARY.

Mr. Crisfield said he was not present yesterday when the Chairman of the Committee on the Judiciary, (Mr. Bowie,) made a report from that committee. It did not appear from the journal but that the report had the concurrence of the whole committee. Such was not the case. Mr. C. said he felt it due to himself that he should express to the Convention his dissent. He especially objected to the time and mode of appointing the Judges proposed; to the principle of re-eligibility, and to having a Judge for each county. He also had other objections of less importance. But he did not propose, at this time, to go into an examination of the subject; at the proper time when this subject should be called up for the consideration of the Convention, he should take occasion to express his opinions at large. For the present he only designed to inform the Convention, and his constituents, that he did not concur in the report.

The President, *pro tem.* Does the gentleman desire that his dissent should be entered on the journal?

Mr. Crisfield. No, sir. I am satisfied with giving this notice.

Mr. Dorsey presented a petition of sundry citizens of Howard District in Anne Arundel county, praying that said Howard District be erected into a new county, to be called "Howard county;"

Which was read, and

On motion of Mr. Dorsey,

Laid on the table.

The President, *pro tem.*, called for reports from committees, notices, resolutions, and motions.

None were offered.

HOWARD DISTRICT

Mr. Dorsey moved that the Convention proceed to the consideration of the report heretofore made by him, from the select committee appointed to consider and report respecting the formation of new counties, in relation to erecting Howard District into a new county to be called Howard county.

This Report had been made the special order of the day for this day.

The President, *pro tem.*, announced the said Report to be the business before the Convention.

THE LEGISLATIVE DEPARTMENT.

Mr. Phelps rose to inquire of the Chairman, whether the unfinished business of yesterday (the Report on the Legislative Department of the Government) had not precedence over the Report of the gentleman from Anne Arundel, (Mr. Dorsey.) He (Mr. P.) had yesterday been compelled, very strongly against his wishes, to take up the former subject, and, having been so, he did not now feel disposed to yield its title to priority. He had also stated the other day, and he now repeated, that he was unwilling to take up this question as to Howard District until the question of representation and apportionment had been settled.

The President, *pro tem.*, replying to the point of order raised by Mr. Phelps, stated the condition of the business upon the calendar, and proceeded to say, that the Convention had yesterday, taken up the Report from the Legislative Department. That report had not been made the order of the day for any particular day. If the report had been allowed to remain where it was left yesterday, after it had been read, it would have come up to-day as unfinished business. But the Convention had thought proper to take it out of its line, and to make it the special order for to-day. It would, therefore, come up after previous special orders should have been disposed of.

Mr. Merrick thought, he said, that the decision of the Chair was correct. The Convention had been brought into the difficulty in which it was now placed, by an error on its own part. And in order that the Convention might clear itself from this difficulty, he would move that all previous orders be postponed, with a view to enable the Convention to proceed to the consideration of the Report of the Committee on the Legislative Department.

Mr. Dorsey briefly opposed the motion to postpone the Howard District report, and suggested that if the report of the legislative committee should be first acted upon, it would be requisite to re-consider portions of its provisions, in order to accomodate them to the action of the Convention upon the other report. He presumed it would not occupy much time.

Mr. Donaldson hoped that the Convention would take up the Howard District report.

Mr. Phelps hoped, he said, that the motion of the gentleman from Charles, (Mr. Merrick,) would prevail. The question involved in the report of the gentleman from Anne Arundel, (Mr. Dorsey,) was an important one, and he, (Mr. P.,) thought that the gentleman was mistaken in supposing that the report would pass *sub silentio*, or or without debate. For his own part, he, (Mr. P.,) was not disposed to give his vote in favor of erecting new counties, until he had first ascertained what the basis of representation was to be. He thought that the argument of the gentleman from Anne Arundel, (Mr. Dorsey,) did not apply, because the report of the legislative committee provided how new counties, made by subdivision, should be represented in the legislative halls. In addition to this, he, (Mr. P.,) would state, that there was a number of gentleman on both sides of the Convention who were anxious to vote upon the second section of the report of the committee on the legislative department, and who were desirous to leave the city. He thought that an opportunity should be extended to them to express their sentiments and to record their votes upon the section. (It was that which related to biennial sessions.) He hoped, therefore, that the report of the committee on the legislative department would be taken up to-day.

Mr. Merrick said it was deeply to be regretted, that so much of the time of the Convention was consumed in discussing the order of business. At the time of the adjournment yesterday, it was manifestly the fixed purpose of the Convention to go on with the report of the committee on the legislative department; and it was only by an error, as he had before stated, that the difficulty had arisen this morning. He hoped that the purpose still existed in the mind of the Convention, to proceed now with this important part of the public business. And he submitted that there was no necessity to act upon the report of the committee relative to Howard District, in anticipation of the report of the legislative committee.

Mr. Dorsey said he had looked at the report of the committee on the legislative department with some care, and he assured gentlemen that they were mistaken in supposing that a re-consideration of the legislative report would not be necessary if it was acted upon before the report of the committee on Howard District. He could turn to the report and satisfy gentlemen that they were mistaken, but he did not wish to take up the time of the Convention. He thought that the Howard District report would occupy but little time, and he hoped that the Convention would go on and dispose of it now.

The President, *pro tem.*, stated the question to be on the motion of Mr. Merrick, to postpone the consideration of the Howard District report, with a view to take up the report of the committee on the legislative department.

Mr. Brown hoped that the motion to postpone would not be agreed to. The best way to get through with the business of the Convention, was to consider and dispose of it in the order in which it came up.

Mr. Jenifer gave notice that if he should be absent, (as he probably might be,) when the report from Committee No. 14, in relation to the establishment of a Board of Works, should come up, he did not desire that the Convention should regard his absence as any objection to taking it up.

HOWARD DISTRICT.

The PRESIDENT, *pro tem.*, again stated the question to be on the motion of the gentleman from Charles, (Mr. Merrick,) to postpone the Howard District report. And the PRESIDENT, *pro tem.*, stated that a vote of two-thirds would be required —the motion being for a suspension of the rules.

Some conversation on the point of order followed between Mr. MERRICK and the PRESIDENT, *pro tem.*, when

The PRESIDENT, *pro tem.*, then decided that, inasmuch as the Convention had taken up and proceeded to consider the report of the gentleman from Anne Arundel, (Mr. Dorsey,) it was competent for the Convention, by the vote of a majority, to postpone its further consideration.

The question, "shall the further consideration of the said report be postponed," was then taken, and by ayes 36, noes 34;

The further consideration thereof, was postponed.

THE LEGISLATIVE DEPARTMENT.

The Convention thereupon, proceeded to the consideration of the report made on the twenty-eighth ultimo, by Mr. JOHNSON, as chairman of the committee on the legislative department of the government.

[For this report, see the date in which it was made.]

Mr. DORSEY said, that he was not in his seat yesterday, being engaged in the court above. He did not, therefore, know on what part of the report the Convention was engaged. He had an amendment which he desired to offer to the first section of the report.

The PRESIDENT, *pro. tem.*, stated that yesterday the report had been read for information only; no progress had been made in it. The first section of the report was now under consideration.

The first section of the report was then read as follows:

Section 1. The legislative power of this State shall be vested in two distinct branches, the one to be styled the Senate, the other the House of Delegates, and both together, "the General Assembly of Maryland."

Mr. DORSEY moved to strike out the first section, and to substitute for it an amendment, (hereafter noticed,) commencing as "article" first.

Mr. D. explained, that, by reference to page 106 of the journal, the Convention would perceive that the word "article" as applied to a clause of the report was informal. The resolution introduced by the gentleman from Baltimore city, (Mr. Presstman,) and which would be found at the page mentioned, provided "that the several committees on the Constitution, be instructed to report by *articles*, such propositions as are to be submitted by them for the adoption or rejection of this body," &c.

His, (Mr. D's,) reason for the motion to strike out the clause itself, was, he thought, that in the old Constitution better. Mr. D. read the two. The provision of the old Constitution, he thought, expressed every thing quite as explicitly, and in fewer words.

Mr. CHAMBERS, of Kent, suggested that he supposed the idea to have been, to make an article of each branch or department of the government, and then to sub-divide the articles into sections.

Mr. PHELPS concurred in the explanation given by Mr. CHAMBERS, and said, that the committee on the legislative department had framed the phraseology of their report, in accordance with that contained in other reports, and had not thought proper to depart from the usual manner of expression.

As to the substitute amendment proposed by the gentleman from Anne Arundel, (Mr. Dorsey,) he, (Mr. P.,) had no objection to it. He felt himself placed, however, in an unenviable position in regard to this report. He was not prepared, in the absence of the chairman of the committee, (Mr. Johnson,) to make a repor himself.

That gentleman came here a few days ago, and was anxious to leave the next day. His report was submitted to the committee, and was just read with the understanding that each member of the committee might dissent from the report, or offer any amendments to it. Subsequently, the chairman of the committee, had stated to him, [Mr. P.,] that he probably might not be here when the report was taken up, and had asked him, [Mr. P.,] to take charge of it in his absence. He had answered generally, that he would endeavor, in the best way he could, to carry out the design of the report.

He concurred with the gentleman from Anne Arundel, (Mr. Dorsey,) that the language of the old Constitution was more concise and expressive than that of the report.

Mr. BOWIE. I accept the amendment then;

Mr. DORSEY, (referring to the resolution on the journal,) submitted that it would be better to arrange the provisions of the report with a view to having them numbered from beginning to end. It would prevent mistakes. He thought that the resolution showed that the intention of the Convention was such as his amendment indicated. He was not tenacious about it, but he thought its effect would be beneficial.

Mr. MERRICK said, he thought it was not material whether the word "article" or "section" was used. Yet, he thought, that perhaps, for the reason suggested by the gentleman from Kent, (Mr. Chambers,) it might be better to use the word "section."

He concurred in the opinion expressed by the gentleman from Anne Arundel, (Mr. Dorsey,) that the words of the old Constitution were preferable to those of the report.

Mr. DORSEY remarking, that the verbal amendment he had proposed, would be applicable to other reports, withdrew that amendment, intending to offer it again hereafter.

The question then was on the motion of Mr. DORSEY, to strike out the said first section of the report, and to substitute the words of the old Constitution as follows:

"The legislature shall consist of two distinct branches, a Senate and a House of Delegates, which shall be styled the General Assembly of Maryland."

The question was taken, and the amendment was agreed to.

The second section of the report of the committee, was then read as follows:

Section 2nd. The senators shall be elected by the qualified voters, for the term of four years, and the Delegates for the term of from the day of the general election."

Mr. PHELPS moved to strike out the said second section, and substitute for it an amendment, of which he had given notice on Saturday last, and which was in the following words:

"The senators shall be elected by the qualified voters of this State, for the term of four years, and the delegates in like manner, for the term of two years from the day of the general election; and the regular session of the General Assembly shall be biennial."

Mr. MERRICK remarked that a motion to perfect a section was in order, before the motion to strike it out, He would, therefore, move to fill the blank in the section with "one."

This proposition, (Mr. M. remarked,) brought up the question of biennial or annual sessions. His own opinion accorded with the views entertained by our ancestors, which was, that it was wise and wholesome—a great preservative of liberty and of the rights of the people, that there should be frequent meetings of their representatives. He did not like the idea of leaving the whole affairs of the State of Maryland—its financial concerns and general interests—in the hands of individuals—public officers—for the period of two years, before the grand judgment of the State should be called to examine and pass upon their acts. He thought the public good required that the Legislature should meet once a year—that the representatives of the people should be elected at short intervals, and should account to their principals for the manner in which they had used their powers. This was a great cardinal principle, which lay at the foundation of all free government. He hoped that this Convention would not set the example of violating that principle. Let the length of the sessions be limited, if the Convention chose, to as short a period as they might think proper. But there was no other way in which the people could get at the doings of their functionaries, except through their representatives. This Convention had met to form a Constitution to last for years, until it should be found unsuited to the times. The Convention, therefore, should look now to the dangers which might threaten the State. One of these dangers was, the unfaithfulness of public servants. God forbid that he should reflect upon any man. But gentlemen were to consider the large sums of money which were passing through the hands of these officers, and should remember that the best and purest men, *had* been tempted and corrupted. These public trusts, therefore, should not be left unaccounted for, for the period of two years. Let the officers of the State feel and know that they were annually responsible for their acts. It would be a great check upon them—a safeguard for themselves, and for the people. He hoped, therefore, that there would be annual elections, and annual convocations of the Legislature. So far as the matter of economy was concerned, it was not to be weighed in the balance, against the great good to be attained.

Mr. PHELPS said, he felt constrained to acknowledge that he felt he occupied a most unenviable position, in regard to this report. The honorable chairman of the committee, (Mr. Johnson,) is not now in his seat, and through the courtesy of that distingushed gentleman, in connection with the position assigned him, upon the committee itself, he felt called upon to exercise at least, some supervisory care over this report.

He regretted to differ with his friend from Charles, (Mr. Merrick.) He always entertained the most profound respect for his opinions. His long and brilliant public services, entitled him to regard, but he could not vote for his amendment. It was suggested to him, (Mr. P.,) upon his right, that his object would be attained, by moving to fill the blank, in the second section of the bill, with two years. He thanked the gentleman for his kindness, but must adhere to his original motion.

He desired, by his amendment, to approach his object, boldly and without cover. The majority of the committee were in favor of biennial sessions of the Legislature, and the report now under consideration, was designed to accomplish that object; yet, without this amendment, or some other similar to it, the report would fail to secure this most important proposition. Important in his estimation, in every sense, and one in which the commonwealth must feel the deepest interest.

The gentleman from Charles (Mr. Merrick,) had insisted upon frequent elections, and upon frequent, and direct accountability to the people. That the representative should be forced, at short periods, to give an account of his stewardship to the people themselves. Now, Mr. President, I fully concur in these opinions. They are in strict accordance with the spirit and genius of our Republican institutions. The very principle contended for is already engrafted upon our Bill of Rights, and is destined to become a part and parcel of the organic law of our land. Frequent elections and frequent and direct accountability (Mr. P.) said, were doctrines which he held in common with his friend from Charles. But what *are* we to understand by these words "these cardinal principle?" These are relative terms, and are surely not intended to designate any precise length of time. These terms, if imperative, should apply alike to all the officers of the Government. All alike should be held to direct and strict accountability. Yet, Mr. President, we now have reports before the Convention providing for the election of Governor for the term of three years, Registers of Wills, and Clerks of the County courts for six years, and the Judges for ten years, and they are in most instances made re-eligible to the same offices. If these most important, and truly responsible offices, can be held in accordance with the spirit and genius of the Government, for these respective terms. If their terms of service are not in conflict with this cardinal principle in the Bill of Rights, with the doctrine of frequent elections, and frequent accountability to the people, he would respectfully, but earnestly inquire, where is the fearful, the awful danger, to be apprehended from the election of Delegates, to the General Assembly, for the term of two years? He must be permitted to say, that these dangers existed alone in the excited imaginations of gentlemen. Your Senators in Congress, as well as in your State, hold their positions for six years, without exciting the slightest apprehension of danger; without alarming the fears of any one. Yet, gentlemen are startled, absolutely horrified, at the momentous consequences, which will befal the State, because, members of the House of Delegates, are not returned each and every year. They would have us believe, that the safety and perpetuity of our republican institutions were put in absolute peril, by this amendment, and that our dearest rights, and brightest hopes would be endangered by its adoption, by this House. Mr. P. said for his part, he had no such apprehensions. He had no doubt the morrow's sun would shine quite as bright, and the sky would be quite as clear, if this provision be incorporated upon the Constitution, as if rejected. Yea, sir, our political horizon will be much brightened, by its adoption, and this Convention, in his opinion, elevated in public estimation. The people not only expect it, but they will demand it at our hands.

The great question at issue, Mr. President, and the only one, entitled to the grave consideration of this enlightened Assembly is, does the public interest require annual sessions of the Legislature? Is the condition of the State such, as to demand the presence of the General Assembly, at the seat of Government once in twelve months? Will the prosperity, and happiness of the people of Maryland be promoted, by the return to annual sessions of the Legislature? These are questions which this Convention is called upon to decide, and it is to be hoped, their decision will result in the good of the Commonwealth.

Mr. P. said he would now call upon honorable gentlemen around him, to calmly and dispassionately examine these propositions, and he called upon them to show the necessity of this constant and ever accumulating amount of legislation.

The great questions connected with the internal improvement policy of the State are now settled, and he hoped once and forever. Your Chesapeake and Ohio canal has already reached Cumberland. The Baltimore and Ohio rail road was stretching rapidly across the Alleghanies, and ere long is destined to tap the Ohio river. Your Tidewater canal and your Susquehanna rail road are already finished, to say nothing of your Washington and Annapolis and Elkridge rail roads. These great internal improvement schemes which for the time had so paralyzed the energies of the people of Maryland and so signally embarrassed the public treasury, require no further legislation. But it is to be hoped they will soon be in a condition to make at least partial returns for the vast amount of the public treasure which they have cost. These subjects were, therefore, he hoped, not again to be agitated in these halls.

The financial condition of the State, at one time, was such as to require annual sessions of the Legislature. But a few years since there was an annual accumulation of interest upon the public debt of from three to four hundred thousand dollars. The public credit was dishonored. The faith and honor of Maryland was a by-word in other and distant lands, and repudiation even in these halls stood unrebuked These dark and damning clouds, Mr. President, have passed away once and forever. A brighter and more glorious sun has dawned upon the people of Maryland. Our public faith is fully redeemed, and we stand at all times ready to meet our engagements. Not only so, but we have some three or four hundred thousand dollars surplus annually, to apply to the extinguishment of the principal of the public debt. From this truthful statement, it is evident that the finances of the State do not require an annual supervision by the Legislature.

Where then, is the necessity of returning to annual sessions of the General Assembly? What is the nature and character of the great and almost entire amount of our legislation? Why, sir, mere local enactments for local and private purposes, and in many instances, at least, are of no public or even private utility.

It has been alleged that at the last session of the Legislature, it being the first under the biennial bill, that more than five hundred bills and resolutions had passed the General Assembly. Be it so; and not unfrequently the number under annual sessions had at least approximated this amount of legislation.

Mr. P. said, he had carefully examined the nature and character of those enactments about which gentlemen talk so much, and he had ascertained that out of this number, there was one hundred and fifty-five acts of incorporation. Nearly one third of the entire legislation of the last year was taken up by enactments of this sort. He had had some experience upon this branch of the public service, having in the Senate of Maryland, been a member of the committee on corporations, and he could testify to the amount of trouble and vexation occasioned by this species of legislation. These bills were always exceedingly lengthy, requiring much time for their consideration, both in committee and before the legislature. There was a committee in this body raised upon this subject, and he felt confident that that committee would provide by a Constitutional enactment, that the legislature hereafter should part forever with the power of passing these laws, and that the power should devolve elsewhere. This could be done even by the passage of a general law, defining the manner and conditions upon which companies could incorporate themselves.

Again, there was out of this number twenty-one laws passed to dissolve that most holy and solemn obligations of the marriage agreement, and that, too, generally upon mere *ex parte* testimony.

The report now under consideration provides that hereafter, the legislature of this State should have no control over this subject, but that the courts should exercise exclusive jurisdiction, in all such cases. If these two propositions be acceded to by the Convention, and in his opinion, they doubtless would be, we get rid at once of over one-third of the entire legislation of the State.

To pursue this subject a step farther, he would remark that out of the vast number of laws passed here at the last session, and to which so much importance is attached, thirteen only were of a general character.

Now, Mr. President, is not this a most startling fact, and does it not demonstrate beyond question, the utter folly of burthening the people of this State, with the great expense incident upon annual sessions of the General Assembly.

Mr. P. said he had regarded the subject of biennial sessions, as an adjudicated question—as a proposition solemnly settled by the people themselves. He believed it was so regarded throughout Maryland, during the canvass of last year. The people throughout the State were called upon at the ballot-box, in 1846, to decide for themselves, the question now under debate. The provisions of the biennial law, were published in every county in Maryland, and its various sections entered largely into the canvass before the people of that fall; and in order to ascertain, beyond question, the sense of the people upon this subject, every voter, when at the polls, was called upon solemnly to record his individual vote for or against this constitutional change. The result is well known. Out of about fifty-five thousand votes polled, near five thousand majority were declared in favor of biennial sessions of the Legislature. Has this Convention any evidence of change of opinion upon the subject? None whatever. Not a petition in the opposition has found its way into these halls. Not a newspaper throughout Maryland, has dared to advocate a return to annual sessions; and gentlemen upon this floor, who are most earnest and violent in their opposition to this amendment, have been forced to admit that no complaint against the measure exists, even among their own constituency.

Fourteen States of this Union have adopted biennial sessions, and among that number are the States of Ohio, Kentucky, Tennessee and Louisiana. Ohio, the third State of the Union in point of population, and he believed in wealth, also has adopted this measure, and Louisiana, with the populous and commercial city of New Orleans as her emporium, has also done so. In fact, almost all the Southern Democratic States, have incorporated this provision upon their organic law. He mentioned this fact to show this House, that this amendment did not stand obnoxious to the charge of being exclusively a whig measure.

In no instance had this provision been adopted elsewhere, and after trial abandoned. This principle is contrary to the progresssve spirit of the age. Maryland alone, should this principle be departed from by this Convention, will stand in the unenviable attitude of what is vulgarly called "taking the back track."

Mr. P. said, he would proceed to consider this amendment, as a retrenchment measure—as a proposition calculated to save to the people of Maryland, thirty thousand dollars annually, for all time to come. It would save the interest of half a million of the public debt. He would ask gentlemen what was the most potent argument used throughout the State, in favor of calling this Convention? He would answer, apart from the city of Baltimore, where increased representation was the all prevailing argument, that retrenchment of the public expenditures, was the watchword every where. Low salaries and the reduction of the number of officers, was the constant cry of the reform party, in all the counties —in every section of the State. Retrenchment and reform was emblazoned upon every banner. These were the watchwords of the party, and they ran *pari possa* every where. It was well known here and elsewhere, that he had opposed this Convention, and he felt now constrained to declare that what he had witnessed in these halls, had but strengthened his conviction of the correctness of his own judgment.

But, Mr. President, as the people have determined this Convention should be called, and that they would have a new government, no man on this floor was more anxious and more sincerely desirous than himself to make a good Constitution, and one which would be well received throughout the State. But to return. What are the evidences upon this floor that public expectation will be gratified with regard to these propositions? What salaried officers are now proposed to be abolished? Ah! Mr. President, where is even the salary of one officer proposed to be reduced? No where—no not one. Not one, sir. The converse of this proposition is too true. The necessity and even expediency of returning to annual sessions of the Legislature at an increase of expense of thirty thousand dollars annually is now strongly urged upon this floor. Gentlemen who would become indignant at being called anti-reformers oppose this amendment. Where, he would again ask, are the evidences within these Halls of a determination to retrench in any manner the public expenditures? He could but repeat this most important inquiry.

Do the reports from standing committees now before us foreshadow the result? He could but again answer no, sir, no. But a few years since it was most eloquently urged upon this floor and elsewhere, that the salary of two thousand a year was ample for a plain republican Governor. What say gentlemen now upon this subject? The Chairman of the Executive Committee, the distinguished gentleman from Queen Annes, (ex-Governor Grason,) has given the answer. The report of that committee proposes to fix the compensation of the Governor at four thousand dollars a year, just double the amount fixed upon during the prevalence of this reform fever. The distinguished gentleman from Cecil, (Mr. Mc-

Lane,) who is at the head of the Committee on the Treasury Department, proposes to create a new officer as Comptroller of the Treasury, with a salary of three thousand dollars a year. The no less distinguished and talented gentleman from Charles, (Mr. Jeniffer,) Chairman of what is familiarly called, here the omnibus committee, has reported in favor of a board of public works at an annual cost of some six or eight thousand dollars a year. But where, he would again ask, are the provisions for retrenching the public expenses? He did not now intend to argue these reports.

Mr. P. said he intended to express at this time no opinion upon any one of these propositions. "Sufficient for the day is the evil thereof." At the proper time and in the proper place, he expected to be able to give a reason for the hope that was within him.

Again, Mr. President, we have heard much said about the great and exceeding expensiveness of our Judiciary system. This has been a fruitful source of animadversion by politicians and especially reformers for many years past; and the cry has been loud and long for retrenchment in this Department of the Government. On yesterday the equally distinguished gentleman at the head of the Judiciary Committee, (Mr. Bowie,) presented his report, and this morning we find it upon our desks. He had had only time to give this report a very hasty glance. He found, however, it proposed one Judge for each county in the State, at a salary of two thousand dollars a year, and six other Judges for the city of Baltimore, with salaries varying from fifteen hundred dollars to twenty-five hundred dollars a year. Also an independent Court of Appeals to consist of three members, with salaries of twenty-five hundred dollars each. Now, Mr. President, according to this report we shall have twenty-nine Judges in Maryland, with an average annual salary of over two thousand a dollars a year, making an annual demand upon the Treasury for this department of the Government of some sixty thousand dollars. Mr. P. said he had not time to pursue this subject further, he would leave that matter to the especial friends of retrenchment and reform upon this floor. He would remark, however, that by an examination of the Treasury report, the annual expenses under the Constitution, under the biennial system, was about eighty-nine thousand dollars, and if these various propositions be incorporated in the new Constitution, the annual demands upon the Treasury, under the Constitution, will not be short of one hundred and fifty thousand dollars. So far, Mr. President, from the public expenditures being diminished by this Convention, the probability now is, they will be increased some sixty thousand dollars annually.

He said, let him in sober earnestness, ask the reform party here, and especially those from the smaller counties, who have all to lose upon the representation question, how they will account for their stewardship here, when summoned before the bar of public opinion? How do you propose to answer for these increased public expenditures? Where shall we look for the practical effects of your retrenchment principles? We see no trace of them in these halls. They are gone—forever gone.

Our labors on this floor, Mr. President, must be submitted to the sober judgment of an enlightened and far-seeing constituency, and the effects it may be, will be felt and judged of by posterity itself. We shall, doubtless, be judged by a righteous judgment. He would forbear saying more.

Mr Jenifer submitted that the fact of making the sessions of the Legislature biennial, would not relieve the Legislature from the applications for acts of incorporation and of divorce, upon which the gentleman from Dorchester, (Mr. Phelps,) had laid so much stress. The gentleman had asked whether any petitions had been presented here, calling for a return to annual sessions. He, (Mr. J.,) might, with equal force, ask whether petitions had been presented here, asking for any thing in relation to the judiciary—the executive—or any other department? The people had sent this Convention here, to act according to their best judgment, and to recommend to their adoption, such provisions as might be deemed best suited to their interests and necessities.

His colleague, (Mr. Merrick,) had very properly stated why there ought to be frequent elections, and especially at the present time, in view of the finances of the State, when millions of dollars came into the treasury to be expended, and when, for a period of two years, under the present system, the offices were left without public accountability.

The gentleman from Dorchester, (Mr. Phelps,) in the remarks he had submitted, had traveled beyond the legitimate ground. He had referred to the different reports of committees, and amongst other things, to the proposed increase of the salary of the Governor. That question had been a matter of grave consideration, and the committee had come unanimously to the conclusion, that the salary should be raised. They had been guided by the true Democratic principle, that the office was one open to the humblest citizen of the State, and that a salary ought to be attached to it, which would be commensurate with its importance.

The gentleman had talked a great deal about expense. The question for the Convention was, whether a few thousand dollars, more or less, were to be brought in conflict with the interests and the exigencies of a whole people. If it was supposed that the length of the sessions would be an obstacle in the way of annual meetings of the Legislature, it would be easy to remove that difficulty by limiting their duration.

He, (Mr. J.,) hoped, therefore, that no such prohibition would, at present, at least, be adopted.

Mr. Donaldson said, that he was one of that majority at the polls, to which the gentleman from Dorchester, (Mr. Phelps,) had alluded as having four years and more ago, settled by the popular voice, that the sessions of the Legislature, should be biennial. He had upon better knowledge and more mature consideration, changed his opinion, and, he believed, that the greater part of that majority, if they had had the same information that he had derived from his experience in our legislation, would now vote for annual sessions. The members of this Convention came freshly from the people of Maryland. They are certainly a fair average of the intelligence of the community, and if they, individually, prefer annual sessions, they may well feel assured that such is the preference of the people themselves. He declared that he knew no other safe or proper rule of action, in his representative capacity, than to following his own conscientious convictions, and to presume that the people would approve of his judgment. If the representative sought in regard to these questions to discover the wishes of his constituents, he would embark, without compass, on a wide sea of conjecture.

His reasons for voting at the polls for biennial sessions, were his dread of too much legislation, and his desire to save the State the expense of the alternate session. Shortly after he was elected a Delegate to the General Assembly, and placed in a position which obliged him to become thoroughly acquainted with the financial laws and their system of administration, in this State. He then felt ashamed of the ignorance in which he had voted for biennial sessions. He became convinced, that as long as the receipts and disbursements of the Treasury were so great, our security required yearly sessions of the Legislature. The Treasurer now receives upwards of $1,200,000 annually, and there is often a balance of $400,000 on hand, from month to month, and on the transactions of the Treasurer, the law, as yet, has not imposed adequate checks. The only control over that officer and his accounts, was in the Legislature. No Treasury could well be in a more exposed condition. We had been remarkably fortunate in the character of our officers, but safety to the State, and justice to our own agents, require that they should not be subjected to such great temptations. All the officers in the State engaged in the collection of the revenue, and the number is very great, and their duties most various, are obliged by law to make their returns to the Legislature, as well as to the Treasurer. The Legislature is the grand inquest of the State, and the knowledge of this brings all these officers up to the line of their duty. This is our great security for their promptness and efficiency. To demonstrate this in detail, would, perhaps, be tedious to the Convention, he merely stated it now, as the result of his own observation and experience.

As to the saving effected by biennial sessions, (Mr. D.,) thought it merely apparent, not real. We need this check on the accounting officers, and the cost of the alternate session, was of little consequence compared with the security obtained. Besides, the public moneys are more loosely and lavishingly appropriated by a Legislature, under the biennial system, where the members are not so soon called to account for their action by the people. This is well illustrated by the proceedings of the Lagislature, at its last session.

He differed with the gentleman from Dorchester, (Mr. Phelps,) in his ideas of retrenchment and economy. True economy is judicious expenditure. The refusal to incur an expense, needed for a proper administration of affairs, is false economy. The gentleman from Dorchester, had complained that articles had been reported here, for the appointment of a Comptroller of the Treasuary, thus establishing a new office.

Mr. D. stated that he considered such an officer, in this State, absolutely necessary. It is impossible for the Treasurer, to administer, with efficiency, all the multifarious duties now imposed upon him; and a Comptroller is also needed as a check upon the Treasurer and Commissioner of Loans. He did not hesitate to express a belief, that if we had had such an officer for the last ten years, we might have secured annually, from ten to twenty thousand dollars more revenue than was secured.

In regard to the excess of legislation, (Mr. D., said,) he objected to it as much as any man could, and he would go as far as any one, in restricting the Legislature, so as to remedy that evil. But, he asserted, the legislation under our biennial system, is as excessive an amount, as when we had annual sessions, and is decidedly worse in quality. If worse in quality, then will there be more need of future change or explanatory supplements. The session being limited, and members being always most anxious to get through their private and local bills, of which there is a great accumulation in the course of two years, the public business is thrust aside, or most carelessly performed. Mr. D. considered this as fully demonstrated by the laws of the session of 1849, to which he particularly referred.

Mr. D. concluded by repeating, that he believed the annual system was very important in regard to our finances, was more truly economical than the biennial system, and really more conducive to well considered and permanent legislation.

Mr. Sellman expressed himself conversant with the whole history of the legislation of the State in regard to this question of biennial sessions. Sometimes it had been used as a stalking-horse—sometimes as an ambling ponny. It had been presented as one of the measures for the restoration and preservation of the State credit, and so far as it had been based upon that consideration, it had due weight with him.

But how stood the matter in regard to the argument of the gentleman from Dorchester, (Mr. Phelps)? If it was a mere question of economy, that gentleman had not carried his argument out as he ought to have done; for, in view of economy alone, why designate two years as the period of the meeting of the legislature? Why not say, once in four, six, eight, or ten years?

But there was another and more important principle at stake—that was to say, the right of the people frequently to supervise the acts of their public servants. He referred to the history of this question under the old Constitution, and stated that the motive which controled its framers in establishing annual sessions, (in preference to other terms which had been proposed,) was the principle of responsibility; for in the language of Jefferson, "where annual sessions ceased, tyranny began." That was the ground upon which yearly convocations of the legislature had been originally placed, and upon which they ought to rest now.

He denied that any evidence had been brought to show that such annual meetings were not necessary. As regarded the fact upon which the gentleman from Dorchester, (Mr. Phelps,) had dwelt, that many of the States had adopted the biennial principle, he, (Mr. S.,) thought the gentleman would find that they were for the most part young States to which speculators had flown—men whose interests would best be promoted by biennial sessions, or rather by no sessions at all. He hoped that the new Constitution would be left on the original ground.

Mr. Spencer said, that there were some difficulties surrounding this question, but which might probably be overcome, so as to secure the vote of the Convention upon some acceptable proposition. He had voted at the polls against biennial sessions. He had voted against them, because, at the time, he considered them a violation of the fundamental principle upon which our government rested.

So long as the people were sovereign, he considered it right and proper that the meetings of the legislature should be annual, and any departure from that rule, would be a departure from the recognised rights of the people.

What was the inducement for biennial sessions? Every one knew it, and it was not necessary, therefore, for him to explain. The State had been led into a system of improvident legislation. He laid the responsibilty of that system at no particular door. He spoke merely of the fact. The result was, that the people were about to be burthened with heavy taxation. Every possible devise was resorted to, for the purpose of alleviating the burthen, and among others, this measure of biennial sessions.

The question which presented itself to the consideration of the Convention was—did that necessity exist now? The people of the State of Maryland had as yet given no expression of opinion, to show that they were dissatisfied with biennial sessions.

The Convention was framing a Constitution, which the people might accept or reject, and if this provision was incorporated in the Constitution, the people themselves might adopt or reject it. There was undoubtedly, a large portion of the people in favor of biennial sessions; and it was a point which gentlemen must consider—whether, by adopting the principle of annual sessions, they might not drive men to vote against the Constitution who would otherwise have voted for it. This was the difficulty which remained to be overcome. On the other hand, the Convention had to determine whether it was necessary to incorporate a provision binding the people to biennial sessions.

To meet this difficulty, he intended to propose an amendment. He would vote in favor of the proposition of the gentleman from Charles, (Mr. Merrick,) provided that the amendment of which, he, [Mr. S.,] now gave notice, should be adopted.

[This amendment is not on Wednesday's journal. It was offered the next day, and will be found among the proceedings. It gave the legislature the right to provide by law for biennial sessions.]

If his amendment was not adopted, Mr. S. said, he would experience great difficulty in departing from the system of legislation, as at present existing.

Mr. Brown had not intended to take any part in this debate, but he thought that the gentleman from Dorchester had expressed himself strongly in reference to the course of the legislature. As he, [Mr. B.,] did not belong to the Senate, he could not say what took place there. The gentleman from Dorchester had a peculiar knack of turning the blame from himself upon others. He appeared to complain of the great number of acts of incorporation that passed last year. Now, the gentleman was on the committee on incorporations in the Senate, and I would be glad to know whether he reported unfavorably upon one single act of incorporation during the session, or voted against one in the Senate? If he did, it never came to his knowledge.

He, [Mr. B.,] was opposed to biennial sessions. He thought that possibly, if we were free from all embarrassments, there might be no need of annual sessions, but while we have an expenditure of $1,200,000 a year, it was right that the legislature should meet annually. He became sick of biennial sessions during the last winter, when there were about eight hundred bills reported, and five hundred and sixty-one passed, besides nearly one hundred joint resolutions, he had never known such an amount of labor performed as was performed by the House of Delegates, last session, in the same length of time. But there he would stop.

By the provisions of the Constitution, any bills, with the exception of money bills, may originate in the Senate. But we were very little troubled by bills originating in that body. While we were laboring, the gentleman from Dorchester was sitting in this hall, amusing himself by talking and laughing with the ladies.

Near the close of the session, the House sat from nine o'clock in the morning until late at night, and there was a continual scramble to get bills through. He believed that the question of biennial sessions was passed in 1846, for the purpose of getting rid of the reform movement. He was in favor of frequent elections, and of a rigid responsibility of the departments to the people.

If the house of delegates could have had time at the last session, there would have been a re-organization of the treasury. The present system is too lax, and does not enforce a proper responsibility. And if this had not been the most fortunate State in the Union, and we had not had the most honest men in the world in the administration of that department, there might have been great frauds perpetrated. The bills concerning our public works of internal improvements occupied most of the time of the Legislature. But for these, the sessions might be terminated in six weeks. He had no objection to the amendment proposed by the gentleman from Queen Anne's, (Mr. Spencer.) He was not entirely satisfied that the State had yet got through her pecuniary difficulties. The failure of two or three crops would disable the farmers from paying the taxes, and in that case, we may find that the "dark clouds" spoken of by the gentleman from Dorchester, might still be hanging over us. He was opposed to all extravagant expenditures, and he was against some of the expenditures which had been incurred by this Convention.

Mr. Wells rose to make a few remarks, and in the outset he would express his regret that the gentleman from Dorchester should have deemed it necessary to make any party allusions. He did not think that party considerations should at any time be connected with the subjects before this Convention. He was himself a party man, but he intended to vote on every proposition submitted here, on its own intrinsic merits, regardless of all party obligations. As he had been anticipated by the gentlemen who had preceded him on his side of the question, in most of the points of argument which had suggested themselves to his mind in reference to this subject, he would not attempt to repeat what had been argued with so much superior ability by those gentlemen, but would confine his remarks to a very few thoughts connected with one or two aspects of the case, which had not, he believed, been discussed by any one. Much stress, Mr. President, has been laid by the gentleman from Dorchester, on the fact that by biennial sessions some money would be annually saved to the Treasury. I will not stop to argue that this is a very narrow view of the subject, or to shew, that if it was right to be governed by such considerations here, that a mere saving of money is not the true principle that should direct the operations of an intelligent economist, who will always act with reference to the truth of experience—that a judicious expenditure of money is the true and only economy. I will not stop, sir, to shew, as I think I could shew, the injurious tendency to which such a doctrine would lead in all the pursuits of life, but I must protest against the application of such a rule as this to our proceedings. Does not the gentleman see, that the necessary result of his argument, if it can apply now, will apply to every article affecting every department of the Government, and that the rule by which he must measure the value of the Constitution which we may form is the rule of mere dollars and cents. Sir, the idea of consulting cheapness in the formation of our Constitution, I utterly repudiate, for there is nothing in our political existence of which I have a greater horror, than I have of a cheap Constitution. Is it possible, sir, that gentlemen, who have been placed in the elevated position of members of this Convention are to be governed by pecuniary considerations?—that they are to be influenced in the estimate which they shall place upon the value of the Constitution which they shall make, b considering its value in money? He trusted not, and hoped, that our action would not be guided by such influences, and that we should rise to the dignity of the exalted position we occupied, not by estimating the value of our work by a standard of dollars and cents, but by the high privileges and the inestimable benefits which it was to confer upon us and upon our posterity whom it was to bind, and by the great security which it was to afford to the lives, the liberty, and the property of our citizens. That was the animating principle with him, and to the obtainment of which, all other considerations should yield. But, sir, the gentleman has told us that a majority of all the States of the Union had adopted the system of biennial sessions of the Legislature.

Mr. Phelps remarked, that he had said fourteen States had adopted that system.

Well, sir, (continued Mr. W.,) there is no great difference in the two statements. The gentleman has said, that because fourteen States of the Union had adopted the biennial system, that we ought to adopt it; but does that necessarily follow? Are there not provisions in the Constitutions of many of the States of the Union that it would be manifestly improper for us to adopt, because they would be entirely unsuited to our condition and in every way injurious to us? Ought not the gentleman then in selecting the examples of our sister States which he would hold up to us as worthy of our imitation, to shew us, in order to make them applicable, that there is a similarity between those States and ours in regard to their commercial and other interests—and in regard to the locality of capital and population? Sir, if he will turn to the Constitutions of States having; like ours, a large commercial emporium, and like ours a large concentrated capital and population, he will find that of those States, New York, Massachusetts and Pennsylvania have annual sessions of the Legislature. And why, sir? Because the relations which those large cities bear to the rest of the State by reason of a great concentration of capital and population, and their great trade and commercial influences affecting as they do every part of the State, render it indispensably necessary for the due preservation, *in equilibrio*, of those diversified interests that make up the sum of human pursuits in those States, that the "meetings of the Legislature should be frequent," as well as for "the redress of grievances and for amending, strengthening and preserving the laws." It has been said that the reason for resorting to biennial sessions when the change was made, was because it was at a time when the State was so deeply involved in pecuniary embarrassment as to cause her failure to meet her engagements, and that this condition of things made it an imperative duty on the part of all to adopt measures of retrenchment in order to wipe off the stain from her escutcheon. But what is our condition now? Our financial difficulties have been overcome, a large surplus is annually in the Treasury, and that reason, therefore, no longer continues to be applicable.

Another reason with me for desiring to go back to annual sessions, and I believe this view of the subject has not been presented by any of the gentleman who have spoken—is to be found in the new condition of things that must necessarily grow out of the formation of a new Constitution. All the great departments—the executive, the legislative and the judicial departments—are to be broken up, and new systems substituted in their places. The tenure of office connected with all of them is proposed to be changed, and the mode of appointment of many is to be very different from what it is now. Is it not obvious then, that as general principles can only be provided for in the new Constitution, the details of the new system must not only devolve on the legislature, but that the Legislature must have frequent sessions, in order to discharge that duty efficiently? For, in the working of all new systems, experience only can test their value and suggest the necessary requisites to accomplish the purposes designed. Absolute changes in those details, will, therefore, be found necessary to perfect some, partial alterations may answer for others, but all, all, will need the work of time in order to make them effectual in rendering "the greatest amount of good to the greatest number."

The gentleman from Dorchester has argued that in the election, which is to be proposed, of the judges and clerks and registers, by the people, for long terms, no apprehension exists that the responsibility of these functionaries to the people, will be weakened by the length of service; and I understand him to offer this argument as an answer to the objection which has been made to the system of biennial sessions, that it will have the effect of lessening the responsibility of the representative to his constituent. But the force of this argument is not apparent to me. Few, I presume, would desire that the judges should be elected annually, since it is only by their election for long terms that their independence, and that purity of official conduct which results from independent action, can be secured. As to clerks and registers, their election for long periods will secure better incumbents and more efficient officers, because a proper knowledge of their duties requires a sort of apprenticeship; and if they were elected every year, you would never be able to get one who was worthy of the station. I conclude, then, that a return to annual sessions, will be rendered necessary, as well to make proper provision for those exigencies which will be created by the adoption of a new Constitution, as to secure the enjoyment by the people in their proper sense, of all their rights, liberties and privileges, the preservation of which constitutes the foundation of all republican governments; and I must remark, that it is very singular, that whilst so much has been said about the rights of the people and the paramount duty of all here to protect the rights that the very first attempt which has been made to guard them in their most material feature, by securing to the people the power of annual supervision over their representatives through the ballot-box, should be met by such determined opposition as I have every reason to believe will be found arrayed against it.

Mr. Morgan replied to the remarks of the gentleman from Dorchester, on the subject of the course pursued by the Legislature in reference to an extra session. As he was a member of the House of Delegates at the time, and had, perhaps, as great an agency in that movement, as any member of that body now upon this floor, he rose to disavow any purpose of connecting the movement with the question of biennial sessions. The proposition for an extra session was introduced either by himself or an honorable friend of his, then a member from Anne Arundel, (he did not recollect which,) under a sense of high public duty in view of the many important measures which necessarily would be passed over in consequence of the constitutional limits which brought the session to a close. The Legislature found itself within two days of a final adjournment with its tables loaded with bills unacted upon—amongst which was one for the re-organization of the treasury department, which had been urged upon successive Legislatures by the then Governor and his predecessors, and without which there was very little security for the public funds, except in the honesty of the treasurer and other bills, such as the organization of a Board of Public Works, in which the State had an interest of some sixteen millions of dollars, and which interest demanded from the Legislature efficient action. There also was the general assessment law, nearly all the sections of which had been considered and passed upon—the provisions of which, although it did not diminish the amount of revenue to be received by the State in the aggregate, relieved the burdensome taxation now imposed upon slave property by a reduction of upwards of one third of its assessed value—a property in which his constituents were largely interested; and their interest, in his opinion, demanded of him the vote he then gave—the effect of which, if that session had been called, would have been to reduce their taxes upon that species of property one-third. These bills were laying on the table, whilst a multitude of local laws were passed without reading—some members being afraid to vote against a measure of another, lest one of his own should be defeated. It was at this period, he repeated, he felt himself called upon by a high sense of public duty, to sustain the measure adverted to, without his, or any human being of that Legislature that he had heard of, connecting it in its operations either in the present or the future, with the question of biennial sessions; and he declared that he believed that such an idea never had place in the mind of any individual, unless perhaps the very sensitive and fertile imaginings of the gentleman from Dorchester might have induced, upon his part, such an opinion.

The gentleman from Dorchester had said that the members of that legislature, had by concert and protracted speeches delayed the public business, to bring biennial sessions into disrepute. Justice demanded that he should confirm what had been said by the gentleman from Carroll, (Mr. Brown,) as to the untiring industry of the House of Delegates—where from early in the morning, until late at night, the members assiduously devoted themselves to the discharge of their public duties.

The gentleman has been entirely misinformed

in relation to the consumption of time. That legislature did, by special rule upon important bills, restrict debate in some cases to five minutes speeches, and even with that restriction, after passing more laws than any two legislatures had heretofore done, found it impossible to get through with the public business—and this he declared, in his opinion, was the result of the measure fastened upon the State, by the gentleman and others who acted with him in the passage of his biennial session bill. If every gentleman here had the experience of the last session of the legislature, which he, (Mr. M.,) the gentleman from Carroll, and the gentleman from Baltimore, had, they would never vote for another biennial session.

A word as to the objections of the gentleman from Dorchester. He says, that frequent elections of members of the House of Delegates are no more necessary, than in the case of judges and other officers elected by the people for a long term of years. His friend had mis-read the old bill of rights, where it is said in reference to the legislature only, "that elections should be free and frequent." In this clause there was no reference whatever to judges; the clause declared that a participation in the legislature, frequently by the people was the foundation of all free government—it defines the rights of the people, by securing the sovereign exercise of their will through their representatives in legislature assembled. It simply secured this great principle, and says, in effect, the sovereign power should often be returned to the source of its emanation.

The judges were clothed with no such power; their duty was to administer, not to make the laws. The one could, therefore, with great propriety, be a perpetual office—whilst the other required a frequent recurrence to the original source of all power—the people. The same reason, therefore, did not apply in the case of a judge, as in that of a representative. He referred to the reforms that had taken place in the British government. Instead of long parliaments which sat at earlier times, triennial parliaments were substituted, which was wrung from the reluctant Charles by his people, for the very reason that induced the insertion of the clause referred to in the old bill of rights by our forefathers. It was true their Parliaments were now elected septenially, yet such was the frame work of their Constitution, that even in England at this day, annual Parliaments were obliged to be held.

The British declaration of rights prohibited a standing army, except by consent of Parliament, nor could the King obtain supplies except by appropriation of that body, and these two provisions are considered the greatest bulwark of Constitutional freedom, because it forced the assembling of the representatives of the people annually, to watch their interest, and to guard against all encroachments and abuse from any and all quarters. It was the assertion of this principle having its origin far back in British history, in order to secure the advance that had been made in liberalizing government, that caused the Convention of '76 to place the present article in the bill of rights; and we are now called upon at this day to go back—to approach nearer to the times when usurpation demanded and forced a change. In throwing out these views he not only expressed his own opinions, but was happy to say that he also uttered the voice of the people he represented, who, by a large vote, had declared against biennial sessions. He believed experience had proven the correctness of their opinions, and that no good had resulted to the State, from the change that had been effected.

Mr. PHELPS said he had been charged with attempting to fasten biennial elections on the Legislature, and he was now charged with attempting to fasten them on the people. Gentlemen who made these charges did him too much honor. The question as to biennial sessions was referred to the people of Maryland; and the question was distinctly put to the voters as they came up to the ballot box, whether they were in favor of biennial sessions or against them; when, out of fifty-five thousand votes deposited, there was found to be a majority of no less than five thousand in favor of biennial sessions. From that moment it ceased to be his bill. The people took the bill off his hands and made it their own. The people of Maryland, whose agents we are, adopted the bill, and now it will be seen whether the people of Maryland will be willing to see their decision reversed by this body. For himself he cared but little. His participation in the proceedings of this Convention would be the end of his political life. When he had retired from this body, and reached his own fire-side, he should not thereafter mingle in political bodies. But it would well become the Convention to pause before they act in opposition to the expressed will of the people. He was no prophet, nor the son of a prophet, but he would venture an expression of his belief, that if the Convention should determine not to adopt the system of biennial sessions, the reformers will find that they will have to be content with the old Constitution for the next half century. He reiterated what he had before said on the subject of the salaries of the officers of Government. The gentleman from Anne Arundel, (Mr. Donaldson,) and the gentleman from Charles, (Mr. Jenifer,) had argued that if the sessions should be made biennial, there would be no check on the Treasury. What check, he asked, is provided by annual sessions? If there was a disposition on the part of the Treasurer to defraud the State, he could make false returns to the Legislature annually, as easily as biennially. Our present Treasurer is faithful and honest, and we have every confidence in him. He was ready to give his vote for that officer.

One word, as to the multiplicity of business at the close of the General Assembly. This press of business did not originate with biennial sessions. The number of bills not acted upon, were quite as large, during the existence of annual sessions. You, Mr. President, and I, are old stagers here, and have had much experience within these Halls. We have, time and again, seen the clerk's desk, at the close of the sessions, loaded with bills, and not unfrequently would a member approach that desk, upon the last night of the session, and upon one motion, refer a shoulder }turn over, for the consideration of the next General Assembly. This, sir, is common in all Legislative bodies, and need not now, for the first time, be brought in judgment against biennial sessions.

He was astonished to find himself standing alone in the advocacy of this proposition. Not a single friend had come forward to say one word to sustain him.

Mr. Gwinn said that he was opposed to the system of biennial sessions. They were attended by a real inconvenience, which was separable from the argument founded on the right to frequent assemblies. The course of practice in this State, and our whole system of legislation brought annually before the House and Senate, a large mass of private business, which necessarily came in conflict with the public business of the body. All who had occupied a seat on the floor of the House of Delegates, know how impossible it is to escape the requirements of private and local legislation. Prohibitions in the Constitution might restrain the General Assembly from considering a large portion of such business. But it cannot close the ear of the Legislature, to the various demands which will, at all times, be made upon its attention. It had been said that much of this petty business would be transferred to the levy courts and county commissioners. There was good and evil both, in such a scheme, but the latter predominated. However, it would depend upon the class of powers transferred. It is not, in general, wise to place private rights at the disposal of a local tribunal. The risk of prejudice is increased, for the examiners are more likely to be partail.

The biennial system does not answer. He could speak for the last legislature, and especially for the delegation from Baltimore, of which he was one. All had been industrious and faithful to their duty, but they could not accomplish the necessary business of the city. More than one hundred city bills remained upon the Speaker's table, when the House of Delegates adjourned. Many were private, but some also were well considered, important bills, submitted to the notice of the Legislature, by able and accomplished jurists—but he could not, in any way, get them fairly before the House.

Perhaps every Legislature did waste time. But does it waste less every two years, than every year? If the accumulation of business always exists at the close of the sessions, whether they be annual, or not—does it follow that there ought to be a double accumulation? He could not see the force of such reasoning.

Mr. Merrick rose to express his entire acquiescence in the amendment proposed by the gentleman from Queen Anne's, to come in a proper place. Should the annual sessions be found, on trial, not to work well, it would give the people an opportunity to return to the biennial system. But he was desirous to see the amendment inserted in its proper place.

Mr. Spencer, (in his seat.) "At the end of the section."

He, (Mr. M.,) did not think that the same accountability of executive officers could be enforced under the biennial system as the annual. The gentleman from Dorchester predicts that the people will not accept of this Constitution if the system be changed from biennial to annual sessions. Now, he hoped, that the Convention would be able to make such a Constitution as the people will approve. And he felt that the only way in which he could act so as to facilitate such a result, was to proceed according to the best of his judgment and under a conscientious sense of duty, in his endeavors to provide for the people a good government, and one which will win for itself the approbation of the wise and the good

The gentleman from Carroll, (Mr. Brown,) had argued that the large amount of money which was annually expended on account of the public debt, was a reason in favor of annual sessions. That was true; but this debt, he trusted, would be liquidated in the course of a very few years; but still we must expect that very large sums will continue to pass through the hands of the treasurer annually, should our great works of internal improvement realize what is expected from them, and these large sums must be again disbursed, all of which will require the annual supervision of the people, acting through their agents, the General Assembly. He thought, therefore, that it would be wise to return to annual sessions.

Mr. Harbine rose and said, it was very far from his disposition to take any part in this debate, but as only the gentleman from Dorchester, (Mr. Phelps,) had spoken in favor of biennial sessions, while several had been heard against them, he felt it his duty, as a friend of that system, to present his views. The precedents that had been cited, proved that biennial sessions were no longer an experiment. It was evident that these precedents had not been without their effect upon gentlemen on the other side of the question, from the efforts made by them to do away their force. He would now endeavor to reply to some of the arguments that had been used in favor of annual sessions and against the present system. The gentleman from Anne Arundel county, (Mr. Wells,) when speaking of States that had adopted biennial sessions, said that they were not circumstanced like us; that Maryland had great commercial and moneyed interests which demanded more legislation. But it only required a reference to the population, wealth and resources of some of these States, to prove that position incorrect. It was also said, that in Massachusetts, New York, and Pennsylvania, where the great commercial citles of our country are located, their trade, navigation, and commerce required annual legislation, and that Baltimore having very extensive interests of the same character, we also must have annual sessions. But when, he would ask, under the present system had the interests of Baltimore suffered for want of additional laws? Missouri has the same systom, and will any one say that her commercial emporium, St. Louis, has suffered from that cause? There, too, is the State of Louisiana. She adopted the biennial system in the year 1845. Has New Orlenns none of these great interests that require so much legislation? Put the trade, commerce, and navigation of Baltimore, against the trade, commerce and navigation of New Orleans, and the scale would preponderate vastly in favor of the latter. If then legislation every two years was sufficient there, it certainly ought to be here. But go to the new States, that have adopted the biennial system, Iowa, Texas, and Arkansas. There, to say the least, enterprise is as vigorous as here, and from the very nature of circumstances they must require more legislation than we, yet they get along very well, and prosper under biennial sessions. Nearly all the recently formed State Constitutions contain the same feature, while not one State that has given it a trial has manifested a desire to go back to annual sessions. The present was the age of "progress," and biennial sessions had become one of its great marks. A few months since, and the State of Kentucky made it part of her system; then the Indiana Convention, which has recently adjourned, adopted the same doctrine, and last in this great march of "progress," came the populous and powerful State of Ohio, whose Convention, though yet in session, has made biennial sessions a part of her organic law. He hoped that Maryland would be the last State to renounce this system, the very last in the language of Webster, to "tread backward."

Another argument was, that after the adoption of our new Constitution, "a thousand and one" questions would require legislation, in order to make our laws conform to the new system, and, therefore, we should return to annual sessions. He did not doubt that much additional legislation would be required, but for how long? Certainly only for a few years, until things became settled under the new system, and then it would cease. Now, because a necessity for additional laws would exist *for a short time*, was to him, [Mr. H.,] not a sufficient cause to justify a provision for annual sessions *all the time*.

He hoped the organic law, that the Convention was now framing, would last for ages, until in the course of "progress," it would be found unfit for the changed circumstances of a future people; therefore, he could not agree to incorporate a provision for annual sessions, which at most, would only be required one or two years. But for this extra amount of legislation, which would only be required for a short time, he was reminded by his colleague, that the sixth section of the present report, made ample provision by authorizing the legislature during the first two sessions under the new Constitution, to sit as long as they might think the public interests required. Those two sessions would afford sufficient time to harmonize the laws with the new system, and fully answered that argument.

Another reason for annual sessions had been urged with great ability, by the gentleman from Charles county, (Mr. Merrick.) It was that frequent elections were the bulwarks of civil liberty—that a frequent recurrence to the people was a fundamental right that ought to be exercised, else their wishes would be disregarded and evil consequences ensue. He agreed that elections should be frequent—but how frequent? That was the question, and there they differed. He asserted that every two years was frequent enough for the happiness and prosperity of the people. On the other side, it was argued that "frequent" means annual, and that once a year is the proper time.

The gentleman from Dorchester, had ably argued that once in two years was often enough; and he would ask, if all proper and useful legislation could not be had by biennial sessions, why the great States that lived under that system, did not abandon it?

Mr. H. referred not to those States which had recently adopted it, but to those that had tried it during a long course of years. In Arkansas, the biennial system was introduced in the year 1836; in North Carolina in the year 1836; in Delaware in the year 1832; in Missouri in the year 1820. If all the evils predicted by the gentleman from Charles county, were to flow from this system, why had not these States abandoned it long, long ago? Does not the fact that they still adhere to it, prove these evils a mere chimera, and that argument naught but the "baseless fabric of a vision?" The position was not only incorrect, but that system must operate well, else the States that adopted it, would not be among the most prosperous and flourishing in the Union.

By another argument, it had been said, that biennial sessions in this State, had caused bad legislation, and under that system business would necessarily have to be pushed and hurried through at the end of the session, without sufficient or even any examination.

But had not this also been the case, when the sessions were annual? Without experience himself, Mr. H. had heard from others, that this evil was caused, not by the want of time to transact all the business, but because at the beginning of the sessions, too much time had been spent over champaigne at dinner, and over oyster suppers. Now, if gentlemen could show him, that under the old system, this same waste of time did not or would not exist, he would concede the argument; but the facts were too well known to expect any such an attempt. There was an abundance of time under the system, as it now existed in this State, to do all the legislation required; yet, if we must have more time, he would rather extend the sessions a little, than have them annual. He would now come to the argument of the other gentleman from Anne Arundel county, (Mr. Donaldson.) It was that the financial affairs of the State, could not be so well regulated, and fraud upon the Treasury so well prevented or exposed, by biennial, as by annual sessions of the Legislature. All agree, that so far there has been no reason to complain of the present system on that score. But if an annual investigation of the finances be necessary to prevent abuses, could it not be done without incurring the expense of a session of the Legislature? Such a thing was certainly possible, and now, while engaged in framing the organic law, is "the day, now's the hour," to provide remedies for defects complained of, and the evils that might arise under the present system. The committee on the Treasury department, would doubtless take all these things under their consideration, and report proper safe-guards. In other States, however, whose Legislatures convene but once in two years, we hear of no frauds upon their Treasuries, and no difficulty in regulating properly their finances; yet it is contended, that for these purposes we must hold annual sessions. Is it possible, that we are so much inferior to them? It could not be—for surely the people of Maryland, are as able to govern themselves as any other people; and if others can regulate and properly conduct their fiscal officers under the biennial system and thus effect a considerable saving of the money of the people, we can do the same.

In regard to the economy of this matter, he would say something. He believed that the rights and liberties of all would be, at least, as well secured and protected by the present system, as by any other: while, at the same time, it would save to the tax payers of this State, some *thirty* or *forty* thousand dollars annually. No one would be less willing for the sake of saving money, to sacrifice the rights of the humblest citizen ; but firmly believing, as he did, that the rights of all would be well defined and protected, he could not withhold his support from that system which would economize the public money.

Annual sessions of the Legislature were productive of one of the greatest curses that could befal a people—instability of the laws. That people are indeed afflicted, whose laws, like the quicksands of the ocean, are not to be relied on. Where the people are unable to tell what their legal rights are, how can the order and interest of society be preserved? Yet, under the annual system, all must admit, that the changes, by amendments and supplements, were so frequent, that even the wisest might be ignorant. Continue the present system, and there would be fewer changes and more stability, because more time would exist to ascertain the precise wants of the people, and if laws worked evil, their defects and the required remedy could be better ascertained before the law making power was again convened.

He could see no good reason to return to annual sessions. Whatever might be the opinion elsewhere, the people of the county he represented, were satisfied with the present system. Change it to annual sessions, and if it does not doom the new Constitution, we may, at least, have some fears of its rejection by the people.

Mr. Thomas said he came here, believing that if any question was settled, it was the very question now under discussion ; and the manifestation on this floor, proves how different is the attitude of the man who has been a legislator and the attitude of the people. The discussion has been all on one side. He had been led to anticipate directly the reverse, and he had gathered this opinion from the expression of the people in his section of the State ; for he did not know, in the community from which he came, a single man who had supposed that we were about to disturb this question, which was regarded as the foundation stone of this Convention ; and he could not believe that those who were anxious to devise any plan by which annual sessions of the Legislature might be fastened on us for ever, as standing in any other position than that of enemies to the new Constitution. This question is looked at differently by the people and legislators. While, on the one side it is believed that the citadel is not safe, unless the sentinel is always on the tower ; on the other, it was the sentiment throughout his part of the country, that there was too much legislation, and the people were all disposed to regard the proceedings of the Legislature as resembling the witches' cauldron in Macbeth :

"Double, double,
Toil and trouble,
Fire burn
And cauldron bubble."

He did not stand here to censure the Legislature without cause. Laws were speedily repealed, because they were hastily enacted, and led to the multiplying of suits and other evils. He intended no charge against gentlemen who were members of the Legislature. He was aware that the mass of public men were unable, without great sacrifices, to leave their private and professional business, and that they were only induced to come to the Assembly from a disposition to benefit their fellow citizens. Scarcely had a law passed and gone into operation, when lawyers have just begun to settle down on the true construction of its provisions, before some philanthropist gets a supplementary law enacted, which has the effect of perplexing the lawyers and dividing public opinion. He believed the great evil we have to complain of is too much legislation, and on coming into this body to meet it, he found gentlemen clogging the question as to a remedy for the evil, with all kinds of matter the most irrelevant. He came first to the Legislature in 1822, and he would ask, whether from that period up to the time when the biennial system was established, it had not always occurred, that a budget of bills was brought forward at the close of every session. He had been a member of the Legislature three times, and he had always found this to be the case. This pressure of business was not the result of the biennial system, but was owing to the indisposition of members themselves, at the beginning of a session, to go to business. During the last four days of the session, more business has been done, than in a month at the commencement. This fact then can be no argument against biennial sessions. If gentlemen who think that the biennial system will not allow sufficient time for legislation, when they come to the proper section which fixes sixty days as the length of the session, should be so disposed, they may so amend it, as to make it ninety days. He would vote against such extension. But he did not wish this section to be put in peril by referring to questions which have nothing to do with it. He would leave them to be considered in their proper place.

He did see some difficulty growing out of the financial condition of the State, until now. The remedy proposed, that the Legislature shall assemble once a year, for the sole purpose of examining the accounts of the treasurer, would inflict on the people an expense altogether disproportionate to the object. We have now a guard in the executive, whose duty it is to supervise the departments. Another remedy proposed, was the appointment of a comptroller. He should vote against such appointment. He was in favor of few officers and sufficiently liberal salaries. But there was a better remedy than either of these. Let the assembly appoint a joint committee, three members from one House and two from the other, to meet here in the alternate years on the first of January, and examine the treasurer's accounts, and then, if the Governor should deem it necessary, he can call an extra session of the Legislature. But if we were to provide that there shall be annual sessions of the Legislature in opposition to the expressed will of the people, for no other purpose than to examine the accounts of the treasurer, it would perhaps peril the Constitution. And we all know that the Legislature acts by committee. The Legislature itself, seldom looks beyond the report of the Committee of Ways and Means. He had said thus much because it is perilous to engraft a provision against which the people have already decided. If we are to go on, inserting provision after provision offensive to some one portion of the State or another, we may find, at last, that all our time here, and the public money expended on this body, have been wasted. If, through the arguments and objections urged by gentlemen on the other side, any evils shall be discovered in the biennial system, proper remedies may be applied.

When the bill to make the sessions of the Legislature biennial, was referred to the people of his county, he was disposed to vote against it; and believes that he did so vote. He then desired to have the Legislature in session every year, that the agitation then in progress, with a view to this Convention, might not be suspended. He did not now distinctly remember what opinion he,at that time entertained on this question, independent of its connexion with his inclination to expedite the session of this Conventien. The Convention was now in session, and he could judge of the measure upon its intrinsic merits. And if he even had, but he had not, doubts as to the policy of this measure, they would be yielded to the judgment of the whole State, which had been distinctly pronounced in its favor.

Mr. Brown briefly expressed his dissent from some of the positions of the gentleman from Frederick. Many of his people are of the opinion, that annual sessions are the safest. His argument has been misunderstood. He said that the people were taxed heavily, and while they were so taxed, there ought to be annual sessions. The gentleman from Dorchester, had talked something about the dark cloud of repudiation having passed away, and that we are now enjoying the sunshine of prosperity. We have, it is true, paid off a good deal of our debt, but we have still much to pay. Should the crops be good, he believed that the time was not distant, when the public debt will be entirely liquidated. But, he thought, the people should have an annual supervision over their affairs, through the Legislature. He had voted against biennial sessions, and he would do so know. Elections should be frequent —the Constitution says "annual." The gentleman from Frederick, says there is too much legislation. He asked if we can stop that by biennial sessions? No—for at a biennial session, there will be twice as many bills passed as at an annual one. He should go for annual sessions as the safest and best.

Mr. Biser rose to say a single word, regretting that after the overpowering eloquence of his colleague, (Mr. Thomas,) he would still be compelled to vote against him. He had listened to the argument with delight, so far as he enlarged on general principles, but when he came to the question of the expediency of biennial sessions, he differed from him. After mixing with the people, as freely and as recently as his honorable colleague, he could not come to the same conclusion. He did, it was true, vote for biennial sessions, when he thought that the embarrassed condition of the State made it his duty to advocate every measure of retrenchment. But it did not then go to the people, as a naked proposition, for it contained a provision making all the annual appointments biennial, so that whether the vote of the people was fairly given in favor of the biennial system, was subject to some doubt. He did not intend to waste the time of the Convention, at this late hour, but as an humble member of the last Legislature, he thought it right to make this statement. He would say that while his distinguished colleague travelled the county once, last fall previous to the September election for delegates to this Convention, he, (Mr. B.,) had travelled it again previous to the gubernatorial election;and he had found none who had even referred to this subject; none at all. The people were every where conscious,that they lived under aConstitution framed amidst the din of battle and the clash of arms. They also knew that out of the sixty articles of which the Constitution consisted, twenty-five had been abrogated,and twenty had been so amended, as to have retained little of their original form; so that only fifteen remained as they came from our fathers; therefore, the Convention question was in favor with the people.

They desired a change in the judiciary system; the election of clerks and registers by the people —a change in the basis of representation, and other important changes. He differed also from his colleague, on the subject of frequent elections, to which he, (Mr. B.,) was friendly; and, he thought, the people of his section of the State would not thank him if he voted against them.

He, (Mr. B.,) was in favor of annual sessions, but desired that they be limited to a much shorter time, than they are under the present Constitution. He was in favor of this as a measure of retrenchment. He regretted that the state of his health would not permit him to say more.

Mr. Buchanan expressed himself exceedingly gratified by the views of the gentleman from Frederick, (Mr. Biser,) which had rendered it unnecessary for any one to say more on that side. He has *travailed* much and his new born delivered. At some other time, he, [Mr. B.,] might take part in the discussion.

Mr. MERRICK rose, at a very late hour, and said a very few words on the necessity which existed for a vigilant supervision of the finances of the State, which would go to ruin, if that vigilance was relaxed. The people ought, therefore, to be annually convened by their legislature, for that purpose.

A committee might be partial, and its report would not give the people that security which would be obtained by the presence of the legislature. Instead of extending the biennial sessions to ninety or one hundred and twenty days it would be better to have annual sessions of half that length.

The amendment of the gentleman from Queen Anne's, (Mr. Spencer,) would enable the legislature to return to biennial sessions, at any time when the public interests may require more prompt legislation.

Mr. THOMAS made a brief reply, in which he argued against giving the power to the legislature, to return to biennial sessions on one hand, while we were restricting them on the other. It was said the legislature might adjourn to meet the next year, to take up the unfinished business. In that case there would be few votes against it.

His colleague, (Mr. Biser,) had travelled his county oftener than he, [Mr. T.,] would, to be President of the United States; but it was a pregnant fact, that he was never in a single instance, called to account for his vote in favor of biennial sessions.

And then the Convention adjourned until to-morrow, at eleven o'clock.

—

Sketch of the Remarks of Mr. BLAKISTONE, *on Wednesday, Feb.* 5, *on the motion of* Mr. BRENT, *of Baltimore, to amend the twenty-first article of the Bill of Rights, in relation to the "free colored population."*

Mr. BLAKISTONE said it was wondrous strange that such a proposition should receive any countenance in a Convention of the State of Maryland. These people are among us, and was it possible that any one here could desire to put them out of the pale of our protection. In this nineteenth century was such a doctrine to be set forth in such an assembly.

Mr. B. read the article as it now stands, and then came the amendment of the gentleman from Baltimore. If ever there was a proposition of doubtful propriety it was that now offered. We have had much talking here about human rights, and the rights of the people. He yielded to no man in his advocacy of the rights of the people, and perhaps he went farther than any member of the Convention for extending them. The free colored population have no political rights here, and never can have any. These people have been placed by the Providence of God among us, and he was for giving them protection. Insert this amendment and they will be thrown at the mercy of the wicked, even of the kidnapper, who will come and steal them in the midst of us; and here you offer him a license to do so, because, when you say certain rights of certain persons shall be protected, you leave all other persons and all other rights, not specifically enumerated, unprotected, and open to violation. *Inclusio unius est exclusio alterius.* The amendment goes even beyond this, and specified their exclusion from the protection the original article was designed to afford. It was the duty of every Marylander to repudiate the doctrine of this amendment. The moment a human being, native, or foreigner, white or black, bond or free, sets his foot upon our soil, he is under the protection of the laws of the State, and when that time shall come when you take away that protection, which he trusted never would, violence and outrage would stalk with unbridled phrensy throughout the land. Looking at it in a political aspect he referred to the efforts which had recently been made to effect a dissolution of the Union. He had no sympathies with disunionists in any quarter, north or south, east or west. He was for the Union as it is, one and indivisable.

He asked the gentleman from Baltimore, if he was willing to pander to this morbid excitement, to this turbulent and unholy spirit? Was he willing to add fuel to the flame of discord, that prevails in our land? Was he willing to give even the semblance of an argument to the northern abolitionists—the professed friends, but the worst enemies of the colored race, against one of the slave holding States of this Union. He could not give his consent to insert a provision saying, that the free colored population should not be protected in their persons and property. He believed the slave holding States of this Union, the best friends of the colored race. In case of necessity, he would be willing to colonize them among their own race in Liberia. There they would have rights which will not be given to them here.

But, this Convention ought to be careful not to fan the flame which a discontented portion of the Union has endeavored to kindle. Let the colored people know that they will find protection here. Let them understand that they are better protected, and better cared for in Maryland than they are in any other State of the Union. Many of them know this already, although there may be some too stupid to understand their own best interests. They, the more stand in need of our protection. There may be some bad among them, as well as some good, but whether they were all good or all bad, they are equally entitled to protection while they remain here. If they distutb the peace of the State, they should be removed, and the legislature has the power to remove them, as the penalty for their misconduct.

But if we cannot get rid of them, while they are here, let the broad mantle of protection be extended over them. He could not see what good could result from this amendment, its only tendency, in his opinion, was to feed the prevailing excitement. If it was ever thought proper to get rid of this class, (these people of color,) in

Maryland, he would do it in the most humane manner by sending them to the Maryland colony in Liberia.

He concluded, by expressing his belief, that if the question were submitted to the people of Maryland, they would be found almost unanimously against the amendment of the gentleman from Baltimore.

—

ERRATA.—In page one hundred, bottom of first column, in the speech of Mr. DAVIS, instead of "1,000,000" as by a typographical error it is printed, read "0,000,000," the cypher being intended to show the amount of legislative encouragement given to agriculture.

In page forty-seven, column two, line thirty, of the sketch of Mr. BLAKISTONE's remarks, instead of "design" read "offspring."

In page ninety, on the amendment of Mr RIDGELY to thirtieth article of the Bill of Rights, adding the words "political trust or employment of any kind whatever"—the word "*rejected*" should read "*adopted.*"

In pages ninety-six and ninety-seven, insert the name of Mr. CHANDLER (as moving to strike out the thirty-fourth article of the Bill of Rights,) instead of Mr. BLAKISTONE.

THURSDAY, February 13, 1851.

The Convention met at eleven o'clock.

Prayer was made by the Rev. Mr. GRAUFF.

The roll was called, and the journal of yesterday was read and approved.

MR. J. U. DENNIS.

On motion of Mr. JOHN DENNIS, it was

"Ordered, That it be entered upon the journal that Mr. JAMES U. DENNIS, is detained from his seat in the Convention by the illness of a member of his family."

There being no reports of committees, motions, resolutions, or notices,

The PRESIDENT, *pro tem.*, announced the unfinished business of yesterday.

THE LEGISLATIVE DEPARTMENT.

The Convention then resumed the consideration of the special order of the day, being the report heretofore submitted by Mr. JOHNSON, chairman of the committee on the legislative department of the government.

The second section of the report was under consideration as follows:

"*Section* 2. The Senators shall be elected by the qualified voters, for the term of four years, and the Delegates for the term of from the day of the general election."

SESSIONS OF THE LEGISLATURE.

And the pending question was on the motion of Mr. MERRICK, to amend the said second section, by filling the blank in the second line, with the words "one year."

Mr. PHELPS rose to a question of order. He had yesterday, he said, submitted an amendment, by way of substitute for the whole section. He desired to know whether the motion of the gentleman from Charles, (Mr. Merrick,) to fill the blank in the second section of the report, took precedence over his, [Mr. P's,] motion to strike out.

The PRESIDENT, *pro. tem.*, said, that the motion to fill the blank, would take precedence over the motion to strike out and insert, because the friends of the original section had the right in the first instance to perfect it.

Mr. DORSEY gave notice that when the question should be taken on the motion of the gentleman from Dorchester, [Mr. Phelps,] he, [Mr. D.,] desired a division of the question, first on striking out, and then on inserting.

Mr. BRENT, of Charles, said, he found himself in a position which was at all times unpleasant to his feelings. He found himself upon this question, differing with his colleagues. For their judgment and opinions, he always entertained the highest respect and esteem; and it was always, therefore, with the greatest diffidence, that he differed from them.

He considered the question now under consideration, as one of grave importance. But important as it was, he would not have troubled the Convention with any remarks, but for the fact of the difference of opinion which he had stated.

He regarded the question of annual or biennial sessions as a financial measure. In that light he should argue it. He believed that a proper principle of economy should lie at the foundation of all governments; and that it was the duty of the representatives of the people upon every occasion so to economise the public expenditures, as to secure the advantages of good government, at as little cost as possible to the public treasury.

The question of biennial sessions was not a new question in this country.. Some of the States of the confederacy had engrafted the principle upon their governments, so far back as the year 1818. And in ten or more of the States that principle had long been in successful operation. In the State of Kentucky, where the Convention called to remodel the organic law, had terminated its labors within some twelve or eighteen months, the principle of biennial sessions had been adopted even without an argument. Under the old Constitution of that State, he believed the sessions of the legislature had been annual. He had referred to the policy of other States, with a view to gather from their experience lights for his own guidance; because he believed it was always the part of true wisdom to avail itself of the experience of others, and engraft it upon its own.

Mr. B. now proceeded to refer to the direct vote which had been given by the people at the ballot box upon this question of biennial sessions, and to the decision which they had made in favor of such a change.

Here then, he said, was the voice of the people of the State of Maryland. He considered himself as their agent—whose duty it was to carry out their wishes thus expressed; and he, for one, must obey their voice.

He understood that it had been stated here yesterday, (when he was not present, for he had been called away by circumstances beyond his control,) that annual sessions were required, because it was necessary that the elections should be frequent—this being a fundamental principles of our government. To sustain this argument, the fifth clause of the bill of rights had been referred to, which declared, "that the right in the people to participate in the legislature, is the best security of liberty, and the foundation of all free government; for this purpose, elections ought to be free and frequent," &c.

Now, what was the meaning of this declaration? Did it mean that elections for the Legislature should be held annually? Surely, that was not the construction to be put upon it. Its import and true meaning evidently was that there should not be a long continuance of the delegated power of the people in the hands of the same Legislators; that there should be no series of sessions of the Legislature without new elections and a fresh infusion, into the Halls of Legislation, of the spirit and temper of the people themselves; it was to secure to this extent, at least, the participation of the people themselves in their legislation; and would not the people participate as freely and fully in their legislation, and have their feelings and wishes as fully reflected in a Legislature, meeting only once in two years (and that early after their election) as they would if that body assembled every year? Most certainly they would, and such was manifestly the only fair and liberal construction which could be given to the article which had been quoted from the Bill of Rights. It meant not to require that convocations of Legislatures should be so very frequent, but that accountability to the constituency should follow speedily upon the exercise of all delegated powers, and each Legislature when it assembled, should come free and fresh from the people, and reflect truly in the lower House, at least, their will and wishes.

Another reason which had been assigned for annual meetings of the Legislature, was that the state of the finances might require it. It was true that the State of Maryland, having been embarrassed from causes to which he need not now particularly allude, had found it necessary to raise from her citizens a large amount of revenue. That revenue went into the Treasury, and it was important that there should be a supervision over the proceedings of the accounting officers—it was proper that the finances should be sufficiently guarded. But what had been the action of the Legislature on this subject? Would the finances of the State be injured or endangered by reason of biennial sessions of the Legislature? The very amendment of the Constitution which had been proposed in 1845-'6, and passed in 1846-'7, required the Treasurer to make to the Governor of the State the very identical Report which he would have made to the Legislature if it were in session. Nor was this Report confined exclusively to the Governor. In the year 1847, the House of Delegates passed a resolution requiring the Treasurer to have twelve hundred copies of this report printed—ten copies to be sent, for circulation, to each member of the Legislature. What was the character of that Report? The Treasurer showed the amounts of money received and the sources from which they were received; explaining what these sources were. The Report referred to each item, and the different tables accompanying the Report showed the persons from whom the amounts were received, and the amounts themselves.

He (Mr. B.) was in favor of imposing the same obligation under the new Constitution. He would even go further, and authorise the Legislature to appoint a committee to come to Annapolis and examine the accounts and vouchers of the report made by the Treasurer during the recess of the Legislature. It was not necessary that the Legislature should meet for the purpose of supervising the Treasurer's accounts. Gentlemen might be assured that if ever it should be the ill-fate of Maryland to have at the head of her financial department a man who was not honest, she would still be defrauded whatever guards she might throw around her Treasury. The finances could be as well guarded and protected by biennial meetings of the Legislature.

Were the liberties of the State to be endangered by biennial sessions? Truly had it been said, that "the world was governed too much." The history of the past—all experience taught us, that there was no danger to be apprehended under a republican government, by the want of being governed. If evil was to fall upon our institutions, it would come not from the few laws which might be passed, but from the many. He might well refer to our own statute book, to sustain this position. He did not know that any law stood upon it, which directly endangered the liberties of the people. But where was the man to be found, within the confines of Maryland, who was so learned in the law, that he could, without long and laborious examination, tell what the laws of the State were, upon every subject which they embraced? It seemed to him that there was a kind of ambition in every man, who came to the Legislature, to do something in the way of law-making. The brains of men were constantly upon the rack to discover what they could do—what more they could make—what changes they could effect upon the statute book—so that when they returned to their constituents, they might be able to answer the enquiry which met them, "what have you done?" by pointing to some act of legislation, the passage of which they had been mainly instrumental in securing. They were not satisfied with telling the people that they had discharged their duty generally—that they had prevented the passage of this or that law, the operation of which might be injurious. Their constituents would tell them that is not what we want. Tell us what you have done for *us*—what law or measure you have caused to be adopted. Every country had its peculiar *mania;* and this was the mania of the State of Maryland. This was a state of affairs which he desired to avoid. He desired that the laws should be free and few, and easily understood. He knew of nothing in Maryland, which had more seriously conduced to the glorious "uncertainty of the law," than this condition of things.

Mr. Spencer. Is not the evil to be attributed as much to the administration of the law?

Mr. Brent. I think not. I think the evil lies mainly in the legislation of the State, for the reasons I have given.

Mr. B. then proceeded to remark, that the experience of the State, under biennial sessions, had not been long. But there had been an interval between two sessions of the Legislature, and what was the condition of the State? Was she not as thriving as before? Were not her fields as productive—her soil as kind and generous—her people as happy—and their rights as well protected, as they had been under annual sessions of the Legislature? Gentlemen knew that such was the fact. The State was as prosperous, and her interests as well guarded, and they would continue to be so under biennial, as under annual sessions. The Legislature, at its last session, had done as much as was required by the interests of the State. There were some measures—such as a general assessment law—which had failed, from want of time perhaps, or some other cause. But gentlemen were to bear in mind, that this was not the first time, that measures had been crowded into the last days of the session, and not been acted upon for want of time.

He believed, then, that biennial sessions would be for the interest of the State. If the Legislature, meeting biennially, could perform the duties required from it, that would be all that was necessary, and an annual saving would be effected of twenty-five thousand dollars. This was an expense which he wished to avoid, and it ought to be avoided, unless there were strong and overpowering reasons, why the money should be expended.

It had been said that perpetual vigilance was the price of liberty. No doubt it was so. But was that perpetual vigilance to be exercised exclusively through the Legislature of the State? If it were so, then the meetings of that body would, of necessity, be perpetual. But it was not the Legislature, which was to be the sole guardian of our liberties. The people themselves were to be vigilant. Their agents were to be vigilant—their Governor, to whose keeping they had confided their honor and their interests, was to be ever upon the watch. There was also another mighty sentinel upon the watch-tower of liberty—that was the giant press. Whenever our institutions were threatened in their strongholds, its voice would be heard from the mountain peaks to old ocean's wave, sounding the alarm and awakening the freemen of the land to action.

Mr. B. then remarked, that his opinion in relation to biennial sessions, were modified by the circumstances that surrounded him. He believed that a Constitution would be passed, and that it would be adopted by the people at the ballot-box. That Constitution would impose very onerous duties upon the Legislature, for some time after its adoption. He should, therefore, vote in favor of two annual sessions, to enable the Legislature to carry out the provisions of the new organic law. And if no other gentleman moved an amendment to that effect, he would do so. He also expressed his intention to urge the adoption of a provision empowering the Governor, when, in his judgment, the exigencies of the State might require it, to call a special session of the Legislature.

For these reasons, he could not vote for the proposition of his able and distinguished colleague, (Mr. Merrick.)

After a brief explanation by Mr. Spencer,

Mr. Chambers of Kent, said, he would endeavor to add a few words, without repeating arguments already urged in favor of biennial sessions.

The reasons assigned for annual sessions, resolved themselves into these two—first, the inability of the Legislature to perform all the duty required by the interest of the State, and second, the want of necessary supervision over the treasury of the State and its officers.

As to the first, it happened that the laws of the session of 1849, the first of the biennial sessions, lay upon the adjoining desk in the service of his next neighbor, and when the accumulation of duty was remarked upon in the course of debate, he had opened to the middle of the volume, and found that more than one half of the whole number of laws, were passed within the last four days of the session. He believed in some of the States, a whole session has not lasted beyond four days. He was aware that many of these laws of 1849, had been in some progress before the day on which they bear date—some of them nearly consummated, but still it was true the great part of the business of every session was performed in the last few days.

He had passed the last thirty winters in this city, with the exception of nine years, while he held a seat in the Senate of the United States, and it was as well known to him, as it was to every one who was conversant with these matters, that in the early part of the session, members were enjoying themselves in social and agreeable indulgencies. He did not allude to this in the way of reproach—not at all. It was characteristic of the species. Man is naturally a self-indulgent and indolent being—essentially a creature of appetite and passion. Some motive must excite him to toil and labor. When it became necessary, the members would and did devote themselves to their serious duties.

The fact that they did so only after a considerable portion of the session had elapsed, proved his position, that less time was necessary than it was now contended was required. With regard to the supervision over the Treasury, and a strict eye upon accounting officers, he must say he had not much faith in the influence of investigating committees, or in the "grand inquest." He asked gentlemen when and where defaulters had been detected and exposed by such committees.

Experience taught us differently. Such defaulters generally had the ability and the means to prepare false and fraudulent accounts and vouchers, to conceal the traces of their frauds. We know numerous instances in banks and other moneyed institutions, in which these frauds have been completely covered over, and concealed by such false vouchers.

It is generally on change or in the street we get the first intelligence of these defalcations. Those who are guilty of them generally make investments--usually for speculation--and according to the trite saying, "ill-gotten gain never benefits its owner," their reckless speculations usually fail, and suicide or flight is most frequently the first intimation of their guilt. He held that the first and great security for the State must be found in the well earned character of the officer, for high moral integrity. Discard considerations of party service and select your man, from a long and intimate knowledge of his virtue and his merit. The next reliance must be on the pecuniary indemnity into which competent sureties have entered for the faithful discharge of his duties. Let no partiality or favoritism prevent a due observance of strict duty by those entrusted with this important branch of service.

The Legislature, as a body, was no match in the contest with a defaulter, in the effort on the one hand to detect, and on the other to evade detection in a course of official malversation. A committee was equally impotent.

He could not then perceive in either of these reasons a ground to annul the deliberate action of the people, who had most deliberately and decidedly expressed their wishes in relation to this particular question, some three years since.

Not a gentleman on this floor has been able to say he has heard the first whisper of discontent, or any desire for change in this respect. Every voter in the State knows we are here engaged in re-modelling the Constitution, and all sorts of suggestions have been made during our three months session, but no voice has reached us advising a return to annual sessions. He believed the judgment passed upon the subject was as much influenced by the belief that excessive Legislation was pernicious as by considerations of economy. For himself, he was much of the opinion very often expressed by an old friend now no more, a former Attorney General of the State. The experience of a long life actively occupied in the business affairs of the world, had induced his strong-minded friend to conclude that it was of much more importance to have the law settled than to have it this way or that—to know what the law was, rather than why it was. He doubted whether the State would suffer by curtailing the usual quantum of legislation to one-half of what it had been.

Mr. Sprigg rose to give notice of an amendment which he desired to offer, as follows:

Amend the said section by striking out all after the word "term," in the second line, where it secondly occurs, and insert in lieu thereof, the following:

"Of one year from the day of the general elections, the General Assembly may continue its first session after the adoption of this Constitution, as long, as in the opinion of the two Houses, the public interests may require it, but all subsequent regular sessions of the General Assembly shall be closed on the fiftieth day from their commencement, unless the same shall be closed at an earlier day by the agreement of the two Houses."

Which was read.

Mr. Brown said it had been repeatedly urged as an argument against annual sessions of the Legislature, that nothing was done for the first three or four weeks of each session. He had had some experience in these matters, and thought that gentlemen were mistaken in the views they had expressed. In the House of Delegates there were but few members who were what might be termed old politicians. They were generally strangers to each other. On the meeting of the Legislature, a Speaker had to be elected, and committees appointed—the latter being a duty imposing much responsibitity, because of the necessity of a judicious selection. This took a week. In the meantime, the members were becoming acquainted with each other, and everything was done, that could be done, to set the machinery of legislation into operation. These delays which could not be avoided in any deliberative body; and for this Convention, more especially, to complain of the waste of time thus caused, seemed very much like Satan rebuking Sin. The committees then went to work, and some two or three weeks might be taken up in maturing important bills for the action of the body. They were then taken up and discussed.

Mr. B. then proceeded to show, in reply to the remarks of Mr. Chambers, of Kent, that bills, which had been acted upon by the lower House, went to the Senate, and it was not until they came back again to the House, that a date was given to them. So that, in fact, many of the bills, which, from their dates, seemed to have passed on the last few days of the session, might have passed long before. He cited the instance of the law calling the Convention, in respect to which, a proposition had been introduced at the commencement of the session, even before the usual messages had been interchanged between the two Houses.

One word as to the treasury. He did not suppose that any gentleman intended to say that the House of Delegates guarded the treasury. He certainly did not intend to say so. But we had established a large system of taxation. It might be necessary that changes in that system should be made, in consequence of injury to some particular interest which it might be proper to relieve. The crops might fail, or some other calamity befal us. If we continued prosperous, no such necessity would arise. But did gentlemen mean to say, that if the necessity come, the relief should not be afforded?

In regard to conferring upon the Governor the power to call the legislature together, he, [Mr. B.,] had only to say, that he never knew any benefit grow out of extra sessions, either under the general or State governments.

He thought it would be better to adopt the amendment of the gentleman from Queen Anne's,

(Mr. Spencer.) Let the annual sessions continue until the people themselves should call for a change. Let a provision to that effect be inserted in the Constitution, and no injury could result.

Mr. Merrick said, that as the amendment indicated by the gentleman from Prince George's, [Mr. Sprigg,] struck him, [Mr. M.,] as very appropriate, and as better than his own, he would withdraw his amendment, and accept that as a modification.

Mr. Weber said, that he rose to make a few remarks in explanation of the vote he intended to give. Hitherto, as a representative in the General Assembly, and as a citizen at the polls, he had voted against the change in the Constitution which substituted biennial for annual sessions. He had done so, because, in the first place, he regarded the proposed change as calculated, if not intended, to postpone and protract the call of a Convention to revise the organic law of the State. And secondly, because he believed in the policy and necessity of frequent elections, in order that the people might hold their representatives to a proper accountability. But the people themselves had removed the grounds of his objections. They had removed the first, by calling this Convention—whether for better or for worse, remained yet to be seen. They had removed the second ground by defining at the polls, what they intended should be understood by the term, "frequent elections," so far as related to elections for members of the legislature. They had defined it to mean "every two years." He held that the people, having all power in themselves, had a right to declare and define the principles of their government. In the words of the declaration, adopted a few days ago, that they "ought to have the sole and exclusive right of regulating their internal government." The people had determined to have biennial sessions, and that was the interpretation which they desired their representatives here, to put on the term, "frequent elections." As one of those representatives, he took this position; although a small majority of his immediate constituents had voted against the change. But he looked to the voice of a majority of the people of the State, and felt, that, as an agent of their's, he was to be governed by their voice.

He was also constrained to adopt this course by the consideration that, during the contest which took place among the people in regard to the call of a Convention to remodel the organic law, he had never heard, in his own county, or seen it stated in the newspapers of any other county in the State, that one of the reforms desired by the people, was the change now advocated. He believed that the position assumed by the people was to be attributed in a great measure, to the fact set forth by the gentleman from Frederick, (Mr. Thomas,) yesterday—that they were satisfied that there was two much legislation.

Again. The people not only desired reform, but they asked also for retrenchment in the expenditures of the Government; and although he did not stand here as the advocate of a cheap government without reference to the fact whether it was to be good or bad; yet he was satisfied in his own mind that it was his duty, if he believed a good Government could be obtained cheaply, to prefer it to a good Government costing much.

The difficulty had been presented that, for two, four, six, or perhaps eight or ten years, after this Convention should have closed its labors—and in the event of the new Constitution being adopted by the people—annual sessions of the Legislature would be necessary; and it was proposed by those who advocated them, to restrict the term for which the Legislature was to remain in session. He was satisfied, from what little experience he had himself had, in legislative life, and from the admission of the gentleman from Carroll, (Mr. Brown,) that much time was loss at the commencement of every session in the organization of committees and in the proper distribution and arrangement of business. If then it was necessary that important measures should be matured to carry out the provisions of the new Constitution, he thought that the great object in view was more likely to be accomplished efficiently and economically if the sessions were for a longer term, rather than by annual sessions of short duration; because, in the latter case, the local business pressing upon the Legislature would prevent, or greatly impede, the formation and adoption of such laws as might be necessary to carry on the new system of Government. If this principle was adopted, the Legislature, at the first session, might attend to the local business, and would then be much better able to form the necessary laws than Legislatures newly assembled and with all the local legislation of the State to attend to. He objected, however, to any amendment which would look to both annual and biennial sessions. He desired that the Constitution should contain a provision declaring that the meetings of the Legislature should be either annual or biennial—one or the other, not both.

Mr. Biser said he was about to make a motion which he would preface with a brief remark or two. The gentleman from Kent, had partly made a convert of him, when he showed that in the last five days of the session of the last Legislature, one half of all the bills of that session were passed—that the half of five hundred and sixty-one bills, making two hundred and eighty, were disposed of in that time. He was happy also that he and his honorable colleague, (Mr. Thomas,) from whom he differed yesterday, were drawing a little nearer together. Now he, (Mr. B.,) was a strict economist, when the public interests required retrenchment; and he found, on looking into the matter, that the expenses of two annual sessions could be so reduced, by lessening the duration of the sessions, as to be less than those of one protracted biennial session, he presumed that the same could be done in an annual session. There would, therefore, be no necessity for making the session extend to fifty days, and when, in order, he would move to strike out fifty and insert thirty days.

Mr. Biser then moved to strike out "fifty" and iusert "thirty."

Mr. Hicks had made an effort, the day before, to obtain the floor, but was unsuccessful, and had he then succeeded would have occupied the Convention somewhat longer than he now designed to do. He rose now only from a stern sense of duty, to add a word if possible to what had already been said and so well said in favor of the proposition now under consideration; nor would he attempt it, at this late stage of the discussion of this substitute, did he not consider it to be one of the most important subjects, connected with our doings here. Important first as a tax-saving measure. *But infinitely more important as a measure*—the failure of which, would, in his opinion, contribute more to jeopard the Constitution which we are now striving to prepare for submission to the people of our agitated State, than anything we may do here. And he now raised the voice of warning, though feeble, and trusted gentlemen upon this floor would reflect well upon this subject and act prudently. He should have contented himself with the able vindication by his colleague of his important measure, together with the valuable aid it received by the able and distinguished members from Frederick and Washington counties yesterday, and by others to-day. But coming from a section of the State where this measure of biennial sessions has been earnestly called for and are very popular, he desired to bear his testimony to that fact, and confirm, if not strengthen, what his colleague had said in that connexion. *We* are engaged. *he spoke of the people of the Eastern Shore—we* are engaged, in helping, *at least*, to pay a debt for which we have never received value; therefore desire to get through as quick as possible and forget it. He voted for biennial sessions, and so did his people *of all parties*, when submitted to the people, four years ago—and unlike the gentleman from Howard District, he intended to vote for it again. The gentleman from Howard District and his friend from Frederick, (Mr. Biser,) seemed to think they have discovered their folly and are retracing their steps, but *he* had began right and intended to keep right. Gentlemen speak of annual sessions of the Legislature as a subject not to be considered by the Convention in connexion with that of expense. Are we not here to make an organic law, to last, he trusted, for ages to come; and are we not to guard all the interests of the people as best we can? He thought; he felt so; but how do some gentlemen propose to do it? Why, sir, by the multiplication of officers, and largely increased salaries. The gentleman from Frederick, (he meant his friend, Mr. Biser,) says he voted for biennial sessions too; and why? Because, he says, the cry of repudiation was then to be heard in our State. So it was; and my word for it, Mr. President, if we choke the wholesome financial measures which have been so wisely concocted and now in successful operation, you will hear it again, for although we are comparatively quiet now, it is not to be forgotten, that we have a debt of sixteen millions of dollars hanging over us, and which, enormous as it is, we intend to pay, if let alone as we now are. The same gentleman (Mr. Biser) has told us that nothing was said during the canvass last summer by the people of Frederick, upon the subject of biennial sessions. Certainly not; and why? Obviously, because they *there*, as everywhere else, considered it a fixed subject, settled by them, and never, as they supposed, to be disturbed again. Had not the people decided this subject of biennial sessions unequivocally, and shall this Convention thus trifle with them? He hoped not. Have your elections once in two years, and your sessions of the Legislature in like manner, and then you save money and morals. He felt that it was most desirable to avoid frequent elections, for all knew as well he does, the demoralizing effect of popular elections; and he thought all ought, with him, go for just so many elections as were really necessary and no more. The people desired repose and relief from the continual excitement of elections, and for himself, he felt a great anxiety on account of the too frequent elections, for the reason that they are demoralizing in their tendency; and therefore he desired to have the popular elections of the State less frequent for the two-fold reason of immorality and expense. As to the argument founded on the necessity for a strict supervision of the Treasury, he would say, that so long as we have officers faithful as now, and in the past, there is no need of such frequent supervision.

We come here, professing to take charge of the public interest, and how do we do it? Why, by multiplying offices and increasing salaries—the last thing the people expect us to do. The people who have so unequivocally decided in favor of biennial sessions, have not sent us here to change the system, rely on it.

Why, gentlemen talk as though we had come here to repeal our entire statutory system. What have we to do with the statutes? Our duty is to frame an organic law, in conformity with our laws already made, and to which all laws, hereafter to be made, must conform. We are not here to prepare a statutory code. If we insert in this Constitution, propositions at variance with the expressed sense of our people, we do not do our duty. He hoped we shall be able to form such a Constitution as will be acceptable to our people. As to his own votes, he would only say, they shall be honestly cast. *He* had repeatedly served in the Legislature *too*, but was ready to admit that his friend from Carroll, (Mr. Brown,) had been in more legislative bodies and had belonged to more parties than he had, and should not controvert what he had said in connexion with the industry of the last Legislature; but he must say, that *he* knew, as had been said in many instances, that weeks of the earlier parts of the sessions were consumed in idleness or pleasure. Some time must be used in electing officers and the other processes of organization, but no one having experience, doubts that much time is lost in amusements on such occasions. If we can send out to the people, such a Constitution as we may reasonably expect them to adopt, we must be careful what the provisions are which we insert in it.

His friend from Frederick, (Mr. Biser,) had said that the cry of repudiation was once heard in Maryland, and that he had then voted for biennial sessions, as a measure of retrenchment. That was true; but now, when our debt is likely to be paid off, if we check those wisely concocted measures of finance, which have been the means of resting our prosperity, rely on it, the people will cry out against us. If he could see the necessity for annual sessions, he, for one, would vote to return to them, but he thought the business could be done just as well by biennial as annual sessions. The Legislature, if industrious, can pass all necessary laws in sixty days, just as well as six months, and if not, they have the power to extend their session, in view of perfecting changes on account of the Constitution now being made, to six months or longer, if found necessary; and then, if the system may be found not to work well, they can but return to annual sessions. But there is no fear as to the result. The proposition of his colleague was a self-evident one, he thought, and ought to carry conviction to the mind of every one; he trusted it would be adopted, as great good would certainly grow out of its adoption.

Mr. SCHLEY said that when the proposition for biennial sessions was before the people, he voted against it, believing that it was a scheme designed to get rid of a Reform Convention. He had been influenced by the opinion, that elections should be frequent, and that the Legislature ought to meet annually to supervise the accounts of the Treasurer. His first objection was removed by the call of the Convention, and his second, by the action of the people establishing biennial sessions. The more he reflected on the subject, the more was he satisfied with the decision of the people on this question. He would now vote for biennial sessions; first, because as a financial measure, it would lessen the burden of taxation; and, secondly, because the people had expressly sanctioned the system. He could bear testimony to what was yesterday said by the gentleman from Frederick, (Mr. Thomas.) He had found no man who had raised his voice against this biennal system. It was, therefore, to be regarded as a settled question; and, in his vote, he intended to act in conformity with the will of the people. Another reason which influenced him, was, that nearly half the States of the Union, had adopted the principle; and lastly, he would vote for it from a thorough conviction that it will, if rejected, put in jeopardy the Constitution itself. The people had reflected on the subject, and had made the change, and it would endanger the Constitution to insert a provision in opposition to their expressed will. He desired to make the new Constitution such as they will approve and adopt. He had merely risen to make these brief remarks, and he would now move the previous question. He withdrew the motion at the request of Mr. DONALDSON, who promised to renew it.

Mr. DONALDSON merely desired to say a few words, by way of explanation. Gentlemen on the other side seemed to have understood his argument, as if he meant that the accounts of the Treasurer alone, were to be subject to the inspection of the Legislature. The check to which he referred, was upon all the accounting officers in the State, including the Treasurer, whose returns where made to the House of Delegates, and there became the subject of various enquiries and orders, which often proceeded from not the most friendly sources. This responsibility, and this apprehension, tended to make those officers prompt, efficient and scrupulous. In regard to the excess of legislation, he repeated that it was his conviction, that the evil was really increased by the biennial system, and, in this connexion, he gave some further illustrations of his views.

Mr. DONALDSON concluded by renewing, (according to promise,) the demand for the previous question.

Mr. BRENT, of Charles, desired to offer an amendment, (which was not now in order.)

Some conversation followed on a point of order, in which Mr. MCHENRY and the PRESIDENT, *pro tem.*, took part.

Mr. SCHLEY now withdrew the previous question, at the request of

Mr. BRENT, of Charles, who, in accordance with the indication he had this morning given, sent to the clerk's table, to be read, an amendment, which he intended to offer when in order, and which is given hereafter.

Mr. B., in accordance with his pledge, renewed the demanded for the previous question.

There was a second, and the main question was ordered to be now taken.

The first question was on the amendment of Mr. SPRIGG, as accepted by Mr. MERRICK.

Mr. DIRICKSON asked the yeas and nays, which were ordered, and having been taken, resulted as follows:

Affirmative—Messrs. Tuck, President, *pro tem.*, Morgan, Donaldson, Dorsey, Wells, Randall, Kent, Sellman, Merrick, Buchanan, Welsh, Constable, Chambers, of Cecil, McLane, Bowie, Sprigg, McCubbin, Spencer, George, Wright, Shriver, Biser, McHenry, Magraw, Gwinn, Brent of Baltimore city, Presstman, Ware, Davis, Anderson, Parke, Shower and Brown—33.

Negative—Messrs. Ricaud, Chambers, of Kent, Mitchell, Dalrymple, Brent, of Charles, Bell, Ridgely, Lloyd, Dickinson, Sherwood, of Talbot, Colston, John Dennis, Dashiell, Williams, Hicks, Hodson, Eccleston, Phelps, Miller, Bowling, Dirickson, McMaster, Hearn, Fooks, Jacobs, Thomas, Gaither, Annan, Stephenson, Nelson, Carter, Stewart, of Caroline, Hardcastle, Stewart, of Baltimore city, Schley, Fiery, Neill, John Newcomer, Harbine, Michael Newcomer, Waters, Brewer, Weber, Hollyday, Fitzpatrick, Smith and Cockey—47.

So the amendment was rejected.

Mr. BRENT, of Charles, now offered the following amendment:

Amend the said second section by striking out all after the words "term of," where they secondly occur in the second line, and inserting in lieu thereof, the following:

"One year from the day of the general election, for the first two years after the adoption of this Constitution, and thereafter for the term of two years from the day of each general election, so that the first two sessions of the

General Assembly of Maryland, after the adoption of this Constitution, shall be annual, and thereafter biennial."

Mr. BROWN suggested to Mr. BRENT, to extend the time to three or four years.

Some conversation followed on the point of order, in which Mr. BROWN and the PRESIDENT, *pro tem.*, took part.

Mr. BRENT declined to accept the modification of Mr. BROWN.

The question then recurred on the motion of Mr. BRENT, of Charles.

Mr. MCMASTER asked the yeas and nays, which were ordered.

Some further conversation followed on a point of order, in which Messrs. THOMAS and PRESSTMAN, took part.

Mr. THOMAS suggested a certain modification of the amendment of Mr. PHELPS, which lead to further conversation upon a point of order.

The question was then taken on the amendment of Mr. BRENT, of Charles, and resulted as follows:

Affirmative—Messrs. Donaldson, Wells, Randall, Kent, Sellman, Brent, of Charles, Merrick, Welch, Constable, Bowie, Sprigg, McCubbin, Bowling, Gaither, Gwinn, Brent of Baltimore city, Presstman, Ware, Davis, Brewer, Waters, Hollyday, and Fitzpatrick—23.

Negative—Messrs. Tuck, President, *pro tem.*, Morgan, Ricaud, Chambers, of Kent, Mitchell, Dorsey, Dalrymple, Buchanan, Bell, Ridgely, Lloyd, Dickinson, Sherwood, of Talbot, Colston, John Dennis, Dashiell, Williams, Hicks, Hodson, Eccleston, Phelps, Chambers, of Cecil, Miller, Spencer, George, Wright, Dirickson, McMaster, Hearn, Fooks, Jacobs, Thomas, Shriver, Biser, Annan, Stephenson, McHenry, Nelson, Carter, Stewart, of Caroline, Hardcastle, Stewart of Baltimore city, Schley, Fiery, Neill, John Newcomer, Harbine, Michael Newcomer, Weber, Smith, Parke, Shower, Cockey and Brown—54.

So the amendment was rejected.

Mr. SPENCER then offered the following amendment:

Amend said second section by striking out all after the words "term of," where they lastly occur, in the second line, and insert in lieu thereof the following:

"One year from the day of the general election, but the legislature shall have the right to provide by law for biennial sessions."

And Mr. S. demanded the previous question on the amendment.

There was a second; and

The main question was ordered to be now taken.

Mr. HARBINE asked the yeas and nays, on the amendment of Mr. SPENCER;

Which were ordered; and

Being taken, were as follows:

Affirmative—Messrs. Tuck, President, *pro. tem.*, Morgan, Donaldson, Dorsey, Wells, Randall, Kent, Sellman, Merrick, Buchanan, Welch, Constable, Chambers, of Cecil, Bowie, Sprigg, McCubbin, Spencer, George, Wright, Shriver, Biser, McHenry, Magraw, Presstman, Ware, Davis, Anderson, Hollyday, Parke and Brown.—30.

Negative—Messrs. Ricaud, Chambers of Kent, Mitchell, Dalrymple, Brent of Charles, Bell, Ridgely, Lloyd, Dickinson, Sherwood of Talbot, Colston, John Dennis, Dashiell, Williams, Hicks, Hodson, Eccleston, Phelps, Miller, Bowling, Dirickson, McMaster, Hearn, Fooks, Jacobs, Thomas, Gaither, Annan, Stephenson, Nelson, Carter, Stewart, of Caroline, Hardcastle, Gwinn, Stewart of Baltimore city, Brent of Baltimore city, Schley, Fiery, Neill, John Newcomer, Harbine, Michael Newcomer, Brewer, Waters, Weber, Fitzpatrick, Smith, Shower and Cockey—49.

So the amendment was rejected.

Mr. PHELPS now withdrew his substitute, and moved to amend the said second section by filling the blank in the second line, with the words "two years."

Some further conversation followed on a point of order, in which Messrs. PRESSTMAN, HARBINE and PHELPS took part.

Mr. PHELPS demanded the previous question on his amendment.

There was a second; and

The main question was ordered.

Mr. HICKS asked the yeas and nays on the amendment;

Which were ordered, and

Being taken, resulted as follows:

Affirmative—Messrs. Ricaud, Chambers of Kent, Mitchell, Dorsey, Dalrymple, Brent of Charles, Bell, Ridgely, Lloyd, Dickinson, Sherwood of Talbot, Colston, John Dennis, Dashiell, Williams, Hicks, Hodson, Eccleston, Phelps, Bowling, Spencer, Dirickson, McMaster, Hearn, Fooks, Jacobs, Thomas, Gaither, Annan, Stephenson, Nelson, Carter, Stewart of Caroline, Hardcastle, Stewart of Baltimore city, Schley, Fiery, Neill, John Newcomer, Harbine, Michael Newcomer, Davis, Brewer, Waters, Weber, Hollyday, Fitzpatrick, Smith and Cockey—49.

Negative—Messrs. Tuck, President, *pro tem.*, Morgan, Donaldson, Wells, Randall, Kent, Sellman, Merrick, Buchanan, Welch, Constable, Chambers of Cecil, Bowie, Sprigg, McCubbin, Wright, Shriver, Biser, McHenry, Magraw, Gwinn, Brent of Baltimore city, Presstman, Ware, Anderson, Parke, Shower and Brown—28.

So the amendment was adopted.

Mr. WELLS offered the following amendment, to come in at the end of the section:

"Whenever the legislature may hereafter determine to substitute biennial for annual sessions; and in the meantime, and until then, said sessions shall be annual, and the members of the House of Delegates shall be elected annually."

Mr. CHAMBERS, of Kent, demanded the previous question on the amendment.

There was a second.

The main question was ordered to be taken.

Mr. HICKS asked the yeas and nays;

Which were ordered; and

Being taken, resulted as follows:

Affirmative—Messrs. Tuck, President, *pro tem.*, Morgan, Donaldson, Dorsey, Wells, Randall, Kent, Sellman, Merrick, Buchanan, Welch, Constable, Bowie, Sprigg, McCubbin, Spencer, George, Wright, Shriver, Biser, Magraw, Brent of Baltimore city, Ware, Anderson, Parke, Shower and Brown—26.

Negative—Messrs. Ricaud, Chambers of Kent, Mitchell, Dalrymple, Brent of Charles, Bell, Ridgely, Lloyd, Dickinson, Sherwood of Talbot, Colston, John Dennis, Dashiell, Williams, Hicks, Hodson, Eccleston, Phelps, Miller, Bowling, Dirickson, McMaster, Hearn, Fooks, Jacobs, Thomas, Gaither, Annan, Stephenson, Nelson, Carter, Stewart of Caroline, Hardcastle, Gwinn, Stewart of Baltimore city, Presstman, Schley, Fiery, Neill, John Newcomer, Harbine, Michael Newcomer, Davis, Brewer, Waters, Weber, Hollyday, Fitzpatrick, Smith and Cockey—50.

So the amendment was rejected.

Mr. MCHENRY offered the following amendment:

Amend said second section, by striking out all from the word "delegates," in the second line to the end thereof, and inserting in lieu thereof, the following:

"For the term of one or two years from the day of the general election, as the people may, by separate vote determine at the first of such general elections."

Mr. McH. said, he had seen great evidence of a change in the public mind, not only in his own county, but in the city of Baltimore.

Mr. McH. demanded the previous question on the amendment.

There was a second, and

The main question was ordered to be now taken.

The yeas and nays were ordered, and

Being taken, resulted as follows:

Affirmative—Messrs. Tuck, President, *pro tem.*, Morgan, Donaldson, Dorsey, Wells, Randall, Kent, Sellman, Buchanan, Welch, Chambers of Cecil, Miller, Bowie, Sprigg, George, Shriver, Biser, McHenry, Magraw, Stewart of Caroline, Gwinn, Brent of Baltimore city, Presstman, Ware, Davis, Anderson, Shower and Brown—28.

Negative—Messrs. Ricaud, Chambers of Kent, Mitchell, Dalrymple, Brent of Charles, Bell, Ridgely, Lloyd, Dickinson, Sherwood of Talbot, Colston, John Dennis, Dashiell, Williams, Hicks, Hodson, Eccleston, Phelps, Bowling, Spencer, Wright, Dirickson, McMaster, Hearn, Jacobs, Thomas, Gaither, Annan, Stephenson, Nelson, Carter, Hardcastle, Stewart of Baltimore city, Schley, Fiery, Neill, John Newcomer, Harbine, Michael Newcomer, Brewer, Waters, Weber, Hollyday, Fitzpatrick, Smith, Parke and Cockey—46.

So the amendment was rejected.

Mr. SPENCER moved the following amendment:

"But the legislature shall have the right to provide by law, for annual sessions."

A motion was made, that the Convention adjourn, but was waived to enable

Mr. THOMAS to give notice that he should, to-morrow, move to amend the twenty-first rule of the Convention, by striking therefrom the words "voting with the majority."

And the Convention adjourned, until to-morrow morning, 11 o'clock.

Remarks of Mr. MERRICK, *(revised) Monday, Feb.* 10, *in relation to taxing property beyond the limits of the State.*

Mr. MERRICK thought it would be best to leave the section as it stood in the report of the committee. He said there were some descriptions of property beyond the limits of Maryland and owned by some of her citizens, which our revenue laws could not reach, and any attempt to tax which would be ridiculous, yet there were other kinds of property, particularly public stocks of other States and counties, equally beyond our limits, which, if owned by resident citizens of Maryland, we could and did make subject to our revenue laws with advantage to our Treasury, as well as to the benefit of the value of our own State stocks. The effect of this clause as it stood would be to leave to the Legislature full discretionary power over the subject, they would exercise that discretion wisely and with due reference to the circumstances which may exist at the time they may be called upon to act—and it is certainly not to be inferred because the Legislature have full power over this subject, and have to choose between a wise policy and a foolish attempt to reach property which cannot be reached—that they will do the foolish thing, as some of the arguments seem to imply. I think very differently of our State Legislatures. By engrafting upon the section the amendment proposed, you tie up the Legislature, and deprive them of the power to do that which may be wise, proper, and salutary, because you fear they might attempt that which is ridiculous. I have heard of an attempt on the part of some citizens of this State to evade the payment of their fair proportion of the taxes necessary for public purposes—by selling their Maryland State stocks which are subjected by our laws to taxation, and purchasing and holding in its place the stocks of other States; this attempt seems to be improper, and one, the success of which should be prevented by subjecting such foreign stocks to taxation equally with our own—but make the amendment now proposed, and you take away from the Legislature the power to do this. He should, for these reasons, vote against this and similar amendments, and for the section as it now stands.

FRIDAY, February 14, 1851.

The Convention met at eleven o'clock.

Prayer was made by the Rev. Mr. GRAUFF.

The Roll was called, but no quorum was present.

Mr. JOHN NEWCOMER moved that there be a call of the Convention—which was ordered.

And the roll of the members having been again called—and a quorum being present,

On motion of Mr. JOHN NEWCOMER, all further proceedings on the call were dispensed with.

The Journal of yesterday was then read and approved.

The PRESIDENT, *pro tem.*, laid before the Convention a communication from the clerk of Kent county court, in obedience to the order of the Convention of the 15th of November, which was read, and, on motion of

Mr. RICAUD, was referred to the committee on the Judiciary.

MOTIONS TO RE-CONSIDER.

There being no morning business before the Convention,

Mr. THOMAS called up the motion, of which he had yesterday given notice, so to amend the twenty-first rule of the Convention as to provide that motions to re-consider might be made by *any* member of the Convention, and not, as at present provided, by members alone who had voted with the majority.

The amendment having been read,

An explanation of its object was made by Mr. THOMAS.

The proposition was opposed by Mr. DORSEY, and sustained by Messrs. PHELPS and THOMAS.

After which the question was taken, and the amendment, by ayes 38, noes 20, was agreed to.

THE LEGISLATIVE DEPARTMENT.

The PRESIDENT, *pro tem.*, announced the special order of the day, being the report heretofore made by Mr. JOHNSON, Chairman of the Committee on the Legislative Department.

BIENNIAL SESSIONS.

The section under consideration at the hour of adjournment yesterday, was the second section of the report as amended.

And the question immediately pending was on the amendment proposed by Mr. SPENCER, to add at the end of the said second section the following:

"But the Legislature shall have the right to provide by law for annual sessions."

Upon this question Mr. SPENCER was entitled to the floor.

Mr. HOWARD called for the reading of the section and of the amendment—which were read.

Mr. SPENCER said his object in moving an adjournment on the day previous, was to give time to consider the amendment which he had offered. It was then late in the day, after three o'clock, and, notwithstanding he considered the question an important one, he was unwilling then to detain the Convention by an argument on the question.

He was in favor of biennial sessions, because the people of the State had so determined, and we had no evidence that a change in public sentiment had taken place.

He was of opinion, that for a few years, there would exist a necessity for annual sessions. If the Constitution, which we are now modeling, shall be accepted by the people, then it will necessarily follow, that we shall require the best wisdom of the State to legislate on the subject, and frequent sessions of the Legislature for a few years. The Constitution will embrace principles; the Legislature which is to follow, must carry out the details. Under such circumstances, he was in favor of leaving a discretion over the subject in the Legislature. Hence, it was, that on yesterday he advocated, for the present, annual, leaving it to the Legislature to provide for biennial sessions. He thought that this discretion might be safely reposed in the Legislature, the peculiar tribunal of the people. If we provide in the Constitution for biennial sessions only, and eave no discretion over it any where, then the people of the State might be put to great inconvenience, growing out of the operations of the new government; to remedy this, he offered his amendment to provide for biennial sessions, but as the Convention indicated, by its vote, a preference for biennial sessions, he had offered the one now under consideration He offered it under the most solemn conviction, that it would prove a shield of defence in case of an emergency, when delay in legislation would be attended with great public inconvenience. If it is opposed, it can only be because we are afraid to trust the representatives of the people. We shall abridge their power, so as to prevent them from altering the Constitution, and it is not likely that the people will exercise the power, for some years to come. In the meantime, great exigencies may arise which may require prompt legislation. Some discretion must be reposed in the Legislature, on a question so important.

It is said that it will be used as a political hobby. There need be no such fear. There is much better ground to apprehend that the Legislature will be afraid to provide for annual sessions even in case of a necessity, than they would recklessly resort to them. Men are more apt to support popular than unpopular measures.

Mr. RANDALL suggested to the gentleman from Queen Anne, (Mr. Spencer,) to add to his amendment, the words "and shall have the power to change the times of the meeting of the Legislature."

Mr. R. said, it was his intention to vote in favor of the amendment of the gentleman from Queen Anne, though he, (Mr. R.,) should prefer it with the addition he had suggested. He should vote for it, because he thought that neither annual nor biennial meetings of the Legislature, ought to be a matter of permanent constitutional law. He thought that the suggestion made yesterday, that a clause should be inserted in the Constitution, providing exclusively for *annual* sessions, might be productive of injurious consequences. Such, also, he, (Mr. R.,) believed would be the case, by providing in the Constitution exclusively for biennial sessions of the Legislature, because it would require a change of what should be the permanent organic law, to suit a matter of mere expediency.

In the course of the discussion, gentlemen had referred to the judgment which they allege had been passed by the people, in favor of biennial sessions, and had stated that this judgment stood unrepealed, and should be obligatory and conclusive upon our action. The vote by the people was cast, to which reference had been made, by about fifty-five thousand voters, but an aggregate vote of twenty thousand more had often been given by the people of this State. How would the twenty thousand men who did not vote, have voted on this subject—none could tell. A small portion of them would have over-ruled the majority of four thousand six hundred, by which this judgment had been given. And it was yet to be determined, (he spoke as to a matter of figures,) whether a majority ofthe people of this State were, are, or ever had been in favor of biennial sessions of the Legislature. We had as much right to conclude, that the twenty thousand citizens who did not vote, were in favor of annual sessions, as that they were in favor of a change to biennial sessions. If the twenty thousand were in favor of a change, why did they not so declare themselves? They did not vote, we may conclude, because they preferred the existing law, providing for annual sessions. To say the least, they were indifferent about it, and hence a majority could not be said to be favorable to this change to biennial sessions.

Another consideration which controled the decision of many voters in favor of biennial sessions, and which had an important bearing in neutralizing the influence of many who would otherwise have opposed it—the embarrassing condition of the finances of the State, at the time this vote was cast. The State had suspended payment in specie or its equivalent. We all know that men were induced, from economy alone—in order to aid in maintaining the faith of the State, to vote for biennial sessions. They determined to make sacrifices of what they had hitherto enjoyed, in order to obtain means to be just. That necessity had now passed away—thanks to the people of the State—to their sterling honesty, and their devotion to the public plighted faith. He was, therefore, yet to be satisfied that, if the question had then been put to the people as an isolated question, there would have been a majority in favor of biennial sessions. Other considerations influenced this vote, as has been stated on this floor. The friends and opponents of reform by Convention, used it to advance their peculiar views, and voted for or against biennial sessions, as it influenced that measure. But, be that as it might, he had nothing more to say on the subject, but to add, that in supporting the amendment of the gentleman from Queen Anne, (Mr. Spencer,) he, (Mr. R.,) believed he was doing nothing inconsistent with any expressed wishes of the people. But had there not been an expressed declaration of the people, opposed to biennial sessions? Now it was not until that famous biennial bill had been passed, and the people had experienced its operation, that they, through their delegates, called this Convention. That measure might have been the very last grievance to fill up the measure of their forbearance, and render intollerant things as they were. Certain it was, that up to that time, no such vote could ever have been obtained in the Legislature, to call a Convention—immediately after the operation of that darling measure of biennial sessions was known, this Convention was called. The reformers saw, or thought they saw, in these biennial sessions, no hope of alterations in the Constitution by th eLegislature, and that a Convention alone could afford them relief.

If the question to be decided was, whether the Convention should insert in the organic law, as a matter of permanent provision, a clause that there should be biennial sessions of the Legislature, and none other—was this Convention to deprive the Legislature, and through the Legislature, the people, of the right to have annual sessions, be the exigencies of the State what they might; and that, too, when in this very bill it was declared that the Governor should have this power? How would this show the inconsistency of those gentleman, who were heretofore maintaining in this Convention, popular rights with so much zeal and eloquence, if they now refused to the Legislature the exercise of this power, and gave it to the Governor? Who had the best opportunity of knowing when, and what legislation was required? The Governor or the Legislature? Those to whom the Constitution has confided the legislative power, or he, whose power that Constitution has declared, shall be forever separated from those of the Legislature? He did not think it could be asserted, that the Governor could possibly have the means which the representatives of the people possessed, of knowing what they desired, or what legislation was necessary or proper for them, or at which time it ought to be enacted. Let the power, therefore, be placed in the hands of those who had been selected to discharge that duty, who were best able to judge of the emergency which might demand its exercise. It did not follow, as a matter of course, that we were to have annual sessions. All he contended for was that they should not be prohibited by the Constitution.

Let the times of the meeting of the legislature, whether annual or biennial, or triennial, be determined by the legislature. Thus you exclude this vexed question from being a Constitution provision—you prevent alterations in the Constitution, merely to change the times of the meetings of the legislature which should be controled by the temporary demands of the State.

Another view of this subject. The Convention would, he believed, endanger the adoption of this Constitution, by permanently fixing annual or biennial in its provisions. Many would vote against it, because their opinion on this subject was opposed by its provision; whereas, their votes for the Constitution might be secured, if the right had been reserved to themselves through the legislature, to change biennial into annual sessions. In this respect the Constitution would be realizing that idea of permanency, which Chief Justice Marshall said, should ever characterise such sacred instruments.

At present, the finances of our State were steadily and smoothly moving on to their consummation—the liquidation of the public debt long within the period contemplated, when that debt was contracted. We enjoy a clear sky and a stormless sea; but the aspect of things might change. Emergencies might arise, requiring the legislature to meet annually—war might be declared—a suspension of specie payments might take place. Having yet a debt of sixteen millions of dollars—the interest of which, had to be annually provided for, in this state of prosperity—how much more arduous would be the duty and more frequent the sessions of the legislature in any such disastrous event. Some sudden blight upon the prosperity of the State, such as a failure of crops, or other signal calamity, might fall upon the State which might imperatively require action upon the part of the legislature.

It was true, that, at present, we were paying off our public debt, and securing it by the sinking fund, even in anticipation of the terms of our contract, and by larger reductions than the exigencies of its present condition required.

He did not mean to intimate, that, in the present state of things, he would change one of the provisions by which this early blessing to our State, of freedom from debt, was being consummated. He hoped they all would be continued in their united influence, to bring about this glorious result.

But might not the emergency in any year arise which would demand a change of the system, perhaps a reduction of the taxes, and yet the faith of the State be preserved—nay, be the means of preserving it. An exigency of this kind or of any other kind might occur, demanding a session of the legislature, when it was inhibited by this clause in the Constitution, and where was the danger or the difficulty which could be apprehended? The legislature, the immediate representatives of the people, were to act on this subject—they best knew the wishes of the people, their wants and their views, and had the strongest motives of duty and interest, to execute them. You now confide that very power to the executive.

For one, he would never consent that the Governor exclusively ought or should exercise the power of calling the legislature together.

He was opposed to this mode of altering the Constitution by the legislature. He hoped there would be no such power given. He was opposed to giving the power to the legislature, of constantly tinkering with the Constitution. It has produced this piece of patch-work, to which gentlemen have referred. He preferred the Constitution should be altered at stated periods, by a Convention to be called in pursuance of a provision to be made in the Constitution, when a majority of the people so expressed their determination by their ballots.

This, he thought, should be the only means of changing it. As matters now stood, nearly one half of the time of the legislature was spent in discussing propositions for changes of the Constitution, and the other half in the consideration of local laws. The result was, that these general laws of the State, which the liberties, interests and property of the people demanded, have been almost invariably overlooked, overshadowed and disregarded, to make way for petty acts of incorporation, and mere unimportant local laws. No stronger evidence of this truth was needed than the fact that, of the whole number of laws, passed at the last session of the legislature, (and to which the gentleman from Kent, Mr. Chambers, had alluded,) about ten only were designed for the promotion of the general interests of the State. Last session, a new assessment law, which would have no doubt, from the increased wealth of the State, greatly enlarged the property to be taxed—bringing, in all probability, a large additional revenue into the Treasury, was laid over for want of time. Maryland was behind most of the States of the Union in her general legislation. The demand for a codification of our laws, is universal in this State, and yet it cannot be done. This general and important interest of the people at large, had been overlooked—whilst local matters and popular harangues, about alterations in the Constitution, by changing the times of their meeting, and whether the sessions of the legislature should be annual or biennial, occupied the time of the legislature. In this proposition of the gentleman from Queen Anne's, (Mr. Spencer,) he, [Mr. R.,] saw a prospect of diminishing the subjects of Constitutional discussion and amendment. Make no provision permanently in it at all, prescribing at what time, or how often the legislature should convene; leave that to the legislature itself, and place it within the control of the people, who can so change it from time to time, as suits their wants and wishes, and the exigencies of the State.

Another view of this matter, as suggested by the gentleman from Dorchester, (Mr. Hicks.) We should take care not to create a prejudice against this new Constitution. That gentleman had urged this view, as a reason why we should not, by the Constitution, make the sessions annual, after the vote of the people favorable to biennial sessions. This view is capable of another application. Do not cause those who favor annual sessions, to be able to make that objection to this Constitution. Nearly one-half of all who voted voted to retain annual sessions. Do you not run the risk of having this vote cast against a Constitution, having in it a provision for biennial sessions alone?

I believe (concluded Mr. R.) that if you place in the Constitution a provision making the sessions of the Legislature biennial, but at the same time leaving it to the people themselves to make them annual, if they should think proper to do so, you remove all objections on both sides, and to that extent increase the chances of the final ratfication of the Constitution.

Mr. Dirickson said:

Regarded in any light, the principle of the amendment of the gentleman from Dorchester,

(Mr. PHELPS,) was one of no slight or trifling importance. Endorsed by the most solemn and unequivocal sanction of the whole people of Maryland, it commended itself with weight and seriousness to the earnest and deep consideration of every member of the Convention. Quite content himself, in listening to the remarks of others, he, (Mr. D.,) would have gladly obeyed the dictates of his own feelings and inclinations—by giving his vote cheerfully and without the utterance of a single word, in accordance with the commands of that sovereign will, so clearly, and so plainly manifested. But the debate which had arisen since the agitation of this subject had been singular in many respects—expressions had fallen, and arguments deduced so novel and surprising in their character, as to require that an answer should be at once, directly, and promptly given. He should shrink from no duty attached to his position as a representative to whom a portion of the community had confided their interests. And however reluctant at all times to assail the opinions and doctrines of others, he should never, for a moment, hesitate to speak fearlessly, whenever in his judgment their interests seemed to demand it. Like the distinguished gentleman from Frederick, (Mr. Thomas,) whose eloquence was heard with so much pleasure—he had long looked upon the biennial policy as part and parcel of the great fundamental law of the land. As having been directly inserted and placed amid its provisions by the irresistable fiat and authority of the very source of all power itself. Sir, this is not the first time the discussion of this subject had been agitated within these halls or disturbed the popular mind. Every one was as familiar with its object, design, and tendency as with any political event of the past or present day. Years ago its policy was tried by the fiery ordeal of public sentiment. It was alike the theme of the hustings and the argument that filled the columns of every newspaper in the land. And eventually it sprang into full vitality and being, consecrated by the direct and distinct sanction of the popular vote. All here knew and well-remembered the peculiar history of the measure. It was useless to trace it distinctly through all its course, or in its every progressive step. Abundant precaution had been taken to prevent the slightest degree of surprise. There was no unwise hurry, no unsafe dispatch. Full time was given for the exercise of the most serious and calm reflection, and for the use of the ablest and soundest discretion. And the result was a manifestation, so triumphant and overwhelming, that no one for a moment could be mistaken in its character. Judgment, final and conclusive, clear and explicit, had been promptly rendered by the only majesty recognized and revered by freemen. And all had bowed deferentially and willingly to such mandate. The Legislature that succeeded the ratification by the people, at once engrafted the provision as part of the organic law, and the record of the times will show how slight and feeble was the resistance then made to that "voice" which our noble old Commonwealth had echoed from every quarter. Under such circumstances and with such historic recollections fresh upon his memory, he had witnessed the undisguised hostility exhibited by very many upon this floor against this great measure of economy and reform, with a feeling of wonder and amazement. "'Twas strange, 'twas passing strange," to see how speedily and completely time, with its despoiling touch, had wiped away every impression and vestage of the recent past, though it had been made even by the sovereign hand. 'Twas wonderful that those who professed to drink "par excellence" from the very fount of Democracy—who worshiped at no other political shrine, and bowed to no other political God—should have so soon not only scoffed at the mandates, but absolutely by their speeches rebuked the very wisdom of the people. Democracy did indeed assume strange guises, and well might the delusive resemblance be at times mistaken for the pure reality.

No one could be suprised at the course which had been taken by the whole distinguished delegation from the county of Anne Arundel; recognising, as they doubtless did, the sacred relation that existed between constituent and representative, they had faithfully and honestly shadowed forth the trust and sentiment that was entrusted to their keeping. Nor was he in the least degree disposed to find fault with the kind and hospitable community around him. They were, after all, like the rest of us, but human beings, endowed with the virtues and the frailties that belong to our common nature; and all history had shown, that the wisest judgments had been discolored and perverted by the "cunning of interest," even when guarded by the most exalted integrity. No doubt, their convictions of propriety sprang from the most conscious exercise of all their reasoning faculties, and surely the views of no section of the State were more legitimately entitled to be heard with deference, within the walls of the capitol. But other gentlemen had opposed the amendment already alluded to, whose views did not seem to be in harmony with the constituency they represented, at least so far as the returns of the vote given upon that subject might indicate. Familiar with that people from whose bosom they had come, it might be that they justified themselves by the belief that a change, great and radical, had been effected—that they were even now anxious to reverse the judgment which they had so recently given with such general and singular unanimity; and though it had already been announced from a high source that every thing was in a state of mutation and revolution—that change was written upon the whole moral and physical world—until some more substantial evidence than mere conjecture had been given, he should be unwilling to believe that the people, like bubbles upon the water, were liable to be blown hither and thither by every passing whim and momentary caprice. Nations and communities, like individuals, might be fickle in their moods and wayward in their course, but they seldom departed from that line of policy which had been sanctioned by the maturest reflections, and in the propriety of which their judgments and their interests alike concurred. We are told, however, that apart from these considerations, and towering vastly above them in importance, are other arguments and reasons that place the policy now under discussion upon very different grounds, and render annual sessions of the Legislature an absolute essential to the perfection and harmony of the new system under which we are soon to begin our onward progress. With much apparent earnestness, we had been referred to our present financial condition and to the immense revenues that were yearly collected and disbursed through the various offices of the government, and with great force and ability it was argued, that at least one careful revision was annually required, both to keep the whole complicated system working in perfect harmony and to secure strict fidelity in the discharge of every duty, to the State. Sir, it was indeed a fact, that the closest vigilance and the most rigid scrutiny should be exercised over all who had our revenue in charge. The great arteries of internal improvement were just beginning to develop themselves and immense as was the sum that already flowed weekly, monthly and yearly into the public coffers. No one could safely predict the extent and magnitude of our resources when once those mighty commercial highways were in full vigor and action. The day, perhaps, was not distant, when, under wise legislation, the patient tax-payer might reap the full harvest of past toiling. The question, however, that now presented itself was not as to the amount or future disposition of the finances, but as to the best and most economical method of guarding them against dishonest appropriation and improvident squandering. Surely for such a purpose it was not essential to assemble together the whole legislative body of the State at an expense enormous and extravagant, when compared with the hundred simpler methods that might be easily devised, better effecting the same purpose and with less than a hundredth part of the expenditure.

As had been suggested by the gentleman from Frederick, (Mr. Thomas,) a committee, (and a legislature only acted after all through a committee,) might be provided by law, whose duty it should be to make the annual investigation at the close of that alternate fiscal year, when the General Assembly was not in session. If this mode was not acceptable, and it was merely suggested as an example, there was not a gentleman present who could not originate a scheme that would accomplish all the purposes desired, and in a manner much more likely to secure full integrity from all the officers, and full justice to the State, than that general supervision, which from the very nature and composition of Legislatures, could only be formally and carelessly effected. It had been well and wisely said, that the cheapest policy was not always the most economical; but surely a measure, commended both by reason and economy, could not fail to address itself with convincing power, to the judgment and prudence of all. Extravagance was the mother of corruption, and the warning page of history had shown that corruption was the poisonous bane that had worked out the downfal of the strongest governments of the earth. Such solemn teachings of the past, could not and, would not be without its legitimate influence upon this body, and he entertained the hope that the most wholesome and proper economy would be every where applied. Not relying, however, entirely upon the argument to which he had just replied, the friends of annual sessions urged against the biennial policy, "the want of time" necessary to the consideration and wise formation of all the laws, which the public and private interests might demand. He regarded this as the most unfortunate and untenable position, which could, by possibility, be assumed. Law-making was the veriest, crying vice of the age, and throughout the whole State, there was complaint, universal, loud and deep, against the countless statutes with which our books are already filled. The familiar maxim, that every one is presumed to know the law, had, in point of fact, long since become obsolete, and no man now dared to express an opinion upon the simplest subject, without the most patient, painful and laborious investigation. Why has order after order been submitted to our consideration asking for a codification and a new arrangement of the laws. Because, sir, our statutes have been one mighty mass of enactment, and repeal, re-enactment and re-repeal—supplement, and supplement upon supplement, until the very brain grows dizzy, in the almost vain attempt to gather from the profound medley what really *is the law*. We have been told that courts and jurists, alike had been baffled as well in the search as in giving a true construction to the mystic line when once discovered.

Such obscurity could only have resulted from too much and too frequent legislation. Ere an enactment had been permitted to test its efficacy, it was ruthlessly assailed, and it might be by a "tinkering" hand, that at once defeated and destroyed its whole original design and object. But beside this reply to the argument alleging "a want of time," it was well known that a very large period of each past session had been occupied and consumed in the passage of private laws—in the consideration and granting of divorces, and in a vast deal of local legislation, which so far as the judgment of the Convention had been shaddowed forth, was designed to be removed entirely from this hall, and given to other and more appropriate jurisdiction. Under such an arrangement, the whole "time" would be given exclusively to the great public wants, and with but little industry and energy, every subject might receive that calm and earnest deliberation so essential to wise and wholesome provisions. Let the Legislature hereafter busy itself, as well in the beginning as at the end of the session. Let it proceed earnestly and at once, in the labor before it, and on the day fixed by the Constitution for its final adjournment, every petition will have been heard and every real want been gratified. He was unwilling to detain the Convention longer with the refutation of an argument which seemed unsustained by reason, and utterly destitute of every principle of propriety. But it had been said, by the zealous opponents of the measure, he was now advocating, and with an air triumphant, that it was anti-democratic in its tendency, and in direct and open violation of the spirit and teaching of that article, in our bill of rights, which, framed in the days of seventy-six, and looking eminently to the "security of liberty" and "the foundation of government," advised, in express terms, both the freedom and *frequency* of elections. No one could be more anxious than himself, to infuse into every department of the government, the genuine essence of pure democracy and perfect equality. No one recurred to the wisdom of our revolutionary fathers, with more unfeigned reverence and entire respect. But why, sir, should so much stress be laid upon the term frequent? It was not a word of isolated, definite and precise meaning; but relative and comparative in its character, and evidently designed to receive such liberal and rational interpretation as the circumstances and necessities of the times seemed to demand. It was inserted in the great charter of our rights, as a wise and noble precept, and not as a rigid and unbending rule, which despite of every change, was to tie all future generations down to one uncompromising line of action. The same process of reasoning that proved that annual sessions were nearer to the meaning and design of the principle taught by the article, than the biennial policy, would apply with equal force, to the adoption of semi-annual sessions; and the argument might be continued until it became apparent to every one, that the attempt to give to the term "frequent," any strict meaning, differing from that which the reason of the times justified, was utterly and perfectly absurd.

The example of annual sessions, we are told, had been established by the earliest founders of the government. But what was their situation? The government itself was in a sort of half chrysalis state—just emerging from the colonial position. The havoc of war was desolating the whole country, and filling it with alarm and terror. Civil discord and intestine commotion agitated every section within our borders; and our very liberties themselves were struggling for that triumph, which was only secured after long years of peril and strife. Surely if ever there was a time when the wisdom, and virtue, and experience of the land should be frequently assembled, it was in that dark and dangerous hour. Then, if ever, wise counselings were demanded—then, in short, the crisis of the times were above all other considerations, and reason and propriety alike dictated the construction and the action taken by our sires. That fearful period had forever passed away, and with the exception of the political excitement, common to our form of government, our good old State was now moving with peace, plenty, and power, in her onward destiny. With the change of events, the reasons for annual sessions had vanished away, and no one could entertain a doubt, but that the highest dictates of economy, imperatively called for the adoption of a policy warranted by the circumstances of the times, and in direct accordance with the popular demand. Gentlemen had further urged, in argument, that the biennial act had been proposed at a time peculiar in our affairs, and engrafted amid the provisions of the Constitution, purely as a measure of saving; and economy; and they had then pointed with honest pride to the well-filled coffers of a surplus treasury, as fully justifying them in seeking to return to that policy of which their judgments approved. It was indeed a glorious truth, that Maryland had emerged in full splendor, from the obscurity that once threatened to cloud her fair fame; and now possessed of an untarnished escutcheon, she stood with noble presence amid the sister sovereigns around her. Under the guidance of a master-hand and courageous heart, a mighty system of revenue had been breathed into full life and action; and the demon of repudiation rebuked and abashed, was made to slink away from our domain forever. The change was great and happy—one worthy of imitation—one worthy of all remembrance. But even in the full tide of prosperity, we should not conceal from ourselves the stern and stubborn fact, that a patriotic people were still toiling manfully under the burthen of millions. The tax collector was wandering in every section of the land, gathering in the hard earned and yet cheerfully paid gold, that the honor or our State might remain unsullied without blemish and without stain. Not a fraction of the taxes had been removed, and every reason of economy that had originated the measure of reform and relief, still remained in full force and vigor. Aye, the very gallantry itself, with which the whole community, as one man, had come to the rescue, furnished additional and powerful motives for making the most strenuous effort to lighten, quickly and effectually, the load so nobly borne. He wished to see the mighty incubus of debt, that was now depressing and weighing down the energies of men, pass speedily off, and he should cheerfully, eagerly aid in every and all reforms consistent with propriety, which would directly or remotely assist in accomplishing this great and paramount result. With him, reform implied economy as well as convenience; and whatever might be the vote he was called upon to give, he should never depart from that principle.

Of the amendment which had just emanated from the honorable gentleman from Queen Anne's (Mr. Spencer,) after the remarks he had already had the honor to submit to the Convention, it was unnecessary for him to speak or notice, by any other than the briefest comment. Its object and design, as expressed directly upon its face, was to give to the Legislature, hereafter to be assembled, "the right to provide, by law, for annual election of delegates to the General Assemhly, and for annual sessions of the Legislature, which shall not continue in session longer than fifty days." It appeared only to differ from other propositions, by shifting the responsibility from ourselves to the Legislature that might follow. It was equally at war with the direct mandate of the sovereign power, and equally liable to all the difficulties and objections previously urged. We are, or should be, as capable of making the decision, as those who are to come after us, and should not, by a mere change of the tribunal, seek to avoid the judgment which we had been emphatically ordered to give. Much had been said in this discussion, and by gentlemen who had participated in its labors, of the embarrassment thrown around the session of the last Legislature from the effect of this very biennial policy; and if he had rightly heard and understood, it had been clearly intimated, that the proposition to recommend the call of an extra session, had been gravely, if not publicly argued by many of that eminent and distinguished body.

Mr. BROWN remarked that he believed the Governor was in favor of the call of an extra session.

Mr. CHAMBERS, of Kent, was understood to inquire whether the Governor was in favor of getting the Legislature to recommend the call, or of calling it himself.

Mr. BROWN said, he had understood that the Governor was inclined to the call, if the Legislature thought proper to recommend it.

Mr. GWINN desired to say, in behalf of a gentleman who was not here to speak for himself, that there were some matters pending before the last Legislature which were believed to be of serious importance. But he (Mr. G.) had never understood that the Governor either desired, or recommended to any set of individuals, that an extra session should be called. The Governor thought that there would be a moral justification for the step in the Legislature, and was prepared to act upon its recommendation; but he had never in any manner interfered, or counseled, or influenced the Legislature in regard to it.

Mr. DIRICKSON resumed. He believed he had properly understood and correctly stated the expressions to which he had alluded—and the moral which the declarations and avowal taught him, was that it might be dangerous to give this power to such a body as this amendment proposed. Had this provision have existed in the present Constitution an extra session might, at this very moment, be holding its sittings and fearfully increasing the already enormous expenditure of the State. Neither the necessities of the times, nor the wants of the community, rendered essential such additional outlay of the common treasure for such a purpose. The power is by the existing Constitution already vested in the Executive—why had it not been exercised. The distinguished officer who then occupied the gubernatorial chair was incapable of shrinking from the discharge of any moral or legal duty imposed by that exalted position, and the irresistible inference is forced upon all that no such extra session was in reality demanded. Sir, we should be careful how we vest this extreme authority in that department of the Government, which from its very numbers cannot by possibility feel that direct responsibility necessarily requisite to its wise and wholesome exercise. Let it remain, as provided by a future section of this report, in the hands where it had been placed by our fathers, to be used only when some high and unusual crisis justified its employment. From the constant mutability and very uncertainty of all things earthly, it must be lodged somewhere, to be wielded in the hour of emergency for the security, the protection, and the prosperity of all. Great and unexpected financial embarrassments might come suddenly upon us—war, with its horrors, menace our liberties—pestilence and famine invade our borders, and insurrection with gory head rear itself in our midst. If such a time should ever come, then would the crisis have arrived when the wisdom and patriotism of the land should be summoned to these, our council chambers; then might this power work the great and legitimate object for which it was properly and wisely designed. With such views and sentiments he could not lend his sanction to the amendment to which he had last alluded. He could not aid in trampling under foot a measure which had been ordained by the people themselves. He could not consent to take a step backward in the great onward march of reform now going on every where within and around us. He wished to see Maryland in the very van of those States that, upon the ruins of old fabrics, were rearing better, purer, and more *economical* governments. That was the kind of reform desired by the people whom he had the honor in part to represent. He believed he knew their wishes and their interests, and in accordance with his constant and earnest aim, he should endeavor at all times, honestly, and faithfully to cling to and sustain them.

Mr. TUCK said:

That he had stated, when advocating the publication of the debates, that he would trouble the Convention as little as any of the speaking profession to which he belonged, and he believed he had been true to his promise.

It would appear, from what his friend from Worcester had said, that the State had been actually convulsed from the Allegany mountains to the ocean, on the subject of biennial sessions.

Mr. T. rather suspected, that in this instance his friend had taken Worcester county for the State. If the excitement spoken of, had swept over the State, it had not reached the lower counties on the Western Shore as far as he was informed. It is true that Prince George's county gave a majority for biennial sessions. But there was no excitement or agitation of the subject before the election, as far as he, [Mr. T.,] knew, or had heard. It so happened, that he participated actively in the canvass of 1846, though not a candidate; and he did not remember to have heard the subject mentioned, and he knew that many persons had not considered the matter at all before they were asked the question at the polls. He knows this, because he heard many say so at the time—and many declined voting on that question for this reason. His county gave a majority for the biennial act; but not more than one thousand, two hundred and fifty voters passed on the question, out of about one thousand five hundred or more, that were polled.

If he, (Mr. T.,) thought that this question were deemed of paramount importance by his constituents—that it was above all others affecting their rights and interests, and had been recently settled by the vote at the polls, he would not now vote for annual sessions. He acknowledged the right of instruction, and the duty of obedience.

But when not instructed, he must suppose that his constituents designed to place some confidence in his judgment, to clothe him with some discretion.

It was his duty to vote now, not as his constituents had voted four years ago, when this Convention was not contemplated by them; but as he, (Mr. T.,) believed, they would decide, if the question were now submitted to them. He was of opinion that they would decide differently if they were here and could see the difficulty we have experienced in forming a Constitution; and the probability that many things will be left to future legislation.

Gentlemen have stated time and again that they would not encumber the Constitution, with what they considered legislative provisions. This, he, (Mr. T.,) said, was his own opinion. Though belonging to a party which receives scant credit with our adversaries, for confidence in the people, he might say for himself, that when he witnessed the efforts that are sometimes made throughout the land, to inflame the passions, and excite the prejudices of the people for political ends, he ever turned with an abiding trust to their intelligence, virtue and patriotism, as the lasting foundations of our republic. He was willing to leave many things to be considered—much to be done by the legislature, who could better ascertain and follow the wishes of the people than we can.

If we lay down correct principles in the Constitution, the people will follow them out. If we furnish a good plan of government, the legislature will fill up the details as may best promote the interest and prosperity of the State.

Mr T. said, he thought that annual sessions would be necessary for some years at least, before the machinery of this new government could be properly set in motion. He was in favor of annual sessions, and short sessions of fifty or sixty days at most. He had, himself, last winter witnessed what he never before saw in legislation. He had seen bill after bill passed without having been read at all; when he was satisfied that very few of the members knew what they were voting upon. This was in consequence of the number of bills before the body. He had seen much confusion and haste at the close of the annual sessions—but nothing to compare with what he saw last winter. He was not a member, but he saw enough as a mere spectator at the lobby, to satisfy him that the biennial bill had been purchased at a fearful cost —the hazard, if not the loss of sound, deliberate, and judicious legislation.

Gentlemen had argued against leaving too much power to the legislature. What is "too much?" Here we may differ. In one breath we are told that we must obey the potent will of the people, because they have expressed it favorably to biennial sessions. In the next breath it is said that the legislature must not be trusted again with this power, although they come from the people.

If we acknowledge this duty ourselves, why shall we impute a different sense of duty to those who may come after us as representatives of the people. They obeyed the people on this subject in 1846; why will they not obey again, if this question goes a second time before that high tribunal as is now proposed by the amendment.

Gentlemen had warned the friends of reform that if this biennial feature is not retained, the Constitution will be rejected by the people. This warning might properly enough come upon those who rejoiced in the name of reformers; but he was at a loss how to account for such a voice from Dorchester and Worcester counties. The gentleman from Dorchester, (Mr. Hicks,) had said sometime ago, if he remembered, that the basis of representation and some other features in the present Constitution, suited him. Mr. T. inferred that if the basis and these other features were materially changed, the rejection of the Constitution would not be disagreeable to that gentleman. The gentleman from Worcester, had said he voted for the Convention in June last, and therefore claimed to be a reformer. Yet, the reformers do not take him as one of their brotherhood. His two Eastern Shore friends might go for triennial sessions without risk of being deemed any better reformers than they would be called if they went even for annual sessions. Annual and biennial sessions have little to do with the question of reform, as it is understood by those who claim to be its peculiar friends. Some of the stoutest reformers here are advocating annual sessions. Carroll county goes for them, as carrying out a cardinal democratic doctrine—"frequent elections and strict accountability;" while Frederick county is divided. Mr. T. supposedthat his friends from Frederick, (Messrs. Biser and Shriver,) considered themselves none the less good reformers because they happened to disagree with their colleagues on this question of legislative sessions.

But suppose the warning be heeded. It may operate the other way at last. Mr. T. was no prophet, and he gave no warnings to others. He had quite enough—may be too much—on hand in endeavoring to keep right himself. He would, however, venture to suggest, that twenty-five thousand five hundred voters cast their ballots in 1846 against the biennial bill. Suppose all, or a large portion of these, were to cast their votes against the Constitution, if they are not gratified by having the annual sessions incorporated as part of the instrument—it may be rejected. We are not to suppose that these twenty-five thousand five hundred are not of the same mind now, any more than we are to presume that the other thirty thousand, who were for biennial sessions, have not changed their opinion. In about fifty-five thousand votes, there was a majority for biennial sessions of about four thousand six hundred. While, therefore, the reformers are taking warning, they had as well remember, that in 1846, there were nearly one half of all the voters—only twenty-three hundred, less than half—opposed to biennial sessions, and that these same, for aught we know, may make this very feature the ground of invincible repugnance to the ratification of the Constitution.

This was not altogether conjecture, for one of the delegates from St. Mary's states that one reason assigned by certain gentlemen in his county, for advocating the Convention was, that it would be a means of getting rid of biennial sessions of the Legislature, and returning to annual sessions.

Mr. T. read from the election returns of 1846, to show the vote upon the biennial bill. Allegany county gave a majority against the bill of 73; Carroll 704; Baltimore county 133; Baltimore city 694—while the majority for it in Washington was 751, and in Frederick only 8; the Western Shore gave a majority against the bill of upwards of 1200 votes; the large majorities for the bill were on the Eastern Shore. The majorities in Prince Georges and Charles were 140 and 159—while the vote in Calvert and St. Mary's shows a majority against the bill of 354. It was a mistake, therefore, to assume that this biennial bill had passed by such large majorities as to leave no room to doubt what the vote of the people would be at this time. On the Eastern Shore it was passed as an anti-reform measure—a device to keep off this Convention. The design having been frustrated, it might be reasonable to say that even there, it was still an open question.

Mr. Brown said that a question had been put to him by the gentleman from Worcester; and the use which that gentleman had made of the answer, rendered it his, (Mr. B's.) duty, to make some reply. The gentleman from Worcester did not appear to him to understand the Constitution. The session of the Legislature is limited to the tenth of March, and the Governor has the power to call an extra session. The question was agitated in the Legislature and obtained only a few votes. It was said that the Governor would have no objection to call the Legislature together, as much business of importance was laid over, which was proper and necessary to carry on the operations of the Government. Such was the fact in relation to that matter. The particular part of the State from which these biennial sessions are urged, made him somewhat suspicious as to the object in view. The effort comes from the Eastern Shore. And he would ask those gentlemen if they intended to vote for the Constitution if these biennial sessions were provided for in it?

Mr. Phelps said, if the gentleman asked him, he would say "yes."

Mr. Brown resumed. If the population basis had prevailed, the gentleman would not. Another project has been agitated in this Hall. Yesterday, he began, from what he had heard, to think that we were to have no sessions of the Legislature at all, but that it would be merely necessary to send a joint committee here annually to transact all the Legislative business. We say we have too much legislation, the people do not think so; he supposed therefore it was intended by way of compromise, to have none at all, except what could be done by a committee. Never, until now, had he heard it laid down as Democratic doctrine, that elections might be too frequent. All the Constitutions which have been framed from the time of Jefferson, contain the clause in favor of frequent elections. He repeated what he had before stated as to the industry of the last Legislature, and particularly of the Baltimore delegation; and concluded with stating that he intended to sustain the Democratic principle of frequent elections and representation by members.

Mr. Dirickson said:

He did not desire to detain the Convention but a single minute, in reply to the remarks which had just fallen. He was always gratified to receive information from any source, though in this particular instance, it was certainly unnecessary for the distinguished gentleman from Carroll, to have given evidence of the possession of such profound Constitutional lore. Wonderful and mysterious as the erudition might seem, he had long been aware of the fact, that the present Constitution contained no provision giving to the legislature the right to call an extra session. Nor did he believe any other gentleman upon the floor, had for an instant, understood him as expressing any opinion or idea inconsistent with that fact.

He was discussing the amendment which had been presented by the gentleman from Queen Anne's, (Mr. Spencer,) proposing to give this power to the legislature, and was arguing as to what might have been the consequences, had a similar clause have been inserted in our present Constitution. After the information which had been as to the feeling of many of the body that last occupied these halls, it was not difficult to imagine that had there have been no organic or constitutional barrier—an extra session might this moment be holding its sittings and additional thousands flowing from the Treasury.

In regard to what he had said in reference to the confusion of our statutes produced mainly by too frequent legislation, he begged leave to adhere to his original opinion. The most eminent jurists of that body had sustained him by the expression of similar sentiments; and however trifling and unimportant that objection might seem to the powerful intellect of the gentleman over the way, he should not be turned aside from his course in seeking to eradicate the difficulty. He could not refrain from congratulating the country and the Convention, that genius had at length been found, before which, that mystery and obscurity of the laws, hitherto baffling so many, would vanish away; and it was possible it might be the evidence, that the age of perfection—the very millennium—was well-nigh upon us.

Mr. Brown said, he did not mean to say that the gentleman from Worcester, did not understand the Constitution, but only that he overlooked some of its provisions.

Mr. Ridgely said he had but a few words to urge against the amendment of the gentleman from Queen Anne's, (Mr. Spencer.) He should confine his remarks to that subject, and not follow the discussion, which had wandered into a consideration of the merits of annual or biennial sessions; a question which he had supposed was determined by the vote of yesterday. Before, however, he proceeded, he would put a single question to the gentleman from Queen Anne's.

Had he rightly understood his amendment, as designing to confer upon the Legislature the power of alternating between annual and biennial sessions at its pleasure?

Mr. SPENCER referred to the language of the proposition, leaving the subject to legislative discretion.

Mr. RIDGELY resumed. He had so understood the amendment, and he regarded it as the most dangerous proposition which had been offered in connection with this subject. What was it? Would gentlemen analyze it; strip it of its seeming deference to the popular will; look it freely in the face? It was nothing more nor less than a special amendatory clause of the Constitution—a power to the Legislature, at its mere pleasure, to alter the fundamental law by a single act of Assembly. It appeared to him, that the effect of the amendment would be to render the constitutional provision adopted yesterday, making the sessions of the Legislature biennial, nugatory and idle; and the Constitution had as well be silent upon that subject, since the Legislature would then have the power now proposed to be conferred upon it. But he regarded the amendment as most objectionable, in view of the power itself, proposed to be granted to the Legislature. In comparison with this proposition, he considered the fifty-ninth article of the old Constitution, odious as it was to conventional reformers, by reason of the construction given to it by those who claimed exclusive legislative control over that instrument, as much to be preferred. This proposition takes away from the people the color of participation on their part, which the fifty-ninth article provides to effect a change in the organic law, by permitting, in this particular, such change to be accomplished by a single legislative enactment; when the fifty-ninth article contemplates the act of two consecutive Legislatures to effect that object. He could go for no such proposition. He was free to confess, that in his judgment, the amendment surrendered an elementary principle of the reform party. What was the cardinal doctrine of coventional reformers? If he had not greatly misunderstood the theory of that party, whig and democrat, it was, that no earthly power, other than the people, ought to make, change, or alter the organic law—that the claim set up by the literal constructionists of the fifty-ninth article for exclusive legislative control over the Constitution, was qualified and determined by the forty-second article of the Bill of Rights; and further, that although no such reservation had been grafted upon the Bill of Rights, yet it would have existed, as an inherent and unalienable right in the people. Was not this the doctrine of conventional reformers? Is it not now our doctrine? Have we not been for twenty years struggling against legislative amendments of the Constitution, and demanding a Convention, and yet it is now deliberately proposed to delegate the very power to the Legislature against which we have so long, so earnestly, and at last successfully contended.

For one, he here avowed, that regarding the people as possesssing the exclusive right to control the organic law, he should never consent to delegate to the Legislature any power whatever to tinker with the Constitution. The honorable gentleman from Queen Anne, had argued that the amendment contemplated the exercise of the power by the Legislature only, when demanded by the popular will; and he had earnestly asked, Were we afraid to trust the people. What security, he would ask, had the people, that this power if conferred upon the Legislature, would be held subordinate to their will? Does the amendment impose any restraints upon the exercise of the power? On the contrary does it not authorise a change of sessions from annual to biennial, or *vice versu*, by a single legislative enactment, and thus practically annihilate the provision of the Constitution for biennial sessions? Nothing is more evident. The honorable gentleman from Queen Anne, has maintained with great earnestness, that the Legislature would not dare to exercise such a power *mero motu*, except upon the prompting of public opinion, because it would sacrifice every member of the body, who had the temerity to oppose the popular wish. It was not, in his judgment, important whether the power would or would not be abused. He was against conferring any power whatever over the organic law upon the Legislature, even in the most unimportant particular, and for a direct Constitutional recognition of this prohibition, by a provision for future Conventions. Yet he would ask, what evidence does the past supply, that such a power would be exercised in conformity with public sentiment? The vice of the argument appeared to him to be in confounding the Legislature and the people. These must be regarded as correlative, as one and the same thing, to justify such conclusions—and he was sure such was not the theory of his friend from Queen Anne. Certainly as he had already intimated, the past was not full of encouragement to the people in this particular, that they should again peril their political fortunes by such a venture. Have not the people, the majority, a large majority, been for years struggling against the very theory which this amendment upholds? Have we not been first respectfully asking, then remonstrating, and now demanding that the Legislature shall be so constituted, as to represent the people? With what success, heretofore, this application has met, the honorable gentleman is well informed; and will he consent to trust the power of altering the Constitution in the hands of the Legislature as now constituted; and can he hold out any reasonable hope to us, that its present basis, will be modified in accordance with the equal political rights of citizens? We have been sent here for a far different purpose, as he understood his duty. We came here to make a Constitution, to be submitted to the people, as the only competent tribunal to breathe life into it, or to change or amend it. Let us then perform our proper office—our whole duty—and not attempt to shift responsibility, or to devolve the people's prerogative upon the Legislature.

The gentleman from Queen Anne's had siad, that the first two or three sessions of the legislature, after the adoption of the Constitution, would be attended with an unusually great amount of public business, growing out of the necessary legislation, to put in proper motion the machine of government. He was disposed to admit the truth of the remark, yet he thought, that exigency amply provided for; first, in the fact that the sixth section of the bill removed all limitation as to the duration of the two first sessions of the legislature, after the ratification of the Constitution; and it was further provided, that the Governor should have the power to call extra sessions, if the public interest demanded it. Certainly it was wiser to trust to the capacity of these means to meet the emergency, to be produced by the accumulation of business for the first two or three years, under the new government, than to venture upon the extreme measnre proposed by the amendment of conferring upon the legislature the power of altering the Constitution; and, indeed, it appeared to him, that the very fact urged by the gentleman from Queen Anne's, that the increase of business would not extend over two or three sessions, was an admission, that biennial sessions would thereafter amply meet the public interests.

If, then, the absence of all limitation upon the two first sessions, as to time, and the power of the Governor to call a special legislature, will more than probably meet the exigency for the period of two or three years, shall we engraft a principle upon the Constitution which recognizes legislative power over it, and that, too, for a purpose comparatively unimportant?

He had not intended to say a word upon the subject of annual or biennial sessions, considering that question closed by the decided vote of yesterday, but the remarks of gentlemen on that subject, he could not permit to pass in silence.

The honorable gentleman from Prince George's, (Mr. Tuck,) had produced the returns of the election held, by which biennial sessions of the legislature was adopted; and had argued from the meagre vote then polled, that the presumption was fair, that it was not a reliable exponent of the popular sentiment—the vote being some twenty thousand short. He had also analysed the vote, and shown that some of the western counties, which were now loudest in favor of biennial sessions, were then against it, including Baltimore county, which cast a majority of one hundred and thirty votes against the law. He would not stop to vindicate the silent votes, or twenty thousand absentees from the polls, from the inference drawn by the gentleman from Prince George's, that if they had voted, the result might have been against biennial session. It was equally fair to presume the reverse—it might have swelled the majority. Such inquiry was entirely speculative; but he would say, that he did not regard that vote as a reliable expression of public opinion, for another and a very different reason. The biennial session bill was, in the first place, a legislative amendment to the Constitution, and was objectionable to Conventional reformers as such.

In the second place, it was originated by the gentleman from Dorchester, (Mr. Phelps,) whose motive was well known. He had always been recognized as an anti-reformer, and from an anti-reform county. It was well understood in the larger counties, that the then movement was intended to put off conventional reform, to defer our hopes and expectations of a Convention. In fact, it was known to be an anti-reform measure—hence, the city of Baltimore, and all the large counties, went against it. That was the reason why that vote—although a majority vote of five thousand—was not a reliabie exponent of public sentiment. Now that we have obtained a Convention; and have no longer distrust of the movement, but, on the contrary, every reason to to recgnise it as a salutary measure of reform and retrenchment, the sentiment of the people is in sympathy with it. For one, as a reformer, it was his theory, never to let go a jot or title of a point once gained, but to struggle on for further acquisition. His friend from Carroll, (Mr. Brown,) had asked the gentleman from Dorchester, (Mr. Phelps,) if he would vote for any Constitution that was formed by the Convention, thereby meaning to test his sincerity in offering the proposition for biennial sessions. That gentleman had answered the question for himself, with frankness. He would now ask his friend from Carroll, to look at the vote of Anne Arundel county, fifteen hundred majority against biennial sessions, and apply the same test to that delegation—all of whom have supported the amendment under consideration, and gone in a body against biennal sessions. It was a pregnant fact, that while every other county in the State, gave a comparatively short vote, Anne Arundel had given fifteen hundred majority against biennial sessions. He repeated, it was a pregnant fact, and he would make no comment upon it. Such was, nevertheless, the infirmity of human nature, that people would vote according to their interests, and if the power was given to the Legislature, to say whether that body should meet annual or biennially, a considerable portion of every session would be employed in the discussion of that question, and the influences—local influences—surrounding the body, would be strung to their utmost capacity; and past experience, and a very superficial knowledge of human nature, indicates very clearly, that annual sessions would soon become the fixed law. His friend from Carroll, had misconceived the meaning of the terms "frequent elections," as used in the bill of rights. The political doctrine meant to be affirmed by that sentiment, was inseparable from all free government. It was proclaimed by our forefathers, in view of the long duration of parliament, without a return of the delegated power to the people. The direct accountability of public servants, and frequent returns of the political power to the constituency, gives an opportunity for change in office, when the people require it. It does not follow that elections should be annual, if the accountability exists, and may be enforced by the public within reasonable periods, so as not to postpone the right to change officers to too great a distance from the appointing power.

He concluded by stating, that for the reasons he had assigned, he should vote against the amendment of the gentleman from Queen Anne. If it had been offered in a different form, as a separate provision, to be separately submitted to the people, and at a different time, he should have hesitated to oppose it, but as a part of the Constitution to be voted upon as an entirety, he could not go for it.

Mr. SPENCER was much surprised at the course of remarks made by the gentleman, (Mr. Ridgely,) from Baltimore county. What change was there in his proposition? And what in it, that the reform party of Maryland had ever opposed? Had they ever taken ground that it was dangerous to trust the Legislature with questions which were essential to the protection of the interests of the people? For what purpose was the Legislature created? Is it not intended to represent the people and to provide laws to promote their happiness, and to meet their necessities? The complaint of the reform party was, that the Legislature had heretofore failed to perform this duty. They would neither pass the necessary laws to reform the abuses of the Government, nor provide for a Convention, to enable the people to do it themselves. For years the people had invoked the Legislature to discharge their duty and to call a Convention. But it was for a long time in vain. The call was made—what reformer will venture to say that the Legislature is not to be trusted with a power, eminently protective of the rights of the people.

Mr. RIDGELY interposed. Under its existing basis, the Legislature would always be distrusted.

Mr. SPENCER replied that it was the basis which was distrusted and not the Legislature. Where did the gentleman from Baltimore county get his construction of the doctrine of the reform party? Now, he (Mr. S.,) had always been identified with the reform party. If he had ever advocated a power in the Constitution to take away the rights of the people, then the gentleman might have taken exception to his course. Instead of doing this, his proposition enlarged the rights of the people. Was that anti-republican? If so, he would only say that he must have studied in the republican school in vain. He examined the construction put by the gentleman from Baltimore county on his amendment as authorising the Legislature to extend their sessions as they might see fit. The gentleman from Baltimore county said that no person acquainted with human nature would give this power to the Legislature, because he would know that the feelings of members would lead them to vacillate between annual, or alternate biennial and annual sessions. He could tell that gentleman, that any member who would take that course would commit political suicide.

Mr. RIDGELY said he had confined his views to the effect of the amendment. He intended nothing personal.

Mr. SPENCER did not suppose that there was any thing intended of a personal character. But his feelings were wounded when he heard a gentleman so respectable, as the gentleman from Baltimore, express himself so strongly with reference to his amendment. He then reiterated what he had before said as to the fifty-ninth article.

Mr. BUCHANAN said:

He was heartily sick of the protracted discussion. He only desired to ask his friend from Queen Anne's, if he would modify his amendment ment so as to limit the duration of session to one half the time now occupied. Of the various arguments which had been made against annual sessions, he had never yet heard any man speak against them, either on the ground of their multiplying legislative business, or avoiding it. When the biennial bill was before the people, the discussion as to its propriety or impropriety turned, in a measure, on the question of finance. It was now brought forward as an argument against the annual system, that it led to so much legislation that the people would never return to it. That might serve for an argument, but it was his opinion that the people would prefer annual sessions, if they could have two annual sessions at no greater cost than one biennial session. This was the aim of his suggestion to his friend from Queen Anne's.

What had experience taught us? The expenses of a legislative session have been about $56,000. He wished to divide this sum, so as to make it sufficient for two sessions, by reducing the duration of each session, one half. As much work could be done in thirty-five days, by an industrious legislature, as in twice that period by one of an opposite character. The people will be satisfied with annual sessions when they see the expenses so restricted, as that two of these sessions could be held at no greater expense than one biennial session.

Mr. SPENCER then (accepting the suggestion of Mr. BUCHANAN,) modified his amendment by adding the words, "which shall not continue in session longer than forty days."

The amendment as modified, read as follows:

"But the legislature shall have the right to provide by law, for annual elections of delegates to the General Assembly, and for annnal sessions of the legislature, which shall not continue in session longer than forty days."

Mr. PHELPS would not have risen to say a word, but for what had fallen from the gentleman from Queen Anne's, as to the effect of the diminution of the term of the session.

Mr. SPENCER interposed and suggested, that, as he wished to have a full attendance when the vote on his amendment was taken, he would suggest to the gentleman from Dorchester, (Mr. Phelps,) to give way for a motion, that there be a call of the Convention. The gentleman could conclude his remarks after the call had been made.

Mr. PHELPS, acceeding to the suggestion, yielded the floor.

Mr. SPENCER moved that there be a call of the Convention; and

It was ordered.

The roll was called.

On the motion of

Mr. SPENCER, the doorkeeper was sent to request the attendance of members, who might be in the city, but were not in their seats.

In the mean time,

Mr. PHELPS resumed. If the House was prepared to vote on the proposition now, he was prepared to vote; but, as there must be some time allowed for the call of the House, he would avail himself of the opportunity to make a few remarks, particularly as to that branch of the amendment which imposes a limitation of the session to forty days. It sometimes happens that very little business can be matured in forty days. The election of a speaker and the officers frequently consumes much time; and then the Speaker must have an opportunity to become acquainted with the members, before he can appoint the committees, after which a considerable period must elapse before the committees can mature the business and report to the House. This objection then, must be fatal to the proposition to limit the session to forty days. With reference to the expenses, he would state, that the itinerant charges of the session, amount to about $5000; and if annual sessions should be determined on, this would be an annual instead of a biennial charge. The objection, therefore, to the annual sessions, would not be obviated by diminishing the length of the session. The gentleman from Anne Arundel thought this power to call the Legislature together was a dangerous power to place in the hands of the Governor, but there is not a single State in the Union in which it is not conferred on the Executive. If war was to be declared against us, or if some great insult should demand instant reprisal, or any sudden financial exigency should occur, he asked, should not the Governor have power to assemble the Legislature?

Mr. RANDALL explained that he was speaking as between the Governor and the Legislature, and had then said he thought it would be better in the hands of the Legislature than in the Governor.

Mr. PHELPS resumed. We all know that the Governor has the power to call an extra session. But if the usual length of the sessions is to be shortened to one half, the greater part of that will be consumed in discussing whether the Legislature shall sit annually or biennially; and forty days might easily be wasted in such a discussion. It was urged by the gentleman from Queen Anne that the Legislature would require some additional time to carry out the general principles established by the Constitution in Legislative details. In reply to this, he reminded the gentleman from Queen Anne that there was now a section in the Constitution which gave the Legislature power to prolong its sessions, for this purpose, to six months, or nine months, or twelve months, or even two years. If new men, fresh from the people, were sent here every two years, they would be quite as competent to make such laws, as to enact all other laws The gentleman from Prince George's, (Mr. Tuck,) said that public sentiment was not disturbed in his county by the biennial question. Whatever it may have been in Prince George, he could say that in most of the counties of the State the biennial bill was circulated and discussed freely, and orators took the stump for and against it. Great efforts were made to defeat the bill, on the ground that it was merely a tub thrown to the whale. It was believed by many that it was intended only to defeat the effort to get up this Reform Convention. Yet, notwithstanding these efforts to prejudice the public mind against the bill, it obtained a large majority in the State.

Further proceedings on the call of the Convention were then dispensed with.

The question then recurred on the modified amendment of Mr. SPENCER.

Mr. S. asked the yeas and nays, which were ordered, and being taken, resulted as follows:

Affirmative—Messrs. Tuck, President, *pro tem.*, Morgan, Donaldson, Dorsey, Wells, Randall, Kent, Sellman, Merrick, Buchanan, Welch, Chambers, of Cecil, Miller, Sprigg, Spencer, George, Wright, Shriver, Biser, McHenry, Gwinn, Presstman, Ware, Anderson, Parke, Shower, Cookey and Brown—28

Negative—Messrs. Ricaud, Chambers of Kent, Mitchell, Dalrymple, Brent, of Charles, Howard, Ridgely, Lloyd, Dickinson, Sherwood, of Talbot, John Dennis, Williams, Hicks, Hodson, Phelps, Bowling, Dirickson, Hearn, Jacobs, Thomas, Gaither, Annan, Stephenson, Magraw, Nelson, Carter, Stewart, of Caroline, Brent, of Baltimore city, Schley, Fiery, Neill, John Newcomer, Harbine, Michael Newcomer, Brewer, Waters, Weber, Hollyday, Fitzpatrick and Smith—40.

So the amendment was rejected.

Mr. SPENCER. I now offer the last of the series of amendments, which I intend to offer on this subject.

The amendment was read as follows:

Add to the end of the section, the follow proviso:

"*Provided*, That the judges of elections in each county and city, when this Constitution shall be submitted to the people for their ratification, shall put the question distinctly to each voter: "are you in favor of annual or biennial sessions of the Legislature?" and the said judges shall record separately on their poll books the answer of each voter to the said question; of which they shall make return in the same manner as prescribed by law, to ascertain the sense of the people on the ratification of said Constitution. And if a majority of the legal voters in the State should be in favor of annual sessions, then at the next meeting of the Legislature, after the ratification of this Constitution, the Legislature shall provide by law for annual elections of Delegates to the General Assembly, and for annual sessions of the Legislature."

The amendment having been read,

Mr. SPENCER demanded the previous question, but withdrew it at the request of Mr. PRESSTMAN,

Mr. PRESSTMAN rose and stated, that he had up to this time voted for all the amendments which had been offered, with a view to defeat the biennial provision. He did not wish the House to understand him, as seeking to avoid the main question, from any other motive; and it would be a change of front in him, if he did not vote for any one of these amendments. It was clear, however, that there was too great a majority in the House, who were resolutely opposed to annual sessions, to be defeated in their object by any parliamentary management. With this impression, he had risen to request his friend from Queen Anne, to disband the little army which had thus far stood by him, in all his efforts. His friend from Queen Anne, had exhausted all the tactics which could be expected from the leader of a forlorn hope. For his part, he was now willing to give the battle up. The amendment now offered by his friend from Queen Anne, was nearly the same as the one which had been offered by the gentleman from Harford, (Mr. McHenry,) for which he, (Mr. P.,) had voted. He thought it would be very embarrassing to the people, if they are required to vote at the polls, not only for the Constitution as a whole, but on this biennial provision, also, in a separate vote. He had promised his friend from Queen Anne to renew the call for the previous question.

Mr. SPENCER withdrew the previous question, and said he disclaimed any intention to make a speech. He could not, however, avoid expressing his surprise, at the course of the gentleman from Baltimore. When that gentleman spoke of an army against biennial sessions, he made a great mistake. He would tell that gentleman, that he was in favor of the biennial system. If the gentleman from Baltimore was inclined to withdraw, there were other gentleman who were coming in to join him. The gentleman from Baltimore county, (Mr. Ridgely,) had said, that if the proposition was put in a shape to be separately presented to the people for their vote, he would be willing to go for it. Others round him had said the same. The amendment he had now offered, differed from that submitted by the gentleman from Harford. The proposition offered by the gentleman from Harford, was to hold over the reference of this question to the people, until the next election after the adoption of the Constitution. But if the gentleman from Harford preferred his own amendment, and would move a reconsideration of the vote by which it was rejected, and would amend it, he, (Mr. S.,) would withdraw his amendment. We are framing a Constitution which is to be submitted to the people. The people having once passed on the question of biennial sessions, there are some gentlemen here who are unwilling to vote against the judgment of the people. But, he believed, there was no gentleman here, who is not willing to let this question be specifically put to the people. He referred to the various objections which had been made, and suggested that the mode presented by the amendment would obviate them all. It should be borne in mind that there is no reservation by which the Legislature can hereafter change the sessions. If a majority of the people are in favor of bienninl or annual sessions, who will oppose their will?

Mr. SHOWER demanded the previous question.

Mr. RIDGELY requested him to withdraw the demand, to enable him, (Mr. R.,) to say a few words in reply to the remarks of the gentleman from Queen Anne, (Mr. Spencer,) who had, unintentionally, no doubt, misstated his, (Mr. R.'s) position.

Mr. SHOWER declined to withdraw.

The question was then taken on the demand for the previous question, and by ayes 31, noes 26, there was a second.

And the main question, (on the amendment of Mr. Spencer,) was ordered to be now taken.

Mr. MITCHELL asked the yeas and nays on the amendment, which were ordered, and being taken, resulted as follows:

Affirmative—Messrs. Tuck, President, *pro tem.*, Morgan, Donaldson, Dorsey, Wells, Randall, Kent, Sellman, Merrick, Buchanan, Welch, Chambers, of Cecil, Miller, Sprigg, Spencer, George, Wright, Shriver, Biser, Stephenson, McHenry, Magraw, Nelson, Stewart, of Caroline, Gwinn, Brent, of Baltimore city, Presstman, Ware, Brewer, Anderson, Weber, Hollyday, Fitzpatrick, Parke, Shower, Cockey and Brown —37.

Negative—Messrs. Ricaud, Chambers, of Kent, Mitchell, Dalrymple, Brent, of Charles, Howard, Ridgely, Lloyd, Dickinson, Sherwood, of Talbot, John Dennis, Williams, Hicks, Hodson, Phelps, Bowling, Dirickson, Hearn, Jacobs, Thomas, Gaither, Annan, Carter, Schley, Fiery, Neill, John Newcomer, Harbine, Michael Newcomer, and Smith—30.

So the amendment was adopted.

Mr. DIRICKSON gave notice of his intention, at the first opportunity, when there should be a full Convention, to move a reconsideration of the vote on the amendment just adopted.

Mr. SPENCER moved to amend the amendment by adding the words "which shall not exceed forty days."

A motion was made that the Convention adjourn.

The Convention refused to adjourn.

Mr. JOHN NEWCOMER moved to amend Mr. SPENCER's amendment, by striking out "forty," and inserting "thirty" days.

Mr. BROWN called for a division of the question, (first on *striking out* forty,) which was ordered.

Mr. DIRICKSON asked the yeas and nays, which were ordered, and being taken, resulted as follows:

Affirmative—Messrs. Ricaud, Chambers, of Kent, Mitchell, Dalrymple, Lloyd, Dickinson, John Dennis, Williams, Hicks, Hodson, Phelps, Bowling, Dirickson, Jacobs, Gaither, Biser, Annan, McHenry, Schley, Fiery, Neill, John Newcomer, Harbine, Michael Newcomer, Waters, Hollyday, Fitzpatrick and Smith—28.

Negative—Messrs. Tuck, President, *pro tem.*, Morgan, Donaldson, Dorsey, Wells, Randall, Kent, Sellman, Merrick, Howard, Buchanan, Sherwood, of Talbot, Chambers, of Cecil, Sprigg, Spencer, George, Wright, Thomas, Shriver, Stephenson, Magraw, Nelson, Carter, Stewart, of Caroline, Gwinn, Brent, of Baltimore city, Presstman, Ware, Davis, Brewer, Anderson, Weber, Parke, Shower, Cockey and Brown—36.

So the motion to strike out was rejected.

The question then recurred on the amendment of Mr. SPENCER.

The yeas and nays were asked and refused.

The question was then taken, and by ayes 32, noes 21, the amendment was adopted.

Mr. DONALDSON moved to amend the second section, (the object of which was to make the elections uniform.)

Mr. D. explained, that his object in offering this amendment was to make the elections uniform. Now they will occur, some in one year, and some in two years, after the adoption of the Constitution. He desired to concentrate all the elections, so as to save expense, which would defeat the object of biennial elections. It would be necessary that the first delegates elected, should be for one year. The Senate would hold on. In the year 1852, the new House of Delegates would meet; and then the elections afterwards, would be every two years. In this way the elections would all take place together, and there would be a considerable saving of expense.

Mr. PRESSTMAN said, that as this was a question which would lead to long discussion, he would like to have it postponed until we get on the subject of biennial sessions. If the proposition should be amended too much, it might be broken down. It is the last straw which breaks the camel's back. Rather than endanger the amendment, if the gentleman from Anne Arundel was a friend of the annual system, he had better withdraw his proposition for the present.

Mr. DONALDSON then withdrew his amendment, indicating that he would hereafter offer it in another form.

And then the Convention adjourned.

SATURDAY, February 15, 1851.

The PEESIDENT of the Convention resumed the duties of Chair this day.

The Convention was called to order by the PRESIDENT at eleven o'clock.

Prayer was made by the Rev. Mr. GRAUFF.

The roll of the members was called.

The Journal of yesterday was read, and having been so amended as to state the fact that the previous question, called by Mr. Spencer on his amendment, had been withdrawn by him, and that it had then been called by Mr. SHOWER, was appended.

OFFICE OF THE ATTORNEY GENERAL, ETC.

Mr. SHRIVER, Chairman of the Committee heretofore appointed on the office of Attorney General and his Deputies, said he was instructed to make a report.

In presenting it, Mr. G. stated, that the committee were unanimously of opinion, that the office of Attorney General and the present mode of appointing Deputies, should be abolished, and that, in lieu thereof, the Governor should be empowered to employ counsel, when, in his judgment, the interests of the State required it; and that in each county, Howard district and the city of Baltimore, respectively, the legal voters should elect a Prosecuting Attorney for the term of three years.

The report was read, as follows:

REPORT.

Section 1st. The Governor shall have power to employ counsel for the State, when in his judgment the public interest requires it; and make suitable compensation from the contingent fund placed at his disposal.

Sec. 2nd. There shall be an Attorney for the State of Maryland in each county, Howard district and the city of Baltimore, respectively, to be styled "the Prosecuting Attorney," who shall be elected by the plurality vote of the qualified voters of each county, Howard district and the city of Baltimore; and who shall hold his office for three years from the day of his election, and until his successor be elected and qualified; and shall be re-eligible thereto, and be subject to removal from office for disqualification, wilful neglect of duty, or misdemeanor in office, by presentment of the Grand Jury, and conviction of a Petit Jury of the county, Howard District or city of Baltimore, in which he shall have been elected.

Sec. 3rd. The fees and commissions to the Prosecuting Attorney shall be the same, as now by law, allowed to the Attorney General and his Deputies, subject to such change, from time to time, as the Legislature shall provide; and to receive any other fee or reward than such as is allowed by law, shall be, upon conviction, sufficient cause for removal from office.

Sec. 4th. That in case of vacancy in the office of Prosecuting Attorney, by death, resignation, refusal to act, disqualification, removal from the county, Howard district, or city of Baltimore, in which he shall have been elected, or upon conviction, as hereinbefore specified, the said vacancy shall be filled by the Judge or Judges of the court having criminal jurisdiction in the county, Howard district, or city of Baltimore respectively, in which said vacancy shall happen, until the next general election thereafter, when the plurality vote of the qualified voters of the county, Howard district or the city of Baltimore, in which said vacancy shall occur, shall elect a suitable person for the residue of the term thus made vacant.

Sec. 5th. No person shall be eligible to the office of Prosecuting Attorney, who has not been admitted to practice the law in this State, and who has not resided for at least one year in the county, Howard district, or the city of Baltimore, in which he may be a candidate for election.

Sec. 6th. All elections for Prosecuting Attorneys, shall be certified to, and returns made thereof by the clerks of the respective counties, Howard district, and the city of Baltimore, to the Judge or Judges of the court having criminal jurisdiction in said counties, Howard district, and the city of Baltimore, and by whom the oath of office shall be administered.

Sec. 7th. The election of Prosecuting Attorneys

shall take place througout the State, on the first Wednesday of October next, and on the same day every third year thereafter; and in case of a tie between two or more persons for said office, then, the Judge or Judges of the court having criminal jurisdiction in the county, Howard district, or city of Baltimore, in which said tie may happen, shall designate which of said persons shall qualify as Prosecuting Attorney.

On motion of Mr. Shriver, the report was ordered to be printed.

BASIS OF REPRESENTATION.

Mr. Merrick said that it was his intention this morning to have made a report from the committee on representation. He desired, however, when he made it, that the other members of the committee should be present. He thought it was the intention of two or three of them to make independent reports. He should be glad to make his own sometime in the course of to-day, but should prefer delaying it until the other members of the committee should be in their seats.

The mode in which the report came in was somewhat peculiar, and for this reason he preferred that it should be made in the presence of the other members of the committee. He would suggest, therefore, that if they should not be in their seats before the Convention passed to the orders of the day, he should be allowed, at some period of the sitting, to move to suspend business, in order that the report might be presented.

Mr. Howard said he hoped that the Convention would accord to the Chairman of the committee, (Mr. Merrick,) the privilege making his report in the manner suggested. The committee had had frequent meetings, and had at last agreed to bring the subject matter of their deliberations before the Convention in a very imperfect shape, because it was the only mode in which the committee could accomplish the object. But it was an important mode. There were two minority reports, besides a partial report of his own, which, with that of the Chairman of the committee, would make four reports altogether.

The President suggested that the Convention would, without doubt, grant to the gentleman the privilege of making his report at any time during the day.

Mr. Merrick. The report which it is my intention to make, is not a report in which the committee, as a committee, concur. It is a report whichI I, as chairman, shall make by the permission and authority of the committee—they having reserved the right to act upon it as they please.

It is only for the purpose of bringing the question before the Convention, according to the usual forms, that the report will be made.

Mr. Smith could not see any good reason, he why the regular business of the Convention d be interrupted for the purpose of receiv- his report.

e gentleman from Charles, (Mr. Merrick,) now present his report, and the minority ts could be made whenever the gentlemen present. In the meantime, the report of the chairman of the committee would take the usual course. It was utterly impossible to understand reports which were read from the clerk's table, owing to the confusion in the Hall.

He, [Mr. S.,] preferred that the gentlemen should hand in their reports, and that they should be printed. They could then be read and understood by the members. The question was a very important one, and this, he thought, would be the best course that could be adopted.

Mr. Chambers, of Kent, now took his seat.

Mr. Howard, speaking for the other member, (alluded to by Mr. Merrick,) and who was not at the moment in his seat, (Mr. Lloyd,) suggested that Mr. Merrick should make his report.

Mr. Merrick, acquiescing in the suggestion, said, he would present his report at this time—prefacing it with the remark that, after long and anxious deliberation, and comparison of views and arguments, the committee had found it impossible to concur by a majority, in any plan whatsoever. Aware of the difficulties which would embarrass the Convention, if they should come before it without some scheme as a basis of action, and should ask to be discharged from the further consideration of the subject, the committee had authorised him, as their too much honored chairman, to present a report which embodied simply his own views.

But, it came in, he repeated, by the permission and under the authority of the committee. At the same time, he was bound to say, that each and every member of the committee, (except himself,) had reserved to themselves the privilege of adhering to their several and respective views and opinions, and had directed him to say, that they desired the Convention not to hold them committed, individually or collectively, to any of the principles or details of the report. And it was solely for the purpose of bringing the subject in an orderly and regular manner, before the Convention, that the committee had authorised this report to be made.

The report which he now presented, varied from the scheme which he, himself, had formerly submitted, and had had referred to the committee on representation. But it varied only in this respect—that, upon further reflection, he had thought it would be well to provide for the representation of fractions in sundry counties. [Mr. M. explained.]

The result in the several counties varied from the result anticipated in the project and tables he had before submitted. This was attributable to the difference in what it was *supposed* would be, and what were now *known* to be the census returns.

Mr. M. now read the report as follows:

REPORT.

Section 1. The legislature shall be formed of two distinct branches, a Senate and a House of Delegates, which together shall be a complete legislature, and shall be styled the General Assembly of Maryland.

Sec. 2. The House of Delegates shall consist

of members to be chosen annually on the first Wednesday of the month of October, by the voters of the several counties of the State, and of the city of Baltimore, according to the number of the population of each of said counties and of the said city of Baltimore, and in conformity with the following rule: That is to say, each of said counties and the city aforesaid, shall elect one Delegate for every four thousand souls it may contain up to twenty thousand, and for any excess in the number of population in any of said counties, or in the city of Baltimore, above twenty thousand, and of not less than eight thousand, there shall be allowed to each county or city having such excess, one additional delegate; and for any excess of population in any of the counties or city aforesaid, above twenty eight thousand, and of not less than sixteen thousand, one other additional delegate shall be allowed to each of the counties or to the city having such excess; and so on, duplicating the number of souls required to be in excess above last the number upon which an additional delegate was allowed, for the allowance of each further additional delegate, to which by such duplicating ratio, any of the counties or the city of Baltimore, may be entitled for the whole number of its population, and for any fractional number of inhabitants in any county or in the city of Baltimore, less than sufficient to entitle the county or city, to an additional delegate, according to the aforegoing rule, and greater than one-half the highest number upon which, according to said rule, delegates or an additional delegate is allowed to said county or city, one additional delegate shall be allowed to the county or city having such fraction.

Sec. 3. The Senate shall consist of twenty-two senators, to be elected every fourth year, at the time, places and in the manner prescribed for the election of members of the House of Delegates; one senator to be chosen by the voters of each county in the State, and two by the voters of the city of Baltimore; but for this purpose the said city of Baltimore, shall be divided or laid off as nearly as may be, into two equal senatorial districts, each of which districts shall separately elect one senator; and the said city of Baltimore shall also be laid off into nine equal electoral districts, for the purpose of electing members of the House of Delegates, and each of said electoral districts shall separately elect one delegate—and it shall be competent for the legislature at their first session after the authoritative promulgation of each decenial census of the people of the United States, or whenever the said city shall, by the further increase of her population, become entitled according to the basis of representation now fixed, to one or more additional delegates, to provide for re-arranging said electoral districts or creating others, for the purpose of such election; but it shall not be competent for the legislature to alter or disturb the arrangement of said districts for any other purpose, nor upon any other occasion, nor to make the number of said districts less than the number of delegates to be elected from said city; and the legislature shall have power at the same decenial periods to alter, for the purpose of equalizing, the senatorial districts of said city, but at no other time.

TABLE

Showing the Population of Maryland, and the number of Delegates to which each County in the State and the City of Baltimore will be entitled, according to the principles of this Report :

Counties, &c.	White Population.	Free Colored.	Total Free.	Slaves.	Grand Total.	Number of Delegates.
Allegany	21,643	412	22,055	724	22,779	6
Anne Arundel	16,542	4,602	21,144	11,249	32,249	6
Baltimore City	141,440	24,668	166,018	2,946	169,054	9
Baltimore County	34,354	3,474	37,828	3,771	41,599	7
Carroll	18,676	963	19,639	976	20,615	5
Caroline	6,096	2,788	8,884	808	9,692	2
Calvert	3,630	1,530	5,160	4,486	9,646	2
Cecil	15,482	2,612	18,094	843	18,937	5
Charles	5,665	913	6,578	9,584	16,162	4
Dorchester	10,788	3,803	14,591	4,281	18,872	5
Frederick	33,300	3,771	37,071	3,912	40,938	7
Harford	14,414	2,778	17,192	2,166	19,358	5
Kent	5,615	3,144	8,759	2,627	11,386	3
Montgomery	9,435	1,311	10,746	5,114	15,860	4
Prince George	8,902	1,138	10,040	11,510	21,550	5
Queen Anne	7,040	3,174	10,214	4,270	14,484	4
St. Mary's	6,226	1,630	7,856	5,842	13,698	3
Somerset	13,417	3,455	16,872	5,588	22,460	6
Talbot	7,085	2,592	9,677	4,134	13,811	3
Washington	26,888	1,852	28,740	2,090	30,830	6
Worcester	12,401	3,012	15,413	3,434	18,847	5
Total	419,039	73,622	492,661	90,355	583,016	102

Mr. BUCHANAN. What will be the whole number of which the House of Delegates will be composed?

Mr. MERRICK. One hundred and two.

I had intended, continued Mr. M., to make some general remarks. But the Convention is not full, and I will reserve them to a more appropriate occasion.

Mr. THOMAS made a suggestion in regard to the form of the report, which led to some conversation between that gentleman, Mr. MERRICK, and Mr. HOWARD.

Mr. DIRICKSON enquired of Mr. MERRICK, by what rule he assigned to Dorchester and Worcester five representatives, and to Somerset six?

Mr. M. again read that portion of the report and explained.

Mr. HARBINE rose to state, that as a member of the committee, the report which had been read by the Chairman (Mr. Merrick) had not his concurrence. He was opposed to the ratio of four thousand, and still more opposed to duplicating that ratio for every additional member above five. That would work injustice to the large counties. Again, in reference to the very large number of which it was proposed that the House of Delegates shall consist, he differed with the Chairman. Sixty or seventy, at the highest, would be amply sufficient. As stated by the honorable Chairman, a majority of the committee were unable to agree upon any basis, and as a matter of courtesy due that gentleman, consented that he should report his own views, reserving to themselves the right to act as each deemed best. No one of the reports now proposed to be made embodied his opinions, or the opinions of a majority of the committee. Having accomplished his object in rising, he would not now go further into the subject.

The President announced that the hour had arrived for taking up the orders of the day.

Mr. HOWARD moved that the consideration of the orders of the day be postponed for the purpose of disposing of the pending question.

The question was taken and decided in the affirmative.

So the orders of the day were postponed.

Mr. LLOYD then rose and said, that he desired, as a member of the committee to present a report; but that as it was not exactly in form, he should hereafter ask leave to withdraw it temporarily, in order to put it in proper form.

The report was received as follows:

RULE OF APPORTIONMENT.

Section 1st. The Senate shall be composed of twenty-one members, for the election whereof, each of the counties of the State and the city of Baltimore shall be one Senatorial District, and elect one Senator.

Sec. 2d. The House of Delgates shall consist of eighty-one members; until the number of sixty-six delegates be attained, every six thousand inhabitants in each of the counties, and the city of Baltimore, shall be entitled to one delegate; and thereafter, twenty-five thousand inhabitants in each of the counties and city of Baltimore shall be entitled to one delegate.

Sec. 3d. If in any of the said counties, according to the present population thereof, there shall be over the said ratio of six thousand, a fraction exceeding three thousand; in that case the said counties shall be entitled to a delegate for said fraction.

RESULT:

Section 1st. The Senate shall consist of twenty-one members whereof the several counties of the State and the city of Baltimore shall elect one Senator.

Sec. 2d. The House of Delegates shall consist of eighty-one members whereof Allegany county shall elect four, Anne Arundel county shall elect five; Baltimore city shall elect twelve; Baltimore county shall elect seven; Carroll county shall elect three; Caroline county shall elect two; Calvert county shall elect two; Charles county shall elect three; Cecil county shall elect three; Dorchester county shall elect three; Frederick county shall elect seven; Harford county shall elect three; Kent county shall elect two; Montgomery county shall elect three, Prince George's county shall elect four; Queen Anne's county shall elect two; St. Mary's county shall elect two; Somerset county shall elect four; Talbot county shall elect two; Washington county shall elect five; Worcester county shall elect three members.

Which was read.

Mr. CHAMBERS said:

He would submit in the form of a minority report, the views which he held in common with two of his colleagues on the committee, (Messrs. Kent and Dennis.) It was the plan adopted in 1836, and then made part of the Constitution, in all respects, except that it adopted the aggregate population as a basis instead of that of federal numbers. By the arrangement of 1836, the present representation was to remain unchanged until after the census of 1860, but this report anticipates the period for its commencement, and proposes its adoption at once. The report would show the instances in which the fractions exceeded one half the number which by the rule adopted would entitle the county to an additional representative, leaving it without advice, for the House to dispose of the question of fractions as it might deem proper.

Mr. CHAMBERS, of Kent, a member of the committee, then presented and read the following report:

The undersigned, a minority of the committee on representation, beg leave to report the following as a proper basis, being the same which was arranged by compromise in 1836, and then made part of the Constitution, with the exception only that the plan now proposed is based upon the gross amount of population instead of federal numbers. The arrangement was designed to go into effect after the census of 1860. The undersigned recommend its adoption at this time as a fair adjustment of a subject which this Convention has indicated as one proper for compromise.

Every county shall be entitled to elect one Senato, and the city of Baltimore shall also be entitled to elect one Senator.

Every county having a population of less than fifteen thousand souls shall be entitled to three delegates; every county having a population of fifteen thousand souls, and less than twenty-five thousand, shall be entitled to four delegates; every county having a population of twenty-five thousand, and less than thirty-five thousand souls, shall be entitled to five delegates; and every county having a population of more than thirty-five thousand souls shall be entitled to six delegates; and the city of Baltimore shall be entitled to the same number of delegates as the county which shall be entitled to the largest representation.

The undersigned herewith submit a table showing the practical operation of the basis they recommend.

E. F. Chambers,
James Kent,
John Dennis,

CENSUS OF 1850.

Counties.	White.	Free Colored.	Total Free.	Slaves.	White, Free and Slaves.	Federal Numbers.	Present number of Delegates.	Proposed number of Delegates.	Fraction, exceeding half the number required for an additional delegate
Allegany . . .	21,752	397	22,149	724	22,873	22,584	4	4	7,873
Anne Arundel .	16,542	4,602	21,144	11,224	32,388	27,891	5	5	7,388
Baltimore City .	141,441	24,625	166,066	2,916	169,012	167,830	5	6	
Baltimore County	34,222	3,600	37,822	3,767	41,589	40,091	5	6	
Carroll . . .	18,676	963	19,639	976	20,615	20,220	4	4	5,615
Caroline . . .	6,096	2,788	8,884	808	9,692	9,370	3	3	
Calvert . . .	3,610	1,520	5,130	4,488	9,618	7,824	3	3	
Cecil	15,482	2,612	18,094	843	18,937	18,263	4	4	
Charles . . .	5,665	913	6,578	9,584	16,162	12,329	3	4	
Dorchester . .	10,788	3,803	14,591	4,282	18,873	17,162	4	4	
Frederick . .	31,595	3,637	35,232	3,261	38,493	37,188	5	6	
Harford . . .	14,414	2,785	17,199	2,166	19,365	18,498	4	4	
Kent	5,595	3,132	8,730	2,627	11,357	10,608	3	3	
Montgomery . .	9,435	1,311	10,746	5,114	15,860	13,815	4	4	
Prince George's	8,902	1,138	10.040	11,510	21,550	16,946	4	4	6,550
Queen Anne's .	7,040	3,174	10,214	4,271	14,485	12,776	3	3	
Saint Mary's .	6,280	1,590	7,870	5,811	13,681	11,359	3	3	
Somerset . . .	13,417	3,453	16,870	5,588	22,458	20,224	4	4	7,458
Talbot	7,087	2,590	9,677	4,134	13,811	12,158	3	3	
Washington . .	26,969	1,885	28,854	2,089	30,943	30,108	5	5	5,943
Worcester . .	11,824	3,593	15,417	3,453	18,870	17,490	4	4	
							82	86	

Mr. Howard requested gentlemen to bear in mind that all the reports looked to a rule. So that which he was about to offer comprehended a rule, and it is intended that this rule shall be applied decennially, so as to operate on every enumeration of the State under the Census of the United States. But the result could not be correct, nor indeed could the rule itself be applied, unless some mode of applying it should be established. In pointing out a mode there, was a danger of coming in conflict with the duties of the committee to which will be referred the task of revising and arranging the articles in the new Constitution. He had therefore thought it would be the most advisable course merely to submit to the Convention a resolution to inquire into the expediency of adopting some mode. This resolution might be sent to the committee on revising the Constitution, and thus the danger of any conflict of views would be avoided. He hoped, therefore, that the resolution which he would now send to the Chair, might be at once put on its passage.

Mr. Howard, a member of the committee, then presented a report (in the form of a resolution), which was read and adopted, as follows:

Resolved. That the committee on amendments and revision of the Constitution be instructed to enquire into the expediency of inserting an article substantially as follows:

That in the year 1862, and every tenth year thereafter, it shall be the duty of the Governor for the time being, to arrange the representation in the House of Delegates, according to the ratio adopted by this Convention, and to declare by Proclamation, the number of Delegates to which each county and city may be entitled according to the new census of the United States. And in said Proclamation, he shall also invite the people of the State, to vote on a day therein to be named, whether or not they desire to hold a Convention for the purpose of altering the Constitution. And in case a majority of those who vote, shall desire that a Convention according to the new basis of Representation, the Governor shall take the same steps to organize the Convention, which were followed as to the present.

All the said reports were ordered to be printed.

There was now no question before the Convention.

Mr. Presstman put an inquiry to Mr. Chambers, of Kent, as to the rule upon which Mr. C. had made his report—and some long explanations, partly personal, followed, under the leave of the Convention. [These remarks will be given hereafter.]

After which,

On motion of Mr. Merrick,

The Convention proceeded to the orders of the day.

THE LEGISLATIVE DEPARTMENT.

The Convention resumed the consideration of the report of the committee on the legislative department.

BIENNIAL SESSIONS.

The pending question was on the adoption of the second section of the report as amended.

Mr. Spencer said, that very few members were in the Hall, but that there were more in the city, and he moved a call of the Convention.

A call was ordered; and

The roll of the members was called.

The doorkeeper was then sent to request the attendance of absent members.

Whilst the doorkeeper was absent on his exploring expedition, (the Convention not being in a condition, *ad interim*, to proceed with the business before it,) a long and desultory debate took place on several points of order. They did not result in any formal decision made, or appeal taken—but in reply to an inquiry by

Mr. Dirickson, as to the construction to be given to that portion of the twenty-first rule, which provides that a motion to reconsider, being once put and lost, "shall not be renewed, nor shall any subject be a second time reconsidered, without the consent of the Convention."

The President intimated his opinion to be, that the words "without the consent of the Convention," implied, without the consent of a majority of the Convention."

Mr. Thomas also desired the opinion of the chair upon this point, whether, if the second section, as amended, should be rejected, any member might move to insert the second section as it would stand *without* the amendment of Mr. Spencer.

The President replied, that, if the section, as amended, should be rejected, it would be competent for the Convention to entertain another amendment, but that the chair could not decide whether the amendment would be in order, until its precise character was known.

All these proceedings had reference to the motion of which Mr. Dirickson had given notice, to move a reconsideration of the vote on the amendment of Mr. Spencer yesterday, by which the question of annual or biennial sessions was to be submitted to the people.

The doorkeeper was still out on his cruise—when

Mr. Spencer moved, that all further proceedings on the call be dispensed with.

Ordered accordingly.

The Convention then got steerage-way on, once more;

And the President announced the recurring question, to be on the adoption of the second section, as amended.

Mr. Thomas said:

He desired to ascertain the sense of the House, whether it will sanction this section as it has now been amended. If the House should be disposed to do that, a motion to reconsider the vote by which it had been amended would be useless. That was his view. He had but few words to say in opposition to the section.

He wished to call attention to the conflicting statements of the state of the public sentiment on this subject. If it was true that public opinion would now sanction annual sessions, he had not that conclusive evidence of the fact, which would induce him to vote against their already expressed opinion.

No man had a higher respect for public sentiment than he had; but he could not shape his course here, exclusively with a view to it. If he was made sensible that public sentiment required him to pursue a course against the dictates of his judgment, that might drive him from public life, and send him into retirement for the residue of his days, but it could never induce him to give a vote against the dictates of his conscience. Such would always be his course. When before the people for election, he had always stated his opinions with all candor and freedom, and had then left it to the people to say whether they would elect him or not. But when the election was over, and he had taken his seat in the legislature, he would then have information to influence his course, which the people at the polls have not, and which he had not, previous to his election, and by that information he had heretofore been, and wonld now be governed. With these views, he desired to frame a Constitution himself, and not to transfer that work to others.

In this Convention, we are divided into two parties—not whig and democratic, but into reformers and anti-reformers. There are men in this body who were always opposed to the idea of a Convention, and who in the legislature, voted against the law by authority of which this Convention was called. He would ask of them whether there must not be a compromise of views that we may stand together here, to make a Constitution. And when it comes to be submitted to the people, our friends must be induced to march up to the polls in an unbroken phalanx for the purpose of sustaining us in our action in this body. It was his great object to produce harmony here, and final action on every part of the Constitution.

If we cannot effect any thing here by compromise, the result will be to send the Constitution to the people at the polls piece-meal. If we take the sense of the people on this one article, he feared we would follow this evil example on other parts of the Constitution. But if we will take the proper responsibility by finally deciding the question, there will be less cause to fear for the ultimate result of our deliberations.

He illustrated what might be the consequence of this proposition to call upon the people to do what we had been sent here to accomplish, by referring to the report which had been made by a magnanimous representative of one of the smallest counties, (Mr. Lloyd, from Talbot.) In that report it was proposed to give to the city of Baltimore the right to send twelve members to the House of Delegates. This was a liberal proposition, coming from a small county. It was less than he would be willing to give to a city of whose wealth and power Marylanders ought not to be jealous or envious, but proud. This delegation to Baltimore, as a part of a measure that is, in other respects, highly beneficial to the less populous counties, may be sustained by their delegates here as a measure of compromise. But suppose we take this article for Baltimore and submit it by itself to the people, and, at the same time, submit for separate action, to the people, that part of this same report which proposes to each county a right to choose one member of the Senate; can any man fail to foresee the consequences. The small counties would vote against an increase of the Baltimore delegation, while the large counties and the city of Baltimore would vote against giving one Senator to each county, without regard to their representative numbers. And in this way, both articles of the Constitution would be rejected. Then, as to the Judiciary, if the Convention think that we ought to abolish the life tenure of the judges and reduce the number in commission, are we to incorporate articles in the Constitution subject separately to the sanction of the popular vote? The same may be said as to every article in the Constitution. If we are to send it out to have separate votes upon each of its provisions, we shall only make confusion worse confounded, and all our labors will be of no public utility. He preferred biennial sessions, but felt but little zeal on that question when compared with that which he avowed against this distracting proposition to call upon the people to do that which we were chosen to perform.

Mr. John Newcomer remarking, that enough had been said, and that he hoped that the Convention would second the motion he was about to make, demanded the previous question.

And on the question being put, "will the Convention second the demand for the previous question?"

No quorum voted.

Mr. Chambers, of Kent, called for the yeas and nays, which were ordered.

And the question was again put, "will the Convention second the demand for the previous question," and was decided in the negative, as follows:

Affirmative — Messrs. Dalrymple, Buchanan, Welch, Dickinson, Phelps, Hearn, Annan, Stephenson, Nelson, Schley, Fiery, Neill, John Newcomer, Harbine, Michael Newcomer, Brewer, Parke and Cockey—18.

Negative—Messrs. Chapman, President, Morgan, Ricaud, Chambers, of Kent, Mitchell, Donaldson, Dorsey, Wells, Kent, Merrick, Howard, Ridgely, Lloyd, Sherwood, of Talbot, John Dennis, Williams, Hicks, Hodson, Miller, Tuck, Sprigg, Bowling, Spencer, George, Wright, Dirickson, Jacobs, Thomas, Shriver, Gaither, Biser, McHenry, Carter, Stewart, of Caroline, Presstman, Ware, Waters, Anderson, Weber, Hollyday, Fitzpatrick, Smith, Shower and Brown —44.

So there was not a second.

The question then again recurred on the adoption of the second section, as amended.

Mr. Spencer said the object at which the gentleman from Frederick, [Mr. Thomas,] aimed was the defeat of this section. In some of the views thrown out by the gentleman, he, [Mr. S.,] entirely accorded; and the proceedings of this day bear testimony, that the sentiment is not peculiar with the gentleman from Frederick—that he is operated upon by high and elevated principles, rising above the reach of party influences. The gentleman from Frederick must be satisfied, that there are other members of this body who are actuated by principles equally high. The man who looks not beyond the sphere of selfish or party considerations, is undeserving of a seat in this body. We should all satisfy ourselves, that the object we have in view is one which must be promotive of the public welfare, and then march boldly to it. He agreed also with the gentleman from Frederick, that the reformers in this body ought to act in union. But when reformers differ among themselves, as to the provisions which ought to be inserted in the Constitution, where is to be the point of compromise? Who is to lead in the attempt to reconcile these differences of opinion? Every man must stand on his own principles. He was one of those who knew no leader. He could not abandon the principles he had adopted from a conviction of their correctness. There are many who consider biennial elections as the proper principle; while there are others who contend for annual sessions; but he was willing, in a spirit of compromise, to make some concession to those who thought differently; and, therefore, he had offered various propositions. The gentleman from Frederick, and his friends, have taken a fixed stand against all compromise, while we who are willing to compromise, have been driven by the course of the gentleman from Frederick, and his friends, to take a separate vote on this question at the polls. It appears, therefore, that there are divisions among us all round. Some of the most distinguished members of reform, and of the whig party, are in favor of biennial sessions, while some of the members of the reform, as well as the whig party, are in favor of annual sessions. This was one of the questions which was not agitated before the people. When things are in this condition, and these conflicting opinions cannot be reconciled, is it not prudent to submit the question for a separate vote of the people? Every gentleman here knows the sentiment of his constituents on the subject of representation. Why then should the question of representation be submitted separately? He concluded with saying that he is not wedded to this proposition. If a proposition should be made for the Legislature to meet annually for the next three years he would prefer it.

Mr. DIRICKSON asked the yeas and nays on the adoption of the second section as amended—which were ordered.

Mr. DORSEY moved to amend the section, as amended, by striking out the words "general election."

Mr. D. thought that the language, as it now stood, was vague and uncertain, and that the amendment would make it more definite.

The question was taken, and the amendment was agreed to.

The question then again recurred, and was taken, on the adoption of the section as amended, and the result was as follows:

Affirmative—Messrs. Morgan, Donaldson, Dorsey, Wells, Kent, Merrick, Buchanan, Welsh, Chambers of Cecil, Miller, Tuck, Sprigg, Spencer, George, Wright, Shriver, Biser, Stephenson, McHenry, Nelson, Stewart of Caroline, Presstman, Ware, Brewer, Anderson, Weber, Hollyday, Fitzpatrick, Cockey, Parke, Shower, and Brown—32.

Negative—Messrs. Chapman, President, Ricaud, Chambers of Kent, Mitchell, Dalrymple, Howard, Ridgely, Lloyd, Dickinson, Sherwood of Talbot, John Dennis, Williams, Hicks, Hodson, Phelps, Bowling, Dirickson, Hearn, Jacobs, Thomas, Gaither, Annan, Carter, Schley, Fiery, Neill, John Newcomer, Harbine, Michael Newcomer, Waters and Smith—31.

So the second section, as amended, was adopted.

And thereupon the Convention adjourned until Monday morning.

MONDAY, February 17th, 1851.

The Convention met at eleven o'clock.

Prayer was made by the Rev. Mr. GRIFFITH.

The roll was called; and, after some time, a quorum being present,

The journal of Saturday, (with the exception of reports, the reading of which, on motion of Mr. Brown, was dispensed with,) was read and approved.

Mr. WELLS, chairman of the committee on accounts, made the following report:

The committee on accounts respectfully report that they have examined and passed the account of Hayward, Bartlett & Co., for repairs, to the furnace, herewith filed, and recommend the adoption of the following resolution:

G. WELLS, *Chairman*.

Resolved, That the President of this Convention, draw on the Treasurer in favor of Haywood, Bartlett & Co., for one hundred and forty-six dollars and thirty-one cents.

Which was read and adopted.

Mr. HARBINE moved that the Convention proceed to the order of the day, but waived the motion at the request of Mr. SOLLERS.

THE CONVENTION AND ITS BUSINESS.

Mr. SOLLERS said he had risen for the purpose of making a motion, which perhaps would come with better grace from another member of the Convention, than from himself. He proposed that a committee should be appointed to examine and consider the rules of the Convention, and to report such alterations and amendments as, in their opinion, would facilitate the business of the Convention.

Mr. GWINN. I second the motion.

Mr. SOLLERS continued He had hitherto taken occasion, he said, to refer to the jarring and discordant elements of which this Convention was composed, and to state that they were such as to prevent any human being predicting when it would be possible for it to adjourn. No programme of settled principles, upon which this body should base its action, had been discussed before the people; and gentlemen had met here without knowing what the people wanted, or what they wanted themselves. What had been the consequence? The Convention was afflicted with that curse which, in olden times, had been visited upon a rebellious people, who attempted to build a tower which should reach to heaven—a confusion of tongues. For his own part, he was opposed to nearly all the reforms, which were contemplated by this Convention, yet he felt that something was due to the wishes and the interests of a disappointed and indignant people. Well might they exclaim, in the language of the Roman orator, "quousque tandem abutere patientia nostra?" From one end of the State to the other, a dissatisfied feeling pervaded the public mind, in regard to the condition of the business of this Convention. They had been three months in session, and were but just upon the threshold of the business for which they had assembled. All the difficult and intricate questions claiming the attention of the Convention, yet remained to be discussed. There was a defect somewhere. It was evident that there was too much speaking. There lay the difficulty, and his object was that a committee should be appointed to revise the rules, with a view to obviate that difficulty.

He thought that if a rule was adopted providing that, if any subject should be referred to the committee of the whole, the debate should terminate at a fixed period, the business of the Convention might be facilitated. After it was reported from the committee of the whole, or perhaps in committee of the whole, after the general debate had terminated, it might be desirable to allow five minutes, or perhaps a still less time, for explanation of amendments. Other changes of the rule, not requisite to be mentioned here, might also be found advisable and proper.

He had made this movement from the sincerest motives and the kindest feelings. Especially had he made it from motives of charity to the reform party in this Convention, who were bringing upon themselves a tremendous responsibility, and heaping coals of fire upon their own heads. Upon them the people would visit the consequences of the state of things which now existed in this Convention.

He had only to request that if the committee should be appointed, the President would not place him, (Mr. S.,) upon it.

Mr. GWINN said:

That he would gladly support the motion of the gentleman from Calvert, or any motion which would facilitate the business of the Convention. In the absence of other means he would himself move, before long, to fix a day for the adjournment of the Convention, distant enough to ensure a full consideration of all the business which it was assembled to perform, and yet sufficiently near to make all absentees sensible of the necessity of their attendance.

Much had been said in relation to the diligence of this Convention. He did not intend to detract from its merits, whatever they might be, but it was certain that it afforded evidences of a longer session, than any body which had ever assembled in any one of the several States, which had resorted to the same means of reforming their Constitution. Our duties and our labors, dignify them as we may, stand in no higher place than those which other Conventions have performed.

He confessed that he was anxious to bring the labors of this Convention to a close. When a member of the last Legislature, he had supported the bill under which it was organised. He did not do this because he considered it just, or equitable, in all its parts,—but for the reason that the reform party of the whole State had committed itself to bills as unequal in their character, from the beginning of the movement, to the day of the passage of the bill in question. He was then hopeful, that, unequal as the representation was, full justice would be done to all sections of the State. In the Legislature, with such inequality, little could be expected. It was composed chiefly of young men, who, properly enough, were unwilling to assume the direction of public opinion in the sections of the State, which they represented. The Legislature, in general, is but the index of the public feeling; and must have attained extraordinary developement before a body, so constituted, will obey its impulse. But it was supposed that this Convention, made up of men distinguished for long and honorable service to the State Government, and from their position and ability, entitled to direct public opinion, would be prepared to assume the responsibility of over-leaping the narrow limits or present interest, and would provide, with a wise foresight, for such a settlement of this vexed question, as would ensure future tranquility in the whole State. He confessed that he had been disappointed—deeply and bitterly disappointed—but he was not less anxious to bring the labors of the body to a speedy and sober conclusion. It would be, after all, but the making of the first step; a small step, it might chance to be—but it would be the beginning of a progress, which should end only in the attainment of full and substantial justice.

The PRESIDENT, (to Mr. Sollers.) Does the gentleman designate any number of which the committee shall be composed?

Mr. SOLLERS said he would submit that point to the judgment of the Chair.

Mr. SOLLERS then took the floor, and disclaimed any intention to detract from the character of the gentleman from Baltimore city, (Mr. Gwinn,) or of any of that delegation, but expressed the opinion that the confusion of tongues of which he, (Mr. S.,) had spoken, had been created in a great degree by that delegation, owing to the amount of talking which they had done.

Mr. GWINN. The gentlemen must remember that we are entitled to one third of the talking. [Laughter.]

Mr. SOLLERS. You are entitled to it, and you have done it. [Laughter.]

Mr. BUCHANAN said he believed the Convention would bear him witness that he had talked but little hitherto, and, for himself, he could promise, that he should talk still less hereafter. I am gratified, (continued Mr. B.,) at the proposition of the gentleman from Calvert, (Mr. Sollers) It meets my hearty approbation. But I think that the gentlemen will perceive that some injustice has been done, which, if report speaks truly of him, he would be the last man to do.

Some time ago the proceedings of this Convention were spoken of as being dilatory elsewhere, and sometimes here. I am free to confess, that the progress of business has been protracted and slow. Nevertheless, I believe that there are men here, who, from first to last, have been influenced by the sincerest and most conscientious desire to discharge their legitimate duties. And I say to my friend from Calvert, (Mr. Sollers,) that, so far as the standing committees are concerned, every one of them has made its reports. These reports are before the Convention; are about to be taken up; and although we are just now, as the gentleman has observed, only on the threshold of the debate; still the work is all cut out, and is here. Let us do it. I, for one, am ready.

I had occasion some time ago, in an incidental debate here, to refer to the labor which had been performed by the committees of this body, and to shew that the last of all complaints which could justly be made against them, was that they had been neglectful of their duty, or slow in its discharge. The results of their labors are now before us, and I believe that if the proposition of my friend from Calvert, (Mr. Sollers,) prevails, we shall do more work within the next five weeks, so far as the perfecting of measures is concerned, than we have done in the whole antecedent period of our session. But I concur entirely in opinion with him, that we must put a stop to this everlasting propensity to talk. And to accomplish that object, some uniform rule will be required.

If one gentleman indulges in remarks, another must have the privilege of reply, and thus instead of closing our labors by the first of April, (after which period, I do not believe that a quorum of this body can be kept together,) we shall not terminate them until September. I cast reflections upon the course of no man, but I have a right to vindicate my own.

During the three and a half months that have elapsed since the meeting of this Convention, I have been absent from my seat only two days. I am here at my post now and at all times, ready and anxious to discharge the duties which have been entrusted to my hands. So far as my personal wishes or interests are concerned, the business of this Convention cannot be disposed of too soon. I will vote for every fair and reasonable proposition which has that most desirable consummation in view.

Mr. JOHN DENNIS said:

That as it seemed to be the order of the day for gentlemen to give their experience, it might not perhaps be considered inappropriate in him to say a very few words on the proposition now under consideration. The Convention would bear him witness that he had obtruded himself but little on its attention—whether, because his natural temperament was such, that he was not troubled so much as some gentlemen, with that raging disease known as the *cacœthes loquendi*, or whether because he did not feel himself as competent to participate in public discussions as others, it was not for him to say. But from the commencement of the session until the present time, with the exception of a short interval after the recess, he had been in his seat.

It had pleased the honorable gentleman who presides over the deliberations of this assembly, with so much dignity, ability and credit to himself, to appoint him upon four very important committees—to wit: The committee of twenty-one, composed of a member from each county, and the city of Baltimore—the committee on qualifications of members to seats—the committee on the apportionment of representation—and the committee of twenty-one called the union committee.

I believe, (continued Mr. D,) that during the sittings of these committees, night or day, I have been absent but once. I am, therefore, responsible for none of the impediments or delays which have attended the transaction of the business for which we assembled. In May last, when the subject of this Convention was mooted, I, in the exercise of my privilege, voted against the call; not that I did not think there might be some improvements made in the Constitution, but because I doubted the propriety and expediency of this mode of action, and, because, from the little experience which I had had in the course of twenty years, I feared the result would be pretty much that, which surrounding events and circumstances now foreshadow.

During the last fall, I took the ground before the people that no man could estimate what the cost of this Convention would be. It was said that it would be some sixty thousand dollars. My answer was, that it might cost that sum—or it might cost one hundred thousand dollars—or that, for aught that could then be foretold, it might cost two hundred thousand dollars. I knew we might anticipate that some long-winded gentlemen would be returned to this body, whose love of speaking, growing by what it fed on, would render it impossible to tell how long we might remain here, or what the cost might ultimately be. Although no prophet, nor the son of a prophet, it seems that these anticipations are likely to be realized. The wide unbounded prospect lies before us—but shadows, clouds and darkness rest upon it.

We are here in chaos, and when we are ever to emerge from the darkness that envelopes us, into the light of day—the powers above alone can tell.

I knew or thought I knew, that this task of making a Constitution would prove more difficult in its execution, than was dreampt of in the philosophy of those whose vision is bounded by the political horizon of twenty-four hours. Instead of finding it a work of such easy execution, it is now discovered it may not inaptly be compared to the labor of Sisyphus.

I told my people that I preferred they would select another delegate in my place; but when they insisted that I should represent them here, I told them of all the difficulties by which we should be met. I told them that the duration of the session would be far beyond any calculation of theirs, or any reasonable expectation of my own, and that it might become requisite for me to return to my home.

I shall vote with all my heart in favor of the proposition of the gentleman from Calvert, (Mr. Sollers,) or of any other that is likely to be attended with beneficial results.

It is high time that something should be done. If something is not done, we may go on *ad infinitum*, and never bring our labors to a close. Let us stop debate, and go to work.

Mr. MORGAN said, that he should, with pleasure, support the proposition of his friend from Calvert, (Mr. Sollers,) but declared, in advance, that he would not vote for the proposition of the gentleman from Baltimore city, (Mr. Gwinn.) The Convention, (continued Mr. M.) will bear me out in the assertion, that I am not one of those at whose door can rest the charge of having interrupted or impeded the proceedings of the Convention, by offering propositions which have led to debate, or by debating such propositions myself. And I must say to my friend from Baltimore city, (Mr. Gwinn,) that the motion of which he has given notice, comes with no very good grace from him. For, I think that the proceedings of the Convention will show that most of the propositions which have delayed its action have emanated from the quarter from which this motion is to come to-morrow.

Mr. GWINN. From myself?

Mr. MORGAN. No—but from the quarter of the State from which this motion is to come to-morrow. I do not intend to say, that the gentleman has interrupted or impeded the progress of the public business. But what does the gentleman now say? He declares, in the presence of this body, that if he had known what would have been the result of our proceedings, his right arm should have withered before he would have voted, as a member of the Legislature, for the bill which authorised the call of this Convention. Sir, does the gentleman intend to say that any one of the propositions which have been maintained here were spoken of in the Legislature? Did the gentleman ever hear the question of representation talked of when the bill was under consideration? Gentlemen were very cautious upon that question, until after the passage of the bill—and yet the gentleman comes here and tells us that his right arm should wither by his side before he would have voted for it, if he had known what now he knows.

Every body knows that certain propositions have been brought in here from Baltimore city, which have been defeated; and now, because, as I suppose, they were not decided as he and his constituents desired that they should be, he rises in his place and proposes to put an end to this Convention. I cannot sympathise with him in such a purpose. I tell my friends here that the people of the State of Maryland, beyond the limits of the city of Baltimore, desire that a Constitution should be formed; and that if the votes and proceedings which may be recorded here should not be in consonance with the views of the people of that city, they may be in accordance with the views of the people of the rest of the State. And for that reason, I shall vote against any motion to bring the session of this body to an abrupt or premature termination. The most important measures before us have yet to be acted upon, and I believe that the confirmation by the people of what we may do here, depends upon the result of these measures.

I have heard much of the dilatory proceedings of the Convention. I have seen the charge in the newspapers and elsewhere. But look at the condition of things. No State in the Union can be cited as an example for our own. A Convention assembled in any other State, under circumstances similar to those by which we are surrounded, would have been placed in the same difficulty. The condition of our people is different from that of the people of any other State.

In one section of the State, we have a large slave interest, and in another section an anti-slavery feeling. We have a large city in our midst, with an overwhelming population, claiming representation according to numbers, and with the counties in opposition to it. We have a commercial and agricultural interest, and all these interests conflicting with each other. And, to crown all, we have an organic law that has remained essentially unchanged for seventy years; so that we have now to engraft upon it all the modifications and improvements, which, through this long lapse of years, have been developed in the science of human government. All these delicate and difficult questions have now to be settled by us, as the people of other States, through their Conventions, have already settled them. I cannot, therefore, concur in the opinion any where expressed, that we have been here doing nothing.

If we now go earnestly to work—if we attend to the business before us, and deliberate calmly and wisely upon it, the people, instead of condemning us for what we have done, or finding fault with the time we have spent, will greet, with their approbation and applause, the Constitution which we may submit to them.

I shall, therefore, vote against the motion of the gentleman from Baltimore city, (Mr. Gwinn,) but in favor of every proposition calculated to expedite the transaction of the public business.

Mr. SOLLERS. I call the previous question.

There was a second.

The main question was ordered, and having been taken, the motion of Mr. SOLLERS was agreed to.

So a committee was ordered to be appointed.

The PRESIDENT. The Chair nominates as the committee, Messrs. SPRIGG, MCLANE, RICAUD, SCHLEY and BUCHANAN.

Mr. MCLANE asked to be excused on the ground of feeble health.

The Convention excused Mr. MCLANE,

And the PRESIDENT appointed Mr. BROWN in his stead.

Mr. SPRIGG asked to be excused, upon the ground of his imperfect acquaintance with parliamentary practice.

The Convention excused Mr. SPRIGG,

And Mr. JOHN DENNIS was appointed by the PRESIDENT in his place.

Mr. DENNIS asked to be excused from service, on the ground that he had already been appointed a member of four committees.

Mr. D. was excused.

The PRESIDENT then said that the House being very thin, the Chair would take further time to complete the committee.

On motion of Mr. HARBINE, the Convention proceeded to the orders of the day.

THE LEGISLATIVE DEPARTMENT.

The Convention resumed the consideration of the unfinished business, being the report of the committee on the legislative department.

The third section was read, as follows:

"*Sec.* 3. The first election for Senators and Delegates shall take place on the first Wednesday of October, eighteen hundred and fifty-one, and on the same day in every second year forever thereafter, the general elections for Delegates, and for one half of the Senators, as nearly as practicable, shall be held."

Mr. DORSEY moved to amend the section by striking out the word "general," in the third line.

Mr. Fiery moved further to amend said section, by striking out in the second line the word "first," and inserting in lieu thereof, "second."

Mr. F. said, this change would be for the convenience of the agricultural portion of the State.

Mr. Sellman desired to move to strike out the "first Wednesday of October," and insert "the second Monday of August."

Mr. Shower called for a division of the question, (on the motion to strike out,) which was ordered.

The question was then taken on the motion to strike out.

But no quorum voted.

Mr. Brown said, he was satisfied that a quorum was in the city, and he would, therefore, move that there be a call of the Convention.

But, by general consent, the question was again taken, and a quorum having voted, the motion to strike out was agreed to.

Mr. Jacobs then moved to fill the blank with the first Monday in November.

Some conversation followed on the part of Messrs. Dirickson, Spencer and Dorsey,

When the question was taken, first on inserting the most distant day, (i. e. the first Monday in November,) and it was agreed to.

The question then recurred on the section as amended.

Mr. Donaldson offered the following substitute for the third section, as amended:

Section 3rd. "The first election for Delegates shall be held on the first Monday of November, 1851, and the Delegates then chosen shall hold their seats for the term of one year only, the Senators heretofore elected, shall hold their seats until the first Monday of November, 1852, when an election shall be held for Senators and Delegates; and thereafter, on the same day in every alternate year, an election shall be held for Delegates, and for one half of the Senators as nearly as may be, unless in accordance with the preceding sections, the Legislature shall provide for the annual election of Delegates."

But on a suggestion by Mr. Dirickson,

Mr. Donaldson waived it for the present.

The fourth section of the report was then read as follows:

"*Section* 4. Immediately after the Senate shall have convened after the first election under this Constitution, the Senators shall be divided by lot, into two classes, as nearly in number as may be. The Senators of the first class, shall go out of office at the expiration of two years, and Senators shall be elected on the first Wednesday of October, 1853, for the term of four years, to supply their places; so that, after the first election, one-half of the Senators may be chosen every second year. In case the number of Senators be hereafter increased, such classification of the additional Senators, shall be made as to preserve as nearly as may be, an equal number in each class."

Mr. Dorsey moved to strike out the first Wednesday, so as to make it conform with the provision of section three.

The amendment was agreed to.

And the section, as amended, was adopted.

The fifth section was then read as follows:

"*Section* 5. The General Assembly shall meet on the first Wednesday of January, 1852, and on the same day in every year, for ever thereafter, and at no other time, unless convened by the proclamation of the Governor, who shall have power to convene the same whenever he may deem it expedient and proper."

Mr. Spencer moved to strike out the fifth and sixth sections and insert as follows:

"The General Assembly shall meet on the first Wednesday next, after the first Monday of January, eighteen hundred and fifty-two, and on the same day in the next year thereafter, to be named and fixed by the Legislature, but all subsequent sessions shall be biennial, and commence on the first Wednesday next after the first Monday of January, eighteen hundred and fifty-four, and on the same day in each alternate year thereafter, and at no other time, unless convened by the proclamation of the Governor, who shall have power to convene the same, whenever he may deem it expedient and proper, and all subsequent regular biennial sessions of the General Assembly, shall be closed on the tenth day of March next ensuing the term of their commencement, unless the same shall be closed at an earlier day by the agreement of the two Houses."

Mr. Spencer said, that in this form, the section would so read as to secure three annual sessions. If, therefore, it was agreed to in this form, he would be willing to move a reconsideration of the vote by which the amendment he proposed on Saturday, was embodied in the second section, so as to make that section a simple declaration that the sessions shall be biennial

Mr. Chambers suggested, that it would be better to make the time the first Wednesday after the first day of January. A great many persons would find it inconvenient to leave their homes on the first day of January. He wished to make another suggestion while he was on the floor. The vote of Saturday was taken when the House was very thin; and it is by no means improbable that when there is a full attendance of members a difference of opinion may be expressed. He would suggest that, in this condition of things, time might be saved if we postponed this question for the present, and went on with some of the other sections of the report.

Mr. Spencer repeated his belief, that if this proposition was adopted, fixing that there shall be three annual sessions, there would be no difference of opinion in the House on the course to be pursued. The vote of Saturday would be reconsidered. At least, such was the opinion of several gentlemen near him who had spoken to him on the subject.

Mr. Smith asked whether the fixing of the time which had been named, might not interfere with the meeting of the House of Delegates?

Mr. Spencer replied, that it would not.

Mr. Biser said, that if he was called on to vote on this question, he should be compelled to vote against the proposition of the gentleman from Queen Anne's. He referred to the speech of the gentleman from Queen Anne's on Saturday in favor of this very amendment, which he is now disposed to defeat. That cogent argument of the gentleman from Queen Anne's still rung in his ears. He had not heard it answered, and unless the gentleman himself would answer it, he could not now consent to change his course.

Mr. Spencer reminded the House that in some remarks he made on Saturday, he had expressly declared that he was in favor of biennial sessions. He had then stated that he would prefer a provision for three annual sessions to enable the Legislature to pass the laws necessary to carry out the requisitions of the new Constitution. But as he could not effect that object, he had no course left him but to move the amendment providing that the question shall be submitted to the people.

Mr. Biser said the gentleman from Queen Anne had also stated that he was in favor of biennial sessions, because the people had decided in favor of them; but that other gentlemen thought that public sentiment was now opposed to them; and the gentleman from Queen Anne had asked if there was any gentleman who would be unwilling to submit the question again to the decision of the people?

Mr. Thomas apologized for rising to trouble the House with any remarks, but as he had been requested by the gentleman from Dorchester, not now in his seat, to look after this question, and as he felt something was due to his colleague who was necessarily absent, he trusted he should be permitted to say a very few words. He regreted that he should have been brought before the House so much more frequently by these circumstances than was agreeable to himself. He desired now to ask a question of the gentleman from Queen Anne for his own information. If he understood the present proposition offered by that gentleman, it seemed to him to conflict both with the views of that gentleman as it did with his own. He had no objection to make to the clause as to the time of the meeting of the two first sessions of the Legislature. But he understood the gentleman from Queen Anne as proposing to strike out the sixth section, which fixes a limitation of the duration of the subsequent sessions, which he did not think was in accordance with the disposition of the House.

He was willing to vote to make it imperative on the Legislature to hold two annual sessions, by way of holding out the olive branch, and he would advise all the friends of reform to take this course. This would be equivalent to the bill as it now stands, which gives to the Legislature the power (which he believed the Legislature would exercise) to sit twice in the first two years. And if he understood this amendment it limits as the bill before us limits, the third session to the 10th of March. We shall then retain the important provision for biennial sessions, commencing with the year 1854. It should be borne in mind that there are propositions to be made, looking to a codification of our laws, to a reform in the practice and of special pleading, and to such other changes as will make the proceedings in our Courts analogous to the practice of the Courts of Law in some of the other States of the Union. If we expect the Legislature to do this work, there will be business much beyond the ordinary business which comes before the Legislature, for its action. Some of the best practioners of law in our State may probably be willing to come to the Legislature to be engaged in this employment which will require great practical knowledge. Now if you subject lawyers of this character to the drudgery of two elections, which must be the case, unless under one election they may attend two sessions, he would put it to gentlemen on this floor, who are entirely competent to give him an answer, whether these gentlemen could be induced to canvas their counties twice over? They might be willing to make sacrifices to be elected once to the General Assembly to assist in reforming our Laws. The first business of the Legislature would be to lay off the new Congressional Districts in the State, under the new apportionment made by Congress under the new census by which this State will loose one representative in that body. They may then proceed to take up the subject of the revision of our laws, with a view to their codification. Before this can be completed, they may adjourn from 1852 to 1853, when they will find it necessary to resume the work for the purpose of completing it. But should it be required by the Constitution that a new election shall intervene between these sessions, half of those gentlemen who had commenced the work might be left at home, the whole task would be recommenced and gone over again. He hoped, therefore, that the friends of reform would accept of the proposition now offered, and thus secure one important article in the Constitution.

Mr. Schley said the argument in favor of annual sessions had been made on the ground that a greater amount of labor than usual would be imposed on the General Assembly, for the purpose of enacting the laws necessary to carry out the provisions of the new Constitution. He thought this was a mistake. He was anxious that there should be a codification of the laws of the State, and the only way in which he thought it ought to be done, would be for the Legislature to appoint Commissioners to examine and codify them. This would be a work requiring much time; it will not be done in 1852 or 1853, and probably not even in 1854. It is not possible for a task of this magnitude to be completed by the first meeting of the Legislature. It is very desirable that some change should be made in the practice, in relation to special pleading. The great objection to the present mode of special pleading is not, as is generally supposed, that it is too special. Let it be stripped of its verbosity, and its antiquated forms, and that may be all which may be found necessary. The only effect of any laborious effort at change, may be to make what is already special, still more special. Apart from these two objects, what other business is there which requires that there shall be annual sessions of the Legislature? The mere laying off of new districts would certainly not be sufficient to warrant annual sessions. He had not risen to take up the time of the Convention in unnecessary debate, and he would detain it no longer. If these were the strongest arguments which could be brought forward by the friends of the annual system, he would still adhere to biennial sessions, believing that they are in accordance with the will of the people.

The question was then stated to be on the motion of Mr. SPENCER, to strike out the fifth and sixth sections, and insert the amendments he had offered.

Mr. BISER called for a division—first on striking out;

Which was ordered.

And the question being taken,

The motion to strike out was rejected.

Mr. JACOBS now moved to reconsider the vote, adopting the third section.

The vote having been reconsidered,

Mr. JACOBS said, his object in the amendment he had offered to the third section, was to make the State elections conform to the Presidential election. Finding he had been mistaken in the day—he now moved to strike out the first Monday in November, and insert "on the Tuesday next after the first Monday, in the month of November."

Mr. SPENCER called for a division on striking out;

Which was ordered.

The motion to strike out was agreed to.

The question then recurred on the motion to insert the day designated by Mr. JACOBS.

Mr. BROWN moved a reconsideration, of the vote striking out from the third section the words, "first Monday in November."

He made the motion, he said, because he had given his vote in favor of the motion to strike out under a misapprehension. The object he had in view, was to keep the State and the general elections free from each other.

Some conversation followed on the part of Messrs. BROWN, THOMAS, DIRICKSON and MITCHELL.

Mr. SPENCER asked the yeas and nays, on the motion to reconsider;

Which were ordered; and

Being taken, resulted as follows:

Affirmative—Messrs. Buchanan, Welch, Lloyd, Dickinson, Sherwood of Talbot, Constable, Chambers, of Cecil, Miller, McLane, Spencer, George, Wright, Thomas, Shriver, Gaither, Biser, Annan, Stephenson, Nelson, Carter, Stewart, of Caroline, Gwinn, Stewart of Baltimore city, Sherwood of Baltimore city, Ware, Harbine, Brewer, Anderson, Weber, Hollyday, Fitzpatrick, Parke, Shower and Brown.—34.

Negative—Messrs. Chapman, President, Morgan, Ricaud, Chambers of Kent, Mitchell, Donaldson, Dorsey, Wells, Randall, Sellman, Dalrymple, Sollers, John Dennis, Hicks, Hodson, Phelps, Sprigg, Bowling, Dirickson, Hearn, Jacobs, Magraw, Schley, Fiery, Neill, Waters Smith and Cockey—28.

So the vote was reconsidered.

The question now recurred on striking out the "first Monday in November," and inserting the amendment of Mr. JACOBS.

Mr. CHAMBERS, of Kent, suggested to the gentleman from Worcester, that it was not worth while to press this question now. There was but a thin attendance, and that it would be impossible to determine to-day, what the sense of the Convention was.

Mr. JACOBS explained that his only object was, in the amendment he had offered, to avoid the multiplicity of elections.

But the sense of the Convention had been expressed, as he supposed, that the State and Federal elections should be held on the same day. He was not anxious to press the question now—and yielding to the suggestions of gentlemen, would withdraw the amendment for the present.

Mr. DIRICKSON gave notice that he should to-morrow move to reconsider the vote of the Convention on the second section of the report.

The fifth section was then again read.

Mr. THOMAS moved to amend the section after the word "every" in the second line, by inserting the word "second."

The question was taken.

But no quorum voted.

Mr. MAGRAW moved that the third, fifth and sixth sections of the report, be passed over informally.

The PRESIDENT. It can be done only by unanimous consent.

Objection was made.

Some conversation followed on the part of Messrs. CHAMBERS, of Kent, THOMAS, and HARBINE.

Mr. SPENCER proposed to amend the section by inserting, in the second line the words "and on the same day in the year 1853."

The question was stated to be on the amendment of Mr. SPENCER.

Mr. SPENCER asked the yeas and nays;

Which were ordered.

Some desultory conversation followed, as to the effect of the amendment, in which Messrs. SPENCER, THOMAS, CONSTABLE, WELLS, PHELPS, BUCHANAN, HARBINE and DONALDSON, took part.

The question on the amendment of Mr. SPENCER was then taken and resulted as follows:

Affirmative—Messrs. Chapman, President, Morgan, Ricaud, Chambers of Kent, Mitchell, Donaldson, Wells, Sellman, Buchanan, Welch, Sherwood of Talbot, John Dennis, Hicks, Hodson, Miller, Sprigg, Bowling, Spencer, George, Wright, Dirickson, Jacobs, Thomas, Shriver, Biser, Annan, Carter, Stewart of Caroline, Gwinn, Fiery, Neill, Harbine, Waters, Anderson, Hollyday, Fitzpatrick, Smith and Cockey—38.

Negative—Messrs. Lloyd, Dickinson, Phelps, Constable, Chambers of Cecil, McLane, Hearn,

Gaither, Stephenson, Nelson, Stewart of Baltimore city, Sherwood, of Baltimore city, Ware, Schley, Brewer, Weber, Parke and Brown—18.

So the amendment was adopted.

The question then recurred on the amendment of Mr. THOMAS, to insert in said section after the word "every" in the second line, the word "second."

Mr. T. then modified his amendment, by moving to amend said section by inserting after the word "day" in the second line, the words "in the year eighteen hundred and fifty-four."

The Convention now became involved in a long conversational discussion, (chiefly verbal and technical,) as to the effect and operation of the amendment, and its probable conflict with the vote of the Convention, already given on the subject of biennial sessions;

Messrs. CHAMBERS, of Kent, THOMAS, PHELPS, BUCHANAN and SPENCER, taking part therein.

And pending the question,

The Convention adjourned until to-morrow morning at eleven o'clock.

—

DEFERRED DEBATE.

The following are the remarks referred to in the last number, made on the presentation by Mr. CHAMBERS, of Kent, of his report on the basis of representation:

Mr. PRESSTMAN desired to inquire of the gentleman from Kent, (Mr. Chambers,) by what rule he and those of the committee who had united with him in the report just submitted, had arrived at the number of representatives to compose the House of Delegates. His reason for propounding the inquiry was, to ascertain the whole scope and object of the report, that it might be fully understood and reflected upon. If it be said that the rule adopted was to settle the basis upon the compromise act, as it was termed, of 1836, he wished to call the attention of the Convention to the fact, that this report sought to make no change in the basis of representation already guarantied by that act, in favor of the principle of popular representation, but that it actually condemned that compromise by seeking to destroy the advantages secured by the federal basis. He wished to be informed what was the reason of this departure in that particular alone from the rule, if it could be so called, in the act of 1836.

He begged to invite the serious reflection of the Convention to the disposition manifested in that report, while it did not yield any thing to the white population of the State beyond what was secured by the act to which he had referred, sought to engraft a provision new in its character in the history of this State, or of any other in the Union, viz: That the aggregate vote of the population, including every negro, free or slave, was to compose the basis. This surely would be regarded as a retrograde movement by the great body of the people of Maryland. As a representative in part of the city of Baltimore, he had early announced his willingness to adjust this question of representation upon a fair principle of compromise. He could not refrain, however, from saying that he regretted to find that any gentleman should desire to settle the basis of representation upon a principle such as that contained in the report just submitted—which not only refused any concession to the people of Western Maryland and to his constituency, comprising of themselves nearly one-fourth of the population of the State—but offended their sense of justice and right, by seeking to place the entire negro population of the State upon an equality with them, so far as constituting the basis of representation. In truth what could be more abhorent, that while Baltimore with her white population, numbering nearly one hundred and forty-two thousand souls, was limited to a representation of six delegates, every slave in Maryland should be considered as worthy to constitute in part the basis of representation. More than that, sir, the county of Kent, with but a five thousand, five hundred and ninety-five white population, has granted her in this report three delegates.

He had sought the information from the gentleman from Kent, perhaps in a manner somewhat irregular, but inasmuch as the gentleman from Charles, (Mr. Merrick,) the distinguished Chairman of the committee, had in presenting his report accompanied it with the expression that each separate report of the committee, as well as his own, looked to the establishment of a rule of apportionment, and such also had been announced by the gentleman from Baltimore county, (Mr. Howard,) as his object in the report he had submitted. These observations had induced him to propound the question.

Mr. CHAMBERS. The gentleman, (Mr. Presstman,) has asked a question "by what rule we have arrived at the number of representatives indicated in the report." The question cannot be more satisfactorily answered, than by again reading the report.

"Every county having a population of less than 15,000 shall be entitled to three delegates; every county having a population of 15,000 and less than 25,000, shall be entitled to four delegates; every county having 25,000 and less than 35,000, to five, and every county having more than 35,000, to six; and Baltimore city the same number as the largest county."

The gentleman's question, he hoped, was answered fully. But the gentleman had gone far beyond asking a question. Indeed, his question seemed to have been put, not at all because he did not comprehend the rule suggested by the report, but merely as a prelude to an assault upon it. It was certainly a very unusual course, when a report on an important measure was made, at the instant of its presentation, before it was printed, or in possession of the House, to commence an attack upon it. The same gentleman had some time since gratuitously assumed the task of protecting the rights and interests of the slave-holding portions of the State, had volunteered and earnestly pressed a measure designed to manifest a very warm feeling toward this interest. This was the first instance in which the rights of the slaveholder, as such, had since then been presented to the consideration of the House, and behold the gentleman is the only member of the body who rises, at a most unusual and untimely moment, to assail the principle of representing the slave population. These remarks are the "first fruits," of this glowing sentiment of singular attachment to our peculiar condition! Why this "hot haste"? Cannot the gentleman restrain his hostility, till the report comes up for discussion? Then is the appropriate period for his denunciation. But why should this principle of representation of the aggregate population be denounced? There was great propriety in adopting federal numbers in the Constitution of the United States, because there was some of the States having no slaves. But as far as relates to internal regulation, there was no motive or consistency in adopting the principle of federal numbers, nor did he fear any sound reason upon which the gentleman could successfully sustain his enmity to this feature of the report. He would be prepared to demonstrate this at the proper period.

Mr. Presstman said that he took occasion to remark, preliminarily to the observations he was about to offer, in reply to the gentleman from Kent, [Mr. Chambers,] that he had sought to evince, at all times, towards that gentleman, and to every member of that body, the most respectful and courteous consideration. He had, however, observed, and was compelled so to declare, that he had not always been met in the same spirit, by the gentleman who had just addressed the Convention. In answer, sir, to a plain and simple inquiry, calculated in no degree to offend the nicest sensibility, he had had a retort made upon him, certainly not very parliamentary in style or manner.

Mr. Chambers interposing, declared it was foreign to his wish, to say any thing personal in its character to the gentleman from Baltimore city; on the contrary, he was among the last gentlemen, to whom he would evince any unkindness of feeling.

Mr. Presstman. He did not suppose that the gentleman had designed to give him personal offence, or to attack his motives. There could not possibly be such an issue between them. In that Convention, composed of Maryland gentlemen, he would be slow to believe that any such intention would be manifested. But he did mean to complain and avow that the gentleman from Kent, both in the manner and matter of his remarks, had not extended to him the same frankness and courtesy, which he had invariably manifested, in discussion, with that gentleman, whose great ability he had so often acknowledged and whose friendship he highly prized. But enough of that, sir. He could not say less in justice to his own sense of propriety.

He had been charged with inconsistency in the position he had assumed, in reference to the report, and the ground he had occupied when he submitted a proposition, intended as a full and complete guaranty to the rights of the slave holders of Maryland to be secured in their slave-property against the possibility of legislative emancipation. Sprung, sir, from a race of slave-holders, he had been impelled alike by a sense of feeling and the dictate of stern duty, to offer his humble aid to guard the institution as it now exist. But, sir, that course has been looked upon with suspicion, and forsooth, his independent action on that subject has been met, not as it should have been, as a token of willingness to dispel all doubt upon this question, vital as some seemed to regard it, but strangely converted into a cause of reproach and mistrust. He could not say that had he anticipated that an effort so entirely free from selfishness, or the expectation of personal advantage on his part, would have been so misconceived by those who represent the slave interest upon this floor, he would have withheld his sentiments and his vote upon that question, but he would say, that if the gentleman from Kent, (Mr. Chambers,) was to be regarded as speaking for that class of delegates, (which, however, he would not assume,) the unanimous vote of this body, to sustain the rights of slave holders, had been most illy deserved.

What, sir, is it inconsistent in a gentleman upon this floor, to seek to guard the property of slave holders, as a chattel interest, if, at the same time, he should refuse to recognize each and every negro as entitled to be ranked with a freeman, in establishing the basis of representation.

Verily, sir, with great deference he would ask, when will wonders cease, if gentlemen will argue such a proposition? In the language of Junius, their "imagination may conceive such a thing, but where shall we find credulity enough to believe it."

As he had often said, he now reiterated, that he had offered that proposition in good faith and for two reasons—first,because, he thought it was right in itself, and would be the means of obtaining the confidence of the slave interest; and secondly, to silence the misrepresentations and slanders, which had been industriously circulated to the prejudice of his constituency. Should the propositions contained in the report of the gentleman from Kent, (Mr. Chambers,) be sustained, what gentleman could doubt, that the new Constitution would be indignantly rejected by more than two-thirds of the freemen of Maryland. Our work would then have been in vain, and the cherished hopes of the people would vanish, and a deep gloom would fasten upon their minds.

Remember, gentlemen in coming to this Convention, composed upon the basis that it is, all our confidence was placed, not in the power to demand and enfore our rights, but in the magnanimity and sense of common justice, which as freemen, and above all, as Marylanders, you would mete out to your common brethren. Surely you will be able to discard in part, if not altogether, the local prejudices which are said to influence, more or less, each and every man in his modes of thinking and acting; and if you are prepared to deny the equality of rights and privileges to each citizen of Maryland, which are now enjoyed in almost every State in the republic, you will honor yourselves by extending the olive branch of reconciliation which may lead to an harmonious adjustment. Do not, as the report of the gentleman from Kent, (Mr. Chambers,) would counsel, shut your eyes and turn a deaf ear to the claims of those, who by every principle of nature, sanctioned by nature's God, are entitled to be considered your equals.

Mr. CHAMBERS said :

The gentleman has by way of boast, it would seem, told us he represents 160,000 constituents. Does he mean to claim any peculiar privilege on this floor on that account? If he expects this he labors under a sad mistake. My constituents, said Mr. C., are few in comparison, and he who now speaks for them, one of the humblest of the members on this floor. But if that gentleman or any other, thinks proper to prefer claims of superiority on the score of a large constituency, he had only to say he claimed a stand on the same platform with the most important personage here—aye, even if the other should represent one hundred and sixty times the number of the gentleman's 160,000. He claimed the same rights, the same privileges, and the same authority here for every individual member, no matter what might be the amount of his constituency.

He hoped the measures of the Convention were not to be carried by "authority"—above all, the authority of numbers not here to speak for themselves, and for whom he assumed the privilege of thinking, their delegates did not always exactly present the true index of sentiment.

As little did he regard the declaration of the gentleman, if designed as a *threat*.

Mr. PRESSTMAN said he did not so design it.

Mr. C. If the good people of Baltimore or any other part of the State prefer the new Constitution to the old one, they will of course vote for its ratification. Those who are not satisfied with it will of course vote against its ratification. But this would not make him adopt a principle he believed to be mischievous, nor abandon one he believed calculated to promote the interest and happiness of the people of the State.

He must be permitted again to say, he could see no propriety in this premature attack upon the report of the minority. Why not assail the report of the Chairman? It assumed the aggregate population. Why not attack the report of the two gentleman, (Mr. Lloyd and Mr. Howard,) who had united in discarding the principle of federal numbers? Federal numbers never had been known as an element in our system of representation till 1836—never. Under such circumstances, he felt it a just cause of remark, that this unreasonable mode of putting a black mark upon the report, to go out with it, to prejudge and prejudice it, had been indulged.

—

Erratum.—In No. 17, page 118, first paragraph, in the remarks of Mr. Buchanan in reply to Mr Biser, substitute the words "although, (according to his own account) he had been a long time in *travail*, he was most happily delivered at last" for these words: "He has *travailed* much and his new born delivered," which, by a typographical error found its way into the Register of that date.

TUESDAY, February 18, 1851.

The Convention met at eleven o'clock.

Prayer was made by the Rev. Mr. GRIFFITH.

The roll of the members was called.

PERSONAL EXPLANATION.

Mr. THOMAS said, that before the House proceeded to the regular business for the day, he desired to correct an error in our published debates, to which his attention had been kindly turned by a friend. He did not habitually read the debates. He very seldom looked at the printed journal. He relied upon his recollection of passing events in this body, and would not have known, but for the information derived from another, that in his absence, language imputed to him without warrant, had been commented on in the course of debate.

It would be remembered by the House, that several days ago, when the subject of apportioning representatives to the Legislature was under consideration, he had said, that the distribution of political power was the most difficult duty that this Convention had to perform. This remark, he supposed, did not admit of but one construction. And he was surprised to hear that the obvious meaning of this language was not apprehended by every one in whose presence it had been uttered.

Now, sir, what is meant by distributing political power, when applied to the action of this body engaged in apportioning representatives to the Legislature? We propose to give to the Legislature a law—making political power. We propose then to give to the voters of the several counties and to the city of Baltimore, the right to elect representatives to this Legislature. And in doing this, in authorising the voters, separately, to direct, by their suffrages, how the political power we are to give to the Legislature shall be exerted, we distribute to each citizen at the polls, in effect, a portion of that political power which the Constitution has conferred upon the Legislature. This, then, is the obvious meaning of his language. He had said nothing about offices or office-holders, and made no reference to the one or to the other.

While he was speaking, immediately after he had used the words he had now explained, he heard the gentleman from Kent, (Mr. Chambers,) say, "and offices." To that language, he made no reply. He considerod it at the time, to be one of those jests that the gentleman pleases sometimes to indulge in, and did not turn from the course of his remarks to notice it in any way.

Mr. T. referred to that part of the report of our debates wherein he is represented to have granted that the gentleman from Kent was right in saying that we were engaged in distributing offices, and said that he was authorised by the reporters, who were setting before him, to say, that there was, in that part of these reports, an error.

Mr. DONALDSON said it was proper for him to say a word upon this subject, because he was one of those who had referred to the expressions of the gentleman from Frederick, (Mr. Thomas,) in that interpretation of them of which that gentleman complained. Mr. DONALDSON referred to page 52 of the Register of Debates, in which the gentleman from Frederick is made, in express words, to assent to the remark of the the gentleman from Kent, (Mr. Chambers.) Such, too, was his, (Mr. D's.,) understanding, at the time; and he had not had the slightest idea of perverting the meaning of the gentleman from Frederick —nothing could be further from his intention or desire. Of course he did not now mean to controvert the statement of that gentleman in regard to the words he used, or his own meaning in using them. He merely rose to show that he, (Mr. D.,) had not intentionally misconstrued the remarks made, or which he supposed had been made by the gentleman from Frederick.

The journal of yesterday was then read and approved.

THE CONVENTION AND ITS BUSINESS.

Mr. GWINN rose and said, that upon consultation with several gentlemen of the Convention, he had decided to modify the resolution of which he had given notice, so far as to put it into the following form:

Resolved, That the Convention will hereafter meet at ten o'clock, and that no motion to adjourn, shall be in order before three o'clock.

The resolution having been read,

Mr. GWINN demanded the previous question.

Mr. STEWART, of Baltimore city, asked the yeas and nays on the adoption of the resolution.

Mr. SMITH requested Mr. GWINN to withdraw the demand for the previous question, for a moment.

Mr. GWINN declined to withdraw.

Mr. CHAMBERS, of Kent, rose to a question of order. He submitted that by a rule of the House, a motion to adjourn was always in order, and that this was a proposition to repeal that rule.

The PRESIDENT. The chair thinks that the last part of the order, will be entirely noperative and void; because every parliamentary body can adjourn at any time it pleases.. If the resolution should be adopted, the Convention could *non obstante*, adjourn the next moment.

Mr. BRENT, of Baltimore city, called for a division of the question.

Some conversation followed on the point of order, as to the divisibility of the resolution under the rule.

The PRESIDENT decided that it was in order to divide the resolution.

And a division was ordered.

The question was then stated to be on the first branch of the resolution, to wit: that hereafter the hour of the daily meeting of the Convention, should be ten o'clock.

The yeas and nays were then ordered.

Mr. SPRIGG. I desire, with the permission of the Convention, to put an enquiry to the gentleman from Baltimore city, (Mr. Gwinn.) Has the gentleman abandoned the pledge which he yesterday gave, that he would to-day offer a resolution pending that the Convention shall adjourn, *sine die*, in five weeks from this time?

Mr. GWINN. My own individual opinions have undergone no change. But, when I rose to offer the resolution now before the Convention, I stated that different gentlemen had expressed their opinion, that the business of the Convention would be better promoted by the substitute. If this substitute should be adopted, and if within a few days, I shall find that it does not facilitate the transaction of the public business, I shall then fall back upon the original proposition of which I gave notice yesterday, and shall introduce it. I have postponed it for the present, in deference to the wishes of others. Is the gentleman satisfied?

The question on the first branch of the resolution of Mr. GWINN, was then taken, and was decided in the affirmative, yeas 44, nays 23.

So the first branch of the resolution was adopted, and the Convention decided that hereafter the daily hour of meeting, should be ten o'clock.

The question then recurred on the second branch of the resolution, (prohibiting a motion to adjourn before the hour of three o'clock.)

Mr. GWINN desired, he said, to withdraw the second branch of the amendment.

The PRESIDENT said, if no objection was made, the gentleman could withdraw it.

No objection having been made,

The second branch of the resolution was withdrawn.

EVENING SESSIONS.

Mr. MITCHELL offered the following order:

Resolved, That after to-day the Convention will meet every evening at half-past four o'clock.

The order having been read,

Mr. MITCHELL demanded the previous question.

Mr. STEWART, of Baltimore city, asked the yeas and nays on the adoption of the order, which were ordered.

There was a second to the demand for the previous question, and the main question was ordered, and having been taken, the resolution, by yeas 33, nays 35, was rejected.

THE RULES.

The PRESIDENT announced the following gentlemen as composing the committee which had yesterday been ordered to be appointed, to revise the rules, and report such alterations and amendments thereto, as they might think expedient.

Messrs. RICAUD, SCHLEY, BUCHANAN, BROWN and MORGAN.

THE LEGISLATIVE DEPARTMENT.

On motion of Mr. FIERY, the Convention resumed the consideration of the special order of the day, being the report heretofore submitted by Mr. JOHNSON, as chairman of the committee on the Legislative department.

The fifth section (see yesterday's Registry,) being under consideration,

Mr. THOMAS had moved to amend it by inserting after the word "day," in the second line, the words "in the year eighteen hundred and fifty-four."

And the pending question was on the adoption of the said amendment.

BIENNIAL SESSION.

Mr. DIRICKSON, (to the President.) Is it now in order for me to make the motion, of which I yesterday gave notice, to reconsider the vote heretofore taken on the second section,

The PRESIDENT. It is in order.

Mr. DIRICKSON. I make the motion.

The PRESIDENT. What is the precise motion of the gentleman?

Mr. DIRICKSON. I desire to move a reconsideration of the vote of the Convention adopting the amendment of the gentleman from Queen Anne, (Mr. Spencer,) to the second section of the report.

Some conversation followed between the Chair and Mr. DIRICKSON, as to the mode by which the object could be attained, when

Mr. DIRICKSON moved to reconsider the vote of the Convention adopting the second section of the report.

The question was taken, and by ayes 32, noes 20, the vote was reconsidered.

Mr. DIRICKSON then moved to reconsider the vote by which the amendment of Mr. SPENCER had been adopted, (i. e. the amendment submitting to the people the question of annual or biennial sessions.

The question was taken, and the vote was reconsidered.

And the question then being on agreeing to Mr. SPENCER's amendment,

Some conversation followed on a point of order.

Mr. SPENCER expressed his desire to withdraw the amendment.

Some conversation followed on the point order.

The PRESIDENT then expressed his opinion that under a liberal construction of the sixteenth rule, the gentleman from Queen Anne, (Mr. Spencer,) might withdraw his amendment.

Mr. SPENCER thereupon withdrew the amendment.

The question then recurred on the adoption of the section.

Mr. WELLS moved to amend the said second section, by adding at the end thereof the following:

"And the sessions of the General Assembly shall be annual."

Mr. WELLS asked the yeas and nays on the said amendment, which were ordered, and being taken, resulted as follows:

Affirmative—Messrs. Chapman, President, Morgan, Donaldson, Dorsey, Wells, Merrick, Buchanan, Welch, Constable, Chambers, of Cecil, McCullough, Sprigg, Shriver, Biser, Gwinn, Brent, of Baltimore city, Sherwood, of Baltimore city, Ware, Anderson, Ege, Shower and Brown—22.

Negative—Messrs. Ricaud, Chambers, of Kent, Mitchell, Dalrymple, Bell, Ridgely, Lloyd, Dickinson, Sherwood, of Talbot, John Dennis, Williams, Hicks, Hodson, Phelps, Miller, Bowling, Spencer, George, Wright, Dirickson, Hearn, Jacobs, Thomas, Gaither, Annan, Stephenson, McHenry, Magraw, Nelson, Carter, Stewart, of Caroline, Stewart, of Baltimore city, Schley, Fiery, Neill, Harbine, Davis, Brewer, Waters, Weber, Hollyday, Fitzpatrick, Smith, Parke and Cockey—45.

So the amendment was rejected.

Mr. PARKE moved to amend said second section by adding at the end thereof, the following proviso:

"*Provided*, That the Delegates shall be elected for one year and the Senators for three years, (one-third of the latter annually, as near as may be,) as soon as a majority of the legal voters of the State, at some general election shall have decided in favor of a change from biennial to annual sessions of the Legislature; and the General Assembly shall have the power to provide by law for taking the sense of the people as aforesaid, and for making all arrangement necessary to carry such change into effect, should a majority of the legal voters determine in favor thereof."

Mr. PARKE said he did not desire to interpose any delay. He was in favor of biennial sessions at present, but that there should be the power in the Legislature, to change the time so soon as the people could be relieved from direct taxation. This, he was inclined to believe, would accord with the feelings of the people themselves.

The question was taken, and the amendment was rejected.

The question then recurred on the adoption of the said section, as amended.

Mr. PHELPS demanded the previous question.

Mr. McHENRY enquired of the chair, whether the action of the Convention would be final, or whether it would again be in order to move a reconsideration.

The PRESIDENT said that, under the rule, it had been the practice to reconsider more than once.

The call for the previous question was then seconded.

The main question was ordered, and having been taken, the section, as amended, was adopted.

The Convention now resumed the consideration of the motion of Mr. THOMAS, to amend the fifth section, as amended, by striking out, in the second line, the words, "in every," and inserting in lieu thereof, the words, "in the year 1854, and on the same day in every second year."

Mr. THOMAS made some explanatory remarks as to the effect of the amendment which he had offered, which was intended to make the bill consistent throughout, stating that it was rendered necessary by the amendment to the fifth section which had been engrafted in it on the motion of the gentleman from Queen Anne, (Mr. Spencer.) He briefly showed what would be the effect of the adoption of the fifth section as it had been amended, without the amendment he (Mr. T.) had now proposed, and then consistency would be restored to the bill by the adoption of his amendment.

Mr. DONALDSON said the whole of the programme of the gentleman from Frederick was entirely consistent with his opinion in favor of biennial sessions. But, as he illustrated in a few explanatory remarks, it was directly in conflict with the amendment he (Mr. D.) had offered.

Mr. CHAMBERS said:

The bill as framed by the committee contemplated annual sessions. A vote of the House apparently decisive, had expressed a preference for biennial sessions. The amendments so far adopted, would require the first election for the first biennial session to be held in the fall of 1852, unless, indeed, it should be designed to have the election sixteen months before the session commenced, instead of four, which he could not presume to be the design. The amendment now offered by the gentleman from Frederick, (Mr. Thomas,) was calculated to foreclose that question. He thought it ought to await the action of a full house. He regarded it as an important question, and thought the elections ought to be thrown upon the even years, so that every alternate election should occur at the same time as the election for electors of President.

It was certainly desirable in every general election to furnish every facility and every inducement to voters to express their opinions. He thought it quite undeniable that a more full expression of popular sentiment could be expected, when in addition to the interest excited by the election for State officers, there would be added the further interest of a Presidential election. To this motive was added another—that of economy. Why incur the unnecessary expense of two elections, when you gain all the advantages, and indeed additional advantages, by having one? Not only would the number of voters be diminished, and the permanent expenses of the counties be unnecessarily increased, but we are now asked to provide for a third annual session of the Legislature to enable us to bring about these mischiefs. He held it to be altogether unnecessary to hold three successive sessions to carry out the details of the provisions to be adopted in the new Constitution. It ought all to be done in a single session—certainly in two.

Mr. THOMAS briefly replied that as the House had already determined as to the time of elections, that question was settled. It had also incorporated the amendment offered by the gentleman from Queen Anne's, to the fifth section, and that without the present amendment, rendered the bill a deformity. He stated that he had agreed to the amendment making it imperative on the Legislature to hold a second session, because he believed that the Legislature would have done so without such provision. His sole object was to make one section in accordance with another, and his amendment would be in strict conformity with the provisions agreed on by the House.

Mr. MERRICK said he certainly preferred that the sessions of the Legislature should be held in even years. If the amendment of the gentleman from Frederick was not adopted, the consequence would be, that the Delegates would be elected eighteen months before the session.

Mr. CHAMBERS. The gentleman from Frederick, (Mr. Thomas,) was mistaken in the fact that the House had passed upon the question of the time of the election. His friend from Anne Arundel, (Mr. Donaldson,) had offered an amendment to the third section, which was intended to settle that question, but being one of importance it was passed over informally in consequence of the absence of a large number of members. It was no great evidence of temerity, therefore, to presume, as he had ventured to do, that the House would provide for an election four months prior to the session, rather than sixteen months before the members elect would take their seats. As the matter stood, without the amendment now for the first time offered, that was the only question. In regard to this amendment, he must again ask, "*cui bono?*" The gentleman had heard his objections, very briefly to be sure, but very distinctly stated; first, that every one who encouraged the exercise of this great prerogative of a freeman—the right of suffrage—should multiply the facilities and inducements to a full expression of popular sentiment; and, secondly, that every motive of economy was disregarded by the proposed measure. He could not but invite the attention of the House to the fact that the gentleman had not even made a beginning to answer these objections.

Mr. THOMAS suggested that if the gentleman from Kent was willing to do so, they might go back to the third section and test the sense of the House by a vote, which would settle the difficulty.

Mr. CHAMBERS. The reason which induced the House to pass informally by the third section is of greater force now. If so important a measure should be determined by so thin a House as we now have, it would of course be reconsidered when absent members resume their seats. He wished the subject still to remain open.

The question was then stated to be the amendment of Mr. THOMAS.

Mr. THOMAS asked the yeas and nays.

Which were ordered; and

Being taken, resulted as follows:

Affirmative—Messrs. Buchanan, Bell, Welch, Ridgely, Lloyd, Dickinson, Sherwood of Talbot, Chambers of Cecil, McCullough, McLane, Spencer, George, Wright, Thomas, Shriver, Gaither, Biser, Annan, Stephenson, McHenry, Magraw, Nelson, Carter, Stewart of Caroline, Gwinn, Brent of Baltimore city, Ware, Harbine, Brewer, Anderson, Weber, Hollyday, Fitzpatrick, Ege, Shower and Brown—36.

Negative—Messrs. Chapman, President, Ricaud, Chambers of Kent, Mitchell, Donaldson, Dorsey, Wells, Dalrymple, Merrick, John Dennis, Williams, Hicks, Hodson, Sprigg, Bowling, Dirickson, Jacobs, Stewart of Baltimore city, Schley, Fiery, Neill, Davis, Waters, Smith, Parke and Cockey—27.

So the amendment was agreed to.

The question then was on the adoption of the said fifth section, as amended;

The question was taken, and

The section as amended, was adopted.

Mr. Chambers, of Kent, gave notice that when there should be a full Convention, he would move to reconsider the vote by which the amendment of Mr. Thomas, had been adopted.

The sixth section was then read as follows:

Sec. 6. The General Assembly may continue their first two sessions after the adoption of this Constitution, as long as in the opinion of the two Houses, the public interest may require it, but all subsequent regular sessions of the General Assembly shall be closed on the tenth day of March next ensuing the time of their commencement, unless the same shall be closed at an earlier day by the agreement of the two Houses.

Mr. Parke moved to amend the section by striking out "two sessions" and inserting "session."

The question was taken; and

The amendment was rejected.

And then the section was adopted.

The seventh section was read as follows:

Sec. 7. No person shall be eligible as a Senator or Delegate who, at the time of his election, is not a citizen of the United States, and who has not resided at least three years next preceding the day of his election in the State, and the last year thereof in the which he may be chosen to represent, if such shall have been so long established, and if not, then in the county from which in whole or in part, the same may have been formed; nor shall any person be eligible as a Senator, unless he shall have also attained the age of years, nor as a Delegate unless he shall have attained the age of twenty-one years at the time of his election.

Mr. Thomas moved to fill the blank in the fourth line, with the words "county, city, or district."

Mr. Dorsey moved to amend the amendment by striking out the word "district."

After a brief explanation between Messrs. Thomas and Dorsey—

Mr. Thomas accepted Mr. Dorsey's amendment.

The amendment thus modified, was agreed to.

And the same words,

On motion of Mr. Thomas,

Were inserted in the fifth line of the section.

Mr. Sprigg moved to amend the seventh section, as follows:

Strike out in the second line, the words "is not a citizen of the United States," and insert, "has not been a citizen of the United States for at least five years"

Mr. Brown. This is an important amendment. I ask the yeas and nays.

Mr. Thomas called for a division of the question, first on striking out.

Mr. Dorsey said:

He was opposed to the proposition of the gentleman from Prince George's, (Mr. Sprigg,) the object of which was, to postpone the rights of naturalized citizens. Was any beneficial object to be effected by it? He saw no reason for such a provision. When the old Constitution was formed it was not considered necessary that either the Governor, a Senator or a member of the House of Delegates, should be a citizen, nor was it considered that voters should be so until the year 1836. That, however, was wrong; and the constitutional amendments of 1836 provided the remedy. But it appeared to him to be altogether unnecessary to require the lapse of five years after naturalization before a naturalized foreigner can be admitted to the privileges of a native born citizen.

He was unwilling to impose unnecessary restraints on naturalized citizens; they ought to have the same rights as natives. There was not the least danger of the State being so overrun by naturalized citizens, as to render them dangerous to the native born population. Maryland held out no such inducements to their settlement in it, in such excessive numbers, as did the new States. If naturalized citizens settle among us and give proof of their attachment to our institutions, by so conducting themselves as to obtain the respect and confidence of the community, their fellow-citizens think proper to elect them to responsible stations, he would not interpose in this respect any restriction to the wishes of the people. He saw no benefit in its interposition—no evil resulting from its omission. He would deem it wrong to put a limit of this kind on the free exercise of the elective franchise, and eligibility to office. In the State of Maine, he believed, there was a restriction of this kind, where the population is made up, in some portions of the State, of English and Irish, and other foreigners, which rendered it necessary, in the opinion of those who framed the Constitution of that State, to impose such restriction.

But in this State, he repeated, we had no ground of apprehension of an excessive or dangerous influx of foreign population; and if the people chose to elect a naturalized citizen to an office of trust and honor, he knew no reason why they should be restricted in their choice.

Mr. Sprigg interposed and said, that if the gentleman from Anne Arundel, (Mr. Dorsey,) would yield the floor for the purpose, he, (Mr. S.,) would relieve the gentleman from the necessity of further discussion.

He, (Mr. S.,) had no intention to excite debate on this or any other question. With the permission of the gentleman, he would withdraw his amendment.

Mr. Dorsey yielding the floor for the purpose;

Mr. Sprigg withdrew his amendment.

Mr. McHenry moved to amend the section by striking out all from the words "United States," to the word "nor" in the seventh line, and inserting "and of this State."

Mr. McH. said, that the requirement of three years residence would be avoided by the adoption of his amendment. He thought the people were always sufficiently jealous of any encroachment on their rights, to keep a strict guard over them; and he would oppose the proposition to impose a restriction, where the choice of the people should be untrammeled. An individual may possess every requisite qualification; may stand well in the estimation of his fellow citizens, and in every respect may be just the man required by the public wishes and the public interests; but because he has not resided in the county exactly the time prescribed, the people are to be debarred from electing him. It did not require a multiplicity of words to show the impolicy of such a restriction; and he would, therefore, refrain from troubling the House with any further remarks.

Mr. Phelps said:

That if the principle was to be admitted that it is wrong in any case, to put a restriction on the right of election, we may as well say at once that a person may be taken from the county of Dorchester, to represent the county of Harford, or from Harford to represent Dorchester, or do away at once, with all qualification on the score of residence. But, to do this, would be in violation of the principles on which our political institutions are founded. It was proper that there should be a certain prescribed term of residence before a citizen is eligible to offices of trust and emolument.

He hoped the amendment of the gentleman from Harford would not prevail. He could see no force in the argument the gentleman had brought forward in support of his proposition.

Mr. McHenry replied, that if the gentleman from Dorchester could see no argument in what he, (Mr. McH.,) had advanced, the gentleman from Dorchester certainly did not meet it with any argument.

Mr. Phelps explained. He had said he did not comprehend the force of the argument of the gentleman from Harford, but he disavowed any intention to use that language in any disrespectful sense.

The question was then taken on the amendment of Mr. McHenry; and

It was rejected.

Mr. Dorsey moved to amend said section by striking out "three" in the third line, and inserting in lieu thereof "two."

Mr. Dorsey said that hitherto twelve months residence had been what was required for a Delegate, and three years for a Senator. It occurred to him that two years would be quite enough for either. If a gentleman well known in the neighboring States of Pennsylvania or Delaware, near the confines of Maryland, and generally respected, should move his residence over the line into our State, it would not be necessary, if he were known and esteemed, that he should have a long residence to qualify him for office. It was only necessary for the candidate to have been a sufficient length of time in the State and county, to know what were the interests of the State and of his immediate constituents. If the people knew him to be properly qualified, no public inconvenience would result from their electing him after a residence of two years. The restriction would operate on the native, equally with the naturalized citizen.

The question was then taken, and the amendment of Mr. Dorsey was rejected.

Mr. Merrick moved to amend said section by filling the blank, in the eighth line, with "thirty."

Mr. Schley moved to fill the blank with "twenty-five."

And the question was first on the longest time.

The amendment of Mr. Merrick was rejected.

And the amendment of Mr. Schley was agreed to.

The section was further verbally amended on motion of Mr. Dorsey.

The section, as amended, was then adopted.

The eighth section of the report was read and adopted, as follows:

Section 8th. No member of Congress, or person holding any Civil or Military office under the United States, shall be eligible to a seat in the General Assembly, and if any person shall, after his election as a member of either House of the General Assembly, be elected to Congress or be appointed to any office, Civil or Military, under the government of the United States, his acceptance thereof shall vacate his seat.

The ninth section was read as follows:

Section 9th. No Priest, Clergyman or Teacher of any religious persuasion, society or sect, and no person holding any civil office of profit under this State, except Justices of the Peace, shall be capable of having a seat in the General Assembly.

Mr. Gwinn moved to amend it by striking out the word "civil" in the second line.

On a question put by Mr. Spencer as to the effect of this amendment, a brief conversation took place, in which Mr. Dorsey, Mr. Gwinn, and Mr. Spencer took part, when Mr. Ridgely suggested that his colleague, (the Reverend Mr. Chandler,) was absent from his seat owing to severe indisposition in his family, and that he wished to be heard on this question. He therefore asked of the courtesy of the House to pass over this matter informally for the present.

The President said, that under the practice of the Convention, unanimous consent would be required to pass over the section informally.

Some conversation followed, after which,

On motion of Mr. McHenry, the consideration of the section was postponed until the other sections of the report should have been considered.

The tenth section of the report was read as follows:

Section 10th. Every Senator and Delegate before he acts as such, shall take and subscribe the following oath or affirmation, viz: "I do solemnly swear, (or affirm as the case may be,) that I will support the Constitution of the United States, and the Constitution of the State of Maryland, and that I will faithfully discharge my duties as Senator, (or Delegate as the case may be,) without prejudice or partiality, and to the best of my ability."

Mr. CHAMBERS, of Kent, (with a view, he said, to avoid the multiplication of oaths,) offered a substitute oath.

Mr. SPENCER moved an amendment.

Some explanation followed between Messrs. CHAMBERS and SPENCER, and STEWART, of Caroline.

Mr. STEWART, of Caroline, moved to strike out the section.

Mr. CHAMBERS, of Kent, acquiescing in a suggestion of Mr. STEWART to that effect, withdrew his amendment.

The question was then taken on the motion of Mr. STEWART,

And the section was stricken out.

The eleventh section of the report was read, as follows:

Sec. 11th. The Senate, upon assembling, shall choose a President and its other officers, and the House of Delegates when assembled shall choose a Speaker and its other officers—each House shall be judge of the qualifications, elections and returns of its members, but a contested election shall be determined in such manner as shall be directed by law.

Mr. DORSEY, (to meet a suggestion of Mr. Chambers, of Kent,) moved to amend the said section by inserting after the word "determined," in the fifth line, the following:

"By the House in which such contests may arise."

The amendment was agreed to.

And the section, as amended, was adopted.

The twelfth section was read and adopted as follows:

Sec. 12th. A majority of each House shall constitute a quorum for the transaction of business, but a smaller number may adjourn from day to day, and may compel the attendance of absent members in such manner and under such penalties as each House may prescribe.

The thirteenth section was read and adopted, as follows:

Sec. 13th. The doors of each House and of committees of the whole shall be open, except when the business is such as ought to be kept secret.

The fourteenth section was read, as follows:

Sec. 14th. Each House shall keep a Journal of its proceedings and cause the same to be published—the yeas and nays of the members on any question shall, at the desire of any five of them, be entered on the journal.

Mr. STEPHENSON moved to amend by striking out "five," and inserting in lieu thereof "two."

The motion was rejected.

Mr. RICAUD moved to amend by striking out the last clause of the section, (in regard to the yeas and nays,

Mr. THOMAS stated that this amendment presupposes the case where a majority of members present may not wish their votes to go out to the world, and therefore do not desire to have the yeas and nays recorded. The number of five is specified, because it is believed that the House could never be in such a condition but that five members could be found ready to second a call for the yeas and nays. He thought the clause a novel one to be engrafted in a written Constitution.

Mr. RICAUD withdrew his amendment.

Mr. CHAMBERS moved to amend the section by providing that the yeas and nays should be ordered on the call of three, (instead of five) members of the *Senate.*

Mr. RICAUD suggested one.

Mr. CHAMBERS, of Kent, accepted the modification.

The amendment, as modified, was adopted.

And the section, as amended, was adopted.

The fifteenth section was read and adopted, as follows:

Sec. 15th. Neither House shall, without the consent of the other, adjourn for more than three days, nor to any other place than that in which the Houses shall be sitting, without the concurrent vote of two-thirds of the members present of both Houses.

The sixteenth section was then read, as follows:

Sec. 16th. The enacting clause of every bill shall be, "Be it enacted by the General Assembly of Maryland," and no law shall be enacted except by Bill.

Mr. DORSEY said, that if change, for the sake of change, was not the order of the day, he should prefer the language of the old Constitution. But if we were to have change, he would move to amend the said section by inserting after the word "the," in the first line, the words "commencement of the first."

Mr. CHAMBERS hoped, he said, that the Convention would stand by the language of the old Constitution so far as practicable.

The amendment of Mr. DORSEY was rejected.

Mr. STEWART, of Caroline, moved to amend the section by adding, at the end thereof, the words,

"And that all laws be passed by original Bill and not as supplement."

Mr. STEWART, of Caroline, pointed out the confusion and embarrassment, which were produced in the laws, by the practice of passing supplementary acts. The original law, embracing every variety of subjects, has been permitted to stand, and supplements have passed, until a very few lines of the original law remain in force. And it is impossible for the people to tell what is in force as law, or what has been repealed. Laws are enacted for all classes of the community, and should be plain and intelligible. All laws should be passed by original bill, and in the language of his amendment should embrace but one subject, and that subject should be described in the title of the law.

Mr. SPENCER said the amendment was one which would produce much difficulty. It would lead to great delay in legislation, and would furnish a crib from which to feed the printers.

Mr. STEWART replied, that the cost of printing, if the benefit and good that would result, was quadruple, should not prevent the passage of the amendment. The gentleman from Queen Anne's, had said that if would create a great crib for the printers. He,(Mr.S.,)knew not why there ought not to be a crib for printers, as well as one for lawyers, for surely the present mode of legislation is one of the latter kind. But in framing a Constitution for a great and growing State, we should not look to any one class of the community alone, but endeavor to secure the greatest good to the greatest number.

Mr. HARBINE expressed himself entirely favorable to the object of the amendment, but he could not see how the difficulty against which it was directed, could be overcome. One-half the members of the Legislature,would not know where to find these laws. If we are to provide for the codification of our system, then indeed this proper reform might be carried into effect. Without such codification, the gentleman from Caroline, could not get at the object of his amendment.

Mr. BROWN said the difficulty with him was this. If the Legislature put all the laws relating to a subject, which have not been repealed, into one, it would amount to a codification, and it would take a long time, perhaps twelve months, [Mr. Schley, in his seat, "twelve years."], to accomplish it.

Mr. SPENCER thought the subject was surrounded with difficulties. If every time we find a defect in a law, the Legislature is to re-enact it, there will be no end of legislation. Almost every law will have to be re-enacted, and the sessions must become interminable. He refered to the insolvent laws, and the attachment system, which would, in such cases, lead to long discussions, so as to protract the sittings of the Legislature.

Mr. STEWART, of Caroline, said that he felt a deep interest in the amendment that he had offered, because he thought it would remedy many of the evils that exist under the present mode of legislation, and work great good to the people of the State.

The gentleman from Queen Anne's, (Mr. Spencer,) has said that the adoption of the amendment, would lead to interminable sessions of the Legislature. He (Mr. S.) did not think so. If the plan he had proposed, had been adopted at the commencement of our State Government, the whole volume of laws, instead of swelling out to its present bulk and requiring a lifetime of study to know them, would not now exceed, three or four hundred pages, and would be understood by the most of the people. The existing evil calls for a remedy, and how else can it be applied except by a provision in the Constitution; and what better time can there be, to commence a new system of legislation than when the new Constitution has been adopted? It has repeatedly been urged, against the amendment, that members of the Legislature could not know what the laws were, and the gentleman from Anne Arundel, (Mr. Dorsey,) has said that they would have to go to a lawyer to get a simple amendment to a law drawn. There could not be no stronger argument in favor of the amendment than this. It is an acknowledgment that incompetent men, under the present system, may draft laws and get them passed in an imperfect form. How, he would ask, could the Legislature pass wise and judicious amendments to laws, when they knew not what the laws were. As well might you expect a man, who knew nothing of mechanics to repair an engine properly, as that the Legislature should amend a law wisely, when they knew nothing of the law that they were amending. Many amendatory supplements, now, require explanatory acts, and thus supplement is added to law, and law to supplement, until it requires judges, lawyers, and jurymen, to find out what the law is. There are many penal statutes that is of vital importance, that they should be understood and yet in many cases, they were so covered up amid supplements and amendments, that it is often difficult to find the true law. If a farmer or mechanic should desire to prove an account to be sent out of the State, or one against a deceased person, he doubted whether they could find the law. The laws are now so voluminous, that but few will incur the expense of their purchase.

The latter part of the amendment has met with the strongest opposition. Is it because it is something new? He was aware that there were many persons averse to change—that prefer old things and customs to new. This is an age of progress and improvement. We cannot look around anywhere in this great and flourishing Union, but what we see improvement and progress. There is no nobility in old usages and customs. Every thing is appreciated for its intrinsic worth.

What, he would ask, does the latter part of the amendment propose? "No law shall be revived or amended by reference to its title only." Is not that right and reasonable? Does not every one know that laws are often amended or revived by reference to their title only? This, then, is to prevent such mode of reviving and amending laws. Then again, "but in such case, all such parts of the act to be revived or amended, that are embraced in the object of the bill, shall be re-enacted and published at length. If this be adopted, the Legislature, before they can revive or amend a law, must have it before them. They must then know what it is they are to revive or amend. It is also proposed to have the laws codified. He was heartily in favor of it, and when they were codified, the amendment he had offered would keep them so. Without it, they would require codifying every ten years.

Mr. SPRIGG moved to amend the amendment of Mr. STEWART, of Caroline, by adding the following:

"And no law enacted by the Legislature, shall embrace more than one object, and that shall be described in its title, and no law shall be revised or amended by reference to its title only."

Mr. DORSEY said he thought it very important the qualifications of the persons employed in this work, should be well ascertained. No man should be permitted to discharge the duty who is not a sound and experienced lawyer. The codification of our system of laws would require great skill and care. The members of the General Assembly were incompetent to the discharge of such a duty. If it was required that the Legislature should go back to the commencement of our legal system, and codify all the laws, the qualifications for such a task would rarely, if ever, be found in any House of Delegates. He referred also to the price of printing the work, as imposing a great expense on the State, and the work, when completed, would be wosre than valueless. Every member of the Legislature would be required to familiarize himself with all its enactments before he would be competent to discharge the duties proposed to be assigned him.

Mr. SCHLEY suggested that the gentleman from Caroline, might better obtain his object by the mode adopted in the Constitution of the State of Missouri, which he read. That he considered to be the only feasible mode by which it could be done. A colleague of his had early in the session, suggested the appointment of a committee to revise the laws, but he could not find it in his file of journals If a commissioner were appointed, and the clause from the Missouri Constitution were added, the amendment might be simplified and made effective.

Mr. SPENCER notified the House that, at a proper time, he, if no other member of the Convention did so, would bring forward a proposition relative to arranging the laws in a system. In this way, he thought, the object of the gentleman from Caroline, might be accomplished. The great labor and expense to which the amendment of the gentleman would lead, was his great objection to it in its present shape.

Mr. STEWART said this was a subject which had not occurred to his mind, at a very recent period. It was one which had given him much reflection. He had no objection to pass over his proposition for the present.

And then, pending the question,

The Convention adjourned until to-morrow morning at ten o'clock.

WEDNESDAY February 19, 1851.

The Convention, pursuant to the order yesterday adopted, met at 10 o'clock.

Prayer was made by the Rev. Mr. GRAUFF.

The roll was called.

Mr. GWINN, (to the PRESIDENT.) I understand there is not a quorum present.

The PRESIDENT. No quorum, sir.

Mr. GWINN. I move that the doorkeeper be sent to notify the absent members to attend.

Ordered accordingly.

Mr. DAVIS moved that the Convention proceed to the orders of the day.

The PRESIDENT stated, that the Convention was not in a condition to proceed to business, no quorum being present.

Mr. DAVIS said, he hoped that fact would be noted on the journal.

After the lapse of a few minutes—a quorum being present,

The journal of yesterday was read, and having been amended as to an error in the statement of Mr. THOMAS' amendment, was approved.

LOTTERIES.

The PRESIDENT laid before the Convention a petition of sundry citizens of the city of New York, praying the Convention to incorporate in the organic law of this State, a provision entirely, and forever prohibiting the drawing of lotteries within the State of Maryland.

The petition having been read,

Mr. DONALDSON moved that it be printed on the journal, (omitting the names, with the exception of the first two or three.)

Mr. SHRIVER moved that the petition be referred to the committee on the legislative department;

Mr. DORSEY expressed himself in favor of the reference, but opposed to the printing of the petition.

It was an innovation upon the practice of the Convention, and would, he thought, open the door to an expense which could not readily be calculated.

Mr. DONALDSON said, his motion to print, embraced only the petition, not the names. The petition was very short, and as to the precedent, he thought it could lead to no difficulty. But few petitions were presented here. This came from a sister State, and as a matter of comity, he thought it well that it should be printed

Mr. BROWN thought it was a doubtful question whether the petition ought even to be received. If it was, the Convention might be called upon to receive petitions upon every other subject which the people of other States might think proper to intrude upon them. The Convention had not honored its own citizens by printing their petitions, and he saw no reason why they should treat petitions from other States with more respect than the petitions of our own people.

Mr. SMITH suggested that the petition was very short, and that the printing could not be a matter worth speaking of.

Whilst on the floor, he desired to present a petition.

The PRESIDENT said, the petition before the Convention must first be disposed of. The gentleman, (Mr. Smith,) could present his petition, after the pending proposition should have been disposed of.

Mr. DORSEY said, he very much misunderstood the question, if the courtesy due from one State to another, had any thing to do with this matter. The petition did not come from the State of New York, but from some persons, lottery dealers or others, in New York. He did not think that the Convention should show greater respect to them, than to their own citizens.

Mr. DONALDSON said, that in making the motion to print, he had not the slightest idea that it would lead to a discussion. It seemed to him that the minds of gentlemen were filled with chimeras. The petition showed one of the great evils of our lottery system—it showed that we were not only doing evil in our own State, but sanctioning it in other States.

Mr. D. gave notice that it was his intention to introduce a proposition, the object of which was to bring the present lottery system to a close.

In speaking of the courtesy which was due, he did not mean to say that this petition came from the legal constituted authorities of the State. He intended merely to say, that this was a case in which laws of our own State, bad in themselves, had a tendency to demoralize the citizens of New York as well as the citizens of Maryland, and he thought that a respectful complaint and remonstrance against them, should be placed upon the journal.

As to loading the journals down with such matter, he did not think that any difficulty was to be apprehended from that source. If the petition had come from our own citizens on a subject of similar importance, he should have moved that it be printed.

Mr. Buchanan said:

He was utterly opposed to the motion of the gentleman from Anne Arundel, (Mr. Donaldson.) It was the beginning of evil; no man could know where it would terminate, if this Convention, from comity, was to be called upon to print the petitions of citizens of other States. Gentlemen might be called upon to present petitions of a very different and very exciting character. Upon what principle of comity, of justice or equality, could his friend get rid of such petitions if this was printed?

Now, he, [Mr. B.,] gave notice, that if this proposition should prevail, he might himself be called upon within a few days to present a petition from people of our own State, relating to a subject of very great interest to them, and which he, in pursuance of this order, if it should be adopted, might ask to be placed on the journal. He should not ask it because he did not think it proper to do so—but if he did so, he could not see how the gentleman from Anne Arundel, [Mr. Donaldson,] could oppose it.

Mr. Brown. I move that the petition be laid upon the table.

Mr. B. did not press his motion—

Mr. Thomas taking the floor.

Mr. T. suggested that, if a petition should be received from the people of a foreign State, because the object of it happened to accord with our own notions of morality, the question must arise, what was the Convention to do, if a petition should be impertinently presented here upon which we chose to judge for ourselves, whether it was moral or not? Upon that ground he hoped that the petition would be rejected altogether.

If the Convention should receive a petition on one subject, because it was believed that the effect was good, it might be called upon to receive petitions upon another, because the people of another State said, that the effect was injurious and pestilential. He hoped the Convention would reject the petition.

Mr. Donaldson. I withdraw the motion to print.

Mr. Brown said, he would now substitute for the motion which he had made to lay the petition on the table, the motion suggested by the gentleman from Frederick, [Mr. Thomas,] that the petition be rejected.

Mr. Thomas now modified his motion, so as to substitute for it a motion, that the petition be laid upon the table.

Mr. Stewart, of Caroline, thought that if this petition should be laid upon the table, and thus slightly passed over, it might be considered disrespectful to the people of the State of New York. He thought that the Convention ought to treat with the utmost respect every petition that came from the other States of the Union.

Mr. Merrick called for the reading of the petition.

Mr. Thomas briefly re-stated the ground of his objection to the petition.

Mr. Merrick thought, he said, that this was an impertinent interference with our business.

Mr. Thomas. I think so, too.

The question was then taken on the motion of Mr. Thomas.

And the motion having been decided in the affirmative,

The petition was laid upon the table.

Mr. Smith presented a petition of sundry citizens of Allegany county, praying that a provision may be engrafted in the new Constitution, that the privilege to sell intoxicating liquors shall not be granted to any person in any part of the State, except the same shall be sanctioned, or approved of by a majority of the voters in the election district where the same is to be sold.

The petition having been read,

Mr. Smith moved its reference to committee, No. 14

Mr. Dorsey moved a select committee.

The motion of Mr. Smith was agreed to, and

The petition was referred to committee No. 14.

The Convention then proceeded to the orders of the day.

LEGISLATIVE DEPARTMENT.

The Convention resumed the consideration of the report of the committee on the legislative department.

When the Convention adjourned yesterday, the following section was under consideration:

Sec. 16th. The enacting clause of every bill shall be, "Be it enacted by the General Assembly of Maryland," and no law shall be enacted except by bill.

Mr. Stewart, of Caroline, had moved to amend the said section by adding at the end thereof, the following words:

"And that all laws be passed by original bill and not as supplement."

And Mr. Sprigg had moved to amend the amendment by adding the following words:

"And no law enacted by the Legislature, shall embrace more than one object, and that shall be described by its title, and no law shall be revised or amended by reference to its title only."

Mr. STEWART, of Caroline, suggested that the section should lie over informally for the present.

Mr. SCHLEY suggested to the gentleman to withdraw his amendment for the present.

Mr. STEWART withdrew his amendment, (intending to offer it again.)

Mr. SPRIGG also withdrew his amendment, with the intention to offer it again in a different place.

Mr. DORSEY moved a reconsideration of the vote on the sixteenth section, with the view to offer an amendment.

Mr. D. explained that his object in offering the amendment, was to prevent a double or doubtful construction of the phraseology of the section, and from a desire that the Constitution, in all its parts, should be as clear and explicit as possible.

Mr. BROWN was in favor of the reconsideration, and said that if the motion should prevail, he would move to substitute the language of the old Constitution.

The vote on the adoption of the section was reconsidered.

Mr. BROWN moved to amend said section, by striking out, in the first line, the words "the enacting clause of every bill shall be," and inserting in lieu thereof, the words "that the style of all laws run thus."

Mr. SCHLEY moved to amend the amendment by striking out the words "run thus," and substituting in lieu thereof, the words "of this State shall be."

Mr. BROWN accepted the modification.

The amendment of Mr. SCHLEY was agreed to.

And the sixteenth section, as amended, was adopted.

The seventeenth section of the bill was read as follows:

Sec. 17th. Any bill may originate in either House of the General Assembly, and be altered, amended or rejected by the other, but no bill shall have the force of a law until it be read on three different days in each House, unless in case of urgency three-fourths of the House, where such bill is depending, shall dispense with this rule.

Mr. PHELPS moved to amend said section, by striking out in the first line, the words, "any bill," and inserting in lieu thereof the following:

"Bills for raising revenue or levying taxes, shall originate in the House of Delegates, but the Senate may alter, amend or reject them as other bills.

Mr. PHELPS said:

In offering the amendment just read, he felt no particular personal interest. He had done so, because he regarded the section, as reported by the committee, as unusual, and contrary to the well recognized principles, in the legislation of the whole country.

The origination of what is familiarly called "money-bills," is confined to the immediate representative branch of the Legislature, in most, if not all, the States of the Union. In fact, *in all the States*, so far as he had examined. The same principle was recognized in the Constitution of the United States.

This is the case, also, in the Parliament of Great Britain. The House of Commons has the sole right of levying taxes, and of proposing measures of revenue. This principle, in this country, was doubtless borrowed from the Constitution of England, and as public opinion, had so long sanctioned it, he saw no reason for departing from it now.

This amendment confined the origination of all bills for levying taxes, or raising revenue, to the House of Delegates, but authorizes the Senate to alter, change, or amend, all such bills. This is a departure from the principles of the present Constitution of Maryland. The tenth section of the Constitution, gives to the House of Delegates, the right to levy taxes, &c., and the eleventh goes on to define, what may, and what may not, be regarded as money-bills, so as the one House should not infringe upon the rights of the other. The construction given to these sections in the Maryland Senate, was always very strict, and denied to that body the right to make the slightest modifications, or the most trifling alteration, in any bill which had for its object, the levying of taxes, or the disposing, in any manner, of the public revenue.

Long experience in the Senate, had convinced him, that there should be, at least, some enlargement of power upon the subject. Bills often came to that body from the House, and for want of power to make perhaps some slight alteration, or amendment, the bill failed to become a law, when the main features of the bill were approved by the Senate.

Mr. PHELPS said, in order to avoid the two extremes, he had proposed this amendment, and if it be engrafted upon the Constitution, the Senate may amend money bills, although they may not originate them. It will doubtless be said, if the Senate possess the power to amend a bill of this character, that they may so change the features of the bill, as to some extent, to conflict with the design of the House, in its origination. If so, when returned to the House for its subsequent action, the House can but reject the amendment, and adhere to the original proposition. The power to amend money bills exists in the Senate of the United States, and is frequently exercised by that body, without injury, so far as he knew, to the public service.

The theory, Mr. President, of our Government is, that in the construction of our legislative bodies, one house should be regarded as the popular branch, reflecting the popular will, whilst the other, is farther removed from the people, and should be more independent, and more conservative in its character. It is true this principle, in these later days, have been much infringed upon, and to some extent at least, both Houses have been merged into popular branches. The subsequent history of the country, will develop the fact, whether this be, or be not, an improvement. For his part he was free to say, he would like to see the Senate what it was designed to be, by the fathers of our country, a highly independent and conservative branch of the Government.

But, Mr. President, although this principle, as before remarked, has to some extent been infringed upon, yet we still recognize two distinct branches of our Legislature, and the House of Delegates is regarded as the popular branch of the Government and, therefore, more immediately responsible to the people for their action.

For this reason, he said, he preferred to confine to the House of Delegates, the power of levying taxes, and of raising revenue, and was unwilling to give to the Senate powers not delegated to it by any other State Constitution, so far as he knew in the whole Union, and not recognized either, in the Constitution of the General Government.

Again, if we admit for the sake of the argument, that both branches of the Legislature is equally popular, and equally dependent upon the people for their power; if we admit that both branches are elevated to their position from the same source, and are equally dependent upon the people for their continuation in office; still he preferred the House of Delegates should exclusively exercise this power. They were emphatically the popular branch of the Legislature. They were elected for a shorter term, and were more immediately, and more distinctly responsible to the people; and besides they were more numerous.

The Senate as now organized, is composed of twenty-one members, and the House of Delgates would therefore, in his estimation, more fully and more truthfully represent the opinions and the wishes of all class of the community, than would the Senate. The power of levying taxes, is perhaps one of the highest prerogatives of a free Government, and should therefore be properly guarded. He was unwilling for his part, to see long established usages in this respect departed from without good and sufficient reasons.

Mr. MERRICK said, he thought the bill had better remain as it was. This notion of denying to the Senate the privilege of originating money-bills, was an obsolete idea. It was behind the times, and originated in a jealousy of an aristocratic branch. There was such a branch in England, and probably there had been similar branches here. But things were all changed. Here we were now all democratic. He saw no necessity for prohibiting one branch of the legislature, any more than the other, from originating laws. Both branches must concur in passing a bill—and both branches ought to have the privilege of originating all such bills, as in their opinion, the interests of the people might require. Let us not keep up obsolete usages, when the reasons which called them into being had ceased to exist.

Mr. DORSEY was opposed to the amendment. He did not think that, in view of what would be the organization of the Legislature of the State of Maryland, or, in fact, of what that organization now was, that such an amendment ought to prevail.

He referred to the principle upon which the restriction as to money-bills had been originally placed in the Constitution, (which was, that the House of Delegates, being then the territorial branch of the Legislature, should alone levy taxes on the people,) and to the inconveniences and delays in legislation which he had himself witnessed from the practical operation of the restrictive clause. He was satisfied that, in this State, there was no necessity for a restriction in either branch. Bills could not become laws except by the concurrence of both Houses; and there was no fear that the legislation would not be equal and impartial.

Mr. PHELPS directed the attention of the Convention to the article of the old Constitution, placing restraint upon the Senate in regard to money-bills. Mr. P. agreed with the gentleman from Anne Arundel, [Mr. Dorsey,] that great inconveniences had arisen under that particular clause; and to get rid of that difficulty, he [Mr. P.] had offered his amendment giving to the Senate the power to change or amend such bills.

It was said, that this restriction was an obsolete idea. But he found that it had been adopted in various new constitutions of different States, within a few years past, [in all of which the Senate was elected by the people.] He thought it highly proper that the immediate representatives of the people should have the sole power to originate money-bills—but that the right to alter, to change and amend them should be given to the Senate. It was not yet certain that the House of Delegates would not remain the territorial branch of the Legislature. The basis of representation had not yet been settled. The Convention, however, could dispose of the amendment as it thought proper. He should be satisfied with the decision, whatever it might be.

Mr. DORSEY suggested that the same reason existed for giving to the Senate the power to originate, that gave them the power to alter or amend; and that, to be consistent, the Convention must adopt the principle of the old Constitution, and leave them no power to do either.

Mr. PHELPS. I will only say, that the Senate of the United States have the power to alter and amend money-bills, and so have the Senates of nearly all the States.

The question was then taken and decided in the negative.

So the amendment of Mr. PHELPS was rejected.

Mr. WELLS moved the following amendment, to come in after the word "House," where it first occurs, in the fourth line, the words:

"Nor shall any bill originate in either House during the last three days of the session."

Some conversation followed, as to the construction to be given to the section as thus amended, when

Mr. DORSEY, [on behalf of Mr. Wells, not at the moment in his seat,] changed the position of the amendment so as to make it come in at the end of the section.

Mr. SPENCER said he should vote against the amendment because we were to have biennial sessions. The legislature must be entrusted with some discretion—and an emergency might arise within the last few days of the session, which might render its exercise necessary.

Mr. BROWN suggested that if the amendment should be adopted, it would change the preceding part of the section. The power to pass a bill in case of urgency would be taken away.

Mr. CHAMBERS, of Kent, said it did not affect that question at all; and gave his construction o the section.

Some conversation followed.

Mr. BROWN said, he would not press his view of the question, though it appeared to him that the amendment tangled up the section.

Mr. MERRICK said, that he thought the three-fourths vote required by the section was an ample guaranty against any improper legislation. The Convention might be satisfied that three-fourths of the Legislature would never concur in any legislation that was not necessary. Why then should their hands be tied up in this manner. Let the bill stand as it did.

Mr. SPENCER assented to the construction put upon the amendment by Mr. BROWN; and explained what his (Mr. S.'s,) understanding of the effect would be. It seemed to him that under this amendment, a bill could not be passed even if the Legislature were unanimously of opinion that the case of urgency had arisen. He thought the section was already protected sufficiently well.

Mr. CHAMBERS, of Kent, explained his construction of the section, and asked the gentleman from Queen Anne, (Mr. Spencer,) to point out in what particular he (Mr. C.) was mistaken.

The simple object of the amendment was to take away all discretion from the Legislature for the last three days of the session, so that no bill might be introduced for the first time; that was to say, if there was an urgent necessity, a law might be completed, but could not be originated. He referred to the irregular manner in which the business of the Legislature was carried on during the last days of the session, and said that not one member in twenty-five knew any thing of the contents of bills brought in under such circumstances until they read them on the statute book.

As regarded the emergencies to which reference had been made; every man and woman in the State knew when the Legislature met, and when it would adjourn. And to suppose that any such great and sudden novelty in the affairs of the State would arise, was, he thought, speculating rather too much upon remote probabilities. We must conduct the affairs of State upon rational probabilities—and there was no rational probability of such an event. Every general rule was attended with some inconveniences. Against these, it was not possible to guard. No human legislation was perfect. Perfection belonged only to One—and that not an earthly Being.

Mr. C. hoped the amendment would be agreed to.

Mr. BROWN still dissented from the construction of Mr. CHAMBERS, and insisted that the amendment if adopted, would take away from the Legislature that discretion which was necessary for the protection of the people.

Mr. MERRICK said, it was true, as the gentleman from Kent, [Mr. Chambers,] had stated, that nothing on earth was perfect—and that the business of the legislature, during the last days of its session, was conducted with irregularity. But that was the fault of the legislators themselves—not of the law. And even that irregularity took place only as to matters of indifferent interest, and not as to matters of grave and general concern. If the amendment should prevail, the legislature would not be able, even by unanimous concurrence, as to the necessity of the case, to bring in a bill whatever the emergency might be. In his experience, he had known such emergencies. He referred to the ten millions bill passed by Congress within the last two or three days of the expiration of its term, to enable the administration to put the country into a state of defence supposed to be necessary by the Navy Island [Caroline] affair.

Might not some strong necessity—of rebellion, insurrection or invasion—arise in our own State? No risk could be run by leaving this discretion with the legislature, unless upon the supposition that that body was corrupt, and that this Convention was immaculate. He repeated that the three-fourths restriction was a sufficient guaranty that no mischievous or improper act would be done—whilst great evil might result from taking away the power.

Mr. PHELPS gave notice, that if the amendment should be adopted, he would move to strike out "three-fourths" and insert "two-thirds;" and also to alter the phraseology of the last line of the bill.

Mr. STEPHENSON called for the reading of the amendment, which was again read.

Mr. SPENCER asked the yeas and nays on its adoption, which were refused.

The question was then taken, and the amendment was rejected.

Mr. PHELPS suggested a verbal amendment, which was rejected.

Mr. STEPHENSON moved to amend said section by inserting after the word "read," in the third line, the word "through."

[So that, Mr. S. said, the bill should be read through each time.]

Mr. MERRICK opposed the amendment. Some of the bills were very long, and took up much time in reading.

Mr. STEWART, of Caroline, moved an amendment to the amendment, providing that the bill should be read "*once through*, and twice by its title."

Mr. MERRICK hoped that his friend from Caroline, [Mr. Stewart,] would see the necessity of leaving these things to the discretion of the legislature.

Mr. SCHLEY suggested that the whole object of the section would be defeated unless some such amendment was inserted. He hoped the amendment of the gentleman from Harford, [Mr. Stephenson] would be agreed to.

After some conversation between Messrs. CHAMBERS, of Kent, and SCHLEY,

Mr. STEWART, of Caroline, withdrew his amendment.

Mr. STEPHENSON asked the yeas and nays on his amendment, which were refused.

The question was then taken, and the amendment of Mr. STEPHENSON was rejected.

Mr. BLAKISTONE moved to amend said section by striking out from the word "other," in the second line, to the end of said section.

Mr. B. said, it would be as well to leave to the Legislature to make their rules of proceeding without incorporating them in the organic law. He merely offered the amendment. He should make no remarks upon it.

The question was taken and the amendment was rejected.

Mr. WELLS said, he was unavoidably absent at the time the question was taken upon his amendment. He understood it had been acted upon as applicable to the end of the section. If in order he would now move to insert the amendment after the word "house," where it first occurred, in the fourth line.

The amendment was read as follows:

"Nor shall any bill originate in either House during the last three days of the session."

The PRESIDENT decided the amendment to be in order on the ground that its effect in that connection would be different from that in the portion of the section to which it had been appended.

The question was taken and the amendment was agreed to.

Some conversation followed as to the effect of the amendment.

Mr. SPENCER to put the matter beyond question, he said, moved further to amend the section by adding at the end, the words:

"As to reading and originating bills."

The amendment was agreed to.

And the section as amended was adopted.

The Convention now resumed the consideration of the sixteenth section as follows, (a motion to reconsider having been made and agreed to):

Section 16th. The enacting clause of every bill shall be, "Be it enacted by the General Assembly of Maryland," and no law shall be enacted except by Bill.

Mr. SPRIGG moved to amend said sixteenth section, by adding at the end thereof, the following words:

"And no law enacted by the Legislature, shall embrace more than one subject and that shall be described in its title, and no law shall be revised or amended by reference to its title only."

Mr. Stewart, of Caroline, moved as a substitute for said amendment, the following:

"All laws shall be passed by original bill and not by supplement, and every law enacted by the Legislature shall embrace but one subject, and that shall be described in the title, and no law shall be revised or amended by reference to its title only; but in such case, all parts of the act to be revised or amended that are embraced in the object of the bill, shall be re-enacted and published at length."

Mr. STEWART, of Caroline, desired, he said, very briefly to explain why he had changed his proposition in one particular. His first idea was that, whenever a law was to be amended or revised, the whole law should be re-enacted and published. He believed that there were a number of gentlemen who were in favor of going to that point. But, from conversation with several members, he had come to the conclusion that it would be impossible to get a law passed to that extent.

The greatest objection urged against it was the expense. No man was more ready to save expense to the State than himself; but when looking to the saving of money, we should at the same time, look to the benefit which might result from its expenditure. And if the people of the State were to be greatly benefitted by the insertion of such a provision in the Constitution, notwithstanding the expense which might attend it, surely it would be prudent and politic that it should be adopted. Mr. S. illustrated this idea.

It seemed to him that, in the aggregate, the result would be, to save to the people of Maryland a greater amount of money, by the adoption of the article as originally proposed by him, than would be expended in the printing of the laws.

After referring to the provisions of the Constitution of Louisiana, as sustaining his own views on the subject, he proceeded to enquire what would be the operation of the new article he proposed. In Louisiana, every law embraced one subject, and the object of the law was expressed in the title page. Any law which might be needed, could readily be found. The law, as it was in actual present existence, might be found. Every citizen might know what the law is; whilst in the State of Maryland, it was exactly the contrary.

He referred to the acts passed by the legislature in 1848-9—numbering five hundred and sixty. Many of these, he explained, were supplements—some supplements to supplements, and here and there an explanation of a supplement, and so on; so that to get any knowledge of the object, it was requisite to go back to the original law itself.

Laws should be few, plain and easy of access. With us, the case was precisely the reverse. They were many, complicated and inaccessible. None but a profound lawyer could tell any thing about them, and even he might easily get confused. It was still more necessary that a knowledge of the laws should be disseminated in the State of Maryland, possessing as she did, a criminal code, which, from its peculiarity in some respects, might be infringed without any violation of the moral law. He instanced the case of the oyster laws—laws relating to the fisheries, wild ducks, etc., and in the last named connection, gave some humorous illustrations.

If the laws were codified, it would be easy to look into the code, and see what the laws were which required revision and correction, and then a law could be passed to amend them. In this way, we should have a pefect law, which the people would be able to understand, without the aid of lawyers. He referred to the objection made by the gentleman from Queen Anne, on the ground of the great cost of printing, and repeated the reply he gave yesterday, that it was as well to have a crib for printers, as one for lawyers. In the framing of a Constitution, we ought not to be looking to see who were to be fed; it is our duty to feed the people by giving them a wholesome code of laws, under which they may be satisfied, and grow in prosperty. By a proper codification and a good index, any man will then be able to find what the law is.

Mr. SPENCER said he believed the proposition of the gentleman from Caroline, was about the same in principle as that offered by the gentleman from Prince George's, (Mr. Sprigg,) except that it was a little more in detail. He compared the two amendments to shew that they were, in fact, one and the same. There was a portion of the proposition, for which he was willing to vote, while he could not give his vote for the other part. He wished to have the amendment divided. Reference had been made to the Constitution and laws of Louisiana, but if he were not mistaken, they were formerly printed in French, that being the language of the inhabitants when it first became part of the United States. The change which had taken place in the character of the inhabitants of that State, combined with other circumstances, furnished good reason for printing them now in the vernacular. But what might be sound policy in the State of Louisiana, might be very imprudent in Maryland. Their position was entirely dissimilar.

Mr. PRESSTMAN asked if all the testamentary system was embraced in the laws which were within the contemplation of the amendment of the gentleman from Caroline?

Mr. STEWART replied that it was all embraced in the laws.

Mr. PRESSTMAN said, that in that case the amendment was altogether impracticable. If a gentleman desired to look into a particular law, it would be necessary for him to examine the whole mass.

Mr. HICKS, (in reply to Mr. Presstman,) said he happened not to be a lawyer. He might, therefore, be considered as perfectly disinterested in this matter. He agreed with the gentleman from Caroline, in all he had said on the subject of simplifying, collating, and codifying our whole body of laws, so as to make it intelligible to the people. A large portion of the people of his county, did not possess a great deal of legal learning, but they were plain, intelligent farmers, merchants, mechanics, &c., perfectly competent to understand common sense matters. Instead of making it necessary to go to these lawyers with a fee of five dollars, ten dollars, or fifty dollars, for lawyears know how to charge, as well as other people, he would put the people in a condition to know for themselves what is the law. He looked upon lawyers as being a highly respectable class of men; had no prejudice against them, though some say they are necessary evils, for we cannot do without them; and he yet would go to them as seldom as possible. The testamentary system had been referred to by the gentleman from Baltimore, (Mr. Presstman.) That system contained several branches, but it would not be necessary to go through the whole system, in order to look into the branch concerning inventories, or the laws of descents, individual wishes to perfect his title to land which he has purchased. Sometimes it is covered with mortgages. He examines the records, and thinks he is going to make out a clear title, when he finds some supplement enacted fifty years back, which at once comes in conflict with his hopes and clouds over what seemed previously to be clear. Then he is compelled to go to the lawyers, and they do not always know every law that has been passed on the subject. As to the charges for printing, he had no doubt that his people would be more willing to pay a small additional tax for the printer, than to give a fee of perhaps five hundred dollars to a lawyer, to tell him what he would understand himself. The money would be well laid out, if it produced the effect of simplifying the law, so that every business man might be able to judge for himself of the validity of his title, when made. He hoped the amendment would be passed, as great good would inure to the people from it.

Mr. SPENCER called for a division on the substitute, which was ordered.

Mr. S. also asked the yeas and nays, remarking that the question was one of infinite importance and that he hoped, therefore, the Convention would give them.

The yeas and nays were ordered.

Mr. HARBINE desired, he said, to move an amendment.

The amendment was not now in order.

Mr. HARBINE briefly stated, that his view of the effect of the amendment of the gentleman from Caroline, (Mr. Stewart,) was not altered. He had heard no reason to change the opinion he yesterday expressed. A state of things might occur, in which it would be highly politic and popular, but that could only arrive after a codification of the statutes of this State, and until then, the amendment, if adopted would produce evil consequences and great confusion in legislation. After a codification of our laws, there were many powerful considerations in favor of the effect of the amendment, and the cost of printing, which seemed to be the main objection to it, would have to give way to these considerations. It would be better to pay to printers large sums of money, in order to make the laws plain to every man, than to pay thrice the sum to lawyers to have them explained and understood. But his object in rising was to say, that if the proposition pending should be adopted he intended to offer an amendment which would postpone its effect, until our statute laws were codified. He regarded a codification as a matter of great public utility, and when the proper period arrived, if no one else did, he would submit a proposition to that effect.

The question was then stated to be on the first branch of the amendment, as follows:

"All laws shall be passed by original bill, and not by supplement."

Mr. SPENCER said he did not ask the yeas and nays on that branch.

Mr. DIRICKSON asked the yeas and nays, and they were ordered.

The question was then taken on the first branch of the amendment, and resulted as follows:

Affirmative—Messrs. Weems, Bell, Lloyd, Dickinson, Sherwood of Talbot, John Dennis, Hicks, Hodson, Constable, Chambers of Cecil, McCullough, Miller, Bowling, Dirickson, Shriver, Gaither, Biser, Annan, Stephenson, Magraw, Nelson, Carter, Thawley, Stewart of Caroline, Schley, Fiery, Neill, Weber, Fitzpatrick, Smith, Ege, Cockey and Shower—33.

Negative—Messrs. Chapman, President, Morgan, Blakistone, Chambers, of Kent, Donaldson, Dorsey, Wells, Merrick, Ridgely, Williams, Phelps, Sprigg, Spencer, George, Wright, Hearn, Gwinn, Stewart, of Baltimore city, Presstman, Harbine, Davis, Brewer, Parke and Brown—24.

So the first branch of the substitute was agreed to.

Mr. CHAMBERS, of Kent, asked a further division on the second branch of the amendment, as follows:

"And every law enacted by the Legislature, shall embrace but one subject, and that shall be described in the title."

Mr. STEWART, of Caroline, said it was due to the gentleman from Prince George, (Mr. Sprigg,) to state that he, (Mr. Stewart,) had taken this branch pretty much *verbatim* for his amendment.

Mr. MERRICK enquired whether it could be possible that this grave body was going to require the Legislature, when it came to revise any of the previous legislation of the State, to re-enact a whole statute.

Mr. THOMAS said he was in favor of the amendment of the gentleman from Caroline, as it was originally offered, if it was the same now. He did not concur with the gentleman from Charles, [Mr. Merrick,] that the whole of a system of laws must be re-enacted if we touch any single branch of it. The testamentary system was one law, but it had many chapters. Should it be thought necessary to amend the chapter which relates to guardians, you do not re-enact the whole system, but merely that law which relates to guardians. You take a single part and not the whole system. If the law concerning guardians were re-enacted, the advantage to the practitioner of law would, in his opinion, be great. He had only practised law for five years, but his short experience had satisfied him that no man, unacquainted with the subject, could believe what amount of labor it required to go through the whole of the testamentary system, with its supplements and additional supplements, when advice was required as to any particular part of it. It would be a great advantage to have the whole of the laws, or any one subject, thrown into one statute. He thought the cost of printing, which had at first struck him as a strong objection, could be materially diminished by a judicious arrangement of the bills, as they might require amendment or not. He noticed the complaint that members of the legislature, not lawyers, sometimes drafted laws which were so loose as to give rise to conflicting constructions by lawyers and judges, in consequence of which they had to be submitted for decision to the Court of Appeals. He expressed his belief that lawyers were quite as ready as other persons to reform the laws, where it was necessary, and he asked if any one supposed that there could not be found lawyers to undertake the codification. He had found some difficulty in deciding on his course, but when he looked at the evils which had resulted from the present practice of legislation, he could no longer hesitate. In illustrating the evils that might grow out of the practice of revising statutes by reference to their titles only, he referred to the fact, that before the year 1798, the salary of the Chancellor was $2200. In 1798, in consequence of the great expense of living here, it was raised to $3400, by an act that was to expire in one year from its enactment. That salary continued to be appropriated year after year, by reviving, by reference to its title only, this Act of Assembly. Members who voted to revive had never read the law. This continued for several years, when this act, increasing the Chancellor's salary, was continued from year to year by an act passed at the close of each session, declaring that all laws that were to expire at the end of the session, should be continued to the end of the next session of the General Assembly.

Mr. MERRICK admitted that there was great truth in much of what had fallen from the gentleman from Frederick, (Mr. Thomas.) There was much confusion in the laws, and it certainly would require great care on the part even of the most skilful lawyer, to say what is precisely the law of the State on many subjects. He did not differ, therefore, with that honorable gentleman as to the existence of the evil of which he had spoken, but he did differ from him as to the proper mode of remedying that evil. The honorable gentleman thinks the laws should be codified, and to effect that object he advocates the pending amendment which contemplates requiring the Legislature whenever they shall amend, alter, or repeal any of the existing laws, they shall re-enact and publish at length all the existing laws on that subject—in short codify to that extent. And it is argued this will require greater care in preparing bills and prevent incompetent persons from attempting to prepare and present them. Now I have two objections to this—the one is that the Legislature are not—no large body can be—competent to the codification of the laws. This Convention has been in session very nearly four months, endeavoring to make a Constitution. We have yet traveled over only a few and a very few pages. How long at the rate we have progressed would it take us to codify the laws of the State? Sir, we could never accomplish it. What is true of us, will be found to be equally true of the Legislature—we cannot, they cannot—from their very nature; both bodies are utterly incompetent to any such task. If left to the Legislature then, there will never be a codification of the laws, and the evils of which the gentleman has complained will, by the mode proposed, be increased rather than diminished, and the necessity the Legislature will be under, if the amendment prevails, of attempting that for which their nature as a body unfits them, will be to make "confusion worse confounded." I hope to see a provision made by this Convention for codifying the laws of the State, but it can only be done by a few of the ablest lawyers of the State, who should be selected for the purpose, and adequately paid for their services in preparing such a code, to be submitted to and receive afterwards, the sanction of the Legislature. In this way this desirable work may be accomplished, but it can be effected in no other way. Besides, it is argued that this amendment will have the effect of preventing or restraining incompetent men from attempting to prepare bills for the legislative action, inasmuch as it will require a thorough knowledge of all previous legislation to prepare a bill embodying all pre-existing laws on the subject. It is desirable certainly, that incompetent persons should not become members of the Legislature, but who is to be the judge of the competency of gentlemen to hold seats in the Legislature besides their constituents? If the people think a man competent, there is an end of that question, and he stands in this Hall the equal of any other. And shall it be said or maintained here that a farmer, a mechanic, or any other that the people may please to elect, shall not be privileged to bring forward such measures as his constituents require, because he is not learned in the laws, and the Constitution requires that he shall maka a collection of all the laws that have ever been passed upon the subject, on which his people want but some partial legislation, and therefore, none but a good lawyer can draw a bill? I trust not. I am very sure the honorable gentleman from Frederick, (Mr. Thomas,) intends no such thing as this. But such will be the scope and operation of the proposition if adopted. Errors and egregious blunders, it is true, do sometimes blur our statute book, but this was a small evil compared with a policy which would disfranchise a portion, probably a large portion, of the members of the Legislature. Besides this, you would be imposing a task upon the Legislature which even those who might be most competent to its performance would rarely and always most reluctantly undertake; it would be requiring a large expense of of time, labor, and money to no good purpose whatever, that he could perceive. He was not disposed to go farther in the discussion. The time was past when he would be apt to feel much enthusiasm about any thing; but he confessed the contemplation of this proposition, in all its bearings shocked him.

Mr. Hicks expressed a hope that he should be excused for entering the arena with the learned gentleman of the bar, who had taken part in this debate; but the discussion appeared to him to have been one-sided. He could not imagine any time more proper than this, when we are approaching the entrance to a new Government, to entertain such a proposition. The Judiciary system is to be thoroughly changed; the orphan's court, as he understood, was intended to be abolished; and the duties of the register of wills to be enlarged. A new state of things was just opening upon us. When, he asked, could there be a more propitious time for the codification of our laws, for he had no doubt that the people would be ready to carry out the proposition? He made a reference to the digest of the laws published some years since, and what it had cost the State, and stated that it had been of very little service in shedding light on the laws of the State, or facilitating the progress of business in our courts. It was not to be supposed that a codification of our laws could be effected in a moment. It would require much time and much industry to complete it. He had no doubt that others of our intelligent citizens besides lawyers would be employed in the work. But there would be no deficiency of able lawyers who would be always ready to give their aid. And then there is the library here from which much assistance may be obtained; and this facility, with the aid of the lawyers, would, he thought, enable any intelligent citizens to perfect a codification. While they are engaged in concocting, and putting the laws together, we ought to provide for the simplification of those now and hereafter enacted; and this would be a step towards codification. Though it may be done gradually, it will be done cheaply and yet efficiently.

Mr. Presstman said he had not supposed when the proposition was submitted by the gentleman from Caroline, that it would meet much, if any favor from the Convention. It had, however, assumed more importance in his estimation, since the discussion, in which the gentleman who had offered it and others, have unfolded their views, and the objects they design to accomplish.

He would call the attention of the gentleman from Frederick, (Mr. Thomas,) to the necessary construction which the courts would be obliged to give to this article, whereby either all laws kindred in their character, would be repealed which were omitted by the negligence of the draughtsman of an Act of Assembly, or not being so repealed, the article if adopted would not reach or carry out in any degree the object of the several gentlemen who have advocated it. If the first result would follow, (and he thought such would be the case in legal contemplation,) he was unwilling to subject the whole legislation of the State to the inexperience and want of general information in matters of law, which must necessarily exist in the body constituted as was the General Assembly.

He meant, certainly, no disrespect to a large class of individuals who were not members of the legal profession, when he said they would not be prepared to offer laws if the effect would be to interfere with prior legislation to an indefinite extent, as would be the case if the amendment now pending prevailed. What, sir, will you thereby virtually deprive the mechanic, the farmer, on the floor of the General Assembly of Maryland, from offering any act without consulting the innumerable volumes of laws to see to what extent they are to be embraced in an act or by omission repealed? He admired the sentiment of the gentleman from Frederick, (Mr. Thomas,) when he said that he would not compliment any one at the expense of what he believed to be true, and that his purpose was to arrest the practice of unskilful persons from preparing Acts of Assembly which if passed produced great mischief, but he, (Mr. P.) would not trust to that—the *argumentum ad modestiam* might not be always a safeguard. If any change is to be made in the insolvent or testamentary systems, surely it ought not be necessary to codify in the act of Assembly, looking to a slight alteration, all that relates to the subject contained in any previous act. The Convention will unquestionably provide for a digest and codification of the laws, and if that was done, would not that in effect accomplish all that could be reasonably desired? Not only is there danger from the inexperience of members of the General Assembly, and on that point he might be allowed to say that, when he was in the Legislature ten years ago, and at that time Chairman of the Judiciary committee, he was certainly incompetent to present any act on an important subject, if the amendment now offered had been a part of the Constitution. Very few eminent lawyers are seldom found in the Legislative branch of our State Government, and such men alone are competent to codify a system of laws. But, sir, at present no great evil results by allowing any member of the General Assembly to take part in the preparation of the laws of the State, especially upon the less important subjects.

Mr. BROWN said he should vote against the amendment. Either the laws must remain as they are, or they must be codified. There were but few men in the legislature who were qualified for the work; and if the Legislature were to embody all the existing laws in a new code, a hundred men would be employed, and would not do it after all so well as three skilful and experienced men. He was therefore against the proposition.

Mr. SPENCER said he was impressed with the importance of the subject, and was apprehensive that the Convention was progressing in a matter which might produce serious evil. He had a strong desire to vote for any proposition, coming from his friend, Mr. STEWART, of Caroline, but he would not support this. It requires the Legislature hereafter, when a law is amended, to re-enact every law bearing on the subject. It was urged, that the purpose was to make the acts of Assembly clear and intelligible to all, so as to supersede the necessity of applying to the lawyers for information. He did not hesitate to say, that if this amendment prevailed, it would have the very contrary result. If we desired to do an act to benefit the lawyers, no scheme could be divined which would redound more to their profit than this. A very few members of the Legislature could be found who would undertake a task of so much difficulty. There would be too much hazard in it. In the enactment of a law, if the Constitution prescribes the mode, it must be strictly followed. If, therefore, an amendment to a public or local law becomes necessary, and this amendment be adopted, then to make such an amendment, you must re-enact, as he had said, every previous Act of Assembly bearing on the subject. In such case, if a single law connected with the subject be omitted, then if the re-enactment be valid, every Act of Assembly which was omitted would be repealed. And, on the other hand, if the law be anulled, because of its failure to re-enact *all* the previous laws existing, then all the legislation on the subject would be lost, together with all the expenses incident to the same. Who can fail to see, in such a state of things, that lawyers would be constantly hanging on the Legislature, to be employed in drafting laws for the members, and that interminable controversies would be carried on in the courts, the result of such legislation?

The gentleman from Frederick illustrated by saying, that if that portion of the testimentary laws, relating to guardians, and wards, required amendment, it would only be necessary to re-enact that portion of the law, which referred to guardians and wards. To do even this, would require great labor, time and expense, in making amendments. Could it be necessary, if it became desirable to amend the law of guardian and ward, so as to require more ample security, that the whole law should be re-enacted in every particular? It was inexpedient and unwise to do so.

But he thought the gentleman was wrong in saying, that it would only be necessary to re-enact that part of the act of 1798, which in its subdivision refers to guardian and ward.—Throughout that whole act, there are parts which bear immediately on the subject. In fact, it is one whole system, testimentary in its character, and if the amendment prevail, there is good ground to contend, that any amendment, would require the re-enactment of the whole system. How is it with the laws of insolvency and of attachment? They each make a perfect system, on the subjects ;to which they respectively refer. And the same may be said of the school system for each of the counties—who, with such a section in the Constitution, would hazard an amendment to alter one of these systems of law, with consequences so alarming, in the event of a failure to provide fully for the evil. Who would undertake a work of such high responsibility, such intense labor and such accurate skill?

But it is proposed to provide in the Constitution for a codification of the laws. Pass this amendment, and until the laws are codified the legislature will be engaged, in the re-enactment of all and every part of every act of assembly, which may require amendment, to be adapted to this Constitution.

This will be done at great expense of time, in the delay of the legislature, and of immense costs for printing. And this, too, at the very time when scientific commissioners will be actually engaged in the very work of arranging the laws.

And again, after the laws have been actually codified, still, whenever an amendment becomes necessary, the same evil of re-enactment is to continue, with its interminable consequences of costs and consequent litigation.

He hoped the Convention would long deliberate, before it adopted such anamendment. He would not enter the ample field of argument which it opened. His purpose being in a plain and practical way to assign the grounds of his opposition.

Mr. STEWART, of Caroline, made some explanatory remarks. The gentleman from Baltimore city, (Mr. Presstman,) had maintained that it would be impracticable to make the laws so plain to every man, "that he who runs may read." He, (Mr. S.,) had seen a commentary in which it was maintained, that according to the original language of the phrase, it should be read "he who reads may run." With this revision, he might well apply it to the laws of the State. He, (Mr. S.,) had not, and would not, promise that his amendment, if adopted, would make every man a lawyer, but, he believed, it would prevent much unwise legislation, and would tend greatly to simplify the laws. Referring to his amendment, he said that he had looked into the Constitution of the State of Louisiana, and had found therein an article, that embraced much of the principle of his amendment. He had examined the laws of that State, since the adoption of the new Constitution, and found the laws plain and easy to understand. He had first been led to investigate this subject, some years since, by reading the life of the Hon. S. W. Downs, at present United States Senator from Louisiana, who was an able and warm advocate of reform in his State for many years, before the Convention of that State, in 1844, of which Convention he was a member. He had the whole banking interest of the State arrayed against him, yet over all opposition he triumphed.

In reply to the statement so repeatedly urged, that the members of the Legislature could not know all the laws of the State, and that the amendment would operate to prevent farmers and mechanics from going to the Legislature, he must say he saw no force in the argument. He denied that it would have that effect. He considered it an acknowledgment, on the part of the opponents to the amendment, that it would produce industry and watchfulness in the Legislature. It was right that legislators should well understand the subject on which they were engaged. It would place the labor of research and investigation upon the members of the Legislature, where it properly belonged.

The gentleman from Dorchester, (Mr. Hicks,) had stated that the members of the bar, knew how to charge. Perhaps they took lessons from the Registers. He, (Mr. S.,) vindicated the profession of the law; and refered to the history of the country, to show that lawyers had always took a prominent part in contests for liberty. They had contributed their means, time and talent, verily, their blood to its procurement. Lawyers might occasionally rail each other, but if others undertook it, they would find themselves in the condition of the man, who interfered with the quarrels of husband and wife, and thereby brought them both upon him. He expressed his great esteem and regard for the gentleman from Queen Anne's, (Mr. Spencer,) and the pleasure he always felt in co-operating with him, but, in this matter, he must differ with him. He thought from the tone and manner of the gentleman from Queen Anne's, that some startling disclosure was about to be made; some dreadful evil would come upon the State by the adoption of the amendment. He, (Mr. S.,) could see no danger. The principle, so far as it had been adopted in Louisiana, had worked well.

Mr. MERRICK asked if the Constitution of Louisiana did not refer to the revisal of laws?

Mr. STEWART replied, that in the Constitution of that State, the word *revised* was used; but, on turning to the debates of the Convention that adopted the Constitution, he found that the word revised, was, on motion of Mr. Lewis, stricken out of the article reported, and the word *revived* inserted, and he could not find where it was afterwards changed, so he inferred that the word revised in the Louisiana Constitution, ought to be revived. However that might be, he preferred the word revived. He could see no difficulty from the operation of his amendment. If gentlemen in the Legislature, were not able to prepare a law, it could be done in the committees. He thought that it would render the fountain pure, and then the stream would flow clear. The honorable gentleman from Frederick, (Mr. Thomas,) has so fully and ably advocated the amendment, and so forcibly portrayed the evils that it is to correct, that he, (Mr. S.,) would not longer detain the Convention.

Mr. THOMAS briefly replied to the remarks of the gentleman from Baltimore city, (Mr. Presstman,) and thanked him for adopting and endorsing his opinions. With reference to the effect of the amendment to repeal all pre-existing laws which might be omitted in codifying the laws, he expressed a willingness to give it that tendency. He was disposed to repeal all laws of a doubtful or occult character. Such, he believed, was the object of codification.

He asked if it was not the practice to repeal all previous laws on the same subject, whenever a new law was enacted? The gentleman from Baltimore city had said, that we could not simplify laws so as that every man who "runs may read." It was his desire that they should be too clear to be misapprehended.

After speaking of the profession of the law in terms of the highest eulogy, he stated that the cause of the multiplicity of suits was the doubt in the minds of lawyers themselves, of the true construction of laws, or because they had only read a portion of the laws relating to the subject. They may have been poring diligently over the laws, and after all, may have missed some supplementary act.

He briefly adverted to the remarks of the gentleman from Charles, (Mr. Merrick,) on the opinion he had expressed that, lawyers only should be employed in the task of codification. Suppose, said he, the gentleman and myself were appointed to revise the system of special pleading. He felt very certain that he would not be competent to the task, unaided by advice from any quarter, and as the gentleman from Charles had been some time out of the practice of the law, he also might feel some diffidence as to his own ability; and how could we expect that the most intelligent persons, not in the profession of the law, would be fit to undertake the task? We are not all like Minerva sprung from the head of Jupiter, ready for the conflict; or like Venus, in all her beauty, rising from the foam of the sea; but we are all men fitted for the duties which are within our sphere. Intelligent gentlemen who have no practical knowledge of the law, would feel themselves insulted if asked to enter on such a task.

On these grounds he would confide the work of drawing the laws to lawyers only, as coming within the range of their professional and habitual studies. He admitted the perfect competency of men of sound judgment and good sense, to pass judgment on bills when they had been prepared, and to decide whether they were such as the interests of society demanded. And hence he was in favor of submitting the code to the legislature for rejection or adoption.

Mr. Merrick explained, and recapitulated his previous remarks. He was most anxious, he further said, that the laws should be condensed and simplified as much as possible and rendered intelligible to the plain good sense of the country. And he had not only suggested, but urged, when last up, the adoption of what he considered the only safe and wise plan for attaining that desirable object even partially; which was the employment of one or more persons, eminent for their industry, legal learning and ability, to codify the laws. These persons should be the most eminent men the profession could furnish, and they should receive such a compensation for their services as would justify them in putting aside all other business, and devoting their whole time, talents and energy to the task; the work, when accomplished, should be of course submitted to the Legislature for their sanction; and, if approved by them, would have imparted to it the binding force of law; but, if not approved and enacted by the Legislature, it would still be worth more than it would cost, as a collection of statutes with the deliberate comments of wise men upon them. But he was opposed, and had so expressed himself, to requiring the Legislature in the course of their ordinary business, to codify each particular branch of the law they might have occasion to touch. Such a requirement would be, in his judgment, fraught with pernicious consequences, and productive of no compensating good whatever. He had said, for the purpose of codifying the laws, none but lawyers, and those the most deeply read and eminent men the State could furnish, should be employed. But he was very far from agreeing that the ordinary business of legislation should be confined to this or any other class, as would, to a great extent, be the effect of the pending amendment if adopted and made a part of the Constitution. No Legislature was competent to the work of codification to any great extent, not because there might not be members of the Legislature competent to such a task, but even if every member in such a body were separately capable of performing such a work, the body would still be incompetent, because of its multitudinous character. There were, also, in every Legislature, a large number of gentlemen, not professional men and not competent because of their different pursuits and habits of thought, to codify or even collate the statutes, who were yet as capable and often even more capable than the lawyers, of performing all the appropriate duties of ordinary legislation. He would not consent to a proposition which should hinder or impede such men in the performance of these duties, by making a prerequisite that they should either be competent to codify or even perform the labor of collating all the statutes on any subject upon which they might deem some legislation necessary. He hoped to see the Legislature left free, as it had heretofore been, to do the will of their constituents, and to change and modify the laws of the State as the progressive changes in the world and the state of society might require.

Something had been said about reflections upon lawyers; it was not, he supposed, it could not have been intended for him. He certainly was one of the last men living, who would cast reflections upon that honorable class of citizens. That was said to be a bird of evil omen, which would befoul its own nest. He had been in early life a lawyer himself, and though for many years exclusively engaged in other pursuits, he still felt some identity with them, and besides those dearest to him of all men on earth, were now engaged in that noble and enobling profession.

This amendment, if adopted, Mr. President, it strikes me, will be making a retrograde movement, taking a step backwards, in this age of progress. Arts, sciences, civilization, religion, are all progressing. The human intellect is progressing and attaining a development, and reaching a dominion never before known to men. Shall legislation alone go backwards? Shall we of Maryland alone, say our legislators can no longer be trusted to make laws for the regulation and government of society, as the ever varying, continually improving condition of society may require? I trust not.

After some conversation,

The question was taken, and

The second branch of the amendment was adopted.

The question then recurred on the third branch of the amendment, as follows:

"And no law shall be revised or amended by reference to its title only; but in such case all parts of the act to be revived or amended that are embraced in the object of the bill, shall be re-enacted and published at length."

And the question being taken,

The result was as follows:

Affirmative—Messrs. Mitchell, Weems, Buchanan, Bell, Welsh, Lloyd, Dickinson, Sherwood of Talbot, John Dennis, Hicks, Hodson, Phelps, Constable, McCullough, Miller, Sprigg, Bowling, Dirickson, Thomas, Shriver, Gaither, Biser, Annan, Stephenson, Magraw, Nelson, Carter, Thawley, Stewart of Caroline, Fiery, Neill, Anderson, Weber, Fitzpatrick, Smith, Ege, Cockey and Shower—38.

Negative—Messrs. Chapman, President, Morgan, Blakistone, Chambers of Kent, Donaldson, Dorsey, Wells, Dalrymple, Merrick, Williams, Spencer, George, Wright, Jacobs, McHenry, Gwinn, Stewart of Baltimore city, Brent of Baltimore city, Sherwood of Baltimore city, Presstman, Ware, Schley, Harbine, Kilgour, Davis, Waters, Brewer, Hollyday, Parke and Brown—31.

So the third and last branch of the amendment was agreed to.

The question then recurred on the adoption of the said section, as amended.

Mr. SPRIGG thereupon withdrew his amendment,

And the Convention adjourned until to-morrow at 10 o'clock.

THURSDAY, February 20, 1851.

The Convention met at ten o'clock.

Prayer was made by the Rev. Mr. GRIFFITH.

The roll of the members was called; and

A quorum being present,

The journal of yesterday was read and approved.

On motion of Mr. STEPHENSON, it was

Ordered, That it be entered on the journal that Mr. SAPPINGTON, is detained from his seat in consequence of the serious indisposition of his family.

Mr. FIERY moved that the Convention proceed to the orders of the day.

The motion was agreed to.

THE LEGISLATIVE DEPARTMENT.

The Convention resumed the consideration of the report of the committee heretofore made by Mr. JOHNSON, on the legislative department of the government.

The question pending at the time of adjournment yesterday,

Was on the adoption of the sixteenth section as it had been amended.

Some conversation followed on a point of order.

Mr. DORSEY moved the following as a substitute for the said sixteenth section:

"The legislature of Maryland, shall, at its next session, if then practicable, and if not, as soon thereafter as it can be done, contract with two learned jurists of this State, distinguished as well for their industry, as professional ability, to codify or digest and abridge the public acts of assembly then in force."

Mr. DORSEY referred to the proposition which had yesterday been adopted, and briefly stated his objections to its various branches. He dwelt especially upon the inconveniences and difficulties which would attend the introduction into the title of a bill, of every subject upon which legislation might have been had, and elucidated his position by reference to the testamentary and other systems.

It seemed to him that the section as it now stood, would lead to inextricable confusion. He explained the import and object of his own amendment, and earnestly urged upon the Convention the necessity and expediency of a codification of the laws under the requirement of an imperative constitutional provision.

Mr. THOMAS rose to call the attention of the House to the character of the amendment of the gentleman from Anne Arundel, (Mr. Dorsey.) It was a proposition not only antagonistic to the article adopted at the instance of the gentleman from Caroline, but it was against another purpose, entertained by many members of the Convention.

The gentleman from Anne Arundel proposes to strike out the section, moved by the gentleman from Caroline, and to insert his own amendment, which is intended to procure a digest and compilation of the laws, and not a codification. A digest and compilation of the laws had already been prepared by Judge Dorsey—not by the member on the floor—but by Judge Clement Dorsey, deceased. That digest was never acted upon by the legislature.

It was admitted by all the members of the profession, to be a very imperfect work. No prudent member of the profession would undertake to say what are our statute laws on any particular subject, after having consulted this compilation of Judge Dorsey alone. For it had been ascertained that laws still in force were often omitted in the digest. And as the legislature had not passed a law declaring that all statutes and parts of statutes not included in that compilation were repealed, the profession of the law and the public had desired a partial and a very small advantage.

We want not a digest but a code; and he was in favor of requiring the legislature to act upon the code, and after adopting it to pass a law repealing every statute in force now not re-enacted in the adoption of the code.

He explained the difference between a code and a digest, to show that the latter mode of legislation would meet the public demand, which required that our statutes should be analysed and that each several element or subject should be incorporated into a statute, and that no incongruous subjects should be mixed up in the same law.

Mr. MERRICK said, he had no pride of opinion on the subject, nor had he any particular anxiety that his own views should prevail. The question as now presented, was different from that which was under consideration yesterday, and gentlemen might express opinions upon it different from those which they expressed yesterday, without any inconsistency. He thought that the proposition offered by the gentleman from Anne Arundel, (Mr. Dorsey,) came nearer to the desires of the Convention, and to the accomplishment of a cherished object on the part of the people themselves, than the section as it now stood. That object was a simplification, codification, and digest of the laws under which they lived, so as to make them plain, and easy of access. It would be far better not to attempt such a work, unless the Convention was sure that the object itself would not be defeated by the manner in which it was attempted to be done.

Mr. M. proceeded to show the impracticability of such a task being performed by the legislature. He compared the two propositions, (that adopted yesterday, and that offered by Mr. Dorsey to-day,) and concluded that the latter proposed to accomplish the object in the only facile mode in which it could be effected. In no other way could a digested system of the statutory laws ever be made. The work was to be prepared by men of eminent ability and skill; but before any binding force could be given to it, it must of necessity come before the Legislature, for re-enactment. If they did not re-enact it, the result would be that the work would still stand, for convenient reference, as an arrangement and digest of the laws of the State.

Mr. Spencer offered the following as a substitute for the entire section:

"The style of all laws of this State shall be: "Be it enacted by the General Assembly of Maryland," and all laws shall be enacted by bill only, and no law enacted by the Legislature shall embrace more than one subject, and that shall be described on its title, and the Legislature shall at its next session after the adoption of this Constitution, or as soon thereafter as it can be done, at the expiration of every five years thereafter, contract with two learned jurists, distinguished for their industry and professional ability, to digest, abridge and condense and codify, the statute laws of this State, and with two other equally distinguished jurists, to simplify and abridge the rules and practice and pleadings, and proceedings of the courts of record of this State, abolishing all special pleading, subject to the approval of the Legislature."

The substitute having been read,

Mr. Constable suggested that the first part of the proposition had already been adopted. The latter part, (that which related to the codification,) was new, and for that he should vote.

Mr. Presstman suggested, that under instruction from the committee on the legislative department, he had made a report embracing the provisions of the amendment of the gentleman from Queen Anne, [Mr. Spencer.]

Mr. Spencer said, he was aware that the chairman of the committee on the legislative department, had reported a section pretty similiar to that offered by himself. The report of the gentleman was in the following words:

"That the Legislature, at its first session after the adoption of the Constitution, shall appoint one commissioner to revise, digest, and arrange the statute laws of the State, civil and criminal, and one commissioner to revise, simplify and abridge the rules and practice, pleadings, forms, and proceedings of the courts of record of this State."

Mr. S. disclaimed any intention to interfere with the duties or proceedings of the committee on the legislative department, but the proposition adopted yesterday, appeared to him to involve great and interminable difficulty; and he thought that if some proposition should be offered, embodying something of the report of the gentleman from Baltimore city, it might be the means of effecting a compromise. With that view he had offered the amendment. It embodied all the unobnoxious parts of the proposition adopted yesterday, and he believed it would disembarrass the whole question. This matter of digesting the laws, was a most important and hazardous undertaking, and it would be dangerous, he thought, to trust it to legislative enactment. The learning and skill requisite for the task, could only be found in the legal profession, and his amendment proposed that mode of proceeding.

Mr. S. then briefly explained the latter portion of his amendment, in regard to the simplification and abridgment of the rules and practice of pleading, &c.

Mr. Schley offered the follow amendment.

"The Legislature at its first session after the adoption of this Constitution, shall appoint one or more commissioners, learned in the law, whose duty it shall be to revise and codify the statutes of this State, and one or more commissioners, learned in the law, whose duty it shall be to revise, simplify and abridge the rules and practice, pleadings, forms and proceedings of the courts of record in this State, and report the same to the Legislature for adoption, and it shall be the duty of the Legislature at the expiration of every subsequent period of ten years after the adoption and promulgation of the code of laws, to have published and promulgated all the statute laws of this State then in force."

Which was read.

Mr. S. said, he had yesterday opposed the latter part of the section, because he thought that it would produce inextricable confusion in the legislation of the State—that it would impose on the Legislature a duty which no one could tell how long it would take to perform. If codifiers should be appointed by the Legislature, and one system of laws be arranged, if a code should be drawn up and formed into articles, the amendment adopted yesterday would carry out the design. After having once had the laws codified, the Legislature would become codifiers themselves, and by a republication of the laws every ten years, the public would know what the laws were. The result would be that the code of laws would be gradually reduced and simplified. He referred to the laws of Missouri, as a beautiful model of a system. He hoped that the friends of the measure would accept his amendment, and adopt it as a part of their own proposition.

Mr. Stewart, of Caroline, said it had been suggested to him yesterday to accept, as a modification of his own proposition, the amendment of the gentleman from Washington county, (Mr. Schley.) He (Mr. Stewart) had declined to accept it, because he thought it might as well be offered as an independent proposition. He was still of that opinion. He regarded it as but one system for the simplification of the laws. If it had not been for the lucid and eloquent defence which the gentleman from Frederick, (Mr. Thomas,) had this morning made of his (Mr. S.'s) proposition, he did not know but that he might have been scared off from his proposition.

But it seemed to him that that was the proper system to be adopted.

He expressed his surprise at the mode of attack which had been introduced against his proposition. If a motion had been made to reconsider the vote taken yesterday, he would have voted for it—not because his views had undergone any change, but because he was willing to see whether any proposition better than his own could be brought forward.

Mr. S. then proceeded to vindicate his own proposition, and to reply *seriatim* to the objections which had been urged against it.

Mr. Spencer expressed his regret that the gentleman from Washington,(Mr. Schley,) had offered his amendment to the 16th section, as amended by the amendment of the gentleman from Caroline. He could vote for it as a distinct proposition, but not in its connection, because the effect would be, that the Legislature before the codification took place, would have to re-enact at much trouble and expense many laws, and after the codification took place, the same evil would continue. Between the gentleman from Washington and himself there was a difference of opinion, as to the construction put on the amendment of the gentleman from Caroline, by that gentleman and the gentleman from Frederick,(Mr. Thomas.) He asked the gentleman from Frederick, if he did not find that though, in amending a law, it would not be required that the whole law should be re-enacted, as the whole of the testamentary system, yet all the parts of the law which related to the subject amended would have to be re-enacted.

Mr. Thomas declined making any further explanation. If he was not understood by the House he could not make himself more clear. He did not decline to answer from any disrespect to the gentleman. If he was opposed to him, he knew how to respect an honest difference of opinion—which it was not important to reconcile, as the House might vote for different reasons. He was unwilling to take the floor too often.

Mr. Spencer stated that he had asked further explanation, because he, and the gentleman from Washington, (Mr. Schley,) understood the gentleman from Frederick differently. They did not comprehend the gentleman from Frederick alike, on the point whether the amendment of a part of any law rendered it necessary to re-enact all the parts of the law applying to the subject, or only a portion of a law.

Mr. Thomas still declined to make any further explanation of his views.

Mr. Schley thought the opposition made to his proposition by the gentleman from Queen Anne's arose from a misunderstanding of its import. To make its object more clear, he turned to the codified laws of Missouri, and showed that the laws were divided in chapters. If one of these chapters was amended it was not necessary to re-enact the whole law. By merely amending the chapter and publishing it as amended, every useful purpose was answered.

Mr. Merrick stated that the fact that gentlemen were unable to agree as to the meaning of the amendment proved, the truth of what he had before said, that the tendency of the amendment was to make confusion worse confounded.

Mr. Brown wished the codification by the legislature not to interfere with that under the amendment.

Mr. Schley suggested that the gentleman could move an amendment.

Mr. Harbine stated, that on a previous day he had said he would offer an amendment to the section under consideration, so as to prevent the operation of the amendment of the gentleman from Caroline, (Mr. Stewart,) until after a codification of the laws. After consultation with gentlemen of more experience, he had concluded to waive that intention. It had been charged that those voting against the proposition of that gentleman were opposed to codification. This was a great mistake. He was as much in favor of it as any man, and did not believe that among those who voted against that proposition, five could be found who were hostile to it. His reason for voting as he did, was because he did not believe the Legislature competent to codify. It was a great work, that could only be properly performed by the most learned lawyers. That was the conclusion arrived at by all other States where the laws had been codified, and in no instance had such work been left to the Legislature. True, one precedent had been cited, in the State of Louisiana. But when examined, that was no precedent at all. There the laws had been first codified by Mr. Livingston, one of the greatest lawyers of his day, and it was only after that, that the Legislature done what was proposed by the amendment of the gentleman from Caroline. Now let our laws be first codified and then he would cheerfully vote for such a proposition; indeed, what he contended for all the time, was to postpone the effect of that proposition until the laws were codified, and then, but not until then, would the case cited and our's, run parallel. Not only was there no precedent cited, but among the varied Constitutions of the several States, he did not believe a single one could be found. And why? Because their sages and statesmen must have supposed such a provision impolitic and fraught with evil. We should accord to others as much wisdom and as sincere a desire for the public weal as we possess; and surely, but for the evil consequences that were thought would ensue, such a provision would have found a place in more than one Constitution. Now, according to the amendment, the Legislature were to codify—for it amounts to that—until the persons appointed by the Legislature had reported a code and the same had been adopted. This would take several years. Mr. Livingston was engaged three years in the great work for the State of Louisiana, and it was said, that in the State of New York, four years were already spent, and the work was not yet completed. From these cases, it would appear to every man who knew the confused and chaotic condition of our legislation from 1692 to the present time, that four or five years must elapse before those engaged for the purpose could report the code. Now, during these four or five years immediately after the adoption of the new Constitution, more legislation would be required than in perhaps any ten years after; and during that time too, we were to have a body highly incompetent, engaged in codifying our statutes. This period was a most unfortunate one for such an attempt; not only because of the number of laws necessarily acted upon, but because of their importance. He agreed with the several gentlemen who had spoken of the evil consequences of legislative codification, while our laws were in their present condition. It would uproot our fundamental laws. Let a code be prepared by persons of sufficient ability, who could devote time enough to it; and, after its adoption, but not before, would the Legislature be competent to perform the duties imposed upon them by the amendment already adopted. They could then see the law at a glance; but now it was often very difficult to find, and still more difficult to ascertain its meaning, when found. He did not agree with those who thought that the amendment by making it more difficult to legislate properly, would prevent an excess of laws and therefore exert a good influence. That would not prevent legislation. As heretofore, those who did not know the laws in existence, would still frame bills. No one likes to confess his ignorance and inability; and self-esteem, as it so often does, would still urge persons to do that which they did not understand. But his colleague had added to the section, as amended, a clause to codify, and that he would most cheerfully sustain. It would make the section more palateable and he would be compelled to swallow the bitter with the sweet.

Mr. Dorsey desired to say a few words in reply to the gentleman from Frederick, (Mr. Thomas,) and in explanation of the substitute which he had moved to the section. He defended the preference which he had expressed for supplements over original bills, because a law, of which the index was imperfect, and which could not be found without great difficulty, when in an original bill, could be found easily when in a supplement,that always giving a direct reference to the bill to which it is supplemental, and, if it could be found through the supplement, why hunt through a mass of original bills to find it? By the supplement, you are referred to the original bill, and then you have the contents of both presented to your view. He referred to the loose and unsatisfactory character of the amendment which was adopted yesterday, and read the following extract from it, "Every law &c., shall embrace but one subject." And yet there can scarcely ever be found a law of any length that does not, of necessity, embrace various subjects. He objected to the amendment, therefore, on that ground. If the meaning was subject matter necessarily brought in connection with each other by the enactment, fifty original bills, might be required to accomplish that for which, without his amendment,a single original bill would be all-sufficient. The expression,"one subject,"appeared to him not to express the meaning of its author,and incapable of being reduced to practice. Then the amendment went on to say, "and that shall be described in the title." Now if there happen to be many of these subjects in the bill, the effect of this provision might be to make the title of the bill of useless and intolerable length. It would be much better for persons to look into the bill itself, and read its enactments through. In reply to what had been said by the gentleman from Frederick, in relation to the salary of the Chancellor, he said he had no doubt that the Legislature did not vote inadvertently, but knew very well what they were voting for. But his strongest objection was to the last part of the amendment, which reads "but in all cases all parts to be revived or amended, that are embraced in the object of the bill, shall be re-enacted and published at length." This would render it necessary to re-enact every clause and portion of the whole law, on which the amendment could operate, though entirely abrogated or constructively repealed by the amendment made. Though such be the obvious construction of the amendment, such surely was not the design of its mover. He thought the whole amendment so loosely put together, that, in its present form, it could not be adopted. He regarded the subject of codification as an entirely independent proposition. He approved of some part of the amendment of the gentleman from Washington, (Mr. Schley,) but not of the other part, and therefore would be compelled to vote against it.

Mr. Stewart, of Baltimore city, said he concurred entirely in the argument of his distinguished friend from Anne Arundel, (Mr. Dorsey,) and had felt its force from the beginning. He, (Mr. S.,) was at all times unwilling to intrude upon gentlemen, who were addressing the Convention, but he had risen for the purpose of asking a question. Suppose a law, thus re-enacted, should be imperfect by the omission of four or five laws, all relating to the same subject-matter—would the re-enacted law, in this imperfect condition, be a constitutional exercise of the legislative power? He looked upon this amendment as vesting in the Legislature a particular and limited authority. They were to re-enact the whole law—all parts of the law were to be embodied in the re-enactment. If, therefore, they should omit several laws, would not that be an imperfect exercise of the legislative power, and would it not render the law unconstitutional?

He also desired to ask the gentleman from Anne Arundel, another question, whether, in the absence of any repealing clause in the re-enacted law, the laws which had been omitted would not remain in full force and vigor, provided there were no conflict between the provisions of the original laws and of those which had been re-enacted? He assumed, in the first place, that the exercise of this power, was the exercise of a special authority, and that the whole law must be re-enacted, or that it would not be worth the paper on which it was printed; and, in the second place, that if there be not a repealing clause in the re-enacted law, any laws which might be omitted, provided they were not in conflict with any portion of the re enactment, would remain in full and vigorous operation, and that the courts must so decide.

Mr. Dorsey resumed, in reply. If he was asked his private opinion, he would reply that, if, in the cases stated, the repealing clause was inserted in the new act, the previous law would be repealed. Or if the amenndments conflicted with each, they would be ineffectual in their operation. And if the repealing clause was not inserted, the pre-existing laws which had been omitted in the codified and re-enacted law would remain in full force.

The amendment does not say that the whole of the laws are to be re-enacted, but only that parts of the law shall be examined and re-enacted, and published at length. He could see no advantage which would be derived from thus re-enacting and publishing these parts of the law, which may have been rescinded by the amendment; and he thought it ought not to be done—that it would lead to endless confusion.

He believed the gentleman from Washington, (Mr. Schley,) did not design to employ any other than competent lawyers in the performance of this task. One of his great objections to a change in the system, was that the instability of laws render them of less efficiency.

On the subject of special pleading, he referred to the change which had been made in that branch of the practice in New York. He had heard it said that the new system worked well there. But it was the very last system (for reasons which he a few days ago had advanced to some,) that he would adopt. From all he had seen or known of its operation, he was on every ground opposed to it. Certainly it would not do in the State of Maryland, to increase the costs of litigation to more than ten times their present amount.

Mr Schley explained that he had no desire to abolish special pleading. So far as his own opinion went, he would much prefer to see it made still more special.

Mr. Dorsey entirely agreed with the gentleman from Washington there. It requires to be made more special. He referred to the simplicity of the present practice in cases where *non assumpsit, non cul, &c.*, were the proper pleas; and argued that it was scarcely necessary to have included special pleading in the amendment of the gentleman from Washington.

It was not necessary to appoint commissioners at a great expense to the State, to change a course of practice which the legislature had it in their power, at any time, to change without putting the State to any expense.

He then explained the nature and object of special pleading. The length, the expenses and all the characteristics of this system of practice in Maryland, differed widely from what they were in the States which were enthusiastic on the subject of progess. Justice was here administered as cheaply as it was in any State where justice is administered in the same way. He put some cases for the purpose of showing how the New York system would work in Maryland. New York had abolished special pleading, and would not permit a defendant to put in the simple plea of "not guility," or *non assumpsit*; but in lieu of this, the plaintiff and defendant are required to put in a brief statement of facts, and that brief statement has led to more litigation than any other mode which has been devised. If the plaintiff or defendant fail to insert every thing required in his statement or answer, his loss is ten times greater in New York than in Maryland.

He read one of these statements, of which a gentleman had furnished him with a copy; and the reading furnished much amusement to the House. He then read the bill of costs appended to the statement from which it appeared that the costs to the defendant for an unsuccessful resistance to a suit—nay, where there was no resistance, no trial, but judgment by default, no jury being required—for $296, amounted to $96 75; while in Maryland they would only have been $6 or $7.

He had also understood that in one case in New York, the answer put in by the defendant covered six thousand pages. And this is under the reformed system by which special pleading has been abolished, and legal proceedings have been simplified.

Mr. Schley repeated that he had not attempted to abolish special pleading.

Mr. Dorsey said, it was a mistake of his. It was the gentleman from Queen Anne's.

Mr. Schley said, the proposition of the gentleman from Queen Anne's was not before the House. He desired to state that his amendment looked only to amending and modifying the present system of special pleading, by which he meant to make it more special, merely stripping it of its antiquated forms and superflous verbiage.

Mr. Dorsey replied, if such were his object his amendment was not limited to its accomplishment. The amendment opened the door to the abolition of all special pleading.

Mr Thomas said:

There was certainly nothing in the present amendment which contemplated the abolition of the system of special pleading. It looked only to the appointment of commissioners to revise and modify the present practice and pleadings. No man would deny that some change was necessary in the old laws which had become liable to great abuses. The first proposition was to codify the laws and submit the work to the legislature; and the second was to revise the system of special pleading and practice, and report the result to the legislature.

He, for one, had never joined in the cry against special pleading. On the contrary, he thought the establishment of the present system one of the greatest efforts of human wisdom. It was probable that so the commissioners would report to the legislature. But he might also be of opinion, that the system had not kept pace with the changes of circumstances, and the progress of public sentiment; and can it be said that we are on dangerous ground, when we desire only to make such changes as will adapt it to the present advanced state of human intellect? He was not, however, going into that branch of the subject. But it could not be denied that puerilities had sometimes been introduced by lawyers, under the idea that they were practising in the art of special pleading.

He could cite instances where enormous costs had been incurred in suits under our forms in Maryland, greater than those in the case from New York, but he would not go into that subject. He left it to the discretion of the legislature, which had the power to correct such evils.

He read the latter part of the amendment of the gentleman from Caroline, and contended that it was not liable to the criticisms made upon it by the gentleman from Anne Arundel, (Mr. Dorsey,) and repeated what he had said before on the subject of the testamentary system, and the continuance of the increased salary of the Chancellor for many years, in consequence of the negligence of the legislature in not examining the annual bills, (to continue in force certain laws,) before they were passed.

He knew from his own experience that it was a practice merely to read the titles of certain bills to continue bills about to expire for another term, without reading more than the titles. He never read these bills taking the word of the chairman of the committee as to their contents.

When gentlemen argued that a branch of a law might not be amended, without re-enacting the whole law of which it was a part, he asked if this was not running counter to the express language of the article we have adopted? And he read that article that the House might judge.

He remarked on the criticism of the gentleman from Anne Arundel, on the word "subject," and said that if it was susceptible of so many constructions, it would have been better for that gentleman to have moved the substitute of a more distinct word by way of remedying the error. He laid down the principle that it requires much mental discipline to be able to analyse any subject embracing a variety of ideas, so as to separate the elements, and collicate and arrange them; stated that there were few minds competent to the task, and applied it to the work of codification.

He could readily conceive how gentlemen desired to have the laws collected and collocated to their hands, because it saved them the great mental processes of searching up all the laws and going through all the decisions of the Courts of Appeals. It was a labor of such magnitude that but few minds could be found capable of performing it. He had seen many a member of the bar who had lost a case, because his mind had not taken in all the points of which it was susceptible; and he had seen judges, who, from the same cause had delivered false decisions. The popular mind calls for a reform in our legal system.

He was ready to adopt any mode best calculated to gratify popular feeling, to which he responded with all his heart and soul, which demands that the laws shall be made so clear that even the unlettered man may know them, and that the "way-faring man, though a fool, may not err therein." He had great respect for the opinions of the gentleman from Anne Arundel as to the codifying the laws, but he could not, on this important subject, consent to abandon his views.

It was so also, as to special pleading: the gentleman from Anne Arundel was so wedded to old forms, that he thought the present system could not be amended. But the popular demand must be gratified.

Let these changes be made now, in the midst of the nineteenth century, in the form of our laws; and let our system of special pleading, which no one desires to abolish, be revised and so modified as to be in accordance with the advanced intelligence of the age; and let the whole system of our laws, of our forms of pleading, and of our rules of practice, be adapted, as they can be, to the condition and circumstances of society as it is now; and let them not remain, as they obviously are in many respects, adapted to the condition the world was in, Anno Domini, one.

Mr. Dorsey made an explanation in reply. He said, he was inclined to question the expediency, much less the necessity of the legislature inflicting on the State, the enormous expenditure of appointing two separate boards of commissioners on the two distinct subjects, under this amendment. He could not allow the construction put upon it, that the commissioners were to make the code, and without submitting it to the legislature, it was to become the law of the land; such an opinion could not for a moment be sustained. The code, until its adoption by the legislature, had no vitality or operation. He had no such intention, as was clear from the subsequent part of the amendment, where it is provided how the legislsture might act with regard to it. The legislature have the power to arrange all the details without any constitutional provision.

He could not pretend to know any thing about the popular feeling on the subject of special pleading. If there really was any such feeling, it was probably got up by politicians to subserve some momentary purpose, and did not originate with the people, and from its nature would soon die away.

It had been asked by the gentleman from Frederick, why, if he objected to the looseness of the words "one subject," he did not propose to substitute a more definite term? He could only answer that he saw no necessity for any attempt on his part, to amend a proposition to which he was altogether opposed. It was certainly no part of his duty to amend the proposition; and, in reply, he would ask, why he did not amend it? Certainly nobody was more competent to do so, than he was. He cited some cases for the purpose of showing that the word "subject" was too loose. It would be better, he thought, to have a variety of subjects, relating to the same object, in one bill, instead of having them scattered through several bills, a separate bill for each separate subject, although relating to one general object. If the act should be either altered or amended, the whole would have to be re-enacted and published at length. He could not see any propriety in this. It was an inconsistency which he thought ought to be avoided.

The question was then stated be on theto amendment of Mr. SCHLEY.

The hour was now growing late, when

A motion was made that the House adjourn, but was withdrawn, and renewed.

The motion by yeas 30, nays 39, was rejected.

A call of the House was ordered, and

The call of the roll had been commenced, when

A motion was made. that further proceedings on the call be dispensed with.

A motion was again made, that the House adjourn; and

By yeas 34, nays 34, was rejected.

So the House refused to adjourn.

After some conversation,

The Convention adjourned until to-morrow at ten o'clock.

FRIDAY, Feb. 21st, 1851.

The Convention met at ten o'clock.

Prayer by the Rev. Mr. GRIFFITH.

A quorum being present, the Journal of yesterday was read and approved.

RULES OF THE CONVENTION

Mr. RICAUD, Chairman of the select committee appointed to revise the rules submitted the following

REPORT:

Strike out the seventeenth rule and insert:

The previous question shall be always in order in Convention, that shall be in this form: "Shall the main question be now put?" It shall only be admitted when demanded by a majority of the members present, and its effect shall be to put an end to all debate and to bring the Convention to a direct vote upon pending amendments and the section of the Constitution then under consideration. On a motion for the previous question, and prior to the seconding of the same, a call of the Convention shall be in order; but after a majority shall have seconded such motion, no call shall be in order prior to a division of the main question.

RULE EIGHTEENTH.

On a previous question there shall be no debate. All incidental questions of order arising after a motion is made for the previous question and pending such motion shall be decided, whether on appeal or otherwise, without debate.

The rules from eighteenth to twenty-eighth, to be altered numerically so as to correspond with this report.

Rule twenty-ninth to be repealed, and the following rule to be substituted:

A motion to postpone to a day certain, to commit, to determine the priority of business or to lay on the table, shall be decided without debate.

RULE THIRTIETH.

Every amendment or motion may be divided into as many parts as it is susceptible of, and separate votes taken on each if required.

Which was read.

On motion of

Mr. MORGAN, it was

Ordered, That it be entered upon the Journal that Mr. Hopewell is detained from his seat in this Convention, in consequence of the indisposition of a member of his family.

Mr. KILGOUR offered the following order:

Ordered, That when this Convention shall adjourn, it stand adjourned over to Monday, the 24th inst., at twelve o'clock, in honor of the anniversary of the birth day of the illustrious George Washington.

The order having been read,

Mr. KILGOUR said:

Mr. President—To-morrow is the twenty-second of February, the birth-day of the illustrious Washington.

It has always been customary, I believe, for bodies of this kind, to suspend business for that day, to pay that respect which is due to his memory. But more particularly has it been determined, by all the Conventions, and Legislative bodies, now in session throughout the country, to pursue this course, on the approaching anniversary of the father of his country, and to make it a day of thanksgiving to kind Heaven for the peace and harmony which now pervade our beloved Union—under the operation of the compromise measures, adopted by Congress, after the tremendous and powerful crisis through which it has passed. I hope the resolution will be unanimously adopted.

Mr. SMITH briefly opposed the adoption of the order, on the ground of the difficulty of procuring a quorum after the adjournment, and of the necessity, in view of the approach of Spring, of proceeding as rapidly as possible with the public business.

Mr. FIERY moved that the resolution be laid on table.

Mr. SMITH asked the yeas and nays which were ordered, and, being taken, resulted as follows:

Affirmative—Messrs. James U. Dennis, Hodson, Phelps, Stephenson, McHenry, Nelson, Thawley, Gwinn, Schley, Fiery, Harbine, Weber, Smith, Parke, Shower, Cockey and Brown—17.

Negative—Messrs. Chapman, President, Morgan, Blakistone, Dent, Ricaud, Chambers, of Kent, Dorsey, Wells, Randall, Sellman, Weems, Merrick, Bell, Welch, Dickinson, Sherwood of Talbot, John Dennis, Williams, Goldsborough, McCullough, Miller, Tuck, Sprigg, McCubbin, George, Wright, Jacobs, Thomas, Shriver, Biser, Annan, Magraw, Carter, Stewart of Caroline, Ware, Davis, Kilgour, Brewer, Waters, Anderson, Hollyday, Fitzpatrick and Ege—43.

So the Convention decided that the resolution should not be laid on the table.

The question then recurred on the adoption of the resolution.

Mr. SMITH asked the yeas and nays, which were ordered and, being taken, resulted as follows:

Affirmative—Messrs. Chapman, President, Morgan, Blakistone, Dent, Ricaud, Chambers of Kent, Dorsey, Wells, Sellman, Weems, Merrick, Buchanan, Bell, Welch, Lloyd, John Dennis, Williams, Goldsborough, McCullough, Miller, Tuck, Sprigg, McCubbin, George, Wright, Jacobs, Thomas, Gaither, Biser, Magraw, Carter, Stewart of Caroline, Brent of Baltimore city, Ware, Davis, Kilgour, Brewer, Waters, Anderson, Hollyday, Fitzpatrick, and Ege—41.

Negative—Messrs. Dickinson, Sherwood of Talbot, James U. Dennis, Hodson, Phelps, Shriver, Annan, Stephenson, McHenry, Nelson, Thawley, Gwinn, Schley, Fiery, Harbine, Weber, Smith, Parke, Shower, Cockey and Brown—21.

So the resolution was adopted.

INSPECTION OF TOBACCO, ETC.

Mr. SELLMAN offered the following order, which was read and adopted:

Ordered, That the Treasurer be requested to report to this Convention the amount of money expended in the purchase of lots and the erection of Warehouses in the city of Baltimore, for the Inspection of Tobacco; and also to report further, whether the purchase of Lots, the erection of Warehouses and the expenses of Inspection are now, or have been at any time heretofore a charge upon the Treasury of the State.

CODIFICATION OF THE LAWS, ETC.

Mr. GWINN rose and gave notice that he would, at the proper time, if the course of the proceedings should authorise it, move a proposition in relation to the matter pending at the adjournment yesterday. He would merely remark, that he did not offer it on his own judgment alone, but upon consultation with other gentlemen.

The amendment was read.

Mr. DORSEY rose and gave notice that he would, at the proper time, offer a proposition as a substitute for the proposition yesterday offered by himself.

The substitute was read.

On motion of Mr. BROWN, the Convention passed to the orders of the day.

THE LEGISLATIVE DEPARTMENT.

The Convention resumed the consideration of the report heretofore made by Mr. JOHNSON, from the committee on the legislative department.

The pending question was on the amendment offered yesterday by Mr. SCHLEY to the sixteenth section. [See yesterday's proceedings.]

Mr. EGE. On that amendment I ask the previous question.

Mr. GWINN called for a division of the question.

The PRESIDENT said that the gentleman from Montgomery, (Mr. Davis,) had yesterday called for a division.

Mr. BLAKISTONE. If the gentleman from Carroll, (Mr. Ege,) insists on the previous question, I shall move a call of the Convention.

Mr. EGE. I do insist. We have been three days wasting the time of the Convention in useless discussions on this question. Gentlemen were as well prepared to vote two days ago as they are now.

Mr. BLAKISTONE. Then I insist on my motion for a call of the Convention.

The question was taken on the motion of Mr. BLAKISTONE, and, having been decided in the affirmative,

The roll was called.

The names of the absentees were then read.

Mr. EGE moved that further proceedings on the call be dispensed with.

Mr. RICAUD said there were some members in the city who desired to vote, but who did not expect that the question would be taken so soon.

After some conversation,

The Convention refused to suspend proceedings on the call.

The PRESIDENT then directed the door-keeper to wait on such of the absentees as were in the city and notify them to attend.

A pause followed, after which

The PRESIDENT stated that the door-keeper had returned, and had notified the absent members, &c.

Further proceedings on the call were then dispensed with,

And the question recurred on the demand of Mr. EGE for the previous question.

There was a second. And the main question (on the amendment of Mr. SCHLEY,) was ordered to be now taken.

Mr. DAVIS withdrew his call for a division.

Mr. GWINN renewed it.

The PRESIDENT stated that the proposition was susceptible of three divisions.

Mr. THOMAS suggested another subdivision, which was ordered.

The first division was stated as follows:

"The Legislature at its first session after the adoption of this constitution, shall appoint one or more commissioners learned in the law, whose duty it shall be to revise and codify the statutes of this State."

Mr. EGE called the yeas and nays, which were ordered.

The question then was taken and resulted as follows:

Affirmative.—Messrs. Chapman, President, Morgan, Blakistone, Dent, Ricaud, Lee, Chambers, of Kent, Weems, Bond, Merrick, Buchanan, Bell, Welch, Lloyd, Dickinson, Sherwood, of Talbot, John Dennis, James U. Dennis, Williams, Hodson, Goldsborough, Phelps, McCullough, Miller, Tuck, Sprigg, McCubbin, Bowling, Wright, Dirickson, Hearn, Jacobs, Thomas, Shriver, Biser, Annan, Stephenson, McHenry, Magraw, Nelson, Carter, Thawley, Stewart, of Caroline, Gwinn, Brent, of Baltimore city, Ware, Schley, Fiery, Neill, Harbine, Kilgour, Brewer, Waters, Anderson, Weber, Hollyday, Fitzpatrick, Smith, Parke, Ege, Shower, Cockey and Brown—62.

Negative—Messrs. Dorsey, Wells, Sellman and Davis—4.

So the first branch of the amendment was agreed to.

The question was then taken on the second branch of the amendment, which was in the following words:

"And one or more commissioners learned in the law, whose duty it shall be to revise, simplify and abridge the rules and practice, pleadings, forms and proceedings of the courts of record in this State."

The result was as follows:

Affirmative.—Messrs. Chapman, President, Morgan, Blakistone, Dent, Ricaud, Lee, Weems, Buchanan, Bell, Welch, Lloyd, Dickinson, Sherwood, of Talbot, John Dennis, James U. Dennis, Williams, Hodson, Phelps, McCullough, Miller, McCubbin, Bowling, George, Wright, Dirickson, Hearn, Jacobs, Thomas, Shriver, Biser, Annan, Stephenson, McHenry, Magraw, Nelson, Carter, Thawley, Stewart, of Caroline, Gwinn, Brent, of Baltimore city, Ware, Schley, Fiery, Neill, Harbine, Kilgour, Brewer, Waters, Anderson, Weber, Hollyday, Fitzpatrick, Smith, Parke, Ege, Shower, Cockey and Brown—58.

Negative.—Messrs. Chambers, of Kent, Dorsey, Wells, Sellman, Goldsborough, Tuck, Sprigg and Davis—8.

So the second branch of the amendment was agreed to.

The question was then taken on the third branch of the amendment, which was in the following words:

"And report the same to the Legislature for adoption."

The result was as follows:

Affirmative.—Messrs. Chapman, President, Morgan, Blakistone, Dent, Ricaud, Lee, Chambers, of Kent, Sellman, Weems, Bond, Buchanan, Bell, Welch, Lloyd, Dickinson, Sherwood, of Talbot, John Dennis, James U. Dennis, Williams, Hodson, Goldsborough, Phelps, McCullough, Miller, Tuck, Sprigg, McCubbin, Bowling, George, Wright, Dirickson, Hearn, Jacobs, Thomas, Shriver, Biser, Annan, Stephenson, McHenry, Magraw, Nelson, Carter, Thawley, Stewart, of Caroline, Gwinn, Brent, of Baltimore city, Ware, Schley, Fiery, Neill, Harbine, Davis, Brewer, Waters, Anderson, Weber, Hollyday, Fitzpatrick, Smith, Parke, Ege, Shower, Cockey and Brown—63.

Negative.—Messrs. Dorsey and Wells—2.

So the third branch of the amendment was agreed to.

The question was then taken on the fourth and last branch of the amendment, as follows:

"And it shall be the duty of the Legislature at the expiration of every subsequent period of ten years after the adoption and promulgation of the code of laws, to have published and promulgated all the Statute Laws of this State then in force."

And the result was as follows:

Affirmative.—Messsrs. Chapman, President, Morgan, Blakistone, Dent, Ricaud, Lee, Chambers, of Kent, Weems, Buchanan, Bell, Welch, Lloyd, Dickinson, Sherwood, of Talbot, John Dennis, James U. Dennis, Williams, Hodson, McCullough, Miller, Tuck, Sprigg, McCubbin, Bowling, George, Wright, Dirickson, Hearn, Thomas, Shriver, Biser, Annan, Stephenson, McHenry, Magraw, Nelson, Carter, Thawley, Stewart, of Caroline, Brent, of Baltimore city, Ware, Schley, Fiery, Neill, Harbine, Davis, Kilgour, Brewer, Waters, Anderson, Weber, Hollyday, Fitzpatrick, Smith, Parke, Ege, Shower, Cockey and Brown—62.

Negative,—Messrs. Dorsey, Wells, Sellman, Goldsborough, Phelps and Gwinn—6.

So the fourth and last branch of the amendment was agreed to.

The question then recurred on the amendment proposed by Mr. SPENCER, as a substitute for the said section, as amended.

Some conversation followed on a point of order.

Mr. DORSEY directed the attention of the Convention to that part of the amendment of Mr. SCHLEY, which proposed that the Legislature should appoint, *one or more*, commissioners to codify, &c.

Mr. DORSEY thought that a provision, so indefinite, ought not to be incorporated into the Constitution. The number of commissioners might be so multiplied, that there would be no responsibility any where, as to the manner in which the work should be done. The result probably might be, that the character of the work might be such as to render it of no value. The expense, under such a system, would probably be double under the plan proposed by himself.

Mr. D. was also opposed to the other part of the amendment of the gentleman, which provided for the appointment of commissioners, in relation to pleadings, &c. He thought that the Convention ought to pause before giving such powers to any commissioners. Under the power thus given, the commissioners might abolish special pleading altogether. The gentleman had stated that he had no such intention.

Mr. D. had no doubt as to the gentleman's intention. But the language of the amendment was unlimited, and gave the power to the commissioners to do as they pleased. Great expense would also be incurred, without the attainment of any commensurate object.

Mr. D. then briefly explained the character of

his own amendment, and the claims to preference which, in his judgment, it possessed.

Mr. BUCHANAN concurred in part, he said, in the opinion expressed by his friend from Anne Arundel, (Mr. Dorsey.) He, (Mr. B.,) thought that the proposition to appoint one or more commissioners, was too indefinite and might lead to difficulty. But he did not concur in the proposition of the gentleman to appoint only two commissioners, no matter how distinguished they might be. It would be safer, (Mr. B. thought,) looking to the grand divisions of the State—the local legislation of the State, and the legal ability of the State, that three should be appointed. At all events, he thought the number should be definite.

He referred to the code of Louisiana, as to the accuracy of which some doubts had been expressed, and spoke of it as a highly valuable and accurate production.

Nor could he agree with the gentleman from Anne Arundel, in the apprehension he had expressed, as to the other portion of the amendment of the gentleman from Washington, [Mr. Schley,] that, in the large discretion given to the commissioners, the system of special pleading would be broken down. There was no danger of that result, in the first instance. But if the commissioners should think that a system could be devised by which justice could be better obtained than by special pleading, let us get rid of it. He hoped that the commissioners might conclude that it would be expedient to get rid of a large portion of the system, if not of the whole. The very reason, therefore, which induced the gentleman from Anne Arundel, to go against that portion of the amendment, would induce him, (Mr. B.,) to go against it.

Mr. TUCK moved to amend the sixteenth section, as amended, by inserting in the second line, after the word "commissioners," the words "not exceeding three,". also by inserting the same words after the word "commissioners," in the fourth line.

The question was taken and the amendment was adopted.

Mr. DENT said:

I have an amendment to offer, the object of which is to refer to the commissioners to be appointed under this section, the forms of conveyancing now in use in this State, that they also may be simplified and abridged. It has been suggested to me, that this matter is otherwise provided for; but I am not aware of any provision for this object, more than exists in the Legislature by non-prohibition. The Legislature also has the same power, with regard to forms of pleadings, rules of practice, &c., in the courts of record. The power of the Legislature, in these matters, is not questioned. But the object of the section proposed, is to place the Legislature under constitutional obligations, to perform the duties specified in the section. I consider the abridgement and simplification of conveyancing, very important and necessary for general convenience; and as it has been determined to appoint a commission to simplify and abridge the forms of pleading and rules of practice in the courts of record of the State, an object of which I highly approve, it will add very little to the labors of that commissioner, to prepare a set of simple and abridged forms of conveyancing, which, when once recognized in a formal manner, will immediately obtain general use.

Mr. D. then moved to insert after the word "State," in the fourth line, the following:

"And also to simplify and abridge the forms of conveyancing, now in use in this State."

The question was taken and the amendment was agreed to.

Mr. CHAMBERS, of Kent, asked the attention of the gentleman from Washington, [Mr. Schley] to the language of his amendment. Was it the purpose of the gentleman to revise and codify the private as well as the public laws?

Mr. SCHLEY. It is not.

Mr. CHAMBERS did not intend, he said, to make any motion himself. He merely called the notice of the gentleman to the words of the amendment, which were "whose duty it shall be to revise and codify the statutes of this State."

Mr. SCHLEY, [acquiescing in the suggestion of Mr. Chambers,] moved to amend his amendment by inserting before the word "statutes," wherever it occurred, the words "public general."

The amendment was agreed to.

Some conversation followed in relation to the propriety of the words "public general," in which Messrs. DORSEY, SCHLEY, THOMAS and CHAMBERS, of Kent, took part.

The substitute amendment of Mr. DORSEY, was then again read, as follows:

"*Section* 16. The style of all laws shall be: "Be it enacted by the General Assembly of Maryland." The Legislature of Maryland, shall at its next session, if then practicable, if not, as soon thereafter as it can be done, contract with two learned jurists of this State, distinguished, as well for their industry as professional ability, to codify or digest and abridge the public acts of Assembly then in force, and every ten years thereafter, and additional code or digest, shall, in like manner, be made of all public acts of the Legislature, passed subsequently to those embraced in preceding codes or digests, and no act of Assembly shall include in its enactments, subjects unconnected with each other, and forming fit subjects for distinct and independent legislation; and the title of every bill shall indicate the nature of its enactments, and no law or any section thereof, shall be continued, revived, amended or repealed by reference to its title only, or the number of the section."

Mr. BROWN said, it was his intention to vote against the substitutes of the gentleman from Queen Anne, [Mr. Spencer,] and the gentleman from Anne Arundel, [Mr. Dorsey,] with the intention of voting for the substitute of the gentleman from the city of Baltimore, (Mr. Gwinn.)

Mr. SCHLEY took two objections to the substitute of the gentleman from Anne Arundel, [Mr. Dorsey,] first, that it proposed *either* a codification or a digest, (i. e. abridgement.)

Mr. Dorsey said, his amendment left it discretionary with the Legislature, to contract either for one or the other, as they might think proper. He, [Mr. D.,] had no doubt what their choice would be.

Mr. Schley said, what was wanted, was a codification.

The second objection to the substitute of the gentleman from Anne Arundel, was that it omitted any provision in relation to pleadings, &c.

Mr. Chambers, of Kent, desired, he said, to see some proposition adopted which might lead to a codification of the laws of the State, under the sanction of the Legislature. He had no preferences as to its paternity; nor had he regarded the question of so much importance as some gentleman had. He had not risen to make an argument, but only a suggestion. It was easier to codify a part of the laws, than the whole of them. It was more likely that an early result would be reached by confining the code, in the first place, to public general laws. If the commissioners should accomplish that portion of the work, the Legislature would very probably make provision for codifying the public local laws. And he suggested to the Convention the propriety of deciding that question. With a view to bring it distinctly before the Convention, he would move an amendment.

The amendment was not now in order.

The question then recurred upon the substitute as offered by Mr. Spencer.

Mr. Buchanan, stated to the Convention that Mr. Spencer had informed him that he had been compelled to leave the city on pressing business, and desired him to ask the Convention to pass over the sixteenth section informally, until he could be present.

The question was then taken on the substitute of Mr. Spencer, and it was decided in the negative.

So the substitute was rejected.

The question then recurred on the substitute of Mr. Dorsey.

Mr. Chambers, of Kent, offered the amendment he had indicated, but, on a suggestion by Mr. Thomas, and after some conversation, withdrew it.

The question, therefore, again recurred on the substitute amendment of Mr. Dorsey.

Mr. Stewart, of Caroline, called for a division on striking out the section, which was ordered.

Mr. Dorsey asked the yeas and nays, which were ordered and, being taken, were as follows:

Affirmative—Messrs. Chapman, Pres't., Morgan, Blakistone, Ricaud, Lee, Chambers of Kent, Dorsey, Wells, Sellman, Weems, Merrick, Williams, Goldsborough, Phelps, Tuck, Sprigg, McCubbin, Hearn, Jacobs, McHenry, Gwinn, Ware, Davis, Kilgour, Waters, Anderson, and Brown—26.

Negative—Messrs. Dent, Buchanan, Bell, Welch, Lloyd, Dickinson, Sherwood of Talbot, John Dennis, James U. Dennis, Hodson, Miller, Bowling, Wright, Dirickson, Thomas, Shriver, Stewart of Caroline, Brent of Baltimore city, Schley, Fiery, Harbine, Brewer, Weber, Hollyday, Fitzpatrick, Smith, Parke, Ege, and Shower—36.

So the Convention refused to strike out.

Mr. Gwinn then offered the substitute of which he had given notice, as follows:

"All laws shall be passed by original bill, and every law enacted by the Legislature, shall embrace but one subject—and that shall be described in the title,—and no law or section of law, shall be revived, amended, or repealed, by reference to its title or section only, and it shall be the duty of the Legislature at the first session after the adoption of this Constitution, to appoint two commissioners, learned in the law, to revise and codify the laws of this State, and the said commissioners shall report the said code so formed to the Legislature, within a time to be by it determined, for its approval, amendment or rejection, and if adopted after the revision and codification of the said laws, it shall be the duty of the Legislature, in amending any article or section thereof, to enact the same as the said article or section would read, when amended; and whenever the Legislature shall enact any public general law, not amendatory of any section or article in the said code, it shall be the duty of the Legislature to enact the same in articles and sections, in the same manner as the said code may be arranged; and to provide for the publication of all additions and alterations which may be made to the said code; and it shall also be the duty of the Legislature to appoint one or more commissioners, learned in the law, whose duty it shall be to revise, simplify and abridge the rules of practice, pleadings, forms and proceedings of the courts of record in this State."

The substitute having been read,

Mr. Gwinn made some remarks (which will be found embodied in a report of some other remarks at a later period of the day.)

Mr. Thomas expressed his hope that no motion would be made to divide the question. The effect of a division would be that the question would first be taken on striking out, leaving them at liberty to insert any article hereafter, and the vote on that motion, should it prevail, would be no indication of the sense of the House on the merits of the particular proposition now offered. For this reason he hoped that there would be no division of the question.

The question was then stated to be on the substitute amendment of Mr. Gwinn.

Mr. Dorsey moved to amend the substitute by striking out the word "general."

The amendment was rejected.

The question recurred on the amendment of Mr. Gwinn.

Mr. Stephenson asked the yeas and nays which were ordered.

Mr. Dorsey called for a division, so as to take the question separately on that portion of the amendment which related to pleadings, &c.

Some conversation followed on a point of order.

On a suggestion by Mr. Tuck,

Mr. Dorsey withdrew the call for a division.

Mr. Chambers, of Kent, gave his views of the

state of the question, under the different amendments which had been adopted.

Mr. CHAMBERS explained, in detail, the various particulars involved in the amendment of the gentleman from Baltimore, to show that it included all the provisions which the Convention, by its previous votes, had expressed a willingness to adopt, except only a portion of the amendment of the gentleman from Caroline. He advocated the system of codification, and would agree to the plan of simplifying the system of special pleading, as it seemed to be the wish of the Convention. He suggested various difficulties which must result, if the Convention adhered to the portion of the amendment which was now omitted. He was aware how difficult it was for gentlemen who had cast their votes in favor of it yesterday, to surrender pre-conceived and pre-expressed opinions. It was a false pride, though common to us all. But he did believe, if persisted in, this necessity to repeal or re-enact every thing in a former law having an "object" in common with the new law, would result in many and great mischiefs. It would require infinite labor and a large share of legal investigation in every case, and very often the result would be, that the new law, by its repealing clause, would operate upon previous provisions never intended to be repealed; or if there were no repealing clause, the new law would not be pursuant to the Constitution for the want of a full enumeration and re-enactment of all the previous provisions having a common object. He denied that after the experience of its mischiefs in a few instances, it would prevent incompetent persons from attempting to draft Acts of Assembly. Every session would bring in new members of that class; and the last to perceive his incompetency would be the incompetent member. Experience of others would never profit such a man. Bad as it might be to have a law drafted so obscurely as to make it difficulty or even impossible to give it operation, it was worse to have this additional mischief, that useful provisions of pre-existing laws should be annulled when no one desired or designed to repeal them.

He illustrated these positions and strongly urged the adoption of the amendment of the gentleman from Baltimore.

Mr. THOMAS made a brief reply, in which he further illustrated the arguments he had made on several previous occasions. He enforced the position he had formerly taken, that parts of some laws ought not to be amended without rendering it necessary to re-enact the whole, because all other parts would be affected by the change of a part. He referred to the acts granting charters to banks and other corporations, which contained a number of conditions and restrictions occupying various sections, and to the practice which prevailed, of lobby members coming here for the purpose of obtaining supplementary acts for the purpose of repealing such sections as were most onerous, and said that our statute books were swelled out by these numerous supplements passed by Legislatures that did not see their effect. He wished to avoid this inconvenient multiplication of laws. He could not see that any obstacles would be thrown in the way of present legislation by the course he recommended. He thought that by it this danger would be avoided, of surprise on the Legislature, when the section to be repealed or amended and the whole act of incorporation, of which it was a part, were printed and laid before the House, having the question of repeal under consideration.

Mr. CHAMBERS thought much difficulty would grow out of the use of indefinite language. An act of Assembly often has a variety of "*objects*." It cannot be necessary to re-enact a whole law, perhaps a long one, and to republish it because a new law changes some one of these objects, or provides a new and additional rule concerning them. He instanced cases that might occur in in regard to the testamentary act, which is almost a volume of itself.

He did not perceive how the proposed prevention of frauds was to be accomplished by it, as suggested.

If, as has been said, members of the Legislature would not look at provisions in a printed volume, lying open before them, containing the laws of a previous session, to learn the character of a bank charter or any other charter, why should we expect them to look at the pages of another document? Nothing but a blind confidence, which closes the eye to all means of information, except from the party confided in, could occasion such gross and culpable neglect of duty. Misplaced confidence under any system will end in fraud. Even in this wonderful age of "progress," that great desideratum was yet to be attained— "a mode to prevent the cunning knave from overreaching the credulous and unsuspecting."

He pointed out various advantages as likely to ensue from the adoption of the amendment of the gentleman from Baltimore.

Mr. GWINN said:

That the gentleman from Kent, had so thoroughly established the unreasonableness and inconvenience of the proposition of the gentleman from Caroline, that he would not recur to any portion of the argument upon that head. He desired, however, to answer an illustration, used by the gentleman from Frederick. Admit that a charter had been obtained, by the person alluded to, which conferred, by way of supplement, extraordinary powers upon any corporation. What did it prove? Why, surely, if the charter went beyond the intention of the Legislature, it demonstrated only that the Legislature had been imposed on, or that the committee, which had charge of that branch of the public business, had not paid proper attention to their work. Nor did he see how the mistake could ordinarily occur. For if a bill repealed an act by its title, or a section by its number, it was not likely that any committee would be so grossly neglectful, as to omit the examination of that which they designed to repeal, and if any thing were added it would speak for itself.

If the whole law were to be re-enacted, worse errors would occur. By a supplement, the only mischief done, was what its terms accomplished. But if the theory of the gentleman was true, and whatever was omitted was repealed—infinitely greater risks would be encountered. If a committee, or the legislature, were likely to fall into error, from ignorance of the prior law, how much more likely would they be to commit mistakes, when the whole existence of the prior law would depend upon their knowledge of it, or sufficient re-enactment of its terms when it was discovered?

He would take the case of another corporation, since the gentleman from Frederick had alluded to the mischief, which supplements to a charter might affect. The laws relating to the Baltimore and Ohio Rail Road Company, fill a considerable volume. They affect every portion of the economy and management of that road.

Now, at the last session of the legislature, a brief law of some dozen lines was passed, prescribing the time of the annual selection of the directors of this company. It was a supplement to the act of 1826, which incorporated the company. Who here can say, what parts of the old act this disturbed, so as to require a republication?

It might incidentally alter the whole relation of the company to the State—its largest stockholder—or it might, as was probable the case, be a measure of mere inconvenience only.

Yet this proposition would have entailed upon the projector of this law, a laborious and difficult analysis of the very numerous acts of Assembly, relating to that Company, in order that all portions connected with it in the old system, might be preserved; or else, by their omission, they would have been constructively repealed. And, if a safer course were pursued, and *the whole* of the law were re-enacted in one grand railroad law, the statute book would be over-loaded. So again, in reference to any other charter. If a bank had a privilege given to it, which was an extension of an old liberty, it would require for its safety that all its old chartered privileges should be re-enacted. He could conceive nothing more cumbrous. than such legislation. The laws of one session would be the same of almost all that had gone before, with the lucubrations of the year added.

In more serious matters the case would be worse. Take the testamentary law; it began in the last century, and its supplements are very numerous. Many of its sections contain provisions, explicable to different classes of objects. The thread of connection is difficult to trace. Suppose that a new inconvenience were to occur if, as a member of the legislature, he was satisfied by his own experience, assisted by the judgment of abler counsel, that this inconvenience could be remedied, he would not have hesitated, under direction and advice, to introduce such an amendment. But if the proposition of the gentleman from Caroline, carries, who would amend such a law? The risk would be too great.

If all the provisions properly belonging to the amendment were not re-enacted, they would be considered as repealed. But to re-enact them might demand a patient analysis of sections, which very few men were capable of performing; and yet, if this were not done, the tenure of property—the most solemn formalities of the testamentary, system—the course of distribution—the probate of claims—the regulation of accounts—might all be disordered, and the most serious and irremediable embarrassments involve the whole system. The only escape would be the re-enactment of the whole law—a labor utterly useless in itself. Public convenience is readily gratified by digests, which derive their authority from the character of the compiler. The plan offered by himself ensured the certainty of the law. He understood that this re-enactment was only intended as a public convenience. But since the whole system would be codified—why, by re-enactment make a partial digest, when the re-enactment itself would be digested in the formation of a code? The code would be made in some three or four years—and the old system or legislation would serve till then. The inconvenience had been endured for nearly two centuries, and it could surely be borne with for four years longer at most.

The objection to the amendment of the gentleman from Washington, (Mr. Schley,) was that it did not provide for a codification of laws passed, after the code of existing laws was framed. It directed that there should be, every ten years, a publication and promulgation of the statute laws of the State, which were then in force. But if there was to be a code, he could not see why subsequent laws should not be codified by the Legislature which passed them.

No commissioners would understand their meaning better, and it was certainly running a useless circuit, for one Legislature to enact a law—another to appoint men to codify it—and a third to accept it as codified—when the first could have engrafted it, on the code itself, by legislating in that way, instead of pursuing the usual forms of a general act. The one plan was as convenient as the other, and more likely to lead to a correct understanding of the law, and to its symetrical growth.

In offering his proposition, he could frankly say, that he did it to achieve a union of conflicting opinions, and he had freely acccepted every suggestion which did not interfere with the main plan.

Mr. Thomas said a few words in reply, in which he said he would not publish the whole statute, but merely the sections in it which were to be amended.

Mr. Dent said:

He would move an amendment to the substitute offered by the gentleman from Baltimore city, (Mr. Gwinn,) the same amendment, which upon his, (Mr. D.'s,) motion, had been engrafted upon the amendment of the gentleman from Washington. He, (Mr. D.,) preferred it should come in at the end of the substitute. There was some doubt which of these amendments would be adopted; he, therefore, wished to see his amendment incorporated upon both propositions. He was sure there would be no opposition.

Mr. Gwinn accepted the amendment of Mr. Dent, as a modification of his own proposition.

The question then recurred on the modified

amendment of Mr. Gwinn, and being taken, resulted as follows:

Affirmative—Messrs. Chapman, President, Morgan, Blakistone, Dent, Ricaud, Lee, Chambers, of Kent, Dorsey, Wells, Sellman, Weems, Merrick, James U. Dennis, Williams, Hodson, Goldsborough, Phelps, Tuck, Sprigg, McCubbin, Hearn, Stephenson, McHenry, Nelson, Gwinn, Brent, of Baltimore city, Ware, Fiery, Harbine, Davis, Kilgour, Waters, Anderson, Hollyday, Cockey and Brown—36.

Negative— Messrs. Buchanan, Bell, Lloyd, Dickinson, Sherwood, of Talbot, John Dennis, Miller, Bowling, George, Wright, Dirickson, Thomas, Shriver, Biser, Annan, Magraw, Carter, Thawley, Stewart of Caroline, Schley, Neill, Brewer, Weber, Fitzpatrick, Smith, Parke, Ege, and Shower—28.

So the substitute of Mr. Gwinn was agreed to.

The question then recurred on the adoption of the section as thus amended.

Mr. Tuck moved an amendment.

After some explanatory conversation on the part of Messrs. Tuck, Gwinn and Chambers, of Kent,

Mr. Chambers, of Kent, suggested that the object avowed in the amendment of the gentleman from Prince George's, (Mr. Tuck,) was accomplished in the amendment of the gentleman from Baltimore city, (Mr. Gwinn) We might not all see through the same spectacles, but he thought that when the Convention met on Monday, in a calmer mood, the fact would be seen to be such as he had stated.

Therefore he moved to adjourn.

The Convention refused to adjourn.

Mr. Tuck withdrew his amendment.

Some conversation followed on a point of order between Mr. Brent, of Baltimore city, and the President.

Mr. Gwinn moved to amend the amendment, by inserting the following words, to precede the said section:

"The style of all laws of this State, shall be: 'Be it enacted by the General Assembly of Maryland,' and."

The amendment was agreed to.

The section, as amended, was then adopted.

And the Convention adjourned until Monday at 12 o'clock.

MONDAY, February 24, 1851.

Pursuant to the order of Friday last, the Convention met this day at 12 o'clock.

Prayer was made by the Rev. Mr. Griffith.

The roll of the members was called, and a quorum being present, the journal of Friday last was read and approved.

The President laid before the Convention the following communication from the Treasurer of the State.

Treasury, *Annapolis*, Feb. 22nd, 1851.

Sir :—In compliance with the order of the Convention of the 21st inst., "requesting the Treasurer to report to them the amount of money expended in the purchase of Lots and the erection of Warehouses in the city of Baltimore, for the Inspection of Tobacco, and also to report further whether the purchase of Lots, the erection of Warehouses and the expenses of Inspection are now, or have been at any time heretofore a charge upon the Treasury of the State."

The Treasurer reports that the amount of expense incurred in the purchase of Lots and Warehouses, and in the erection of Warehouses, including payments on account of Interest on the several loans which have been negotiated for them, are :

For Insurances and other incidental expenses,	$722,994 43
Of which has been paid,	559,304 76
Leaving due a balance of	$163,689 67

He further states, that none of the expenses, either on account of the purchase of Lots, the erection of Warehouses, or of Inspection are now, or have at any time heretofore, been a charge on the Treasury of the State.

Very respectfully, your obedient serv't.,
D. Claude, Treasurer.

Hon. Jno. G. Chapman, Pres't. of Con.

Which was read, and

On motion of Mr. Donaldson,

Referred to the committee on Inspections.

RULES OF THE CONVENTION.

Mr. Ricaud called up the report heretofore made by him as Chairman of the select committee on the rules.

And the Convention proceeded to the consideration thereof.

The report was adopted, without debate or amendment, precisely in the form in which it was reported, (as published in Friday's proceedings.)

On motion of Mr. Brown, the Convention passed to the orders of the day.

THE LEGISLATIVE DEPARTMENT.

The Convention resumed the consideration of the special order of the day, being the report heretofore made by Mr. Johnson, from the committee on the legislative department of the government.

The eighteenth section of the said report being under consideration in the words following :

"*Section* 18. No bill shall become a law unless passed in each House by a majority of the whole number of members elected, and on the question of its final passage, the ayes and noes shall be recorded."

Mr. Phelps moved to strike out said 18th section, and substitute in lieu of it the following.

Section 18th. "No bill shall become a law unless it receive the concurrent vote of a majority of the members present in both Houses."

Mr. P. briefly explained the object of his amendment. He desired to make the section conform to the twelfth and fourteenth sections of the report.

Mr. WEEMS said he had intended to offer a substitute for the eighteenth section, which he would now read.

Mr. W. read his proposed amendment; but

Mr. DONALDSON having suggested that the substitute was properly an amendment to the twenty-first and not to the eighteenth section,

Mr. WEEMS withdrew his substitute for the present.

The question then recurred on the amendment of Mr. PHELPS.

Mr. DONALDSON opposed the amendment. He had thought, in looking over the report of the legislative committee, that if any of its sections met with the general apprebation of the Convention, this certainly would. To his judgment it was the most valuable provision in the whole report.

There was in fact no inconsistency between this section and the other sections to which the gentleman from Dorchester, (Mr. Phelps,) had referred. By the 12th section, a majority of each House shall constitute a quorum for the transaction of business; it is on the single question of the final passage of the bill that this 18th section requires the affirmative vote of a majority of all the members elected; all antecedent questions may be decided by a majority of a quorum. By the 14th section the yeas and nays must be recorded on any question, on the demand of five members; by the section under consideration, the yeas and nays must be recorded on the final passage of a bill, whether demanded or not.

He believed that no one who had had any experience in our State Legislature, could fail to have observed the great evils which had arisen from the want of such provision. Hundreds of laws were passed by the mere silent assent of the great body of legislators, often passed by their titles, and of their contents most of those who permitted them to pass were utterly ignorant. Their first knowledge of them was derived from the printed volume of the statutes; and no votes having been recorded, every member was enabled to escape from responsibility for the injurious results of such legislation. The evil would be cured by this provision. Under the present system, also, members frequently absented themselves for the very purpose of ensuring success to measures, which they dared not vote in favor of; and this was an important part of most of the log-rolling, which had inflicted so much injury on our own, as well as other States. He knew one case, where, by such management, a most injurious, and most unpopular change was made in the Constitution of our State, by thirty-five votes of the House of Delegates, little more than one-third of the number elected, confirming the act of a previous session. Adopt this 18th section and such absenteeism, whether fraudulent or not, could work no such evil effect; indeed, absenteeism, which was one of the curses of our Maryland Legislatures, would itself be cured, for the presence of members would be absolutely necessary to carry through effectually the business of legislation. It would also act as an admirable check upon hasty and excessive legislation, of which we had heard so much well-founded complaint. He hoped there was no doubt of its adoption.

Mr. SPENCER said, if he thought that the other provisions, which, he took it for granted, were to be inserted in the Constitution, would not be placed there, he should attach more weight to the remarks of the gentleman from Anne Arundel, (Mr. Donaldson,) than under present circumstances he could attach to them. He (Mr. S.) took it for granted that it was the intention of the Convention to incorporate in the Constitution provisions by which appropriations of the public money, and pledges of the public credit, for works of internal improvement, would be arrested. If so, the direct effect would be to arrest the system of combination and log-rolling on which the gentleman had based his argument, that the vote of a majority of the whole body ought to be required. He (Mr. S.) thought that great inconveniencies would result from the adoption of the section as it stood in the report. The proposition of the gentleman from Dorchester, (Mr. Phelps,) seemed to him a wise and salutary provision, and he (Mr. S.) should vote for it.

Mr. BROWN said, he did not like the language of the section as it stood, and that he felt disposed to vote for the amendment of the gentleman from Dorchester, (Mr. Phelps.) Gentlemen were to bear in mind that combinations were made *against* the passage of bills, as well as in favor of their passage; and though the section as it stood in the report might prevent some bad legislation, yet, as a whole, he thought it would do more harm than it would do good. As at present advised, he should prefer to take the language of the old Constitution. If he should find that he was mistaken in his opinion, he should change his vote accordingly.

Mr. JENIFER thought that if there was one single section, in the whole bill under consideration, which, more than another, was wholesome, salutary, and conservative, it was this; and he thought that if the section should be struck out, and nothing of an equivalent character be inserted, the legislation of the State would be worse hereafter than it had been heretofore.

Mr. DONALDSON replied to the remarks of the gentleman from Queen Anne's, (Mr. Spencer,) and stated, that he did not mean to confine his objections to the single class of bills, to which that gentleman referred. Our dearest rights and interests, and the welfare of the whole community, were involved in a great many other laws passed, or which might be passed by the legislature. The bill to which he himself had before referred, as having passed by the votes of little more than a third of the members elected to the House of Delegates, was the incorporation of a lottery grant into the Constitution. Often, too, special acts were passed, which produced great injustice to persons who knew nothing of any purpose to apply for them.

In regard to the inconvenience of the section proposed, he said, that the same provision was in the New York Constitution, and he had never heard of any difficulty arising therefrom in that State, although the interests represented in her legislature were of such great variety and magnitude. This was, in fact, the true method of securing the attendance of members. Reference had been made to the thinness of this Convention in which important questions were, from day to day, decided by mere majorities of quorums. The fact, he must say, was discreditable. But, the action of the Convention was, after all, only advisory. The people by their votes were to adopt or reject what was done here; and if the work were good, it would matter little whether it came from the hands of few or many. The legislature, on the other hand, made laws, which, of their own efficacy, regulated the rights, and affected the interests of the people; and those laws ought not to pass without the express consent of a majority of the people's representatives.

Mr. D. insisted further on the evils of log-rolling, which could not, perhaps, be entirely prevented, but which might be greatly checked. By the decision of the Convention, that a bill should relate to one object only, which should be expressed in its title, a blow had been already struck at that vicious system of legislation; and a still more effective blow would be struck by the adoption of the section under consideration. He therefore hoped that the amendment of the gentleman from Dorchester would not prevail.

Mr. Phelps said, he had no particular objection to the latter clause of the section, (that which provided for the taking of the yeas and nays on the final passage of bills,) but he thought that its effect would be to retard the business of the legislature, and to embarrass its proceedings.

As to the section itself, if such a provision had been inserted in the old Constitution, the result to the State of Maryland, would have been repudiation and insolvency. To sustain this position he referred to the meagre vote by which various important measures had been passed—the majority in some cases being only one or two, not of the whole number elected, but of the number present.

Mr. Spencer would vote for the section, he said, if he could believe for a moment that its effect would be, to cause all bills before the legislature, to be more thoroughly examined and considered, or if he could feel justified in expecting from it any of the beneficial operation which was claimed for it. In his judgment, no such result would follow.

He referred also to his own experience as sustaining the assertion that, when action was taken upon great public measures, the attendance in the legislature was always full.

Mr. Biser said, that if he had been called upon to select one provision in this bill, better calculated than any other, to promote the public interest, this was the section to which he should have pointed. Caution was the parent of safety. At home and abroad—in this Hall and out of it, he was a majority man, and he intended to vote in favor of the first branch of the section. The absence of such a provision had been the source of serious evil to the legislation of the State.

He was also in favor of the last clause of the section—believing, as he did, that it was a saving and salutary provision. He believed that it would obviate much mischief in the legislation of the State.

Mr. Weems suggested that it was in the power of any member of the legislature to call for the yeas and nays which, if the call was sustained by a small number of members, must be ordered. It seemed to him, therefore, that there was no nececsity for making an imperative rule, that the yeas and nays should be taken on every law, or resolution, however unimportant or local its object might be. Such a rule would greatly retard the business of the legislature.

He moved, therefore, to amend the section by striking out the words "and on the question of its final passage, the ayes and noes shall be recorded."

The President. That amendment will take precedence of the substitute.

Mr. Biser. I call for a division on striking out.

Mr. Spencer said, he never could consent to vote for striking out the provision which related to the yeas and nays.

Mr. Blakistone moved an amendment confining the operation of the restriction to bills appropriating money or imposing a tax upon the people.

Mr. B. said, that, in his judgment, these were the only laws which absolutely required the vote of a majority of all the members elected. In ordinary matters of legislation, he thought such a provision unnecessary.

He hoped the gentleman from Calvert, (Mr. Weems,) would accept the amendment as a modification of his own proposition.

Mr. Weems. I cannot do so. The amendment does not at all suit my views.

Mr. Blakistone withdrew the amendment.

Mr. Gwinn said he could not agree to vote for the proposition just read by the gentleman from St. Mary's (Mr. Blakistone). He did not suppose that any member could be influenced in his course by a call of the yeas and nays on a question, but the call possessed the advantage of placing the responsibility where it ought to rest. There is a great inconsistency in saying that a majority of the members is a quorum competent to transact business, and yet requiring the yeas and nays only on the final vote. This he considered as unjust in its operation. A majority of a *quorum* may have amended a bill and put it in a shape in which it will pass, why then should there be required a *majority* of the whole House to pass it? If the rule is to be made applicable at all, it should be applicable in all the stages of the bill. Nor could he understand why members who were absent, from sickness or any other necessity, should be always considered as opposed to a bill. The true secret and protection of legislation must be in the honor and conscience of the individual member. All questions should, in his opinion, be determined by a majority of the *quorum* who may be present. Absenteeism cannot always be prevented, as it frequently proceeds from causes beyond the reach of legislative power, and ought not to be permitted to influence the fate of a measure.

Mr. Spencer moved to amend said eighteenth section, by striking out, in the second line, the words "which number of," and the word "elected."

Mr. Phelps accepted the amendment.

Some conversation followed.

Mr. Weems expressed a hope that the time would never occur, in this hall, when any bill involving important public interests, would be permitted to pass without a call for the yeas and nays. This, he thought, was sufficiently guarded against, by the provision which had been adopted that the yeas and nays shonld be taken on the call of five members of the House, and one member of the Senate. But it was not necessary that they should be taken on every local and private bill. As the section now stands, he believed it is required that the ayes and noes, shall be taken on all bills without discrimination. He thought it would be better that a majority of all the members elected, should be required on all laws of public concernment, and that, in such cases, the vote should be taken by yeas and nays. He hoped the agricultural interest, on this floor, would vote for such a provision as that, no bill of a public character should be permitted to pass the Legislature without the vote of a majority of the whole number of members elected.

Mr. Morgan suggested that his friend from Calvert, would not be able to gain his object, without some modification of his amendment. How was he to ascertain whether a majority of the whole number of members elected, had voted without taken the ayes and noes.

Mr. Weems explained that it would be easy for the speaker, when he counted the House, to ascertain whether a majority of the whole number of members had voted.

Mr. Morgan said it would not consume much more of the time of the House to take the yeas and nays, than was consumed in dividing the House. He agreed that every one who had had much experience in legislation, must see the propriety of adopting some such provision. He had himself known a bill passed by a vote of only twenty-four members, that being the majority of forty-six, which was a quorum of the House, and that a very important bill. It would be better, he thought, to insert a provision in the Constitution, than to leave the matter to be settled by the Legislature, many of whom cared little about the responsibility of their acts. Such a provision embodied the only conservative principle, and the only guard against negligent legislation. He wondered that any one could be found to sanction the principle of passing laws, without reading more than the title. There ought to be a guard against such infractions.

Mr. Jenifer said, that forty-six members of the House constituting a *quorum*, twenty-four would be a majority of a *quorum*, and eleven being a *quorum* of the Senate, six was a majority of that *quorum*. He could not suppose that the Convention would be willing that important bills should be passed by so small a number without the vote being taken by yeas and nays. But the fourteenth section of this bill provides that the yeas and nays shall be ordered on the call of five members of the House, and of one member of the Senate. As to the fact, whether a majority of all the members elected had voted, the Speaker could always decide that point. He thought that he provision in the fourteenth section, to which the had referred, is a sufficient protection of the public interests.

Mr. Phelps said he was not particularly tenacious of his own amendment. He was perfectly willing to accept the amendment of the gentleman from Queen Anne's, (Mr. Spencer.) The principle that a majority of the members present should pass laws had been engrafted on the Constitutions of nineteen States, yet a cry was raised against this proposition, as if some terrible encroachment was about to be made on the usual course of legislation. He was indifferent whether any more laws were passed or not. If there was not another law passed in the next hundred years, he believed no harm would result. He would withdraw his amendment and accept that of the gentleman from Queen Anne's.

Mr. Chambers entirely concurred with the committee in the whole section as it stands. He had hoped his friend from St. Mary's would have admitted that the vote by yeas and nays was always the mode of testing the sense of a legislative body. He would say, in reply to the gentleman who was such a stickler for majorities, that twenty-four members, although the majority of a *quorum*, was not a majority of the whole House.

The question was then stated to be on the amendment of Mr. Weems, striking out from the section the following words:

"And on the question of its final passage, the ayes and noes shall be recorded."

Mr. Weems asked the yeas and nays, which were ordered, and being taken, resulted as follows:

Affirmative— Messrs. Dent, Weems, Lloyd, Phelps, Stewart of Baltimore city, Sherwood of Baltimore city, Ware, Shower and Brown—9.

Negative—Messrs. Chapman, President, Morgan, Blakistone, Ricaud, Lee, Chambers of Kent, Donaldson, Dorsey, Wells, Kent, Jenifer, Bell, Ridgely, Dickinson, Sherwood of Talbot, Colston, John Dennis, James U. Dennis, Williams, Hodson, Goldsborough, Miller, Tuck, Sprigg, McCubbin, Spencer, George, Dirickson, Jacobs, Gaither, Biser, Annan, McHenry, Magraw, Nelson Carter, Thawley, Stewart of Caroline, Gwinn, Schley, Fiery, Neill, Harbine, Kilgour, Brewer, Waters, Weber, Hollyday, Fitzpatrick, Smith and Parke—51.

So the amendment was rejected.

The question then recurred on the amendment of Mr. Spencer.

The question was taken, and the amendment was rejected.

And the eighteenth section was then adopted.

Mr. Fitzpatrick offered the following amendment to the report:

"The Legislature shall have power to provide by law, for exempting from execution not more than five hundred dollars worth of the household furniture or other property belonging to each jamily in this State."

Mr. Morgan called the attention of the gentleman from Alleghany, (Mr. Fitzpatrick,) to the fact that a similiar provision had been reported by Mr. Presstman.

Mr. Fitzpatrick said the provision in the report alluded to, was not as specific as his own proposition. But he would withdraw it, and gave notice that he should hereafter offer it as an additional section.

Mr. Sprigg moved to amend said report by inserting as the nineteenth section, the following:

"The House of Delegates shall have the sole power of impeachment in all cases, but a majority of all the members, must concur in an impeachment; all impeachments shall be tried by the Senate, and when sitting for that purpose, they shall be on oath or affirmation, to do justice according to the law and evidence, but no person shall be convicted without the concurrence of two-thirds of all the Senators."

Mr. Chambers expressed a wish that the words "not otherwise provided for in this Constitution" should be stricken out. He thought that there was no other tribunal competent to try cases of impeachment but the Senate. They were in a thousand instances founded on charges which had no legal definition. The appropriate duties of the ordinary courts of law and of juries were not at all applicable to such cases. They ought to be tried only before a tribunal which is discharged from all the technicalities by which the ordinary courts are bound.

Mr. Sprigg said he would accept the amendment suggested by the gentleman from Kent, and would modify his amendment accordingly.

Mr. McHenry moved to amend the amendment of Mr. Sprigg by striking out the words "two-thirds," and inserting in lieu thereof "a majority."

Mr. McHenry was sorry the amendment he had now submitted had not been offered by some other gentleman. He believed it would be found impossible ever to get two-thirds of the Legislature to agree to the dismissal of an unworthy officer. He would be happy to take the sense of the Convention on his amendment.

Mr. Tuck replied that the agreement of two-thirds was required in most, or all of the other States. The object of the two-third rule was to protect the accused party against party or political hostility. That was the original cause of the provision. If, in ordinary cases, where an individual is accused of crime, it is required that a jury of twelve men must agree on a verdict, he did not see why there should not be an agreement of two-thirds in cases of impeachment, which are also of a criminal character. He therefore, thought it would be much the best way to let it remain two-thirds.

Mr. Weems, after requesting that the amendment should be read, suggested the insertion of the word "elected" after "members." It would then accord with the rest of the section.

Mr. McHenry said this would make the provision still more stringent. The gentleman from Prince George's (Mr. Tuck,) says that these are criminal cases, and that they should be treated in a way analagous to others of the same character. But impeachment cases are not always founded on criminal acts. Very frequently, they merely look to the removal of officers who have become inefficient or incompetent. Even if a majority had the power to make these removals, he did not think they would be made as easily as they ought to be. Every facility ought to be rendered for the removal of incompetent public officers. Except in times of great party excitement, all the the public sympathies would be in favor of the accused; and it was his object to obtain some security for the public interests.

Mr. Jenifer was of opinion that if the amendment prevailed, impeachment, instead of being a criminal prosecution, would be a party or political persecution. You insert a provision in the Constitution that these public officers shall be elected by the people, and then you insert another provision giving a party majority the power to remove them from office by impeachment. The subject had been already discussed on a former occasion. He hoped the amendment would not prevail.

Mr. Neill reminded the House that this subject was likely to come up again for discussion, when the judiciary report shall be before the Convention. There was some portion of that report which contained a provision of this character. He would, therefore, suggest it as the better course to postpone the consideration of this question, until the report of the judiciary committee shall be up for consideration.

Mr. Sprigg accepted the suggestion, and the section was informally laid over.

The nineteenth section was then read as follows:

Section 19*th*. No money shall be drawn from the Treasury of this State but in consequence of appropriations made by law, an accurate statement of the receipts and expenditure of public money shall be attached to and published with the laws after each regular session of the General Assembly.

Mr. Ridgely moved to amend said section by inserting after the word "law" in the second line, the following:

"And every such law shall distinctly specify the sum appropriated, and the object to which it is to be applied."

The question was taken, and the amendment was agreed to.

Mr. Ridgely (to avoid all ambiguity, he said,) moved to amend the section by adding at the end thereof, the following words:

"Provided, that nothing, herein contained, shall operate to prevent the Legislature from placing by appropriation a contingent fund at the disposal of the Executive."

Mr. Spencer stated, that he felt some hesitation about voting for this amendment. He hoped the gentleman from Baltimore county, (Mr. Ridgely,) would refrain from pressing it at this time. If he were urged now, he could not consent to vote for it, and he would feel himself compelled to ask for the yeas and nays.

Mr. RIDGELY replied, that he was as much opposed to the principle of placing the public money at the disposal of the executive as any one. But it has always been the practice to leave a sum in his control to meet such contingencies as may arise. And it was usual to place funds within his reach in case of any sudden exigency; and as the legislature would be the judge of the nature of the exigency, which it was impossible for this Convention to foresee, and to provide for, he could not see what evil could result from the adoption of the provision. The legislature only can be competent to judge of the exigency when it shall take place.

Mr. SPENCER admitted the full force of the remarks of the gentleman from Baltimore county; but we must bear in mind that we are now establishing a new government, and it becomes us to proceed with great care. Heretofore, experience has taught us that modes have been devised of getting round the Constitution. We ought to guard against such practices hereafter. We have imposed many restrictions on the legislature as to the appropriation of money, and if we now permit the legislature to place, at their discretion, a contingent fund without limit, at the disposition of the executive, it might open the door to great abuses hereafter. He saw so much cause for apprehension in this amendment, that he should not only vote against it, but he must call for the yeas and nays on the question. But if the gentleman would place a limit on the amount, or if he could obtain from the Governor any information as to the usual amount required, and would limit it to that amount, he would vote for it.

Mr. DONALDSON said, he could tell the gentleman from Queen Anne's, that the usual amount annually granted was $5,000, and had recently been $6,000. The executive cannot abuse the grant, as he must render his account of expenditures annually, to the legislature.

Mr. SPENCER moved to amend said amendment by adding at the end thereof, these words, "not exceeding six thousand dollars per year."

Mr. McHENRY expressed his opionion that there was no necessity to give any specific power to the Legislature; but, he believed, that when Congress made appropriations for contingent expenses, the objects for which the appropriations were made were specified, so that the grant should be for specific objects.

Mr. DONALDSON explained that the appropriations by Congress were not always specific.

Mr. McHENRY thought this proposition would be an anomaly in any Constitution. We came here to reform evils, but instead of imposing restrictions on the Legislative and Executive departments, we are opening the door for the entrance of new abuses. He would prefer to see this power of appropriation put in another form, where it would not be liable to abuse. Under it, as it now stands, the Governor may go on to make extravagant expenditures. We are now commencing a new government—we are entering on a new state of things, and he desired to see an entire emancipation from the customs and traditions of the past.

Mr. BROWN would not vote for any restrictions. He thought there had been very good legislatures heretofore, and he did not doubt that there would be as good ones hereafter. All the acts of this body appeared to him to have a tendency to abolish legislation altogether. It was only necessary to look back at the various restrictions which have already been imposed on the Legislature, to be assured of this.

He would like to know how much further this Convention intended to go. We ought to be careful lest while stopping one hole in the Constitution, we make two fresh holes. He was very willing to impose restrictions on the Governor, but he was not disposed to go to the extent of depriving the Legislature of all power. Under such a pressure of business as there was at the last session of the General Assembly, the new restriction requiring the ayes and noes to be called, could not be enforced without great risk to important measures. While, on the one hand, you tie up the Legislature so as not to originate any business during the last three days of the session, you now come forward with this new restriction, which will lead to a great consumption of time. You may almost as well abolish all legislation at once. He begged gentleman who were thus eager after change, to pause awhile, and reflect on what may yet be brought forward. We have not yet done with this legislative report. He himself expected to make some proposition before it was disposed of. The House had established biennial sessions—he had voted for annual ones. You are restricting the Legislature until they will have nothing on there hands. He thought the Legislature as trustworthy as this body is, and that we ought not to tie down their hands.

Mr. McHENRY thought that it was a singular mode of protecting the Legislature by giving more power into the hands of the Executive.

Mr. BROWN replied that this proposition gave power to the Legislature.

Mr. McHENRY rejoined. We should labor to throw power into the hands of the people, who only are worthy of entire confidence. They are trust-worthy; but he was not disposed to put too much trust in mere agents. He admitted the necessity of employing agents, but he was desirous that they should be employed under a faithful and vigilant supervision.

Mr. DONALDSON suggested that there were a large number of accounts which the Governor settled. There would be difficulty attending a constitutional provision of a particular amount for this contingent fund. It might prove either too large or too small, according to circumstances, which we cannot foresee. It must be left to the Legislature to make the sum appropriated correspond with the necessity. If the sum we now fix should be too large for the necessities of some particular year, then there would be a tendency and a temptation to spend the whole of it, which would lead to extravagance and favoritism. On the other hand, exigencies might occur which would make the sum fixed entirely inadequate, and thus, much inconvenience might be produced. There is but little danger of collusion between the Executive and the Legislature, in order to sanction extravagance in the former; and the liability to account for these expenditures in detail, is a sufficient check on abuses. Such has always been the practice, and it has led to no evil result.

The question was then stated to be on the amendment of Mr. SPENCER.

Mr. SPENCER withdrew it.

The question then recurred and was taken on the amendment of Mr. RIDGLEY, and it was agreed to.

And the question recurring on the section as amended,

On motion of Mr. SPRIGG, said section was further amended by adding, at the end thereof, the following:

"And the Governor shall report to the Legislature at each session, the amount expended and the objects and purposes for which said amount was incurred."

And the section, as amended, was then adopted.

The twentieth section was read, as follows:

Sec. 20th. No divorce shall be granted by the General Assembly, nor any tax or other burden be levied on the persons or property of the people, for the support of any religious sect or denomination.

No amendment having been offered, the section was adopted.

The twenty-first section was read, as follows:

Sec. 21st. No loans shall be made upon the credit of this State which are not redeemable at the pleasure of the State, except such as may be authorized by an Act of Assembly, passed at one session and ratified and confirmed at the next succeeding regular session of the General Assembly.

Mr RIDGELY explained that this section together with some other subjects, were referred to the committee on municipalities, and they had deliberated on it, and come to an agreement to report some propositions to the Convention. As it was thought the object of the committee could be as well accomplished, by proposing their resolutions in the form of amendments to the legislative report, as by making a separate report, he would now move their adoption as a substitute to the amendment now under consideration.

Mr. RIDGELY moved to amend said report by striking out the twenty-first section and substituting in lieu of it the following:

"The credit of the State shall never be given or loaned in aid of any person, association, municipality or corporation, nor shall the legislature contract any debt, which shall singly, or in the aggregate exceed a half million of dollars, for which purpose a vote of three-fourths of all the members elected to both branches of the General Assembly shall be necessary, provided that the State may contract debts exceeding that amount, to repel invasion, suppress insurrection, and if threatened, to provide for the public defence."

Mr. GEORGE offered as a substitute for said section and substitute, the following:

Article 1. The amount of debts, hereafter contracted by the legislature, shall never exceed one hundred thousand dollars, except for the defence of the State, unless such debt shall be authorized by a law providing for the collection of an annual tax or taxes sufficient to pay the interest on such debt as it falls due, and also to discharge the principal of such debt within fifteen years from the time of contracting the same. And the taxes laid for this purpose shall never be repealed, or applied to any other object, until the said debt and the interest thereon shall be fully discharged.

Art. 2. The assent of two-thirds of the members elected to each branch of the legislature, shall be requisite to every bill appropriating the public money, or pledging the public faith, for local or private purposes; and the legislature shall not have the power to make appropriations, loans, or subscriptions to any work of internal improvement.

A motion was made to adjourn;

But withdrawn to enable,

Mr. DONALDSON to suggest that gentlemen who had amendments to offer, should now offer them, that they might appear upon the journal.

Mr. HODSON gave notice that he should offer at the proper time, the following as a substitute for the twenty-first section:

"Nor shall the legislature borrow money for internal improvements, without first taking the sense of the people through the ballot box; and any county or the city of Baltimore, who may cast a majority of votes against the proposition, shall be exempt."

Mr. TUCK, gave notice, that he should offer at the proper time, the following as a substitute for the twenty-fourth section:

"No senator or delegate of the assembly, if he shall qualify as such, shall hold or execute any office of profit, or receive the profits of any office exercised by any other person during the time for which he shall be elected."

Mr. DENT said:

We have adopted the twentieth section of this report, rather hastily I think. It reads thus: "No divorce shall be granted by the legislature, nor shall any tax, or other burden be levied on the persons or property of the people, for the support of any religious sect or denomination." The section embraces two subjects, so very distinct and dissimilar, that they should in my opinion, be provided for in two sections.

If in order, I therefore move a reconsideration of the vote on this section.

The motion not being now in order,

Mr. DENT gave notice that he should move a reconsideration of the vote on to-morrow.

Mr. D. said, the subjects embraced in the section had no connection with each other.

The motion was entered on the journal.

Mr. WEEMS gave notice that he should offer at

the proper time, the following as a substitute for the twenty-first section:

"No bill appropriating money or pledging the faith and credit of the State for works of internal improvement, shall become a law, except it be passed by a vote of two-thirds of the whole number of representatives in each branch of the legislature."

Mr. BREWER also gave notice that he should offer at the proper time, the following, as a substitute for the twenty-first section:

"*Section* 21. No loans shall be made upon the credit of this State, which are not redeemable at the pleasure of the State; and which may not be necessary to the payment of the existing public debt; nor shall any taxes be imposed upon the assessable property of the State, nor upon the inhabitants thereof, for any new schemes of improvement, (or for any other purpose, other than for the current expenses of the State,) except such as may be authorised by an act of assembly passed at one session by a two-third vote of the two Houses of the legislature, providing therein for taking the sense of the people thereupon at the next election thereafter, and ratified and confirmed at the next succeeding session of the General Assembly, in case a majority of the qualified voters of the State shall have declared in favor of the said act of Assembly."

And then the Convention adjourned until to-morrow, at 10 o'clock.

TUESDAY, February 25, 1851.

The Convention met at ten o'clock.

Prayer was made by the Rev. Mr. GRIFFITH.

The roll of the members was called.

A quorum being present, the journal of yesterday was read, and having been amended,

On motion of Mr. JENIFER, in that part which had erroneously attributed to him the motion to adjourn, was approved.

EDUCATION.

Mr. SMITH, chairman of the committee on education, submitted the following report:

Section 1st. A permanent and adequate school fund shall be established by the Legislature, so soon as the financial condition of the State shall justify it, the present fund for the support of free and common schools, and all money, stock and other property which may hereafter be appropriated for that purpose, or received into the treasury, under the provision of any law heretofore passed to augment the said fund, shall be securely invested and remain a perpetual fund, and the income thereof, shall be annually appropriated to the support of public schools, and it shall not be competent for the Legislature to borrow, appropriate or use the said fund or any part thereof, for any other purpose, under any pretence whatever.

Sec. 2nd. It shall be the duty of the Legislature, so soon as it may be compatible with the provisions of the aforegoing section, to establish a uniform system of common school education.

Sec. 3rd. There shall be elected by the qualified voters of the State, every year, a Superintendent of education or common schools, whose duties and compensation shall be prescribed by the Legislature.

Sec. 4th. For the preparation of teachers for such schools, it shall be the further duty of the Legislature to establish a Normal School for the education of persons who may desire to become teachers of common school, and that each county shall be entitled to its distributive share, according to its present disposition by law.

Mr. S. in presenting the report, stated that it had not been unanimously concurred in by the committee, and that the members dissenting from it reserved the right to present their own views.

The report was read and ordered to be printed.

Mr. CARTER, presented an account of James H. Fountain clerk of Caroline county court, for services rendered under the order of the Convention.

Which was read, and

On motion of Mr. CARTER,

Referred to the committee on accounts.

On motion of Mr. HARBINE, the Convention proceeded to the orders of the day.

THE LEGISLATIVE DEPARTMENT.

The Convention resumed the consideration of the report of the committee on the legislative department.

Mr DENT, in pursuance of the notice he had yesterday given, moved a reconsideration of the vote by which the twentieth section had been adopted, as follows:

"*Section* 20. No divorce shall be granted by the General Assembly, nor any tax or other burthen be levied on the persons or property of the people, for the support of any religious sect or denomination."

Mr. DENT said he had not made the motion for the purpose of having the provisions of the section rejected, but for the purpose of having them provided for in two separate sections. As the section now stands, it presented an amalgamation of subjects and objects entirely distinct and unconnected with each other.

The PRESIDENT intimated his opinion, that the section might be divided into two distinct sections without the necessity of a motion to reconsider. It would not be in order, without such a reconsideration, to change the *structure* of the section; but a mere motion to divide, might be made.

Mr. DENT submitted a motion in accordance with the suggestion of the chair, and the section was divided into two sections, as follows:

"*Section* 20. No divorce shall be granted by the General Assembly.

"*Sec.* 21. No tax or other burthen shall be levied on the persons or property of the people for the support of any religious sect or denominate."

THE PUBLIC CREDIT, ETC.

The twenty-first section was then read as follows:

"*Section* 21, (of the Report.) No loans shall be made upon the credit of this State, which are not redeemable at the pleasure of the State; except such as may be authorized by an act of Assembly passed at one session and ratified and confirmed at the next succeeding regular session of the General Assembly."

Mr. RIDGELY, in pursuance of the notice he had yesterday given, moved the following as a substitute for the said section:

"The credit of the State shall never be given or loaned in aid of any person, association, municipality or corporation, nor shall the Legislature contract any debt, which shall singly, or in the aggregate exceed a half million of dollars, for which purpose a vote of three-fourths of all the members elected to both branches of the General Assembly shall be necessary, provided that the State may contract debts, not exceeding that amount, to repel invasion, suppress insurrection and if threatened, to provide for the public defence."

Mr George, in pursuance of the notice he had yesterday given, offered the following articles as a substitute for the said twenty-first section, and for the substitute of Mr. RIDGELY:

"*Article* 1. The amount of debts, hereafter contracted by the Legislature, shall never exceed one hundred thousand dollars, except for the defence of the State, unless such debt shall be authorized by a law providing for the collection of an annual tax or taxes sufficient to pay the interest on such debt as it falls due, and also to discharge the principal of such debt within fifteen years from the time of contracting the same. And the taxes laid for this purpose shall never be repealed, or applied to any other object, until the said debt and the interest thereon shall be fully discharged.

"*Art.* 2. The assent of two-thirds of the members elected to each branch of the Legislature, shall be requisite to every bill appropriating the public money, or pledging the public faith, for local or private purposes; and the Legislature shall not have the power to make appropriations, loans or subscriptions, to any work of internal improvement."

And the question was first on the amendment of Mr. GEORGE.

Mr. DORSEY moved to amend the original section of the bill, by striking out the following words:

"Which are not redeemable at the pleasure of the State."

Mr. D. said, he was not pertinacious about the adoption of this amendment; but it seemed to him that if he we ever contemplated borrowing money, it ought to be borrowed upon the best possible terms; and if we made the loans redeemable at the pleasure of the State, we should have to pay more than if we made them payable after a certain time.

The PRESIDENT stated that the proposition of the gentleman from Anne Arundel, (Mr. Dorsey,) being a proposition to perfect the original section, would have precedence over the substitutes proposed.

The question was then taken and the amendment of Mr. DORSEY was agreed to.

The question then recurred on the substitute of Mr. GEORGE.

Mr. MCHENRY called for a division, so that the question should first be taken on the motion to strike out.

Mr. RIDGELY accepted the substitute of Mr. GEORGE as a modification of his own proposition.

Mr. JOHN DENNIS moved to amend said amendment by striking out these words, "the amount of debts, hereafter contracted by the Legislature, shall never exceed one hundred thousand dollars," and insert in lieu thereof, "the Legislature hereafter shall contract no debt."

Mr. GEORGE accepted this amendment.

Mr. RIDGELY asked the yeas and nays on the substitute.

Mr. SPENCER remarked that a suggestion had been made to him, that the words of the substitute "for the defence of the State," were too latitudinous. To obviate this objection he would move an amendment. He did so to meet the wishes of other gentlemen who desired to support the proposition, if the amendment he offered was agreed to.

Mr. SPENCER then moved further to amend said amendment, by striking out these words, in second line, "except for the defence of the State," and inserting in lieu thereof "except in case of war, to repel invasion, and to suppress insurrection."

Mr. SCHLEY said, he should vote against the amendment of the gentleman from Queen Anne, (Mr. Spencer,) not because he, (Mr. Schley,) differed as to the object to be attained by it, but because he thought it was already attained by the words "defence of the State." He was opposed to the multiplication of words in the Constitution. He desired that they should be as pithy, concise, and brief as possible.

The question was then put on the amendment of Mr. SPENCER,

But no quorum voted.

Mr. MITCHELL stated that he could not vote, because he had paired off with Mr. HOLLYDAY.

The question was then again taken, and, having been decided in the negative,

The amendment of Mr. SPENCER was rejected.

Mr. DONALDSON offered the following as a substitute for the substitute:

"The aggregate amount of debt or liability hereafter contracted by the Legislature shall never exceed the sum of one hundred thousand dollars, except in case of war, to repel invasions, or suppress insurrections, unless the same shall be authorised by a law for some single object, distinctly specified therein, passed by a vote of two-thirds of all the members elected to each branch of the Legislature, which law shall provide ways and means, exclusive of loans, to pay the interest of said debt or liability and discharge the principal thereof, within twenty years from the passage of the law, but new loans may be made if necessary, and new bonds issued in pursuance of law, for the payment of either principal or interest of the debt now existing."

Mr. DONALDSON briefly explained the substitute offered by him. He said that the proposition of the gentleman from Queen Anne's (Mr. George,) as amended at the suggestion of the gentleman from Somerset, (Mr. Dennis,) did in effect destroy the power of the Legislature to make use of the credit of the State for even the most beneffcient purpose, and, in so many words, forbade appropriations, loans, or subscriptions to any work of internal improvement. Whatever our circumstances might be hereafter, however manifest might be the advantages to the community of a particular project, however unanimous might be the wishes of the people concerning it, and however abundant might be the receipts of the Treasury from the works already constructed, no such application of those receipts could be made by the Legislature; although all our debt may have been paid off, and all our tax laws repealed. When he considered, that not very many years would pass before we should realise such a state of things, if the present tax-system were in the meantime left undisturbed, as he hoped and presumed, he could not but foresee, that the entire destruction of this power of appropriation might hereafter produce serious inconvenience, and perhaps detriment to the State. The works of internal improvement now yield, unfinished as they are, about $200,000 annually to our Treasury, and that sum will soon be greatly increased. Those works might hereafter, perhaps, be made much more productive of revenue to the State, and much more advantageous to the trade of the community, if their capacity were enlarged, or tributary works were constructed. He did not advocate laying taxes for those purposes; but after our debt was paid, if surplusses not derived from taxation were in the Treasury, he would desire that the Legislature should have the power to use them in the manner which it deemed most beneficial. Yet he was not for leaving this power unrestricted. He wished to guard it from abuse in the most stringent manner. He thought that his substitute imposed such restrictions, as would effectually prevent abuse, yet would preserve a power that might be beneficially used in cases of manifest propriety.

That substitute required the concurrent vote of two-thirds of the members elected to each branch of the Legislature, for any law creating a debt or liability. Such a vote could never be obtained, unless the necessity of such a law were apparent. Even in the times of our wildest extravagance, when all our heavy debts were incurred, although a mere majority of a quorum in each house was requisite to pass a law, the loan bills were almost all carried by bare majorities. They never could have been carried, had two-thirds of all the members elected, been requisite. Yet none of those bills provided resources for paying the interest or principal of the debt created; in their delusion, the legislators of that time seemed to think that means for complying with the State's engagements, would drop down from heaven. If the imposition of a tax, which was the only provision then in their power, for the payment of the debt, had formed part of those bills, they would never have passed even by bare majorities. Now this substitute required, that the law creating any debt should provide ways and means, exclusive of loans, for the liquidation of the debt, principal and interest, within twenty-years. The ways and means must be either taxation, or certain revenue derived from property of the State, or from the State's interest in works of internal improvement. With those checks on the power to create debt, and with the past experience of our legislation to warn us, he believed there could be no danger of extravagance, or improvident enterprises, in future.

In regard to the last clause of the substitute, which authorised new loans to be made, if necessary, for the payment of the principal or interest of the debt now in existence, he said, that its purpose was, first, to provide for any temporary deficiency, proceeding from the unequal distribution of the receipts and expenditures of the Treasury—the smallest receipts coming in at the time when the expenditures are largest, and *vice versa*—or from an extraordinary casualty, which might possibly in some year befall our public works; and, secondly, to enable the Legislature, at or after the periods when the principal of any of our loans became redeemable, if funds for the purpose are not in the Treasury, to make new loans, and from the proceeds redeem those that have come to maturity. The terms of the loans are, irredeemable until after a certain date, and then redeemable at the pleasure of the State. Now, it may well happen, that the relative value of money may fall in the market before the greater part of these loans are redeemable; in which case a sum of money adequate to the discharge of the principal of those loans may be procured at a lower rate of interest than we now pay, and the difference in the interest would, of course, be so much saved to the State.

Mr. BROWN said that at first sight, the amendment of the gentleman from Anne Arundel, (Mr. Donaldson,) struck his mind favorably, but that upon reflection, and aided by the explanations which the gentleman himself had given, he, (Mr. B.,) was opposed to it. He argued that the only way to open the eyes of the people and to let them understand what their pecuniary condition was, to raise money by loan, when it must be raised, and to levy a tax for the payment of the interest and the ultimate liquidation of the debt. The people then knew what their Legislature was doing. And if, as the gentleman had predicted, it should hereafter, come to pass that large amounts of money were realized by works of internal improvement, it should be returned to the pockets of the people who had paid, by taxation, a large amount of money for these very works. The proposition of the gentleman from Queen Anne's, (Mr. George,) contained a guard which was acceptable to him, (Mr. B.) He hoped we were not about to forget the lessons which we had learned. It might be that events, not now foreseen, might take place greatly affecting the receipts from our works of internal improvement, and by which the supply from that source might be arrested. At all events, whenever there was a surplus of money in the treasury, he thought that all of it, over and above what might be required for the education of the people, should go back into the pockets of those who had had to raise it.

Mr. SPENCER replied to the argument of Mr. DONALDSON, that there would be a large surplus revenue from the public works. If such a state of things was to arise, what necessity was there that that revenue should be pledged to meet any ry debt which might be incurred? If there was to be an excess of revenue, there would be no necessity to pass a law for the creation of a debt. The appropriation of the credit of the State for purposes of internal improvement had been the great flood gate by which the State had been inundated with debt, and it was now proposed to reverse the principle. He believed that as great evil would fall upon the State by a converse rule as by the operation of the original rule itself.

Mr. MERRICK said:

He thought there was much sound sense and wisdom in the proposition of the gentleman from Anne Arundel, (Mr. Donaldson.) He was quite willing to deny to the legislature the power of appropriating in future, to works of internal improvement, the actual money or the credit of the State, if gentlemen would be content with that—but there were other great purposes for which it was wise and expedient, the legislature should have power to raise money by the use of her credit. There was yet a heavy public debt to be paid off, and a proper use of such a power by the legislature, would, in all probability, greatly facilitate this interesting object and materially lighten the burthens of taxation. No observant man could mistake the indications every where given of the great change now in progress, in the monetary affairs of the world. We had passed through a period of long and distressing scarcity of money, and consequent depression of prices, and things were now rapidly tending in the other direction. Confidence was being restored, credit revived, money becoming plenty and cheap, and labor and all the productions of labor, were rising in price. This was likely to be carried farther than usual, with such oscillations, because there was now a new additional and powerful cause acting in concurrence with the ordinary causes, which was the great actual augmentation of the precious metals which was taking place from the gold mines of California. The amount already added to the solid currency from that source, was very large. But supplies from that source were going on to increase in geometrical progression; to what extent it might go, none could calculate—for the mines were found every day to be more and more extensive, and the supply of metal less and less capable of exhaustion.

The consequence was and must be a fall in the value of money, and depression of the rate of interest. Already this has taken place to a great extent. But a few years since, stocks, government stocks, (which are the things most sensitive to such changes, and give most decisive indications of their approach or advent,) were below par; even the six per centum loans of the United States could not be negotiated at par. Now, behold, they are freely commanding twenty per cent. premium. This state of things would go on progressively until probably in a few years, good government three per cent. stocks, would be worth par.

The amendment of the gentleman from Anne Arundel, (Mr. Donaldson,) proposes to leave with the legislature, the power to turn this new state of things to the advantage of the State, in her financial affairs—by paying off, should the opportunity offer, her outstanding debts and liabilities, by new loans at a less rate of interest, and thus saving to the tax-paying people, the difference between the high and the low rate of interest. Thus, suppose the State debt now to be ten millions of dollars; to pay the interest on which, at six per cent., the people have to be taxed annually, to the amount of six hundred thousand dollars. If you can now, or at any time hereafter, before this debt is paid, make a loan of the same amount, at three per cent., the annual interest of which, would be but three hundred thousand dollars, and with this loan pay off the present debt, is it not plain that you would save to the people, the three hundred thousand dollars, the difference between the interest you now pay, and that you would have to pay, on the new three per cent. loan—and could, therefore, reduce the taxes one half.

It is the valuable and important power to do this, that I wish to reserve to the legislature. Suppose interest should not fall so low as three per cent., the saving would still be in the same proportion for any greater or less fall in the rate of interest. Besides, a revenue was now coming from our works of internal improvement—the actual receipts from that source being during the last year, more than two hundred thousand dollars. This must augment, and in his judgment as well as that of many others, this augmentation must be great and rapid. But every little increase of the revenue from this source, would be necessary to insure a sufficiency to pay the interest, and any new loan of the character suggested, and thus place the State in a condition to relieve the people from all taxation—a consummation must devoutly to be wished; and he was most anxious to give to it every facility—at least, he could consent to throw no obstructions in the way, by tying up the hands of the legislature, and depriving them of this valuable and important power.

Mr. DONALDSON said:

The gentleman from Queen Anne's, (Mr. Spencer,) had enquired what necessity there could be to create a debt, if the money was already in the treasury. There might be surplus money in the treasury, annually, to double the amount of the interest on the loan proposed to be made, thus furnishing a large sinking fund for the redemption of the principal within a reasonable time; and yet there might not be enough, without the aid of a loan, to accomplish the object desired as early as it ought to be accomplished. A public work of importance might readily be completed in a couple of years, by means of such a loan, whilst the loan would be paid off in the course of ten or fifteen years. Without the loan, the revenues, on which it would be based, could not be made available to construct the same work within a shorter period than the whole ten or fifteen years.

The gentleman from Queen Anne's, had once been chairman of the committee on ways and means in the House of Delegates, and he surely knew enough of finance to understand that.

A few words in reply to the gentleman from Carroll, (Mr. Brown.) He, [Mr. D.,] had certainly expected when that gentleman rose, that he would take the same side with himself. That gentleman had yesterday treated us to a philippic in relation to our chaining down the legislature.

Mr. Brown interposed, and said, he had yesterday stated, that he would go to chain down the legislature in relation to this very matter.

Mr. Donaldson continued. The gentleman yesterday had delivered a philippic against the Convention, because of the checks it was imposing upon the legislature. He had declared that the legislature was the people's body, that through it the people expressed their wishes, that it was their voice, and that these restraints upon it were in the last degree improper; he had confidence in the people, and the people's delegates, and was ready to trust them. On this theme, he was so warm, so earnest, so vehement, that he became almost eloquent. He was then willing that a mere majority of a quorum should pass laws affecting our dearest rights and interests; yet now he would not trust the same legislature, although two-thirds of the whole number elected were requisite for the passage of a law, and although the scope of that law was restricted by certain important conditions. This is chaining down the legislature with a vengeance.

Mr. D. said, that no man could be more opposed than himself to wild schemes of internal improvement. He repeated, that he would not advocate the imposition of taxes, for the purpose of making such expenditures. It was better, in general, to leave such undertakings to private capital and enterprise. But he conld not consent to deprive the State of the power to use her own surplus receipts hereafter, in the manner which might, at the time, be most conducive to her prosperity. Gentlemen ought not to let themselves be frighted from their propriety, by the alarming apprehensions which had been indulged, in regard to this subject. It was the part of statesmen to restrict a power, so as to prevent its abuse; but not to destroy the power, if, under proper guards, it could be uesd beneficially.

Mr. McLane said, he supposed that the restriction which was contained in the bill, was a lesson we had derived from experience; and that it was now proposed to engraft upon the legislation of the State some provision which would for the time to come, prevent the recurrence of the evils under which we were now laboring.

He concurred in the opinion expressed by the gentlemen from Carroll, (Mr. Brown,) that the necessity of taxation was, after all, the great security which we possessed against abuses by the legislature, of the power to contract debts.

I believe, (continued Mr. McL.,) that no gentleman who listens to me this day, entertains a doubt, that, if, at the time we became involved in our present enormous debt, those who contracted it, had been compelled at the same time to provide by taxation for its payment, that debt never would have been created. Does not every man know, that when this system was commenced, it was represented and believed, that the revenues to be derived from our great system of internal improvements—for great I conceive it to be—would more than pay the interest on the debt and would open to the State a career of prosperity and success, not easily computed? If gentlemen will look back to the elaborate reports made at the time, and to the constant calculations presented to the public, they will find that every man dreamed that he was about to reach a new *El Dorado*. Taxation was to exist no longer—public debt was to become an obsolete idea. These works were to bring upon us a flood-tide of prosperity and advancement, which was to know no ebb, which was to be felt to all time, and throughout all the various interests of the State.

What was the result? I am not one of those who would depreciate these works. But I think that the imagination which can now look forward to so early a fruit from them, is about as vague and insubstantial, as thatwhich in the first instance led us astray. There are, within the sound of my voice, men who will live to realize that many of these calculations are as empty and as deceptive, as those which tempted us to the creation of the debt; though some of them will, no doubt, be realized.

The gentleman from Anne Arundel, [Mr. Donaldson,] always able, and always ready, has submitted a proposition; and what is it? He proposes to confer upon the Legislature, the power to contract debts for public works—mere public works. And they are to provide for the payment of the debts, not by taxation, but by other means. And what other means does the gentleman contemplate? The revenue to be derived from the public works. Well—some ten or fifteen years hence, we may realize some five, or six, or perhaps more, hundred thousand dollars a year, from these works; some grand scheme uniting the interests of all parties, may be brought before the Legislature, and we may be told that no taxation is to grow out of it. We have an income of five or six hundred thousand dollars a year, and, therefore, there can be no apprehension that we shall ever suffer taxation for the payment. And the Legislature—yes, two-thirds of both branches—not from any improper motive, but from a just appreciation of public sentiment, at the time, and from an honest conviction that they are promoting the public interests, may pass the bill; and in two or three years afterwards, it may be discovered that the work is to cost quadruple the amount which was estimated, and a debt would then be created. Have we had no lessons on that point? How much were our public works estimated to cost when the eight million bill was passed, under all the allurements which surrounded it? What, I say, was the estimate? Three millions for the construction of the Baltimore and Ohio Railroad, and three millions or a little more for the construction of the Chesapeake and Ohio canal to Cumberland. Let us look back to the estimate, and then see what has been the cost. Three millions of dollars? Why, sir, the Baltimore and Ohio Railroad has already cost six or seven millions of dollars.

Mr. MERRICK interposed, and said that the gentleman was mistaken in supposing that the estimated cost of the Baltimore and Ohio Railroad, was only three millions of dollars. It was three millions from the State—three millions from the city of Baltimore, and other income from private subscriptions.

Mr. McLANE, (continuing.) The gentleman can notice hereafter any thing I may say. The state of my health is such, that I cannot say the little I desire, with any satisfaction to myself, and I am not in a condition to answer his enquiries. If the fact is as the gentleman states it to be, so much the worse. It was not a true estimate. May not the same thing happen again? What public work is ever estimated at its actual cost? I never heard of such a case, nor do I think it will ever occur. The Legislature and the people will, therefore, find themselves involved in a debt greater than was at first contemplated, on account of the cost and extravagance of the work. Then difficulties may arise in the course of trade, and our public works may cease to yield a revenue. The debt is contracted upon the gronnd that we have funds coming into the treasury to pay the interest, and by the progressive increase of the funds from these works, to reimburse the principal. But trade stops or falls off—or is diverted into other channels. Rival works spring up. We do not continue to receive the income upon which we had calculated. Will not taxation follow? And will not the public be drawn into a debt, in the course of a few years, which will be an incumbrance upon them and their posterity, to the end of time, for ought that we can see, just as we of this generation are incumbered now? It seems to me that our great security lies in a rigid adherence to this principle—that when our law-givers create a debt, the burthen of which is to rest upon us and our posterity, we should know and understand that we are to be taxed for its redemption. We shall then scrutinize the law closely, and see that we are not unwarily betrayed into such a commitment of the public funds. Can any injury result from the adoption of this principle? It prevails elsewhere. If the construction of a great public work should be demanded by the interests of the State, and the money should be expended, my word for it, the people will pay the tax when once convinced of the necessity of the work. But I hope that this Convention will never put it in the power of the Legislature, led on by flattering, perhaps fanciful, calculations as to the success of public works, to contract a debt to-day, counting upon resources which may melt away to-morrow, and thus leaving a heavy tax upon the people. It is this against which I protest.

I will say one word in relation to the second clause of the proposition of the gentleman from Anne Arundel, (Mr. Donaldson,) to which, as he explains it, I cannot see any great objection. But I am afraid of the consequences; and more so when I reflect on the remarks of gentlemen in the course of this debate—when we are told that we ought to give to the Legislature the power to make these contracts because money is becoming very valuable—that the interest of money will fall soon to three per cent.—that we may pay our existing debt, now bearing interest at six per cent., by taking advantage of the rise of money; and that, therefore, it is wise to give the Legislature the power to do it.

I am not of that school of financiers who attach much credit to this view of the subject. I think that the lesson taught by the younger Pitt, at a moment when he was tempting the British nation into a large amount of public debt for the prosecution of the war with France, should not be lost upon us. If gentlemen would read his speeches and refer to the national history of that day, they would be led to think that in a very few years the whole public debt of England would be paid. Look at the fact. I think that the general rule is a sound one, that money is always worth its real value, and, if by the fluctuations incident to it, a man gives six dollars for a hat one day and three dollars the next, it is just the same thing; he is paying the same value for the hat when he gives three dollars for it as when he gives six. And the notion which is started as to the rise or diminution in the value of money—(I speak with no disrespect to the argument of the gentleman on the other side, for whom I entertain a high esteem,)—but I assure him, that all such notions have gone into the category of political alchemies. The rule is not a sound one; and any nation which expects to pay its public debt by borrowing money at three per cent. to get rid of a debt at six, will find that it has made no bargain. I hope, therefore, that the Convention will look to this as a great and grave subject. Some gentlemen have come here with one idea of reform and some with another. I confess, that one great duty which I felt it incumbent upon me to discharge when I came here was, to place some salutary restriction on the power of the Legislature as to the creation of a public debt. I live in a State of which I feel sincerely proud, whether I regard the past or the present, or look forward to the future—a State abounding in all the elements of prosperity—a great and growing commonwealth—fettered and tied down by a debt which at one period almost jeoparded her reputation, but which was rescued by the exertions of many enlightened and patriotic men, and probably by none more so than the gentleman from

Anne Arundel, (Mr. Donaldson.) That is its only drawback—its only evil; a great debt incurred under the most promising auspices and the most flattering inducements and calculations of prosperity. And, here we are, at this hour, laboring under this great incubus. Let us prevent its recurrence for the time to come. Is there anything so tempting to individuals, States or communities as the contraction of debt? Do we not all know—every one of us—that our judgments will be tempted into flattering speculations, not doubting that, in the course of a few months or years, we may double our ventures? The same feeling enters into States. I desire to guard against all such temptations. Let us say to the Legislature, if you choose to construct public works, we require you, at the same time that you create the debt, to lay such a tax as will pay the interest and the principle; for then, and not otherwise, you will be under a just responsibility to your constituents.

At a moment in public affairs when upon this whole nation—as well as upon the States—a vast burthen of debt was resting heavily, I urged, in my humble way, and, of course, only through private channels, that a great measure of relief should be proposed by which the General Government would assume all the debts of the States upon one single condition—that the States should incorporate in their fundamental law, an irrepealable provision that no State debt should ever again be contracted without the imposition of a tax for its liquidation. I believe that such a measure would have been wise for the country—wise for the government of the Union, wise for the governments of the States. I repeat now, that the great bane of our prosperity is the contraction of large debts under tempting circumstances; and that the greatest security we can afford to the people will be, that these debts shall no longer be contracted unless the urgency is so great as to justify a system of taxation to pay for it.

I have felt it my duty to myself and my constituents, earnestly to invoke the Convention not to leave open this door—but, looking to it as the great medium by which the evils that afflict us have crept in upon the State, to close it now and forever, that we may relieve ourselves and our posterity from the apprehension of their recurrence.

Some explanations passed between Mr. McLane and Mr. Merrick—after which

Mr. Merrick said, his only object in the remarks he had made, was to show that there were great fluctuations in the value of money; and that a change was now taking place in that value, to the advantage of debtors, that is, the rate of interest—the price of money was falling, and would probably become very low. The honorable gentleman says, money always maintains its own value. That may be so when considered separately; but the proper mode of considering it, seems to me to be, to view it relatively. And the very illustration which the gentleman gives, proves its great relative fluctuation, and the position I have assumed, to be correet. He says he knows he can at one time purchase a hat for three dollars, and at another time he will have to give six dollars for the same or a similar hat; and this difference I contend, if it arise from the state of the money market, proves the fluctuations in the value of money. Like every thing else, the value of money is regulated by the relations between supply and demand.

If money becomes abundant, the supply of all other things purchased with money remaining the same, the price of these other things will rise in proportion to the increase in the supply of money; and if the supply of money be doubled, the three dollar hat will command six dollars—three dollars is still three dollars, and six dollars is still six dollars—but it now requires six dollars to procure the same amount of property, or the products of labor, as three dollars would before command. This is certainly true, and the great confusion of ideas, the apparent conflict of facts and consequent difficulty in ascertaining the truth in such cases, arises from the fact, that there are most frequently various causes operating to affect values and prices; some known, and some unseen and unknown at the time. The supply of a particular product of industry may increase more rapidly than the increase of the supply of money, though both are increasing; and of course, in that case, the value or price of that product would not increase. So there may be greater facility or economy introduced in the production or manufacture of any article of commerce, simultaneously with the influx of a greater supply of money—of course the money price of the article so more cheaply produced, does not rise. And so might a thousand instances be cited of interfering circumstances which modify or destroy the effect of the general law, and seemingly, but in the seeming only, contradict it. The law is fixed and certain, and operates as unerringly as gravitation; and as well may it be said, that the laws of gravitation are not unerring, because some heavy body is upheld by a counteracting force; as it may be said that superabundance of money will not occasion low rates of interest, and an advance in the prices of other articles, of which the supply continues the same, because in some instances other causes of sufficient force are operating to prevent this result.

I have said, this change in the relative value of money and stocks, and other articles of commerce, was now taking place, and was likely to increase to great extent; and we all see the evidences of the fact every where around us. A state of the money market has arisen, and is about to arise, greatly advantageous to debtors, and I wished the State, therefore, to be left with power to turn to the benefit of her tax-paying people, the advantages this change will offer. We have passed through a season of severe money pressure—great depression of prices. The pendulum is now oscillating to the other side, and I desire to leave the Legislature power to take advantage of this favorable oscillation. Credit has, for a long time been depressed; stocks have been low; the Legislature have, all along, had this power; and to deprive them of it, to fetter their hands now, would be about as wise as it would be for a tobacco planter, who has, during the long course of years in which tobacco has been so low as not to pay the expense of production, continued the cultivation of it, to abandon the cultivation now, when the article has become very high and will rapidly enrich its producers. I illustrate by tobacco planters, because it is apt to the purpose, and there are many gentlemen around me engaged in its cultivation.

Tie the hands of the Legislature as fast as you please, in regard to contracting *further* debt, or engaging in other works of internal improvement, but leave them the power to take advantage of the coming change in affairs, by paying off as much of her existing debt as they can, by new stocks bearing a less rate of interest. Every dollar we can save, is important to the people, and if the opportunity offers, as I believe it will, I wish to see the Legislature have the power to substitute for our present six and five per cent. stocks, stocks bearing only three or three and a half per cent., thus saving several hundred thousand dollars annually, until the whole debt is paid off.

Mr. Jenifer desired to offer an amendment, (which was not now in order.)

Mr. J. gave notice of his intention to offer it at the proper time. He believed that the time might come when it would be extremely important that such a power should be in the hands of the Legislature. Its exercise might be important to the prosperity of the State. At the same time it was necessary to guard such a power as rigidly as possible. The past experience of the State demonstrated the necessity of this. It might be possible that danger might be apprehended to the State from the very prosperity which would result from these works, if the state of things which gentlemen anticipated should be realised. He would therefore place proper restrictions upon the power, though he believed that its judicious exercise might be attended with benefit to the State.

Mr. J. then read his amendment.

Mr. Spencer said, the gentleman from Charles, had indicated no opposition, by his argument, to any portion of the proposition of the gentleman from Anne Arundel. The proposition met with his entire opposition. He looked upon it, as one of the most dangerous he had encountered. It positively opens the door to further speculation in works of internal improvement, and is advocated by the mover, for that very reason. In the Constitution which we are about to amend, no such express power is found. It was assumed by construction. And now when the people are sore upon the subject, and wholly opposed to all such schemes, and actually expect at our hand, a restriction on the legislature in this particular, the gentleman from Anne Arundel proposes, by express provision, to give the Legislature the power to do so. Adopt his section, and the Legislature will have the power to subscribe to any work, and to provide the ways and means at their discretion, to support it. I beg the gentleman to turn to the Constitution, and lay his finger, if he can, on any part of it, which authorized the Legislature to embark in such works. From the very beginning of this system of legislation the power had, by many, been denied. He, [Mr. S.,] had at all times denied that the Legislature could make appropriations of money or State credit, for such purposes. And when the Legislature found it necessary to impose a direct tax upon the people, the unprecedented outrage was practised of inserting a provision in the law, denying to the people the benefit of the wisdom and learning of the court of appeals, on the constitutionality of the law. Yes, sir; by the act of Assembly imposing the tax, the court of appeals were directed not to entertain any question as to the constitutionality of the law.

The gentleman from Cecil, had eloquently pictured the delusions under which the people voted when this system was imposed upon. He had beautifully painted its evils, and he, (Mr. S.,) would not follow in the same field. He would content himself, by saying, he was opposed to the whole system of internal improvements, whether there be a surplus in the treasury or not. He was opposed to it because it opened the door to abuse and corruption. It was well known, that they had already assumed a party cast, and were used for party purposes by the legislature. Originally, the Governor had the appointment, with the advice of the Senate, of the State's agents. The power was taken from him and given to the legislature, and in order to prevent it from passing out of the hands of the party then in the ascendant, by an act of the legislature, the agents then in office were to continue in, until removed by a concurrent vote of the Senate and House of Delegates. Every body understands the effect of such legislation.

It was not his purpose now to dwell on the evil of the system. He had been always opposed to it. It needed no argument now to expose it, and he was well satisfied that this Convention, instead of authorising the legislature to encourage them, would inhibit the authority of the Legislature altogether.

Mr. Thomas expressed his readiness to vote for the amendment of the gentleman from Queen Anne's, (Mr. Spencer.) To that extent he was willing to go; but nothing less than that would satisfy the people he represented. If there was any one sentiment against which, over all others, they felt an unmitigated hostility, it was that of the power exercised by the legislature to make appropriations for the construction of roads and canals. And in this sentiment he had fully and uniformly concurred, from the year 1827 to this hour; and such was the feeling of the leading men of the part of the State which he represented. And the confidence which his constituents felt in the accordance of his sentiments with theirs, had been the cause of the honor he now enjoyed in being their organ on this floor.

He had never considered the construction of roads and canals as coming within the legitimate duties of government. To cherish the interests and protect the rights of the people constituted its great duties. And in the performance of those duties, he would ever be ready to render all the assistance in his power. But never would he give his consent that the legislature should embark in magnificent schemes of internal improvement, which must always result in fixing an onerous tax on the people; and this, he said, in the face of all the glowing descriptions of the inestimable blessings which would result from binding all the remote regions of our wide spread country in one. He had never given a vote for an appropriation for such a purpose, until the State was so deeply involved by the extent to which they had been carried, that it was deemed necessary to carry the works through, to give her a chance of extrication.

It was when the Delaware and Chesapeake canal was before the House, that he took the responsibility of differing from his constituents, and voted in favor of a small appropriation. He was a representative in the House of Delegates in 1827, and his name was not to be found on the record during that session in favor of any appropriation of the kind. He recollected a conversation he had, at that time, with a gentleman from Baltimore who came here for the purpose of getting the act incorporating the Baltimore and Ohio rail road through the legislature. After listening to the extravagant descriptions of the advantages to be derived from this work, the favorable estimates as to its cost, and the time when it could be completed, he well remembered his reply to the gentleman, after he had stated that he only asked an appropriation of $500,000. "If the capitalists of your city are so well convinced of the great profits which must accrue from this work, how happens it that they have not embarked in the enterprise?" He was aware that gentlemen who engage in speculative undertakings, sometimes deceive themselves, but it was generally found that those works which promise the greatest amount of risk and the least amount of profit, are the branches of the system which fall to the share of the government.

He stated that he could not support the amendments offered by the gentlemen from Anne Arundel and from Charles. He could not, under any combination of circumstances, however flattering might be the prospect of revenue, consent that the legislature should have the power to loan the capital of the State for the construction of any public work, road or canal, which could have a local and partial interest.

He could vote for no proposition which, in any event looks to the embarkation of the capital of the State, in any project of internal improvement. It might so happen that a large surplus may be in the treasury, which cannot be applied to the payment of the public debt which is not redeemable for many years, and the treasury may, in consequence, be placed in a perilous situation. And is it difficult to see how, in such case, the public money might be expended? And if the legislature under such circumstances should appropriate this surplus money to the construction of public works, and a sudden reverse should take place, or the works should be stopped, and just when the treasury is exhausted a large amount of State bonds, or interest on the debt, should fall due, the consequence would be new taxation.

So far from there being any desire among the people that the legislature shall have power to appropriate money for roads and canals, that it is the universal wish that the money may be honestly applied to the payment of the public debt and not to the construction of improvements. We have now a considerable surplus in the treasury. If it be suffered to accumulate, it will be larger next year, and still larger the following year; and are we to empower the legislature to expend this surplus on any of these great schemes of internal improvement, which are now the topic of conversation? Are we to throw this surplus out of the treasury to be scrambled for by schemers and stockholders?

He was against any such projects, with all his heart and soul. If ever the time should come when the State internal improvement stocks shall become equal in value to the State bonds, he would be very willing to exchange all the stock held by the State in these internal improvement companies for the bonds of the people. But the amendment of the gentleman from Anne Arundel looks to a perpetual connection between the State and these institutions.

There was great plausibility, he admitted, in another idea thrown out by the gentleman from Charles which was very tempting, but the few expressions from the experienced and able statesman and financer, the gentleman from Cecil, would effectually counteract its influence. The doctrine of the gentleman from Charles looked to the convertion of us into a company of stock-jobbers. It was well said by the gentleman from Cecil, that all these projects were delusive in a great degree. If we could be certain of borrowing at three per cent. to pay off a debt bearing an interest of six per cent., with the certainty that the relative value of money and labor would not change its standard, there might be some reason for such a movement and posterity might be left to pay the debt thus created for the payment of the previous debt. But as the gentleman from Charles ought to perceive, we may happen to borrow when labor and produce are high and money low, and when we have to pay, labor and produce may have fallen one hundred per cent. beyond the value at the time when we became borrowers. It was well understood that experienced capitalists can foresee the fluctuations in the money market, and are always on the alert to take advantage of the changes; and they are always ready to flock round the Treasury when the bonds of the State are at the highest market rate. He was opposed to giving the Legislature the power to deal in stocks of any sort; while he was anxious that we should promptly discharge every dollar due from the State either for the interest or the principal of the public debt. And he fervently hoped that the day was not very far distant when a report of a committee of ways and means in the House of Delegates, or the annual message of the Governor of the State, could cause a rise or fall of public securities in the market.

Mr. Merrick wished to make a remark or two only in reply. The gentleman from Frederick, (Mr. Thomas,) has said that a "low rate of interest was accompanied by, and proved the low price of labor and of the productions of industry." Now this position, Mr. M. considered essentially erroneous and the very reverse of the fact. A low rate of interest procured the abundance of money, and abundance of money always and inevidently produced enhancement of the price of labor and an increase in the price of all the productions of labor; this was plain to the simplest understanding; was proved by every man's experience, and as certain almost as a mathematical truth. As regarded supply and demand and relative values—money and all other articles of commerce, the productions of industry, occupied antagonistical positions—might be considered as being in opposite sides of a balance, whenever one side went down the other must of necessity go up. Whenever money becomes plenty and easy of procurement, other things would increase in their money price. These truths had been illustrated a thousand times, and were illustrated by the facts with which we were now surrounded; money is becoming plenty, the rate of interest is falling, or what is the same thing, interest bearing stocks are rising in the market, and labor, and all the products of labor, are consequently rising, and have greatly risen in price. Look at your two great staples—cotton and tobacco—they are both worth more than double the money they would have commanded a year ago. Look at the price of slaves, a direct evidence here of the value of labor; they are now worth and will command nearly double the price they have sold for a year since. The position assumed by the honorable gentleman is therefore erroneous, and this error runs through his whole argument and destroys therefore all its force. But the gentleman, (Mr. Thomas,) has said, if he could be *certain* of the results, he would be willing to borrow at three per cent. and pay off debts bearing six per cent. interest. Can any thing in nature be more certain in its results than such an operation? Even if the gentleman's theory about relative values and fluctuations in prices, were correct, still it would not affect the results of such an operation. Suppose the time to have arrived when the State owing ten millions of dollars of six per cent. bearing debt, and therefore paying annually six hundred thousand dollars interest, when the rate of interest is but three per cent., and she can therefore borrow other ten millions at three per cent, and pay off with it her six per cent. debt, upon this new loan she will thereafter have to pay but *three* hundred thousand dollars annually for interest, and her other debt will be extinguished. Will she not *certainly* and inevitably have made or saved the sum of *three* hundred thousand dollars annually—the sum of the difference between the interest on the new loan and the interest she has heretofore paid and would still have had to pay upon the old six per cent. debt had it not been extinguished in this way? This again is certain as mathematics and figures can make any thing, and entirely independent of all fluctuations in prices and values, let them rise and fall as they will, or be governed by what laws you please. This operation once performed, the gain to the State of the three hundred thousand dollars annually is certain, and will be so as long as it is certain that three and three make six, or that three is the half of six. Let us illustrate by the case of an individual. Suppose some member of this Convention to owe his neighbor on bond at six per cent. interest, fifty thousand dollars, and has therefore to pay him three thousand dollars annually. Another neighbor has and is willing to lend this debtor fifty thousand dollars on his bond at an interest of three per cent. He borrows of this latter neighbor and pays off the first, and thereafter has to pay for interest but fifteen hundred dollars annually! Has he not profitted, gained by the operation, or rather saved by it one half the interest on his old debt, fifteen hundred dollars a year? Nothing could be plainer nor more certain.

He would concur with the gentleman in restricting the power of the Legislature in any way, no matter how closely, so as to prevent all further appropriations to works of internal improvement. He knew such a restriction would be desirable and acceptible to his constituents—and no matter what might be his individual opinions, knowing their wishes, it was his duty, as it would be his pleasure, to carry them into effect. But he was anxious to see the power left with the Legislature to avail themselves of the good times, which were coming and to come, for debtors, to relieve, as far as possible, the people of Maryland from the burthens they had so long nobly and heroically borne. He was fully and sincerely opposed to the contracting of any further debt, whatsoever, by the State. But there was a large debt yet to be paid off, and for its speedy payment he wished to see that line of policy pursued, which it appeared to him was equally dictated by plain common sense, and the maxims of an enlightened political economy.

Mr. Thomas wished to say a few words. Supposing that the State could borrow at a lower rate of interest for the purpose of paying off a debt at a higher rate, still he would oppose the transaction, because the lender would require that the loan should run for a long period, and the stock would be an instrument for speculation in the market. He repeated what he had before said, as to the relative value of money and labor, and the effect of the fluctuations to which they are liable. In his retirement, he said, that he had perused the message of the late Governor of Maryland, and, (he spoke with the highest personal respect towards that gentleman,) he could not but feel astonished at the doctrines put forth in that message, in which he recommended a continuance of taxation. Now he, (Mr. T.,) had always supposed that when there was any surplus in the Treasury, if there were no bonds which required payment, the surplus ought to be guarded against, by the reduction of taxes. It appeared by the report to the Legislature, that there was a surplus in the treasury. It would have been proper, in these circumstances, as there are no bonds payable for many years to come, that the taxes would have been diminished. He referred to the period when, after the war of the revolution, the general government bound itself for a large sum, to enable her to assume the debts of the States. For that purpose three per cent. bonds were issued by the United States. Afterwards, when the treasury was full to overflowing, the holders of these bonds, seeing that the surplus in the National Treasury would have to be applied to their redemption, came to the government and demanded their redemption at the rate of one hundred dollars and upwards, for fifty dollars loaned. He was surprised that the late Governor and the Legislature did not reduce the surplusage in the Treasury, by repealing such taxes as the necessities of the State did not require to be continued. He wished the gentleman from Queen Anne, so to modify his amendment, as to provide that hereafter the Legislature may, whenever a surplus shall again appear to be in the treasury, reduce it in the manner he had indicated. There was no reason why the Legislature should not have repealed a portion of the taxes, but the temptation to new investments in works of internal improvement, carried them away. It was the doctrine which prevailed among the people, that where no debt calls for payment, any surplus in the treasury ought to lead to the reduction of taxes to that amount. He hoped the gentleman from Queen Anne's, would extend his proposition, which, as it now stands, might be made to sanction the raising of any sum He was of opinion, that all these golden expectations from the Chesapeake and Ohio canal, would not be realized for a quarter of a century, and this impression made him still the more cautious concerning these public works. He referred to a section in the old law, which explicitly provides that when the debt is paid, the surplus shall be assigned to the counties for their benefit, and explained its operation and the past treatment of its obligations by the Legislature. No matter how the daring pilot may disregard the dangers ahead, he thought a careful course to be the most prudent, and would, by relieving the tax-payers, when we can encourage them to prompt and cheerful compliance with a system, believed by us all to be unavoidable.

Mr. Merrick rose to say, that having been alluded to by name, in connection with the remarks gentlemen had made on the general subject of internal improvements, he felt called upon to remark, that though he did not wish now, nor was this the proper time, to enter upon a discussion of that large subject, it was his intention to avail himself of the first suitable opportunity which should present itself, to give a detailed and corrected history of the progress of the legislation on that subject, so far at least, as he had been connected with it. He was, to a large extent, responsible for the legislation of that character, which had taken place whilst he held a seat in the halls of legislation. He was prepared to meet that responsibility, and to throw from himself much unjust censure, which had been heaped upon him; but he was not responsible for the mismanagement of those who had charge of the works themselves, and the application of the States' money—neither was he responsible for the changes and mutilations which had been made by succeeding Legislatures, in the laws he had been instrumental in passing, with the valuable aid and support of yourself, Mr. President, in the other branch of the Legislature. But of all this I will speak fully when the appropriate occasion shall arise. I will, therefore, content myself now, with saying in reference to the system of internal improvements, of which I have been the steady and uniform advocate—as the lustre of the diamond cannot be destroyed by the dust which may accummulate upon it, nor the brilliancy of the sun be long hidden by the vapor which may float before his disc, so cannot the magnificence, the benificence, nor the wisdom of that system of internal improvements be destroyed, nor long obscured by the clouds which ignorance, prejudice or partizan zeal, may have temporarily heaped from it.

A very considerable revenue was now actually being paid into the treasury from those works of internal improvement—that revenue would greatly and rapidly increase It was desirable it should be first applied to the extinguishment of the public debt on that account contracted, but let it be so applied in the manner most advantageous to the State, and her tax-paying people. This was what he had been all along contending for, and should contend for to the last. He would not now say how soon it might be, but this he would say, if the revenues of the State from these sources were applied according to a wise political economy, the day was not distant when all the taxes might safely be dispensed with.

Mr. Donaldson said he must again beg the indulgence of the Convention, that he might reply to some of the arguments which had been advanced by other gentlemen. He felt impelled to do so because his views had been somewhat misunderstood, and he had thus been placed in a position very differerent from that which he really occupied. From the course of those who opposed his proposition, it would be supposed, that he was in favor of leaving to the Legislature the most unrestrained license to embark in the wildest speculations and schemes of internal improvement. But, in fact, he came here with the fixed determination, as far as his exertions could avail, to check the Legislature in its future action upon such subjects. He had always thought that the imposition of such restrictions was one of the most beneficial reforms that this Convention could make. He thought so still, and he considered his present action consistent with that opinion. With almost all that had been so ably said by the gentleman from Cecil, (Mr. McLane,) he cordially agreed, and his warnings proceeded from a wisdom which truly read the history of the past. He, (Mr. D.,) was in favor of restriction, so as to remedy the abuse complained of; but he thought it improper and unwise to destroy utterly a power which might hereafter be used with great advantage to the community. He thought that his substitute would effect all desirable restriction, whilst it preserved the power. He had stated before, that in the days of the wildest and most extravagant speculation, when the whole country seemed possessed with a mania for grand projects, which were to be accomplished, as was dreamed, without placing any burdens on the property of the people—even then, but small majorities in the Legislature, and sometimes mere majorities of quorums, had carried through the bills for internal improvement, loans and subscriptions. If two-thirds of all the members elected had been required, as by this substitute, those bills could never have passed, and we should never have contracted the debts which now press upon us. What danger can there be then for the future, after the warnings of the past, when such a restriction is imposed, and when, also, the law creating a debt must itself provide for the payment of the whole debt, principal and interest, either by taxation or by revenues actually secured? There could be none; and no gentleman had attempted to answer this argument. He believed it unanswerable.

Gentlemen had spoken as if he, (Mr. D.,) was in favor of appropriating surplusses in the treasury to other objects beside the payment of the public debt, before that debt was extinguished. He had never dreamt of such a thing. In the resumption law, which he himself had drafted, all surplusses are expressly appropriated to the extinguishment of the principal of the State debt. That he considered the true disposition to make of them. But if the present tax system remain undisturbed, it will not be a great number of years before we shall be entirely relieved from taxation on account of our debt; and we shall then have in the treasury, derived from public works, surplusses of which some use or other must be made. He hoped we were not making a Constitution for ten years only, but for half a century at least; and we must look to what will be our situation hereafter, and not take away from the Legislature all power of applying funds in the treasury to purposes, which may be manifestly proper and conducive to the welfare of the State.

The gentleman from Frederick, (Mr. Thomas,) had censured the last message of Governor Philip F. Thomas, in which a continuation of the system of revenue now in operation was recommended, on the ground "that every consideration of duty, economy and sound policy exacts the most rigid adherence to its provisions, until the last dollar of the public obligation is redeemed and cancelled." Mr. D. said he took the occasion to say, that he most cordially concurred in that recommendation, and he thought such a course most just to the creditors, most safe for the State, and really most advantageous to the property holders who paid the taxes. In regard to the great rise which gentlemen spoke of as likely to be produced by the State's purchasing her own stock in the market, he thought that it never could take place to the extent apprehended. It seemed to be forgotten that there were other stocks beside those of the State of Maryland. The stocks of Maryland were no better secured than those of the U. States, of New York, Massachusetts, Ohio, and others, the market value of which would have much to do in regulating that of our own State. These last would prevent ours from rising to such an indefinite amount. He considered, that we could make no better investment than in our own debt, and that the application of surplusses to that purpose would benefit all property in the State, by hastening the entire relief from all taxation.

If the question now were, whether we should establish such a system of internal improvement as we long ago embarked in, he would agree with the gentleman from Frederick, in his opposition to it. But, as that gentleman declared, that he had heretofore avoided additional appropriations to complete works before commenced, in order to save the sums the State had previously expended on them; so he, (Mr. D.,) considered, that future appropriations, made from surplusses in the treasury, might be properly applied towards making those works more efficient and productive.

The gentleman from Carroll, (Mr. Brown,) was for the re-payment of those surplusses into the pockets of thepeople. Mr. D. looked upon that as impracticable; but thought that the same end might be accomplished much better by expenditures for the benefit of the whole community, which might be ensured by the provisions of his substitute.

The gentleman from Queen Anne's, (Mr. Spencer,) had asked, whence, under the old constitution, was derived the power of making such appropriations as had been made, and he spoke of his substitute as giving a power not heretofore possessed by the legislature. Mr. D. declined going into an argument in regard to a matter, which a long course of legislation, and universal acquiescence therein had thoroughly settled. Presuming that such a power existed in the absence of any thing in the constitution forbidding it, his present proposition restricted it, as he believed, within salutary limits.

The last clause of his substitute had been misconstrued by the gentleman who opposed it. At present, the law gives power to borrow, to supply a temporary deficiency in the revenue, and that was the main purpose of that clause. But another purpose was, that the State might avail herself of any favorable change in the value of money, in order to pay off old loans which had become redeemable, if new loans of the same amount could be made at a lower rate of interest. He did not mean, that it would be any benefit to the State to borrow money to buy up in the market at a premium, her stocks which were not yet redeemable, in order to substitute stocks, bearing a lower rate of interest. That process would come within the censure of the gentleman from Cecil, (Mr. McLane,) of whose financial ability he expressed the highest opinion. He concurred entirely in the views of that gentleman as to such a process. The error of Mr. Pitt as referred to, was, that he issued large quantities of government stocks at a low rate of interest receiving for them, a much less amount than their nominal value. These stocks could only be redeemed afterwards, by paying the full nominal value, and the rate of interest could not be lowered when money became plenty. If he had borrowed money at its real market value, that is, bearing a high rate of interest, he might, in more prosperous times, when the market rate was lower, have saved money to the State by making new loans to substitute for the old. Although it was of no advantage, to borrow at a low rate of interest for the purpose of buying up at a premium stocks not yet redeemable; yet, if those stocks had become redeemable, and so could be discharged at par, and the cash for their redemption was not in the treasury, it certainly would be a great saving to the State, to borrow the sum necessary to redeem them, at a lower rate of interest, than we should have to pay if the old loan continued unredeemed. If the money was actually in the treasury, of course apply it to the discharge of the debt; no new loan would then be necessary or proper. Money certainly bears a higher rate of interest at one time than at another, and a man who contracts a debt when money is scarce, is benefitted, if money should be abundant at the time when his debt becomes payable. Of this, Mr. D. gave a familiar illustration.

Allusion had been made to the sinking fund of Mr. Pitt. It was, indeed, an extraordinary delusion of that great man, though not confined to him. He had looked upon a sinking fund as if it were some magical machine for generating money, and which of its own efficacy, independently of taxation, could pay off a public debt. Such a notion seemed to have prevailed among many in our own State. But, in fact, our sinking fund was nothing more than the appropriation at stated periods of a portion of the proceeds of taxation, or other revenue, to the redemption or extinguishment of so much of the principal of the debt. Any other notion of it was a fallacy, and one of a most dangerous kind.

Mr. D. concluded, by saying, that he really could not see that the dangers apprehended by gentlemen would arise from the adoption of his substitute, and he would, therefore, adhere to it.

Mr. Grason regretted that he came into the Convention so late, as to be prevented from hearing the gentleman from Anne Arundel, and other gentleman who had preceded him. He wished, however, to state his objections to the proposition. The amendment of his colleague, (Mr. George,) was intended to prohibit debts from being hereafter incurred for works of internal improvement, while that of the gentleman from Anne Arundel, (Mr. Donaldson,) provided, that a part of the surplus revenue might, in a certain contingency, be applied to the extension of such works. How easy would it be for the Legislature, under the influence of speculative and visionary men, to pass a law for that purpose, and to provide, that after the payment of the public debt, the surplus in the treasury should be applied to the construction of railroads and canals. It had been estimated that the public debt would be extinguished in twelve years, but many events might occur to defeat so desirable an object. Within the period assigned for the payment of the State debt, the United States might be involved in a war, and, in that case, our efforts for that purpose, would be arrested for an indefinite period. The gentleman from Anne Arundel, seemed to think that the time would come when we shall have no other use for the public money, but to invest it in internal improvements; but, he believed, that no new works would result in advantage to the State. We cannot carry the Chesapeake and Ohio canal beyond Cumberland, and our railroads had already been extended beyond the limits of the State. He wished now, while the people of the whole State were suffering under the burden of a public debt, that the Legislature should be deprived of the power of involving the State in future difficulties. Should there be a large surplus revenue hereafter, of which there was very little prospect, it might be applied to the use of the counties in relieving them from their annual county assessments. Unless restrictions were imposed on the Legislature, to prevent appropriations for works of internal improvement, he was satisfied the people would reject the Constitution.

Mr. Brown briefly stated his opinion that we ought to leave the Legislature untied in reference to this subject of appropriations; although there were some matters in which he would feel no objection to impose restrictions on the Legislature.

Mr. Donaldson explained.

Mr. Jenifer, in a very few remarks, defended the late Governor of Maryland against the imputations of the gentleman from Frederick as to his political opinions. Differing as he did from the ex-Governor in his general political views, there was no act of his, during his administration, which had done so much to sustain the political reputation of the State, as the message which had been animadverted upon. He happened to be abroad at the time, and he knew the effect which was produced by it on our credit in the European market. The stocks of the State immediately rose. If any one act of that gentleman's political life ought to be selected above all the rest for its wisdom, it should be this, which stemmed the tide of ruin.

Mr. Thomas said that nothing had fallen from the gentleman from Charles to change his, (Mr. T.'s,) opinion on the subject. He hoped that we would, by paying our debts, hasten the day when nothing said here by a Governor of the State, or by a member of the House of Delegates, could affect, in any way, the value of stocks abroad. He knew very well how speculators could use these matters so as to make fortunes. They were of no advantage to holders of these securities who held them as permanent investments. Although the surplus money in the treasury might sometimes be employed to buy stocks when it could be done with advantage to the State, they could never be used to continue a system of internal improvements; and it was on this point that he differed from the late Governor, although he did so with the greatest respect for him personally. He did not see, however, how the message could have affected the price of stocks in the hands of holders, who looked to the dividends on these State bonds as a means of support for themselves and their heirs. This class of holders would get their quarterly or semi-annual dividends from the treasurer, whether the bonds were above or below par in the markets in this country or in Europe, and he would do nothing, he would say nothing, that would interfere with that wise policy of the State which put the punctual payment of such dividends beyond the reach of all doubt or uncertainty.

Mr. Chambers expressed an unwillingness to allow one branch of the remarks of the gentleman from Frederick to pass without comment.

Nothing, in his opinion, could be more pernicious than to inculcate the idea that we were to relax in our efforts to discharge the public debt. He not only agreed with the proposition that honesty required a community as well as an individual to pay his just debts when he had the means, but he insisted that it required the earnest effort to procure the means.

He differed altogether with the gentleman on another point. He considered it the crowning act of the late Governor's political life, that regardless of popular clamor, he had so manfully, so faithfully and so judiciously recommended a perseverance in the system of taxation, for the purpose of discharging the obligations of the State.

Every one knows and feels the force of habit. Nothing is more repulsive to our nature than to be compelled to return to a system of restraint, abstinence and privation after having escaped from this system to one of indulgence in ease and luxury. The descent from toil and labor and privation to ease, abundance and extravagance, is natural enough, and quite a comfortable transition to most persons. But to reverse the operation is a terrible task. This may be said of communities as well as individuals. We become familiar with what we have for a long time indulged in, and to those who have no experience with greater indulgencies, their absence occasions much less regret than to those who have been accustomed to enjoy them.

He instanced the people of England. They esteem themselves the happiest people under the sun, and enjoying a more perfect condition of civil and political liberty than any other nation on the face of the earth.

They have long lived under the system which prevails; they are accustomed to the burdens imposed upon them, and their condition and habits in all other respects conform to these circumstances. Yet if the heavy taxes, on every comfort of life, which they pay, should be imposed on the people of this State, it would produce an outbreak of feeling that would sweep from the political stage, every man who should have participated in bringing about such a state of things. We all knew with what extreme difficulty our present system of taxation was introduced. When his friend over the way, (Governor Grason,) had the firmness first to recommend a resort to taxation, neither the committee of finance nor the Legislature would back him, though of his own politics.

Mr. Spencer explained that he as chairman of the committee of ways and means recommended a compliance with the opinion of the Governor, but the committee did not agree with him.

Mr. Chambers meant no unkind allusion. It proved the want of nerve to do an unpleasant thing, though necessary to prevent the degradation of the State. We were now happily and rapidly relieving ourselves of these oppressive embarrassments, and it was with deep regret he heard distinguished gentlemen suggest a partial abandonment of the only means of ultimate and early exoneration. He had risen only to enter, as he did, his humble protest against any such notions as unwise and perilous, involving, as he thought they did, a very possible condition in which after being once removed, these taxes might again become necessary.

Mr. Thomas said, as regards the credit and honor of the State, he was ready to go with any gentleman, to any extent, to maintain them unsullied. The effect of the argument of the gentleman from Kent, would be to raise the value of stocks to the profit of the speculators in stocks, but would produce no advantage to the State, or to those who hold stocks as a permanent investment. Speculators watch very astutely every movement of this government, in order to ascertain the character of the financial policy which is likely to be adopted. If there should be a surplus in the Treasury, the reduction of taxes does not follow. Speculators, who know that the public debt will not be redeemable for many years, will foresee that the Government will be compelled to buy its bonds at their market value, and stock gamblers will refuse to sell unless they bear a price much above that. And in this way stock gamblers will profit. Rather than pursue a policy leading to such results, he would prohibit the Treasurer from buying up any of the stock at a dollar above par, for if that was done, as soon as the bonds were due, the State would have faithfully fulfilled its engagements. By paying the public debt in this mode, we would be able to alleviate the burdens of the people who had been heavily taxed for its payment. He was astonished to hear the gentleman from Kent assert, that the people of England fancy themselves to be one of the happiest people in the world. There may be some thirty thousand who hold all the public securities and all the lands in England, who are contented. But it was not the case that all the residue of the people was so. To show the contrary, he described the scenes that are constantly passing before us, when numbers of her people are casting off their dearest ties, and abandoning their *natale solum*, after groaning and suffering under taxes, piled on each other, like Pelion on Ossa, and Ossa on Olympus, and leaving behind them the bones of their fathers, to find homes in a foreign land.

Mr. Chambers said, the expressed, and therefore known, unwillingness of the gentleman from Frederick, (Mr. Thomas,) to be interrupted, had alone prevented him from correcting the very odd error into which he seemed to have fallen. That gentleman seemed to labor under the mistaken idea, that the opinion of the superior happiness and liberty of the English people, to which he had alluded, was his, [Mr. C.'s] opinion. One moment's thought must have caused the gentleman to see that it was quite impossible it should be so, because it would make the illustration defeat the argument. It was because it was the opinion of the English people themselves, and because familiarity with their condition and their burdens, led them so to think, when, in fact, it was not so; that is, precisely because their opinion was erroneous, that the case illustrated the truth of what he had urged. Certainly that gentleman, and every one who knew him, must know, that in his opinion, no people on the wide surface of the habitable globe, had so much cause of thankfulness for the measure of civil, political and religious freedom, as the American people; yet he re-asserted the same fact—the English people do think themselves the most happy and most free. The imigration into this country, is said to prove that they feel their rulers and measures to be tyrannical and oppressive and for this cause leave the country. He differed with that gentleman. It was very true many of those who came to our country, expressed this opinion, after they were here, and had some experience of our greater political privileges, and our greater abundance in all the necessaries and comforts of life. But these were not fair exponants of the general sentiment of their countrymen, any more than a class—and not a very small one—in our own country, who are ever dissatisfied with the existing government, and anxiously and vehemently urging changes. Emigration ever did, and ever will follow an exce s of population.

Whenever the inhabitants of one country become so numerous that the production is insufficient to sustain them, labor must of necessity become cheap, while food becomes scare and dear, and they will migrate to another country to find better wages and better food, as certainly as water will seek a level. We were receiving emigrants from all other quarters of populous Europe, as well as from England, and must expect to do so while land and its products were abundant, and labor in demand to an extent unknown in Europe.

Our own people were continually migrating to the new States and territories, in some instances as rapidly as they were emigrating from the old country into this. While, therefore, he admitted that our free institutions constituted *one* element, in the aggregate of motives to immigration, it did not weaken at all the force of his position.

In relation to the matter of government stocks he must enter his dissent to the views of the gentleman from Frederick, and express his concurrence with those explained by his friend from Anne Arundel, (Mr. Donaldson.) Contractors for loans, like all other traders, will of course make the best bargain they can.

The purchaser of stock looks to its security and its productive value or dividend. If he can get the stock of the State of Maryland, on as good or better terms—reference being had to these considerations—he will buy Maryland stocks. If he can purchase the stock of other States believed to be equally safe and equally productive on better terms, he will purchase these.

There is nothing in the case of stocks to distinguish them from other articles of traffic. The supply and demand will determine the price. The error lies in treating the subject as if the were no stocks in the market but Maryland State stock, whereas the supply of other stocks is sufficient to enable purchasers always to select. He deprecated the abandonment of the system to which we had now accommodated our prices of land, labor and production, as well as our domestic and social habits, until our emancipation was complete. It would also advance our credit in the event of a necessity to employ it hereafter. He illustrated this view, by contrasting the prudent, economical debtor, who anticipated the day of payment, with the man of indulgence and extravagance, who with much larger pecuniary means, was always just in "at the last gasp," or perhaps a little behind the stipulated time. He regretted to hear a contrary opinion urged. It was to be feared if we entered upon this easy downward path of repealing taxes, we should be in the condition of the passenger on the railroad, who in going down the inclined plane cut loose the fastenings, and was hurried with such rapid impetus into the mire below, that he could neither extricate himself nor be reached by his friends.

Mr. Spencer said, the reference which had been made to him by the gentleman from Kent, (Mr Chambers;) and the gentleman from Anne Arundel, (Mr. Donaldson,) made it necessary for him to make a response It had been said that at the December session of the Legislature of eighteen hundred and thirty-nine, Governor Grason had, with great firmness and integrity of character, in his annual message, recommended the imposition of a direct tax to meet the exigencies of the State, resulting from her internal improvement works. But that the committee of ways and means, of which he, (Mr. S.,) was Chairman, had not recommended in their report to the Legislature such a tax and had not sustained the Governor. It was true that he had the honor, at that important session of the Legislature, to be the Chairman of that committee, and he was fully sensible, as he had occasion before to say to this body, of the high and patriotic position then taken by Governor Grason and Mr. McCubbin, then the treasurer of the State. As the Chairman of the committee of ways and means, he made every effort in his power to provide for a direct tax, but it was impossible. On the ninth day of January, the Legislature having been in session only ten days, and before any time had been allowed for any action, by the committee of ways and means, General Ridgely, of Anne Arundel, a leading whig, and the year before, the Speaker of the House, submitted a set of resolutions repudiating the sentiments contained in the message of Governor Grason, and declaring that the Legislature do not concur in the opinion of the Governor, that a direct tax is necessary, but on the contrary would hold such a measure premature, unwise and burdensome to the people of this State. [See page 52 of the Journal of House of Delegates, session 1839.]

On the eleventh day of the same month, he, (Mr S,) being chairman of the committee of ways and means, and with the approval of three other members of that committee, submitted to the Legislature a counter set of resolutions, approving the course of the Governor, setting forth the condition of the finances; the resources of the State; its plighted faith; the obligations of the Legislature to meet it, and the impropriety in the Legislature, to intercept the action of the committee of ways and means, on the subject. [See page 68, of same journal.]

On the same day, Mr. LeGrande of Baltimore, and a Democrat, offered others, declaring that whilst it is the duty of the Legislature to provide adequate means for the support of Governments, "those ends may for the present be attained without a resort to direct taxation." [See page 70, of same journal.]

These resolutions elicited in the House a warm and excited debate, and after various discussions, another distinguished Whig, Mr. Tuck, now a member of this Convention, submitted on the twenty-third of January, another set of resolutions, denouncing in very strong terms the message of Governor Grason, and declaring "that this Legislature does not concur in the suggestion of the message, that the revenue should be increased by a direct tax laid on the real and personal property of the people." [See page 126, of same journal.]

It will readily be perceived, how completely the committee of ways and means were embarrased. The entire whig party in the House, stood firm to a man in opposition to Governor Grason's message. At the same time, although the democrats had a majority in the House, there was a small division of them, who, with the whigs, opposed a direct tax. Every effort was made to induce a small portion of the whig party to act with and support the committee of ways and means. Three distinguis ed gentlemen from Baltimore, and he mentioned it with infinite pleasure, for it did them great honor—Messrs. Grafton Dulany, J. V. L. McMahon and William Schley, visited in person the whig members and appealed to them to come to the rescue of the chairman of the committee of ways and means, as he was ready to report a tax, if he could carry it. It was urged, that it could then be done, free from party influence. That the governor, a democrat; the treasurer, a whig, and the chairman of the committee of ways and means, a democrat, had supported, and were in favor of it, and it only required a small support from whig members, to carry a measure which should rise above party. It was urged that the measure would have to come and that it had better come at once. But the appeal was in vain The committee could not get support sufficient to carry the measure and it was driven to resort to the best expedients which could be carried under the circumstances, and to assign the best reasons that could be furnished, for pursuing such a course.

A temporary expedient was adopted, but with it went forth the annunciation in the report of the committee, that upon the faith which capitalists, at home and abroad, gave to our acts of assembly, they "have been induced to subscribe their money. In this manner, the debt has been created. The money has been actually borrowed and distributed through the State, in payment of officers, contractors and laborers, who have been employed on the public works."

"The professed design was an advancement of the common prosperity of the people. So far, the end contemplated has failed, and the State is called upon to redeem its obligations."

"We must so act as to prove, that what we owe, we intend to pay. Every principle of honor, virtue and patriotism, compels us to such a course. It is not the characteristic of an American to mould his principles to subserve his selfishness. What he would require of another, he will perform himself. His principle is to exact nothing but what is right, and submit to nothing that is wrong."

"When General Jackson was the President of the United States, he insisted upon a payment of a debt due by the French Government. In enforcing the claim, the friendly intercourse between the two nations, were for a while arrested. We were upon the verge of war. Great as was the opposition to his administration, on other subjects, upon this question the hearts of all united. Though the controversy was with France, our ancient ally, when we were struggling for political liberty and independence, still as the demand of the government was just, past friendship was forgotten, and the course of the administration ardently sustained. The chivalry of the nation was aroused, and nothing but an unconditional payment of the debt would have been tolerated. It must not be said of us, that what we exacted of France, we will refuse to others."

"If the period has arrived, when to pay the interest on this debt, all other resources have failed except direct taxation, we must resort to it."

Tha,tin the opinion of the committee, "there is no necessity to provide for a direct tax, at present, but they cannot disguise the fact, that after the year 1841, it will be inevitable, unless the Chesapeake and Ohio canal company, and the Baltimore and Susquehanna railroad company, shall contribute largely to the payment of the interest on the public debt."

[See report of committee of ways and means—Session 1839.]

Mr. Brown demanded the previous question, but waived it at the request of

Mr. Donaldson, between whom and Messrs. Spencer and Chambers, of Kent, some explanations passed.

Mr. Brown renewed the demand for the previous question.

There was a second.

And the main question was ordered to be now taken.

Mr. Grason enquired, if it would now be in order to move a call of the House.

The chair, at this time, was occupied by Mr. Blakistone.

The President of the Convention rose and said, that under the new rule, a call of the House was not in order, after the main question had been ordered.

Mr. Spencer said, that the vote on such a question ought not to be taken without a full House. He moved, therefore, a reconsideration of the vote ordering the main question, with a view to move a call of the House.

The motion was not entertained.

The question then recurred on the main question, [being the substitute amendment of Mr DONALDSON.]

Mr. McHENRY asked the yeas and nays thereon, which were ordered, and being taken, resulted as follows:

Affirmative — Messrs. Chapman, President, Blakistone, Ricaud, Lee, Chambers, of Kent, Donaldson, Dorsey, Wells, Kent, Merrick, Jenifer, Williams, Goldsborough, Sprigg, McCubbin, Waters and Smith—17.

Negative—Messrs. Dent, Sellman, Weems, Buchanan, Bell, Ridgely, Lloyd, Dickinson, Sherwood, of Talbot, Colston, John Dennis, James U. Dennis, Hodson, Phelps, Constable, Chambers, of Cecil, Miller, Spencer, Grason, George, Wright, Jacobs, Thomas, Gaither, Biser, Annan, Sappington, McHenry, Magraw, Nelson, Carter, Thawley, Stewart of Caroline, Gwinn, Stewart of Baltimore city, Sherwood of Baltimore city, Ware, Schley, Fiery, Neill, John Newcomer, Harbine, Michael Newcomer, Kilgour, Brewer, Weber, Fitzpatrick, Parke, Shower and Brown—50.

So the substitute amendment of Mr. DONALDSON, was rejected.

The question recurred on the substitute amendment of Mr. GEORGE, [accepted by Mr. RIDGELY.]

Mr. STEWART, of Baltimore city, and Mr. RIDGELY, asked the yeas and nays, which were ordered.

Mr. DONALDSON called for a division of the question, which was ordered.

And the question was then taken on the first article of the substitute, and the result was as follows:

Affirmative — Messrs. Chapman, President, Blakistone, Dent, Hopewell, Ricaud, Lee, Chambers, of Kent, Donaldson, Dorsey, Wells, Kent, Sellman, Weems, Jenifer, Buchanan, Bell, Ridgely, Lloyd, Dickinson, Sherwood, of Talbot, Colston, John Dennis, James U. Dennis, Williams, Hodson, Goldsborough, Phelps, Chambers, of Cecil, Miller, McCubbin, Spencer, Grason, George, Wright, Thomas, Gaither, Biser, Annan, Sappington, McHenry, Magraw, Nelson, Carter, Thawley, Stewart, of Caroline, Gwinn, Stewart, of Baltimore city, Sherwood, of Baltimore city, Ware, Schley, Fiery, Neill, John Newcomer, Harbine, Michael Newcomer, Kilgour, Brewer, Waters, Weber, Fitzpatrick, Smith, Parke, Shower and Brown—64.

Negative — Messrs. Merrick, Constable and Sprigg—3.

So the first article of the substitute was agreed to.

The question recurring on the adoption of the second article of the substitute,

Mr. STEWART, of Baltimore city, asked a subdivision thereof, which was ordered, so as to include to the word "and" in the fourth line.

The question was taken and the result was as follows:

Affirmative—Messrs. Chapman, President, Blakistone, Dent, Hopewell, Ricaud, Lee, Chambers of Kent, Donaldson, Sellman, Weems, Merrick, Jenifer, Buchanan, Bell, Ridgely, Lloyd, Dickinson, Sherwood of Talbot, Colston, John Dennis, James U. Dennis, Williams, Hodson, Goldsborough, Phelps, Chambers of Cecil, Miller, Sprigg, McCubbin, Spencer, Grason, George, Wright, Hearn, Jacobs, Thomas, Gaither, Biser, Annan, Sappington, Magraw, Nelson, Carter, Thawley, Stewart of Caroline, Gwinn, Stewart of Baltimore city, Sherwood of Baltimore city, Ware, Schley, Fiery, Neill, John Newcomer, Harbine, Michael Newcomer, Kilgour, Waters, Weber, Fitzpatrick, Smith, Shower and Brown—62.

Negative—Messrs. Dorsey, Wells, Constable, McHenry, Brewer and Parke—6.

So the first branch of the second article of the substitute was agreed to.

The question then recurred, and was taken on the last branch of the second article of the substitute.

And the vote resulted as follows:

Affirmative—Messrs. Chapman, President, Morgan, Blakistone, Dent, Hopewell, Ricaud, Lee, Chambers of Kent, Sellman, Weems, Merrick, Jenifer, Buchanan, Bell, Ridgely, Lloyd, Dickinson, Sherwood of Talbot, Colston, John Dennis, James U. Dennis, Williams, Hodson, Phelps, Constable, Chambers of Cecil, Miller, Spencer, Grason, George, Hearn, Jacobs, Thomas, Gaither, Biser, Annan, Sappington, McHenry, Magraw, Nelson, Carter, Thawley, Stewart of Caroline, Gwinn, Stewart of Baltimore city, Sherwood of Baltimore city, Ware, Schley, Fiery, Neill, John Newcomer, Harbine, Michael Newcomer, Kilgour, Brewer, Waters, Fitzpatrick, Smith, Parke, Shower and Brown—61.

Negative—Messrs. Donaldson, Dorsey, Wells, Kent, Goldsborough, Sprigg, McCubbin and Weber—8.

So the last branch of the second article of the substitute was agreed to.

The question recurred on the section as amended;

And decided in the affirmative.

So the section, as amended, was adopted.

Mr. MERRICK offered an amendment which was decided out of order.

Some conversation followed on a point of order.

Mr. McHENRY moved a re-consideration of the vote adopting the said section, as amended.

Mr. McH. gave notice that, if the motion was re-considered, he would offer the following amendment:

Section 21. The General Assembly shall have power to provide by law for borrowing such sums of money as may become necessary to fulfil the obligations of the State, contracted previously to the adoption of this constitution, to defray the expenses of repeling invasion, or of suppressing insurrection, and to meet any temporary deficiency in the revenue; but for no other purposes whatever. All loans made under this authority shall be payable and paid within twenty years, and those to meet temporary deficiencies within two years, from the respective dates thereof.

Sec. 22. The credit of the State shall not, in any manner be given or loaned to, or in aid of any individual, association or corporation.

Sec. 23. This State shall never embark in works of internal improvement, nor in pecuniary adventures of any kind.

And then the Convention adjourned until to-morrow at ten o'clock.

WEDNESDAY, Feburuary 26, 1851.

The Convention met at ten o'clock.

Prayer by the Rev. Mr. Griffith.

The roll was called, and the journal of yesterday was read and approved.

ALLEGANY COUNTY.

Mr. Smith, from the select committee on new counties, submitted the following

REPORT:

When that part of Allegany, lying south and west of a line beginning at the summit of Big Back Bone, or Savage Mountain; where the Mountain is crossed by Mason and Dixon's line, and running thence by a straight line to the middle of Savage river, where it empties into the Potomac river, thence by a straight line to the nearest point or boundary of the State of Virginia; then with said boundary to the Fairfax Stone, shall contain a population of ten thousand, and the majority of electors thereof shall desire to separate and form a new county, and make known their desires by petition to the Legislature, the Legislature shall direct at the next succeeding election, that the judges shall open a book at each election district in said part of Allegany county, and have recorded therein the vote of each elector, "for or against," a new county, in case the majority, (or two-thirds) are in favor, the said part of Allegany county, to be declared an independent county, and the inhabitants whereof shall have and enjoy all such rights, and privileges as are held and enjoyed by the inhabitants of the other counties in this State.

Mr. Smith said, he made the report, with the concurrence of the committee, at this time, because it was connected with the report of the committee on the Legislative Department now under consideration.

The report was read, and ordered to be printed, and laid on the table, to be called up hereafter.

INTOXICATING DRINKS.

Mr. Harbine, presented a petition of sundry citizens of Washington county, praying that provision may be made in the new Constitution, that the privilege to sell intoxicating liquors shall not be granted to any person in any part of the State, except the same shall first be sanctioned, or approved of by a majority of the votes in the election district where the same is to be sold.

Which was read, and

On motion of Mr. Harbine,

Referred to committee No. 14.

THE LEGISLATIVE DEPARTMENT.

The Convention, resumed the consideration of the report of the committee on the Legislative Department of the Government.

THE FINANCES.

Mr. Jacobs inquired of the Chair, whether it was now in order to move an additional article?

The Presieent said, it was in order.

Mr. Jacobs moved to amend said report by inserting as the twenty-second section, the following:

"The present financial system of this State, shall remain inviolate until the State debt and interest thereon are fully paid; or the sinking fund be sufficient for the payment thereof, after which the Legislature shall provide by law for the annual distribution amongst the counties and city of Baltimore of this State, of the nett revenues of the several works of Internal Improvements, in the proportion which by taxation they shall have contributed to the same."

The amendment having been read—

Mr. Jacobs said that his motive in offering it was to show to the people the sincerity of the purposes of this Convention, that they intended to adhere to the present financial system until the debt was paid—and that it was intended, after the debt should have been paid to secure to them something in return for the taxes they had contributed. The people whom he represented looked to the adoption of some such provision with great solicitude; and good faith to the people, generally, required, he thought, that something of this sort should be inserted in the Constitution.

Mr. Donaldson called for a division of the question.

The President said, in the judgment of the Chair the amendment was susceptible of two divisions.

Mr. Brown suggested that the amendment, in his opinion, went further than the gentleman from Worcester, (Mr. Jacobs,) designed that it should go. If the gentleman designed that there should be no reduction of taxes until the entire debt was paid, then it would follow that there must be a large surplus in the Treasury. The system, it seemed to him, (Mr. B.,) would not work well. He should be compelled to vote against it.

Mr. Jacobs I do not propose that the present system shall continue in force beyond the time when the sinking fund shall be swelled to an amount sufficient to meet the payment of the State bonds, as they may, from time to time, become due. Immediately after the debt shall have been paid off, the distribution, proposed by my article, will commence. Hence, after the debt is paid, there can never be any surplus in the treasury, for any length of time, under the proposed distribution.

Mr. Dorsey suggested to the gentleman from Worcester, (Mr. Jacobs,) to modify his proposition by inserting the words "until the debt and interest are fully paid, or the sinking fund shall be found sufficient for payment thereof."

Mr. Jacobs accepted the modification.

Mr. Thomas said he had yesterday expressed an earnest opposition to the course of policy in relation to our finances, which was foreshadowed in some gentlemen's speeches, and which is this morning proposed in the amendment of the gentleman from Worcester, (Mr. Jacobs.) He would, this morning, say in a few words, why he must vote against this proposition. Before he did so, he had something to say on a question mooted yesterday in this hall.

He was not here when the honors were distributed yesterday to those who were entitled to the credit of rescuing Maryland from the disgrace of a public bankruptcy. He humbly conceived, that when all the facts were known, no one would deny to him some portion of that commendation which had been given altogether to others. To some of these facts he would refer, especially as they would tend to remove every shadow of suspicion from the minds of members, that he was less jealous than another, of the honor of the State. We may differ as to the mode in which public faith may be maintained, but those differences should not lead us to entertain apprehensions and distrusts of each other, that have no foundations.

It was well known to the Convention that he had been chosen President of the Chesapeake and Ohio Canal company in 1839. Prior to that, the State of Maryland had contracted a debt of more than seven millions to pay for stock taken in the canal company and to raise money to be loaned to the same company to prosecute its great undertaking. The acts of the General Assembly of Maryland, authorizing State bonds to be issued for these purposes, each and all contain sections requiring the canal company to mortgage to the State all their incomes and the whole work they were constructing, to secure the punctual payment of the interest on the loans thus made by the State, and on the State bonds issued to raise means to pay for this canal stock for a stated period of years. At the time he became their President, the annual interest, payable from the canal company to the State, exceeded four hundred thousand dollars. The whole income of the company was not sufficient to keep that part of the canal which was then finished, in repair, and to pay the salaries of its officers. Thus circumstanced, the officers of the company had no means to pay the interest due to the State but by selling the bonds of the State itself, for whatever they would bring in the market. And, in this way, when two millions of dollars were advanced by the State to construct the canal, about one million five hundred thousand dollars would be expended in the further construction of the work, and the other five hundred thousand would be sold in the market to raise means to be paid into the State treasury. If these bonds to pay interest had been sold by the treasurer of the State, the true character of these financial arrangements would have been obvious. But under the arrangements that were made, a delusion prevailed on this subject. The people believed that the large sums of public money which had been expended for internal improvements, could not, in any event, lead to taxation. And the purchasers of the bonds felt secure of the punctual payment of their dividends, under the belief that the mortgages given by the canal company to the State, had been executed by a company having ample means to comply with its pecuniary engagements. This financiering, Mr T. said, was deceptive; but he did not impute intentional wrong to any one who had been concerned in it. When these contracts were entered into by the canal company and the State, he had no doubt but that the parties to them fully believed that the canal would be completed at an early day, and that then its incomes and profits would be abundantly adequate to the fulfilment of its contracts. He thought otherwise, and took measures as soon as he had time, fully to understand the affairs of the company to arrest this whole proceeding. At that time a corps of Engineers were locating a route for the canal west of Cumberland with a view to its extension to the Ohio. They were withdrawn. The idea of extending the canal to Ohio river was abandoned. If it had been possible to keep the financial system in operation, which was relied upon to pay the interest on bonds of the State issued to construct the canal, the bonds to be issued for that purpose, would have exceeded thirty millions of dollars. Having taken measures to limit the undertaking of the company to the completion of the canal from tide-water to Cumberland, he addressed a letter to the gentleman from Queen Anne's, who was then Governor of Maryland, urging him to call an extra session of the Legislature, that measures might be adopted to put the financial affairs of the State in order, and place them on some sure and stable foundation. He then thought and said, that taxation, and taxation alone, was the rightful remedy. After his letter to the Governor had been received by him, they had a personal conference on this subject, when there was no difference between them as to the stern necessity which existed for an interposition of the Legislature. But the Governor thought it would not be expedient to call an extra session of the Legislature he preferred to wait for a regular annual session of that body, the time for commencing which being then near at hand. Having detailed these facts, he asked whether no credit was due to the citizen of Maryland who had taken upon himself high responsibility to arrest a proceeding that must have eventuated but for that interruption in the contracting of a public debt that would have frustrated every plan since devised to maintain the honor of Maryland.

It was well known that he had opposed the internal improvement policy that had caused our financial difficulties. He differed now as to the manner in which our financial affairs were to be conducted, and he was not to be deterred in the pursuit of his objects by the possibility that he might encounter the hostility of those elsewhere, who contributed nothing but frothy declamations about State faith towards the maintenance, unsullied, of State honor.

He was opposed to the amendment of the gentleman from Worcester, and would vote against any proposition to impose such restriction on the legislature as would leave them no power to reduce the taxes, when the state of our treasury would fully justify such a measure. His principal objection to such a course, was founded in the belief, that, it would cause the public securities to rise in the market much beyond their nominal value, and in that way afford opportunities to stock-jobbers, to make large profits and interfere seriously with the policy of the State, intended to pay the public debt through the medium of the sinking fund. Our treasurers habitually purchased Maryland stocks with the proceeds of the sinking fund. The amount of stocks of that character, due and payable was very limited. The largest portion of the State would not be due for twenty, thirty and forty years. Was it then wise policy to compel our legislature to keep the present tax system in full operation, when it was notorious that the surplus annually accruing in the treasury, would soon be, if it was not now, much greater in amount than the bonds of the State outstanding and due. He denied that it would be good policy to deny to the legislature, power to touch this tax system before the whole debt is paid off. We have an increasing income from the public works. That may increase in a few years and swell this surplus revenue. And in that event, the treasurer would have on hands large sums of money to be applied to the purposes of the sinking fund. This State of our finances would be known to stock-jobbers; and could any one fail to foresee that that class of citizens holding large amounts of State securities, that the treasury had not a right to redeem without consent of the holder, until they were due, would demand for their prices high above this nominal value. To him this seemed very clear, and he would undertake to predict that if the policy indicated by this amendment, was enforced upon the legislature that it would be found hereafter that we had paid eighteen or twenty millions, instead of fifteen million of dollars for our State bonds. Such a result he depricated.

He regarded these debts of the State as obligatory on the people of Maryland. They are to be paid, but we are under no obligation to provide for their payment before they are due. Those who hold our securities as a permanent investment, and look to their dividends from that source as a means of support, will be satisfied if we take care to provide for the punctual payment of those dividends, and are ready to redeem the principal when it is due. For these purposes our State financial system has been made abundantly adequate by the Legislature. And he had no reason to doubt that the Legislature, if the whole subject is left as it ought to be, to their discretion, would be derelict to their duties in this respect.

He had said this to explain the vote he was to give. He could not agree to detain the house by saying more in support of propositions that appeared to his mind so obvious and indisputable.

Mr. CHAMBERS said, when this subject was unexpectedly started yesterday, he had ventured to enter his protest against the policy of an early reduction of taxes. The gentleman from Frederick had to day renewed the subject with an elaborate argument.

He should not waste words or the time of the Convention by an effort to show the duty of providing for the *interest* on the public debt. No man he supposed could be found to deny that duty, or oppose its performance. It would place him in a position odious in public estimation.

The gentleman from Frederick had advanced two propositions, first that the fact of the Treasurer's being in the market would necessarily swell the price of our stock to an inordinate sum; secondly, that it would be the means of securing large fortunes to speculators and stock-jobbers.

Mr. THOMAS repeated his positions, in order to set the gentleman right.

Mr. CHAMBERS said he understood the positions assumed by the gentleman, and supposed he had correctly stated them, and he desired to express his entire dissent from each of them. He would reiterate the views he had yesterday expressed, that the considerations which connect themselves with stock operations are not those assumed by the gentleman from Frederick. The elements which enter into the estimate of the value of stock are such as he had before asserted. Men are governed in their transactions in this article of traffic by the same influences which control their action in their traffic in in other articles. It was subject to the same general law which governs in all matters of trade. The proportionate amount of demand and supply would regulate the price.

So it was with land or its products; when abundant, a man would go into the market and invest his money so as to produce the most profit by his purchase. If an individual wanted a farm, he would make its productiveness and its conveniencies the criterion of its value. There might be an exception to this rule, where a person of large wealth indulged his fancy or his taste, or a convenient location of his family, but he spoke of cases generally. A stranger having no local preferences or social feelings to divert him from the ordinary motives of purchasers, would never buy a farm for one hundred dollars per acre, when he could obtain one of as good quality, as conveniently situated, in regard to "mill, market, and church," equally productive and equally improved, at half the price. Nor would it be an inducement sufficient to change his purpose, that some wealthy neighbor was known to be desirous to purchase the first named farm. So with government stock, if there was but a very limited amount in the market, its value as a means of investment would undoubtedly increase, to an extent beyond other articles of which the supply was more abundant. But government stocks were plenty, and a purchaser had ample room for selection. A man of money, therefore, desiring to invest, would ascertain first the perfect security of the investment, and next the annual product or dividend. Whether Mr. A., Mr. B., the Treasurer, or any body else, desired to purchase that stock, would form a very inconsiderable element in estimating the prudence or propriety of the investment, especially if it were to be permanent. If only for a temporary purpose, it might be some additional motive to know that a demand for the particular stock always existed, and to that extent might, to a small amount, enhance its cost.

But safety and productive value, would be the ruling causes of value, because they would always secure purchasers.

He enlarged upon the view, to prove that our State stock could not be forced to an unnatural price in the market, for the reason that the Treasurer was authorized to purchase.

Now the gentleman has stated his second proposition, but what proof has he offered to sustain it? We were yet to learn, why or how, stock-jobbers were to realize overgrown fortunes by the fact that the Treasurer was one of the numerous bidders, in the market, for State stock. He confessed himself unable to perceive the "modus operandi."

This class of men, as he understood the matter, made their fortunes very much after the fashion of dealers in other departments of trade. They devoted all the energies of their minds, to the acquisition of information, as to events and circumstances which experience taught them would effect the value of money

All the political events of the day were closely scaned. They were early advised of the threatened troubles and excitements of governments, the disturbed relations of nations, the consequent probable preparations for such emergencies; the prospect of war or peace; for loans and subsidies; then again they accurately estimated the surplus or deficiency in crops, in cotton. bread-stuffs, and so on; the probable state of commercial operations, imports and exports, and all the various facts which occasioned an increase or diminution in the value of money. This being ascertain, they operated accordingly. If money became cheap and worth for its loan or use, say three per cent. per annum, why of course a six per cent. stock was worth more than par. If money was to be so scarce, by the relative value of other articles, as to command eight per cent., then a six per cent. stock was not worth par. Thus the "bulls and the bears," were up and down by turns. A reference to English government stocks, would show that the prices were ruled by considerations such as he had mentioned. Consols were affected materially by a political rumor. True the quotation per share or per cent. was very small, but like the half-pence sterling in the pound of cotton, this very small per cent. amounted in the aggregate to millions of dollars.

Yet these rumors did not make them less secure, or less productive. Money, like every thing else, had a *relative* value—and when scarce it would procure more in exchange, for other commodities, and when abundant it would procure less. If all this were so, how was it to increase or diminish the emoluments of stock-jobbers, that our Treasurer was authorized to purchase, and had the means to pay for our State stock.

Before quitting this subject, he would address a word of advice on this subject, to that class of persons who had, as he supposed, the deepest interest in this matter. He alluded to the agricultural portion of the community—the owners of land and negroes. They might be well assured they were the very last who would be benefitted by a remission of taxes.

The gentleman from Frederick strongly advised an early diminution of taxes, reducing the revenue to the lowest amount necessary to pay interest and current expenses. Let no such notion be adopted. Let us not be deluded by doubtful or delusive expectations.

We have heard the opinions of those who should best know, that the receipts from the works of internal improvement are most precarious and uncertain. Experience teaches us, that accidents may befal our canal and railroads.

They have heretofore, and without expensive or destructive accidents, failed to produce the rich dividends confidently anticipated. They may do so again. When other sources of revenue have been abandoned, in reliance on the golden streams which are to flow into the treasury from these sources, we may suddenly find these streams have ceased to flow. What comes next? Of course a tax on land and negroes. What has always been the first object of taxation? Land and negroes, most certainly. Aye, and in the proposed system of excision and paring off and paring down of taxes, what is to be the very last item to which the scapel is to be applied? Why, of course, our land and negroes.

Look at the *projet* read to you the other day, from the official proceedings in Baltimore under the imposing title of "reform and *repeal*." Do you find there any suggestion of repealing taxes on land and negroes? No, indeed—quite otherwise. The "odious stamp tax," and all other taxes paid in common by the mercantile and other classes are to be *repealed*, but the tax on land and negroes is the legitimate source of permanent revenue. He warned this great interest of the danger of thus exposing it to a continuance of the ungenerous and unjust exclusiveness which had singled them out, as the peculiar objects of taxation.

This public debt was a universal "mortgage," an incumbrance upon all our estates. Every man should be anxious to see it discharged and released. Every dollar raised for the purpose of discharging the public debt should be regarded, as so far a satisfaction of this mortgage. No man could desire to have his property pass to his children thus heavily incumbered with liabilities. It ought to be constantly kept in mind that our property with this lien upon it, was lessened by that amount, and every dollar that was placed in the treasury to pay the public debt, went just so far to increase the actual value of our property. Every man knew, that if his farm was mortgaged for a particular sum, it was worth to him precisely to the amount of that sum less than its par value. It was precisely the same thing with regard to the whole property of the State, which was incumbered with the public debt, of which he repeated, the items of land and negroes would in any event, pay a large proportion, and if a system of early repeal should be unfortunately adopted, they would be made to pay nearly the whole.

He had thus given his views on the general question, discussed by the gentleman from Frederick, without reference to the particular motion now before the chair. Indeed, he had not heard this proposition read, as the gentleman had just commenced his remarks as he entered the Hall.

Mr. THOMAS, in reply, said, there was one proposition on which he was desirous not to be misunderstood. The gentleman from Kent had laid it down as a principle that the price of the stocks in market, depends on the relation which the demand bears to the supply, and that the presence of the State treasurer in the market cannot, in any way, influence the value of stocks. He admitted that the treasurer could not regulate the price of all stocks. But the amount of the surplus in the hands of the treasurer, might be disproportioned to the amount of such stock in the market, as the treasurer was in the habit of purchasing.

Although the law did not compel the treasurer to purchase Maryland stocks only, it was the practice of the treasurer to do so; and as the amount of Maryland stocks in the market that were due was limited, a large surplus for their purchase would cause an unreasonable elevation in their price.

He was aware that there was no law in this State, which confines the treasurer to the purchase of any particular stock; and he was surprised that the treasurer should be allowed to deal in any other than our State stocks. Not that he meant any insinuation against the present treasurer, for a man more honest never filled the office. But he was opposed to the principle that the treasurer of the State shall be permitted to deal in the stocks of Mississippi, Arkansas, or Canton, or in all of these, without any restriction. He thought it was the duty of the legislature to prescribe how far he might go. He, himself, had been informed that the treasurer had expressed himself sensible, that this large discretion should never be exercised. Purchases with the sinking fund, had always been made in Maryland stocks only. Assuming, then, that the treasurer is limited, he (Mr. T.,) would place himself in a position to meet the argument of the gentleman from Kent. He would ask, if there is any portion of the debt of the State, which has yet thirty-nine years to run in the market, on reasonable terms? The gentleman from Kent argues that we ought to apply the surplus money to pay the State debt. When? That is the question. According to the stipulation in the bond. Because a man does not make sacrifices to enable him to pay debts, which, according to contract, will not become due for many years, is he to be regarded as one who runs counter to all the proprieties of life, and to every moral principle? Is the State to be called on now, to pay a debt, which does not fall due until the year 1890? If we agree to do this, all the advantage of the act will accrue to speculators in stocks, but no profit could result to the State.

But enough had been said on this topic. The subject had been discussed over and over, until the Convention had become weary of it. Every man must have made up his mind how he will vote.

Mr. JENIFER said that the question before the House had been lost sight of, which was not unusual, and he should not now follow in this discussive debate, had not the distinguished gentleman from Frederick, (Mr. Thomas,) a second time referred to matters which appeared entirely irrelevant to the question now under consideration. That gentleman had, in his speech of yesterday, referred to the last message of the late Governor Philip Francis Thomas, and had reiterated to-day his unqualified disapprobation of that part of it which recommended to the Legislature "not to rescind any portion of the taxes until the public debt was paid." That it was not in accordance with his, (Mr. T's.,) understanding of the views of the party to which he belonged. Mr. J. said he did not mean to question the gentleman's sincerity when he declared that he would go as far as any man to preserve and protect the faith of the State, when, at the same time, he was in favor of a reduction of the taxes and a disturbance of that system of revenue upon an adherence to which, the good faith and credit of the State so much depended. Mr. J. said, he differed in political views, generally, with the late Governor of Maryland, but he was willing to "render unto Cæsar the things that are Cæsar's," in doing which, the distinguished gentleman from Frederick, could not take it amiss if *his* gubernatorial policy were brought in contrast with that of the late Governor. Mr. J. said he would not question the motives of the gentleman, but his councils and his measures were apppropriate subjects for animadversion. What was the condition of the finances of Maryland and her credit when the gubernatorial term of the gentleman from Frederick expired? What are they now, upon the expiration of the term of the late Governor, Philip Francis Thomas?

Mr. J. said he would refer to the reports of the Treasurer and messages of the Governor, for the condition of affairs at the period to which he desired to call the attention of the House.

In December, 1844, when the gubernatorial term of the gentleman from Frederick was about to expire, after calling the attention of the Legislature to the financial embarrassments of the State, and the deficit in the revenue to meet the demands upon the Treasury, he says:

"These defalcations in the revenue are to be imputed in a great degree to the palpable insufficiency of the whole taxes levied, even if punctually paid. As long as our tax laws have this obvious aspect, we may expect a large portion of the public dues will be withheld, in the belief that the attempt to pay the public debt will at no distant day be abandoned." Again: "Another fatal error was committed in failing to enforce the law against the first delinquents." In this state of things others were encourged to follow the example of the delinquents; "and now, instead of three, we have seven counties, within whose boundaries the tax laws are not all enforced." "No one in the defaulting counties, it appears is willing to encounter the odium of becoming the collector of the tax levied to pay the interest on our internal improvement debt."

Mr. J. said, these gloomy forebodings pervaded the whole message, and he retired from the Chair of State, leaving to his successors a Treasury embarrassed; the laws unexecuted; the credit of the State prostrated at home and abroad. He concludes his message as follows: "In the retirement to which I go, I shall hail, with exultation, the evidence of wisdom and patriotism on on the part of yourselves, and your successorss, which will lift my native State into the rank which she has a right to occupy among her sisters of the Union."

Mr. J. said he would call the attention of the House to the other side of the picture. He had successors whose "wisdom and patriotism," and energy and zeal, did lift the State into the rank which she had a right to occupy. These successors were Governor Pratt, and Governor Philip Francis Thomas, under whose administration that system of revenue was adopted, which in the langauge of the latter Governor, will "prevent the possibility of a relapse to her former cheerless and degrading condition," and which the distinguished gentleman from Frederick desires now to disturb. How stood matters when Governor Pratt's term, which immediately succeeded the one and preceded the other, expired. Mr. J. said he would refer to the message of the late Governor to the Legislature at December session, 1847, in which he says: "the condition of the finances as represented in the annual message of the Governor, and the report of the Treasurer, is a subject of profound congratulation. While it has been the privilege of my distinguished predecessor, (Governor Pratt,) by his assiduity, firmness, and ability to rescue Maryland from the vortex of insolvency in which he found her engulphed, and to elevate her to that proud position before the world, which the character of her people entitle her to occupy, it will be my more humble aim to discharge the functions of the executive office with fidelity as to ensure stability in the revenues, inspire increased confidence in the honor and integrity of the State, and to prevent the possibility of a relapse to her former cheerless and degrading condition." This is the best testimony, Mr. J. said, coming as it did from a political opponent and his immediate successor, that could be offered to the "wisdom and patriotism" of Governor Pratt. Mr. J. said there was one fact he took this opportunity to refer to. It was his lot during the gloomy administration of the gentleman from Frederick, to be on the other side of the Atlantic. He, like every other American in Europe, deeply and sensibly felt the taunts and denunciations which were unceasingly cast upon the credit and honor of the States.

He felt for all, but most for his native State, Maryland; and when the cheering message of Governor Pratt, announcing that the credit of Maryland was redeemed, first caught his view, he then felt again as an American—as a Marylander—without reproach. None, save those who have experienced similar emotions, can appreciate them. It was the absorbing question of the day Maryland having taken the lead, the other States would soon follow. To Governor Pratt and those who co-operated with him, is the credit due. What now is her condition? And to what state of prosperity, under judicious legislation, and administration, she may expect to arrive, may be anticipated from the Treasurer's report, and the last message of Governor Philip Francis Thomas, who after reviewing the various sources of revenue and the public debt, thus expresses:

"It will then be seen that $375,000, at least, may be safely apppropriated to the annual payment of the main debt, while a balance will always remain on hand, more than sufficient to cover any unforeseen contingency. That amount, together with the increasement of the sinking fund, regularly invested, will extinguish the entire public debt, in thirteen years from the first day of December, 1851." This estimate, however, proceeds upon the hypothesis that in the mean time, no attempt will be successfully made to disturb the existing system of taxation, and that it will be left in all its integrity, to work out the relief which it is so certain to afford.

"Allow the system to continue untouched for at most fifteen years longer, and Maryland will present the anomalous and enviable spectacle of a commonwealth liberated from debt, supported without taxation, and possessed of an annual surplus revenue of from three to five hundred thousand dollars."

Mr. J. said he would make no apology for reading thus copiously from these messages. The extracts showed the true financial condition of the State at the respective periods referred to; and from the attention of the House, he saw that the facts were interesting to all.

The gentleman from Frederick has protested against the messages of Governors, having an effect upon the stock market, as producing an unsound state of things.

Mr. J. considered it the duty of the chief Executive officer of the State, to present the true condition of the finances, and to recommend such measures as he deemed best calculated to promote the great interests of the State.

The gentleman from Frederick, had in his message expressed his opinions of the embarrassed condition of the revenue. They were of a desponding character—the effect of which was felt at home and abroad, and did produce depression in the State stocks and State credit. His two immediate successors presented a different state of things. Instead of repudiation, insolvency, rebellion against the laws, which were then anticipated, they left her redeemed from the stain which had rested upon her, rescued from the "votex of insolvency in which they found her engulphed." Was not this an appropriate topic for an Executive message? Is it not cheering to every citizen of Maryland, after being so heavy pressed down by taxation, to learn from the proper source, that there is a prospect, and at no distant day, of being entirely relieved from those burdens,and with a sufficient revenue, without taxation, to meet all future proper demands upon the treasury?

The gentleman from Frederick, (Mr. Thomas) as also the distinguished gentleman from Cecil, (Mr. McLane,) doubt the realization of the extinguishment of the State debt within the period anticipated, and have expressed their distrust in the estimate of receipts from the sources from which it is to be effected.

If the message of a Governor, in relation to the finances of the State, is calculated to produce an inflated tendency in the stock market, how much depression may be produced by the expression of the desponding remarks of those two distinguished gentlemen who have filled so many high and honorable stations?

But, Mr. J., said, he did not apprehend any injury to the credit of the State, as long as the present system of revenue was adhered to, and the treasurer's reports continued to present such favorable results.

Mr. Thomas said that those who did not know him intimately, might have supposed that the gentleman from Charles, (Mr. Jenifer,) was about to present something from the message of which he had read a part variant materially from opinions, Mr. T. had expressed here to-day. But of that he had felt no apprehensions notwithstanding the trouble the gentleman had taken to look over these old documents.

There was nothing in that message inconsistent, in any degree, with what he had now said. To construe rightly the paragraph that had been read, it would be proper to read also other parts of that document,and parts of the two messages from the same department of our State government, for the years 1842 and 1843. Those messages all contained paragraphs earnestly urging the Legislature, to provide the means to maintain the faith of the State. And the paragraph read by the gentleman, rightly construed, gave one of the strongest reasons that could be addressed to those who were anxious to maintain unsullied the public faith. The paragraph the gentleman had read, was equivalent to the declaration that if energetic measures for that object, were not promptly adopted, there might be reason to apprehend that the public mind would receive the impression, that the Legislature had not the courage to do its duty. And in that event the desire to repudiate might become too strong to be controled. This was the obvious meaning of that part of the message, which had been read to the House, when taken in connection with other parts of the same paper, and with the two preceding messages.

He was surprised to find that the gentleman had searched for this message to see whether there was any thing in it incompatible with the opinions expressed to Gov. Grason, in the letter that had been alluded to. The letter was written when he, (Mr. T.,) could not foresee that any portion of the people of Maryland, would concur with him in the opinions therein expressed. The message was published after the system of taxation had been sanctioned by the Legislature. It was not to be presumed, that he would when surrounded, as chief magistrate, by hosts of friends, shrink from advocating a policy which the Governor of the State had repeatedly urged, and the people had sanctioned. When it was very certain that he, in his retired office in Washington, had boldly set his face against the financial policy that avoided all resorts to taxation in any event.

Being up, Mr. T. said he would briefly reply to the closing remarks of the gentleman from Kent. That gentleman had appealed to the representatives of the agricultural interests, to rally against the proposed power in the Legislature to reduce, if it becomes necessary, our State taxes. He knew the influence of that gentleman over the judgments of many members on this floor. But he did not anticipate that this appeal could have much effect on any portion of this Convention. The gentleman knows—this Convention know—that the legislative power of the State is in the hands of those who are chosen by the agriculturalists. The commercial interests of Baltimore, have but five members of a House of Delegates composed of eighty-two members. The same interest has but one member in the Senate; and yet the gentleman would have us to withhold from the Legislature, the power to reduce taxes in a certain contingency, under the apprehension that in making such reduction, the interests of Baltimore would alone be consulted.

Mr. Brown said, he had no fear that any gentleman would attribute to him a disposition not to pay the State debt and interest. It was sufficient for him to say, that his name would be found recorded in favor of every proposition, for a tax, the object of which was to maintain the faith of the State. But the amendment of the gentleman from Worcester, [Mr. Jacobs] would prevent the Legislature from taking off any of the taxes, until the debt and interest were both paid.

Mr. Jacobs interposed and explained that such was not the effect of his proposition, as he had excepted the modification of the gentleman from Anne Arundel, (Mr. Dorsey.)

Mr. Brown was not aware, he said, that the gentleman had accepted the modification.

When the question of the State debt and finances had sprung up, he (Mr. B.,) had gone to the State Treasurer, for information, upon two points —first, as to the times when the debt of the State would fall due—and secondly, at what price he had purchased the last bonds, from the moneys in the sinking fund. He (Mr. B.,) found that the price at which the purchase had been made, was one hundred and two and half.

Mr. B. then proceeded to argue that the inevitable result of the accumulation of a large sinking fund, would be to enhance the price of the bonds, and that the result of prohibiting the Legislature from reducing taxes, would be to tax the people of Maryland for the benefit of the bond holders. The greater the surplus and the more money there was in the sinking fund with which to purchase the bonds of the State, the higher would be their market value.

It seemed to him that the better course would be to leave the matter to the legislature. He was willing to apply the sinking fund to the purchase of our bonds at something like *par* value, as fast as the fund was competent to that purpose. But he had no idea of anticipating the payment of our debt, so as to run up its value to fifteen or twenty per cent. above *par*. Legislation of this character was neither wise nor just. He was in favor of leaving the Legislature unfettered—to reduce the taxes when, in their discretion, they should think that the reduction could safely be made.

Mr. Donaldson said:

The gentleman from Carroll, (Mr. Brown,) had given us some facts, he, [Mr. D.,] would give a few more facts, and he thought that all taken together would wear an aspect different from that given by the partial statement of that gentleman. It was certainly true, that six per cent. Maryland stocks were now purchased at two and a half per cent. premium, for the increase of the sinking fund. But the gentleman must remember, that for a considerable portion of our debt the State realized at the time of issuing the loans a large premium, ranging even as high as twenty per cent; nor must he forget, that for a long period, when our stocks were very much depreciated in the market, we bought for the sinking fund greatly below par. Thus the sinking fund has so far gained largely in the whole transaction, and has extinguished a considerable part of the public debt on most advantageous terms. It is not probable, that we shall ever lose a greater amount by the payment of premiums for our own stock, than we have gained by receiving premiums, and purchasing again at a discount, for the sinking fund. We have no right to complain of having to pay the premium we now do.

The best investment, he said, was in our own debt; and all surplusses ought to be applied, as they now are by law, to the purchase and extinguishment of that debt. The apprehensions indulged in, of an unlimited rise in our stocks, to be produced by our purchasing for extinguishment, were unreasonable. The Maryland stocks were not, and would not be, the only public securities in the market. The stocks of the United States, of New York, Massachusetts, Ohio and some other States, would furnish as safe investments as our own, and would prevent our own rom rising much, if any thing, above their real value.

The gentleman from Carroll seemed to think, that we should one day have to throw the whole amount of stocks in the sinking fund at once into he market, in order to pay off the public debt.

Mr. Brown explained, that he only meant to say, that an amount of money was to be invested annually for that fund.

Mr. Donaldson continued. He was glad that he had misunderstood the gentleman. But the sum annually invested would make but a small impression on the stock market of the United States. As for the re-issue of State bonds, after their purchase for the State, that was forbidden by law; all such bonds were registered, and then cancelled.

In regard to relief from taxation by a gradual reduction, which the gentleman from Frederick, (Mr. Thomas,) advocated with such zeal in preference to applying surplusses to the redemption of the principal of the debt, until the whole was extinguished, Mr. D. declared himself utterly opposed to such a course. He thought it unwise and dangerous.

If one tax law was repealed, another might be. Contests would arise between different interests, and if the work were once commenced no one could say where it would end. If one brick was taken out another would follow, and then another, until the whole structure would tumble about our heads and perhaps overwhelm the credit of the State in its ruins. Whatever are the imperfections of the present system, the people have become content under it, and it would be hazardous to agitate the question of repealing any part of it. The people now most cheerfully pay the taxes, which provide the interest of the debt, and large surplusses for the redemption of the principal. They now pay them with ease. In this State of things, we should relieve ourselves of as much of the debt as possible; for we cannot be certain that such great prosperity will remain uninterrupted, and a time might possibly occur when the payment would be found more difficult. The plan of the gentleman from Frederick, of constantly reducing taxation so as to prevent surplusses, would, of course, have the effect of indefinitely prolonging the existence of our debt, and of taxes for the payment of its interest. It seemed to him, (Mr. D.,) that it was of much greater advantage to the property holders themselves, to continue the taxes at their present amount, so that they may be entirely relieved of all taxation in the course of ten or a dozen years, than to reduce the rate of taxation by a few cents at a time, from year to year, and so greatly prolong the date of final exemption. He believed that the former policy, if considered as fixed, would add to the present value of all the property in Maryland. The sooner the whole of this debt is discharged, the better for us all. When it is discharged, a very great impulse will be given to our prosperity, and men of capital will not be deterred from coming amongst us, or embarking their means in our enterprises. Such a course, then, is demanded by our own interests. In this connection, he said that the method of stating the amount of our public debt ought to be changed, so as to exhibit to the people, how much it had been reduced in every year. At present, the same amount of debt was stated every year, and although the amount of the sinking fund is also stated, the result is not, in general, correctly understood. Only the amount of principal which has not been extinguished by the sinking fund should be stated as the existing debt, and the sinking fund should be classed as so much extinguished debt. It would then be evident to all, how rapidly we are, from year to year, paying off the principal of the debt, and the people would fully realise the prospect of discharging the whole by a not very distant date, and would therefore pay their taxes with even greater cheerfulness than before.

It was intimated that very extravagant estimates had been made of future receipts from the internal improvements. He himself had certainly indulged in no wild speculations on the subject. He had stated no particular sum as his own estimate. The gentleman from Cecil, (Mr. McLane,) had spoken of $500,000 annually. In their present unfinished condition they yielded to the State $200,000, and were constantly increasing in productiveness; and when the debt was paid off, there certainly would be large receipts from this source, to be disposed of in some manner or other. He would take occasion to state, that he had not made any calculation on receipts from the Chesapeake and Ohio Canal. On that point he agreed entirely with the gentleman from Frederick, (Mr. Thomas). To more than seven millions of our money, and all the interest thereon, that work was,

> A gulf profound as that Serbonian bog,
> Betwixt Damiata and Mount Casius old,
> Where armies whole have sunk;—

He feared the entire amount was irrecoverably gone.

Mr. D. then said, that some remarks of the gentleman from Frederick, (Mr. Thomas,) made it proper that he should speak of a matter somewhat personal to himself. He would not have risen for the purpose, but being on the floor, he thought it well not to let the occasion pass. That gentleman had used the expression, that he was not present when the honors were shared in relation to restoring the credit of the State. When the gentleman from Dorchester, (Mr. Phelps,) in the course of argument the other day, had spoken of him, (Mr. D.,) as having done more to restore the credit of the State than any other person except Governor Pratt, he, (Mr. D.,) thought, that to make any public disclaimer of his title to such an honor, would in itself be assuming too much importance to himself. In private, he had told that gentleman, how much he had exaggerated the merit of any act of his, (Mr. D.'s,) and what injustice he had unintentionally done to others. Afterward, when the gentleman from Queen Anne's, (Mr.Spencer,) claimed that his colleague, (Governor Grason,) had taken the first and boldest step, by advising the imposition of the direct tax, he (Mr. D.,) had interposed to say, that he, (Mr. D.,) had not pretended to claim for himself any credit whatever. He had never estimated what he himself had done at any considerable value. All the most important part of the work had been accomplished by others, before he came upon the field of action. The gentleman from Frederick had informed us of his own claims, of which he, (Mr. D.,) had not before been aware. In regard to others, public records showed us who had been most prominent in the cause of State faith. Governor Grason, in his message, had first publicly recommended the direct tax; it was a bold and noble act, when the circumstances are considered. The late Robert W. Bowie, of Prince George's, deserved, perhaps, more praise than any other man; for by his independence and energy, in the face of opposition and clamor, the law imposing the direct tax was carried through the Legislature. That was the most difficult task of all. Then Governor Pratt and Chancellor Johnson, the first by his recommendations and influence, and the latter by his indefatigable exertions as chairman of the ways and means in the House of Delegates, secured the passage of supplementary tax laws, by which our Treasury was brought into a condition to meet the just demands of our creditors. When he, (Mr. D.,) came to the Legislature, it fell to his lot to occupy a position, which rendered it necessary for him to become acquainted with the condition of our finances. Finding that the measures previously adopted had fully accomplished their object, it was his duty to announce the fact, and to demonstrate to others, as well as he could, that the State might safely resume the payment of interest as her debt. That was all he had done. Any honest man, in his position, would have done the same thing. It had not been necessary for him to propose new burdens on the people; the odium of that had been encountered by those who preceded him; and he had only endeavored to make the previous laws more efficient in their operation. His name had been connected with the final act, which was the consummation to which the labors of others had brought us, and thus a credit had been conferred upon him, which he knew that he never deserved. All he could claim was, to have felt and to feel for the honor and good faith of the State as if they were his own—and such must be the feeling of every true son of Maryland.

Mr. Presstman rose, he said, not to participate at any length in the discussion, but to inquire of his friend from Anne Arundel. (Mr. Donaldson,) if he could state what amount was paid into the Treasury, arising from the auxiliary tax laws, as they are familiarly termed. and of the whole sum, what proportion was paid by the city of Baltimore? His object in propounding the question was this, that it might have its due weight in the distribution of honors which had been spoken of in connection with the maintenance of the State's credit. He thought it would appear from the Treasurer's report, that nearly two-thirds of the revenue arising from the acts of 1844, which had been suggested by Governor Pratt, was collected in that city. He did not mean in the smallest degree to take from the deservedly energetic and talented executive to whom he had referred his just share of the public esteem to which he was entitled, for the part he bore in that crisis of the State's history. But this much he was bound to say, that there were other public men in the councils of the State, sustained by patriotic constituencies to whom the meed of praise is also due, and first among the foremost in his estimation, was the lamented Robert W. Bowie, of Prince George's, the distinguished chairman of the committee of ways and means, who in 1841, brought forward the direct tax system of the State. No man need desire a higher eulogy than the annals of the State furnishes of his zeal, energy, patriotism and ability. He had had the honor of being himself an humble member of that committee, and he could speak advisedly of the patient toil which that distinguished gentleman underwent both in the committee and in the House. He could not see the justice with which either the executives of the State or the Legislatures prior to 1844, were to be held as having failed in view of all the circumstances to discharge their duty upon the subject of State credit, because in their repeated efforts they had not matured a system which time alone could adequately suggest. It required much more sterness of purpose in his opinion, to meet the responsibilities involved in the system of direct taxation as adopted in 1841, and amended in 1842, by which twenty-five cents on every $100 worth of real and personal property was levied throughout the whole State, than to add thereto auxiliary taxation which bore mainly upon a single portion of the State, and that section most unequally represented in the General Assembly of the State. Besides all this, the Convention will remember that prior to the year 1844, the doctrine was almost universally held in Maryland, that under the thirteenth article of the bill of rights, the Legislature was forbidden to lay any tax for the support of government, except it was general in its operation, and bore alike upon every description of property. He hazarded nothing in saying that in the year the direct tax system was adopted. such was the view of the members of the General Assembly, as is abundantly shown by the basis established in that act. No man had the courage at that time to "cut the gordian knot" of constitutional restriction supposed to exist, and which was subsequently boldly done by Governor Pratt; and he might perhaps in view of the exigency in which the State's faith was involved, be disposed to forget these nice distinctions, and rejoice that he had "assumed the responsibility" at that time. But, sir, it ought not to be forgotten that in the gloomy darkness which overshadowed the financial affairs of the State, no backward step was taken from the policy first adopted in 1841; and there was one other gentleman to whose course he might refer with pride and pleasure, to whom something of these large honors was due, who as chairman of the committee of ways and means of the House of Delegates, in 1842, suggested a considerable increase of the direct tax of 1841—he alluded to the honorable R B. Carmichael, of Queen Anne's. In that proposition he was supported by the entire delegation of the city of Baltimore. It failed except so far as an increase of five cents, which was the maximum to which the direct tax has ever reached. A single word would explain his opposition to the proposition now before the Convention. While he yielded to no man in his determination to sustain untarnished the State's credit, and would not for a single moment desire to see repealed a single revenue act which was necessary to its support, he was unwilling to bind up the Legislature of the State to the extent of forbidding any change of a system which in some of its parts bore most unjustly, as he thought, upon the commercial metropolis, which he had the honor, in part, to represent, when the necessity which prompted their adoption might no longer require their continuance. The city of Baltimore was engaged in a severe struggle of commercial rivalry with the northern cities, and she should be as much unfettered in the race of competition as could possibly be allowed.

Mr. Spencer said—whether the State of Maryland had sustained a profit or loss by the sale of her stocks? what is the present condition of the treasury? what stocks the treasurer may now purchase? what are the causes of the fluctuation in the stock market? or who are the parties to be benefitted by stock operations?—were not questions before the Convention. He desired to ask the attention of the House only for a few moments, while he assigned the reasons which would influence his vote. He had before said, that he should look with extreme jealousy to any action of this body which interfered with the finances of the State. He deeply regretted that the subject had ever been introduced here. He was sorry that the present proposition had been brought forward. He should vote against it. We had met here to form a Constitution; and it was never anticipated that we would interfere with the financial operations of the State. Such an idea had never entered into the mind of any man. The financial arrangements of the State properly belong to the Legislature, who come fresh from the people, and are to be regulated by circumstances of which we have no fore-knowledge. Adopt the principle of interference with the system of finance here and you cut off all the power of the Legislature over the subject forever, let what exigency may call for their action. They would not be able to make a new assessment for the valuation of property. The financial system embraces the existing assessment and taxation. They stand together and form one system.

They depend upon each other, and it will not do to say, if you put this inhibition in the Constitution, that the Legislature could provide for a new assessment. If they could do so, they would have jurisdiction over the whole subject, and hence, could direct such mode of assessment, embracing valuation and other matters, as they thought best to adopt. And who will say, that if, in a new assessment, a depreciated valuation were adopted, it would not affect the amount of the revenue as much, as if the rate of tax were diminished. And this would defeat the object of the provision. He was opposed entirely to all action on the part of this Convention which looked to closing the doors of legislation on this subject. He was unwilling to admit, that the system was so perfect that future legislation may not take place, wisely and justly, on the subject. There was now, one very important item of wealth which escaped taxation, unless it had been reached by recent legislation, of which he had never heard. He meant rent charges. He, with Hon. J. A. Pearce, had raised the question, and it had been decided by the Court of Appeals that they were not embraced in our tax laws. Inhibit all legislation on the subject, and wealth will very soon find conveniences for investments not now covered by the laws. But for other reasons, equally strong, he was wholly opposed to the proposition. He knew many respectable men—men of the purest virtue and highest intelligence, who are utterly opposed to the accumulation of a large surplus in the treasury. Because it will tend to legislative corruption and induce an application of the surplus means to other purposes than the extinguishment of the State debt, which is beyond the reach of the State for many years, and not redeemable at the pleasure of the State. There are other equally virtuous and intelligent citizens who hold that it is the duty of the present generation to provide an ample fund to meet the interest on the State debt, but as all the benefit of the public works is to be felt in the future, *that future* should provide for the payment of the debt from the profits of the work.

It was not necessary for him at this time to indicate his opinion. Whenever the proper time should arrive for the explanation, he would be prepared to make it, but it was not in place now and here. We are here to make a Constitution. We have nothing to do with a tax system. He would now say, that if you adopt so many unexpected articles, you may prevent the adoption of the Constitution by the people. If such a principle as is now offered, be admitted it would go as far towards the defeat of the Constitution, as any proposition can.

Many held the doctrine that we ought not to impose any tax beyond what necessity requires. There are many who calculate that if the estimate of the treasurer be correct, there will be in the year 1852, a great surplus, and if we leave that surplus to accumulate, year after year, it will open the way for gross frauds and corruptions. He implored the Convention, therefore, not to suffer itself to be drawn away from the path of duty, by the interposition of extraneous subjects. Let us put as strong a guard against involving the State in debt, or against new works of internal improvement. We may go the utmost length, in reference to those subjects, and rest assured that it will be sustained by the voice of the people. But he would again implore it not to meddle with the tax system. He was in favor of the payment of the public debt, but he was opposed to meddling with the tax system.

And in conclusion he would say, that he thought whilst the gentleman from Anne Arundel, (Mr. Donaldson,) was enumerating the gentlemen, who were entitled to such high honor for the part they had born, in sustaining the State's credit, he might, with some propriety, have referred to Col. Carmichael, of Queen Anne's. Mr. Bowie, it is true, reported the first tax law, but it was wholly inadequate. Col. Carmichael succeeded him, as chairman of the committee of ways and means, at its next session. He recommended an increase in the rate of tax, even a much larger rate than was carried by the legislature, and under that rate it is, that our treasury has proved so flourishing.

He begged further to say, that he had never intended to intimate to the gentleman from Kent, (Mr. Chambers,) that the legislature had the nerve at the session of eighteen hundred and thirty-nine, to provide for a direct tax. On the contrary, it had not the nerve. He had desired to sustain the course indicated by the Governor, but the legislature would not sustain him, (Mr. S.)

Mr. Donaldson said, he had no intention of detracting from the merit of Mr. Carmichael, or any body else, nor had he pretended to enumerate all those who had assisted in retrieving the credit af the State. But the gentleman from Queen Anne's, (Mr. Spencer,) was mistaken in assigning to Mr. Carmichael the honor of establishing our system of direct taxation. The law establishing that system, was carried through the Legislature at March session, 1841, by the late Robert W. Bowie, and what the Legislature did the next session, when Mr. Carmichael, was chairman of ways and means, was to add five cents of tax on the hundred dollars to the twenty cents provided by the first law.

Mr. Spencer interposed to say that he did not mean to be understood as claiming for Mr. Carmichael the credit of establishing the system, but as adding to the amount of taxes so as to make it more efficient. Mr. C. had himself proposed to raise the rate even higher than twenty-five cents.

Mr. Donaldson said, that Mr. Carmichael certainly deserved credit for a course so manly, and he awarded it to him cheerfully.

Mr. Chambers. The gentleman from Anne Arundel, was called upon by the gentleman from Baltimore, [Mr. Presstman,] to answer a question. Is it his intention to answer it? for, if so, I have another question to ask him.

Mr. Donaldson. The gentleman from Baltimore rose immediately on my taking my seat, for the purpose, as he said, of asking me a question. After asking it, he made a speech himself, and, in conclusion, again put the question to me, and called for a reply. As bound, in courtesy, I was about to answer, but was anticipated by the gentleman from Queen Anne's, who got the floor.

Mr. Chambers. The question I ask is, what is the ratio between the value of the works of internal improvement, to the city of Baltimore, and her expenditures therefor, as compared to the ratio between the value of the same works to Kent county, and the taxes paid by that county?

Mr. Donaldson. In answer to the gentleman from Baltimore, he would say, that though the taxes are uniform, the greater portion of revenue is of course derived from that part of the State where the most wealth is concentrated, and where the largest business is transacted. The rich man pays a larger amount of taxes than the poor man, yet the tax is uniform, and each pays in proportion to his substance. This comparison applies to Baltimore and the other parts of the State. In reply to the gentleman from Kent, he had only to say, that every member of this Convention must be sufficiently conversant with the history of our internal improvement system, and its operation, to answer the question for himself.

Mr. Merrick made some remarks, which will be published hereafter.

Mr. Brown said the real question before the Convention was, will you, by putting this feature in the Constitution, let this revenue go into the sinking fund, or you will leave it in the hands of the Legislature, to invest as they may think best? If a provision on the subject is inserted in the Constitution, the question will be settled for many years to come, and you will, by an unalterable provision, fix a high grade of taxation on the State. And you will do that rather than leave it to the people, acting through their legislature, the discretion to act as circumstances may render necessary. He had said, a few days ago, that there was a strong disposition in this body, to tie up the hands of the Legislature. He was in favor of the payment of the debt; but he would not vote for preventing the Legislature from relieving the people from these burdens.

Mr. RIDGELY said that the course which the debate had taken, rendered it necessary that he should say a word in explanation of the vote he was about to give against the pending amendment. Gentleman who advocated the proposition, claim to be the especial friends and guardians of the credit of the State, and urge the adoption of the article suggested by the gentleman from Worcester, as a necessary restraint upon the Legislature, to prevent the possible interruption of the process now going on, of accumulating the sinking fund for the ultimate discharge of the public debt. It is insisted, that the present finance system ought to be maintained unchanged by constitutional obligation, less, per chance, the Legislature may relax the tax laws, and thus, if not jeopard the prompt payment of accruing interest, at least postpone to a late period the ultimate discharge of the public debt. The effect of the argument in favor of this proposition, is to place those who opposed it in a false position; inasmuch, as occupying an attitude adverse to the theory contended for, they are seemingly obnoxious to the imputation of apathy concerning the faith of the State, if not to a still greater reproach. He could not, therefore, impelled as he was, to vote against the amendment, by a sense of its general impropriety, as a provision of the Constitution, consent to cast a vote unexplained, which might, in the slightest degree, qualify his fealty to the honor and credit of the State. He yielded to no gentleman in the Convention in honest and earnest zeal for the maintenance of the State's faith to the public creditor, nor did he believe that a sane man could be found in Maryland, who would, even remotely, put that faith in peril by the modification of the finance system under existing circumstances. Such, he was sure, was the common sentiment of the people of Maryland who had ever manifested on this subject a sensibility and concernment which had rather guided than followed the legislation of the State. There was no danger that such a people would consent to relax any of the revenue laws until there was evidently no longer a necessity for their continuance; yet he hoped, that if a state of circumstances should arise, when these laws might be modified without prejudice to the public creditor, that the Legislature might not be prevented by a constitutional prohibition from relieving the people from unnecessary burthens. He hoped the subject would be left, were it properly belonged, with the Legislature, which frequently meeting and coming fresh from the people, would always be ready to carry out such a system of finance as the exigencies of the treasury, fluctuating from time to time, by circumstances, might require. Certainly, the honor of the State had heretofore been amply vindicated by that body, and might be safely trusted in the hands of the people. Was there any necessity to graft a provision on the Constitution to stimulate the honesty or to awaken the honor of the people of Maryland, touching the public debt? Why, he would ask, had it become necessary to bind the people to a system of finance, never to be modified, no matter what circumstances might arise, for a period of ten, perhaps of fifteen years, when no man could forsee defects in the system itself, or casualities which might intervene, and which were inseparable from all human schemes, however well devised.

He could see no practical good likely to grow out of such a proposition; he was willing to trust the poeple through the legislature, with the public faith. Nobly, honorably, triumphantly had they stood up to this just responsibility without any constitutional obligations heretofore existing; and although pressed heavily by tax laws, had cheerfully, promptly and with alacrity in every quarter of the State, come up to their whole duty. Shall they now be distrusted, when the dark hour of their trial is passed, and the end is as clear to their vision as the brightness of the noon day? Is it now necessary to place a provision in the Constitution to quicken the sense of honor and honesty of the people of Maryland? No, sir. There is a higher, a holier impulse, than the mandate of a written Constitution, which has heretofore, and will continue to animate the people to maintain the financial policy of the State, now in successful progress, until the last dollar of the public debt is discharged, principal and interest. That, sir, is the law of moral duty, of public virtue. There is nothing more uncertain, or precarious, than systems of finance.

Who could say, that the works of internal improvements of the State, all now in active and successful operation, would not return large resources into the treasury, to be applied in aid of the sinking fund. It had been conceded in this debate, that these works were already largely increasing the revenues, and if the anticipations of some gentlemen were only in a remote degree realized in this respect, could there be a rational doubt, under such circumstances, about the propriety of relaxing the existing tax laws? He could not think so. He did not, however, wish to be considered as indulging any very sanguine expectations as to the revenues to arise from these sourees; yet he firmly believed, that from this time forward, they would yield largely to the treasury.

On yesterday the House had passed a Constitutional provision, which, in his judgment, had done much to appreciate the credit of the State. It had, by a very decided vote, declared that all connexion between the State and new projects of internal Improvement, was forever forbidden—that no public debt of any kind should hereafter be created, except by a vote of two-thirds of all the members elected to both branches of the legislature; a result, which, looking to the probable structure of the House of Delegates, it was almost impossible to procure. That measure, he regarded as the most important and salutary of the session, as it was calculated to inspire the public creditor, with increased confidence in the security of his bonds To-d y a proposition was introduced, now under consi eration, which seemed to distrust the stability of the finance system of the State, in as much as it contemplated a constitutional obligation, to impel the performances of a duty, which the people had promptly met, by mere legislative enactments.

This proposition, he was sure, would be voted down, not that there was any disposition to relax any of the existing laws, but because a majority of this House believe it not only to be an act of supererogation, so far as regarded the certainty of the continuance of such laws, whilst the necessity existed for them, but also because the subject itself was in its very nature unfit to be made a part of the organic law; a subject, modification in which, would obviously be necessary from time to time, as circumstances might require. The Constitution now to be made, it was to be hoped, would endure long after the public debt was discharged, and until perhaps it was forgotten.

The future was full of justifiable hope, for a reduction of taxes, and it would, therefore, be unwise to establish, by constitutional law, a permanent system of finance, to thus fetter the hands of the legislature, in total disregard of the probable ability of the State to meet all her obligations, as she had heretofore done, by proper legislation; he had deemed it to be his duty to state the reasons, which influenced his vote, that he might not be subject to the imputation of a want of zeal for the preservation of the honor of the State.

Mr. Davis had no wish to enter into the merits of the question under consideration; but in this "rendering unto Cæsar the things that are Cæsar's," he thought it the duty of even the humblest member upon this floor, to give any facts in his possession, and which had not been adverted to.

He was inclined to this, because his friend from Anne Arundel, in echoing the sentiment of the gentleman from Frederick, [Mr. Thomas.] had described, the Chesapeake and Ohio canal, as the great Serbonian bog, in which so large a portion of the resources of the State had been sunk.

It will be recollected that Mr. Thomas, who had that morning claimed so much credit for having been the first to suggest the means of extricating the State from her financial difficulties, was, in the years '39-'40—the President of the canal company—that having exhausted the means hitherto provided for the completion of the canal, he applied at the session of '40, for further aid from the State, to that work—that the legislature refused this application—that after the adjournment of the legislature, he, as President of the company, had issued a large amount of scrip which the committee of ways and means of the next legislature pronounced to be without any basis whatever. The amount of this currency thus issued, run up from $500,000 to $700,000. The committee stated that they declined to say any thing about the propriety of issuing this amount of scrip immediately after the refusal of the legislature to appropriate the amount which the gentleman asked for to complete the canal.

[Here Mr. D. read an extract from the report.]

He, [Mr. D.,] was not here to defend the Chesapeake and Ohio Canal company. He had personally but little interest in it. But it had been assailed, and justice ought to be done it; and considering the large investment the State had made in that great work, he thought it would be much more noble and patriotic for gentlemen, instead of pre-judging its results, now that it was just completed, at least to give it a trial. These assaults and predictions could now do no good; there only effect was to injure the credit of a great State work. He could not see the propriety of speaking of it in this tone.

Mr. D. would now say a word to the gentleman from Baltimore, [Mr. Prestman.] The gentleman had asked with a point and tone, which showed that he designed the question for effect, whether Baltimore had not contributed two-thirds of the whole revenues of the State? He would, by way of reply, ask that gentleman, what part Baltimore had had in bringing about the necessity for this taxation?

Mr. Presstman replied, that Baltimore had at that time only two representatives in the House of Delegates, and he thought it not likely they could corrupt the whole legislature.

Mr. Davis. Yes, but two delegates, Messrs. Cushing and Jones—and without intending any disparagement to other gentlemen, they were quite as good representatives as Baltimore has had since that time. But Baltimore, it seems, was not satisfied with what these gentlemen could do; she called town meetings.

Mr. Presstman begged leave to explain. He had never intended to go into the subject of internal improvements.

Mr. Davis resumed. Why is the gentleman so restless? Cannot he stand the probe? Will be not suffer the truth to be told? He, [Mr. D.,] proposed to read a scrap of history. He would call the attention of the gentleman from Baltimore, to a letter signed Jesse Hunt, mayor of Baltimore, recommending a town meeting to send a committee to Annapolis, lest the act granting a loan of $2,000,000 to the Chesapeake and Ohio canal, should fail. And this committee—this numerous delegation—[Mr. Chambers, (in his seat.) Representation according to population]—were sent here to represent to the Legislature, that the interest of *Baltimore* and the State, required the passage of the loan bill.

Mr. Presstman rose to explain, stating that not a single word had been said by him in relation to internal improvements.

He knew perfectly well why this discussion was kept up, and every one knew, whoever instigated the gentleman from Montgomery, that it was intended for the benefit of the counties. But, he denied that he ever introduced this matter of inetrnal improvements. He was not responsible for it.

Mr. CHAMBERS interposed a remark, that although the gentleman from Baltimore had not addressed him, he gave him an expressive glance which could not be misunderstood. His friend from Montgomery needed no prompting from him. He has mentioned facts which he did not know before. The gentleman from Baltimore was alone responsible for this debate. The gentleman from Baltimore rises and tells us, that Baltimore has borne two-thirds of the whole taxation of the State, and this led to the discussion concerning which he appears so sensitive.

Mr. PRESSTMAN wished it to appear that when he referred to the auxiliary taxation, no one had risen to contradict him. Whatever collateral inferences might be deduced from his remarks, no one could say that he had introduced the subject of internal improvements. He would ask whether Col. Merrick, of Charles, had not introduced and carried through the legislature, the internal improvement act?

Mr. DAVIS resumed. The question propounded by the gentleman from Baltimore is one of those skilful manœuvres, which he so well understands, and which is intended to divert him, [Mr. D.,] from his purpose.

The gentleman from Charles is fully able take care of himself. He should not interfere between him and the gentleman from Baltimore. But he would have the gentleman from Baltimore to understand that he, and he alone, was responsible for his course in this Convention, and what he said in debate, and he held himself responsible for it. The gentleman insinuated that he was prompted.

Mr. PRESSTMAN said, he had certainly meant no personal offence by the remark.

Mr. DAVIS was glad of it. The gentleman had asked with point, if Baltimore had not paid two-thirds of the taxes of the State.

He, (Mr. D.,) asked, in return, what share Baltimore had contributed to create the necessity for these taxes? The gentleman answered, and this led to the discussion which followed. Mr. D. also read an extract from a report of the Board of President and Directors of the Baltimore and Ohio Rail Road Company, in which the completion of the canal is used as a measure necessary to the prosperity of the State and to the city of Baltimore.

He had only risen to show, in reference to this great work, this Serbonian bog, as it had been called, which had swallowed up so much of the resources of the State, and from which, according to the gentleman from Frederick and the gentleman from Anne Arundel, the State was never to derive any revenue, where the responsibility of these lost appropriations ought to rest, and having accomplished his object, he would conclude his remarks.

Mr. TUCK made a few remarks, which will appear hereafter.

Mr. HARBINE demanded the previous question.

Mr. DORSEY took the floor, and requested the gentleman from Washington county, (Mr. Harbine,) to withdraw the demand, to enable him, (Mr. D.,) to say a few words.

Mr. CHAMBERS, of Kent, made a similar suggestion or enquiry.

Mr. HARBINE refused to withdraw, remarking, that if he did so, the debate would be interminable.

Mr. MERRICK now sent to the Clerk's table the amendment which he had indicated his intention to offer,

And which was as follows:

Strike out, in the second line, the word "inviolate," and insert "inviolable," and after the word "sufficient," in the fourth line, insert, "by its regular accumulations," and after the words "payment thereof," insert "by the time it becomes redeemable."

Mr. DORSEY enquired of the Chair, whether the demand for the previous question had been sustained? because, if it had not, he desired to state some facts which he knew were not in the possession of the Convention.

The PRESIDENT stated that the previous question had not been sustained. The question would be put so soon as the state of the question before the Convention had been ascertained.

The question, "is there a second to the demand for the previous question," was then taken, and the vote stood, ayes 32—noes 34.

So there was not a second.

Mr. DORSEY said he should not have said a single word on this subject if he had not thought it incumbent on him to define his position, and to warn the Convention against the dangerous suggestions of the gentlemen from Carroll and Frederick counties, that the next session of the Legislature was the time to commence the repeal of our taxes. These suggestions, Mr. President, have alarmed me and induce me to concur in the proposition of the gentleman from Worcester, as the best means of counteracting them. He thought the proposition of the member from Worcester would be better without the amendment suggested by the gentleman from Charles, (Mr. Merrick.) Who, it is asked, is to judge of the sufficiency of the sinking fund? The Legislature only, are the exclusive judges thereof, and no judicial tribunal can inquire into the correctness of their decision. The proposition of the gentleman from Worcester is the true course for this State to pursue. The people at present pay their taxes without murmur or complaint; congratulating themselves that in the course of ten or twelve years, under the present financial system of the State, its credit and honor being fully redeemed, its entire public debt being fully paid or its payment, at the earliest period, which, by the terms of its creation was practicable, so provided for, that all public taxes or burdens should be discontinued and the State receiving an annual income of some hundred thousand dollars from its works of internal improvement, to be appropriated as it saw fit. He apprehended there was some misapprehension as to the powers of the Treasurer in the management of the sinking fund. If the stocks of this State rose so unreasonably high as was feared, (but for which fear, as to any large amount there was no foundation,) the Treasurer had full power to invest (if more advantageous to do so,) the accumulations of the fund in any safe stocks; as for example those of New York, Massachusetts, Virginia, &c., and hold on to the same until our public debt, becomes payable, when,by a sale of such stocks, it might be paid in full. In the meantime, as soon as the sinking fund becomes sufficient to pay the public debt at its maturity, the Legislature might order all that part of the sinking fund, consisting of the bonds of the State in the Treasurer's hands, to be bought in and cancelled; leaving with the Treasurer, the stocks, which he held of other States, equal in amount with the remaining debt of the State, (the annual interest on the former being adequate to the payment of that accruing on the latter,) until it became payable, when by a sale of the former the latter could be extinguished, and the State released from its entire public debt. If the existing, well adjusted revenue system be abandoned or impaired in its efficiency, by the changes advocated by the gentlemen from Carroll and Frederick, it is impossible to forsee the disastrous consequences that may result. Once tear down in the manner proposed one of the pillars on which our revenue fabric rests, and in all human probability the whole building will fall to the ground; and the State be involved in perplexity, embarrassment, and dishonor equal to that from which it has so recently extricated itself.

Baltimore, or rather the mayor and city council thereof, according to the extracts read from its proceedings, by the gentleman from Montgomery, has already unfurled the banner of repeal and reform, and called upon all persons without distinction of parties, to rally around it. And according to one of the daily newspapers of the dominant party in Baltimore, shown me a few days ago by my friend from Montgomery, if believed, a large majority of the people of Baltimore, entertain the same views as those avowed by the mayor and city councils.

The excitement for reform is now over; it no longer furnishes electioneering politicians with the means of elevating themselves to office at the people's expense. Some substitute must by them be found for it; and let this Convention but intimate the propriety of a repeal of any portion of the public taxes, and by the time the Constitution goes into operation, you will have the popular feeling excited to the highest pitch, by representations, that our system of taxation is unnecessary, unjust and intolerably oppressive upon the people: different evidences of its injustice and oppressiveness being assigned in every portion of the State.

The system of log-rolling, as it is called, will prevail; combinations will be formed by the delegation from Baltimore, with that from other portions of the State. First, one tax, and then another will be abolished, until those which remain, become unequal, partial and odious in the eyes of the people, when the whole system will sink into ruin, and the honor and credit of Maryland will fall, even lower than it did in 1839.

The gentleman from Baltimore, has told us that he is opposed to such results; but, if once giving countenance to them, as his remarks would indicate, he will be unable afterwards to resist the current of popular opinion, and must in the end, be overwhelmed by the torrent, which he now, undesignedly, has contributed to excite. Of his means to sustain himself, or the precise nature of the course he means to pursue, he has left us to conjecture.

The amendment of the gentleman from Charles (Mr. Merrick,)that the sinking fund should accumulate till 1890, has nothing to rest on, and is wholy unnecessary. Long before that time it would amount to more than double what will be required to pay the debt. The Legislature, when they find the sinking fund sufficient to pay the debt,may safely repeal all the taxes. Some gentlemen had fallen into a mistake, in supposing the sinking fund could only be invested in Maryland State stock. There was no such restriction existing; it may, by the Treasurer, be invested in any State stocks. Part of it originally consisted of Bank stocks, Mr. M'Cubben, a former Treasurer, had wisely deemed it best to buy up the stock of Maryland, at reduced prices, and the same course, as far as practicable, has ever since been pursued. The gentleman from Carroll (Mr. Brown,) complains that the Treasurer had bought some stock at two and a half per cent. above par. That stock was not purchased from necessity, but because the Treasurer faithfully performed his duty, in making the most advantageous purchase he could for the State. More than $1,000,000 of our State stock was then due, but bore only from four and a half to five per cent. interest, and, therefore, the purchase of the stock of the States, bearing six per cent. interest, was the more profitable investment, though made at two and a half per cent. above par, and for that stock the State received twenty per cent. above par.

If we once begin to repal the taxes, Baltimore will demand the repeal of the stamp act, auction duties, &c., &c. The cry of repeal once being raised in that city, the influence of which pervades every cove and inlet in the State, will extend alike to the counties and involve in the great vortex of repeal, all the taxes of the State.

Mr. Presstman desired not to be misunderstood, as going for a repeal of the tax law. There would not be found a man slower than he should be, to repeal any law now on the statute book. Never, in any addresses to the people of Baltimore, had he spoken against it—on the contrary, in the only address in which he had spoken on the subject, he had expressed himself in favor of the tax system. Therefore any insinuation that he would go before the people of Baltimore to oppose it, was unjust.

Mr. Dorsey said the explanation was unnecessary. He had long known the gentleman from Baltimore, and believed him, unless impelled by some popular torrent which he could not resist, incapable of voting otherwise than he believed to be right, and that he would sustain the faith of the State. But unless he was able to stem the torrent of popular sentiment, which was somewhat problematical, his assurances, however sincere, could not remove the danger, and was insufficient security against it. While repeal and reform continued to be the watch cry of the city councils, we cannot safely trust to mere personal pledges. If the gentleman from Carroll was right, in his opinion, that the Treasurer ought not to buy any stocks above par, the sinking fund would remain inert and valueless; it would, in fact, in the ordinary acceptation of the term, cease to be a sinking fund. We cannot extinguish the debt, when above par, as our six per cent. stock shares, will be under our present revenue system, because the Treasurer can only purchase stock at par. The fund, therefore, could never accumulate, by making interest capital, bearing interest as it should do, and the investment would be a loss. He should vote for the proposition as it stands. The people of Maryland are willing to pay the public debt, and look with anxiety and pleasure, to the period when they will be released from all taxation on account of it; and they, ere long, will be relieved, if we restrict the Legislature from creating new debts, and leave the Treasurer at liberty to use his own discretion in the management of the sinking fund. He should be at liberty when our own stock cannot be obtained on reasonable terms, to purchase other stocks of other States of the Union, whose willingness and ability to pay is as indubitable as our own, when he can do so at a fair price.

Mr. Jacobs declined to withdraw the amendment,

And, pending the question,

The Convention adjourned until to-morrow at ten o'clock.

THURSDAY, February 27, 1851.

The Convention met at 10 o'cleck.

Prayer was made by the Rev. Mr. Griffith.

The roll was called and the journal of yesterday was read and approved.

THE COLORED POPULATION.

Mr. Gaither presented a petition of sundry citizens of Frederick county, praying that an article be inserted in the new Constitution, compelling all free persons of color, annually, to give bond, with responsible security, to the State of Maryland, for their good behaviour, and in default thereof to leave the State.

Mr. Michael Newcomer. I should like to have that petition read.

The petition was read, and

On motion of Mr. Gaither, was referred to the committee on the colored population.

Mr. Biser presented the petition of William H. Shield and forty-seven other citizens of Frederick county, praying for the erection of a new county, composed of Hauvers, Catoctin, Middletown, Petersville and Jefferson districts of said county, and the seat of justice to be decided by a majority of the legal voters of the contemplated county;

Which was read, and

On motion of Mr. Biser,

Referred to the commitee on new counties.

Mr. Shriver presented a petition of one hundred citizens of Catoctin district, in Frederick county, protesting against the creation of a new county from parts of Frederick and Washington counties, &c.;

Which was read, and

On motion of Mr. Shriver,

Referred to the committee on new counties.

BASIS OF REPRESENTATION.

Mr. Neill rose and offered the following resolution:

Ordered, That the committee on Representation be instructed to report articles for the Constitution, giving to each of the counties of the State, and to the city of Baltimore, a right to elect one Senator to compose the Senate of Maryland, and making a House of Delegates, to consist of sixty-one members, to be apportioned among the several counties, according to their population, and to the city of Baltimore a representation not larger than that given to the largest county.

The resolution having been read,

Mr. Neill said:

It is obvious, Mr. President, that this question of representation is one which has engrossed the meditations of every member of this Convention from the time of its first organization. We have had full, free and frequent communication with each other in regard to it. The course which every gentleman will take, seems to be pretty well understood. We have now been in session upwards of one hundred days. And upon this, the most grave and exciting subject that is to engage our attention, nothing has been done, unless the reports of individual members of the committee on representation, various and conflicting as they are, may be deemed something.

It is not my purpose to make any remarks calculated to draw forth the protracted debate which I know the subject will produce. Believing that the mind of every member of this body is made up, and believing it to be both right and necessary that there should be some expression of the opinion of the Convention in relation to this question, I demand the previous question on the adoption of the resolution.

Mr. Buchanan. I second the demand.

Mr. Presstman. Do I understand that the resolution *instructs* the committee to report this project?

Mr. Neill. Yes, sir.

Messrs. Buchanan and Blakistone called the yeas and nays on the adoption of the resolution; which were ordered.

Mr. Chambers, of Kent, called for a division of the amendment.

Which was ordered.

The PRESIDENT was about to put the question on the demand for the previous question, when

Mr. BUCHANAN asked that the several branches into which the resolution was to be divided should be read.

The divisions were read.

Mr. PRESSTMAN then moved that there be a call of the Convention.

The call was ordered.

The roll of the members was then called.

Mr. SPENCER rose in his seat and stated, that he had paired off with Mr. DIRICKSON until Saturday next, being himself engaged with business connected with the Court of Appeals.

And then,

On motion of Mr. CHAMBERS, of Kent, all further proceedings on the call were dispensed with.

Mr. BUCHANAN now enquired, as a question of order, whether it was in order to call for a division of a proposition while the demand for the previous question was pending?

The PRESIDENT decided the motion to be in order.

The question was then taken on the demand for the previous question.

And there was a second.

And the main question was ordered to be now taken.

The PRESIDENT indicated his opinion that the pending proposition was susceptible of three divisions.

They were accordingly ordered.

Mr. McLANE called for the reading of the proposition.

Which was again read.

The question was then stated to be on the first branch of the amendment, as follows:

" *Ordered*, That the committee on Representation be instructed to report articles for the Constitution, giving to each of the counties of the State and to the city of Baltimore, a right to elect one Senator, to compose the Senate of Maryland."

The roll was then called.

The name of

Mr. MAGRAW having been called, that gentleman rose and said, that he hardly knew how to vote. He supposed, however, that it would make no difference which side of the question he took, and he should, therefore, vote "aye."

The result of the vote was then announced as follows:

Affirmative—Messrs. Chapman, President, Morgan, Blakistone, Dent, Hopewell, Ricaud, Lee, Chambers of Kent, Dorsey, Wells, Kent, Weems, Bond, Sollers, Buchanan, Bell, Ridgely, Lloyd, Dickinson, Sherwood of Talbot, Colston, James U. Dennis, Crisfield, Dashiell, Williams, Hodson, Phelps, Miller, Tuck, McCubbin, George, McMaster, Fooks, Jacobs, Sappington, McHenry, Magraw, Nelson, Carter, Thawley, Neill, Michael Newcomer, Kilgour, Brewer, Waters and Fitzpatrick—41.

Negative—Messrs. Merrick, Welch, Chandler, Constable, Chambers of Cecil, McLane, Wright, Thomas, Shriver, Gaither, Biser, Annan, Stewart of Caroline, Gwinn, Stewart of Baltimore city, Sherwood of Baltimore city, Presstman, Ware, Fiery, John Newcomer, Harbine, Weber, Slicer, Parke, Shower and Brown—26.

So the first division of the resolution was adopted.

The second division of the resolution was read.

Mr. PHELPS said, he would like to go in favor of the number of sixty-one for the House of Delegates; but he was not prepared to base the representation upon population. He asked, therefore, another division.

The PRESIDENT expressed his opinion that the amendment, was susceptible of this sub-division.

And it was ordered accordingly.

The question was then stated to be on the following branch:

"And making a House of Delegates to consist of sixty-one members."

The yeas and nays were taken and resulted as follows:

Affirmative—Messrs. Wells, Kent, Buchanan, Bell, Welch, Chandler, Ridgely, James U. Dennis, Hodson, Phelps, McMaster, Shriver, Biser, Annan, Sappington, Nelson, Gwinn, Stewart of Baltimore city, Presstman, Ware, Fiery, Neill, John Newcomer, Harbine, Michael Newcomer, Brewer, Weber, Slicer, Fitzpatrick and Parke.—31.

Negative—Messrs. Chapman, President, Morgan, Blakistone, Dent, Hopewell, Ricaud, Lee, Chambers of Kent, Donaldson, Dorsey, Weems, Bond, Sollers, Merrick, Jenifer, Lloyd, Dickinson, Sherwood of Talbot, Colston, Crisfield, Dashiell, Williams, Constable, Chambers of Cecil, Miller, McLane, Tuck, McCubbin, George, Wright, Fooks, Thomas, Gaither, Stephenson, McHenry, Magraw, Carter, Thawley, Stewart of Caroline, Kilgour, Waters, Shower and Brown—41.

So the second branch of the amendment was rejected.

Some conversation followed on a question of order,

After which,

The next division of the amendment was stated to be as follows:

"To be apportioned among the several counties according to their population."

And the question having been taken,

The vote resulted as follows:

Affirmative—Messrs. Buchanan, Bell, Welch, Chandler, Ridgely, Lloyd, Constable, Miller, McLane, Shriver, Gaither, Biser, Annan, Sappington, McHenry, Magraw, Nelson, Gwinn, Stewart of Baltimore city, Sherwood of Baltimore city, Presstman, Ware, Fiery, Neill, John Newcomer, Harbine, Michael Newcomer, Weber, Slicer, Fitzpatrick, Parke, Shower and Brown—33.

Negative—Messrs. Chapman, President, Morgan, Blakistone, Dent, Hopewell, Ricaud, Lee, Chambers of Kent, Donaldson, Dorsey, Wells, Kent, Weems, Bond, Sollers, Merrick, Jenifer,

Dickinson, Sherwood of Talbot, Colston, James U. Dennis, Crisfield, Dashiell, Williams, Hodson, Phelps, Chambers of Cecil, Tuck, McCubbin, George, Wright, McMaster, Fooks, Jacobs, Thomas, Carter, Thawley, Stewart of Caroline, Davis, Kilgour, Brewer and Waters—42.

So this branch of the amendment was rejected.

The next division of the amendment was stated to be as follows:

"And to the city of Baltimore a representation not larger than that given to the largest county."

And the question having been taken,

The result was as follows:

Affirmative—Messrs. Chapman, President, Morgan, Blakistone, Dent, Hopewell, Ricaud, Lee, Chambers of Kent, Dorsey, Wells, Kent, Weems, Bond, John Dennis, James U. Dennis, Crisfield, Dashiell, Williams, Hodson, Phelps, McCubbin, McMaster, Fooks, Jacobs, Sappington, Nelson, Carter, Fiery, John Newcomer, Kilgour and Waters—31.

Negative—Messrs. Donaldson, Sollers, Merrick, Jenifer, Buchanan, Bell, Welch, Chandler, Ridgely, Lloyd, Dickinson, Sherwood of Talbot, Colston, Constable, Chambers of Cecil, Miller, McLane, Tuck, George, Wright, Thomas, Shriver, Gaither, Biser, Annan, McHenry, Magraw, Thawley, Stewart of Caroline, Gwinn, Stewart of Baltimore city, Sherwood of Baltimore city, Presstman, Ware, Neill, Harbine, Michael Newcomer, Brewer, Weber, Slicer, Fitzpatrick, Parke, Shower and Brown—44.

So this branch of the amendment was rejected.

The question was then stated to be on the adoption of the resolution as amended.

Mr. MERRICK remarked, there was no manner of use in instructing the committee on representation, to bring in the report contemplated by this proposition, as such a report had already been brought in. He, therefore, moved a re-consideration of the vote adopting the first branch of the amendment.

Mr. NEILL concurred in the propriety of this suggestion.

The question, "will the Convention reconsider the said vote?" was taken,

And decided in the negative, without a division.

So the vote was not re-considered.

Some conversation followed on a point of order as to the state of the question under the several votes given by the Convention, when

The SECRETARY, under instructions from the PRESIDENT, read the minutes of the journal, to show the exact position in which the votes of the Convention had left the question.

Mr. MERRICK now again called the attention of the Convention to the fact, that, under the existing state of the question, the reference of such instructions to the committee was a mere repetition of what had already been done. The committee on representation had already made a report, providing for the election of one senator from each of the counties, and one from the city of Baltimore. Was it not childish to be doing that which had already been done?

The PRESIDENT. That is a question which the Convention must decide for itself.

Mr. MERRICK, continuing. The gentleman from Kent, (Mr. Chambers,) and the gentleman from Talbot, (Mr. Lloyd,) have both reported *projets* like this, and I will ask whether it is consistent with the dignity and the character of this body, thus to multiply reports and propositions identically the same?

Mr. SPENCER, (to the chair.) Is this in order?

Some conversation followed.

Mr. MERRICK. I move a re-consideration of the vote.

Mr. THOMAS, (to the chair.) Is the motion debateable?

The PRESIDENT. It is not. The previous question is not yet exhausted.

Mr. THOMAS. I ask the yeas and nays on the motion to re-consider.

Some further conversation followed on a point of order, in which Messrs. BROWN, MCLANE, THOMAS, and the PRESIDENT took part, after which

The question was taken on the resolution as amended, and it was adopted.

The question then recurred on the motion to reconsider, (the previous question being exhausted.)

Mr. MERRICK recapitulated the State of the question, and remarked that nothing remained of the proposition before the Convention, but the first branch instructing the committee on representation to report a bill giving one Senator to each county and to the city of Baltimore. This proposition had already been passed upon affirmatively. He moved, therefore, a re-consideration, for the reason that it was idle, and worse than idle, in his judgment, to give instructions to a committee to do that which two of its members had already done. He hoped, therefore, that the reconsideration would be agreed to. The mover himself, (Mr. Jacobs,) had suggested that this course ought to be pursued.

Some further conversation followed on a point of order between Mr. CHAMBERS, of Kent, and the PRESIDENT.

Mr. JENIFER said, that he should not himself have been in favor of moving such a proposition; but the resolution had been adopted, and a motion to reconsider might leave the committee in an uncertain and embarrassed State, looking to their conflicting views upon this question of representation. He should, therefore, vote against the re-consideration—because the resolution itself embraced a principle which he intended to support. The instruction, he thought, was a guard; it settled at least the point that there was to be one Senator to the city and to each county. The committee on representation had come to no conclusion. They could not agree, and the question was, whether the Convention would adopt its own views, or refer the matter to the committee without instructions. If it was to go to the committee at all, let it be accompanied with instructions.

Mr. MERRICK. I withdraw the motion to reconsider.

Mr. THOMAS. I renew it.

Mr. THOMAS said he should vote against the proposition in the form in which it was offered. He could not consent to take it as an isolated proposition. If we send back this subject to the committee it will lead to interminable motions to amend. He would vote for the reconsideration, for the purpose of embracing both branches of the Government in one resolution.

Mr. MORGAN (to the Chair.) Is it in order to move the previous question?

The PRESIDENT. The motion is in order.

Mr. MORGAN. I move it.

SEVERAL VOICES. Move to lay the motion to re-consider on the table.

Mr. MORGAN. I will substitute a motion to lay on the table for the previous question. But, before I do so, I desire to say, that I make the motion because I forsee that the debate is to be interminable, unless arrested by one of these processes which the rules of the Convention place within our reach. Ideas have been thrown out by gentlemen, which, if persisted in, can lead to no practical result, but the discussion may consume an indefinite length of time. I move that the motion to re-consider be laid upon the table, and on that motion I call for the yeas and nays

Some conversation followed as to the effect of the motion, on the part of Mr. BROWN, Mr. CHAMBERS, of Kent, and the CHAIR.

The yeas and nays were ordered.

And the question, "shall the motion to re-consider be laid upon the table," was then taken, and the result was as follows:

Affirmative—Messrs. Chapman, Pres't., Morgan, Blakistone, Dent, Hopewell, Ricaud, Lee, Chambers of Kent, Wells, Kent, Weems, Bond, Sollers, Jenifer, John Dennis, James U. Dennis, Crisfield, Dashiell, Williams, Hodson, Phelps, Tuck, McCubbin, McMaster, Fooks, Jacobs. Sappington, Stephenson, Nelson, Thawley, Kilgour, and Waters—32.

Negative—Messrs. Donaldson, Buchanan, Bell, Welsh, Chandler, Ridgely, Lloyd, Dickinson, Sherwood of Talbot, Colston, Constable, Chambers of Cecil, Miller, McLane, George, Wright, Shriver, Gaither, Biser, Annan, Magraw, Stewart of Caroline, Gwinn, Stewart of Baltimore city, Brent of Baltimore city, Sherwood of Baltimore city, Presstman, Ware, Fiery, Neill, John Newcomer, Harbine, Michael Newcomer, Brewer, Weber, Slicer, Fitzpatrick, Parke, Shower, and Brown—40.

So the Convention decided that the motion to re-consider should not be laid upon the table.

And the question recurred on the motion to reconsider the vote of the Convention, adopting the first branch of the order.

The PRESIDENT proceeded to count.

Mr. SHRIVER demanded the yeas and nays.

Mr. STEWART, of Caroline, said, that, in addition to the reasons assigned by the gentleman from Frederick, (Mr. THOMAS,) he, (Mr. S.,) had voted against the proposition because he was opposed to giving instructions to committees upon any thing. If the principle was adopted on one subject, they might be called upon to give instructions upon all. He desired also to remark that the vote he had given was not to be considered as the expression of his opinion upon any of the propositions, but merely as refusing to give instructions.

The question was then taken.

The PRESIDENT stated that the motion was rejected—yeas 32, noes 33.

Mr. PRESSTMAN called for the yeas and nays.

The PRESIDENT said it was too late, the result having been announced.

Mr. SHRIVER said, he had called for the yeas and nays, before the question was taken.

The PRESIDENT said the chair had not heard the gentleman.

Some conversation followed, when

The PRESIDENT suggested that gentlemen desiring the yeas and nays, might accomplish their object by another motion to reconsider the vote on the resolution.

Mr. PRESSTMAN renewed the motion to reconsider.

Mr. BROWN called the yeas and nays, which were ordered.

Mr. CHAMBERS, of Kent, submitted as a point of order to the chair, that a motion to reconsider having just been disposed of, there must be some intervening action, before another motion to reconsider could be entertained. Self-protection required this. Otherwise, it would be in the power of every one of the one hundred and three members of the Convention, to move a reconsideration, one after the other, and thus prevent definitive action on any proposition.

The PRESIDENT. Under the rule as it now stands, a motion to reconsider may be made a dozen times.

Mr. CHAMBERS, of Kent. If the motion to reconsider should prevail, it brings back the question to the proposition, whether the Senate shall be composed of one Senator from each county, and from the city of Baltimore. I do not desire to say a word in relation to the chairman of the committee, but I now state that every word the chairman has said—

Mr. PRESSTMAN interposed to a question of order, that it was not competent to review the remarks of the gentleman from Charles, [Mr. Merrick.] or to refer to what had occurred.

Mr. CHAMBERS. Then I will not refer to the gentleman from Charles.

Mr PRESSTMAN. We will see to what the gentleman does refer.

Mr. DENT, (to the President.) Is this a renewal of the motion to reconsider.

The PRESIDENT. It is.

Some conversation followed on the point of order, between Mr. DENT and the PRESIDENT.

The PRESIDENT said, that a majority of the Convention could, under the rule, give consent to another motion to reconsider. And the Chair would put the question in that form. The question was not debateable.

Mr. BLAKISTONE submitted a further question on the point of order.

The PRESIDENT repeated his decision, expressing the opinion that the rule was unwise, but that, nevertheless, it *was* the rule, and it was the duty of the chair to execute it.

The question was then stated to be, "Will the Convention give its consent that the motion to reconsider be again made."

Some conversation followed between Mr. BUCHANAN and the CHAIR.

The question was then taken and the result was as follows:

Affirmative—Messrs. Donaldson, Kent, Sellman, Merrick, Buchanan, Bell, Welch, Chandler, Ridgely, Lloyd, Dickinson, Sherwood of Talbot, Colston, Constable, Chambers of Cecil, McLane George, Wright, Thomas, Shriver, Gaither, Biser, Annan, Magraw, Gwinn, Stewart, of Baltimore city, Brent, of Baltimore city, Sherwood, of Baltimore city, Presstman, Fiery, Neill, John Newcomer, Harbine, Michael Newcomer, Brewer, Weber, Slicer, Fitzpatrick, Parke, Shower and Brown—42.

Negative—Messrs. Chapman, President, Morgan, Blakistone, Dent, Hopewell, Ricaud, Lee, Chambers of Kent, Wells, Weems, Bond, Sollers, Jenifer, John Dennis, James U. Dennis, Crisfield, Dashiell, Williams, Hodson, Phelps, Tuck, McCubbin, McMaster, Fooks, Jacobs, Sappington Stephenson, Nelson, Thawley, Stewart of Caroline, Kilgour and Waters—32.

So the Convention consented that the motion to reconsider should be again made.

Whereupon the question recurred on the motion to reconsider the vote by which the said first branch of the resolution had been agreed to.

Mr. STEWART, of Caroline, demanded the previous question.

There was a second.

And the main question was ordered to be now taken.

Mr. SHRIVER asked the yeas and nays on the main question, (i. e. the motion to reconsider,) which were ordered, and being taken, resulted as follows:

Affirmative—Messrs. Donaldson, Sellman, Merrick, Buchanan, Bell, Welch, Chandler, Ridgely, Lloyd, Dickinson, Sherwood, of Talbot, Colston, Constable, Chambers, of Cecil, Miller, McLane, Grason, George, Wright, Thomas, Shriver, Gaither, Biser, Annan, McHenry, Magraw, Stewart, of Caroline, Gwinn, Stewart, of Baltimore city, Brent, of Baltimore city, Sherwood, of Baltimore city, Presstman, Ware, Fiery, Neill, John Newcomer, Harbine, Michael Newcomer, Brewer, Weber, Slicer, Fitzpatrick, Parke, Shower and Brown—45.

Negative—Messrs. Chapman, President, Morgan, Blakistone, Dent, Hopewell, Ricaud, Lee, Chambers, of Kent, Dorsey, Wells, Kent, Weems, Sollers, Jenifer, John Dennis, James U. Dennis, Dashiell, Williams, Hodson, Phelps, McCubbin, McMaster, Fooks, Jacobs, Sappington, Stephenson, Nelson, Thawley, Kilgour and Waters—29.

So the vote was reconsidered.

The question recurring on the adoption of the resolution.

Mr. McHENRY moved that the resolution be laid upon the table.

The question was taken and decided in the affirmative, without a division.

So the resolution was laid upon the table.

MOTIONS TO RECONSIDER.

Mr. MORGAN. I rise to ask information of the Chair. If I should now make a motion that the consent of the House be given to enable me to make a motion to reconsider, would that motion be in order.

The PRESIDENT. The Chair can give no other construction to the rule, in the shape in which it now stands.

Mr. MORGAN. Then it is high time it should be changed; otherwise this Convention may move for weeks and months, round the same circle, without the power to extricate itself, or to take one single step towards the final disposition of any subject-matter, that may come up for its consideration.

I give notice that I shall to-morrow move to amend the twenty-second rule, by striking out that portion of it which permits a motion to reconsider, after having been once made and decided, to be again made by the consent of the Convention; and I hope that the Convention, on all sides, will give me its aid towards removing this obstacle, at least, from our path.

The motion was entered on the journal.

The Convention thereupon passed to the orders of the day.

THE LEGISLATIVE DEPARTMENT.

The Convention resumed the consideration of the special order of the day, being the report heretofore made from the committee on the Legislative department of the government.

The question pending at the time of adjournment yesterday, was on the amendment of Mr. JACOBS. [See yesterday's proceedings.]

Mr. JACOBS withdrew the amendment offered by him on yesterday, and substituted in lieu of it the following:

"The Legislature shall not repeal the taxes now imposed for the payment of the public debt, until the revenues and funds of the State, shall be sufficient to ensure its ultimate extinguishment within the period limited for its payment; and when the public debt is paid, the surplus revenues derived from the public works of the State, after defraying the necessary expenses of the government shall be distributed according to the mode provided by the resolution, No. 47, of the General Assembly, of December session, passed 1833."

Mr. JACOBS said:

Mr. President.—On the day before yesterday, we adopted two sections as a substitute for the original twenty-first section reported by the committee on the legislative department, and I voted with great pleasure for both of them; because, in my opinion, they imposed such restrictions upon the future Legislatures of this State, as past experience has proved to be necessary, and the whole public mind required, as a guarantee against similar legislation in future. So far as those sections go, I approve of them entirely; for they declare,

First, "The Legislature, hereafter, shall contract no debt, unless they provide for its payment by a tax, levied at the time; which tax shall never be diverted to any other purpose." This taxing accompaniment will be the best security against contracting debt in future, that we could possibly have ; for whilst, in case of foreign invasion or domestic insurrection, it might become necessary to contract debt, in which emergency, the power is not denied, yet for purposes of mere policy, the power would be inoperative, because of the responsibility of delegates to their constituents and the aversion of the people to taxation.

Second, "Two-thirds of the Legislature shall be requisite to appropriate public money, and the Legislature shall not have the power to make appropriations, loans or subscriptions to any work of internal improvement." I say I voted for both of these sections, but they do not go far enough; we want some indemnity for the past, as well as security for the future, and that was the object designed to be secured, by the amendment I offered yesterday.

Gentlemen thought that amendment susceptible of improvement and the section I offer now, in lieu of the one proposed on yesterday, embodies those improvements, while it retains the original provisions, looking to the stability of our financial system until a time when the sinking fund shall be increased to an amount large enough to anticipate the payment of the State bonds at the periods when they shall severally become due ; after which, it requires a distribution amongst the counties and city of Baltimore, of the nett revenues of the public works according to the mode provided in resolution No. 47 of the General Assembly of December session passed 1833. It was because of the mode of distribution, that I preferred this substitute. By the resolution of 1833, No. 47, the whole of the nett revenues of the internal improvements would be distributed as follows : One half would be divided into twenty parts and given to each county and Baltimore city equally, while the other half would be divided between the counties and city of Baltimore, according to their respective white population. This would give to the counties a larger share than they would obtain on the principle of distribution according to taxation as proposed on yesterday.

Sir, I regret the necessity for such a provision in the Constitution as much as any gentleman in this Convention can, but I am not to be swerved from a course I deem just and right, because, forsooth, it argues a want of confidence in the Legislature of the State. This is not the arena or the occasion for an exhibition of those very delicate shades of refinement that forbid the exercise of prudence on a matter of such grave interest to the people of this State.

I heard it argued yesterday, that the Legislature had always been a safe depository of the public trust, and might well claim our confidence in the future management of the finances of the State. Sir, what some gentlemen approve, I disapprobate, and there lies the issue. If, as it is argued, the present financial system of the State, will, with the aid of the sinking fund, pay our debt in twelve years, is it not good policy, to secure inviolate that system until the expiration of that time? Some say the treasury will be in a state to admit a reduction in the taxes in a very short time, and it would be hard the Legislature should be debarred giving any relief. They would have a reduction of five cents two years hence, and a reduction of five more two years after that, but they would continue the remaining fifteen cents till 1890, to meet the payment of the last bonds then due. I would like to know the difference in paying twenty-five cents on the $100 for twevle years, and then be entirely released from direct taxes—and a payment, by taxation, equal in amount but varied in rate, and interspersed through a lapse of forty years. Could we hear the response of the people of this State, I am very sure it would be in favor of continuing the twenty-five cent tax until the whole debt is paid or the sinking fund increased sufficiently to pay it when due. Not that the people love taxation, but if the money must be paid, they would sooner do it, in a reasonable time, than transmit, with their property to future generations, this eternal and inalienable tax.

Continue the present tax of twenty-five cents on the one hundred dollars until the proposed time, and our people will pay it cheerfully, because they would the sooner be released from taxation altogether, and the sooner share the benefits of what they have already paid. But adopt the other plan, and change, alter, raise and lower the taxes, to suit the policy of every administration, and the theory of every tyro in finance, who may hold a seat in the legislature; and you will certainly do one of two things—you will exasperate the public mind, by a constant vacillation in your revenue laws, or you will inure the whole state to a system of taxation that is to be perpetual. I am opposed to perpetual taxation. I never want our people to recognise it, as the settled policy of the State, nor would I wantonly tantalize their most ardent desires for exemption from taxation entirely.

I well remember the struggles and remonstrances made by the people of my county, before yielding to the present tax laws; that county was one of the seven referred to on yesterday, by the gentleman from Frederick, (Mr. Thomas,) who repudiated the *justice* and *equity* of those tax laws, devised by, and under the administration of Mr. Pratt.

That gentleman then held a warm place in the affections of the people of Worcester county, but in his fixed and steady purpose to maintain the faith of the State, he found it necessary to recommend a system of tax laws, considered oppressive and unjust, by the people of that county, and this caused the love of many to wax cold towards him. Moved by high patriotic motives, we yielded to the burdens of taxation, only to throw them off at the earliest practical moment.

We have lived to see the policy of that gentleman developing itself in a manner flattering to his far-seeing judgment, and likely to consummate the object proposed, and we would adhere to that policy, and that system of taxation until the last dollar is paid. I would hold to the present financial system of the State, until it has worked out its high destiny, of restoring the people of old Maryland once more, to that proud position they once occupied. Aye, more; I would engraft upon this Constitution a guaranty that those taxes shall be returned to the people, when the public works become remunerative, according to the mode prescribed by my amendment. Shall we neglect this amendment, and deceive the reasonable expectation of the people? Continue to sport their confidence? Ever allure them by a course of duplicity into hopes never to be realized? I trust this is not the determination of this Convention, but that we shall evince our sincerity and good faith towards the people of this deeply indebted State, by engrafting this section upon the Constitution, to be submitted to their judgment.

Mr. Donaldson called for a division of the question;

Which was ordered.

Mr. Sollers rose to enquire of the gentleman from Worcester, (Mr. Jacobs,) what the meaning of this provision was? As he, (Mr. S.,) understood it, the tax-laws were not to be repealed until a sufficient fund should have been provided to extinguish the debt. Who was to be the judge of that sufficiency?

Mr. Jacobs said: The legislature, I presume.

Mr. Sollers continued. It seemed then, he said, to be unnecessary. If it was not intended to bind the legislature against passing any law to repeal the taxes, for what purpose had it been offered? Was it done to gratify bond holders? He could not think so. He did not believe that any gentleman representing an agricultural district, would introduce any proposition, prejudicial to the interests of his own constituents, or calculated to promote the interests of bond-holders and stock-jobbers.

What then was the object of this proposition? Was it intended as a mere expression of opinion on the part of this Convention that we did not intend to repudiate? Why, who dreamed of such a thing? That day—the darkest in our history—when "the heaven's were hung with black"—had long since passed. And no man at this hour would stand up and advocate any thing like the doctrine of repudiation. He could not understand the purpose for which the proposition had been offered.

If it meant that the legislature was to pass no law to repeal the tax-laws, notwithstanding that there might be a large surplus annually flowing into the treasury, then he was opposed to it. He would not, he dare not go before a down-trodden constituency, and tell them that although there was a large accumulation of money in the treasury, wrung from their hard toil and the sweat of their brows, yet the organic law forbid us relieving them from a burthen which was crushing them. Gentlemen of the counties, (asked Mr. S.,) can *you* do this?

He spoke of the peculiar position of himself and of the people whom he represented, to whose benefit these gigantic works had in no degree contributed. Yet they were paying for them annually more than they were able to pay—and now a demand was made for a constitutional provision prohibiting the Legislature from repealing the tax-laws although some of the burthens they imposed might well be taken off.

It was not often that the gentleman from Kent, (Mr. Chambers,) found it necessary to resort to *ad captandum* arguments. But there certainly was some savour of such an argument in the remarks which the gentleman made the other day, when he appealed to the farmers here and told them that the last taxes to be taken off would be the taxes on the land. He, (Mr. S.,) declared that the very first bill which reduced the taxes would take off some five or ten cents from the land tax. The very same influences which were brought to bear for the establishment of the system which the gentleman from Baltimore city, (Mr. Presstman,) had yesterday designated the auxiliary taxes, would again operate to continue them whilst the necessity for taxes existed—and *these* were the very last which the farmers would consent to repeal.

We were told that this was a solemn pledge to the people of Maryland and to the world, that under no circumstances should the tax laws be repealed, and that the faith of the State should be maintained inviolate. No man was more disposed to maintain the faith of the State than he was. But where in the history of the world had a system of finance been found so perfect, that it was not susceptible of improvement? There were certain gentlemen who seemed to take into their own peculiar keeping the faith and credit of the State—to regard it as exclusively the work of their own hands, and to consider it almost a sacrilegious act for any man to touch it. Gentlemen must pardon him. But he knew of no work of mere human wisdom which, in the change of time and circumstances, might not require to be changed. And was he to be told that, although there might be surplus millions in the Treasury, they were not to be touched, and that the enormous taxes now weighing heavily upon the people were to be continued, even when they could safely and properly be relaxed? He, for one, could not go home and teach such a doctrine to a constituency who had so honestly and so freely paid the taxes which the State, in the hour of her need and her peril, had imposed upon her.

Mr. Gwinn said, that he was opposed to the first branch of the proposition offered by the gentleman. He could not see the wisdom of keeping up the present system of taxation, until the whole public debt was paid off. Under the estimates of the Treasurer, the sinking fund would absorb it in about fifteen years. But what need was there for the continuance of the present system in all its parts, in order that this result might be accomplished in so brief a time. Taxation was, indeed, designed to meet the current interest, and to provide for the payment of the principal of our obligations. But it was surely only right that this burthen should be as equally distributed, as was consistent with the terms of our obligations.

The works of internal improvement were not designed for the benefit of the present generation only. This result could never have been anticipated even, because their extent and character made it evident that the main advantage would be derived from the future. And, although the responsibility which we assume, imposes on us the duty of taking our fair share of the burden we have created, yet those who derive the chief advantage our investment, should also contribute to the discharge of the liability.

Again, it would seem reasonable that this scale of taxation should be gradually reduced. The gradation would maintain the equipoise in the value of property in this State, which would else be suddenly disturbed if the whole burden were removed at once. Prudence, no less than justice, would require reductions running through a series of years. He would gladly provide for a diminution, following a certain per centage; say five cents in the hundred dollars, in every period of three years, until the whole debt was discharged. But he could not support the proposition as it now stood. It was not necessary to the credit of the State, for there was no risk following upon gradual reduction in taxation.

Mr. Jenifer now offered the following amendment, (which he had yesterday indicated his intention to offer to the then pending proposition of Mr. Jacobs.)

Amend the first branch of the amendment by adding, at the end thereof, the words "except by an act passed at one session, submitted to the people and re-enacted at the next succeeding session of the Legislature."

Mr. Jenifer did not see the necessity for the insertion of any restriction in the organic law. He saw no necessity, either for restricting or for urging on the Legislature in reference to taxes. If the question was to be taken now, he would wish to make the first proposition so as to prevent any restriction on the Legislature, to take off the taxes, when, in their discretion, they may think it ought to be done. He was opposed to taking off the taxes, until the debt was paid; but when the debt was paid, he would wish taxation to cease. He was not so clear on the point that the last tax which would be repealed, would be the tax on land. If the modification he had suggested was adopted, he would vote for the proposition; if not, he must vote against it.

The auxiliary tax, as it was called, did operate more on Baltimore than any other part of the State, but it should be recollected that she received nearly all the benefits from these works of internal improvement, and if that tax should be repealed, the burden must fall more heavily on the property of the counties, and on those which never expected to derive any direct interest from these works. Much had been said of the large amount of taxes paid from Baltimore. She necessarily pays the largest portion from her wealth and population, but much less in proportion than the advantages derived from being the termini of these great works. Her commerce is enlarged—her wealth increased—her city becoming a rival to the first of the Union—these facts should satisfy gentlemen, that no injustice will be done to Baltimore, by a continuance of these auxiliary taxes until the final extinguishment of the public debt. Then she will receive her fair proportion of the nett revenues arising from these works, and all the advantages they were intended to bestow. For these reasons, (Mr. J. said,) he should not be for disturbing the present system of revenue at any point until the entire liquidation of the public debt.

After some conversation on a point of order, between Mr. Sollers and the Chair,

The question was taken on the amendment of Mr. Jenifer,

And it was rejected.

The question then recurred on the adoption of the first division of Mr. Jacobs' amendment, which was read as follows:

"The Legislature shall not repeal the taxes now imposed for the payment of the public debt, until the revenues and funds of the State shall be sufficient to ensure its ultimate extinguishment within the period limited for its payment."

Mr. Brown asked the yeas and nays;

Which were ordered.

And being taken, resulted as follows:

Affirmative.—Messsrs. Chapman, President, Blakistone, Ricaud, Lee, Chambers, of Kent, Donaldson, Wells, Crisfield, Dashiell, Williams, Hodson, Phelps, Bowling, McMaster, Fooks, Jacobs and Waters—16.

Negative.—Messrs. Morgan, Dent, Hopewell, Sellman, Weems, Sollers, Jenifer, Buchanan, Bell, Welch, Chandler, Ridgely, Lloyd, Dickinson, Sherwood, of Talbot, Colston, James U. Dennis, Constable, Chambers, of Cecil, Miller, McCubbin, Grason, George, Wright, Thomas, Shriver, Gaither, Biser, Sappington, Stephenson, Nelson, Carter, Thawley, Stewart, of Caroline, Gwinn, Stewart of Baltimore city, Brent, of Baltimore city, Sherwood, of Baltimore city, Ware, Fiery, Neill, John Newcomer, Harbine, Michael Newcomer, Kilgour, Brewer, Weber, Slicer, Parke, Shower, and Brown—52.

So the first division of the amendment was *rejected.*

The question then recurred on the second branch of the proposition;

As follows:

"And when the public debt is paid, the surplus revenue derived from the public works of the State, after defraying the necessary expenses of the government, shall be distributed according to the mode provided by the resolution No. 47, of the General Assembly of December session, passed 1833."

Mr. Gwinn said that the rule fixed in the second branch was based on a resolution that applied to the school fund. In that view, it was wise enough as a sort of compromise, only for the reason that it was perhaps the easiest way that could be devised of settling a mooted question.

It was now, however, proposed to give it a much wider meaning, by providing that the fund indicated in the second branch should be divided into two parts—one of which should be distributed among the counties and city of Baltimore according to their white population, and the other half to be divided into twenty parts, allowing one to each of the counties in existence in 1833, and one to the city of Baltimore.

It seemed to him that if such distribution were ever to occur, it should be made in the same proportion in which the fund was contributed. He would refer to the table marked [statement G.] in the Treasurer's report of 1849. The amount of the whole yearly levy for the State was $477,-276—and of this Baltimore city contributed $175,762, or more than one-third of the gross amount of the whole revenue. Now with what reason is it urged, that Baltimore should, after making contribution of a fund, which was not required by the necessity of the case, receive back only eleven-twentieths of what it had paid, and not the whole sum which it contributed. The same injustice would result to the counties relatively also. Why should Frederick county, which pays eight times as much as Calvert, receive back only one-half of its contribution—and one-twentieth of the gross sum—when it has contributed in a far different proportion. It was certainly an extraordinary idea, and though it might work to the advantage of the small counties, it could not be supposed that they would obtain this benefit by injustice to the larger counties and to the city of Baltimore.

The question was taken and resulted as follows:

Affirmative—Messrs. Chapman, Pres't., Morgan, Blakistone, Dent, Hopewell, Ricaud, Lee, Chambers of Kent, Sellman, Weems, Bond, Sollers, Colston, James U. Dennis, Crisfield, Dashiell, Williams, Hodson, Phelps, McMaster, Fooks, Jacobs, Carter, Thawley, Fiery, John Newcomer, Kilgour, Brewer, and Waters—30.

Negative—Messrs. Donaldson, Wells, Buchanan, Bell, Welch, Chandler, Ridgely, Lloyd, Dickinson, Sherwood of Talbot, Constable, Miller, McCubbin, George, Wright, Thomas, Gaither, Biser, Annan, Sappington, Stephenson, McHenry, Nelson, Gwinn, Stewart, of Baltimore city, Brent of Baltimore city, Sherwood of Baltimore city, Presstman, Ware, Schley, Neill, Harbine, Michael Newcomer, Weber, Slicer, Fitzpatrick, Parke, Shower and Brown—39.

So the seeond branch of the amendment was rejected.

Mr. Jacobs. I have one other proposition which I desire to submit. And I move the previous question on its adoption.

The amendment was read as follows:

"The Legislature shall at its first session after the adoption of this Constitution, and from time to time thereafter, diminish by law, the direct taxes of the State, to a minimum, equal only to pay the interest on the present State debt; and no law shall hereafter be passed to raise money by taxation with a view to the payment of any part of the principal of the State debt."

There was a second to the demand for the previous question.

And the main question was ordered to be now taken.

Mr. Jacobs asked the yeas and nays, which were ordered.

Mr. Brewer called for a division of the question, which was ordered.

And the question was taken on the first branch of the amendment as follows:

"The Legislature shall, at its first session after the adoption of this Constitution, and from time to time thereafter diminish by law, the direct taxes of the State, to a minimum, equal only, to pay the interest on the present State debt."

And the question having been taken, the result was as follows:

Affirmative—Messrs. Weems, Bond, Constable, Miller, McMaster, Fooks, Jacobs, Thawley, Michael Newcomer, Brewer, Parke, and Shower—12.

Negative—Messrs. Chapman, Pres't., Morgan, Blakistone, Dent, Hopewell, Ricaud, Lee, Chambers of Kent, Donaldson, Wells, Jenifer, Buchanan, Bell, Welch, Chandler, Ridgely, Lloyd, Dickinson, Sherwood of Talbot, Colston, James U. Dennis, Crisfield, Dashiell, Williams, Hodson, Phelps, McCubbin, Grason, George, Wright, Thomas, Shriver, Gaither, Biser, Annan, Sappington, Stephenson, McHenry, Nelson, Carter, Stewart of Caroline, Gwinn, Stewart of Baltimore city, Brent of Baltimore city, Sherwood of Baltimore city, Presstman, Ware, Fiery, John Newcomer, Harbine, Waters, Anderson, Weber, Slicer, and Fitzpatrick—54.

So the first branch of the amendment was rejected.

The question was then put on the second branch of said amendment being in these words "and no law shall hereafter be passed to raise money by taxation, with a view to the payment of any part of the principal of the State debt."

Mr. Jacobs asked to withdraw the last branch of said amendment, but the Chair stated, that the yeas and nays having been commenced being taken by the Clerk, the Convention must proceed in taking the vote.

And the question was taken and resulted as follows:

Affirmative—Mr. Fooks—1.

Negative—Messrs. Chapman, President, Morgan, Blakistone, Dent, Hopewell, Ricaud, Lee, Chambers of Kent, Donaldson, Wells, Sellman, Weems, Sollers, Jenifer, Buchanan, Bell, Welch, Chandler, Ridgely, Lloyd, Dickinson, Sherwood of Talbot, Colston, James U. Dennis, Crisfield, Dashiell, Williams, Hodson, Phelps, Miller, McCubbin, Grason, George, Wright, McMaster, Hearn, Jacobs, Thomas, Shriver, Gaither, Biser, Annan, Sappington, Stephenson, McHenry, Nelson, Carter, Thawley, Stewart of Caroline, Gwinn, Stewart of Baltimore city, Brent of Baltimore city, Sherwood of Balt. city, Presstman, Fiery, John Newcomer, Harbine, Michael Newcomer, Kilgour, Brewer, Waters, Weber, Slicer, Fitzpatrick, and Brown—66.

So the second branch of the amendment was rejected.

The twenty-second section of the report was then read, and, no amendment having been offered, was adopted as follows:

Sec. 22nd. No extra compensation shall be granted or allowed by the General Assembly to any public officer, agent, servant, or contractor after the services shall have been rendered, or the contract entered into, nor shall the salary or compensation of any public officer be increased or diminished during his term of office.

The twenty-third section of the report was then read as follows:

Sec. 23rd. No county now established by law, shall ever be reduced by the establishment of any new county, to a population of less than thousands, nor shall any new county be hereafter established with a population of less thousand.

This section was informally passed over.

The twenty-fourth section of the report was then read, as follows:

Sec. 24th. No senator or delegate shall, during the term for which he shall have been elected, be appointed to any civil office in this State, which shall have been created, or the salary or emoluments of which shall have been increased during such term; and no senator or delegate, during the time he shall continue to act as such, shall be eligible to any civil office.

Mr. HARBINE suggested that the gentleman from Prince George's, (Mr. Tuck,) had given notice of an amendment which he intended to offer. [It appeared that Mr. T. had been unexpectedly called from the city by sickness in his family.]

After some conversation,

The section was informally passed over.

The twenty-fifth section of the report was read and adopted, as follows:

Sec. 25th. Each House may determine the rules of its own proceedings, punish a member for disorderly or disrespectful behaviour, and with the consent of two-thirds, expel a member but no member shall be expelled a second time for the same offence.

The twenty-sixth section of the report was read and adopted, as follows:

Sec. 26th. Each House may punish by imprisonment, during the session of the General Assembly, any person not a member, for disrespectful or disorderly behaviour in its presence, or for obstructing any of its proceedings, or any of its officers in the execution of their duties; provided, such imprisonment shall not at any one time exceed ten days.

The twenty-seventh section was read, and no amendment having been offered, was adopted, as follows:

Sec. 27th. The members of each House shall, in all cases, except treason, felony or breach of the peace, be privileged from arrest during their attendance at the sessions of the General Assembly, and in going to and returning from the same, allowing one day for every thirty miles such member may reside from the place at which the General Assembly is convened.

The twenty-eighth section of the report was read and adopted, as follows:

Sec. 28th. No senator or delegate shall be liable in any civil action or criminal prosecution, whatever, for words spoken in debate.

The twenty-ninth section of the report was read, and no amendment having been proposed, was read as follows:

Sec. 29th. The House of Delegates may inquire, on the oath of witnesses, into all complaints, grievances and offences, as the grand inquest of the State, and may commit any person, for any crime, to the public jail, there to remain until discharged by due course of law—they may examine and pass all accounts of the State relating either to the collection or expenditure of the revenue, or appoint auditors to state and adjust the same—they may call for all public or official papers and records, and send for persons whom they may judge necessary in the course of their enquiries concerning affairs relating to the public interest, and may direct all office bonds which shall be made payable to the State, to be sued for any breach of duty.

The thirtieth section of the report was read and adopted as follows:

Sec. 30th. In case of the death, disqualification, refusal to act, expulsion or removal from the county or district for which he shall have been elected, if any person shall have been chosen as a Delegate or Senator, or in case of a tie between two or more qualified persons, a warrant of election shall be issued by the Governor, or person exercising the functions of Governor for the time being, for the election of a Senator or Delegate, as the case may be, to supply the vacancy, of which not less than ten days notice, exclusive of the day of notice and day of election, shall be given; provided, however, that unless a meeting of the General Assembly may intervene, or the vacancy shall occur during the session of the General Assembly, the election to fill the same shall take place on the day of the ensuing general election.

The thirty-first section of the report was read, and no amendment having been offered, was adopted as follows:

Sec. 31st. The senators and delegates shall receive such compensation for their services as may be allowed by law; but no law increasing or diminishing the compensation shall be made to take effect until after the general elections next ensuing the passage thereof. No book or other printed matter not appertaining to the business of the session, shall be subscribed for, for the use of the members, or be distributed among them.

The thirty-second section of the report was read, as follows:

Sec. 32nd No law passed by the General Assembly shall take effect until the expiration of days, from the closing of the sessions at which it may be passed, unless it be expressly declared on the face of the law, that it shall take effect on or after a different day; and no law of a public nature shall take effect until the same shall be published.

Mr. PHELPS moved to fill the blank in the second line with "ninety."

The amendment was agreed to.

And the question recurring on the adoption of the section, as amended—

After some explanatory conversation on the part of Messrs. BROWN, HARBINE, PRESSTMAN, SOLLERS and CHAMBERS, of Kent,

Mr. CHAMBERS, of Kent, moved to amend said section by adding at the end thereof, these words, "in such mode as the Legislature may direct."

Mr. RIDGELY submitted that the last paragraph was superfluous, and moved, therefore, to strike out the following words:

"And no law of a public nature shall take effect until the same shall be published."

The question was first taken on the amendment of Mr. CHAMBERS, of Kent.

And the amendment was agreed to.

The question then recurred on the motion of Mr. RIDGELY.

Mr. RIDGELY withdrew his motion.

And the question recurring on the adoption of the section, as amended,

On a suggestion by

Mr. STEWART, of Caroline, the words "or after" be stricken out.

Mr. PRESSTMAN explained that the insertion of the words "or after," was a mere typographical error.

And then the article, as amended, was adopted.

The thirty-third section of the report was read, as follows:

Sec. 33rd. The General Assembly shall have full power to exclude from the privilege of voting at elections or of being elected to either House, or of being elected or appointed to any civil or military office in this State, any person convicted of perjury, bribery, or other infamous crime.

Mr. PRESSTMAN referred to a discussion in the earlier part of the session, when the report on the elective franchise was pending, when something was said about the effect of constitutional disfranchisements upon the commission of offences, and whether in case of pardon by the executive, or fulfilment of the punishment allotted, would restore a party to his civil rights.

The gentleman from Calvert, (Mr. Sollers,) seemed to have some doubt upon this point and at his suggestion, qualifying terms had been employed. He had instanced at the time the offence of duelling among other violations of the law, and thought that the pardoning power might not be sufficient to restore the rights of the party.

He, [Mr. P.,] had thought that every offence was purged by pardon or the actual fulfilment of the sentence of punishment. It was of importance enough to have the matter well understood and if he was wrong in his view, or if there was any uncertainty, the section had better be amended. He did not favor in any manner, a perpetual disfranchisement for any offence.

Mr. SOLLERS explained, that his idea was, that the provision should be amended, so that after a person convicted of an infamous crime had been pardoned by the executive, the disqualification should be removed. There might be cases where it would be the duty of the executive to exercise the prerogative of pardon. An innocent person may have been convicted, and proof of his innocence may have subsequently come to light. The Governor should in such case pardon the convicted: and yet, as the clause stands, he may be deprived of the right of voting.

Mr. SOLLERS moved to amend said section by adding at the end thereof, these words, "unless such person shall have been pardoned by the executive."

The question was then taken, and

The amendment was agreed to.

The question then recurring on the adoption of the section, as amended,

Mr. STEWART, of Caroline, moved further to amend said section by striking out in the second line, these words, "the privilege of voting at elections, or of."

He, (Mr S.) objected to the amendment, because it was already included in the report on the elective franchise, in nearly the same terms. It cannot produce any effect even if we insert it here. How can the legislature prevent the people from electing any person they may think proper to represent them. All they would have the power to do, would be to prevent him from being qualified.

Mr. CHAMBERS, of Kent, moved to amend said section by striking out in the second and third lines, these words, "being elected to either House or of being elected or appointed to," and inserting in lieu thereof "holding."

Mr. C. explained to the gentleman from Caroline, (Mr. Stewart,) that the report of the committee on the elective franchise was an absolute and unconditional constitutional provision. This left the matter to the discretion of the legislature. It would be better, he thought, not to disturb the language of the section in this particular.

Mr. JOHN NEWCOMER moved to strike out the section, believing, he said, that the provision in the report on the elective franchise to be sufficient.

The amendment was not now in order.

Mr. STEWART, of Caroline, asked the gentleman from Kent, whether if this amendment were adopted, it would not require that the legislature should pass a special act for each particular case?

Mr. CHAMBERS, of Kent, replied that the legislature have the power, and can exercise it at their discretion; and the legislature will still have the power whether this provision shall be in the Constitution or not.

Mr. STEWART, of Caroline, said he was opposed to the proposition. He did not think it right to place any restriction on the people, as to the person they should elect as their representative.

Mr. WEEMS said, he had not that perfect understanding of the import of the section, which he wished to have before he gave his vote. He was now asking for information of those who were more skilled in legal matters, what was meant by *infamous crime?* Now, he might consider it infamous, if a gentleman were to spit in his face. And if he were to knock down the person who committed the outrage, that might be considered as infamous in him. He wanted something more definite in the phraseology, such as perjury, felony, &c.

Mr. CHAMBERS, of Kent, said, the words used were technical words in common law, and in common law treatises; and to strike them out might involve us in difficulty. It depended on the punishment affixed by law to a crime.

Mr. WEEMS resumed. He was opposed to too many technicalities in the Constitution. The people are complaining of them. These terms are beyond their comprehension. A great majority of the people are not in a situation to refer to law books. Many who have capacity to comprehend, have no means of reference to books, and cannot understand the meaning of these terms. As far as it could possibly be done, he would wish to expunge all technicalities. He did not like to oppose any thing coming from such a high source as the gentleman from Kent, but he did desire to see the organic law made as comprehensible to the masses as it could be. The explanations of the gentleman were not satisfactory to his mind, as he could have wished. Let the organic law be so plain, that he who runs may both read and understand it.

Mr. PRESSTMAN thought it was due to the committee, to say, that the construction they put upon the phrase "infamous crime," was the same as that which the gentleman from Kent, (Mr. Chambers,) had indicated. It meant, he thought, most unquestionably, no other offence, at least, than such as were punishable capitally or by imprisonment in the penitentiary, though strictly speaking, some offences punishable under certain acts of Assembly might not be deemed infamous at common law. There could not be any room to enlarge the catalogue of infamous crimes beyond those he had specified. As to the idea that the Constitution can be free from technicalities it is wholly out of the question. To courts of law, any other than technical words defining crime would be mere jargon. There is scarcely a man in Maryland, outside of the legal profession, who in cases of homicide, knows the precise distinction between murder in the first and second degrees, and manslaughter. Neither Solon, Lycurgus, nor any of the greatest lawgivers in the world, ever yet found a mode of framing laws so simple and plain, that "a wayfaring man, though a fool," might understand them. Should any man succeed in that effort, he would enrich himself beyond the cunnings of all the inventors of patent medicine. To discover that would be to discover the philosopher's stone. Lawyer's become acquainted with these terms by study and practice—they are the tools of their trade, and by them all things are made comparatively easy. So a farmer may make himself perfectly intelligible to another farmer by the use of terms and phrases which are only familiar to those engaged in agriculture. It is so in all other pursuits as well as in the science of the law, and they are indispensable.

Mr. WEEMS, in reply, said he had never entertained the idea that the Constitution could be made so simple as to be comprehensible to a fool. He knew that could not be done, because we are told that if you bray a fool in a mortar with a pestle, his foolishness will not depart from him. So that whether we insert techicalities or any thing else, the fool will not understand. His object was to make the Constitution plain to men of ordinary intellect; he was not making war against technicalities which, he had no doubt, were found useful. The gentleman from Baltimore was a lawyer, and was familiar with these expressions. But he, (Mr. W.,) said he was not a lawyer, nor were a majority of the people lawyers, but he did not object to the desire of the gentleman from Baltimore to retain technicalities in the courts of law. He, (Mr. W.,) had already stated his inexperience in Constitution making. He had not even ventured to suggest a single article; he left the work to those who had more practical knowledge of the business. But when articles were presented to him for his opinion, then he was required to call his judgment into action, and he would act independently; and when he felt a doubt, he would seek for further information. No one had a greater respect for the profession of the law than he had. But he had noticed with deep regret, that when a plain man, as he was, rose to say any thing in this body, the lawyers immediately begin to put questions to him, until they embarrass him. He, however, was not to be deterred from seeking information to guide him right in his votes. He would merely say in conclusion that he would like some other words in this case, or he would like to hear a more satisfactory explanation as to the extent of the meaning of those which were used.

Mr. SOLLERS expressed a wish that the gentleman from Baltimore would show him where it was laid down that a man must have been in the penitentiary before his crime could be called infamous? He understood him to say that whether it was an "infamous crime" or not, must depend on the sentence of a court. It must be very well known to gentlemen round him, that courts do not always decide the same way. He believed that even the Court of Appeals had decided both ways. At the beginning of a term, he had known a court to decide one way, and before the end of the term, decided the other way. It was his wish to put a restraint on the courts, so far as this matter goes.

Mr. PRESSTMAN expressed his regret that the gentleman from Calvert, (Mr. Weems,) would for a moment suppose that he had not heard any views or suggestion he might make, or any other member, with the most entire respect and courtesy. Indeed, he would take occasion to say, as that gentleman had disclaimed any unkind imputation, that he entertained for him the highest respect, as well for his intelligence as his strict integrity. And he must have been understood in a way far different from that he intended, if any gentleman thought that by the denial of legal and technical knowledge to many of those around him, sufficient to frame a Constitution in all its parts, he would wish to arrogate any superiority to the profession of which he was an humble member. Among the most esteemed and valued friends he had in that body, and in whose judgment upon many weighty matters he had often to rely, were gentlemen not bred to the law.

To intelligent men he never had any fear of speaking the truth; it is only the ignorant who profess to know every thing. Lawyers bow with deference to the superior attainments of others, who have devoted their lives to a particular calling.

To draught a law or frame a Constitution is in many respects peculiarly appropriate to lawyers, though to pass upon its expediency or fitness for the wants of the people required sound common sense, which belonged to no class exclusively.

He repeated what he had said, of the certain definition of the term, infamous crime. He had tried cases where witnesses was objected to as incompetent to testify, having committed an infamous crime; the courts and lawyers readily understood the term. The party in order to testify, must have purged himself of the offence by having served out the punishment allotted, or produce the evidence of pardon.

Mr. Sollers said, he was not satisfied with the explanation of the gentleman from Baltimore. It appeared then, that the courts had to determine this question. What is, and what is not an infamous crime, is a rule of court, to be decided by the *dictum* of the court. But if it so happen that the court disagree, who is to decide? Take the case of a duel; it is an assault with intent to kill, but although no one is hurt, yet the accused may be convicted of an infamous crime and must pay the penalty And yet, would any man pretend to say that such a person ought to be regarded as infamous? According to the definition of the gentleman from Baltimore, however, he might be held so by the decision of the court.

Mr. Constable objected to the phrase *infamous crimes*, because its meaning was uncertain, and there might be a want of uniformity in its application, arising from a diversity of opinion as to import, which would operate injustice.

He also thought it objectionable as investing the legislature with an indefinite power to extend these disabilities. Whatever might have been the *crimes* known as *infamous* at common law, and he believed there were none below the grade of felony, it was obvious that they might be multiplied indefinitely by statute. Thus *forgery*, which was not a *felony* at common law, and hence not embraced in the class of offences which it denounced as *infamous* had been made so by act of parliament.

In the same manner, assault and battery and other trivial *misdemeanors*, may be made *infamous crimes*; and those who commit them be subjected to the harsh disabilities imposed by this section. This phrase then, was liable to be extended both by *legislation* and *construction*, and if done by the *latter*, the same crime when committed by different persons might not always be visited with these disabilities. In order to obviate this objection, though not that resulting from legislative extensions, which could only be avoided by a specific enumeration of the offences intended to work these disabilities, he would move to substitute the word, *felony*, for the phrase, *infamous crimes*.

The amendment was not now in order.

The question was then stated to be on the amendment of Mr. Chambers, of Kent, and having been taken,

The amendment was agreed to.

Mr. Constable then offered his amendment, (as above indicated.)

A brief legal discussion, technical and colloquial in its character, here took place; in which it was contended, by Mr. Constable, that if the infamy of an offence was decided by the fact of confinement in the penitentiary, under the fifth amendment to the Federal Constitution, the offence of assault and battery is infamous, because it is presentable in the United States courts by a Grand Jury, and punishable by confinement in the penitentiary. He also stated, that in Harford county, a man who had been convicted of an infamous crime twenty years before, and had served out his imprisonment, was rejected as an incompetent witness.

Mr. Chambers dissented from this view, that assault and battery, and misdemeanor, could be classed among infamous crimes.

Mr. Presstman insisted that the gentleman from Cecil, (Mr. Constable,) had raised this question as an argument, which did not express his real sentiments, and contended that the term "infamous crime," exists in the law books with a technical meaning, including treason, felony and all offences which come within the "*crimen falsi*" of the Roman law. To avoid uncertainty, the committee had designated some offences by name, and then added the word "infamous" to cover the rest. Because the courts may commit errors, was not a sufficient reason for changing the language of the books.

The question then recurred and was taken on the amendment of Mr. Constable.

The amendment was agreed to.

The question then recurred on the amendment of Mr. Stewart, of Caroline.

Mr. Chambers said, the gentleman from Calvert, (Mr. Weems,) had asked what was to be understood by the words "infamous crime," and had remarked that to spit in the face of a gentleman would be an "infamous crime."

Mr. Weems explained. He did not say it would be. He put the matter hypothetically. He repeated what he had before said.

Mr. Chambers said, let it be so. He then went into a technical argument to show that the term was known to common law and to lawyers.

It was very desirable to use definite language, and when words had acquired a known meaning, the more technical the better. Nothing produced more confusion than the use of words of various significations. He instanced the word "clever," which in different locations indicated very different qualities, such as intelligence in one place, honesty in another, and fine social habits in a third. He denied that assault and battery was at common law regarded as amongst "infamous crimes," nor was it so classed by the fifth section of the amendments to the Constitution of the United States, as had been said by the gentleman from Cecil, (Mr. Constable.) That section did not mention the crime of assault and battery at all, and the idea, that because an indictment was necessary in the case of an "infamous crime," and also in "assault and battery," therefore assault and battery was an infamous crime, was quite untenable. That fifth section had nothing to do with the question. That gentleman had also spoken without his usual consideration when he said "forgery" was not a crime at common law. He read from Blackstone's commentaries to show what was intended by "infamous crimes," and also to prove that forgery was a common law offence.

Mr. CONSTABLE reiterated what he had before said in reference to the subject.

Mr. McHENRY hoped that the amendment would be adopted. The language of the Constitutution should be such as will be intelligible to all, not merely to the legal profession, who could not at all times comprehend it; for we have had to-day some proof of the glorious uncertainty of the law. He hoped, therefore, that the terms adopted, would be intelligible to those who usually constituted our Legislatures. There was, in the good old times of merry England, a Parliament which obtained the name of the Blessed Parliament, and this was because not a single lawyer had a seat in it. It was, by no means, impossible that we should one day see in this State a Blessed Legislature.

Mr. PRESSTMAN, (interrupting,) said. The gentleman could find no man in the State, out of the profession, who could define felony.

Mr. McHENRY replied that he had only meant to show that there were great discrepancies of opinion among the lawyers, as to the words first used. Probably there would be difficulty in getting at a correct aud precise definition of any word.

Mr. PHELPS said that this same provision was in the report on the Elective Franchise. In that report the provision went no further than to place the power in the hands of the Legislature. It was so in that report, and he thought the Legislature should have the same power here.

Mr. STEWART, of Caroline, said it was generally unnderstood that the committees appointed early in the session, would report on the subjects referred to their charge. They had various duties assigned to them; and the duty assigned to one committee ought not to be permitted to run into the duty of another. This clause had been inserted in the report on the Elective Franchise; and, if gentlemen would turn to that report, they would find an amendment which, included all which he had moved to strike out. It is similar; and the advantage of having all the laws on one subject included in one bill, must be apparent to all. No man looking for the provision against bribery would think of turning to the legislative report to find it. If it related to the subject of voting at elections, he would naturally turn to the report on the Elective Franchise; and, if he could not find it there, he would probably come to the conclusion that there was no provision in the Constitution concerning it.

Mr. PHELPS said that the report of the committee on the Elective Franchise had not been finally disposed of, but had only been gone through with in committee of the whole. There had been, as yet, no action on it on the part of the House on the Elective Franchise report. Nothing had been decided in reference to it. It depends on the action of the House whether it shall be a part of the fundamental law or not. If the clause of disfranchisement should not remain in the report on the Elective Franchise, it ought to be in this. If it should be determined to insert the clause of disfranchisement, the Legislature need not to pass any law on the subject, because it will be contained in the Constitution. He hoped the section would remain as it is.

The question then again recurred, and was taken on the amendment of Mr. STEWART, of Caroline, and by ayes 25, noes 27,

The amendment was rejected.

The question recurred on the section as amended.

On motion of Mr. BRENT, of Baltimore city,

Said section was amended by inserting after the word "person" in the fourth line, these words, "who may hereafter be."

The amendment was agreed to.

The section, as amended, was then adopted.

Mr. McHENRY gave notice that on to-morrow he should move to reconsider the 21st section of the report.

And the Convention adjourned until to-morrow at ten o'clock.

FRIDAY, February 28, 1851.

The Convention met at ten o'clock.

Prayer was made by the Rev. Mr. GRIFFITH.

The roll was called, and

The journal of yesterday was read and approved.

THE COMPROMISE.

The PRESIDENT laid before the Convention the following communication from His Excellency the Governor of Alabama:

EXECUTIVE CHAMBER,
Montgomery, Ala., Feb. 18, 1851.

Hon. J. G. CHAPMAN:

SIR: I have the honor to acknowledge the receipt of yours of the twelfth of December, with the accompanying "Report of the committee of the Maryland Reform Convention, on the late acts of Congress, forming the compromise, &c." Maryland has spoken frankly and patriotically. I sincerely hope her voice may receive a harmonious response from the North, the East and the West—the South will be true to the Union so long as the "sacred charter of our rights" is respected and honored, and the general government manifests a willingness and ability, "to enforce the laws made for our protection."

I have the honor to be, with great respect, your obedient servant,

H. W. Collier.

Which was read.

THE SCHOOL SYSTEM OF ALABAMA.

The President also laid before the Convention the following communication from His Excellency, the Governor of Alabama:

Executive Chamber,
Montgomery, Ala., Feb. 6, 1851.

Hon. J. G. Chapman:

Sir: During my absence from the Seat of Government, your letter of the twenty-fifth of November, was laid upon my table, instead of being sent to my residence, Tuscaloosa, as my Secretary should have done; and consequently, did not meet my eye until within the last week. I now answer it as a mere apology for my seeming neglect.

Our educational system may be seen by a reference to the laws of Alabama, which are deposited in the department of State, of the several States. We have a University endowed with $250,000, six per cent. State stock, a small annual revenue from rents, &c.

We have a sixteenth section school fund, amounting to more than $1,000,000, invested in six per cent. State stock. This fund being in common, but to the townships in proportion to the sum, at which their respective sixteenth section sold, is doing but little good, especially in the poor districts where it is most needed.

In Mobile and the larger towns, the common school system of education, if properly managed succeeds very well, but in the sparsely populated parts of the State, it has not hitherto promised very beneficial results.

The lands given us by Congress, for the establishment of a "Seminary of Learning," have not yielded one-half the sum at which they could have been sold, owing to the unwise and extraordinary legislation in respect to them. But the fund is now well secured. The same remark will apply to many of the sixteenth sections.

I am sure this information will be worth nothing to the Convention, even if it had not adjourned. Even as a matter of history, it is hardly worth reading.

With great respect, I have the honor to be, your obedient servant,

H. W. Collier.

Which was read, and

Referred to committee No. 14.

LICENSE SYSTEM.

The President also laid before the Convention a petition from sundry citizens of Washington county, praying that provision may be made in the new Constitution, that the privilege to sell intoxicating liquor shall not be granted to any person in any part of the State, except the same shall first be sanctioned or approved of by a majority of the votes in the district where the same is to be sold.

Which was read.

Mr. Dorsey said, this was an important subject, and he moved the reference of the petition to a select committee, to be composed of seven members.

Ordered accordingly.

KENT COUNTY.

The President also laid before the Convention a report from the clerk of the Levy court of Kent county, in relation to the fees allowed the Attorney General and his Deputies by said county.

Which was read, and

Referred to the committee appointed on the Attorney General and his Deputies.

Mr. Jacobs expressed a desire to change his vote on the second branch of the substitute amendment, which he had yesterday offered.

The President said, that the result would not be changed by the change of the gentleman's vote; but that the unanimous consent of the Convention would be required to enable the gentleman to make the change.

No objection having been made,

The vote of Mr. Jacobs was changed on the said proposition, from the affirmative to the negative.

THE LEGISLATIVE DEPARTMENT.

Mr. Dorsey, who had been absent from his seat yesterday, for a considerable portion of the day, in consequence of indisposition, expressed a desire to move certain amendments to sections twenty-seven, thirty, thirty-one and thirty-three, of the report of the legislative department, which had been passed upon. And he desired to move a reconsideration of these sections with a view to move the amendments.

Mr. D. was proceeding to explain the character of his amendments, when

Mr. Thomas suggested that it would be better that the sections should be reconsidered separately—that the Convention might the better understand the several propositions of the gentleman from Anne Arundel, (Mr. Dorsey.)

Mr. Dorsey, accepting the suggestion, moved a reconsideration of the vote, by which the twenty-seventh section of the report had been adopted.

The vote was reconsidered.

Mr. Dorsey then moved to amend the said section by striking out in the second line, the words "breach of the peace," and inserting in lieu thereof "other criminal offence."

Mr. D. said, it seemed to him to be proper that, if members of the legislature were to be subjected to arrest for treason or felony, they ought also to be subjected to arrest for receiving stolen goods, knowing them to be stolen, and for other offences.

Mr. Thomas suggested that the object of the gentleman would be accomplished by striking out the words "breach of the peace," and inserting the words "or other criminal offences."

Mr. Dorsey accepted the modification.

The amendment was agreed to.

And the section, as amended, was adopted.

Mr. DORSEY then moved a reconsideration of the vote, by which the thirtieth section had been adopted.

The vote was reconsidered.

Mr. DORSEY moved to amend the said section by striking out in the second line the word "district," and inserting "city," and in the first line after the word "disqualification," inserting "resignation," and in the fourth line by inserting the word "such," between the words "more," and "qualified."

Mr. BROWN suggested to Mr. DORSEY to insert "city" instead of "district," in the second line.

Mr. DORSEY accepted the suggestion.

And the amendment was agreed to.

Mr. DORSEY then moved further to amend said section by striking out from the word "issued," in the fifth line, to the end of said section, and inserting in lieu thereof, the following:

"By the Speaker of the House of Delegates or President of the Senate, as the case may be, for the election of another person in his place, and in case of such resignation or refusal to act, being communicated in writing to the Governor, by the person making it, or such death occur during the legislative recess, and more than ten days before its termination, it shall be the duty of the Governor, to issue a warrant of election to supply the vacancy thus created in the same manner that the said Speaker or President might have done during the session of the legislature, of which election not less than ten days notice shall be given, exclusive of the day of the publication of the notice, and of the day of election; provided, however, that unless a meeting of the General Assembly may intervene, the election thus ordered to fill such vacancy shall be held on the day of the ensuing election for delegates and senators."

Mr. D. said, his object was to give to the Governor the power of ordering elections, when the parties elected, died, or resigned. But in the other cases—such as disqualifications, removals, &c.—it seemed to him that the legislature was the proper branch to decide upon such cases.

The amendment was agreed to.

And the section, as thus amended, was adopted.

Mr. DORSEY moved a reconsideration of the vote by which the thirty-first section of the report had been adopted.

The vote was reconsidered.

Mr. DORSEY moved to amend the said section by striking out the words "the general," and inserting the words "their elections."

Mr. D. said, that he made this motion in accordance with what had been sanctioned by the House in some of the preceding articles of the report.

The amendment was agreed to.

The question recurring on the section as amended;

Mr. JOHN NEWCOMER expressed his desire to offer a substitute for the section.

Whilst Mr. N. was preparing the substitute,

The section was informally passed over.

Mr. DORSEY now moved to reconsider the vote by which the thirty-third section of the report had been adopted.

Mr. D. explained that he made this motion with a view so to amend it, as to make more definite the crimes for which persons should be excluded from voting, or holding office, &c.; and also that the Convention should itself exercise powers which were appropriately their own, instead of leaving their exercise to the Legislature.

The question was taken on the motion to reconsider, and by yeas 22, noes 36,

The Convention refused to re-consider the vote.

So the amendment of Mr. DORSEY was not entertained.

MOTIONS TO RE-CONSIDER.

Mr. MORGAN, in pursuance of the motion he had yesterday given, moved to amend the twenty-second rule by inserting after the word "re-considered," in the fourth line, the words "on the same day."

Mr. M. stated that, after reflection, he had decided to offer the amendment in the form in which he now presented it, instead of that which he had yesterday indicated.

After some explanations between Messrs. MORGAN and BROWN,

The question was taken and the amendment was agreed to.

So the rule was amended accordingly.

THE LEGISLATIVE DEPARTMENT.

The Convention then passed to the orders of the day, and resumed the consideration of the report of the committee on the Legislative Department of the Government.

The Convention resumed the consideration of the thirty-first section (which had been informally laid over.)

Mr. JOHN NEWCOMER, pursuant to the notice he had given, now moved to strike out the said section and insert the following:

"The members of the Legislature shall receive three dollars per diem, as a compensation for their services, and the sum of one dollar for every ten miles they shall travel, once going to and once returning from their place of meeting, on the most usual route. No book or other printed matter not appertaining to the business of the session shall be subscribed for, for the use of the members or be distributed among them."

Mr. MITCHELL called for a division of the question—which was ordered.

And the question was first on striking out.

Mr. JOHN NEWCOMER asked the yeas and nays, which were ordered, and being taken, resulted as follows:

Affirmative—Messrs. Mitchell, Bell, Sappington, Stephenson, Nelson, Thawley, Hardcastle, Fiery, Neill, John Newcomer, Harbine, Michael Newcomer, Slicer and Parke—14.

Negative—Messrs. Chapman, Pres't., Morgan, Blakistone, Dent, Hopewell, Ricaud, Lee, Chambers of Kent, Donaldson, Dorsey, Wells, Sellman, Weems, Bond, Jenifer, Buchanan, Welch, Chandler, Ridgely, Lloyd, Colston, James U. Dennis, Crisfield, Phelps, Chambers of Cecil, Miller, McLane, Grason, Wright, McMaster, Hearn, Fooks, Jacobs, Thomas, Shriver, Gaither, Biser, McHenry, Gwinn, Brent of Baltimore city, Sherwood of Baltimore city, Presstman, Ware, Kilgour, Brewer, Waters, Weber, Hollyday, Fitzpatrick, Shower, and Brown—51.

So the Convention refused to strike out the section.

Mr. Stephenson moved to amend the said section by adding, at the end thereof, the words "at the expense of the State."

Mr. Chambers, of Kent, had no objection to the amendment, he said, but suggested that the object proposed to be effected, and which he desired to see effected, would be accomplished by the language as it now stood in the section.

Mr. Stephenson submitting, he said, to the better judgment of the gentleman from Kent, (Mr. Chambers,) withdrew his amendment.

Mr. Presstman moved to amend the said section by inserting after the word "law," where it occurs in the second line, the following:

"And that each county of the State and the city of Baltimore, shall defray the per diem and mileage of the members of the General Assembly elected, by said county or city, in a manner to be provided by law.

The amendment was rejected.

Some conversation followed, on a suggestion made by Mr. Chambers, of Kent, as to the construction of the section as it read with the words "the general," stricken out under the motion of Mr. Dorsey.

Mr. Phelps moved a re-consideration of the vote adopting the amendment, and

The question being on agreeing thereto;

Mr. Thomas suggested to the gentleman from Anne Arundel, [Mr. Dorsey,] to insert, in lieu of the word "general," in the fourth line, the words "for Senators and Delegates."

Mr. Dorsey accepted the suggestion.

No question had been taken on the amendment, when

Mr. Grason moved to amend the said 31st section by striking out the first four lines in said section to the word "thereof" inclusive, and inserting in lieu thereof the following:

"The Senators and Delegates shall receive a per piem of four dollars, and such mileage as may be allowed by law."

Mr. Grason expressed his conviction that great advantage would result, if the *per diem* of the members of the Legislature should be fixed by constitutional provision. It was a perpetual theme of debate in the Legislature, and much valuable time was consumed by it. For his own part, he had always found that those gentlemen who were the most loud and earnest in favor of the reduction of the pay, were as glad to receive it as any others. [Laughter.] Four dollars a day was but a small compensation; and if it was reduced to three, members would either have to leave Annapolis without paying their bills, or draw on their private resources.

The President stated that the amendment of the gentleman from Queen Anne's (Mr. Grason,) was not now in order, the amendment of the gentleman from Anne Arundel, (Mr. Dorsey,) being before the Convention.

Mr. Dorsey waived his amendment for the present, to allow the gentleman from Queen Anne's to offer his.

So the question was on the amendment of Mr. Grason.

On a suggestion made by Mr. John Newcomer, in relation to mileage,

Mr. Grason modified his amendment so as to make it read "and the mileage now allowed by law."

Mr. Brown suggested that it would be better to leave the subject to the discretion of the Legislature, to act as the facilities and changes in the mode of travel might render proper.

Mr. Grason again modified his amendment in accordance with this suggestion.

The question was then taken,

And the amendment was agreed to.

Mr. Grason moved further to amend the said 31st section, by inserting in the fifth line, after the words "shall be," the words "purchased or."

The amendment was agreed to.

The question then recurred on the adoption of the section as amended.

Mr. Harbine moved to reconsider the vote of the Convention on the amendment offered by Mr. Grason, and just adopted, for the purpose of offering the following amendment:

Strike out the words "such mileage as may be allowed by law," and insert in lieu thereof "the sum of one dollar for every ten miles they shall travel in going to, and once returning from, their place of meeting, on the most usual route."

Mr. H., in explanation, said, that this was the language adopted in the Constitution of the State of New York, and of a number of the Western States, that had recently formed new Constitutions. The same reason which applied to fixing the *per diem*, applied also to the mileage.

Mr. Blakistone said he should vote against the proposition. The gentleman from Washington, (Mr. Harbine,) who had introduced it, was one of the favored few. That gentleman had a rail road to travel on. Other gentlemen had steamboat communication. But in his, (Mr. B.'s,) section there was neither rail road nor steamboat, and they had to avail themselves of any means they could, to get here—omnibusses—wagons—go-carts, or any thing else. And the amendment would operate very unjustly upon them.

Mr. John Dennis had voted, he said, against this, because he thought that the language of the section, as it stood, was most appropriate. He alluded to the fluctuations which might take place in the value of money, so that the sum of four dollars a day, which might be enough at one time, might not be so at another; and he thought that the whole subject ought to be left to the representatives of the people. As to t he s u ffic ency or insufficiency of the compensation, he had not a word say. It was an electioneering hobby at home, and if the calibre of any man was so slight that he could not stand a shot on this matter, he ought to stay at home.

Mr. GRASON argued that it would be impossible for the Legislature to modify the *per diem* of members according to the various fluctuations in the value of stocks or in the supposed value of money. He declared, that his only object in the amendment, was to take away the opportunity and excuse for popular harangues upon the subject of saving the people's money by reducing the pay of their representatives. He knew something of the people of the State of Maryland; and whilst they were opposed to the expenditure of money for useless or extravagant purposes, yet they were willing to pay a full and sufficient compensation to their public servants. In the city of Annapolis, it was impossible for a man to live like a gentleman for less than three or four dollars a day. He was in favor of fixing the sum at four dollars a day, that being the usual compensation; that amount, he believed, was satisfactory to the people. But, he repeated, his main object was to get rid of the debates.

Mr. BUCHANAN said that he always listened with pleasure to the remarks of the gentleman from Queen Anne's, (Mr. Grason,) and never failed to derive instruction whenever that gentleman addressed the Convention. He, (Mr. B.,) concurred entirely with him, that the *per diem* should be fixed in the Constitution. But there was a good deal of reason in what had fallen from the gentleman from Washiugton, (Mr. Harbine,) in relation to mileage.

His friend from Queen Anne's, (Mr. Grason,) anticipated that there might be, as there had hitherto been, debates in the Legislature on the subject of *per diem*. The gentleman, by his amendment, had disposed of one of the bones of contention, by providing that the *per diem* should be fixed in the Constitution. But how was it in relation to mileage? That was left to the law making power. This opened the door wide; discussions would arise upon this which would embrace the whole subject matter, and thus we should find ourselves in the same difficulty. He would vote for the amendment in any event; but he would be glad if the gentleman from the coinage of his brain, would submit a proposition which would enable the Convention to act upon the subject of mileage, so as to leave the Legislature no room for discussion.

Mr. GRASON said, the two subjects were different. The *per diem* might easily be fixed with relation to a general estimate of the value of money. But as to mileage, the circumstances which should control it, were constantly changing. The gentleman from St. Mary's, (Mr. Blakistone,) had furnished some useful information on the subject.

He, (Mr. G.,) thought it would be very difficult to fix the mileage in the Constitution. It would be better to leave it to the legislature. The question of mileage was not so likely to be introduced into the House of Delegates as a topic of debate, as the question of *per diem* was.

Mr. HARBINE dissented from this opinion, and appealed to our legislative history, to show that the idea that mileage would not be the subject matter of debate, was not borne out. He referred to some of the new States—Iowa, Texas, &c.—in whose Constitutions such a provision had been inserted to show, that, if it was practicable there, where the facilities of communication must necessarily be less than with us, it was also practicable here.

He shewed that it was not quite so easy a matter for gentlemen from his county, (Washington,) to travel hither as the gentleman from St. Mary's (Mr. Blakistone,) supposed. He admitted, that there might be isolated cases, like that of the gentleman, in which such a rule would bear hard.

This, he, (Mr. H.,) regretted; but it was a result inseparable from the operation of all general rules. He insisted that the mileage was higher than it should be, and that it ought to be reduced. He declared that this was no Buncombe movement, and that every single reason which would justify the insertion of a constitutional provision, fixing the *per diem*, applied with equal force to the mileage. If ten cents was not enough, say fifteen. But, whatever the mileage was, let it be fixed.

Mr. KILGOUR said, he thought the matter too small to be the subject of debate in this Convention. At all events, it was too small for him to appreciate. Probably, he might never be able to do so, until he took a lesson in the Washington county school of economy. As to this sum being sufficient, it might be perhaps for those who traveled the distance once only.

But for himself, he had some attractions at home, [laughter,] and was glad at times to escape from the dull, tread-mill round of labors, which their duties imposed.

From first to last, efforts had been made in this Convention, to fix upon the people of the State of Maryland, a character for parsimony—nay, for actual meanness—which did not belong to them. The people, themselves, would disown it. It was unworthy of them. They were enlightened and liberal-minded, and did not always desire to weigh the services of their public agents, to the nicety of a hair. If it were so, probably some gentlemen in the legislature, perhaps, even some gentlemen in this Convention, would be found to receive more than they deserved.

Every public servant should be paid a just and fair compensation. The people of Maryland were willing to pay it, and those who desired to cry down their character in this respect, were doing that for which the people themselves would not thank them. He moved that the amendment be laid upon the table.

The PRESIDENT stated that the amendment of the gentleman from Washington, (Mr. Harbine,) was not in order, without a motion to reconsider the amendment, which had just been engrafted on the bill.

Mr. HARBINE moved a reconsideration of the vote.

The question was taken, and

The Convention refused to reconsider.

The PRESIDENT suggested to Mr. HARBINE, that he could accomplish his object, (i. e. to have a vote taken on his amendment,) by moving it as an additional section.

Some conversation followed.

Mr. HARBINE said, that the ideas of some gentlemen were very much inflated; and, that if there was any meanness in such a proposition, it was at least one which other States of the Union had not thought it beneath their dignity to adopt. He was not, however, tenacious about it. He had introduced it for the purpose of arresting debate in the legislature. He would, therefore, withdraw it, not because he thought the proposition too small to engage the attention of the Convention, but because he was not tenacious enough to adhere to it.

So the amendment was withdraw.

Some conversation followed on a point of order, between Mr. PHELPS and the CHAIR.

Mr. DENT moved to amend said thirty-first section, by striking out the last paragraph in said section, from the word "thereof," in the fourth line.

The motion was rejected.

The section, as amended, was then adopted.

CLERGYMEN, ETC.

Mr. THOMAS called the attention of the Convention to the fact, that, on a former day, the ninth section of the report of the legislative committee, had been informally laid over, owing to the unavoidable absence of the gentleman from Baltimore county, (Mr. Chandler.) That gentleman being now in his seat, he, [Mr. T.] would move that the Convention resume the consideration of the section.

The motion was agreed to.

The section was read as follows :

Sec. 9th. No Priest, Clergyman or Teacher of any religious persuasion, society or sect, and no person holding any civil office of profit under this State, except Justices of the Peace, shall be capable of having a seat in the General Assembly.

Mr. CHANDLER said :

Mr. President—Permit me, through you sir, to thank this Convention for the courtesy which they have been pleased to extend to me in deferring action upon this article until my return. Their kind feelings thus manifested towards one as humble as I feel myself to be, I can assure them is duly appreciated.

I propose sir, to strike out all in the ninth article, that refers to ministers, priests, and teachers of religion, as entirely unnecessary and unjust.

Sir, I offer this amendment with no little embarrassment.

First, because, having been detained from my seat in this body for the last two weeks, by serious illness in my family, I have had no opportunity whatever, for making the necessary preparation, to support by proper argument the amendment which I now propose.

Secondly, Because, of the unnecessary jealousy entertained by many in reference to ministers of the gospel.

Thirdly, Last, though not least, the strong feelings, prejudices, and talents, arrayed on the other side of this question.

But feeling, as I do, that my position is just, I shall, though I may stand alone, advocate this amendment.

Mr. President, I believe, in these United States, and in the States separately, we profess to admire a Democratic form of Government?

Sir, what are we to understand by a Democratic form of government?

It guarantees, if I mistake not, *equal rights* and *privileges*, not to a *favored few*, but to the *whole people*. Yet the article under consideration proposes *deliberately*, to disfranchise a very large and respectable class of our fellow-citizens.

Sir, if this self-denying, and self-sacrificing class of our fellow-citizens are to be cut off without ceremony from the right to participate in the affairs of Government, then I trust, that in your wisdom and magnanimity, you will introduce some organic provision in the Constitution, by which they shall forever hereafter, be exempt from the burthen of taxation, to support a Government, in which you thus solemnly declare they have no *right* to participate.

But sir, it seems strange, that from every quarter of this House, we hear it proclaimed in language beautiful and eloquent, by honorable gentlemen of profound erudition—"Equal rights and privileges to all." Then after this flourish of trumpets in behalf of popular rights, we see those same gentlemen calmly uniting their strength, to blot from political existence a numerous and influential class of our fellow-citizens, as wholly unworthy of all confidence and even dangerous to the Commonwealth.

Have gentlemen considered that twenty States of this Union have never adopted this obnoxious and oppressive provision in their Constitutions, and that another has since stricken it from their organic law—making in all, twenty-one States that, at the present time, have no such proscriptive measure. And yet we have heard of no internal commotion, or threatened danger to these States. On the contrary they get on as prosperously and as harmoniously, as States which have adopted this anti-republican provision.

But, sir, what great offence, what high crime have this class of our fellow-citizens committed, that they should be deprived of one of the dearest privileges of American born citizen—that of eligibility to office? Have they committed high treason? Have they been guilty of highway robbery? Are they murderers? No, sir; none of these crimes have been alleged against them; still in the opinion of the honorable committee, who made and presented this report, they are guilty of a crime, which should forever disfranchise them as citizens of this enlightened Commonwealth?

Sir, what is that crime? It is this. They have bowed in humble adoration to the God who made them; they have believed in his Son Jesus

Christ as their Saviour, and having drunk at this pure, unadulterated fountain of true happiness, they have ventured to point their fellow men to the same chrystal fountain. In other words, they have ventured to teach the way of life and salvation. And for this offence they must be stricken from the political firmament and consigned to eternal oblivion, so far as all preferment is concerned, in the civil government.

Mr. President, a little more than eighteen hundred years ago, the lawyers and doctors assumed the responsibility of casting reflections upon the Saviour of the world. They charged him with being a wine bibber and a glutton, the friend of publicans and sinners. The Saviour himself said, "If they do these in the green tree, (meaning himself,) what will they not do in the dry?" (referring to his followers.) "As they have despised me, so will they also despise you."

Sir, the lawyers, doctors, scribes and Pharisees did not cease to exist with that age; but to the prosent time they say to Christ's ministers, "Stand aside, we are more holy than thou," or at any rate, beyond all controversy, we are more *worthy* to fill all civil offices; *you* are not to be *trusted*; that is a settled polnt.

But, Mr. President. perhaps you may think that I am under the impresslon that honorable members upon this floor, who favor this oppressive measure, and who wish, by constitutional provision, to disfranchise a large portion of our fellow citizens, are wholly destitute of principle. No, sir! In the language of one of Virginia's distinguished statesmen, John Randolph, they have *seven* principles at least, *the five loaves and two fishes;* nor are they destitute of generosity; they divide, with a good grace, the five loaves and two fishes amongst *themselves*, and then write in large capitals the words, *equal rights and privileges to all;* and this inscription, when written, is nailed up to every sign post along the road that leads to higher office and and a greater division of the spoils. And these words, *equal rtghts and previleges to all*, are trumpeted forth, to deceive that class of our fellow citizens who are not even permitted to gather up the fragments or partake of the crumbs that fall from the lordly tables of those who consider *themselves worthy* to rule.

Sir, this prescribed class of our citizens, are not ao stupid as not to see through such deception. They know their rights, and if they do not maintain them, it is because they love peace, and had rather suffer loss than engage in contention and strife.

But I may be told that ministers are engaged in a higher and more noble calling, and that they should not leave their profession to make laws. Very well! But is this any reason why you should say in your Constitution ihat they are *unworthy* of a lower calling? that they have no *right* to participate in the affairs of government? Why, the thing is absurd, perfectly absurd!

You might tell me with the same propriety that the man who has no knowledge of letters, though he have other qualifications, ought not to be elected President, and therefore some provision should be introduced in the Constitution of the United States to render such an one ineligible.

Sir, I ask if this would not be a direct reflection upon the sovereign people themselves. Are the people not capable of being their own guardians? Why then say to them, you shall never elect a President who cannot write his name? Why say to them you shall not do that which they never intended to do. In proscribing ministers of the gospels you are in effect saying to the people, you are not capable of choosing for yourselves; we have the matter in hand; we will choose for you.

But why single out this particular profession? Why not as well proscribe lawyers? Do they not leave their profession and their clients to suffer? while they come to the Legislature to engage in law making? Why not proscribe doctors? Do they not leave their patients to linger and die while they are in the Legislative Halls? Why not proscribe the farmer? But for the farmer *all professions* would languish and die. And is he to be taken from his lawful pursuit to engage in the work of Legislation? Why sir, this eternal hatred to ministers or teachers of religion? Why should they be proscribed and crushed to the earth more than any other profession? Why, Mr. President, according to the hypothesis contended for on the other side, that every man should stick to his profession, then, sir, you ought not to occupy the honorable position you do, as the presiding officer of this body, nor should you ever think of coming to the Legislature, however much your constituents might desire it. But as a *General*, sir, you should be training soldiers *for the war, which we may expect in a few years with Great Britain.* The language used playfully by the honorable gentleman over the way, (Governor Grason,) on yesterday may yet be prophetic.

Sir, the fact cannot be disguised that the Stars and Stripes must soon wave over Cuba! Then we shall have *war* with *England, France, Russia, Prussia, Austria, all the world and the rest of mankind, and the Eastern Shore of Maryland.*

Mr. President, let us look for a few moments calmly at this subject. As you pass along your streets you see a poor unfortunate man in the gutter, beastly intoxicated. That man is eligible to the office of Governor! On the other side you see another equally intoxicated, who feels called upon, by every consideration to *defend his most sacred honor;* and for this purpose measures off the proper distance, and *fights a duel with the lamp-post for flying around* the *corner* and *knocking* him *down*, when he was *passing peaceably by. That man* is *eligible* to a seat in the *General Assembly!*

But walking on a little farther, we meet two gentlemen passing along accompanied by a little army of bright eyes and happy faces. They interfere with no one, but quietly proceed towards the house of God. Their mission is one of peace and good will to men. Let us inquire who they are. They are the minister and the Sabbath school teacher, both *proscribed* as *unworthy* to participate in the affairs of civil government.

In conclusion, Mr. President, permit me to say that I have not offered this amendment, or these remarks from any ambitious motives. I am here now, sir, not by my own choice, but by the earnest solicitations of a *noble* and *generous* constituency.

I do not think that ministers ought to neglect their flocks to go the Legislature; but neither do I think, that you have the right to *disfranchise* them as *free-born American citizens*. Sir, it is the *principle* for which I contend. Ministers have *rights* in common with other citizens. And now sir, I have discharged what I have conceived to be my duty, very imperfectly, it is true. I thank you sir, and through you the honorable body, for the respectful attention with which they have listened to my remarks.

Mr. Jenifer disclaimed any intention to enter into the argument on this question. But he thought the gentleman from Baltimore county was mistaken in some of his views. The provision in the Constitution does not exclude clergymen, more than others who fill civil offices, from sitting in the Legislature. All persons who fill civil offices are equally excluded. There was therefore nothing oppressive in this exclusion. A minister of the gospel has a high mission; his functions are of a class which lift him above the ordinary business of political life; and it must lessen the usefulness of his position and distract his duties when he enters into political strife. The gentleman says the ministers ought to be relieved from taxation. He, (Mr. J.,) did not know that clergymen were taxed.

Mr. Chandler. They were. His tax last year amounted to twenty dollars on his property.

Mr. Jenifer. Aye, for property—not as a clergyman. If the idea of the gentleman, that property should be exempt from taxation were carried out, there would be a speedy falling off of the revenue for the support of the State. Any man who desired to escape the payment of taxes would only have to join the class of privileged persons and he would escape.

Of all forms of government, that which comprised a religious element, was the most to be depricated. Where religion had become united with political rule, there had always been the greatest amount of tyranny and despotism, and the least possible exercise of freedom. The moment you permit the ministers of religion to assume political power, their whole character is changed. Whilst in the exercise of their religious duties exclusively, they command the respect and veneration of all good men, no matter of of what denomination; transfer them to the arena of party contest, let them mingle in the heated contests of the day, and they cease to be the humble and christian dispensers of those blessings, which belong to their high mission. The Legislature is no place for ministers of the gospel. The pulpit is the appropriate sphere for their teachings.

Mr. J. said, it would not be understood that he, by any means, objected to them or any other citizen being members of a Convention like this to frame a Constitution for the State. He was gratified to see the reverend gentleman from Baltimore county, here in this body, and to receive the benefit of his advice, and if all clergymen would conduct themselves in the dignified, charitable and unexceptionable manner, as he has done, his, [Mr. J's,] objection would be greatly lessened. But this cannot be expected; religious and political professions are incompatible amidst the frailty of human nature; and the high respect he entertained for the clergy, would prevent him from permitting them to be placed in a situation, where their usefulness would be impaired.

Mr. Chandler made some further remarks in which he complained, that while other professions were permitted to hold seats in the legislature, by a solemn declaration, clergymen are disqualified. He thought, as a matter of conscience, that it was better that ministers of the gospel should not become members of the legislature; they have higher occupations—occupations which demand the entire devotion of their time and talents. But his objection was to the adoption of the principle of disqualification in the Constitution.

The great Apostle of the Gentiles said, all things may be lawful, but all things may not be expedient. The clergy do not desire to be placed in a position in which they are denied the rights and privileges of American citizens. He perfectly agreed with the gentleman from Charles, (Mr. Jenifer,) as to the impropriety of a union between Church and State. Against such union the clergy were united; and they now complained, that, by this very provision, the government is interfering with the clergy, and will not leave them alone. He denied the statement that where religious governments prevailed the worst consequences follow. It was true that under the mask of religion, those who are falsely called religious, have persecuted and destroyed their fellow creatures, but these are not members of the true christian church. It would be as reasonable to repudiate the metallic currency of the United States, because some of it has been counterfeited, and to close all our banks and refuse to receive silver and gold coins. While we affect to leave all men free, to oppress none, and to extend to every one liberty to worship God according to the dictates of his own conscience, we, in the same instrument, disqualify all who are the ministers of religion, for the enjoyment of the rights which all other citizens enjoy.

Mr. Jenifer said,

In reply to the worthy gentleman's remark, "that those religious governments which persecuted, did not belong to the true christian church," he did not know what the gentleman calls the true christian church. But, if he would go back a little into the history of the church, he would find from its earliest period to the present day, that all denominations were alike, when political power was placed in their hands. Presbyterians, Roman Catholics, Episcopaleans, down to the Mormons, all had been guilty of the greatest oppression and tyranny. One of the greatest curses inflicted on mankind, had been by religious fanaticism, united with the power of political rule. And even in our day, in this glorious land of freedom, that spirit attempts to ride over the laws and Constitution.

Mr. CHANDLER said, that was fanaticism, not religion.

Mr. JENIFER. It was religious fanaticism, and the same spirit which seeks to justify a violation of the Constitution of the United States, by a superior law of conscience.

If any religious sect had a right to complain it was the Quakers and other friends, conscientiously scrupulous of bearing arms. They pay a tax for carrying on war against their conscience.

In the section of the bill now under consideration, and which the reverend gentleman has moved to strike out, judges, clerks and all other civil officers, are placed upon the same footing with clergymen. It is not deemed consistent with a proper discharge of their respective duties that they should hold seats in the legislature. There is no exclusion for conscience sake. It is because the positions they have assumed, of their own free will, render the discharge of legislative duties incompatible.

Mr. CHANDLER called attention to what had taken place in the State of Rhode Island, referring to the character and conduct of Roger Williams, who was the first minister and Governor of the State, and who was the first to proclaim the doctrine of an unfettered conscience and of the right to worship as they might think right. Religion and fanaticism are as opposite to each other as night is to day. He presumed the gentleman had reference to the abolitionists, who have taken leave of religion and morality, and of common sense also. They had shaken hands with common sense. If the church were made up of such persons as these, he would be willing to quit it. He regarded the abolitionists as the greatest curse of our country.

Mr. CHAMBERS desired, in few words, to assign the reasons, or some of them, which would influence his vote, and he believed many others. He did not exactly accord with the gentleman from Charles, (Mr. Jenifer,) in his apprehensions of religious despotism. He did not, however, mean to interpose between the contending parties on the subject of persecution, &c. The gentleman before him, (Mr. Chandler,) had made the most of his case. He had asked "if they were excluded from seats in the legislature, he and his clerical brethren, because they were murderers or drunkards, or were they hated because they preached the Gospel?" Why, does the gentleman forget that we judges are in the same category? Does he, or can he, for a moment suppose that because a man is a judge, *therefore* he is considered a murderer or drunkard, or becomes hateful? Certainly he cannot. The reason is obvious, the one station is supposed to be inconsistent with the other. He regretted to find the gentleman disdain to keep company with the judges.

Mr. CHANDLER, (in his seat,) said he certainly did not.

Mr. CHAMBERS. They were all in the same sentence, each equally excluded and for similar reasons. The contemplation of the Constitution was, that their peculiar avocation was not calculated to qualify them to fill the office of a legislator as well as others. The people had a right to select, as their agents in different departments, those best qualified to fill the various stations assigned to them. An astronomer would not go to a ploughman to assist him in calculating an eclipse or the distance to a star—nor would a farmer apply to an astronomer to plough his field or seed his grain. "Every man to his trade," was an old rule and a good one. He supposed it quite obvious, that the appropriate duties of a clergyman were altogether unlike those of a politician, and that it is proper to encourage the usefulness of each, at all events not to do anything calculated to destroy their usefulness. He then described what he regarded as the appropriate duties of a minister of the Gospel of peace and salvation. He professes to have a mission from his Divine master—a mission of love and charity. His great duty is to contend against the lusts of the world—he renounces its pomps and vanities—he seeks honor of God, not of men, and lays up his treasure in Heaven, not on earth. His high and holy office is with the souls of men, not with their political favors; he is sacrificed to the world and its honors and its emoluments, and they are sacrificed to him. His whole object and aim is to lead sinners to the fountain of eternal life. Would you arrest such a man in his holy calling and place him in a legislative hall, where every man is a political antagonist to one portion, and a political partizan to the rest—amongst men whose leading motive is to acquire worldly distinguishment and preferment, and to acquire them at the expense of the political destruction of contending parties—amongst those whose passions and prejudices are continually kept alive by the anticipation of earthly honors and emoluments, and whetted by continual opposition and frequent defeat? Political assemblies, composed of party men—and such are generally those which occupy our legislative halls—present the least possible aid in the cultivation of the cardinal christian graces of love and charity to our fellow man, to say nothing of their influence on the "first and great commandment." Why then take the messenger of "peace on earth and good will to man," to place him where his labors would be confined, not to conversions from sin to holiness, but from one political doctrine to another? Ministers who rightly appreciated their condition and their duties, never would make these temporal honors and profits an object of pursuit.

Mr. CHANDLER here said, the gentleman from Kent and himself agreed on that point. *He* also thought that ministers should not come to the legislature, but should pursue the work to which they are called. But he desired that it should be left to the people at the ballot box, to say if they would elect ministers, and to the ministers, if elected, to act according to the dictates of their own consciences. What he was opposed to, was, the insertion of a disqualification in the organic law as a principle.

Mr. CHAMBERS resumed. The gentleman then admits, that the removal of the disqualification would not introduce into the legislatute those ministers who have a just and conscientious appreciation of their religious duties and obligations. If, therefore, he should succeed in his amendment, the effect is to be, that we admit those only who are either ignorant, or regardless of their solemn vows and duties.

Now, would the gentleman, or would the Convention, be willing to put into the Constitution a provision, directing in terms that ministers, unworthy of the character they bear, and none others, should be considered proper candidates for these responsible offices? Certainly not. Then why should they adopt a provision, the necessary and practical effect of which, would be precisely the same? The gentleman had used one expression, the force of which he could not have duly considered. He had deplored the exclusion of his clerical brethren from the participation of the "loaves and fishes"—the significant expression by which John Randolph defined office and emolument.

Did the gentleman mean to intimate that ministers of the gospel were to be influenced by such sordid motives, as to neglect the spiritual interests of immortal souls to secure the paltry sum of four dollars a day? Or did he suppose the Convention capable of being influenced by a desire to secure it for laymen exclusively? Surely not.

He would remark, in answer to what the gentleman had said about lawyers, that it would have been more candid, if he had stated, what he and every other minister must know, that the persons alluded to in the texts he has referred to, were "Doctors of Divinity"—teachers of Divine law—not such persons as are now known by the term lawyers.

Having passed his whole life at the bar and bench, he might be permitted to add a word in defence of lawyers as a body. He would remark to the gentleman, that he who assailed them would be apt to get a hornet's nest about him in the first place, and would fail to enlist public sentiment in the next. There were, undoubtedly, bad men in the profession. So there were bad men in every profession and department of life. But as a body—as a class—they were entitled to as much respect as any other class of citizens. It was, perhaps, not saying more than history and fact would justify, to assert that they were the authors and effective promoters of all the great political movements which had ameliorated the condition of man, in his civil and political relations; the pioneers in all the great struggles for freedom against tyranny. It was, then, so far from being true, that this long standing provision, which excludes preachers from the legislative hall, originated in the want of proper regard and respect for the ministerial office, that the motive was to preserve it pure and blameless.

It was asked, why not protect them? We did give them the protection best suited to their wants—protection against the vices, the snares, the temptations incident to political life. We have too much need for their valuable services, in restraining our own violations of the pure precepts which would make saints of sinners, too much interest to have them possess the virtues they should teach to us, to expose them to the contaminating influences of a life of politics. Their duty is to advocate the interests of their master, not their own—to warm our hearts with love to God, not devotion men—to inspire us with hopes of heaven, not of office—to minister to the poor, the humble, the sick, the dying, and to talk to them of the vanity of all things temporal; not to company with the rich, the great, the influential men of the world, and court their aid, to robe themselves in the glittering baubles of this world's honor, or fill their pockets with the mammon of unrighteousness.

Mr. Chandler, in reply, adverting to what the gentleman from Kent had said on the subject of cutting the clergy horizontally, said the gentleman had stated that the bad ministers would be thrown on one side of the line, and the good on the other, if his amendment should prevail. But he thought the argument did not make against the proposition, because, if the amendment did not prevail, the clergyman who was not conscientious about the matter, could now, if elected, present his credentials to the church and take his seat, because then he would have a right to it. He could not but be struck with the affectionate regard which the gentleman from Kent expressed for ministers of religion. He said they stood on too high a platform. He presumed that the gentleman supposed they must wear long faces and a sanctimonious aspect, which would be outraged by their association with members of the Legislature. And in what light did the gentleman place legislators? It would appear that they are all covered with mud and dust, and he would not let us come into the body and mix with such corruption. He certainly felt some surprise at the acknowledgment. But he would beg leave to remind the gentleman from Kent, that those who formed the Constitution of the United States did not feel the force of such scruples as the committee who prepared the Legislative Report did, on this subject. That Constitution was formed by some of the wisest men the country had ever produced, yet it contained no such disqualifying provision. And although it was not of frequent occurrences, it was well known that ministers of religion had had seats in Congress; and, if he was not mistaken, there was one, or perhaps two ministers in Congress, at this time.

Mr. Chambers. Yes, there is Mr. Palfrey.

Mr. Chandler. He is an abolitionist.

Mr. Chandler now modified his amendment so as to strike out to the word "and" in the second line of the section.

Mr. Buchanan said:

Before the vote was taken on this proposition he desired to put a few questions, and to make a remark or two to his friend and colleague, (Mr. Chandler,) for whom he took the opportunity to say, he entertained the highest personal regard.

It so happened, said Mr. B., that during the address of his friend, he, [Mr. B.,] was so circumstanced, (being in the temporary occupancy of the Chair,) as to render it impossible for him with propriety to put a question to his friend, which, if at the time he could have put, would have saved him the necessity of saying any thing at present.

His colleague had remarked, that some eighteen hundred years ago, the doctors and the lawyers persecuted the Saviour.

Now, as to the doctors, said Mr. B., whether doctors of divinity as was intimated by the gentleman from Kent, or doctors of medicine, as was charged by his colleague—he had nothing to say—no defence to make. He was uninformed on the subject; and besides, the doctors are generally able to take care of themselves. But as to the lawyers, so gallantly defended by his friend from Kent, [Mr. Chambers,] he, [Mr. B.,] desired to know of his colleague, who was Joseph of Arimathea? He, [Mr. B.,] was aware that his colleague was an accomplished Bible historian, and he called upon him out of the fullness of his biblical knowledge to instruct the Convention in this—who was Joseph of Arimathea?

He was, (said Mr. B.,) a lawyer—a counsellor. Who was it, he would ask his colleague—who, in that dread hour, when the sun was darkened, and the vail of the temple was rent in twain, and the earth did quake, and the graves were opened—that stood firmly and faithfully by the side of his crucified Redeemer? It was Joseph of Arimathea, a lawyer,

Who was it when all the followers of the Saviour had fled in alarm, saving only his mother and a few faithful women—whilst the pierced body still hung upon the accursed cross—that went boldly unto Pilate and craved the body of his God? It was Joseph of Arimathea, a lawyer.

Who was it that took down the body of the Saviour from the cross at the risk of his own life, wrapped it in fine linen, and laid it in his own new sepulchre, hewn out in the rock? It was Joseph of Arimathea, a lawyer. Beware then, after the high example, how you traduce the lawyers as a class.

These are the questions in kindness I desired to put, and these the remarks I desired to make.

Mr. Jenifer briefly congratulated the gentleman from Baltimore county, for his research into the history of the lawyers, which had carried him back nearly to the commencement of the world.

Mr. Bell. I rise not to defend the lawyers, but to say a word or two on the subject of physicians. He would not go as far back as his honorable colleague, but if he did, he thought the comparison would not be unfavorable to the physician. He only desired to say a word in reply to his respected colleague on his left, who had addressed the Convention a short time before, and hinted at the impropriety of professional gentlemen neglecting their special duties and engaging in politics. He desired to state a subject within his own knowledge. He was himself a physician of long experience; he had attended, he thought, faithfully to his calling, and to his patients, but it sometimes so happened that he was compelled to leave them, being called off on business for a few days; yet on his return, to his great astonishment he mostly found them improving, he thought faster than if he had been in constant attendance—they having taken the advantage of his absence in recruiting their health. He, therefore, felt no conscientious scruples in leaving his patients, and holding a seat in this body. And he doubted if lawyers and physicians were more frequently absent, whether their clients and patients would be much the losers.

The question was then declared to be on the modified amendment of Mr. Chandler.

Mr. C. asked the yeas and nays,

Which were ordered, and

Being taken, resulted as follows:

Affirmative—Messrs. Bond, Buchanan, Bell, Welch, Chandler, Colston, Fooks, Shriver, Biser, McHenry, Thawley, Stewart of Caroline, Hardcastle, Fiery, John Newcomer, Harbine, Michael Newcomer, Kilgour, Brewer, Waters, Weber and Parke—22.

Negative—Messrs. Chapman, President, Morgan, Blakistone, Dent, Hopewell, Ricaud, Lee, Chambers of Kent, Mitchell, Donaldson, Dorsey, Wells, Sellman. Weems, Merrick, Jenifer, Ridgely, Lloyd, James U. Dennis, Crisfield, Dashiell, Phelps, Constable, Chambers of Cecil, Miller, McLane, Grason, George, Wright, McMaster, Hearn, Jacobs, Gaither, Sappington, Stephenson, Nelson, Gwinn, Sherwood of Baltimore city, Ware, Hollyday, Slicer, Fitzpatrick, Shower and Brown—44.

So the amendment was rejected.

The ninth section was then adopted.

Mr. Merrick moved a reconsideration of the vote on the twenty-first section, (that which relates to loans on the credit of the State,) with a view to offer an amendment, (of which he had heretofore given notice.)

The President, *pro tem.*, (Mr. Blakistone,) finding that notice of a motion to reconsider had been made on a former day by Mr. McHenry, stated that fact.

Mr. McHenry made the motion to reconsider. He did so, he said, with the concurrence of the mover of the amendment, which had been adopted, and of other gentlemen who had voted for it, and with the intention to move, if the motion to reconsider prevailed, that the consideration of the section should be postponed, until after the other sections of the report had been disposed of.

After some conversation,

The question was taken on the motion to reconsider.

But no quorum voted.

The question was again taken.

But no quorum voted.

Mr. Kilgour moved a call of the House.

Mr. Presstman enquired of the Chair, how many members were present?

The Chair replied, fifty-one.

The question was taken on the motion of Mr. Kilgour;

And decided in the negative.

So a call of the Convention was refused.

Mr. Merrick asked the yeas and nays, on the motion to reconsider;

Which were ordered, and

Being taken, resulted as follows:

Affirmative—Messrs. Chapman, President, Morgan, Blakistone, Dent, Hopewell, Ricaud, Chambers of Kent, Mitchell, Donaldson, Dorsey, Wells, Kent, Sellman, Weems, Bond, Merrick, Jenifer, Buchanan, Bell, Colston, James U. Dennis, Crisfield, Phelps, Constable, Chambers of Cecil, Miller, George, Jacobs, Thomas, Shriver, Biser. Sappington, Stephenson, McHenry, Nelson, Thawley, Stewart of Caroline, Gwinn, Presstman, Michael Newcomer, Kilgour, Hollyday, Parke and Brown—44.

Negative—Messrs. Lee, Ridgely, Lloyd, Grason, Wright, McMaster, Fooks, Gaither, Hardcastle, Stewart of Baltimore city, Sherwood of Baltimore city, Ware, Fiery, John Newcomer, Harbine, Brewer, Weber, Slicer, Fitzpatrick, Shower and Cockey—19.

So the vote was reconsided.

Mr. Merrick then moved to amend the said section by adding at the end thereof the following:

"But it shall be competent for the legislature at any time, when it can do so, to pay off its outstanding bonds, or any part thereof, by an issue of other bonds or stocks bearing a less rate of interest and for no greater amount than the amount redeemed or paid off."

Some conversation followed between Messrs. Thomas and Merrick, as to the propriety of laying the section over informally for the present.

Mr. Constable offered the following, as a substitute for the original section:

1. The legislature shall have no power to contract debts or borrow money except to repel invasion or suppress insurrection.

2. They shall have no power to authorise any subscription on the part of the State to the capital stock or shares of any canal, rail road, plank road, turnpike, banking, exchange, insurance, manufacturing or mining corporation, or of any other corporation or association whatsoever; nor shall they invest or embark any of the funds of the State, either directly or indirectly, in any trade, business or adventure of mining, manufacturing, commercial and marine, or of any other description whatsoever.

3. They shall not be authorised to loan the credit of the State, in any form or for any purpose whatsoever.

4. They shall have no power to appropriate money for any purpose, or to any object for which they are not authorised to raise the sum so appropriated by a general State tax.

5. They shall be authorised to impose State taxes for the following purposes, and none other whatsoever: For the defence of the State, payment of the principal and interest of the public debt, to defray the necessary expenses of the government, for the improvement and preservation of the public property, and for the establishment of a uniform system of public schools throughout the State, adequately endowed to educate every white child within its limits.

6. They shall have no power to except from the operation of any law, imposing a general State tax, any other property than that owned by the State, or by a county, city, or other municipal corporation and burial grounds; nor shall they by law or otherwise enter into any contract or other expedient, or devise to exempt, or which shall operate as an exemption or suspension, wholly or partially of any other property, or body corporate, or of any person worth over two hundred dollars, from contribution, rateably and equally to such general tax, according to his or its actual worth in real or personal property.

The consideration of the section was then postponed until Tuesday next.

The thirty-fourth section of the report was then read as follows:

Sec. 34. The General Assembly may confer upon   of the several counties, such powers of local legislation and administration as they may prescribe, provided, however, that all laws conferring such powers shall be general in their nature, and shall extend to all the counties of the State.

Mr. Phelps, moved to amend said section by filling the blank in said section with these words "the Levy court or commissioners of the tax as the case may be."

Mr. John Newcomer moved to insert "the county courts."

Mr. Presstman moved to strike out the section. (It was, he said, wholly impracticable, if intended for the city of Baltimore.)

Mr. John Newcomer withdrew his amendment.

Some explanatory conversation followed, on the part of Messrs. Phelps, Dorsey, Presstman, Chambers, of Kent, Brown and Ridgely.

Mr. Presstman said it seemed to be the general impression of the Convention, that the city of Baltimore was not to be reached by the section. If this was so, he should not press his amendment.

Mr. Phelps withdrew his amendment.

The question then recurred on the motion of Mr. Presstman to strike out the section.

Mr. Gwinn offered an amendment, (not to be found on this day's journal, but which will be found in the proceedings of the succeeding day.) Its general object was to give to the Mayor and City Council of Baltimore the exclusive right to open streets, &c.

Mr. Gwinn briefly explained the necessity of the amendment.

Mr. Presstman said he was more satisfied than ever that the section of the report could not have any application to the city of Baltimore. If so, he would regret to see the amendment of his colleague prevail—not because he was opposed to it, but because it would give the appearance that the whole section was intended to apply to the city of Baltimore.

Mr. Chambers, of Kent, dissented from this view, and did not understand that the same general feature of the law did not apply to the city of Baltimore as well as to other portions of the State.

Mr. GWINN said he could obviate the difficulty suggested by his colleague, as to his, (Mr. G's.,) amendment, in a moment. And he modified his amendment with that view.

Mr. PRESSTMAN suggested to his colleague that the amendment might perhaps be better introduced at another time and in another form.

The object and construction of the section were further explained by Messrs. CHAMBERS, of Kent, PRESSTMAN, DORSEY and GWINN.

Mr. GWINN expressed his intention to insist on the amendment here, because, he said, he knew of no other place in which it could properly be introduced.

But Mr. G., on the suggestion of Mr. PRESSTMAN, decided to offer the amendment as an additional section.

Thereupon, the Convention adjourned until to-morrow at ten o'clock.

SATURDAY, March 1, 1851.

The Convention met at ten o'clock.

Prayer was made by the Rev. Mr. GRIFFITH.

The Roll of the members were called.

LICENSE LAWS.

The PRESIDENT announced the following gentlemen as the members composing the select committee of seven, yesterday ordered to be appointed on the subject of the license laws:

Messrs. DORSEY, HARBINE, FOOKS, WRIGHT, DENT, WEBER, and DASHIELL.

Mr. DORSEY asked to be excused from service. It was usual not to put upon these committees gentlemen who were opposed to the applications. He concurred in part with his friend from Cecil in his opposition. He, (Mr. D.,) thought there should be a general law, and not a separate law for any particular district or neighborhood. As he was opposed to this and could not discharge the duty in such a way as would enable the petitioners to have their case fully considered, he hoped he might be excused from service.

The Convention excused Mr. DORSEY.

Mr. DONALDSON was appointed by the PRESIDENT to supply the vacancy.

THE LEGISLATIVE DEPARTMENT.

The PRESIDENT announced the unfinished business of yesterday, being the report of the committee on the Legislative Department of the Government.

Mr. THOMAS offered the following substitute:

"The General Assembly may provide for the election or appointment of such county officers as may be required, and are not wholly authorised by this Constitution, and prescribe their powers and duties; but their tenure of office, mode of appointment, and the character of their powers and duties shall be uniform throughout the State."

The substitute having been read,

Mr. THOMAS said, he did not want to discuss the amendment. He merely submitted it. He supposed the Convention would forsee that there were many officers whose appointment the Convention would not undertake to prescribe.

Mr. SHRIVER asked the yeas and nays.

Mr. CHAMBERS, of Kent, said he supposed that the question of electing Levy Courts, or that item in the organization of the police of the State now known to some of the counties as Levy Courts, and existing in some form in every county, must at some time be decided upon by the Convention. If there was a settled purpose, as he supposed there was, to have this done by election, why not now say so? The question had to be acted upon, and the action of the Convention was now embarrassed for the want of knowing how these tribunals were to be organised. He did not desire to introduce the question if it would lead to any difficulty. But if there was such a settled purpose on the part of the Convention as he had supposed, to adopt some plan, he thought it had better be done. With a view, therefore, of testing the sense of the Convention, he had prepared an amendment as a substitute. He did not desire to debate it, nor was he solicitous as to what the decision of the question might be.

The substitute indicated by Mr. C. was read as follows:

"The General Assembly shall avoid partial and local legislation as far as practicable; and may confer upon the Levy Court of each county, the members of which shall be elected by the people of their respective counties, by general ticket and not by districts, such powers of local legislation and administration as may be necessary, and all laws conferring such powers shall be general in their nature, and extend to all the counties of the State."

Mr. THOMAS said, that the difference between his proposition and that of the gentleman from Kent, (Mr. Chambers,) was very material.

Mr. CHAMBERS. Oh, very.

Mr. THOMAS proceeded to state that his amendment proposed to leave to the Legislature the passage of laws providing for the appointment of such county officers as the Convention might not expressly authorise. Mr. T. specified some of them.

His reason for desiring the adoption of this amendment was, that in the past legislation of the State, there had been a continual change in the mode of appointing even the Levy Court Judges. At another stage of the proceedings, he desired to go to the extent which the gentleman seemed to contemplate in another particular. He, (Mr. T.,) would be glad to see a provision in the Constitution denying to the Legislature the power to make that a crime in one county which was a mere misdemeanor in another.

Mr. CHAMBERS, of Kent, suggested that the proposition of the gentleman from Frederick, (Mr. Thomas,) so far as it went, was precisely his proposition.

Some explanatory conversation followed between Messrs. THOMAS and CHAMBERS, of Kent, as to the extent of the difference between the two propositions.

Mr. MERRICK suggested that there was no sort of incompatibility between the two propositions. Both were excellent. Let them go together. If they did so, it seemed to him that they would receive the almost unanimous vote of the Convention.

After an explanation by Mr. DAVIS as to the effect of the proposition,

Mr. DORSEY urged the propriety of leaving the matter to the Legislature. They would make such provision as they deemed right and proper, and the Convention, he thought, should not check or control their action in this respect. The local situation of each county and of the parts of counties were subjects to be considered by the Legislature, and he was for leaving them untrammeled. If the design was to abolish all local legislation, and to say that all elections should be general, the provision would interfere unjustly with the Legislature, and impose restrictions upon the community which should not be imposed We should be much better protected by leaving the power there than elsewhere. And such a mode, it appeared to him, would do justice to every part of the State.

Mr. MERRICK then offered the following amendment, as a substitute for the said section:

"The Levy Courts or Commissioners of the several counties of the State, shall be elected by general ticket and not by districts, by the voters of the respective counties; and said commissioners shall exercise such powers and duties only as the Legislature may prescribe, but such powers and duties as shall be uniform throughout the State—and the General Assembly may provide for the election or appointment of such other county officers as may be required, and are not provided for by this Constitution, and prescribe their powers and duties, but their tenure of office, their powers and duties and mode of appointment shall be uniform throughout the State."

Mr. THOMAS. I will accept that. It is precisely the idea I was aiming it.

Mr. CHAMBERS, of Kent. It does not answer the proposition I had in view. But I do not desire to create any difficulty. And I will, therefore, accept it.

CONSTABLE moved to strike out the words "or appointment," [but withdrew the motion.]

After some conversation on the part of Messrs. THOMAS, CHAMBERS, of KENT, CONSTABLE, and BUCHANAN,

Mr. CHAMBERS, of Kent, moved to strike out the words "or commissioners."

Mr. BLAKISTONE suggested that, if uniformity was going to be provided for, the time of election and the tenure of office should be fixed.

Mr. JOHN NEWCOMER opposed the suggestion.

Mr. DAVIS suggested some considerations why the provision proposed would operate injuriously.

The question was then taken on the motion of Mr. CHAMBERS, of Kent, to strike out the words "or commissioners."

The amendment was rejected.

The question recurred on the amendment of Mr. MERRICK.

Mr. CRISFIELD moved to amend the amendment, by striking out the words "Levy Courts or," [so as to let it stand "commissioners."]

Mr. RIDGELY said, he saw what the idea which the gentleman from Kent, (Mr. Chambers,) desired to carry out was, and it was a very proper one. To remove all difficulty, he would offer a proposition, that all these particular authorities should be known by one name throughout the county.

Mr. RIDGELY then moved to amend said amendment, by striking out these words: "the Levy Courts or Commissioners of the several counties of the State," and inserting in lieu thereof, the following:

"That the county authorities now known as levy courts or county commissioners, shall hereafter be styled commissioners, and;"

Mr. THOMAS said, that the proposition was acceptable to him.

Mr. MERRICK accepted the amendment as a modification of his own proposition.

Mr. CRISFIELD suggested that instead of the words "county commissioners," the words "commissioners of county" should be inserted.

Mr. RIDGELY said, the idea was the same.

Mr. CRISFIELD withdrew his amendment to strike out the words "Levy Courts or."

Mr. McMASTER moved to strike out the words "by general ticket, and not."

Mr. DORSEY seconded the motion of Mr. McMASTER, and stated his objections to the general ticket system.

Mr. PHELPS replied, and stated that no such evils as the gentleman spoke of had, within his knowledge, attended the general ticket system.

Mr. WRIGHT moved the previous question.

The PRESIDENT proceeded to ascertain whether there was a second.

Mr. BUCHANAN desired to submit an amendment.

The PRESIDENT said it was not in order.

Mr. BLAKISTONE moved a call of the Convention.

The PRESIDENT stated that no motion was in order while the Convention was dividing.

And the question having been taken, the Convention refused to second the demand for the previous question.

Mr. McHENRY indicated his desire to offer an amendment.

Mr. CHAMBERS, of Kent, suggested that it would be better that the vote should be taken on the single question of Districts or Counties, and that other amendments should come in afterwards.

Mr. McHENRY said, that a committee of which he was a member, had had under consideration a general plan of local organization. It seemed to be almost the only subject which had been entrusted to the keeping of that committee. The amendment before the Convention took one branch of that subject (relating to County Commissioners) out of the hands of the committee, thus dislocating and throwing into confusion the whole subject. If the Convention thought proper to annihilate one of its committees in this way, well and good. He had no objection to it.

Mr. McHenry then moved to amend the thirty-fourth section in the report, by inserting after the words "General Assembly," the words "shall pass no special or local act, but," and filling the blank in the first line, with the words "local authorities." Also insert before the word "powers" in the second line, the word "additional."

After a few words by

Mr. Dorsey, in reply to the remarks of Mr. Phelps—and by

Mr. Bell—in favor of the general ticket system, of the evils of which, as here spoken of, no knowledge had (he said) come to his possession.

The question was taken on the first branch of the amendment of Mr. McHenry;

And it was rejected.

And the question was taken on the second branch of the amendment of Mr. McHenry;

And it was rejected.

And the third branch of the amendment of Mr. McHenry, inserting the word "additional," was rejected.

The question then recurred on the motion of Mr. McMaster, to strike out the words "by general ticket and not."

Mr. McMaster asked the yeas and nays, which were refused.

The question was then taken, and the amendment was rejected.

The question then recurred on the amendment of Mr. Merrick.

Mr. Davis moved to amend said amendment by adding at the end thereof the following proviso:

"Provided, This article shall be so construed as not to prevent the Legislature from passing any law or laws to open the public roads when two or more counties are interested."

The amendment was rejected.

The question recurred on the amendment of Mr. Merrick as amended.

Mr. Weems called for a division, which was ordered.

The question was taken on the first branch of the amendment, in these words:

"That the county authorities now known as Levy Courts or County Commissioners, shall hereafter be styled "Commissioners."

The first branch of the amendment was agreed to.

The question recurred on the second branch of the amendment, as follows:

"And shall be elected by general ticket, and not by districts, by the voters of the respective counties."

Mr. Dorsey asked the yeas and nays, which were ordered, and, being taken, resulted as follows:

Affirmative—Messrs. Chapman, President, Blakistone, Dent, Hopewell, Ricaud, Lee, Chambers of Kent, Mitchell, Sellman, Weems, Bond, Merrick, Buchanan, Bell, Welch, Ridgely, Lloyd, Colston, Crisfield, Dashiell, Phelps, Constable, Chambers of Cecil, Miller, McLane, Grason, George, Wright, Hearn, Thomas, Shriver, Gaither, Biser, Sappington, Stephenson, Thawley, Stewart of Caroline, Hardcastle, Gwinn, Sherwood of Baltimore city, Ware, Fiery, Neill, Jno. Newcomer, Harbine, Michael Newcomer, Davis, Kilgour, Weber, Hollyday and Shower—52.

Negative—Messrs. Donaldson, Dorsey, Wells, Randall, Kent, James U. Dennis, Bowie, McMaster, Fooks, McHenry and Slicer—11.

So the second branch of the amendment was adopted.

The third and last branch of the amendment was then adopted as follows:

"And said commissioners shall exercise such powers and duties only as the Legislature may prescribe, but such powers and duties shall be uniform throughout the State; and the General Assembly may provide for the election or appointment of such other county officers as may be required, and are not provided for by this constitution, and prescribe their powers and duties, but their tenure of office, their powers and duties and mode of appointment shall be uniform throughout the State."

The second amendment was then adopted as a substitute for the thirty-fourth section of the report.

The thirty-fifth section of the report of the committee was then read as follows:

Sec. 35th. Every bill passed by the General Assembly, when engrossed, shall be presented by the Speaker of the House of Delegates, in the Senate Chamber, to the Governor for the time being, who shall sign the same, and thereto affix the great seal in the presence of the members of both Houses; every law shall be recorded in the office of the Court of Appeals of the Western Shore, and in due time be printed, published and certified under the great seal to the several county courts in the same manner as has been heretofore usual in this State.

Mr. Grason moved to amend the section by striking out all of said section to the word "Houses," inclusive, in the fifth line, and inserting in lieu thereof, the following:

"Every bill when passed by the General Assembly, and sealed with the great seal, shall be presented to the Governor, who shall sign the same in the presence of the presiding officers and chief clerks of the Senate and House of Delegates."

Mr. G. explained the inconveniences attendant upon the obligation that the Governor should sign bills in the presence of the two Houses, &c. It was the object of the amendment to obviate those inconveniencies.

Mr. Phelps expressed his concurrence in the views of the gentleman from Queen Anne, (Grason,) and thought that the proposition would be an improvement on the section as it stood in the bill.

The amendment was agreed to.

The second branch of the section was then adopted.

And the section, as amended, was adopted.

The thirty-second section of the report was read, and no amendment having been offered thereto, was adopted, as follows:

Sec. 36th No person who may hereafter be a collector, receiver or holder of public moneys, shall have a seat in either House of the General Assembly or be eligible to any office of profit or trust under this State, until he shall have accounted for and paid into the Treasury all sums for which he may be liable.

The thirty-seventh section of the report was read, as follows:

Sec. 37th. All laws and parts of laws not inconsistent with this Constitution, shall continue in force according to their respective provisions, subject, neverthless, to be altered, amended or repealed by the General Assembly.

Mr. CHAMBERS, of Kent, suggested the propriety of striking out the last part of the section.

Mr. DORSEY objected to the motion.

Mr. THOMAS suggested that the whole section be stricken out.

Some conversation followed between Messrs. CHAMBERS, of Kent, THOMAS and DORSEY, when

Mr. PRESSTMAN, following the suggestion of Mr. THOMAS, moved to strike out the section.

Mr. CHAMBERS, of Kent, accepted the motion as a modification of his own proposition.

Mr. DORSEY insisted on the propriety of retaining the section, but moved to amend it by adding at the end thereof the following proviso:

"Provided such amendment, alteration or repeal be not inconsistent with the fundamental principles of natural justice and right, or the provisions of the constitution of the United States, or of the State of Maryland."

The amendment of Mr. DORSEY was rejected.

And the motion of Mr. PRESSTMAN was agreed to.

So the section was stricken out.

Mr. PHELPS then moved to amend said report by inserting as the thirty-seventh section, the following:

Sec. 37th. Any citizen of this State who shall, after the adoption of this Constitution, fight a duel with deadly weapons, or send or accept a challenge to fight a duel with deadly weapons, either in or out of the State, or who shall act as second, or knowingly aid or assist in any manner those offending, shall be deprived of holding any office of trust or profit under this State."

Mr. PHELPS asked the yeas and nays, which were ordered, and being taken, resulted as follows:

Affirmative.—Messrs. Chapman, Pres't, Dent, Lee, Chambers, of Kent, Donaldson, Randall, Kent, Bell, Ridgely, James U. Dennis, Crisfield, Dashiell, Phelps, McMaster, Hearn, Fooks, Shriver, Gaither, Biser, Stephenson, Thawley, Hardcastle, Sherwood, of Baltimore city, Ware, Fiery, Neill, John Newcomer, Harbine, Michael Newcomer, Davis, Weber and Slicer—32.

Negative—Messrs. Blakistone, Hopewell, Ricaud, Mitchell, Dorsey, Wells, Weems, Bond, Merrick, Buchanan, Welch, Lloyd, Colston, Constable, Chambers, of Cecil, Bowie, Grason, Wright, Thomas, Sappington, McHenry, Gwinn, Brent, of Baltimore city, Presstman, Kilgour and Hollyday—29.

So the amendment was agreed to.

Mr. PHELPS moved further to amend said report, by inserting as the thirty-eighth section thereof, the following:

"*Sec. 38th.* No lottery grant shall ever hereafter be authorised by the Legislature of this State."

The amendment was adopted.

Mr. PHELPS moved further to amend said report by inserting as the thirty-ninth section of said report, the following:

"*Sec. 39th.* All property, both real and personal, of the wife, owned or claimed by her before marriage, and that acquired by gift, devise, or descent, shall be her separate property, and laws shall be passed by the Legislature, more clearly defining the rights of the wife in relation to her separate property."

This amendment, as originally offered, was modified on the suggestion of

Mr. HARBINE, who thought that the words "or claimed," should be stricken out.

Mr. PHELPS accepted the modification.

The question was taken and the article was adopted.

Mr. DORSEY moved a reconsideration of the vote adopting the said last amendment.

The motion to reconsider was briefly spoken to by Messrs. CHAMBERS, of Kent, PRESSTMAN, DONALDSON, MITCHELL, RANDALL and PHELPS, when

The question was taken and the motion to reconsider was agreed to.

Mr. CRISFIELD moved to strike out the whole of the said section and insert the following:

"The General Assembly shall pass laws necessary to protect the property of the wife from the debts of the husband during her life, and for securing the same to her issue after her death."

Mr. PHELPS modified his original proposition in accordance with the suggestion of Mr. CRISFIELD.

And the amendment of Mr. PHELPS, as thus modified, was agreed to.

Mr. GWINN now renewed the proposition heretofore offered, but withdrawn by him, in the ollowing words:

"The Mayor and city Council of Baltimore shall have the exclusive right to open and close all streets, lanes and alleys within the limits of the said city; but nothing in this section shall be construed to prevent the Legislature from passing any general law directing the process which shall be had in such cases, or from prescribing a general rule of compensation to the parties who may be injured thereby."

Mr. GWINN explained the object and effect of the amendment.

Mr. BELL moved to amend said amendment by adding at the end thereof the following proviso:

"Provided, that all persons in the city petitioning for opening or closing such streets, lanes or alleys, shall pay all the expenses that may accrue for the same."

Mr. RIDGELY moved to postpone the consideration of said section and amendment, (with a view to its more mature consideration.)

Determined in the affirmative.

Mr. FITZPATRICK moved to amend said report by adding at the end thereof, as an additional section, the following :

"*Sec.* 41*st*. The Legislature shall, at the second session after the adoption of this constitution, provide by law for exempting from execution not more than five hundred dollars worth of the household furniture, or other property belonging to each family in this State."

Pending the question on this amendment,

The Convention adjourned until Monday morning at 10 o'clock.

MONDAY, March 3, 1851.

The Convention met at ten o'clock.

Prayer by the Rev. Mr. GRAUFF.

The journal of Saturday was read.

THE LEGISLATIVE DEPARTMENT.

The Convention resumed the consideration of the special order of the day, being the report of the committee on the legislative department of the government.

HOMESTEAD EXEMPTION.

The pending question was on the following amendment, offered on Saturday last by Mr. FITZPATRICK, as an additional section to the report:

"*Sec.* 41*st*. The Legislature shall at the second session after the adoption of this Constitution provide by law for exempting from execution not more than five hundred dollars worth of the household furniture, or other property belonging to each family in this State."

Mr. STEWART, of Caroline, moved to amend said amendment, by striking out the word "five," and inserting in lieu thereof "seven."

Mr. PRESSTMAN said, he did not see the gentleman from Allegany, (Mr. Fitzpatrick,) who had offered the amendment, in his seat. Perhaps, it would be well that the amendment should be passed over informally for the present.

Mr. WEBER said, his colleague, (Mr. Fitzpatrick,) had no desire that the proposition should be passed over, in consequence of his absence.

Mr. MITCHELL said, it struck him, that if this proposition was agreed to, it would be impossible for a poor man to get any credit; and credit was as necessary as money to a poor man—in fact, more so. He was in favor, as every man who knew him would testify, of doing all he could for the poor. But if the sum of five hundred dollars should be exempted—if he was only worth that sum or less, who would take his note? No one—because he would have no sort of guaranty for the payment. Upon this ground, and upon no other, he should oppose the proposition.

Mr. MCMASTER. To carry out the view of the gentleman from Kent, (Mr. Mitchell,) I move to strike out "five" hundred, and insert "one" hundred.

Mr. SHRIVER. I call for a division of the qnestion.

Which was ordered.

The motion to strike out was rejected.

Mr. HARBINE desired to enquire of the gentleman from Caroline, (Mr. Stewart.) whether his amendment made it obligatory on the legislature to exempt from execution, seven hundred dollars worth of property. The original proposition was that any sum not exceeding five hundred dollars should be exempted.

Now, if he understood the proposition of the gentleman from Caroline, (Mr. Stewart,) it made it obligatory on the legislature to exempt seven hundred dollars. He, [Mr. H.,] thought that this matter ought to be left to the legislature. Without any such provision, the legislature had the right and the power to exempt property from execution. The fact that they did not do it, rendered it probable, that they did not think it requisite that it should be done. He thought that the original proposition was the best.

Mr. STEWART, of Caroline, said, that the objection which he had to the section as it now stood, was that it left the matter vacillating and uncertain. One year $200 might be exempted—another year $300—and so on. It would be a constant subject of change and discussion. If any thing was to be done, he thought that the amount ought to be fixed, and that the Legislature should have no power to change it. Whatever the amount was it should be certain.

As to the objection of the gentleman from Kent, (Mr. Mitchell,) it was true that a poor man might not under this article obtain any more credit than if he had nothing, but he would certainly be so much better off. By this amendment, this amount would be secured to the party and his family.

Mr. WRIGHT (very imperfectly heard by the reporter,) was understood to express his concurrence in the views expressed by the gentleman from Kent, (Mr. Mitchell,) and he, (Mr. W.,) trusted that the Convention would not fix upon any sum to be exempted.

He referred to an act which had heretofore been passed by the Legislature, exempting property from execution to the amount of $50. The law created much feeling all over the State of Maryland, and petitions flowed in from all quarters, and that familise were left houseless and unprovided for, because no one would trust them; and that they were prevented from obtaining credit by the very steps which the Legislature had taken for their protection. He hoped that the views of the gentleman from Kent, (Mr. Mitchell,) would be carried out—that no steps would be taken: but that the whole matter would be left to the Legislature to make such provision as the exigencies of the time might call for.

Mr. MITCHELL said, he understood perfectly the object his friend from Caroline, (Mr. Stewart,) had in view. It was to benefit the poorer class of our citizens. But his friend was mistaken. He (Mr. M.) assured him, that the very thing which the gentleman desired to do would recoil injuriously upon those whom he wished to protect. He (Mr. M.) knew that the gentleman had a very good heart, and that he did much towards the support of a number of persons in his own region. He (Mr. M.) felt sure that his friend would not take the note of such a man if this law should go into operation.

Mr. Stewart, of Caroline, said he would say a word in reply to the complimentary allusion which had been made to him by the gentleman from Kent, (Mr. Mitchell.)

He, (Mr. S.,) had not yet been able to satisfy his own mind whether it would be better for the mass of the people, that there should be a homestead exemption or not. All he said, was, that if the Convention should determine to adopt such a principle, they should fix the amount in the article, and should not leave it to the legislature, to be a constant subject-matter of contention. He cared not, whether the sum was fifty, five hundred, or seven hundred dollars; but, whatever it was, let it be fixed in the Constitution—that the legislature might neither go below, nor above it. He was free to say, that he thought such a provision would operate beneficially throughout the State.

Mr. Phelps said, it seemed to him that such a provision engrafted upon the Constitution, would be of no value. Under the old Constitution, the legislature had from time to time exempted property from execution. He cited a case. If the legislature had the power to do this under the old Constitution, they would equally possess the power under the new one.

He, however, was opposed to the principle. He knew that such a provision had been engrafted on the Constitutions of many of the new States, and it might work well in a new country where the property of a person was chiefly his land, and where the exemption applied literally to the *homestead*. But here, the state of things was different. Our citizens were occupied in all the various ramifications of business, and he did not see that any good could grow out of such a provision. He confirmed the view taken by the gentleman from Kent, (Mr. Mitchell,) and expressed the opinion that the provision would embarrass the very class for whose benefit it was intended.

Mr. Mitchell, (to the Chair.) Is it in order to move to strike out the whole of the section?

The President. It is not in order.

Mr. Mitchell. I move that the subject matter be laid upon the table.

Mr. Harbine. I call for the yeas and nays.

Mr. Mitchell. At the request of gentlemen near me, I withdraw the motion to lay on the table.

Mr Dorsey, in confirmation of the statement made by the gentleman from Queen Anne's, (Mr. Wright,) cited the Act of the General Assembly, passed the sixteenth of February, 1821, entitled "an Act for the relief of poor and distressed families, in cases of execution for debt and distress from rent." By this law, the bed, bedding and wearing apparel, or other necessary articles of housekeeping were exempted from execution.

Mr. McLane. Is that law now in force?

Mr. Dorsey. It is not. In the following year, (February 4, 1822,) when the practical operation of the law had been tested, the legislature passed an act by which it was repealed.

He recollected something of the effect of this law. The opinion was universal among the poorer classes, that it was the most imprudent, impolitic and inconvenient measure that could be adopted for them. They could not get credit for their families even where they were almost starving. They could not rent houses—they could get credit for nothing which their families might need, until security could be obtained. The poorer classes, dissatisfied with it, as he understood, almost to a man, came forward and demanded of their representatives the repeal of the law, and it had been repealed as he had shown.

Mr. McMaster, (to the President.) Is a substitute in order?

The President. Not at this time.

Mr. Stewart, of Caroline, withdrew the amendment offered by him, and moved to amend the amendment by striking out the words "not more than"

The question was taken and the amendment was rejected.

Mr. McMaster offered the following substitute.

"That the Legislature shall, at the second session after the adoption of this Constitution, provide by law for the exemption from execution of one hundred dollars worth of Household Furniture or other property belonging to each family in this State."

Mr. Kilgour asked the yeas and nays, which were refused.

The question was then taken on the substitute of Mr. McMaster, and it was rejected.

The question recurring on the adoption of the amendment as offered by Mr. Fitzpatrick,

Mr. Harbine asked the yeas and nays, which were ordered, and, being taken, resulted as follows:

Affirmative—Messrs. Blakistone, Dent, Hopewell, Weems, Bond, Merrick, Buchanan, Bell, Ridgely, Dashiell, Constable, Chambers of Cecil, McLane, Shriver, Gather, Biser, Annan, Stewart of Caroline, Sherwood of Baltimore city, Ware, Schley, Fiery, John Newcomer, Harbine, Mich'l Newcomer, Kilgour, Weber and Smith—28.

Negative.—Messrs. Chapman, President, Lee, Chambers, of Kent, Mitchell, Donaldson, Dorsey, Wells, Jenifer, Welch, Colston, James U. Dennis, Crisfield, Hicks, Phelps, Sprigg, Grason, Wright, McMaster, Hearn, Fooks, Jacobs, Sappington, Stephenson, Thawley, Hardcastle, Gwinn, Stewart, of Baltimore city, Brent, of Baltimore city, Presstman, Hollyday and Slicer—31.

So the amendment was rejected.

Mr. Brent, of Baltimore city, then moved to amend said report, by adding at the end thereof as an additional section, the following:

"In all cases where the head of a family shall die or become insolvent owning a dwelling house or homestead furniture in a dwelling house or other property, not exceeding hundred dollars, said house, homestead furniture or other property shall be exempt from administration or liability to creditors, but shall thereupon belong in equal parts to the family of said deceased or insolvent, and in the event that said dwelling house, homestead furniture or other property, shall exceed the value of dollars, then there shall be a preferred lien on the said property to the amount of dollars, for the equal benefit of his or her said family."

The amendment having been read,

Mr. BRENT said, the object of his amendment was to exempt furniture or dwelling houses. It seemed to him that this could be done effectually in seven or eight lines in the Constitution, without referring the matter to the legislature. He thought the amendment would dispose of the whole question.

Mr. JENIFER said, if he understood the amendment it was confined exclusively to persons owning houses or furniture. To supply the defect which, he thought, existed in the amendment, he offered an amendment to this effect:

"Or other property owned by the decedent at the time of his death."

Mr. BRENT, of Baltimore city. I accept the modification.

The PRESIDENT. Does the gentleman from Baltimore city, (Mr. Brent,) move to fill the blank with any particular sum?

Mr. BRENT. Not now, sir.

The PRESIDENT. It will be too late when the question has been taken.

Mr. BRENT. I move to fill the blank with five hundred dollars.

Mr. HEARN rose to a question of order. He was understood to enquire whether this was not essentially the same proposition which had been already voted down. If so, he submitted that it was not in order.

The PRESIDENT. The Chair thinks the proposition is different from that which has been already voted down, and that it is in order.

The question then recurred and was taken on the motion of Mr. BRENT, of Baltimore city, to fill the blank with $500.

But no quorum voted.

Mr. SCHLEY. I would like to hear the whole proposition read; [and it was read.]

The question was then again taken on the motion to fill the blank with $500—and by yeas 24, noes 31, it was rejected.

Mr. JOHN NEWCOMER moved to fill the blank with $300.

Mr. HICKS. I move to fill the blank with $2000.

The question was taken first on the highest number.

Mr. SCHLEY asked the yeas and nays which were ordered, and being taken, resulted as follows:

Affirmative—Messrs. Chambers of Kent, Bond, Crisfield, Hicks, Phelps, Hearn, Fooks, and Gaither—8.

Negative—Messrs. Chapman, Pres't., Blakistone, Dent, Hopewell, Lee, Mitchell, Donaldson, Dorsey, Wells, Weems, Jenifer, Buchanan, Bell, Ridgely, Colston, James U. Dennis, Dashiell, Constable, Chambers of Cecil, McLane, Sprigg, Bowling, Grason, Wright, McMaster, Jacobs, Shriver, Biser, Annan, Sappington, Stephenson, Thawley, Stewart of Caroline, Hardcastle, Gwinn, Stewart, of Baltimore city, Brent of Baltimore city, Sherwood of Baltimore city, Presstman, Ware, Schley, Fiery, John Newcomer, Harbine, Michael Newcomer, Kilgour, Weber, Hollyday, Slicer, and Smith—49.

So the Convention refused to fill the blank with $2000.

Mr. WEEMS moved to fill it with $600.

Mr. CRISFIELD asked the yeas and nays.

Mr. WARE moved that the whole subject matter be laid upon the table.

Mr. BRENT, of Baltimore city, asked the yeas and nays; [which were ordered.]

Mr. CRISFIELD (to the Chair.) To what does the motion to lay on the table apply?

The PRESIDENT. To the whole proposition of the gentleman from Baltimore city, (Mr. Brent.)

Mr. CRISFIELD. Very well. If that is the case, I am ready to vote for the motion.

The question, "shall the subject matter be laid upon the table," was then taken, and resulted as follows:

Affirmative—Messrs Chapman, Pres't.. Chambers, of Kent, Mitchell, Donaldson, Dorsey, Wells, Buchanan, Colston, James U. Dennis, Crisfield, Dashiell, Hicks, Phelps, Grason, Wright, McMaster, Hearn. Fooks, Jacobs, Gaither, Sappington, Stephenson, Thawley, Hardcastle, Stewart of Baltimore city, Sherwood of Baltimore city, and Ware—27.

Negative—Messrs. Blakistone, Dent, Hopewell, Lee, Weems, Bond, Merrick, Jenifer, Bell, Ridgely, Constable, Chambers of Cecil, McLane, Bowling, Shriver, Biser, Annan, Stewart of Caroline, Gwinn, Brent of Baltimore city, Presstman, Schley, Fiery, John Newcomer, Harbine, Michael Newcomer, Kilgour, Weber, Hollyday, Slicer, and Smith—31.

So the Convention decided that the subject matter should not be laid upon the table.

The question then recurred on the motion of Mr. WEEMS, to fill the blank with $600.

Mr. THAWLEY moved $50.

The motion of Mr. WEEMS was rejected.

The question then recurred on the motion of Mr. JOHN NEWCOMER to fill the blank with $300.

Mr. N. asked the yeas and nays, which were refused.

And the question being taken, the vote stood—ayes 24; noes 22.

No quorum voting.

Mr. BRENT, of Baltimore city, asked the yeas and nays which were ordered, and being taken, resulted as follows:

Affirmative—Messrs. Chapman, Pres't., Blakistone, Dent, Hopewell, Weems, Bond, Merrick, Jenifer, Bell, Ridgely, James U. Dennis, Constable, Chambers of Cecil, McLane, Sprigg,

Bowling, Shriver, Gaither, Biser, Annan, Stephenson, Gwinn, Brent of Baltimore city, Sherwood of Baltimore city, Schley, Fiery, John Newcomer, Harbine, Michael Newcomer, Kilgour, Weber, Hollyday, Slicer, and Smith—34.

Negative—Messrs. Lee, Chambers of Kent, Mitchell, Donaldson, Dorsey, Wells, Buchanan, Colston, Crisfield, Dashiell, Hicks, Phelps, Grason, Wright, McMaster, Hearn, Fooks, Jacobs, Sappington, Thawley, Stewart of Baltimore city, and Presstman—22.

So the blank was filled with $300.

The question then recurred on the amendment.

Mr. Brent, of Baltimore city, expressed the hope that the amendment would prevail. It seemed to him but a small boon to give to the family of deceased or insolvent persons. He admitted that cases might occur, even under the terms of the proposition, where a family might not obtain relief; but it seemed to him impossible to lay down any other safe rule than this. It would, however, operate upon the major part of the hard cases of insolvency, and would rescue from the grasp of a heartless and griping creditor the small pittance of $300 for the benefit of his family.

Mr. Mitchell. It strikes me that if a man owns a house he would be relieved under this proposition, but that if he be a poor devil who only rents one, (laughter,) he would not.

Mr. Brent, of Baltimore city. The gentleman is entirely mistaken in his construction of the proposition. And Mr. B. explained.

Mr. Presstman expressed his regret that the proposition of his colleague, (Mr. Brent,) was such as could not meet with his, (Mr. P's.,) concurrence. Far from it. He should be glad if it did so. He did not believe that it would be acceptable to the city of Baltimore, although upon that point a difference of opinion might well be entertained. He referred to the report which he had himself made, providing for the abolishment of imprisonment for debt. This, he thought, would be sufficient relief.

If, in addition to this measure, the Convention should think proper to withdraw from responsibility, the property of a debtor, to the extent of three hundred dollars, it would bear upon the working classes of the city, so as to cripple them to a considerable extent. He referred to the case of the law, of the operation of which, the distinguished gentleman from Anne Arundel, (Mr. Dorsey,) had given his experience. That was one of the most unpopular laws that ever went into operation.

As regarded the proposition to abolish imprisonment for debt, the barbarity of the existing law, although that had undoubtedly had its weight upon his mind, was not the prominent consideration. He was in favor of doing away with credit. He was in favor of permitting an honest mechanic, when he did his work, to be paid for it. He considered the law in its present form, as "keeping the word of promise to the ear, and breaking it to the hope." He was not influenced by considerations, looking to the debtor, so much as he was by the great interests of the creditor, who was now deceived—who expected to be paid, but, under the insolvent laws was deluded.

The proposition of his colleague, he thought, was open to many objections. He, [Mr. P.,] proceeded to point out objections to its phraseology. He suggested that it could not be construed by the courts with any degree of certainty —that it was indefinite, and might be construed to mean not the immediate family only, but grand-daughters and grand-sons, and all embraced in the legal term "family," It made no discriminations between meritorious and worthless children; and was open also to other objections.

Desiring to stand right before the community, he should feel constrained to vote against the amendment.

Mr. McMaster moved to amend the proposition by striking out the words "administration or."

Mr. Chambers rose, to present to the Convention an idea which had not yet been suggested, and but for which, he would not have said a single word. The hypothesis on which this amendment has been defended, is, that when a heartless, griping creditor endeavors to oppress the poor and desolate widow of a deceased debtor, the law should interpose for her protection. On this ground he would be one of the last men in the world to raise an objection to it.

He would always be ready to interfere between the hard and unfeeling creditor, who does not want the money due to him, and the bereaved widow, whom he attempts to oppress.

But he asked gentlemen who took this ground, to look at the case in a more correct point of view. When a poor man dies insolvent, is it to be taken for granted, that his creditors are all wealthy? Not at all. He buys his soap, his candles, his sugar, and all his household necessaries, at some small store in his neighborhood; and the person from whom he buys, is just as poor as he himself is; that person too depends on what is owing to him, as a means of keeping up his supply, and when he suffers a loss, it bears heavily upon him. He thought it was wrong to permit this.

The law can lay its hand on the person, if living, or it can take his property. But here the person of the poor is rescued from the power of the law, and this amendment casts off the poor and suffering creditor from any chance of indemnifying himself from the property. The principle was antagonistic to the policy of our insolvent laws. It would also operate injuriously on the poor, generally, because it would restrain persons from giving credit to those who have but small means.

If the creditor is just as poor as the debtor, the one is as much deserving of legal protection as the other. Why, would you take from a poor man five dollars, and give it to another who is equally poor, perhaps, but not more so than himself. He would willingly agree to any proposition where it could be made to appear that the debt of the deceased insolvent was due to a man of ample means who would not suffer from the loss, to relieve the widow from the oppression of the creditor; but, as he had before stated, in these cases it generally occured, that the creditor was just as poor, and as deserving of protection, as the debtor himself.

He thought it better to leave it for the legislature to act as occasion might require, than to place this broad, unqualified provision in the Constitution.

Mr. Grason would prefer leaving the subject to the legislature, but as it appeared to be the general wish to insert some provision of this kind into the Constitution, he would make no objection. In his opinion, the family of a deceased debtor ought to have something secured to them as a means of temporary subsistence. It is not merely harsh creditors, but the law itself which leaves families in the most destitute condition. Administrators are compelled to take an inventory of every thing; and every article of furniture, and even the provisions are sold for the benefit of creditors.

It had been said, that laws exempting property from execution, operated to the injury of the very persons they were intended to benefit, because they deprived them of credit. But credit was generally given to laboring men on account of their industry and good conduct, and not on account of a few articles of furniture and provisions, which no family could dispense with. He would like to know if a merchant, or any other person, trusted a poor man with the view of selling his bed from under him, or of depriving his family, as soon as he was dead, of the few articles which their immediate necessities required. Credits which were to be followed by such sacrifices, were of no benefit to any one, and if creditors expected to secure the collection of their debts by such means, it was necessary that some legal provision should be made to keep them within the bounds of humanity.

Mr. Hicks expressed his belief that gentlemen who were advocating this amendment, were proceeding under a mistake. He thought the mover of the amendment, who he did not recollect, was influenced by the best motives, but would find it did not affect the object he desired. By an existing law, the family of a deceased debtor is already protected against his creditors. Property to a certain extent is now reserved for the benefit of a family, and other provisions have been made, all to the injury of honest creditors. He thought this was all wrong. He referred to a case which occurred while he was at home. An insolvent person died, possessing but little property, and leaving two children. His whole estate would not pay twenty-five cents in the dollar. A short time before his death, the grandfather of the children had died, and by his death, they had become possessed of some thousands of dollars, and they were well provided for whilst the honest mechanic and merchant suffered. The father had been trusted on the faith of his industrious habits, but owing to his death the creditors lost three-fourths of their honest due, and the children had ample means, and at that he felt much gratified. He did not doubt that there were heartless creditors in Queen Ann's, as well as in Dorchester. In fact he knew of a case of *ca. sa.* which occurred in that county, of great hardship. There were indeed hard cases every where. He was very willing to vote to abolish imprisonment for debt. But while we were making these provisions for the benefit of the insolvents, we are injuring honest creditors. He knew that, after the bill which had formerly passed on the subject, there were numerous petitions sent to the legislature, shewing that the effect of it had been to injure the credit of the poorer classes, and to bring about a material diminution of their comforts. The blacksmith and other mechanics will not give credit where there is no reasonable security that they will be paid. There are numbers who are now willing to trust a man who has an honest reputation, but let this amendment be adopted, and they will say that if he dies there will be no chance of recovering their debt, and this will make them reluctant to give credit to poor men. There are also many dishonest men in the State, who will be benefited by this provision. He was in favor of benefiting the poor, but he did not think this proposition would place them in a better condition than now. Indeed, they must be the principal sufferers, as it shuts out important advantages to them and in fact to all classes. Mr. H. closed by saying, he hoped the amendment would not be adopted.

Mr. Brent, of Baltimore city, desired briefly to notice one or two of the objections made to his amendment. His colleague, (Mr. Presstman,) objects to the word "family," which he seemed to think was too indefinite, and would be construed to include collateral relations.

Mr. Presstman explained. He had said distant relations, meaning grand-children, &c.

Mr. Brent. Suppose it does embrace grandchildren. The object is to include all those who are near him, forming part of his family at home, and not those who are remote.

Mr. Crisfield wished to put a question to the gentleman from Baltimore city. If a man leave a wife, a child and a child of a widowed daughter, how would the property be divided?

Mr. Brent. It would be equally divided. There was no reason why there should not be an equal division. His friend from Baltimore city, (Mr. Presstman,) says further, that there is no discrimination between a meritorious and an unworthy child. Not so. It only protects them all alike from the grasp of the debtors. The father can discriminate between his children. His friend says further, that there may be the abolition of imprisonment for debt, which is protection for property against the creditor. That merely protects the person from confinement and ignominy. This provision is intended to relieve the property when the debtor is no longer within the reach of the law. Again, it is said, that this amendment protects the property against the claims of poor mechanics. He was the last man in the world to propose any plan which would injure mechanics. But if this proposition be inserted in the Constitution, the honest mechanic who trusts the poor man, will give him credit with a full knowledge of the existence of this law. If he is disposed to credit a man who has no property, he will do it with his eyes open to the consequences. In reply to the gentleman from Kent, (Mr. Chambers,) who had expressed his readiness to vote for a proposition which would only screen the poor debtor from the heartless and grasping creditor who could afford to lose the debt, such a clause could not be inserted in the Constitution. It would be ridiculous to attempt it. A homestead ought to be always reserved. As to the property which may be left by a deceased debtor, the wife and children ought to be secured to the extent of three hundred dollars. He knew of cases where creditors, just after the death of the debtor, had forced the widow and children out of the house and sold the property. The Act of Assembly which had been passed last year, and which the gentleman from Dorchester had referred to, reserves only one hundred and fifty dollars, and that is exclusively to be paid out of her distributive share. He pointed out the unjust operation of this Act, by which a widow *without children* could obtain from the insolvent estate of her husband seventy-five dollars, while a widow *with children* could obtain nothing.

Mr. Gwinn offered the following substitute:

"The Legislature shall provide for the exemption of property, real and personal, belonging to any person dying insolvent, or taking the benefit of the insolvent laws, to an amount not exceeding three hundred dollars, from the proceedings of creditors, and in case of such dying insolvent, or of insolvency during life, the said property so exempted, shall go in the first instance to the wife or widow, and then according to its nature, go as now directed by the statutes of descent or distribution; provided, always, that the provisions of this section shall only apply to a father, mother, sister, brother, husband, or wife, or child, or grand child of the said person so dying or becoming insolvent."

Mr. Crisfield objected to the amendment of the gentleman from the city of Baltimore, (Mr. Brent,) and also to the substitute for that amendment offered by the other gentleman from that city, (Mr. Gwinn.) That substitute would not meet the object which the gentleman himself had in view, certainly not the object the Convention had in view. The object, as he understood it, was to secure a homestead for the head of every family beyond the reach of creditors; but the substitute was to provide some thing in lieu of a homestead; it was to exempt from execution real and personal property to a certain amount; but this was only to be done in case of a person dying insolvent, or becoming insolvent, which he supposed meant petitioning for the benefit of the insolvent laws; and the right of property was not to be vested in the person himself, but in his wife or widow, and heirs or nearest of kin. It was not a benefit conferred on the person himself; he was to receive no benefit from it; he must die or become an insolvent petitioner, before there should be any exemption. This was not what was designed; and is not sustained by any of the reasons which might be urged for a homestead exemption, which he supposed was designed for the benefit of the debtor himself, to attach him to the soil and prevent emigration by securing him a permanent abode. But he could see no reason for any exemption at all, either in the shape of a homestead exemption or otherwise. He thought the tendency of all such laws was to injure the class which they were designed to benefit. They destroyed credit; and credit was beneficial to all classes; and to that portion of the community designed to be effected by this proposition, credit was indispensable. It was better to leave every man to himself; protect all from fraud and oppression; encourage industry; secure the rights of property; and facilitate credit. These objects are best accomplished by providing the most certain, expeditious, and convenient means of applying all his property to the fulfilment of the owner's obligations. Legislation will never make men industrious, prudent, or skilful in the management of their affairs. Exemption of any portion of the debtor's property from execution, encouraged idleness and improvidence, and lead to poverty. He differed from the gentleman from the city of Baltimore, (Mr. Brent,) in his construction of the act of the last session; that act secured to the widow, property to the value of $150; at all events, if she have children; which he knew to be the practical construction of it. The case referred to by the gentleman from Queen Anne's, (Mr. Grason,) could never have occurred; because the law already exempts from execution articles of domestic use such as that gentleman referred to, the necessary bedding for the family, and the implements of trade. He hoped that both propositions would be rejected.

Mr. Gwinn said:

That he designed his amendment to operate in favor of the immediate family of the debtor. The debtor himself will be sufficiently protected by the security which the Constitution will afford to his personal liberty, and by the necessaries which are now preserved by the amenity of the law from the hands of the creditor. But where there is a wife or children, it is only right that the law should set apart something from the assets of the debtor for their immediate wants. It is but analagous in principle to that rule of equity, which gives a wife a right to receive a portion of the shares in action, which pass to the trustee of an insolvent husband. Law should have its charities as well as rigor. The ends of justice are often better served by clemency than harshness.

Mr. Dorsey opposed the proposition, which he believed would lead to endless difficulties, and might frequently be productive of flagrant injustice. He thought, as the gentleman from Baltimore city, (Mr. Presstman,) did, that the term family was too indefinite, and might embrace those whom it was never intended to benefit. Another objection was that the proposition was so prepared, that it might operate but little to the advantage of those who ought to be the especial objects and favorites of the measure. It is true, it strips the creditors without pretext of justice or right, of three hundred dollars, even though it may reduce them to penury and destitution. It does not, as its apology, require that the family shall be in a destitute condition without other means of support, before this three hundred dollars shall be taken from the creditors. The widow, if there be one, may, in her own right be possessed of a thousand acres of land, with valuable negroes, &c., and yet under the proposition before us, the creditors must be robbed for her benefit, of the three hundred dollars to be secured to her, &c. Can an apology be offered, for thus plundering creditors to increase the means of a wife and children already in affluence? Yet, this may be the result of the measure now proposed for our adoption. And it does not necessarily follow that the family of a deceased or insolvent, are a wife or children. It may be that his family are his father or mother, brothers or sisters, uncles or aunts, &c., all of whom have fortunes of their own; yet for them the three hundred dollars must be wrested from the impoverished needy creditors.

If this be a necessary article of our organic law, may Heaven forefend us against Constitutions and Conventions. Surely we could not desire to perpetuate such flagrant injustice as this, by putting it out of the power of the legislature to alter or control it.

But, suppose there are no wife or children, is it intended that this proposition shall embrace uncles, aunts, or any other persons who may happen to reside with him, though they may be all rich and independent? Are the creditors thus to be deprived of their hard earnings, to be given to those who are richer than they are?

He thought the Convention ought not for a moment to listen to such an amendment. The power to regulate these things is now in the legislature. He was disposed to leave it there, and let the legislature act as circumstances may call for; it never would of itself adopt such a proposition as this.

If we put this provision in the Constitution we shall have tied up the hands of the legislature, so that they will have no power to modify or change the law, no matter how urgent may be the necessity, or universal the popular sentiment in favor of the change.

He then remarked on the difficulty which would attend the practical operation of such a provision. The three hundred dollars is to be equally divided, between the wife and children. If the latter be infants, as most probably would be the case, not a particle of their portions could be used for their support or education, until all the expense and trouble must be incurred, of having a guardian appointed by the orphans court to each infant; and the expenses would consume the whole subject-matter—"the play not be worth the candle."

The deceased or intestate, might leave a dozen children, most of whom might be living at the time of the death or insolvency with their relations; yet though equally destitute, they would get no part of the plunder.

He thought if any thing was to be done on the subject, it would certainly be the wisest plan to leave the legislature to act untrammeled in the matter, and he had no fear of its perpetrating such an enormity as that now proposed for our adoption. The evils resulting from the measure before us, can but be indistinctly foreseen. It would lead to frauds innumerable; annihilate the credit of the poor man, and leave him without the means of rescuing his family from destitution and want.

Upon these grounds, and upon every principle of justice and common honesty, he was opposed to the amendment now before the Convention.

Mr. Jenifer moved that the whole subject-matter be laid upon the table.

Mr. Brent, of Baltimore city, asked the yeas and nays,

Which were ordered.

Mr. Buchanan called for the reading of the proposition and amendment;

Which were read.

Mr. Brent, of Baltimore city, to meet objections made against the proposition, as originally offered by him, modified his proposition to read as follows:

"In all cases where the head of a family shall die or become insolvent, owning a dwelling house or homestead furniture, or other property, or where an execution is levied upon the property of any debtor, the said house, homestead furniture or other property, shall be exempt from administration or liability to, or seizure by creditors; provided, said property, real or personal, does not exceed the sum of   in value, but the same shall thereupon belong in equal parts to the wife and descendants of said descedant or debtor, and in the event that said property, shall exceed the sum of   in value, then there shall be a preferred lien on said property to the amount of   dollars, for the equal benefit of the said widow or descendants; provided, nothing herein shall affect creditors existing at the time of the adoption of this constitution."

The question then recurred on the motion of Mr. Jenifer:

"Shall the whole subject-matter be laid upon the table?"

And the result was as follows:

Affirmative—Messrs. Chapman, President, Ricaud, Lee, Chambers of Kent, Mitchell, Donaldson, Dorsey, Wells, Jenifer, Ridgely, Colston, James U. Dennis, Crisfield, Dashiell, Hicks, Phelps, Sprigg, Bowling, Wright, McMaster, Hearn, Fooks, Jacobs, Gaither, Thawley, Hardcastle, Stewart of Baltimore city, Presstman, and Ware—29.

Negative—Messrs. Blakistone, Dent, Hopewell, Weems, Bond, Buchanan, Bell, Welch, Chambers of Cecil, Grason, Shriver, Biser, Annan, Sappington, Stephenson, Stewart of Caroline, Gwinn, Brent of Baltimore city, Sherwood of Baltimore city, Schley, Fiery, John Newcomer, Harbine, Michael Newcomer, Kilgour, Weber, Hollyday, Slicer and Smith—29.

A tie vote.

So the subject-matter was not laid on the table.

Mr. Ridgely said:

He had voted to lay the proposition on the table, because he thought it too important to be hastily disposed of, especially when there is danger, that we may come to an unwise decision. Therefore, he was disposed to leave the matter to be disposed of by the legislature. He thought there was a great deal of force in the remarks of the gentleman from Anne Arundel, (Mr. Dorsey,) and that the proposition now offered, might operate unjustly.

The amendment as it was originally offered by the gentleman from Allegany, (Mr. Fitzpatrick,) appeared to have been the form which was the least objectionable.

Mr. Ridgely gave notice of the following amendment:

"Laws shall be passed by the legislature to protect from execution, a reasonable amount of the property of a debtor."

Mr. Brent defended his construction of the act of assembly. He did not desire to leave this subject to the discretion of the legislature. It was his wish to settle the question at once, and secure this small boon to the families of deceased debtors.

Mr. Crisfield said he had ventured to differ with the gentleman from the city of Baltimore, [Mr. Brent,] in his construction of the act of the last session of the General Assembly; and notwithstanding the great attainments and elevated position of that gentleman, he must be allowed to say that he still differed. The gentleman's idea is that if the distributive share of the widow should be less than $150, she would not, under the first section of that act, be entitled to take that sum. The gentleman had not read the whole section; he would read it; and the mere reading, he thought would be decisive of the question at issue, between them. Mr. C. here read the first section of the act as follows:

"That, in all cases hereafter, when letters of administration or testamentary shall be issued by any of the orphans courts in this State, and an inventory and appraisement of the personal estate of the person deceased shall have been returned, by the executor or executrix, administrator or administratrix, to the orphans court of the county, &c., the widow of such deceased person shall have the right to take to herself, and apply to her own use, and the use of her children, such household and kitchen furniture, or other personal property as she may choose; provided, the said deceased died seized of no real estate; provided the same shall not exceed in value, according to the inventory and appraisement aforesaid, the sum of one hundred and fifty dollars; and provided further, that the amount of personal property so selected to be taken by her, shall be deducted from her distributive share of of said personal estate."—[1849, ch. 543, sec. 1.]

There could be no misunderstanding as to the import of this statute. By the plain words of the law, the widow was entitled to the sum of $150 "in all cases hereafter;" and the effect of the last proviso was simply to prevent her from taking that sum in addition to her distributive share. She is entitled to $150 in all events; when her distributive share exceeds that amount, that sum is to be deducted from the share.

Mr. Brent in reply, stated that the construction of the act was purely a legal question, and he did not desire to discuss it any farther here, but would agree to argue a case stated, for the satisfaction of the gentleman, [Mr. Crisfield,] so that the courts might decide who was right.

The question then recurred on the amendment of Mr. McMaster, to strike out the words "administator or."

The amendment was rejected.

Mr. Ridgely now offered his substitute as above given.

The question was taken.

No quorum voted.

Mr. Brent, of Baltimore city, asked the yeas and nays, which were ordered, and being taken, resulted as follows:

Affirmative—Messrs. Chapman, Pres't., Blakistone, Hopewell, Lee, Chambers of Kent, Mitchell, Donaldson, Dorsey, Wells, Weems, Merrick, Bell, Welch, Ridgely, Colston, James U. Dennis, Crisfield, Dashiell, Hicks, Phelps, Sprigg, Bowling, Wright, McMaster, Hearn, Fooks, Gaither, Sappington, Stephenson, Thawley, Stewart of Caroline, Hardcastle, Stewart of Baltimore city, Sherwood of Baltimore city, Presstman, Ware, and Kilgour—37.

Negative—Messrs. Dent, Ricaud, Bond, Jenifer, Buchanan, Grason, Jacobs, Shriver, Biser, Annan, Gwinn, Brent of Baltimore city, Schley, Fiery, John Newcomer, Harbine, Nichael Newcomer, Weber, Hollyday, Slicer, and Smith—20.

So the amendment was adopted.

Mr. Donaldson then moved that the whole subject matter be laid on the table.

Mr. Kilgour asked the yeas and nays which were ordered, and being taken, resulted as follows:

Affirmative—Messrs. Chambers of Kent, Mitchell, Donaldson, Dorsey, Wells, Merrick, Jenifer, Hicks, Phelps, Sprigg, Wright, McMaster, Hearn, Fooks, Jacobs, Gaither, Annan, and Presstman—18.

Negative—Messrs. Chapman, Pres't., Blakistone, Dent, Hopell, Ricaud, Lee, Weems, Bond, Buchanan, Bell, Welch, Ridgely, Colston, James U. Dennis, Crisfield, Dashiell, Bowling, Grason, Shriver, Biser, Sappington, Stephenson, Thawley, Stewart of Caroline, Hardcastle, Gwinn, Stewart of Baltimore city, Brent of Baltimore city, Ware, Schley, Fiery, John Newcomer, Kilgour, Weber, Hollyday, Slicer, and Smith—39.

So the subject matter was not laid on the table.

Mr Dent offered the following substitute:

"The Legislature at its first session after the adoption of this Constitution, shall make some provision by law, exempting a reasonable amount of the property of the heads of families from seizure or sale for the payment of any debt, or liability thereafter contracted."

The question was taken.

No quorum voted.

Mr. Dent explained that his proposition differed from that of the gentleman from Baltimore county in this respect: That his, (Mr. R's,) is too general in its provision, while his, (Mr. D's.,) substitute looks to a provision for a special class. The proposition of the gentleman from Baltimore county makes no discrimination of cases, but proposes to confer the benefits of such a provision on all alike, without regard to any circumstances or conditions, except that the party in whose favor it is to operate, must be a debtor. He had understood that the object contemplated by such provision was a humane and charitable object. It was intended as a boon of charity by the law, and there is no doubt, in looking to this object, it is our duty so to provide as to prevent the greatest amount of suffering and want to the debtor, and those helpless ones who may be dependant on him, and at the same time work the least amount of evil to the creditor. The heads of families are the parties in whose favor we would discriminate. They will be the most worthy and the most needy recipients of such a favor. It will not be pretended that the man without any family, with no one to provide or care for but himself, stands in an equal degree entitled to such legal exemption as the man who has a wife and helpless children dependant entirely upon his efforts for all the necessaries of life. He therefore proposed to authorize the Legislature to discriminate and make such provision as would confer the greatest amount of benefit on the most needy and meritorious class, and at the same time avoid screening, by the law, the property of him who has no responsibilities or cares but for himself.

Mr. Phelps said, this proposition could not be regarded as one of charity. Individuals had the unquestioned right to dispose of their own property as might seem to them right and proper. They might indulge a spirit of munificence and liberality if they please, but this Convention has no right to provide for the wants of one family at the expense of another. A. may die justly indebted to B. five hundred dollars, and the family of the former be quite as dependant upon this sum as that of the latter, and yet if this proposition be engrafted upon the Constitution, the one must be impoverished for the benefit of the other. The principle in his estimation was radically wrong and could not receive his sanction.

Mr. Ridgely did not think there was any substantial difference between this proposition and what had already been adopted.

The yeas and nays were ordered and taken on the amendment of Mr. Dent, and the result was as follows:

Affirmative—Messrs. Blakistone, Dent, Hopewell, Chambers of Kent, Mitchell, Donaldson, Jenifer, Colston, Sprigg, Bowling, McMaster, Hearn, Fooks, Stephenson, Gwinn, Sherwood of Baltimore city, Schley, Fiery, John Newcomer, Harbine, and Michael Newcomer—21.

Negative—Messrs. Chapman, President, Lee, Dorsey, Wells, Randall, Weems, Bond, Merrick, Buchanan, Bell, Ridgely, James U. Dennis, Crisfield, Dashiell, Hicks, Phelps, Chambers of Cecil, McLane, Grason, Wright, Jacobs, Shriver, Gaither, Biser, Annan, Sappington, Thawley, Stewart of Caroline, Stewart of Baltimore city, Presstman, Kilgour, Weber, Hollyday, Slicer and Smith—34.

So the amendment was rejected.

The question then recurred on the adoption of Mr. Ridgely's amendment as an original proposition.

Mr. Randall offered the following substitute:

"That the Legislature shall pass such laws as may be required to secure to the widow and infant children of deceased debtors, out of their personal estate, some provision for their support in preference to creditors."

Mr. Randall thought, he said, that the benefit of the proposition should be confined to the families of deceased debtors. The debtor may by his own means, or by the aid of friends in his life-time recover himself. This reservation for the benefit of his family out of the deceased's estate, was nothing unusual, as such provision had been made in some of the States.

The reasons for the legal rights secured to widows out of real estate in preference to creditors, regarding the times when they originated, require such additional provision now to be made for the widow and infant children out of the personal estate, viz: the protection of the most helpless in society. In the early ages, when dower was awarded to widows, personal property was of very little consequence.

It was centuries ago, when the entire personal property of the subject was probably little more than his cattle, horse and accoutrements. Personal property was then worthy of little or no *consideration*. The widow's right of dower, a life estate in one-third of the landed property, was an interest in what, at that time, was ninety-nine hundredths of all the property of the realm. But circumstances have changed; and now, personal property in England and in this country, is perhaps equal in value to the real estate. On the same principle which gave dower, therefore, in these early ages, we ought now to give (to widows and children, over creditors,) an interest in the personal estate. Thousands die now, whose whole estate consists of personal property, and that too, perhaps, derived from the wife or accumulated from her savings and industry. Is it just that creditors should enjoy the whole—that she and her children should be deprived of every cent of property, at a time when they were also deprived of their husband and father? Moreover, public policy demands that at such a time as this, there should be some provision set apart for the necessary and temporary support of the deceased's family. *He* did not know what was the policy which caused the original proposition to be made, but he thought it should be our policy to deduct from the estate to be divided among creditors for the benefit of the widow and infant children of a deceased alone. It would be better that a few creditors have their dividends of the estate diminished, than that these widows and children should be thrown on society for maintenance and education.

And where would be the injustice of such a course? The creditors will all know beforehand what the law requires, that this part of the personal estate of a deceased man shall be set apart for his widow and children. They will act upon this knowledge, and give credit accordingly. The reserved property will be assigned as a preference claim, for the benefit of the most interesting portion of society, and generally, will be only a small deduction, from the claims of creditors who know that this claim would be allowed, as against them, when they gave credit to the former proprietor, in his life-time. You therefore, do no wrong when you adopt such a provision

If there can be any danger of wrong it is where you give property to the living debtor and take it from his creditors. Frauds too are most apt to result from such a provision which a debtor may at any time make for himself out of what should be the means of his creditors. This does not apply to the case of a deceased man's family.

Mr. MERRICK suggested that the proposition be modified, so as to embrace "infants."

Mr. RANDALL said, he was willing to take that modification which would render the proposition stronger.

Mr. CRISFIELD moved to strike out the word "additional."

Mr. C. thought this proposition was a more objectionable one. He read the proposition. The Legislature must pass laws to give the widow additional means. Already if she has no children, the widow is entitled to one half of the personal estate. If she has children she will have one third. This proposition gives her and the infant children a preference above all other persons. If the benefit is to be conferred to infants, what is to become of grown children. Surely it is not intended by the mover of the amendment to give to the families a larger proportion of means than the law now provides. He would suggest to the gentleman so to amend the proposition as to leave it to the Legislature.

Mr. RANDALL referred to the act of Assembly, granting $159 to widows, and after briefly defending his proposition, intimated his willingness to accept the amendment.

Mr. CRISFIELD suggested a modification.

Mr. RANDALL modified his amendment, to meet the views of Mr. CRISFIELD.

The question on the modified amendment of Mr. RANDALL was taken, and the vote stood—ayes 18, noes 36.

So the amendment was rejected.

Mr. RIDGELY called the previous question.

There was a second. And the main question was ordered to be now taken; [which main question was, on the adoption of the substitute of Mr. RIDGELY in place of the original proposition.]

Mr. RIDGELY asked the yeas and nays, which were ordered, and being taken, resulted as follows:

Affirmative—Messrs. Chapman, Pres't., Blakistone, Hopewell, Lee, Weems, Bond, Bell, Ridgely, Colston, James U. Dennis Crisfield, Dashiell, Chambers of Cecil, Bowling, Grason, Shriver, Gaither, Biser, Sappington, Stephenson, Thawley, Stewart of Caroline, Gwinn, Brent of Baltimore city, Sherwood of Baltimore city, Schley, Fiery, John Newcomer, Harbine, Michael Newcomer, Kilgour, Weber, Hollyday, Slicer, and Smith—35.

Negative—Messrs. Dent, Chambers of Kent, Mitchell, Donaldson, Dorsey, Wells, Randall, Merrick, Jenifer, Buchanan, Welch, Hicks, Phelps, Sprigg, Wright, McMaster, Hearn. Fooks, Jacobs, Annan, Stewart of Baltimore city, and Presstman—22.

So the substitute of Mr. RIDGELY was adopted as the original proposition.

Mr. MITCHELL gave notice that he would, when there should be a full Convention, move a re-consideration of the vote just taken.

AN IMPRESSIVE SCENE.

It was now three o'clock, and the members of the Convention, in various quarters of the Hall, were giving strong evidences of a disposition to make a precipitate retreat into the open air.

Mr. MERRICK rose, and pointing in the most solemn manner to the clock, said—

Mr. President and Gentlemen of the Convention:

[The earnest tone of invocation in which the words were spoken, arrested the retreating movement, and the PRESIDENT, calling the Convention to order, and recognising the right of Mr. MERRICK to the floor said—

The gentleman from Charles will proceed with his remarks.]

Mr. MERRICK continued. Sirs, I feel it to be my duty to call the attention of this body to a most grave and important subject—one which has engaged the most devout attention of philosophers, statesmen, and patriots, in all ages of the world—whose interest has never flagged, and whose influence upon the destinies of mankind can scarcely be exaggerated. It is no less a matter than the necessity which, at this period of the day, every gentleman feels and understands, of recruiting the powers of weak, exhausted human nature. [Laughter.] I move that this Convention do now adjourn. [Roars of laughter.]

And thereupon the Convention adjourned until to-morrow at ten o'clock.

TUESDAY, March 4, 1851.

The Convention met at ten o'clock.

Prayer was made by the Rev. Mr. GRAUFF.

The roll of the members was called.

No quorum was present.

The PRESIDENT sent the doorkeeper to notify the absent members who were in the city, to attend the Convention.

After the lapse of some time,

The doorkeeper returned and made his report to the Chair.

The PRESIDENT informed the Convention that the doorkeeper had discharged the duty assigned him.

Mr. MICHAEL NEWCOMER. I move that the Sergeant-at-Arms be sent to bring in the absent members who are in the city.

Mr. BOWIE. Oh! what is the use? They will be here presently.

Mr. MICHAEL NEWCOMER. I adhere to my motion.

The PRESIDENT put the question on the motion.

Fifteen members not voting in favor thereof, (as required by the rule,) the Convention refused to send the Sergeant-at-Arms, to bring in the absent members.

A pause followed.

Mr. WEBER then moved that there be a call of the Convention.

The call was ordered.

The roll of the members was then called,

And the names of the absentees were again called.

The PRESIDENT announced that a quorum was now in attendance.

The journal of yesterday was then read.

On motion of Mr. FIERY,

It was so amended, as to state the fact, that the motion to lay on the table the amendment of Mr. BRENT, of Baltimore city, in relation to the homstead exemptions, was made by Mr. WARE, and not by Mr. FIERY, as erroneously stated.

And then the journal was approved.

EXEMPTION FROM EXECUTION.

Mr. RIDGELY moved a reconsideration of the vote, by which the following proposition offered by himself, had yesterday been adopted:

"Laws shall be passed by the legislature to protect from exemption, a reasonable amount of property of a debtor."

It has occurred to me, (said Mr Ridgely) upon reflection that the word "*reasonable*" amount, is a very indefinite term. The legislature would be under no restraint whatever in fixing the amount to be exempted under this provision. If the motion to reconsider should be agreed to, I shall propose to amend the article by inserting the words, "not exceeding in value the sum of five hundred dollars."

He designated this as a limitation upon the legislature, beyond which they shall not go.

Mr. WELLS desired to call the attention of the gentleman from Baltimore county, (Mr. Ridgely,) to the fact, that the gentleman from Kent, (Mr. Mitchell) had yesterday given notice of his intention to move a reconsideration of the vote; that gentleman was not now in his seat. He, (Mr. W.,) would suggest to the gentleman from Baltimore county, (Mr. Ridgely,) that it would be better to waive the motion until the gentleman should be present.

Mr. RIDGELY said, he had no objection. If the House should agree to reconsider, he would then offer his amendment, and it could lie on the table for the present.

Mr. DORSEY enquired of the gentleman from Baltimore county, (Mr. Ridgely,) what he proposed to do with the fund—leave it in the hands of the debtor, or what disposition would he make of it?

Mr. RIDGELY. I leave that matter in the hands of the legislatnre.

The question was then taken,

"Will the Convention reconsider the said vote?"

No quorum voted.

Mr. WARE asked the yeas and nays,

Which were ordered, and

Being taken, resulted as follows:

Affirmative—Messrs. Chapman, President, Blakistone, Dent, Hopewell, Ricaud, Weems, Buchanan, Bell, Welch, Ridgely, Lloyd, Colston, James U. Dennis, Dashiell, Chambers of Cecil, Miller, McLane, Grason, Wright, Shriver, Annan, Ware, Schley, Fiery, Neill, John Newcomer, Harbine, Michael Newcomer, Weber, Hollyday, Shower, Cockey and Brown—34.

Negative—Messrs. Lee, Chambers of Kent, Donaldson, Dorsey, Wells, Jenifer, Hicks, Bowie, Sprigg, McMaster, Hearn, Fooks, Biser, Sappington, Stephenson, Thawley, Stewart of Caroline, Hardcastle, Gwinn, Stewart of Baltimore city, Brent of Baltimore city, Presstman, Slicer and Smith—25.

So the vote was reconsidered.

Mr. MITCHELL now being in his seat—

Mr. RIDGELY moved to amend the said amendment by adding at the end thereof, the words:

"Not exceeding in value the sum of five hundred dollars."

Mr. HOLLYDAY moved to strike out "five" and insert, "three" hundred.

The question was taken, and

The amendment was rejected.

Mr. HICKS moved to strike out "five hundred," and insert "one thousand" dollars.

Mr. MITCHELL. I regret very much that this question has been brought up to-day. I gave notice yesterday of my intention to move a reconsideration of the vote, when the Convention should be full. As things are now, we may go on voting upon sums of two hundred, and five hundred, and one thousand—and nothing will be decided.

The question was stated to be on the amendment of Mr. HICKS.

Mr. HICKS asked the yeas and nays;

Which were refused.

The question was then taken, and

The amendment of Mr. HICKS was rejected.

Mr. THAWLEY moved to strike out "five hundred," and insert "one hundred."

Mr. STEPHENSON called a division of the question, on striking out;

Which was ordered.

Mr. PRESSTMAN desired to offer a substitute.

The proposition was not now in order.

Mr. JOHN NEWCOMER desired to offer an amendment.

The PRESIDENT said, it was not in order at this time.

Mr. JOHN NEWCOMER. The gentleman from Baltimore county, (Mr. Ridgely,) has fixed the *maximum* limit of five hundred dollars. I desire to have a *minimum* limit, and I will say one hundred dollars. I give notice of my intention to offer this amendment, when it is in order.

The question was taken on the motion to strike out, and

Was decided in the negative.

So the Convention refused to strike out.

Mr. GRASON demanded the previous question.

There was a second.

Mr. JOHN NEWCOMER. Is my amendment now in order?

The PRESIDENT. It is not. No motion is in order pending the demand for the previous question.

There was a second;

And the main question was ordered to be now taken.

The question was then stated to be on the amendment of Mr. RIDGELY, adding at the end of his own proposition the words, "not exceeding in value the sum of five hundred dollars."

Mr. HEARN, (to the President.) Is it in order now to move that the subject-matter be laid upon the table?

The PRESIDENT. It is in order.

Mr. HEARN. I make the motion.

The question was taken, and

The Convention decided that the subject-matter should not be laid upon the table.

The question then recurred on the amendment of Mr. RIDGELY.

Mr. DORSEY asked the yeas and nays,

Which were ordered, and

Being taken, resulted as follows:

Affirmative—Messrs. Blakistone, Dent, Hopewell, Ricaud, Weems, Buchanan, Bell, Welch, Ridgely, Lloyd, Colston, Dashiell, Constable, Chambers of Cecil, Miller, McLane, Bowie, Sprigg, Grason, Shriver, Gaither, Biser, Annan, Sappington, Stephenson, Stewart of Caroline, Gwinn, Brent of Baltimore city, Sherwood of Baltimore city, Ware, Schley, Fiery, Neill, John Newcomer, Harbine, Michael Newcomer, Weber, Hollyday, Cockey and Brown—40.

Negative—Messrs. Chapman, President, Lee, Chambers of Kent, Mitchell, Donaldson, Dorsey, Wells, Merrick, Jenifer, Hicks, Wright, McMaster, Hearn, Fooks, Thawley, Hardcastle, Stewart of Baltimore city, Presstman, Slicer, Smith and Shower—21.

So the amendment was agreed to.

The question then recurred on the adoption of the article as thus amended.

Mr. MITCHELL, (to the Chair.) Is not an amendment in order?

The PRESIDENT. It is not. The previous question is yet in operation.

Mr. PRESSTMAN. Is the vote we are about to take, the final vote?

The PRESIDENT. Certainly.

Mr. PRESSTMAN. Is it not competent for me to move to strike out the article adopted yesterday, and which now comes up as an original proposition, and to move to insert, in lieu thereof, another proposition.

The PRESIDENT. It is not in order. If the gentleman will refer to the seventeenth and eighteenth rules, he will see that the point is very plain.

Mr. PRESSTMAN. I should like to hear the rules read.

Some conversation followed on the point of order.

The question then recurred on the adoption of the amendment as amended.

Mr. BOWIE asked the yeas and nays,

Which were ordered,

And being taken, were as follows:

Affirmative.—Messrs. Blakistone, Hopewell, Ricaud, Weems, Bond, Buchanan, Bell, Welch, Ridgely, Lloyd, Colston, Dashiell, Chambers, of Cecil, Miller, McLane, Bowie, Sprigg, Grason, Shriver, Gaither, Biser, Annan, Sappington, Stephenson, Stewart, of Caroline, Gwinn, Brent, of Baltimore city, Sherwood, of Baltimore city, Ware, Schley, Fiery, Neill, John Newcomer, Harbine, Michael Newcomer, Weber, Hollyday, Cockey and Brown—39.

Negative.—Messrs. Chapman, President, Dent, Lee, Chambers, of Kent, Mitchell, Donaldson, Dorsey, Wells, Merrick, Jenifer, Hicks, Wright, McMaster, Hearn, Fooks, Thawley, Hardcastle, Stewart, of Baltimore city, Presstman, Slicer and Smith—21.

So the article, as amended, was adopted.

Mr. HICKS. I now give notice that at a convenient and proper time, I shall move to re-consider the vote just taken, for the purpose of offering an amendment which I suppose it will not be improper for me to read. I indicate this intention because we are here taking away the means and the money of private individuals. That we have a right to use the public money of the State, I do not controvert; but that we have the right to say what portion of any man's money shall be taken from him by force of arms, (for it is too tantamount to that,) is a proposition to which I cannot subscribe. Whilst we are at work on this matter, I think it would be better that we should work understandingly and safely, as discreet and reasonable men should act.

Mr. H. then gave notice that, if the motion hereafter to be made to re-consider the vote, should prevail, he would offer the following proposition:

"And that any man who may hereafter die or become insolvent, in this State, leaving an estate less than five hundred dollars, in every such case, the sum of five hundred dollars shall be provided by the Legislature for the support of his family,"

THE LEGISLATIVE DEPARTMENT.

The Convention passed to the orders of the day, and resumed the consideration of the report of the committee on the Legislative Department.

The Convention passed to the consideration of the twenty-first section, (postponed until this day.)

The question before the Convention was on the amendment offered by Mr. Merrick on Friday the 28th ult., to come in at the end of said section, as follows:

"But it shall be competent for the Legislature, at any time when it can do so, to pay off its outstanding bonds or any part thereof, by an issue of other bonds or stocks bearing a less rate of interest and for no greater amount than the amount redeemed or paid off."

Mr. MERRICK said he had promised the Convention when he presented the amendment that he would not trespass on their patience by any further discussion of the subject, unless such discussion should be rendered necessary by others. He believed the merits of the question had been fully elaborated by previous debates, and he would therefore now content himself with simply recalling to the mind of the Convention the true nature of the question at issue.

It was this: It was admitted by all, and had been several times stated by himself and others, that a great change was about to take place in the monetary affairs of the world. To what extent this change was to go, none could foresee or calculate with any certainty—it was certain only that the change was in progress. That from the action of ordinary causes, as well as because of the great and unexpected augmentation of the amount of precious metals, the relative value of money was to be greatly depreciated, to be accompanied and followed, as the shadow follows the sunbeam, by a low rate of interest—possibly in a few years as low as three per cent. even in this country.

The State of Maryland has a large outstanding debt, bearing interest at the rate of six per cent. If the state of things anticipated should arise, the State, if the amendment prevails, would have the power, through her Legislature, to exchange her outstanding debt, which bears this high rate of interest, as it becomes redeemable, for a debt at the lower rate of interest—say three per cent.; and thus secure to the State the difference between the two rates of interest, three and six per cent. upon the amount of her debt so converted. The saving would be, supposing the whole debt could be so converted, three hundred thousand dollars per year, and in the same proportion upon such a commission of any amount of said debt less than the whole. Without this amendment, under the sweeping restrictions imposed on the power of the Legislature, by the section as it now stands, the Legislature will have no power to do this; and you will be obliged to continue the payment of six per cent. per annum, upon all that part of your outstanding debt which is now or may become redeemable, when you have not the cash in hand to pay it off, although thousands of others may be ready and anxious to lend you the amount at *three* per cent. interest. Would it not be wise to give the Legislature power to turn to the advantage and relief of the people of the State, this condition of the money market, should it arise as anticipated—taking care, as the amendment does, that the gross amount of the State's debt, shall not be increased, by providing that the new stock to be issued, shall not be for any greater amount than the amount of debt redeemed, and shall bear a *less* rate of interest. It is a power which cannot be abused, and if used can be used only for beneficial purposes. The case is precisely similar to that of an individual who owes on his land some fifty thousand dollars, bearing six per cent. interest. He has not the money to pay off this debt, but he has other neighbors or friends, who are willing to lend him the fifty thousand dollars at *three* per cent., would not every one say he was blind to his interests, if he did not take the loan at *three* per cent. interest, and pay off the debts bearing *six* per cent. interest? It is not proposed to require the Legislature to do this, but to leave them the *power* to do so, if that state of things should arise which will enable them to do so; and the circumstances and condition of the State is such, as to make it wise and proper at the time. In my judgment, this salutary power should be left with the Legislature; and this is the whole question the Convention have now to decide. They must understand it; can judge of it; and, therefore, I forbear any further remarks.

Mr. McLane spoke at some length on the subject of financial operations. The remarks will be published hereafter.

Mr. Merrick said:

He was glad to find so few points of difference between himself and the honorable gentleman from Cecil, (Mr. McLane,) and the wonder was that there should be any, after the statements and admissions of the honorable gentleman. He admits that by the operation I have before explained we shall save three per cent. per annum upon the amount of State debt which may be so converted. That is the great and the single object of the amendment. If circumstances arise in which that object can, in whole or in part, be accomplished, the amendment proposes to give power to the Legislature to accomplish it—should those circumstances not arise, then the amendment will be inoperative, and can do no harm. It is one of those rare propositions which will give power for good but none for evil. The gentleman admits the good, if it could be accomplished; he also admits the approach of that state of things which will favor its accomplishment—why not then give the power? The honorable gentleman has gone into a long argument upon general subjects of finance, and the fluctuations in values and exchanges about which there is no dispute, no differences of opinion, and upon which we may discourse as long and as eloquently as we please, and at the end, find ourselves just where we started. I have proposed to bring the mind and judgment of the Convention to bear upon a single and plain proposition in the science, (if you so please to call it,) of finance; which is, that if you can exchange a six per cent. bearing debt for a a three per cent. debt, you save three per cent. by the operation. Nothing could be plainer nor more simple. And believing, for the reasons assigned, that that state of relative values and exchanges is about to arise which may enable you to effect such an operation, I propose to give the Legislature power, if they can accomplish it, to do that most desirable thing. The correctness of my facts are admitted—the approaching depreciation in the value of money is admitted—the consequent fall in the rate of interest is admitted, and the great probability that the object might in whole or in part be accomplished is not controverted. And yet the measure is opposed; and we are told that the approaching season of prosperity, is to be followed by another period of revulsion and distress, when money will again become high and scarce, and the productions of labor and industry low. Well, sir, I admit all that, and have stated it over and over again on this floor before. Every man who has been at all observant of the history and progress of commerce and exchanges, knows that those fluctuations are constantly recurring—have frequently occurred before, and as certainly as like causes, under similar circumstances, produce like effects, will occur again—and again, in future. The causes of these fluctuations are not always visible, and seem mysterious often to the common eye, yet they depend upon fixed principles, which principles are easily understood; but great knowledge, and close observation, and ripe judgment, are necessary to know how to estimate or justly appreciate the modifying effect upon those principles of concomitant, concurrent, and conflicting circumstances. The revulsion of 1837 has been adverted to as standing alone. That is a mistake; there have been other, and as great or greater revulsions before. I will not stop to give the instances; they can be seen by reference. But what of all this? Far from furnishing any argument against the proposition I have made—they but prove its propriety and wisdom—but prove the probable occurrence of that very state of things in which the power I propose to give the Legislature, can be used greatly to the benefit of the tax-paying people of Maryland.

I have not denied that these fluctuations take place. I have not denied that money is at one time plenty and cheap, and at another time scarce and dear. On the contrary, I have affirmed, from the first, both propositions. But what I have and do insist upon, is, that seeing and knowing that these fluctuations do take place, and also seeing and knowing that that change is in rapid progress and likely to go to great extent, which leads to high prices of stocks and other things, and a very low rate of interest—that it becomes us, as wise statesmen, Maryland being largely indebted, to leave with the Legislature the power to make the approaching change subservient to her interests, and to avail of it to the relief of her people, by an exchange, as far as it can be done, of her outstanding debt, bearing a high rate of interest, for other stocks bearing a *less* rate of interest. This done, what does the argument amount to, which goes to show that things will afterwards again change, and interest become high? That change will not effect us. Our exchange will have been made, and we shall be paying interest only at the rate of three per cent., when the common rate may be six again. Should this happen, it will only prove the wisdom of the measure; and its possibility, or even probability, is therefore no argument against it, but the reverse. No danger, no possibility of danger, attends this proposed grant of power to the Legislature. Already there is in the new Constitution, the prohibition upon the contraction of any larger debt, or new debt, whatever; also, the prohibition upon lending or advancing the credit of the State, in any way or for any purpose; and this proposition is simply to give power to exchange the existing debt for one *less* burthensome.

The gentleman has said, that a large part of our State debt is not redeemable now, and will not be so for years to come. I know that is so; but I also know that some of it is now redeemable, and more of it will become redeemable next year, and we have not the cash wherewith to pay it off. To that extent then, the principle of economy I have been advocating, could now be applied, or can be applied when the rate of interest shall fall a little more, perhaps at the very next meeting of the Legislature.

Besides, these stocks not now redeemable, are not always to remain so; and those not now redeemable, may become so at a time. when, in the course of its oscillations, the pendulum of values and exchanges may be at the same extreme of the arc, that it now is approaching, and we may not have in hand the cash to pay or redeem that stock with, at the time. Let the Legislature then have the power to make the saving operation I have explained, and which has not been, and cannot be, denied to be legitimate, proper and beneficial, under such circumstances.

The honorable gentleman has said, that it is in contemplation, and fully calculated upon by the authorities of the State, to pay off the whole of our public debt, in twelve or fifteen years. I have good reason to know that is so. Having myself had some, not altogether insignificant, part in the formation of the sinking fund of the State, I am not ignorant of its power, its amount, nor the additions to be made to it. All this is well—is glorious, and I rejoice from the bottom of my heart, at the bright prospect of the early extinguishment of the debt. But does this furnish any argument against facilitating the means of that early extinguishment? Rather let us, while we rejoice in the hope and prospect of that glorious result, contribute by every means in our power to expedite, and make more certain that desirable consummation.

The doctrine has been presented and denounced, "that a national debt is a national blessing." Who has ever advanced any such a doctrine here? I know that doctrine has been been advanced in England, and strenuously maintained there, where there may be some truth in it—at least, it may be true with reference to those who there consider themselves the nation, namely: the King or Queen and Lords. It tends to give stability to the throne, and aristocracy, by binding the money power, by the ties of interest to the existing order of things. It renders capital the ally of tyranny—and combined, they have the power, and use it, too, of oppressing the millions for the benefit of the few.

But who has ever advanced or maintained such a doctrine on this side of the Atlantic? I confess I have never heard it, and if advanced it would not and could not be tolerated for an instant. We want no artificial ligaments of this sort here, to bind the people to the government, or give it stability. Ours is a government of the people themselves—it is their own, and lives and has its being in their affections only; its principle is equality of rights and duties and privileges to all; it loathes and scorns all wrong and oppression of any. Far, therefore, from needing or desiring the combination of the money power with the government in the form of a national debt, they should and do dread it as the worst enemy to the vital principle of the republic. Money is a most powerful lever in the affairs of men. It is of infinite use as a subordinate agent —but it is no less powerful as a means of oppression—and ruthless always is the tyranny sustained by it.

There is not, there cannot be a voice here then, for a continuance of a national nor a State debt, one moment longer than necessity requires. The object sought after, most anxiously desired by us all, is the early and final extinguishment of our public debt. But we desire to see it paid off by the most ready and facile mode.

If we can so arrange now as with fairness and justice to the public creditor, to reduce by one-third or one-half the amount of annual interest we have to pay, such an arrangement would certainly expedite, or at any rate, greatly facilitate the final payment—and the twelve or fifteen years to elapse, according to the estimates referred to by the gentleman, before the final payment of this debt, is a very long time to be paying a double, or much too great a rate of interest, when a little wisdom now, and good management hereafter might avoid it.

The honorable gentleman has said, that altho' he foresees the approaches of a season of abundance of money, and low rate of interest—yet, he also sees in the signs which are to produce thereafter, another season of great depression, and he gives as those signs, the great importations into the country, and the fact that many of the States of the Union, especially, in the west, are again eagerly embarking in systems of internal improvement.

He may argue correctly, and I believe does, except that I am strongly persuaded, the recurrence of another revulsion is much more distant than the gentleman seems to suppose; but that it will come, I have no doubt, if not with the regularity, at least with the certainty of the reflux of the tides of the ocean. I hope our statesmen in the west and elsewhere, will forsee its approach in time, and provide against its consequences. But what is that to us now, for our present objects and purposes? Tutored in the school of experience, we have guarded against all danger to our State from such causes, by the restrictions already engrafted upon the Constitution we are making. All our great works of internal improvement are completed, or nearly so, and we are in future to embark in no others. We shall, therefore, be in the proud and happy position of dreading no consequences from such a revulsion, let it come when it may. But all this again has nothing to do with the present argument. We have now only to deal with a simple proposition to leave with the Legislature power to save, if they can, a portion, and it may be a very large portion, of the interest we are now paying on our public debt, and of relieving to the extent they may so save in our annual expenditures, the tax-paying people of the State, from the purpose of taxation. This is the single, simple, naked proposition the Convention have to decide, and with them I now leave it.

Mr. George enquired of the Chair, whether it was in order for him to withdraw the proposition he had heretofore offered, and to submit in lieu thereof a substitute.

After some enquiry as to the state of the question, and some conversation on the point of order,

The President stated that such a motion was in order.

Mr. George thereupon withdrew his amendment, and offered the following in lieu thereof:

"No debt shall hereafter be contracted by the Legislature, unless such debt shall be authorized by a law, providing for the collection of an annual tax or taxes, sufficient to pay the interest on such debt as it falls due, and also to discharge the principal thereof within fifteen years from the time of contracting the same; and the taxes laid for this purpose shall not be repealed, or applied to any other object, until the said debt and the interest thereon, shall be fully discharged; and the amount of debts so contracted and remaining unpaid, shall never exceed one hundred thousand dollars. Nor shall the Legislature hereafter appropriate the public money, or pledge the public faith for the use of individuals, associations or corporations; or make appropriations, loans, or subscriptions to any work of internal improvement; but the Legislature may, without laying a tax, borrow any amount never to exceed fifty thousand dollars, to meet temporary deficiencies in the Treasury, and may contract debts to any amount that may be necessary for the defence of the State."

Mr. G. said, that the object was to let the Convention take its choice between this proposition and the substitute of the gentleman from Cecil, (Mr. Constable.)

Mr. Merrick then moved to amend said amendment, by adding at the end thereof, the following:

"And they may at any time, when it may become practicable to do so, redeem and pay off the whole or any portion of the outstanding stocks or bonds of the State, by an issue of other stocks or bonds for no greater amount than the stock or bonds redeemed and bearing a less rate of interest."

Mr. Constable intimated his intention hereafter to offer some propositions by way of amendment.

Mr. Jenifer suggested to his colleague, (Mr. Merrick,) the propriety of fixing some limitation. The question, as it appeared to him, was merely whether it will be better for us to pay an interest of six per cent. on our bonds for ten years, or of three per cent. for twenty or thirty years. He read the amendment to show that it justified this construction. He thought there could be no difficulty in paying off the public debt, as it was called, by gaining an extension of time. The only question is, whether it is not better to pay off such bonds as are, or as they may become due, and then empower the Legislature to convert the six per cent. bonds into three per cent stocks at a period not longer than ten years. The State would derive not benefit, as was conclusively shown by the gentleman from Cecil, (Mr. Mc-

Lane,) if we agree to pay the same aggregate amount of interest, whether we pay it in fifteen years or in thirty years. The question then was not the payment of the public debt, because the conversion of the bonds, no matter in what manner, does not extinguish the debt. But, Mr. J. said, the only one was, whether we should postpone to a longer period of time, the payment of the debt, by the purchase of three per cent. or other less rate of interest than the six per cent. bonds. He agreed with the gentleman from Cecil, (Mr. McLane,) that it was better and safer to let the present system continue as it now works. Mr. J. said he should be in favor of authorising the Legislature or Treasurer to borrow, upon short time, sufficient funds to pay off any deficit which might arise on account of the interest.

Mr. Chambers congratulated himself on the fact, that the distinguished gentlemen who had spoken on the subject, had concurred in the views he had the honor to submit a few days since, as to the propriety of a vigorous effort to pay off the public debt as promptly as possible. The amendment of the gentleman from Charles only authorises the Legislature to re-issue bonds when it can be done at the par value of the existing debt. There cannot be more than a million at six per cent. exchanged for a million at the reduced per cent. The only objection to this conversion of stock from a larger to a smaller interest, seemed to be that the period limited for the discharge of the new debt, might be extended to an unreasonable length.

However the valuation of money and other articles might fluctuate, there could be no difference of opinion as to the advantage of paying a small rate of interest in preference to a large rate. If on the very same day one man receives six dollars for his one hundred, and another receives three for his hundred, most certainly the receiver in one case gets double the value as well as double the sum for the use of his money. Of course no holder of a bond bearing six per cent., would exchange it for a bond of the same security at a lesser interest, unless extension of time or some other element to increase its value was offered as the inducement. The bonds at six per cent. could therefore only be converted when at maturity, for stock on time at a reduced rate of interest.

But we have now some portion of our public debt actually due, and payable at the pleasure of the government, and more might become due at a period which would allow an issue of new stock, at lower interest, on reasonable time, without extending the period at which the large portion of the debt is redeemable. Why not allow the government the advantage, in the mean time, of converting the portion of the debt actually due into stock bearing less interest? Every one who heard his remarks a few days since, would know his earnest anxiety to get rid of the public debt at the shortest possible period, yet he could perceive nothing in the proposed plan which was in collision with this view, provided there was a reasonable limit to the credit to be given on the new stock. He therefore would offer, and ask the gentleman from Charles to accept, a provision by which the new stock should be redeemable, at the pleasure of the government, not later than seven years after it is issued.

Mr. Merrick wished to say one word on the subject of the limitation proposed, upon the time the new stock would have to run. He thought it objectionable, for the reason that it would impair the value of the new stock in the market, and would not be productive of any good effect whatever. If that state of the money market we anticipate should arise, this new stock, if negotiated at all, can, consistently with its objects, only be negotiated when interest shall be at a very low rate, suppose about three per cent. It can only be at some such low rate, the arrangement as contemplated by the amendment, of paying off a stock "bearing a high rate of interest, by the issue of a similar amount of stock bearing a low rate of interest" can be accomplished. If this end be accomplished, and your six per cent. stocks redeemed, and your stocks outstanding bear interest only at the rate of three per cent, there will in the event of future fluctuations causing a rise in the value of money, be no difficulty, if the State has the money, in redeeming this three per cent. stock, though its redemption be not stipulated for in the bonds; the very change in the values adverted to will make this redemption easy—for the reason, that if money becomes more valuable, say worth six per cent. a year, State bonds bearing only three per cent., *must fall below par*; and therefore, if the State should have the means of redeeming them, at a time when this state of things exists, they can be purchased by your fiscal agents below par, and thus another large profit or saving may be made for the State.

Mr. Chambers asked if his friend from Charles did not see, that if money rise above par just at the moment when the State is called on to pay its bonds, it would have to pay more than par for them. These fluctuations are sometimes sudden and always unavoidable in any market.

Mr. Merrick said he would authorize the Legislature to issue bonds bearing the lowest rate of interest. No one calculates that the interest of money is going to fall so very low as one or two per cent. We know its oscillations are continually going on. This amendment looked to nothing more than to authorize the Legislature to borrow at the lowest rate of interest, to pay off a debt bearing a high rate of interest. All that he now sought for was to compare opinions with other gentlemen, and then to adopt the plan which in the view of the Convention would be the wisest.

Mr. McLane replied. His remarks will be given hereafter.

Mr. Spencer read the proposition of his friend from Queen Anne's, (Mr. George,) and referred to the amendments and arguments since presented, and contended that if the amendments were adopted, the legislature might authorise the payment of one bond of a million, by the substitution of another bond of the like value, and appropriate the money in the treasury to other purposes. The proposition of his colleague requires it to be appropriated to the discharge of the public debt and interest, and to no other purpose, and that the legislature shall create no new debt.

He contended that the appropriation of money for other purposes did not involve the creation of a new debt. On the contrary, he contended that it would not. The legislature could at any time, pay off a million by substituting another million bond. He contended that there was no probability of the success of any plan looking to the convertibility of stocks, as no man would give up a bond bearing six per cent interest for one bearing three per cent.

Besides, the State has no power to redeem the debt at its pleasure. The holder of a bond, bearing six per cent interest, would not consent to accept payment, when money was at a depreciated value. His loss would be certain; no good could come from the amendments, but great harm.

Mr. MERRICK expressed his surprise, that gentlemen on all sides, should continue to argue as if the question pending, was a bill directing the proposed negotiation to be actually made—whereas it was a proposition merely to leave the power with the legislature, to cause this pecuniary negotiation to be made hereafter, if the propitious circumstances so often spoken of and explained, should arise; and they, the legislature, should in their wisdom upon a view of all the concommitant circumstances, judge it to be for the advantage and interest of the State to do so. He was no less surprised to find such strong manifestations of a fixed purpose to strip the future legislatures of all salutary power, of all ability to conduct and regulate the affairs of the State, in such manner as wisdom and patriotism might, under circumstances hereafter to arise, (and of which, knowing nothing about them, of course, this Convention cannot judge,) conduce to the happiness and well-being of the people of the State.

Is there to be no faith, no confidence placed in those who are to compose our future legislature? Is all wisdom, all virtue concentrated, in this Convention? Who are to be our future legislators? Are they not to be the same men that are now here, or there descendants, or the descendants of other citizens of the State equally wise, equally virtuous, equally patriotic, with the members of this Convention? Gentlemen must calculate upon a melancholy degeneracy, a sad falling off in the old Maryland stock, if those who are to compose our legislators in future, are to be utterly unworthy of all trust and confidence. I thought the age was progressive. Man was advancing in morals, science and learning—and far from becoming in future less wise and patriotic, were to be expected to improve upon their ancestry.

In response to the gentleman from Cecil, (Mr. McLane,) who had argued that the pending proposition would continue existing taxes beyond the period which would otherwise be required for the payment of the public debt, he must say that such an argument appeared to him strange indeed. It was not so intended; it could have no such effect. Its end and object was to save money to the State; to relieve the people from their burthens, and to give them to some extent present relief. We now raise by taxation, from the pockets of the people, some six hundred thousand dollars a year for the payment of the interest on the public debt. If the exchange of stocks the amendment proposes to give the Legislature power to make, can be effected, and your whole debt of ten millions bearing *six* per cent. interest, can be exchanged for a debt of the same amount bearing interest at the rate of *three* per cent. only, we certainly would save by that exchange *three hundred thousand dollars* a year; and instead of raising annually by taxation *six* hundred thousand dollars a year to pay the interest—*three* hundred thousand dollars only would be required for that purpose; and *one half* the present taxes might be repealed. This is the object; and this would be the effect. If not to the whole extent, to as great an extent as the exchange could be effected by the Legislature. Far then from continuing taxes beyond the period during which under the existing state of things they would be required—this measure contemplated gives immediate relief to the people, by dispensing with the necessity for a large portion of them. No man could be more anxious than he was to see the public debt extinguished, and he was anxious to see every means used which could fairly and honestly tend to expedite and facilitate that result, and accomplish it with the least possible amount of taxation. It was a high and holy duty, incumbent upon every one, to lessen the burthens of the people, as far and as soon as could be made consistent with the public faith and honor. As tending to this end, he had moved the pending proposition. To that end it would operate, if it operated at all, and it could operate to none other. He would now leave the matter with the Convention.

Mr. BROWN. I think this question has been sufficiently discussed, and I am anxious to get on with the business. I move the previous question.

Mr. CHAMBERS, of Kent, sent to the Clerk's table the amendment he had indicated, and which was as follows:

" *Provided*, That such new bonds or stocks shall be made redeemable within seven years from the time of their being issued."

Mr. MERRICK accepted the amendment as a modification of his own proposition.

Mr. JENIFER suggested another amendment to his colleague, (Mr. Merrick,) which led to some conversation between the two gentlemen. Mr. M. explaining that the object of his colleague would be accomplished by the amendment in its modified form.

Mr. CONSTABLE requested Mr. BROWN to withdraw the demand for the previous question, to enable him, (Mr. C ,) to say a few words in reply to the gentleman from Queen Anne's (Mr. Spencer.)

Mr. BROWN assented.

So the demand for the previous question was withdrawn.

Mr. CONSTABLE spoke at length in reply. His remarks will be given hereafter.

Mr. GRASON rose, he said, not with a view to object to the propositions of the gentleman from Cecil, (Mr. Constable,) but to answer the objections which had been made to the proposition of his colleague. The gentleman from Cecil, is unwilling to confer power upon the Legislature, to contract debts to the amount of one hundred thousand dollars, because, to that amount, the money might be applied to any purpose whatever. If the gentleman would examine the articles, submitted by his colleague, (Mr. George,) he would find that it could not be applied to the use of societies, corporations, or to purposes of internal improvement. His colleague had not enumerated the objects to which it might be applied, because it was impossible to forsee all the contingencies which might occasion a deficiency in the treasury. It was obvious, however, that the current revenue might occasionally be insufficient to pay the interest on the public debt, and meet the necessary expenses of the State. The statehouse or the tobacco-warehouses, might be destroyed by fire and the Legislature should have the power to borrow a limited amount to meet such contingencies as they arise. The gentleman from Cecil apprehends that the Legislature, if this power were conferred, would enter into every kind of wild speculation; but as the amount of debt to be contracted was limited to one hundred thousand dollars, and was to be accompanied by a tax, and could not be applied to the use of corporations or to the purposes of internal improvement, there could be no danger of an abuse of the power. If the immediate representatives of the people could not be trusted to this limited extent, it would be better to abolish the Legislature.

Mr. DONALDSON said the amendment of the gentleman from Charles, (Mr. Merrick,) was suggested, he believed, by a clause of the section which he, (Mr. D.,) had proposed some days before, and which the Convention had rejected. The purpose of that clanse he had explained at the time, to be mainly to provide for a temporary deficit of revenue, if any such should occur. The treasurer now, under an Act of Assembly, had the power to make such a loan, and he considered it important to the credit of the State that the power should not be taken away. He had before explained how, on account of the inequality of the expenditures of different quarters there might be a deficiency at the particular day when money was needed, although the whole year might show a large surplus. If some great calamity were to happen to our public works in the course of any year, and we are bound to consider such contingencies, we might find the power to borrow absolutely necessary, to save the public faith, and yet, the sum borrowed, could so soon be repaid out of accruing revenue, that the levying a new tax would be useless and absurd. These considerations. however, had had no weight with the Convention. Under the influence of a panic, proceeding from the recollection of former extravagance—gentlemen must excuse him for saying so—the power had been entirely destroyed. Time would probably show who was right on that point.

But he had stated that another purpose of the last clause of the section he proposed, was to enable the State to redeem its loans when they became payable, in case there were not adequate funds in the treasury, by borrowing at a lower rate of interest if money were then abundant. The gentleman from Cecil, (Mr. McLane,) had then misapprehended the purpose of that clause, supposing it to mean that money should be borrowed at a low rate of interest, to buy up the State loans not yet due and at premium in the market. He agreed with that gentleman that such a course would be bad financiering. He now understood that gentleman to say that if loans, when they became redeemable, were discharged, as they could be, at par, with money borrowed at a lower rate of interest, the State would of course be the gainer by the difference in the interest.

Mr. McLANE assented. He had so said this morning.

Mr. DONALDSON continued:

This part of his proposition was now urged as a separate amendment by the gentleman from Charles, (Mr. Merrick.) He, (Mr. D.,) considered it well that such a power should be given, but with great deference to that gentleman, he must say, that its importance had been very much overrated. We never could save any great amount of money by the operation contemplated; for the simple reason, that the mass of our debt was not redeemable until the years 1870 and 1890. Before the first named period, he hoped that all our debt would be extinguished; for, if our tax system remain untouched, the sinking fund and the surplusses will have absorbed the whole. It was only, then, to so much of our debt as was now redeemable, or would soon become so, that the amendment could apply; and the gain to the State, in any case, could not be very considerable. As a matter of course, the holders of our stock would not surrender the stock for par when it commanded a premium in the market, and we could not commute for a lower rate of interest until the time fixed for redemption. The gentleman from Charles had probably forgotten at what distant dates most of our loans were payable.

There was much force in what the gentleman from Cecil said on the danger of protracting the the time of final payment of the debt by new loans, even at a lower rate of interest than the old. It might lead to a reduction of taxes, and he agreed that such a result would more than counteract the benefit to be derived from the saving in interest. To meet this view, it was better to place some limit of time, as suggested by the gentleman from Kent, (Mr. Chambers,) within which the new loans should certainly be redeemable.

Mr. D. declared his great satisfaction at the strong expressions of the gentleman from Cecil, in favor of continuing in full force our present system of taxation until our whole debt is discharged. He himself had taken occasion a week ago to express his views on that subject, in answer to the gentleman from Frederick, (Mr. Thomas,) and his friend from Kent, (Mr. Chambers,) had ably supported the same side of the question. Mr. D. repeated what he had before asserted on this point, and said, that if it were fully realised that all our debt would be discharged in the course of ten or twelve years, the present value of every rood of land in the State would be increased, in spite of the taxes we have to pay.

In regard to the system of internal improvement adopted by this State, and the consequent burdens of taxation, he took the liberty of differing in some degree from the gentleman from Cecil, who seemed tolook upon them as evils of such tremendous magnitude. He, himself, when he considered the peculiar position and circumstances of Maryland, did not hesitate to say, that in spite of all the money recklessly wasted on projects that should not have been entertained, and in spite of all the taxation we had suffered, the whole result had been beneficial to the State. Those public works which were already productive of great benefit to the State, and which he considered absolutely essential to her future prosperity, would not have been undertaken, if they had depended solely on private capital and enterprise. If they had not been undertaken, Maryland would have sunk into insignificance among her sister States. Nor has the pressure of debt been without its advantages to us, not only in testing the public virtue, but in giving valuable lessons for the future. The system would have been an almost unmixed benefit, if the true financial principle had been followed, of providing in the laws creating the debt, substantial ways and means for its liquidation. As the State then had no receipts from internal improvements, taxation should have been at once resorted to. Then extravagance and speculative schemes would have been effectually checked. Still, taking matters at the worst, the whole result was, in his opinion, beneficial.

Mr. Dorsey without intending to make any extensive remarks, could not but notice some of the strange propositions which he had heard, as to the effect of the conversion of stock, and the calculations which had been made of the early extinguishment of the public debt. He had never felt any great horror of a mere public debt. The only real ground of dread is, when a State has a heavy debt, which it is unable to pay. The State was now in such a condition, that if the amendment proposed the other day by the gentleman from Worcester, had been adopted, he should have said we were in a state of happy exemption from all disquietude upon the subject. He knew that a great part of the debt would not be payable until 1870 and 1890, and he also knew that all the calculations which had been made of the actual payment of the entire public debt were somewhat problematical. Some of the persons who hold Maryland debt, will hold on to their bonds, and reject all offers for their redemption; but the number of such is not large, and they interpose no serious obstacle to the State's emancipation from its public debt. The great body of the bond holders are mere speculators, who hold the debt not as a permanent investment, but as an article of traffic, a subject for speculation, and on offering them a shade above the market price, the stock is at your service and is thereby redeemed. The State will, therefore, meet with no difficulty in redeeming the great portion of its debt,as soon as it possesses the means of doing so.

He desired the sinking fund or rather its income and accumulations to be used for that purpose, as it heretofore has been as long as the holders of the State debt, would, by sale or redemption, permit the operation. When the impracticable stockholders, (if he might so call them,) put an end to the operations of the sinking fund in Maryland stocks its investments should be made in State stocks of Massachusetts, New York, Virginia, etc., until the amount thereof purchased, was adequate to the payment of the Maryland debt as its maturity, and in the meantime, to keep down the interest thereon. At that desirable epoch, he regarded our State debt as paid; it then would cease to excite dread or apprehensions in the minds of the most timorous. He stated that the value of State stock, mainly depended on the remoteness of the period at which it was redeemable. The more remote that period, the higher the market price of the stock.

He, therefore, was in favor of the power proposed to be given by the gentleman from Charles. But his desire for its adoption had been nearly extinguished,by an amendment he had accepted, which, he believed, had almost wholly paralized its original efficiency.

Mr. McLane enquired of Mr. Dorsey, if he could name any instance in which such a financial operation as that contemplated by the gentleman from Charles, had ever taken place?

Mr. Dorsey could not, at the moment, call to mind any such instance, as he was not very conversant with stock operations, never having been engaged in them, but had no doubt there had been many such, for reasons most obvious.

He then illustrated his statement by putting a supposititious case of a transaction between two individuals; and stated that he had seen accounts of such transactions, but could not now specify time. He repeated that the value of the State bonds depended on the time they had to run. He had seen in a recent publication of the price of stocks, that a five per cent. stock which had a long time to run, was selling at a higher price than a six per cent. stock redeemable in a shorter period. This he had seen, and he supposed others also had seen it.

He presumed the five per cent stock had a long time to run, and that the six per cent. stock was payable now or in some short period. He objected to the limitation of seven years, because he conceived it was too short a period. He did not think the debt could be paid in twelve or fourteen years, not because the State would not be able to pay it before that time, but because all the holders of the bonds will not sell or receive the money for them. But the gentleman from Cecil asks if we have a surplus in the Treasury what do we mean to do with it? And then he goes on to express his fears that it will be dissipated in unwise speculations. Not so. He, like the gentleman from Carroll, (Mr. Brown,) had too much confidence in the Legislature to feel any such apprehensions, and the constitutional provisions already adopted rendered such indiscretions morally impracticable. He then went into a view of the operation of the sinking fund. The moment that fund becomes adequate to the public debt and interest thereon as it accrues, the Legislature will repeal all our taxes, and not wait until 1870 or 1890; when our debt is redeemable.

He admitted that States, like individuals, were bound to discharge their obligations. When debts become due, every individual strives to pay them; and when he finds difficulty for the moment his notorious solvency and punctuality, enable him to borrow for the purpose. He had no such idle terror of debt, that he would not be perfectly willing to give his bond for ten thousand dollars, bearing an interest at three per cent., and at the same time lend the same amount on a bond bearing six per cent., to a person of as unquestioned solvency as himself.

If the State by extending the time of payment, could issue bonds at an interest of five per cent., and receive in exchange its own bonds at six per cent., the exchange would be a beneficial operation. And here Mr. D. read a statement which he had prepared, to show the immense gains by such an operation after a long period of years upon the just principles of compound interest.

By carrying on the calculation, it would be seen what would be the effect of the sinking fund, before the debt becomes due. The people of the State are not now discontented about the taxes. They all agree that it is better to continue them until the means of paying the public debt have been provided, when taxation should terminate. He repeated that he had entire confidence in the virtue and discretion of the Legislature, under the restrictions we have already imposed on it, and he thought that power should be vested in them to make such appropriations as future events might render indispensably requisite. He would, therefore, vote for the amendment under consideration.

Mr. D. then said that he was now enabled to point the gentleman from Cecil to one instance where a six per cent. stock before it became due, to the best of his recollection, and that of his friend from Baltimore, was converted into a five per cent. stock. It was the stock of the city of Baltimore.

The question was then stated to be on the amendment of Mr. Merrick.

Mr. Dorsey moved to amend the amendment, by striking out the words "seven years."

Mr. D. said, he saw no object in retaining these words They paralysed and destroyed the object of the amendment.

The amendment was rejected.

And the question was then taken on the amendment of Mr. Merrick,

And it was rejected.

The question then recurred on the substitute of Mr. George.

Mr. Constable asked a division of the question upon striking out.

A division was ordered accordingly.

Mr. McHenry moved to amend said amendment, by adding at the end thereof these words, "or meet the just liabilities of the State incurred previously to the adoption of this Constitution."

This amendment Mr. Constable accepted.

Some explanations followed, in which Messrs. McLane, Spencer, Constable, and Thomas, took part.

On a suggestion by Mr. McLane,

Mr. Constable further modified his amendment, by retaining that portion of the proposition of Mr. George, which is in the following words:

"But the Legislature may without laying a tax borrow an amount never exceeding fifty thousand dollars to meet temporary deficiencies in the Treasury."

Mr. Thomas expressed his preference for the proposition of Mr. George. He also called attention to the amendment which had been offered by Mr. McHenry and accepted as a modification by Mr. Constable, and which he (Mr. T.) regarded as an objectionable and perilous proposition.

And then, without taking any question the Convention adjourned until to-morrow at ten o'clock.

WEDNESDAY, March 5th, 1851.

The Convention met at ten o'clock.

Prayer was made by the Rev. Mr. Grauff.

The roll of the members was called, and a quorum being present, the journal of yesterday was read and approved.

LICENSE SYSTEM.

Mr. Sellman presented a petition of sundry citizens of Anne Arundel and Calvert counties, praying that the privilege to sell intoxicating liquors shall not be granted to any person in any part of the State, except the same shall be first sanctioned, or approved of by a majority of the votes in the election district where the same is to be sold.

Which was read, and

On motion of Mr. Sellman,

Referred to the select committee appointed on that subject.

DESECRATION OF GRAVE YARDS.

Mr. Davis presented a petition of George L. L. Davis, of the city of Baltimore, for the protection of "grave yards."

Which was read, and

On motion of Mr. Davis,

Referred to committee No. 14.

THE LEGISLATIVE DEPARTMENT.

The Convention resumed the consideration of the special order of the day, being the report of the committee on the legislative department of the government

The question pending before the Convention on yesterday, being on the adoption of the amendment offered by Mr. CONSTABLE, and amended on the motion of Mr. McHENRY.

Mr. BROWN moved to strike out the words "or to meet the just liabilities of the State incurred previously to the adoption of this Constitution"

[These words were yesterday proposed by Mr. McHENRY and accepted by Mr. CONSTABLE, as a modification of his proposition.]

Mr. McHENRY said, he did not desire to detain the Convention, nor was he so arrogant as to suppose that any remarks which he could submit, would counter-balance the force of the opposition which the distinguished gentleman from Frederick, (Mr. Thomas,) had yesterday made. He, (Mr. McH.,) must, however, be permitted to disclaim any intention to authorise the State to borrow money for schemes of stock-jobbing. He doubted whether the words of the amendment conveyed any such signification. No man in the State, or out of it, was more opposed than himself, to the corruption and iniquity of stock-jobbing and trading with the public money. He read and explained his amendment. In the event of such a convulsion as had swept over the country in 1837, again occurring, it was probable that a deficit in the treasury of the State far exceeding fifty thousand dollars might take place. It was to meet a case of that kind, as any other case in which the faith of the State was justly, and properly pledged, that he had offered his amendment. If any gentleman of more experience than himself, would suggest a form of words which would meet the object he had in view, and would not be liable to the exceptions taken to his own, he, (Mr. McH.,) would cheerfully adopt it. They had all the same object at heart—the maintenance untarnished of the faith and honor of the State.

Mr. BROWN said, that no man would question the purity of the motive, or the singleness of the object of the gentleman from Harford, (Mr. McHenry.) But in his, (Mr. B.'s) judgment, the amendment would bear a construction which the gentleman himself did not intend should be put upon it. It seemed to him, (Mr. B.,) that the amendment gave to the Legislature the power to adopt the very course indicated in the amendment of the gentleman from Charles, (Mr. Merrick,) and which had been voted down by the Convention.

He, (Mr. B.,) could not vote for the proposition of the gentleman from Cecil, [Mr. Constable.] so long as this provision remained in it. If the gentleman would strike out this provision, he [Mr. B.,] would vote for the amendment rather than for the proposition of the gentleman from Queen Anne, [Mr George.]

Mr. CONSTABLE expressed his desire again to modify his amendment, by striking out the provision offered by the gentleman from Harford, [Mr. McHenry,] yesterday, and accepted by himself. He, [Mr. C.,] would withdraw that branch of the amendment, if no objection was made.

Mr. McHENRY said, there would be no objection on his part.

Some conversation followed, after which

Mr. CONSTABLE modified his proposition by striking out the words "or to meet the just liabilities of the State, incurred previously to the adoption of this Constitution?

Mr. McHENRY now moved to amend the amendment of Mr. CONSTABLE, by inserting the following in place of the words just stricken out:

"Or absolutely necessary to enable the State to discharge in good faith its just liabilities incurred previously to the adoption of this constitution."

Mr. McH. said, it seemed to him that if there was any force in the meaning of words, the amendment as now modified by him, could not be liable to the objections urged against it yesterday by the distinguished gentleman from Frederick, (Mr. Thomas.)

Mr. THOMAS remarked that, as special reference had been made to him by the gentleman from Harford, (Mr. McHenry,) he, [Mr. T.,] would respond simply by saying, that he could not vote in favor of the proposition. He did not deem it necessary to enter again upon a statement of the objections which he had indicated. He preferred the amendment of the gentleman from Queen Anne's, [Mr. George.]

Mr. McHENRY said:

He had hoped, that the gentleman from Frederick, (Mr. Thomas,) would find that the amendment, as now modified, was free from the objection which had been urged yesterday. He was sorry that so important a proposition had so feeble an advocate as himself. He could only express the hope that it would recommend itself to the favor of the Convention, and he would ask the yeas and nays on its adoption.

Mr. GRASON rose, he said, to call the attention of the Convention to the question as it now stood. It would be remembered that the two articles submitted by his colleague, [Mr George] had been adopted by an almost unanimous vote. But many members of the body, upon reflection, were apprehensive that the restraints placed upon the legislature were not sufficient, and, therefore, it was suggested to his colleague, that it might be advantageous that the articles might be reconsidered, with a view so to amend them, as to prevent the legislature in the most positive terms, from again embarking in any wild or extravagant schemes For his own part, he was satisfied with the two articles in the form in which they had been adopted; because, in the course of his experience, he had found that when men were anxious to obtain too much, they were apt to obtain less than they originally asked.

It seemed to him that the restrictions imposed by the amendment of his colleague, were sufficient to secure the people from the imposition of further burthens. He was satisfied that, if these articles had been a part of the original Constitution, the State would not at this day have been incumbered with one cent of debt.

But as it was a matter of great importance to prevent the legislature from contracting a large amount of debt, and knowing that the motion to reconsider would be made, he was disposed to accede to the wishes of gentlemen who desired greater restrictions, rather than risk the whole provision. To his mind, the most important object to be accomplished by the call of this Convention was to place restrictions upon the legislature—to prevent them hereafter from involving the State in pecuniary difficulty. But he did not wish to treat the legislature, as a captured enemy—refusing to them, even the honors of war.

The proposition of his friend from Cecil, (Mr. Constable,) actually treated the legislature as if they were a foreign enemy; the gentleman was afraid to trust them with any expenditure of the public money. And it was his, (Mr. G's.,) opinion that the propositions of the gentleman from Cecil, [Mr. Constable,] even in their original shape, were much more likely to involve the State in difficulty than the proposition of his, [Mr. G's..] colleague.

With all the interest which he felt in this matter of legislative reform, he did not wish to embarrass and tie down the legislature by Constitutional provisions in such a manner as to stop the wheels of the government. He was disposed to believe that the objection to the proposition of his colleague, if any could be raised against it, was that it was too stringent.

He, [Mr. G.,] would himself have been willing to go to the extent of one hundred thousand, instead of fifty thousand dollars, to meet deficiencies in the treasury, not fearing that any prejudicial results would have followed from the adoption of this more extended limit.

The question which the Convention had now to decide, was whether they would take the proposition of his colleague, [Mr. George,] as modified, or would take the various propositions of the gentleman from Cecil, [Mr. Constable,] and with them, the amendment of the gentleman from Harford, [Mr. McHenry.]

He, [Mr. G ,] understood that the true meaning of the amendment of the gentleman from Harford, was, that the legislature might impose taxes, for the purpose of redeeming the public debt, hitherto contracted. The gentleman seemed to act under the supposition that no provision had been made for the payment of that debt. Yet we had heard from various quarters of the Convention, and amongst others, from the gentleman from Anne Arundel, (Mr. Donaldson,) whose intimate knowledge of the financial condition of the State was well known, that, in the course of twelve or fifteen years, the payment of this debt would be accomplished under the provision now made for the purpose. There was, therefore, no necessity for making any provision to pay off the debt hitherto contracted.

Mr. McHenry interposed, and turning to Mr. Grason, made a remark apparently in explanation, of which nothing was heard by the Reporter.

Mr. Grason then proceeded to examine *seriatim*, the propositions of Mr. Constable—remarking at the outset, that he, [Mr. G.,] objected generally to them, because, notwithstanding the ability of the gentleman by whom they were drawn, they were complicated—and it would be impossible for any man but a lawyer to comprehend their full extent and operation.

Reading the first, second, and third branches of the substitute of Mr. Constable, Mr. G. expressed the opinion that all these details were provided for, and the whole ground covered by the proposition of his colleague.

The fourth proposition of the gentleman from Cecil was, that the Legislature shall have no power to appropriate money for anypurpose, or to any object for which they are not authorised to raise the sum so assessed by a general State tax. It seemed to him, (Mr. G.,) that this section was somewhat obscure. He took it for granted that the Legislature at present had no power to appropriate the public money for any purpose for which they might not raise a tax. But, according to the language of the gentleman from Cecil, it might happen that an appropriation was needed of one thousand or fifteen hundred dollars for the payment of some particular services. The question would then come up before the Legislature, whether they had the right to levy a tax upon the people to pay this sum. He thought that this was rather obscure—too minute—and that it was better provided for in the amendment of his colleague.

The next branch, as to the imposition of State taxes for the defence of the State, and the payment of the principal and interest of the public debt, was provided for in the amendment of his colleague.

"To defray the necessary expenses of the Government," was another object provided for in the same section. This was a branch under which, he thought, more abuses might creep in, than could under the amendment of his colleague.

The sixth and last article related to the exemption of property from taxation. He thought that the Legislature should have the power to exempt from the operation of any system of taxation property simply enough for the purposes of public worship, &c.; he meant churches and burial grounds. Yet, as he construed the proposition of the gentleman from Cecil, (Mr. Constable,) it did not exempt churches.

The fifth section gave the Legislature a general power to establish a system of public schools, adequately endowed, throughout the State. There was a general feeling throughout the State, by men who were zealous upon the subject, that private resources were not sufficient to keep up these schools, but that it was necessary for the Legislature to resort to the public Treasury, and take from it money raised by taxation for the establishment of a more general system. There was nothing in his colleague's proposition which prohibited the Legislature from making appropriations for public schools. But at the same time it contained no invitation or incitement to that end. The Legislature would be prompt enough to apply the public funds to purposes of education without any suggestion in the Constitution. The danger rather was that they would run into the contrary extreme, and that there would be as great a rage for schools now as there was for internal improvements twenty years ago.

He objected to such a provision on another ground—which was, that we already had in particular counties ample funds for the purpose. It was so in Queen Anne's. Mr. G. explained the operation of the school system there—and showed that a school house was built in every primary school district—by taxes levied upon the people residing in such districts, and with their consent. Would a county so situated be willing to adopt a general school system by taxation, in addition to what they had already borne, for the purpose of educating children in the different parts of the State?

There were other objections, of considerable force, which struck his mind in reference to the various propositions of the gentleman from Cecil. He, (Mr. G ,) had already pointed out such as he considered the main objections. The others were subordinate. The Convention must decide which of the two amendments it would take. He was satisfied that the proposition of his colleague covered every inch of ground that ought to be covered; and, he repeated, that if it had any defect at all, it was that it restricted the Legislature too much. He believed it a matter of high importance that salutary restraints should be imposed on the Legislature, but the Convention should take care not to go so far as to incur any danger of arresting the operations of the Government. He thought it would be better to be satisfied with the proposition as it stood.

Mr. Constable made some observations to shew what were his views on the subject of the power which ought to be confided to the Legislature with regard to appropriations. His remarks will be published hereafter.

Mr. Grason made some remarks which will be published hereafter.

Mr. Merrick remarked that he did not rise to inflict a speech. The Convention had already listened to-day, to speeches from two able and learned gentlemen, and he thought that with the lights which had been shed upon the question by them, and by other gentlemen in the course of the general debate, the Convention must now be ready to vote. He, therefore, demanded the previous question.

Mr. Bowie requested the gentleman from Charles, [Mr. Merrick,] to withdraw the demand, to enable him, [Mr. B.,] to say a very few words. He would, if required, renew the motion.

Mr. Merrick acquiesced.

So the previous question was withdrawn.

Mr. Bowie said, he had intended to take no part in this discussion, and to content himself with giving a silent vote. But, in looking over the proposition, he found its phraseology to be such as would prevent him giving it his support.

He took it for granted that the Convention, on all sides, was pretty well united in desiring to prohibit the Legislature from running the State into any great public debt. That was the main object in view. In accomplishing this end, the Convention should take care to use no language which would prevent the Legislature making appropriations that might be absolutely necessary to defray necessary expenses, or for any other necessary purpose. The Statehouse, as had been suggested, might be burnt down; and it would cost sixty or seventy thousand dollars to rebuild it. So with the Penitentiary—the Maryland Hospital—the asylum for the Deaf and Dumb—or the Blind Asylum. All these were public property, and large sums of money would be required to re-build them. Great principles of public policy, of benevolent and philanthropic action, were involved in these establishments, and they should not be left to suffer. Yet, according to his view of both the propositions, all these objects would be entirely defeated, unless they fell within the limit of the one hundred thousand, and the fifty thousand dollars.

Another objection to the phraseology of the amendment of the gentleman from Queen Anne's, [Mr. George,] was, that the Legislature should not appropriate money for the use of individuals, &c. Now, if the proposition was adopted in this form, the Legislature could not appropriate one cent to the payment of a claim no matter how just it might be. Surely, the Convention did not intend any such thing. He was sure that his friend from Queen Anne's could not entertain such an idea. And yet, under the proper, legal construction of the amendment, we must come to this conclusion.

Why should we lay a tax at the same time that we raised a sum of one hundred thousand dollars? It might be wanted for the purposes which had been indicated by the gentleman from Queen Anne's, and there were others which he, [Mr. B.,] could designate. Why not allow the State to borrow the money upon the general credit of the treasury, without laying a tax? It could be done, and it seemed to him that there was no necessity for laying a tax when we raised one hundred thousand dollars, any more than there was when we desired to raise fifty thousand dollars to meet a *deficit* in the treasury.

He was willing to impose all proper restrictions upon the Legislature. He would not authorise them, under any circumstances, to lend the credit of the State to private associations or companies, or for works of internal improvement. But he thought that the Convention had gone as far as the public safety demanded or public policy required, when they had reached that point. Nor did he believe it requisite to specify the objects for which these appropriations should be made. The necessity of a specific grant was not the same with a State as with the federal government. He was willing to specify the prohibitions, but could see no necessity for a specific grant of powers. He thought the proposition of the gentleman from Cecil, [Mr. Constable,] in this respect, went too far.

He, [Mr. B.,] had drawn up an amendment, which, it seemed to him, would accomplish the objects aimed at by both these propositions, divested of the objections he had indicated. It was not now, he believed, in order, but he would read it as a part of his remarks.

Mr. B. read the amendment.

Mr. McLane invited the gentleman from Prince George's, [Mr. Bowie,] to give his view of the terms "just liability," employed in the amendment of the gentleman from Harford, [Mr. McHenry.]

Mr. BOWIE said, he could well conceive, with the gentleman from Harford, that some legislation might be necessary to consummate an engagement already entered into, upon the faith of the State, in relation to these works of internal improvement. He was not ready at this moment to specify There were a great many contigencies which might take place, rendering such an appropriation necessary; and the Convention should not impose restrictions upon the Legislature, which would prevent them, in the exercise of an honest discretion, from making such an appropriation, if it should be required.

Mr. B. renewed the demand for the previous question, but, with the consent of Mr. MERRICK, waived it.

Mr. GRASON made some remarks which will be published hereafter.

Mr. DONALDSON gave notice that he would, at the proper time, offer an amendment, [which was read, and will be found hereafter.]

Mr. DONALDSON said:

He hoped there was no doubt about the adoption of the amendment he proposed. He considered it essential for the purpose of making perfectly sure the fulfilment of the State's obligations. It was most probable, that we never should have to borrow for the purpose of paying the interest of the debt, at any quarter; but that such a necessity should occur, was by no means impossible, and in maintaining the State faith, there should never be any uncertainty. He had stated several times before, that on account of the great inequality of receipts and expenditure, at the different quarters, we might have a considerable surplus of revenue in the whole year, and yet a deficiency at a particular quarter. By the temporary failure of some of the public works, or by the occurrence of some unforeseen casualty, there might be a deficiency at some quarter of more than fifty thousand dollars, which was the extreme fixed in the article of the gentleman from Queen Anne's [*Mr.* George.] The treasurer now had the power, conferred by the Legislature, to make a loan for such a purpose, according to the actual necessity. He thought that power should not be abridged.

Mr. D. said, he had no intention of again arguing the propriety of restricting the *Legislature*, to the extent proposed in this article. That the Convention had settled in opposition to his views, whether wisely or not, would be hereafter seen. But he could not help remarking, that it seemed to him a mere mockery, to provide, as this article did, for levying a tax to pay off, in the course of fifteen years, a debt, which, in the aggregate, should not exceed one hundred thousand dollars. Such a debt could be paid off without taxation, in less than a year. Our annual surplus now, is more than three hundred thousand dollars. He supposed that it was contemplated to have all the financial machinery of a regular sinking fund, to absorb this immense sum of one hundred thousand dollars, in fifteen years; and until that was effected, we could not even re-build the State-house, the Hospital, or the Tobacco warehouses, in case they should burn down. It really would be a great deal better, in his opinion, to take away entirely the power to borrow in any event, than to put such a provision as this, in our Constitution, which was now seriously proposed.

Mr. SPENCER. One word as to the term of fifteen years. The gentleman from Anne Arundel, seemed to regard this proposition as frivolous. So it would be in different circumstances. But the State of Maryland is largely in debt—to the amount of millions. If the State was out of debt, one hundred thousand would indeed be nothing. But this one hundred thousand dollars, when added to the millions already outstanding, helps to make the debt more onerous. He thought it right that the restriction should be inserted in the Constitution. The limitation of fifteen years had been fixed on, owing to the peculiar situation in which the treasury now stands.

The question was then stated to be on the amendment of Mr. MCHENRY.

Mr. MCLANE referred to the latitude of construction of which, in his judgment, the amendment was susceptable, and invited the gentleman from Harford, [Mr. McHenry,] to state what, in his view, this "just liability" was.

Mr. MCHENRY replied that he could only answer for his own intention and object. These, he supposed, he had sufficiently explained, in the remarks he had before made. He referred again to the contingency of a revulsion, such as had occurred in 1837, when all the sources of revenue might be stopped. He also declared that he had in view the payment of any *just* claim against the State, whatever its extent might be.

Mr. MCLANE felt himself less disposed, he said, to support the proposition under the explanation of its object made by the gentleman who offered it, than he had been before, and indicated his intention to vote against it.

Some explanatory conversation followed between Messrs. BOWIE and MCLANE.

The question then again recurred on the amendment of Mr. MCHENRY.

The yeas and nays were ordered.

The question was then taken and the result was as follows:

Affirmative — Messrs. Chapman, President, Blakistone, Dent, Hopewell, Ricaud, Lee, Chambers, of Kent, Donaldson, Dorsey, Wells, Randall, Weems, Merrick, Crisfield, Goldsborough, Bowie, Sprigg, Bowling, McMaster, McHenry, Schley, Fiery, John Newcomer, Davis and Smith—25.

Negative—Messrs. Sellman, Bond, Jenifer, Buchanan, Bell, Welch, Chandler, Ridgely, Lloyd, Colston, Dashiell, Hicks, Constable, Chambers, of Cecil, Miller, McLane, Spencer, Grason, George, Fooks, Thomas, Shriver, Gaither, Biser, Annan, Sappington, Stephenson, Thawley, Stewart, of Caroline, Gwinn, Stewart, of Baltimore city, Brent, of Baltimore city, Presstman, Ware, Neill, Harbine, Michael Newcomer, Weber, Hollyday, Slicer, Parke, Ege, Shower, Cockey and Brown—45.

So the amendment was rejected.

The question then recurred on the modified amendment of Mr. CONSTABLE.

Mr. CONSTABLE again modified the amendment by striking out the words "without paying a tax."

The words were, Mr. C. said, unnecessary.

The question then was on inserting the amendment of Mr. CONSTABLE, in lieu of the first paragraph of the amendment offered yesterday by Mr. GEORGE.

Mr. WEEMS asked the yeas and nays which were ordered, and being taken, resulted as follows:

Affirmative—Messrs. Blakistone, Dent, Hopewell, Sellman, Weems, Bond, Merrick, Buchanan, Welch, Chandler, Lloyd, Colston, James U. Dennis, Dashiell, Hicks, Constable, Chambers, of Cecil. Miller, McLane, McMaster, Hearn, Fooks, Gaither, Stephenson, McHenry, Hardcastle, John Newcomer, Michael Newcomer, Parke, Shower and Brown—31.

Negative—Messrs. Chapman, President, Ricaud, Lee, Chambers, of Kent, Mitchell, Donaldson, Dorsey, Wells, Randall, Jenifer, Bell, Ridgely, Crisfield, Goldsborough, Bowie, Sprigg, Bowling, Spencer, Grason, George, Thomas, Shriver, Biser, Sappington, Thawley, Stewart, of Caroline, Gwinn, Stewart, of Baltimore city, Sherwood, of Baltimore city, Presstman, Ware, Schley, Fiery, Neill, Harbine, Davis, Kilgour, Weber, Hollyday, Slicer, Smith, Ege and Cockey—43.

So the amendment was rejected.

The question then recurred on the amendment of Mr. GEORGE.

Mr. DONALDSON, moved to amend said amendment by striking out all after the word "improvement," to the end thereof, and insert the following:

"But without laying a tax, debts may be contracted to any amount that may be necessary to provide for the punctual payment of the interest of the public debt now existing, or in case of war, or to suppress insurrection."

Mr. CHAMBERS, of Kent, suggested certain divisions of the question on the amendment of Mr. GEORGE.

Mr. C. referred to the provision prohibiting appropriations of money for the use of individuals. He concurred in the spirit of the proposition which was, that the legislature should not mix itself up with private enterprise. But as the provision now stood, it would continually embarrass the legislature.

He suggested several cases in which difficulties might grow out of it, and said, that if these difficulties could be removed, he would vote for the amendment. He preferred it to the proposition of the gentleman from Cecil, [Mr. Constable.]

Some explanations as to the just interpretation of this branch of the proposition took place, between Messrs. GRASON, CHAMBERS, of Kent, SPENCER and THOMAS.

Mr. CHAMBERS, of Kent, moved to amend the amendment, by striking out the word "individuals."

Mr. THOMAS asked the yeas and nays,
Which were ordered, and
Being taken, resulted as follows:

Affirmative—Messrs. Chapman, Pres't, Blakistone, Dent, Ricaud, Lee, Chambers of Kent, Donaldson, Dorsey, Wells, Randall, Sellman, Weems, Jenifer, Ridgely, Crisfield, Hicks, Goldsborough, Constable, Bowie, Sprigg, Bowling, Spencer, McMaster, Fooks, McHenry, Schley, Fiery, Neill, Harbine, Davis and Kilgour—31.

Negative—Messrs. Merrick, Buchanan, Bell, Welch, Chandler, Lloyd, Colston, James U. Dennis, Dashiell, Chambers of Cecil, Miller, McLane, Grason, George, Thomas, Gaither, Biser, Annan, Sappington, Stephenson, Thawley, Stewart of Caroline, Hardcastle, Gwinn, Stewart of Baltimore city, Presstman, Ware, John Newcomer, Michael Newcomer, Weber, Hollyday, Slicer, Smith, Parke, Ege, Cockey and Brown—37.

So the amendment was rejected.

The question then recurred on the amendment of Mr. DONALDSON.

Mr. THOMAS asked the yeas and nays,
Which were ordered.

Some explanations followed as to the construction of the amendment, by Messrs. SPENCER, THOMAS, MCLANE and DONALDSON.

The question was then taken on the amendment of Mr. DONALDSON, and the result was as follows:

Affirmative—Messrs. Chapman, Pres't, Dent, Ricaud, Lee, Chambers of Kent, Donaldson, Dorsey, Wells, Randall, Sellman, Merrick, Jenifer, Crisfield, Hicks, Goldsborough, Bowie, Sprigg, Bowling, Spencer, Grason, George, McMaster, McHenry, Schley, Fiery, Neill, John Newcomer, Davis, Kilgour, Weber, Slicer and Smith—32.

Negative—Messrs. Hopewell, Weems, Buchanan, Bell, Welch, Chandler, Ridgely, Lloyd, Colston, James U. Dennis, Dashiell, Constable, Chambers of Cecil, Miller, McLane, Fooks, Thomas, Gaither, Biser, Annan, Sappington, Stephenson, Thawley, Stewart of Caroline, Hardcastle, Gwinn, Stewart of Baltimore city, Brent of Baltimore city, Presstman, Ware, Harbine, Michael Newcomer, Hollyday, Parke, Ege, Cockey and Brown—37.

So the amendment was rejected.

Mr. DAVIS then moved to amend said amendment by inserting after the word "corporations" in the twelfth line, these words, "except for purposes of education."

Mr. DAVIS called the attention of the Convention to the fact that by this proposition, the Legislature were deprived of any power to make appropriations for the purpose of education. In his part of the State, the people generally were desirous to have a system of education established. And now we are here, blocked up by this provision, which prevents any appropriation for any kind of improvement, even for the education of the children in the State.

The question was stated to be on the amendment of Mr. Davis.

Mr. D asked the yeas and nays,

Which were ordered.

Mr. Ege suggested to the gentleman from Montgomery, [Mr. Davis,] so to modify the phraseology of his amendment as to say "for common school purposes." The term "education" was very indefinite.

Mr. Davis declined to modify. The word "education" comprehended, he thought, the object he had in view.

Mr. Ege. The term "education" comprehends much more than I desire. I shall be constrained to vote against the amendment.

The question was then taken on the amendment of Mr. Davis,

And the result was as follows:

Affirmative.—Messrs. Chapman, President, Blakistone, Dent, Hopewell, Ricaud, Lee, Chambers, of Kent, Donaldson, Dorsey, Wells, Randall, Sellman, Weems, Merrick, Jenifer, Ridgely, James U. Dennis, Crisfield, Dashiell, Hicks, Goldsborough, Constable, McLane, Bowie, Sprigg, Bowling, Spencer, McMaster, Fooks, Biser, Annan, Stephenson, Stewart, of Caroline, Hardcastle, Schley, Fiery, John Newcomer, Harbine, Davis, Kilgour, Weber, Slicer and Smith—43.

Negative.—Messrs. Buchanan, Bell, Lloyd, Colston, Miller, Grason, George, Thomas, Gaither, Sappington, McHenry, Thawley, Gwinn, Stewart, of Baltimore city, Brent, of Baltimore, Presstman, Ware, Neill, Michael Newcomer, Hollyday, Parke, Ege, Cockey and Brown—24.

So the amendment was agreed to.

The question recurred on the adoption of the amendment as amended.

Mr. Presstman desired to enquire of the gentleman from Montgomery, [Mr. Davis] whether it was the object of his amendment to give to the Legislature, without limit, the power to appropriate the public money for schools.

Mr. Davis said that the gentleman from Baltimore city, [Mr. Presstman] was as capable of interpreting the language of the amendment as he, [Mr. D.,] was.

Mr. Presstman suggested that the gentleman should answer affirmatively or negatively.

Mr. Davis said he had no hesitation in saying, that he did wish the Legislature to appropriate a sufficient sum for that purpose—sufficient to educate every child in the State of Maryland, without a single exception.

Mr. Presstman. My object is answered. I wish the Convention to understand that the appropriation is to be without limit.

Mr. Thomas moved a re-consideration of the vote just taken. He regretted the necessity of trespassing upon the time of the Convention, but he felt it his duty to call the attention of gentlemen to the fact that the mode of representation in Maryland was not based upon the popular will of the people of Maryland. Without particular reference to the past, he could say, that every one in Maryland knew that the funds of the public treasury, for purposes of education, had not been fairly apportioned.

Mr. T. went on to say that he was not willing to have his vote on the journal on this question without explanation. If there was any prospect that justified the expectation that there would be a fair republican apportionment of representatives in the Legislature, he might feel less hostile to a proposition to confer upon that body a power like that proposed. But foreseeing that no Legislature will be organised by this Convention that will give to the majority of the people the power to make our laws, he was not disposed to encourage an expenditure of the public money for purposes of education. Without this article in the Constitution, the Legislature would have power to do this, but he would not encourage the exercise of this power. He would, if he could, take the power away, and leave to the several counties and to the city of Baltimore authority to establish schools within their respective limits. In support of this, his position, he explained the manner in which education funds had heretofore been disposed of by the State Legislature. Maryland had advanced a large sum to defend the country during the revolutionary war, which had been paid to the State by the United States. That part of this fund which had been received from the General Government, and which was set apart for the purposes of education, had not been fairly distributed. It was divided between the counties and the city of Baltimore, not according to population, but by an arbitrary rule, that gave to Frederick with her population of thirty-five thousand white inhabitants, very little more than the smallest county in the State. The State had derived also a considerable revenue by a tax of twenty cents on the hundred dollars of bank stock, the largest portion of which tax was paid by citizens of Baltimore city and of the western counties. The income of the State from this source had been divided by the Legislature into equal parts, and one part had been given to each of the counties and to the city of Baltimore, without the slightest regard to the great inequality that existed in the population of these several communities. This he thought was not right. If there there is any fund that ought to be distributed according to the white population of the State, it is the fund intended for education. The Legislature in making such a distribution ought to feel that every white child in the State is equally an object of its regard, no matter where its residence may be in the State, from the sea beaten beach of Worcester, to the Western boundary of Allegany. This had not been the case heretofore. Some of the small counties have a school fund more than they want, while other counties are compelled, and Baltimore city is compelled, to tax heavily the property of the people within their limits, to maintain a system of common schools. Seeing this, he was disposed to restrict the legislative power on this subject. And would prefer that each county and city should provide and maintain its own system of common schools. Admonished by the past injustice of the Legislature on this subject, and having no reason to hope for better in the future, he must vote against any article like that before us. At the same time he protested earnestly against being considered hostile to the great cause of education On that subject he had a zeal always warm He would, if he could, send a ray of intelligence—that Promethean fire from Heaven, to illumine every darkened mind on earth.

Some explanation here took place, as to the construction of the amendment of the gentleman from Queen Anne's, [Mr. George.] as amended by the gentleman from Montgomery, [Mr. Davis.] whether it gave an unlimited or merely limited power to the Legislature, to appropriate the public money for the purposes of education.

Mr. Presstman thought that the construction of the amendment by the gentleman from Queen Anne's, [Mr. Spencer,] could not be sustained. He here read the amendment, and commented upon the limitations contained in it, so far as the one hundred thousand dollars was allowed in the first branch, for certain objects, and fifty thousand dollars allowed in the latter branch, to supply a temporary deficit. It was undoubtedly the object of the gentleman from Montgomery, and so avowed, that appropriations, for educational purposes, should be the exception to the operation of these restrictions as to amount. Most unquestionably, such was the clear and manifest reading of the amendment as adopted. He desired to make a single remark upon the expediency and justice of the proposition, in the view which he had stated.

The maintenance of a public school system in this State, to further the great objects of education, found no greater advocate than himself But, sir, what sort of a system is best calculated to produce the end in view, with justice to all, may well admit of doubt. He was admonished by the past, that in the distribution of the school fund, a due regard was not had to the relative population of the counties and the city of Baltimore. As for the past, perhaps, that was beyond remedy, but he protested against the power to impose taxes upon the people of the State, where an unfair distribution was likely to follow. Here is an effort to introduce a State system to be supported out of the general treasury. To this theory, in whole or in part, first and last, he was utterly opposed. Let each county and city levy taxes for the support of their own public school system. While Baltimore city had contributed, by a tax on the bank stock of corporations, situated within its limits, and owned almost exclusively by her citizens, a very large share of the school fund, she receives in return a mere pittance. Her present school system was one of great cost to the inhabitants of that city but she did not seek legislative aid. The precedent once set, would be a dangerous one, of endowing schools and colleges throughout the State. Those who are now here struggling to secure some acknowledgement of the rights of the majority, could hardly be expected to place the Treasury of the State, swelled by a new system of taxation, under the control of the representatives of a small minority of the people of the State.

Mr. Brown said, he should vote for the motion of the gentleman from Frederick to reconsider. He believed there was a committee on education; and it would be better to postpone this whole subject until we have a report from that committee. The amendment removes all restriction from the Legislature Under it they may borrow money; and he could not agree to the imposing of a tax for the support of a system of education. The county of Carroll had raised a fund of from fifty to sixty thousand dollars as a school fund, and had just put the schools in operation. And he could not consent to give power to the Legislature to apply the money out of Treasury and even to go so far as to create a new debt for the purpose of establishing a system of education. He knew it was a popular movement, but it was a dangerous one. The subject was new, and started suddenly on the Convention; and we ought not to act hastily upon it. Let us first pay off our debt before we go into new expenditures. He could not go for a splendid school system. He was for educating the children, as they were in Carroll There was an academy at Carroll, which was the worst managed of all the schools

Mr. Spencer said, he intended to vote for the motion of the gentleman from Frederick to reconsider. He felt himself compelled to vote yesterday for the amendment proposed by the gentleman from Montgomery as he found it, because he thought that the modification as it previously stood, excluded the power to make an appropriation for education. The section tied up the Legislature from making appropriations for the benefit of individuals, so that no individual could be educated nor schools supported by public appropriations. He was not willing to tie up the hands of that body, so that no appropriation could hereafter be made for education. He would prefer now that the motion of the gentleman from Frederick should prevail. Not because his mind had undergone any change, as to the legal effect of the amendment. On the contrary he was of the opinion still, that it would not bear the construction given it by the gentleman from Frederick. There was no unlimited power given to the Legislature by this amendment. It would bear no such construction. He then read the section as it stood, with the amendment of the gentleman from Montgomery, and stated his own view of the proper construction which it warranted.

There was a limitation to the amount of one hundred thousand dollars, to any appropriation which could be made, and that appropriation the Legislature could apply for any purpose, except for the restraining clause which follows, which expressly leave them the power to appropriate for education. The true meaning of the section as amended is that the Legislature shall not have the power to create any debt above one hundred thousand dollars, except to supply a temporary deficit in the Treasury of fifty thousand dollars, or to provide for defence in time of war or insurrection It was limited to three specific objects. But as there was a difference of opinion as to the construction of the motion, he was willing that it should be reconsidered to be made more clear, by an amendment he intended to offer.

Mr. Thomas insisted that if the gentleman

from Queen Anne's, (Mr. Spencer,) had carefully examined the section, he would have given no such construction to it. It was the duty of every one in debate to analyze and distribute the elements of a proposition until he had made the whole perfectly comprehensible. And he thought he could, by that process, make it clear as any proposition in Euclid, that the gentleman from Queen Anne's was wrong.

It proposed to confer on the Legislature a power to borrow not exceeding one hundred thousand dollars, on certain conditions touching the taxes that were to be laid to pay any debt that might be contracted in pursuance of that power. This article further authorised the Legislature to borrow fifty dollars, to meet temporary deficits in the treasury, without imposing taxes to pay such debts. In addition to these powers to contract debts, he contended that the section under consideration gave to the Legislature power to appropriate money without limit, and to pledge the faith of the State without limit, for purposes of education. He conceded that the power to borrow money for any purposes, was limited. But insisted, that as the taxing power was unlimited, and as this section gave an unlimited power to appropriate and pledge the faith of the State for education, that the restrictions touching the power to create a State debt, would not check the wildest extravagance in the expenditure for education to associations, corporations or individuals.

He then took up the section, as amended, read and examined it, and contended that it gave to the Legislature an unlimited power to appropriate money from the treasury for education.—Looking at the construction of the section, he insisted that no language could be clearer. He presumed that the true effect of the proposition would, by and by, be permitted to appear in the action of the Legislature under it; for no one supposed that the sum of one hundred thousand dollars would be sufficient for the establishment of a system of education. The gentleman from Montgomery, (Mr. Davis,) had very frankly told the Convention that his object was to educate every child in the State. Yes, they are all to be educated from this great fountain here. The proposition of the gentleman from Cecil, (Mr. Constable,) to limit the taxing power of the Legislature, was rejected, because the Convention could not see what exigency might arise hereafter, to render it necessary to exercise this taxing power. Under the section, as now amended, the Legislature would have the right to pledge the faith of the State without issuing bonds and they might go on to make contracts to build colleges and establish a splendid system of education, and then the people throughout the State would feel themselves called on to sustain this system, based, as it would be, on the plighted faith of the State. If the State House should happen to be burned, the Legislature would not be compelled to create a debt for re-building it, but would pledge the faith of the State and enforce a tax on the people to re-construct the building, and thus redeem the pledge. In like manner they could build colleges, academies and seminaries of learning, and thus redeem the pledge. They would do this the more readily, because they would know that no man of high principle would hesitate to contribute to a tax to redeem the pledged honor of the State.

Mr. Davis felt the peculiar position in which he was placed, but at the risk he knew he had to encounter, in meeting three such able opponents as had taken the floor against his amendment, he would venture a few words in reply.

The gentleman from Frederick, [Mr. Thomas] objected to the amendment, because Frederick county had raised a large school fund, and would contribute her unequal share. So, says the gentleman from Baltimore city, [Mr. Presstman.] has Baltimore done; and he will not consent that Baltimore shall be taxed to educate the children in the counties.

Well, sir, what has the unequal distribution of the present school fund, which the gentleman complains of, to do with propositions now before the Convention? What are we here for, but to reform the past, and provide for the future? My proposition is prospective in its character. It is only to save something from this general locking up of the resources of the State, to aid in carrying out a system of common school education, as is recommended by the committee upon education, of which he was a member.

He had told his people that he should endeavor to introduce into the Constitution a provision for the establishment of a system of education; and if he stood alone, he should strive to obtain it.

Had the gentleman from Frederick read the report on education, he would have seen that a uniform system was provided for, and intended to apply to the whole State alike, not excepting the rich and populous county of Frederick, and the city of Baltimore; and had he have expected this question to come up to-day, he would have been prepared to prove, that it is far cheaper to educate the children of the State, than to maintain them in ignorance. Go to your jails, your penitentiaries, and your alms houses, and you find them filled with the ignorant and unlettered. In a report which he had seen from the penitentiary at Philadelphia, it was stated that the per centage of those who had passed through their common schools, was very small—while that of those, who could not read or write, was overwhelmingly large.

Gentlemen need not fear that the legislature will make any very large appropriation for this purpose. The difficulty was to get them to make any provision at all. At the proper time, if not now blocked up, he intended to indicate a plan for this object.

He was gratified at the large vote in favor of his amendment. He hoped the motion of the gentleman from Frederick to reconsider would not prevail.

Mr. Merrick made some remarks which will be published hereafter.

Mr. Ege obtained the floor.

And the Convention adjourned, until to-morrow, at ten o'clock.

THURSDAY, March 6, 1851.

The Convention met at ten o'clock.

Prayer was made by the Rev. Mr. GRAUFF.

The roll of the members was called; and

A quorum being present,

The journal of yesterday was read and approved.

Mr. BISER presented a petition signed by five hundred and fifty-three citizens of South Western portion of Frederick and South Eastern part of Washington counties, asking for the formation of a new county, embraced within the following boundary, to wit: beginning at the mouth of Catoctin Creek, and running thence up said creek to Magruder's Bridge, crossing said creek, thence with the old Middletown and Sharpsburg road to Getting's Store, on the Red Hill, then North West with the road to the Turnpike at Keedysville, then with the middle of said road to Antietam creek at Mumma's Mill, then with the middle of said stream to the bridge near Sherrick's, then with a straight line to the Potomac river, at or opposite Reynold's Mill Dam, then with the Potomac to the beginning, including an estimated population of ten thousand inhabitants and twelve hundred voters.

Which was read, and

Referred to the committee on New Counties.

LICENSE LAWS.

Mr. KENT, presented a petition of sundry citizens of Anne Arundel county, praying that a provision may be made in the new Constitution, that the privilege to sell intoxicating liquor shall not be granted to any person in any part of the State, except the same shall first be sanctioned or approved of by a majority of the votes in the election district where the same is to be sold.

Mr. HOLLYDAY, presented a petition of sundry citizens of Allegany county of similar import.

Mr. DONALDSON, presented a petition of sundry citizens of Howard District in Anne Arundel county, of similar import;

Which were severally read, and

Referred to the select committee already appointed on that subject.

[Mr. D. remarked, that the petition presented by him, came from a number of respectable persons, many of whom were not what was generally called temperance men—that was to say, they were not members of any temperance society.]

BASIS OF REPRESENTATION.

Mr. LLOYD rose and said, it would be remembered by the Convention, that, about three weeks ago, several reports had been made from the committee on representation. No question had been taken on these reports. He moved, therefore, that they be made the special order of the day, for Tuesday next.

Mr. MERRICK, (chairman of the committee on representations,) said, he would be very glad to accommodate his friend from Talbot, [Mr. Lloyd] but his, [Mr. M.'s,] private business would render it indispensably necessary, that he should be absent next week. If the Convention preferred to proceed with the consideration of that question in his absence, he must acquiesce. But as he had had charge of the subject, and as it was one in which he had taken much interest, he would be glad to be present when it was acted upon.

Mr. LLOYD expressed his desire to meet the views of the gentleman from Charles, [Mr. Merrick.] His, [Mr. L.'s,] only object was, that an early day should be fixed for the consideration of the question.

Mr. MERRICK suggested Monday week. By that time, he said, he should be in his place.

Mr. BOWIE, (to the Chair.) Will this question, if it should be made the special order, supersede the consideration of the report of the committee on the executive department of the government?

The PRESIDENT said, that would depend on the order of business on the calendar.

Having referred to the calendar, the President stated that the report of the committee on the executive department, had been made the special order of the day, for the second Tuesday in January, and its consideration had from time to time been postponed, by the general consent of the Convention. In the judgment of the Chair, therefore, the report on the executive department, would, as the next special order, have precedence over other business.

Mr. MERRICK thought it necessary and proper, that some day not too near, should be fixed upon for the consideration of this question, in order that all the members of the Convention might be notified to attend. It was important that any decision which might be made, should be the deliberate judgment of a majority of the Convention. He hoped, therefore, that the Convention would give notice of the day on which the question would be taken up, and that that day would be adhered to.

The PRESIDENT stated that the motion of the gentleman from Talbot, (Mr. Lloyd,) being simply a motion relating to the priority of business, was not debateable.

Mr. BOWIE said, he had supposed it was the intention of the Convention, deliberately expressed, to take up the report of the executive committee, immediately after the report of the Legislative committee should have been disposed of. His friend from Queen Anne, (Mr. Grason,) chairman of the committee on the executive department, was ready to proceed with the consideration of that report. We did not know how long it might occupy—perhaps four or five days. He would suggest to the gentleman from Talbot, (Mr. Lloyd,) to wait until that report should have been disposed of.

Mr. LLOYD, expressing his desire to accommodate gentlemen, withdrew his first motion, and substituted for it a motion to make the report of the committee on representation, the special order of the day for Monday week.

Mr. Blakistone suggested Thursday week, as the boat from the Eastern Shore came up on that day.

Mr. Thomas expressed the hope that the gentleman from Talbot, (Mr. Lloyd,) would adhere to his original motion. It was impossible to accommodate the action of this body to the various and conflicting private engagements of its members. He, [Mr. T.,] could not be here next week. Let each gentleman who was compelled to be absent, pair off with some other gentleman of opposite opinions.

Mr. Merrick said, he could not possibly be here next week.

Mr. Dorsey suggested that there was another special order, besides that which had been alluded to by the Chair, and which he, [Mr. D.,] believed had precedence of the report of the committee on the executive department. He alluded to the report which had been made in relation to Howard district.

The President, on enquiry, stated that the report alluded to by the gentleman from Anne Arundel, [Mr. Dorsey,] had been simply made the order of the day, [in parliamentary phrase,] and not a *special order* for any particular day.

Mr. Gwinn submitted to the Chair, whether the consideration of a special order might not be postponed, by a vote of a majority of the Convention.

The President indicated the opinion that a vote of two-thirds would be required to postpone the consideration of a special order.

Mr. Lloyd, [to the Chair.] If I should now move that the report of the committee on representation be made the special order of the day for Tuesday next, will it come up immediately after the report on the executive department shall have been disposed of?

The President. It will.

Mr. Lloyd. I make the motion.

Mr. Merrick moved to make the report the special order for Tuesday week. It was impossible, he said, that gentlemen should receive notice, and be here by the time designated in the last motion of the gentleman from Talbot, [Mr. Lloyd.]

The President stated, that the question would be taken first on the most distant day.

And the question was stated to be on the motion of Mr. Merrick, to make the report of the committee on representation, the special order of the day for Tuesday week.

Mr. Ware asked the yeas and nays, which were ordered, and being taken, resulted as follows:

Affirmative — Messrs. Chapman, President, Blakistone, Dent, Hopewell, Ricaud, Lee, Chambers, of Kent, Donaldson, Dorsey, Wells, Randall, Kent, Sellman, Weems, Merrick, James U. Dennis, Crisfield, Dashiell, Hicks, Hodson, Goldsborough, Eccleston, Bowie, Sprigg, Bowling, McMaster, Fooks, Sappington, Stephenson, Thawley, John Newcomer, Davis and Kilgour—33.

Negative—Messrs. Bell, Welch, Ridgely, Lloyd, Colston, Chambers, of Cecil, McCullough, Miller, Spencer, George, Thomas, Gaither, Biser, Annan, Stewart, of Caroline, Hardcastle, Gwinn, Stewart, of Baltimore city, Sherwood, of Baltimore city, Presstman, Ware, Schley, Fiery, Neill, Harbine, Michael Newcomer, Weber, Hollyday, Slicer, Smith, Parke, Ege, Cockey and Brown—34.

So the motion of Mr. Merrick was rejected.

The question then recurred on the motion of Mr. Lloyd, fixing Tuesday next.

Mr. Dent moved to amend the motion, by making the report the special order of the day for the first Monday in April.

Mr. D said, that some time ago, many gentlemen were anxious to postpone the consideration of this subject, until after the other business of the Convention had been disposed of, who were now anxious to take it up.

The question was stated to be on the amendment of Mr. Dent.

Mr. Kilgour moved to amend it by designating *Monday week.*

Mr. Wells asked the yeas and nays,

Which were ordered.

Mr. Ricaud moved that there be a call of the Convention.

A call was ordered.

The roll of the members was called, and the names of the absentees were then called over.

The Doorkeeper was sent to notify the absent members who were in the city to attend.

After some time the doorkeeper returned, and the President informed the Convention that all the members in the city, not sick, had been notified to attend.

Further proceedings on the call were then dispensed with.

The question then recurred on the motion of Mr. Kilgour, designating Monday week, and being taken,

The result was as follows:

Affirmative.—Messrs. Chapman, President, Blakistone, Dent, Hopewell, Ricaud, Lee, Chambers, of Kent, Mitchell, Donaldson, Dorsey, Wells, Randall, Kent, Sellman, Weems, Sollers, Merrick, Jenifer, James U. Dennis, Crisfield, Dashiell, Hicks, Hodson, Goldsborough, Eccleston, Bowie, Sprigg, McCubbin, Bowling, McMaster, Fooks, Sappington, Stephenson, Thawley, John Newcomer, Davis and Kilgour—37.

Negative.—Messrs. Welch, Chandler, Ridgely, Lloyd, Colston, Chambers, of Cecil, McCullough, Miller, Spencer, Grason, George, Thomas, Gaither, Biser, Annan, McHenry, Stewart, of Caroline, Hardcastle, Gwinn, Stewart, of Baltimore city, Brent, Sherwood, of Baltimore city, Presstman, Ware, Schley, Fiery, Neill, Harbine, Michael Newcomer, Weber, Hollyday, Slicer, Smith, Parke, Ege, Cockey and Brown—37.

A tie vote.

So the motion of Mr. Kilgour was rejected.

The question then recurred on the motion of Mr. Lloyd, designating Tuesday next.

Mr. JENIFER enquired of the Chair, whether the effect of this motion would be to postpone all other special orders.

The PRESIDENT said there was only one special order.

Mr. DAVIS interposed, and said that more than one hour had already been spent, and he would move that the Convention proceed to the orders of the day.

Mr. NEILL moved that the consideration of the orders of the day be postponed, for the purpose of acting upon the question now pending before the Convention.

Mr. DAVIS asked the yeas and nays,

Which were ordered.

Some conversation followed on a point of order, in which Messrs. THOMAS, SPENCER, MERRICK and the PRESIDENT took part.

The question was then taken on the motion of Mr. NEILL,

And the result was as follows:

Affirmative.—Messrs. Buchanan, Bell, Welch, Ridgely, Lloyd, Colston, Constable, Chambers, of Cecil, McCullough, Miller, Spencer, Grason, George, Thomas, Gaither, Biser, Annan, McHenry, Magraw, Stewart, of Caroline, Hardcastle, Gwinn, Stewart, of Baltimore city, Sherwood, of Baltimore city, Presstman, Ware, Schley, Fiery, Neill, Harbine, Michael Newcomer, Weber, Hollyday, Slicer, Parke, Ege, Cockey and Brown—38.

Negative—Messrs. Chapman, Pres't, Blakistone, Dent, Hopewell, Ricaud, Lee, Chambers, of Kent, Mitchell, Donaldson, Dorsey, Wells, Randall, Kent, Sellman, Weems, Sollers, Merrick, Jenifer, James U. Dennis, Crisfield, Dashiell, Hicks, Hodson, Goldsborough, Eccleston, Bowie, Sprigg, McCubbin, Bowling, McMaster, Fooks, Sappington, Stephenson, Brent, of Baltimore city, John Newcomer, Davis, Kilgour and Smith—38.

A tie vote.

So the motion of Mr. NEILL was rejected.

And the Convention passed to the orders of the day.

THE LEGISLATIVE DEPARTMENT.

The Convention resumed the consideration of the report of the committee on the legislative department of the government,

The question pending before the Convention on yesterday, being on the motion of Mr. THOMAS to reconsider the vote of the Convention on the amendment submitted by Mr. DAVIS, and adopted by the Convention, inserting in the amendment offered by Mr. GEORGE, as the twenty-first section of the report, these words, "except for purposes of education," to come in after the word "corporations," in the twelfth line.

Mr. EGE was entitled to the floor.

He desired, he said, to call the particular attention of the Convention to the proposition which had yesterday been adopted on the motion of his friend from Montgomery, (Mr. Davis.) He, (Mr. E.,) considered the amendment as inappropriate, and as not coming up to that high principle whch he, and as he believed, a majority of the people of Maryland, desired to see engrafted on the Constitution of the State. He alluded to the principle of education.

His design in now addressing the Convention was, to show that the amendment of the gentleman from Montgomery was out of place here, and that his object could be accomplished in a different and a better form.

It was out of place, because in point of law, or under the rule of common sense, the proposition of the gentleman from Queen Anne's, (Mr. George,) to which that of the gentleman from Montgomery was an amendment, did not forbid the application of moneys by the Legislature to the purposes of a general or common school system of education. It only forbid appropriations or grants to the use of individuals, associations, or corporations, an object which he earnestly desired to see accomplished. And unless the committee on education by their report, and the gentleman from Montgomery, (Mr. Davis,) by his amendment, desired that individuals, corporations, or associations, coming particularly under the head of academies and colleges, should be benefitted by this provision, he, (Mr. E.,) could see no good reason for its adoption.

The committee on education should have reported a definite proposition for the action of the Convention, not smothering this great principle under the operation of previous laws, but adopting it as a fundamental provision of the organic law which should confer benefits and blessings upon generations yet to come.

Mr. SMITH, (chairman of the committee on education,) interposed, and desired to say a word in explanation.

Mr. EGE yielded the floor for that purpose.

Mr. SMITH desired to say, that the proposition now before the Convention, had nothing to do with the report of the committee on education. It was not at all connected with it, nor was the report of the committee now the subject-matter of discussion before the Convention. He thought that the gentleman ought not to involve the subject in any difficulty of this kind.

Mr. EGE resumed. Certainly, he said, he designed no reflection on the chairman of the committee on education, or on the committee itself. His main object was to show the connection of this great principle of common school education with the highest and best interests of the people, through the length and breadth of the State.

The amendment of the gentleman from Montgomery, (Mr. Davis,) as appended to the proposition of the gentleman from Queen Anne's, (Mr. George,) was in the following words:

"Nor shall the Legislature hereafter appropriate the public money, or pledge the public faith for the use of individuals, associations, or corporations, *except for purposes of education.*"

Under what rule? Under the rule which had been reported to the Convention by the committee on education—and which he should show operated unjustly and unequally, and did not confer the advantages which the framers of the law themselves intended to bestow.

If he was right in the general proposition which he laid down that, independent of this particular clause, it would be in the power of the Convention to declare in another part of the Constitution that the Legislature should have the right to appropriate money for the specific purposes of education, then he could not see the object of the gentleman from Montgomery in placing his amendment where he now desired it to be. But even if he, (Mr. E ,) was wrong in this position, he had prepared an amendment in terms so broad that its intent could not possibly be misapprehended—an amendment which, in his judgment, would obviate every difficulty, and which he would now read as a part of his remarks.

Mr. E. then read his amendment, (of which the reporter has not a copy.)

He desired now to show to the Convention that the appropriations made by former Legislatures were not such as came within the rules of justice, or common sense, and that they were not even in accordance with the intentions of the framers of the laws themselves. He did not conceive that the amendment of the gentleman from Montgomery, or the report of the committee on education came up to the point which the Convention desired to attain, and which the people themselves, so far as his, (Mr. E.'s,) (knowledge enabled him to speak, intended to reach. He desired to show that the relative population of the counties and of the city of Baltimore, was not represented either by population, black and white—or so as to receive, either under the report of the committee on education, or of the amendment proposed by the gentleman from Montgomery, the benefits which they were entitled to receive—but that the system operated with signal injustice and inequality.

Mr. Brown rose to a point of order, concerning the relevancy of the debate.

After a brief conversation thereon,

Mr. Ege, (having been decided to be in order,) proceeded with his remarks.

He proposed, he said, to take the school fund appropriated to the different counties of the State, and to show the gross inequality that existed in its distribution. He proposed to show that many of the counties of the State, received a proportion of the fund upon principles not just in themselves, and against which he came here to contend.

He hoped to see a principle adopted in the Constitution for the establishment of a general system of common school education, by which general knowledge should be diffused among all clases of our citizens, whether living on the low lands of the bay shore, or in the pure mountain regions of the west.

But he would now proceed to show the inequalities that existed in the application of the public funds. Take, for example, the counties of Kent and Anne Arundel proper. They received more than one fourth of all the taxes they paid into the treasury, whilst the county which he, [Mr. Ege,] had in part the honor to represent, (Carroll,) received only eight hundred dollars. Even this small sum was more equally distributed among the people in his county, than perhaps the money received by any other county in the State. Still, he believed, it was not properly distributed, because particular localities were the exclusive recipients of its benefits.

Mr. E. then read the following statement:

TABLE,

Showing the White population of each County and Baltimore City, with the amounts of the Academy and College fund, and the Free School fund, annually distributed amongst them.

Counties.	*White Population.* 1850.	*Academy Fund.*	*Free School Fund,* 1851.
Allegany, .	21 643	$800	$2,588 63
Anne Arundel	16,542	3,800	3,335 86
Baltimore c'y	141,440		5,525 53
Baltimore co.	34,354	800	3,047 83
Carroll, . .	18,676	800	3,144 03
Caroline, .	6,096	800	2,227 15
Calvert, . .	3,630	800	2.015 02
Cecil, . .	15,482	800	2,856 40
Charles, .	5,665	800	2 141 07
Dorchester,	10,788	800	2.842 62
Frederick, .	33,300	1,200	4,473 08
Harford, .	14.414	800	2,931 24
Kent, . .	5,615	800	2,370 70
Montgomery,	9,435	1,000	3,636 42
Pr. George's,	8,902	800	2,722 77
Queen Anne's	7,040	800	2,636 59
St. Mary's, .	6,226	800	2,411 57
Somerset, .	13,417	800	2,754 93
Talbot, . .	7,085	800	2,861 39
Washington,	26,888	800	3,559 65
Worcester,	12,401	800	2,832 81
Total, .	419,039	$19,600	$62,915 29

Note.—The Free School fund is distributed as follows: One-half to each county, and Baltimore city, equally; and the other half amongst said counties and city, in proportion to their white population.

Such were the inequalities and such the injustice of this system. He wared against it. He desired that it should be brought to an end. He wanted to see a general system adopted in place of that partial and miserable one which was now in operation, by which a select few received the benefits of academic and collegiate education to the detriment of the great mass of the children of the State.

Let academies and colleges be left to private enterprise, or to corporations that were able to maintain themselves by their own efforts. Let them not draw their sustenance from the public treasury, whilst industry, energy, enterprise and learning itself were left to slumber. He desired to see the State cleansed from this foul leprosy which had so long been eating into its vitals, and no effort of his should be wanting to secure its extermination.

He desired to see the whole available school fund of the State appropriated, not according to local. county, or sectional interests, but according to population, in order that equality in its distribution might be preserved as nearly as possible. He desired that every child in Maryland should be educated; and. if the school fund should not be sufficient for that purpose, then he was in favor of making every voter in the State contribute to the object, as one of the holiest and most interesting, that could engage the attention of civilized men.

Mr. DAVIS interposed, and desired to ask a question.

Mr. EGE yielded the floor.

Mr. DAVIS. Did I understand the gentleman to say, that every voter in the State should contribute to a school fund?

Mr. EGE. I do say so—and I make the declaration in the utmost sincerity, and under a full conviction of the responsibility which attaches to it?

Mr. DAVIS. I only wished to be sure that I understood the gentleman correctly.

Mr. EGE. You did, sir.

Mr. SOLLERS, (in his seat.) A poll tax!

Mr. EGE. It is immaterial to me by what name it is called; and, I care not what opprobrium may be attempted here or elsewhere to be cast upon me for the principle I have avowed.

Mr. DAVIS. I intended no opprobium, and expressed no opinion. All I desired was to be certain that I was not mistaken as to the position which I understood the gentleman to assume.

Mr. EGE. I am well aware that this is not a popular doctrine. I care not for that. I believe it to be right, and I am not disposed to yield my own convictions of truth and duty, because they may not chime in with the popular voice, or even with the sentiments of my own immediate constituents. I must act for myself.

I know the responsibility under which I speak, and I shall not shrink from meeting it. The principle is one which, if carried into practical operation would destroy many heart-burnings, and forever save the feelings of honest penury from cruel and unnecessary wounds. The poor man's son could then stand proudly by the side of the rich man's son, and say "I am your equal." It would benefit the poor man by securing education to his children at a much cheaper rate than it can be obtained under the present system. The appropriation of this pittance to so noble a cause, will be an honor to the poor man, and a declaration that no superiority is acknowledged by the mere accident of wealth or station. He should demand it for every reason dear to him as a citizen, father, and patriot—that a pure fountain of truth, justice, and equality, may take the place of the turbid and unequal stream now flowing through the State.

It only remains for me to say that I have not brought forward this proposition upon the mere impulse of the moment. It has been a matter of anxious deliberation with me, and it may not perhaps have escaped the remembrance of the Convention that, at an early stage of its proceedings, I introduced a resolution embodying the principle I now advocate.

Mr. SPENCER. The motion is to reconsider the vote. and it had nothing to do with the various subjects which were now under discussion. He would not discusss the subject of education, or the manner in which appropriations should be applied. When those questions come up. in their proper order, he would be ready to go into their discussion. His object was to make a few remarks only, in reply to what had yesterday fallen from the gentleman from Frederick. In answer to a remark from the gentleman from Baltimore, (Mr. Presstman,) he, (Mr S.,) had said that the Legislature would be restricted by the amendment of his colleague, (Mr. George,) from going beyond one hundred thousand dollars. and he had given his views to that effect. The gentleman from Frederick stated that he could show, with the clearness with which a proposition in euclid could be demonstrated, that a different construction was the true one. After all, however. the gentleman from Frederick had not convinced him that he had given a wrong construction. But it appeared that there were differences of opinion on the subject among gentlemen in the House, and this had brought him to the conclusion that something might be done by way of compromise. He intended to give his vote in favor of the motion to reconsider, and if that motion should be decided in the affirmative, he would then be prepared to offer a proposition which he would now indicate, in order that the two sections shall not hereafter stand in opposition to each other. And then he intended to offer an additional section. He briefly stated what would be the effect of the propositions to which he had referred, and which he read.

Mr. DAVIS proposed briefly to state what he thought would be the effect of this motion. He would take the opportunity to explain himself. His amendment was brief and simple, being contained in the few words, "except for purposes of education." Nothing could be more plain. All can understand it. The vote in favor of the proposition yesterday was nearly as two to one. But notwithstanding this decided expression of the sense of the Convention, the potential voice of the gentleman from Frederick is heard this morning, asking that the vote of yesterday shall be re-considered, because he finds himself in the awkward position of having his name on the record as opposed to the education of the people. Here, however, he hoped the gentleman from Frederick would be allowed to stand; and there, as far as he could do it, he, (Mr. D.,) intended to keep him. He called the attention of the House to a very able report on the subject of education which was made to the Legislature some years ago by a gentleman of distinction, who was always regarded as *par excellence*, a Democrat and a Reformer; he meant Judge Legrand. It appears from that report, that in this State of Maryland, there are fifteen thousand seven hundred and fifty-four persons above the age of twenty-one, who can neither read nor write. It was to save something for the education of this numerous class that his motion was intended to provide.

Mr. CHANDLER here suggested the propriety of postponing the further discussion of this subject until after the vote of the House had been taken on the motion to reconsider. The discussion of the subject of education would then be more properly before the House.

Mr. DAVIS thanked the gentleman from Baltimore county for his suggestion, in which he, (Mr. D.,) concurred; but the gentleman would see that what he had said had been forced from him. If the motion to reconsider should prevail, the opponents of the system of education would then move to reject the whole proposition to relieve the gentleman from Frederick, and those who were now on the record with him against the proposition He repeated what he had said yesterday, that with the aid of the statistics at hand, were the Convention disposed to listen to them, he would be able to prove that a great expense would be saved to the State by the adoption of a system of education, because, as has been justly said, ignorance is the parent of idleness—idleness of vice and immorality, with its concomitant crime—and crime with all its attendant expense, of loss first—then detection, conviction, and punishment—unless the party gets "scot free" to perpetrate other injuries and depredations.

The question was then stated to be on the motion to re-consider the vote adopting the amendment of Mr. DAVIS.

Mr. PRESSTMAN asked the yeas and nays, which were ordered, and being taken, resulted as follows:

Affirmative—Messrs. Bell, Welch, Lloyd, Colston, Constable, Chambers of Cecil, McCullough, Miller, Spencer, Grason, George, Thomas, Shriver, Gaither, Biser, Annan, Sappington, Stephenson, McHenry, Thawley, Hardcastle, Gwinn, Stewart of Baltimore city, Brent of Baltimore city, Sherwood of Baltimore city, Presstman, Ware, Schley, Fiery, Neill, John Newcomer, Michael Newcomer, Weber, Hollyday, Slicer, Parke, Ege, Cockey and Brown—39.

Negative—Messrs. Chapman, President, Blakistone, Dent, Hopewell, Ricaud, Lee, Chambers of Kent, Mitchell, Donaldson, Dorsey, Wells, Randall, Weems, Merrick, Chandler, James U. Dennis, Crisfield, Dashiell, Hicks, Hodson, Goldsborough, Eccleston, Bowie, Sprigg, McCubbin, Bowling, McMaster, Fooks, Davis, Kilgour, and Smith—31.

So the vote was re-considered.

The question then recurred on the adoption of the amendment of Mr. DAVIS.

Mr. GRASON made some remarks which will appear hereafter.

Mr. CHAMBERS rose to correct impressions which might be made, by what had been said, on the minds of those who had not investigated the history of the school fund. The origin of the school fund, dated a long way beyond the birth day of Carroll county. The first legislation in relation to this subject, will be found to have been more than a century since.

A word or two in reference to the colleges—he meant the two colleges which were made the university, in 1784. By their charters in 1782 and 1784, the Legislature had engaged to endow the colleges, if individuals would advance the funds necessary to establish them. The condition was complied with, and in 1784 the endowment was granted.

Thus was produced a state of things, which in the view of those who had charge of the colleges, brought them completely within the principles established in the supreme court of the United States, in the case of the Dartmouth college, and others of a similar class. In these cases it had been declared that such contracts were inviolable by the State. It happened, however, subsequently, that persons occupied seats in these legislative halls, who entertained notions in regard to the education of our citizens, very different from those entertained by our intelligent and judicious ancestors. Such notions, as we now hear from some quarters, obtained the ascendancy, and the colleges were deprived, arbitrarily, as they supposed, of these endowments. At the time this alleged violation of their constitutional rights was perpetrated, there was on our statute book a law by which the State could be sued, by any of her citizens having a just claim against the State. The colleges supposed they could avail themselves of this law, to bring the matter fairly before the supreme court, and after a long course of fruitless effort, to obtain justice by an appeal to the Legislature, were preparing to adopt the only remedy left them, and institute suit

The law was then repealed, and the opportunity of contesting the power of the Legislature thereby denied. Subsequently, at a late period, and under the influence of a higher sense of justice and legal obligation, a compromise was effected, and an annual sum granted to the colleges, which was given and accepted expressly as a satisfaction in full, for their very large demands. The terms of the resolution granting the annuity and the acquittance executed by the colleges, would prove this. Such was a brief history of the transactions between the State and these colleges.

A friend near him, [Mr. Randall,] had just offered him the book containing the charter, subscription list, and early proceedings of Washington college, by which it would appear that the contributions toward the establishment of that institution, amounted to ten thousand pounds.

Mr. EGE asked the gentleman to read the resolution.

Mr. CHAMBERS said the resolution was not before him, but he would read what was immediately under his eye. It was the first item on the list of subscribers, and is in the words following:

"His Excellency, *George Washington*, Esq, General and Commander-in-Chief of the armies of the United States, as an earnest of his good-will, fifty guineas."

Mr. EGE said:

That when he asked the gentleman from Kent, to read the resolution to which he had referred, he had no idea that the gentleman would throw out such a mere cobweb. He had always thought and he still did think, that the appropriations for these colleges were unwarranted.

As to the gentleman's construction of the law of contract, which he intimated had been violated, he, [Mr. E.] thought that the gentleman from Kent, would find it a difficult task to have such a contract inserted in the new Constitution. He did not suppose that this Convention would settle the question on the ground that General Washington had subscribed fifty guineas towards the endowment of these colleges. It was certainly a noble example, which he hoped the county of Kent would follow. But he did not wish that a tax should be imposed by the legislature for the purpose of education. Let the people of the counties themselves support their own schools. He was not to be moved by any sarcasms which might be thrown out about the city of Baltimore. He felt pride in Baltimore, in her wealth, her growing population and her spirit of enterprise. And what would the State be without Baltimore? The appropriations which gentlemen here are so desirous to obtain, are not desired by the people, nor are they in accordance with the spirit of the age in which we live. He hoped that a system of education might be established, without the imposition of any tax on the people by the legislature, which would redound to the honor and interests of the State.

Mr. Davis desired to say a word only in reply to the gentleman from Queen Anne's, (Mr. Grason,) who had said that he, (Mr. D.,) did not comprehend the language of his colleague's amendment. He admitted that he had no other power of comprehension than the little common sense, the God and nature had given him. Still he believed that he had rightly comprehended the amendment of the gentleman's colleague, (Mr. George,) and the gentleman's colleague, (Mr. Spencer,) had, himself, yesterday admitted, that his, [Mr. D's.,] comprehension of it was correct.

The gentleman from Queen Anne's insisted that the proposition was only intended to exclude corporations from obtaining the public money. But the language of the amendment went further, stating that no *individuals* nor *associations*, as well as corporations, shall have any use of the public money. The children of the State shall have no education, if it is to be given them thro' the medium of a corporation, because corporations are odious to the gentleman. But in the zeal of the gentleman to strike down corporations he also prevents any person from obtaining any benefit from the public money, even for the economical and benevolent purpose of educating the poor children of the State, should it either come through individuals or associations,as well as corporations. How else can it come? He was unable to see. He did not pretend to be a prophet —but in this instance he had proved a true one, for he now saw that the gentleman from Queen Anne's, [Mr. Spencer] was about to vote against his, [Mr. D's.,] amendment. And to relieve the gentleman from Frederick, and those who voted with him, against an amendment to save something to educate the children of the State, this proposition is now to be rejected.

Mr. Spencer said, the gentleman from Montgomery had no right to impute to him motives for the course which he might pursue. Had the exposition of his colleague been made yesterday, he would not have voted for the amendment of the gentleman from Montgomery. He then briefly explained the view he took of the amendment of his colleague. His only object was to have a more intelligent proposition offered and adopted.

Mr. Grason suggested that in the hurry of debate, the attention of the Convention was not sufficiently directed to the language of the proposition. It was never intended to prevent appropriations for the purposes of education, but was merely an inhibition of appropriations for the building of corporations.

Mr. McHenry explained his understanding of the proposition of the gentleman from Queen Anne's. It prevents the Legislature from contracting loans for the use of corporations, associations or individuals, except for educational purposes. He was disposed to go as far as any one for the support and extension of education by taxation. But he was decidedly opposed to the State's incurring any debt or pledging, in any form, its credit, for any purposes, except in extreme exigencies. He was not disposed to tax posterity for the education of the children of the present day. The men of this generation should not grudge the cost of educating their own and their neighbors' little ones, nor attempt by State loans, or other devices, to transfer to posterity the burdens which are properly our own.

Mr. Sherwood, of Baltimore city, desired to say a word or two on the amendment of the gentleman from Montgomery, (Mr. Davis.) Although he should vote against the proposition, as a part of the article to which it was sought, in his judgment, improperly to be attached, he did not think in doing so, that he would incur the censure of hostility to a general system of popular education. On the contrary, it was his attachment to the system, and his desire for its further success, that prompted his opposition to the amendment at this time. He had been too long the ardent advocate of public instruction, to be now found doing any act to retard its progress, or to weaken its usefulness, by withholding from it, in any proper manner, the fostering care of the State. With emotions of pleasure he contemplated its advancement, and with native pride he saw school-houses dotting every section of the State, like so many beacon lights, to guide the young mind safely into moral and intellectual havens; and he rejoiced to say, that the city of Baltimore was more wealthy in these ornaments than in all her other proud monuments. He, in common with the constituency, which, in part, he represented in this Convention, regarded public education as an indispensable auxilliary to Baltimore's rapidly increasing prosperity; nor will she ever be so unmindful of her duty and interests, as to abandon an experiment which some twenty years of private and public devotion, has crowned with the most gratifying success. No one desired more than he, to see it enjoying that standard of eminence to which its usefulness entitled it, and would ultimately place it, if improvident or partial legislation did not interpose its sectional feeling, to disturb the harmony that should characterize the entire system. The proposed amendment, he thought, would not meet the objects claimed for it by its immediate friends; it was of very questionable utility; and he, therefore, preferred to have the merits of the whole subject discussed and disposed of, when the report of the committee on education, (now on the desks,) should come up for consideration. That, he conceived, with great deference to the opinions of others, to be the appropriate time to secure to educational purposes, the necessary constitutional safeguards, as well as to obtain a more equitable distribution of the present and prospective munificence of the State. He would observe, that under existing laws, Baltimore city did not enjoy her fair proportion of the school fund, and it was to protect her in the future, that he objected to the amendment of the gentleman from Montgomery, which, to his mind, looked rather to a perpetuation, than to a rerorm of existing abuses.

Mr. S. referred to the progress of public schools in Baltimore city, from their origin to the present period, compared the annual expenditures incurred for tuition in the several cities, and alluded, in terms of commendation, to the last annual report of the school commissioners of Baltimore, in which he found interesting data to encourage the friends of popular education here and elsewhere. He earnestly declared that he never could be found refusing his aid, whenever legitimately demanded, to a system that had proved itself, under all disadvantages, so admirably adapted to the cultivation of the mind, and so essential to the preservation of the moral, social and political happiness of the whole State. He would add, for himself, and in behalf of his colleagues, that if gentlemen inferred from the vote they should give on this proposition, that they were opposed to general education, they will have drawn an erroneous conclusion. So far from opposing, their opinions ran in a contrary direction. They were firm as any could be in their determination to extend the benefits of education, and to secure an equality of rights to all.

The question was then stated to be on the adoption of the amendment of Mr. Davis.

Mr. Davis asked the yeas and nay, which were ordered.

The roll was called.

Before the decision was announced,

Mr. Sollers rose and asked if it was in order for him now to assign his reasons for the vote he had given?

The President said it was not in order.

Mr. Sollers then said, he must ask the unanimous consent of the Convention to say a few words.

The President put the question, and the Convention gave its unanimous consent, that Mr. Sollers should assign his reasons for his vote.

Mr. Sollers desired permission to explain the vote he was about to give, for without such explanation it might possibly be misconstrued. No man desired more sincerely than he did, to see every child in the State educated, for it never could be too often repeated, that upon the virtue and intelligence of the people depends the perpetuity of our institutions. But at the very moment when we are restricting the Legislature in every possible way to prevent the contracting of debt for works of internal improvements, at the very moment when we are interposing constitutional barriers to protect the people from mad and ruinous schemes, a proposition is introduced which grants to the Legislature the unrestrained, unlimited, indefinite right to contract any amount of debt for purposes of education, and to establish any system no matter how gigantic, embracing the establishing and endowing of colleges and academies in every county in the State. Said Mr. S. I am opposed to all this, he wanted something tangible to act on; he did not want to act in the dark. Whenever the revenues derived from the works of internal improvement, about which we hear so much shall be sufficient to the establishment of public schools, he desired their application to that purpose; but until the public debt was entirely discharged. and until we had a fixed and certain revenue, he was opposed to all schemes, which might in any possible way again involve the State in debt.

The result of the vote was then announced as follows:

Affirmative.—Messrs. Chapman, Pres't., Blakistone, Dent, Hopewell, Ricaud, Lee, Chambers of Kent, Mitchell, Donaldson, Dorsey, Wells, Randall, Kent, Weems, Merrick, James U. Dennis, Crisfield, Dashiell, Hicks, Hodson, Goldsborough, Eccleston, Bowie, Sprigg, McCubbin, Bowling, McMaster, Fooks, Biser, Davis, and Kilgour—31.

Negative.—Messrs. Sellman, Sollers, Bell, Welch, Chandler, Ridgely, Lloyd, Colston, Chambers, of Cecil, McCullough, Miller, Spencer, Grason, George, Thomas, Shriver, Gaither, Annan, Sappington, Stephenson, McHenry, Magraw, Thawley, Stewart of Caroline, Hardcastle, Gwinn, Stewart of Baltimore city, Brent of Baltimore city, Sherwood ot Baltimore city, Presstman, Ware, Schley, Fiery, Neill, John Newcomer, Michael Newcomer, Weber, Hollyday, Slicer, Parke, Ege, Cockey, and Brown—42.

So the amendment was rejected,

Mr. Spencer moved to amend said amendment by striking out all from the word "dollars," in the ninth line to the word "but," in the thirteenth line, and inserting in lieu thereof the following:

"But the Legislature shall not contract any debt for the use of individuals, associations, or corporations, except for public schools, and then only to the extent and in the manner that may be provided for in this Constitution."

Some explanations as to the construction of the amendment passed on the part of Messrs. Spencer and Sollers.

Branching from these explanatory remarks—

Mr. SOLLERS concluded his explanation.

Mr. BROWN demanded the previous question—and gave notice that he would not withdraw it. It was time that the debate should be brought to close.

Mr. EGE asked Mr. BROWN to withdraw, to enable him to make a few remarks.

Mr. BROWN declined to withdraw.

The question was then taken on the demand for the previous question, and there was not a second.

The question then recurred on the amendment of Mr. SPENCER.

Mr. MERRICK intimated that a proper time, when a suitable occasion should offer, and that he supposed would be when the report of the committee on public works came up for consideration, he intended to show that if the provisions of the act of 1836 had been complied with, the evil day which had caused us so much sorrow, would not have come on Maryland. It was in the contemplation of the Convention, he believed, when the report of the committee on education shall be taken up for discussion, to adopt some mode for the support of public schools, which will be free from the objections of gentlemen who oppose the present proposition.

Mr. EGE replied to the charges which, at least by construction, were made against him and those who voted with him, in the course he was pursuing with reference to the subject of education. He could only say that he was taking his course on his own personal responsibility to his constituents, and that the charge of demagogueism, so far as he was concerned, fell harmless. He repelled the idea that this Convention was a humbug, and expressed a hope that no gentleman would permit himself to be driven by the mere fear of ridicule from an honest perseverance in the line of duty. He knew not why local and popular rights should be withheld on no better ground than that they are advocated by a certain class of political men.

He came here for the purpose of sustaining certain prominent principles, and of these, education was one which he intended to stand by to the last, against any force which might oppose him; nay, if he stood alone in the Convention. If his people were to say that his course did not meet their approbation, he would yield obedience to their voice and resign his seat here. As to the question of the election of judges, he reminded gentlemen that the judges of Israel were elected by the people. And he asked, whether any one, of any party, could be found to vote for a judge whom he deemed incompetent to perform the duties of his office. He referred to the satisfactory result of the application of the elective principle to the people of New York, and asked why it should be assailed as demagogueism when we are only attempting to introduce the same principle here which had been successful there? He was of opinion that justice was rendered without perversion in other States of the Union where judges were elected by the people, and that the fountains of justice was quite as pure there as they are in this State. It had been alleged that every thing is to be done here by party influence, and that the cry is, "stick to your party!" He was of no party here, and he left others to pursue that course which was thought right; and let his acts to be judged of by his own constituents. This Convention had been called into existence by the voice of the people. It was at first opposed by those in power. But the clarion of Reform sounded from the western hills of Maryland until power began to tremble. The people have called for reform in a voice of thunder, which will make itself heard here. He concluded with stating, that when he rose he merely designed to show the unequal operation of the amendment of the gentleman from Montgomery.

Mr. SOLLERS briefly explained.

The question then again recurred on the adoption of the amendment of Mr. SPENCER.

Mr. DORSEY called for a division on striking out,

Which was ordered.

Mr. MCHENRY said that the objection which, in his opinion, lay against the amendment of the gentleman from Montgomery, would be also against the amendment of the gentleman from Queen Anne's, (Mr. Spencer.) The true mode is to draw the money required for the object, at the time when wanted, from the people by taxation. The gentleman from Calvert was right in his opinion, that the people are opposed to the contraction of any further debt by the State. The amendment of the gentleman from Queen Anne's might, if adopted, lead to serious embarrassment. He, (Mr. McH.,) desired to prevent the Legislature from exercising any power to loan the credit of the State for any object. He intimated that he had an amendment which he proposed to offer.

Mr. MCHENRY then moved to amend said amendment, by adding at the end thereof, the following:

"The credit of the State shall not, in any manner, be given or loaned to or in aid of any individual, association or corporation, nor shall the General Assembly have the power, in any mode, to involve the State in the construction of works of internal improvement, or in any enterprise which shall involve the faith or credit of the State."

Mr. SPENCER, (some members not being present, he said, when he offered his amendmet,) repeated his explanation of it, and gave notice of his intention, if it should prevail, to follow it up with another amendment, which he read.

Mr. SOLLERS suggested to Mr. MCHENRY a modification of his amendment, which is embodied in it as given above.

The question was then stated to be on the said amendment, as modified.

Mr. MCHENRY asked the yeas and nays,

Which were ordered, and

Being taken, resulted as follows:

Affirmative—Messrs Chapman, Pres't, Blakistone, Dent, Hopewell, Dorsey, Wells, Kent, Sellman, Weems, Sollers, Merrick, Bell, Welch, Chandler, Ridgely, Lloyd, Colston, James U. Dennis, Dashiell, Hicks, Hodson, Goldsborough, Eccleston, Chambers of Cecil, Miller, Sprigg, Bowling, McMaster, Fooks, Shriver, Biser, Sappington, Stephenson, McHenry, Magraw, Stewart of Caroline, Hardcastle, Schley, Fiery, Neill, John Newcomer, Michael Newcomer, Kilgour, Ege, Cockey and Brown—46.

Negative—Messrs. Ricaud, Lee, Chambers of Kent, Mitchell, Donaldson, Randall, Crisfield, Bowie, McCubbin, Spencer, Grason, George, Thomas, Gaither, Annan, Thawley, Gwinn, Stewart of of Baltimore city, Sherwood of Baltimore city, Presstman, Ware, Harbine, Davis, Weber, Hollyday, Slicer, Smith and Parke—28.

So the amendment was agreed to.

The question then recurred on the adoption of the amendment, as amended.

Some conversation followed on a point of order, [arising out of some confusion as to the state of the question.]

To obviate the difficulty in which the Convention had become involved—

Mr. CHAMBERS, of Kent, moved a reconsideration of the vote by which the modified amendment of Mr. McHenry had been adopted.

Mr. THOMAS suggested that the object [which was to get at the the judgment of the respective propositions of Messrs. Spencer and McHenry,] could be attained by a division of the question.

Mr. CHAMBERS, of Kent, assented and withdrew his motion to reconsider.

Mr. SOLLERS moved to amend said amendment by striking out the first branch thereof—being that portion of the amendment offered by Mr. SPENCER.

The question then recurred on the second branch of the said amendment.

Mr. SOLLERS moved to amend by adding at the end thereof, these words:

"Or making any appropriations therefor."

The amendment was agreed to.

The question then recurred on the adoption of the second branch of said amendment, as amended.

Mr. THOMAS asked the yeas and nays,

Which were ordered, and

The question having been taken, the result was as follows:

Affirmative—Messrs. Chapman, Pres't, Blakistone, Dent, Hopewell, Ricaud, Lee, Chambers of Kent, Mitchell, Donaldson, Dorsey, Wells, Randall, Kent, Weems, Sollers, Merrick, Welch, Chandler, James U. Dennis, Dashiell, Hicks, Hodson, Goldsborough, Eccleston, Constable, Bowie, Sprigg, McCubbin, McMaster, Fooks, Sappington, Stephenson, McHenry, Hardcastle, Schley, Fiery, Neill, John Newcomer, Michael Newcomer, Davis, Kilgour and Cockey—42.

Negative—Messrs. Bell, Ridgely, Lloyd, Colston, Crisfield, McCullough, Miller, Bowling, Spencer, Grason, George, Thomas, Shriver, Gaither, Biser, Annan, Thawley, Stewart of Caroline, Gwinn, Brent of Baltimore city, Sherwood of Baltimore city, Presstman, Ware, Harbine, Weber, Hollyday, Slicer, Smith, Parke, Ege and Brown—31.

So the second branch of the amendment, as amended, was adopted.

Mr. SPENCER then moved as a substitute for the amendment just adopted, the following:

"The legislature shall not hereafter appropriate the public money, or pledge the public faith, or make loans or subscriptions to any association corporation or work of internal improvement; and they shall not use or appropriate the proceeds of the internal improvement companies, or of the State tax now levied, or which may hereafter be levied, to pay off the public debt, to any other purpose, until the interests and debt are fully paid."

Mr. CRISFIELD gave notice that at the proper time, he should offer the following amendment:

Strike out after the word "dollars," in the tenth line, to the word "the" in the thirteenth line, and insert:

"Nor shall the legislature hereafter create any debt, or pledge the credit of the State, except for the purpose of education, as hereinafter may be provided, to or for the use of any association or corporation, or for or on account of any work of internal improvement, but after the payment of the public debt as provided by law, the revenue which may accrue from the State's investments in works of internal improvement, may be appropriated to the improvement of existing, and the construction of additional works."

The question then recurred on the amendment of Mr. SPENCER.

Pending the question on this amendment;

The Convention adjourned until to-morrow at ten o'clock.

DEFERRED DEBATE.

In Convention, Feb. 11, 1851.

Remarks of Mr. DASHIELL on his amendment to the preamble of the bill of rights, proposing to add the words "representing the counties and city of Baltimore."

Mr. DASHIELL said:

That the gentleman from the city of Baltimore, (Mr. Gwinn,) desires to know what theory, he, (Mr. D.,) proposed to inculcate by the amendment he had offered. He would say, the amendment itself, developed his theory; and he was somewhat surprised at the inquiry. The remarks also which he had made at the introduction of his amendment gave a further and fuller exposition of the same. What further explanation the gentleman desired, he could not conjecture, unless he wished, at this time, to enter upon the discussion of the great question of representation. The amendment which he had proposed; contains nothing but a plain and notable fact, which he presumed the gentleman would not undertake to dispute or deny; and from that fact, but one true theory can be deduced, and all others are spurious. Now, the gentleman from the city of Baltimore, with a suspicious fear, seems to discover in the amendment, a phantom, and starts at it, as if it were his "evil genius." Ah, Mr. President, truth, that mighty and faithful reality, is sometimes startling, and calculated to inflict much terror; and it is manifest the gentleman betrays much of its power working upon him, and evidently to his disquietude.

Mr. D. said, that he was aware that his amendment conflicted much with the fond notions of some, in regard to the question of representation, and among that number was the gentleman from the city of Baltimore. He knew there was an effort being made to obliterate county distinctions in regard to representation, and already notice had been given for districting the State, regardless of county lines, for that purpose.

The next monstrous notion he expected to hear announced, would be to elect delegates to the General Assembly, by a general ticket system throughout the whole State. Then would soon follow an obliteration of all other county distinctions recognised by the present Constitution. And then, indeed, the counties of old Maryland, which have had, and enjoyed rights, powers and privileges for two centuries, will be shorn of the same, and will experience the sore penalty of their wickedness, for bending their "knees to Baal." The city of Baltimore in a short time will have half of the population of the State; and recognise in her the potency of numbers—cease to protect the counties from her power; and she will have the ability to yield the government of Maryland. Then, whether for weal or wo, the counties will be compelled to submit. They will no longer have an existence, for their separate and distinct interest, to be represented in the halls of legislation. Who is prepared to lend a hand to effect this dangerous innovation? Is there a delegate here, representing any of the counties of this State, willing to give away, or to barter for a mere "mess of pottage," for party consideration, the dearest interest of his constituents? Is there a delegate here with his sword drawn, ready to commit such an atrocious suicide? He fain hoped the contrary.

Mr. D. said, the gentleman from the city of Baltimore contends that we are not here as "delegates of the counties, but of the State of Maryland." If this be the fact, then the delegates from the counties are as much the representatives of the city of Baltimore, as those of her own choice. She has, according to that theory, the whole delegation of Maryland representing her upon this floor. Why then all of this outcry from Baltimore, for more representation? Why then those treasonable threats we see almost daily made by a public press in that city, because she is denied a larger representation? If the whole delegation of Maryland represent her in the legislative department of the government, all must acknowledge she is now amply represented.

But, said Mr. D., he believed that theory would be modified, or entirely abandoned, when the question of representation came up for discussion. Upon a failure to district the State, for the purpose of representation, which he anticipated would occur, he thought there would be many, who now deny his theory in regard to county distinction, who will then become even clamorous in its favor, and perhaps also for county superiority.

Why, (exclaimed Mr. D.,) this anxious desire to do away county distinctions? Why this eagerness to adopt a new mode of representation? Ah, Mr. President, it is because of the hope entertained, that if such a thing can be achieved, of getting admitted into the Legislature of your State, the Herculean power of Baltimore city. Sir, it is to obtain power and the mastery, that such schemes are concocted. Yield to those wild notions and extravagant demands of some, and you will have the anomaly of our city within a State, occupying but a few acres of its territory, with a large population, heterogeneous in its nature, and turbulent in spirit, governing that State. Sir, tell me not, that to concentrate political power, sufficient to control the government of a State, in a single city of the same, there need be no apprehensions of misrule and tyranny. Tell me not, that a single city, possessing the power over other communities, would be less liable to practice tyranny, than a single individual. The old adage, "the greater the number of tyrants, the greater the amount of tyranny," would be fully realized and felt, upon such an event. Much more, Mr President, would I prefer the category under another old maxim, "*that one tyrant is better than many.*"

But, said Mr. D., the example of other States will, no doubt, be urged in favor of this new mode of representation, and for abolishing that old and well-tried system, adopted by our patriotic forefathers, and under which we have lived and prospered for about two hundred years. Sir, the example of those States, is not a proper example to affect us in the adjustment of this question. Our cases are not at all similiar. We have a small State with a large city, which will soon number and contain half of our population, and they have large States, with large cities, the population of which can never exceed one-eighth of that of the whole State. The adoption of the principle of representation based upon population alone, will never, in those States, concentrate a preponderance of political power in a single city. But it will be readily seen, that our situation is vastly dissimilar, and experience must induce us to adopt a different rule in the distribution of legislative power. The old adage, "that circumstances alter cases," must be applied to that principle, for which we have an example in other States, and to which some are so warmly attached, or we shall sacrifice justice, and open the door for oppression, by the adoption of a principle in the apportionment of representation, which is in no way suited to our case.

Mr. D. said, he could not agree to the theory advanced by the gentleman from Baltimore city, although in one point of view it may be regarded as a strong argument against the demands of Baltimore city, and the larger counties, for an increase of representation, which he positively opposed. He regarded the delegates in this Convention, as the representatives of the different counties and the city of Baltimore, which elected them, and from whom they derive their authority; and he regarded them also, in the aggregate, as the representatives of the whole State? Each delegate here is the representative of his immediate constituents, *particularly*, and of the State *generally*. He did not look upon the counties as sovereignties, for such a notion would be vain and foolish—the State herself has hardly a principle of sovereignty left her; but he did hold they were separate and distinct communities, and were recognized as such by the Constitution under which we now live. As communities, they are entitled to a separate and distinct representation in the Senate and House of Delegates of the State. Geographically, they are separate and distinct from each other, and have separate jurisdiction. They have also different and dissimilar interests, and the economy of the government has provided for it a representation in the legislative department of the same. Some have an agricultural interest of a grain growing nature; others, that of tobacco; and others have interests combining agriculture, mining and manufactural; and Baltimore city an interest purely manufactural and commercial. The arts and sciences are dispersed throughout the State, and like precious jewels in the hands of owners, having an intrinsic value wherever they be at, but susceptible and subject to change of location. From these different interests and sources, the State derives her revenue, and the people gain a livelihood, amass wealth, and obtain trade.

These are the interests which demand our fostering care, and therefore, should be distinctly represented in the Legislature of our State.

Mr. D. said that his amendment contained a principle which had been the fixed policy of Maryland from the year 1650 up to the present moment. That principle is county representation. He was sure this was no strange theory—no heterodoxy—but a well k own fact, and a principle which has been tenaciously adhered to in all times past, and should be, in all times to come. These "civil divisions," known as counties, were carved out of the territory of the colony, and erected by "orders in council," and of the proprietary's Governors, and were deemed as separate and distinct communities, and entitled to a separate representation. But two counties, Allegany and Carroll, derive their existence from the present government of the State, and they were formed out of the territory of other counties, but with the free and full consent of all parties. Two others, Washington and Montgomery, were erected out of Frederick county by the Convention which formed the Constitution in 1776. All the rest derive their origin from quite a different source, and far anterior to the present government of the State. A notable fact which he would recur to, although known to all in this Convention, but which will grate hard upon the ears of some, is, that from their first introduction to about the year 1824, they lived in perfect peace, harmony and contentment, and until demagogues commenced their work of mischief among them, they were recognised as equals, regardless of the difference in territory and population which have always existed. In 1836 the Legislature of that year. whose acts in relation to a change in the Constitution will prove a curse to the counties in all future time, yielded to the principles and demands of demagogues, and stamped upon the counties of this State the abominable heresy of political inequality. That year will ever be looked upon and held in memory, as the beginning of our downfall. By the change effected then in the Constitution, the smaller counties were robbed of their just rights in the election of Governor, and also of their just right in the lower branch of the Legislature. These invaluable rights, and that just equality which were secured to them in the compact of government entered into in 1776, are now lost and can never be regained. The apology given for this yield of power by the smaller counties was, "that it was for the sake of peace and to allay excitement." But the receivers, having tasted of it then, are still unsatisfied and their desire for more have become insatiable. Our strength having been impaired by the loss incurred then, and party feelings and selfishne-s begetting in us divisions now, we are much weakened in our capacity to resist further aggression. Can we indeed successfully resist it?

Mr. D. said, this county system now extant, was introduced in our mother country as far back as the ninth century, and has for its author the same distinguished law-giver who established trial by jury. It has been well tried by the ordeal of time, and found to be substantial and invaluable. One of its great virtues was political equality; and fluctuations in population and wealth, did not disturb its equilibrium. In it there was no room for complaint, emulation and strife, and political jealousy had no existence among them. From this wholesome example, this county system was established in this country in all of the colonies, and has remained to this day; but in some States its worth has been greatly impaired, by the rash hand of innovation.

Mr. D. adverted to the situation of the counties of this State in 1774, at which time, he said, the proprietary's government ceased to have effect. The proprietary's Governor, although remaining in the colony, yet he was powerless, and the government had not the ability to sustain itself. The people were incensed against the mother country on account of acts of oppression, and were at that time openly engaged in making preparations for revolt. Yet, the proprietary's governor was unable to surpress insurrection and did not dare to attempt it.

He contended that whenever a government ceased to have power to inforce itself, it had no longer existence. He said the Convention which assembled in 1774, had no authority under the government then existing; but it was the creature of the people,and the result of their sovereignty. Upon the fall of the old government, all the rights and powers of the people yielded up in its establishment, reverted back to them, and again they possessed the freedom and ability to form a new government. The counties then being separate and distinct communities, with well established lines of demarkation as to territory, and accustomed to rights and powers, separate and distinct from each other, elected, each one for itself, "a committee of observation," to whom was intrusted the internal management of its affairs. Under this new mode of government they continued separate and distinct from each other, until called upon by the "sons of liberty," to unite in holding a Convention on the twenty second day of June, 1774. In that Convention they were represented equally, and recognized as equals, and were looked upon as parties competent to enter into confederation and agreement.

Each county sent its committee to represent its wishes and views; and the heading of its proceedings as found upon the third page of the journal reads thus: "At a meeting of the committees *appointed by the several counties* of the province of Maryland," &c. which shows plainly the principle adopted then is the same contended for now by my amendment, and is our true theory, and should be still perpetuated. As a further evidence in favor of county distinction and equality, and as parties to the work then to be performed, I will read the very first act of that body which shows beyond all doubt in what capacity they were acting. It reads thus: "It being moved from the chair to ascertain the manner of dividing upon questions, it was agreed, that on any division *each county have one vote*, and that all questions be determined *by a majority of counties.*" This Convention after a session of three days adjourned, and its interesting proceedings can be found on pages 3, 4, and 5, of the journal.

In November 21st, following, another Convention assembled, and continued its session for four days, but there not being a full attendance it passed the following resolution and adjourned. "*Several of the counties* not being fully represented, from the want of sufficient notice of the time of this meeting, resolved that this meeting will adjourn to Thursday, the eighth December next; and that a letter be wrote to those counties, earnestly to request them to send *their deputies* to attend punctually on that day, as matters of very great importance,"&c. [See page 5, of the journal.]

The Convention met again on the day appointed, viz: eighth December, 1774, and among its deeply interesting proceedings, may be found on pages eight and nine of its journal, the following resolutions:

Resolved, That it is earnestly recommended by this Convention, to the people of this province—that the determinations of the *several county committees be observed and acquiesced in:* That no persons, except members of the committees, undertake to meddle with or determine any question respecting the construction of the association entered into by the continental Congress; and that peace and good order be inviolably maintained throughout this province.

Resolved, unanimously, That it is recommended to the committees of each county, to raise, by subscription, or in such other voluntary manner as they may think proper, and will be most agreeable to their respective counties, such sums of money, &c., &c., &c.; and that the committees of the respective counties, lay out the same in the purchase of arms and ammunition for the use of such county, to be secured and kept in proper and convenient places, under the direction of the said committee.

Resolved, unanimously, That it will be necessary that a provincial meeting of deputies chosen by the several counties of this province, should be held in the city of Annapolis, on Monday the 24th of April next, &c.; and, therefore, we recommend that the several counties of this province, choose deputies as soon as conveniently may be, to attend such meetings, &c.

That Convention met according to the time appointed, and another met also in July following, 1775, the latter of which adopted articles of association which contains a kind of provisional government, and a confederation of the counties.

See page nineteen to thirty-six of the journal.

In those articles of association, on page thirty, the following provision for future Conventions is made: "And on the same day, or the next, to which the said delegates are empowered to adjourn, the said electors also choose, by ballot, five of the most discreet and sensible of such freemen, as aforesaid, of their county, to be delegates for the same, in any provincial Convention to be held for this province, within one year then next following, with full power and authority to such delegates or any three or more of them, to appear and *act for such county* in such Convention; and to consent and agree to, *and bind such county* to perform and execute all such matters and things as such Convention or *a majority of the counties* of this province shall determine," &c.

The next Convention was called under the "Articles of Association," and assembled on the 7th of December, 1775. It transacted much business of importance, all tending to carry out the object and principles of the "Association." Among its proceedings may be found, on page eighty-five of the journal, a settlement by ballot of the *rank of counties*, and Somerset, the county I have in part the honor to represent, stands as first in the catalogue. This was a proud and lofty position, and well may she yet contend for those great principles of county equality, when only by lot she was made the "chief among equals."

The sixth Maryland Convention was held on the 8th of May, 1776, and its session was laborious and protracted, continuing until Saturday the 6th of July following, to the very noon of night. During its session, on page one hundred and eighty-four of the journal, provision was made for calling a new Convention for the express purpose of forming a new government. In that Convention, the counties were to be represented upon the usual footing of perfect equality, anticipating a division of Frederick county in three counties, which was done. Baltimore town and Annapolis were recognised as boroughs; and a representation of only half that allowed to a county, was reluctantly conceded to each. The resolution says, "nor shall the resolution be understood to *engage or secure* such representation to Annapolis or Baltimore town, but temporarily; the same bring, in the opinion of this Convention, properly to be modified, or taken away, on a material alteration of the circumstances of those places, from either a depopulation or a considerable decrease of the inhabitants thereof."

It will be seen by this, Mr. President, that the right was reserved to take away the representation of Annapolis and Baltimore, under certain circumstances; but no such right was given, reserved or acknowledged to have the like effect upon the counties under any circumstances whatever. Their right to political existence and equal representation, was reserved to each, and whenever it is changed, modified or abolished, it must be done by their own free consent, or acquiesance. Under this agreement they entered into the compact of government in 1776, and have remained until this day. But some of them have suffered by their rights being impaired by a change made in the Constitution in 1836, in which they have acquisced.

Mr. McMahon, in his history of Maryland, in speaking of the system of representation adopted in the Constitution of 1776, says:

"With reference to the several counties of the State, the *principle* of our present system of representation in the House of Delegates, is perfect equality, because of distinct county interest, without regard to difference in territory or population."

And again he says: "This system imparts to the State the character of a confederacy of counties, and unless so regarded, it has no governing principle."

And again he says, when speaking of this probable permanency. "There is, however, one alteration of it, relating only to the representation of the city of Baltimore, which, it is believed, the justice and magnanimity of the State will yet accord to her. This proposes *merely* to increase the number of her delegates to *four*, so as to place her on an *equality* with the counties. It received the sanction of the Legislature at the session of 1824, but was not confirmed as the Constitution requires, at the ensuing session. * * * On that occasion it was resisted, not so much on account of its immediate objects and effects in raising the representation of Baltimore to an *equality* with that of the several counties, as for its *supposed tendency to extend the hand of innovation to the whole system, and to strengthen her claims for a farther increase.* Without regarding it as the beginning of *innovation*, it was difficult to find an argument of justice or expediency, upon which the bill could be resisted. By the very grant of a partial representation, this city is admitted as *a distinct member* of the *quasi-confederacy*, having *distinct interest*" &c.

And now, Mr. President, after having examined into the history of this State thoroughly, only a small portion of which I have found it convenient to cite as authority, but leaving an abundance still behind, I have come to the conclusion, that the present government is constituted of a confederacy of counties, each one being a party to the compact, and that each county has yet reserved rights, among which is the right to *political existence and individuality.*

FRIDAY, March 7, 1851.

The Convention met at ten o'clock.

Prayer was made by the Rev. Mr. GRAUFF.

The roll was called, and a quorum being present, the journal of yesterday was read and approved.

Mr. JOHN NEWCOMER presented a petition of sundry citizens of Washington county, praying that a provision may be made in the new Constitution, that the privilege to sell intoxicating liquor shall not be granted to any person in any part of the State, except the same shall first be sanctioned or approved of by a majority of the votes in the district where the same is to be sold.

Which was read, and

Referred to the select committee already appointed on that subject.

HOWARD COUNTY.

Mr. DORSEY rose and asked the Convention at this time to take up and consider the report heretofore presented by him, in relation to making Howard District a county. He did not intend himself to discuss it, he said, and he had no reason to suppose that it would occupy more than a few minutes of the time of the Convention.

Mr. BROWN suggested that the unfinished business of the morning hour of yesterday, would come up to-day as a matter of course.

The PRESIDENT replied, that the unfinished business of the morning hour would come up as a matter of course; but that it might be postponed by the vote of a majority of the Convention.

Mr. DORSEY said, the report would probably not occupy more than five minutes.

Mr. BROWN replied, that it was probable that the unfinished business could be disposed of in the same length of time. He hoped that the Convention would dispose of that in the first instance.

The PRESIDENT inquired, whether the gentleman from Anne Arundel, (Mr. Dorsey,) persisted in his motion.

Mr. DORSEY. I should like to have the sense of the Convention upon it. And he made the motion accordingly.

Mr. PRESTMAN intimated his opinion that the report would lead to discussion.

Some conversation followed on a point of or- of order.

Mr. DORSEY asked the yeas and nays on his motion, which were ordered, and being taken, resulted as follows:

Affirmative—Messrs. Chapman, Pres't., Blakistone, Dent, Hopewell, Chambers of Kent, Mitchell, Donaldson, Dorsey, Wells, Randall, Kent, Sellman, Weems, Dalrymple, Sollers, Bell, Ridgely, Crisfield, Dashiell, Hicks, Hodson, Goldsborough, Eccleston, Sprigg, McCubbin, Bowling, Grason, McMaster, Fiery, John Newcomer, and Davis—33.

Negative—Messrs. Ricaud, Lee, Lloyd, Colston, Chambers of Cecil, McCullough, Miller, Spencer, George, Fooks, Thomas, Shriver, Gaither, Biser, Annan, Sappington, Stephenson, Magraw, Thawley, Hardcastle, Gwinn, Sherwood of Baltimore city, Presstman, Ware, Schley, Neill, Michael Newcomer, Weber, Hollyday, Slicer, Parke, Ege, Cockey, and Brown—32.

So the Convention determined to proceed to the consideration of the said report.

The report was read as follows:

The select committee apointed to consider and report respecting the formation of New Counties in this State, beg leave to make the following report, and recommend its adoption as an article of the constitution about to be formed:

THOS. B. DORSEY, *Chairman.*

Article. That part of Anne Arundel county called Howard District, is hereby erected into a new county to be called Howard county; the inhabitants whereof shall have, hold and enjoy all such rights and privileges as are held and enjoyed by the inhabitants of the other counties in this State: and its civil and municipal officers at the time of the ratification of this constitution shall continue in office until their successors shall have been elected or appointed, and shall have qualified as such; and all rights, powers and obligations incident to Howard District of Anne Arundel county, shall attach to Howard county.

The question was then stated to be on the adoption of the report.

Mr. WARE said, that before the question was taken he should like to know the census of Anne Arundel county proper, and Howard District.

Mr. DORSEY said, he had not the census before him; but he understood upon good authority, that the population of the district was some twelve or thirteen thousand.

The question was then taken and the report was adopted.

BASIS OF REPRESENTATION.

Mr. SPENCER moved that the Convention resume the consideration of the unfinished business of the morning hour—which motion was agreed to.

The Convention thereupon resumed the consideration of the motion submitted yesterday by Mr. LLOYD, making the several reports from the committee on representation the special order of the day for Tuesday next.

Mr. GWINN asked the yeas and nays, which were ordered.

Mr. WELLS, (to the Chair.) Is it in order to move another day?

The PRESIDENT. It is in order to move any other day that has not yet been named.

Mr. WELLS. I move Wednesday week.

The yeas and nays were ordered.

Mr. PRESSTMAN said, he did not see the necessity of being pertinacious as to a particular day, or of taking the yeas and nays on each day named. The Convention could designate some day most acceptable to it, without the delay consequent upon this process.

Mr. SOLLERS, (to the Chair.) Is an amendment in order? I wish to move an indefinite postponement.

The PRESIDENT. A motion to postpone indefinitely is not in order at this time. The proposition is to fix a day certain for the consideration of the question.

Mr. SAPPINGTON addressed the Chair.

The PRESIDENT now stated that the pending question was not debateable, and the Chair would not entertain discussion.

Mr. HOPEWELL. Is it in order to move to lay the motion on the table?

The PRESIDENT. The motion is in order.

Mr. HOPEWELL. I make it.

The question was taken, and the Convention decided that the motion should not be laid on the table.

The question then recurred on the motion of Mr. WELLS, to designate Wednesday week, and being taken, resulted as follows:

Affirmative — Messrs. Chapman, President, Blakistone, Dent, Hopewell, Ricaud, Lee, Chambers, of Kent, Mitchell, Donaldson, Dorsey, Wells, Randall, Kent, Sellman, Weems, Dalrymple, Bond, Crisfield, Dashiell, Hicks, Hodson, Goldsborough, Eccleston, Sprigg, McCubbin, Bowling, Grason, McMaster, Fooks, Sappington, Stephenson, McHenry, Thawley, Schley, Fiery, John Newcomer, Davis and Kilgour—37.

Negative — Messrs. Sollers, Bell, Welch, Ridgely, Lloyd, Colston, Chambers, of Cecil, McCullough, Miller, Spencer, George, Thomas, Shriver, Gaither, Biser, Annan, Magraw, Hardcastle, Gwinn, Sherwood, of Baltimore city, Presstman, Ware, Neill, Michael Newcomer, Weber, Hollyday, Slicer, Parke, Ege, Cockey and Brown—31.

So the reports from the committee on representation was made the special order of the day, for Wednesday week.

THE LEGISLATIVE DEPARTMENT.

The Convention proceeded to the special order of the day, being the report of the committee on the legislative department.

The pending question was on the substitute amendment offered yesterday by Mr. SPENCER in the following words:

"The Legislature shall not hereafter appropriate the public money, or pledge the public faith, or make loans, or subscriptions to any association, corporation or work of internal improvement; and they shall not use or appropiate the proceeds of the internal improvement companies, or of the State tax now levied, or which may hereafter be levied to pay off the public debt, to any other purpose, until the interest and debt are fully paid."

Mr. SPENCER moved the question be taken by yeas and nays.

Mr. SPENCER said, that he had yesterday offered this as a substitute for the amendment of the gentleman from Harford, [Mr. McHenry.] He now withdrew it. He did so in consequence of a conversation with that gentleman, in which he, (Mr. McH.,) had agreed to accept the latter part of the substitute as a modification of his own proposition.

Mr. McHENRY accepted this modification.

Mr. CRISFIELD now offered the following amendment, of which he had yesterday given notice:

Strike out after the word "dollars," in the tenth line, to the word "the," in the thirteenth line, and insert:

"Nor shall the legislature hereafter create any debt, or pledge the credit of the State, except for the purpose of education, as hereinafter may be provided, to or for the use of any association or corporation, or for or on account of any work of internal improvement, but after the payment of the public debt as provided by law, the revenue which may accrue from the State's investments in works of internal improvement, may be appropriated to the improvement of existing, and the construction of additional works,"

Mr. C. said, he had yesterday given notice of his intention to offer this amendment, and he now offered it, because, as the matter now stood, it appeared to him, that the legislature would be precluded from giving any aid to the improvement of the internal condition of the State, and from assisting the development of her resources.

He wished it to be distinctly understood, that no gentleman was more opposed than he was, to increasing the public debt. He saw no necessity for it. No new debt, in his opinion, ought to be contracted; except some great emergency, as the public defence for instance, should require it, and it was not likely that such an emergency would arise.

But he thought the ordinary revenue of the State, derived from that system of *indirect* taxation now in force, and which must for reasons other than financial, be maintained, with that derived from our investments, other than for works of internal improvements, was quite sufficient for the ordinary expenses of the government and should be so applied. He could see no good reason why the revenue to be derived from the State's investments in works of internal improvements, after the payment of the public debt, should not be applied to the improvement of the works already constructed, and to the construction of new ones where the public interest may require.

Improvements were greatly needed in his own section of the State. His constituents had been severely taxed on account of the works already constructed, and had secured no direct benefit from them; and more than one half of the State was in the same condition. He was not willing to preclude his constituents from all hope of advantage from their large expenditures, by withholding from the legislature all power of appropriation for this object. He hoped that at some time, far distant though it might be, his people would be compensated, at least in part, for their contributions, by having the navigation of their rivers improved, their swamps drained, and the facilities of inter-communication increased.

But, he added, he did not intend to inflict a speech on the Convention; the general subject, he thought, had been sufficiently discussed, and he would trouble the Convention no further than to ask that his amendment might be read before the vote was taken.

The amendment having been recorded,

Mr. Sollers remarked that he had but a word to say. He understood that the sense of the Convention had been expressed yesterday distinctly and emphatically upon this proposition. He could not imagine any thing more dangerous than this very amendment of the gentleman from Somerset, (Mr. Crisfield.) If there ever was an accumulation in the treasury, (a matter problematical in his opinion,) arising from the revenues received from our works of internal improvement, he did not desire to see them appropriated to works hereafter to be made. If there was one single question upon which the judgment of the people had been passed, it was that the Legislature of the State was never again to be permitted to contract another debt for any such purpose. If there was one reform which they had demanded, it was this: He warned the Convention to take heed what it did with this proposition, introduced as it was for the purpose of defeating the action which had yesterday been deliberately taken.

Mr. Crisfield said he could not conceive by what process the gentleman from Calvert, (Mr. Sollers,) could arrive at the conclusion just announced, that this was a project for the creation of additional debt. The amendment declared, in the most distinct terms, that no debt should be created for internal improvement, or for the use of any association or corporation, except for the purposes of education. The purpose of the amendment was, and its effect will be, to prevent the creation of new debts; and he really was surprised to hear a different object and effect attributed to it. But while he desired to prevent the increase of debt, he did not desire that those portions of the State, which had not yet received any direct benefit from the vast sums which had been expended on works of internal improvement, should forever be precluded from enjoying any of the fruits of those expenditures. If these works fulfil the promises of their projector, large revenues will come into the treasury from that source; and he would ask what is to be done with the money after the payment of the public debt? It will not be required, and ought not to be used, for the ordinary expenses of the government. Must it lie idly in the treasury? Was it to remain as a fund on which politicians might speculate? He hoped not. There had been quite enough of folly and extravagance, to say nothing of corruption, already in the management of our affairs. Let us, as far as possible, remove all temptation out of the way of those who may hereafter be called to administer them.

The improvement of the social condition of the people, and the development of the numerous sources of wealth which abound in every quarter of the State, are objects worthy the patronage of the State, and next after the education of her people, should claim the attention of the government. Here were purposes highly useful and beneficial, and quite sufficient to absorb all the revenue which will be received from the source referred to; and he hoped the Legislature would not be prohibited from devoting it to them. And this amendment too, he would add, addressed itself quite as strongly to the justice of the government as to that wise and liberal policy which should actuate it. As already remarked, a large part of the State, without any direct advantage to itself hitherto received, has contributed equally with the rest to pay for these works, and it would be exceedingly unjust if it should be forever prohibited from receiving back, in the shape of similar works, to be made for its convenience and benefit, some remuneration for its large outlays. He hoped his amendment would be adopted.

Mr. Blakistone said, he should vote against the proposition of the gentleman from Somerset, (Mr. Crisfield,) and he, (Mr. B.,) would briefly assign his reasons for so doing. Ever since the first appropriation had been made for works of internal improvement, the promise had been held out to the people, that when those works should have been completed, they would confer immense benefits upon the whole people—that every portion of the State was to be ornamented with school-houses—and that there would be money enough to defray the expenses of the government, and all local expenses, without the necessity of sending the tax-gatherer round to collect the taxes If the proposition of the gentleman from Somerset should be defeated, it was his, (Mr. B.'s,) intention to offer an amendment to carry out in good faith this expectation. So far as his section of the State was concerned, there was no need for internal improvements. They were blessed with canals, natural canals, rivers and streams sufficient for all their purposes. They had a direct communication with Baltimore—they had a direct communication with the District. They wanted no roads and canals, and the only benefit, if any, which they were to receive from the works now constructed, would be from the revenues they would yield after the public debt should have been paid.

According to the proposition of the gentleman from Somerset, (Mr. Crisfield,) the whole of these revenues, contrary to the pledge of the State, might be diverted by the Legislature to purposes which might be in conflict with the interests of certain portions of the people. His, (Mr. B.'s,) plan was, that after the debt was paid, the stock of these internal improvement companies, so far as pledged at the time of the appropriation, should be given to the counties in proportion to the sums they might have paid into the State treasury for the redemption of the State debt.

His second proposition was, that after the State debt should have been paid off, or if the sinking fund should be sufficient to meet the debt as it became redeemable, it should be the duty of the Legislature to appropriate the surplus revenues among the several counties and the city of Baltimore equally, having a just regard to the amount paid into the treasury by each, and taking into consideration the advantages and disadvantages resulting to each from the works of internal improvement, after deducting so much as might be required to meet the current expenses of the State and to provide for any sudden exigency that might arise. This, he thought, would carry out the good faith of the State ot the people in every portion of it.

If a provision should be engrafted on the organic law, giving power to the Legislature to appropriate to purposes of internal improvement, in any section of the State, a fund which had been pledged for the specific use of the people of Maryland, it would produce feelings of dissatisfaction and discontent, not to be quelled by the eloquence of gentlemen here, or by their high-sounding appeals to the patriotism of the people beyond these walls. Their confidence in those to whom they had entrusted their interests and their destinies, would be irrecoverably lost. And if it were not for the intense vigilance and jealousy with which the people, guarded the honor of the State, and for the love which, as her own children, they bore her, they would almost feel justified in declaring that they would not pay at all. But he would not go so far as to say that they would do *that*. For however badly this Convention might behave, he did not believe that the people could be induced to follow their example. [Laughter.]

Mr. B. then read his amendment, (which will be found in a later portion of the day's proceedings.)

Mr. Crisfield. The gentleman from St. Mary's, (Mr. Blakistone,) complains that the adoption of my proposition would be a violation of the public faith—that the proceeds to be derived from these public works are pledged for purposes of education. Will the gentleman tell me what portion of these revenues are pledged, and whether he, himself, in the amendment he indicates, does not propose to establish a new rule of distribution which sets at naught the very pledge to which, I suppose, he has reference?

Mr. Blakistone. I allude to the tax law of 1840. The last section of that act is in the following words:

Chapter 23, Session 1840 and 41.

Section 64. And be it enacted, That it shall be the duty of the treasurer of the Western and Eastern Shores respectively, to keep an accurate account of the moneys that are paid into the treasury by the city of Baltimore, Howard district, and the several counties in this State, under the provisions of this bill; and the said city, district and counties respectively, be authorised, through their corporate authorities, levy courts or commissioners respectively, to commute the sums of money so paid by them into the treasury, into so much of the State's stock in the Chesapeake and Ohio canal company, as may equal the amounts respectively paid by them, whenever the said canal company shall be able to pay six per cent. upon the said stock, and the treasurer of the Western Shore is hereby directed to cause the necessary transfers of stock to be made to the said city, district, or counties respectively, and they shall be considered stockholders in said canal company, and thereafter be entitled to receive the dividends that may accrue on the amounts of stock so held by them respectively.

Now, (remarked Mr. B.,) I want to carry this law fully out, and not to authorise the Legislature to divert these funds to any purpose whatsoever.

The question was stated to be on the substitute of Mr. Crisfield.

Mr Dorsey said, he was in favor of striking out the amendment of the gentleman from Harford, (Mr. McHenry,) as now amended, because, however much he, (Mr. D.,) might have been disposed to sustain it in the first instance, he could not possibly vote for it in the modified form it had now assumed. If he understood the language of the amendment, the effect of it would be that if there should be half a dozen persons holding the stock of the State of Maryland, due in the year 1890, and who refused, before that time, to sell out to the agent of the State, who had charge of the sinking fund, not one dollar of the half million of money which we might be receiving annually for twenty or twenty-five years, could be appropriated or used for any purpose, until this handful of obstinate stock-holders should be paid. It seemed to him that the Convention should not adopt any such constitutional provision. It might have the effect of placing beyond the control of the Legislature, some ten or fifteen millions of dollars, which they could not touch. Although the State might have money enough before the years '63 or 4, to pay off every dollar of debt which she owed, and was willing to pay it, yet from that time to the year 1890, the money must remain in the treasury idle and useless, and could not be appropriated to any purpose whatsoever If there was any meaning in language, this was the meaning of the amendment. He must, therefore, vote against it. Gentlemen would perceive, that it placed the subject in a very different point of view from that in which it stood under the amendment of the gentleman from Harford, (Mr. McHenry.) It would be unreasonable thus to tie up the hands of the Legislature.

He, (Mr. D.,) was in favor of the substitute of the gentleman from Somerset, (Mr. Crisfield.) As he, (Mr. D.,) understood that proposition, the money, after the payment of the debt, might be appropriated, and he could readily suppose a case, where such an appropriation might be requisite and proper. He instanced the case of the opening of the channel of a river, &c.

He thought that the Convention was disposed to show, by its action, an entire want of confidence in the Legislature, to regard them as possessed neither of intelligence, patriotism, nor honesty, and to leave them the power to do nothing, either for good or for evil.

Mr. Brown remarked that the discussion on this question had, in his judgment, lasted long enough. And he gave notice that hereafter, on all occasions, when he thought the discussion had been ample, he should test the sense of the Convention, as he now did, on the demand for the previous question.

The question "will the Convention second the demand for the previous question," was then taken, and decided in the negative.

So there was not a second.

The question then recurred on the amendment as amended.

Mr. Spencer said, that however great his respect might be for the ability of the distinguished gentleman from Anne Arundel, (Mr. Dorsey,) who had made the criticism on his, (Mr S.'s,) amendment, as accepted by the gentleman from Harford, he could not subscribe to the correctness of that gentleman's construction. He, (Mr. S.) held that it embodied no such proposition as the gentleman had indicated. He should not, however, discuss it. He held that his amendment looked to the payment of the public debt, and allowed the Legislature to appropriate money in any way, either by the creation of a sinking-fund or by any other process, looking to the extinguishment of the debt. But it restricted the Legislature from appropriating the revenues for any other purpose.

Inasmuch, however, as there was a diversity of opinion on the subject, he would, in order to relieve the question from all embarrassment offer a modification of his proposition which would dispose of the objection, and which his friend from Harford had agreed to accept.

As regarded the substitute of his friend from Somerset, (Mr. Crisfield,) he, (Mr. S.) was opposed to it for several reasons. In the first place, it invited the State to engage in these works of internal improvement; and he, (Mr. S.,) was not willing to put into the hands of the Legislature any power of that character. In the second place, he was opposed to it; inasmuch as the Legislature would possess the discretion, under the amendment as it now stood, to appropriate money for public schools.

Mr. McHenry moved to amend the amendment by adding at the end thereof, the following:

"Or the sinking fund shall be equal to the amount of the outstanding debt."

The amendment was agreed to.

The question then recurred on the adoption of the substitute of Mr. Crisfield.

Mr. Brown asked the yeas and nays, which were ordered, and being taken, resulted as follows:

Affirmative.—Messrs. Ricaud, Lee, Chambers of Kent, Mitchell, Donaldson, Dorsey, Wells, Randall, Kent, Sellman, Crisfield, Sprigg, McCubbin, and Davis—14.

Negative—Messrs. Chapman, Pres't., Blakistone, Dent, Hopewell, Weems, Dalrymple, Bond, Sollers, Jenifer, Bell, Welch, Ridgely, Lloyd, Colston, Dashiell, Hicks, Hodson, Goldsborough, Eccleston, Chambers of Cecil, McCullough, Miller, Bowie, Bowling, Spencer, Grason, George, McMaster, Fooks, Thomas, Shriver, Gaither, Annan, Sappington, Stephenson, McHenry, Magraw, Thawley, Hardcastle, Gwinn, Sherwood of Baltimore city, Presstman, Ware, Schley, Fiery, Neill, John Newcomer, Michael Newcomer, Weber, Hollyday, Slicer, Parke, Ege, Cockey, and Brown—55.

So the substitute was rejected.

The question then recurred on the adoption of the amendment as amended, and it was decided in the affirmative.

So the amendment as amended, was adopted.

The question then recurred on the amendment of Mr. George, as the twenty-first section of the report, as amended, and was decided in the affirmative.

So the amendment of Mr. George, as amended, was adopted.

Mr. Blakistone then moved to amend said report by inserting as an additional section, the following:

"That it shall be the duty of the Legislature so soon as the public debt shall have been fully paid off, to cause to be transferred to the several counties and city of Baltimore, stock in the internal improvement companies, equal to the amount respectively paid by each towards the erection and completion of said works, at the then market value of said stock. It shall further be the duty of the Legislature after the public debt shall have been fully paid off, or the sinking fund shall be sufficient to redeem the same at maturity, to appropriate such portions of the annual revenue of the State stocks in the internal improvement companies of this State, (after deducting so much, together with the other annual revenues of the State as may be necessary to meet the current expenses, and any sudden exigencies that may arise;) equally among said counties and the city of Baltimore, having a just regard to the several amounts paid by each into the State Treasury; and the advantages and disadvantages resulting to each respectively from the construction of said works of internal improvement. The said stocks and revenue when paid over, to be under the direction and control of the county authorities of the several counties, and the Mayor and City Council of Baltimore, respectively to be by them applied to purposes of education, and such other purposes as the said county and city authorities may deem proper."

The amendment having been read—

Mr. Ridgely said, that it presented two propositions, and he called for a division. He desired also to ask the gentleman from St. Mary's, (Mr. Blakistone,) who had offered the amendment, by what rule he determined the appropriations which the relative parts of the State should receive, from the revenues derived from the public works?

Mr. Blakistone said, he proposed to leave that matter, exclusively to the Legislature to be decided, he presumed, by a sort of compromise, or conciliation from one part of the State towards another, like the Constitution which this Convention might adopt. He presumed that Baltimore would receive more than other parts of the State, because she had paid more. So with the large counties. He thought, however, that St. Mary's ought to receive a little more in proportion, because she had derived no benefit from the construction of the works.

Mr. Spencer. I have risen merely to indicate the vote I shall give. I shall vote against the proposition. And I shall vote against all kinds of prospective legislation.

Mr. Dent demanded the previous question.

There was a second,

And the main question was ordered, (being on the amendment of Mr. Blakistone.)

Mr. Weems asked the yeas and nays,

Which were ordered.

And the question was then taken on the first branch of the amendment in the words fowlloing:

"That it shall be the duty of the legislature so soon as the public debt shall have been fully paid off, to cause to be transferred to the several counties and the city of Baltimore, stock in the internal improvement companies, equal to the amount respectively paid by each towards the erection and completion of said works, at the then market value of said stock."

And the result was as follows:

Affirmative—Messrs. Chapman, Pres't, Blakistone, Dent, Hopewell, Dorsey, Wells, Randall, Kent, Weems, Dalrymple, Bond, Jenifer, Bell, Welch, Ridgely, Colston, Dashiell, Hicks, Hodson, Goldsborough, Eccleston, Chambers of Cecil, Miller, Bowie, McCubbin, Bowling, McMaster, Fooks, Gaither, Annan, Stephenson, Thawley, Presstman, John Newcomer, Michael Newcomer, Weber and Slicer—37.

Negative—Messrs. Ricaud, Lee, Chambers of Kent, Donaldson, Lloyd, Crisfield, Sprigg, Spencer, Grason, George, Thomas, Shriver, Biser, Sappington, McHenry, Hardcastle, Gwinn, Ware, Schley, Fiery, Neill, Davis, Hollyday, Parke, Ege, Cockey and Brown—27.

So the first branch of the amendment was adopted.

And the question recurred on the second branch of the amendment.

And the result was as follows:

Affirmative—Messrs. Chapman, Pres't, Blakistone, Dent, Hopewell, Chambers of Kent, Randall, Kent, Weems, Dalrymple, Bond, Jenifer, Colston, Dashiell, Hicks, Hodson, Goldsborough, Eccleston, Bowie, Sprigg, McCubbin, Bowling, McMaster, Fooks, Stephenson, Thawley, Hardcastle, John Newcomer, Michael Newcomer and Davis—29.

Negative—Messrs. Ricaud, Lee, Donaldson, Dorsey, Wells, Bell, Welch, Ridgely, Lloyd, Crisfield, Chambers of Cecil, McCullough, Miller, Spencer, Grason, George, Thomas, Shriver, Gaither, Biser, Annan, Sappington, McHenry, Gwinn, Sherwood of Baltimore city, Presstman, Ware, Schley, Fiery, Neill, Weber, Hollyday, Slicer, Parke, Ege, Cockey and Brown—37.

So the second and last branch of the amendment was rejected.

IMPRISONMENT FOR DEBT.

Mr. Presstman. In the early part of the session, I was instructed by the committee on the legislative department, to report certain provisions, as additional articles to the report now under consideration. It is rather remarkable that every one of these provisions, with one exception, has already been adopted. The article which concerned the abolition of the relation of master and slave as it now exists in this State, was taken possession of by the gentleman from Charles, (Mr. Jenifer.) I have no desire to reclaim it under the fugitive slave law. [Laughter.] All I have to say, is, that I am glad it has been adopted.

The next article directed the legislature at its first session after the adoption of the Constitution, to appoint a commissioner to revise, digest and arrange the statute laws of the State, civil and criminal, and a commissioner to revise, simplify and abridge the rules and practice, pleadings, forms and proceedings of the courts of record of this State.

This was taken possession of by my colleague. I am happy that he had the opportunity of doing so. It was also adopted.

The next provision gave power to the legislature to protect by law from forced sale, a certain portion of the property of all heads of families. This principle was adopted on the suggestion of the gentleman from Baltimore county, although I, myself, changed my mind and voted against it.

The only remaining proposition is in these words:

"No person shall be imprisoned for debt."

I should be glad if I had been saved the trouble of offering this provision also. It becomes my duty, however, (no member of the Convention having been kind enough to come to my relief,) to ask the attention of the Convention to it. As we all know, it involves a very important principle; still I do not believe that there is any necessity for a protracted discussion upon it. I am sure, that gentlemen, whether in favor of the abolition of imprisonment for debt, or opposed to it, will scarcely be influenced by any discussion here.

They have formed their opinions deliberately. It is not probable that debate will change them. I am satisfied that a majority of the members of this body, are fatigued with the long and almost uninterrupted discussion which has taken place; and that they will not desire to extend it, at all events, on a subject which is so well understood. I hope, therefore, that the proposition may be put to the vote. As the report emanates from myself, I cannot call the previous question. It would not be courteous in me to do so. I can only express the hope that the Convention will feel disposed to take the question up with as little delay as possible.

The PRESIDENT then stated the question to be on the adoption of the section, reported by Mr. PRESSTMAN, as an additional article to the report of the committee on the legislative department.

Mr. JENIFER said he had no desire to steal the thunder of his friend from Baltimore city upon this question of master and slave, and it was to prevent such proceeding by others that he, (Mr J.,) had the proposition returned to the committee No. 14, and also, he, (Mr. J.,) as chairman of that committee, was prepared to report an article on that subject, in which the committee was unanimously agreed. Yet, to ensure a unanimous vote in the House, it was agreed to adopt the proposition of the gentleman from Baltimore city, believing, that by so doing, no objection would come from that section of the State, which otherwise might be apprehended.

Mr. PRESSTMAN asked if his friend from Charles believed him to be doubtful on this subject?

Mr. J. replied that his friend from Baltimore city was too sincere and honorable to be distrusted upon any question.

Mr. BOWIE said that he disclaimed the credit which his friend from Charles, (Mr. Jenifer,) had given to him in reference to that section of the Constitution which deprives the Legislature of the power to abolish the relation of master and slave in this State. He was as perfectly willing to accord to his friend from Baltimore city, (Mr. Presstman,) the credit of having first offered this provision of the Constitution, and coming, as it did, from that portion of the State which had been supposed to be rather unfriendly to the institution of slavery, he, (Mr. B.) hailed it, at the time, as a harbinger of peace and security to the people of this State on a subject of the deepest and most vital importance to them. When his friend, the gentleman from Charles, (Mr. Jenifer,) moved to take up the report of the committee on that subject, of which he was chairman, and asked the Convention to proceed at once to a consideration of it; he, (Mr. B.,) prefering infinitely the proposition of the gentleman from Baltimore city, to the report of the committee, was anxiously expecting that gentleman to move it as a substitute for the report of the committee; but the gentleman from Baltimore city did not do so, and the Convention were about to adopt the article as it was reported from the committee. At this stage of the proceedings, he, (Mr. B.,) availed himself of the opportunity of adopting the proposition of his friend from Baltimore city, (Mr. Presstman,) and moved it as a substitute for the report. It was subsequently accepted by the committee and adopted by a unanimous vote of the Convention. This, said Mr. B., was the history of the matter, and he was quite willing that the gentleman from Baltimore city, (Mr. Presstman,) should have all the credit of the movement.

Mr. SCHLEY said, that, as the gentleman from Baltimore city, (Mr. Presstman,) was appropriating to himself the credit of all these subject-matters, it was right and proper that the "honors," which were about to be dealt out, should be fairly distributed.

Mr. S. then referred to the journals to show that the first notice of a proposition relative to the codification of the laws, was submitted by Mr. FIERY.

In relation to the rights of married women—

Mr. PRESSTMAN, (interposing) There are no married women in my report, sir. [Laughter.]

Mr. SCHLEY, nodding a good-humored acquiescence, took his seat.

The question then recurred on the adoption of the section abolishing imprisonment for debt.

Mr. DENT demanded the previous question.

There was a second,

And the main question was ordered to be taken.

The yeas and nays were demanded by a dozen voices,

And were ordered.

And the main question, [on the adoption of the report,] was ordered,

And having been taken, resulted as follows:

Affirmative—Messrs. Chapman, Pres't, Blakistone, Dent, Hopewell, Ricaud, Lee, Wells, Randall, Sellman, Weems, Dalrymple, Bond, Jenifer, Bell, Welch, Ridgely, Lloyd, Colston, Dashiell, Hicks, Hodson, Goldsborough Eccleston, Chambers, of Cecil, McCullough, Miller, Bowie, Sprigg, McCubbin, Bowling, Spencer, Grason, George, Thomas, Shriver, Gaither, Biser, Annan, Sappington, Stephenson, McHenry, Thawley, Gwinn, Sherwood, of Baltimore city, Presstman, Ware, Schley, Fiery, Neill, John Newcomer, Michael Newcomer, Davis, Kilgour, Weber, Hollyday, Slicer, Parke, Ege, Cockey and Brown —60.

Negative.—Messrs. Chambers, of Kent, Donaldson, Dorsey, McMaster and Fooks—5.

So the amendment of Mr. PRESSTMAN was adopted as an additional article.

Mr. BLAKISTONE. I believe we have now finished the legislative report. I move that the Convention proceed to the consideration of the executive report.

Mr. RIDGELY. I have another article to offer to the legislative report. I do not intend to invite discussion. I ask that the amendment may be read, and I call the previous question.

The amendment was read, as follows:

"The Legislature, at the first session after the adoption of this constitution, shall provide for the substitution of salaries in place of the fees and perquisites of office, now payable to the clerks and registers of the several courts of law, equity and probate in this State, and for reducing and regulating the rates of fees, costs and legal charges in said courts."

There was a second to the demand for the previous question.

The main question was ordered,

And having been taken, the amendment of Mr. RIDGELY was agreed to.

Mr. SPENCER moved a re-consideration of the vote taken this morning, adopting the first branch of the amendment offered by Mr. BLAKISTONE, as an additional section to the report.

Mr. SPENCER said, the amendment requires that the internal improvement stock should be disposed of in a certain way. It takes the internal improvement companies, out of the hands of the State authorities, and places them under the control of the counties. Wherever the most stocks would be found, there the works could be contracted. If there was a disposition on the part of the Convention, to take the control from the State, let it be so understood. But he now made the motion to reconsider the vote, because he desired to have the deliberate sense of the Convention on the propriety of adopting the principle of the amendment. He was certain it was not understood.

Mr. BLAKISTONE expressed his fear that the Convention was falling into the old track. After a question has been adopted by a solemn vote, and by an overwhelming majority, these motions to reconsider on the part of those who stand in a minority, are the cause of immense and unprofitable delay. Last week a vote was taken by which a proposition made by the gentleman from Queen Anne's, [Mr George,] was adopted. He, [Mr. B.,] concluded, as a matter of course, that that question was disposed of, when suddenly a motion was made to reconsider the subject. From that moment, we have gone backwards, and we are now precisely where we were eight days ago, and if we continue to go on in this way, the Convention will be found sitting here from June till January, and from January till June, and after all no Constitution will be made. It had been intimated to him that the city of Baltimore, is hereafter to have the control of the internal improvements of the State. This he did not believe.

But, [said Mr. B.,] if she has contributed to their erection, as it is claimed she has done, let her have the benefit of them to that extent. He was willing. All that he would ask is, that the counties should receive their fair proportion. Baltimore should only have the proportion she pays into the revenue. She does not contribute more than the counties do. He believed she only paid in one-third of the whole amount. It had been thrown out that if Baltimore gets the public works under her control, she will stop the canal. But she would have too great an interest in that work, to permit her to do this, because she must have some five or six millions before she could have the control. It would not be very wise in her to stop the canal when she can make ten per cent. on her capital embarked in that work, if the calculations of its projectors shall ever be realised. She may perhaps apply to the Legislature for a cross-cut to Baltimore: and this might be very wise in her, and she might apply her own means to its completion. He had no objection to this He was a Marylander, and he would be willing that Baltimore shou'd have her share. He held in his hand a law of the Legislature known as the tax bill, which shows the existence of a contract between the counties and the city. If Baltimore helps to pay the debt of the State, let her have the benefit of the these internal improvements. The people have contributed liberally towards these public works, and he diverted that the revenue from them should not be divided to other purposes than those specified in the contracts. Many seem to think that Baltimore will have a controling interest over these works, but this he doubted. To talk of her shutting up the canal even if she had the power, is to talk of that which in the nature of things, is scarcely possible. After she has contributed millions to this magnificent work by a tax upon her people, the idea of her closing the canal is too absurd to be believed.

Mr. B. concluded by moving the previous question.

There was a second.

The main question was ordered to be now taken, [being on the motion to reconsider.]

Mr. BLAKISTONE asked the yeas and nays, which were ordered, and being taken, resulted as follows:

Affirmative—Messrs. Ricaud, Lee, Chambers, of Kent, Mitchell, Donaldson, Jenifer, Lloyd, Crisfield, Dashiell, Hicks, Goldsborough, Chambers, of Cecil, Miller, Sprigg, McCubbin, Bowling, Spencer, Grason, George, Thomas, Shriver, Gaither, Biser, Annan, Sappington, Stephenson, McHenry, Magraw, Hardcastle, Schley, Fiery, Neill, Hollyday, Parke, Ege, Cockey and Brown—37.

Negative—Messrs. Chapman, President, Blakistone, Dent, Hopewell, Dorsey, Wells, Randall, Kent, Sellman, Weems, Dalrymple, Bond, Sollers, Bell, Welch, Ridgely, Colston, Eccleston, Bowie, McMaster, Fooks, Thawley, Gwinn, Brent, of Baltimore city, Sherwood, of Baltimore city, Presstman, Ware, John Newcomer, Michael Newcomer, Davis, Weber and Slicer—32.

So the vote was reconsidered.

The question then recurred on the amendment of Mr. BLAKISTONE.

Mr. JENIFER said:

The amendment had better lie over, that it might be printed, and that the members might have an opportunity to examine it. He had voted for it, but he had strong doubts about it. He moved it lie over until to-morrow.

If the question was taken now, he must vote against it.

Mr. WEEMS moved to postpone its consideration until Wednesday next.

Some conversation followed, and several suggestions were made, that the matter should again come up to-morrow.

Some conversation followed, and several suggestions were made that the matter should again come up to-morrow.

Mr. WEEMS said, he must necessarily be absent to-morrow, and he hoped, therefore, that the Convention would either act on the question to-day, or postpone it until next Wednesday, by which time, he would be here. He desired to record his vote upon it.

Mr. WEEMS said:

That he had the honor of a seat in the legislature when the tax law was passed. He claimed to be the author of the sixty-fourth section of the law as it now stood. He offered this section as an amendment to the original bill and it was accepted by Mr. BOWIE, chairman of the committee of ways and means, by whom the bill was reported. It was his, [Mr. W's.,] deliberate opinion that the bill would not have become a law at that session, had not this section been adopted. The people expected that the faith of the State, as pledged by that law, would be redeemed. He was in favor of carrying out the provisions of the law.

Here Mr. W. read the sixty-fourth section, and stated, in conclusion, that he agreed in all which had fallen from the gentleman from St. Mary's, (Mr. Blakistone,) as to the propriety of carrying out the provisions of the law faithfully.

Mr. CHAMBERS said, the practice which had, of late become prevalent, was likely to lead to difficulties. A gentleman rose, presented a proposition, assigned all the reasons he could find to sustain it, and before he quit the floor, moved the previous question. No room for explanation or correction was allowed.

Now he supposed many gentlemen had voted entirely on the faith of what had fallen from his friend from St. Mary's, [Mr Blakistone.] He had, with his usual animation and earnestness, urged the absolute and binding force of the law of 184–, in regard to the mode of distribution. His remarks would lead us to believe, what the gentleman seems to suppose is the fact, that the law of 1841, is the only, or at all events, the earliest one on this subject.

No mistake could be greater. There were other and earlier laws, pledging portions of these funds, with equal solemnity. He did not mean to go into the subject a large. A gentleman from Charles, [Mr. Merrick,] not now present, had examined this subject, and had given us, on a former occasion, the evidence of his investigations. We ought to wait and receive more full information, and he therefore urged a postponement of the subject.

Mr. THOMAS said he hoped the question would be postponed. There are other pledges of this internal improvement fund, than that which had been referred to by the gentleman from St. Mary's. He adverted to the joint resolution concerning the two million of loan to the Chesapeake and Ohio canal company, in which he said there was a rule laid down for the distribution of the revenue from that source, different from the rule now proposed. He referred also to the important question which had arose between Washington county and the Baltimore and Ohio railroad company. It had been agreed that a large sum was to be given to Washington county, in case the railroad did not pass through it. The case instituted to recover that sum, went to the court of appeals. The court decided that the Legislature had not the power to make a contract of this kind with the counties.

Mr CHAMBERS explained that the court had decided that that was not a contract of binding force; not that the parties had not power to make a contract.

Mr. THOMAS said he was not now going to argue the question. He thought the effect of making this transfer, ought to be well considered before going into it. There was an antagonism of interests growing up out of our system of internal improvements, which ought to be weighed before a provision was inserted in the organic law on the subject. A constitutional provision cannot be changed, and the parties, even if disposed, might thus be debarred from making a compromise, which the law and the joint resolution he had referred to would not forbid.

Mr. THOMAS then moved to postpone the consideration of the motion to Wednesday week.

Mr. WEEMS assented.

Mr. BLAKISTONE designated Monday week.

Mr. THOMAS said that day would be acceptable to him.

Mr. MCHENRY suggested that the bill and amendments should, in the interval, be printed.

Mr. WEEMS accepted the suggestion as a part of his motion.

Some conversation followed.

Mr. JOHN NEWCOMER called for a division of the question—first on postponement.

The consideration of the amendment was postponed to Monday week.

The question recurring on the motion to print, It was taken and agreed to.

Mr. LEE gave notice that, at the proper time, he should offer the following as an additional section to the report:

"*Sec.* 42. The General Assembly shall, at its second session after the adoption of this constitution, provide by law against the sale of any real estate to satisfy any judgment or other lien in cases where the yearly rents and profits, beyond the payment of taxes, and the necessary repairs, are sufficient within the space of seven years, to satisfy or pay such judgment or other liens."

Mr. CHAMBERS renewed the motion which he gave on the seventh of February, that he should, on Monday week, move to reconsider the vote of the Convention on the amendment offered by Mr. DORSEY, and adopted by the Convention, as an amendment to the thirty-third article.

On the day on which the bill should be taken up, Mr. C. said, he proposed to press the question.

Mr. CRISFIELD said, he rose to give notice of his intention to move a reconsideration of the vote just taken, to abolish imprisonment for debt, with the view of amending and perfecting that measure. Imprisonment for debt in this State was already nearly nominal, and rarely existed practically, except with the consent of the debtor, or in cases of frauds; but if the people desired to abolish it entirely, he was willing. He wished, however, to throw such guards about the abolition, as were necessary, to prevent frauds, and secure the honest appropriation of all the debtors property for the payment of his creditors. With that view he should move a reconsideration at the proper time. His purpose was not to defeat the abolition of imprisonment for debt; but in relieving debtors he wished the rights of creditors to be protected.

Mr. PRESSTMAN said, that when the proposition for the abolition of imprisonment for debt was originally introduced by him from the legislative committee, he did not suppose that if the principle was recognized, it would, in any manner, prevent any gentleman from proposing additional sections, looking to the punishment of frauds in the subject matter of the contract, or in providing any change or alteration in the present system of insolvency, to meet the altered state of things, whereby the assets of insolvents might be distributed. But why, sir, is there any necessity for the reconsideration of the naked principle which this Convention has adopted by a vote so decisive, as any abandonment of the position is hardly to be expected. The gentleman from Somerset, (Mr. Crisfield,) may now, or at any time, propose to engraft upon the Constitution provisions controlling the whole subject, or requiring that the Legislature shall, at their first session after the adoption of the new Constitution, enact such laws as will carry out his general design, which he, (Mr. P.,) understood not to be, in any degree, hostile to the general principle, except so far as to meet cases of fraud. It would be almost impossible in a Constitution, to define specifically what should be deemed fraud. This was a work of detail and ought properly to be left to the wisdom of the Legislature.

Mr. CHAMBERS moved a reconsideration. He had voted with the minority, against adopting the provision in its present unqualified and unconditional form. It might be very proper to adopt the principle of the provision, but it required guards and modifications, which could not be enacted by the Legislature under the broad and sweeping terms of the article as now adopted. In fact, there could not be said to exist, at this time, in our State, such a thing as involuntary imprisonment for debt, except where fraud was established; and in that case he did not think it wise to dispense with it. Having been denied the opportunity of assigning his reason, previously to the vote, he had moved the reconsideration to enable him to do so in the fewest words possible, and now withdrew his motion.

The PRESIDENT, *pro tem*, (Mr. Spencer,) stated that all this debate had been out of order.

Some conversation followed.

Mr. BOWIE, (for the purpose of making an explanation,) moved that the Convention reconsider the vote on the motion postponing the consideration of the legislative report.

Mr. BOWIE thought there was no occasion for a reconsideration of the vote just taken on the abolishment of imprisonment for debt. He could not see the necessity for any amendment. He rejoiced that such a provision had been engrafted in the Constitution, and he hoped the friends of the measure would not place it in jeopardy by consenting to a re-consideration. It is said that the provision is too general in its terms, and that some limitations might be inserted which would provide against the perpetration of fraud by dishonest debtors; but he thought, that such limitations would be altogether out of place, if inserted in the Constitution. Such was not the case in those States where imprisonment for debt had been abolished. The general principle alone was inserted in their Constitution. The Constitution ought not to be encumbered with such matters of detail as was contemplated by the motion of the gentleman from Somerset, (Mr. Crisfield.) It was competent, at all times, for the Legislature to provide by law for the punishment of frauds. They are as fully competent to perform this task, as the Convention would be, and he thought it much more proper that they should do it. Let the broad principle be inserted in the Constitution, and we shall then have discharged our duty; and let us leave it to the Legislature to make all necessary rules to guard against frauds He hoped, therefore, that the provision would stand as it now is, and that no re-consideration of it would prevail.

Mr. BOWIE then withdrew the motion.

Mr. JENIFER, by unanimous consent, made the following report from committee No. 14:

Art. 1. No person holding an office or appointment under the Constitution or laws of this State, (mere members of the legal profession not being regarded as such office-holder,) no member of the General Assembly of Maryland, no person holding any office or appointment thereunder, or under either branch thereof shall under any promise or expectation of a fee, reward, or compensation of any nature or kind, for so doing, advocate before the General Assembly or either branch thereof, or any member of the same a claim of any other person, against the State; or with such legislative body, or any of its members, use advise recommendation, or persuasion for the allowance or payment of any such claim, or the adoption of any legislative action for that purpose; and any person herein offending shall be guilty of a high misdemeanor, and on conviction thereof, on indictment in a court of law, shall be fined a sum not less than five hundred dollars; and be imprisoned for at least six months, and shall thenceforth cease to hold the office or appointment of which he may be then the incumbent.

Which was read.

THE EXECUTIVE DEPARTMENT.

Mr. GRASON announced his readiness to proceed with the report of the committee on the Executive Department of the Government.

Some conversation followed as to the order of proceeding; after which

The SECRETARY proceeded to read the report of Mr. GRASON, Chairman of the Committee on the Executive Department, and which was as follows:

Section 1. The Executive power of the State shall be vested in a Governor, whose term of office shall commence on the first Monday of January next ensuing his election, and continue for three years, or until his successor shall have qualified by taking the oath herein prescribed.

Sec. 2. The persons qualified to vote for delegates to the General Assembly, shall meet on the first Wednesday of October, in the year eighteen hundred and fifty-three, and on the same day and month in every third year thereafter, at the places where they are entitled to vote for delegates, and elect a Governor; the election to be held in the same manner as the election of delegates, and the returns thereof, under seal, to be addressed to the Speaker of the House of Delegates, and enclosed and transmitted to the Secretary of State, by whom or by the Executive, they shall be delivered to the said Speaker at the commencement of the session of the Legislature next ensuing said election.

Sec. 3 And the Speaker of the House of Delegates shall then open the said returns in the presence of both houses, and the person having the highest number of votes, and being constitutionally eligible, shall be the Governor, and shall qualify in the manner herein prescribed, on the first Monday of January next ensuing his election, or as soon thereafter as may be practicable.

Sec. 4. And if two or more persons should have the highest and an equal number of votes, then one of them shall be chosen as Governor by the joint ballot of the Senate and House of Delegates; and all questions in relation to the legality and number of votes given in the election of Governor, and in relation to the returns of said election, shall be determined by the House of Delegates.

Sec. 5 The State shall be divided into three districts; the eight counties of the Eastern Shore to be the first; Baltimore, Harford, Carroll, Frederick, Washington and Allegany counties, the second; and St. Mary's, Charles, Calvert, Prince George's, Anne Arundel and Montgomery counties, and the city of Baltimore, the third; and the Governor elected from the second district in October last, shall continue in office during the term for which he was elected; his successor shall be chosen from the third district, and then a Governor shall be taken from each district in regular succession.

Sec. 6. A person to be eligible to the office of Governor, must have attained the age of thirty years, and been for ten years a citizen of the United States, and must have been for seven years next preceding his election a resident of the State, and for two years a resident of the district from which he was elected.

Sec. 7. In case of death or resignation of the Governor, or of his removal from the State, the General Assembly if in session, or if not, at their next session, shall by joint ballot elect some other qualified resident of the same district, to be the Governor for the residue of the term for which said Governor had been elected.

Sec. 8 And in case of any vacancy in the office of Governor during the recess of the Legislature, the President of the Senate shall discharge the duties of said office till a Governor is elected by the two Houses; and in case of the death or resignation of said President, or of his removal from the State, or of his refusal to serve, then the duties of said office shall, in like manner, and for the same interval, devolve upon the Speaker of the House of Delegates, and the Legislature may provide by law for the case of impeachment or inability of the Governor, and declare what person shall perform the executive duties during such impeachment or inability; and for any vacancy in said office, not herein provided for, provision may be made by law, and if such vacancy should occur without such provision being made, the Legislature shall be convened by the Secretary of State for the purpose of filling said vacancy.

Sec. 9. The Governor before entering upon the duties of his office, shall take the following oath:

Sec 10. The Governor shall be commander-in-chief of the land and naval forces of the State, and may call out the militia to repel invasions, suppress insurrections, and enforce the execution of the laws; but shall not take the command in person without the consent of the Legislature.

Sec. 11. He shall take care that the laws be faithfully executed.

Sec. 12. He shall nominate, and by and with the advice and consent of the Senate, appoint all civil and military officers of the State whose appointment or election is not otherwise herein provided for.

Sec. 13 And in case of any vacancy during the recess of the Senate in any office which the Governor has power to fill, he shall appoint some suitable person to fill said office, whose commission shall continue in force till the end of the next session of the Legislature, or until some other person is appointed to the same office; and the nomination of the person thus appointed during the recess, or of some other person in his place shall be made to the Senate within thirty days after the next meeting of the Legislature.

Sec. 14. And no person, after being rejected by the Senate, shall be again nominated for the same office at the same session, unless at the request of the Senate; nor shall he be appointed to the same office during the recess of the Legislature.

Sec. 15 All civil officers appointed by the Governor and Senate, shall be nominated to the Senate within fifteen days from the commencement of each regular session of the Legislature; and their term of office shall commence on the first Monday of May next ensuing their appointment, and continue for one year, (unless they are sooner removed from office,) or until their successors respectively, qualify according to law.

Sec 16. The Governor may suspend or arrest any military officer of the State, for disobedience of orders, or other military offence, and may remove him in pursuance of the sentence of a court martial; and may suspend or remove any civil officer whose tenure of office is not placed beyond his control by some other provision of this Constitution.

Sec. 17. The Governor may convene the Legislature or the Senate alone, on extraordinary occasions; and whenever, from the presence of an enemy, or from any other cause, the seat of Government shall become an unsafe place for the meeting of the Legislature, he may direct their sessions to be held at some other convenient place.

Sec 18. He shall from time to time, inform the Legislature of the condition of the State, and recommend to their consideration such measures as he may judge necessary and expedient.

Sec. 19. He shall have power to grant reprieves and pardons, (except in cases of impeachment,) and to remit fines and forfeitures for offences against the State; but shall in every case in which he exercises this power, report to either branch of the Legislature, whenever required, the petitions, recommendations and reasons, which influence his decision.

Sec. 20. For contingent expenditures, not provided for by law, he may draw from the treasury such sums of money as the public service may require, provided that the whole amount shall not exceed   thousand dollars in any one year; and he shall inform the Legislature, at the commencement of each regular session, of the amount of the sums so drawn, the purposes to which they were applied, and the names of the persons to whom they were respectively paid.

Sec. 21. And the Governor shall reside at the seat of government, in order that he may constantly attend to the duties of his office, and shall receive for his services an annual salary of four thousand dollars.

Sec. 22. The Secretary of State shall be appointed by the Governor, by and with the advice and consent of the Senate, and shall continue in office, unless sooner removed, till the end of the term for which the Governor, appointing him, was elected, or until his successor shall qualify, and shall receive such annual compensation as may be fixed by the Legislature.

Sec. 23. And he shall carefully keep and preserve a record of all official executive acts and proceedings, and shall lay the same before either branch of the Legislature whenever required, and shall perform such other duties as may be prescribed by law, or as may properly belong to his office.

Mr. SPRIGG offered a substitute for the report of the gentleman from Queen Anne's, (Mr. Grason,) which substitute was read as follows:

Sec. 1. The supreme executive power of this State shall be vested in a chief magistrate who shall be styled the Governor of the State of Maryland.

Sec. 2. The first election for Governor, in pursuance of this constitution. shall be held at the same time and places of electing electors of President and Vice President of the United States in the year eighteen hundred and fifty-two, and at the same time and places in every fourth year thereafter; and every free white male citizen, possessing the legal qualifications of electors of this State, shall be entitled to vote for Governor.

Sec. 3. The returns of every election for Governor, until otherwise provided by law, shall be made out, sealed up and transmitted to the seat of government, and directed to the Speaker of the House of Delegates, who shall, during the first week of the next session of the Legislature thereafter, open and publish them in the presence of both Houses of the Legislature; and the person having the highest number of legal votes, and being constitutionally eligible, shall be declared by the Speaker, under the direction of the Legislature, to be Governor; but if two or more persons shall have the highest, and an equal number of votes, one of them shall be immediately chosen Governor by joint vote of both Houses of the Legislature. Contested elections for Governor shall be determined by both Houses of the Legislature.

Sec. 4. The Governor shall hold his office for the term of four years from the first Monday of January, eighteen hundred and fifty-three, and for the same term, and from the same day, in every fourth year thereafter, and until his successor shall be duly qualified.

Sec. 5. No person who shall be hereafter elected Governor of this State, in pursuance of the provisions of this constitution, and shall act as such, shall be again eligible until, and after the expiration of the next succeeding six years; he shall be, at least thirty years of age, a native born citizen of the United States, a citizen of this State for ten consecutive years and an actual resident of the gubernatorial district from which he may be taken, three whole years next preceeding his election.

Sec. 6. The first Governor elected under the provisions of this constitution, shall be taken from the counties of Saint Mary's, Charles, Calvert, Prince George, Anne Arundel, (including the City of Annapolis,) Montgomery and the City of Baltimore; which said counties and city, shall, together constitute and be known as the First Gubernatorial District; at the second election he shall be taken from the counties of Cecil, Kent, Queen Anne, Caroline, Talbot, Dorchester, Somerset and Worcester, which said counties shall, in like manner, together constitute and be known as the Second Gubernatorial District; and at the third election he shall be taken from the counties of Baltimore, Harford, Carroll, Frederick, Washington and Allegany, which said counties shall, in like manner, together constitute, and be known, as the Third Gubernatorial District.

Sec. 7. He shall, at stated times, receive a compensation for his services, which shall not be increased or diminished during the term for which he shall have been elected, which compensation shall be dollars per annum.

Sec. 8. No person holding the office of Governor, shall hold any other office or commission civil or military. nor receive the perquisites, or any part of the perquisites, of any other office.

Sec. 9. He shall be the Commander-in-Chief of the army and navy of this State, and of the militia, except when they may be called into the service of the United States; and shall, (by and with the advice and consent of the Senate,) appoint and commission all the officers of the militia; and all commissions shall be in the name and by the authority of the State of Maryland, be sealed with the seal of the State, signed by the Governor, and attested by the Secretary of State; and the seal of the State heretofore used as such, shall be the future seal of this State and be kept by the Governor and used by him officially.

Sec. 10. He may by proclamation, should the public exigencies require it, convene the Legislature at the seat of Government, or at a different place, should the seat of Government be at the time visited by any infectious disease, or be in the actual possession of a public enemy; and when assembled he shall, in writing, state to them the purposes for which they were assembled; but they shall transact no legislative business other than that for which they were so especially assembled. He shall reside at the seat of Government, and the city of Annapolis shall continue to be the seat of Government of this State.

Sec. 11. He shall, from time to time, give to the Legislature information in writing, of the state of the Government, and recommend to their consideration such measures as he may deem expedient.

Sec. 12. He shall take care that the laws be faithfully executed.

Sec 13. He shall have power to grant *nolle prosequies* and, after conviction to grant reprieves, commutations and pardons, for all offences, except treason and cases of impeachment, upon such conditions, restrictions, and limitations as he may think proper, subject, nevertheless, to such regulations as may be provided by law relative to the manner of applying for pardons; and, under such rules as the legislature shall prescribe, he shall have power to remit fines and forfeitures. In cases of treason, he shall have power by and with the advice of the Senate, to grant reprieves and pardons; and he may, in the recess of the Senate, suspend the execution of the sentence until the next meeting of the Legislature, to which he shall report the case, and the Legislature shall either pardon or commute the sentence, direct the execution of the sentence, or grant a further reprieve. He shall annually communicate to the Legislature the number of *nolle prosequies* granted during the year, and also each case of reprieve, commutation and pardon granted for the same time, and he shall state the name of the convict, the crime of which he was convicted, the sentence and its date, and the date of the commutation, suspension, pardon or reprive.

Sec. 14. He shall have power to fill all vacancies in the civil offices of the government which may occur during the recess of the Legislature; and all such appointments, so made, shall be valid and remain good to the end of the first session of the Legislature thereafter.

Sec. 15. He shall nominate and by and with the advice and consent of the Senate, shall appoint all officers of the State whose offices are, or may be created by law, and whose appointment shall not be otherwise provided for by the Constitution and form of government, or by any law not inconsistent with the Constitution and form of government.

Sec. 16. He may remove any of the civil officers of the Government, of his appointment, upon satisfactory evidence of any malfeasance in office, but shall report every such case to the Legislature at the next session thereafter.

Sec. 17. He may call out the militia to repel invasion, suppress insurrection, and to enforce, if needs be, the execution of the laws.

Sec. 18. There shall be a contingent fund of dollars placed at the control of the Governor, to be expended by him for such purposes only as may appear to him necessary to the faithful discharge of his duties, and he shall report annually to the Legislature the amount expended, the object and purposes for which said amount so expended, was incurred.

Sec. 19. The Governor before he enters upon the duties of his office shall, in the presence of both Houses of the legislature, take and subscribe the following oath: I do solemnly swear or affirm upon the Holy Evangily of Almighty God that I will support the Constitution and laws of the State of Maryland, so help me God.

Sec. 20. There shall also be a Lieutenant Governor, who shall be chosen at every election for Governor, by the same persons, and in the same manner, and from the same gubernatorial district, who shall continue in office for the same time and possess the same qualifications. In voting for governor and lieutenant governor, the electors shall distinguish for whom they vote as lieutenant governor. (The lieutenant governor shall, by virtue of his office, be president of the Senate, and shall, when the Senate is equally divided give the casting vote.) In case of the death, resignation, removal from office, inability or refusal of the governor to serve, or of his impeachment, or absence from the State, the lieutenant governor shall exercise the power and authority appertaining to the office of governor, until another be chosen at the periodical election, and be duly qualified, or until the governor impeached, absent or disabled, shall be acquitted, return, or disability be removed.

Sec. 21. Whenever the government shall be administered by the lieutenant governor, or he shall be enabled to attend, as President of the Senate, the Senate shall elect one of their own members as President for the time being; and if during the vacancy of the office of governor, the lieutenant governor shall die, resign, refuse to serve, or be removed from office, or be unable to serve, or if he shall be impeached, or be absent from the State, the President of the Senate for the time being, shall, in like manner, administer the government until he shall be superseded by a governor, or lieutenant governor. The lieutenant governor shall, whilst he acts as President of the Senate, receive for his services the compensation which shall be allowed to the Speaker of the House of Representatives and no more; and during the time he shall administer the government as governor, he shall receive the same compensation which the governor would have received for the same time. The President of the Senate for the time being, shall, in like manner, during the time he shall administer the government receive the same compensation which the governor would have received. If the lieutenant governor shall be required to administer the government, and shall, whilst in such administration, die, resign, or be absent from the State during the recess of the legislature, it shall be the duty of the Secretary of State to convene the Senate for the purpose of choosing a President for the time being.

Sec. 22. There shall be an Attorney-General of the State, who shall be appointed by the Governor, by and with the advice and consent of the Senate; and there shall be a Secretary of State, who shall also be appointed by the Governor, by and with the advice and consent of the Senate, both of whom shall continue in office during term of service of the Governor, by whom they shall be so appointed; subject nevertheless, to removal for cause, and the Secretary shall keep a fair register of all official acts, and proceedings of the Governor, and shall, whenever required, lay the same and all papers, minutes and vouchers relative thereto, before the Legislature, or either House thereof; and shall perform such other duties as may be required of him by law. He shall receive as compensation for his services, such sum per annum, as the Legislature may by law allow; but which shall neither be increased or diminished during the term for which he shall have been appointed.

Sec. 23. The Governor shall, in no case whatever, have the power to remit any portion of the principal or interest of any debt or debts which may be due to this State, except in cases of fines and forfeitures.

Sec. 24. Nominations to fill all vacancies that may occur during the recess of the Senate, and which the Governor has the power to make, shall be made to the Senate at least twenty days before the end of the next session thereafter; and should any nomination so made, be rejected by the Senate, the same individual shall not again be nominated during the session, except at the request of the Senate, to fill the same office; nor be appointed to the same office during the recess of the Senate. And should the Governor fail to make nominations to fill any vacancy existing during the session of the Senate, which vacancy may have occurred during its recess, such vacancy shall not be filled until the next meeting of the Senate.

Sec 25. A Treasurer and Comptroller of public accounts shall be elected by the joint ballot of both Houses of the Legislature at its January session, eighteen hundred and fifty-three, and at every (quarternian) session thereafter; and in case of a vacancy in either of said offices, during the recess of the Legislature, such vacancy shall be filled by the Governor, which appointment shall continue until the close of the next session of the Legislature thereafter.

Sec. 26. The Governor shall transact all executive business with the officers of Government, civil and military, and may require information in writing from the officers of the executive department upon any subject relating to the duties of their respective offices.

Sec. 27, Whenever the Governor shall, with the consent of the Legislature, be out of the State in time of war, at the head of any military force thereof, he shall, nevertheless, continue Commander-in-Chief of the military force of the State.

The substitute having been read,

The question recurred on the original report of Mr. Grason, which was taken up by sections.

And the first section was taken up as follows:

Sec 1 The Executive power of the State shall be vested in a Governor, whose term of office shall commence on the first Monday of January next ensuing his election, and continue for three years, or until his successor shall have qualified by taking the oath herein prescribed.

Mr. Dorsey moved to amend said report of the committee on the Executive Department, by inserting after the word "Governor," in the second line, first section, the following:

"To be chosen by an electoral college, consisting of one elector from the city of Baltimore, and one from each of the several counties of the State, which election of Governor shall be by ballot, and the person receiving a majority of all the electoral votes hereby authorised to be given, shall be declared duly elected; and the number of ballots or votes which each elector shall put into the ballot box, shall be as follows: The elector from the city of Baltimore, shall give six votes; from Baltimore county, four votes, from Frederick county, four votes; from Anne Arundel county three votes; from Washington county, three votes; from Allegany county, two votes; Somerset county, two votes; Worcester county, two votes; Prince George's county, two votes; Carroll county, two votes; Harford county, two votes; Cecil county, two votes; Dorchester county, two votes; Charles county, two votes; Montgomery county, two votes; Queen Anne's county, one vote; St. Mary's county, one vote; Talbot county, one vote; Kent county, one vote; Caroline county, one vote; and Calvert county, one vote.

Mr. Grason made a few remarks, (which will be published hereafter.)

The question was stated to be on the amendment of Mr. Dorsey.

Mr. Chambers, of Kent, called for a division of the question so as to allow a distinct vote to be taken as to the mode of electing the Governor—whether it should be by the popular vote or by college.

The division was ordered.

Mr. DORSEY said, he had on a former occasion expressed his reasons for desiring a change in the mode of electing a Governor. He would not trespass on the time of the Convention by repeating them.

Mr D. then made a few remarks as to the increase of power which Baltimore would obtain after the next census.

Mr. MITCHELL said:

That as far as he understood the history of the State, the counties of St Mary's and Kent were the original State. In consideration of this fact, he would suggest as an act of generosity and grace on the part of the Convention, that each of these counties should be allowed twenty votes. [Laughter]

The question then recurred, and was taken on the first branch of the amendment of Mr. DORSEY, in these words:

"To be chosen by an electoral college."

Mr. WARE asked the yeas and nays,

Which were ordered,

And being taken, resulted as follows:

Affirmative—Messrs. Chapman, Pres't, Chambers of Kent, Dorsey, Wells, Kent, Bond, Sprigg, McCubbin and Fooks—9.

Negative—Messrs. Blakistone, Dent, Hopewell, Ricaud, Lee, Mitchell, Donaldson, Randall, Sellman, Weems, Dalrymple, Sollers, Jenifer, Bell, Welch, Ridgely, Lloyd, Colston, Dashiell, Hicks, Hodson, Goldsborough, Eccleston, Chambers of Cecil, McCullough, Miller, Bowie Bowling, Spencer, Grason, George, McMaster, Thomas, Shriver, Gaither, Biser, Annan, Sappington, Stephenson, McHenry, Magraw, Thawley, Hardcastle, Gwinn, Brent of Baltimore city, Sherwood of Baltimore city, Presstman, Ware, Schley, Fiery, Neill, John Newcomer, Michael Newcomer, Weber, Hollyday, Slicer, Parke, Ege, Cockey and Brown—60.

So the first branch of the amendment of Mr. DORSEY was rejected.

The rest of the proposition of Mr. DORSEY fell, the first branch having been rejected.

Some conversation followed in relation to the order of proceeding.

Mr. DORSEY moved an amendment, (as to the day of the election,) which amendment, he said, had been made necessary by the action of the Convention in relation to the day of the meeting of the legislature. As originally reported, the bill was all right. The charge had been made since.

Mr. GRASON was not, he said, in the Convention when the time was fixed for the meeting of the legislature. He would prefer the second Wednesday in January.

Mr. DORSEY accepted the modification.

The amendment was agreed to

The question was then stated to be on the motion of Mr. GRASON to strike out three years, (as the term of the governor,) and insert four.

Mr. JENIFER briefly sustained the motion.

Mr. SPENCER called for a division of the question on striking out;

Which was ordered.

The yeas and nays were asked and ordered, and

Being taken, resulted as follows:

Affirmative—Messrs. Chapman, Pre'st, Blakistone, Dent, Hopewell, Ricaud, Lee, Chambers of Kent, Mitchell, Donaldson, Dorsey, Wells, Randall, Kent, Weems, Dalrymple, Bond, Jenifer, Bell, Welch, Ridgely, Crisfield, Dashiell, Hicks, Hodson, Goldsborough, Eccleston, Bowie, Sprigg, McCubbin, Bowling, Spencer, Grason, George, McMaster, Fooks, Thomas, Gaither, Annan Sappington, Thawley, Hardcastle, Schley, Fiery, Neill, John Newcomer, Davis, Weber, Hollyday, Slicer, Ege and Cockey—51.

Negative—Messrs. Lloyd, Colston, Chambers, of Cecil McCullough, Miller, Shriver, Biser, Stephenson, McHenry Magraw, Gwinn, Brent of Baltimore city, Sherwood, of Baltimore city, Presstman, Ware, Michael Newcomer, Parke and Brown—18.

So the motion to strike out was agreed to.

The question then recurred on the motion of Mr. GRASON to insert "four" years.

Mr. EGE moved "two years."

The question was taken on the motion to insert "four" years, and

The result was as follows:

Affirmative—Messrs. Chapman, Pres't, Blakistone, Dent, Hopewell, Ricaud, Lee, Chambers of Kent, Mitchell, Donaldson, Dorsey, Wells, Randall, Kent, Weems, Jenifer, Crisfield, Dashiell, Hicks, Hodson, Goldsborough, Eccleston, Bowie, Sprigg, McCubbin, Spencer, Grason, George, McMaster, Fooks, Thomas, Annan, McHenry, Sehley, Fiery, Neill, John Newcomer, Davis, Hollyday and Slicer—39.

Negative—Messrs. Dalrymple, Bond, Bell, Welch, Ridgely, Lloyd, Colston, Chambers of Cecil, McCullough, Miller, Bowling, Shriver, Gaither, Biser, Sappington, Stephenson, Hardcastle, Gwinn, Brent of Baltimore city, Sherwood of Baltimore city, Presstman, Ware, Weber, Parke, Ege, Cockey and Brown—27.

So the motion to insert "four" years, was agreed to.

And then the Convention adjourned until tomorrow at ten o'clock.

DEFERRED DEBATES.

Remarks of Mr Constable, March 4th, on the motion made by him to strike out a portion of the amendment of Mr. George. [See proceedings of March 5]

Mr. CONSTABLE was understood to say, that, when the Convention, on Friday last, reconsidered the section proposed by the gentleman from Queen Anne's, (Mr. George,) he, (Mr. C.,) had offered a substitute, with the understanding that the subject would be postponed to a future day, when he hoped to be able to take some part in the discussion. In this, however, he was disappointed, as ill health still admonished him to abstain from mingling in debate. Without then attempting to open a discussion of the several important propositions contained in his substitute—for he did not even intend to propose them for consideration at this time—he would endeavor very brifly to state some of his objections to the *first* branch of the *present* amendment of the gentleman from Queen Anne's, and for which he proposed to offer the *first* ot his propositions as a substitute. And he was gratified to find that there was now far less disagreement between the views of that gentleman, as shown by the remodeling *this morning* of his amendment, and those expressed in his, [Mr. C's.,] substitute. Indeed, the section as now amended by that gentleman, was not only essentially different, but in one respect, [and that quite important,] was a counter proposition. The whole of the *second* branch of the original, as submitted by that gentleman, and once adopted by the Convention, was *left out* of the section as amended by him this morning, while the *first* branch of it was so modified as to render it much less obnoxious. In fact, the article as now amended, approximated nearer to his, [Mr. C's.,] substitute than to the original of the gentleman from Queen Anne's. But there still remained one point of difference between them, and which he, [Mr. C,] regarded as of essential importance. The *first* branch of the section, as now amended by the gentleman, proposed to limit the power to contract debt by fixing a *maximum* of one hundred thousand dollars, while the original conferred the power without such limitation; both, however, required that a tax should be imposed sufficient to pay the accruing annual interest and discharge the principal in fifteen years. Now, while he thanked the gentleman from Queen Anne's for this concession, still it did not come up to what he, [Mr. C.,] considered as the proper and necessary restriction of the power. For, said Mr. C., I regard the withholding from the Legislature of all power to contract debt except in the emergencies of invasion or insurrection, as the only true and reliable safeguard. He also adverted to the fact that this branch of the amendment contained no specification of the *objects* for which debts might be contracted, and remarked that he did not know that he would object to the power to negotiate temporary loans, when necessary, to meet an unexpected deficit in the revenue, although he feared that this very facility for supplying such deficit might sometimes have a tendency to cause one. Such was the general course with individuals, and the same might be indicated in regard to States. But here the power is not confined by any *declared purpose* and may consequently be exerted for any and every object within the whole range of legislative action.

Not only was it objectionable in this respect, but the professed limitation of the powerby at *maximum* amount of any such debt, as that it shall not, at any time, exceed one hundred thousand dollars, he regarded as delusive. A much larger authority lurks under the words of this grant, than many may suppose. Any amount that the people will endure to be taxed for may, in a series of years, be borrowed under this amendment. The contracting of one such debt—the borrowing at one time of one hundred thousand would not exhaust the power, but only operate as a temporary suspension of it until the revenue raised by taxation, or derived from some other source, should discharge the debt. And why may not this be done every year? Thus a succession of debts within the amount specified, be contracted and paid off during each year by a trifling tax, until millions had been borrowed and improvidently squandered. Any authority which might bring about such a condition of things, was not only to be deprecated, but was scarcely less objectionable than a power to borrow in any one year, a sum not exceeding one hundred thousand dollars, without the condition that a tax should be imposed when the debt was contracted. In either case, the Legislature might exert the power with equal facility, and he feared to an improper extent. In both cases the burdens on the people who have to pay might be onerous, and as little relished as their present heavy taxes. The chief difference consisting rather of the time when they shouldbe taxed,than as to the amount—whether, immediately, the small sum necessary in each year to re-emburse the principal and interest, or a larger amount at a future and remote time.

Such a consideration, Mr. C. said, was not, in his judgment, a sufficient restraint on this power. Wherever it exists, as in the counties, where the amount borrowed is paid by taxes imposed during the year, it has never been regarded as an obstacle or check on the power to borrow and contract debt.

Mr. C said, that he desired the most stringent and effective limitation of this power—that nothing but the highest public exigencies should call it into being. He would, therefore, move to strike out the first branch of the section as amended by the gentleman from Queen Anne's, with a view to substitute the following:

"*The Legislature shall have no power to contract debts or borrow money, except to repel invasion or insurrection.*"

Mr. C. remarked, in conclusion, that the other propositions of which he had given notice in his substitute, related to the general powers of *taxation* and *appropriation* for State purposes, to a proper enumeration of the *purposes* as well as the *subjects* of the *former*, and the appropriate limitation of the *later*. These he should not now present or attempt to discuss, for the reason already indicated, but he would offer them for consideration when the subject again came before the Convention.

SATURDAY, March 8th, 1851.

The Convention met at ten o'clock.

Prayer was made by the Rev. Mr. GRAUFF.

The roll was called, and the journal of yesterday was read, and several corrections having been made therein, not affecting any matters erroneously set forth in the Register, was agreed to.

Mr. CRISFIELD presented a petition of Edward Burford, and sixty-two others, citizens of Somerset county, to restrict the issuing of licenses to sell liquor, unless the same be approved by a majority of the voters of the election district, in which the license is to be used.

Mr. RIDGELY presented the petition of seventy citizens of Baltimore county, praying constitutional protection against the sale of spirituous liquor, without the assent of a majority of voters in the neighborhood, and

Mr. WEBER presented a petition signed by one hundred and seventy-two citizens of Allegany county of similar import;

Which were severally read, and

Referred to the select committee already appointed on that subject.

GOVERNOR'S TERM OF OFFICE.

Mr. BUCHANAN rose and said:

He was detained from his seat in the Convention on yesterday from indisposition

He had been informed that, in his absence a vote of the Convention had been taken, establishing quadrennial elections of Governor. To this, Mr. B. said, he was altogether opposed, and if he had been present, would assuredly have voted against the proposition.

One of the great objects of the people, as he understood it, in demanding the convocation of the Convention, was that the terms of services of public functionaries might be abridged rather than enlarged. Mr. B. was in favor of the present term of three years. Mr. B. then gave notice that at the proper time he would move a re consideration of the vote of yesterday, for the purpose of offering an amendment, providing for election of Governor every three years.

The motion was entered on the journal.

CLERKS, REGISTERS, ETC.

Mr. DAVIS gave notice of his intention to move a reconsideration of the vote of yesterday, on the first section of the report of the committee on the Legislative Department, and adopted by the Convention, in relation to the fees and perquisites of office, now payable to the Clerks and Registers of the several courts of law and equity, &c.

The motion was entered on the journal.

THE EXECUTIVE DEPARTMENT.

The Convention resumed the consideration of the unfinished business of yesterday, being the report made by Mr GRASON, as chairman of the committee on the executive department.

The pending question was on the adoption of the first section of the said report.

After a verbal amendment made,

On motion of Mr. GRASON,

The section was adopted.

The second section of the report was then read as follows:

Sec. 2. The persons qualified to vote for delegates to the General Assembly, shall meet on the first Wednesday of October, in the year eighteen hundred and fifty-three, and on the same day and month in every third year thereafter, at the places where they are entitled to vote for delegates, and elect a Governor; the election to be held in the same manner as the election of delegates, and the returns thereof, under seal, to be addressed to the Speaker of the House of Delegates, and enclosed and transmitted to the Secretary of State, by whom or by the Executive, they shall be delivered to the said Speaker at the commencement of the session of the legislature next ensuing said election.

Mr. G. offered as a substitute for said section, the following:

Section 2. The first election for governor, under this constitution, shall be held on the first Wednesday in November, in the year eighteen hundred and   and on the same day and month in every fourth year thereafter, at the places of voting for delegates to the General Assembly, and every person, qualified to vote for delegates shall be qualified and entitled to vote for governor; the election to be held in the same manner as the election of delegates, and the returns thereof, under seal, to be addressed to the Speaker of the House of Delegates, and enclosed and transmitted to the Secretary of State, and delivered to the said Speaker at the commencement of the session of the legislature next ensuing said election.

Mr. G. said, that the substitute contained no new provisions, but it was merely made a little more simple and clear. He had left out the time at which the first election for governor under the new Constitution should take place, because the Convention was thin, and the question was one which he desired should be discussed when there was a full attendanae.

Mr. DONALDSON suggested to the gentleman from Queen Anne's, (Mr. Grason,) to leave blank the *day* of election as well as the year.

Mr. GRASON assented.

Mr. GWINN suggested that the month also should be left blank.

Mr. GRASON again assented.

Mr. DORSEY suggested that the amendments and new sections intended to be proposed by the gentleman from Quenn Anne's, (Mr. Grason,) should be printed.

This led to some conversation in which Messrs. GRASON, BRENT, of Baltimore city, JENIFER, DORSEY, SPENCER and THOMAS, took part.

Mr. GRASON finally moved that the consideration of said section, and substitute be informally passed over.

Ordered accordingly.

The third section of the report was read as follows:

Sec. 3. And the Speaker of the House of Delegates shall then open the said returns in the presence of both Houses, and the person having the highest number of votes, and being constitutionally eligible, shall be the Governor, and shall qualify in the manner herein prescribed, on the first Monday of January next ensuing his election, or as soon thereafter as may be practicable.

Mr. DORSEY moved to amend said section by striking out the words "Speaker of the House of Delegates," and substituting in lieu thereof "President of the Senate."

Some explanation as to the propriety of the amendment, passed between Messrs. DORSEY and GRASON.

The question was then taken, and

The vote stood ayes 31, noes 32.

So the amendment was rejected.

Mr. BRENT, of Baltimore city, moved to amend the said third section in the first line, by striking out the words "the Speaker of the House of Delegates," and inserting, "Secretary of State for the time being."

Mr. B. briefly explained the amendment.

Messrs. GRASON and SPENCER opposed it.

Mr. BRENT, not desiring, he said, to excite debate, and feeling no solicitude as to the adoption of the amendment, withdrew it.

Mr. DORSEY moved to amend the section by inserting before the word "votes" in the third line, the word "legal."

Mr. GRASON opposed the amendment as unnecessary.

The amendment was agreed to.

Mr. GRASON moved further to amend said section by striking out in the fourth line the words, "first Monday," and inserting in lieu thereof, "second Wednesday."

The amendment was agreed to.

And the third section, as amended was adopted.

The fourth section of the report was then read as follows:

Sec. 4. And if two or more persons should have the highest and an equal number of votes, then one of them shall be chosen as Governor by the joint ballot of the Senate and House of Delegates; and all questions in relation to the legality and number of votes given in the election of Governor, and in relation to the returns of said election, shall be determined by the House of Delegates.

Mr. DORSEY moved to amend said section by inserting after the word "Governor" in the fifth line, the words "his eligibility."

Some explanation followed on the part of Messrs. DORSEY, GRASON, JENIFER and CRISFIELD.

Mr. CRISFIELD moved as a substitute for said amendment to insert after the word "election," in same section and fifth line, these words, "and in relation to the qualifications of the persons voted for as Governor."

The substitute of Mr. CRISFIELD was rejected.

The question recurred on the amendment of Mr DORSEY.

Further explanations passed on the part of Messrs. BRENT, of Baltimore city, GRASON, BOWIE, BROWN and DORSEY.

The question was then taken, and

The amendment of Mr. DORSEY was agreed to.

Mr. BRENT, of Baltimore city, then moved to amend said section by adding at the end thereof the following:

"And if the person receiving the highest number of votes should not be constitutionally eligible, then the Governor shall be chosen by the joint ballot of the Senate and House of Delegates."

Mr. GWINN offered as a substitute for said amendment, to come in at the end of said section, the following:

"And in case that the person receiving the highest number of votes, shall not be constitutionally eligible, it shall be the duty of the Governor for the time being, or in case of the vacancy of the said office, for the Speaker of the House of Delegates to issue writs for a new election."

The substitute was sustained by Mr. GWINN, and opposed by Mr. BRENT, of Baltimore city.

Mr. GWINN said he offered the amendment as a substitute for that of his colleague, (Mr. Brent.) The contingency provided for, was certainly remote, but if it required any notice in the Constitution, it was only right that the means adopted to remedy the evil should be in consistency with the spirit of the Constitution, on which it was engrafted. Until 1836, the Governor of Maryland was elected by the joint vote of the two Houses of the Legislature. This feature in the system was long opposed by all who thought that the people of the State should, by a direct vote, appoint the chief executive officer of the Commonwealth. He did not think it wise, when this result had been attained with such exteme difficulty. to adopt any provision, which would,in any contingency, defeat the good effects of a struggle so protracted, and place the Executive power in the hands of that body, from whose grasp it had been wrested with such difficulty.

If the amendment had contemplated only the case of a vacancy arising by death or resignation during the term, it would have been liable to great objection, but still, its advocates could then have argued the inutility of renewing an exciting contest for supremacy during the few remaining months of the official term. But the proposition now introduced, has no such justification. It is the case in which the people have, through fraud or misapprehension, been induced to cast their suffrage for one who was not constitutionally eligible, or have equally divided in their preferences for rival candidates. In such instances it would seem that there was paramount reason for permitting them to exercise again the privilege of which they had been defrauded, without aid, upon their part. Certainly, there is no justification for taking from them the privilege of correcting their mistaken confidence, or in case of an equal vote, of determining, in a more deliberate manner, their preference for one or the other of the two candidates who may have received their suffrages.

The only inconvenience resulting, would be the interregnum which would result. This could easily be provided for; and he had no objection to permit the Legislature to appoint some one who should under certain restraints, exercise the ordinary executive functions, until a new election could be held. The period, needful for preparation, would be necessarily a very brief one, and no mischief could result.

After a few remarks by Mr. DORSEY—

Mr. GWINN said, that the gentleman from Anne Arundel, did great injustice to the argument he had made. By necessary preparation for the election of a Governor. was not meant provision for electioneering purposes; nor had he supposed that in this Convention, there was any reason for such a disclaimer

The mind of the gentleman seemed busy with the images of corruption and evil influence, which he had dwelt upon in the early part of the Convention, and he had construed "preparation" to mean banners, music, and transparencies—the secret struggles of political clubs—and all the machinery which parties put in operation for their support. Whatever effect such arrangements may have upon the popular mind, he certainly had not intended to allude to them in the Convention.

By "preparation," speaking in the hearing of a grave constitutional assembly, he had meant only that full and reasonable notice of the election about to occur, which would be sufficient to enable the people of the State to exercise a deliberate judgment in the choice of an executive. No one could properly misconstrue such a purpose. There were reason and advantage in parties, wherever formed; but no party man could so far forget the dignity which properly attached to combinations embracing the whole people of a State, as to imagine that their honor or success lay in the management of petty shows, or in small electioneering details.

Mr. DORSEY opposed the substitute of Mr. GWINN, and sustained the amendment of Mr. BRENT.

Mr. DENT gave notice of an amendment which he would hereafter offer.

After an explanation by Mr. SPENCER,

Mr. GWINN called the yeas and nays on his substitute,

Which were ordered, and

Being taken, resulted as follows:

Affirmative—Messrs. Lloyd, Chambers of Cecil, McCullough, Miller, Shriver, Sappington, Stephenson, McHenry, Gwinn, Sherwood of Baltimore city, Presstman, Ware, Michael Newcomer, Weber, Parke, Ege and Brown—17.

Negative—Messrs. Chapman, President, Blakistone, Dent, Hopewell, Lee, Chambers of Kent, Donaldson, Dorsey, Wells, Dalrymple, Bond, Merrick, Jenifer, Buchanan, Bell, Chandler, Ridgely, Crisfield, Dashiell, Hicks, Hodson, Goldsborough, Eccleston, Bowie, McCubbin, Bowling, Spencer, Grason, McMaster, Fooks, Thomas, Gaither, Annan, Thawley, Brent of Baltimore city, Fiery, Neill, John Newcomer, Davis, Hollyday, Slicer and Cockey—42.

So the substitute of Mr. GWINN was rejected.

The question then recurred on the amendment of Mr. BRENT, of Baltimore city,

And it was agreed to.

Mr. GRASON moved further to amend the said section by striking out the words "ballot by the Senate and House of Delegates," in the third line, and inserting in lieu thereof, "vote of the Senate and House of Delegates, the said vote to be taken *viva voce.*"

The amendment was agreed to.

Mr. DENT moved further to amend said section by inserting between the word "the," and "House," in the sixth line of said section these words "by the joint vote of the Senate and."

Mr. D. said, he offered this amendment for the purpose of having the provision as to questions of eligibility and contested elections of Governor, conform to the previous provisions in relation to the same officer.

The question was then taken.

No quorum voted.

Mr. GWINN asked the yeas and nays.

Some explanation passed on the part of Messrs. DENT, GRASON, THOMAS, JENIFER, SPENCER, and BLAKISTONE.

The yeas and nays were asked and ordered, and being taken, resulted as follows:

Affirmative—Messrs. Blakistone, Dent, Hopewell, Lee, Chambers of Kent, Mitchell, Donaldson, Dorsey, Wells, Kent. Dalrymple, Bond, Merrick, Crisfield, Dashiell, Hicks, Hodson, Goldsborough, Eccleston, Bowling, McMaster, Fooks, Fiery, John Newcomer, and Davis—25.

Negative—Messrs. Jenifer, Buchanan, Bell, Chandler, Ridgely, Lloyd, Colston, Chambers of Cecil, Miller, Bowie, McCubbin, Spencer Grason, Thomas, Shriver, Gaither, Biser, Annan, Sappington, Stephenson, McHenry, Magraw, Thawley, Hardcastle, Gwinn, Brent of Baltimore city, Sherwood of Baltimore city, Presstman, Ware, Schley, Neill, Michael Newcomer, Weber, Hollyday, Slicer, Parke, Ege, Cockey, and Brown—39.

So the amendment was rejected.

The fourth section as amended was then adopted.

The fifth section of the report was read as follows:

Sec. 5. The State shall be divided into three districts; the eight counties of the Eastern Shore to be the first; Baltimore, Harford, Carroll, Frederick, Washington, and Allegany counties, the second; and St. Mary's, Charles, Calvert, Prince George's, Anne Arundel and Montgomery counties, and the city of Baltimore, the third; and the Governor elected from the second district in October last, shall continue in office during the term for which he was elected; his successor shall be chosen from the third district, and then a Governor shall be taken from each district in regular succession.

Mr. GRASON moved to amend by inserting the word "Howard," after the words "Anne Arundel."

The amendment was agreed to.

Mr. GRASON suggested that the section should be informally laid over.

Some conversation followed.

Mr. JENIFER moved to amend said section by inserting after the words "Eastern Shore," the words "and Harford county," and by striking out from the word "first," in the second line, to the word "and," where it occurs in the fifth line, and inserting in lieu thereof the following: "Baltimore city, Baltimore and Carroll counties, the second, and St. Mary's, Allegany, Washington, Frederick, Montgomery, Anne Arundel, Prince George's, Calvert, Charles and Howard counties, the third."

Mr. J. briefly explained his amendment.

Mr. THOMAS moved to amend said section by striking out all of said fifth section to the word "third," in the fifth line, and inserting in lieu thereof, the following:

"The State shall be divided into four districts, Allegany, Washington, Frederick, Carroll and Baltimore counties to be the first; Harford and the eight counties on the Eastern Shore, the second; St. Mary's, Charles, Prince George's, Anne Arundel, Howard and Montgomery counties, the third, and Baltimore city the fourth districts."

The amendment was briefly explained by Mr. THOMAS.

Mr. DORSEY offered the following amendment:

Strike out in fifth section, second line, "Baltimore, Harford," and insert "St Mary's,Charles, Calvert, Prince George's, Anne Arundel, Howard, Montgomery," and after the word "and" in third line, strike out' St. Mary's,Calvert,Charles Prince George's Anne Arundel and Montgomery," and insert "Baltimore and Harford."

Mr. D. proceeded to explain the object of his amendment, but yielded to a motion that the Convention adjourn.

A motion was made that the when the Convention adjourns, it adjourn to meet at twelve o'clock (instead of ten,) on Monday, so as to allow time for members to arrive by the cars.

The motion was agreed to,

And the Convention adjourned until Monday at twelve o'clock.

MONDAY, March 10, 1851.

Mr. BLAKISTONE, (the President *pro tem.*,) called the Convention to order at 12 o'clock, being the hour to which the Convention stood adjourned this day.

Prayer was made by the Rev. Mr. GRAUFF.

The journal of Saturday was read.

Some conversation followed, arising out of the fact that a substitute amendment, offered by Mr. DORSEY, to the fifth section of the report, had not been entered on the journal.

A point of order arose as to whe her the amendment was received as in order, or was only offered as a notice of amendment. The result was that the amendment was ordered to be entered on the journal.

Mr. JENIFER, chairman of committee No. 14, asked leave to report back the petition from citizens of Allegany county, praying that the Convention "provide in the new constitution that the privilege to sell intoxicating liquors shall not be granted to any person in any part of the State, except the same shall first be sanctioned or approved of by a majority of the voters in the election district where the same is to be sold," and that the same be referred to the committee already appointed on that subject. Also, the petition from citizens from Washington county, on the same subject, be referred to the same committee.

Also, that the petition of Wm. B. Shield and forty-seven other citizens of Frederick county, praying for a new county, composed of Hawvers, Catocton, Middletown, Petersville and Jefferson districts of said county," be referred to the committee on new counties.

Also, that the petition for the protection of grave yards from desecration, be referred to the next General Assembly of Maryland.

And that committee No. 14 be discharged from the further consideration of the same.

Which was read.

The report of the committee was concurred in, and the several petitions therein mentioned, were severally referred as recommended in said report.

Mr. SOLLERS presented an account of Edward M. Wise, Messenger to His Excellency, the Governor of Maryland.

Which was read, and

Referred to the committee on accounts.

THE EXECUTIVE DEPARTMENT.

The Convention resumed the consideration of the report heretofore made by Mr. GRASON, from the committee on the executive department of the government.

The question was on the fifth section, and the amendments thereto pending.

On a suggestion by Mr. GRASON, the section was informally passed over for the present.

The Convention then proceeded to the consideration of the sixth section of the report, as follows:

Sec. 6. A person to be eligible to the office of Governor, must have attained the age of thirty years, and been for ten years a citizen of the United States, and must have been for seven years next preceding his election a resident of the State, and for two years a resident of the district from which he was elected.

Mr. GRASON moved to amend said section by striking out "ten," in the second line, and inserting "seven," and by striking out "seven," in the third line and inserting "five," and striking out "two," in the fourth line, and inserting "three."

Mr. BUCHANAN moved to amend by striking out "seven," in the second line, and inserting in lieu thereof "five"

The PRESIDENT, (*pro tem.*,) stated that the question would be on the largest number first.

Mr. DORSEY said he had intended to offer an amendment somewhat, but not exactly similar to that of the gentleman from Queen Anne's, (Mr. Grason.) It seemed to him that the Convention should not make odious distinctions between naturalised and native-born citizens, which were unnecessary. He was, therefore, in favor of the amendment of the gentleman from Baltimore county, (Mr. Buchanan.) He thought that restrictions enough would be imposed by that amendment. No discriminations, he thought, should be drawn except such as might be required by the interests of the people, or important objects of public policy He thought there was no such object in the present case, and he should therefore vote for the amendment of the gentleman from Baltimore county.

Mr. Brown gave notice, that when in order, he would move to strike out, in the second line, the words "been for ten years," and insert the word "be," [so as to permit any man who had been a resident of the State for seven years to be eligible.]

Mr. Spencer. Say ten years.

Mr. Brown. It will shut out native Americans—those who are here in the country, coming from another State into Maryland.

Mr. Spencer. Not at all.

Mr. Brown, [resuming.] A foreigner, then, cannot be elected Governor, unless he has been a resident of the State for ten years. I think that is enough.

Mr. Spencer gave notice that at the proper time, he should offer the following amendment, strike out in sixth section, from the word "year," in the second line, to the word "and," in the fourth line, and insert these words, "and been for ten years a resident citizen of this State."

Mr. Grason thought, that practically, it was a matter of very little importance whether the Convention decided upon the term of ten, seven or five years. It was not probable that any foreigner would ever be nominated or elected Governor of the State of Maryland. Still, he thought it was their duty to show to the people that this Convention was not making a provision with the express object of bringing in a man who had not been for ten years a citizen of the United States. He had, in the first instance, designated the period of ten years, but, upon subsequent reflection, had thought it better to designate seven At the same time, he repeated, that so far as the practical operation of the section was concerned, he was indifferent as to the term.

Mr. Chambers said, he must express his regret at these unceasing, persevering efforts to shape our Constitution, as if we were in an especial manner providing for a particular class of persons—a class of foreigners and strangers. The current seemed continually to become deeper and wider as we proceeded. This instance exemplified the remark. An intelligent committee in the calm quiet of their committee room, had unanimously reported these restrictions. They had deemed it proper to require of foreigners a reasonable period of time for a residence amongst us, to enable them to acquire a knowledge of our peculiar institutions, and to undergo a probation before they could be admitted to the chief executive office, but the continually growing demand for the privileges of these people, the accession of new advocates and the defeat of opposition to them, was now leading the Convention to overrule the well considered caution of the committee. He thought it time to call a halt in this progress.

He had yet to learn that in any State in this Union, a foreigner had been made Governor. Why should Maryland desire to go ahead of the rest of the American world in this respect? Was it to invite foreigners to come amongst us? It could scarcely be supposed they could propose to themselves such a motive for their emigration. He supposed no man here expected, that he or his children or his children's children, would live to see the day when a foreigner, in ten years after his coming into the country, would be made chief magistrate of the State.

He was willing to pay any just tribute to the merits of foreigners, but such a provision as is now advocated, is an indirect imputation of incompetency, upon our own citizens. Had there every been a dearth of our own people, that we must invite foreigners to fill this station? Certainly there was no evidence of scarcity in native material at present, nor any prospect of a future diminution. He preferred the proposition reported by the committee, and as no advantage could result from any high bidding on the one side or the other, he hoped the house would not consent to change it. There being neither necessity nor advantage to recommend it, why change it for the mere sake of change?

Mr. Brown read the fourth section of the second article of the Constitution of the State of Pennsylvania, in the words following:

"He, [the Governor.] shall be at least thirty years of age, and have been a citizen and an inhabitant of this State, seven years next before his election; unless he shall have been absent on the public business of the United States, or of this State."

Mr. Buchanan said he did not know what the gentleman from Kent, (Mr. Chambers,) meant by "high bids." He was unable to say whether the gentleman intended to apply his remarks to his venerable colleague, (Mr. Dorsey,) who had favored the amendment offered by him, (Mr. B.,) or to some other person.

I can only say, continued Mr. B., that however disconcerted the gentleman from Kent may feel at the undoubted indications of a liberal tendency on the part of the gentleman from Anne Arundel, [Mr. Dorsey,] we who desire to advocate liberal doctrines here, are altogether satisfied with his position on this question, and welcome his advent with pleasure. The grounds assumed by the honorable gentleman from Anne Arundel, in his argument just submitted to the Convention, are liberal, equitable, and patriotic. He is opposed to odious and ungenerous distinction between the native born and the naturalized citizen. And this we hold to be the true doctrine.

Although, said Mr. B., this remark of "high bids" was made by the gentleman from Kent, *sotto voce*, and apparently without any specific meaning—still it had its object. The design of the gentleman doubtless was *gently* to *insinuate* to the public that, there were gentlemen here ready to "bid high" for popularity.

Now an imputation of this sort, Mr. President, [said Mr. B.,] made by another with reference to the gentleman from Kent himself, would have been, as we all know, repelled with quite sufficient point. He must, therefore, not be surprised if others are not disposed quietly to submit to such intimations when applied to them. Does not the gentleman from Kent perceive, said Mr. B., that his intimation of "high bids" is quite broad enough to involve his friend from Anne Arundel, [Mr. Dorsey,] who here advocates the liberal doctrine—and yet it is surely to be presumed, that a gentleman of the advanced age of the honorable gentleman from Anne Arundel, would not turn upon his heel for any office in the State.

If my friend from Kent, really designed an imputation invidous, in the remark which he made, I can only say, coming from him, it is in very bad taste. For myself, said Mr. B., the mover of this amendment, I claim to stand as far removed from any unworthy influences here, as the honorable gentleman from Kent possibly can. I ask nothing—I desire nothing—but the consciousness of having endeavored faithfully to discharge my duty here as a representative of the people. My part here is to act upon my best judgment of what is proper to be done, uninfluenced by any one. What effect a particular act or vote may have on my personal popularity, I stop not to enquire and care not to know.

This amendment, said Mr. B., was offered by me mainly for the reasons which have been assigned by the gentleman from Anne Arundel, (Mr. Dorsey,) that is to say to guard, against invidious and odious distinction between native born and naturalized citizens. Such distinctions are in my judgment illiberal, *impolitic* and unjust.

My friend from Queen Anne, [Mr. Grason,] said Mr. B., thinks that there is not the least proability that a man of foreign birth will be elected Governor of Maryland, and that, therefore, the restriction is unimportant. If this be the fact, I cannot conceive why it is that my excellent friend so tenaciously adheres to it. Why not obliterate it at once? If there is no danger there is no need of the restriction.

Mr. President, [said Mr. B.,] our present Constitution contains no such objectionable provisions, as that which is now proposed. We are going back instead of forward—we are becoming more restrictive instead of becoming more liberal. We came to this Convention avowedly to enlarge the privileges of the people, and now we desire to be engaged in an effort to contract them.

Suppose a naturalized citizen should be elected Governor of the State—where the harm? Where the danger? Have we not confided our dearest interests to them in other days, and where have they shown themselves faithless or ungrateful? I shall vote for the amendment.

Mr. Chambers said with regard to the good or bad taste of his remarks, which had formed the principle subject of the lecture just administered by the gentleman from Baltimore county, [Mr. Buchanan,] he had only to remind that gentleman that it was a subject on which he should not be too dogmatical. One of the most ancient adages we have, has taught us to believe that "taste is not a matter for argument" He was quite willing to submit to the House the decision of the question of taste. Another attempt of the gentleman was rather amusing. He had gratuitously given to his remarks about "bidding" a personal application to his venerable friend from Anne Arundel, [Mr. Dorsey.] Why, asked Mr. C., can any one suppose that at his time of life, that gentleman is preparing for a race in the field of popularity? We all know it is quite impossible. But to the subject. He had said, and he repeated, our course was downward in this matter. The current was continually setting more and more strongly down hill. Did not the votes on the elective franchise bill show that? The gentleman from Baltimore county, he believed, went in every case for enlarging the privileges of foreigners. Did not the history of the present bill confirm the existence of this tendency? In the quiet of their chamber the committee had matured a system, which they thought reasonable, and he believed, properly so thought. It is introduced here, and the moment the idea is suggested that an alteration may be made, enlarging the privileges of the foreigner, that moment the eloquence of gentlemen is put in requisition to resound the popular note—"no distinction," "no proscription," "no exclusion." It was his decided opinion that sound reasons existed for a distinction in the matter.

Our system of government is a complicated one. Educated as we are in the midst of these institutions and familiar with their operations, we do not appreciate this fact. But it is made evident by the observation of the almost universal errors that prevail on this subject abroad. It is not at all understood by foreigners. Anything approaching to an accurate knowledge of our system is confined to persons connected with affairs of government at home, whose official duties make it necessary to know something of the nature and proceedings of other governments. Of this class none emigrated to this county. Of this class even, we constantly witness instances of the greatest misconception of the practical operation of our complex federative system.

It was not likely then, that under such circumstances foreigners, who came here at mature age, with habits of thought formed and fixed, could without a reasonable period for experience as well as probation, be qualified to administer the office of Chief Magistrate, as well as one who, equal in all other respects, had a perfect acquaintance with all the peculiarities of our condition.

Again, it is one most important item in the duties of a Governor to make selections from the citizens of the State for the various offices. Strip him as you may of his present patronage, still it is quite impossible to avoid the necessity of leaving with him the sole power to appoint, in some instances. and the power to appoint *ad interim* in many of the most important

To do this usefully, he should know well the character of those who are to be selected. A fitness for some of these high offices, is not to be evidenced but by a course of life and conduct pa-sing over many years. The very language of our Constitution, pays respects to this principle, by requiring a given age as a qualification. The man who has passed his life amongst us, knows the character, and has observed the course of life, of his prominent fellow citizens.

Has the foreigner the same advantage? Can the man who is here but since yesterday, be possibly able to exercise an equally sound judgment, in selecting persons for office? Is the State as likely to be well served in the various departments, which his appointees are to fill?

It must be obvious, that in executing such a trust, he must either act without sufficient information, or he must be the *lccum tenens* for some party favorite, whose opinions govern the Governor.

If, however, these arguments were not conclusive, he had one more question to propound. Why, if no distinction should be made—why require any residence at all? Why not admit the foreigner to hold office just so soon as he is a naturalized citizen? The argument is abandoned, and the whole principle surrendered, by a short time. as effectually by a longer time. We have natives enough, and are likely always to have enough, to preside over us; let us not intimate a fear, or a doubt, of their ability to fulfil this high trust, without calling in the aid of foreigners.

Mr. SPENCER said, the section, if amended, as proposed, would discriminate between foreigners and the native-born In order to prevent this, he would submit a modification, which would effect all that the committee had in view. Whilst it required a proper residence, it made no discrimination between the classes of citizens. It put all on the same footing.

Mr. DORSEY stated that he did not regard the allusion of the gentleman from Kent as having reference to him. He believed himself discharging his duties as independently of all views to popularity as any member in this Convention. He certainly desired to retain and deserve the good opinion of his fellow citizens. But he would never swerve from that course pointed out by a sense of duty, to win popular favor. It was said that this proposition is an invitation to foreigners to occupy the gubernatorial chair of the State. He did not so regard it. But suppose it were so to be regarded. That invitation assumes as a condition precedent to its acceptance, that the accepted must be eminently distinguished for his patriotism, intellectual acquirements and many other virtues which should adorn the station. He had not the slightest objection to extend the same invitation to every qualified citizen of the State, whether native-born or naturalised.

He referred to the old constitution of 1776, to show that in the choice of Governor, there was no express requisition of citizenship—it contained no restriction of this kind. The foreigner is there placed on an equality with the native. And no inconvenience has heretofore ever resulted from that equality. We have never had a foreigner in the gubernatorial chair. But if, at any time hereafter, some eminently qualified foreigner should reside among us, who, in a time of war, should save our State from conquest and desolation, rendering it services above all price, by successfully leading the sons of Maryland in the field of battle, and who should be as pure and patriotic as Lafayette, and he residing five years among us after being naturalised, and being eminently possessed of every valuable and intellectual acquirement, beloved and trusted by the people, were proposed by them as a candidate for Governor, would you shut the doors of office against him? He would impose no such restriction when no danger would result from its non-existence—no benefit follow its imposition. He would leave the people to elect him who was the object of their choice.

He was disposed to say, that the same residence of five years after naturalization, should be required of a native citizen of another State, to qualify him to fiill the office of Governor of Maryland It had been said that five years was not a sufficient time to enable a foreigner to obtain that knowledge of the interests of the State which is necessary. He appealed to gentlemen whether a naturalized foreigner whom the people would be willing to select, might not be as likely to be qualified within that period. as many of own own aspirant citizens now are? We ought to put all on an equal footing.

Mr. D here read the clause from the old Constitution, relating to this subject, and said that he had lived seventy-five years uuder this Constitution, which interposes no barrier between foreigners and the gubernatorial chair, yet no foreigner h ad ever occupied that chair. Still, he thought, it was an omission in that Constitution, and he was therefore willing to impose a restriction to a residence of five years after naturalization. If we take the amendment of the gentleman from Baltimore county, [Mr. Buchanan,] and place foreigners on a footing with the citizens of the other States of the Union, it would be amply sufficient. He thought that the office of Governor was not the only important branch of our government. The Legislature is quite as much so; and if we intend to be consistent in our cousre here, we ought to have required a somewhat similar restriction as to residence, in relation to members of that body, as we now require in the case of the Governor. Yet this had not been done. He would not propose such an amendment, because he thought it was unnecessary. He referred to a naturalized foreigner with whom he was acquainted, who was worthy and intelligent, and who, with himself, had once represented the city of Baltimore in the Legislature, and no inconvenience had resulted from it. He stated that a foreigner was not disqualified to hold the highest station in the courts of the United States or of this State, and as both the Legislature and the judiciary were left open to naturalized foreigners, as well as natives, why was it thought necessary to raise this excessive distinction as to Governor? He was quite willing to impose reasonable restrictions, sufficient to give an opportunity for candidates to learn all of a local character, that it is necessary for them to know, wisely and faithfully to discharge their duties.

He was afraid the gentleman from Kent, in his unwillingness to change any of the features in the old Constitution, may be looking beyond the present question, and may desire hereafter to retain what, in this progressive age, we may not think it necessary to retain. He referred to the Constitutions of different States, on the subject of qualifications for office, commenting on them as he proceeded, and stating that although he had referred to them, he should disregard their local prejudices, the causes for them not existing in Maryland. This body should not be controlled by what has been done by other States, dissimilarly situated, but act independently, and solely with reference to the feelings and interests of our own State. He would not consent to impose any unreasonable unnecessary restrictions on the popular will

Mr. GRASON said he had already suggested that the restriction ought to be limited. The people were not likely to elect a Governor who had not been a resident of the State for seven years. In reply to the gentleman from Anne Arundel, (Mr. Dorsey,) that no such restriction was provided for in the legislative branch, he would suggest that there will probably be some discrimination of the same kind, in reference to the Legislature. But he would remind the gentleman from Anne Arundel, that the executive powers were confided to a single person, while the powers of legislation were distributed among a considerable number. In time of war the Governor is invested with important powers, and is at all times commander of the land and naval forces of the State. Without some such restriction as was proposed, the Governor might be a recently naturalized citizen, and commanding our forces while we were waging a war with the country that gave him birth. He referred to the provisions of the federal Constitution, which required the President to be native citizen; and Senators of the United States to be citizens for nine years. Our naturalized citizens had never complained of these discriminations. They wished to be admitted to the general rights of citizenship, but were not unreasonable enough to expect, as soon as they landed on our shores, to fill the highest offices of government. He was not disposed to require a very long residence, and had fixed the time according to what he supposed to be the general sentiment of the people.

Mr. DORSEY said:

This could not properly be considered as a constitutional restriction, because the legislature has the power to control it. The legislature can pass an act authorising a foreigner to hold real estate; so that the fact of an individual being by the constitution recognised as holding real estate does not of necesssity, prove him not to be a foreigner. There ought to be a discrimination. He wished that all persons who were citizens of the United States, and residents of Maryland, should participate in the honors of the State, if the people desired so to elevate them.

He was not opposed to the provisions of the Constitution of the United States in regard to the qualifications of a President of the United States. What would be the population settling our immense Western wilds could not be foreseen, and where danger may be rationally apprehended, it ought to be against. But, in reference to Maryland, there are no grounds of apprehension, and therefore, no such restrictions should be imposed on the rights of the people.

As to the remark of the gentleman from Queen Anne's, (Mr. Grason,) that danger might occur in case the gubernatorial chair should be filled by a foreigner against the country of whose birth a war might be waged, he replied, that if this was a good objection, it was not provided against by the amendment of the gentleman from Queen Anne's. The Governor cannot take the command of the army and navy, without the authority of an act of the legislature.

He did not believe that if such a case occurred, the Governor would turn traitor. There have been traitors among natives, as well as adopted citizens, and our revolutionary war shows they were more frequently among the former than the latter, and there would be no greater danger of treason, if a naturalized foreigner filled the Chair. He hoped the amendment of the gentleman from Baltimore county, would be adopted.

The question was then taken first on striking out "ten" years;

And by ayes 36, noes 22,

It was agreed to.

The question was then put first, on the motion of Mr. GRASON, to insert "seven," in place of the word "ten" stricken out.

Mr. DORSEY called the yeas and nays,

Which were ordered, and

Being taken, resulted as follows:

Affirmative—Messrs. Blakistone, Pres't *pro. tem.*, Dent, Hopewell, Ricaud, Lee, Chambers of Kent, Donaldsan, Randall, Kent, Dalrymple, Bond, Brent of Charles, Jenifer, Colston, Crisfield, Dashiell, Hicks, Hodson, Goldsborough, Eccleston, Sprigg, McCubbin, Grason, Dirickson, McMaster, Fooks, Stephenson, Ware and Davis—29.

Negative—Messrs. Dorsey, Wells, Sollers, Buchanan, Bell, Welch, Lloyd, Dickinson, Chambers of Cecil, Miller, McLane, Spencer, Shriver, Gaither, Biser, Annan, Sappington, McHenry, Nelson, Hardcastle, Gwinn, Stewart of Baltimore city, Sherwood of Baltimore city, Schley, Fiery, Neill, John Newcomer, Michael Newcomer, Kilgour, Weber, Hollyday, Slicer, Parke, Cockey and Brown—35.

So the Convention refused to insert "seven."

The question recurred on the amendment of Mr. BUCHANAN to insert "five."

Mr. BROWN gave notice that he would, at the proper time, offer a substitute, which was taken *verbatim* from the Legislature of the State of New York.

He (Mr. B.) liked that provision much better than any he had seen.

The substitute was read.

Some conversation followed.

The question then recurred on the amendment of Mr. BUCHANAN, inserting "five" years,

Mr. BISER asked the yeas and nays, which were ordered, and being taken, resulted as follows:

Affirmative—Messrs. Blakistone, President, *pro tem*., Dent, Hopewell, Ricaud, Lee, Chambers of Kent, Donaldson, Dorsey, Wells, Randall, Kent, Bond Sollers, Brent of Charles, Jenifer, Buchanan, Bell, Welch, Lloyd, Dickinson, Colston, Crisfield, Dashiell, Hicks, Hodson, Goldsborough, Eccleston, Constable, Chambers of Cecil, Mc Lane, Sprigg, McCubbin, Spencer, Grason, Dirickson, McMaster, Fooks, Shriver, Gaither, Biser, Annan, Sappington, Stephenson, Magraw, Nelson, Hardcastle, Gwinn, Ware, Schley, Fiery, Neill, John Newcomer, Michael Newcomer, Davis, Kilgour, Hollyday, Parke, Cockey, and Brown—61.

Negative—Messrs. Miller, McHenry, Stewart of Baltimore city, Sherwood of Baltimore city, Weber and Slicer—6.

So the amendment was agreed to, and the blank was filled with "five."

Mr. GRASON moved to amend said section, by striking out in the third line the word "seven," and inserting "five," and in the fourth line the word "two," and inserting in lieu thereof "three."

Mr. SPENCER in accordance with the notice given, then moved to amend said sixth section, by striking out from the word "year," in the second line, to the word "and," in the fourth line, and inserting in lieu thereof these words, "and been for ten years a resident citizen of this State."

Some explanatory conversation as to the interpretation of this amendment followed, on the part of Messrs. SPENCER, DORSEY, and SOLLERS.

Mr. GWINN opposed the amendment of Mr. SPENCER.

Mr. GWINN said, that he should vote against the amendment of the gentleman from Queen Anne's, [Mr. Spencer.] He could not agree to the necessity of restricting the people of the State in the selection of their chief executive officer. They were not likely to overlook the claims of a native citizen, and to honor with their confidence any individual, recently naturalized, unless there existed strong reasons for the preference. And if there were such, in the superior qnalities or services of such an individual, the people should be left at liberty to confer on him what office they pleased. Besides the whole theory of naturalization, as understood in this country is, that it places the foreigner, who has complied with the requirements of the law on the same footing with those who were native-born. And there was, in truth, no reason for departing from the principle which this establishes in the case of our chief magistrate. It was true that there are certain limitations in the Constitution of the United States, which confine the choice of candidates for the Presidency to natural born citizens.—There may be an argument made in favor of this limitaiion: because the President is, in fact, from the existence of his veto power, one of the coordinate branches of the National Legislature; and upon his action may depend the integrity of the whole system. And to prevent a possible, though not probable danger, it was well to affix this single limitation to the office.

Mr. SPENCER said, that after the views presented by the gentleman from Baltimore city, (Mr. Gwinn,) he [Mr. S.] wondered that the gentleman did not offer an amendment.

Mr. GWINN said he would do so, and he offered an amendment.

MR. SPENCER suggested that the gentleman's amendment did not sustain his argument.

MR. GWINN indicated the perfect consistency of the two.

MR. DORSEY expressed his dissent from the views of the gentleman from Queen Anne's, [Mr. Spencer,] as well in his construction of his amendment, as on the expediency of its adoption.

Mr. SPENCER modified his amendment, by inserting before the word "citizen" the word "resident" citizen.

An explanatory conversation passed between Mr. SPENCER and Mr. GWINN, on the subject of the amendment proposed by the latter.

Mr. DORSEY dissented both from the law and the argument, of the gentleman from Queen Anne's. He referred to the proceedings of the Convention in an earlier period of the session, when it was decided by an overwhelming majority, that naturalization only conferred civil rights, but did not impart political privileges. In the same way we may give the citizen of another State, residing amongst us, who is a native of the United States, civil rights, but exclude him from political office. We can, if we please, confer all these rights on unnatural ized foreigners, as far as concerns our State government. He would be willing to take the amendment, which made no difference between naturalized foreigners, and the natives of other States of the Union. He would fix the term of five years for residence for each.

Suppose one of our distinguished citizens, of other states, as for example, Clay, Cass, Dickinson, Webster, or any other eminent citizen, should remove into our State, and it became the wish of the people of this State to show their gratitude for noble patriotic public services, and to pay honor to them in their declining years, by placing them in the Gubernatorial chair, would you, by a Constitusional provision, say that they should be ineligible unless they had resided in the State for the term of ten years? He thought the amendment of the gentleman from Baltimore county could not work any evil, and he believed no one would refuse to honor so distinguished citizen, because he had resided but five instead of ten years in the State.

Mr. WEBER desired to ask a single question. If he understood the amendment, it would require that a foreigner shall reside in the State fifteen years, and a native citizen of another State ten years, before he shall be qualified for the office of Governor. If he comprehended the force of the language employed, it certainly called for the term of residence which he had stated. He thought that the proposition of the gentleman would produce the very evil which he had stated it to be his intention to obviate.

The question then recurred on the amendment of Mr SPENCER.

Mr. GWINN asked the yeas and nays, which were ordered, and being taken, resulted as follows:

Affirmative—Messrs Blackistone, President, pro tem., Dent, Hopewell, Ricaud, Lee, Chambers, of Kent, Donaldson, Bond, Brent, of Charles, Jenifer, Crisfield, Dashiell, Hicks, Hodson, Goldsborough, Eccleston, Sprigg, Spencer, Dirickson, McMaster, Fooks, Jacobs, Stewart, of Baltimore city, and Davis—29.

Negative—Messrs. Dorsey, Wells, Kent, Sollers, Buchanan, Bell, Welch, Lloyd, Dickinson, Colston, Constable, Chambers, of Cecil, Miller, McLane, McCubbin, Grason, Shriver, Gaither, Biser, Annan, Sappington, McHenry, Magraw, Nelson, Hardcastle, Gwinn, Ware, Schley, Fiery, Neill, Jno Newcomer, Michael Newcomer, Kilgour, Weber, Hollyday, Slicer, Parke, Cockey and Brown—39.

So the amendment was rejected.

Mr. GWINN withdrew his amendment.

Mr. BROWN then moved to strike out the 6th section in said report, and substitute in lieu of it the following:

"No person except a citizen of the United States, shall be eligible to the office of Governor, nor shall any person be eligible to that office, who shall not have attained the age of thirty years, and who shall not have been five years next preceeding his election, a resident within this State, and for three years a resident of the district from which he was elected.

The substitute having been read,

Mr. WARE moved for a division of the question on striking out.

Mr. SOLLERS asked the gentleman who moved the amendment, to state the difference between this substitute and the proposition as it stood.

Mr. BROWN explained.

Mr. SOLLERS submitted that the only difference was in the taste and the wording.

Mr. SPENCER submitted that a substantial difference existed; and he explained.

Mr. SOLLERS persisted that there was no substantial difference between the two propositions.

Mr. BROWN asked the yeas and nays,

Which were ordered, and,

Being taken, resulted as follows:

Affirmative—Messrs. Constable, Chambers, of Cecil, McCullough, Miller, McLane, Shriver, Biser, McHenry, Magraw, Gwinn, Stewart, of Baltimore city, Michael Newcomer, Weber, Slicer, Parke, Cockey and Brown—17.

Negative—Messrs. Blackistone, President pro tem., Dent, Hopewell, Ricaud Lee, Chambers, of Kent, Donaldson, Dorsey, Wells, Randall, Kent, Bond, Sollers, Brent, of Charles, Jenifer, Buchanan, Bell, Welch, Lloyd, Dickinson, Colston, Crisfield, Dashiell, Hicks, Hodson, Goldsborough, Eccleston, Sprigg, McCubbin, Spencer, Grason, McMaster, Fooks, Gaither, Annan, Sappington, Hardcastle, Ware, Schley, Fiery, Neill, John Newcomer, Davis, Kilgour, Dirickson and Hollyday—46.

So the Convention refused to strike out the sixth section.

The sixth section was then adopted.

The seventh section of the report was read as follows:

Sec. 7. In case of death or resignation of the Governor, or of his removal from the State, the General Assembly if in session, or if not, at their next session, shall by joint ballot elect some other qualified resident of the same district, to be the Governor for the residue of the term for which said Governor had been elected.

Mr. GRASON moved to amend the said section. by striking out in the 3d line "by joint ballot," and inserting in lieu thereof, the words, "by the joint vote."

The seventh section as amended, was then adopted.

The eighth section of the report was then read as follows:

Sec. 8. And in case of any vacancy in the office of Governor during the recess of the Legislature, the President of the Senate shall discharge the duties of said office till a Governor is elected by the two Houses; and in case of the death or resignation of said President, or of his removal from the State, or of his refusal to serve, then the duties of said office shall, in like manner, and for the same interval, devolve upon the Speaker of the House of Delegates, and the Legislature may provide by law for the case of impeachment or inability of the Governor, and declare what person shall perform the executive duties during such impeachment or inability; and for any vacancy in said office, not herein provided for, provision may be made by law, and if such vacancy should occur without such provision being made, the Legislature shall be convened by the Secretary of State for the purpose of filling said vacancy.

Pending this section—

The Convention adjourned until to-morrow at ten o'clock.

TUESDAY, March 11, 1851.

The Convention met at ten o'clock.

Prayer was made by the Rev. Mr. GRAUFF.

The roll was called, and the journal of yesterday was read.

LICENSE LAW.

Mr. ANNAN, presented a petition of sundry citizens of Frederick county, praying that provision may be made in the new Constitution to prevent the sale of intoxicating liquors. except the same shall be approved of by a majority of the votes in the election district where the same is to be sold.

Which was read, and

Referred to the select committee appointed on that subject.

On a request to that effect made in his behalf, by the PRESIDENT, (pro tem.,) Mr. BLAKISTONE.

Leave of absence for Wednesday and Thursday of this week, were granted to HENRY G. WHEELER, official reporter of the Convention.

THE EXECUTIVE DEPARTMENT.

The Convention resumed the consideration of the special order of the day, being the report heretofore made by Mr. GRASON, chairman of the committee on the executive department of the government.

The pending question was the eighth section of the report:

Section 8. And in case of any vacancy in the office of Governor during the recess of the Legislature, the President of the Senate shall discharge the duties of said office till a Governor is elected by the two Houses; and in case of the death or resignation of said President, or of his removal from the State, or of his refusal to serve, then the duties of said office shall, in like manner, and for the same interval, devolve upon the Speaker of the House of Delegates, and the Legislature may provide by law for the case of impeachment or inability of the Governor, and declare what person shall perform the executive duties during such impeachment or inability; and for any vacancy in said office, not herein provided for, provision may be made by law, and if such vacancy should occur without such provision being made, the Legislature shall be convened by the Secretary of State for the purpose of filling said vacancy.

On motion of Mr. GRASON,

Said section was amended by striking out in the 3d line the words "by the two Houses," and inserting in lieu thereof "as hereinbefore provided."

And the section, as amended, was adopted.

The ninth section of the report was then read as follows:

Section 9. The Governor before entering upon the duties of his office, shall take the following oath:

Mr. GRASON moved to amend said section by adding at the end thereof, the following:

"I do solemnly swear (or affirm,) that I will faithfully discharge the duties of the office of Governor, and will to the best of my ability, preserve, protect, and defend the Constitution of Maryland."

The question was put,

Mr. DENT suggested that no quorum was present.

The PRESIDENT, *pro tem.*, directed the Secretary to count the Convention.

The count having been made,

A quorum was declared to be present.

The question having been stated to be on the amendment of Mr. GRASON,

Mr. G. explained that he had not inserted the words "the Constitution of the United States," because that was a separate oath which all officers of the United States were obliged to take, when they entered upon their duties

Mr. DORSEY enquired whether, under the old Constitution, the oath did not include the oath to support the Constitution of the United States. If not, it was a very appropriate oath, and both, he thought, should be embraced.

Mr. GRASON said, he did not recollect the exact legal provisions. But he knew that separate oaths were taken, first to support the Constitution and laws of the State. There was then a separate oath to support the Constitution of the United States, and another in relation to the belief in the Christian religion.

Mr. DORSEY invited Mr. GRASON to refer him to the clause of the old Constitution. It seemed to him that the oaths might be put together in a few words.

Mr. GRASON said, the Convention should bear in mind, that this provision looked to the oath to be taken by the Governor of the State of Maryland, as such, and he, (Mr. G.,) thought that the oath should not be blended with the oath to support the Constitution of the United States. The Constitution of the United States, required every State officer, before he entered upon the discharge of his duties to take an oath to support that Constitution. It was not necessary, therefore, to insert it here. Still he had no particular objection to it.

Mr. DORSEY enquired, whether there was not another oath, which required the incumbent to swear that he would not receive the profits of any other office held by any other person? To give an opportunity for examination of these several oaths, he suggested that the section should lie over informally.

Mr. GRASON said, he thought there was in the bill of rights a provision requiring such an oath, as the gentleman referred to. He hoped, however, that the Convention would not put in this executive oath, every thing which might be required by other parts of the Constitution. The effect would be so to complicate and extend the section as to make it cumbersome.

Mr. DORSEY said, he would not ask any delay but, if he should hereafter deem it necessary, he would move a re-consideration.

The question was then taken on the amendment of Mr. GRASON.

But no quorum voted.

Mr. GWINN asked the yeas and nays.

Mr. DONALDSON sugggested, that some time since the gentleman from Kent, (Mr. Chambers,) had proposed that a general form of oath should be adopted for all officers. This, Mr. D. thought, was in the legislative report—and the question had gone over so that the whole matter might be made to accord. His impression was that such was the understanding. He suggested the propriety of not multiplying oaths The gentleman from Kent, (Mr. Chambers,) was not at the moment in his seat—and he, (Mr. D.,) thought that the section should lie over.

Mr. GRASON thought, he said, that in addition to the general oath, it might be proper to take the oath here prescribed. The Constitution of the United States imposed an oath upon the President nearly in the same words, and embraced in two lines.

Mr. SPENCER explained the previous action of the Convention on the subject of oaths, and confirmed the opinion expressed by the gentleman from Anne Arundel, [Mr. Donaldson,] in regard to the intention of the gentleman from Kent, [Mr. Chambers,] to offer a general oath, and suggested that the matter should lie over for the present.

Mr. GRASON acquiesced.

And the section was informally laid over.

The tenth section was read, and no amendment having been offered, was adopted in the following words:

Sec. 10. The Governor shall be commander-in-chief of the land and naval forces of the State, and may call out the militia to repel invasions, suppress insurrections, and enforce the execution of the laws; but shall not take the command in person without the consent of the Legislature.

The eleventh section was read, and no amendment having been offered, was adopted in the folowing words:

Sec. 11. He shall take care that the laws be faithfully executed.

The twelfth section of the report was read as follows:

Sec. 12. He shall nominate, and by and with the advice and consent of the Senate, appoint all civil and military officers of the State whose appointment or election is not otherwise herein provided for.

Mr. GRASON moved to amend the said section by adding at the end thereof, the following:

"Unless a different mode shall be prescribed by the law creating the office."

Mr. CRISFIELD said, he had intended to offer an amendment to the same purpose. But he suggested to the gentleman from Queen Anne's, [Mr. Grason,] to substitute for the language of his amendment that adopted in the old Constitution, [which Mr. C. read.]

Mr. GRASON said, he preferred the language of his own amendment, and stated that these amendments had been prepared with great care and upon consultation with very eminent lawyers.

Mr. CRISFIELD said, he offered no amendment. He simply made the suggestion.

Mr. GRASON said, he thought the object of both propositions was the same.

The question was then taken, and the amendment was agreed to.

And the section, as amended, was adopted.

The thirteenth section of the report was read as follows:

Sec. 13. And in case of any vacancy during the recess of the Senate in any office which the Governor has power to fill, he shall appoint some suitable person to fill said office, whose commission shall continue in force till the end of the next session of the Legislature, or until some other person is appointed to the same office; and the nomination of the person thus appointed during the recess, or of some other person in his place shall be made to the Senate within thirty days after the next meeting of the Legislature.

On motion of Mr. GRASON,

Said section was amended by inserting after the word "until," in the fourth line. the words "the same or," and by striking out the word "the," in the fifth line, and inserting the word "every."

On motion of Mr. HOLLYDAY,

Said section was further amended, by striking out in the sixth line, the word "some," and inserting the word "any."

The section, as amended, was then adopted.

Mr. CHAMBERS, of Kent, called the attention of the gentleman from Queen Anne's, [Mr. Grason] to the language of the thirteenth section, which provided that "in case of any vacancy during the recess of the Senate in any office which the Governor has power to fill, he shall appoint some suitable person to fill said office, *whose commission shall continue in force until the end of the next session of the Legislature, or until some other person is appointed to the same office.*" And he, [Mr. C.,] suggested a difficulty which might grow out of it. Suppose the case of a nomination by the Governor being rejected by the Senate—and where there was a failure during the session of the Senate to agree to any nomination of the Governor. What would be the condition of the Governor's appointee during the recess?

Mr. GRASON thought, he said, that the suggestion of the gentleman from Kent, [Mr. Chambers,] would apply more properly to the fourteenth than to the thirteenth section. He, [Mr. G.,] would state why the words had been inserted as they stood in the report. In the Constitution as it now was, the commission was to be continued in force until the end of the next session of the Legislature. Judging from his own experience, it occurred to him that it might happen that persons thus appointed during the recess might be incompetent and might be turned out by the Governor before the Legislature met, and some other person be appointed. This provision was made to enable the Governor to turn out a person of his own appointment, if he should be found to be incompetent during the recess of the Legislature.

The next section, [No. 14] brought up, he thought, the question suggested by the gentleman from Kent, [Mr. Chambers] Under that section some difficulty might arise. He thought that the fourteenth section would present the question more properly.

The PRESIDENT, (*pro tem.*,) to Mr. CHAMBERS. Does the gentleman move to reconsider the vote by which the fourteenth section had been adopted?

Mr. CHAMBERS said it struck him that some difficulty might occur. He took it for granted that the intention of the Convention was, that the appointments made by the Governor *ad interim*, should cease with the termination of the session. The difficulty on his mind was, that this provision went to continue in office the person appointed by the Governor, not only until the end of the session, but until another appointment should be made. Of course, this was only the suggestion of the moment. So far as he could, at this moment, appreciate the object of the gentleman from Queen Anne's, (Mr. Grason,) he, (Mr. C.,) doubted whether the language of the fourteenth section controlled the language of the thirteenth. In other words, he thought it was doubtful whether the fourteenth section would correct the mischief of the thirteenth.

Mr. GRASON said that he had, in the first instance, misunderstood the enquiry of the gentleman from Kent, (Mr. Chambers.) He, (Mr. G.,) now thought that there might be a difficulty which the fourteenth section would not, as he had at first supposed, sufficiently meet. He thought that an amendment should be made to that section. There was now a general provision in relation to all appointments, that the incubents should continue in office until their successors should be appointed. The object had been to prevent detriment to the public interests from interregnums, whether arising from the refractory temper of the Governor or the Senate, or both.

Mr. CRISFIELD said he had very imperfectly heard the remarks of the gentleman from Queen Anne's, (Mr Grason,) but it seemed to him, (Mr. C.,) that under the section as it now stood, the Senate might, under some circumstances, be precluded from any participation in the appointing power. He supposed such a case, and asked how such a provision would work? Such a case might occur. Under the old constitution it was specially guarded against.

Mr. C. read the fifteenth section of the act of 1836, (amendatory of the constitution,) as follows:

"The Governor shall have power to fill any vacancy that may occur in any such offices during the recess of the Senate, by granting commissions which shall expire upon the appointment of the same person, or any other person, by and with the advice and consent of the Senate, to the same office, or at the expiration of one calendar month, ensuing the commencement of the next regular session of the Senate, which ever shall first occur."

This provision, he, [Mr. C.,] thought, was much less liable to lead to mischief than the section. He had no doubt that the object of the gentleman from Queen Anne's, (Mr. Grason,) was precisely the same as that contemplated in the act of 1836.

He thought that the section as it stood, might be perverted—that it was open to doubt and misconstruction, and might be construed to give to the Governor the exclusive power of appointment. To obviate this difficulty, he would offer an amendment which was substantially a copy of the act of 1836.

The PRESIDENT, *pro. tem.* The gentleman must move to reconsider before he can offer his amendment.

Mr. CRISFIELD then moved to reconsider the vote of the Convention just taken on the thirteenth section, to enable him to move the following as a substitute for said section.

The amendment of which Mr. C. intended to offer, if the motion to reconsider should prevail, was then read as follows:

"The Governor shall have power to fill any vacancy that may occur during the recess of the Senate, in any office to which the Governor has the power of appointment, by granting a commission, which shall expire upon the appointment of the same person or any other person, by and with the advice and consent of the Senate, to the same office, or at the expiration of one calendar month, ensuing the commencement of the next regular session of the Senate which ever shall first occur."

Mr. GRASON compared the section with the amendment as offered by the gentleman from Somerset, [Mr. Crisfield.] and argued that it was not open to the exceptions taken against it by that gentleman. Its object simply was, to guard against vacancies. There were some offices which it was extremely important should not be left vacant.

Mr. SPENCER could not see the difficulty in this section which his friends on the other side saw in it.

He gave his construction of it, and submitted that by looking at the bill in all its parts—by comparing the effect of one section upon the other, (noticing specially the twelfth, thirteenth, and fifteenth,) it would be found that every object had been attained.

Mr. CHAMBERS, of Kent, dissented from the construction put upon the amendment by the gentleman from Queen Anne's, (Mr. Spencer,) and submitted that the language of the section did not carry out the idea of the committee: and he suggested that the whole difficulty might be obviated by inserting after the word "office" in the fifth line, the words "which ever shall first occur."

Mr. GRASON replied to the objections taken by Mr. CHAMBERS, and expressed the opinion, that, it was scarcely possible that the mischievous results which that gentleman supposed might occur from the adoption of the section could be realized.

He, [Mr. G.,] was not disposed, however, to be tenacious in a matter of this kind.

Mr. CHAMBERS, of Kent, remarked that the amendment he had indicated, could, at least, do no harm.

Mr. GRASON supposed a case in which injury to the public service might result from the amendment, and insisted on the importance of some provision guarding against vacancies which might occur from a collision between the executive and the Senate. It was not likely that such cases would occur often; but it was well to guard against the possibility of them.

Mr. Brent, of Baltimore city, desired a reconsideration for another object.

He read the twelfth section, and said, that the appointing power was vested in the Governor and the Senate concurrently. Now, the thirteenth section provided only for cases of vacancy during the recess of the Senate. But he submitted that a case might occur—and had occurred under the old Constitution, and under the Constitution of the United States—where a new office had been created at the end of the session. Could the Governor fill that office during the recess? As the thirteenth section now stood, he could not, either under that or the twelfth section. To remove this doubt he should hereafter (if the reconsideration prevailed,) offer an amendment.

Mr. Grason said, that probably the gentleman from Baltimore city, (Mr. Brent,) was right in his construction, but he, [Mr. G.,] would call the attention of the gentleman to the particular words of the thirteenth section.

Some conversation followed.

The question was then taken,

And the vote by which the thirteenth section had been adopted, was reconsidered.

Mr. Chambers, of Kent, then moved to amend the section by inserting after the word "office," in the fifth line, the words "which ever shall first occur."

The question was taken, and

The vote stood ayes 33, noes 17.

No quorum voting.

The question was again taken, and

The vote stood ayes 39, noes 21.

So the amendment was agreed to.

Mr. Crisfield said, he would now offer his amendment, as a substitute for the section. The amendment of the gentleman from Kent, (Mr. Chambers,) would not do away with the difficulty, he, [Mr. C.,] saw.

The substitute was again read.

The question was then taken, and

The substitute was agreed to.

The question then recurred on the adoption of the said substitute, as the thirteenth section of the report.

Mr. Brent, of Baltimore city, said, that as the substitute of the gentleman from Somerset, (Mr. Crisfield,) had been adopted, it would be necessary for him, [Mr. B.,] to move an amendment, which he probably might not have offered, if the proposition had been allowed to stand in the original form.

Mr. B. then moved to amend said substitute by inserting after the word "appointment" in the fourth line, the following:

"Or in case any office or appointment shall be created by law, and shall not be filled during the session of the Senate."

The amendment was read, and the pending question was stated to be on the adoption thereof

Mr. Brent explained its object.

Mr. Dorsey suggested that the substitute of Mr. Crisfield covered more ground than the gentleman supposed.

Some explanation followed on the part of Messrs. Brent, Dorsey, and Crisfield, when

Mr. Dorsey waived his objection.

Mr. Brent stated that the object of his amendment was to obviate a difficulty that had arisen under the old Constitution (referred to hereafter).

Mr. Crisfield had not been aware, he said, that any such difficulty had arisen under the provision of the old Constitution. And he thought that some such amendment as the gentleman from Baltimore city had offered, properly guarded, should be adopted.

Mr. Grason expressed his regret that the section had not been permitted to stand as amended. The section of the old Constitution retained the old debateable grounds which had been acted upon in different ways by different Governors. As the section was now amended, he thought that its language was not susceptible of any misconstruction.

Mr. Brent, of Baltimore city, to show that difficulties had arisen on this question, read the following extract from a letter addressed to him by Thos. H. O'Neal, Esq., Secretary of State:

State Department,
Annapolis, Feb. 27, 1851.

Hon. R. J. Brent,

Attorney General:

Sir:—By the direction of the Governor, I respectfully call your attention to the following point, which you will please submit in writing, at an early day:

By the act of 1836, (amendatory of the pre-existing Constitution,) chapter 197, sec. 14, the appointing power is vested in the Governor, to be exercised by and with the advice and consent of the Senate. By the 15th sec. the Governor is authorized to fill vacancies which may occur, during the recess of the Senate.

The practice heretofore obtaining in this Department, in the appointment of new Justices of the Peace, has been to confine such appointments, during the recess of the Senate, exclusively to cases of vacancy; thereby seeming to view the power of the Governor as limited by a strict construction of the 15th section of the act of 1836, before referred to.

Notaries Public, Commissioners to take acknowledgments of deeds, &c. out of the State, Auctioneers in the city of Baltimore, and other similar officers, created by law, come within the operation of the 14th section, aforesaid; and the number and location of said officers, in most cases, are left discretionary with the Executive. It frequently occurs that additional appointments, during the recess of the Senate, are required by the public interests, and yet it is a matter of doubt with the Executive as to whether or not he is restricted to the filling up of actual vacancies, occasioned by death, removal, removal out of the place designated by law, resignation, refusal to qualify, or any other recognized cause of vacancy.

The extract having been read,

Mr. Brent said that the object of his amendment was to obviate this difficulty.

Mr. CRISFIELD moved to amend the amendment of Mr. BRENT, by inserting after the word "law," "within twenty days next before the recess of the Legislature."

The question was then taken and decided in the affirmative, ayes 27, noes 25.

So the amendment of Mr. CRISFIELD was agreed to.

The question recurred and was taken on the amendment of Mr. BRENT,

And it was agreed to.

And the thirteenth section, as amended, was then adopted.

The Convention then resumed the consideration of the fourteenth section.

On motion of Mr. DORSEY,

Said section was amended by striking out the word "and," in the first line.

And the section, as amended, was adopted.

Mr. SPENCER rose to an explanation. On page 164 of the register of debates, he is reported in the following words:

"Mr. SPENCER explained that he, as chairman of the committee of ways and means, recommended a compliance with the opinion of the Governor, but the committee did not agree with him."

He was not understood by the reporter. He did not say the committee did not agree with him. He said that the Legislature would not sustain him. *But* a majority of the committee were willing to go with him.

The fifteenth section of the report was then read, as follows:

Sec. 15. All civil officers appointed by the Governor and Senate, shall be nominated to the Senate within fifteen days from the commencement of each regular session of the Legislature; and their term of office shall commence on the first Monday of May next ensuing their appointment, and continue for one year, (unless they are sooner removed from office,) or until their successors respectively, qualify according to law.

Mr. GRASON moved to amend the section by striking out, in the fifth line, the words "one year," and inserting in lieu thereof, "two years."

The question was taken, and the amendment was agreed to.

Mr. GRASON moved further to amend the section by striking out, in the last line, the words "according to law."

Some conversation followed on the part of Messrs. GRASON and DORSEY.

The question was then taken on the amendment.

But no quorum voted.

The question was again taken, and the vote stood, ayes 46, noes 6.

So the amendment was agreed to.

Mr. CHAMBERS, of Kent, suggested to the chairman of the the committee (Mr. Grason,) to insert the words "unless otherwise provided for."

The section, Mr. C. said, was drawn upon the theory that all officers were appointed by the President and Senate, and were to hold their offices for two years. But there might be an office the term of which would be longer; and to provide for such a contingency, he suggested that the words he had designated should be inserted.

Some conversation followed.

Mr. GRASON had no objection, he said, to the amendment, but submitted to the gentleman from Kent, (Mr. Chambers,) whether the word "biennially," inserted after the word "appointed," in the first line, would not answer the purpose?

Mr. CHAMBERS assented.

On motion of Mr. GRASON, the said amendment was agreed to.

On motion of Mr. DORSEY,

Said section was amended by striking out in the fifth line, the word "or," and substituting the word "and"

On motion of Mr. CHAMBERS, of Kent,

Said section was further amended by striking out in the fifth line, the words "they are."

Mr. DORSEY moved further to amend said fifteenth section, by adding at the end thereof, the following:

"Unless the appointment be made to fill a vacant office, when the appointee's term shall commence as soon as he shall have qualified."

Which was read.

Mr. DORSEY withdrew said amendment.

The said fifteen section was then adopted as amended.

The sixteenth section of the report was then read as follows:

Section 16. The Governor may suspend or arrest any military officer of the State, for disobedience of orders, or other military offence, and may remove him in pursuance of the sentence of a court martial; and may suspend or remove any civil officer whose tenure of office is not placed beyond his control by some other provision of this Constitution.

Mr GRASON moved to amend said section by adding at the end thereof, the following: "or the law creating the office."

Mr. CHAMBERS would enquire of the chairman, what was in contemplation of the committee, when in this sixteenth section they say, the Governor may remove all civil officers whose tenure of office is not placed beyond his control by an express provision of the Constitution.

If it was intended to introduce here, or to countenance the practice of removal from office for political opinion, he should regret the success of any such design. He had not anticipated any attempt to insert a provision, which could imply the right of the executive, to remove from office, without just cause, officers who received their appointment from the joint action of the Governor and Senate. He was unwilling to make those who were thus deliberately appointed, and who should prove themselves competent, and faithful, dependent upon the breath of the Governor. A power to cut short the political existence of a meritorious officer, in the midst of the term for which he was appointed, by the mere *ipse dixit* of a party Governor, was a dangerous incentive to mal-administration. It should be controled.

It was said the same power had been given in the new article introduced into the Constitution of 1836. If so, it still left the question now to be considered, whether it was proper. But it was never practically so considered. The power to remove had never been exercised, but in the case of inferior officers, on complaint, and for misconduct, or incompetency. An attempt to exercise it, would have been visited by an indignant public sentiment. A deliberate introduction now of such a clause might possibly be regarded as an invitation, or at least an inducement, to exercise such an odious power, and lead to gross abuse.

He was not aware that any other portion of the bill had provided any adequate restraint upon the mischievous indulgence of this prerogation; of this, however, the chairman could inform the House. Some guard ought to be introduced.

Mr. GRASON said, that the gentleman from Kent, had commented on the power of the President of the United States, to make removal from office. That subject was discussed in the first Congress under the Constitution, and it was then decided, Mr. Madison concurring, that the power of removal, if not expressly limited, was incidental to the power of appointment. The gentleman from Kent, contended that it was now proposed to confer a new and dangerous power on the Executive, but if he had examined our present Constitution, he would have seen that this power had been conferred by the original provisions of 1776, and had never been subsequently modified. The power of removal properly belonged to the Executive, in relation to annual or biennial appointments, and if it did not exist in some branch of the government, public officers might retain their commissions, after they had notoriously betrayed their trust, or proved themselves incompetent to the discharge of their duties. He had, however, prepared an amendment for the purpose of obviating some of the objections of the gentleman from Kent.

The amendment was then agreed to.

Mr. GRASON then offered the following amendment, (suggested to him, he said, by the explanation of the gentleman from Kent, (Mr. Chambers,)

Amend the section by striking out all after the word "remove," in the fourth line, to the end of said section, and insert in lieu thereof the following: "all civil officers who are appointed biennially by the Governor and Senate."

Mr. PRESSTMAN expressed his conviction that after the forcible views presented by the honorable Chairman of the Committee, the Convention would see the propriety of letting the section stand without further amendment, than the modification which the Chairman had prepared. On the subject of the doctrine of removal from office he dissented entirely from the view of the gentleman from Kent. The power of removal, he (Mr. P.) insisted had always been in the hands of the Governor. It was a power which every President of the United States exercised when he came into office. And if the power was not in the hands of the Executive, the effect would be that any subordinate must remain in office, whether he was able to perform the duties or not. Each of the political parties removed persons of opposite sentiments from office, and the common excuse set up, when enquiry was made, was that it was for cause. He had seen men of the most respectable standing, of the highest class of business men, skilful and industrious, struck down, and removed, as it was alleged, for cause, He would say it was not for cause. The Councils of the city of Baltimore have been in the practice of removing their officers. They are all removable by the will and power of the Executive, and so it is throughout the country generally. And there was as much money too in the hands of the city officers, who have been removed, as can be found any where. He liked to see a strong Executive. It was not asking too much, to ask that either party should possess the power.

He objected to the principle of the gentleman from Kent. The power is not only sustained by the Constitution of 1836, but by the Constitution of the State of 1776, and he believed that when the gentleman from Kent looked back to that instrument, and saw what had been done by our ancestors, who are so much revered by that gentleman, that he would be induced to withdraw his objection. He (Mr. P.) was of opinion that the Governor ought to have the power to remove any incompetent persons. The abuse of the power is one thing, and the existence of it for wise purposes another. Those who to-day may be disposed to deny its very existence, will approve perhaps to-morrow of its exercise, under a flimsy pretence of *cause* to justify a political end.

Mr. CHAMBERS said, he had not discovered the precise point of his remarks, to which the gentleman from Baltimore city was opposed. He did not understand the gentleman to deny any one of his propositions. He did not know of any instance, in which the Governor of Maryland had removed a person from office.

Does the gentleman know of any case?

Mr. PRESSTMAN replied that he did not at the moment call any case to his recollection. But every one knew that the existing government of the United States had removed many persons from office. He did know cases in Maryland where parties had been removed on account of incompetence in the performance of their duties. But removals of this kind did not grow out of the Constitution. The question we are discussing is as to the power, not its application.

Mr. CHAMBERS. If the Governor has ever removed an officer before the expiration of his term, on the ground of a difference in political sentiments, he was yet to learn the fact. With some acquaintance with the history of the State for the last forty years, he had no recollection of such a case. The power of removal, in the case of inferior officers, as a conservative power, was defensible. An officer might be found utterly incompetent, might become demented, or guilty of gross crime, and in such cases his removal might be very proper. The original Constitution gave the power of removal in cases where a civil officer was not appointed during good behaviour, but in the very next section, it provided that all such officers should be appointed annually. The result was, that the Governor could only remove officers, who were annually appointed, and these were of his own appointment. There was no danger of removal for political opinion in such a state of things; and in point of fact, as far as he was informed, removals had only occurred in the case of justices of the peace and officers of that grade, who had been subject to charges for incompetency or misbehaviour.

He had heard, that at one time, the question was mooted, whether the Governor, under the amendments of 1836 had power to remove clerks and registers, who had beeen appointed by his predecessors, and whose term of office had not expired. But the attempt was not made and he supposed never would be made, because he thought no Governor would subject himself to the just and universal indignation which such an attempt must incur He submitted to the gentleman, and to the house, whether any one act could be imagined, which would occasion greater excitement or greater odium throughout the length and breadth of the State, than that of an edict of the Governor, revoking the commissions of the clerks and registers, granted by his predecessor, for no other reason but that of a difference in political opinion.

He was aware, that in the Federal government, officers had been removed on such grounds. With regard to a certain class of officers such as those representing the Government abroad and others necessarily intrusted with the confidence of the Executive, in the discharge of such duties as were political in their nature, it might be necessary. We had no such class in the State.

It was true, that when the Government was wielded by the powerful arm of General Jackson, appointments were revoked, as well as made, from party considerations. Some of the best and wisest men in the nation resisted the power, and denied it to be found in the spirit of the Constitution. But there was no appeal from his decisions. It had ultimately grown into familiar practice, and it was now pursued, as much by one party as the other. In this respect he believed they were pretty much alike.

He trusted never to see any such practice introduced into Maryland. As he wished never to live under such a dispensation, so he must refuse his assent, to any provision in the Constitution, which, by recognizing such a power, seems to invite its exercise. We now know how it has been elsewhere abused, and therefore how it may be here abused. He hoped a consideration of the subject would induce the Convention to shape the provision in such a way, as to secure officers, who were competent, faithful, useful, and acceptable to the community, from being sacrificed merely because their best and honest convictions led them to adopt a particular class of political opinions.

Mr. Presstman replied,

That some of the ablest statesman in the Union, had maintained the right of the Executive to make removals from office. He then referred to the advocacy of that doctrine by Mr. Calhoun, then opposed to the administration, in the case of the removal of Mr. Duane from the cabinet. Under all parties from the beginning of the federal government, by the elder Adams, Jefferson, &c., down to this day, the power of making removals from office has been exercised.

As to the State of Maryland, the removals have not been very numerous, but the power has never been doubted.

He then called the attention of the gentleman to the case of Col. W. R. Stewart, of Baltimore city, who was removed from the office of commissioner of lotteries, and stated at some length the particulars of that removal.

The gentleman from Kent has demanded to know when this power was exercised—neither of us have command of the files of the Executive Chamber at this moment. He did not doubt an examination would sustain his position.

Mr. Jenifer said:

It was too late at the present day to charge upon one party or the other, removals from office without cause. He believed it had long been conceded, if not a fixed fact, that political reasons are sufficient.

He did not think that either his friend from Kent, (Mr Chambers) or from the city of Baltimore, (Mr. Presstman,) eloquent as they both were, would succeed in reversing the principle which had been in practice ever since it had been proclaimed, and just acted on by a distinguished functionary in a sister State, [Governor Marcy, of New York, who happened at this moment to be within the bar of the Convention.]—"That to the victor, belonged the spoils."

The question was then taken on the amendment of Mr. Grason,

And it was agreed to.

The section as amended was then adopted.

The seventeenth section was then read as follows:

Sec. 17. The Governor may convene the legislature or the Senate alone, on extraordinary occasions; and whenever from the presence of an enemy, or from any other cause, the seat of government shall become an unsafe place for the meeting of the legislature, he may direct their sessions to be held at some other convenient place.

No amendment having been offered,

The section was adopted.

The eighteenth section was read,

No amendment having been offered, was adopted in the words following:

Sec. 18. He shall from time to time, inform the legislature of the condition of the State, and recommend to their consideration such measures as he may judge necessary and expedient.

The nineteenth section was read as follows:

Sec 19 He shall have power to grant reprieves and pardons, (except in cases of impeachment) and to remit fines and forfeitures for offences against the State; but shall in every case in which he exercises this power, report to either branch of the legislature, whenever required, the petitions, recommendations and reasons, which influence his decision.

Mr. Dorsey moved to amend said section by

inserting after the word "impeachment," in the second line the following:

"And in cases where he may be deprived of such power by some provision of this Constitution, or express legislative enactment."

Mr. Dorsey said there were some cases in which he thought it indispensible for the Legislature to hold this power If the Legislature should think it right to deprive the Governor of the power of extending pardon in a case where its exercise would be injurious to the public interest, it would be proper that they should have the power to do so. There ought to be this restrictive power somewhere; the Constitution had vested it in the Legislature, and there it should remain. And it was with this conviction that he had proposed this amendment. By the Constitution of 1776, the pardoning power is conferred on the Governor, with this express limitation; and by the act of 1782, ch. 42, this power of restriction was exercised by the Legislature. Have your Governors of late years become so pure, so eminently trustworthy, that they should be clothed with all powers, as well legislative as executive? Such appears the tendency of our proceedings, and of *modern democracy*; it formed no part of the democracy of olden times.

Mr. Spencer stated that he had contemplated an amendment in some respects similar to that which the gentleman from Anne Arundel had offered. And if the gentlemen would modify his amendment, by striking out the words "an express legislative enactment," he [Mr. S] would vote with him. But he was not willing to give the Legislature an indefinite power to be exercised at their discretion.

A division of the amendment was ordered.

Mr. Sollers gave notice of an amendment, which he would offer when in order.

Mr Ridgely stated that if he understood the amendment proposed by the gentleman from Anne Arundel, it purposed to place in the hands of the Legislature the authority to restrict the pardoning power in the Governor, whenever in their discretion, they may see fit to do so. If therefore, he understood the amendment rightly, if it was adopted, it would be idle to give the Governor the power at all. It was idle to give the Governor the power to pardon offences if that power was liable to be restricted at the discretion of the Legislature, who may thus entirely take away the power from the Governor. It would, under such a constitutional provision be perfectly competent for the Legislature, by a single enactment, to divest the Governor entirely of the pardoning power, and thus render this proper constitutional prerogative a mere shadow He did not think the Convention was disposed to give such a power into the hands of the Legislature He concurred with the gentleman from Queen Anne's. [Mr. Spencer] in the views he had expressed. He was willing to vote for a restricting power in the Legislature in such cases as are specified in the Constitution. He expressed a hope that the question would be decided, and that the House would never consent to give the Legislature an unlimited authority to restrict the power in the hands of the Executive, but only in reference to the cases restricted in the Constitution.

Mr. Dorsey contended that the gentleman from Baltimore county, (Mr. Ridgely,) had assumed more than he could sustain. The Governor has no constitutional power. He did not offer his amendment with a view to deprive the Governor of the pardoning power. But to leave the pardoning power in the same condition it always heretofore existed It appeared to him very important that there should be a power in the Legislature—an authority as there always heretofore had been—to restrict its abuse whenever there is danger of its exercise to the public injury. He referred to the possibility of abolitionists persevering in abducting our slaves and attempting to murder their masters when seeking to recover them, and the Governor of the State being tinctured with abolitionism, an event by no means impossible, under the present mode of electing him, were induced to grant *nolle prosequis* in all such cases, would you deprive the Legislature of the authority always heretofore possessed by it under our present constitution, of prohibiting the pardoning power from being exerted. He insisted that in such a case, the power ought to be in the hands of the Legislature, to restrict the Governor. He believed there was no danger that the power of the Legislature would be exercised except in extreme cases, where its necessity was apparent.

The question was then taken on the first branch of said amendment, being in these words, "and in cases where he may be deprived of such power by some provision of this constitution."

And it was agreed to.

The question recurred on the second branch of the proposition.

Mr. Dorsey. This is a very important question. I call for the yeas and nays.

The yeas and nays were ordered.

Mr. Crisfield expressed his willingness to go for the amendment, if its operation was limited to future cases.

Mr Crisfield desired to ask the gentleman from Anne Arundel if he intended that after an individual had been convicted of a crime, and had gone to the penitentiary, the right of the Governor to pardon was not complete? Was it his intention that in such a case where the punishment of the crime is inflicted, the Legislature may interfere to check the pardoning power in the hands of the Executive? If the gentleman from Anne Arundel would confine his amendment to such cases as may hereafter occur, which may arise after the passage of the act creating the offence, he would be willing to vote for it But without some limitation, he could not give it his support

Mr. Grason adverted to what he regarded as a defect in the amendment of the gentleman from Anne Arundel, and referred to the debates in the New York Convention, and the opinions expressed by Kent, Spencer, and other eminent judges, that the pardoning power ought to be vested in the Executive, notwithstanding its liability to abuse in his hands He also took up the Constitution of the United States, and read the clause which gives the pardoning power to the President of the United States. This section is the same in effect, but is not so well expressed as in the Constitution of the United States. He hoped the Convention would not consent to take away the pardoning power from the Governor. If he can pardon in cases of murder and the highest crimes known to our laws, why is he not to be permitted to pardon in cases of bribery? For it would be recollected, his colleague had introduced a restriction on the Executive power to pardon in cases of bribery. He hoped no authority would be conferred on the Legislature to restrain or take away this power

Mr. SPENCER said he was opposed to the principle of leaving so delicate a power to be exercised, subject to the discretion of the Legislature. He would not vote for such an amendment. The gentleman from Anne Arundel (Mr. Dorsey) had referred to the possibility that some abolition excitement may spring up, and that in such contingency, it might be important that the Legislature should have the power to say whether persons engaged in it should be subjects of the pardoning power or not. There was no man, who would go farther than he (Mr. S.) in punishing agitators of this kind, and yet he could not yield to the force of such an argument. We must remember, that this is a subject, which of all others is most calculated to excite feeling and prejudice. It is a charge which necessarily excites the passions of men, and under such a state of feeling, public indignation might be directed against an innocent man, and his conviction be the result. In such cases he preferred to leave the pardoning power in the hands of the Executive, who would never pardon unless he were fully satisfied that the conviction had been brought about under the influence of excitement and unjust prejudice. He was opposed to the amendment of the gentleman from Anne Arundel.

His friend and colleague, [Mr. Grason] referred to his [Mr. S.'s] amendment, withholding from the Executive the power to pardon in cases of bribery. He explained his purpose in offering that amendment, and drew a distinction between an offence committed from a sudden impulse, or in a moment of thoughtlessness, and a crime coolly and deliberately planned and carried out.—He had voted for the first branch of the amendment of the gentleman from Anne Arundel, in order to leave the question open to the Convention.

Referring again to the offence of bribery, he stated that it was always perpetrated with deliberation The bribe must be deliberately offered. The party offering must have previously arranged his plans, sought out his object, and acted deliberately. In no case where a man calmly and deliberately conceives a criminal purpose and carries the design into execution, ought the pardoning power to be exercised He was therefore willing to restrain the Executive in granting pardons, in cases of convictions against an individual for giving bribe, unless he was satisfied that the convictions were the result of persecution and without evidence. He would discriminate too, between the one who gave and the receiver of a bribe. They were generally humble, poor and uneducated men, who were seduced by the temptations which were offered to them—temptations, which under the circumstances of penury and want, they could not resist.

Mr. DORSEY said, that he was struck with the force of the proposition of the gentleman from Somerset, (Mr. Crisfield,) and had modified the second branch of his amendment, to meet the views of that gentleman. As any legislative restriction, after the perpetration of the crime, of the pardoning power, would be somewhat in the nature of an *ex post facto* law. With reference to the objections of the gentleman from Queen Anne's, he would reply, and he was sure the gentleman from Carroll, (Mr. Brown,) would agree with him, there ought to be some confidence reposed in the Legislature. He had heard of the pardoning power, or one somewhat analogous, having been abused in the hands of the Executive. Even since we have met here, a case had occurred, in which the Governor had thought proper to release the sum of eight hundred and fifty-three dollars due on a debt to the State, from a collector of taxes, thus indirectly levying taxes to that amount upon the people, a power which he.(Mr. D.,) had, under like circumstances, never heard of, as having been exercised before; and the recurrence of which he hoped the Convention would take care to prevent.

In the case to which he had referred, the Governor could not have acted from any political feeling, because the collector was a whig, backed, however, by an opposite and powerful influence. The reasons assigned by the collector. in his application for the release, was that in 1844 and 1845, when he was appointed collector, there was an indisposition in tax payers, to pay their taxes, and that money was scarce in those years. Every member of this body knew the indiscreet manner in which the pardoning power had been exercised; and he had heard many complaints on the subject—a general desire prevailed that it should be restrained. He had proposed no new restriction. He had left the power to be exacted as it has existed from 1776. He did not propose to add any restriction, but would merely leave the Governor in the position, in which he has in been since the year since the year 1776; and yet he was told that we must not touch the power of the Governor; and one would imagine, from the manner in which this declaration is made, that even the Constitution itself has no power to control it. Sir, the Governor possesses no pardoning power, but as given to him by the Constitution. Here Mr. D read the section from the Constitution of 1776.

Because it was supposed that this power had been abused, complaints have been made again and again, and he knew that these complaints came from all portions of the State He had moved his proposition without reference to any political party. He had nothing to do with political parties. He did not care whether the Governor was a whig or a democrat. But complaints had been made, and if he was sure that whig Governors would always hereafter be elected, he would still desire that he should be subjected to this restriction, because the Executive is always in more danger of error from the influences brought to bear on him, than from the free exercise of his own judgment.

The gentleman from Queen Anne's, [Mr. Spencer,] was opposed to his proposition, because he thinks that the excitement and prejudice in the minds of the jury, when cases of a certain class come before them may lead to an unjust verdict. He, [Mr. D.,] during the time he had been on the bench, had always found juries most humane and conscientious, and he had not known of any conviction, not warranted by the law and the testimony save one. In case such conviction should take place, it was in the power of the court to grant a new trial, and, if the court thought the conviction improper, it was ever ready to do so. But he believed the jury competent to form a correct judgment from the nature of the discussions and proofs before them. But how is it with the Governor? He has not before him all the evidence which is before the Court. What information he has is generally derived from the persons convicted or his friends, who are applicants for the pardon, and who represent the case in the form most favorable to their wishes. He thought that the Governor should use greater caution and circumspection in the granting of pardons. And there are cases in which the Governor ought not to have the power to pardon. There are many complaints against the unqualified exercise of the power. Some wish it to be restricted in one case, and some in another. The Governor was generally found too ready to pardon, not indeed so much so as a Governor of Pennsylvania, who if newspaper statements be true, granted to a political favorite a pardon, for an offence subsequently to be committed.

After a few words by Mr. Brent, of Baltimore city,

Mr Dorsey said he had only intended to say that, under the Constitution of 1836, Baltimore as it now is, or in a few years will be, has practically obtained the exclusive power to elect the Governor.

He did not propose, he repeated, to add any new limitations to this power. On the contrary, he increased the power in the hands of the Executive, by limiting the means of restriction in conformity with the views of the gentleman from Somerset, [Mr. Crisfield.] He had no doubt that the power would be discreetly exercised. The gentleman from Baltimore said that it was not a sufficient reason for taking away the power because it had sometimes been abused, but it was a good restricting it; for appointing a controlling authority by which its abuse might be prevented.

Mr. Dirickson wished to enquire of the gentleman from Anne Arundel, if it was intended to take away the pardoning power from the Executive, with reference to any other class of crimes except impeachment?

Mr. Dorsey replied. Where the Legislature may think it proper.

Mr. Dirickson. One other question. Is it left in the discretion of the Legislature to create new crimes?

Mr. Dorsey replied, it was not intended to confer any new power on the Legislature, but merely to enable them to exercise the power they already possessed.

Mr. Buchanan expressed a readiness to take from the Executive all the patronage which devolved on that department, even to the appointment of Secretary of State, and confide it directly to the people, but he never would consent to deprive the Executive of the benign prerogative of mercy.

This power of pardon, (said Mr. B.,) must rest somewhere. It exists in every government and cannot safely be dispensed with in any.

It has been said that punishment should tread upon the heels of the transgressor, and that to convict and punish the *guilty* should be the object of every government. This is true, but a no less important object of every government, should be to protect, sustain and shield the *innocent.*

If the guilty alone could suffer, then, indeed, there might be some pretext for the effort to dispense with the prerogative of pardon, but when we remember the infirmities of our nature, the imperfection of our laws, the difficulty of correctly applying them, the possibility—nay, the probability of mistake, we see at once that the innocent may be involved as well as the guilty. And it is for the protection of the innocent, that the pardoning power is chiefly designed.

I repeat, then, Mr. President, (said Mr. B.,) that the power to pardon should rest in some department of the government. It should rest in a department of high and undivided responsibility. Where can it be with more propriety reposed than with the Executive?

The duty of the Executive is to see that the laws shall be faithfully executed, and that the administration of the laws shall never become an engine of oppression.

The power to pardon in all countries, rests with the Executive. In England, it belongs to the Crown. The King by his coronation oath is bound to exercise justice in mercy. And in that country it has been said by an able writer, that there are cases in which the exercise of the pardoning power is at once beneficial to the Crown which bestows, and just to the party who receives it. It is in many cases the only mode in which a party can be protected from the consequences of an improper verdict and judgment.

In the government of the United States, (said Mr. B.,) the power to pardon is confided to the Executive *exclusively.* By the Constitution of the United States, the President shall have power to grant reprieves and pardons for offences against the United States in all cases, except in cases of impeachment. Even in cases of treason he may grant reprieves and pardons, without control or limit. This power has been exercised by the various Presidents of the United States ever since the adoption of the Constitution. No harm has been found to grow out of it—nor has any effort at any time been made to withhold it from the national Executive. The great object of the framers of the Constitution of the United States in confiding this power to the Executive alone, was to consolidate responsibility. Alexander Hamilton, says: "that as the *sense* of responsibility is always strongest in proportion as it is undivided, it may be inferred that a single man would be most ready to attend to the force of those motives which might plead for a mitigation of the rigor of the law, and least apt to yield to considerations which were calculated to shelter a fit object of its vengeance."

In most of the States of the Union, the power to pardon, said Mr. B., is confided exclusively to the Executive departments. It is true that in the Constitutions of some of the States, provisions are inserted requiring the Executives to report to the Legislature; but in most of the States the power to pardon belongs exclusively to the executive departments.

Mr. President, (said Mr. B.,) the proposition here as I understand it, is to divide the responsibiliy of the exercise of the pardoning power, between the executive and the legislative branches of the government. It is in effect to say to the Executive, you can grant pardons and reprieves, but you are to do so only in concurrence with or in subordination to the Legislature.

Why is this? Why this distrust of the Executive? Gentlemen express the fear, (said Mr. B.,) that favoritism or prejudice may find their way into the Executive chamber. Have gentlemen never heard of favoritism finding its way into the halls of Legislation. May not the Legislature be sometimes in danger of being operated on by motives or feelings inauspicious to the just and merciful exercise of this prerogative. No, Mr. President, (said Mr. B.,) if we desire to have this power safely confided, let it be left in the hands of the Governor to be exercised on his responsibility alone.

Mr. Hamilton well says: "The reflection that the fate of a fellow creatures depends on the sole fiat of the Executive, would naturally inspire scrupulousness and caution. The dread of being accused of weakness or connivance would beget equal circumspection, though of a different kind. On the other hand, as men generally derive confidence from that number, they might often encourage each other in an act of obduracy, and might be less sensible to the apprehension of censure for an injudicious or affected clemency. On these accounts one man appears to be a more eligible dispenser of the mercy of the Government, than a body of men." This, Mr. President, (said Mr. B.,) is the best doctrine, and an adherence to it, will guard us against difficulty and danger.

A word only, (said Mr. B.,) to his friend from Queen Anne's, (Mr. Spencer,) and he would have done. That gentleman and myself, have for many years borne the most intimate and friendly relation towards each other. A kinder heart does not animate a human bosom than does his. And yet, Mr. President, (said Mr. B.,) it seemed to me that to-day, an entire change came over the feelings of my friend. Of all men else I should have calculated on him to battle for the privilege of pardon, for the prerogative of mercy. But if I understood him correctly, he was not disposed without much restriction to vest this power with the Executive. In a case of clear and undoubted guilt, [said Mr. B.] my friend, if I understood him correctly, would not leave the power of pardon in the hands of the Executive.

That might perhaps be well if it could be surely known when guilt *did actually* exist with nothing to alleviate. But how are we to be sure of this undoubted, unredeeming guilt. May there not be false accusations, perjured witnesses, misled juries, inaccurate judgments, inefficient counsel? May there not be mitigating, justifying circumstances?

Can you imagine no case, Mr. President, [said Mr. B.] in which, although the rigor of the law might demand the offender, the shield of justice should protect the victim?

You cannot with safety, [said Mr. B.,] restrict or divide this power to pardon Under its exercise, there is no fear that the guilty will escape. And by it the innocent may be protected.

Mr. Spencer replied that he was always pleased to hear the eloquent bursts of his friend from Baltimore county. That gentleman had known him for a long time, and he seemed to think that he, [Mr. S.,] had lost some particles of those kind qualities which he had imbibed from being so long in instructive association with him. But his friend from Baltimore county did him injustice. He, [Mr. S.,] had not deviated from his course. He had said on a former occasion that there was one class of offences in relation to which he would take away the power of the Executive to pardon. What was that class of offences? It was bribery. And his aim was to prevent pardon from being extended, not to the person who received, but to him who gave, the bribe. It was against the individual whose circumstances placed him beyond the reach of corruption, but who went about with a preconceived purpose to corrupt others, that he would arm the law with its utmost terrors. It was in reference to these persons that he would withhold the pardoning power from the Executive. If such an offence, calmly determined on, and perpetrated with entire deliberation, were brought home to a man, would his friend from Baltimore county tell him, that such a man was a fit subject for the pardoning power? No. That power should be exercised towards those who have been inconsiderately and under some sudden impulses, hurried into a violation of law. This was the position he had taken and occupied. He would stand by that part of the amendment of the gentleman from Anne Arundel, which restricts the pardoning power in all cases provided in the Constitution. But he would never give his vote for the second branch which gives the Legislature unlimited authority to restrict this power in the hands of the Executive in relation to other cases.

Mr. Dorsey, by consent, modified his amendment to meet the view of Mr. Crisfield, by adding the words "passed before the perpetration of the crime."

Mr. Sollers, (to the Chair.) Is it in order to move the previous question?

The PRESIDENT, *pro tem.* It is.

Mr. SOLLERS demanded the previous question.

There was a second. The main question was ordered to be now taken, (being on the second branch of the amendment of Mr. DORSEY,) in these words, "or express legislation passed before the perpetration of the crime"

The question was then taken, and the result was as follows:

Affirmative—Messrs. Blakistone, President, pro tem., Dent, Hopewell, Chambers of Kent, Donaldson, Dorsey, Wells, Randall, Kent, Dalrymple, Bond, Sollers, Brent of Charles, Crisfield, Hodson, Sprigg, Bowling, and Davis—18.

Negative—Messrs. Ricaud, Lee, Jenifer, Buchanan, Bell, Welch, Chandler, Ridgely, Lloyd, Dickinson, Sherwood of Talbot, Dashiell, Hicks, Eccleston, Constable, Miller, McLane, McCubbin, Spencer, Grason, Dirickson, McMaster, Fooks, Shriver, Gaither, Biser, Annan, Sappington, Stephenson, McHenry, Magraw, Nelson, Hardcastle, Gwinn, Stewart of Baltimore city, Brent of Baltimore city, Ware, Schley, Fiery, Neill, John Newcomer, Harbine, Michael Newcomer, Kilgour, Brewer, Weber, Hollyday, Slicer, Parke, Ege, and Brown—51.

So the last branch of the amendment was rejected.

The question then recurred on the section as amended—and it was adopted.

Mr SOLLERS, (who had called the previous question under a misunderstanding of its effect,) desired to offer the amendment of which he had given notice.

Mr. DONALDSON [with a view to offer amendments contemplated by him] moved a re-consideration of the vote just taken.

Mr. DIRICKSON asked the gentleman to state what the amendments were.

Mr. DONALDSON explained.

The question was stated to be on the motion to reconsider.

Mr. JENIFER said:

He should oppose the motion to reconsider, notwithstanding the disposition he always felt to show courtesy to gentlemen in motions of this kind.

He thought that the Convention, so far as it had gone, had shown too great a disposition to restrict the Executive, and to take away from him powers which belonged to him, and which the interests of the State did not require should be lodged elsewhere. It seemed as if the Convention designed to make an automaton of the Governor, and nothing more.

Mr. SOLLERS said:

That if the gentleman from Charles, (Mr. Jenifer,) thought that he wished to strip the Executive of any power, he was mistaken. He did not belong to that new fangled school which went for cutting down every thing. His only object was to guard the power against abuse. He then stated a case of extreme hardship, in which the executive had been deceived by numerously signed petitions from Calvert, into granting a *nolle prosequi*, by which a man against whom a suit and judgment for the crime of forgery had been obtained by a young lawyer, who died very suddenly, escaped from the law, and an imputation was cast on the reputation of the young gentleman who had obtained the judgment, that he had received the money from the forger and dissipated it.

That was the reason for the amendment which he had proposed requiring the publication of the names of the signers of petitions asking for the pardon of criminals.

Mr. JENIFER referred to a case of a different character, to show that such publication might act injuriously.

The question was then taken, and

The motion to reconsider was agreed to.

The Convention then adjourned until to-morrow at ten o'clock.

WEDNESDAY, March 12th, 1851.

The Convention met at 10 o'clock.

Prayer was made by the Rev. Mr. GRAUFF.

The journal of yesterday was read, and, after being amended,

On motion of Mr. CRISFIELD, by substituting the word "recess," for the word "adjournment," in the amendment offered by him, was approved.

DOORKEEPERS.

Mr. SAPPINGTON submitted the following order:

Ordered, That a select committee be appointed and instructed to enquire and report to this House whether or not it would not be expedient to discharge some of the doorkeepers and committee clerks.

On motion of Mr. SAPPINGTON, the special committee was ordered to consist of three members.

Mr. MAGRAW moved to lay the order on the table.

Mr. SAPPINGTON asked for the ayes and noes,

And they were ordered.

The question was then taken on the motion of Mr. MAGRAW, to lay the order on the table, when it was decided in the negative, as follows:

Affirmative—Messrs. Blakistone, President *pro tem.*, Dent, Hopewell, Ricaud, Lee, Chambers, of Kent, Donaldson, Kent, Dalrymple, Sollers, Brent, of Charles, Jenifer, Chandler, Dashiell, Hicks, Eccleston, Sprigg, Bowling, Grason, Dirickson, McMaster, Annan, Magraw and Kilgour—24.

Negative.—Messrs. Dorsey, Wells, Sellman, Lloyd, Dickinson, Sherwood, of Talbot, Chambers, of Cecil, Miller, McCubbin, Spencer, Shriver, Gaither, Biser, Sappington, Nelson, Hardcastle, Gwinn, Stewart, of Baltimore city, Brent, of Baltimore city, Ware, Schley, Fiery, John Newcomer, Harbine, Michael Newcomer, Brewer, Weber, Hollyday, Slicer, Parke, Cockey and Brown—32.

So the Convention refused to lay the order on the table.

The question was then taken on the adoption of the order, when it was decided in the affirmative.

So the order was adopted.

The PRESIDENT, *pro tem.*, then appointed Messrs. SAPPINGTON, ANNAN and RICAUD to compose the committee under said order.

On motion of Mr. RICAUD, he was excused from serving on said committee.

And Mr. DIRICKSON was appointed in his room.

Mr. DIRICKSON asked to be excused from serving on said committee.

Mr. BROWN moved to reconsider the vote by which the order had been adopted. He then withdrew the motion.

Mr. SOLLERS renewed the motion to reconsider.

Mr. SAPPINGTON asked for the ayes and noes,

And they were ordered.

The question was then taken on the motion to reconsider,

And decided in the negative, as follows:

Affirmative.—Messrs. Blakistone, President *pro tem.*, Dent, Hopewell, Lee, Dalrymple, Sollers, Brent, of Charles, Jenifer, Buchanan, Welch, Dickinson, Sherwood, of Talbot, Colston, Dashiell, Hicks, Hodson, Eccleston, Chambers, of Cecil, Tuck, McCubbin, Bowling, Grason, Dirickson, McMaster, Annan, Magraw, Gwinn, Stewart, of Baltimore city, Presstman, Ware, Kilgour, Waters and Brown—33.

Negative.—Messrs. Ricaud, Chambers, of Kent, Donaldson, Dorsey, Wells, Randall, Sellman, Bell, Chandler, Ridgely, Crisfield, McCullough, Sprigg, Spencer, Shriver, Gaither, Biser, Sappington, Nelson, Hardcastle, Schley, Fiery, Neill, John Newcomer, Harbine, Michael Newcomer, Davis, Brewer, Weber, Hollyday, Slicer, Parke and Cockey—33

So the motion to reconsider was not agreed to.

And the question being on the motion of Mr. DIRICKSON to be excused from serving on the committee, it was decided in the affirmative.

On motion of Mr. ANNAN, he was excused from serving on said committee.

Mr. BISER presented a petition of two hundred and eighty-six citizens of Frederick and Washington counties, remonstrating against the creation of a new county from parts of the aforesaid counties.

Which was read and referred to the committee on new counties.

INTOXICATING LIQUORS.

Mr. CHAMBERS presented a petition of sundry citizens of Cecil county, praying that provision may be made in the new Constitution, to prevent the sale of intoxicating liquors, except the same shall be approved of by a majority of the votes in the election district where the same is to be sold; and

Mr. MAGRAW, presented a petition of sundry citizens of Harford county of a similar import.

Which were severally read, and

Referred to the select committee already appointed on that subject.

COMMITTEE OF ACCOUNTS.

Mr. WELLS from the committee on accounts, submitted a report, accompanied by the following resolution:

Mr. WELLS, chairman of the committee on accounts, submitted the following report:

The committee of accounts respectfully report that they have examined the accompanying claims numbered 1, 2, 3, 4, 5, 6 and 7, amounting to the sum of $357 52, and recommend the adoption of the subjoined resolution.

G. WELLS, *Chairman.*

Resolved, That the accounts herewith filed, be paid by the orders of the President of the Convention, on the Treasurer of the State, in favor of the persons entitled to receive the same, for the amounts due to them respectively.

Which was twice read and adopted.

EXECUTIVE DEPARTMENT.

On motion of Mr. GRASON, the Convention resumed the consideration of the orders of the day, being the report on the executive department.

The question being on the nineteenth section as amended,

Mr. SOLLERS moved to amend said section by striking out from the word "case," in the third line to the end of said section, and inserting in lieu thereof, the following:

"Before he exercises the power of granting reprieves and pardons, cause to be published at least thirty days in some newspaper published at the seat of government, and in some newspaper published in the county where the person petitioning for a reprieve or pardon resides, if there be any, the petition of such person, and the names of all persons signing such petition, and the publication aforesaid shall be made at the expense of the State, or the party petitioning as the Governor may determine."

Mr. SOLLERS said, it was that reprieves and pardons had been sometimes granted improperly; because petitions, numerously and respectably signed, had been sent to the Governor, on which he had decided the case without much examination. It may be that persons will be more cautious in signing such petitions, if it be required that the petitions and signatures shall be published.

Mr. RIDGELY did not think the amendment would reach the object which the mover intended. It gave the right to pardon, in the first place, and provided for the publication of the petitions afterwards.

Mr. SOLLERS modified his amendment to obviate this objection.

Mr. BREWER suggested the possibility of no newspaper being published in the county. He therefore moved to amend the amendment, by inserting these words, "and if there be no newspaper in said county, then a copy of said petitions, together with the names of the petitioners, to be set up at the court house door of said county."

Mr. PRESSTMAN suggested that the party might be sent to the penitentiary, before the Executive could issue the pardon. It would be better to grant the pardon before the accused is subjected to the ignominy of going to the penitentiary. There might be a provision that the court should delay the sentence, until the decision of the Executive on the case should be known.

Mr. SOLLERS replied that the ignominy was not in the punishment, but in the conviction. He thought such a case would be of rare occurrence. If there was any disposition to grant a pardon, the Executive could issue a respite.

Mr. STEWART, of Baltimore city, suggested to the gentleman from Montgomery, (Mr. Brewer,) the propriety of withdrawing his amendment. He was satisfied from the information before the committee on printing, that there was no county in which there was not a newspaper printed.

Mr BREWER then withdrew his amendment.

Mr. PRESSTMAN suggested a modification of the amendment, by adding at the end thereof, the following:

"And that sentence of the court shall not be executed where the court is satisfied that the convicted party has applied for Executive clemency, until the Governor shall have acted upon the application."

Mr. SOLLERS was about to accept, when

Mr. TUCK suggested, before the gentleman from Calvert, accepted the modification, the propriety of so amending the amendment as to make it read that the party shall have previously applied for a pardon and notified the court of such application.

Mr. KILGOUR said there might be cases of wrong which would not be reached by the amendment as it stood. He moved the following amendment:

"Amend said amendment by inserting after the words "signing such petition," these words "unless recommended for pardon by the court and jury before whom convicted."

Mr. SOLLERS accepted the amendment of the gentleman from Baltimore city, and modified his amendment accordingly.

The question was then taken on the amendment offered by Mr. KILGOUR, and it was rejected.

Mr. GRASON objected to the amendment of the gentleman from Calvert, which required the publication of the names of all who signed petitions for pardon. Applications of this kind were often made in letters, which sometimes had more influence than the names attached to petitions. He objected to the publication, on account of the difficulty and expense. In the case of Turner, it was understood that the petitions were signed by three thousand persons. It would take several numbers of the largest newspaper to contain the names and petitions in that case. There might be cases in which it would be improper to publish the names.

A person committing a crime, might be willing to give testimony against his accomplices, on condition of first receiving a *nolle prosequi*, and of not being publicly known as a witness till his associates were arrested. He had himself granted a *nolle prosequi*, in a case of this kind, at the request of the President of the Frederick county Bank.

Again, a person, perhaps a female, suffering from cold or hunger, might steal as much wood or provisions as would supply their immediate wants. There might be cases of this kind, in which the court and jury and the whole community would invoke the pardoning power Why should there be a necessity for keeping such an offender in prison to await the publication of the names and petitions?

There was another class of cases—the escape of a slave from his owner, is made felony by an act of assembly. If arrested and committed to jail, he cannot be delivered to his master without a *nolle prosequi*, which is usually granted on condition of his being sent out of the State. In such cases, why should any delay or expense be incurred, by a publication of the names and petitions in the newspapers?

Mr. SOLLERS said:

The objection of the gentleman from Queen Anne's was based on the ground of inconvenience. The object of the amendment was to guard against the escape of criminals from punishment by means of petitions, which did not embody the public sentiment and came from irresponsible sources. By such means many a criminal may go "unwhipped of justice," especially on the eve of an election. He desired to prevent this evil, by requiring the publication of the names of those who signed such petitions.

Mr. BRENT, suggested that there should be a provision for the publication in a Baltimore paper, and that it should not be confined to a paper printed in Annapolis.

He hoped the gentleman from Calvert, would agree to introduce after the words "if there be any," the words "or elsewhere in the discretion of the Governor."

Mr. SOLLERS accepted the amendment and modified his amendment accordingly.

Mr. GWINN offered as a substitute for the said amendment, the following:

"And the Governor shall before proceeding to grant any pardon or *nolle prosequi*, (unless where the same is granted for reason of public policy,) give a reasonable notice of the application of such pardon or *nolle prosequi*, and of the grounds on which the said pardon or *nolle prosequi* is prayed "

Mr. GWINN said:

That he thought that the Governor should be required to give a reasonable notice of such applications, but that it was improper to fix the precise period which should be required for such notice. It would necessarily vary according to circumstances.

If the offence were newly committed, in a thickly settled community, the briefest notice would suffice to excite public attention, and to prevent imposition upon the Executive, or upon the prerogative of pardon. But in other cases, where the neighborhood was sparsely settled, a greater length of time might be required.

Again, this right of pardon does not extend to recent cases only, but to offences long since committed. After an individual has been some years in the penitentiary, he is to some extent lost sight of in the community. If an application is made in his behalf, the lapse of time, the death of witnesses, the forgetfulness of men, would make it impossible to act upon the case with the same facility, as if he were recently arraigned or convicted. In all these different cases, the degree of notice varies with the particular instance brought to the consideration of the Governor, and it should be left to his conscience to determine what was sufficient information to the public. After all he must finally determine for himself; and, however strong the resistance may be, he can under the power granted, exercise his discretion. If the object is to make him amenable to public opinion, the end will be accomplished by that comment, which must ensue, if the notice of application, which he directs, should be insufficient for public remonstrance.

There is no reason to prescribe the way in which this notice shall be given. It is not proper to say that it shall be in a newspaper only, because in thinly settled sections, the end may be attainable only by proclamation. The Governor will always conscientiously determine upon the means, which are sufficient to inform the public of the application made for clemency.

The question was then taken, and the substitute of Mr. Gwinn was rejected.

The question recurred on the adoption of the amendment, as amended.

Mr. Spencer moved for a division of the question, (upon striking out,) which was ordered.

And the Convention refused to strike out.

Mr. Gwinn then read a substitute which he proposed to offer.

Mr. Sollers referred to a class of thieves against whom he was anxious to guard. They were the receivers of stolen tobacco; and were well known to the Executive Department. He referred to a case in which one of these depredators, whose guilt was notorious, who had got up a petition to the Governor, and obtained a *nolle prosequi*, when, had the fact of his application been known in his neighborhood, every respectable person there would have petitioned against it. Worse than that, this man was afterwards made a justice of the peace. He desired to protect the Governor against these deceptions.

After a few explanatory remarks between Messrs. Tuck and Gwinn, in reference to the substitute of the latter,

Mr. Gwinn moved his substitute, when

Mr. Brent asked for the previous question.

The previous question was then ordered.

The question was then put on the substitute offered by Mr Gwinn, and it was negatived.

The question recurring on the amendment of Mr. Sollers, as amended,

Mr. Spencer moved for a division of the question.

The question was then put on striking out, and it was decided in the negative—ayes 27, noes 29.

Mr. Donaldson moved to amend the section by inserting after the word "pardons," in the first line, the words "after conviction."

He said, every one must acknowledge that the power of granting pardons before trial and conviction, was liable to great abuse; but to his mind the abuse of it seemed so certain and the benefits derived from its used, so insignificant, that he thought it ought to be entirely taken away. The power of pardoning after conviction he would still retain. There were many cases where it could be used beneficially, and the cause of justice was in fact promoted by its judicious exercise. It was sometimes necessary to protect innocence against the prejudice and excited pass ons which have usurped the place of judgment; facts might come to light after conviction, which if known before trial, would have produced an acquittal; a man might be technically guilty of a criminal charge, and yet the circumstances might be such as would make it unjust or peculiarly harsh, that he should suffer the penalty by law affixed to that crime; and the subsequent conduct of a convicted man might be such as to call for some mitigation of his punishment. This reserved power of mercy in the Executive, when properly exercised, gives greater certainty to the administration of justice by our courts and juries. Even that power should be more checked, than it is by the sections under consideration, and he proposed, if not cut off by the previous question, to offer another amendment, requiring the Governor to report all these cases to the Legislature, whether called upon or not. But in regard to the amendment now proposed, he would say, that he did not know of a case in our present state of society in which a pardon, before conviction, would be productive of any benefit worth estimating, when compared with the evils arising from the exercise of such a power. The only just ground for exercising the power, was for the protection of innocence. And what innocent man, when suspicion is once attached to his name, would not court, rather than evade, a trial? If evidence enough, of whatever sort, could be produced against him to cause a grand jury to present him a fair, and open trial was his only protection from the tongues of calumny. If a false and malicious accusation could be entirely smothered by a pardon, then there might be some reason for retaining the power, but the slightest whisper of such a charge is caught up by the public press and spread far and wide. In these times, there is no power to seal the accuser's lips, and he who seeks, by the interposition of the Executive, to shield himself from trial, fixes on his character a stain that cannot be effaced.

Mr. D. called upon those who opposed this amendment, to state the cases which justified such an interposition, that they might be tested, to see whether there was any thing to outweigh the great public policy of permitting the administration of justice to take its course until judgment was rendered. This is a matter in which all good citizens are deeply concerned, and the manner in which the pardoning power had been abused, is a subject of general complaint. To place these restrictions upon it, would be a reform which might not commend itself to the politicians, but which certainly would be acceptable to the people. They are willing that mercy should temper justice, but not that justice should be superseded in her office.

Mr. D. said, in conclusion, that the great majority of State Constitutions contained the qualification he now proposed to attach to the pardoning power, and in many States it had been in force for a great number of years.

Mr. Grason, in reply to the urgent call of the gentleman from Anne Arundel, for reasons, would say, that if "reasons were as plentiful as blackberries," it was not pleasant to give them on compulsion. He would, however, state such as occurred to him. Suppose a man bears a challenge, and the fact is admitted and known to every one, would it be necessary to have a trial, as the gentleman suggests, if the circumstances were such as to justify a *nolle prosequi?* Would it be necessary to pay counsel for defending him from a charge which he admitted to be true? Take another case—a poor woman may be keeping house, without a particle of fuel to protect herself and children from the cold, and may take a few sticks of wood under the pressure of absolute want. The circumstances may be known to all, and all may wish the Governor to interpose; but the gentleman from Anne Arundel would have her imprisoned, and subjected to the delay and torture of a public trial, in order that the Governor should be prevented from abusing his powers. Numerous cases might be stated, but as the gentleman had only asked for a single reason, it was needless to say more on this point. Mr. G. then read an extract from a speech of Chancellor Kent, on the subject of pardons. He was aware that the Governor might err in exercising this power, and sometimes in *not* exercising it. He believed that he had himself erred in several instances, in which he had refused applications for pardon. Lawyers and judges seemed to think that the real facts of a case can only be ascertained by a trial before the court and jury; whereas it was notorious that material facts, which were known to the whole community, and which would decide the guilt or innocence of a prisoner, were shut out by the rules of evidence or concealed by the prevarication of witnesses. Gentlemen seemed to believe that courts and juries could never be deceived in the investigation of a criminal offence; and that it was presumption in the Executive to look behind the record for mitigating circumstances. He could state a number of cases to show the incorrectness of such an opinion. He had another objection to the amendment of the gentleman from Anne Arundel. The amendment requires the Governor to report every case to the House of Delegates. Suppose a runaway slave to be arrested, and a *nolle prosequi* to be granted at the instance of the owner—what advantage could be derived from a communication of the facts to either branch of the Legislature? The bill now provides that every case of pardon shall be reported, with all the petitions and reasons, whenever required by the Senate or House of Delegates. He wished the Governor to have an opportunity of giving his reasons, for he could then justify himself against unfounded imputations. He had no doubt that the gentleman from Anne Arundel wished to improve the section, but the amendment was calculated to produce an opposite effect, and the Convention ought to consider it carefully before they adopt it.

Mr Spencer was opposed to the amendment of the gentleman, (Mr. Donaldson,) because it would deprive the Executive of the power to grant a *nolle prosequi*. He was disposed to leave this attribute untouched in the hands of the Executive. He had no doubt that the power is liable to abuse, but it often happens that truth comes to light after trial and conviction. He stated the case of a man who was convicted of an offence and was recommended by the jury to mercy. But the Governor happening to be present at the trial, was thoroughly convinced of his guilt. A new trial was granted in consequence of some irregularity in the indictment, and some lost evidence which the man on his first trial urged, would prove his innocence if it could be found, having come to light, his entire innocence of the crime was proved. Numerous cases of this kind were always occurring to require the exercise of this important power in the hands of the executive. He could call the attention of the Convention to other cases. Take a man whose character stands well, he did not mean of adventitious character, but one moving in any sphere of life, esteemed for his general amiability of demeanor, throw him suddenly into a scene of strong excitement, where he is suddenly provoked by some violent attack on his honor, and, under a momentary provocation, he seizes a stick and inflicts a blow which fatally wounds the traducer of his character. Public sympathy is with him, but he has violated the law. In such a case would you deprive the Governor of the power of granting a *nolle prosequi*, when it is known that he must otherwise be brought to trial, and that the facts being proved in evidence, he must be convicted? Would you say he should not be pardoned before conviction? Would you compel him to stand in the felon's box, to hold up his hand like a felon, and be consigned to a felon's doom? He would leave the power where it has always been. He could cite cases of a school master, a parent, a master of a family, inflicting incautiously a blow which inadvertently caused death. Yet every one knew that nothing could be further from the intention of the parent, and the effect of that blow would be to carry that parent in sorrow to his grave. And would you add to his agony by making him stand in the felon's box?

Mr. Brent, of Baltimore city, asked for the previous question.

The previous question was ordered.

Mr. Donaldson asked for the yeas and nays, which were ordered.

The question was then taken on the amendment of Mr. Donaldson,

And decided as follows:

Affirmative.—Messrs. Lee, Chambers, of Kent, Donaldson, Dorsey, Wells, Randall, Kent, Sollers, Crisfield, Dashiell, Hicks, Eccleston, McMaster, Gaither, Davis, Weber and Smith—17.

Negative.—Messrs. Blakistone, President, *pro tem.*, Hopewell, Ricaud, Sellman, Brent, of Charles, Jenifer, Buchanan, Bell, Welch, Chandler, Ridgely, Lloyd, Dickinson, Sherwood, of Talbot, Chambers, of Cecil, McCullough, Miller, McLane, Bowie, Tuck, Sprigg, McCubbin, Bowling, Spencer, Grason, Dirickson, Fooks, Biser, Annan, Sappington, McHenry, Magraw, Nelson, Hardcastle, Gwinn, Brent, of Baltimore city, Presstman, Schley, Fiery, Neill, John Newcomer, Harbine, Michael Newcomer, Kilgour, Brewer, Waters, Slicer, Parke, Cockey and Brown—51.

So the amendment was rejected.

The question then being on the section,

Mr. SPENCER asked for the ayes and noes,

And they were ordered.

The question was then taken and decided, as follows:

Affirmative.—Messrs. Blakistone, President, *pro tem.*, Dent, Hopewell, Ricaud, Sellman, Dalrymple, Sollers, Brent of Charles, Jenifer, Buchanan, Bell, Welch, Chandler, Lloyd, Dickinson, Sherwood, of Talbot, Chambers, of Cecil, Miller, McLane, Bowie, Tuck, Sprigg, McCubbin, Bowling, Spencer, Grason, Dirickson, McMaster, Fooks, Shriver, Biser, Annan, Sappington, Magraw, Nelson, Hardcastle, Gwinn, Stewart, of Baltimore city, Brent, of Baltimore city, Presstman, Schley, Fiery, Neill, John Newcomer, Harbine, Michael Newcomer, Brewer, Hollyday, Slicer, Parke, Cockey and Brown—52.

Negative.—Messrs. Lee, Chambers, of Kent, Donaldson, Dorsey, Wells, Randall, Kent, Crisfield, Dashiell, Hicks, Hodson, Eccleston, Gaither, McHenry, Davis, Waters, Weber and Smith—18.

So the the nineteenth section was adopted.

Mr. GRASON moved that the Convention proceed to the consideration of the second section, which was passed over on Saturday last in consequence of the absence of the gentleman from Prince George's, (Mr. Sprigg.) The Convention was now as full as he expected it would be during the rest of the week.

Mr. CHAMBERS said that the vote of a full House would be required for the adoption of this section, and unless the House was full, a motion to reconsider would be made after every important question was voted on.

Mr. DORSEY said he had risen to give notice of some amendments which he proposed to offer as additional sections. He did not know what objection the gentleman from Queen Anne's could have to hear them read. He did not care about pressing them now.

Mr. GRASON said he had no objection to hear them.

The PRESIDENT *pro tem.* Does the gentleman offer his amendments now, or only give notice of his intention to offer them hereafter?

Mr. DORSEY said he would rather move them now.

The PRESIDENT *pro tem.* The gentleman from Queen Anne's has precedence.

Mr. GRASON repeated that the House was as full now as it had been for some weeks, or as it may be again. The second section was an important one and many gentleman wished to have it acted on.

Mr. DORSEY read the following amendments which he proposed to offer when he could have the opportunity:

Article. "The Governor shall in no case remit any portion of the principle or interest of any debt due to the State, except in cases of fines and forfeitures."

Art. "It shall be the duty of the Governor semi-annually, and oftener if he deem it expedient, to inspect the bank book, books of accounts, and other proceedings of the treasurer."

Mr. BOWIE hoped the bill would be gone thro' before we go back.

Mr. GRASON was satisfied that the bill would not be gone through in two days. And on Saturday the House will be too thin to take any important vote. He had notified the Convention on Saturday that he would call up this section on Tuesday or Wednesday.

Mr. JENIFER thought it would expedite business to go through the bill first.

Mr. GRASON supposing the gentleman from Charles had not heard him, repeated what he had said.

Mr. SPENCER asked for the ayes and noes on the motion,

And they were ordered.

The question was then taken on the motion of Mr. GRASON,

And decided as follows:

Affirmative—Messrs. Jenifer, Bell, Welch, Dickinson, Sherwood of Talbot, Chambers of Cecil, Spencer, Grason, Shriver, Biser, Sappington, McHenry, Nelson, Hardcastle, Gwinn, Stewart of Baltimore city, Brent of Baltimore city, Ware, Neill, John Newcomer, Harbine, Michael Newcomer, Brewer, Weber, Hollyday, Slicer and Parke—28.

Negative—Messrs. Blakistone, Pres't, *pro. tem.*, Dent, Hopewell, Lee, Chambers of Kent, Donaldson, Dorsey, Wells, Kent, Sellman, Dalrymple, Brent of Charles, Lloyd, Crisfield, Dashiell, Hicks, Hodson, Eccleston, Miller, McLane, Bowie, Tuck, Sprigg, McCubbin, Bowling, Dirickson, McMaster, Fooks, Gaither, Annan, Schley, Fiery, Davis, Kilgour, Waters, Smith, Cockey and Brown—38.

So the Convention refused to take up the second section.

Mr. DORSEY moved to amend the report by inserting the following as the twentieth section.

Section 20. The Governor shall in no case remit any portion of the principal or interest of any debt due to the State, except in cases of fines and forfeitures."

Mr. D. disclaimed any intention to occupy the time of the Convention. The object of the amendment he had now offered was to restrict the Governor from granting releases to collectors, for their neglect of duty in not collecting and paying over public taxes as required by law; the granting of such releases operating as an inducement to collectors as well as tax payers not to pay with the promptitude and punctuality which were essentially necessary. It would also tend to a postponement of the payment of the public debt, and the granting of such a release, was in its effect, to the extent of the sum released, equivalent to a new levy of taxes upon the people.

He hoped that every effort would be made to render the present tax system effective. If the proposition which he now offered were adopted, there would be some reasonable prospect of the payment of the public debt in twelve or fourteen years. But if the proposition were rejected, he could not foresee at what period the debt would be paid.

The question was then put, and

The amendment was adopted as an additional section.

Mr. DORSEY then moved further to amend the report, by inserting the following as the twenty-first section:

"*Section* 21. It shall be the duty of the Governor semi-annually, and oftener if he deem it expedient, to inspect the bank book, books of accounts and other proceedings of the Treasurer."

Mr. D. said, one of the objections made to biennial sessions was, that the treasurer would not be called on to report the state of the treasury as often as he should, and that this might lead to frauds or malversation in office.

The amendment provides that the Governor shall semi-annually inspect the bank book, books of accounts and other proceedings of the treasurer. The duties thus imposed on the Governor were neither inappropriate nor onerous. Nothing then can be done by the treasurer over which the Governor will not exercise a supervision, more effectual than that resulting from annual sessions of the legislature.

The money is deposited in the Farmers' Bank of Maryland, and the Governor will be subjected to no serious inconvenience in the duty now assigned him. And if the treasurer should commit any abuse of his trust it will be detected. The Governor will have sufficient leisure for this inspection, and its exercise would supersede the necessity of appointing a comptroller at a salary of $3,000, as is proposed in the report of the committee on the treasury department. If we are to have a comptroller for the purposes proposed in the report, the treasury must be removed to the city of Baltimore.

The question was then put, and

The amendment was adopted as an additional section.

Mr. TUCK moved to amend the report, by inserting the following as the twenty-second section:

"*Section* 22. Before granting any pardon or *nolle prosequi*, the Governor shall cause such notice as he may deem expedient, by publication in some one or more newspapers, that an application has been made, and that the same will be considered on or after a day to be named in said notice."

Mr. T. defended his proposition in some remarks which will be published hereafter.

The question being put,

The amendment was agreed to.

The twentieth (printed) section being under consideration,

Mr. GRASON said, there was a section in the legislative report, nearly the same in effect as this section. He, therefore, moved to strike out the section.

The motion was agreed to,

And the twentieth section was stricken out.

The twenty-first section being under consideration as follows:

"And the Governor shall reside at the seat of government, in order that he may constantly attend to the duties of his office, and shall receive for his services an annual salary of four thousand dollars."

Mr. DIRICKSON moved to strike out the section, and insert in lieu of, the following:

"*Section* 21. The Governor shall be in attendance at the seat of government during the sessions of the legislature of the State, and shall receive for his services an annual salary of two thousand dollars."

Mr. D made some remarks which will be published hereafter.

Mr. GRASON desired, before the amendment proposed by the gentleman from Worcester was received, to move an amendment, by striking out the following words in the section, "in order that he may constantly attend to the duties of his office."

Mr. JENIFER was opposed to the amendment of the gentleman from Worcester, (Mr. Dirickson.) At the very moment when we have imposed additional duties on the Executive, by requiring him to examine the bank books, and in other respects also, he thought it wrong to reduce his salary. The people have already expressed their approbation of a rate of salary suitable to the dignity of the office and the character of the State. He desired to give to every man a salary in proportion to the importance and value of the office he fills. And it is proposed further that the Governor shall remove his residence from this city. He would warn the gentleman from Worcester against touching Annapolis, endeared as it is to the citizens of this State by its hallowed associations. Let the Governor act as he feels disposed. Give him an adequate salary, and leave him free to do as he will. He was opposed also to the amendment offered by the gentleman from Queen Anne's.

Mr. DORSEY intended to move to amend the substitute of the gentleman from Worcester, by striking out the words "during the sessions of the Legislature of the State," and inserting in lieu thereof the following words, "during the session of the Legislature, and in the recess thereof be in the city of Annapolis, during the first week of every other month of his term."

Mr. D. went into a brief explanation of the duties of the Governor, and stated that they were not such as to require his constant residence at Annapolis.

The question was then put on the amendment offered by Mr. GRASON, and it was adopted.

The question being on the amendment submitted by Mr. DORSEY,

Mr. BISER moved a call of the House. The salary of the Governor was before the Convention, and when it was formerly under consideration he happened to be absent from his seat; and it had given him so much trouble to explain the reason of his absence, that he was desirous to prevent other gentlemen from having the same trouble.

Mr. SPENCER hoped the gentleman from Fredrick would withdraw the motion, as it would only lead to a useless consumption of time.

Mr. BISER said he had shown as little disposition as any one to consume the time of the House by useless notions. He then withdrew his motion.

Mr. SPENCER expressed his hope that the Convention would not specify any particular time when the Governor shall be in Annapolis, and thus leave the inference to be made that it may not be necessary for him to be here at all times.

Mr. DORSEY was of opinion that it is necessary for the Governor to be here, while the Legislature is in session. But in the recess of the Legislature, he did not think it necessary. It is known that he has heretofore occasionally been absent for a week, or perhaps a month, at a time, so that his duties do not compel his constant presence, yet you require him to be here at all times ready to discharge his duties. He has to discharge the functions of his office; and whether he performs the duty here or while he is absent from Annapolis, is of no consequence. It is rather to be preferred, that he should not give hasty opinions and decisions, as soon as business is brought before him; but that he should take a a little time for deliberation, before he replies to applications, and his replies, if he is absent, can be transmitted through the Secretary of State. There have been complaints, that although the Governor may reside here, he is not to be found at the Government house. It is with a view to relieve him from these complaints, and to fix where and when he may be found, that this amendment is offered. He will, perhaps, have fewer duties to attend to after the new Constitution is established. And if he attends here during the first week in every month, after the legislative session terminates, it will be quite sufficient.

Mr. BRENT, of Baltimore city. If a requisition should be made on the Executive by the Governor of another State, is the messenger to be compelled to run all over the State to find him?

Mr. DORSEY. There will be no occasion for that. The mails travel very rapidly. It is not necessary that the Governor should remain here on that account. Sometimes these requisitions call for deliberation, which causes delay. And it often occurs that it is necessary for the Governor to take legal advice upon the subject, and some days may elapse before his opinion can be obtained. He did not think the salary of the Governor should be fixed so high, as to make the office desirable for the sake of the emolument. Therefore he held it to be proper to reduce it.

Mr. GRASON would first consider the question, whether the public interest required the Governor to reside at the seat of government. In the commencement of our government, the Governors lived in Annapolis, but in the course of time, they generally remained at their private residences during the recess of the Legislature. This was the custom till the law of December session, 1837, required the Governor to reside at the seat of government. He then enumerated the various duties of the executive. The mere examination of claims and accounts against the State occupies considerable time. While he [Mr. G.] was in office, no account was paid until it received his examination and approval; and he had no doubt that the investigation and rejection of improper claims, had saved more to the State than the whole amount of his salary. A duty of this kind could not be performed by the Governor if he remained at his own residence during the recess of the Legislature.

Mr. BROWN moved the previous question.

Mr. McHENRY asked for the ayes and noes on the motion, and they were ordered.

Mr. BROWN then withdrew his motion.

Mr. DIRICKSON addressed the Convention. His remarks will be published hereafter.

Mr. BRENT of Baltimore city, was opposed to the introduction of Yankee notions into a Maryland Constitution. This is a Southern State, and he never desired to see her Constitution framed with a view to small economy, but to principles. The gentleman from Worcester says he is a reformer, and he calls on all reformers to unite with him in whittling down the salaries of our public officers. But he would tell the gentleman from Worcester, that the people of Maryland want no *penny wise* policy. The issue presented, is non-residence at Annapolis, and low salary, or residence and fair salary; whether the public duties shall be neglected at a small cost, or whether they shall be faithfully performed for adequate compensation. He would suppose that his friend from Worcester should some day be clothed with this honor, and a murder, startling the whole community, like that recently committed in Kent county, had taken place, and it was necessary that a reward should be offered for the detection of the murderer without delay, would he like that the messenger from Kent county should be hunting for him among his friends in Worcester, to issue the proclamation, and in the mean time the murderer should make his escape? Or, if a requisition should be made on him by the Governor of another State, would it be proper to be running all through the State to find the Governor, before any step could be taken? And as he understood the proposition of the gentleman from Worcester, it was to reduce the salary of the Governor to two thousand dollars. Where would the gentleman from Worcester find a competent person to take the labor and responsibility of the office for that sum? He hoped no such proposition would find favor with the Convention.

Mr. DIRICKSON said it would be the very way to get a fit person to take the office.

Mr. SOLLERS did not approve such notions as

those thrown out, by the gentleman from Worcester, who stands forward here as the friend of the sovereign people, a large portion of whom are poor. In England, where the institutions are aristocratic, and where the wealthy only obtain public employments, it may be very proper to cut down salaries. But here the very object of giving salaries sufficient to support those who are in office, is to prevent the poor from being excluded.

Mr. DIRICKSON asked whether two thousand dollars, and a residence wherever the home of the Governor may be, is not equal to four thousand dollars, and a residence during the whole year in Annapolis.

Mr. SOLLERS resumed. The people ask for no such reduction of salary. Let the gentleman take off the two thousand dollars from the salary, and how far would it relieve the people of the State of their burdens? How much would it diminish the annual taxation? Something is due to the dignity and character of the State. It was an expression of public sentiment which caused the salary to be raised.

The gentleman from Worcester said, that, in his county the people asked for a reduction of the salaries of public officers. In my county, (said Mr. S.,) not a man desires it.

Mr. BUCHANAN desired to say but three words to put himself on the record. It was clear to him that the Governor of Maryland ought to reside at Annapolis—that he ought to be a gentle man, and that he should receive a salary sufficient to support the dignity of the office. Admitting all these propositions, he should go for the highest salary.

Some further remarks were made by Messrs. SOLLERS and FIERY at a late hour.

Mr. DIRICKSON briefly explained.

Mr. KILGOUR moved that the Convention adjourn.

The motion was decided in the negative, when

On motion of Mr. MAGRAW,

The Convention adjourned.

THURSDAY, March 13, 1851.

The Convention met at ten o'clock.

Prayer by the Rev. Mr. GRAUFF.

The journal of proceedings of yesterday, was read and approved.

The SECRETARY announced that Messrs. BRENT, of Charles, and CRISFIELD, were appointed members of the special committee ordered on yesterday in relation to doorkeepers, in the room of Messrs. DIRICKSON and ANNAN, who had been excused from serving.

EXECUTIVE DEPARTMENT.

The Convention resumed the order of the day, being the report on the executive department.

The twenty-first section of the printed report being under consideration, and the question being on the motion of Mr. DORSEY, to amend the amendment to the section submitted by Mr. DIRICKSON, by striking out "during the sessions of the legislature of the State," and inserting in lieu thereof, the following:

"During the session of the legislature, and in the recess thereof, be in the city of Annapolis, during the first week of every other month of his term."

Mr. STEWART, of Baltimore city, moved a call of the House;

Which was ordered.

Pending said call,

Mr. DORSEY withdrew his amendment.

Mr. FIERY moved to suspend all further proceedings under the call,

But the motion was decided in the negative.

The PRESIDENT, *pro. tem.*, informed the Convention that the doorkeepers had returned, and reported that they had notified the absent members.

The question then recurred on the amendment submitted by Mr DIRICKSON.

Mr. PHELPS asked for a division of the amendment, and that the vote be first taken on inserting these words, "the Governor shall be in attendance at the seat of government during the sessions of the legislature of the State."

Mr. DIRICKSON asked for the ayes and noes on both branches,

And they were ordered accordingly.

Mr. PHELPS withdrew his motion for a division of the amendment.

Mr. DIRICKSON renewed the motion.

The question was then taken on the first branch of the amendment.

And it was decided as follows:

Affirmative.—Messrs. Lee, Dorsey, Dalrymple, Bell, Lloyd, Dickinson, Sherwood, of Talbot, Crisfield, Dashiell, Eccleston, Dirickson, McMaster, Fooks, Gaither, Sappington, Nelson, Carter, Hardcastle, Schley, Fiery, John Newcomer, Harbine, Davis, Brewer, Slicer, Smith, Cockey and Brown—28.

Negative.—Messrs. Blakistone, President, *pro tem.*, Dent, Hopewell, Chambers, of Kent, Mitchell, Donaldson, Wells Randall, Kent, Sellman, Sollers, Brent, of Charles, Buchanan, Welch, Chandler, Williams, Hicks, Hodson, Phelps, Chambers, of Cecil, Miller, McLane, Bowie, Tuck, Grason, Shriver, Biser, McHenry, Magraw, Gwinn, Stewart, of Baltimore city, Presstman, Ware, Kilgour, Waters, Weber, Hollyday and Parke—37.

So the first branch of the amendment was rejected.

The question then recurring on the second branch of the amendment, as follows:

"And shall receive for his services an annual salary of two thousand dollars,"

Mr. CRISFIELD asked if it was not a motion to strike out and amend?

The PRESIDENT, *pro tem.* It is.

Mr. CRISFIELD then asked for a division of the question, so that it may be first taken on striking out.

Mr. MITCHELL wished to give a reason for his vote. He came here with a view to the retrenchment of unnecessary expenditures. He was a reformer. He had heard it said that the first gentleman in the United States is Millard Fillmore Now he wished to make the Governor of Maryland a gentleman of the first class. He would therefore give him a high salary that he may be so.

Mr. DIRICKSON withdrew the second branch of his amendment, and moved to amend the twenty-first section by striking out the words "four thousand," and inserting in lieu of them, the words "two thousand."

Mr. CRISFIELD asked for a division of the question and that it be first taken on striking out.

Mr. DORSEY moved to amend the twenty-first section by inserting after the word "government," in the first line, the following words, "during the sessions of the General Assembly, and in the recess thereof, shall be in the city of Annapolis during the first week of every other month of his term."

Mr. JENIFER said it would be necessary, he presumed, in order to comply with this provision, that the Governor should carry a reporter about with him to make a record and report of all his movements.

Mr. DORSEY replied that the amendment gives public notice of the times at which it is the duty of the Governor to be at the seat of government. It did not appear to him to be necessary that the Governor should always reside at the seat of government. From the foundation of our State government in 1776 until 1836, he was not compelled to have his residence here. But in the year 1836, this new duty was unnecessarily imposed on him. The Governor needs not to be always at Annapolis. He did not wish, in the least degree to detract from the manner in which the gentleman from Queen Anne's, (Mr. Grason,) had performed his duty while he was Governor. But the executive chamber was a warm, comfortable room, well supplied with the newspapers, books and documents, and had always a good fire in it, and he thought that the walk to it every morning was but necessary exercise, and to sit there a few hours daily, was no great sacrifice, and that the daily visits to it by the Governor, would have been paid if business did not require them. As to what was said by the gentleman from Baltimore about the murder in Kent county, he, (Mr. D.,) thought the delay and trouble of getting a proclamation issued might be as great, in cases of this kind, if the Governor, though required to reside here constantly, but is occasionally absent, or if he is only here at stated intervals. He knew it was the opinion of some that the Governor should be always on the spot. But what would be the great inconvenience if the business was sent, or persons had to go, to Frederick, where the home of the present Governor is, or to Easton, where the ex-Governor lived. The only object is, that the people might know where he is to be found, then no inconvenience can result.

It is said there are many accounts which require to be examined daily. This statement, he apprehended, must be received with many grains of allowance, nor are they so numerous as to make it necessary to give an increased salary, and to require a constant residence here, in order that the Governor may be enabled to perform this duty. He could not understand what great number of accounts there could be. There can be no money drawn from the treasury, unless it has been previously appropriated by law, and if the Governor has other accounts to pay, which are not the subjects of specific appropriation, but are paid out of the contingent fund—the fewer they are the better. But if there are these accounts to settle, it is better that they should not be paid too hastily; but that they should be subjected to as much delay as is necessary for their full and deliberate examination. Applications, in the absence of the Governor, may be always sent to the Secretary of State, or may be forwarded to the Governor himself, and he can direct the Secretary of State to pay attention to them. And as to the individual who traveled from Allegany bare-footed to see the Governor, there would be no new difficulty thown, in the way of such persons, by the adoption of this amendment, which would only require of the person a change in the time, or direction of his journey.

In relation to the public debt, he desired to say, that from information which had come to his knowledge since that subject was discussed here, he had reason to believe that the debt will not be paid off so soon as some gentlemen seem to have imagined Their calculations were based on the assumption, that the debt could be all bought up at par. But the gentleman from Carroll, told us that the debt could only be purchased at a premium, and such was unquestionably the fact. In that case the money in the treasury will not be sufficient to pay the debt at the time anticipated. And if we, with this fact before our eyes, sitting here as a Convention to form a Constitution, increase the salaries of our public officers, we shall still further protect the payment of the debt. He had about as much southern feeling as he desired to have, but he had no wish to expend the public money, for the mere purpose of showing our ostentatious hospitality. If the Governor thinks it proper to give entertainments, he can pay for them out of his salary. But it would be wrong for this Convention, by sanctioning this practice, to hold out encouragement to extravagance. He liked to see the Governor hospitable; and he had no doubt that his friends from Baltimore, where money was plentiful, and he supposed easily acquired, as a thousand dollars was no more thought of than as many cents are in the country, would be ready enough to vote him the largest salary, as the means of keeping up expensive hospitalities. But it ought to be remembered, that throughout the country, at present, there is a great amount of poverty and distress. He did not know, if salaries were to be increased, why the increase should be confined to the Governor. The judges have as good a claim to share in the benefit of the operation. The judges of the courts of appeals have far more incessant labor to endure—more responsible duties to perform. For every thing that could elevate the value of their services, their claims to adequate salary, are not inferior to those of your Governors, yet the clamor of your self-sacrificing, patriotic electioneering politicians, has been that the expense of your judiciary is inexordinately high and ought to be reduced for the sake of the "dear people."

The Legislature are the peculiar guardians of the public purse. They come here biennially from the people, and return to them again, for the most part for re-election. They bring with them the views and wishes of the people, and return to them responsible for their conduct. We, on the other hand, never expect to come here to another Convention; therefore we stand, in a measure, independent of and not responsible to the people. He would rather leave it to the Legislature to fix the amount of salaries. The salary of the Governor was raised by the Legislature to $4200. But afterwards, when the attention of the people was called to the subject, it was reduced to the sum of $3000. For aught that he knew, it might be the wish of the people that it should so remain, and to them only belongs the right to change it. He was disposed, therefore, to leave the salary to be fixed by the Legislature, who were far more economical and mindful of the wishes and interests of the people, than this Convention, of which he had the honor to be a member.

In reply to the disparaging remarks made of the New England States. Mr. D. spoke in terms of the highest eulogy of the condition of the New England States, and described the impressions made upon him, by an observance of their wealth, their superior intellectual acquirements, their refinement and habits mingled with a system of economy, their morality, their commercial enterprize their system of common schools and the immense number of their churches, in 1807, when he traveled through that country on horseback, for the benefit of his health; and during his slow and entire journey, from Marblehead to Baltimore, he never saw a drunken man, and gave his opinion that the people there were in advance of us in intelligence, in morality, and in all the conveniences and comforts of life at least—being a century ahead of the people of the South, and even of those of old Maryland.

Mr. SOLLERS asked if this happy condition of New England, resulted from the abolition of slavery?

Mr. DORSEY said he believed not.

Mr. SOLLERS. The northern people say so.

Mr. DORSEY supposed that the gentleman from Calvert, did not intend to endorse all northern opinions. He then proceeded to remark on the attacks which had been made on the judiciary, on account of their extravagance. He had heard that a distinguished politician on the Eastern Shore, had declared that five hundred dollars was salary enough for any man. He had heard that a gentleman, a member of this body, not very far from him, had asserted that the judges are now paid too much. We shall make a bad beginning of our reforms, if we raise the salary of the Governor. It may be, however, that he is entitled to it, if it be true, as is said of him here, that he represents the people of Maryland, more fully than the General Assembly. He was against trusting to much power in the hands of a single individual, or idolatrously worshiping or eulogising him because he was Governor, or for the purpose of obtaining an office. He would much rather trust to the General Assembly, the fixing of the salaries of all public officers. He thought that under his amendment, the Governor may live more economically, and that we may obtain better men, who will consent to take the office when they are not bound to live during the whole term in this city. As the sessions of the Legislature are not to extend beyond sixty days, the Governor will not be compelled to be in Annapolis but a short time, and therefore his salary may be reduced below what it is in the report, without injury to him.

Mr. BROWN said, that he had never heard the salaries of the judges complained of. He had been attacked for voting to raise the salary of the Governor; and a person had come to him, and offered to do it for $1600 a year. The people of his county did not wish to interfere with the salaries of the judges. Their desires ran in another direction. They only asked that the judges may be elected by the people. They were opposed, as he was, to all life offices.

Mr. DORSEY said if the people of Carroll were not sensitive, at the time the gentleman referred to, on the subject of the salaries of the judges, they have become so since, if the information he had on the subject was correct.

Mr GRASON would state the reasons which induced the committee to fix the salary of the Governor at four thousand dollars. He had yesterday spoken of the necessity for the residence of the Governor at Annapolis. The gentleman from Anne Arundel has replied, and he, (Mr. G.,) would say a few words in answer to what had been said by that gentleman Formerly, in consequence of the continued absence of the Governor, a steward was employed, at a salary of two hundred dollars, to take charge of the Governor's house and furniture. But notwithstanding this, it was found that many things were lost in consequence of the negligence of the steward or the depredations of other persons. On this account, as much would be lost by the absence of the Governor as would be saved by a reduction of his salary. It was admitted by all, that the salary ought to be sufficient for the dignity of the station. The committee wished to allow a liberal compensation, not for the purpose of encouraging extravagance, as many supposed, but to enable the Governor to pass through his term of office without impairing his private resources. The salaries in Wisconsin and Indiana had been referred to as the proper standard, but what might be sufficient in those remote States, where living was cheap, would be inadequate in Maryland, where it had always been the custom to extend the hospitality of the Government House to visiters from every part of the State as well as from foreign countries. This custom has existed too long to be disregarded; and if the gentleman from Washington, who wishes to reduce the salary to $2000, were placed in the executive chair, he would find it impossible to resist the example of his predecessors. No Governor can save any thing out of his salary. Whatever he receives, is distributed in some form or other among the people of the State. But the gentleman from Anne Arundel complains of the heavy taxes under which the people are suffering, and desires to relieve them from their burdens by taking away a part of the Governor's salary. This would, indeed, afford considerable relief, as it would appear, by an accurate calculation, that each tax payer would save annually at least one-fifth of a cent. But a few weeks ago, the gentleman viewed our system of taxation in a different light. He then described the prosperity of the State in glowing colors; and spoke of the alacrity with which the people of every county, and especially of his own district, paid their taxes; and of the regret they would feel at any reduction of their burdens till the public debt was entirely extinguished. The gentleman compares the salaries of the executive and judges, and, of course, is of opinion, that the superior abilities of the latter entitle them to a higher compensation. Admitting this superiority, in deference to the gentleman from Anne Arundel, it must be remembered that judges have been appointed for life, and have never been under the necessity of increasing their expenses, or changing their residence; whereas the Governor is elected for a short time, and subjected to great additional expenses, which do not always cease with a termination of his salary. And what, after all, is a salary of $4000. The clerks of many of the counties receive as large a compensation, and the cashiers of banks half as much, without being under the necessity of increasing their expenses or neglecting their private business. Why, then, should we reduce the compensation of the Governor, whose salary is expended in hospitality, while the profits of other offices are added to the private fortune of the incumbents. The Governor of Maryland is exposed to an expense, from which the Governors of other States are exempt. Ships of our own navy, as well as foreign vessels of war, frequently anchor in Annapolis roads; and whatever might be the opinion of members, the people of the State expected the hospitality of the State to be exercised on every such occasion, and that the Governor should incur the necessary expense. The gentleman from Calvert, (Mr. Sollers,) had clearly shown, that a material reduction of the salary would exclude men of limited means from the office. The proposition to reduce the salary to $2000, ought to be entitled a bill to prevent a man, without a fortune, from being Governor of the State.

Mr. Phelps vindicated the part of the Eastern Shore, which he represented from the charge of desiring to establish the doctrine that five hundred dollars was a sufficiently high salary for any public officer. He and his colleagues were in favor of the reduction of the number of officers, but they were equally in favor of giving sufficient compensation to those who were necessary.

Mr. Tuck would not prolong the discussion. He believed that the opinion of the Convention was that the salary of the Governor should be liberal, and that he should reside in Annapolis. He moved the previous question.

Mr. Chambers requested the gentleman from Prince Georges to withdraw the motion for a moment to enable him to offer an amendment.

Mr. Tuck waived the motion for the moment.

Mr. Chambers then moved to amend the section by striking out "four thousand," and inserting in lieu thereof "thirty-six hundred."

The previous question was then seconded.

The question being on the first branch of the amendment on striking out,

Mr. Sappington called for the ayes and noes on the question, and they were ordered.

The question was then put on striking out, and decided as follows:

Affirmative—Messrs. Dent, Lee, Chambers, of Kent, Dorsey, Dalrymple, Brent, of Charles, Lloyd, Dickinson, Sherwood, of Talbot, Crisfield, Dashiell, Williams, Eccleston, Phelps, Dirickson, McMaster, Fooks, Shriver, Gaither, Biser, Sappington, Nelson, Carter, Hardcastle, Schley, Fiery, John Newcomer, Harbine, Davis, Brewer, Weber, Slicer, Smith, Parke, Shower and Cockey—35.

Negative—Messrs. Blakistone, President, *pro tem.*, Hopewell, Mitchell, Donaldson, Wells, Randall, Kent, Sellman, Weems, Sollers, Jenifer, Buchanan, Bell, Welch, Chandler, Hicks, Hodson, Chambers, of Cecil, Bowie, Tuck, Grason, McHenry, Magraw, Gwinn, Stewart, of Baltimore city, Brent, of Baltimore city, Presstman, Ware, Kilgour, Waters, Hollyday and Brown—32.

So the motion to strike out was agreed to.

The question was then put on the motion of Mr. Chambers to insert $3,600, and it was decided as follows:

Affirmative—Messrs. Blakistone, President, *pro tem.*, Dent, Hopewell, Chambers, of Kent, Mitchell, Donaldson, Wells, Randall, Kent, Sellman, Weems, Sollers, Brent, of Charles, Jenifer, Buchanan, Bell, Welch, Chandler, Lloyd, Dickinson, Sherwood, of Talbot, Hicks, Hodson, Phelps, Chambers, of Cecil, Miller, Bowie, Tuck, Grason, Shriver, Biser, McHenry, Magraw, Gwinn, Stewart, of Baltimore city, Brent, of Baltimore city, Presstman, Ware, Kilgour, Brewer, Waters, Hollyday and Brown—43.

Negative—Messrs. Lee, Dorsey, Dalrymple, Crisfield, Dashiell, Williams, Eccleston, Dirickson, McMaster, Fooks, Gaither, Sappington, Nelson, Carter, Hardcastle, Schley, Fiery, John Newcomer, Harbine, Davis, Weber, Slicer, Smith, Parke, Shower and Cockey—26.

So the blank was filled with "thirty-six hundred"

The question then being on the adoption of the section as amended,

Mr. Dirickson asked for the ayes and noes on the question, and they were ordered.

The question was then taken and decided as follows:

Affirmative—Messrs. Blakistone, President, *pro tem.*, Dent, Hopewell, Chambers, of Kent, Mitchell, Donaldson, Wells, Randall, Kent, Sellman, Weems, Sollers, Brent, of Charles, Jenifer, Buchanan, Bell, Welch, Chandler, Lloyd, Dickinson, Sherwood, of Talbot, Crisfield, Williams, Hicks, Hodson, Phelps, Chambers, of Cecil, Miller, Bowie, Tuck, Grason, Shriver, Biser, McHenry, Magraw, Gwinn, Stewart, of Baltimore city, Brent, of Baltimore city, Presstman, Ware, Kilgour, Brewer, Waters, Hollyday and Brown —45.

Negative—Messrs. Lee, Dorsey, Dashiell, Eccleston, Dirickson, McMaster, Fooks, Gaither, Sappington, Nelson, Carter, Hardcastle, Schley, Fiery, John Newcomer, Harbine, Weber, Slicer, Smith, Parke, Shower and Cockey—22.

So the 21st section as amended was adopted.

Mr. Dorsey moved to reconsider the vote just taken, for the purpose of moving to amend the section as follows—to strike out in the third line, an annual salary of "thirty-six hundred dollars," and insert in lieu thereof the following words: "as shall hereafter be prescribed by the Legislature."

Mr. Davis said, he felt no particular interest in the exact amount at which the Governor's salary might be fixed, but it seemed there were gentlemen now occupying high positions in the State, who had felt an interest in the subject—whose aspirations and success showed that they had felt an interest in it—and who had taken occasion to place upon record their opinion as to what the exact amount ought to be. He held in his hand the Journal of the House of Delegates of December session, 1845, at which time Mr. Lowe, the present Governor of Maryland, was a member from Frederick county.

Mr. McHenry called Mr. Davis to order.

Mr. Davis. The gentleman from Harford will please to reduce his point of order to writing.

Some conversation followed, and

While Mr. McHenry was reducing his point of order to writing, the chair decided Mr. Davis to be in order.

Mr. Davis resumed: All he had proposed to do, he said, when interrupted, was to read from page 327 of the Journal of the House of Delegates where it would be seen, the report from the Committee on Retrenchment being under consideration, and the question being upon the section fixing the Governor's salary, that Mr. Lowe moved to strike out 3000 and insert 2000. The question was taken by ayes and noes, and resulted as follows: Ayes 53, noes 21—Mr. Lowe voting in the affirmative. At a subsequent period of the consideration of that report, the section fixing the salary of the Secretary of State being under consideration, Mr. Lowe moved to strick out 1200 dollars and insert 1000—determined in the affirmative. So it seemed that Mr. Lowe, who doubtless then looked forward to the Gubernatorial chair, which he now fills, thought that 2000 dollars was a sufficient salary for the Governor of Maryland, and 1000 dollars enough for the Secretary of State.

He (Mr. D.) had only risen to present this recorded evidence of the opinion of the present Governor of Maryland, which certainly ought to be entitled to some weight; and he commended it to his friends, who now thought that the salary of the Governor ought to be fixed at 4000 dollars, and the salary of the Secretary of State at 1500 dollars. He would not further occupy the time of the Convention.

Mr. Dorsey did not think this a proper tribunal to fix the compensation for the Governor. It was a fit subject for the Legislature to act on. He thought that the sum now fixed was excessive. The gentleman from Queen Anne's [Mr. Grason] had stated that a good deal of public property had been taken away from the Government House when in charge of the steward, by visiters in the absence of the Governor and his family. If so, that was the fault of the Governor. He ought to have selected a more vigilant steward, who would have taken more care of the property. We ought not to set up the Government House as a palace open to public inspection; and the Governor should have placed the charge of the property in more faithful hands. The people would not be willing to pay a negligent steward, nor a Governor who neglected his duty. He did not think the Government House, in the absence of the Governor and his family, ought to be thrown open to visiters to inspect it, and as is alleged, abstract or destroy its furniture. The gentleman from Queen Anne's also says that he took great care of the public property and plate, and handed it over to his successor. But it ought to be known that in most cases, either from wear and tear, or from some other cause, it passed into the hands of the successor in a worse condition than if it had even passed through the hands of the steward. And the accounts of the Treasurer will show that the appropriations for furnishing the Government House have been larger since the Governor has been compelled to reside here, than they were before. It appeared, therefore, that the residence of the Governor here had increased, not diminished, the appropriations after every new election of a Governor.

Mr. Shriver asked what the course of Mr. Lowe in 1845, had to do with the question before that Convention?

Mr Dorsey said, that as the legislature have had the power to raise the salary of the Governor, they ought also to have the power to reduce it. Ought they not to have the power to diminish it? He thought the vote should be reconsidered that the matter may be left to the legislature.

Mr. Grason said, he had voted for the $4,000, and he had also voted for $3,600. The legislature could not raise or diminish the salary after this provision shall have gone into operation. We have provided that members of the legislature shall receive four dollars a day. He thought it better that the provision should remain as it is.

Mr. DORSEY asked for the ayes and noes on the motion to reconsider,

And they were ordered.

Mr. SMITH gave notice that he would move hereafter to reconsider the vote by which this section was adopted, for the purpose of taking the sense of a full House as to the reduction of the Governor's salary.

The question was then taken on the motion to reconsider,

And decided as follows:

Affirmative—Messrs. Lee, Dorsey, Crisfield, Dashiell, Eccleston, Dirickson, McMaster, Fooks, Gaither, Sappington, Nelson, Carter, Hardcastle, Schley, Fiery, John Newcomer, Harbine, Davis, Smith, Parke, Shower and Cockey—22.

Negative—Messrs. Blakistone, Pres't, *pro. tem.*, Dent, Chambers of Kent, Donaldson, Wells, Sellman, Brent of Charles, Jenifer, Howard, Buchanan, Bell, Welch, Chandler, Lloyd, Dickinson, Sherwood of Talbot, Williams, Hicks, Hodson, Phelps, Chambers of Cecil, Miller, McLane, Bowie, Tuck, Grason, Shriver, Biser, McHenry, Gwinn, Stewart of Baltimore city, Brent of Baltimore city, Kilgour Brewer, Waters, Weber, Hollyday, Slicer and Brown—38.

So the Convention refused to reconsider the vote.

Mr. BRENT, of Baltimore city, gave notice that he should on to-morrow move to reconsider the thirteenth section of the report, for the purpose of correcting an omission.

He called the attention particularly of the gentleman from Somerset, (Mr. Crisfield,) on whose motion the section had been amended, to its present defective condition, in consequence of which, the Governor would be without the power of appointing, during the recess, certain officers whose services were indispensible for the public convenience.

There were numerous applications before the Governor for appointment out of the State of Maryland, to take the acknowledgment of deeds; some of these were from California, and it was important that such appointments should be made. But as these are considered by the Governor who is a strict constructionist, to be new offices, he feels himself debarred by the terms of the existing Constitution from making the appointments. The Governor has also the power to appoint in his discretion, twenty auctioneers in Baltimore, and these are biennial appointments. But if twelve of these should be appointed, and the thirteenth is to be appointed during the recess, with his construction that this thirteenth is a new appointment, the Governor will be restrained from making it.

The public interests, therefore, require some modification of this section. He would, therefore, give notice of his intention to move a reconsideration of the thirteenth section for the purpose of moving the following substitute. As the Constitution now stands, not one of the applications before the Governor can be complied with, and this amendment will supply the *casus omissus*.

The substitute was read as follows:

"In all cases where the Governor has the power by the Constitution or laws to make any appointment to office, or in case any vacancy shall occur during the recess of the Senate, in any office to which the Governor has the power of appointment, he shall have power in the recess of the Senate to make such appointment or fill such vacancy, by granting a commission which shall expire upon the appointment of the same person or any other person by and with the advice and consent of the Senate, to the same office, or at the expiration of one calendar month ensuing the commencement of the next regular session of the legislature which ever shall first occur."

Mr. CRISFIELD made some remarks, which will be published hereafter.

The twenty-second section was then read, when

Mr. DORSEY moved to amend the section by adding at the end thereof, the words, "before his appointment."

Mr DORSEY said, the salary ought to be fixed before the appointment; otherwise, party feelings and prejudices may influence the appointment. He thought, therefore, that the legislature ought to fix the salary before they make the appointment.

Mr. CHAMBERS. It would be better to do it now.

Mr. DORSEY. I have no objection.

Mr. CHAMBERS then moved to amend the section by striking out in the fifth line, the words, "such annual compensation as may be fixed by the legislature," and inserting in lieu thereof, these words, "one thousand dollars"

Mr. JENIFER moved twelve hundred dollars.

Mr. GRASON said:

The salary had not been fixed because the committee could not tell who might fill the office. If he was a single man, eight hundred or a thousand dollars might be sufficient. If he was a lawyer with a family, it would not be enough. If we fix the amount in the Constitution, it cannot be changed, and we may thus debar men of respectability from accepting it.

Mr. DIRICKSON said, after this question was disposed of, he intended to move to strike out the whole section.

Mr. PARKE asked for a division of the question, and that it may be first taken on striking out.

The question was then put on the motion to strike out,

And it was agreed to.

The question recurring on the motion of Mr. CHAMBERS.

Mr. McHENRY moved fifteen hundred dollars.

Mr. DORSEY asked what was the present salary as fixed by law?

Mr. BOWIE. One thousand dollars.

Mr. GRASON said the clerk of the council who formerly performed the duties that are now assigned to the Secretary of State, received fifteen hundred dollars a year, besides the perquisites of his office, which increased his annual compensation to about two thousand dollars. The Secretary of State at first received a salary of two thousand dollars, which was afterwards reduced to one thousand dollars. He thought that less than fifteen hundred dollars would not be sufficient to induce a competent person, with a family, to accept the appointment. Other public officers, who have lighter duties to perform, receive a higher rate of compensation. By fixing the salary at one thousand dollars, a competent person will be prevented from filling the office.

Mr. JENIFER entirely agreed with the gentleman from Queen Anne's, that it will be impossible to fi d a competent man here all the year, without giving him an adequate salary. He would, hereafter, have additional duties to perform, and he ought to be properly paid. He would withdraw his motion to insert twelve hundred and would vote for fifteen hundred dollars.

Mr. CHAMBERS had no wish to be illiberal. He was not a Governor, never was Governor, and was never likely to be Governor. He knew no more of these matters than he learned from the laws prescribing the duties of the Secretary, but he was not aware of any very important or responsible duties which devolved upon him.

Mr. JENIFER interrupted. Keeper of the records.

Mr. CHAMBERS. By the Constitution as amended in 1836, the Secretary of State would succeed the Governor in the event of a vacancy during the recess of the Legislature, but now it will not be so, and he is but the keeper of the records The present salary is one thousand dollars, and no difficulty had been found in obtaining the services of competent persons. The duties of the office did not materially interfere with the pursuit of professional or other duties. Why then this increase?

He was an advocate for liberal but not profuse salaries. A vast deal had been heard about reform and *retrenchment*, but he found, when a practical occasion arose here, he was about as near the mark as those who claimed to be *par excellence*, the *elite* of this retrenchment party. He did not mean those who preferred such claims here, but out of doors it was quite a different affair to play this game before the dear people, quite another to act it out in this Convention.

As to the duties of the Governor, which he might get the Secretary to perform for him, he would only remark, that the Governor's salary was designed as a fair compensation for all his duties, and if he chose to relieve himself of any portion of them by putting them on the Secretary, it would be a proper subject of arrangement and contract. If he performs a part of the Governor's duties, let the Governor pay him a part of his salary. The State is not to pay twice for it.

Mr. JENIFER put an interrogatory to the gentleman from Kent, (Mr. Chambers,) which, with the reply, could not be heard.

Mr. GRASON said that any one acquainted with the facts, knows that there are many duties which the Governor is not required to perform. This officer is not the Governor's secretary, but the Secretary of the State. He, (Mr G.,) could not undertake to enumerate all the duties which he had to perform, but he knew that they were numerous and important. He was satisfied that the gentleman from Kent was disposed to give a proper salary, and that he would, on a little reflection, be willing to allow more than a thousand dollars. The Secretary of State was obliged to live here. When he, (Mr. G.,) came into the office of Governor, the salary of the Secretary of State was two thousand dollars. And with that salary, Mr. Cornelius McLane, one of the most competent men in the State, was willing to accept it; but if the compensation were fixed at one thousand dollars, he believed the office would be generally held by incompetent persons.

Mr. CHAMBERS desired to ask the gentleman from Queen Anne's a single question. Was it not formerly the practice to charge a fee on every military commission which issued from the Governor? And when copies of records are required, is not a fee demanded for the copies?

Mr. GRASON replied that when he was in office, no charge was made for copying papers or for issuing commissions.

Mr. DASHIELL stated that when it was in order he intended to move a substitute for the section.

Mr. DORSEY said the Secretary ought to be the confidental friend of the Governor. The gentleman from Queen Anne's had not stated the present emoluments of the office The gentleman from Kent, thinks there are none but those arising from military commissions. He did not know how that was. But he knew there was no difficulty in getting a Secretary of State. But if we are to look for a distinguished man who would take the office on the calculation of a contingency by which he might become Governor, we shall not be very likely to find one. He knew the gentleman who filled the office, was fully competent. He is a surveyor in Frederick county, of high reputation for his intell igence and business habits. The duties of the office do not entirely prevent the Secretary from pursuing any other avocation. He can practice law, and he, (Mr. D.,) knew that this had been done. We have had very good Secretaries for a thousand dollars; and he thought the duties of the office would hereafter be less, unless the Governor inappropriately impose some of his own duties upon the Secretary. He will indeed be a mere clerk to the Governor. We can get just as good an officer for one thousand dollars, as we can for fifteen hundred dollars; and if he ever becomes Governor, he will receive the Governor's salary. The State is still struggling with the weight of her public debt, and there is no necessity to give a higher salary. He thought it ought to be fixed at a thousand dollars.

Mr. LEE asked for the ayes and noes on the motion of Mr. McHENRY, and they were ordered.

The question was then put on the motion of Mr. McHENRY, to insert $1500, and it was decided as follows:

Affirmative — Messrs. Wells, Randall, Kent, Sollers, Jenifer, Howard, Buchanan, Hicks, Hodson, Grason, McHenry, Magraw, Brent of Baltimore city, Presstman, Ware, Kilgour and Hollyday—17.

Negative—Messrs. Blakistone, President, *pro tem.*, Dent, Lee, Chambers of Kent, Donaldson, Dorsey, Sellman, Weems, Brent of Charles, Lloyd, Dickinson, Sherwood of Talbot, Crisfield, Dashiell, Williams, Eccleston, Phelps. Chambers of Cecil, Miller, McLane, Bowie, Tuck, Dirickson, McMaster, Fooks, Gaither, Biser, Sappington, Nelson, Carter, Hardcastle, Gwinn, Schley, Fiery, John Newcomer Harbine, Davis, Brewer, Waters, Weber, Slicer, Smith, Clarke, Shower, Cockey and Brown—47.

So the Convention refused to insert "fifteen hundred dollars."

The question being then on Mr. JENIFER's motion to insert $1200.

Mr. LEE asked for the ayes and noes on the question, and they were ordered.

The question was then taken on Mr. JENIFER's motion, and decided as follows:

Affirmative—Messrs. Donaldson, Wells, Randall, Kent, Sellman, Weems, Sollers, Brent of Charles, Jenifer, Howard, Buchanan, Welch, Hicks, Hodson, Miller, Bowie, Tuck, Grason, Biser, McHenry, Magraw, Gwinn, Brent of Baltimore city, Presstman, Ware, Kilgour and Hollyday—27.

Negative—Messrs. Blakistone, President, *pro tem*, Dent, Lee, Chambers of Kent, Dorsey, Bell, Lloyd. Dickinson, Sherwood of Talbot, Crisfield, Dashiell, Williams, Eccleston, Phelps, McLane, Dirickson, McMaster, Fooks, Shriver, Gaither, Sappington, Nelson, Carter, Schley, Fiery, John Newcomer, Harbine, Davis, Brewer, Waters, Weber, Slicer, Smith, Parke, Shower, Cockey and Brown—37.

So the Convention refused to insert "twelve hundred dollars."

Mr. JOHN NEWCOMER moved to insert "eight hundred dollars."

The question was first taken on the motion of Mr. CHAMBERS to insert "one thousand dollars," and it was agreed to.

Mr. BOWIE moved to amend the section so as to make it read "a Secretary," instead of "a Secretary of State."

He stated that in 1836 when the Secretary of State was created, it was provided that in case of a vacancy in the Gubernatorial chair by death or otherwise the Secretary of State shall act as Governor, until a Governor shall be appointed. He is now merely a recording Clerk, and as we have now cut him down to that, it will be but proper to call him by his right name.

Mr. CHAMBERS suggested that it was necessary to retain the name, as papers going abroad must in some cases, have the attestation of the Secretary of State. Secretary and Clerk are ordinary terms, but the Secretary of State is an officer, whose name signifies that he is attached to the Government. It would appear that the motion is intended as a reflection on the course of the Convention in fixing the salary too low. But the Convention thought differently.

Mr. JENIFER. If he is not Secretary, he will no longer be responsible to the State, but only to the Governor.

Mr. GRASON. If the salary is insufficient, the title should be left to make up the deficiency.

Mr. BOWIE. Very well. I withdraw the motion.

Mr. DASHIELL moved to amend by striking out the 22d section, and inserting the following as a substitute:

"The Secretary of State shall be elected by the qualified voters of the whole State, at the same time the Governor shall be elected, and his term of office shall be the same as for Governor, and his salary shall be one thousand dollars per annum."

Mr. DASHIELL said the Secretary of State was an important officer of the State of Maryland.—We have voted him a thousand dollars a year. According to the theory of the reformers, of whom he claimed to be one, every public officer should be elected by the people, from the Governor downwards. The Secretary of State is in the confidence of the Governor, and stands in the place of a Lieutenant Governor. He occupies an important position, and ought to be elected by the people. He would ask that the question on his motion should be taken by ayes and noes.

Mr. PHELPS moved to amend the amendment by adding at the end, "exclusive of electioneering expenses." If he is to go through the State to electioneer for his office, he will want to be paid his expenses.

He withdrew the amendment.

Mr. JENIFER interposed an objection, that an individual belonging to a county on one side of the State could scarcely be known to the people of the counties at the other extremity.

Mr. GRASON said it might so happen that a Governor would be elected from one party and a Secretary of State from another. The Secretary then might not keep the secrets of the Governor. They might require separate apartments, and a sergeant-at-arms to keep them at peace.

The yeas and nays were then ordered on the motion of Mr. DASHIELL.

Mr. CHAMBERS said, he had hoped some one would have risen promptly to rebuke the most exceptionable suggestion thrown out by the gentleman from Charles, (Mr. Jenifer.) It deserved rebuke. He for one could not allow it to pass without condemnation. The people not to know all about every body and every thing! The people have no business to vote because they know nothing about it! How strange. Why the approved doctrine is, that every man in every part of the State is perfectly well informed and competent to judge of the fitness of any candidate, whether for a clerkship or any thing else. Aye, knows better than those who have passed a lifetime in learning the duties of the office and in association with those who are aspirants to it. But it is said the people ought not by their votes to decide a matter about which they can know nothing. This was most monstrous doctrine! He went for the rights of the people, the eternal and immortal people, their inalienable, indisputable rights—rights which could not be taken away, modified or controled—rights which they alone and nobody else possessed. It is their special, their exclusive privilege, to vote for whom they please, for what they please, and whether they know any thing about it or not!

It was thought of old that *labor viginti annorum* was requisite to know the law, but it is now ascertained, that every man, whatever have been his capacity or his means of information, or his want of either, is perfectly competent to decide the relative of those who are proposed to fill your highest judicial stations. If they know nothing about the man or his duties, it is their *inestimable privilege* still, to decide. He could allow no encroachment on this exclusive right of the people.

Mr. JENIFER said, the gentleman from Kent was evidently trying to run him down in the race of popularity. But he, (Mr J.,) was determined not to be beat. He intended to run neck and neck with the gentleman from Kent to the end of the session, and to prove himself a better republican.

The question was then taken on the motion of Mr. DASHIELL, and decided as follows:

Affirmative—Messrs. Blakistone, President, *pro tem*, Dent, Hopewell, Lee, Buchanan, Bell, Dashiell, Hicks, Eccleston, Phelps, Miller, Dirickson, McMaster, Gaither, Sappington, Nelson, Carter, Ware, Fiery, John Newcomer, Harbine, and Smith—22.

Negative—Messrs. Chambers of Kent, Mitchell, Donaldson, Dorsey, Wells, Randall, Kent Sellman, Weems, Sollers, Brent of Charles, Jenifer, Howard, Welch, Lloyd, Dickinson, Sherwood of Talbot, Crisfield, Williams, Hodson, Chambers of Cecil, McLane, Bowie, Tuck, Grason, Fooks, Shriver, Biser, McHenry Magraw, Hardcastle, Gwinn, Stewart of Baltimore city, Brent of Baltimore city, Presstman, Davis, Kilgour, Brewer, Waters, Weber, Hollyday, Slicer, Parke, Shower, and Brown—45.

So the Convention refused to accept the substitute.

Mr. DIRICKSON made some remarks, which will be published hereafter.

Mr. MITCHELL had but a single word to say. He had made enquiry on this subject this morning, and he had satisfied himself that it was impossible for the Governor to discharge his duties without assistance, and he ought to have a confidential officer, who should be well paid, and appointed by himself. If you abolish this office, and as you have already fixed the salary of the Governor at thirty-six hundred dollars, and being obliged to spend that sum or more, in entertaining his personal and political friends, he will have no time left to do the work of his office.

Mr. SHRIVER said the Convention had had a lecture from the gentleman from Worcester on the subject of retrenchment, but it came from that quarter with a bad grace. The gentleman from Worcester was himself prominent in fastening upon us this batch of officers at the beginning of the session. And only yesterday, when he was appointed on a Committee to enquire into the propriety of dispensing with some of the superfluous clerks, he asked and was allowed to decline the service. The Secretary of State, a gentleman of as much purity of character and industry as any gentleman of the Convention, is busily employed, and without intermission. He works every day from nine o'clock in the morning until nine at night, writing letters in reply to applications to the Governor.

Mr. DIRICKSON. Why does not the Governor answer them himself?

Mr. SHRIVER replied that he had not time.—Copies are kept of all letters which are written. If the gentleman from Worcester chose to call at the office of the Secretary, he might see for himself that it was no sinecure. There is a great variety of duties to perform. As he believed the subject had been sufficiently discussed, and every gentleman's mind was made up as to his vote, he would ask for the previous question.

He withdrew the call for the previous question at the request of the gentleman from Worcester, Mr. DIRICKSON.

Mr. DIRICKSON made some remarks, which will be published hereafter.

On motion of Mr. GRASON, the twenty-second section was further amended by striking out the word "the," in line one, and inserting in lieu thereof, the word "a."

The twenty-second section, as amended, was then agreed to.

REDUCTION OF CLERKS.

Mr. SAPPINGTON asked leave of the Convention to make a report from the special committee to whom was referred the resolutions offered by him yesterday.

Mr. CHAMBERS moved that the rules be suspended for the purpose of enabling the Convention to receive the report.

The motion was agreed to,

And the rules having been suspended,

Mr. SAPPINGTON made the following report, which was read.

The committee appointed to enquire and report to this House whether or not it would be expedient to discharge some of the committee clerks and doorkeepers, ask leave to report, that in their opinion, from the advanced condition of the business of this Convention—most of the committees having made their reports—it is no longer necessary or expedient to retain the services of the whole number of committee clerks. For this reason they recommend that the number be reduced. They conceive further, that the duty implied devolves upon them to designate who of said committee clerks should be retained—Mr. John W. Rider was appointed by a separate order of this Convention clerk to the President and also to the committee on Accounts. His services will be required during the entire session of the Convention. Of the other committee clerks, they recommend that Messrs. Geo. S. King, Samuel Peacock and Joseph Morritz, be retained.

They do not think that any of the doorkeepers should be discharged, as their services are still required.

In accordance with the above views, they recommend the adoption of the following resolution:

Resolved That it being no longer necessary to retain in this Convention the services of the whole number of committee clerks heretofore appointed, the following only be and are hereby retained, that is to say, John W. Rider, Geo. S. King; Samuel Peacock and Joseph Morritz.

J. SAPPINGTON, *Chairman.*

Mr. CRISFIELD, from the minority of said commtitee, submitted the following

REPORT:

The undersigned, a member of the committee to whom was referred the enquiry, "whether or not it would be expedient to discharge some of the doorkeepers and committee clerks," begs leave to report, that he finds there are three doorkeepers; two for the Hall of the Convention and one for the Senate Chamber, which is daily used for the accommodation of the members of the Convention and its committees. He is of opinion, that two doorkeepers are necessary for the Hall, and that, as long as the Senate Chamber is used as it has been during the whole of the session, a doorkeeper for that apartment is absolutely necessary for the protection of the public property, and for the accommodation of the committees and members of the Convention. The undersigned, therefore, thinks it would not be expedient to discharge any of the doorkeepers.

The undersigned finds that there are in the employment of the Convention a Post Master and seven committee clerks, one of whom performs the duties of clerk to the President as well as those of clerk of the committee on accounts, and keeps all the accounts of the Convention. His services are indispensible in the opinion of the undersigned.

The labor to be performed by the committee clerks of the Convention, has not been great or arduous at any time, and it might well be doubted whether the number orignally employed was not greater than was necessary; but, however that may have been, it is certainly true, the labor for which committee clerks are necessary, is now over, or nearly performed. The undersigned is of opinion that there is not now, and it is not likely there will be during the residue of the session, labor to employ more than one half of the present number of committee clerks. He is therefore of opinion, that the public business would not be injured by dispensing with the services of three of the present clerks. The undersigned, however, wishes it to be distinctly understood, that in announcing this opinion, he does not intend to depreciate the characters and services of these officers; as far as he knows, or has been informed, each of the clerks of this body has faithfully performed every service which has been required of them. The undersigned thinks a portion of them may be dispensed with, not because they are incompetent or unfaithful, but because their services are unnecessary.

The undersigned thinks it no part of the duty of the committee to indicate which of the clerks can best be discharged. The resolution does not require the expression of any opinion on that subject.

J. W. CRISFIELD.

Which was read.

The question being on the adoption of the resolution.

Mr. TUCK moved to lay the resolution on the table.

Mr. CHAMBERS suggested, whether it would not be the better course to have a day fixed for the discharge to take place, in order that those who will be discharged, may make their arrangements for leaving.

Mr. BRENT said, he would now offer a substitute for the resolution, and would ask that it should be laid on the table with the reports and resolution, and that they may all be taken up tomorrow. He did not think that any of these clerks should be discharged.

The substitute was read as follows:

"*Ordered*, That on and after Monday next, no clerk, doorkeeper, or other officer be entitled to compensation when absent, unless upon leave of absence, granted by the Convention.

Mr. TUCK, again moved to lay the reports, resolution and substitute on the table.

The question being put, the motion was decided in the negative.

Mr. HICKS moved to postpone said reports and substitute until the first Monday of May next.

Determined in the negative.

Mr. BROWN moved to postpone said reports and substitute until to morrow.

Determined in the negative.

Mr. CHAMBERS, of Kent, moved to amend the report of the majority committee, by adding at the end of the resolution, the following:

"And that the persons whose services are dispensed with, be allowed their per diem to Monday next, the 17th inst."

Mr. HICKS moved as a substitute for said reports and substitute, the following:

Ordered, That the reports of the committee appointed to enquire into the propriety of discharging some of the clerks and doorkeepers, be recommitted to the said committee, with instructions to said committee to write the names of each committee clerk and each doorkeeper, upon a separate piece of paper, and placed in a hat or box, and that the first three names drawn out be the clerks or doorkeepers to be discharged.

The PRESIDENT ruled the substitute to be out of order.

Mr. PRESSTMAN moved the previous question, and being seconded.

The question was put on the adoption of the amendment as offered by Mr. CHAMBERS, of Kent, and

Determined in the affirmative.

The question was then put,

"Will the Convention accept the substitute as offered by Mr. BRENT, of Baltimore city?"

Mr. SAPPINGTON moved the question be taken by yeas and nays, and being ordered, appeared as follows:

Affirmative— Messrs. Blakistone, President,

pro tem., Dent, Hopewell, Mitchell, Wells, Weems, Sollers, Jenifer, Dashiell, Williams, Hicks, Hodson, Eccleston, Phelps, McLane, Bowie, Tuck, McMaster, Magraw, Carter, Gwinn, Stewart of Baltimore city, Brent of Baltimore city, Presstman, Ware, Kilgour and Waters—27.

Negative—Messrs. Lee, Chamber of Kent, Donaldson, Dorsey, Randall, Sellman, Brent of Charles, Howard, Buchanan, Bell, Welch, Lloyd, Dickinson, Sherwood of Talbot, Crisfield, Miller, Grason, Dirickson, Fooks, Shriver, Biser, Sappington, McHenry, Nelson, Hardcastle, Fiery, John Newcomer, Harbine, Brewer, Weber, Hollyday, Slicer, Smith, Parke, Shower, and Brown—36.

So the Convention refused to accept the substitute.

The question was then put on the adoption of the report of the majority of the committee.

Mr. Chambers, of Kent, moved the question be taken by yeas and nays, and being ordered appeared as follows:

Affirmative—Messrs. Lee, Chambers of Kent, Donaldson, Dorsey, Randall, Sellman, Brent of Charles, Howard. Buchanan Bell, Welch, Lloyd, Dickinson, Sherwood of Talbot, Crisfield, Miller, Grason, Fooks, Shriver, Biser, Sappington, McHenry, Nelson, Carter, Fiery, John Newcomer, Harbine, Brewer, Weber, Hollyday, Slicer, Smith, Parke, Shower and Brown—35.

Negative—Messrs. Blakistone, President, *pro tem.*, Dent, Hopewell, Mitchell, Wells, Weems, Sollers, Jenifer, Dashiell, Williams, Hicks, Hodson, Eccleston, Phelps, McLane, Bowie, Tuck, Dirickson, McMaster, Magraw, Gwinn, Stewart of Baltimore city, Brent of Baltimore city, Presstman, Ware, Kilgour Waters—27

So the report of the majority committee was adopted.

The Convention adjourned until to-morrow morning at 10 o'clock.

FRIDAY, March 14, 1851.

The Convention met at ten o'lcock.

Prayer by the Rev. Mr. Grauff.

The journal of yesterday having been read,

CORRECTION.

On motion of Mr. Chambers,

A correction was made in page 442, in the amendment offered by him, to the resolution of the special committee, to allow such clerks as may be dispensed with, their per diem to Monday next, by adding the word "inclusive."

He explained his object to be, to remove any doubt as to the time when the *per diem* should cease.

There being no objection, the correction was made, and

The journal was then approved.

NEW COUNTY.

Mr. Shriver presented a petition of eighty voters of Middletown, Hawver's, and Catoctin districts in Frederick county, remonstrating against the creation of a new county from parts of Frederick and Washington counties.

Which was read, and

Referred to the committee appointed on New Counties.

INTOXICATING LIQUORS.

Mr. John Newcomer, presented a petition of sundry citizens of Washington county, praying that provision may be made in the new Constitution, that the privilege to sell intoxicating liquors shall not be granted to any person in any part of the State, except the same shall first be sanctioned or approved by a majority of the votes in the election district where the same is to be sold.

Which was read, and

Referred to the select committee appointed on that subject.

BASIS OF REPRESENTATION.

Mr Smith said:

He rose to submit an order, accompanying which, was a tabular statement which he desired to have printed. This statement contained various views which he, in conjunction with other gentlemen, had been preparing on the subject of the basis of representation.

He hoped this document would be printed and put in the hands of gentlemen as speedily as possible, in order that it might be examined. He thought it important that the Convention should see at a glance, all the various projects on the subject.

He then offered the following order,

Which was agreed to.

Ordered, That the committee on Printing, be directed to have printed for the use of the Convention, in one tabular form, the various plans for a basis of representation of the House of Delegates.

REDUCTION OF CLERKS.

Mr. Brent, of Baltimore city, enquired whether it was now in order to move to reconsider the vote by which the order discharging a portion of the committee clerks was yesterday adopted?

The President, *pro tem.*, replied that such a motion was in order.

Mr. Brent, then submitted the motion to reconsider.

Mr. McHenry moved to lay the motion to reconsider on the table.

Mr. Phelps hoped his friend from Harford would withdraw the motion to lay on the table. Yesterday the previous question was sprung, and no opportunity was afforded to say a word. He gave notice that if the motion to reconsider was laid on the table, he would renew it to-morrow.

Mr. Brent, of Baltimore city, asked for the

ayes and noes on the motion to lay the motion to reconsider on the table, and

They were ordered.

The question was then taken,

And decided as follows:

Affirmative.—Messrs. Lee, Chambers, of Kent, Donaldson, Dorsey, Randall, Sellman, Buchanan, Welch, McLane, Fooks, Shriver, Biser, McHenry, Nelson, Schley, Fiery, Neill, John Newcomer, Harbine, Brewer, Weber, Slicer, Smith, Parke, Shower, Cockey and Brown—27.

Negative.—Messrs. Blakistone, President, *pro tem.*, Dent, Hopewell, Wells, Dalrymple, Jenifer, Ridgely, Dickinson, Sherwood, of Talbot, Crisfield, Dashiell, Williams, Hicks, Hodson, Eccleston Phelps, Bowie, Tuck, Sprigg, Bowling, Grason, Wright, Dirickson, McMaster Gwinn, Brent, of Baltimore city, Sherwood of Baltimore city, Presstman, Ware, Davis and Waters—31.

So the Convention refused to lay the motion to reconsider on the table.

The question then recurring on the motion to reconsider,

Mr. TUCK said he had yesterday moved to lay this subject on the table. He thought there was an impropriety in discharging officers without notice. He would not go so far as to call it injustice; but he thought that when, out of the six gentlemen who have been employed by us, a portion is about to be dispensed with, the whole of them ought to have an opportunity of being heard. He could not be supposed to know what had passed in the committee on this subject; but he presumed that it was because they happened just now to be absent from the city, that the three whose names had been reputed as those to be discharged, had been selected. If the other three clerks had happened to be absent, they perhaps would have been the three selected for removal.

So far as he knew, these clerks had been generally here, and ready to do whatever gentlemen asked of them. They have only been absent when leave has been given them by the President. He did not see how the selection of three out of the six clerks to be discharged, could be made, without leaving something like an imputation on them. Every one would naturally come to the conclusion that we have retained the three clerks who are the most competent. And, as the fact had doubtless been published this morning in the Baltimore Sun, the injurious impression will spread over the State, and the action of this Convention will be every where understood to be a reflection on the gentlemen who are discharged. He thought it would have been the most proper mode to let these six gentlemen have arranged between themselves, by lot, or in any other way, which of them should go out, and which should remain.

If any charge were substantiated against the three selected, he would go for their instant removal. We employed them for the whole session, and it has been our fault, not theirs, that they have not had much to do. We have done very little ourselves.

Mr. JENIFER had listened to the gentleman from Prince George's, but he could not agree with that gentleman, that all clerks had been always attentive to their duties. He had voted against the resolution yesterday, and he had also voted against laying the motion to reconsider on the table to-day, because he did not think it right to discharge officers without some notice. He was astonished, however, to hear the gentleman from Prince George's say, that all the clerks had discharged their duties with entire satisfaction—for he, (Mr. J.,) had heard frequent complaints, yet he had none to make himself, although he had to perform much of the duties of the committee of which he was chairman, nor had he expressed any dissatisfaction as regards that committee clerk. He thought the proper course would be to notify the absent ones that hereafter, that they should not leave without permission.

Mr. BROWN stated that he had voted for the resolution yesterday, and he should vote for it again to-day; for these reasons, first, that there is nothing for these clerks to do. When the Constitution comes to be engrossed, it ought to be done in the very best style, because it will have to be deposited among the public archieves; and he believed there could not be found in Annapolis, a dozen person who were capable of doing it as it should be done. It will most probably be the case, that we shall have to get a person specially for the work and pay the extra charge out of the treasury. We do not want these committee clerks; and the question is, shall we pay away two or three thousand dollars for services which are of no use to us. He had thought, when these clerks were appointed, that the Convention would terminate its sitting in the month of February, and all these officers he knew must have expected to terminate their labors long before this time. There was no reflection intended on any of these clerks. If they had been the best clerks in the world, we could have had no further use for them. He would vote for the resolution. He would even go further, and dispense with the services of some of those who were retained.

Mr. BRENT reminded gentlemen that the expense of discussing this matter, would eat up more than the amount which would be saved by dismissing these clerks. Strict economists should not prolong this discussion. Why did not the gentleman from Carroll, take the same stand when the previous order was under consideration, Another remark: In the month of November, an order which was introduced authorizing the appointment of clerks, was voted down. Then on the 14th of the same month, an order was passed appointing the present six clerks by name. How then can gentlemen who voted on that platform, now turn about and vote for a partial removal of some of these clerks? He agreed with the gentleman from Charles, (Mr. Jenifer,) that some of these clerks had absented themselves from their duties. As the House had refused to the committees leave to report their reasons on any subject referred to them, these clerks may have supposed that there was no occasion for their regular attendance here. But they ought to be all required to attend. He believed they were all deserving men, and he had no doubt would do whatever duties were required of them or assigned to them.

Mr. BROWN explained that on looking back to the platform, he found that the gentleman from Baltimore voted for these clerks, and he, (Mr. Brown,) against them. The gentleman from Baltimore says, we are wasting time. He agreed with him that we are wasting time, but he thought these unnecessary clerks ought to be cut off.

Mr. BUCHANAN moved the previous question, and the motion being seconded,

Mr. BUCHANAN asked for the ayes and noes on the motion to reconsider, and they were ordered.

The question was then taken, and decided as follows:

Affirmative.—Messrs. Blakistone, President *pro tem.*, Dent, Hopewell, Wells, Dalrymple, Jenifer, Dickinson, Dashiell, Williams, Hicks, Hodson, Eccleston, Phelps, Bowie, Tuck, Sprigg, Bowling, Dirickson, McMaster, Gwinn, Brent of Baltimore city, Sherwood of Baltimore city, Presstman, Ware, Davis, Kilgour and Waters—33.

Negative.—Messrs. Lee, Chambers, of Kent, Donaldson, Dorsey, Sellman, Buchanan, Welch, Ridgely, Sherwood, of Talbot, Grason, Wright, Fooks, Shriver, Biser, McHenry, Nelson, Carter, Schley, Fiery, Neill, John Newcomer, Harbine, Brewer, Weber, Slicer, Smith, Parke, Shower, Cockey and Brown—30.

So the Convention refused to reconsider.

Mr. BISER present a petition signed by 392 citizens of Frederick county, praying for a new county to include all the districts of Middletown Valley, in Frederick county, and such parts of Washington county, as lie contiguous to said districts, and their counter petition for a new county to be composed of Jefferson, Petersville, Middletown and Cacoctin districts of Frederick county, and Pleasant Valley, part of Boonsboro' and Sharpsburg in Washington county.

Which was read, and

Referred to the select committee on new counties.

ORDER OF THE DAY.

On motion of Mr. GRASON the Convention resumed the consideration of the order of the day, being the Report on the Executive Department.

The 23d section having been read,

Mr. GRASON moved to amend said section by striking out in the 2nd and 3rd lines of said sections, these words "and shall lay the same before either branch of the Legislature whenever required."

Mr. G. confessed that in inserting the words which he now moved to strike out, he committed the error of borrowing from some of the modern Constitutions. He had generally been very cautious how he borrow from any of them, but he unfortunately did so on this occasion. He had now submitted the motion to strike out the words because the Secretary of State was not the proper officer to answer the demands of the Legislature.

On reflection, he was opposed to making the Secretary of State the medium of communication between the Governor and the Legislature.

Some conversation here took place between Messrs. CHAMBERS and GRASON on the subject of the duties which the Secretary of State is required to perform by the act of Assembly, and those, the performance of which custom has imposed on him.

Mr. BOWIE asked if there was any provision making it the duty of the Governor to allow the records to be open to the inspection of persons.

Mr. GRASON replied in the negative.

Mr. BOWIE thought it necessary that the records of the Executive department should be open to general inspection. But his friend from Queen Anne's seemed to think that copies of the records ought to be furnished without cost. He [Mr. B.] thought it the duty of the Secretary of State to furnish the General Assembly with copies whenever they might be called for, but in reference to private applications, a compliance could only be considered as a matter of courtesy. He did not know that it was the duty of the keeper of the records to supply the Legislature with copies of the records, unless there was an official call for them. He would suggest the propriety of amending the section by inserting the words "and shall be laid before each branch of the Legislature when required." He was against striking out that part of the section, and hoped the Convention would not agree to the motion of the gentleman from Queen Anne's.

The question was then put on the motion of Mr. GRASON, but a quorum did not vote.

Mr. GRASON objected to the amendment of the gentleman from Prince George's, because its meaning was doubtful and obscure. The gentleman from Prince George's seemed to suppose that unless the Governors were required by the Constitution to submit the executive records to the inspection of the Legislature, he might refuse to communicate information respecting his official acts and proceedings. It was true that the President sometimes declined complying with the calls of Congress, on the ground that a communication of the intelligence required, was inconsistent with the public interest. But the executive proceedings of Maryland were always open to the inspection to either branch of the Legislature, and to every member who desired information. But he had no objection to the amendment, if properly modified.

After a few words from Messrs. BOWIE, CHAMBERS and GRASON, in explanation,

Mr. DORSEY suggested an amendment by striking out the word "and" in line 2, and inserting in lieu thereof, the words "the Governor."

Mr. GRASON withdrew his amendment.

The question was then taken on the amendment of Mr. MCLANE, and it was agreed to.

The question then recurred on the adoption of the section as amended, and,

It was adopted.

The Convention had now gone through with this bill.

Mr. GRASON said it would be in the recollection of the Convention, that on Wednesday last, the second section of the report had been postponed, because there was not a full Convention He was ready to go on with it at this time. It was, however, a matter for the Convention to determine whether they would proceed with the consideration of the section at this time, or would further postpone it until there was a more full attendance.

Mr. DORSEY suggested that time spent in passing upon important questions whilst there was so sparse an attendance, would be lost, inasmuch as a reconsideration of the question was sure to be moved, when there was a more full attendance.

Mr. BRENT, of Baltimore city, said he took it for granted that no important question could be passed upon here without an effort to reconsider when there should be a more full attendance. He suggested that the Convention should take up the motion he had yesterday made to reconsider the vote of the Convention on the 13th section, for the purpose of enabling him to offer a substitute.

The Convention thereupon proceeded to the consideration of the motion to reconsider the vote on the said 13th section.

Mr. CRISFIELD said he was opposed to the motion of the gentleman from the city of Baltimore, [Mr. Brent,] to reconsider the 13th section. The object of the motion to reconsider, is to allow the mover to offer a substitute for the 13th section, which will be found in the journal of yesterday That substitute, if adopted, would authorise the Governor, in all cases, where he has power to make any appointment to office, to make such appointment during the recess of the Senate, no matter when such office may have been created, or when the vacancy proposed to be filled, may have occurred. The question then is, one of preference between the 13th section as it stands, and the substitute proposed to be offered.

As it now stood, the 13th section provided for cases of vacancy occurring during the recess of the Senate; temporary appointments might be made by the Governor, to fill such vacancies to terminate at the expiration of thirty days after the commencement of the succeeding session, or on the appointment of the same, or some other person, to the same office, by and with the advice of the Senate. The section also provided for another class of cases—new offices created less than thirty days before the termination of the session, which might be filled in the recess, in the same manner as vacancies occurring in the recess. The object of this latter provision, was to afford the Governor time for reflection and examination, before he should be obliged to make his appointments. If a law should pass creating a new office more than twenty days before the close of a session, the Governor must make his nomination to the Senate before the adjournment, the presumption being that within that time, he can satisfy himself, who is the proper person to be appointed. Here then, were two classes of appointments, which might be made by the Governor during the recess, by granting temporary commissions which would run into the next session, and afford ample time for the Governor and Senate to perform their respective functions, before they would be vacated. Was there any other class of cases for which additional provision was necessary?

The object of the 13th section, as it now stood, was to restrain the Governor within the just limits of his authority, and secure to the Senate its constitutional right of passing on all appointments. All agree that the Senate is properly a part of the appointing power. The necessity of its co-operation exercises a powerful influence over the Governor. It is a powerful check on a spirit of favoritism in the Governor, and tends to prevent the appointment of unfit persons, from prejudice, want of information, family connexion, personal attachment, or a desire for popularity. Hence, the Constitution authorised the Senate to act upon all appointments. But this provision would be idle and ridiculous if it may be evaded. The 13th section as it now stood, would prevent all evasion. As long as that stands, no appointment by the Governor can continue for a longer period than the interval between the sessions, and thirty days during the succeeding session. It was therefore essential to preserve the substance of that section, in order to secure to the Senate the full exercise of its constitutional authority.

Now what is the substitute which the gentleman from Baltimore city proposes, and to let in which the reconsideration is moved? It is, as already observed, to authorize the Governor in all cases where he has power to make an appointment to office—to make such appointment in the recess of the Senate, no matter when the office was created or the vacancy occurred. What is the effect of this? If an office be created, or a vacancy occur during the session of the Senate, the Governor would not be under any constitutional obligation to fill it during the session; and if he failed to fill it, the office need not remain vacant, until the next session. Suppose, in the recess, he make a temporary appointment, and at the next session he make a nomination to the same office, and it is rejected; the Governor would have power, after the close of the session, to make another appointment; and so on from session to session. By a little adroitness, the Governor might preclude the Senate from all participation in the appointments. All he need do to secure to himself practically the sole power of appointment, unchecked by the Senate, is to make, at each recurring session, a nomination which will be rejected, and thus be enabled to keep his favorite in office, during his entire term, without the consent, and possibly in defiance of the wishes of the Senate. The substitute, if adopted, would enable an unscrupulous Governor to evade the provisions of the Constitution.

The difference between the propositions was this: The section proposed to be stricken out, guarded the appointing power, and secured to the Senate the full exercise of the authority conferred on it by the Constitution to pass on all appointments; the section proposed to be inserted, would enable a Governor, who might be so inclined, to concentrate in his own hands practically, the sole power of appointment, and destroy the power of the Senate.

The Convention should be careful how the appointing power was guarded ; it was a power capable of infinite mischief in thoughtless or corrupt hands.

Mr. C. thought the question now to be decided was, whether the appointing power should be committed to the Governor, without limit or restraint; or whether the Senate should be secured in the exercise of a negative on his nominations, which all admitted was necessary and proper. He hoped the motion to reconsider would not prevail.

Mr. BRENT, of Baltimore city, proceeded to oppose the amendment submitted by the gentleman from Somerset, (Mr. Crisfield,) which he read, as follows :

"The Governor shall have power to fill any vacancy that may occur during the recess of the Senate, in any office to which the Governor has the power of appointment, by granting a commission which shall expire upon the appointment of the same person or any other person, by and with the advice and consent of the Senate, to the same office, or at the expiration of one calendar month ensuing the commencement of the next regular session of the Senate, whichever shall first occur."

He thought this amendment did not provide for all cases, it merely limiting the power of appointment to two classes--first, when a vacancy occurred during the recess, (and about this there could be no dispute, for it was contained in the old Constitution ;) and, secondly, where a law should be passed creating offices within twenty days prior to the adjournment of the Senate. The amendment did not apply to cases where an office should be created more than twenty days before the adjournment of a session. The act of 1837 allowed the Governor to appoint commissioners out of the State, *ad libitum*, for the acknowledgment of deeds. He might appoint thousands of commissioners out of the State, but they would be new appointments and not vacancies to be filled. The amendment of the gentleman would not enable the Governor to make these appointments in the recess of the Senate, the necessity for which was now increased, as in future they were to have biennial sessions. It was very evident that the section would have to be amended to meet this class of cases. The Governor, under this section, would not even have the power of creating new auctioneers, though the revenue of the State might be increased thereby; and the Convention must very clearly see, that the vote by which the thirteenth section was adopted should be reconsidered. He wished to see whether this body would tie up the Governor as the gentleman from Somerset proposed, or whether they would give him a large discretion, to act upon his responsibility to the State and to the power of impeachment.

The gentleman from Somerset anticipated that the Governor would fraudulently withhold his appointments until the Legislature should adjourn. If that functionary should withhold appointments purposely, to make temporary commissions; if he should do this from corrupt motives, he would be liable to impeachment, and he, (Mr. B.,) was prepared to vote for a clause to this effect. But he could not presume that the Governor would act in this way. The gentleman thought that some remedy should be applied. Reconsider the vote by which this section was adopted, and then let them consider what remedy was necessary.

Mr. CRISFIELD replied to the remarks of Mr. Brent. The thirteenth section, it was said, did not authorise to make appointments in the recess, to new offices which had been created more than twenty days before the adjournment. That was true; and he contended that it was not proper to give the Governor such power. So far as depended on him, no such power should be given to that officer. He wished to limit the power of the Governor, and guard against all abuses by requiring his nominations to be submitted to the action of the Senate at the earliest reasonable period. By the thirteenth section, as it now stood, twenty days were allowed the Governor in all cases of newly created offices, to submit to the Senate, for approval, the names of proper individuals to fill them; and this, considering the limited extent of the State, and the general acquaintance which the Governor usually has in every portion of it, was certainly ample time for him to examine the character, and acquaint himself with the fitness of every individual who desired any office within his gift. The limitations of the thirteenth section, were indispensable to secure to the Senate the just exercise of the power delegated to it by the Constitution. If the doctrine advocated by the gentleman from Baltimore city be true, what would be the result? If the Legislature should create an office on the first day of its session, the Governor would have three months nearly, in which he might make his selection and nomination of the individual proper to fill it; and yet for his own purposes, he might postpone the appointment till after the close of the session, and for two years defeat the action of the Senate, whose privilege and duty it was to pass on all appointments. Such would be the practical effect of the gentleman's views. Was the Convention prepared to sanction them? If it was, then he hoped some one would move that the power of the Senate, in this respect, be stricken out altogether, and absolute authority over appointments be given to the Governor. Let such a proposition be presented to the Convention, and let it be seen how many of that body would favor it.

Mr. C. said the gentleman from Baltimore city, [Mr. Brent,] contended that under the 13th section the Governor had no power to appoint in the recess, when appointments are to be made according to the discretion of the Governor, with or without limit as to number, and he [Mr. B.] had instanced commissioners under the act of 1837, to take acknowledgments of deeds out of the State, &c., and the case of auctioneers, notaries public, &c. The 13th section was the identical provision of the existing Constitution; and he had never heard a complaint until now, that the Governor could not make these appointments during the recess. He was not prepared to admit the construction of the laws referred to, given by the gentleman from Baltimore city, and he believed a different construction had always until now, prevailed in and out of the Executive department. These offices were created by law, not by the Constitution; and the law could prescribe the manner in which appointments to them should be made, whether by the Governor in the recess or not. It has always been conceded that the Governor could fill them during the recess; but if that was an enormous construction, the law could be changed at the next session of the Legislature. And it should be remarked too, that the people of Maryland, were little interested in this class of offices; appointments to them were made mostly for the benefit of the appointees, and as a privilege or a license to carry on the business to which they relate. The public interest would not suffer if no appointments could be made in the recess. But to obtain a mere ideal advantage, which at most benefits individuals, and not the public generally, to enable the Governor to make appointments under laws which may be changed next winter, appointments which in no sense effect the public interest, and that too, when every Executive which had preceded the present, had acted on a different construction, the gentleman from Baltimore city would give to the Governor, what would be destructive of the rights of the Senate, and practically would be an unlimited power over all appointments.

The gentleman had said, that he (Mr. C.) spoke as if the persons who might wield the executive power, were not to be upright men. Mr. C. must say, that he had no very exalted opinion of the purity of public men. All government was a satire on human nature, and was made necessary by the vices and ambition of men. He was not disposed to trust to the mere goodness of individuals. It was prudent to guard against every danger. He would, if he could, by positive restraints, render it impossible for men to do wrong He could not assent to the opinion advanced by the gentleman, that the character of the person who might happen to be Governor, his purity and patriotism might safely be relied on, as a sufficient guaranty against the dangers apprehended. If this doctrine be true, there was no necessity at all for constitutional restraints. And he must be permitted to say, he was surprised to hear such sentiments promulgated. They were a remnant of the antiquated idea of the infallibility of rulers. They do not belong to this land, nor to this age; and especially they do not suit gentlemen, who claim to be *par excellence*, the friends of the people. He could not subscribe to them. He was not willing to trust to the character of any individual, however pure and exalted that character might be, as the only defence against the aggressions of power. He had always been taught to believe, and his experience justified the lesson, that the only security for popular liberty is to be found in the express requirements of a written Constitution. The gentleman has said something of impeachment; it is idle to talk of impeaching a Governor of one of the States of this Union. It was scarcely worth while to insert such an article in the Constitution. The power of impeachment never had been, and never would be successfully enforced against an individual occupying such an elevated and influential position But the danger feared would be the legitimate result of the powers conferred upon him; and how could he be impeached for what the Constitution authorized him to do?

The power proposed to be given to the Governor, was a dangerous one, it was liable to be evaded, or perverted to a mischievous use, and he hoped, therefore, no reconsideration would be had for the purpose of adopting it; but if the section should be reconsidered, he would then offer an amendment, which in his opinion would accomplish every proper end, without encountering the dangers which threatened from the adoption of the gentleman's proposition.

Mr. Brent proposed to answer the extraordinary position assumed by the gentleman from Somerset. Because that gentleman did not construe the Constitution as the Governors of Maryland had done, and because there was no necessity, in his opinion, for putting this doubt to rest, therefore, he thought that the vote ought not to be reconsidered. He would say, that this was a very extraordinary position. The gentleman had said that the practice, in the State of Maryland, had been for the Governor to make original appointments in the recess of the Senate. He, (Mr. B.,) would say, that if there had been such practice, it had been erroneous, with all due deference to the better judgment of the gentleman from Somerset. Mr. B. asserted, that if any Governor, under the act of 1837, had, in the recess of the Senate, appointed commissioners of deeds out of the State, it was done in violation of plain law. What is the law? It was as follows:

"*Sec.* 1. Be it enacted by the General Assembly of Maryland, That the Governor, by and with the advice and consent of the Senate, be and he is hereby authorised to name, appoint and commission one or more commissioners in each or such of the other States or territories of the United States, or in the District of Columbia, as he may deem expedient, which commissioners shall continue in office during the pleasure of the Governor, and shall have authority to take the acknowledgments and proof of the execution of any deed, mortgage, or other conveyance of any lands, tenements or hereditaments lying or being in this State; any contract, letter of attorney or any other writing, under seal, to be used or recorded in this State, and such acknowledgment or proof taken or made in the manner directed by the laws of this State, and certified by any one of the said commissioners before whom the same shall be taken or made, under seal, which certificate shall be endorsed on or annexed to said deed or instrument aforesaid, shall have the same force and effect and be as good and available in law, for all purposes, as if the same had been made or taken before some one of the judges of the United States courts or of the courts of record of the several States."

It would be seen that the law merely authorized the Governor to name and appoint the commissioners, by and with the advice and consent of the Senate. He had no power, therefore, to appoint these commissioners. But suppose the Governor had construed the law wrong, that he had no power to make these appointments, he was not going to yield his opinion because gentlemen of the Convention thought differently. If the gentleman wished to fetter executive power, let the vote by which the article was adopted be reconsidered, and then they could consider whether restraints should be applied. He, (Mr. C.,) could then submit his amendment, which proposed that the Governor should have no power to appoint commissioners to take deeds, notaries public, or auctioneers, although the revenue of the State might be benefitted by it. The gentleman presupposed that the Governor of Maryland, having the power to make original appointments, would purposely make appointments and withhold the nominations, for the purpose of making temporary appointments. He, (Mr. B.,) did not think the Governer would do this. If the gentleman proposed an amendment free from exception, he would vote for it.

Mr. B. said that his purpose was to improve this class of cases. He had no other object, and repudiated any other object. If a law should be passed twenty-one days before the termination of a session; and if the Governor should be unable to make a nomination for the office to the Senate before it adjourned, then, by the gentleman's amendment the public interests were to be disregarded. If the gentleman would show him how he could restrict the Governor, and at the same time safely leave the offices unfilled, then he would vote with him after the adoption of the clause should be reconsidered; but he did not wish to see the public interests put in jeopardy. He wished to see the offices filled by temporary appointments rather than not filled at all. If they should have a Governor corrupt or negligent enough not to fill offices which had been created not more than twenty days before the termination of a session, or to fill offices authorized by permanent law, then the public interests were to be disregarded, and the offices left vacant, whatever might be the necessity of filling them, merely from an apprehension that the Governor might commit fraud.

His, (Mr. B.'s,) substitute only proposed that during a recess, when a vacancy should occur, or an original appointment is to be made for the first time, the Governor shall fill the vacancy and make the appointment.

Mr. Donaldson said there were but few offices to which the remarks of the gentleman from Baltimore city, (Mr. Brent,) would apply, and to remedy an inconvenience in regard to them, it was proposed now to put all offices, great and small, in the hands of the Executive solely. The amendment indicated by the gentleman from Baltimore, would enable the Governor to fill all offices and keep them filled, in despite of the Senate, whose right of confirmation might become a nullity if the desire of usurpation and the boldness to usurp existed. He explained this and illustrated it by examples. In this he agreed with the gentleman from Somerset. And what was the inconvenience sought to be remedied? The present Governor, whether he had a constitutional right to appoint, in the recess of the Senate, commissioners to take acknowledgments of deeds, auctioneers and notaries public; on the ground that no vacancy in any such offices had occurred during the recess. By law, twenty auctioneers may be appointed, but it is seldom that the full number apply, and afterward, during the recess, some one or two may make application. The number of notaries public and of commissioners to acknowledge deeds is unlimited, and the necessity for some particular appointment develops itself during the recess. Now, in these cases, the practice of all our previous Governors had been to make such appointments in the recess, and the practical construction had been given to the Constitution that vacancies in such offices had accasioned when the appointments became necessary. Yet, if there is really any doubt, let the matter be set right by Act of Assembly, by which those officers were created. They were not officers designated in the Constitution, and the Legislature might make rules for their appointment, consistently with the old Constitution, and with the fifteenth section of the present report on the executive department. Mr. D. said he had no particular objection to the reconsideration, though he thought it hardly worth while; but if the section were reconsidered, he hoped the purpose of the gentleman from Baltimore might be carried out by an amendment less comprehensive and dangerous than that which he had already suggested.

Mr. Grason remarked that some reference had been made to the course pursued by him. He had no recollection of having made any appointments of commissioners during the recess of the Senate. He always held the opinion that the Governor had not the power to make these appointments during the recess, and he certainly would not have made an original appointment after the adjournment of the Senate.

Mr. Donaldson suggested that if there was any doubt on the subject, it would be better to reconsider the section and amend it.

The question "will the Convention re-consider the vote by which the said thirteenth section was adopted?" was then taken, and decided in the affirmative—ayes 32; noes 44.

So the vote was re-considered.

Mr. Brent, of Baltimore city, then moved the following as a substitute for said section:

Sec. 13. In all cases where the Governor has

the power by the Constitution or laws, to make any appointment to office, or in case any vacancy shall occur during the recess of the Senate, in any office to which the Governor has the power of appointment, he shall have the power in the recess of the Senate, to make such appointment or fill such vacancy by granting a commission which shall expire upon the appointment of the same person or any other person, by and with the advice and consent of the Senate, to the same office, or at the expiration of one calendar month ensuing the commencement of the next regular session of the Legislature, whichever shall first occur."

The substitute having been read.

Mr. CRISFIELD said, that before the question was taken upon it, he believed it would be in order to perfect the original proposition.

The PRESIDENT, (*pro tem.*,) assented.

Mr. CRISFIELD then moved to amend the original thirteenth section by adding at the end thereof, the following:

"And the Governor may in the recess of the Senate, appoint and commission, subject to the limitations aforesaid, an additional number of such officers as are authorised by any law existing at the time of the appointment, which in its terms do not limit the number of such class of officers or of which the number limited has not been filled."

Mr. BRENT, of Baltimore city, said, it seemed to him that the amendment was the same as his own.

Mr. CHAMBERS, of Kent, (addressing himself to Mr. BRENT, of Baltimore city,) enquired, whether the gentleman was not satisfied that, under the language of his amendment, the Executive officer might forbear to make appointments. He, (Mr. C.,) did not know that any Governor would be guilty of such misconduct, but did the amendment of the gentleman from Baltimore city, [Mr. Brent,] guard against it? If the the amendment of the gentleman from Somerset, [Mr. Crisfield,] met this objection, why did not the gentleman from Baltimore city also guard against it?

Mr. BRENT, of Baltimore city. Let the amendment of the gentleman from Somerset, [Mr. Crisfield,] be again read.

The amendment having been again read—

Some explanations as to its object and effect followed, on the part of Messrs. McLANE, CRISFIELD, and CHAMBERS, of Kent.

Mr. HOWARD suggested that the object of the amendment of the gentleman from Somerset, [Mr. Crisfield,] was reached by the twelfth section which had been adopted.

Some conversation followed on a point of order, between Mr. SPENCER and the PRESIDENT [*pro tem.*]

Mr. SPENCER said, he should be compelled to vote against the section altogether, because, if amended as proposed by the gentleman from Somerset, [Mr. Crisfield,] if the Governor were to discharge his duty and were to make a nomination to the Senate within one calendar month after the commencement of the session, and the Senate should happen not to confirm the appointment, or should postpone action on the nomination,—no matter how important it might be that the office should be filled—there would be a vacancy.

Mr. CRISFIELD desired to ask the gentleman from Queen Anne's, [Mr. Spencer,] a question. Was not the section as amended, on his [Mr. C.'s] own motion, so far as the commentary of the gentleman was now concerned, in the same words as those of the existing Constitution?

Mr. SPENCER replied in the affirmative.

Mr. CRISFIELD enquired then, whether any such difficulty as that to which the gentleman referred had ever existed under the present Constitution?

Mr. SPENCER said, he had listened to the question with proper respect, as he always should to any enquiry which gentlemen might think proper to submit to him, in reference to any remarks he might make. But, in reply to the enquiry of the gentleman, he, [Mr. S.,] would ask, whether any man could have contemplated that ten years ago, the Legislature would have violated its imperative and sworn duty so far as to fail ,during the whole session to elect a Senator of the United States? And now when he, [Mr. S ,] pointed out a defect in the proposition which might lead to serious difficulty, the gentleman met his objection by asking him whether this was not a copy of the provision of the old Constitution. He, [Mr. S.,] was not to wait until such a case had arisen. If he could see any contingency in which a difficulty might arise, it surely was right and proper that the Convention should provide against it. He did say with all respect to the proposition and to the mover of it, that it did not place things in a better condition than that in which they were under the provision as reported from the committee. On the contrary, he thought it was worse.

Mr. CRISFIELD explained the object and operation of his amendment.

Mr. BRENT, of Baltimore city, moved as a substitute for said amendment, the following,to come in at the end of said thirteenth section:

"And in all cases whereby existing laws or any law hereafter to be passed,there are appointments to be made according to the discretion of the Governor, with or without limit as to number, then in such case, the Governor may in the recess of the Senate, grant temporary commissions as aforesaid."

Mr. BRENT said, this amendment would meet all the difficulties which had been suggested.

Mr. CRISFIELD said, that so far as he could understand the amendment from merely hearing it read, he had no objection to it. He would ask that the amendment, as now offered by the gentleman from Baltimore city, (Mr. Brent,) and the whole section might be again read.

They were accordingly read, whereupon

Mr. CRISFIELD said he would accept the amendment of Mr. BRENT, as a substitute for his own proposition.

Mr. McLane suggested that the original section, as it came from the committee, had been rather marred than improved, by the amendments which had been made.

Some conversation followed as to the state of the question, in which Messrs. McLane, Crisfield and Jenifer took part

And some further explanations followed between Messrs. Crisfield and McLane, as to the effect and operation of the amendment.

Mr. McLane thought the gentleman would not accomplish his object, by the proposition he had offered. He referred to the discussion which had taken place on the question of the power of appointment, during the recess, in relation to Federal offices, and adverted to the opinion given by Mr. Wirt, when attorney general, in the case of the appointment of a collector on Lake Erie, that the President had the power to fill the vacancy during that recess; an opinion which he, (Mr.McLane,)considered as having had stronger basis to rest upon than the provision in our Constitution conferring the power on the Governor. He regarded the power of the President of the United States, and the power of the Governor of Maryland, as precisely parallel in reference to this subject. He therefore saw no necessity for either of these propositions. He thought the section as it came from the committee preferable to either of them. He did not think the term of an appointment should of necessity expire within thirty days after the meeting of the Legislature If the appointment made by the Governor was an improper one, the Senate could at any time reject it.

He was not aware that the Governor had the power to appoint, during the recess, and that if the nomination was rejected by the Senate, he could fill the office again with the same person, until the gentleman from Anne Arundel, (Mr. Donaldson,) suggested it. If the Governor had any such power, it ought to be taken away from him.

Mr. Donaldson explained what he had said

Mr. Brent referred to the opinion of the Attorney General, Charles Lee, as directly opposite to that given by Mr. Wirt, as to the power of the President to appoint a commissioner, (an original appointment,) during the recess of the Senate If there was a doubt existing on the subject, it ought to be removed by the action of this Convention.

Mr. Chambers concurred in the general course of the remarks of the gentleman from Cecil — But there was still room for doubt whether the temporary appointee would not hold on after a rejection by the Senate. The language is express that the appointee shall continue to hold the office till a new appointmens is made. No new appointment is made until a nomination is confirmed. He could not suppose the Convention designed to have the temporary appointee fill the office after his rejection, and yet if other persons were afterwards nominated, who were also rejected, there would be no new appointment, and then the language of the proposed section might be relied on to justify the temporary appointee to continue. He stated what he considered to be the practice of the General Government, under the Constitution of the United States. Where a knowledge of a vacancy first came to the President in the recess, it was regarded as "occurring in the recess." He would be willing to take the section with the simple addition of the word "occurring," and adding a provision that the temporary appointment should cease with the next session of the Senate.

Mr. Grason called the attention of the Convention to the article as it was reported, and the substitute proposed for it. According to the bill as it now stood, a person appointed in the recess, must be nominated to the Senate within thirty days from the commencement of the session, and if rejected, his appointment terminates; and of course his commission cannot be continued or renewed after the adjournment. The fourteenth section expressly provides that no person, rejected by the Senate, shall be appointed during the recess.

The objection to the substitute is, that it only provides for vacancies that "*occur during the recess.*" These words are used in the existing Constitution, and have been susceptible of different constructions. Under one Executive, the construction has been, that *any* vacancy in the recess, is considered as *occurring* at the time; and under a different administration it was supposed that no vacancy could be considered as *occurring during the recess*, unless it originated after the adjournment of the Senate. Under the latter construction, the most important offices might remain vacant, in case of the death or resignation of the incumbents immediately before the adjournment.

In preparing the bill, the committee had wished to avoid the use of the doubtful terms which are now attempted to be revived.

The gentleman from Kent, (Mr. Chambers,) was extremely anxious to guard against any possible abuse of power by the Governor, but as regards the abuse of power, on the part of the Senate, he appeared to entertain no apprehensions whatever. There might be abuses of power by the Senate as well as the Executive, and appointments might fail from a difference of opinion respecting the persons nominated. In case of a difference between the Executive and Senate, and a consequent failure to make an appointment, the Governor ought to have the power during the recess to fill the vacancy, not by appointing persons who had been rejected, but others who were not liable to objection.

Mr. McLane rose to reply to the gentleman from Kent on two points—the one a difference of principle, and the other of interpretation. The law of the United States provided, in case that a vacancy was found in the recess of the Senate, the President may fill it in the recess.

Mr. Chambers objected that this was too broad an interpretation. The practice is this: if the President has first heard of a vacancy in the recess, it is the construction that it occurred when the President heard of it. But the President has no power to fill any office which was vacated during the session, in the recess.

Mr. McLane contended that where any vacancy is found to exist in the recess, the President fills it in the recess.

Mr. Chambers did not mean his remarks to apply to a certain class of appointments which come under a new system of laws.

Mr. McLane replied that this was the very class to which this exercise of power bears reference. The practice of the General Government as he had stated it, is in accordance with a construction put on the power, and sustained by the ablest statesmen and writers in the United States, and arises from the necessity of the case. And it had led to no ill results, but exclusively to good. And, he asked, why would not gentleman profit by the lessons of experience! Why deny to the Governor of the State, the same power which the United States Constitution gives to the President of the United States. Why should we throw out of our institutions that privilege which has been found indispensibly necessary in the administration of the General Government? Cases of great emergency may arise, and you deprive the Governor of the power to act as the necessity of the cases demands, lest a fraud should be perpetrated. The gentleman from Kent supposes that under this section an appointment made in the recess may continue until the end of the session, or a new appointment is made. He presumed the original section did not mean this, but only until the Senate should appoint. It was never intended that he should hold to the end of the session, but only until there is a new appointment. If there is ambiguity, he was willing to adopt any language which would remove it.

Mr. Chambers repeated what he had before said, as to the practice under the Constitution of the United States. Certainly General Jackson in the plentitude of his power, had largely advanced upon any previous practice. But he did not admit the propriety of his new precedents. He never did and never could approve the re-appointment of Mr. Gwynn, after his nomination had been once rejected, and on a second nomination laid on the table. But a manifest difference was to be noticed between the condition of the United States, and the State of Maryland. The vast extent of the former might require a large part of a session of Congress, to pass away after a vacancy had occurred, before a knowledge of the fact could reach the President. The Senate may have adjourned in the *interim*. In that case, for all pratical purposes, the vacancy did occur in the recess, that is to say, when the President first became informed of it. In Maryland such a thing was not to be expected; with the facilities for rapid communication, it was scarcely possible. But why further discuss this question? There was doubt expressed, therefore, he assumed there was room for doubt. A very few words would remove it, and make it as plain as a pike-staff. Why then this unwillingness to change a letter, a cross or a dot?

Mr. Grason and Mr. Chambers mutually explained.

The question was then taken on the amendment of Mr. Brent, of Baltimore, (as accepted by Mr. Crisfield.)

No quorum voted.

A long conversation followed on points of order.

The question was then again taken on the said amendment.

But no quorum voted.

Mr. Presstman moved that there be a call of the Convention.

The motion was not insisted upon, a quorum having been ascertained to be present.

The question on the amendment was then again taken, and it was rejected.

The question then recurred on the adoption of the thirteenth section, as amended.

Mr Grason offered as a substitute for said section, the following:

"*Section* 13. In case of any vacancy during the recess of the Senate, in any office which the Governor has power to fill, he shall appoint some suitable person to fill said office, whose commission shall continue in force till the end of the next session of the Legislature, or until some other person is appointed to the same office, whichever shall first occur, and the nomination of every person thus appointed during the recess or of any other person in his place, shall be made to the Senate within thirty days after the next meeting of the Legislature."

Some conversation passed between Messrs. Chambers, of Kent, and Grason, arising out of a change in the phraseology suggested by the former gentleman.

The question recurred on the substitute of Mr. Grason.

Mr. Chambers, of Kent, moved to amend the said substitute, by adding the words he had suggested to Mr. Grason,) as follows:

In the first line, after the word "vacancy," insert the words "may happen."

The amendment of Mr. Chambers, by ayes 28, noes 27, was agreed to.

The question recurred on the adoption of the substitute of Mr. Grason.

And it was adopted.

And the section, as amended, was adopted.

Mr. Thomas, by permission of the Convention, withdrew the amendment offered by him on Saturday, the 8th instant, to the fifth section of the report, and substituted the following:

"The State shall be divided into four districts. Allegany, Washington, Frederick, Carroll and Baltimore counties, to be the first; St. Mary's, Charles, Prince George's, Anne Arundel, Howard and Montgomery counties, the second; Baltimore city the third; Harford and the eight counties on the Eastern Shore, the fourth district."

MOTIONS TO RECONSIDER.

Mr. Chambers, of Kent, gave notice of his intention to move a reconsideration of the twenty-second rule for the purpose of introducing the following amendment:

"Whenever a question shall have been decided by yeas and nays, no motion to reconsider shall prevail, unless there shall be cast in favor of a reconsideration a larger number of votes than those of the majority or original vote."

Mr. Brown moved that the Convention take up for consideration the second section of the report of the committee on the Executive department, for the purpose of making it the order of the day for Thursday next."

Pending the question on this motion,

The Convention adjourned until to-morrow morning at ten o'clock.

SATURDAY, March 15th, 1851.

The Convention met at ten o'clock.

Prayer was made by the Rev. Mr. Grauff.

The roll of the members was called.

There was no quorum present.

Mr. Phelps moved that there be a call of the Convention.

Five members having sustained, the motion, (as required by the rule,) a call of the Convention was ordered.

The roll was called.

And the names of the absentees were then again called.

When the name of Mr. Chandler was called,

The President, *pro tem.*, rose and stated to the Convention, that he had been requested by Mr. Chandler, to inform the Convention, that he had been called home by the illness of a member of his family.

The doorkeeper was sent to notify the absent members to attend; and, in a short time, he returned and stated, through the President, *pro tem.*, that he had perform his duty.

Subsequently the doors were locked, and the Sergeant-at-arms, was sent to bring in the absent members.

After some proceedings, and a good deal of fun, (no quorum having been obtained,)

The Convention adjourned until Monday morning at ten o'clock.

MONDAY, March 17, 1851.

The Convention met at ten o'clock.

At a quarter before twelve o'clock,

Prayer was made by the Rev. Mr. Grauff.

No quorum was present.

Mr. Phelps rose and said, it was intimated by gentlemen near him, that a quorum was in the city. By calling the roll, and sending the doorkeeper to notify such members as might be in the city to attend, it was probable that the attendance of a quorum might be obtained.

The roll was accordingly called.

Thirty-four members only answered to their names.

Mr. Phelps moved that the doorkeeper be sent to notify the absent members to attend.

Mr. Bowie. Of what use will it be? There is no quorum in the city.

Mr. Phelps. I understood there was.

Mr. Bowie. Oh, no! Only four or five members came down by the cars. I move, (addressing the Secretary in the absence of the President, *pro. tem.*,) that this Convention do now adjourn.

Mr. Shriver moved that the names of those present be entered on the journal, and that the Secretary put the question on the motion to adjourn.

The Secretary stated the question to be on the motion to adjourn.

Mr. Phelps asked the yeas and nays, which after some conversation on a point of order, were taken, and

Were yeas 18, nays 25.

So the Convention refused to adjourn.

And, the motion having been renewed and decided in the affirmative,

The Convention adjourned until to-morrow morning at ten o'clock.

TUESDAY, March 18, 1851.

Prayer was made by the Rev. Mr. Griffith.

Mr. Ware rose and moved, that in the absence of the President of the Convention, Mr. Buchanan, of Baltimore county take the Chair.

The motion was unanimously agreed to.

Mr. Buchanan thereupon took the Chair.

The roll of the members was called.

Forty-seven members answered to their names.

After some time, fifty members were reported to be present.

Not a quorum.

Mr. Smith said that there were, to his knowledge, other members of the Convention in the city not now in their seats. He would, therefore, move that there be a call of the Convention.

The roll was called and a quorum was ascertained to be present.

THE PRESIDENT.

Mr. Bowie rose and stated that a letter had been received from General Chapman, President of the Convention, stating that he was detained from the Convention by a serious accident. It would, therefore, be necessary to go into the election of a President, *pro tem.* And he, (Mr. B.,) moved that the Convention now go into an election.

The question was taken,

And the motion was agreed to.

Mr. Bowie nominated Mr. Williams, of Somerset.

Mr. Shriver nominated Mr. Buchanan, of Baltimore county, (the present Chairman.)

Mr. DIRICKSON enquired whether any motion had been made as to the mode by which the election should take place—by ballot or *viva voce?*

The CHAIRMAN said no motion had been made. Does the gentleman submit any?

Mr. DIRICKSON. I have none to make.

Mr. BOWIE. I move that the election take place *viva voce.*

The motion was agreed to.

Mr. SHRIVER moved that the Secretary announce the names of the nominees, (which being done,)

Mr. SMITH moved that tellers be appointed to count the votes.

Ordered accordingly.

Mr. PHELPS moved that the tellers be appointed by the Chair.

Ordered accordingly.

The CHAIRMAN appointed the following gentlemen tellers to count the votes:

Mr. MAGRAW, of Harford.

Mr. PHELPS, of Dorchester.

The tellers took their seats and the Secretary proceeded to call the roll.

Mr. JENIFER, when his name was called, remarked that it would give him pleasure to vote for Doctor WILLIAMS, but as the Presidents, *pro tem.* had hitherto been taken from the smaller counties, he preferred to vote on the present occasion for a gentleman from one of the upper counties, and should therefore vote for the gentleman from Baltimore county, (Mr. BUCHANAN.)

The roll having been called through,

The result of the vote was announced as follows:

Whole number of votes, fifty-three.

Of which number—

Mr. BUCHANAN received thirty-four, and Mr. WILLIAMS, nineteen.

So Mr. BUCHANAN, having received a majority of all the votes cast, was declared duly elected PRESIDENT, *pro. tem.*

Whereupon, the PRESIDENT, *pro. tem.*, took the Chair, and, after a brief pause, rose and addressed the Convention as follows:

Gentlemen of the Convention:

I acknowledge with deep sensibility the honor you have conferred upon me, in calling me to administer the duties of this Chair during the regretted absence of the presiding officer of your choice. I speak with unaffected sincerity when I say, that this signal mark of your confidence and respect was not less merited, than unexpected by me. Yielding, however, to no man in a stern patriotic purpose to accomplish the great objects which have brought us together, I shall endeavor to discharge the duties of this station in such a manner as may best promote these objects and secure their final consummation. In this earnest and honest effort, I shall rely confidently, gentlemen, on your forbearance and support.

It is not inappropriate to the occasion to say, that since I have had the honor of a seat in this Convention, it has been my good fortune to move on harmoniously, and in the kindest interchange of fraternal regard with all its members. I have had but one aim—one end—one hope. I have known no party. I have cast from me, as unworthy and polluted things in such an assembly as this, all party considerations. I have looked with a single eye to the honor and the welfare of proud old Maryland—the Shibboleth of our policy—the glorious centre of all our hopes and all our affections! I have endeavored solely and simply to secure to her the adoption of such a Constitution, as her enlightened and patriotic children have a right to expect at our hands. Nor has my confidence in the ultimate realization of that result, been in any degree shaken. I do conscientiously believe, that notwithstanding the portentous clouds which have at times darkened our horizon, there exists an inflexible determination here to give a triumphant issue to our labors, by the formation of a Constitution which will be acceptable to the people, and under whose benignant provisions the State may rapidly advance towards the fulfilment of the high destiny that awaits her.

The work is before us. Gentlemen, let us accomplish it.

The journal of Saturday last and of yesterday, were then severally read and approved.

MOTIONS TO RE-CONSIDER.

Mr. CHAMBERS, in pursuance of the notice he had heretofore given, moved to reconsider the twenty-second rule of the Convention, for the purpose of introducing the following amendment:

"Whenever a question shall have been decided by yeas and nays, no motion to re-consider shall prevail, unless there shall be cast in favor of a re-consideration a larger number of votes than those of the majority on the original vote."

Mr. C. said, he took it for granted, that it was not necessary for him to say any thing in favor of this change of the rule. Its object simply was to prevent a thin Convention from over-ruling the decision of a Convention more full. Common honesty, it seemed to him, required the change.

Mr. McLANE said, he was sorry he could not vote in favor of the proposition of the gentleman from Kent, (Mr. Chambers.) It might lead to a vast deal of embarrassment, and was not exactly in place, he thought, in such a body as this. Of all bodies, that which had assembled for the purpose of forming a Constitution should, as regarded votes and re-consideration of votes upon propositions which might from time to time come before it, be as free as possible.

On going back to the Convention which formed the Constitution of the United States, and probably there could be no better model, either as regarded the instrument itself, or the character of the body which framed it, it would be found that the constant practice was to take up a subject to-day, vote upon it, lay it aside, take up another, and, after considering that, go back by a motion to reconsider to that subject which they had in the first instance partially disposed of. Such was the practice of that body, not only as regarded cardinal principles, but the details of measures. And it was absolutely necessary that it should be so.—The motion of the gentleman from Kent (Mr. Chambers) would very much deprive the Convention of all the benefits resulting from such a practice. So far as his [Mr. McL's.] knowledge extended, no such rule as the gentleman proposed was to be found in any deliberative or legislative body, unless perhaps it might have been in some of the colonial or provincial Legislatures. The only distinction in relation to motions to reconsider had been, that such a motion should be made by a member who had voted with the majority; and this had been a sufficient security against any improper use of the power to reconsider. This Convention had varied that rule, because it had found it requisite to do so for its own security. He was willing to go back to the original vote, so far as to require that motions to reconsider should be made by members voting with the majority; but he was opposed to the adoption of any new restriction from which he conceived great inconvenience might result. And Mr. McL. put a case in illustration.

He found that in the Convention which framed the Constitution of the State of Massachusetts in 1820-21, a motion had been made similar to that of the gentleman from Kent, [Mr. Chambers.] The rule was debated by some most eminent men; and, after a good deal of discussion, a motion was made by Mr. Morton to strike out the whole rule, and insert "one which should allow of reconsideration, when as many members voted for it as were in favor of the original measure, provided they were a majority of the members voting on the question of reconsideration—notice to be given—and one reconsideration of the same question only to be allowed." Let us see how Mr. Webster treated the proposition. He [Mr. McL.] read from page 27, of the debates of the Convention.

"Mr. Webster thought, that of all the various propositions which the occasion had elicited, that now before the Convention was the most extraordinary. It appeared to him to be in many respects objectionable. In the first place, what is meant by requiring as many votes to reconsider a motion, as were in favor of the original measure? Suppose the questions were on the adoption of an amendment—a vary small number, for example five, might be in favor of it, and all the rest against it. Yet, in this case, by the proposed rule, the vote was necessarily to be reconsidered. The honorable gentleman had drawn his motion as if *affirmative* votes only could be reconsidered, and has made no provision at all for the reconsideration of *negative* votes. Again, according to this provision, a motion for reconsideration might be made and discussed for a week; then put to the vote, and although carried affirmatively by a majority, have no effect, and be declared a nullity because the majority was not large enough.

"He begged leave to dissent entirely, and most widely, from all such modes of proceeding. All rules respecting reconsiderations, were intended and adopted for the purpose of ascertaining, under what circumstances, and by whom, a motion for reconsideration might be brought forward. But when once brought forward, it must, of course, like all other motions, be decided by a majority. Nobody, he believed, ever before heard of a rule, by which a motion to reconsider when once regularly made, was not to be decided like other motions. It might well be doubted whether the Convention could prescribe any such rules; rules by which anything, more than a majority of members should be required for the decision of any question regularly before it.

"Mr. W. proceeded to say, it was with great unwillingness that he troubled the Convention again on this occasion, but he would indulge the hope, that after the failure of so many attempts to qualify the right of moving to reconsider, in any manner acceptable to the Convention, gentlemen would be more inclined to adopt the usual limitation—the restriction of the right to some member voting with the majority. No other qualification was so simple, or so easily understood, and none better secured the right against abuse."

Mr. W. then went on, (continued Mr. McL.,) to advocate the adoption of the general rule, as applied in most cases—that was to say, that the motion to reconsider should be made by a member voting with the majority.

The rule proposed by Mr. Morton, which was the same as that now offered by the gentleman from Kent, (Mr. Chambers,) was voted down, without even the form of a division, and ultimately the Convention, on the motion of Mr. Webster, adopted precisely the rule which he, (Mr. McL.,) had indicated at the outset of his remarks; that was, simply requiring the motion to be made by a member voting with the majority.

We had had that rule here, but it was changed. He confessed that he desired as much latitude as possible, and he thought that such also should be the general desire of the Convention. A decision might be made on a question to-day, when there might be a thin attendance. It might become important to have the decision of a full House.

They were acting here on the formation of a Constitution which was to endure, he hoped, so long as any of those, who assisted in framing it might exist. And it was important that every part of it should be well considered. If a mistake was made to-day, the Convention should have an opportunity without any great formality to go back to the proposition and rectify that mistake. When the Convention came to the final vote, there would probably be a full attendance, and any error which might have been made could be corrected.

He thought that the gentleman from Kent, (Mr. Chambers,) would not obtain his object by the proposition he had offered. He thought the amendment which had been made to the rule on the motion of the gentleman from Frederick, (Mr. Thomas,) was a good one. The Convention had not wasted time under it, nor did he think that there need be any apprehension on that score.

Mr. Chambers said he felt some degree of

mortification, as well as surprise, at the opposition to the proposed change or addition to the rule. He had supposed if any proposition could be offered, which would receive universal consent, it was this. It seemed to him to be dictated by the plainest principles, not of generosity only, but of common fairness and propriety. What was it? Why nothing more nor less than this, that after a majority had deliberately adopted a measure, it should not be defeated and annuled by a minority. He thought the fairly expressed will of the majority ought to prevail. If this republican doctrine was sound any where, it certainly was here in this body. He must be permitted to say, that he could not perceive the accuracy of the conclusions to which the argument of the gentleman from Cecil, had conducted him. With the gentleman's argument, he found no necessity to battle, but his, (Mr. C.'s,) perceptions must be strangely oblique, if they justified the result at which that gentleman had arrived. The argument was that in a body like this, there should be a full and perfect opportunity to reconsider every measure which might have been adopted. No one has gainsaid this. We have a rule granting leave to reconsider, more liberal and of broader extent than ever prevailed, so far as he knew and believed, in any Convention or legislative body, in any State in this Union. It allows a reconsideration to be moved, at any period of the session, however remote from the day of the original vote, by any individual, whether in the majority or minority. The gentleman had found a debate, in the proceedings of the Massachusetts Convention of 1820, on this subject of reconsideration, and supposed he also found there a proposition like this, and that it was rebuked by Mr. Webster. Sir, said Mr. C., there is not more difference between light and darkness, than there is between that case and this. In that case, as it is read by the gentleman, for he had not seen it, the rule proposed for reconsideration was, that the motion must be made on the *same* or the *next day* after the vote taken. Here it may be reconsidered at any period of the session. The rule there required as many members of the Convention to be present, at the time of the reconsideration, as at the time when the original vote passes. In our rule no such requirement is found.

The object of Mr. Webster seemed to be, as far as he could collect it from the gentleman's reading, to have the rule conform to the rule which obtains in Congress. Where the motion to reconsider was confined to the same or the next day, there could not well be surprise, and that was what he wished to avoid. The same members would be apt to be present; at all events they would know that a reconsideration might be moved within that period, and after remaining to the close of the succeeding day, would be secure against surprise. But how is it here? We have one hundred and three members. They may all be present, and on a contested question, in a full house a proposition is carried, and an article of the Constitution adopted, by a vote of seventy-six to twenty-seven. The yeas and nays are recorded, showing this to be the sentiment of the house. At the expiration of three months after this vote, there are fifty-five members attending; a case not impossible, because it has actually and repeatedly occurred. One of the twenty-seven moves, after a day's notice, for a reconsideration, and it is voted for by twenty-seven members, then being a majority, and the vote of the seventy-six is overuled by the vote of twenty-seven; it may be the same twenty-seven, who, when the house was full, constituted barely a fourth of the whole number of votes given. Was this proper? Was it consistent with fair dealing? Was there anything in the Massachusetts Convention, or any other Convention like it? He thought not. But, says the gentleman, we may expect a full Convention when a final vote on a proposition is to be taken. What security have we for this? Nay, what reasonable expectation have we? We have taken final votes, and most important votes; we have waited and postponed from time to time, but have we had a full house? The journal would sadly contradict any such statement. We all knew that members were continually absent, attending to their professional and domestic concerns, and the prolonged session of the body would further increase the motives to be absent. He had no motives, personal or political, to gratify. He was in his chair all day, every day. His particular views were as little likely to be injuriously affected by the existing state of the rule, as those of any other individual. His sole object was to secure the Convention against the effects of excited feeling, which might lead an accidental majority, to yield to other influences than such as prudence and sound discretion would suggest, and do what was wrong in itself.

His amendment only applied to votes taken by yeas and nays, [always the index of a fixed purpose,] and simply protected such a vote from a reversal by a smaller number of votes, at any subsequent time.

Mr. C. here read from the proceedings of the Massachussetts Convention, [which had been handed to him from Mr. McLane,] and insisted that Mr. Webster had not said one word in opposition to the views which he, [Mr. C.,] had advocated. The state of the rule there, does not make it a case of resemblance or comparison in the particular to which his amendment applied. Mr. Webster's rule was, on the contrary, decidedly more stringent than ours would be after the amendment should be added to it.

He alluded to the various instances of motions for reconsideration—and the extended discussions which have been had since the presentation of the first report—the report from the committee on the elective franchise—and to the small number of attending members, to show the danger of reconsidering with a thin House.

He was a thorough-bred republican, at least in one respect. He thought a decision of the majority, fairly expressed, ought to prevail and not be subject to reversal by a subsequent vote of the minority. He had, therefore, thought it best to guard against this danger; but, if a majority of the Convention chose to authorise such a state of things, be it so. He could submit with as good grace as other folks. He could not, however, believe it would add much unction to their work—the new Constitution. He repeated his surprise at the opposition, the more particularly, because, when he gave notice of his intention to move it, he thought there were manifestations of approbation from all parts of the Hall.

Mr. McLane said, that the tone rather than the substance of the remarks of the gentleman from Kent, (Mr. Chambers,) induced him, (Mr. McL.,) to trespass a few moments longer upon the time of the Convention. He had not stated, nor insinuated, that the learned gentleman had found a precedent for his motion in the proceedings of any previous Conventions which had been held. He, (Mr. McL.,) was sure that the gentleman could not find a case in which a motion had been successfully made to engraft such a provision on the rules of proceeding. The gentleman was entitled to the merit of an original invention; and he, (Mr. McL.,) freely conceded that merit to him. It was true that a proposition identical, as he understood, with this had been introduced into the Massachusetts Convention, and had been deemed so objectionable on all sides as to have been voted down without a division. If, therefore, the gentleman from Kent, [Mr. Chambers,] had seen the notice of such a proposition in the Convention of Massachusetts, and was aware of the fate to which it was consigned, he must have had some courage undoubtedly to introduce such a proposition here, with any expectation that it would be successful. Surely he, (Mr. McL.,) did not mean to say, that the gentleman obtained his proposition from the Massachusetts or any other Convention. What he had said was, that such a rule never had, so far as his knowledge extended, been adopted in any legislative body or Convention—unless a precedent might be found in the provincial legislatures—a source to which he thought very few would be disposed at this day to go for parliamentary rules, or rules relating to the freedom of debate, or of action.

He had referred the gentleman to the Convention which formed the Constitution of the United States, where it would be found that the right of re-consideration and the practice were alike free.

Some conversation passed between Messrs. Chambers, of Kent, and McLane; after which

Mr. McLane resumed his remarks. He meant to say, that the practice of the Convention which formed the Constitution of the United States was uniform, in daily going back, for purposes of re-consideration, to questions which had been passed upon.

Mr. Bowie, [in his seat.] Without limitation as to time?

Mr. McLane. Without limitation as to time, so far as I know.

Mr. Chambers, of Kent. We will have the authority here, so that we may be certain.

Mr. McLane continued. He thought that if the gentleman would look to the Madisonian papers, or to any other authority professing to give the proceedings of the Convention, he would find that all these strict parliamentary rules were dispensed with. He did not mean to say that there were no written rules. He meant to say, that no question was disposed of at any one time, until the Convention came to take the vote on the close of the whole question.

In relation to the evil spoken of by the gentleman from Kent—the right of a minority to control the majority—he, [Mr. McL.,] did not differ with that gentleman. But he wished that the gentleman would carry the principle a little further into graver matters, rather than into mere matters affecting the rules of proceeding in this body—that he would agree to form a Constitution upon a basis by which the majority, and not the minority, should have the control of the Government. He, [Mr. McL.,] could not, therefore, dissent from the view expressed by the gentleman on this point. He, [Mr. McL.,] meant to say this: if the gentleman was afraid of the rule as it now stood, let him go back to Mr. Webster's rule and provide that a re-consideration shall only be moved by a member voting in the majority. What he, [Mr. McL.,] objected to, was that, after a vote had been taken, no matter how the opinions of gentlemen might have changed, no matter how egregiously they might have erred in the decision they had made, they could not go back and rectify the error, unless there were the same number of members here who voted in the first instance.

Mr. Chambers went into an examination of the proceedings in the Massachusetts Convention, insisting on the marked difference between that case and the one now before this House; and that nothing said by Mr. Webster, was intended to oppose the principle now proposed. The first amendment proposed to the Massachusetts rule, was by Mr. Bliss, "that no vote of the House should be reconsidered, except on motion of one of the majority." It was objected that this "would preclude any one who was absent, or did not vote, from moving a reconsideration." To this Mr. Webster replied, "it was proper it should operate in that manner." "No one should be absent, flattering himself he might remedy any mischief by moving a reconsideration." "He wished every subject to be thoroughly discussed, but he wished it to be done according to the rules of legislative bodies." "Every member conversant with the proceedings of deliberative assemblies, must have observed the inconvenience from the practice of frequently reconsidering votes which have been passed."

The rule was subsequently reported in such a form as to require as *many members of the Convention* to be present when a reconsideration is voted for, as were present when the original vote passed. Was that what is now proposed here? Not at all—nothing like it. What was the objection there? Hear it: "The House is now very numerous—gentlemen would be from inevitable accident called home, and the members of the House regularly decreasing. It would also be in the power of persons opposed to reconsideration, to keep out of the House, and in that way to gain their object." Yes, sir, one man by keeping out of the House might thereby prevent a reconsideration, though a number very much larger than that by which the original vote was carried, were ready and anxious to reconsider.

It was this which occasioned the strong remark of Mr. Varnum. A rule was then proposed "to allow of re-consideration, when as many members voted for it as were in favor of the original measure, provided, they were a majority of the members voting on the re-consideration—notice to be given and one re-consideration only to be allowed."

The defects in this rule as stated by Mr. Webster, and which induced him to declare it the most extraordinary of all propositions submitted, were amongst others, that on a question of adopting an amendment to the Constitution "a very small number, for example five, might be in favor of it and all the rest against it, yet in this case, by the proposed rule, the vote was *necessarily* to be re-considered." Again he said: "the rule as proposed was drawn as if *affirmative* votes only could be re-considered." Did these objections, Mr. C. asked, did either of them apply here? Most certainly not. An equal number of members need not be present, an affirmative or a negative vote may be re-considered, and he would add, a majority will have its decision enforced. All that had been quoted from Mr. Webster, was said in relation to the particular rule there discussed. He was for restricting the right of reconsideration, greatly more than it would be restricted by our rule, with the amendment now before us. The language on page 28—too long to quote at large—will be found to design any thing but a commendation on the facilities of re-consideration. But we were not left to grope through an argument to find Mr. Webster's views. After succeeding in convincing the Massachusetts Convention of the correctness of his views, he embodied them in a condensed form in the shape of a rule in the following words—to be found on page 29—"when a motion has been made and carried, in the affirmative or negative, it shall be in order for any member of the majority, to move for a re-consideration thereof, on the same or succeeding day." And on page 30, this rule was adopted, by a vote of two hundred and fifty to one hundred and twenty. This is precisely the rule of Congress, which we have thought it right and proper, greatly to enlarge. This rule, it will at once be seen, restricts the right to reconsider greatly more than the rule here would do, even when amended as now proposed. He trusted, that, however, in the first remarks he had made, without the book to consult, he had misapplied some of the remarks there used, he had now fully satisfied the Convention that he was not proposing a measure which would make a reconsideration more difficult than Mr. Webster's did.

The gentlemen from Cecil does not deny or propose to remedy the evils against which this proposition is directed, but rests his opposition on the ground of its "novelty." Why certainly it is novel. And why novel? Simply for the reason that the existing rule is novel, entirely novel, not known or adopted in any Convention or legislature, whose history is known to us. And was it not ' of course," that modifications of this "novel" rule must be "novel" also. He did not suppose that in this presence, the argument *per se*, that a measure was novel, should condemn it.

The gentleman had referred to the rule said to be adopted in the Convention which formed the Constitution of the United States. No other evidence had been furnished of the existence of any such rule, except what was said of it by one of the members in the course of debate in Massachusetts. He could not, of course, admit or deny what was the character or purport of a rule of which neither he or the gentleman were informed. So much for the proposed alteration of the rule, about which he cared but little, but wished it understood.

The gentleman from Cecil had commented on his, (Mr. C.'s,) profession of republicanism, intimating a want of consistency in not carrying out the principle of "the right of a majority to rule." He did understand the allusion, not being aware he had on any occasion here advocated the doctrine that a minority should control the majority. He had expected the majority of this Convention to make the new Constitution. He held they were bound to do so, and he, for one, was ready and constantly had been, to employ himself in this duty. He was every hour of every day in his chair, and intended so to be, to the neglect of other urgent and important duties, to accomplish this very purpose. It was very true that those who were so loud in their demands for reform, cannot now determine amongst themselves, what is the reform needed. That was no fault of his, nor should the fault be at his door, if no Constitution was made. He was always ready to vote, and if out-voted to submit.

He was not, therefore, to be impeached by anything he had done here when he claimed to be a republican. He was one—one of the old stamp—had been so all the days of his life. The first political speech he ever made, the first vote he ever gave, were made and given in and for that school, and there he had remained in it to this day. This was dating, perhaps, beyond some gentleman who had attached themselves to later schools of republicanism, and which, because later, were of course improvements; as the book-makers say of their new editions, "revised, corrected and improved." These new editions sometimes command a higher price, but they do not always contain better matter. He was a republican in nothing more sternly than in the doctrine, that in every question properly for decision, a majority should govern.

Mr. Brent, of Baltimore city, said that much time had, undoubtedly, been consumed in deciding questions of reconsideration, but still more time, he thought, had been consumed in reconsidering the rules of the Convention, because, no sooner was one set of rules adopted, than it was immediately met by a motion to reconsider. He thought, however, that the great evil was not in the rules, but in a difficulty which the amendment of the gentleman from Kent, (Mr. CHAMBERS,) did not propose to remedy.

Mr. B. here referred to the habit of gentlemen to read the newspapers when the debates were going on, thus not listening to what might be said. [Several gentlemen rose and asserted their ability to read the newspapers and listen, at the same time, to everything that was said.]

Mr. BRENT continued. All he could say then, was, that gentlemen had a finer capacity than he possessed.

Mr. B. then referred to the case of the thirteenth section of the executive report, which had been reconsidered, and in which, after the reconsideration, on the motion of the gentleman from Kent, [Mr. Chambers,] the proposition had been restored just as it stood before. The result was, that the same mischief was left in the new Constitution which was found in the old one. He referred to the proposition which allowed the Governor to make temporary appointments during the recess where they were not cases of vacancy. There was the case of an original proposition passed for want of proper attention. It was reconsidered, and then restored as it stood before. Unless the Convention could enforce gentlemen to attend to what was going on—to keep the current of the debate and thus enable themselves to vote understandingly—no rule would prevent the consumption of time in motions to reconsider.

What was the proposition of the gentleman from Kent, [Mr. Chambers]? That the majority must govern. The rule was a very good one for the Convention, but would not do for the people. Gentlemen were not willing to apply it to the people. He would like to see gentlemen consistent—these Jeffersonian republicans, who were born in the doctrines of the Jeffersonian school—he would like to see them carry out these principles, as he, (Mr. B.,) did, among the people. Did Jefferson sanction the doctrine that the minority of the people were to govern? He would like to see the gentleman carry out the doctrines of that eminent man in all respects.

Mr. B. then examined the proposition of Mr. CHAMBERS—gave his, [Mr. B's,] understanding of its effect, and argued that it ought not to be adopted. Members might from better information, from conscientious conviction of the error of their decision, change their minds, and desire to reconsider the decision they had made. They should not be deprived of the opportunity to do so.

Mr. CHAMBERS replied. His remarks will be published hereafter.

Mr. PRESSTMAN said:

That he should not enter upon any of these nice distinctions which had been drawn on either side in the course of this debate. He did not know that it was important to the settlement of this question, whether the proposition had been sustained, or voted down in the Convention of Massachusetts, or whether the gentleman from Kent, (Mr. Chambers,) had adhered more closely to the Jeffersonian track than the gentleman from Cecil, (Mr. McLane,) or the gentleman from Baltimore city, (Mr. Brent,) or whether, when the gentleman from Kent brought forward his amendment, (from the most honest motives as he, [Mr. P.,] did not doubt,) the almost unanimous sentiment of the Convention was in favor of its adoption. He did not know how the gentleman had arrived at that conclusion.

Mr. CHAMBERS, of Kent. By a general exclamation. I heard at least a dozen voices cry out in its favor.

Mr. PRESSTMAN, continuing, said, that he was in the Convention at the time the notice was given, and no such exclamations had reached his ear. He had no doubt that the gentleman was sincere and honest in his course—that he believed that the existing rule had worked mischief, and that his amendment would work good.

He, [Mr P.,] desired to call the attention of the Convention to the plain, practical fact. There were now upon the journal, propositions which had passed by immense majorities, as to which motions of reconsideration had been intimated, and which, if not reconsidered, might, in the opinion of some gentlemen lead to a good deal of harm.

In this connection, Mr. P. cited the case of the single provision abolishing imprisonment for debt, where the naked principle had been adopted, without any of these controling provisions which, in the judgment of some gentlemen, could alone obviate the ruinous effects which would result from its adoption. That proposition had passed by an affirmative vote of sixty-five—against a negative vote of some five or six. This was one prominent measure in respect to which a motion to reconsider was pending. That motion had been indicated by the gentleman from Kent, (Mr. Chambers.)

It was to be borne in mind that, although the gentleman from Kent had, no doubt, in his eye the future and not the past proceedings of the Convention, yet, as the gentleman from Cecil, (Mr. McLane,) had stated, the gentleman from Kent, (Mr. Chambers,) was not here arguing for the restoration of the rule as it originally stood. If the gentleman's proposition had sought merely to restore the rule which provided that no member should move a reconsideration, except he had voted with the majority, he, (Mr. P.,) could see some good reason for it.

But the gentleman proposed an entirely different thing. He had gone, in his, [Mr. P's,] judgment one step too far, and had submitted a proposition, the effect of which, would be to delay, rather than facilitate the business of the Convention. He did not believe that the gentleman desired any such result.

He, [Mr. P.,] thought that a majority of the Convention might be willing to restore the old rule; but this was entirely a new proposition for which the gentleman had not been able to produce a single precedent in any legislative body.

He, [Mr. P.,] was one of those who were in favor of the application of the previous question. He hoped it would be freely used. It was at any time, in the power of the Convention to get rid, by its application, of any subject-matter before it, whenever they believed that the discussion had been sufficiently extended, to enable the members to give an intelligent vote.

Some further remarks were made by Messrs. CHAMBERS and PRESSMAN which will be published hereafter.

Mr. BRENT, of Baltimore city, said, that when he called attention to the fact that but few members were listening—although it appeared to be the case that some were listening who were, at the same time, reading newspapers—it was with no unkind motives, and was intended as no reflection upon any member of the Convention. On the contrary, it was intended as a strong illustration of the evil to which he had referred.

Mr. B. proceeded to illustrate his objection to the amendment proposed, by supposing that one hundred and three members, being the whole number, should be present, and that they should be so equally divided that fifty-two should be in favor of the proposition and fifty-one against it. If one of the fifty-two should change his opinion and desire a reconsideration, there would be but fifty-two desiring the reconsideration; and inquired whether it was just and proper that the majority should not have the right, in that contingency, to reconsider.

Mr. CHAMBERS, of Kent, said, that as that was a possible, though not a very probable case, he would modify his proposition so as to allow an equal number of votes to reconsider.

Mr. BRENT proceeded to show that with a less number, the same thing might happen. There being sixty-one members present, for example, if to-day thirty-one were in favor of a proposition and thirty against it; and if to-morrow one of them should change, there would still be but thirty-one in favor of a reconsideration. He was in favor of the rule recommended by all parliamentary experience, and had no doubt that the amendment was carried inconsiderately.

Mr. MCLANE, of Cecil, wished to place himself right; not feeling that justice had been done to his argument by the gentleman from Kent. When he had risen this morning to interrupt the harmony of the majority, by whom the gentleman from Kent seemed to suppose that he was supported, he had not the least conception whether there was a majority for or against the proposition. It was not his custom to reflect whether in any proposition he thought it to be his duty to make, he should be sustained by the majority, or should be found in the minority. He arose for the purpose of expressing his views upon the question before the House; and, having done that, he was content to leave the question with the Convention. The gentleman from Kent had greatly the advantage of him, if he deemed it an advantage, in starting much earlier in the career of Jeffersonian republican. They had started very wide apart, and if he were to judge from what he had seen, they were likely to end just as far apart as when they started. Either one or the other had totally mistaken the Jeffersonian policy; and they must remain the antipodes of each other in respect to that policy. They seemed to be upon different *radii* of a circle, and their distance seemed to be widening as they go. When they come to leap off from that circle to the great ocean beyond, whatever their lot might be, he suspected that neither would be much inclined to dispute about Jeffersonian politics. They would have other cares to engross their attention.

The gentleman had misconceived his argument, and had not done justice to the authorities he (Mr. McL.) had cited. He had not spoken of the rule as it now stood. He had conceded that the rule was an improper one. He thought it prudent and wise to go back to the original rule—the universal rule of every parliamentary body—and to require the motion to reconsider te be made by a member who voted in the majority. His objection was to the mode of correcting the evil. He would now proceed to call the attention of the Convention to the rule proposed in Massachusetts.

The rule reported by the committee, in the Massachusetts Convention, was as follows:

"No motion for the reconsideration of any vote shall be sustained, unless made on the day on which such vote passes, and a return of the Convention be then made and entered on the journal, when the question was not taken by yeas and nays; every such motion shall lie on the table one day before it shall be taken up for consideration, and shall not be taken up, unless as many members are present in Convention, as were present when such vote passed, and not more than one motion for the reconsideration of any one question shall be sustained.

The record shows that Mr. Danna moved to strike out a clause requiring the same number of members to be present when the motion for reconsideration was sustained, as were present on passing the original vote. He considered the rule too strict, and referred to the Convention which framed the Constitution of the United States, in which the right of reconsideration was exercised with the greatest freedom. Mr. Sibley thought it wonld be impossible ever to reconsider a motion, if this rule prevailed. It would be in the power of persons opposed to reconsideration, to keep out of the house, and in that way to gain their object. After a long discussion, the restriction was voted down; and then Mr. Morton made the motion to amend "by striking out the whole rule and inserting one which should allow of reconsideration when as many members voted for it as were in favor of the original measure, provided they were a majority of the members voting on the question of reconsideration—notice to be given, and one reconsideration of the same question only to be allowed."

The proposition, as originally introduced, has been more stringent than Mr. Morton's amendment, since it had required a majority. It was now, however, placed upon the same principle with that amendment, requiring only an equality of votes upon the reconsideration, with the number originally in favor of the measure.

Mr. CHAMBERS suggested that there was still this difference, that his own amendment allowed a reconsideration as often as the Convention might choose, whereas the amendment moved by Mr. Morton in the Massachusetts Convention, authorized a reconsideration once only.

Mr. McLane replied that he did not object to that, but to the number required for reconsideration. The two rules were identical in that respect, and the present amendment was open to all the objections taken to the other. Mr. Webster, in speaking of the amendment moved by Mr. Morton, said that he "thought, of all the various propositions which the occasion had elicited, that now before the Convention was the most extraordinary. It appeared to him to be in many respects objectionable. In the first place, what is meant by requiring as many votes to reconsider a motion, as were in favor of the original measure? Suppose the question were on the adoption of an amendment—a very small number, for example, five, might be in favor of it, and all the rest against it. Yet this case, by the proposed rule, the vote was *necessarily* to be reconsidered. The honorable gentleman had drawn his motion, as if affirmative votes only could be reconsidered and had made no provision at all for the reconsideration of negative votes. Again, according to this provision, a motion for reconsideration, might be made and discussed for a week; then put to the vote, and although carried affirmatively by a majority, have no effect, and be declared a nullity, because the majority was not large enough He begged leave to dissent entirely and most widely from all such modes of proceeding. All rules respecting reconsideration, were intended and adopted for the purpose of ascertaining under what circumstances, and by whom a motion for reconsideration might be brought forward. But when once brought forward, it must of course, like all other motions, be decided by a majority. Nobody, he believed, ever before heard of a rule by which a motion to reconsider, when once regularly made, was not to be decided like other motions. It might well be doubted whether the Convention could prescribe any such rules—rules by which any thing, more than a majority of members, would be required for the decision of any question regularly before it."

Such was the language of Mr. Webster in the Massachusetts Convention, upon a question identical with that now under consideration. By making the change proposed, infinite confusion would result. It would be impossible to go back and reconsider, with no matter how strong motives, without rescinding the rule. It was tying up the hands of the Convention, and placing a matter once decided upon, beyond their reach. He did not question the evil effects of the rule as it now stood; but he disapproved of the remedy proposed. He would adopt Mr. Webster's suggestion, and re-enact the rule which was orginally adopted by the Convention, rescinding the amendment by which a member voting in the minority was allowed to move to reconsider. He considered this one of the most important rules of the body; and especially important as it was their purpose and object to frame a Constitution to endure for many years unchanged; and not merely to legislate—their acts and the mischievous effects resulting from them being capable of easy correction. He could not give the amendment his approbation.

Mr. Bowie said, that it seemed to him that one of two things ought to be done; either to go back to the original rule which required that a member voting in the majority should move a re-consideration; or to adopt some such provision as that proposed by the gentleman from Kent. His own opinion was that the better way would be to adopt the original rule as reported by the committee on rules. He was not present when the motion was made by the gentleman from Frederick to amend the rules, by allowing a member who voted in the minority to move a reconsideration If he had been present, he would have opposed it; foreseeing that it would lead to irreparable mischief. The whole evils which had occurred, grew entirely out of that rule. There was some restraint upon the power of reconsideration as long as it was confined to those voting in the majority; but the very moment any member was allowed, whether voting in the majority or in the minority, to move a reconsideration, all restriction was abandoned, and all the evils resulted, to which allusion had been made. What on one day was decided by a large majority of the members of the Convention, might be overthrown the next day by a mere minority.

He professed to be a reformer. He was as anxious as any gentleman in the Convention, to see great questions of reform carried in this body. He did not wish to see those measures jeoparded by a minority vote of the House. The effect of the rule as it stood was undoubtedly to allow a minority to undo what the majority had done. No matter how wholesome and judicious the law or regulation of reform might be, which should be adopted by the majority, if the friends of the reform would chance to be absent, on another day, the anti-reformers could repeal it. The Convention ought to be guarded and to take care not to allow any rule to place it in that position. This was the effect of the rule established upon the motion of the gentleman from Frederick; as it allowed a gentleman voting in the minority to move a reconsideration. It was not probable that a reconsideration could take place without sufficient grounds under the old rule; which was that prevailing in all deliberative bodies in all the States of the Union, everywhere, except in the Reform Convention of Maryland. He would undertake to say that there was no deliberative body upon the face of the globe, where such a rule had been adopted for a moment. Believing that the true plan was to go back to the original rule, he would propose as a substitute, if the gentleman from Kent, [Mr. Chambers,] would accept it, the following resolution:

"*Resolved*, That so much of the rule as allows a member voting in the minority to move a reconsideration of the question, shall be and the same is hereby rescinded."

Mr. Jenifer considered the question too simple to require a prolonged discussion. It was whether a minority should be allowed to adopt or reject measures which had previously been decided to the contrary by a larger vote. It had been very clearly pointed out that the rule would allow a small proportion of the Convention when it happened to be thin, to reverse the action of a very large and overwhelming majority, and thus, that majority might be taken by surprise.

The gentleman from Baltimore city, (Mr. Brent,) acknowledged that he had misunderstood the rule, and was corrected. He misunderstood it again, and was again corrected. He had been reminded of the familiar saying—

> " A man convinced against his will,
> Is of the same opinion still."

The gentleman from Baltimore city had said, that there were no precedents for this. There was the best of all precedents, in the very act about to be adopted in the Constitution, that it should require a majority of all the members elected to each branch of the legislature, to pass any law which with a *viva voce* vote on all questions of importance would greatly restrain the loose and neglected manner in which many laws had heretofore been passed.

He hoped no article of the new Constitution would be adopted, unless it had a majority of the whole number of the members of the Convention.

The object of that rule was to prevent a minority from adopting a bill and passing it. That was not the case with the Convention. A question might be considered and fully discussed, and might be dicided upon in the morning, and later in the day, when but fifty-two were present, the same measures might be over-ruled. He would not pretend to say, or to intimate, that there was a single member of the Convention who would intentionally take advantage of such circumstances; but the Convention should place itself in a position so as not to be subject to this continual vacillation. In regard to the idea that the Convention would be tying up their hands, and have no opportunity to discuss the measures, the simple motion to reconsider would open the whole question to debate. If the motion to reconsider should be grounded upon considerations which ought to have weight, it would always be in the power of members, to bring those arguments before the Convention.

Mr. Bowie would very cheerfully go for the rule proposed by the gentleman from Kent, (Mr. Chambers,) but that it violates a fundamental principle which he could not disregard. He held that a quorum, being a majority of the body, had a right to pass any law they pleased. A majority in any legislative body, ought always to prevail. But the rule of the gentleman from Kent, required something besides a majority. Although there might be a decided majority in favor of reconsideration, yet if that majority was not equal to and did not exceed that which passed the measure, the motion to reconsider would be lost. He was utterly opposed to such an innovation upon the great cardinal principle, that the majority should rule, and he believed the innovation would be fraught with dangers and with infinite mischief. To get rid of all this, he proposed to go back to the original rules, so as to allow no one to move a reconsideration, who had not voted in the majority. Much mischief had already been done, by allowing the minority to overrule what the majority had done, and this proposition was to go back to the original question.

Mr. Phelps raised the question of order, whether this amendment could be introduced without one day's notice, the amendment proposing to change another rule from that under consideration.

Mr. Bowie remarked that the notice having been given to the Convention, that the rules would be considered to-day, the House had jurisdiction over the whole subject.

Mr. Chambers said that to obviate the necessity of discussing a question of order, he would state that he should decline under any circumstances, to accept the proposition, one contingency existing as at present. That portion of the rule with which gentlemen were dissatisfied, had been adopted at the suggestion of a distinguished gentleman from Frederick, not now in his seat, (Mr. Thomas.) He should be very unwilling to have the rule rescinded in the absence of that gentleman. There was no such pressing necessity as to require action upon it, in the absence of the gentleman who had suggested it.

To meet the case which had been shown to be possible, that there would be 52 upon one side and 51 upon the other, and but one member should change his opinion, he had modified his proposition so that whenever a question should have been decided by yeas and nays, no motion to reconsider should prevail unless there should be cast in favor of the reconsideration, a number of votes at least equal to the number of votes given by the majority on the original question.

He would suggest the propriety of allowing the question of a change in the rule, lie until the arrival of the gentleman from Frederick, when it would be taken up and acted upon.

Mr. Gwinn moved the previous question.

Mr. Chambers moved that the whole subject lie upon the table for the present.

Mr. Gwinn thereupon withdrew the call for the previous question.

The question being taken upon laying upon the table, it was agreed to—ayes 38; noes not counted.

Mr. Dorsey rose for the purpose of giving notice of his intention to offer an amendment to the 17th rule—it being the rule which authorised the call for the previous question. He said that he had noticed much inconvenience resulting from the manner in which the rule was made to operate. Many members after making speeches, were in the habit, without allowing an opportunity to reply to their arguments, of moving the previous question. His amendment, if adopted, would prevent this.

Mr. D. read his amendment as follows:

"But no member who has discussed any subject before the Convention, shall be permitted to move the previous question thereon, until at least two or more members have had an opportunity of replying to the mover of the previous question."

Mr. Wright presented a petition of sundry citizens of the State, praying that provision be made in the new Constitution, that the privilege to sell intoxicating liquors in small quantities shall not be granted to any person in any part of the State or city, except the same shall first be sanctioned or approved by a majority of the voters in the county, election district or ward where the same is to be sold;

Which was read, and

Referred to the select committee already appointed on that subject.

Mr. Hicks gave notice that on to-morrow he should move to reconsider the vote of the Convention on the resolution adopted in relation to dispensing with the services of certain committee clerks.

Mr. Crisfield, from the minority of the committee on the Judiciary, submitted following

REPORT:

Sec. 1. There shall be a Court of Appeals, which shall have, use and exercise all and every the powers, anthorities and jurisdictions of the existing Court of Appeals, and such additional power, authority and jurisdiction as may be conferred by this Constitution, and laws made pursuant thereto; and its judgments shall be final and conclusive in all cases whatever.

Sec. 2. The Court of Appeals shall hold its session at the seat of Government, at least twice in every year, or oftener, if required by law; no judgment of reversal shall be rendered, except with the concurrence of at least three of the judges thereof; and in every case decided, an opinion in writing shall be filed, and provision shall be made by law, for publishing reports of cases argued and determined in the said court.

Sec. 3. The Judges of the present Court of Appeals, shall be Judges of the Court of Appeals hereby established; and shall hold their offices during good behaviour, and subject to removal as now provided; and they shall have and be entitled to receive, at stated periods, the salaries hereinafter provided, which shall not be diminished, during their continuance in office; and from and after the period, when the number of said Judges shall be reduced to four, by death, resignation or removal, the Court of Appeals shall be composed of one chief judge, who shall be styled chief justice of the State of Maryland, and three associate judges.

Sec. 4. The Judges of the Court of Appeals to be appointed in pursuance hereof, shall be citizens of the United States, and shall have resided in this State at least five years next before the time of their respective appointments, and shall continue to reside herein, while they act as Judges; they shall be selected from among those who are most distinguished for integrity, wisdom and sound legal knowledge, and appointed by the Governor, by and with the advice and consent of the Senate; and shall hold their offices during good behavior, removable for misbehavior, on conviction in a court of law, or shall be removed by the Governor, upon the address of the General Assembly; provided, that two-thirds of the members of each House concur in such address; and shall each, at stated times, receive for their services a salary of twenty-two hundred dollars per annum, which shall not be diminished during the time of their continuance in office.

Sec. 5. There shall be a clerk of the Court of Appeals, and he shall be appointed by the judges of the said court; he shall be a citizen of the United States and shall have resided in this State at least five years next before the time of his appointment; and shall hold his office for the term of seven years, and until his successor shall be appointed and qualify, and he shall qualify in the manner, perform the duties, and be entitled to the fees of the clerks of the said court on the Eastern and Western Shores, until otherwise provided by law.

Sec. 6. This State shall be divided into eight judicial districts, in manner and form following, to wit: St. Mary's, Charles and Prince George's counties, shall be the first district; Anne Arundel, Howard, Calvert and Montgomery counties, shall be the second district; Frederick and Carroll counties, shall be the third district; Washington and Allegany counties shall be the fourth district; Baltimore city shall be the fifth district; Baltimore, Harford and Cecil counties, shall be the sixth district; Kent, Queen Anne's, Talbot and Caroline counties, shall be the seventh district; and Dorchester, Somerset and Worcester counties shall be the eighth district; and there shall be appointed as hereinafter directed, one person, having the qualifications hereinafter prescribed, for each of the said judicial districts, except the fifth, to be judge thereof; the said judges shall be styled district judges, and shall respectively hold a term of their courts at least twice in each year or oftener, if required by law, in each county, composing their respective districts; and the said courts shall be called district courts for county in which it may be held; and shall have, hold and exercise, in the several counties of this State, all and every, the powers, authorities and jurisdictions which the county courts of this State now have, hold and exercise, or which shall hereafter be prescribed by laws made pursuant to this constitution; and the said judges in their respective districts, shall have, use and exercise all the powers, authorities and jurisdiction which the Chancellor of Maryland, as a judge in equity now has, uses and exercises, and the said Judges shall also be judges of the Orphans' courts of the several counties, composing their respective districts and shall have, hold and exercise, all and every, the powers, authorities and jurisdiction which the Orphans' courts of this State now have, hold and exercise, or which hereafter may be conferred by law.

Sec. 7. There shall be appointed as hereinafter provided, four persons having the requisite qualifications, for the fifth judicial district, to be Judges thereof; who may sit jointly or separately as the exigencies of business may require; and the said judges shall be styled district judges, and shall hold a term of their court at least twice in each year, and oftener if required by law; and the said court shall be called the district court for the city of Baltimore, and shall have, hold and exercise in the said district, all and every, the powers, authorities and jurisdictions, which Baltimore county court, sitting for said city, Baltimore city court, and the Chancellor of Maryland, as a judge in equity, now have, hold and exercise therein ; and the said judges shall also be judges of the Orphans' court for Baltimore city, and have, hold and exercise, all and every, the powers, authorities and jurisdictions appertaining and belonging to the said Orphans' court within said city; and the number of judges authorized by this section may be increased by law, when such increase shall be required for the dispatch of business in the said district, and such additional judges shall have the same powers, authorities and jurisdictions in all respects as are conferred by this section on the judges directed to be appointed; and the Legislature may establish within the city of Baltimore, a court of limited criminal jurisdiction for the trial of offences not punished capitally, which may be committed in the said city; define its powers and prescribe the number, tenure, mode of appointment, and compensation of the judges thereof, which shall be paid by the city of Baltimore.

Sec. 8. The Judges of the District Court shall respectively hold at least two terms in the city of Baltimore, and in each county comprising the judicial district as courts of law, at least two terms, for the transaction of Equity business within an intermediate day for the return of process: and at least four sessions of the Orphans' court in each county; or oftener, if required by law.

Sec. 9. The General Assembly may, by law, not inconsistent with this Constitution, establish and define the jurisdiction of the courts of this State, prescribe rules of practice, and the course of business therein; and determine the number of terms of said courts, and the time and place of holding the same ; but no law shall be passed to confer original jurisdiction in any case what ever, on the court of Appeals, or to require said court to sit elsewhere than at the seat of government; or to give Justices of the Peace jurisdiction in any case, when the matter or thing in controversy exceeds one hundred dollars in value; and all laws regulating and determining the jurisdiction of the Courts or Justices of the Peace; and for the administration of justice, shall, as far as practicable, be uniform throughout this State.

Sec. 10. The judges of the several Judicial Districts shall be citizens of the United States, and shall have resided five years in this State, and two years in the Judicial District for which they may be respectively appointed, next before the time of appointment, and shall reside therein while they continue to act as judges; they shall be selected from among those who having the other qualifications herein prescribed, are most distinguished for integrity, wisdom and sound legal knowledge, and appointed by the Governor, by and with the advice and consent of the Senate, and shall hold their offices during good behavior, removeable for misbehavior on conviction in a court of law, or shall be removed by the Governor, upon the address of the General Assembly, provided that two-thirds of the members of each House shall concur in such address; and the said judges shall each receive a salary of twenty-five hundred dollars per annum, and the same shall not be diminished during the time of their continuance in office; and no judge of any court in this State who has a salary fixed by law shall receive any perquisite, fee or reward in addition thereto, for the performance of any judicial duty.

Sec. 11. If from sickness or any other unavoidable cause, any of the district judges shall be unable to hold the regular term of his court, his place may be supplied by a judge from another district to be selected by the Governor, or by a person of integrity and sound legal knowledge, to be appointed by the Governor as may be provided by law; and such judge, or the person so appointed, shall have and exercise for the time being. the same power, authority and jurisdiction, as the judge whose place is thus supplied, and shall receive such compensation as may be provided by law; and if any district judge shall be interested in any cause pending in any court of which he is judge, he shall not sit in the same, but upon a suggestion in writing of the interest of the judge, verified by affidavit, the said cause shall be transferred to some county of an adjoining judicial district, to be heard and determined, or the same proceedings may be had as are provided for in the case of the sickness of a judge; and the Legislature shall provide rules to carry this section into effect.

Sec. 12. No suit shall be commenced in, or removed from any court to the court of chancery in this State, after official notice shall have been given of the adoption of this Constitution by the people of this State; but all causes which may be pending in the said court at the time of the said notice shall be proceeded with in the said court, and determined according to the usual course of business therein; provided the same can be done in five years from the time aforesaid; and at the expiration of five years from the time of the giving of the said notice, the said court and the office of Chancellor, shall be, and hereby are abolished. If a vacancy shall occur within the period aforesaid, in office of Chancellor, or of Register in Chancery, successors to them respectively shall be appointed as now provided for, to serve for the unexpired portion of said term, who shall have, and exercise the powers, authorities and jurisdiction, and perform the duties, and receive the salary, fees and emoluments respectively appertaining to said offices. If at the end of the said term of five years, any cause or business shall remain in said court unfinished, the General Assembly shall provide a method for the final determination thereof; and also for the disposition and safe keeping of the records of the said court.

Sec. 13. There shall be one register of wills, and one clerk of the district court, in each county of this State and the city of Baltimore, who shall be citizens of the United States, and shall have resided in the State five years, and in the county in which he may be voted for two years, before the election, and shall be elected by a plurality of the qualified voters of the county or city, and shall perform the duties and be entitled to receive the emoluments and fees, appertaining to the said offices respectively. They shall be commissioned by the Governor, and shall hold their offices for the term of six years; and until their successors shall have been elected and qualified; the time, place and manner of holding said election, and making returns thereof, and the mode of determining contested elections for said officers shall be prescribed by law, and in case of the death, resignation or disqualification of any Clerk or Register, a new election shall be held as aforesaid, at the next general election for delegates to the General Assembly; and in the mean time the judge or judges of the district in which said vacancy may occur, shall immediately appoint a person having the qualifications aforesaid to fill said vacancy; and the person so appointed shall be Register of Wills, or Clerk as the case may be, for the county or city for which he may be appointed; and shall hold said office, discharge the duties, and be entitled to the fees and emoluments thereof, according to law, until the election and qualification of his successor; and the Clerk for the district court for Baltimore city shall in addition to his other duties in like manner perform the duties and be entitled to the fees of the clerk of Baltimore city court; and the General Assembly shall have full power to enlarge, alter or change the powers and duties of the said Clerks and Registers, prescribe the mode of qualifying, and fix, determine or alter their fees or compensation.

Sec. 14. Justices of the Peace of this State for the several counties and the city of Baltimore, shall be elected by the qualified voters of the county or city for which the election may be held, and shall hold their offices for the term of two years, and until their successors shall have been elected, and shall have qualified; and the General Assembly shall, by law, prescribe the number of Justices of the Peace for each county and city; their duties and emoluments; the time, place, and manner of holding elections, the mode of making returns thereof, rules for determining contested elections; for certifying the election and qualifications of the persons elected; and for filling vacancies which may occur; but no person shall be a Justice of the Peace for any county or city, who shall not be entitled to vote therein at the time of his election.

Sec. 15. Constables, Coroners and Elizors shall be appointed as now prescribed by law, or in such manner as the General Assembly may direct.

Sec. 16. Sheriffs shall be elected in each county, and in the city of Baltimore every fourth year, that is to say, two persons for the office of Sheriff for each county, and two for the said city, the one of whom having the highest number of votes of the qualified voters of said county or city, or if both have an equal number, either of them, at the discretion of the Governor, to be commissioned by the Governor for the said office, and having served for four years, such person shall be ineligible for the five years next succeeding; bond with security, to be taken every year as usual, and no sheriff shall be qualified to act before the same be given. In case of death, refusal, disqualification or removal out of the county before the expiration of the four years; the other person chosen as aforesaid shall be commissioned by the Governor to execute the said office for the residue of the said four years, the said person giving bond with security as aforesaid. No person shall be eligible to the office of sheriff but a resident of such county or city respectively, and who shall have been a citizen, of this State at least five years preceding his election, and above the age of twenty-one years. The two candidates, properly qualified, having the highest number of legal ballots, shall be declared duly elected for the office of sheriff for such county or city, and return to the Governor with a certificate of the number of ballots for each of them.

Sec. 17. The General Assembly shall have power to tax clerks of the District Courts, Registers of Wills and the clerk of the court of Appeals; but all such taxes shall be in equal proportion, as far as praticable, according to the actual value of said office respectively.

Sec. 18. The Judges of the several county courts, Baltimore city court and the Orphan's Court of the several counties, Justices of the Peace, Registers of Wills and clerks of county courts of the several counties and Baltimore city court who may be in office at the time of the adoption of this Constitution, shall remain in office, and continue to discharge the duties of their respective offices, until the appointment or election and qualification of the Judges, Justices of the Peace, Registers of Wills and Clerks, provided for by this Constitution and no longer; and the first election of Clerks, Registers, Justices of the Peace and Sheriffs, and all other officers, whose election by the people is provided for in this article of the Constitution, shall take place throughout this State on of in the year eighteen hundred and fifty-two.

Sec. 19. To facilitate the dispatch of business in the Orphans' courts of this State, the General Assembly shall by law prescribe rules of practice in the said courts; enlarge and define the powers and duties of registers of wills, and authorise them to pass such orders as may be necessary and proper, to bring any cause, suit or business depending in the said courts to a final hearing, and determination; but no order, act or proceeding of the registers of wills of a judicial nature, shall be final and conclusive until ratified, and confirmed by the court.

ESTIMARES:

1st. Of the cost of the Judiciary system, here by proposed:

Four Judges of the Court of Appeals at $2,200 each, - - - -	$8,800 00
Eleven District Judges at $2,500 each, - - - - - - -	27,500 00
Whole cost per annum, when in full operation, - - - - -	$35,300 00

2nd. Of the cost of the present Judiciary of this State, including the supposed cost of two hundred and sixty-nine Justices of Magistrates' courts, which are reported to be now in commission, as estimated by the committee on Judiciary, - $98,100 00

3rd. Of the cost of the system reported by the said committee, as estimated by themselves, - - 61,000 00
Add for one Judge for Howard county, now established, - - 2,000 00

$63,000 00

The system now submitted proposes to do the same work for a sum, scarcely more than half the cost of the system reported by the committee, and a fraction only above one-third of what the committee estimate to be the cost of the present system; and it is submitted with a far greater probability of having it well and promptly done.

But this illusion to the estimated cost of the present system, must not be understood as an admission of the correctness of the committee's estimate; on the contrary, that estimate, is believed to be extravagant and far above the actual cost. The committee best understand the cost of their own scheme, and therefore their estimate of its cost $61,000, is assumed to be correct.

Which was read, and

On motion of Mr. CRISFIELD,

Ordered to be printed.

Mr. BOWIE gave notice that on to-morrow he should move to take up the amendment moved by Mr. CHAMBERS, of Kent, to the rules, and the substitute moved by him for said amendment.

Mr. SCHLEY inquired if there was any business before the Convention?

The PRESIDENT, *pro tem.*, replied that there was no business before the Convention.

Mr. GWINN moved that the Convention proceed to the consideration of the report of the committee on the elective franchise.

Mr. SCHLEY moved to take up, for consideration, the report of the committee on the Attorney General and his deputies.

The PRESIDENT, *pro tem.*, stated that the Chair, in reply to an inquiry from the gentleman from Washington county, had said that there was no subject before the Convention. The report of the executive committee had not yet been disposed of, and was therefore the first business in order, unless postponed to some future day.

Mr. McLANE said, that as the chairman of that committee was absent, he would move that the further consideration of this subject be postponed until his return.

Mr. SCHLEY said that his only object for submitting his motion was, that the Convention might have something to do. If the report of the executive committee was the order of the day, he did not wish to interfere.

The question was then taken on the motion of Mr. McLANE that the further consideration of the report of the committee on the executive be postponed,

And it was agreed to.

So the further consideration of the report was postponed.

The question then recurred on the motion of Mr. SCHLEY, that the Convention proceed to the consideration of the report of the committee on the Attorney General and his deputies,

And being put, it was decided in the affirmative.

THE ATTORNEY GENERAL AND HIS DEPUTIES.

The Convention accordingly proceeded to the consideration of said report,

Which was read.

The bill was then considered by sections;

When the first section was read, as follows:

Sec. 1. The Governor shall have power to employ counsel for the State, when, in his judgment, the public interest require it, and make suitable compensation from the contingent fund placed at his disposal.

Mr. DORSEY remarked that he had had no opportunity, before this morning, of reading the bill under consideration. He objected to this section, as placing in the power of the Governor the authority to make suitable compensation, out of the contingent fund, to such persons as might be employed in legal causes concerning the State, and thought that such compensation should be allowed by the Legislature for such services rendered the State. He would reduce to writing an amendment of this nature.

Mr. SCHRIVER said, that if he had been correctly informed, claims for legal services had never been paid out of the contingent fund, but direct from the treasury. Under resolutions emanating from the Legislature, the Governor, from time to time, had been directed to make such compensation as he might think proper, to persons employed in legal causes by the State, and to draw upon the treasury for the amount of such compensation.

Mr. DORSEY stated that he was very unwilling to consume the time of the Convention, by questions of this character, and he would therefore, refrain from submitting his amendment.

Mr. CRISFIELD enquired if the question was on the adoption of the first section?

The PRESIDENT, *pro. tem.*, replied in the affirmative.

Mr. CRISFIELD said:

That he thought there should be an Attorney General, but he would not have him appointed as he now is; but would have him appointed for a term to continue as long as as the Governor's term. If a Governor should be elected for four years, he would allow the Attorney General's term, to continue for the same length of time. He would have the Attorney General to be an officer of the State Government, whose duty it should be to advise every part of the government, and the State's Attorneys in the different counties, and should receive a salary. He would not let him hold office during good behavior, and would only allow him to appoint prosecuting attorney's in the different counties. He would make him an officer whose duty it should be to give legal advice to the Governor—perhaps to act for the Government in the higher courts, and would strip him of the patronage now exercised under law.

With the view of giving him time to prepare an amendment to meet the views he had presented, he would move that the first section be informally passed over. The other sections were disconnected from it, and could be perfected, without reference to this first section.

Mr. SHRIVER was desirous of having the sense of the Convention on this subject, as it would decide whether a majority were in favor of the creation of the office of Attorney General, or whether they were opposed to it. To his mind, it was very clear that the office was entirely useless and unnecessary.

Mr. CRISFIELD said that he desired that the Attorney General should be an officer who should receive a salary. If the Legislature should think, upon the performance of any unusual service, that he should receive additional compensation, they could give it to him.

He would not allow the Governor to employ as many counsel as he might think fit, nor would he allow him to give them such compensation as he might deem proper.

With a view to move such an amendment, and to allow him time to prepare it, he had submitted his motion to pass over this section informally. If the Convention was opposed to having such an officer, and opposed to the views he had expressed, it could signify its opinion by refusing to agree to his motion.

Mr. McLANE suggested to Mr. CRISFIELD that he could move his amendment when the second section should come up for consideration, and stated that he should vote against continuing the office of Attorney General.

Mr. SHRIVER thought that the office, if created, should be provided for in the first section, and its duties defined and salary fixed. The question of the creation of the office would arise, and he wished to have it disposed of, as a test question, on the first section.

Mr. BOWIE concurred with the gentleman from Somerset that there should be such an officer as Attorney General, and thought that the Convention ought to provide for the appointment of such an officer. The idea of giving to the Governor the right to employ as many counsel as he pleased, to prosecute in the courts in and out of the State, in any cause in which the State was concerned, was conferring on him too much power.

There should be but one officer, and although he was opposed to having an officer for life or during good behaviour, he did not see the least inconvenience or impropriety in allowing every Governor to appoint his own Attorney General. This would create rotation in office, which seemed to suit the people and the republican notions of the present age.

He was opposed to permitting the Attorney General to appoint deputies in the different counties, which he thought might be done by the tax and levy courts. He thought this would produce a wholesome result, although he had no objection to electing the deputies by the people.

He did not regard the situation of Prosecuting Attorney as an office, but looked upon the person holding it, as a professional gentleman, practicing his profession for the State, and would give him no more fees than now allowed by law. As to electing these officers by the people, he saw no necessity for so doing; though he had no insuperable objection to such a course, as he went very generally for electing all officers by the people.

If he thought, however, that these were really offices which the people desired to fill, he would be in favor of electing by the people.

He was of the opinion that the Governor had better appoint the Attorney General, and that it would be proper for each county to take care of its own officers, by appointing competent persons who could attend to the interests of the State.

Mr. DIRICKSON said that he was willing to vote for the motion to pass this section over informally as a matter of courtesy to the gentleman who made the motion; but if it was meant as a test question as to whether there should be an Attorney General or not, he would vote against it.

Mr. CRISFIELD said that he would not consider it unkind if the gentleman should vote against his motion. He certainly desired that an amendment such as he had indicated, should be brought before the Convention, but he had not the time to prepare it now. He preferred it to the one indicated in the bill. He could see no evil in passing over the section informally, unless the majority had determined to adopt the particular scheme contained in it, in which event they could just as well vote upon it now as at any other time.

The question was then taken on the motion of Mr. CRISFIELD, to pass over the first section informally, when on a division of the Convention no quorum voted.

Mr. GWINN asked the yeas and nays,

Which were ordered,

And being taken were as follows:

Affirmative—Messrs. Morgan, Lee, Chambers of Kent, Donaldson, Wells, Weems, Brent of Charles, Jenifer, Crisfield, Dashiell, Hicks, Hodson, Eccleston, Phelps, Bowie, McMaster, Fooks, Sherwood of Baltimore city, Presstman, Weber, Hollyday, Slicer and Smith—24.

Negative— Messrs. Buchanan, President, *pro tem.*, Dorsey, Welch, Dickinson, Sherwood of Talbot, Miller, McLane, George, Wright, Dirickson, Shriver, McHenry, Magraw, Nelson, Carter, Hardcastle, Gwinn, Brent of Baltimore city, Ware, Schley, Fiery, Neill, John Newcomer, Harbine, Brewer, Fitzpatrick, Parke, Shower and Cockey—29.

So the motion was not agreed to.

The question now being on agreeing to the first section,

Mr. McHENRY moved to amend said section, by inserting after the word "State," the words "at such rates of compensation as the General Assembly may prescribe," and by striking out the words "and make suitable compensation from the contingent fund placed at his disposal."

Mr. McH. remarked that he was unwilling to give the Governor any such discretionary power as was proposed in the bill. It seemed to him that the past practice of the General Assembly, in entrusting to the Governor a contingent fund of considerable amount and applicable at his pleasure, was at variance with the principles which had been cherished as fundamental in representative governments. Now, it was proposed to go further. It was proposed to authorise the Governor to make use of this fund, in a manner such as would avoid all responsibility; for he might employ as many counsel as he pleased, and give them such compensation as he pleased, without answering to any one, and without being limited to the amount of the contingent fund in his hands any deficiency in which, under the provision of the bill as reported, the Legislature would be bound to make good. Such a power —so unrestricted and vague, violated that essential characteristic of all limited constitutional government, the absence of all control by the executive over the purses and property of the people.

He was opposed to giving the Governor the entire control of a contingent fund of any considerable amount, and much more averse to entrusting to any one individual, irresponsible power over the entire funds of the State. He desired that these should be most carefully guarded by the Constitution they were now framing.

Mr. Dirickson could not perceive how rates of compensation, as proposed by the gentleman's amendment, could be established.

Mr. McHenry said, that he would modify his amendment so as to meet the acceptance of the gentleman.

He altered his amendment so as to strike out the words, "and make suitable compensation from the contingent fund placed at his disposal," and to insert in lieu thereof, the words:

"For whose services such compensation shall be made as the legislature may allow."

Mr. Dirickson said:

He had offered the substitute now under consideration, because he regarded the legislature as the appropriate and regularly constituted guardian of the public treasury, and he wished so far as possible to confide the payment of all money to their keeping exclusively.

They came at all times fresh from the bosom of the people, and must necessarily feel in an eminent degree, their direct and immediate responsibility. Whilst then by such an arrangement, the common fund would be safely preserved from unwise and improvident squandering—no one could doubt but that a body of Maryland gentlemen, of which the legislature would be composed, would always compensate those who had rendered the State a service with a generous and liberal hand. There was not within the limits of the Commonwealth, a jurist, however eminent, who would not willingly risk her justice—not a counsellor who would not trust her long established and well known character with entire and unlimited confidence.

The objection urged that by such an arrangement there would necessarily be some delay in the payments, seemed of slight importance. All knew that the profession every where were compelled to wait with patience the reward of their studious labors and toilings, and a delay so inconsiderable as that which might occur during the interval between the legislative sessions, could not be urged successfully for an instant against the general propriety of the proposition. By the adoption of this substitute in addition to the considerations already advanced—the whole responsibility would be entirely removed from the hands of the Executive, and he would thus be relieved from a position frequently of the utmost delicacy. Necessarily a full statement of all the services renderod would be regularly forwarded to the legislature, and they, after a calm and deliberate inspection would, he doubted not, render the most equitable and liberal payment.

Any one who would give himself the trouble to examine the statement of the various sums which had been paid for the services of counsel during the past years, would feel with him, the necessity of some such provision as that which he had submitted, and with the most serious earnestness, he commended it to the favorable consideration of every member of the Convention.

Mr. Presstman made some remarks, which will appear hereafter.

Mr. McHenry said that his only reason for not accepting the modification of the gentleman from Worcester, (Mr. Dirickson) was, the lawyer, like any other workman, should know beforehand what amount he was going to receive for his services. By allowing the Legislature to prescribe rates, that object would be accomplished.

Mr. Dirickson desired to know if the gentleman could give to the Convention some idea as to how the rates could be prescribed for services hereafter to be rendered?

Mr. McHenry replied that the Legislature could prescribe rates for certain kinds of services. Fees were fixed for other kinds of services; and he could not see why the fees of attorneys should not be fixed. Not being conversant with legal phrases, he was willing to substitute any other word for "rate." He was open to suggestion and conviction.

Mr. Shriver desired to say that the committee who prepared this report were unanimous in opinion. They desired that any wholesome amendment should be made. He would say that the principle of the abolition of the office of Attorney General, and the election by the people of Prosecuting Attorneys should not be lost sight of. The gentleman from Hartford had said that his objection grew out of his opposition to an unlimited contingent fund. There was no unlimited contingent fund, nor ever had been; for it had always been limited and fixed by the Legislature. For the last two years it had been twelve thousand dollars.

He objected to the amendment because it was impossible for the Legislature to fix any rate of compensation. No one could anticipate the amount of labor to be performed by counsel.—Such a course would be unjust, both to the State and the individual who rendered the service. He desired the responsibility to rest upon the head of one individual; he did not wish it to rest upon the entire body composing the Legislature of Maryland. Look at the past history of the legislation of the State, and it would be found that it never had fixed the compensation of attorneys. That responsibility had always been thrown upon the Governor. The Legislature when recognising the existence of something being due, left it to the judgment of the Governor to make such compensation as he thought proper. The treasury was safer in the hands of the Governor than in the hands of the Legislature. If there was a necessity for the Legislature to reduce the contingent fund, let them do it, and then the Governor would be compelled to pay less compensation for the services of competent persons. By the vote just taken, refusing informally to pass over the first section, the Convention had determined that they would not have an Attorney General.

Mr. Jenifer, Mr. McMaster and Mr. Donaldson, severally disclaimed that in voting against the motion to pass over informally the first section, they voted against the creation of the office of Attorney General. They did not consider it a test question.

Mr. Dorsey said, he was in favor of the proposition of the gentleman from Worcester, (Mr. Dirickson.) He could not suppose that there would be any difficulty in getting counsel. As to the objection that some time would elapse before they could get paid, he did not suppose that would make much difference. There would be no kind of difficulty in getting the best counsel in the State. He disagreed, with the gentleman from Frederick, (Mr. Shriver.) The Legislature had heretofore fixed the value for professional services of their counsel, and they are perfectly competent to do so again. It is peculiarly proper that they should perform this duty. They hold the purse strings of the State; and avoiding extravagance, they will appropriate for this purpose what liberality and justice demand. Mr. D. in reply to the gentleman from Baltimore, (Mr. Gwinn,) then stated some facts in relation to the contract for the construction of the Annapolis and Elkrige railroad, and the difficulties to which it gave rise, which resulted in a reference of the case to Judge Legrand, by whose award it was decided. It being stated that the power of compensating for legal services ought not to be confided to the Legislature in consequence of its conduct in that case.

Mr. Magraw rose to a question of order, on the ground that this matter of Mr. McCullough was not relevant, and that as Mr. McCullough has a brother in the Convention, it was not proper to be commenting on the case here.

Mr. Gwinn said, that he had first referred to this case. He regretted that it had been brought here again.

Mr. Dorsey was proceeding to reply, when Mr. Magraw again raised the point of order.

Mr. Dorsey resumed. The Legislature would have been recreant to their duty, if they had allowed one dollar of this claim which amounted to about forty-eight thousand dollars. At their last session the Legislature voted down the claim by a vote of almost two to one. The Convention ought to suffer this matter to rest with the Legislature. He should think the Governor would be well satisfied that the control of this subject should be out of his hands. The Legislature is the appropriate tribunal to fix the amount of compensation to be paid to the legal officers. There was no ground for the apprehension expressed that under such circumstances, no distinguished lawyer would consent to be employed in the service of the State. It was an unmerited reproach to the profession to say so. He believed no lawyer would refuse to act in any case for the State, because he might not be paid until his services were rendered and could thus be estimated.

He would be willing to trust to the liberality of his client, as is ordinarily done, unless their penuriousness be such that a previous contract as to compensation be deemed a necessary precaution. Such conduct in the State is not to be predicated. He was very sure no lawyer would have any hesitation in trusting such a client as the State of Maryland. If the power be left in the hands of the Governor it may be abused; extravagant fees may be given to incompetent favorites. Charges of such partiality the Governor should seek to avoid.

The appointing power as to counsel should generally rest, with the Governor when the necessity for its exercise arises, the Legislature being rarely in session. But as a general rule; as the payment of counsel must come from the pockets of the people, it is but reasonable that they should, through the Legislature, fix the amount of compensation, and if they deem it expedient, select the persons to be retained as counsel.

Mr. Chambers did not mean to discuss the subject properly before the House, nor did he mean to say one word in defence of, or in opposition to, the claim of Mr. McCullough. He did not perceive how the justice or injustice of that claim could influence the proposition for the action of the Convention. He rose to say a word in vindication of those gentlemen who acted as arbitrators by the authority of the State. They were all his friends, and with one of them, particularly, he claimed relations of kind, social intercourse, which, in the absence of the two gentlemen from Queen Anne's, who were more intimately connected with him, made it proper to say a word in reply to what had fallen from his friend from Anne Arundel.

He was utterly at a loss to conceive, on what just grounds the claim of those arbitrators to remuneration could be resisted. The Legislature, by a deliberate resolution, without a word of previous consultation or arrangement with them, had appointed those gentlemen to act as referees upon a claim then pending before that body. In pursuance to this appointment, amounting to a request, these gentlemen had been occupied for many weeks in taking testimony and hearing arguments for and against the claim. The Attorney General had been directed to superintend the interests of the State, and amongst the items reported in a document on our files, was one of fifteen hundred dollars paid to that officer by the State, in part for his services in resisting that claim before the arbitrators. Eminent counsel were engaged before them in sustaining the claim, and their laborious service is not denied. That they gave an award, in exact conformity to their honest judgment upon the proofs before them, has never been doubted, and he ventured to assert, never would be doubted, by any man acquainted with the deservedly high standing of those gentlemen. They were second to none in all the feelings of honor and integrity that could exempt men from the remotest suspicion of favoritism. Having then faithfully labored at the request of the State, and having concluded their labor, by an honest decision upon the matter submitted to them, it appeared to him as a necessary consequence, they were justly entitled to a fair compensation for their services. It was no answer to this claim to say that other proofs ought to have been laid before them, or other arguments, or other matter which might have altered the character of their award. This is no af fair of the arbitrators—it was no part of their duty to hunt up proofs—their duty was to decide on such as were presented. Even if their opinion differed from those who were asked to make them just compensation, it would still not lessen the force of their claim to be remunerated for the money, time and labor expended for, and at the instance of the Legislature. These gentlemen were the last to make claim which was not sanctioned by every principle of law and equity. If, in a transaction like this, individuals had been substituted for the State, there could be no doubt of a right to recover upon a *quantum meruit* in a court of law.

Mr. Crisfield stated it to be his intention to sustain the amendment of the gentleman from Worcester, (Mr. Dirickson.) The power in the hands of the Legislature would be a check on the Governor. But he had not risen to speak on that point. What he desired to say, was in reference to the section itself, and the state of opinion in the Convention. The House had, by its vote which had been just taken, solemnly determined that there shall hereafter be no Attorney General.

Mr. Presstman asked on what ground the gentleman from Somerset made such statement.

Mr Crisfield replied that the gentleman from Frederick, (Mr. Shriver,) as well as himself, had proposed to the Convention that the vote on passing over the section shou d be considered as a test vote, and the House had determined as he had stated.

Mr. Presstman insisted that the chairman of the Committee, (Mr. Shriver,) had no right to make such a proposition to the Convention.

Mr. Sriver said he took this question to be settled by the decision of the House.

Mr. Jenifer said he had not voted from such a consideration.

Mr. Shriver. The gentleman from Charles voted with the minority.

Mr. Crisfield resumed. However any particular gentleman may have understood the vote, the general understanding was, that there should be no Attorney General hereafter. He had so understood it, and he was at a loss to conceive the reason which induced the Convention to come to this conclusion. He wished it were otherwise. He thought the office of Attorney General one of great importance.; indeed, his duties were indispensible. He was an officer of the law; his duties were defined by law; he was appointed by the Governor, by and with the advice of the Senate; and he was responsible to the laws and to the public for the faithful discharge of his duties. Vast and important interests were committed to his care; he represents the State in the courts of law, and prosecutes or defends all her interests, depending in the Courts. He is a conservator of the peace, and it is his business to see that the peace, government, and dignity of the State are not violated, and crimes do not go unpunished. He is the adviser of the Governor, of the Legislature, and of every executive officer; his opinion in the first instance, fixes the construction of all laws; ascertains the powers and duties of the different departments of the government; directs the proper mode of executing the laws, and what are the rights of the State. He is in fact, in some sort, a general director of the internal affairs of the State, and exercises a large influence over every department. He has also important and delicate duties to perform, growing out of the intercourse of this State with the other States of the Union; and in reference to rights conferred, and duties imposed on this State by the Constitution of the United States. He has also other duties deeply effecting the public interest. An officer who is thus appointed, and whose responsibility is thus fixed and determined by law, whose duties are so varied and so important, is to be dispensed with, and the office abolished And what is proposed to be substituted in his place? Why it is proposed to authorise the Governor to employ such counsel, as in his judgment the public interest requires,and pay them according to his discretion, out of the contingent fund of the executive department. The number of counsel, who may be selected, is without limit. The Governor may employ one,or one hundred counsel. His discretion is the only limit. And the powers of the counsel is equally without limit. Their duties are wholly undefined They are under no public responsibility. They are to be simply counsel—not even required to be lawyers—and it is not expressed on what subjects they are to give counsel, whether of a legal or political character. In the next section, Prosecuting Attorneys are provided for; and there is nothing in the section or the article under consideration, to prevent the Governor from assigning to the counsel to be selected by him, all the duties which the Prosecuting Attorneys are expected to perform.

Again, the compensation these counsel are to receive, is limited only by the extent of the contingent fund. The scheme would be greatly more expensive than the present system. In addition to the fees provided by law for the Attorney General, there have been paid large sums to that officer, and others, for services which are not embraced within the range of his regular duties. Mr. C. read a report from the treasurer, from which it appeared there had been paid for legal services in the last thirteen years, in addition to the fees provided by law, the sum of $22,948. If the measure now in consideration should be adopted, who doubts that the expense would be greatly increased.

Mr. C. said he would continue the office, but not on the present footing. He would appoint the Attorney General as he is now appointed, but his term should be limited to four years, which is the duration of the Governor's term. He should be appointed by the Governor, because intimate official relations which must exist between the Governor and his legal adviser, requires that they should be personally agreeable to each other, and that entire confidence should prevail between them. The public service require this. He also desired to see the Attorney General deprived of all patronage. He should not have, as he now has, the power of appointing deputies in every county of the State. He should also receive a compensation from the Treasury fixed by law. Thus restricted, he desired the office of Attorney General to be continued, for the reasons already intimated.

While he was up, he would add that the entire article under consideration, was vague and uncertain, in all its provisions. There were no duties assigned to the Prosecuting Attorneys—no restrictions—no responsibilities imposed upon them. What were they to do? What were they not to do? There was nothing definite—nothing certain—there were no duties—no restraints prescribed. The article as reported, was unmeaning, and ought not to pass. Mr. C. said he could not vote for it.

Mr. Gwinn said that the main question now presented by the report of the committee, on the office of the Attorney General and his deputies, and by the amendments offered thereto, was, as to the necessity for an Attorney General. By one clause of the system proposed (and in this, at least, all appear to agree,) the deputies are to be elected by the voters of tneir respective counties, and of the city of Baltimore. These officers are entrusted with the duty of prosecuting in all criminal cases, arising in the State of Maryland, and, if they are competent, the interests of the commonwealth, within their districts, can be attended to without the assistance of any general officer. Their *incompetency* cannot be presumed, because they will be elected by the people, who are most deeply interested in preserving the peace and good order of the State.

Much has been said concerning the necessity of having some adviser to the State, to overlook its interests. But it is well to consider what these interests are, in order to a better understanding of this alleged necessity. There certainly are many occasions in which Executive officers require advice. But where they have a local character only, they ought properly to address themselves to the person acting for the State within their county, who is bound to render this service.

If any question arise, affecting the State at large, whether it be a construction of a tax law, or of an act of assembly, involving any of the duties of the Executive, or in any question of a similar nature on which the General Assembly desire information, it is certainly proper that the State should have a conscientious adviser, upon whose judgment the Governor or the legislature can rely.

Where is the responsibility for the determination they may adopt? On the Executive, or on the legislature only. When they ask advice, they are bound in their own justification, to obtain the best counsel the learning of the State can afford. If they act upon improper. or insufficient advice, they will not be sheltered from censure, because it *was advice*, and this necessity of choosing will impose a wholesome restraint.

The rule will work another advantage. It will place responsibility where it properly belongs—upon the Executive, and upon the Legislature—and not upon the Attorney General. As to the compensation, it might be observed, that the Governor seemed to be the fittest person to make the compensation which any one acting for the State should receive. There were difficulties in the way of leaving the subject to the Legislature. It is never in a situation to estimate, with the same certainty, as the Executive, the value of the labor which has been performed.

Mr. McLane submitted some remarks, which will be published hereafter.

Mr. Pressman also made a few remarks, which will be published hereafter.

Mr. Jenifer gave notice that at the proper time he should offer the following, as a substitute for the first section of said report:

"There shall be an Attorney General appointed by the Governor, by and with the advice and consent of the Senate, whose term of office shall expire with that of the Governor, and whose duty and compensation shall be regulated by law."

And then, pending the question on the amendment offered by Mr. Dirickson,

The Convention adjourned until to-morrow morning at ten o'clock.

Erratum—In the inaugural address of Mr. Buchanan, Tuesday, March 15th, the words "unexpected by me," should read "anticipated by me."

DEFERRED DEBATE.

POWER OF APPROPRIATION.

Remarks of Mr. Grason, *March* 5, 1851, *in reply to* Mr. Constable.

Mr. Grason wished, he said, to make a brief reply to the gentleman from Cecil. The first objection of the gentleman was as to the original proposition of his friend and colleague, (Mr. George.) He, (Mr. G.,) thought, that in connection with the provision of a two-thirds majority, and the levying of a tax when the debt was contracted, would be a sufficient security. The gentleman from Cecil objected to the restriction of the power of appropriating public money for private and local purposes, because it was in effect an admission that the power now existed in the Legislature to make such appropriations. After this power had been exercised for so many years by the Legislature, and acquiesced in by the people, it was too late to say that a clause to regulate and restrict its application conferred the power. To illustrate this point, Mr. G. made references to various appropriations which had been made, at different periods, for private and local purposes. He, (Mr. G.,) had objected to the provision in the amendment of the gentleman from Cecil, authorizing appropriations for the necessary expenditures of the Government. He had made that objection because these expenditures were not sufficiently defined by the word "necessary." The courts had decided that the word admitted of a larger latitude of construction than he was willing to permit, embracing such expenditures as were for convenient purposes. Under such an interpretation as this, the Legislature might consider themselves empowered to appropriate money to any amount they might think fit, for such expenses of State as they might determine to be necessary. He had no great objection to granting this power, provided the objects for which the appropriations were to be made should be clearly specified so as to guard against any abuse. The gentleman from Cecil objected further to the proposition of his friend and colleague, [Mr. George,] that there was no safety in voting for the last branch of it, although he indicated a willingness to do so, because the first part of the proposition might not afterwards be adopted; and he desired that the two branches should be taken together. And in consequence of these objections, the gentleman from Cecil had thrown all his great powers into the scale against the proposition.

—

CREDIT OF THE STATE.

Remarks of Mr. Grason, *March* 5, 1851, *on the amendment of* Mr. George.

Mr. Grason said:

That if the propositon of his colleague could be fairly interpreted as it had been by the gentleman from Prince George's, [Mr. Bowie,] it would present a serious objection to its adoption, because its effect would be to prevent the payment of any just and proper claim against the State. But he did not think it could be properly susceptible of such interpretation. The intention of the amendment of his colleague was to prevent the Legislature from loaning the public money or the public credit for the use of individuals or associations, but not that the Legislature should not have the power to pay any just debts due to individuals. He was neither a lawyer nor a judge, but to him it appeared quite clear that the amendment could have no such effect. The gentleman from Prince George's said it would prevent any appropriations for hospitals and universities. The universities stood on a different foundation, and would not be touched by the amendment. And as to the various hospitals which have sprung up in the city of Baltimore, he would like to be informed how they became State institutions. He did not know the amendment of his colleague would prevent any further appropriations for them. But if it would, he had no objection. The amendment suggested by the gentleman from Prince George's would let in a number of claimants on the Treasury. Internal improvement companies might bring in a number of claims. The proposition of his colleague would not prevent the Legislature from redeeming the pledged faith of the State; and he would go against the adoption of any amendment of doubtful construction. The people had decided against any more internal improvements by the State. Wherever lateral roads are necessary they can be constructed by capitalists and others who have an interest in making them.

—

Remarks of Mr. Grason, *March* 6, 1851, *on the amendment of* Mr. Davis, *in relation to appropriations for purposes of Education.*

Mr. Grason had only a few words to say in reply to the gentleman from Montgomery, [Mr. Davis.] He did not desire to be understood as occupying a position opposed to some plan of education; but he was opposed to taxing the people for the purpose of creating an expensive system, or for establishing or extending corporations for the purpose. But the gentleman from Montgomery was mistaken as to the meaning of the proposition of his friend and colleague. What are the words of the amendment?

Here Mr. Grason read the amendment.

It was not intended to prohibit the Legislature from establishing a plan of education. He knew that the subject would come up in a report from the committee on Education. His colleague had no more idea of preventing an appropriation for education, than for training the militia, or any other indispensable object. It was intended to restrict the Legislature, so as to prevent the approprtation of money for the use of corporations, associations or individuals, but not to prevent the education of the children in the State. But how did the amendment of his colleague read, after the amendment of the gentleman from Montgomery was attached to it? It then not only empowers, but actually invites the Legislature to create corporations for the establishment of a great system of education. Although he entirely agreed in the great principle laid down by the gentleman from Montgomery, he was directly opposed to, and indeed he did not know that the gentleman intended his proposition to have that effect, the creation of these corporations. We have now two colleges in the State; and with these he would not interfere; but he would neither vote for establishing nor extending corporations for the purpose of building up an extravagant system, and he would vote against it now. Not, he repeated, that he was opposed to the principle, and he would go with the gentleman from Montgomery in the adoption of any general measure. But he was opposed to the creation of any more corporations.

—

GOVERNOR'S TERM OF OFFICE.

Remarks of Mr. Grason, March 7, 1851.

Mr. Grason said the report of the committee was framed under the impression that the Convention would provide for annual sessions. But as biennial sessions had been determined, it was now necessary to make an alternation in the bill. It was of the utmost importance that the Governor should come into office, while the Legislature was in session; and, therefore, it was necessary to reduce his term to two years, or extend it to four. It was doubtful which term ought to be preferred In two years, he would acquire the experience which would make his services more valuable, just at the time he was going out of office. On the other hand, by doubling the term, he might continue in power after he had lost the public confidence. He would move to strike out three, and insert the longest term, and if the blank were not filled with four, he should then move to fill it with two.

—

NOLLE PROSEQUIS.

Remarks of Mr. Tuck, *March* 12, 1851.

Mr. Tuck. The power of granting *nolle prosequis* is an executive prerogative, and always exercised unless restrained by the Constitution. He was in favor of expressly recognising the power in Maryland. It had always been possessed by our Governors. That it had been abused, he did not deny. But all powers may be denied or restricted for this reason. The question is, on which side lies the greater chance of evil. Cases of hardship must occur. That of Bromwell had been referred to. Mr. T. was in the Legislature at that time, and being well acquainted with the facts, could speak with certainty. Very strong recommendations were presented to the Governor, predicated upon his age, his long confinement, which was impairing his health, and perhaps hastening his death, the condition and wants of his family, &c. The character of the offence was such, that the Governor thought he ought not to interfere. He had been in jail some eighteen months or two years awaiting his trial. His case had been removed to Harford county—many of the witnesses resided on the eastern shore. He had been carried to Bel-Air two or three times and demanded his trial. The State was never ready on account of the absence of witnesses. His health was failing and a physician had certified that his continued confinement might end in incurable disease, if not in death. His case was brought before the Legislature, and by an almost unanimous vote in both branches, a resolution was passed authorising the city court of Baltimore to discharge him on his own recognisance. The object was to let him go away. He did so, and I believe has never been here since. He thought this was a case for the exercise of such a power. He would, therefore, vote for its retention by the Governor. But he thought that it should be guarded, and would prepare and offer, at a proper time, an amendment requiring that public notice should be given of the application, in order that the Governor might be better informed of the facts of the case than he could be by an *ex parte* application. To prevent injustice to the public, he thought the power could not be too carefully guarded against abuse.

—

SALARY OF THE GOVERNOR.

Remarks of Mr. Dirickson, Thursday, March 13.

Mr. Dirickson moved the following as a substitute:

Sec. 21. The Governor shall be in attendance at the seat of government during the sessions of the legislature of the State, and shall receive for his services an annual salary of two thousand dollars.

Mr. Dirickson said that the substitute which he had just had the honor to submit, was in his humble judgment both eminently proper in itself and in entire harmony with that spirit of retrenchment and reform, which had breathed this very Convention into existence. He had hoped, nay believed, that it would have been received by all with a warm and cordial welcome, and at once promptly sanctioned by a most decided and unequivocal vote. Sir, all, or well nigh all, around me are professed reformers, and we here not only to shaddow forth the embodied sentiment of Maryland, upon the great elementary principles of government, but to apply ourselves earnestly, industriously, sternly if need be, to the abolition of old abuses, and to the entire obliteration of every custom and provision, organic or otherwise, which has been without benefit and without essential good—feeding with an insatiable appetite upon the common treasure gathered from the whole body politic. The time had arrived when we should lay aside the useless, worn out and cumberous machinery of the past, and looking around upon this great confederacy, learn such lessons of political wisdom as will enable us to keep pace with the very foremost. Surely—surely whilst others are moving onward in every social improvement, we shall not be found wedded to our idols, standing still midway the glorious destiny that awaits us.

Tell me not then that the substitute now under consideration is a bold and reckless innovation, because forsooth it seeks to remove a restriction from the Constitution, which can no longer be sustained either by argument or the examples of other States. What was there so peculiar in the condition or extent of Maryland, to require that her chief executive officer should reside permanently and constantly at the seat of government, when so many of her sisters, with territory immensely larger, and with revenues scarcely smaller, had no such constitutional requirements, and yet were advancing in prosperity with a rapidity which we could scarcely realize. The general duties and obligations attached to the official position, were, if not precisely the same, with slight exceptions, very similar in every section of the Union, and if all could be discharged with propriety and alacity elsewhere, why not with equal promptness and fidelity here? It was not rational for an instant to suppose, that any gentleman could be selected for so exalted a position without some permanent residence, and wherever that abiding spot might be, within the limits of our commonwealth, there might he, under all emergencies, be sought and found with as much certainty as though his home, as now directed, was at the very capitol itself. It was true, as had been said, that we had just imposed additional duties upon the office, by requiring that its future occupant should make certain periodical examinations of the accounts of the treasurer; but so long was the interval between these prescribed examinations, and so small would be the portion of time consumed in the investigations, that the objection to the proposition now under piscussion, based upon that fact, seemed really of the slighiest possible importance, and he was sure could not bear a feathers weight against the many benefits that would necessarily flow from its adoption.

Should the Convention concur in these views and desire to assimilate in this respect the instrument we are framing, to those that are working so happily around us, the treasury would not only be relieved from the large expenditure now essential to the preservation of the government house, and adjacent property, but, that very property itself from being a burthen would doubtless be disposed of, and the proceeds added to the profitable capital of the State.

Trifling and insignificant as this economy might seem, it was due to a patient and patriotic people, that the spirit of retrenchment should be every where felt, consistent with the proper and faithful discharge of all the public interests, and he should gladly co-operate with reformers at all times in applying it to every department of the government.

Some there were who might regard the continuance of this gubernatorial residence and establishment as in some sort essential alike, to the dignity and to that character of hospitality which our noble old State had ever borne. He did not so regard it.

He believed the exalted reputation of Maryland could not be so easily marred. It was above and beyond any influence which could spring by possibility from such a source And thus believing no feeling of false pride could turn him aside from that clear and unswerving line of duty owed to that constituency, who had so generously confided their interests in part to his keeping.

But the substitute under consideration proposes not only the abolition of the restriction as to residence, but the reduction of the salary of our Executive from the present extravagant compensation, to the more moderate and yet liberal sum of two thousand dollars annually. Strange as it may seem, a careful examination tests the fact that Maryland with a limited territory, with a sparse and small population—with a debt of millions—with enormous taxation clinging to every species of property—still continues recklessly to pay her Governor a salary equalled by but few of her sister States, however superior they may be in all the elements and resources of wealth. Look to Connecticut giving to her chief magistrate the annual sum of eleven hundred dollars, and then for a moment glance your eye over the long line of distinguished names that have graced that position and guided her destiny with such unexampled success.

Turn to the Constitution of Massachusetts and to those of the thriving communities around her —or if unwilling to learn lessons of wisdom from the North, open the volume that contains the organic code of our own Southern sisters, and even there, with but few exceptions, our liberality seems, indeed, the grossest extravagance.

If we invoke the wisdom of the West, the same result becomes still more manifest. The great and growing State of Illinois with an area of square miles more than five times our own; and with a rapidly increasing population, amounting already to well nigh a million—rewards her Executive with the sum of fifteen hundred dollars.

Why, then, in view of all these examples, this enormous and most unwise extravagance upon our part? Other communities are as well governed—as prosperous and as happy! Why not like them let our liberality be ever tempered with a proper and wholesome economy—aye, sir, with an economy in character with our condition.

But we have been told by those who wage uncompromising warfare against this substitute, that its adoption as part of the organic law has the direct and unavoidable tendency of placing this high position entirely in the hands of the wealthy and the opulent. Was such indeed the case, he should have been the last to have desired to foster such a provision upon the Constitution. Respect for himself—respect for his own position, and for all simularly situated, would alike have forbidden it. Happily such an argument, or rather mere assertion, was sustained neither by reason, nor by past experience or present observation. All around us, in every section of the country, there had been, and were now bright and shining examples, utterly refuting, and with a power which language cannot express, such an objection. However successful we had been in linking the names of the pure and the intellectual with our own executive chair, justice requires us to say that other communities have not perhaps been less fortunate, even where the salaries were much inferior to the sum specified in the substitute. It was a fact well known to every member of the Convention, and to well-nigh every individual in the State, that it was this very provision requiring a permanent residence at the capital, which had attached to the Gubernatorial station such enormous expenditure, by surrounding it with extravagant customs, scarcely consistent with the simplicity of our republican institutions. And when he sought its abolition, he was influenced not only by a desire to effect a wholesome retrenchment, but to bring that exalted position within the reach of merit and intellect, however humble their pecuniary condition. If as seemed to be abundantly shown by the practical workings of other States, every official act could be discharged without the abandonment of home and pursuits, not inconsistent with the duties and the dignity of the post, why should the useless and unnecessary sacrifice be required? However gentlemen might characterize such a policy as penny-wise, he believed it to be sound in all its features, and such as would meet with the approbation of the people. Whilst he desired at all times to exhibit a spirit of proper liberality, he nevertheless regarded extravagance as the worst of follies, and he invoked this body of reformers, to begin at once, and at the very fountain-head, this great work of retrenchment for which we are assembled.

—

OFFICE OF SECRETARY OF STATE.

Remarks of Mr. DIRICKSON, *Thursday March* 13.

Mr. DIRICKSON then moved to strike out the twenty-second section, [abolishing the office of Secretary of State.]

Mr. DIRICKSON said,

That he had made the motion to strike out the section of the report just read; because, after the gravest reflection, he believed that no such officer was essential to the faithful and full administration of the government. With great pleasure and with entire attention, he had listened to the distinguished gentleman from the county of Queen Anne's whilst speaking of the duties and importance of this officer, and yet, frankness compelled him to say, that he had heard no argument which had removed the settled conviction that this official position was utterly and entirely useless. Maryland was in no condition longer to cherish and sustain more *sine cures*. The time had arrived when gentlemen should cease to cling to old establishments simply because they were old, unless it could, at the same time, be clearly shown that they were wise and useful. It had been said, that this officer, with all his high sounding title, was often but little else than a mere clerk to the Executive, and was constantly and busily employed in the issuing of military commissions and in the preparation of such other documents as his Excellency might direct. Sir, but yesterday this Convention fixed the salary of the Governor upon the most liberal if not exorbitant scale, and surely, with such a compensation, it was not requisite to employ others to do the labors that seemed properly to belong to the executive chamber. Let our chief executive officer, as in other States, become a working Governor. Let every department be pruned of the *sine cures* that have so long been fastened to them, and then will the calls of the tax-gatherer become lighter and lighter, and then will all begin to feel and realise the beneficial effects of this Convention.

He had no desire, at any time, "to read a lecture" to the body of which he was a member, but no remarks could deter him from urging upon their consideration the necessity of wielding the blade of retrenchment, wherever consistent with the public interests it might, with propriety, be applied. The honorable gentleman from the county of Frederick, had been pleased, in the discussion, to allude to the vote which he had given in the beginning of the session to effect the complete organization of the Convention; however foreign such an allusion might be to the present subject of debate, he desired briefly to reply, that he had given that vote believing that the officers then selected were essential to the despatch of the business we are here to perform, and it was proper to add, that the belief was sanctioned by the judgments and the votes of many of the most eminent and experienced of the body. It was also true, as had been said, that he had been excused from serving upon "the committee to enquire into the expediency of dispensing with certain officers," but he little thought he should ever have been called upon, here or elsewhere, to defend himself from such a charge. Prompted by the highest sense of propriety, he had asked to be relieved from the committee, and, at the time, avowed his views to be purely and solely upon the ground of the delicacy of his position. One of those officers was from his own county—his personal friend—he had stated it frankly, and the Convention had readily and cheerfully excused him from a situation the delicacy of which, all at once saw and appreciated. He did not desire to say more—nay, should not have said thus much, but that the charge of inconsistency having gone forth, 'twas proper the reply should bear it company. He was entirely willing that an impartial community, in view of all the facts, should decide the issue.

In conclusion, he again urged the importance of the motion to strike out, now before them. He begged reformers to aid him with their votes and to stand by him in the great work of retrenchment.

—

APPOINTMENTS TO OFFICE.

Remarks of Mr. Crisfield in reply to Mr. Brent, of Baltimore city, March 13.

Mr. CRISFIELD stated in reply, that his object in amending the section was to prevent the Senate from being deprived of their share in making the appointments. As the section stood previous to that amendment, he thought it capable of a construction which would have diminished the power of the Senate in relation to appointments; and he desired that the Senate should have their full share in all appointments. He was not aware of the difficulty which the gentleman from Baltimore had pointed out. But if it really existed to such an extent, as to place the Executive in difficulty and embarrass the public convenience it ought to be remedied, and he should interpose no objection.

The CHAIR, (Mr. Tuck,) said the notice should be entered on the journal, and the motion could then stand over until to-morrow. The substitute would also be printed on the journal.

Mr. CRISFIELD, in reply to the gentleman from Queen Anne's, (Mr. Spencer,) explained the object of the amendment, and added that if the Senate failed to perform its duty, it was responsible to the people of the State. There was no danger, in his opinion, of such failure; but if it should fail, the force of public opinion was a sufficient corrective. As to the failure of the Legislature to elect a United States Senator, in 1842, Mr. C. did not know that the gentleman of Queen Anne's, (Mr. S.,) ever condemned that failure. Indeed, he supposed—and he thought he had some reason for the supposition—that the gentleman from Queen Anne's did not condemn that failure. The House of Delegates had a majority who were of the political faith of the gentleman, but that majority did not prefer that gentleman for that high station; and Mr. C. had never heard, that the gentleman was dissatisfied at the refusal of the Senate to go into the election. But whether that gentleman condemned or not, it was very certain the Senate was sustained by public sentiment, and at the next election, the majority of the House was of the same party with the Senate, and has been ever since.

Mr. Spencer said the gentleman from Somerset, in his reference to the session of 1842, had mistaken the facts. There was no gentleman on his, (Mr. Spencer's,) side, who did not regret the failure to elect a United States Senator at that time. The lower house was democratic, and voted to go into the election, but the Senate refused. He had always, privately and before the people, denounced the course of the Senate on that occasion.

Mr Crisfield said his memory was not remarkable for accuracy; but he had supposed the facts to be as he had stated them.

Mr. Spencer. The gentleman is entirely mistaken.

WEDNESDAY, March 19th, 1851.

The Convention met at ten o'clock.

Prayer was made by the Rev. Mr. Griffith.

The roll was called, and a quorum being present, the journal of yesterday was read and approved.

THE COMMITTEE CLERKS.

Mr. Hicks, in pursuance of the notice he had yesterday given, moved a reconsideration of the vote of the Convention on the resolution heretofore adopted, dispensing with the services of certain committee clerks.

The question was stated to be on the motion to reconsider.

Mr. Hicks said he presumed it would be a useless consumption of time to say anything in support of this motion. The members of the Convention had had the subject in their minds, and were no doubt prepared to do justice towards a number of individuals here, who could not make their own defence. He was sure that it was unnecessary for him to urge the propriety of the reconsideration, for he believed it was conceded on all hands, that the vote should be reconsidered, in order to do justice towards individuals to whom injustice would otherwise be inevitably done. He hoped that the motion would prevail. The Convention could then take such action as it might think proper.

The President, (*pro tem.*,) stated the question, and the negative vote apparently prevailing;

Mr. Hicks desired to say one additional word. He earnestly requested gentlemen to reflect upon what they had done. The Convention, from the earliest period of its session, had been constantly in the habit of reconsidering votes upon subject-matters which had been passed upon. Surely no question could be more deserving of the calm judgment and considerate action of the Convention than this. It concerned individuals—highly respectable gentlemen, for such he knew them to be—whose characters had been implicated by the action of this body—not designedly, but not the less certainly. And he was sure that there was sufficient good feeling here to prevent injury being done to any individual in the State of Maryland, however humble his position might be. It was with this view that he had moved the reconsideration. He was no more interested in the matter than any other member of the Convention. The only interest that he had was to see justice done all. It was not a mere matter of dollars and cents to these individuals. It was a matter of character and feeling; and he was sure that every gentleman who regarded the subject in this light would cheerfully vote to reconsider—to re-instate these gentlemen—to put them upon an equal footing with their fellows in this body—and then to take such further action as might seem right and proper.

Mr. Gwinn said, he thought that the Convention ought to retrace the steps it had taken with reference to the committee clerks. He was aware that the change had been made upon grounds of economy—but it had been construed as a public censure—and in justice to them such an imputation ought to be refuted by the action of the Convention itself.

Mr. Jenifer said that he had voted against discharging the clerks; but as the committee had reported that there was no business sufficient for their occupation, and as the act had been done, he could not see that any wrong had been committed whatever. No imputation was intended by the Convention, and it had so declared. Although he voted against discharging these clerks, inasmuch as the Convention had thought proper to do so, and as he believed there was not sufficient business to occupy them, he should vote against the motion to reconsider.

Mr. Hicks said:

That his friend from Charles, (Mr. Jenifer,) was correct in saying that no reflection was designed to be cast on the clerks who had been discharged. He hoped he was not understood as imputing to the Convention any such motive. On the contrary, he had said, that he believed the Convention had no such design. But he would inquire whether it did not in fact reflect upon these individuals?

Now, it was least in his thoughts, to charge this honorable body with a design to reflect, as he had before remaked, upon the humblest individual in the State of Maryland; but did not this seem to be a reflection upon the clerks who were discharged? Was it not an invidious distinction between those who were discharged and those acting in the same capacity who were retained? He hoped they would reinstate the clerks, and if it should be ascertained that there was no necessity for their services, let them resign.

Mr. Hicks asked the yeas and nays on the motion to reconsider;

Which were ordered, and

Being taken, resulted as follows:

Affirmative—Messrs. Morgan, Weems, Dickinson, Crisfield, Williams, Hicks, Hodson, Eccleston, Phelps, Bowie, Spencer, Dirickson, McMaster, Magraw, Carter, Hardcastle, Gwinn, Stewart, of Baltimore city, Brent of Baltimore city, Sherwood of Baltimore city, Ware, Kilgour and Waters—23.

Negative—Messrs. Buchanan, President, *pro. tem.*, Lee, Dorsey, Brent of Charles, Jenifer, Howard, Welch, Chandler, Sherwood of Talbot, Chambers of Cecil, Miller, McLane, Wright, Fooks, Shriver, Sappington, Nelson, Schley, Fiery, Neill, John Newcomer, Harbine, Brewer, Weber, Hollyday, Slicer, Fitzpatrick, Smith, Parke and Cockey—30.

So the Convention refused to reconsider their vote on the said resolution.

Mr. Bowie, (in accordance with the notice given by him on yesterday,) moved that the Convention take up for consideration the amendment offered by Mr. Chambers, of Kent, to the twenty-second rule, and the substitute offered by him therefor.

Determined in the affirmative.

Mr. Bowie then moved to lay said amendment and substiiute on the table.

Determined in the affirmative.

Mr. Dorsey, (in accordance with the notice given by him on yesterday,) moved that the Convention take up for consideration the amendment offered by him to the seventeenth rule.

Determined in the affirmative.

On motion of Mr. Dorsey,

The amendment was laid on the table.

REPORT ON THE ATTORNEY GENERAL.

On motion of Mr. Bowie,

The Convention then resumed the consideration of the unfinished business of yesterday, being the report submitted by Mr. Shriver, as Chairman of the committee on the Attorney General and his Deputies.

The question pending before the Convention on yesterday, being on the motion of Mr. Dirickson, to amend the first section of said report, striking out all after the word "it" in the second line of said section, and substituting in lieu thereof the following:

"For whose services such compensation shall be made as the legislature may allow."

Mr. Bowie said he would not detain the Convention long. As he understood the report of the committee, it abolished altogether the office of Attorney General. The first section authorized the Governor to employ counsel for the State whenever the public interests may require. What were to be the powers, and what the duties of this counsel when employed by the Governor? The report was entirely silent upon that subject. It delegated no powers—defined no duties. He looked upon the powers and duties of the office of Attorney General just as well settled, as those pertaining to the office of Judge, or to any other office known to the Constitution and the laws. When the office of Attorney General was created in 1776, by the Constitution, it was the office known to the common law, with all the powers and duties attaching and belonging to that office according to the principles and rules of common law. That Constitution did not undertake to define the duties or the powers, but simply said that there should be an Attorney General appointed by the Governor, whose office should be during good behaviour. It was therefore the office known to the common law, and as such, just as well known and defined—just as thoroughly settled as the powers and jurisdiction of a judge under the common law.

It was very important to have an Attorney General. No State could well dispense with such an officer. All business in which the State was concerned, whether of a civil or of a criminal character, belonged *exofficio* by the principles of common law to that office. It was his duty to superintend all public business; to try all causes of the King of England in the Courts of that realm; to superintend the administration of criminal jurisprudence; and to attend to the execution and issuing of all State process. All opinions and all indictments were submitted to his inspection, for his approval or condemnation. Witnesses were admitted to, or excluded from the grand jury; bail and recognizances in criminal cases, were to be taken, and their validity and regularity to be examined into by that officer. Was it possible that the Convention should yield to the principle that such an office would be abolished in Maryland? Whose duty would it be to attend to the prosecution and investigation of subjects connected with criminal jurisprudence? Whose business would it be to attend to the preservation of the rights of the people, or the process of the State, if this office should be abolished? Nobody's! Would it be said that a Constitutional provision simply giving the Governor the right to employ counsel, would vest in the counsel those high powers and duties? He would have no more authority *exofficio*, than the counsel employed in any other manner, or by a private individual. The relation of attorney and client would exist, and nothing more; and that even would be confined to the particular case, and there would be no further power inherent in him by virtue of his office. It would only extend to the particular contract made by the Governor, to be superseded by that Governor whenever he might choose to retain or employ any other counsel. Inherently, the office of counsel for the State, would have attached to it no powers and no duties whatever.

Such was not the case with the office of Attorney General. That office was as old as the common law itself, though not known perhaps by that name. The king's sergeant, the king's counsel, and the king's solicitor, were the titles by which the chief law officer of the crown was known in England, and constituted the foundation of the office, as now held by the Attorney General. By names the office was not known prior to the reign of Charles the second; but the king's counsel was known to have had all the functions, and all the duties afterwards given to the Attorney General, in the reign of Charles the second. As was known to every lawyer in the Convention, the powers and duties of the Attorney General, were just as clearly settled by the common law, and by English statute law, as the powers and duties of the judge himself. Why then, he repeated, should that office be abolished? He objected to the report upon the ground, that while it abolished the office of Attorney General, the want was not supplied by adequate provisions for any other officer, with the like *ex officio* powers. He regarded these powers as essentially necessary to the preservation of the sovereignty of the State; intimately identified and inseparably connected with the very idea of sovereignty itself.

Besides the powers given to this officer by the common law, there were several statutes in Maryland, which had superadded other duties and obligations. From the year 1776, to the year 1816, the powers and duties of this officer, remained precisely as at common law. The Attorney General in Maryland, had all the prerogatives, rights, duties, and powers, which the Attorney General in England ever had. In 1816, however, the Legislature had thought proper to abolish altogether the office of Attorney General. The act of 1816, chapter 247, confirmed by the act of 1817, chapter 269, was simply a sweeping clause abolishing altogether that part of the Constitution, which created the office of Attorney General. But at the very same session in which this latter act was passed, another law had passed, re-establishing the office, superadding particular duties, and defining its powers. But this law was simply declaratory, adding nothing that did not exist before, and requiring duties which grew out of the nature of his office, and the relation he held to the sovereign power of the State. The duties, however, were imposed in the form of an act of Assembly. By various succeeding acts of Assembly, the Attorney General was required to superintend the execution of all the revenue laws of the State; to approve the bonds given by public officers of the State, and by collectors of the direct tax; to approve corporation bonds, bonds of insurance companies, and bonds of railroad companies, involving millions upon millions. He was to examine them, and to give his opinion upon them, to the Governor and the Treasurer, whenever required. All these powers are given to him, besides those common law powers, by act of Assembly. What was now to become of this large class of useful and necessary powers, if the office itself should be abolished? Where were they to be lodged? Did the report lodge them in the counsel to be employed by the State? Far from it. It simply said that the Governor might employ counsel, without defining any duty or power whatever, leaving them limited to the particular case in which he should be employed. He would submit it to the Convention, whether they were willing to abolish so important an office, without making some provision for these cases. If gentleman did not choose to call the officer Attorney General, they might call him what they pleased, provided the necessary powers were given to him.

The gentleman from Cecil, [Mr. McLane,] seemed to have taken up the idea that the office was unnecessary, and had drawn a parallel between the office of Attorney General of the United States and that of Maryland. One received only $4,500 and was required to perform all the duties performed by the other, at a salary of $8 or $10,000. What had all this, he asked, to do with the office of Attorney General? If the fees were too large, they should be diminished. If the salary was too large it could be reduced to a proper and reasonable amount. But he could see no reason why the office itself should be abolished, or that it was unnecessary, because these enormous fees had been paid to that officer. The gentleman from Cecil had gone on to show that various sums of money had been appropriated as extra compensation to the Attorney General and his deputies. What had this to do with abolishing the office altogether? He would not say that the Governor had lavishly squandered away the public money by giving too large fees to counsel. He would neither affirm nor deny it. He knew nothing about the facts in relation to it, and the circumstances under which these fees were paid. He would state, however, that in all these cases there had been special acts of the Legislature to warrant the acts. During the few years that he had had the honor of a seat in the Legislature, he had a distinct recollection of being called upon repeatedly to vote upon resolutions authorising the Governor to employ additional counsel for particular cases. The very case in which the Attorney General was sent to New York, was authorised by a special act of the Legislature; and he would undertake to say that in no instance had these extra appropriations been made, except in pursuance of resolutions passed by the General Assembly authorising the Governor to make this expenditure of the public money. He had never done it of his own accord. But all this had nothing to do with the question under consideration. It was not now for the Convention to sit in judgment upon the proceedings of the Executive. He supposed there was not an honorable lawyer in the State, who would not claim the right at least to measure the value of his own services; and there would not be a Governor who would pay more than he thought the services to be worth.

His objection to the first article, which was now under consideration, was, that it abolished the office of Attorney General, an office which he thought was essentially necessary. No state in the Union was without such an officer, whose duties were to prosecute in the name of the State, not only in all criminal cases but in all civil suits. In hundreds of cases, the execution of criminal laws would be frustrated, if there was no such officer as an Attorney General, or some one clothed with that power in the different counties of the State. There was no stage from the very commencement of the issuing of the writ, to the close, that it was not the duty of the Attorney General to supervise the administration of justice in behalf of the State. Unless such an office should be continued, the administration of the law would inevitably suffer. The mere appointment of counsel by the Governor would not remedy the evil, because that counsel would not be clothed with these powers and duties.

As to the mode of appointment, he was indifferent about it. His own impression was that the Attorney General ought to be appointed by the Governor; that every Governor, at the commencement of his term of service, ought to have the right to select his Attorney General for the term of four years. He saw no necessity for throwing that officer before the people, although he had no great objection to it, and if it could be the will of the majority of the Convention that the Attorney General should be elected by the people, he would throw no impediment in the way of it. He should be in favor also of taking away from the Attorney General the power of selecting his deputies which seems so much to be objected to. But while he might consent to the election by the people, he believed it proper to have an eye to the interests of the various portions of the State. He was opposed to the election by the people by general ticket, because he believed that if appointed by general ticket, the city of Baltimore would elect the Attorney General to the end of time. He would prefer to have the State divided into districts, giving each district one term. Regarding the Attorney General as the confidential adviser of the Governor, it seemed to him more proper that he should be selected by the Governor. The selection of a new Governor every four years, would create such a rotation in the office of Attorney General as would satisfy the most ultra reformer in the State.

Mr. Brent, of Baltimore city, said,

Considerations of false delicacy shall not withhold the reasons for the vote which I am called on to give.

Before giving those reasons, I feel at liberty, with a view to correct erroneous impressions, some of which have appeared in the public prints, to refer to the causes which prevented me from resigning my seat in this Convention, when I was honored with the commission of Attorney General.

It has been said, that as a member of the committee on credentials and qualifications, I reported against the competency of any person to sit in this Convention who held any office of profit under the State government. This is wholly untrue.

My report is on file, and will show that I admitted the competency of clerks, registers of wills, and all other State officers, except judges, to hold seats in this Convention.

Therefore, the retention of my seat in this Convention under present circumstances, is *not inconsistent* with my own report on credentials and qualifications.

By the advice of judicious friends, I was averse to troubling my constituents with a special election to fill my place if it could be avoided consistently with the public interests and my duty. Finding that my office could be conducted by deputy, according to law, I felt that the public interests would be perfectly safe when confided to the integrity and ability of the friend whom I have selected. So much for the charges against *my* inconsistency.

In voting upon the office which I now hold, I shall vote for three objects and for any measures which will effect those objects, viz:

First, I shall vote to supersede the present Attorney Generalship.

Secondly, To elect, by popular vote, the Prosecuting Attorneys for each county and the city of Baltimore.

Thirdly, To elect, by popular vote, throughout the State, an Attorney General, with a fixed salary, in order that while the local attorneys superintend the local business of the State, the Attorney General may superintend all matters of general interests, such as advising the Governor, arguing causes in the courts of appeals, &c.

These are the views which I have formed conscientiously, and I shall conscientiously endeavor to carry the mout by my votes.

Mr. Spencer regretted that he could not support the amendment offered by the gentleman from Cecil. He was apprehensive it would bring upon the State innumerable evils.

That gentleman had looked back to the very alarming expenditures in extra compensation paid to Attorney General and special counsels, employed in a variety of cases in which the State of Maryland was interested. By adopting this proposition, he feared the door would be opened for a scene of corruption in the legislature, to be avoided at all times.

If it was the intention of the Convention to abolish the office of Attorney General, something fixed and precise ought to be adopted as the course to be pursued hereafter. He should in that case, infinitely prefer the section reported by the committee, to the proposition of the gentleman from Cecil. He would prefer, if the office of Attorney General should be abolished, that the Governor, under his high responsibility should have the power of employing special counsel, and of regulating and controling the fees, rather than that it should be thrown before the legislature. If the proposition of the gentleman from Cecil should be adopted, the legislature must do one of two things—either pass a law authorizing the Governor to do the very thing which this section now authorised him to do—or refuse to pass such a law and compel the Governor in each particular case in which he shall have occasion to employ counsel, to leave to them the right to adjudge the fees to be paid. In the latter case, who would be willing to be employed to transact any important business, with an uncertainty as to the fee to be allowed by the legislature? There would be counsel willing to go before the legislature by their friends, and by appeals and other inducements, expect to induce the legislature to pay a large fee.

But other highly distinguished gentlemen, would not, under any circumstances, go before the legislature and be compelled to resort to log-rolling and intrigue, in order to obtain a suitable fee. The services of such men would be lost to the government, by the amendment.

He was entirely opposed to the abolition of the office of Attorney General. He fully agreed with the sentiments of the gentleman from Baltimore city, (Mr. Brent,) and would vote for such a proposition, to allow the people of Maryland to elect their own local officers for their local business.

He regarded the office of Attorney General with the same high opinion as the gentleman from Prince George's, (Mr. Bowie.) He wished the salary to be fixed and certain. He believed that the State would save by the adoption of this course. If there was no Attorney General the Governor would be authorized to employ such counsel as the exigencies might require, or as a resolution of the legislature might direct. The result would be, that in each instance, special counsel would be employed. If the Governor should have occasion at one time to consult a lawyer, A would be employed. In another case, at another time, B would be employed. To try a case in the courts, C would be employed, and to try another, D would be employed. In each case, enormous sums of money would be required.

Without intending to find any fault with the officers of the government, he would say, that during the last year, nearly five thousand dollars had been paid in extraordinary cases. These extraordinary cases were constantly occurring. There was one which would necessarily soon come up, of great interest to the State of Maryland.

At the present moment there were incarcerated in the State prison of Pennsylvania, two individuals for having actually arrested fugitive slaves belonging to a gentleman in Cecil county. By the laws of Pennsylvania, if a female escaped from a slave State, and should give birth to a child in Pennsylvania, the child by its birth would be free. No such doctrine prevailed here, and here was a question to be decided between the States of Maryland and Pennsylvania.

It would have to go to the supreme court of the United States for examination. He mentioned this merely as an instance in which the services of counsel would be required. There would be innumerable cases constantly arising, and many would grow out of the very Constitution which they were framing. If these cases were left to be managed by special counsel to be employed for each case, large sums of money would annually be drawn from the treasury to pay for these services. Instead of this, an Attorney General, with a certain and fixed salary, could try all these cases, as the Attorney General of the United States was required to try all cases in which the United States are concerned. However difficulty the task, or however voluminous the documents necessary to consult, when the Attorney General of the United States was asked for his opinion by the President of the United States, he never received an extra fee for it. Whether the case related to the extreme south, or west, or north, if the United States were interested, the Attorney General tried it at length without compensation. So it would be with the Attorney General of this State. If his compensation was fixed, he would have to perform all the duties required, while it would be a saving to the State in a financial point of view.

He had no apprehension, in case the election of the Attorney General should be made by general ticket, and in the districts, although they were not required by the Constitution to come from the districts, that the city of Baltimore would be able to command the Attorney General at all times. Strong and powerful as the city was, he did not believe she would ever undertake to do so. If she did, it would be found that the people of the counties would rise, *en masse*, against her. He had never found, in the gubernatorial elections, that when the person selected was not exactly from that city, but was identified with the city, that it had any influence whatever upon the city. He had never found the city of Baltimore undertaking to assume the right to select the public officer, to be voted for by the people. At the same time, he had no objection to the proposition suggested, and if the gubernatorial elections were to be from districts, the same reasons would exist why the Attorney General should be elected in the same way. He would therefore vote for the proposition.

He had not been here yesterday when the gentleman from Anne Arundel [Mr. Dorsey] made some remarks in reference to the claims of Messrs. Carmichael, Dulany and Emory, which had been before the Legislature of Maryland. He considered these remarks, so far as they tended to depreciate this claim, unjust, though he imputed no unkind motive.

Mr. S. here proceeded to explain the claim, and to show that it had not been rejected by the Legislature, and should not be prejudged by the Convention; but on the contrary, it had been in effect acknowledged by the Legislature. He would take occasion further to say, in reference to the claim of Mr. McCullough, in his opinion, the State was as much bound to refuse the judgment of the referees in his favor, as they would be by the opinion of the Court of Appeals. It had been judged by a special Court, who were entitled to as much respect as the Court of Appeals.

Mr. Gwinn said that he did not intend to allude to the case of the gentlemen who had acted as arbitrators in the McCullough case. He did not understand that an aspersion had been cast upon their conduct, either by any here, or in the Legislature; and their high character rendered a defence unnecessary He intended only to make a very brief reply to the argument of the gentleman from Prince Georges, (Mr. Bowie.)

He has criticised the report of the committtee as a misapprehension of the true character of the Attorney General, and has said, if we attempt to change his character as an officer of the common law, it is necessary to prescribe his duties in the Constitution, or by legislative act. The Attorney Generalship, as known to the English law, is a very different office from that provided for in our system. In England, the King is the source of all judicial and executive authority. The judges and Attorney General who represent a delegated portion of his sovereign executive authority, are common law officers, because a parliamentary creation of the office of judge or Attorney General would have been a limitation upon the common law authority of the crown. But in Maryland the case is widely different. We have no *common law officer whatever*, and the Attorney General cannot exist unless the office is recognised by the Constitution or by some public law. He may have, if you please so to call them, *common law powers*, but these are but the general and necessary powers of every State, incidentally deputed, and not by the force of the common law a part of the office itself.

The first mention made of the office, the gentleman tells us, is in the time of Charles II. Certainly, no more conclusive answer could be afforded to an argument founded upon its existence as common law.

Much had been said about corruption which would result if counsel designated were left to make his claim upon the Legislature. He thought it certainly much wiser that the Executive should have the power, but it is wiser to trust to the general care and diligence of the Legislature in examining such occasional claims as may arise, and to the character of the person employed by the Executive, than for the fear of such abuse to continue such an officer in our State Government. Since, if their counsel is of their own selection, they will have no shelter from the effects of an improper decision.

Can it be said, that when such emergencies arise, proper counsel cannot be obtained, if the whole bar of the State is open to their choice? But the objection is taken that such counsel would not be subject to the responsibility of a sworn officer. In the usual relations of attorney and client, though involving large amounts of property, and even life itself, such checks have not been deemed needful; and it cannot be supposed that a higher guarantee would be required for the service of the State.

Some stress has been laid upon the extra fees which have been paid by the State during the past twelve years; and the argument is that it would be wiser to pay a certain salary than such irregular fees. The sum, though considerable, does not amount to an average of more than two thousand a year, which is about the compensation which some seem to think sufficient for the performance of the duties of an Attorney General. Yet, this system obtained while there *was* an Attorney General, and, yet it is alluded to as a consequence of the want of one. The argument is certainly extraordinary.

Mr. McLane said, that he had been drawn into the discussion on yesterday. He would very gladly escape from it; but some remarks made by the gentleman from Prince George's, [Mr. Bowie,] required a reply. In saying that he desired to escape from the discussion, he would not be understood as entertaining any doubts as to the opinions he had expressed yesterday; because those opinions had been the result of a deliberate examination.

He believed there was a great principle at the foundation of this proceeding, and unless his objection was removed, he could never give it his assent. The Convention was assembled for the purpose of making a new Constitution for the people; and the public had a right to expect that the new Government would not be more expensive than the present. In the creation of that new Government, no officer would be continued who was not indispensably necessary to its wise and efficient administration. Unless it could be shown that the office of Attorney General was of this character, which had not been shown to his satisfaction—he should feel bound to resist the continuance of that office. The gentleman from Prince George's had referred to the amounts paid during the last twelve years, as stated by himself, (Mr. McL.,) on yesterday. His object had been to show that the office of Attorney General was entirely useless; for otherwise this large amount of money would not have been paid for extra compensation. There had been twelve or fifteen cases to which, by the argument of the gentleman from Prince George's, it was the duty of the Attorney General to attend. The cases of special legislation were not included in that paper, in a single instance, because it was not the duty of the Attorney General by virtue of his office, to give his attention to these cases without any compensation whatever. Yet it would be found with that office, existing with all its rigor, that this large amount of money had been paid by those officers.

Was it not a fair deduction, to say that the office was useless, and that some other system ought to be adopted which would be of more advantage to the State? He had adverted to abuses, and did not think it necessary to do so. He had simply referred to the fact, that if while there had been an Attorney General, it had been necessary to employ officers at an expenditure of $23,000 in twelve years, his services ought to be dispensed with. Unless it could be shown, upon grounds not hitherto brought before the Convention, that the office was necessary, he must continue to be opposed to its continuance.

What were the duties of the Attorney General, and upon what grounds was he to be retained? The reference of the gentleman from Prince George, to the acts of Assembly, explaining the duties of the Attorney General, had opened to his mind an entirely new consideration; and had satisfied him more than any thing else, that the office was now entirely unnecessary. The office was originally created under the Constitution; and the gentleman supposed that the Attorney General so created by the Constitution, was like the Attorney General under the common law in England. The case where the Attorney General had resided upon the Eastern Shore, without attending personally to criminal prosecutions at all, would be similar to the office of Attorney General in England.

Anterior to the act of 1817, the duty of the Attorney General would be essentially different from those of the Attorney General of England, where it was the duty to take care of the interests of the crown in all civil causes. He hardly knew of a civil case here, in which the Attorney General had rendered any assistance. According to the document to which he had referred, the Attorney General attended in no case to the interests of the State in a civil suit, without being paid for it, independently of the fees and perquisites of his office. He knew of no such case. He supposed the act of 1817 to be intended in some degree to remedy this defect. It was not necessary now to call attention to that act, as it had been subsequently repealed by the act of 1821, in which the duties of the Attorney General were defined. The act of 1821, provided as follows:

"That from and after the passage of this act, the Governor shall nominate, and by and with the advice and consent of the council, appoint and commission a person of sound legal knowledge, who shall be styled Attorney General of Maryland, and who, previous to, and during his acting as such, shall reside in this State; and it shall be the duty of the said Attorney General, to prosecute and defend on the part of the State, all cases now depending, or which may hereafter be brought in or removed to any of the counties of this State, by or against the State, or wherein the State shall or may be interested, in the same manner, as the Attorney General heretofore was accustomed to do, or could do; and he shall have, exercise, and use all and every the powers and authorities in and relating to the same, as the Attorney General heretofore had used and exercised, or can have, use and exercise in similar cases; and he shall give his opinion and advice whenever he shall be required by the General Assembly, or either branch thereof, by the Governor and Council, or by the Treasurer of the Eastern and Western Shore, or any deputy he may appoint, on any matter or subject depending before them."

The object of this act was to define the duties more particularly, and to give the Attorney General the authority to appoint deputies. All the duties were provided for in this act; and were all transferred to the Prosecuting Attorneys of the several counties and of the city of Baltimore. The Attorney General had nothing to do with it, according to the scheme now proposed.

The proposition of the chairman of the committee, would dispose of the entire first branch of the act of 1821, and devolve the duties now nominally discharged by the Attorney General, upon the county prosecutors. Who could doubt that under this system, an intelligent people, in any part of the State, would select individuals quite competent to the discharge of these duties? What would be the remaining duties of the Attorney General? To give his opinion and advice whenever required so to do by the General Assembly, or by either branch thereof, by the Governor and council, or the treasurer of the Eastern or Western Shore, upon any question pending before them. He would ask the Convention if they were now prepared to continue this office of Attorney General, for no other purpose than to give opinions.

The gentleman from Queen Anne's, had spoken of the salary What gentleman, it had been asked, would take the office for $2500 a year, or for less than that amount? He doubted whether it would be taken by a competent person, for less than $3000. The system under which they were now acting, was other than that. Taking $23000, the amount paid for the last twelve years, it would amount to but $1700 per annum, so that it seemed that the Governor and the State, had had the benefit of the best talent and most eminent counsel in the State, at $1700. Upon every principle, therefore, the office was shown to be entirely useless, and experience had proved that a fixed salary would not dispense at all with the objection he had stated.

He was willing to concede that this amendment was not stringent enough or broad enough to remedy the evil entirely. The argument of the gentleman over the way, (Mr. Spencer,) was founded upon abuses that might creep in, under this amendment, in the Legislature. The gentleman supposed that every case that occurred was to be presented to the Legislature and decided *per se*. That was not his intention. He intended to have the Legislature take up the subject and prescribe regulations at once, by which the Governor would be bound. when he came to select counsel. They would prescribe some general rule by which the compensation should be regulated by the government. That was his intention, and this would prevent the abuses which the gentleman had suggested. If that gentleman required that the amendment should be more strict, if he would make suggestions as to the mode, he, (Mr. McLane,) would cheerfully adopt them. He would gladly put it out of the power, either of the Governor or of the Legislature to abuse the power, should either of them be disposed so to do, which he did not believe would ever be the case. He could, therefore, see no difficulty growing out of it. The office of Attorney General was no longer the constitutional office. It was an office of the law, and if the bill was passed, the Legislature might create the office of Attorney General just as it had already been created. It might be done now, by Act of Assembly, as well as in 1821; and, he thought it important to prevent it. When the second section should come under consideration, he would offer an amendment to prevent it. In the mean time, he could see no benefit to result from the appointment of an officer with a fixed salary of $1700, $2800 or $3000, unless it could be shown that the duties of that officer could thus be most economically discharged. The abuses of the Legislature, which could be guarded against, would constitute no objection to his proposition.

Mr. Spencer said that every one would acknowledge that it was the duty of the Convention to adopt a Constitution which would limit the expenses of the State as much as possible, and which would exclude all useless offices. The question now arose, is the office of Attorney General a useless one? And this was the point with which he took issue with the gentleman who had preceded him, (Mr. McLane.) That gentleman's whole argument showed, the history of the State showed, that the State of Maryland required the assistance of legal advice. The whole history of the State showed that there had not been a period when she had not required it. The only difference between the gentleman and himself was this: How is the State to have this assistance?

Should the Governor have the privilege to select special counsel in all times and all cases, or should the State have a responsible law adviser upon whom it could rely? This was the question. The reason why his learned friend was opposed to this, was not because the State did not require counsel, but his argument was that the office had been abused. If the office had been abused, why did not his learned friend suggest a mode by which the abuses could be corrected, rather than the abolition of the office itself? Any other office in the State might be abused, and did it follow that because the office was abused,therefore it should be abolished? No; wisdom would seem to suggest that to avoid abuse, they should provide a check to prevent it.

What had been the abuse complained of in reference to the office of Attorney General? It was not that that officer had not performed his cuty, nor that the State had not derived essential service from his learning and ability. The fault complained of was that the Legislature had not defined the mode of paying him for services rendered; that in leaving the rate of payment open and uncertain, abuses had crept in, and large sums had been appropriated for the payment of services which were unreasonable and uncalled for. Now he would go with his friend for the correction of these abuses, and how could they be corrected?

All admitted that the State might require legal services and law advice. Let them have a responsible officer to take care of the interests of the State, and give him a fixed salary, beyond which they could not go. By this means they would prevent abuses, and secure to the State the services which it had at all times required. At this very moment, many cases arise in prospective, and there was now a great and important case pending in the State of Maryland, by and through one of her citizens, and the State of New York, growing out of the case of Mr. Lee, of Frederick. He had arrested one of his slaves. This slave, under a process, had been taken out of Mr. Lee's hands by Judge Edwards, of New York,as he was in the act of bringing him home and under a decision of the Judge, delivered out of custody.

The Attorney General or some other lawyer, would have to go to New York and take the case to the highest court of that State, even to the Supreme court of the United States, if necessary. The case was now actually pending, aud was to have been argued at the last February term of the Supreme court of New York. The Attorney General had now been notified to attend that court in May next for the purpose of arguing the case. So it would be at all times, and such cases would always arise, more especially since the passage by the Congress of the United States of the act protecting the right of the master to slave property. It should be made the duty of the law officer of the State to try all cases in which the State has an interest, and, in such cases, as might be necessary, to employ assistant counsel. In this way they could correct abuses.

His friend had said that there would be no necessity for an Attorney General, because the deputy attorneys throughout the counties, no doubt, would be selected for their learning, wisdom and position. The gentleman should recollect that the emoluments of these offices in the counties, are very small, and the question was yet to be determined whether they will command the consideration of men of the character of which he has spoken, particularly when, in addition to the limited pay, the offices are to be of short tenure.

The gentleman had also said, in reference to the Attorney General of the State of Maryland, that when that officer resided on the Eastern Shore, he took no part in the office of Attorney General. The gentleman would allow him to say that he was mistaken. The Attorney General did not prosecute in any county regularly, but whenever the public interest was at stake, and whenever the Governor had occasion to require a legal opinion or his counsel, he was always at hand. It was true that when he appeared in the court of appeals, and tried any peculiar case, as shown by the record, extra compensation was allowed him. But this resulted from defect in the mode of payment, not from the system itself.

The gentleman from Cecil had said, that about $1700 per year, had been paid by the State for some years past to counsel, in addition to what had been paid to the Attorney General by regular fees. He had no doubt that this estimate was correct. He, (Mr. S.,) believed that if the people of the State were allowed to have an Attorney General, with a salary of $2000 per annum, and each county and the city of Baltimore, to elect their local attorneys, it would be much more economical than the system now pursued, or the one recommended by the amendment to the bill. He did not believe that there would be any difficulty in obtaining able men for $2000 per year. He thought that distinguished men could be obtained for $1500 per annum.

He was of the opinion that the Attorney General should have nothing to do with the prosecution of ordinary cases in the courts, but should merely give advice to the Governor, and try cases brought up to the court of appeals, by the deputies of the counties.

Fifteen hundred dollars per annum, he repeated, would secure the most distinguished men. They had the most eminent men as judges at $2 500 a year, whose duty it was to try all cases, and who were obliged to be from home at least six months in the course of a year.

Mr. Chambers, of Kent. Nine months.

Mr. SPENCER. The gentleman from Kent says, that they have to be away from home nine months. Mr. S. said, that believing $1500 would procure the services of a capable person as Attorney General, he would be willing to vote for that sum for his annual compensation.

Mr. CRISFIELD stated his purpose in rising was not to prolong the debate, but simply to give notice of a substitute which he intended to propose, when in order, for the first section. Before doing this, however, he desired to notice a single view taken by the gentleman from Cecil, (Mr. McLane.) That gentleman's argument was, that this office was unnecessary. He had read to the Convention an amendment which the chairman of the committee who reported this article proposed to offer, by which the power of the prosecuting attorneys would cover all the duties of Attorney General, except those for advising the executive department. There were other classes of cases which these officers must be called upon to examine. There were cases continually arising in the land office, growing out of State laws, which must be attended to, as also civil and chancery cases. What did the gentleman propose? That when these cases arose, the clerk should inform the Governor who will delegate some individual to attend to the interests of the State. This showed that the services of a legal officer were necessary to the State, and the question then was—and the bill was based upon the hypothesis that the services of counsel were necessary—whether they were to have the duties performed by an officer who was an officer of law, whose duties would be prescribed by law, who would act under the responsibility of an oath, and who would receive a fixed salary, or whether they were to have an individual to be selected by the Governor, under no responsibility, guided by no law, and with no duty defined, and to receive an unlimited amount of compensation? On one hand, the duties would be undefined, and the compensation unfixed; on the other hand the duties would be defined and the responsibility known.

It seemed to him that the arguments of both sides admitted that some individual was necessary to perform some portion of the duty which the Attorney General heretofore had been required to perform He thought it was better to have an Attorney General, than to adopt the mode suggested by the gentleman from Cecil.

If the Attorney General received last year $9000, why not devise some scheme to prevent this amount from accruing to him? They could limit the amount. The argument had been urged that $1700, in addition to the fees, had been paid for extra compensation. These fees would continue to be given until the law should be altered, so as to give to the Attorney General a certain salary. The Legislature had given this sum regularly themselves: if not directly they had directed the Governor to do it. Unless they restrained the Legislature, these expenditures would still go on. Economy was a sufficient reason why they should have an individual as Attorney General, who would receive a fixed compensation and be required by law to perform such duties as should be assigned to him by law. This would certainly be better than to have a class of individuals irresponsible to the State.

Mr. C. then read his substitute, which he said was based upon the act of 1821, as follows:

Section 1st. The Governor, by and with the advice and consent of the Senate, shall appoint one person of integrity and sound legal knowledge, who shall be a citizen of the United States, and shall have resided at least five years in this State, before the time of his appointment, who shall be styled Attorney General of Maryland; he shall reside in this State while he continues to act as such; shall hold his office for the term of four years, and shall qualify by taking such oath as may be prescribed by law, and it shall be his duty to prosecute and defend, on the part of the State, all cases which at the time of the adoption of this Constitution and thereafter, may be depending in the courts of appeals by or against the State, or wherein the State shall be interested, in the same manner as the Attorney General is accustomed to do, or can do, and he shall have, exercise and use all and every the powers and authorities in and relating to the same, as the Attorney General now has, use, and exercises, or can have use and exercise, in similar cases, except such as are herein conferred upon the State's Attorneys, to be provided for hereafter, and he shall give his opinion in writing whenever required by the General Assembly or either branch thereof, the Governor, the Treasurer, or any State's Attorney, on any matter or subject depending before them, and when required by the Governor or the General Assembly he shall aid any State's Attorney in prosecuting any suit or action brought by the State in any court of this State; and he shall commence and prosecute or defend any suit or action in any of said courts, on the part of the State, as the General Assembly, or the Governor, acting according to law, shall direct to be commenced, prosecuted or defended, and he shall receive for his services an annual salary of dollars, but he shall not be entitled to receive any fees, perquisites or rewards whatever, in addition to the salary aforesaid, for the performance of any official duty; or have power to appoint any agent, representative, or deputy, under any circumstances whatever.

Mr. JENIFER said, that the bill as reported and the amendments and substitutes offered, all provided for a law officer of the State as necessary. This seemed to be conceded on all sides. The questions which arise were, whether he should be called an Attorney General or mere counsel employed by the Governor; whether he should be appointed or elected, and what compensation he should receive. These embraced the general views of the amendments. An objection had been urged to the appointment or election of an Attorney General upon the ground of expense. The gentleman from Cecil, [Mr. McLane.] had assumed that one of the objects of calling the Convention, indeed he had said, the greatest object was economy, which he denominated the platform of the Convention—that economy was the great basis upon which the Convention was called. He (Mr J.,) would admit this was one object, and if they would examine the different bills reported, they would find that it had been carried out as far as it could go. With all the bills reported, economy had been the order of the day. But this was not the only object of the Convention. Its object was also to take away the life tenure of the offices of the judges and others. This was one great complaint of the people—it was also to restrain within proper limits the legislative and Executive departments of the Government.

In regard to economy, how was it? It was provided by the substitutes of the gentleman from Cecil and of the gentleman from Worcester, that the Governor should employ an officer whenever he might think proper. Consequently, the person employed must have a salary, or other compensation.

Suppose it should become necessary that the Governor should employ counsel to the Supreme Court of the United States to go to New York, to Pennsylvania or anywhere else, for the purpose of arguing a case; for each and every case the counsel must be paid, and he is not limited to one counsel, he may employ half a dozen at one time, or at different times. Another case may arise, and another, until the compensation allowed would exceed the amount the Legislature would give an Attorney General. The enormous amount paid the Attorney General had been referred to. He ventured to say, that that amount would be very great economy compared with the appointments of counsel by the Governor, unlimited as to the amount of compensation they were to receive, except by the amount of the contingent fund at his disposal.

It had been said, that at the present time it was not necessary to have an Attorney General. If at any time from the formation of the Government, to the present time, that necessity had existed—now was the time to have a law officer to protect the great interests of the State.

The gentleman from Queen Anne's, (Mr. Spencer,) had referred to the fugitive slave case in New York. Mr. J. thought that the Attorney General should, very properly, go there and argue the case. The State would not then have additional expenses to pay, except such as might be provided for by law—the compensation should be liberal but defined.

Why not say that the Attorney General should have a proper salary, and make it his duty to go when called on by the Governor. In regard to economy, they would see that if they gave the Attorney General $2500 or $2000 per annum, for which the best talent might be engaged, having State's attorneys throughout all the counties, economy would be better accomplished and they would have a law officer respected, whenever duty called him, as the law officer of the State.

In regard to the mode of appointment, he agreed with the gentleman from Prince George's, (Mr. Bowie,) that the appointment should be made by the Governor, and for four years. Mr. J. was of the opinion that the officer should be responsible to the State for the duty performed, but if the power should be given to the Governor alone, he did not see that there would be any responsibility upon the part of the individual employed, because he would not be recognised by law.

As to the mode of appointment, some gentlemen were in favor of election by the people. He ventured to say, that throughout the counties it had scarcely been heard of. He had never heard it mentioned before he came to the Convention. This bill provided that there should be a State Attorney in each county, to be elected by the people of the county. He believed that this power should be placed in the hands of the Governor and Senate.

He had seen it published throughout the papers, that a certain party desired to take from the Governor all responsibility and patronage. And it had been charged upon gentlemen of the lower counties and the Whig party. He said it was a little remarkable, as far as he had seen by the votes and in discussion, that it was the Democratic party who were afraid to trust the Governor with power, and were for curtailing it most. He disavowed for himself being of either party in this great question of reform, and was in favor of placing confidence in the Governor whom the people elected, and also in the Senate. He did not desire to force upon the people what he believed they did not require. He was for appointment by the Governor, by and with the advice and consent of the Senate; the compensation to be regulated either by the Convention or by the Legislature, as might be deemed most expedient. If it should be decided that the Attorney General should not be appointed by the Governor he would take the other alternative, and have him elected by the people. He believed that the manner in which it was proposed to regulate the compensation of this officer by the amendment of the gentleman from Somerset, [Mr. Crisfield,] was a good one, as it would prevent cavil hereafter.

The importance of an Attorney General at the present time had been referred to by the gentleman from Queen Anne's, not only in the case of New York, but in the case of Philadelphia also. The legislature of Ohio had lately passed a law which might bring up great and important questions, for the consideration of the legislature of Maryland, and the opinions of her State officers. That State had passed a law expressly nullifying a law of Congress, by making it a penalty to assist in capturing fugitive slaves. He knew it had been said that the Governor could employ the best counsel to go to these places; but the consequence would be a much larger expense. Therefore, with regard to economy and the great interests of the State, he believed there should be an Attorney General, whose duty it should be to guard the interests of the State at home, and in the Supreme court of the United States, and elsewhere, whenever his services should be required. He would give him a liberal salary, and then he would have no right to charge beyond it, leaving it to the equity and justice of the legislature, to make him extra compensation whenever it might be thought proper he should receive it.

If economy were the sole object, it appeared to him that the appointment of an Attorney General for the State, with a fixed salary, would accomplish that object and comport more with the dignity and honor and interest of the State, than a power vested in the Governor, to employ counsel whenever he deemed it expedient, and at what compensation he pleased. For these reasons he should vote for the appointment of an Attorney General.

Mr. Brent, of Charles, said that the subject presented to the consideration of the Convention, was whether the office of Attorney General, as it now exists in the State, should be retained in the Constitution we have been delegated to form. The plan of the committee proposed to abolish that office, and substitute in place of it State's Attorneys, to be elected by the people in the several counties and the city of Baltimore. From the consideration and thought he had given to the subject, he believed it to be the proper plan, and was prepared to give it his support. The provisions of the second section of the reported bill, rendered the appointment of an Attorney General for the State at large unnecessary, and the arguments submitted on the other side had failed to convince him he was in error. No objection had been made to the main features of this section, but it was contended that in addition to a State's Attorney to be elected in each county and the city of Baltimore, there should also be an Attorney General for the State at large.

The gentleman from Prince George, had gone into an historical inquiry, to show that this was a common law office. He believed that it had its origin in England, during the time of Charles, the second. Many of its duties are derived from the common law, but in this State they are chiefly prescribed by the act of 1817. The various tax and revenue laws of the State, also require certain services to be rendered by that officer. His appointment is provided for in the Constitution, but his duties have been designated by the Legislature. It was not, however, important for him to stop and enquire whether this was an officer at common law or not. An examination of that question in connection with the subject, as presented by the bill of the committee, he thought needless.

What are the duties of that officer? To attend to all cases and suits where the State of Maryland is directly concerned, either in interest or in guarding and enforcing her criminal laws. He is in fact the attorney of the State, in every case where she is the real and not the nominal party. Not being able to attend to every State's case arising within her limits, he has exercised the right of appointing his deputies, of whom acting within the limits of the commission from the Attorney General to them, the same duties are required as of him. He is not the confidential adviser of the Governor, but the Governor of the State has the right to require from him his written opinion upon any subject in which the legal rights and interest of the State are involved.

Mr. B. went on to remark that the Attorney General of the State is not a salaried officer. His compensation is derived from fees, and the amount depends upon the number of cases in which he is professionally engaged. In most of the counties of the State, the emoluments of the office are small, and it is only in the city of Baltimore that the profits of the office are large; being rendered so by the number of criminal cases constantly occurring there, and which will always be an incident to a large and populous city. The fees of the Attorney General and his Deputies, are paid by the county or city, where the several cases are prosecuted, unless by the judgment of the Court they are to be paid by the party convicted. From the remarks of one of the honorable gentlemen from Baltimore, not now in his seat, it might be inferred, although he did not design so to be understood, that the Attorney General of Maryland was paid by that city. If he resides there and prosecutes in criminal cases originating in that city, he is chiefly paid from her treasury. A former Attorney General of the State resided upon the Eastern Shore, and no part of his income was received from Baltimore—the profits of the office there went to his deputy.

It is said if the office of Attorney General is abolished, the interests of the State will suffer. Undoubtedly this is true, unless his duties are deputed to others. What is proposed in the bill under discussion? Why, instead of having this officer for the State at large, it is proposed that each county and the city of Baltimore, respectively, shall elect a "State's Attorney," to be clothed with the same powers and duties, which the present Attorney General is required to exercise, circumscribed only by the limits of the county or city, in which they are elected Every case in which the State is interested within her own territory, must arise in some one of the counties, or the city of Baltimore.—There then will be an attorney under the plan proposed, as well as under the present, to guard and protect her rights. The argument did not seem to him to be sound. But it is assumed that these attorneys will not expect to follow their cases to the Court of Appeals. He, Mr. B., thought it would be their duty to try them there, as well as in the Court below. The deputies under the late Attorney General were required and expected by him to do so. He believed and hoped that the people would elect good and competent men. It was an office of high importance to their peace and welfare as citizens, and he had no doubt they would take care to fill it properly. If attorneys are to be selected in the several sections of the State, to take charge of all her cases originating, or for trial there, he could not understand how their duty to the State as counsel would be discharged until they had followed the case to its termination.

There was an omission it seemed to him in the bill, but this he thought could be easily supplied.

The Governor, as he had before remarked, had now the right to call upon the Attorney General for his written opinion upon questions of interest to the State. It was desirable that the Executive should have the right to claim the opinion of some legal officer, upon questions of law that might arise from time to time in the discharge of his department of the Government. He suggested that he should be authorised to call upon any one of the State's Attorneys, for an opinion in the same manner as he can now claim the opinion of the Attorney General. This he thought could be done without inconvenience, and would remove one of the objections urged against the discontinuance of the office.

It was true, that cases might arise, beyond the limits of the State, in which her rights and interests were involved, requiring that they should be represented and guarded by able and distinguished counsel. This very condition of things is intended to be provided for by the first section. It authorises the Governor "to employ counsel for the State when in his judgment the public interest requires it." With the restrictions proposed in the amendment of the gentleman from Cecil, he, (Mr. B,) would not hesitate in giving him the power. But the fact that such cases will arise is no reason for the continuance of this office. They have arisen, and the late Attorney General, whose ability no man doubted, was not required to appear in them all. When he did appear in any one of them he was liberally paid as he ought to have been, from the treasury of the State. Other distinguished gentlemen were employed in more instances than one. Mr. B. here referred to the printed table of fees paid by the State to counsel in the last twelve years. This then, (he continued,) can be no reason for retaining this office, and the section only authorises the Governor to do that which has been done whilst the office existed. Moreover, how often would these cases occur? From the history of the past it could not be presumed that they would occur often.

He had heard no one object to the election of State's Attorneys in the counties and city of Baltimore. The determination of the Convention seemed to be unanimous upon that point. You are then to have a State's Attorney in every section of the State, and what duty is left to be performed by an Attorney General? It is however proposed that there should be an Attorney General with a fixed salary, who is to be, it is said, the confidential adviser of the Governor. This is the creation of a new office with an old name The Attorney General is now paid by fees. The one proposed to be appointed under the new Constitution is to receive a salary to be paid from the treasury of the State. If you have the office, inducements must be offered to the distinguished talent of the State to fill it. The salary must be a large one. Upon the ground of a proper economy he could not vote for the proposition.

In conclusion, he saw no necessity for continuing this office. Its duties are in fact to be performed by the officers proposed to be elected in the second section of this bill. The interests of the State, in all cases in which she is concerned, would not be left unprotected The power to the Governor to employ counsel, when the interest of the State requires it, will secure counsel to the State in all those cases which do not arise within her limits. He should therefore vote for abolishing the office.

Mr. MORGAN had listened to the discussion with a great deal of interest, and would say that he had come to a different conclusion from the gentleman who had just taken his seat. What was that gentleman's objection to the amendment proposed by the gentleman from Somerset, (Mr. Crisfield,) and how did he propose to obviate that objection? He had said that the Attorney General was not required by the State, because by the article which was before them, the duties of that officer might be performed by the deputies of the respective counties. This was subject to two objections. First—the irresponsibility of these officers discharging the duties of an Attorney General. Secondly—the extra compensation at the discretion of the Governor, or the Legislature, paid to counsel for duties that would be performed by that officer. Now, as to the first objection, he did not concur with his friend from Charles, (Mr. Brent,) that deputies elected in the counties, were always proper persons to follow suits to the court of appeals. There were no doubt some exceptions, among which he was happy to include his friend from Charles. It was well known to every member, that the class of prosecutors were not men of that legal attainment, of that knowledge of the law, who would be proper to follow these cases to the court of appeals. Many of the cases brought to that court, were very important either in the principle to be decided, or the amount involved in the result. He meant no disrepect to these officers, but public duty required that he should speak plainly, and say that it was obvious to the Convention, that should they follow these cases to the court of appeals, that the interests of the State would require that some assistance should be given them in that court. It then resolved itself into this, that counsel other than the prosecuting officer, would be necessarily employed to protect the interest of the State, and in that event extra compensation would be necessarily allowed. Surely his friend from Charles did not mean to say that the prosecuting attorney should follow such cases here, and that the only compensation for his trouble, time, expense of travel, and trying them, should be the $3,33 1-3 cents, now allowed by law. He could not attend to the cases for that fee. He must then receive extra compensation, and as he had before said, many of them would require assistant counsel, who also would receive extra compensation, and this compensation must be, from its nature, uncertain, undefined and unlimited at the time of the rendition of the services, and when fixed, would possibly be ascertained by the party inclinations of the Governor or Legislature, that paid for them. This he considered a strong reason why the present article should not pass, as it opened the doors of the treasury to favoritism, and to a wasteful extravagance of the public money.

Again, what does this bill propose? In the execution of the laws of the State, and the conflicts arising out of them, and in the innumerable instances that required professional advice, it deprived the Governor of the counsel of an Attorney General, and made twenty or thirty deputies elected in the counties at a distance from the seat of government, certainly not eminently qualified to give advice, many of them neither personally or professionally known to him, his advisers and consultors. He asked the Convention, could the Governor have confidence in such consultations, and would the important interests of the State be as wisely and sedulously guarded as under a different system? For his part he could see no good that could result from such a system, except it be to create employment for the benefit of attorneys, without any compensation fixed or limited by law.

Instead of placing the duties of the office of Attorney General in the hands of twenty or more deputies, place them in the hands of one man responsible to the Governor, convenient to him for consultation at all times, and selected from amongst the eminent minds of the State for his knowledge of the law and his capacity to discharge business. This officer should be the adviser of the Governor—his duties should be prescribed by law, and his salary should be fixed and he should be prohibited from receiving any extra fee or allowance for his attention to State business, other than that allowed by law. He would also make it his duty to attend to all cases arising out of the State, in which the interest of the State might be concerned. These cases were continually arising, and would continue to arise, and if gentlemen would take the trouble to look at the treasurer's report, transmitted under an order of this Convention, they would see the enormous expense incurred under the present system in the prosecution of this class of cases; in one or two instances, the amount paid to attorneys, running up to some five or six thousand dollars in each case. This was the result, the inevitable result of your system, and would never receive his sanction or approval.

The amendment of the gentleman from Cecil, (Mr. McLane,) proposed that the attorney employed by the State was to apply to the Legislature for compensation. His friend from Baltimore, (Mr. Gwinn,) had sufficiently answered that argument, though he conceived him rather inconsistent. Yesterday he understood the gentleman to object to the counsel applying to the Legislature, because he did not think that body could estimate properly the value of the services performed, but to-day he has said that he was in favor of allowing the Legislature to fix the compensation.

Mr. Gwinn explained and said, that the arguments which he had used, were not capable of this contradictory interpretation.

Mr. Morgan resumed. He understood his friend now to draw a distinction between what might be considered just claims, and improper claims, and that as to the latter class, attorneys employed to prosecute them by the State, could not from the prejudice attending upon them, receive a just compensation from the Legislature. This was conceding the whole argument, for a claim that might be considered a proper one before investigation might afterwards turn out to be a very unjust one, to be allowed or to be prosecuted—but the correctness, or incorrectness of the claim did not lessen the labor of the counsel employed to investigate it—and those which might be decided to be wrong, would possibly require labor, thought, learning and application in proportion to the contingency of success or defeat. He therefore concurred with the gentleman, that the Legislature could not know what amount of time, labor, application and diligence, which counsel brought to the investigation of such cases, and that they were not the proper agents to form an opinion of the value of the services rendered. In illustration of this argument, his friend on yesterday referred to the McCullough case, and although it was well known that both himself and the gentleman had opposed that claim in the Legislature, yet he understood him to say, that he would have voted for the compensation that was claimed by the distinguished counsel who investigated it.

Mr. McCullough interposing, objected to this claim being brought before the Convention. There must, he said, be one of two objects in bringing this question up—either to retard the progress of the Convention, or to forestall public opinion upon the claim.

Mr. Morgan said:

That he had no design to force the claim upon public opinion. The peculiar relation of the gentleman from Cecil to the claimants had not occurred to him. He certainly had none but the kindest feelings towards either that gentleman or the claimants. He had no agency in bringing it up in this debate, but now that it had been brought in and used by way of argument, he meant no disrespect when he said, that he knew perfectly well when he was in order, and that he meant and intended to use it as a fact for what it was worth in this debate.

Mr. McCullough said, that in his observations, he had no reference to the gentleman.

Mr. Morgan said:

His object was not to argue the merits of the claim—with that we had nothing to do. But his friend from Baltimore had said, that the legislature was not the proper agent to pay attorneys, because they refused compensation in some cases where compensation should be given. He cited this claim as a fact, to prove his argument. He agreed with the gentleman in his conclusions, and no stronger fact could have been brought forward to sustain his views than this very case.

What was that case? Mr. McCullough was a contractor for a la ge portion of the Annapolis and Elk Ridge rail road, he claimed from the State some fifty or sixty thousand dollars, for services rendered outside of his contract. The legislature recognized the equity of some part of the claim by passing an act under which a board of commissioners composed of three distinguished lawyers were appointed, who were required to hear the case and to make an award thereon—they entered upon the discharge of their duties, the claimants appeared by counsel, and the State was represented by the Attorney General and after a laborious investigation of some month or more a full hearing of argument upon both sides, they made their award, and up to this day although these commissioners have knocked at the doors of the legislature for a just compensation for the services which, by law, they had imposed upon them, not one dollar have they received.

Now, he would ask the gentleman from Cecil, if that was a proper body to adjust the claims of lawyers, who might be sent to prosecute a case in any State or before the Supreme Court of the United States? He must say that in his opinion he thought it was not. He meant no disrespect to the Legislature, but the duties of an Attorney and the impossibility of having correct information before them in reference to those duties, made them not the proper sources to apply to for compensation. He also objected to the Governor having an unlimited use of the funds of the State for that purpose—and was in favor of making this an office under the Constitution with a fixed salary, that the Legislature might know, that the people might know, what amount the Attorney received for his services.

Again, it had been said by the gentleman from Cecil [Mr. McLane,] that we should not make the Government we were about to frame more expensive by affixing a salary to the office by Attorney General; that such a salary was unknown to the existing Constitution. Was such an argument sound on the score of economy? In that view it made no difference whether the money was taken from the Treasury of the State by constitutional provision or by appropriation of law, if the amount for the same services appropriated by law was equal to the amount fixed by the Constitution. If the Governor had heretofore paid Attorneys nothing, if the Legislature had paid them nothing, if unlike all past experience in the Government of the State, their services could be dispensed with, then the gentleman's argument was correct. But what are the facts? Gentlemen have now upon their desks a statement of moneys paid to Attorneys for the last twelve years, amounting in the aggregate to twenty-one thousand dollars and upwards, and if, as is proposed under this bill, the opinions required by the various Governors during that time, and which were furnished free of charge by the Attorney General had been paid for, this sum would possibly have been doubled—so that the system itself is infinitely more expensive in its demands upon the Treasury than the one contended for by him, (Mr. M.,) for it is admitted on all sides that these Attorneys will be required and that they must be paid in some manner—no one has intimated that they could be dispensed with.

But, (said Mr. M.,) we should have an Attorney General, for the very reason which the gentleman from Cecil gives that we should not—that of economy. Without paying for any advice during the last twelve years given to the Governors by the Attorney General, it has cost the State, as he before said, upwards of twenty thousand dollars in fees for the legal profession, it is fair to assume that the average cost will be the same hereafter. To this sum you must add similar fees for every opinion required by the Governor in the execution of every law upon which he has a doubt, the aggregate of which would be larger than a salary per annum, that would command the best legal talent of the State. He contended, therefore, that in the practical operation of the government, it was not subject to the objection of being more expensive, but would be a saving to the treasury—would inform the people how and in what manner their money was drawn from it, and divest the Legislature and the Governor, of the power to reward or disallow, at the public expense, the claims of either friend or foe.

The gentleman from Cecil had asked, what salary should be given this officer? He seemed to think that such talent could not be obtained as should be, for the salary proposed. He would undertake to say that for two thousand dollars, or for twenty-eight hundred dollars, the services of the most able men could be procured. It was a duty not at all inconsistent with the business of any lawyer, and one which would, by no means, occupy his time to the neglect of other professional duties; but would he cavil upon a grave constitutional question, about one or two hundred dollars in the salary of an officer? He thought not. It was argued that the Governor must necessarily employ the services of deputy attorneys, and that he could require their opinions when advice was needed. Could gentlemen be serious, when addressing this argument in the hearing of this Convention? Were these deputies so skilled, so eminent, so profound, that no doubt has occurred to the mind of any one as to their capacity to give advice to the chief officer of your State, in the discharge of his high, difficult and important duties? Next fall each county in the State and Baltimore city, will elect an officer of this description, not one of whom the Governor would possibly place the value of an iota upon his opinion, and yet you would make them his advisers in your organic law. And thus you would deprive the Governor of any efficient counsel, so that if he should not be a lawyer himself, he could not with any confidence in his course, know what course to pursue upon all cases of doubtful action. The result would be that the people of Maryland, would have to select for their Governors none but lawyers, as no other class could bring the learning you require to a discharge of the duties of Governor. This, to his mind, was an objection which gentleman had not and could not answer.

Under the existing laws of the State, there was an Attorney General. The amount of fees paid to this officer for the last two or three years was excessive to which the gentleman from Cecil had objected. That gentleman had argued as if the present laws were to continue in force hereafter. And had brought to bear all the evils of the old system, to defeat the one proposed in the new. Had not the gentleman from Somerset, [Mr. Crisfield,] proposed to restrain him from receiving extra compensation, and to define his duties? Had he not in his amendment made it obligatory upon him, to attend to all cases in which the State might be interested, and that he should not receive one dollar of the public money beyond that prescribed by law as his salary?—How then can the argument of the gentleman from Cecil avail him, that although they should appoint an Attorney General. he would hereafter receive extra compensation? This had been done under past laws, and would continue to be done under the system advocated by that gentleman. It was the very evil which he, (Mr. M.) desired should be remedied in the Constitution we were now framing, by fixing the salary and cutting of all extras.

But, says the gentleman, he does not contemplate that the Legislature should pay these counsel for their services, as they have heretofore been paid. He says that the Legislature shall prescribe some rule or schedule of allowances by which these services shall be regulated. Now, can the Legislature ever know what are the services that are to be performed? Its members, perhaps, throwing aside the humanity of which they are common partakers, with their fellow-men, and investing themselves with the presence of Divine wisdom, or catching a ray of that future knowledge of things denied by obdurate man to an all knowing divinity, might have knowledge and information sufficient to prescribe a law to meet every case that might arise, but until such celestial knowledge is vouchsafed unto them, he looked upon all such expectations as entirely out of the question. A case for instance occurs in the State of New York, or any other State: to fix a fee for attention to such a case the Legislature should know before the case arises, how many days or weeks it would take to try, what trouble and investigation it would require before trial, whether it would be disposed of speedily upon the law, or whether by the evidence its continuation would be long, and its expense and labor in proportion to its length This knowledge would necessarily be required, if the sum paid the attorney was in proportion to the services rendered—and this was the only criterion by which they could render any compensation at all. The Legislature, therefore, could not in the nature of things, know what amount to pay. In this point of view he looked upon the proposition of the gentleman from Cecil, as utterly out of the question.

Gentlemen had asked what were the duties of this officer? Had they listened to the able argument of his friend from Prince George's, (Mr. Bowie,) who had shown what were his duties both under the statute and the common law? He would not again repeat that argument. Under the statute law many and responsible duties were thrown upon him in reference to the revenue of the State, where, if competent and proper attention was not given, the State might seriously suffer. Charter privileges, corporations, your internal improvement companies and insurance laws, more or less, throw additional duty and responsibility upon him. He has also been a common law officer in England from the days of Charles down to the present time; has been recognised as such, not only there, but in nearly all the States of this Union, both in their old and new Constitutions. In England he has exhibited all informations and prosecutions for the Crown in matters criminal, and in all cases touching the King's inheritance or revenue, his advice and professional aid is required. In this country he is the great conservator of the public peace, so that those who may outrage the laws of the society under which they live, may be brought to such punishment as the public morals and the dignity of the State may demand. In all questions affecting the property of the State, under its laws it is his duty to watch and protect her interest—to give his advice whenever required by the Executive of the State, at all times and upon all laws. These were some of the duties incident to the office of Attorney General, and he should hesitate a long time before he could be induced to part with an officer whose services the experience of every enlightened government had taught to be necessary.

He should vote against the amendment which abolished this office. Because it left the employment and pay of numberless attorneys at the discretion of the Executive or Legislature, instead of fixing it by law and giving the people some idea of what the expenditures of the State are. He looked upon it as sound public policy that the expenses of government should be ascertained and limited as far as the same can be by law, and not left to either the discretion or caprice of any public officer or agent. He should vote to retain the office because he believed the public interest required it, not only on the score of economy, but because the welfare and protection of society would be guarantied to its members by having an officer whose duty it was to maintain and vindicate the laws that sustain it.

Mr. Howard. The question now before the Convention may be confined within a very narrow compass. It is on an amendment offered by the gentleman from Cecil, (Mr McLane,) as to certain powers to be granted to the Legislature under the first section of this report. We have heard gentlemen after gentlemen, this morning, rising in rapid succession and presenting amendments and substitutes which were all out of order. And what is all this miscellaneous debate to end in? We can come to no conclusions as to the disposition of the matter before us. All this debate, instead of bringing us nearer to the point, only draws us away from the question. There appears to be an antagonistical principle at work which defeats all action on the part of this Convention. Is there to be an Attorney General? Gentlemen differ on that question. What are the duties of the office? Gentlemen differ as to that. Those of us—I rank myself with those who go for the amendment of the gentleman from Cecil—who are in favor of abolishing the office of Attorney General, may yet be inclined to vote for some of the other propositions which may be submitted. Some gentlemen desire to have a salaried officer; but how much they would give him no one has said. If it shall be proposed that he shall have fixed salary, and shall perform all the duties which the State shall require of him, then we shall understand it.

It seems to me, sir, that all the propositions which have been made resolve themselves under two general heads. Will the service of the public be better done, and will it be cheaper done, under the system proposed in the report of the gentleman from Frederick, (Mr. Shriver,) than under the amendment of the gentleman from Cecil? I think not. I think nothing will be gained by the adoption of this section as reported by the gentleman from Frederick. Shall we have an Attorney General? And if so, ought he to be appointed by the Governor, or shall he be elected by the people? I believe that the idea that he should be elected by the people is the most objectionable, and if we are to vest the appointment in the Governor, it will be just as safe to trust him, without the appointment of an Attorney General, with a discretion to employ counsel when required on behalf of the State, out of the profession at large.

The gentleman from Charles, (Mr. Jenifer,) has referred to a record which shows that when the Governor requires legal services in any particular locality, he will take his counsel from that locality. And this is much the best way. Why should he send the Attorney General all over the State, when the best counsel perhaps in the State may be on the very spot, at their own residence there? I would therefore give the Governor the power to select counsel at his discretion. And I believe this will be a cheaper mode than the employment of an Attorney General.

Unless [Mr. H. continued,] we tie up the Legislature from giving compensation to counsel, that body can most properly determine the amount of the fee in proportion to the character of the case. He saw there had been cases in which extra fees had been allowed. He referred to the employment of the Attorney General in Pennsylvania, when he had to take three trips to that State.—And he asked how we could send the Attorney General out of the State, and yet tell him that we would hold him to his salary, and would make him no extra allowance. This could not be done; and the consequence would be that cases of application for additional compensation, would be every session before the Legislature.

Mr. Spencer rose for explanation. He stated that he had said, in reply to the gentleman from Cecil, (Mr. McLane,) who suggested that we could not get an Attorney General competent to perform the duties of the office for two thousand dollars, or even twenty-five hundred dollars, that a competent Attorney General might be obtained for two thousand dollars, and perhaps for fifteen hundred dollars. He said that if the Attorney General was only required to give his opinions at home, and to try cases within the State, he believed an efficient and able one could be had for fifteen hundred dollars.

Mr. Howard, in reply, said that if an Attorney General agreed to take the office for fifteen hundred dollars, he would come to the Legislature for additional compensation. It was impossible that we could get a competent man to go over the State, and to argue cases in the Supreme court of the United States, where it was not unusual to pay a thousand dollars for an argument on any such terms. He regarded it as the most unreasonable proposition that could be advanced.

He believed the business of the State could neither be more cheaply nor better performed by an Attorney General. If we have such an officer, his salary will go on, whether he is employed or not. But in the way now proposed, the counsel in the service of the State would only be employed, when their services were wanted, and would only be paid when employed. Thus the State would be put to no expense beyond what the necessity of the case required.

Mr. Dorsey rose and said:

He was desirous to make some response to the remarks which had been made by the gentleman from Queen Anne's. Any one who should read the debates, would be led to suppose from the character of those remarks, that he, (Mr. D.,) had been making a wanton attack on persons for whom he felt the most sincere respect. Certainly it had been very far from his intention to say a word which could leave an unfavorable impression concerning them.

Mr. Spencer here explained that he had expressly stated that nothing, he was aware, which had been said by the gentleman from Anne Arundel, was intended to have a personal bearing; but that, as the gentleman had said, that the contractors had no claim against the State, that declaration was calculated to prejudice the claim in public opinion.

Mr. Dorsey said:

He did not refer to that part of the gentleman's remarks only, but to what he had said in reference to the court of appeals. The observations, which he, (Mr. D.) had made, were not intended to prejudice the claim, but were in reply to what had fallen from the gentleman from Baltimore city, (Mr. Gwinn,) who had referred to this matter to show that the legislature was either not competent, or not to be trusted to settle the amount of compensation to be allowed for legal services rendered. The gentleman seemed to think it so just a cause of complaint against the legislature, that they had not paid the gentlemen employed in this case, that they ought not to be trusted to fix the compensation for legal services. He understood the gentleman from Baltimore city, to say that the legislature had refused to make any compensation to the gentlemen employed, for their services.

Mr. Gwinn replied that the application was unfavorably reported on by the committee.—Whether it was acted on by the House, he did not know. If it was, it must have been on the last day of the session.

Mr. Dorsey said he had necessarily assumed, from the previous remarks of the gentleman, that the Legislature had rejected the claim; and if it were so, they had only done their duty, and exercised a power expressly reserved in the law for the appointment of arbitrators, who were, of course, apprised of it before they consented to act. He was prepared to give a history of the case, but he would only say, that in view of all the circumstances, the subject was discussed last session, and the claim of McCullough was rejected by a vote of nearly two to one in the House of. Delegates. The chairman of the committee who had voted for the claim before, voted against it afterwards when the vote was forty-five to twenty-four against it. The clause of the Act of Assembly on which he had founded his opinion, that the Legislature was justified in refusing this claim of the arbitrators Mr. DORSEY here read. Under this law the Legislature were to determine whether they would pay or not. Believing, as he conscientiously did, that the State had not a shadow of interest in the matter, and that there was no claim on the State, he stated what he did. The State determined not to pay the arbitrators, because Mr. McCullough was bound to pay them. He thought, therefore, that from this case, the ground could not, with propriety, be taken, that it was right to refuse the power to the Legislature to fix the compensation for legal services.

He did not intend to make any remarks with reference to the Attorney General. He would give his vote for the report. The gentleman from Queen Anne's says we can get an Attorney General for $1500. He, [Mr. D.] knew that for many years past, it had been the practice to make such appointments from political favorites, and thus it was that not always were men of the most distinguished talents selected. It is true, we have had Luther Martin, who conferred more honor on the office than he derived from it. We also have had Roger B. Taney, now Chief Jus tice of the Supreme Court of the United States. And Mr. Pinckney held the office temporarily, until another distinguished individual was competent to fill it. It comported with his conscience to hold it awhile, and it was given to him by the State, on account of his professional pre-eminence, and as an acknowledgment for great services which he had rendered the State, in obtaining a large claim which she had in Europe.

But if the appointment of an Attorney General is to be made now, as it has been for some years past, the State will need some additional counsel. The Attorney General will have to attend to all the business of the State on the Eastern Shore, and before the Supreme Court of the United States. He believed it would be found that the cases of the State before the United States Supreme Court, were never trusted entirely to the Attorney General. He recollected very well that when he was Attorney General, he felt very much gratified at the appointment of Roger B. Taney, to aid him in carrying on a case concerning the right to tax merchandize imported from foreign countries, before the bale was broke. It was so also, in the case of Mr. McCullough, in the Bank of United States.—Cases of this importance, and at this distance from home, were never entrusted to the Attorney General alone. It was never contemplated that they should be. It was no part of the duty of the Attorney General, to travel all over the United States. If such a salary as is spoken of, were allowed him, it would not be expected that he would be required to represent the State in courts out of the State of Maryland, without additional compensation. The salary itself would be no adequate compensation.

The gentleman from Queen Anne's, thinks that upon the terms he has mentioned, the State can obtain very distinguished men. He, (Mr. D ,) doubted if distinguished men could be obtained at any such a salary as the gentleman had named. A man who is competent to fill the office with credit to himself and advantage to the State, never would accept the office at the salary named. If there were only the ordinary duties, men might be found to take it, but not with all these extraordinary duties out of the State, in the performance of which, he would have to make great sacrifices.

He did not agree in the idea, that it was the duty of the Attorney General, as such, to take more care of the interests of the State, than could be expected of any other counsel to whom they may be committed. He had been nearly fifty years at the bar and on the bench, and he could say from his own personal knowledge, had never witnessed any deficiency in zeal or efforts on the part of counsel specially employed by the State. Other counsel will take just as much care of the interest of the State as the Attorney General. He takes the oath of office prescribed by the Constitution; but there is also another oath which no lawyer will violate, and which he takes when he becomes a member of the profession. And no man can be selected by the Governor who would not regard that oath as obligatory on his conduct, as would be the oath of the Attorney General.

He thought then, that there was no real necessity for the appointment of an Attorney General. In the cases which may arise in the counties, the Governor could look among the professional talent of the county or adjoining counties, and appoint counsel resident, as it were, on the spot, and he could do this for less compensation than the Attorney General would require, were he to discharge the duties.

If an important criminal case were to be tried and it was requisite that the State should have very able counsel, the Governor can obtain it, and will have the power to obtain it under this section. Counsel may be taken from among the distinguished men in Baltimore and elsewhere, and taken into the districts, if the Governor should think proper; although it would not be necessary, when in the district itself or its adjoining districts, distinguished counsel could be found fully competent to conduct the case. And these could be obtained at less expense than would be allowed to the Attorney General if he attended there. It had not beenunusual when the Attorney General of the United States who has now a salary of $6,000 a year, to be allowed additional compensation whenever he was sent to a distance and was long detained or rendered important services to the Union.

When the late Attorney General, Reverdy Johnson filled that office, he was sent to New York or Philadelphia, by General Taylor to attend to the interests of the United States in momentous cases about to be tried which had been previously tried and decided against the United States. He was successful, and saved to the United States some ten or twelve millions of dollars When he returned, General Taylor, expressed his high gratification at the manner in which the Attorney General had performed the duties entrusted to him, and asked him to state what was the amount of extra compensation, to which, according to usage, he was entitled. Mr. Johnson replied, that he had examined the law on the subject, and had satisfied himself that he had but discharged his duty as Attorney General, was not entitled to receive and would not receive any compensation for the services rendered, other than his salary.

Mr. JENIFER asked whether Messrs. Pinkney and Rush did not receive large extra fees?

Mr. DORSEY said, he could not answer the question. He had said that it was the practice to receive additional fees. His friend before him, (Mr. Howard,) said it was always usual.

Mr. SCHLEY referred to the section which prohibits the increase or diminution of the salary of a public officer while he remains in office.

Mr. DORSEY said:

This still further demonstrates the impropriety of attempting to obtain an Attorney General at the low salary of one thousand five hundred dollars. The State could never expect to get, at such a salary as that, men like Luther Martin, Pinkney or Taney, who conferred more honor on the office they filled, than did the office on them.

He admitted that it was not now the same honor to fill the office as it was formerly. And his own appointment, perhaps, might in some degree have contributed to that result. But be the cause what it may, the fact, he thought, could not be denied that at the present day the honor of being Attorney General of Maryland, was not sufficiently great to induce the distinguished members of the profession to seek the appointment.

If it is necessary to send counsel to distant parts of the State, to attend to the public business, it would be cheaper to find persons on the spot competent to the discharge of these duties, and who would take care to see that justice was done to the State.

Mr. SPENCER said, I never contemplated, in proposing to give the Attorney General a salary of fifteen hundred dollars, that he was to perform duties beyond the limits of this State, when required, as well as within it, for that sum. I do not hesitate to express my belief that you cannot get an officer at such a salary, to attend to his duties at home, and also go to New York, or any other state of the Union, or to the Supreme court of the United States. If an officer were to undertake to do it, he would involve himself in debt. No, I calculate the fifteen hundred dollars as the emolument within the State of Maryland. This was the position I occupied.

Mr DORSEY. My answer was this, that I do not think it follows from necessity—that it is morally certain that the Attorney General, if selected by the people, would be taken from among the most able and distinguished lawyers in the State—that in great and important cases, such as the one I have already referred to, or where the sovereignty or important pecuniary interests of the State of Maryland are deeply involved and are about to be tried in the Supreme Court of the United States, of the Court of Appeals, or in some other court of the United States, it is desirable that the State should be represented by a member of the bar of distinguished eminence; that such an one would be found in the Attorney General of this State is not at the present day a matter of even moral certainty. The interests of Maryland, therefore, require that the Governor should be permitted to seek him in any part of the State where he is to be found, and not be restricted to the employment of an Attorney General not exactly of that order of talent requisite for the occasion.

I stated that I thought the Attorney General of this State had not been, for the last thirty years or more, of that eminent professional ability which distinguished them in olden times, when a Martin, a Pinkney or Taney occupied that post, and conferred more honor on the office than the office did on them.

Mr. SPENCERR. The gentlman's answer is just what I expected; and when I say this I mean no disrepect to the gentleman. I mean to say it is the only answer that can be given. One of two things must take place, the Attorney General, if we have one, must be either appointed by the Governor or elected by the people. The argument of the gentleman appears to me to be this: that if the Governor had the appointment, then he would not obtain the services of the ablest and most profound lawyers. If he is appointed by the Governor, then the force of the argument of the gentleman is this: that the very Governor who appoints an Attorney General will select a feeble and unsuitable man, but if on the other hand, he is to be required to select special counsel in each case in which he may require advice, then he will go to some *particular part* of the State; perhaps to Anne Arundel county, or to Baltimore city, or some other *particular place*, where he will find and select some very distinguished lawyer.

Mr. DORSEY, (in his seat.) Or, to Queen Anne's county.

Mr. SPENCER. I am glad to find the gentleman looks to Queen Anne's, but I fear he will find an order of men there *far behind those of Anne Arundel.* I have no doubt they will compare well with the rest of the State.

Mr. President, I apprehend if an Attorney General is appointed by the Governor, he would be as cautious in selecting him, as he would be in selecting special counsel.

But, again, if the Governor is not to appoint, then the people will elect. Here I apprehend that inasmuch as there is a probability of the people being required to elect, the gentleman looks into futurity and is afraid that the people will not select an efficient officer, but one that would be utterly inefficient to try a cause. He thinks the people cannot be trusted, and the Governor cannot be trusted, with the selection of an Attorney General; and at the same time he says the Governor will select able counsel, if he is deprived of an Attorney General.

I apprehend no such thing. On the contrary, I believe that if the people are called upon to select an Attorney General, they will select an efficient and able man. And therefore it is, I say, the gentleman's argument proves nothing, for it proves too much. I take the ground that it is demonstrated clearly and without the possibility of misrepresentation, that the Attorney General—the law officer of the State, represents the sovereignty of the State, and therefore when you attempt to strike down this officer, you aim a blow at the sovereign rights of the people. And when you do that, you commit a most serious offence, for there is a great distinction between reforming abuses and practicing innovation. I say that when you attempt to strike down that officer, you step on the ground of innovation, and there is no reform in that. I hold to the doctrine that if there be a necessity for counsel, it ought to receive the approval of the people themselves.

In conclusion, I repeat what I have before said, that I would allow the Attorney General a salary of fifteen hundred dollars a year, for his services within the limits of this State; but if the Governor chooses to send him beyond those limits, then I would be willing to leave it to the Governor, to judge of the discretion and propriety of saying what compensation should be allowed that officer, for extra services on account of being sent abroad. That is the position I take.

The gentleman from Anne Arundel, seems to think that the Attorney Generals of modern days are not equal in ability and talent to the Attorney Generals of olden times and of the old school. Sir, I do not think that all the wisdom and learning belong to former days. although I am proud to know that we have had so many brilliant judicial men, such as the Chief Justice of the United States, who was once Attorney General of Maryland. No, I do not believe that all the learning and talent belong to the men of other days. I believe there is to be found, in this State, counsel equal to any of former times. And there are men rising up every day, in different parts of the State, who would do honor to the station, and I do not believe that the office is to go a begging. I believe that if you adopt a wise provision in the Constitution, there will be no lack of able and highly competent men, ready and willing to accept the office of Attorney General of Maryland, and, therefore, it is, I am opposed to the amendment.

Mr. Dorsey said. A word in explanation of what I have already said, as to which there appears some misconception, though I think my remarks would be justified and correctly understood, without saying anything. I did not mean to say that there were not now distinguished and able men at the bar of Maryland. I stated their were men in it, as able and distinguished as any in the United States, as lawyers. I have had an intimate acquaintance, for a great many years, with gentlemen of the bar, and I think I can say this with perfect safety, as distinguished and able men. There are men that, if my life depended upon it, I would unhesitating trust myself in their hands, but I do not say that such as are fit to be Attorney Generals, abound throughout the State. I said that of late years Attorney Generals were frequently appointed, not bacause they were the most able men in the State, in point of legal attainments, but from motives of political partiality or something of that description, upon no other principle, Mr. President, can I account for my elevation to that office, which I held for a few years, some thirty years ago.

As to the remarks made by the gentleman as to the high dignity of, and profound respect shown to the Attorney General, as representing the sovereignty of the State, and the importance thereof in the discharge of his official duties for the State. I would merely say that I have always regard substance more than form. I have ever considered that in a court of justice, the argument of any other lawyer has just as much weight in the decision of a cause, as the argument of the Attorney General himself. It will do well enough for gentlemen in this body, to talk about the dignity and sovereignty of the State, as represented in the Attorney General, and on southern principles and feelings to gratify our own conceits. But when you come to apply them to matters of litigation, they are wholly disregarded in the adjudications of courts of justice.

The idea, therefore, of the sovereignty of the State, being in the Attorney General, or its having an influence upon the rights of the State before a judicial tribunal, exists only in the imagination of a visionary dreamer. It deserves not the weight of a feather in this Convention.

Now, the gentleman from Queen Anne's, [Mr. Spencer,] asks me whether I think that, if it were left to the people to choose an Attorney General, they would not always make a good selection? That is not my opinion. But I say if the office is to be continued, I would leave it to the people as soon as I would leave it to the Governor—judging from the past. I would have much more confidence that abler men would be selected by the people than by the Governor. I believe it would be the pride of the people to have one of the most distinguished men in this State appointed Attorney General, and such a man would be voted for and elected, if his appointment was considered without reference to political party motives, or the interference and corrupting influence of electioneering politicians. I think the first lawyers in the State, if tendered to them by the people, without an effort on their part to obtain it, would accept the office.

I am, therefore, not liable to the insinuated charge, that I am against trusting the people. On the contrary, I am in favor of trusting the people rather than executive patronage and favoritism.

Mr. SHRIVER said:

It was my intention to have responded to some of the objections which have been urged to the adoption of the first section as reported by the committee, but as the whole subject has been so fully and ably discussed, and as the Convention seem anxious for a vote on this question, I deem it improper to consume more time, and will content myself by reading the second section as I propose to amend it.

[Mr. S. read the section as proposed to be amended.]

That section when amended, taken in connection with the first, will, I think, answer most of the objections made to the first section as reported by the committee.

Mr. PHELPS called for the reading of the amendment,

Which was read.

The question was stated to be, first, on the amendment of Mr. DIRICKSON.

Mr. DIRICKSON with the consent of the Convention so modified said amendment, as to insert the word "thereafter," between the words "may" and "allow."

Mr. D. asked the yeas and nays,

Which were ordered, and

Being taken, resulted as follows:

Affirmative—Messrs. Lee, Chambers of Kent, Donaldson, Dorsey, Wells, Weems, Brent of Charles, Crisfield, Dashiell, Williams, Hicks, Hodson, Eccleston, Phelps, Dirickson, McMaster, Fooks, McHenry, Carter, Stewart of Baltimore city, Schley, Fiery, Neill, John Newcomer, Harbine, Weber, Hollyday, Slicer, Fitzpatrick and Smith—30.

Negative—Messrs. Buchanan, President, *pro. tem.*, Morgan, Jenifer, Howard, Bell, Welch, Chandler, Dickinson, Sherwood of Talbot, Chambers of Cecil, McCullough, Miller, McLane, Bowie, Spencer, Wright, Shriver, Sappington, Nelson, Hardcastle, Gwinn, Brent of Baltimore city, Sherwood of Baltimore city, Ware, Kilgour, Brewer, Parke, Shower and Cockey—29.

So the amendment was agreed to.

The question then recurred upon the adoption of the substitute as offered by Mr. MCLANE, on yesterday for the first section of the report, being in these words:

"In cases required by the public interest, the Governor shall have power to employ counsel under such regulations as the legislature shall prescribe."

Mr. JENIFER then moved to strike out the said first section and substitute the following—

"There shall be an Attorney General appointed by the Governor, by and with the advice and consent of the Senate, whose term of office shall expire with that of the Governor, and whose duty and compensation shall be regulated by law."

The question was then stated to be on the substitute of Mr. JENIFER.

Mr. SHRIVER asked the yeas and nays, which were ordered.

Mr. GWINN called for a division of the question on striking out—but, after some conversation as to the effect of the motion, withdrew it.

Mr. SPENCER renewed it.

A long conversation followed as to the state of the question, and the effect of the amendment.

The question was then taken on the motion to strike out, and the result was as follows:

Affirmative—Messrs. Morgan, Wells, Sellman, Weems, Jenifer, Crisfield, Williams, Hodson, Eccleston, Phelps, Bowie, Spencer, Brent of Baltimore city, Kilgour, Hollyday, Smith, and Shower—17.

Negative—Messrs. Buchanan, Pre't., *pro tem.*, Lee, Chambers of Kent, Donaldson, Dorsey, Brent of Charles, Howard, Bell, Welch, Chandler, Dickinson, Sherwood of Talbot, Dashiell, Chambers of Cecil, McCullough, Miller, McLane, Wright, Dirickson, McMaster, Fooks, Shriver, Sappington, McHenry, Magraw, Nelson, Carter, Hardcastle, Gwinn, Stewart of Baltimore city, Sherwood of Baltimore city, Ware, Schley, Fiery, Neill, John Newcomer, Harbine, Brewer, Weber, Slicer, Fitzpatrick, Parke, and Cockey—43.

So the Convention refused to strike out.

The question then recurred on the substitute amendment of Mr. MCLANE.

The PRESIDENT, (*pro tem.*,) said, that the substitute was not in order—the Convention having refused to strike out.

Mr. WEEMS desired to offer a substitute.

The PRESIDENT, (*pro tem.*,) said, it was not in order.

Mr. CHAMBERS, of Kent, called the attention of the Chair to the twenty-second rule.

The PRESIDENT, (*pro tem.*,) reconsidered his decision, on consulting the rule, and declared the substitute of Mr. MCLANE to be in order.

Mr. WEEMS then said, he should offer a substitute for the section, and that, before it was read, he would say a few words.

Mr. W. said, he was opposed to the abolition of the office of Attorney General, and notwithstanding his unwillingness to participate in the discussion of the bill now under consideration, he would, if in order, offer a substitute for the first section. Before doing so, however, he desired to occupy the floor for a few moments, while he stated very briefly the reasons by which he had been influenced. In looking over the tabular statement, showing the amount paid by the Executive to counsel during the year 1850, he found the sum to be very little less than six thousand dollars. This, in his judgment, was a very important item of expense, one in which his constituents as well as the whole people of the State were interested. For one, he had always thought the Attorney General a very necessary and important officer, as the adviser of the Governor and Treasurer of the State. He considered him the proper person to defend any citizen of the State who might be arrested and put upon his trial for an alleged crime beyond the limits of the State. This bill provides for the election of Prosecuting Attorneys by the people in the several counties and city of Baltimore, by which arrangement, (continued Mr. W.,) the duties of the Attorney General will be very much mitigated.

I make no objection to this portion of the report. I sincerely hope it may work well. I cannot, however, concur with the committee in their views as set forth in the first section of this report. I would prefer continuing this office, and letting the Governor, with the advice and consent of the Senate, appoint the Attorney General, whose term of office should be the same as that of the Executive. By this arrangement I think much expense may be saved to the State, and the Governor relieved of much trouble and inconvenience. Having expressed my humble views, I now offer the following as a substitute for the first section:

"The Governor, with the advice and consent of the Senate, shall have power to appoint an Attorney General for the State, whose term of office shall be years; and it shall be the duty of said Attorney General to attend to all cases in which the State may be concerned, and the annual compensation to said officer shall be two thousand dollars, for services rendered within the limits of the State; it shall also be his duty to attend to any case beyond the limits of the State, whenever required so to do by the Governor, and for services performed out of this State, he shall receive such additional compensation as may be allowed by the Legislature at its first session after such services shall have been performed."

The question was then taken, and the substitute of Mr. WEEMS was rejected.

The question recurred on the substitute of Mr. McLANE.

Mr. CRISFIELD moved to amend said substitute by adding at the end thereof, the following:

"But no law shall be passed to establish the office of Attorney General."

Mr. C asked the yeas and nays on the amendment, which were ordered, and being taken, resulted as follows:

Affirmative—Messrs. Buchanan, President, *pro tem.*, Lee, Chambers of Kent, Donaldson, Dorsey, Brent of Charles, Jenifer, Bell, Welch, Dickinson, Sherwood of Talbot, Dashiell, Eccleston, Chambers of Cecil, McCullough, Miller, McLane, Wright, Dirickson, McMaster, Fooks, Shriver, Sappington, McHenry, Magraw, Nelson, Carter, Gwinn, Stewart of Baltimore city, Brent of Baltimore city, Sherwood of Baltimore city, Ware, Schley, Fiery, Neill, John Newcomer, Harbine, Brewer, Weber, Hollyday, Slicer, Fitzpatrick, Smith, Parke, and Cockey—45.

Negative—Messrs. Morgan, Wells, Sellman, Weems, Howard, Chandler, Crisfield, Williams, Hodson, Phelps, Bowie, Spencer, Kilgour and Shower—14.

So the amendment of Mr. CRISFIELD was agreed to.

The question then recurred on the adoption of the substitute of Mr. McLANE, as amended.

Mr. SHERWOOD, of Baltimore city. I have listened with great attention to this debate, Mr. President, and was in hopes that it would not be necessary to inflict any remarks of mine upon the patience of this Convention; but I find that I must ask your indulgence for five minutes. However anxious gentlemen here may be to bring the labors of this body to a speedy close, allow me to say, that no member of it feels a greater interest in the progress of the public business than myself. The question now before us has been literally "talked to death." It has been so repeatedly altered and realtered, amended and re-amended, that, notwithstanding all the rich displays of legal lore—notwithstanding the elaborate opinions expressed by gentlemen learned in the law, I cannot but come to the same conclusion that Benjamin Franklin came to when sitting by the side of Thomas Jefferson at the time of the adoption of the Declaration of Independence. The anecdote is historical, and no doubt familiar to all here—but, old and familiar as it may be, I shall here repeat it, as most applicable to the present condition of the business of the Convention. It is this: When the Declaration of Independence was under discussion, and Mr. Jefferson was writhing under the criticisms that were being made on some of its parts, Franklin, by way of consoling him, told the story of John Thomson, who was about to set up business for himself as a hatter, and who consulted his acquaintances on the important subject of his sign. The one he had proposed to himself was this: "John Thompson, hatter, makes and sells hats for ready money," with the sign of a hat. The first friend whose advice he asked, suggested that the word "hatter" was entirely superfluous; to which he readily agreeing, was struck out. The next remarked, that it was unnecessary to mention that he required "ready money" for his hats—few persons wishing credit for an article of no more cost than a hat, or if they did, he might sometimes find it advisable to give it. These words were accordingly struck out; and the sign then stood, "John Thomson makes and sells hats." A third friend who was consulted, observed, that when a man looked to buy a hat, he did not care who *made* it; on which two more words were stricken out. On showing to another the sign thus abridged to "John Thomson sells hats," he exclaimed, "why, who the devil will expect you to give them away?" On which cogent criticism, two more words were expunged; and nothing of the original sign was left but "John Thomson," with the sign of the hat.

Now, there has been a great consumption of time on this subject, and it does seem to me that it has already been decided by the vote just taken on the amendment of the gentleman from Charles, [Mr. Merrick,] that we shall have no Attorney General; and we seem to have done much the same thing as was done in regard to John Thompson's sign—struck out everything that has been presented for our consideration, and left nothing but a name and a sign! And yet my friend insists upon restoring that which has been stricken out, and thus revive an office which I think has been pronounced by the deliberate votes and determined action of this Convention, as useless and unnecessary—at least it has been so determined to my entire satisfaction.

I would not have attempted on this occasion,

or on any other, to obtrude myself on the intelligence and wisdom of this Convention, did I not feel constrained to do so by a sense of duty. I have been a quiet but attentive member, and have endeavored to act on all the questions that have been brought before us, so far as my judgment led me, correctly and fairly. If there is any gentleman in this body, worn out after an enduring and long protracted patience, it is myself. I wish to see more acting and less speaking; but if *talking* is to be the order of the day—if *speeches* are to be the only results of the labors of this Convention—if *words* are to repay the people for the treasure expended in their efforts to procure a reform of the abuses that press heavily and unequally upon them—I will not stand idly by

"And see bold deeds achieved by other's hands;"

but will hereafter endeavor to do my share of the *talking*, to inflict as many *speeches* as the most eloquent, and to contribute my full quota of *words* in the discussion of all subjects that may come up. I hope, however, for a better state of things.

Pending the question,

The Convention adjourned until 10 o'clock tomorrow morning.

END OF VOLUME I.